THE OXFORD HANE

MESOAMERICAN ARCHAEOLOGY

THE OXFORD HANDBOOK OF

MESOAMERICAN ARCHAEOLOGY

Edited by

DEBORAH L. NICHOLS

and

CHRISTOPHER A. POOL

OXFORD

UNIVERSITY PRESS

OXFORD
UNIVERSITY PRESS

Oxford University Press is a department of the University of Oxford.
It furthers the University's objective of excellence in research, scholarship,
and education by publishing worldwide.

Oxford New York

Auckland   Cape Town   Dar es Salaam   Hong Kong   Karachi
Kuala Lumpur   Madrid   Melbourne   Mexico City   Nairobi
New Delhi   Shanghai   Taipei   Toronto

With offices in

Argentina   Austria   Brazil   Chile   Czech Republic   France   Greece
Guatemala   Hungary   Italy   Japan   Poland   Portugal   Singapore
South Korea   Switzerland   Thailand   Turkey   Ukraine   Vietnam

Published in the United States of America by
Oxford University Press
198 Madison Avenue, New York, NY 10016

© Oxford University Press 2012

First issued as an Oxford University Press paperback, 2016

Library of Congress Cataloging-in-Publication Data
The Oxford handbook of Mesoamerican archaeology / edited by
Deborah L. Nichols and Christopher A. Pool.
p. cm.
Includes bibliographical references and index.
ISBN 978-0-19-539093-3 (hardcover); 978-0-19-023080-7 (paperback)
1. Archaeology—Mexico.   2. Archaeology—Central America.   3. Indians of Mexico—
Antiquities.   4. Indians of Central America—Antiquities.
5. Excavations (Archaeology)—Mexico.   6. Excavations (Archaeology)—Central America.
7. Mexico—Antiquities.   8. Central America—Antiquities.   I. Nichols, Deborah L.
II. Pool, Christopher A.   III. Title: Handbook of Mesoamerican archaeology.
F1219.O88 2012
972'.01—dc23
2011047914

ISBN 978-0-19-539093-3

1 3 5 7 9 8 6 4 2
Printed in the United States of America
on acid-free paper

CONTENTS

....

Beliefs and Rituals

Art and Iconography, Calendars, Writing, and Literature

Contributors

GUILLERMO ACOSTA OCHOA (Universidad Nacional Autónoma de México)

RANI T. ALEXANDER (New Mexico State University)

FABIO ESTEBAN AMADOR (National Geographic Society)

PHILIP J. ARNOLD III (Loyola University, Chicago)

BÁRBARA ARROYO (Museo Popol Vuh Universidad Francisco Marroquín, Guatemala)

ANTHONY F. AVENI (Colgate University)

JAIME J. AWE (Institute of Archaeology, Belize)

CHRISTOPHER S. BEEKMAN (University of Colorado, Denver)

FRANCES F. BERDAN (California State University, San Bernardino)

GEORGE J. BEY III (Millsaps College)

RONALD L. BISHOP (Smithsonian Institution)

RICHARD E. BLANTON (Purdue University)

JEFFREY P. BLOMSTER (George Washington University)

GREG BORGSTEDE (University of Pennsylvania)

ELIZABETH M. BRUMFIEL (Northwestern University)

MARCELLO A. CANUTO (Yale University)

DAVID M. CARBALLO (Boston University)

THOMAS H. CHARLTON (University of Iowa)

ARLEN F. CHASE (University of Central Florida)

DIANE Z. CHASE (University of Central Florida)

OSWALDO CHINCHILLA MAZARIEGOS (Museo Popol Vuh Universidad Francisco Marroquín, Guatemala)

JOHN CLARK (Brigham Young University)

ROBERT H. COBEAN (Instituto Nacional de Antropología e Historia, Mexico)

GEORGE L. COWGILL (Arizona State University)

ANNICK DANEELS (Universidad Nacional Autonoma de México)

CARRIE DENNETT (University of Calgary)

LORI BOORNAZIAN DIEL (Texas Christian University)

CHRISTINA ELSON (American Museum of Natural History)

SUSAN TOBY EVANS (Pennsylvania State University)

GARY M. FEINMAN (Field Museum)

JAMES L. FITZSIMMONS (Middlebury College)

PATRICIA FOURNIER G. (Instituto Nacional de Antropología e Historia, Mexico)

MANUEL GÁNDARA (Escuela Nacional Antropología y Historia, Mexico)

SERGIO GÓMEZ CHÁVEZ (Instituto Nacional de Antropología e Historia, Mexico)

NIKOLAI GRUBE (Universität Bonn)

DAN M. HEALAN (Tulane University)

JOHN S. HENDERSON (Cornell University)

KENNETH HIRTH (Pennsylvania State University)

KATHRYN M. HUDSON (Cornell University)

EDUARDO DE JESÚS DOUGLAS (University of North Carolina)

ROSEMARY A. JOYCE (University of California, Berkeley)

JOHN JUSTESON (State University of New York at Albany)

DOUGLAS J. KENNETT (Pennsylvania State University)

REX KOONTZ (University of Houston)

MICHAEL LOVE (California State University, Northridge)

BLANCA MALDONADO (Colegio de Michoacán)

PATRICIA A. McANANY (University of North Carolina)

GEOFFREY McCAFFERTY (University of Calgary)

SHARISSE McCAFFERTY (University of Calgary)

EMILY McCLUNG DE TAPIA (Universidad Nacional Autonóma de México)

RANDALL McGUIRE (State University of New York at Binghamton)

DEBORAH L. NICHOLS (Dartmouth College)

MICHAEL A. OHNERSORGEN (University of Missouri, St. Louis)

MICHEL R. OUDIJK (Universidad Nacional Autonóma de Mexico)

SHOSHAUNNA PARKS (University of North Carolina)

JEFFREY R. PARSONS (University of Michigan)

DOLORES R. PIPERNO (Smithsonian Institution)

JOHN M. D. POHL (University of California, Los Angeles)

HELEN PERLSTEIN POLLARD (Michigan State University)

CHRISTOPHER A. POOL (University of Kentucky)

MARY E. PYE (New World Archaeological Foundation)

KATHRYN REESE-TAYLOR (University of Calgary)

F. KENT REILLY III (Texas State University)

PRUDENCE M. RICE (Southern Illinois University)

WILLIAM M. RINGLE (Davidson College)

CYNTHIA ROBIN (Northwestern University)

EUGENIA ROBINSON (Montgomery College)

NELLY M. ROBLES GARCÍA (Instituto Nacional de Antropología e Historia, Mexico)

ROBERT M. ROSENSWIG (State University of New York at Albany)

SILVIA SALGADO GONZÁLEZ (University of Costa Rica)

VERNON L. SCARBOROUGH (University of Cincinnati)

EDWARD SCHORTMAN (Kenyon College)

MAËLLE SERGHERAERT (Université Paris, Panthéon-Sorbonne)

ALFRED H. SIEMENS (University of British Columbia)

BRUCE D. SMITH (Smithsonian Institution)

MICHAEL E. SMITH (Arizona State University)

MICHAEL W. SPENCE (Western Ontario University)

TRAVIS W. STANTON (University of California, Riverside)

REBECCA STOREY (University of Houston)

YOKO SUGIURA Y. (Universidad Nacional Autónoma de México)

SABURO SUGIYAMA (Aichi Prefectural University and Arizona State University)

KARL A. TAUBE (University of California, Riverside)

EMILY UMBERGER (University of Arizona)

PATRICIA URBAN (Kenyon College)

JAVIER URCID (Brandeis University)

MARCIE L. VENTER (Missouri State University)

DAVID WEBSTER (Pennsylvania State University)

E. CHRISTIAN WELLS (University of South Florida)

JASON YAEGER (University of Texas at San Antonio)

CHAPTER 1

MESOAMERICAN ARCHAEOLOGY: RECENT TRENDS

DEBORAH L. NICHOLS AND CHRISTOPHER A. POOL

Where the Rockies meet the northern outliers of the Andes, Middle America rises out of the sea: its plateaus form one of the roofs of the world. Their ground still pulses with the seismic shocks that gave them birth . . . and the ancient prophets of this land spoke of five great periods of time, each destined to end in disaster. (Wolf 1959: 1)

WITH its mountain highlands, snow-capped volcanic peaks, and tropical lowlands, Mesoamerica is a land of geographic and cultural contrasts first settled by humans in the distant past of the last ice age. Like the Andes of South America; Egypt and Mesopotamia; and China and the Indus River Valley, Mesoamerica became a setting for major evolutionary transformations: the development of agriculture and the formation of cities and states, traditional hallmarks of civilization. Mesoamerica also was one of the places where encounters with Europeans most dramatically shaped the course of history and the modern world (Carrasco 2001a: ix).

Mesoamerica as a culture area stretches some 3,000 kilometers, encompassing part of northern Mexico, all of central and southern Mexico, Belize, and Guatemala and parts of Honduras, Nicaragua, and Costa Rica—an area of some 912,500 square kilometers (Figure 1.1).

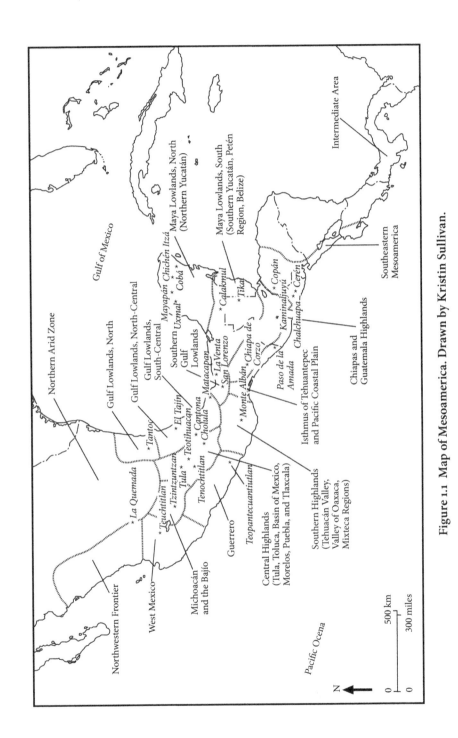

Figure 1.1 Map of Mesoamerica. Drawn by Kristin Sullivan.

Although the region was never politically unified, its prehispanic societies shared a number of cultural practices and beliefs that Paul Kirchhoff (1943) first enumerated (Evans, this volume; Gándara, this volume). As Kirchhoff defined it, Mesoamerica as a culture area did not begin to develop until people started to cultivate domesticated maize in the Archaic period (Figure 1.2). The boundaries of Mesoamerica were never fixed, and goods, raw materials, people, and their ideas moved across fluid borders both within Mesoamerica and beyond (McGuire, this volume; Schortman and Urban, this volume).

No single handbook can cover all the recent trends in Mesoamerican archaeology. Foundational to the present handbook is the sixteen-volume *Handbook of Middle American Indians*, "the most ambitious treatment of a culture area yet produced by anthropologists" (Marcus and Spores 1978: 85). More recently, Carrasco (2001b) and Evans and Webster (2001) have provided encyclopedic coverage of

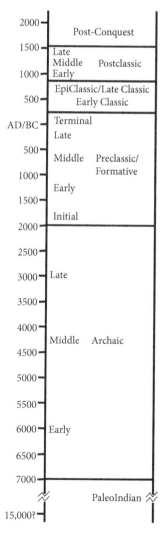

Figure 1.2 Timeline of Mesoamerica. Drawn by Kristin Sullivan.

the region in English, Manzanilla and López Luján (1995–2000) reviewed ancient Mexico in four volumes, and there are a number of books that synthesize the archaeology of particular ancient cultures and regions of Mesoamerica.

This handbook contains essays written by scholars from different disciplines who are active in Mesoamerican archaeology. We wanted coverage of important areas and time periods in a historical and evolutionary framework to be complemented by topical essays that capture significant theoretical and methodological contributions as an update to the archaeology volume in the *Supplement to the Handbook of Middle American Indians,* published over three decades ago (Sabloff 1981). Even with more than seventy chapters, we still recognize gaps in coverage because of page limitations and because we also gave authors considerable leeway in how they would approach their topics. Nonetheless, in addition to presenting a picture of Mesoamerican archaeology in the early twenty-first century, we also see the handbook as a catalyst for future investigations.

Paradigms: Ecology, Evolution, and Practice

Mesoamerican archaeology enjoys a rich record of material remains, prehispanic texts for some periods and places, and colonial documentary sources and ethnographies. Benefiting from the engagement of scholars in anthropology, art history, geography, history, linguistics, and the natural sciences, archaeological research in Mesoamerica encompasses diverse intellectual perspectives and research methods, ranging from highly humanistic to scientific laboratories with nuclear reactors. The field has been shaped by various paradigms and has also contributed to their development. Paradigms, or what Gándara (this volume) calls "theoretical positions," define a discipline's subject matter, its goals and methods, and how it constitutes and evaluates knowledge. The concept of Mesoamerica itself grew out of the paradigms of historical particularism and culture history.

Along with culture history and the expansion of national archaeology programs, cultural ecology, neo-evolutionism, and materialism framed long-term problem-oriented projects in the 1960s and 1970s that were important in shaping contemporary Mesoamerican archaeology (Bernal 1980; Nichols 1996; Sabloff and Ashmore 2001; Willey and Sabloff 1980). Although cultural ecology and evolution provide approaches to structural causes of change and a framework to understand how society and ecology are interconnected, many researchers find these theories too limiting to analyze social change (Brumfiel 1992). Following larger trends in social theory, in the 1980s agency and practice began to receive increasing attention in Mesoamerican archaeology. The focus is on people and their goal-directed actions, not cultural systems, as the agents of change; cultural systems, thus, are outcomes of negotiations between social actors pursuing their goals. In the early 1990s successive Distinguished Lectures in Archaeology for the American Anthropological Association (Trigger 1991; Brumfiel 1992; Cowgill 1993) raised these points and drew on Mesoamerica to illustrate them. Practice theory (Bourdieu 1977; Ortner 1984), Giddens's (1979, 1984) theory of structuration, political economy (Roseberry 1988; Hirth 1996), and feminism (Brumfiel 2006; Conkey 1997) are seen as offering ways to think about dialectical relationships between culture and social life, on the one hand, and rational self-interest, on the other, and to alternate between subject-centered and system-centered analyses, thus widening the door to other approaches, incorporating social identity, materiality, ideation, and embodiment (Brumfiel 1992: 559; Clark 2000; Cowgill 1993: 557–559; R. Joyce 2001; Wilk 1996: 144).

Along with the development of interpretive and postprocessual archaeology, however, processual archaeology itself broadened (Preucel and Mrozowski 2010). At the opposite end of the theoretical spectrum, other archaeologists, especially those working on the origins of agriculture and hunter-gatherers, found behavioral ecology to be a powerful approach (Kennett and Winterhalder 2006). Cultural ecology and cultural evolution continue to be influential (e.g., Evans 2008; Feinman and Manzanilla 2000); selectionist or Darwinian evolution has been applied primarily to change in material culture, especially pottery (e.g., Neff 1992, 1995; Pool and Britt 2000, but see Neiman 1997). Marxism was more widely embraced in Latin America than in North America, but a deep commitment to culture history has remained strong in Mexico and Central America, along with what Gándara (this volume) calls critical processualism. Social archaeology has a presence but it has not been as influential as in some other places in Latin America (Chinchilla, this volume; Lorenzo 1976; Lumberas 1974; Matos Moctezuma 1979; Oyuela-Caycedo et al. 1997; Politis 1999). The view of archaeology as a means of social change has longer roots in Mesoamerica, especially Mexico, than its more recent expression in North America.

The period from the 1980s has been one of "theoretical diversification," accompanied by the development of thematic archaeologies (Gándara, this volume; Hegmon 2003; Trigger 1995, 2006), among them bioarchaeology, gender archaeology, feminist archaeology, ethnoarchaeology, and household archaeology, as well as historic, postcolonial, salvage, cognitive, and landscape archaeology, and so forth. Archaeology has expanded off land and into the water in Mesoamerica (Leshikar-Denton and Luna Erreguerena 2008). Middle-range theory that developed with processual archaeology in the 1970s has become well established, especially in the form of ethnoarchaeology and actualistic research (Trigger 1995). Thematic archaeologies have had more resonance among Latin American archaeologists than processualism or postprocessualism per se (Gándara, this volume). The revolutionary breakthroughs in Maya epigraphy have brought the Classic Maya into the written pages of history (Grube, this volume).

Many Mesoamerican archaeologists have become eclectic or pragmatic about theory, borrowing what they find useful (Gándara, this volume; Lesure 2011a;

Trigger 2006). Most are not extreme relativists, and comparative studies remain important. The growth in tourism, protection of archaeological zones, and state involvement in archaeology research also have very significantly shaped archaeology in Mesoamerica (Awe, this volume; Chinchilla, this volume; Henderson and Hudson, this volume; McCafferty et al., this volume; Robles 2007, this volume; Martínez Muriel 2007). In the 1980s archaeology began to be incorporated into some development projects, as in the case of Copán (King 1985: 379), aided in part by the expanded availability of UNESCO funding. Although words from Maya, Mixtec, Nahuatl, Zapotec, and so on, have labeled archaeological cultures and sites, indigenous and local communities often are not the major beneficiaries of archaeotourism (Castañeda 1996). In recent years some agreements have been reached on profit sharing and allowing access to archaeological sites for religious practices (Chinchilla, this volume; Ivic de Monterroso 2004; Montejo 1999, 2002; Parks and McAnany, this volume).

National archaeology programs have grown throughout Mesoamerica, but foreign archaeologists are still heavily involved. Chinchilla (this volume) concludes that Trigger's (1984) typology of colonial, national, and imperialist archaeological traditions, although it has some utility, has masked complex historical experiences. Throughout the region, states regulate foreign (and national) archaeologists and collaborations of foreign and local archaeologists have risen (e.g., García-Bárcena 2007). The national archaeology programs of Mexico and Central America share some aspects in common but each is also distinct, shaped by separate histories and needs.

ECOLOGY AND ENVIRONMENT

Archaeology offers a long-term perspective on human-environmental interactions, and Mesoamerican archaeology continues to advance understandings of these complex relations (Fisher et al. 2009; McClung de Tapia, this volume). Worldwide concern about climatic change has prompted the development of new paleoclimatic models in the physical sciences—some are so new that archaeologists have not yet assessed their implications. The effects of climatic shifts have been most discussed for the Maya lowlands (Scarborough, this volume), but this may change. Stahle et al. (2011) created the first annually resolved record for Mesoamerica based on a 1,238-year record of bald cypress tree rings. They determined that the 897–922 A D drought that some think contributed to the collapse of Classic Maya kingdoms in the southern lowlands had also extended into the Central Highlands (Gill 2000; Love, this volume; Scarborough, this volume; Webster, this volume).

Volcanic eruptions continue to shape Mesoamerica and in some instances they prompted significant relocations of prehispanic populations (Plunket and Uruñela

2006; Santley et al. 2001; Sheets 2008). The scale of human landscape modifications significantly increased with the advent of cultivation, and much research by archaeologists focuses on the causes and consequences of anthropogenic changes. Advances in molecular and micro- and macrobotanical analyses have produced new understandings of the early development of agriculture. It appears that people who lived in the Central Balsas region had domesticated maize ca. 6900–6600 BC and by the Middle Archaic there is evidence of land clearance in the seasonally dry lowlands, most likely from slash-and-burn farming (Kennett, this volume; Piperno et al., this volume; Pohl et al. 2007). Despite alterations from farming and urbanism, much of the region sustained intensive agriculture throughout prehispanic times (Scarborough, 2009, this volume). In fact, some of the most severe degradation took place in the face of Spanish imperialism and declining populations and was due to the introduction of foreign animals, plants, new crops, and new technologies (Alexander, this volume; Fournier and Charlton, this volume; Scarborough, this volume).

Environmental studies have moved away from a focus on ecosystem equilibrium (McClung de Tapia, this volume). Mesoamerican archaeologists have recently incorporated concepts of historical ecology, landesque capital, resilience and complexity theory, and complex adaptive systems to look at recursive human-environmental relations (Alexander, this volume; Fisher et al. 2009; Scarborough and Burnside 2010). We anticipate that Mesoamerican archaeology will draw even more on heavily on the "new ecologies" (Biersack 2006).

SETTLEMENT AND LANDSCAPE

Mesoamerican archaeology played a leading role during the twentieth century in the development of settlement-pattern research at both the regional and community levels. Data generated by settlement-pattern research have proven robust and can be analyzed and interpreted in new ways. Systematic surveys of regions and sites are ever more critical for salvage and cultural-resource management in Mesoamerica.

New technologies have revolutionized pedestrian survey and mapping methods with global positioning systems (GPS) and total mapping stations, and Google Earth has facilitated siteless surveys (e.g., Parsons and Morrett 2004). Geographic information systems (GIS) make it possible to integrate and analyze different types of spatial data, although accessibility and the integration of databases pose considerable challenges (Snow et al. 2006).

Mesoamerican archaeologists were among the first to integrate aerial photography with settlement-pattern surveys (Siemens, this volume; Nichols 2006; Sanders et al. 1979). New remote-sensing methods have been employed to discover sites and other landscape features, to map sites, and to find buried features (e.g., Chase et al. 2011; INAH 2010a, 2010b, 2010c). Cost remains a major impediment to using such applications more frequently.

Large-site mapping and regional settlement-pattern studies have shown the importance of prehispanic cities in Mesoamerica and their diverse forms, making urbanism a rich topic in Mesoamerican archaeology (Blanton, this volume; A. Joyce 2009; Manzanilla and Chapdelaine 2009; Manzanilla 1997; Mastache et al. 2008; Sanders et al. 2003; Sanders and Webster 1988, 1989; Smith 2007). The Aztec imperial capital, Tenochtitlan, was not the archetype of Mesoamerican urbanism, although it was its most populous expression. Many urban centers, especially in the tropical lowlands, were more dispersed (e.g., Stark 2008). Although there is less consensus about the causes of this diversity, cities can be understood only within their larger societal context. Thus there has been a shift away from typological definitions to an emphasis on function, and multiscalar approaches, which view cities as the result of social action at various spatial scales from households and rural hinterlands to macro-regions, are encouraged (Blanton, this volume; Smith 2008).

Archaeological and textual data provide complementary perspectives, and researchers have incorporated both to analyze regional political and economic hierarchies, especially during the Postclassic (Pohl, this volume). Macro-regional approaches, including modifications of world systems theory and core-periphery models, seek to understand larger scales of interaction (e.g., Blanton and Feinman 1984; Santley and Alexander 1992; Smith and Berdan 2003; Rosenswig 2010). Debates about the nature of interregional interactions have sometimes become very contentious in part because of the nature of core-periphery models that see the actions of rulers in the core as determinative of peripheries. If a social network, however, is the unit of analysis, the focus shifts to seeing how a network operates at different scales with diverse agents acting in different contexts and locales (Schortman and Urban, this volume; Gómez and Spence, this volume). Network analysis can take advantage of isotopic and DNA studies of bones and teeth and source studies of artifacts and raw materials (Bishop, this volume; Gómez and Spence, this volume; Spence and White 2009). Schortman and Urban advocate seeing borderlands as innovative places of cultural hybridity in order to move away from the passive periphery view.

Influenced by practice theory, Giddens's (1984) theory of structuration, and Ingold's (2000) elaboration of Heidegger's "dwelling," Mesoamerican archaeologists have invoked the concept of landscape as both a cultural and natural product to understand how people created and experienced space as places and how places are socially, politically, and ritually charged. Landscape includes all built spaces created by human activity, ranging from sacred precincts created as cosmograms that shaped and expressed the moral order of society (Aveni, this volume; Blanton, this volume; Reese-Taylor, this volume) to quotidian places and spaces of houses and outdoor work areas (Robin 2002).

ECONOMY AND POLITICAL ECONOMY

The earliest economies of Late Pleistocene foragers in Mesoamerica were those of generalized hunter-gatherers (Acosta, this volume). Much had changed between then and 1502, when Christopher Columbus encountered a large canoe of Maya merchants in the Bay of Honduras. By the sixteenth century the complex economies of Mesoamerica involved intensive agriculture, specialization, markets, merchants, and tribute and taxes (Berdan, this volume; Scarborough, this volume). Significant advances have been made in understanding ancient Mesoamerican economies and the intertwining of politics, economics, and, more recently, religion (Wells, this volume).

Applications of sourcing studies, isotopic analyses of human bones and teeth, soil chemistry studies, and micro- and macrobotanical analyses provide valuable data for archaeologists and encourage multidisciplinary research. Mesoamerican archaeology has incorporated these approaches, along with experiments, ethnoarchaeology, and residue analysis to understand the technology, context, intensity, and scale of craft production and the presence of marketplaces (Bishop, this volume; Clark, this volume; Maldonado, this volume; Pool and Bey 2007; Rice, this volume; Wells, this volume; Spence and White 2009). Most craft workshops in Mesoamerica were independent and residentially based, but some specialists worked directly for wealthy households or were attached to temples and palaces. Members of elite families sometimes engaged in the production of wealth goods.

Household archaeology, political economy, and gender theory have encouraged much more dynamic understandings of the domestic economy (Hirth 2009; McAnany 2010). Household workshops often are typified as small scale, but in Mesoamerica by the Classic period they employed techniques of mass production to produce large volumes of goods. A recent volume by Hirth (2009) challenges this and other stereotypes of households and the domestic economy (Brumfiel and Nichols 2009; Carballo, this volume). Rather than seeing elites as the only rational actors and craft specialization as a product of elite strategies of legitimation, Hirth argues that craft specialization grew out of household economies. Households engaged in intermittent crafting and multicrafting to increase production and moderate risks. Viewing crafting and manufacturing in this light conceptualizes them as household strategies and opens the door to seeing them in wider contexts.

Ethnohistorians such as Frances Berdan mined documentary sources to reveal that Postclassic societies were not simply "command economies" (Berdan et al. 1996). Changing views of premodern economies and methodological advances have contributed to a recent upsurge in archaeological studies of Mesoamerican markets and marketplaces with a greater emphasis on agents and strategies while recognizing that economies always exist in a context (Blanton 1996; Blanton and Fagher 2008, 2009; Dahlin et al. 2007; Feinman and Nicholas 2004; Garraty and

Stark 2010; Hirth 1998, this volume; Hodge et al. 1992, 1993; Minc 2009; Nichols et al. 2002). Archaeological studies also have challenged the notion that Mesoamerica's incorporation into the world system after the defeat of the Aztec Empire resulted in the rapid replacement of prehispanic technologies and economies (Fournier and Charlton, this volume; Rodríguez-Alegría 2008).

SOCIETY AND POLITY

Understanding society and polity in ancient Mesoamerica entails the consideration of both agency and structure. Social identity, ethnicity, gender, households, communities, and neighborhoods are recent foci of attention, along with recognizing that ancient states took multiple forms in Mesoamerica. In just a few decades Mesoamerican archaeology has moved from almost no research on gender to volumes on the topic that cover sexuality; how gender intersects with class, status, and age; and how women, as well as men, exercised power (Joyce, this volume). Gender was not simply a dichotomy in ancient Mesoamerica, and gender hierarchies in ancient states, including those of Mesoamerica, varied considerably. The lack of large animals put a premium on human labor and the complementary contributions of women and men. Often in Mesoamerica class and age were more important and this has encouraged consideration of gender parallelism and complementarity (Joyce, this volume). The primacy of place in notions of ethnicity persisted into postcolonial times (Alexander, this volume; Berdan et al. 2008).

Once it arose, the distinction between noble and commoner in Mesoamerica was important, but stratification had multiple dimensions and this created a continuum of social differentiation (Brumfiel and Robin, this volume). People of different statuses belonged to corporate and ethnic groups. Some see lineages as being an important form of corporate group; others feel the "house society" model is most apt (Gillespie 2000; McAnany and Houston 2003; Watanabe 2004). To apply the house concept too widely, however, is no more useful than defining lineages too narrowly. Along with corporate groups, ethnicity crossed class divisions and in contrast to older essentialist notions, today scholars see ethnicity, which in ancient Mesoamerica was often rooted in place, not biology, as strategic and variable as it defined access to land and territory (Berdan et al. 2008). Brumfiel and Robin (this volume) point out that such social modules created interdependence among people and groups of widely different social positions that came together or separated in different situations.

Over its long history, Mesoamerica has been home to various political formations, from kinship-based mobile bands to expansionist states and empires. Hierarchical prehispanic polities took different forms, only partly as a consequence of their development in highland or lowland environmental settings. Networks of interaction were important, and there were cycles or episodes of expansion, contraction, and regeneration of states (Feinman, this volume; Cowgill, this volume; Marcus 1998). Causes of these changes are less clear. Understanding the nature of political rituals and of ideology and belief systems that underpinned notions of rulership has been advanced through studies of texts and archaeology (e.g., Pohl, this volume; Sugiyama, this volume).

Many Postclassic states were small, but they formed alliances and confederations that warrant more study by archaeologists (Pohl, this volume). There is less consensus about the nature of early complex societies and variations in the forms of Classic-period states. Some variation can be explained by different strategies of city-state systems and regional or territorial states, but Teotihuacan exhibited attributes of both (Trigger 2003; Charlton and Nichols 1997; Yoffee 2005). Blanton and colleagues' (1996) dual processual theory and concepts of network and corporate strategies have been highly influential. Debate about what models best fit lowland Classic Maya polities, theater states, galactic polities, segmentary states, city-states, ritual-regal cities, and regional states stem in part from real differences among Classic-period polities in size and scale (Demarest 2004, 2009; Chase and Chase, this volume; Chase et al. 2009).

Beliefs and Rituals

The study of Mesoamerican beliefs and rituals in archaeology has become more sophisticated and broader in approach. Prehispanic people of Mesoamerica believed in a layered universe through which cosmic forces, deities, ancestors, shamans, and cycles of time moved. They engaged in rituals and ceremonies to balance oppositions (Reilly, this volume). Rich information from ethnographic and documentary sources is of great value, and continuities help with interpretation, but there are tensions between the direct historical approach and comparative theoretical analyses in the study of ancient religion. Chroniclers focused on documenting "state" religion and public ceremony, even as they burned books, destroyed temples to build churches, and banned non-Christian ceremonies and rituals. But household archaeology has extended the study of beliefs and practices to the domestic sphere. Figurines are a common class of artifacts that chroniclers had little discussed. Scholars have taken both contextualist and universalistic approaches to understanding them (Lesure 2011b). Recent work explores the social meanings of figurines and the agency of the people who made and used them, and there now are multiple examples of embodied approaches (e.g., Halperin et al. 2009). Even after ritual practitioners became specialists in the Preclassic, houses continued to be places of ritual where individuals and households created and sustained their social identities and their place within society and the cosmos with the use of rites and ceremonies. Dedication and termination rituals indicate that commoner houses and palaces as well as temples, possessed life cycles like the people who occupied them (Plunket 2002).

The importance of ancestors across the social spectrum is manifested by burials in houses and household shrines that represent liminal spaces as "connections between the different levels of existence" (Plunket 2002: 8). The dead continued to influence the living (Fitzsimmons, this volume; McAnany 1994). Yet important differences developed in Mesoamerica; royal tombs are well known for the Classic Maya, and archaeologists are still searching to find one in central Mexico (Sugiyama, this volume). State religion and political ritual will continue to receive attention as the associated monumental works still invoke power. Beliefs and ritual practices were dynamic in Mesoamerica; the shift to an agricultural lifeway brought water and agricultural fertility, cyclic rituals, and reckoning time into high relief (Aveni, this volume). Hierarchical polities conjoined religion and politics; ritual practitioners developed writing and became specialized priests (Reilly, this volume). Cults were one of the ways ideas and practices spread between societies in prehispanic and more recent times (Pohl, this volume; Bey and Ringle, this volume).

IMAGES AND TEXT

The development of village lifeways changed how individuals and groups experienced "things" and initiated changes in human cognition with new technologies and uses of symbols and the creation of new media (Cowgill 1993; Renfrew 1998). Four notational systems had developed by the Late Middle Formative/Preclassic, with Zapotec being the best represented (Justeson, this volume; Urcid, this volume). The presence of some shared signs and conventions indicates interactions among these regions and that all developed from the same script. Justeson (this volume) feels that the evidence is even stronger today that Mesoamerican writing grew out of Olmec iconography.

The Late Formative/Preclassic saw the beginnings of urban elite, artistic representations that expanded in the Classic period out of which imperial and international art styles developed in the Postclassic (Koontz, this volume; Pye, this volume; Bey and Ringle, this volume). Mesoamerican archaeology benefits from the approaches of art historians to images, texts, art, and artifacts (e.g., Diel, this volume; Kubler 1970, 1975; Pasztory 2005). The revolution in Maya epigraphy has put the Classic Maya on the pages of history and has demonstrated the value of linguistic approaches to decipherment (Coe 1992; Grube, this volume; Houston et al. 2001). There has been an explosion in the decipherment of texts. These texts provide rich information about rulers and rulership, associated beliefs and rituals, and interpolity relations, wars, gift exchanges, marriages and royal visits. Even where we lack such a corpus of deciphered texts, glyphs, work on other scribal traditions, and colonial documents have provided a window on ancient ideology and the complex changes of the Colonial period.

Colonial and postcolonial periods were once the exclusive domain of historians and ethnohistorians. Well in advance of most of Mesoamerican archaeology, the late Thomas Charlton launched historic archaeology in central Mexico in the 1960s; without his efforts we would know little about rural Aztec life after 1521. Texts and archaeological remains provide complementary perspectives; each involves different methods and approaches and different strengths and challenges, but one should not be subordinate to the other (Fournier and Charlton, this volume). Expanding collaborations among archaeologists and historians, and ethnohistorians and ethnographers, are highly productive in developing more nuanced understandings of both the Postclassic and early Colonial periods (e.g., Alexander, this volume; Hodge 1997; Kowalewski et al. 2009).

MODELS OF CHANGE

The Mesoamerican past was dynamic, rich, and complex. The greatest challenges for Mesoamerican archaeology are explaining change and managing the archaeological record for the future. Most Mesoamerican archaeologists fall into a middle ground of processualism and postprocessualism akin to Michelle Hegmon's (2003) "processual plus." There are theoretical tensions and debates, although the most contentious debates do not always fall along a processual versus postprocessual divide. The field has not fragmented as some feared; perhaps the truce is temporary, but theoretical pluralism or pragmatism characterizes Mesoamerican archaeology today.

Approaches to change include culture history, cultural evolution and ecology, evolutionary ecology, functionalism, action theory, and social practice. The culture history of the long Paleo-Indian period, from initial colonization until the end of the Pleistocene, before the concept of Mesoamerica is even relevant, remains poorly known. The archaeological record of the Archaic period (ca. 8000–2000 BC) is still very fragmentary, and this hinders understanding both of the change from foraging societies to kin-based villages and of the development of early hierarchical polities. It now appears that important differences developed early between hunter-gatherers in the semi-arid highlands and seasonally dry lowlands. Explanations of why foragers began to cultivate and domesticate crops cover a gamut from demography and risk reduction to prestige competition.

Social differentiation within and between kinship-based villages began soon after their founding in the Early Formative/Horizon, and understanding the dynamics of complex societies from that point forward has been the principal focus of Mesoamerican archaeology. Hierarchical polities took multiple forms and trajectories (Sanders and Webster 1978; Flannery and Marcus 1983). Archaeological recognition of the large range of middle-range societies and even states and empires is often not straightforward and this contributes to a number of debates, for example, about the Gulf Coast Olmec, Teotihuacan's foreign relations, and the Toltec state (Chase et al. 2009). Early state formation was not free of conflict (Spencer 2010).

Archaeologists have employed various theoretical frameworks, political economy, and action and practice theory to consider agency, sources of power and strategies to acquire them, and actions of agents (Blanton et al. 1996; Brumfiel 2000; Clark and Blake 1994; Earle 1997; Pool 2007). Agency is also important in ecology and complex adaptive systems. Blanton and colleagues' (1996) dual processual model distinguishes corporate and network or exclusionary strategies, and it offers one way of conceptualizing political practices. Researchers in Oaxaca applied action theory to meld cultural evolution and agency (Balkansky 2002; Marcus and Flannery 1996; Spencer and Redmond 2001). Actor-based approaches seek to shift the focus from top-down structures to human agency of culturally and historically contingent, goal-oriented individuals (Clark 2000). Influenced by Mauss's (1950) "spirit of the gift," Clark and Blake (1994; Clark 2000) developed an explanation of the origins of hereditary ranking in early Mesoamerica as resulting from political actors ("aggrandizers") competing for prestige and esteem.

Concerns, not insignificant ones, have been raised about too much focus on elite agency and implicit assumptions of western individualism and economic rationalism in rational choice models (Drennan 2000; Gero 2000). To address this, practice, structuration, and feminist theories approach social institutions as emergent social forms among "differently positioned actors" who are simultaneously embedded in history and are also producers and reproducers of history (Brumfiel 2000; also A. Joyce 2009; Joyce, this volume). Social institutions structure the actions of individuals so as to naturalize the existence of such structures until something calls the structures into question (Canuto and Yaeger, this volume; A. Joyce 2009). Cowgill (2000) cautions that actors are not only guided by rational calculations and urges greater attention to the ideational realm (Trigger 2003). Drennan (2000: 194) worries about "overreaching" human agency in understanding "long-term social reorganizations whose study is the special province of archaeology."

While we see social formations, households, communities, towns, cities, polities, states, and empire in Mesoamerican archaeology as ongoing processes, they also did not exist in isolation but were linked in larger networks. Mesoamerican archaeologists have long recognized alternations between periods of macro-regional centralization and fragmentation usually characterized as cycles, although Cowgill (this volume) prefers "episodes" because interval lengths are varied within and between regions (Kowalewski et al. 1989; Marcus 1998). Such alternations between centralization and fragmentation are not unique to Mesoamerica, but the Classic Maya collapse has drawn much attention and debate. Analyses on a site-by-site and area-by-area basis have helped clarify the changes, their variability, and multiple causes (Demarest et al. 2004). The term "collapse" may be problematic, but the sustained population reduction over large areas of the southern Maya lowlands and disappearance of royal dynasties and their ideology of kingship was unlike any other "fragmentation" in prehispanic Mesoamerica (Cowgill, this volume; Webster, this volume; cf. McAnany and Yoffee 2010).

Most Mesoamerican states were small; large regional states that persisted for more than a few generations were exceptions but are important to understand. Most imperial rule was hegemonic, although the Tarascan Empire was more integrated politically than the larger Aztec Empire (Chase et al. 2009; Pollard, this volume; Smith and Sergheraert, this volume). In the socioenvironmental setting of Mesoamerica, with its technological restrictions, human labor was the critical resource that encouraged collective action through the development of complex socioeconomic arrangements and ideologies (Blanton et al. 2010; Feinman, this volume). This helps explain a paradox of prehispanic Mesoamerica, a world region with limited transportation technology where autochthonous civilizations developed that supported numerous cities; some very large, dense rural populations; and interactions and economic integration on a far larger scale than its political systems.

The defeat of Tenochtitlan in 1521, which ended the Aztec Empire, and the conquest of other parts of Mexico and Central America can no longer be explained by the brilliance and heroism of Hernán Cortés as Cortés had claimed (Oudijk, this volume). Seen through the eyes of Tlaxcallan and other allies, the conquest looks very different (Hassig 2006; Oudijk and Restall 2008). The decline in population following the introduction of European diseases and Spanish colonialism shaped Mesoamerica's subsequent history, even as scholars debate the numbers (Storey, this volume). However, archaeology shows that these processes worked in variable ways (Alexander, this volume). Lessening the divide between the Postclassic and Colonial periods will better position Mesoamerican archaeology to contribute to more comprehensive understandings of historic changes.

Today's theoretical pluralism in Mesoamerican archaeology grew from larger intellectual trends of the late twentieth century and from empirical research documenting the diversity and complexity of Mesoamerica's past. Some challenges continue because researchers need to develop bridges to connect theories of whatever stripe with the archaeological and documentary records, to harness the digital age to make data and findings more accessible, and to engage local communities (Geurds 2007; Robles 2000). A continued commitment to empirical research and the conservation of sites and collections is needed to ensure that a rich archaeological record exists for the theorists of the next century.

Looking to the Future

When the archaeology supplement to the *Handbook of Middle American Indians* was published thirty years ago, there were few hints of the developments that lay ahead in archaeological theory and practice. For the most part, the articles

reflected prevailing concerns among North American archaeologists with ecological explanation and systems theory (e.g., Coe 1981; Flannery et al. 1981; MacNeish
1981; Sanders 1981; cf. Lorenzo 1981), as well as regional survey and chronological
synthesis (Blanton and Kowalewski 1981; García Cook 1981). Jones and colleagues
(1981), in their summary of the Tikal project, highlighted important results on
demography and subsistence, on the one hand, and epigraphy and rulership, on the
other, giving just a small taste of what lay ahead on the epigraphic front. Blanton
and Kowalewski (1981) sounded a divergent note in cautiously suggesting that
human-to-human relations were more centrally involved in systemic changes in
the Valley of Oaxaca than were human-environmental relationships, and Blanton
(1981) mounted a challenge to cultural-ecological explanations for "The Rise of
Cities" in his chapter of that title, calling for "new and better theories of cultural
evolution." Millon's (1981) discussion of Teotihuacan governance and ideology pre-
figured much of the recent research there.

In short, the archaeology supplement bore the earmarks of the prevailing processual paradigm of the time and the continued concern for culture history. The
theoretical pluralism that marks today's Mesoamerican archaeology could hardly
have been conceived at the time. The foundational literature of practice theory,
structuration theory, world-systems theory, and selectionist archaeology were
new, only recently translated into English, or still being written (e.g., Bourdieu
1977; Dunnell 1980; Giddens 1979; Wallerstein 1974, 1979; Wolf 1982). We close this
introductory chapter, then, with a few observations on those areas of archaeological theory and practice that we see as important in the near future, fully recognizing that our crystal ball is no better than that of our predecessors.

Making the Most of Theoretical Diversity

Just as a long tradition of interdisciplinary engagement among researchers in archaeology, art history, ethnohistory, ethnology, and linguistics has enriched Mesoamerican
studies, so, too, may an embrace of diverse theoretical paradigms. In the most opti-
mistic scenario, multiple perspectives would be brought to bear on complex problems
ranging from the origins of agriculture or the development of social complexity to
the construction of social identities in specific historical contexts. There is, however, a
danger that such theoretical pluralism may devolve into opportunistic cherry-picking
to support a pet idea about the past. Moreover, theoretical orientations should and do
shape the kinds of data that may be collected and how those data are to be incorporated into—or excluded from—a narrative about past societies. Thus, if theoretical
pluralism is to be more than pragmatic opportunism or adaptive noncommitment
(see Gándara, this volume) attention needs to be devoted to strategies for evaluating
claims made from divergent orientations and integrating them into a multifaceted
picture of the phenomena we hope to understand or explain.

One approach is to relegate a particular theoretical position to a specific class
of phenomena: cultural ecology to understand human-environmental interactions;

microeconomics to understand domestic economies and subsistence strategies; political economy to understand macro-regional relations of core and periphery; agency theory to understand social relations or political strategizing; and feminist theory to understand the construction of gender. Indeed, theoretical eclecticism often takes such an approach. Most theoretical perspectives, however, lay some claim to elucidating a broader range of phenomena and some aspect of social or cultural change.

Another approach conducive to theoretical inclusivity is one that considers the social, temporal, and geographic scales of the phenomena that a particular perspective seeks to explain. For example, Pool and Britt (2000), following Braun (1995), suggested that behavioralist and agentic approaches offered more satisfactory explanations for ceramic variation partitioned at smaller social and temporal scales in the Tuxtla Mountains, while selectionist perspectives offered insights into the aggregate outcomes of individual choices in larger social entities and across longer time spans. Also concentrating on the issue of scale, Lesure (2011a) asks how well divergent perspectives contribute to narratives about the past at multiple spatial and temporal scales. Contrasting developmentalist (processual, evolutionary) and historicist (both cultural-historical and agent-centered) narratives, Lesure argues for "scaling up" accounts from local to "macro-regional" scales to assess the stability of developmentalist narratives. In either case, attention to scale offers a productive line of inquiry into the fundamental question of how individual and collective decisions acted upon in the short-term result in large-scale variation and long-term change in the phenomena under consideration.

Improving Time-Space Frameworks

Attention to the empirical adequacy of theoretical perspectives at multiple scales underscores the need for continuing work to improve chronologies and to align them between regions. As the labels of Preclassic (or Formative), Classic, and Postclassic indicate, the most widely used Mesoamerican chronological scheme derives from a relative chronology that charted stages of cultural development marked by changes in material culture (Archaic and Paleo-Indian, as currently used, were added later). Events were placed relative to the Maya Classic period, which offered the potential for absolute dating in its Long Count inscriptions, but whose correlation with the Western calendar was still uncertain in the early twentieth century. With the advent of radiocarbon dating, it became evident that the "Classic" stage used to anchor the sequence did not align well temporally through all regions. The general resolution was to treat Preclassic, Classic, and Postclassic as periods—blocks of time with no necessary relationship to a stage of development—but the stage labels stuck, and discussions ensued about whether the period that by then had been designated Classic within a particular region began earlier or later than had been assumed. The picture is even messier within the basic periods, with early, middle, and late divisions variously demarcated in different areas and a proliferation of terms such as "Protoclassic," "Middle Classic," "Epiclassic," or "Terminal Classic" used inconsistently to capture developments that played out in different regions at varying geographical scales. An alternative system of chronological nomenclature of periods and phases without stage connotations proposed for the Basin of Mexico was modeled on Rowe's (1960) chronology for the Central Andes, but it has found only partial acceptance (e.g., Sanders 1981).

While confusing to initiates, the customary chronological terms are unlikely to change, and they do little damage except when archaeologists content themselves with assigning materials to the broadest periods. More important is that work continues to refine regional and local chronologies such that the timing of events and tempo of change can be more adequately assessed and correlated between sites and regions. What do we mean by improvement? An obvious form of improvement is one of ever-finer divisions in regional chronologies as Clark and Cheetham (2005) have done for the Early Formative ceramic sequence for the Soconusco, which they aligned with phases of similar duration in other parts of Chiapas. Ceramics are not the only class of artifacts that can be used productively for chronological purposes, and it is the combination of variation across artifact classes within an assemblage (including art and architecture) that provides the most precise division of phases.

Even in cases where temporal resolution of phases based on artifact assemblages is destined to be poor, greater accuracy in fixing the timing of events represents a significant improvement. Advances in radiocarbon dating, particularly through atomic mass spectrometry and improved calibration curves, have been instrumental in refining chronologies in the past two decades, and there still need to be more radiocarbon dates with better stratigraphic control in most areas of Mesoamerica. When radiocarbon dates offer inadequate resolution we must turn to alternative methods, including thermoluminescence, archaeomagnetism, and obsidian hydration sequences properly calibrated with respect to source material, local environmental conditions, and an independent archaeometric method. Fixing the timing of events more accurately does not necessarily relate to pinpointing phase transitions, though it may do so. The changes we identify as temporal boundaries between phases and periods rarely, if ever, happened overnight or even were completed in a generation. What is most important, and what phase-based chronologies attempt imperfectly to chart, is when things happened and how rapidly they changed. With that information in hand, we can better approach the questions of history and process that draw our attention.

ACKNOWLEDGMENTS

We thank the Dickey Center for International Understanding and the Claire Garber Goodman Fund of Dartmouth and the University of Kentucky for their support. Deborah L. Nichols extends her appreciation to the William J. Bryant 1925 Professor of Anthropology. Kristin Sullivan provided invaluable assistance with translations, illustrations, and managing the flow of paperwork. Alex Rahmann, Steven Quinchia, and Alex Tarzy helped with references. We thank Stefan Vranka at Oxford University Press for inviting us to edit the handbook and for gentle prodding. Thanks also to Sarah Pirovitz at Oxford and to Molly Morrison at Newgen North America who oversaw editing and production. We greatly appreciate the care and attention of Linda Gregonis, who prepared the index. We greatly appreciate the efforts of Molly Morrison at Newgen North America who oversaw editing and production and Linda Gregonis who prepared the index. Last, but most important, we thank all of the contributors and our families.

References

Ashmore, Wendy. 2000. "Decisions and Dispositions": Socializing Spatial Archaeology. *American Anthropologist* 104:1172–1183.

Ashmore, Wendy. 2009. Mesoamerican Landscape Archaeologies. *Ancient Mesoamerica* 20:183–188.

Balkansky, Andrew K. 2002. *The Sola Valley and the Monte Albán State: A Study of Zapotec Imperial Expansion*. Museum of Anthropology Memoir 36, University of Michigan, Ann Arbor.

Berdan, Frances F., Richard E. Blanton, Elizabeth Hill Boone, Mary G. Hodge, Michael E. Smith, and Emily Umberger, eds. 1996. *Aztec Imperial Strategies*. Dumbarton Oaks Research Library and Collections, Washington, DC.

Berdan, Frances F., John K. Chance, Alan R. Sandstrom, Barbara Stark, James Taggert, and Emily Umberger, eds. 2008. *Ethnic Identity in Nahua Mesoamerica*. University of Utah Press, Salt Lake City.

Bernal, Ignacio. 1980. *A History of Mexican Archaeology: The Vanished Civilizations of Middle America*. Thames and Hudson, London.

Biersack, Aletta. 2006. Reimagining Political Ecology: Culture/Power/History/Nature. In *Reimagining Political Ecology*, edited by Aletta Biersack and James Greenberg, pp. 3–40. Duke University Press, Durham.

Blanton, Richard E. 1981. The Rise of Cities. In *Supplement to the Handbook of Middle American Indians Vol. 1 Archaeology*, edited by Jeremy A. Sabloff, 392–402. University of Texas Press, Austin.

Blanton, Richard E. 1996. The Basin of Mexico Market System and the Growth of Empire. In *Aztec Imperial Strategies*, edited by Frances F. Berdan, Richard E. Blanton, Elizabeth Hill Boone, Mary G. Hodge, Michael E. Smith, and Emily Umberger, pp. 47–84. Dumbarton Oaks Research Library and Collections, Washington, DC.

Blanton, Richard E., and Lane F. Fagher. 2008. *Collective Action in the Formation of Pre-Modern States*. Springer, New York.

Blanton, Richard E., and Lane F. Fagher. 2009. Collective Action in the Evolution of Pre-Modern States. *Social Evolution and History* 8:133–166.

Blanton, Richard E., and Lane F. Fagher. 2010. Evaluating Causal Factors in Market Development in Premodern States: A Comparative Study, with Critical Comments on the History of Ideas about Markets. In *Archaeological Approaches to Market Exchange in Ancient Societies*, edited by Christopher P. Garraty and Barbara L. Stark, pp. 207–226.

Blanton, Richard E., and Gary M. Feinman. 1984. The Mesoamerican World System. *American Anthropologist* 86:673–682.

Blanton, Richard E., Gary M. Feinman, Stephen A. Kowalewski, and Peter N. Peregrine. 1996. A Dual-Processual Theory for the Evolution of Mesoamerican Civilization. *Current Anthropology* 37:1–14.

Blanton, Richard E., and Stephen Kowalewski. 1981. Monte Albán and After in the Valley of Oaxaca. In *Handbook of Middle American Indians Supplement Volume 1, Archaeology*, edited by J. A. Sabloff, pp. 94–116. University of Texas Press, Austin.

Bourdieu, Pierre. 1977. *Outline of a Theory of Practice*. Cambridge University Press, Cambridge.

Braun, David P. 1995. Style, Selection, and Historicity. In *Style, Society, and Person: Archaeological and Ethnological Perspectives*, edited by Christopher Carr and Jill E. Neitzel, pp. 123–140. Plenum Press, New York.

Brumfiel, Elizabeth M. 1992. Distinguished Lecture in Archaeology: Breaking and Entering the Ecosystem—Gender, Class, and Faction Steal the Show. *American Anthropologist* 94:551–567.

Brumfiel, Elizabeth M. 2000. The Politics of High Culture: Issues of Worth and Rank. In *Order, Legitimacy, and Wealth in Ancient States*, edited by Janet Richards and Mary Van Buren, pp. 131–139. Cambridge University Press, Cambridge.

Brumfiel, Elizabeth M. 2006. Methods in Gender and Feminist Archaeology: A Feeling for Difference—and Likeness. In *Handbook of Gender in Archaeology*, edited by Sarah Milledge Nelson, pp. 31–58. Altamira Press, Oxford.

Brumfiel, Elizabeth M., and Deborah L. Nichols. 2009. Bitumen, Blades, and Beads, Prehispanic Craft Production and the Domestic Economy. In *Housework: Craft Production and Domestic Economy in Ancient Mesoamerica*, edited by Kenneth G. Hirth, pp. 239–251. Archaeological Papers of the American Anthropological Association, no. 19. Wiley-Blackwell, Hoboken, New Jersey.

Canuto, Marcello A., and Jason Yaeger. 2000. *The Archaeology of Communities: A New World Perspective*. Routledge, London.

Carrasco, David. 2001a. Preface. In *The Oxford Encyclopedia of Mesoamerican Cultures: The Civilizations of Mexico and Central America*, edited by Davíd Carrasco, pp. ix–xvii. Oxford University Press, Oxford.

Carrasco, Davíd, ed. 2001b. *The Oxford Encyclopedia of Mesoamerican Cultures: The Civilizations of Mexico and Central America*. Oxford University Press, Oxford.

Castañeda, Quetzil E. 1996. *In the Museum of Maya Culture: Touring Chichen Itzá*. University of Minnesota Press, Minneapolis.

Charlton, Thomas H., and Deborah L. Nichols. 1997. The City-State Concept: Development and Applications. In *The Archaeology of City-States: Cross-Cultural Approaches*, edited by Deborah L. Nichols and Thomas H. Charlton, pp. 1–15. Smithsonian Institution Press, Washington, DC.

Chase, Arlen F., Diane Z. Chase, and Michael E. Smith. 2009. States and Empires in Ancient Mesoamerica. *Ancient Mesoamerica* 20:175–187.

Chase, Arlen, Diane Z. Chase, John F. Weishampel, Jason B. Drake, Ramesh L. Shrestha, Clint Slatton, Jaime Awe, and William E. Carter. 2011. Airborne LiDAR, Archaeology, and the Ancient Maya Landscape at Caracol, Belize. *Journal of Archaeological Science* 38:387–398.

Clark, John E. 2000. Toward a Better Explanation of Hereditary Inequality: A Critical Assessment of Natural and Historic Human Agents. In *Agency in*

Archaeology, edited by Marcia-Anne Dobres and John Robb, pp. 92–112. Routledge, London.

Clark, John E., and Michael Blake. 1994. The Power of Prestige: Competitive Generosity and the Emergence of Rank Societies in Lowland Mesoamerica. In *Factional Competition and Political Development in the New World*, edited by Elizabeth M. Brumfiel and John W. Fox, pp. 17–30. Cambridge University Press, Cambridge.

Clark, John E., and David Cheetham. 2005. Cerámica del formativo de Chiapas. In *La producción alfarera en el México antiguo, Volumen I,* edited by Beatriz Leonor Merino Carrión and Ángel Garcia Cook, pp. 285–433. Instituto Nacional de Antropología e Historia, México City.

Coe, Michael D. 1981. San Lorenzo Tenochtitlan. In *Supplement to the Handbook of Middle American Indians*, edited by Jeremy A. Sabloff, pp. 117–146. University of Texas Press, Austin.

Coe, Michael D. 1992. *Breaking the Maya Code*. Thames and Hudson, New York.

Conkey, Meg W. 1997. Programme to Practice: Gender and Feminism in Archaeology. *Annual Review of Anthropology* 26:411–437.

Cowgill, George L. 1993. Distinguished Lecture in Archeology: Beyond Criticizing New Archeology. *American Anthropologist* 95:551–573.

Cowgill, George. 2000. "Rationality" and Contexts in Agency Theory. In *Agency in Archaeology,* edited by Marcia Anne Dobres and John Robb, pp. 51-60. Routledge, London

Dahlin, Bruce H., Christopher T. Jensen, Richard E. Terry, David R. Wright, and Timothy Beach. 2007. In Search of an Ancient Maya Market. *Latin American Antiquity* 18:363–384.

Demarest, Arthur. 2004. *Ancient Maya: Rise and Fall of a Rainforest Civilization.* Cambridge University Press, Cambridge.

Demarest, Arthur. 2009. Maya Archaeology for the Twenty-First Century: The Progress, the Perils, and the Promise. *Ancient Mesoamerica* 20:233–240.

Demarest, Arthur A., Prudence M. Rice, and Don S. Rice, eds. 2004. *The Terminal Classic in the Maya Lowlands: Collapse, Transition, and Transformation.* University Press of Colorado, Boulder.

Drennan, Robert D. 2000. Games, Players, Rules, and Circumstances: Looking for Understandings of Social Change. In *Cultural Evolution: Contemporary Viewpoints*, edited by Gary M. Feinman and Linda Manzanilla, pp. 177–196. Kluwer/Plenum, New York.

Dunnell, Robert C. 1980. Evolutionary Theory and Archaeology. In *Advances in Archaeological Method and Theory*, Vol. 3, edited by Michael B. Schiffer, pp. 35–99. Academic Press, New York.

Earle, Timothy. 1997. *How Chiefs Come to Power: The Political Economy in Prehistory.* Stanford University Press, Stanford.

Evans, Susan T. 2008. *Ancient Mexico and Central America: Archaeology and Culture History.* 2nd ed. Thames and Hudson, London.

Evans, Susan T., and David L. Webster, eds. 2001. *Archaeology of Ancient Mexico and Central America: An Encyclopedia.* Garland, New York.

Feinman, Gary M., and Linda Manzanilla, eds. 2000. *Cultural Evolution: Contemporary Viewpoints.* Kluwer Academic/Plenum, New York.

Feinman, Gary M., and Linda M. Nicholas. 2004. Unraveling the Prehispanic Highland Mesoamerican Economy: Production, Exchange, and Consumption in the Classic Period Valley of Oaxaca. In *Archaeological Perspectives on Political Economies*,

edited by Gary M. Feinman and Linda M. Nicholas, pp. 167–188. University of Utah
Press, Salt Lake City.

Fisher, Christopher T., J. Brett Hill, and Gary M. Feinman. 2009. Introduction:
Environmental Studies for the Twenty-First Century. In *The Archaeology of
Environmental Change: Socionatural Legacies of Degradation and Resilience*, edited
by Christopher T. Fisher, J. Brett Hill, and Gary M. Feinman, pp. 1–14. University of
Arizona Press, Tucson.

Flannery, Kent V., and Joyce Marcus, eds. 1983. *The Cloud People: Divergent Evolution of
the Zapotec and Mixtec Civilizations*, Academic Press, New York.

Flannery, Kent V., Joyce Marcus, and Stephen Kowalewski. 1981. The Preceramic and
Formative in the Valley of Oaxaca. In *Archaeology: Supplement to the Handbook of
Middle American Indians*, edited by Jeremy Sabloff, pp. 48–93. University of Texas
Press, Austin.

García Cook, Angel. 1981. The Historical Importance of Tlaxcala in the Cultural
Development of the Central Highlands. In *Archaeology: Supplement to the
Handbook of Middle American Indians*, edited by Jeremy A. Sabloff, pp. 244–276.
University of Texas Press, Austin.

Garraty, Christopher P., and Barbara L. Stark, eds. 2010. *Archaeological Approaches to
Market Exchange in Ancient Societies*. University of Colorado Press, Boulder.

García-Bárcena, Joaquín. 2007. Law and the Practice of Archaeology in Mexico. *SAA
Archaeological Record* 7(5):14–15.

Gero, Joan M. 2000. Troubled Travels in Agency and Feminism. In *Agency in
Archaeology*, edited by Marcia-Anne Dobres and John Robb, pp. 34–39. Routledge,
London.

Geurds, Alexander. 2007. *Grounding the Past: The Praxis of Participatory Archaeology in
the Mixteca Alta, Oaxaca, Mexico*. CNWS Publications, Leiden, The Netherlands.

Giddens, Anthony. 1979. *Central Problems in Social Theory*. Macmillan, London.

Giddens, Anthony. 1984. *The Constitution of Society: Outline of the Theory of
Structuration*. Polity Press, Cambridge.

Gill, Richardson B. 2000. *The Great Maya Droughts: Water, Life, and Death*. University of
New Mexico Press, Albuquerque.

Gillespie, Susan D. 2000. Lévi-Strauss: Maison and Société à Maisons. In *Beyond Kinship:
Social and Material Reproduction in House Societies*, edited by Rosemary Joyce and
Susan D. Gillespie, pp. 22–52. University of Pennsylvania Press, Philadelphia.

Halperin, Christina T., Katherine A. Faust, Rhonda Taube, and Aurore Giguet, eds.
2009. *Mesoamerican Figurines: Small Scale Indices of Large-Scale Social Phenomena*.
University Press of Florida, Gainesville.

Hassig, Ross. 2006. *Mexico and the Spanish Conquest*. 2nd ed. University of Oklahoma
Press, Norman.

Hegmon, Michelle. 2003. Setting Theoretical Egos Aside: Issues and Theory in North
American Archaeology. *American Antiquity* 68:213–243.

Hirth, Kenneth G. 1996. Political Economy and Archaeology: Perspectives on Exchange
and Production. *Journal of Archaeological Research* 4:203–239.

Hirth, Kenneth G. 1998. The Distributional Approach: A New Way to Identify
Marketplace Exchange in the Archaeological Record. *Current Anthropology*
4:203–240.

Hirth, Kenneth G. 2009. Craft Production, Household Diversification, and Domestic
Economy in Prehispanic Mesoamerica. In *Housework: Craft Production and
Domestic Economy in Ancient Mesoamerica*, edited by Kenneth G. Hirth, pp. 13–32.

Archaeological Papers of the American Anthropological Association, no. 19. Wiley-Blackwell, Hoboken, New Jersey.

Hodge, Mary G. 1997. When Is a City-State? Archaeological Measures of Aztec City-States and Aztec City-State Systems. In *The Archaeology of City-States: Cross Cultural Approaches*, edited by Deborah L. Nichols and Thomas H. Charlton, pp. 209–228. Smithsonian Institution Press, Washington, DC.

Hodge, Mary G., Hector Neff, M. James Blackman, and Leah D. Minc. 1992. A Compositional Perspective on Ceramic Production in the Aztec Empire. In *Chemical Characterization of Ceramic Pastes in Archaeology*, edited by Hector Neff, pp. 203–231. Monographs in World Archaeology, no. 7. Prehistory Press, Madison, Wisconsin.

Hodge, Mary G., Hector Neff, M. James Blackman, and Leah D. Minc. 1993. Black-on-Orange Ceramic Production in the Aztec Empire's Heartland. *Latin American Antiquity* 4:130–157.

Houston, Stephen D., Oswaldo Chinchilla Mazariegos, and David Stuart, eds. 2001. *The Decipherment of Ancient Maya Writing*. University of Oklahoma Press, Norman.

Ingold, Tim. 2000. *The Perception of the Environment: Essays on Livelihood, Dwelling, and Skill*. Routledge, London.

Instituto Nacional de Antropología e Historia (INAH). 2010a. Archaeologists Locate the Entrance to Teotihuacan Tunnel. Electronic document, http://www.inah.gob.mx/index.php/english-press-releases/59-findings/94-archaeologists-locate-the-entrance-to-teotihuacan-tunnel- (accessed August 21, 2011).

Instituto Nacional de Antropología e Historia (INAH). 2010b. Descruben túnel de Teotihuacan. Electronic document, http://www.youtube.com/watch?v=PPp72MhGIJE&feature=related (accessed August 21, 2011).

Instituto Nacional de Antropología e Historia (INAH). 2010c. Robot en túnel de Teotihuacan. Electronic document, http://www.youtube.com/watch?v=4By4Wf_SPXA&feature=related (accessed August 21, 2011).

Ivic de Monterroso, Matilde. 2004. The Sacred Place in the Development of Archaeology in Guatemala: An Analysis. In *Continuities and Changes in Maya Archaeology: Perspectives at the Millennium*, edited by Charles W. Golden and Greg Borgstede, pp. 295–308. Routledge, New York.

Jones, Christopher, William R. Coe, and William A. Haviland. 1981. Tikal: An Outline of Its Field Study (1956–1970) and a Project Bibliography. In *Archaeology: Supplement to the Handbook of Middle American Indians*, edited by J. A. Sabloff, pp. 296–312. University of Texas Press, Austin.

Joyce, Arthur A. 2009. Theorizing Urbanism in Ancient Mesoamerica. *Ancient Mesoamerica* 20:189–197.

Joyce, Rosemary. 2001. *Gender and Power in Prehispanic Mesoamerica*. University of Texas Press, Austin.

Kennett, Douglas J., and Bruce Winterhalder, eds. 2006. *Behavioral Ecology and the Transition to Agriculture*. University of California Press, Berkeley.

Litvak King, Jaime. 1985. Mesoamerica: Events and Processes, the Last 50 Years. *American Antiquity* 50:374–382.

Kirchhoff, Paul. 1943. Mesoamérica. Sus Límites Geográficos, Composición Étnica y Caracteres Culturales. *Acta Americana* 1 (1):92–107.

Kowalewski, Stephen A., Andrew K. Balkansky, Laura R. Stiver Walsh, Thomas Pluckhahan, John F. Chamblee, Verónica Pérez Rodríguez, Verenice Y. Heredia

Espinoza, and Charlotte A. Smith. 2009. *Origins of the Ñuu: Archaeology in the Mixteca Alta, Mexico*. University of Colorado Press, Boulder.

Kowalewski, Stephen A., Gary M. Feinman, Laura Finsten, Richard E. Blanton, and Linda Nicholas. 1989. *Monte Albán's Hinterland, Part II: Prehispanic Settlement Patterns in Tlacolula, Etla, and Ocotlán, the Valley of Oaxaca, Mexico*. Museum of Anthropology Memoir 23. University of Michigan, Ann Arbor.

Kubler, George. 1970. Period, Style and Meaning in Ancient American Art. *New Literary History* 1(2):127–144.

Kubler, George. 1975. *The Art and Architecture of Ancient America: The Mexican, Maya, and Andean People*. 2nd ed. Penguin Books, Middlesex.

Leshikar-Denton, Margaret E., and Pilar Luna Erreguerena. 2008. *Underwater and Maritime Archaeology in Latin American and the Caribbean*. Left Coast Press, San Francisco.

Lesure, Richard G. 2011a. Early Social Transformations in the Soconusco: An Introduction. In *Early Mesoamerican Social Transformations: Archaic and Formative Lifeways in the Soconusco Region*, edited by Richard G. Lesure, pp. 1–24. Cotsen Institute of Archaeology, University of California, Los Angeles.

Lesure, Richard G. 2011b. *Interpreting Ancient Figurines: Context, Comparison, and Prehistoric Art*. Cambridge University Press, Cambridge.

Lorenzo, José Luis. 1976. La arqueología Mexicana y los arqueólogs noreamericanos. Cuadernos de Trabjo, Apuntes para la Arqueología 14. Departmento de Prehistoria, Instituto Nacional de Antropología e Historia, Mexico, D.F.

Lorenzo, José Luis. 1981. Archaeology South of the Rio Grande. *World Archaeology* 13:190–208.

Lumberas, Luis. 1974. *La arqueología comoe cienca social*. Ediciones Histar, Lima.

MacNeish, Richard S. 1981. Tehuacan's Accomplishments. In *Archaeology: Supplement to the Handbook of Middle American Indians*, edited by Jeremy Sabloff, pp. 31–47. University of Texas Press, Austin.

Manzanilla, Linda. 1997. *Emergence and Change in Early Urban Societies*. Plenum Press, New York.

Manzanilla, Linda, and Claude Chapdelaine. 2009. *Domestic Life in Prehispanic Capitals: A Study of Specialization, Hierarchy, and Ethnicity*. Memoirs of the Museum of Anthropology, No. 46. University of Michigan, Ann Arbor.

Manzanilla, Linda, and Leaonardo López Luján, eds. 1995–2000. *Historia Antigua de México*. 4 vols. Instituto Nacional de Antropología e Historia, México, D.F.

Marcus, Joyce. 1998. The Peaks and Valleys of Ancient States: An Extension of the Dynamic Model. In *Archaic States*, edited by Gary M. Feinman and Joyce Marcus, pp. 59–94. School of American Research Press, Santa Fe.

Marcus, Joyce, and Kent V. Flannery. 1996. *Zapotec Civilization: How Urban Society Evolved in Mexico's Oaxaca Valley*. Thames and Hudson, London.

Marcus, Joyce, and Ronald Spores. 1978. The Handbook of Middle American Indians: A Retrospective Look. *American Anthropologist* 80:85–100.

Martínez Muriel, Alejandro. 2007. The State Control on Archaeology in Mexico. *SAA Archaeological Record* 7(5):16–19.

Mastache, Alba Guadalupe, Robert H. Cobean, Ángel García Cook, and Kenneth G. Hirth, eds. 2008. *El Urbanismo en Mesoamérica, Urbanism in Mesoamerica*, Vol. 2. Instituto Nacional de Antropología e Historia, and Pennsylvania State University, Mexico, D.F., and University Park.

Matos Moctezuma, Eduardo. 1979. Las corrientes arqueológicas en México. *Nueva Antropología* 3(12):7–26.

Mauss, Marcel. 1950. *Essai su le don*. Presses Universitaires de France, Paris.

McAnany, Patricia. 1994. *Living with the Ancestors*. University of Texas Press, Austin.

McAnany, Patricia. 2010. *Ancestral Maya Economies in Archaeological Perspective*. Cambridge University Press, New York.

McAnany, Patricia, and Stephen D. Houston. 2003. Bodies and Blood: Critiquing Social Construction in Maya Archaeology. *Journal of Anthropological Archaeology* 22:26–41.

McAnany, Patricia, and Norman Yoffee, eds. 2010. *Questioning Collapse: Human Resilience, Ecological Vulnerability, and the Aftermath of Empire*. Cambridge University Press, Cambridge.

Millon, René. 1981. Teotihuacan: City, State, and Civilization. In *Archaeology: Supplement to the Handbook of Middle American Indians*, edited by Jeremy Sabloff, pp. 198–243. University of Texas Press, Austin.

Minc, Leah D. 2009. Style and Substance: Evidence for Regionalism within the Aztec Market System. *Latin American Antiquity* 2:343–374.

Montejo, Victor D. 1999. The Year Bearer's People: Repatriation of Ethnographic and Sacred Knowledge to the Jakaltek Maya of Guatemala. *International Journal of Cultural Property* 8(1):151–166.

Montejo, Victor D. 2002. The Multiplicity of Mayan Voices: Mayan Leadership and the Politics of Self- Representation. In *Indigenous Movements, Self-Representation, and the State in Latin America*, edited by Kay B. Warren and Jean E. Jackson, pp. 123–148. University of Texas Press, Austin.

Neff, Hector. 1992. Ceramics and Evolution. In *Archaeological Method and Theory*, vol. 4, edited by Michael J. Schiffer, pp. 141–193. University of Arizona Press, Tucson.

Neff, Hector. 1995. A Role for "Sourcing" in Evolutionary Archaeology. In *Evolutionary Archaeology: Methodological Issues*, edited by Patrice Teltser, pp. 69–112. University of Arizona Press, Tucson.

Neiman, Fraser D. 1997. Conspicuous Consumption as Wasteful Advertising: A Darwinian Perspective on Spatial Patterns in Classic Maya Terminal Monument Dates. In *Rediscovering Darwin: Evolutionary Theory and Archaeological Explanation*, edited by C. Michael Barton and Geoffrey A. Clark, pp. 267–290. Archaeological Papers of the American Anthropological Association, No. 7. Arlington, Virginia.

Nichols, Deborah L. 1996. An Overview of Regional Settlement Pattern Survey in Mesoamerica. In *Arqueologia Mesoamericana: Homenaje a William T. Sanders*, 2 vols., edited by A. Guadalupe Mastache, Jeffrey R. Parsons, Mari Carmen Serre Puche, and Robert S. Santley, Vol. 1, pp. 59–96. Insituto Nacional de Antropología e Historia, Mexico, D.F.

Nichols, Deborah L. 2006. Archaeology on Foot: Jeffrey Parsons and Anthropology at the University of Michigan. In *Retrospectives: Works and Lives of Michigan Anthropologists*, edited by Derek Brereton, pp. 106–135. Michigan Discussions in Anthropology, Vol. 16. University of Michigan, Ann Arbor.

Nichols, Deborah L., Elizabeth M. Brumfiel, Hector Neff, Mary Hodge, Thomas H. Charlton, and Michael D. Glascock. 2002. Neutrons, Markets, Cities, and Empires: A 1,000-Year Perspective on Ceramic Production and Distribution in the Postclassic Basin of Mexico. *Journal of Anthropological Archaeology* 21:25–82.

Ortner, Sherry. 1984. Theory in Anthropology Since the Sixties. *Comparative Studies in Society and History* 26:126–166.

Oudijk, Michel R., and Matthew Restall. 2008. *La conquista indígena de Mesoamérica: El caso de Don Gonzalo Mazatzin Moctezuma*. Secretaria de Cultura del Estado de

Puebla/Universidad de las Américas Puebla/Instituto Nacional de Antropología e Historia, Puebla.

Oyuela-Caycedo, Armando Anaya, Carol G. Elera, and Lido M. Valdez. 1997. Social Archaeology in Latin America: Comments to T. C. Patterson. *American Antiquity* 62:365–374.

Parsons, Jeffrey R., and Luis Morrett. 2004. Recursos acuaticos en le subsistencia Azteca: Cazadores, rescadores, y recolectores. *Arqueología Mexicana* 12(8):28–43.

Pasztory, Esther. 2005. *Thinking with Things: Toward a New Vision of Art*. University of Texas Press, Austin.

Plunket, Patricia. 2002. *Domestic Ritual in Ancient Mesoamerica*. Cotsen Institute of Archaeology Monograph 26. University of California, Los Angeles.

Plunket, Patricia, and Gabriela Uruñuela. 2006. Social and Cultural Consequences of a Late Holocene Eruption of Popocatépetl in Central Mexico. *Quaternary International* 151:19–28.

Pohl, Mary E. D., Dolores R. Piperno, Kevin O. Pope, and John G. Jones. 2007. Microfossil Evidence for Pre-Columbian Maize Dispersals in the Neotropics from San Andrés, Tabasco, Mexico. *Proceedings of the National Academy of Sciences USA* 104:6870–6875.

Politis, Gustavo. 1999. Latin American Archaeology: An Inside View. In *Archaeology in Latin America*, edited by Gustavo C. Politis and Benjamin Alberti, pp. 1–13. Routledge, London.

Pool, Christopher A. 2007. *Olmec Archaeology and Early Mesoamerica*. Cambridge University Press, Cambridge.

Pool, Christopher A., and George J. Bey III, eds. 2007. *Pottery Economies in Mesoamerica*. University of Arizona Press, Tucson.

Pool, Christopher A., and George Mudd Britt. 2000. A Ceramic Perspective on the Formative to Classic Transition in Southern Veracruz. *Latin American Antiquity* 10:139–161.

Pool, Christopher A., and Lisa Cliggett. 2008. Introduction: Economies and the Transformation of Landscapes. In *Economies and the Transformation of Landscape*, edited by Lisa Cliggett and Christopher A. Pool, pp. 1–16. Altamira Press, Walnut Creek, California.

Preucel, Robert W., and Stephen A. Mrozowki. 2010. *Contemporary Archaeology in Theory: The New Pragmatism*. 2nd ed. Wiley-Blackwell, Malden, Massachusetts.

Renfrew, Colin. 1998. Towards a Cognitive Archaeology. In *The Ancient Mind: Elements of Cognitive Archaeology*, edited by Colin Renfrew and Ezra Zubrow, pp. 3–12. Cambridge University Press, Cambridge.

Robin, Cynthia. 2002. Outside of Houses: The Practices of Everyday Life at Chan Nòohol, Belize. *Journal of Social Archaeology* 2:245–268.

Robin, Cynthia, and Nan A. Rothschild. 2002. Archaeological Ethnographies: Social Dynamics of Outdoor Space. *Journal of Social Archaeology* 2:159–172.

Robles, Nelly García. 2007. The Practice of Archaeology in Mexico: Institutional Obligations and Scientific Results. *SAA Archaeological Record* 7(5):9–11.

Robles, Nelly García. 2000. The Management of Archaeological Resources in Mexico: The Case of Oaxaca. Electronic document, http://www.saa.org/AbouttheSociety/Publications/TheManagementofArchaeologicalResourcesinMexi/AuthorsNote/tabid/1095/Default.aspx (accessed 19 August 2011).

Rodríguez-Alegría, Enrique. 2008. Narratives of Conquest, Colonialism, and Cutting-Edge Technology. *American Anthropologist* 110:33–43.

Roseberry, W. 1988. Political Economy. *Annual Review of Anthropology* 17:161–185.

Rosenswig, Robert M. 2010. *The Beginnings of Mesoamerican Civilization: Interregional Interaction and the Olmec*. Cambridge University Press, Cambridge.

Rowe, John H. 1960. Cultural Unity and Diversification in Peruvian Archaeology. In *Men and Cultures*, edited by Anthony F. C. Wallace, pp. 627–631. Selected Papers of the Fifth International Congress of Anthropological and Ethnological Sciences. University of Pennsylvania Press, Philadelphia.

Sabloff, Jeremy A., ed. 1981. *Archaeology: Supplement to the Handbook of Middle American Indians*. University of Texas Press, Austin.

Sabloff, Jeremy A., and Wendy Ashmore. 2001. An Aspect of Archaeology's Recent Past and Its Relevance in the New Millennium. In *Archaeology at the New Millennium: A Sourcebook*, edited by Gary M. Feinman and T. Douglas Price, pp. 11–32. Kluwer Academic/Plenum, New York.

Sanders, William T. 1981. Ecological Adaption in the Basin of Mexico: 23,000 B.C. to the Present. In *Archaeology: Supplement to the Handbook of Middle American Indians*, edited by Jeremy Sabloff, pp. 147–197. University of Texas Press, Austin.

Sanders, William T., Alba Guadalupe Mastache, and Robert H. Cobean. 2003. *El urbanismo en Mesoamérica/Urbanism in Mesoamerica Vol. 1*. Instituto Nacional de Antropología e Historia, and Pennsylvania State University, Mexico, D.F., and University Park.

Sanders, William T., Jeffrey R. Parsons, and Robert S. Santley. 1979. *The Basin of Mexico: Ecological Process in the Evolution of a Civilization*. Academic Press, New York.

Sanders, William T., and David Webster. 1978. Unilinealism, Multilinealism, and the Evolution of Complex Societies. In *Social Archeology: Beyond Subsistence and Dating*, edited by C. L. Redman, M. J. Berman, E. V. Curtin Jr., W. T. Langhorne, N. M. Versaggi, and J. C. Wanser, pp. 249–302. Academic Press, New York.

Sanders, William T., and David Webster. 1988. The Mesoamerican Urban Tradition. *American Anthropologist* 90:521–546.

Sanders, William T., and David Webster. 1989. "The Mesoamerican Urban Tradition": A Reply to Smith. *American Anthropologist* 90:460–461.

Santley, Robert S., and Rani Alexander. 1992. The Political Economy of Core-Periphery Systems. In *Resources, Power, and Interregional Interactions*, edited by Edward Schortman and Patricia Urban, pp. 23–50. Plenum Press, New York.

Santley, Robert S., Steven Nelson, Bentley K. Reinhart, Christopher A. Pool, and Philip J. Arnold III. 2001. When Day Turned to Night: Volcanism and the Archaeological Record from the Tuxtla Mountains, Southern Veracruz, Mexico. In *Environmental Disaster and the Archaeology of Human Response*, edited by Garth Bawden and Richard M. Reycraft, pp. 143–162. Anthropological Papers No. 7, Maxwell Museum of Anthropology, University of New Mexico, Albuquerque.

Scarborough, Vernon L. 2009. The Archaeology of Sustainability: Mesoamerica. *Ancient Mesoamerica* 20:197–204.

Scarborough, Vernon L., and William R. Burnside. 2010. Complexity and Sustainability: Perspectives from the Ancient Maya and the Modern Balinese. *American Antiquity* 75:327–363.

Sheets, Payson. 2008. Armageddon to the Garden of Eden: Explosive Volcanic Eruptions and Societal Resilience in Ancient Middle America. In *Central America and Mesoamerica*, edited by Daniel Sandweiss, pp. 177–196. Dumbarton Oaks, Washington, DC.

Smith, Michael. 2007. Form and Meaning in the Earliest Cities: A New Approach to Ancient Urban Planning. *Journal of Planning History* 6:3–47.

Smith, Michael. 2008. *Aztec City-State Capitals*. University Press of Florida, Gainesville.

Smith, Michael E., and Frances Berdan, eds. 2003. *The Postclassic Mesoamerican World*. University of Utah Press, Salt Lake City.

Snow, Dean R., Mark Gehegan, C. Lee Giles, Kenneth G. Hirth, George R. Milner, Prasenjit Mitra, and James Z. Wang. 2006. Cybertools and Archaeology. *Science* 311:958–959.

Spence, Michael W., and Christine White. 2009. Mesoamerican Bioarchaeology: Past and Future. *Ancient Mesoamerica* 20:233–240.

Spencer, Charles S. 2010. Territorial Expansion and Primary State Formation. *Proceedings of the National Academy of Sciences USA* 107:7119–7126.

Spencer, Charles S., and Elsa M. Redmond. 2001. Multilevel Selection and Political Evolution in the Valley of Oaxaca 500–100 BC. *Journal of Anthropological Archaeology* 20:195–229.

Stahle. D. W., J. Villanueva Diaz, D. J. Burnette, J. Cerano Pareds, R. R. Heim Jr., F. K. Fuey, R. Acuna Soto, M. D. Therrell, M. K. Cleaveland, and D. K. Stahle. 2011. Major Mesoamerican Droughts of the Past Millennium. Electronic document, *Geophysical Research Letters* 38: L05703, doi:10.1029/2010GL046472 (accessed September 9, 2011).

Stark, Barbara L. 2008. Polity and Economy in the Western Lower Papaloapan Basin. In *Classic Period Cultural Currents in Southern and Central Veracruz*, edited by Phillip J. Arnold III and Christopher A. Pool, pp. 85–119. Dumbarton Oaks Research Library and Collection, Washington, DC.

Trigger, Bruce G. 1984. Alternative Archaeologies: Nationalist, Colonialist, Imperialist. *Man* 19:355–370.

Trigger, Bruce G. 1991. Distinguished Lecture in Archaeology: Constraint and Freedom—A New Synthesis for Archaeological Explanation. *American Anthropologist* 93:551–569.

Trigger, Bruce G. 1995. Expanding Middle-Range Theory. *Antiquity* 69:449–458.

Trigger, Bruce G. 2003. *Understanding Early Civilizations: A Comparative Study*. Cambridge University Press, Cambridge.

Trigger, Bruce G. 2006. *A History of Archaeological Thought*. 2nd ed. Cambridge University Press, New York.

Wallerstein, Immanuel. 1974. *The Modern World System, Vol. 1: Capitalist Agriculture and the Origins of the European World-Economy, 1600–1750*. Academic Press, New York.

Wallerstein, Immanuel. 1979. *The Capitalist World Economy*. Cambridge University Press, Cambridge.

Watanabe, John M. 2004. Some Models in a Muddle: Lineage and House in Classic Maya Social Organization. *Ancient Mesoamerica* 15:159–166.

Wilk, Richard R. 1996. *Economies and Cultures: Foundations of Economic Anthropology*. Westview Press, Boulder.

Willey, Gordon, and Jeremy Sabloff. 1980. *A History of American Archaeology*. W. H. Freeman, San Francisco.

Wolf, Eric R. 1959. *Sons of the Shaking Earth*. University of Chicago Press, Chicago.

Wolf, Eric R. 1982. *Europe and the People without History*. University of California Press, Berkeley.

Yoffee, Norman. 2005. *Myths of the Archaic State*. Cambridge University Press, Cambridge.

PART I

THEORY, METHOD,
AND PRACTICE IN
MESOAMERICAN
ARCHAEOLOGY

CHAPTER 2

A SHORT HISTORY OF THEORY IN MESOAMERICAN ARCHAEOLOGY

MANUEL GÁNDARA

MESOAMERICAN ARCHAEOLOGY, THEORETICAL IN SPITE OF ITSELF

Some Mesoamericanist archaeologists may still identify with the character created by Flannery (1976: 2), the archetypical "real Mesoamerican archaeologist": "beer drinker, hell raiser, pub crawler, satyr, nymphomaniac and great story teller," who gets bored with theoretical discussions, dislikes statistical sampling, and loves to dig "telephone booths" using artificial levels (1976: 3, 6–7, 132, 286). While this might be an already extinct species, the portrait still rings true. Alas, the fast advance in Mesoamerican archaeology has been attributed, among other factors, to our avoidance of "sterile, purely methodological exercises," less important than learning about the past: "the subject is people, not archaeology or its practitioners" (Blanton et al. 1993: 7).

But writing even a short history of Mesoamerican archaeology is impossible without reflecting about it to answer three questions: what *is* "Mesoamerican archaeology"? When did it start? Are there periods or trends along its development?

As for the first question, the term "Mesoamerica" itself reflects a clear theoretical persuasion, derived both from American historical particularism and Europe's culture history and diffusionism (Harris 1979 [1968]: 323–339). While Paul Kirchhoff was a committed Marxist (García Mora 1996: 227, 1979; Kirchhoff 1979), the only indication of this in his classic 1943 article (Kirchhoff 2009: 3) is the insistence on intensive agriculture as one of the main defining features of "high cultures" (2009: 13). He cautioned that his delimitation applied only to the sixteenth century and that research was needed before projecting it to the past (Kirchhoff 2009: 1). His advice was not followed: for many colleagues this is just a conventional term, to be used interchangeably with its older cousin, "Middle America," even when their boundaries do not match: Middle America normally encompasses *all* of Mexico and Central America.

Also, talk about *Mesoamerican* hunters and gatherers makes for a convenient terminology but stretches the scope of the concept: they obviously lack intensive agriculture. So, using Kirchhoff's term in a looser, geographical way, a practice I will follow here, already implies a theoretical stance.[1]

The second question requires a criterion to define the beginning of the discipline. The range of dates spans from 1790, for Matos (2002: 10) the birth of Mexican archaeology; to 1935, for Dunnell (1986: 25) the professionalization of archaeology in the United States. Willey and Sabloff (1980: 18) and Daniel (1976: 111), also disagree: the first set of researchers like 1840; the second seems to prefer the 1870s (in England), with the onset of formal schooling, learned societies, and other markers of the start of the discipline as a scientific field in Europe. These differences reflect again differences in theory, evident also regarding the third question, about periods (as previously noticed by Schuyler [1971]): some authors see four (Willey and Phillips 1968: 18), while other see only three (Schmidt 1988: 404), or a different three (Dunnell 1986: 25).

For our purposes, I will use the concept of the "theoretical position." Without entering into its details (but see Gándara 2008), it defines a discipline's subject matter; what goals are considered legitimate, desirable, and achievable; how to go about achieving them; and how is this knowledge constructed and evaluated. Two key elements allow us to differentiate theoretical positions: their cognitive goals and their "ontology"—the way they conceive the reality studied. Here I will attempt to identify the most important theoretical positions in Mesoamerican archaeology, briefly commenting on occasion about some substantive theories.

Thus, the first real theoretical position would be historical particularism, centered on the cognitive goal of *description*, and going from the late 1890s to the 1950s, the "foundational period," followed by neoevolutionism and Marxism with their variants, championing some form of *explanation*, roughly from the late 1950s and onward, in the "theoretical self-awareness period," and finally, in a "theoretical diversification" period, with postprocessual archaeologists pursuing *hermeneutic Interpretation* (from the 1980s onward), and the flourishing of "thematic archaeologies." I will stop around the 1990s, because the recent past is dealt with by Nichols and Pool (this volume).

1. Some do away not only with Kirchhoff's criteria, but also with his credit: for example, Susan Evans does not even mention him in her popular introductory book (Evans 2004).

PRECURSORS

Before the professionalization of archaeology, travelers, explorers, and early scholars were already registering, excavating, and reporting archaeological sites (Willey and Sabloff 1980; Bernal 1979; Matos 2001; due to space constraints, only major references are mentioned, but see "For Further Reading," at the end of the chapter for additional sources). Their questions were the founding ones: How old is this heritage? Who built it? Their main legacy were the first detailed accounts of Mesoamerica's rich heritage, sparking the interest that led eventually to the consolidation of institutions and the beginnings of our discipline.

I shall only mention two highlights: the first is the "founding of archaeology" in Mexico in 1790; Matos (2002) has convincingly argued that León y Gama's work on the monoliths of Coatlicue and the Piedra del Sol started an academic tradition (León y Gama 2009 [1790]): the excavation had a measure of control, but more importantly, the analysis, drawings, and interpretation were promptly published from a university setting. And there was a clear political motivation: in Europe the merits of the Spanish conquest had been challenged, arguing that the conquered people were simple and primitive. For León y Gama the complexity of the monoliths evidenced the high degree of development of their creators. This was also one of the first initiatives of heritage preservation, years earlier still despised and destroyed, since it was considered pagan and "monstrous" (Matos 2002).

The second highlight would be Leopoldo Batres's commission by President Porfirio Díaz to dig and reconstruct buildings in Teotihuacan, as a part of the Centennial of the Independence celebrations in 1910. Archaeology was openly used to build a national identity, even at the expense of the technical quality of the work (Mastache and Cobean 1988: 42; Matos 1998: 55; Bernal 1979: 141). So we find already two of the constants of Mexican archaeology: its intricate connection to politics and the weight of heritage preservation. These are shared in Central America but not necessarily with our North American Mesoamericanist colleagues.

THE FOUNDATION: CULTURE HISTORY

Professionalization happened around the 1900s. With Boas, archaeology became part of the curriculum in blooming anthropology departments that were created at a fast pace by his students. Boas wanted to document cultural variability at a time when the expansion of capitalism was quickly destroying it. This meant organizing variability in space (areas defined on linguistic and cultural terms) and in time (Harris 1979 [1968]: 218–260; Kardiner and Preble 1961: 134–159). But since for many areas there were few historical or linguistic data, archaeology, through the

comparison of stylistic traits (and their patterning), was to construct the equivalent of linguistic groups.

Change in time was important (and archaeologists could not hide it even if
they wanted to). Boas disliked evolution, but he wanted to know the depth as well
as the internal dynamics within culture areas. Middle America was one of them,
so Boas must have been delighted when the Mexican government invited him to be
part of a trinational committee that would start a graduate program in archaeology and ethnography. Together with Seler and Engerrand, who represented Prussia
and France, he founded the International School of Archaeology and Ethnography
(de la Peña 1996: 46). Amazingly, the school functioned for nine years, starting in
1911, in the midst of the Mexican Revolution.

Seler and Engerrand surely made contributions: Seler's "ancient history"—the
study of ethnohistorical sources as well as iconography and art history—was to
become a trademark of Mexican archaeology. But the curriculum was basically
Boasian and would mark later professionalization programs in the region.

Boas promoted Manuel Gamio's work at Azcapotzalco in 1911 that later became
his Ph.D. dissertation at Columbia University. This excavation is widely heralded
as the first "stratigraphical" excavation in Mexico (e.g., de la Peña 1996: 48, foot-
note 6; Willey and Sabloff 1974: 90–91). This is inaccurate. While stratigraphy was
dutifully recorded *post factum*, the excavation itself proceeded by metric intervals.
Thus, it was not really stratigraphical (Mirambell 1988: 4). This comes as no surprise, since the "Wheeler-Kenyon method" of true stratigraphical excavation was
not perfected until the 1930s (Barker 1993; Harris 1989).[2]

Gamio's true claim to fame, however, was the inception of the "Mexican school
(in the sense of style) of archaeology" that would eventually include some of the
greatest Mexican archaeologists: among them, Caso, Bernal, Acosta, Sáenz, Ruz,
Noguera, and the early Piña Chán. Without renouncing culture history, he was
keenly aware of the social responsibilities of archaeology and the opportunities it
afforded for regional development. He was the first to attempt an interdisciplinary, holistic approach in his Teotihuacan Valley project (Gamio 1922), a study that
spanned from the prehispanic past to the present. He even set up training programs and workshops at the site for the local population: concerned with the mar-
ginalization of indigenous and rural populations, he thought archaeology could
help: tourism, craft shops, and, more importantly, the use of the knowledge gained
about prehispanic agricultural techniques to enrich and reinforce current practices.
Gamio later fell from political favor and would eventually abandon archaeology to

---

2. This confusion has subsisted. In the United States both techniques were considered
to be practically interchangeable up to 1973 (see Hole and Heizer 1973:188). Real stratigraphy
was probably introduced from England into Mexico during the 1950s, creating a deep cleav-
age in Mesoamerican archaeology: many archaeologists would contend even today that there
are sites "with no stratigraphy," for which metric intervals are appropriate. Lorenzo (personal
communication, 1973) loved saying that "there is always stratigraphy; what sometimes is lacking is an archaeologist." Later specialists would prove him right (see Harris 1989).

concentrate on the "Indian issue" (de la Peña 1996). But his work would be influential for the creation, in 1938, of the National School of Anthropology (Cárdenas 1993), and, in 1939, of the National Institute of Anthropology and History, with Alfonso Caso as its first director (Olivé 1995).

"Stratigraphical" work in the highlands and epigraphical work in the Maya region soon showed the chronological depth and internal diversity of the area. It is in this milieu that Kirchhoff produced his delimitation of Mesoamerica in 1943. His exact sources are difficult to trace, since he chose not to use references (2009: 3 [re-impression of the 1960 publication of his article]), and it definitely does not show his true orientation (Kirchhoff 1979). But the methodology is clear: you map, compare, and aggregate linguistic and cultural traits into cultural areas; then you trace their development in time, trying to establish contacts, influences, and cultural borrowings that can explain the differences and similarities found. That was to be the archaeologist's job, using ceramic types as the equivalent of cultural norms for delimiting "cultures" and "periods." Since culture was shared, archaeological sites were thought to be homogeneous, making it unnecessary to sample or otherwise control for variability. Under this "normative view," as Aberlee (1960) later called it, culture was a mental phenomenon.

Methodologically, Dunnell (1986: 29–32) claims that corroboration of the ceramic sequences gave culture history its empirical grounding. He is right in that this was not a mindless inductivism, as was later claimed. But he forgets the second component to the equation: ethnic identification. In cases where the direct historical approach was not applicable, typological comparison and patterning would have to do. Hypotheses were the result, not the starting point of research. However, problem orientation started around this time, even if it was restricted to culture-historical problems, such as the identification of Tula, Hidalgo as the "Tollan" of the historical sources (Jiménez Moreno 1941). The aim was "historical explanation" but the real cognitive goal was description or culture-historical narration (Binford 1972 [1968]).

Only in the late 1940s cultural ecology, cultural materialism, and British environmental archaeology introduced a new conception of the environment that went beyond being a mere backdrop, and culture became more than a list of traits. This explains why earlier particularists rarely took paleoenvironmental samples—and some still do not to this day: you can build cultural areas and periods without them.

THEORETICAL SELF-AWARENESS

Criticism of culture history started earlier in the United States (with authors such as Steward and Meltzer, Klukhohn, White, and Taylor, among others [Dunnell 1986; Gándara 1983]). It went almost unnoticed in our region. The impact was felt only when Willey and Phillips introduced settlement archaeology, which borrowed some elements from cultural ecology. After their successful work in Belize and in Perú (Willey 1953), several young archaeologists tried to apply their ideas in Mesoamerica. The most influential would be, without a doubt, William Sanders (e.g., 1952, 1953, 1957).

Sanders combined cultural ecology with what he had learned from Pedro Armillas when he came to Mexico. Armillas, Palerm, and Wolf were deeply interested in one of the theories that Julian Steward had helped popularize: that of "the Asiatic mode of production." Research was to be organized around explicit problems to be solved by long-term research: it was thus that in the 1960s that the projects in the Basin of Mexico were planned (Wolf 1976).

Archaeology was becoming self-aware. In the United States, Willey and Phillips (1968) called for a profound revision of culture history, in order to approach the level of explanation that was sorely missing. In Mexico and Central America the process had a different origin (Gándara, López, and Rodríguez 1985): Armillas, and later José Luis Lorenzo, had introduced the ideas of Vere Gordon Childe, who had almost single-handedly created his own brand of neoevolutionism from a Marxist perspective. This orientation, at once academic and political, was well received in Mexico and other countries: it was congruent with the growing political commitment of archaeologists that in some cases had fled from their countries' political repression. Archaeologists with a leftist orientation applauded Childe's approach. In the United States, coming out of McCarthyism, this would be unthinkable. And there was also the idea that you should never mix science with politics, which many still believe.

Thus, in the early 1960s, there were two separate but parallel developments: in the United States the new processual archaeologists led by Binford were challenging culture history (Binford and Binford 1968), while in Mexico and other countries of the region there was an attempt to revise culture history within a Marxist foundation (Lumbreras 1974). In both areas, of course, the bulk of the practitioners were still particularist in orientation. In the United States this eventually meant a schism and a sometimes bitter separation between the "traditional" and the "processual" archaeologists. In Mexico this was not as violent, but there was definitely a sense that Mexican archaeology was no longer unified: Lorenzo had introduced digging techniques and paleoenvironmental studies he had learned in England, which were not well received by some of his more traditional colleagues. He and Armillas argued for *real* stratigraphical excavation, and more precise recordings of finds, including paleoenvironmental data. The community reacted by saying that those applied only to preceramic sites. Armillas and Lorenzo replied by calling their colleagues "piramidiots." While the tension continued, a sort of truce was established, but Armillas had to leave Mexico after an argument with Caso over Sanders's work (Lorenzo 1981: 23).

Methodologically, the highlights of the 1960s are the long-term, problem-oriented regional projects: MacNeish in Tamaulipas and later in Tehuacán (Byers and MacNeish 1967–76); Sanders in the Basin of Mexico (Sanders et al. 1979), Millon in Teotihuacan (Millon 1973); and Flannery in Oaxaca (Flannery and Marcus 1983), to name a few. Interestingly, at that time, local archaeologists were more involved in monumental reconstruction than in long-term research. Only in the 1970s do we see regional, long-term attempts like the Tula Project (Matos 1974a, 1974b) and the Puebla-Tlaxcala Project (García Cook and Merino 1988).

This panorama diversified further in the 1970s: systemic-processual archaeology was making a mark (thanks to Flannery [e.g., 1968, 1975, 1976]); but in Mexico the slaughter of students in the brutal repression of their movement in 1968 had left a deep scar: it radicalized almost everyone. Colonialist, "indigenista" anthropology and nationalistic archaeology were questioned. Marxism was seen as the congruent position to take (Warman 1970).

This radicalized atmosphere limited the impact of processual archaeology in Mexico and other countries of the region: other than Jaime Litvak (1986) (who was actually closer to Clarke [1968] than to Binford), and some of Litvak's students, the rest either practiced traditional archaeology (reinforced with settlement archaeology) or embraced Marxism, vindicating Childe's contribution (Lorenzo, Pérez Gollán, and García-Bárcenas 1974).[3] The leaders of the position, especially Bate (1977) and his students made important theoretical contributions: "Latin American social archaeology" was to become a very influential orientation, not only in Mexico but also over the entire continent. Unfortunately, for some, this became more of a fashion than a true commitment and years later the trend was partially reversed.

Mesoamerican archaeology adopted some sort of neoevolutionist model and a materialist conception of culture: both cultural ecologists and systemic archaeologists used Service's sequence of "bands, tribes, chiefdoms and states" (Sanders and Price 1968; Flannery 1975 [1972]). Marxists challenged the orthodox sequence of modes of production, which lumped almost everything into the "primitive communism period" and a questionable "Asiatic mode of production" (Gándara 1986); Bate (1986) introduced a new sequence of socioeconomic formations, a theory on hunter-and-gatherer economic cycles, as well as a new formulation for the problem of the origins of class society in the Americas that centered on the control of labor, not of land (Bate 1984).

Explanation was the goal. Cultural ecologists and processualists made a huge theoretical contribution, of which here I can only mention some highlights. Of the first, Sanders gave us one of the earlier models for the rise of the state in the Central Highlands (Sanders and Price 1968); he later abandoned it to produce a much more ambitious theory (Sanders et al. 1979). Of the systemic processualists, Flannery suggested theories about the origins of agriculture (1973) and the state (1975) (both of potential universal application); later he proposed a local theory for the origins of the Zapotec civilization (Flannery and Marcus 1983). Blanton produced a model for the rise of Monte Albán (1978) and a general model for Mesoamerica (Blanton

---

3. Although he was one of its pioneers, Lorenzo was later disenchanted with it (1981); unfortunately, it is hard to evaluate his criticisms, because his text lacks references.

et al. 1993). In other cultural subareas (like the Maya or the Olmec) the focus was different (Marcus 1983: 454–457), but regional studies began to generalize. However, it would be in the field of epigraphy that contributions would start to mount.

THEORETICAL DIVERSIFICATION

The 1980s saw a growing skepticism with the processual, neopositivist model of explanation (Renfrew et al. 1982) as well as a generalized distrust of "prime mover theories," which, it was claimed, were all refuted (e.g., Wright and Johnson 1975; Earle 1978); some scholars set out to find alternate models of explanation, while others challenged explanation itself as the proper goal for archaeology. After a rapid succession of positions, in England Hodder finally settled for interpretive archaeology in the 1990s (Hodder 1995). He and his students posited *hermeneutic understanding* as the legitimate cognitive goal of the discipline, and culture was seen again as a mental phenomenon (meanings rather than behavior or praxis).

While this "antiprocessual" approach eroded processual archaeology in the United States, its impact was less clearly felt in Mesoamerican archaeology. The same happened with other alternative approaches (evolutionary, cognitive, and critical archaeology), perhaps precisely because none of their champions worked here. More important and widespread in all of Latin America was the position that can be called "epigonal or critical processualism," loosely shared by authors like Renfrew, Flannery, Blanton, Feinman, and others (see below). An important trend was the attempt to create a unified vision for Mesoamerica, which had somehow segmented or specialized in specific areas (Feinman and Nicholas 2000). Using theories brought from political science, sociology, and French and British historiography, like the "world system" model, there was an effort to create a new synthesis. Evolutionary steps or levels were questioned, arguing that we should concentrate on processes; characterization of internal variability and heterogeneity were recognized as important as explanation of origins (e.g., Blanton et al. 1996; Feinman and Marcus 1998). "Agency" became the buzzword, and grand scale theory was temporarily set on hold, but we still got Marcus and Flannery's study (1996) of the rise of Zapotec civilization, Blanton's related but alternative theory (Blanton et al. 1999; Smith 2000), and several local and regional syntheses.

In Mexico and Central America Marxist archaeology continued (e.g., Bate 1998), despite the fall of "real" socialism, with important contributions from American Marxists (e.g., Patterson 1994; McGuire 1992). Processual archaeology never really caught up in the region, and interpretive archaeology's constituency was only beginning to grow. This period also saw the rise of the "thematic archaeologies." These do not pretend to be whole theoretical positions, but instead study only a portion of the social spectrum or else specialize on some technical aspect of the discipline. They have a considerable constituency in Mesoamerican archaeology and are making important contributions. They include ethnoarchaeology, settlement-pattern archaeology (now landscape archaeology), archaeometry, gender archaeology, archaeoastronomy, and bioarchaeology, among others. The epigraphic tradition became prominent: in less than two decades it revealed much of the political and military history of the Maya, in a breakthrough of unparalleled pace (e.g., Martin and Grube 2002).

A Guarded Eclecticism

This sketch is, of necessity, a simplification. Except for the leaders of each theoretical position, most archaeologists are more easygoing about theory. They do not suffer when some of the pieces they snatch from different positions are not totally congruent with the rest. Since most are quite responsible professionals, they pick up new techniques and tricks, no matter their origin, if these techniques make their work more reliable and efficient—*provided they are within budget*. They also borrow freely from other positions' terminology: we see an increasing use of concepts like "world system," "long duration," or "habitus" in texts written in the most otherwise orthodox culture history tradition, just as previously "political economy," "mode of production," or "productive forces" were tossed around to spice up a classic particularistic monograph. Purists would call this "theoretical eclecticism." It may be. But their "explanations" still come from the toolbox of the culture historian: diffusion, influence, contact, invasion, and so on, "just so" stories where things "gradually" change.

This interesting phenomenon merits attention by historians, philosophers, and sociologists of science. It is as if archaeology grows not via scientific revolutions but more by accretion, into a kind of "guarded eclecticism" that still maintains a culture history foundation. Again, apart from the adamant position leaders, the rest seem to be content to be "without a label": some maybe because of the high originality and individuality of their work (e.g., Manzanilla 1997a, 1997b, 1997c; López Austin and López Luján 1996); others would openly claim to be "atheoretical," a naïve way of admitting they are actually culture historians. But most do not really lose their sleep over theoretical name tags.

Maybe this had to do with the distrust many Mesoamerican archaeologists have for theory. Or with the infrastructure that is required: you clearly will not adopt processualism without the proper labs, computers, and budgets. So you train students to produce what is feasible to produce; without doubt, eclectic culture history is cheaper and easier to do. Or perhaps people feel it is more compatible with the national responsibility we have for heritage, which processualism tends to look down on as "culture-resource management."

Whatever the cause, this leaves us with an interesting question: could it be that the "wait and see" attitude of many Mesoamerican archaeologists toward theory is actually an adaptive move? If this were the case, we are here to see a culture-historical, guarded eclecticism, for a long time.

ACKNOWLEDGMENTS

Thanks to Alejandro Villalobos (ENAH), for his continued support, and to Gabriela Uruñuela and Patricia Plunkett, (UDLA-P) for their kind advice.

FOR FURTHER READING

In addition to references in the text, and without pretense of exhaustiveness, the reader may find the following useful:

On precursors of professional Mesoamerican archaeology—Mexico: Matos (1998, 2002, 2009); Guatemala: Navarrete (2000); Gutiérrez (1996); Honduras: Lara (2006); Latinoamerica: (Oyuela-Caycedo 1994; Oyuela-Caycedo et al. 1997).

On the Mexican School of Archaeology: Matos (1972); Litvak (1975); Lorenzo (1981); Vázquez (1996) (these include references to the main representatives of the School); on the influence of President Cárdenas's progressive government on the School, see Rodríguez and Olivo (2008).

On the criticism of culture history: Dunnell (1989), with references to critics before Binford.

On Armillas and Lorenzo: Rojas (1991); Litvak and Mirambell (2000); on Litvak: Benavides et al. (2004).

On Marxist archaeology: Trigger (1980); Spriggs (1984); Gándara (1995); for criticism and replies: Oyuela-Caycedo et al. (1997); Politis (2003, 2006); Benavides (2001); Patterson (1997). Some examples of empirical applications in Mesoamerica during the period of interest: Nalda (1981); Fournier (1995); López et al. (1988). In Latin America: Sanoja and Arenas (1979); Vargas (1981); Ortiz (1981).

Some representative examples of thematic archaeologies: ethnoarchaeology: Parsons and Parsons (1990); Williams (1999); landscape archaeology: Ashmore and Knapp (1999); Thiébault et al. (2008); archaeometry: Leute (1987); Manzanilla and Barba (1990); gender archaeology: Wright (1996); Joyce (1999); archaeoastronomy: Iwaniszewski (1994); Aveni (2003); bioarchaeology: Tiesler and Cucina (2003).

REFERENCES

Aberle, David. 1960. The Influence of Linguistics on Early Culture and Personality
    Theory. In *Essays in the Science of Culture: In Honor of Leslie White*, edited by
    Gertrude Dole and Robert Carneiro, pp. 1–49. Crowell, New York.

Ashmore, Wendy, and Bernard A. Knapp. 1999. *Archaeologies of Landscape:
    Contemporary Perspectives*. Blackwell Publishers, Malden, Massachusetts.

Aveni, Anthony. 2003. *Skywatchers*. University of Texas Press, Austin.

Barker, Philip. 1993. *Techniques of Archaeological Excavation*. 3rd ed. Routledge, New
    York.

Bate, Luis F. 1977. *Arqueología y materialismo histórico*. Ediciones de Cultura Popular,
    Mexico.

Bate, Luis F. 1984. Hipótesis sobre la sociedad clasista inicial. *Boletín de Antropología
    Americana* 9:47–86.

Bate, Luis F. 1986. El modo de producción cazador recolector, o de la economía del
    salvajismo. *Boletín de Antropología Americana* 13:5–32.

Bate, Luis F. 1998. *El proceso de investigación en arqueología*. Crítica/Grijalbo Mondadori,
    Barcelona.

Benavides, Antonio, Linda Manzanilla, and Lorena Mirambell, eds. 2004. *Homenaje a
    Jaime Litvak*. INAH/IIA-UNAM, México

Benavides, Hugo. 2001. Returning to the Source: Social Archaeology as Latin American
    Philosophy. *Latin American Antiquity* 12:355–370.

Bernal, Ignacio. 1979. *Historia de la arqueología en México*. 1st ed. Editorial Porrúa,
    Mexico

Binford, Lewis R. 1972 [1968]. Some Comments on Historical versus Processual
    Archaeology. In *An Archaeological Perspective*, edited by Lewis R. Binford,
    pp. 114–121. Seminar Press, New York.

Binford, Lewis R., and Binford, Sally R. 1968. *New Perspectives in Archeology*. Aldine,
    Chicago.

Blanton, Richard E. 1978. *Monte Albán*. Academic Press, New York.

Blanton, Richard, Gary M. Feinman, Stephen Kowalewski, and Peter Peregrine. 1996.
    A Dual-Processual Theory for the Evolution of Mesoamerican Civilization. *Current
    Anthropology* 37: 1–31.

Blanton, Richard, Stephen Kowalewski, Gary M. Feinman, and Laura Finsten. 1993
    [1981]. *Ancient Mesoamerica: A Comparison of Change in Three Regions*. 2nd ed.
    Cambridge University Press, New York.

Blanton, Richard, Gary Feinman, Stephen Kowalewski, and Linda Nicholas. 1999.
    Ancient Oaxaca: The Monte Albán State. Cambridge University Press, Cambridge.

Byers, Douglas, and Richard S. McNeish, eds. 1967–76. *The Prehistory of the Tehuacán
    Valley*. University of Texas, Austin.

Cárdenas, Eyra, ed. 1993. *50 años. Memoria de la ENAH*. INAH, Mexico

Clarke, David L. 1968. *Analytical Archaeology*. Methuen, London.

Daniel, Glyn. 1976. *A Hundred and Fifty Years of Archaeology*. Harvard University Press,
    Cambridge, Massachusetts.

De la Peña, Guillermo. 1996. Nacionales y extranjeros en la historia de la arqueología
    mexicana. In *La historia de la antropología en México*, edited by Mechthild Rutsch,
    pp. 41–82. Universidad Iberoamericana/Plaza y Valdez/INI, Mexico

Dunnell, Robert. 1986. Five Decades of American Archaeology. In *American Archaeology, Past and Future: A Celebration of the Society for American Archaeology, 1935–1985*, edited by David J. Meltzer, Don D. Fowler, and Jeremy A. Sabloff, pp. 23–49. Smithsonian Institution Press, Washington, DC.

Dunnell, Robert. 1989. Philosophy of Science and Archaeology. In *Critical Traditions in Contemporary Archaeology. Essays in the Philosophy, History and Sociopolitics of Archaeology*, edited by Valerie Pinsky and Alison Wylie, pp. 5–9. University of New Mexico Press, Albuquerque.

Earle, Timothy K. 1978. *Economic and Social Organization of a Complex Chiefdom: The Halelea District, Kauai, Hawaii.* Museum of Anthropology, University of Michigan, Ann Arbor.

Evans, Susan T. 2004. *Ancient Mexico and Central America: Archaeology and Culture History.* Thames and Hudson, New York.

Feinman, Gary M., and Joyce Marcus. 1998. *Archaic States.* School of American Research Press, Santa Fe.

Feinman, Gary M., and Linda Nicholas. 2000. New Perspectives on Prehispanic Highland Mesoamerica. In *The Ancient Civilizations of Mesoamerica. A Reader*, edited by Michael Smith and Marilyn Masson, pp. 205–235. Blackwell, Malden, Massachusetts.

Flannery, Kent V. 1968. The Olmec and the Valley of Oaxaca. In *Dumbarton Oaks Conference on the Olmec*, edited by Elizabeth Benson, pp. 79–110. Dumbarton Oaks, Washington, DC.

Flannery, Kent V. 1973. The Origins of Agriculture. *Annual Review of Anthropology* 2:271–310.

Flannery, Kent V. 1975 [1972]. *La evolución cultural de las civilizaciones.* Anagrama, Barcelona.

Flannery, Kent, ed. 1976. *The Early Mesoamerican Village.* Academic Press, New York.

Flannery, Kent V., and Joyce Marcus. 1983. *The Cloud People: Divergent Evolution of the Zapotec and Mixtec Civilizations.* Academic Press, New York.

Fournier, Patricia. 1995. *Etnoarqueología creámica otomí: maguey, pulque y alfarería entre los hñahñú del Valle del Mezquital.* UNAM, México.

Gamio, Manuel. 1922. *La población del Valle de Teotihuacán.* Secretaría de Agricultura y Fomento, Dirección de Antropología, México.

Gándara, Manuel. 1983. La vieja "nueva arqueología" (primera y segunda partes). *Boletín de Antropología Americana, Reimpresiones*, 59–158.

Gándara, Manuel. 1986. El modo de producción asiático: ¿Explicación marxista del origen del estado? In *Origen y formacion del estado en Mesoamerica. Homenaje a Ignacio Bernal*, edited by M. y. L. A. Serra P. UNAM, México

Gándara, Manuel. 1995. El análisis de posiciones teóricas: aplicaciones a la arqueología social. *Boletín de Antropología Americana* (27):5.20.

Gándara, Manuel. 2008. *El análisis teórico en ciencias sociales: aplicación a una teoría de origen del estado en Mesoamérica.* ENAH, México.

Gándara, Manuel, Fernando López, and Ignacio Rodríguez. 1985. Arqueología y marxismo en México. *Boletín de Antropología Americana* 11:5–17.

García Cook, Ángel, and Lenor Merino. 1988. El proyecto Puebla-Tlaxcala. In *La antropología en México: panorama histórico: vol. 5. Las disciplinas antropológicas y la mexicanística extranjera*, 1st ed., pp. 149–178. Instituto Nacional de Antropologâia e Historia, México

García Mora, Carlos. 1979. Paul Kirchhoff, el instigador. *Antropología y Marxismo* 1:7–10.

García Mora, Carlos. 1996. La creatividad científica a través de los papeles de un etnólogo (a propósito del archivo personal de Paul Kirchhoff). In *La historia de la antropologia en Mexico,* edited by Mechthild Rutsch, pp. 225–245. UIA/Plaza y Valdéz/INI, México.

Gutiérrez, Edgar. 1996. *Posiciones teóricas en la arqueología de Guatemala.* Universidad de San Carlos, Guatemala.

Harris, Edward C. 1989. *Principles of Archaeological Stratigraphy.* 2nd ed. Academic Press, London.

Harris, Marvin. 1979 [1968]. *El desarrollo de la teoría antropológica: historia de las teorías de la cultura.* 3rd. ed. Siglo XXI, Madrid.

Hodder, Ian, ed. 1995. *Interpreting Archaeology: Finding Meaning in the Past.* Routledge, London.

Hole, F., and R. Heizer. 1973. *An Introduction to Prehistoric Archaeology.* 3rd ed. Holt, Rinehart and Winston, New York.

Iwaniszewski, Stanislaw. 1994. Archaeology and Archaeoastronomy of Mount Tlaloc, Mexico: A Reconsideration. *Latin American Antiquity* 5:158–176.

Jiménez Moreno, Wigberto. 1941. Tula y los toltecas según las fuentes históricas. *Revista Mexicana de Antropología* 5:79–83.

Joyce, Rosemary. 1999. Gender at the Crossroads of Mesoamerican Archaeology. *Latin American Antiquity* 10:433–435.

Kardiner, Abram, and Edward Preble. 1961. *They Studied Man.* 1st ed. World Pub. Co., Cleveland.

Kirchhoff, Paul. 1979. Etnología, materialismo histórico y método dialéctico. *Antropología y Marxism* 1:11–13.

Kirchhoff, Paul. 2009. *Mesoamérica. Sus límites geográficos, composición étnica y caracteres culturales.* Al fin liebre, Jalapa.

Lara, Gloria. 2006. La investigación arqueológica en Honduras: lecciones aprendidas para una futura proyección. *Revista Pueblos y Fronteras Digital.*, vol. 2. UNAM. México. Electronic document, http://www.pueblosyfronteras.unam.mx/a066n2/misc_02.html (accessed November 2009).

León y Gama, Antonio. 2009 [1790]. *Descripción histórica y cronológica de las dos piedras.* INAH, México.

Leute, Ulrich. 1987. *An Introduction to Physical Methods in Archaeology and the History of Art.* CVH Publishers, New York.

Litvak, Jaime. 1975. *Posiciones teóricas en la arqueología mexicana, en Balance y perspectiva de la antropología en Mesoamérica y el norte de México, XIII Mesa Redonda.* Sociedad Mexicana de Antropología, México.

Litvak, Jaime. 1986. *Todas las piedras tienen 2000 años.* Trillas, México.

Litvak, Jaime, and Lorena Mirambell, eds. 2000. *Arqueología, historia y antropología. In Memoriam. José Luis Lorenzo Bautista.* INAH, México.

López Austin, Alfredo, and Leonardo López Luján. 1996. *El pasado indígena.* 2nd. ed. Fideicomiso historia de las Américas/El Colegio de México/Fondo de cultura Económica, México

López, Fernando, Patricia Fournier, and Clara Paz Bautista. 1988. Contextos arqueológicos y contextos momento. El caso de la alfarería otomí del Valle del Mezquital. *Boletín de Antropología Americana* 18:99–131.

Lorenzo, José L. 1981. Archaeology South of the Rio Grande. *World Archaeology* 13:190–208.

Lorenzo, José L., José Pérez Gollán, and Joaquin García-Bárcena. 1974. *Hacia una arqueología social.* Instituto Nacional de Antropología e Historia, México.

Lumbreras, Luis G. 1974. *La arqueología como ciencia social*. Histar, Lima.

Manzanilla, Linda. 1997a. Early Urban Societies: Challenges and Perspectives. In *Emergence and Change in Early Urban Societies*, edited by Linda Manzanilla, pp. 3–39. Plenum Press, New York.

Manzanilla, Linda. 1997b. Recapitulation and Concluding Remarks. In *Emergence and Change in Early Urban societies*, edited by Linda Manzanilla, pp. 275–285. Plenum Press, New York.

Manzanilla, Linda. 1997c. Teotihuacán: Urban Archetype, Cosmic Model. In *Emergence and Change in Early Urban Societies*, edited by Linda Manzanilla, pp. 109–131. Plenum Press, New York.

Manzanilla, Linda, and Luis Barba. 1990. The Study of Activities in Classic Households. Two Case Studies from Coba and Teotihuacan. *Ancient Mesoamerica* 1:41–49.

Marcus, Joyce. 1983. Lowland Maya Archaeology at the Crossroads. *Latin American Antiquity* 49(4):829–833.

Marcus, Joyce, and Kent V. Flannery. 1996. *Zapotec Civilization: How Urban Society Evolved in Mexico's Oaxaca Valley*. Thames and Hudson, New York.

Martin, Simon, and Nikolai Grube. 2002. *Crónica de los reyes y reinas mayas*. Planeta, México.

Mastache, Guadalupe, and Robert Cobean. 1988. La arqueología. In *La antropología en México: panorama histórico: vol. 5. Las disciplinas antropológicas y la mexicanística extranjera*, 1st ed., pp. 39–82. Instituto Nacional de Antropología e Historia, México

Matos, Eduardo. 1972. *Manuel Gamio: Arqueología e Indigenismo*. Secretaría de Educación Pública, México.

Matos, Eduardo. 1974a. *Excavaciones en la microarea: Tula Chico y la Plaza Charnay*. Colección científica 15. Instituto Nacional de Antropología e Historia, México

Matos, Eduardo, ed. 1974b. *Proyecto Tula*. INAH, México.

Matos, Eduardo. 1998. *Las piedras negadas*. CONACULTA, México.

Matos, Eduardo, ed. 2001. *Descubridores del pasado en Mesoamérica*. Océano, México.

Matos, Eduardo. 2002. *Los comienzos de la arqueología Mexicana: en respuesta Carlos Navarrete*. El Colegio Nacional, México.

Matos, Eduardo. 2009. Introducción. In *Antonio León y Gama: Descripción histórica y cronológica de dos piedras*, edited by Eduardo Matos, pp. xi–xvi. Instituto Nacional de Antropología e Historia, México.

McGuire, Randall. 1992. *A Marxist Archaeology*. Academic Press, New York.

Millon, René. 1973. *The Teotihuacán Map*. University of Texas Press, Austin.

Mirambell, Lorena. 1988. La excavación estratigráfica. In *Colección biblioteca del INAH*, edited by Carlos García Mora M. d. l. L. del Valle, pp. 81–94. Instituto Nacional de Antropología e Historia, México

Nalda, Enrique. 1981. México prehispánico: origen y formación de las clases sociales. In *México, un pueblo en la historia*, edited by Enrique Semo. UAP/Nueva Imagen, México.

Navarrete, Carlos. 2000. Palenque, 1784: el inicio de la aventura arqueológica Maya. *Cuadernos del Centro de Estudios Mayas* UNAM 26.

Olivé, Negrete J. C., ed. 1995. *INAH. Una historia*. Instituto Nacional de Antropología e Historia, México.

Ortiz, Lenin. 1981. *El pasado antiguo de Ecuador*. Consejo Provincial de Pichincha, Pichincha.

Oyuela-Caycedo, Augusto, ed. 1994. *History of Latin American Archaeology*. Avebury, Hampshire, England.

Oyuela-Caycedo, Augusto, Armando Anaya, Carlos G. Elera, and Lidio Valdez. 1997. Social Archaeology in Latin America? Comments to T. C. Patterson. *American Antiquity* 62(2):465–474.

Parsons, Jeffrey R., and Mary H. Parsons. 1990. *Maguey Utilization in Highland Central Mexico: An Archaeological Ethnography.* Memoirs of the Museum of Anthropology No. 82. University of Michigan, Ann Arbor.

Patterson, Tom. 1994. Social Archaeology in Latin America: An Appreciation. *American Antiquity* 59:5331–5537.

Patterson, Tom. 1997. A Reply to A. Oyuela-Caycedo, A.Anaya, C. G. Elera and L. M. Valdez. *American Antiquity* 62:375–376.

Politis, Gustavo. 2003. The Theoretical Landscape and the Methodological Development of Archaeology in Latin America. *Latin American Antiquity* 14:115–142.

Politis, Gustavo. 2006. El paisaje teórico y el desarrollo metodológico de la arqueología en América Latina. *Arqueología Suramericana/Arqueología Sul-Americana* 2:168–175.

Renfrew, Colin, Michael J. Rowlands, and Barbara Abbott Segraves. 1982. *Theory and Explanation in Archaeology: The Southampton Conference.* Academic Press, New York.

Rodríguez, Antonio, and O. Olivo. 2008. *La arqueología mexicana en la revolución social: la arqueología indigenista durante el cardenismo.* ENAH, México.

Rojas, Teresa, ed. 1991. *Pedro Armillas: vida y obra.* CIESAS/INAH, Mexico.

Sanders, William T. 1952. Estudios de patrón de asentamiento del poblado de Xochicalco. *Tlatoani* 1(2):32.

Sanders, William T. 1953. Anthropogeography of Central Veracruz. *Revista mexicana de estudios antropológicos* 13 (2–3):27–78.

Sanders, William T. 1957. Tierra y agua. PhD dissertation, Department of Anthropology, Harvard, Cambridge, Massachusetts.

Sanders, William T., Jeffrey R. Parsons, and Robert S. Santley. 1979. *The Basin of Mexico: Ecological Processes in the Evolution of a Civilization.* Academic Press, New York.

Sanders, William T., and Barbara J. Price. 1968. *Mesoamerica; the Evolution of a Civilization.* Random House, New York.

Sanoja, Mario, and Iraida Vargas Arenas. 1979. *Antiguas formaciones y modos de producción venezolanos.* 2nd ed. Monte Avila, Caracas.

Schmidt, Paul. 1988. Los aportes de la arqueología estadounidense. In *La antropología en México: panorama histórico: vol. 5. Las disciplinas antropológicas y la mexicanística extranjera,* edited by C. García Mora, 1st ed., pp. 473–505. Instituto Nacional de Antropología e Historia, México

Schuyler, Robert L. 1971. The History of American Archaeology: An Examination of Procedure. *American Antiquity* 36:383–409.

Smith, Michael. 2000. Two Perspectives on the Rise of Civilization in Mesoamerica's Oaxaca Valley. *Latin American Antiquity* 11:87–89.

Spriggs, Matthew, ed. 1984. *Marxist Perspectives in Archaeology.* Cambridge University Press, Cambridge.

Thiébault, Virginia, Magdelena García, and María Antonieta Jiménez Isarraraz, eds. 2008. *Patrimonio y paisajes culturales.* El Colegio de Michoacán, Zamora.

Tiesler, Vera, and Andrea Cucina 2003. Sacrificio, tratamiento y ofrenda del cuerpo humano entre los Mayas del Clásico: una mirada bioantropológica. In *Antropología de la eternidad,* edited by Anres Ciudad, María Humberto Ruz Sosa, and María Josefa Iglesias, pp. 337–354. Sociedad Española de Estudios Mayas/Centro de Estudios Mayas/UNAM, Mexico.

Trigger, Bruce G. 1980. *Gordon Childe, Revolutions in Archaeology*. Columbia University Press, New York.

Vargas, Iraida. 1981. *Investigaciones arqueológicas en Parmana* (Vol. 20). Biblioteca de la Academia Nacional de la Historia, Caracas.

Vázquez, Luis. 1996. *El Leviatán arqueológico. Antropología de una tradición científica en México*. CIESAS/Porrúa, México.

Warman, Arturo. 1970. *De eso que llaman antropologia mexicana*. Editorial Nuestro Tiempo, Mexico.

Willey, Gordon R. 1953. *Prehistoric Settlement Patterns in the Virú Valley, Peru*. U.S. Government Printing Office, Washington, DC.

Willey, Gordon R., and Phillip Phillips. 1968 [1958]. *Method and Theory in American Archaeology*. University of Chicago Press, Chicago.

Willey, Gordon R., and Jeremy A. Sabloff. 1974. *A History of American Archaeology*. 1st ed.. W. H. Freeman, San Francisco.

Willey, Gordon R., and Jeremy A. Sabloff. 1980. *A History of American Archaeology*. 2nd ed.. W. H. Freeman, San Francisco.

Williams, Eduardo. 1999. The Ethnoarchaeology of Salt Production at Lake Cuitseo, Michoacán, México. *Latin American Antiquity* 10:400–414.

Wolf, Eric R. 1976. Introduction. In *The Valley of Mexico: Studies in Pre-Hispanic Ecology and Society*, edited by Eric R. Wolf, pp. 1–9. University of New Mexico Press, Albuquerque.

Wright, Henry T., and Gary A. Johnson. 1975. Population, Exchange, and Early State Formation in Southwestern Iran. *American Anthropologist* 77:267–289.

Wright, Rita. 1996. *Gender and Archaeology*. University of Pennsylvania Press, Philadelphia.

CHAPTER 3

MEXICO'S NATIONAL ARCHAEOLOGY PROGRAMS

NELLY M. ROBLES GARCÍA

HISTORICALLY, the teaching of archaeology in Mexico was concentrated on diverse aspects of Mesoamerican archaeology. Although from its birth American archaeology oriented and nurtured it, Mexico's enormous archaeological heritage forced the formation of its own school in 1911, which was founded as the Escuela Internacional de Arqueología (International School of Archaeology) by the Mexican government, under the auspices of universities from the United States, France, and Germany and directed by Eduard Seler. Unfortunately the effort did not last long, and it was canceled in 1920. Subsequently archaeology was taught through conferences at the National Museum and through informal courses at the National University (Bernal 1992: 154).

With the establishment in 1939 of the Instituto Nacional de Antropología e Historia (INAH), the school was revived as a department of the INAH in 1942 called the Escuela Nacional de Antropología e Historia (ENAH). The school has been responsible for the teaching of anthropology in Mexico, including the creation of syllabi for use in other schools (Litvak 2000: 32). In its origins, the ENAH was influenced by schools of thought such as the historical particularism of Franz Boas and later the Mexican expression of environmental archaeology developed by Pedro Armillas, which today is called the American school of cultural ecology. At the time, environmental archaeology was considered to be one of the great antagonists of traditional Mexico's nationalist archaeology that dominated the country for several decades.

If in Mexico the teaching of anthropology examined different theoretical visions of archaeology, the practice was concentrated on solving the problems of Mesoamerican archaeology, otherwise called the "Mexican School of Archaeology."

The Mexican School of Archaeology had as its initial model Manuel Gamio's interdisciplinary research that he conducted in the Valley of Teotihuacan from 1917 to 1922. This project presented Gamio's interdisciplinary vision of anthropological science with the dual objective of enhancing knowledge of the living and of past indigenous societies as well as of improving the quality of life of the people who have inherited those traditional cultures. Gamio's project is well known for the effort that he made in gathering broad data on anthropological aspects for the Valley of Teotihuacan, in contrast with other projects that focused strictly on archeological sites and scientific methods more than on the humanities (Matos 1983: 10).

Alfonso Caso y Andrade continued and consolidated the Mexican School of Anthropology, on both the national and international levels. Starting in 1930, with the Monte Albán project, in Oaxaca, Caso expanded interdisciplinary archaeological studies and, in addition, established the formal features of the monumental restoration of Mexican archaeology.

ARCHAEOLOGY AS ANTHROPOLOGY

Teaching archaeology in Mexico as a project was multidisciplinary right from its start. In its beginnings, the Mexican School of Anthropology was concerned with the comprehensive formation of anthropologists, who, in addition to their particular interests in archaeology, were required to have solid knowledge of other disciplines. Thus, archaeology in Mexico originates in the humanities environment, within the study of anthropology whose five branches of specialization (archaeology, linguistics, physical anthropology, social anthropology, and ethnography) are intimately connected to allow for the integral comprehension of humanity as a cultural entity. Students from all fields take a series of core subjects in the first four semesters before specializing. From its origin in 1942 until the end of the 1980s, the ENAH was characterized by generations sharing core anthropological subjects that guaranteed a holistic vision of Mexican anthropology. Anthropologists, and in particular archaeologists trained at the ENAH and other schools that followed it, were required to know the other anthropological disciplines, thus preventing the dangerous isolation of anthropologists from other social sciences that explain humans as a social being.

ARCHAEOLOGY AND THE MEXICAN STATE

The teaching of anthropology from the outset was linked to the nationalism concept of the Mexican state and this has greatly shaped the profession in Mexico. On the one hand, this has provided free and easy access to schools in Mexico. On the other hand, archaeology often became an object of tension, due to the fact that it was the state, and not necessarily science, who dictated the priorities in the subject (Gándara 1992: 23).

The participation of the state in Mexican archaeology has been especially focused on how the material remains of ancient cultures were exhibited. In this sense, the monumental archaeological zones have been the results of political bias in the historic images promoted by the state that favors monumental projects. Thus, the state creates a spectacular image of the prehispanic past that benefits the Mexican state itself.

Fortunately archaeologists were in charge of executing the monumental restorations and reconstructions that we see today. This fact ensured the fidelity of the existing data and in many cases a great respect for the authenticity of the monuments.

In the same way, certain research topics have been, if not imposed, at least suggested by the state, as was the case in the 1970s when the remains of the Aztec emperor Cuauhtémoc were discovered. This was done with the objective of showing the grandeur of the last Aztec emperor, but the research was biased to such a point that the archaeologists fell into unnecessary disrepute.

The participation of the state in archaeology created a tendency toward a monumental interpretation of Mexican history. Showing the ceremonial centers, pyramids, temples, ball games, plazas, and so on represents only a selective part of the evidence. The archaeological components of the common people, their houses, markets, agricultural terraces, burials, and so on are not shown. Monumental archaeology always showed an archaeology of power in the elite components of the prehispanic cities.

ARCHAEOLOGY AND CONSERVATION

The other important dimension of teaching of archaeology in Mexico has been the restoration of the vestiges of archaeological heritage. From its beginnings as part of the eagerness to show the greatness of the prehispanic past, the teaching of archaeology remained linked (even legally) to the works of conservation of the cultural heritage. As part of the INAH, the ENAH is obliged to conserve archaeological heritage; in Mexico the archaeologist is legally responsible for restoring all material evidence. In addition, until recently, archaeologists had brilliant careers in the field of restoration, so that part of education was received directly in the field through participation in their projects.

For years this reality generated an interesting controversy between the theoretical and the practical positions of archaeology in Mexico. On the one hand, starting with the social movements in 1968, an academic sector with a Marxist basis emerged with a very critical style that simply could not find a comfortable place among the representatives of the Mexican School of Archaeology and on the other, those of a long career in the field bordering on self-teaching. The groups of archaeologists of one and the other positions have never since confronted one another as they did in the decades of the 1970s and 1980s (Guerrero 1982: 97).

Contemporary Teaching of Archaeology

The teaching of archaeology in Mexico through the ENAH is carried out within the National Educational Program of the Ministry of Public Education (ENAH, 2011). That means it is contemplated fundamentally as education provided by the state that therefore is free for citizens. The basic program grants a degree that is equivalent to a Bachelor of Arts.

At this level, archaeology is studied for nine semesters. After that, the student must present a thesis to obtain his or her degree. The resulting diploma opens the doors to a formal market in this field. This degree acknowledges the fact that the archaeologist may now carry out research projects following the methods that the profession demands.

The universities that offer archaeology programs in Mexico share a basic premise that true archaeology is done in the field. Thus after four semesters, most students search for opportunities to initiate their experiences in the field in different national projects. Normally each student receives at least three opportunities to participate in field projects and learn basic excavation techniques. Based on these opportunities, that student finally makes a decision as to his or her field of specialization. After the nine semesters, all students are ready to become members of an archaeological team, particularly in jobs that practice the basic techniques of survey, excavation, and analysis of the archaeological materials. The analysis of materials entails additional studies of regional specialization normally obtained directly in a project laboratory.

Today, the archaeology that is taught at the ENAH has been transformed from the point of view of subjects and priorities in certain study plans. Although the study of Mesoamerica continues to be the central issue, it is no longer the exclusive subject matter. Today, the modern teaching of official archaeology in Mexico offers both theoretical and methodological elements for the study of past civilizations. The education currently provided by the ENAH covers complex theories, including postprocessual approaches that provide the possibilities of revision of aspects involved in explanation and interpretation of past and present social phenomena. This allows the modern archaeologist to study, understand, and compare the social phenomena of world cultures.

Recently, the offerings of archaeology study programs have grown considerably in Mexico. In addition to the ENAH, at least six state universities started academic programs in archaeology. The University of Yucatán (UADY) offers a specialization in its regional archaeology (www.antropologia.uady.mx/programas), and one

well-known private university (UDLAP) (www.udlap.mx/ofertaacademica/licen-
ciaturas/arqueologia), offers a degree in archaeology that begins with two years of
study of the four subdisciplines of anthropology (UDLAP 2011). It is also important to point out that at least two universities (University of the State of Mexico,
UAEMEX, 2011 [www.uaemex.mx/CUTenancingo/Arque.html and the University
of San Luis Potosí, UASLP, 2011 [www.uaslp.mx/spanish/academicas/ccsh/T])
clearly state that one of their objectives for the study of archaeology is attention to
contemporary problems in which archaeological heritage is immersed today. This
last point leads us to delve more deeply into the new trends.

New Trends

Every day contemporary science demands important variations in assessing theories and methodological approaches toward archaeology. Mexico's archaeologists,
as well as students, find themselves immersed in a new array of archaeological specialties that seek answers about past cultures through evidence associated with different kinds of contemporary environments. A summary of these new tendencies
is presented here; these trends, without a doubt, have modified the archaeological
arena, as well as the teaching of new archaeologists in Mexico.

Salvage and Rescue Archaeology

Since the 1970s and even before, archaeology in Mexico was involved in situations
that publicly jeopardized the integrity of archaeological heritage. The presence
of archaeologists is almost necessarily continuous with the construction of large
works of infrastructure. On this note, the 1978 discovery of the Aztec Coyolxauhqui
monolith in the heart of Mexico City, due to the introduction of electricity, initiated a methodological quandary within Mexican archaeology.

What to do with these findings and the organization for research? How to
establish adequate contacts at the right level with business, with official agencies,
and with private owners? These questions resulted in a specialization in salvage
and rescue archaeology (Pérez Castellanos and Esparza 1995). Archaeology is part
of large infrastructure projects such as the enormous subway lines in Mexico City,
gas ducts, oil ducts, highways, dams, refineries, and so on, for archaeologists and
the state to determine the potentiality of the land for the presence of sites and
archaeological materials before the land can no longer be accessed.

"Rescue" and "salvage" have been elevated as legal terms in order to designate
required and urgent works in the field. Rescue is understood as those urgent actions

in which the destruction of the archaeological elements is imminent, and therefore the archaeological project must adjust itself to the circumstances and timetable of the infrastructure project and proceed to recover threatened remains.

Salvage, on the contrary, implies a series of preventive actions during planning and management to avoid the destruction of archaeological heritage. In this case, the archaeologist's work is oriented toward establishing the archaeological potential of the layout, axis, or area to be impacted, in such a way that alternatives can be established to avoid destruction of the sites.

Salvage and rescue have prompted the development of appropriate methodologies by agencies of the INAH. It is in this environment of salvage and recovery archaeology where the most archaeology students consolidate their training in Mexico, because these are open and temporary projects that require large teams of archaeologists for a specified period of time.

Cultural-resources management

Cultural-resources management is another important specialization in Mexico, because it involves methodologies and theories a bit distinct from academic archaeological projects. It arose from the need for comprehensive attention to the sites that were opened for public visits a long time ago but that nevertheless have not as yet been promoted to their maximum capacity for social management (Robles García and Corbett 2010: 111). Archaeological-resources management in Mexico responds, in the first instance, to demands by international entities for better attention toward sites declared by the UNESCO to be on the World Heritage list. Nevertheless, the development of this subject has tended to become generalized, and today it constitutes an important aspect of research for the social management of archaeological heritage. The archaeological techniques in this specialty are clearly oriented toward aspects of interpretation for the comprehension by the public users of the archaeological spaces.

Thus this speciality pays attention to diverse conditions and values of sites and archaeological objects and focuses on the educational values of archaeology and other societal values, such as the possession of the land, and the users in general of archaeological heritage. This specialization in many ways once again melds archaeology with other specialties in anthropology as it deals with contemporary society in the development of the management plans for sites. It forces archaeologists to consider the priorities of a site in terms of its social function, before its priorities in academic research. This has become an increasingly popular specialty among archaeology studies. Similar to what happened with rescue and salvage archaeology, the official institutions have been forced to establish administrative space for the development of cultural-resources management. In addition, due to its own characteristics, it establishes the need for the use of new technologies as tools to meet its objectives.

Cultural Legislation

It is probably within the sphere of cultural-resources management, more than in archaeology per se, that research about cultural legislation in Mexico was developed. This is because it touches a sensitive reality created by the contradictions between the public and private rights. In Mexico, by legal definition, archaeological monuments (considered both as sites as well as objects) belong to the Mexican state. There is no possibility of making them private (Olivé Negrete and Cottom 1997: 11).

Although apparently simple and direct, this reality creates a latent tension between society and the Mexican state. Therefore, due to the vertical application of the legislation as it exists at present, the practice of archaeological research can lead to permanent legal conflict and social negotiation. Various legal experts have created a specialization revolving around revision of the legal framework where culture, and, therefore, archaeology, becomes a very important component. Its research framework is contemplated from the broad sense of the right to culture through to the particularities of the right for use and enjoyment of archaeological property. Given the relevance of this discussion, the archaeologists who are in the formative stage have found important elements in this subject for their political formation and vocation. Therefore, they have also adopted it for academic development. Although it does not enjoy enormous popularity, the subject, little by little, acquires more followers in the field of archaeology, anthropology, and history. Other specialities that have expanded in Mexican archaeology include underwater archaeology, historical archaeology, and landscape archaeology.

In conclusion, the teaching of archaeology in Mexico has gone, in a few decades, from the rigid transmission of a traditional framework of professional activity based on state precepts, to a liberalization of ideas and the adoption of new aspects of critical thought from international tendencies. This allows new archaeologists to have multidirectional growth, which tends toward specialization in each of the new fields.

Without impinging on a holistic starting point as far as anthropological specialties go, and without detriment to the extraordinary history of great heritage values, the training of archaeology students in contemporary Mexico equips them with tools by which they confront not only the practical challenges in the field but can also permit them to make theoretical and methodological proposals that advance integral archaeology within the international field.

Despite the fact that archaeologists today all recognize the enormous labor of the ENAH in carrying out the consolidation of the profession and entering into the modern world, its very nature forced it to establish the channels of interaction with the emerging schools along the length and width of the country and the world. As a consequence, the national programs for teaching archaeology are no longer the product of one single institution, and they do not keep or reproduce a single line of research. The diversity of educational projects, in which luckily the central value of the study of Mesoamerican archaeology has not been lost, guarantees that new generations of archaeologists will have the enormous advantage of academic discussion, the diversity of ideas as a basic premise and, in that sense, the addition of valuable elements from different spheres of specialization chosen by each student.

In this way, the well-informed Mexican archaeologist will be one who completely understands the brilliant past of the profession, will be open to the adoption of techniques and methodologies to confront the contemporary conditions of the archaeological heritage, and will be able to project and anticipate the solutions for social challenges in order to better perform the profession in a world context.

References

Bernal, Ignacio. 1992. *Historia de la arqueología en México*. 2nd ed. Editorial Porrúa, S.A., México.

ENAH. 2011. Escuela Nacional de Antropología e Historia, Licenciatura: arqueología. Electronic document, http://www.enah.edu.mx (accessed July 5, 2011).

Gándara, Manuel. 1992. *La arqueología oficial Mexicana, causas y efectos*. Colección Divulgación. INAH, México.

Guerrero, Francisco Javier. 1982. La Escuela Nacional de Antropología e Historia, el desarrollo científico y la lucha revolucionaria en México. In *Cuatro décadas de la Escuela Nacional de Antropología e Historia*. Colección Cuicuilco, ENAH, pp. 96–106. Instituto Nacional de Antropología, México.

Litvak King, Jaime. 2000. La Escuela Nacional de Antropología: sus tradiciones y su adaptación a nuevas condiciones. In *Memoria, 60 años de la ENAH*, edited by Eyra Cárdenas Barahona, pp. 31–42. Instituto Nacional de Antropología, México.

Matos Moctezuma, Eduardo. 1983. Manuel Gamio. *La arqueología Mexicana*. Colección argumentos, ideas de nuestro tiempo. UNAM, México.

Olivé Negrete, Julio C., and Bolfy Cottom. 1997. *Leyes estatales en materia del patrimonio cultural*. Instituto Nacional de Antropología e Historia, México.

Pérez Castellanos, Leticia, and J. Rodrigo Esparza L. 1995. Historia y perspectivas de la arqueología de salvamento en México. *Actualidades Arqueológicas, Revista de Estudiante de Arqueología de México* No. 1.

Robles García, Nelly M., and Jack Corbett. 2010. Heritage Resource Management in Mexico. In *Cultural Heritage Management: A Global Perspective*, edited by Phyllis M. Messenger and George S. Smith, pp. 111–123. University Press of Florida.

UADY. 2011. Universidad Autónoma de Yucatán, anthropology. Electronic document, http://www.antropologia.uady.mx/programas (accessed July 5, 2011).

UAEMEX. 2011. Universidad Autónoma del Estado de México. Electronic document, http://www.uaem.mx/CUTenancingo/Arque.html (accessed July 5, 2011).

UASLP. 2011. Universidad Autónoma de San Luis Potosí. Electronic document, http://www.uaslp.mx/spanish/academicas/ccsh/T/ (accessed July 5, 2011).

UDLAP. 2011. Liceniatura en Arqueología. Electronic document, http://www.udlap.mx/ofertaacademica/licenciaturas/arqueologia (accessed July 5, 2011).

CHAPTER 4

ARCHAEOLOGY IN GUATEMALA

NATIONALIST, COLONIALIST, IMPERIALIST

OSWALDO CHINCHILLA MAZARIEGOS

PROFESSIONAL archaeology in Guatemala began with the creation of an archaeology department at the Universidad de San Carlos in 1975. Yet Guatemalan archaeologists have inherited a long tradition of description of ancient sites, along with speculation about their inhabitants that goes back to the Colonial period. The scale and abundance of archaeological sites have stimulated protracted interest within the country and abroad, attracting considerable international attention. In an influential paper, Bruce Trigger (1984) outlined three types of archaeology that respond to specific social and political contexts around the world: nationalist, colonialist, and imperialist. All three have played a role in the development of archaeology in Guatemala. Nationalist motivations—the search for the ancient origins of the Guatemalan nation—can be traced back to the Colonial period, and they reappear strongly in nineteenth- and twentieth-century archaeological discourse. As Trigger noted for Mexico, Guatemalan archaeology also incorporates features of a colonialist archaeology "practiced by a colonizing population that had no historical ties with the peoples whose past they were studying" (1984: 360). In both countries, indigenous peoples have had little participation in the study of their ancient past until recently. Yet Trigger himself noted that this description does not account for the complexities of Mexican society and history—a remark

Figure 4.1 View of a ruined compound at the site of Utatlán. Illustration from the 1834 archaeological expedition, sponsored by the Guatemalan government. Lithograph by Julián Falla.

that applies equally well to Guatemala. Moreover, the third of Trigger's types has impacted both Guatemala and Mexico, albeit to a different scale. In Trigger's terminology, imperialist archaeology is practiced by researchers from politically and culturally dominant states in countries that fall under their hegemony.

The historiography of archaeology in Guatemala is still in its infancy. Accounts of Maya archaeology are mostly concerned with the development of ideas in North America and Europe, where strong traditions of Maya research developed since the nineteenth century (Brunhouse 1973, 1975). Few authors delve into the sociopolitical events that have conditioned the work of foreign scholars in the country, their interaction with Guatemalan students, and the intellectual currents that have influenced the latter. Guatemalan archaeology has also been overlooked in general surveys of Latin American archaeology (Oyuela-Caycedo 1994; Politis 2003). This chapter describes selected stages in the history of Guatemalan archaeology, based on previous overviews by the author (1999b) and by Luján Muñoz (1972).

COLONIAL ROOTS

The seventeenth-century chronicler Francisco Antonio de Fuentes y Guzmán exemplifies the peculiar conditions that have shaped the development of archaeology in Guatemala. Fuentes y Guzmán stands out among contemporary writers in the Spanish colonies for the degree of attention that he paid to ancient material remains. The description of archaeological sites was a major objective of his chronicle, *Recordación Florida* (1969–72). In an early example of patriotic archaeological discourse, he viewed material remains as a way to endow Guatemala with an ancient history that would place it on a par with Mexico (Chinchilla Mazariegos

1999a). His approach may find explanation in the absence of substantial written sources about the indigenous kingdoms found by the Spanish conquerors in
Guatemala. Unlike Mexico, where sixteenth-century witnesses left a substantial
amount of documentation on the Mexica and related peoples, the documentary
record available for Guatemala was very small. Fuentes y Guzmán wrote descriptions of Copán, Zaculeu, Kaminaljuyú, and other ruined sites, while using the few
written sources that were available—written by Spanish and indigenous authors
in the sixteenth century—to outline the Pre-Columbian history of the country.

Fuentes y Guzmán's ideas were deeply rooted in his creole patriotism—the
desire to exalt the country and its inhabitants, while justifying the Spanish conquest and the rights to the land of their descendants (Martínez Peláez 2009;
Saint-Lu 1978). However, the Colonial period also witnessed an alternative trend
that saw the ancient sites as sources of information for an intriguing intellectual
question: the origin of the Indians (Huddleston 1967). Where did these peoples
originate, and how were they related to the ancient peoples of the Old World?
This was the question that prompted the Spanish colonial governor of Guatemala
to send expeditions to the site of Palenque between 1784 and 1786 (Castañeda
Paganini 1946; Navarrete 2000). The expeditions were aimed to test the prevailing
view that Palenque was built by Old World immigrants: Romans, Carthaginians,
or even Spaniards. The Italian-born architect Antonio Bernasconi, in charge of the
first expedition, flatly rejected such assumptions, concluding that the site was built
by the forebears of the contemporary Indians. However, throughout the Colonial
period and well into the nineteenth century, many observers denied the capacity of
the indigenous peoples to build such sophisticated cities.

Figure 4.2 Pre-Columbian sculptures assembled at the Agúna coffee plantation on the
Pacific piedmont of Guatemala, with indigenous workers. Unknown photographer, late
nineteenth or early twentieth century.

The Epitome of American Civilization

In the wake of Fuentes y Guzmán's example, archaeology became part of early nationalist projects in Guatemala shortly after independence. In 1834, the government of the state of Guatemala ordered explorations at the ruins of Copán, Iximché, and Utatlan, which were considered as major capitals of prehispanic kingdoms (figure 4.1). The explorations were part of a broad effort to write the history of Guatemala, starting with the indigenous kingdoms that flourished before the Spanish conquest. In the political rhetoric of the independence period, they were characterized as the fathers of modern Guatemala, and as examples worth following. One of the earliest instances of state-sponsored archaeological research in the New World, this effort was clearly related to a nationalist program that also envisioned the creation of a geographic atlas, effectively providing the emergent state both with a historical depth and a geographic shape (Anderson 1991; Chinchilla Mazariegos 1998).

Like the Guatemalan nationalists, John L. Stephens, a U.S. traveler and writer, sought proof of the high achievements of ancient indigenous peoples, while taking no heed of their modern descendants. His descriptions of the ruins of Copán and Palenque—the first to present detailed and precise information about these and other Classic Maya sites—were aimed at proving the antiquity of American civilization, broadly understood as that of his own, booming country, vis-à-vis the great civilizations of the Old World. For Stephens, the great Maya sculptures would be best displayed in Central Park in New York City, and he took steps to secure for this purpose the monuments of Copán and Quirigua (Ortega y Medina 1953, 1990; Preston 1992). While Stephens's plans failed, the idea of exporting the Quirigua stelae lingered on. In the mid-nineteenth century, when British colonial interests and trade loomed large in Central American economies, British diplomats made serious studies of the feasibility of acquiring the monuments (Aguirre 2005).

Eventually, it was a British gentleman, Alfred P. Maudslay, who took Maya exploration a step further. His magnificent photographic records and descriptions of sculptures and buildings at major Maya sites provided a sound basis for the interpretation of their inscriptions and iconography (Graham 2002; Maudslay 1889–1902). The decipherment of the Maya calendar, achieved in the late nineteenth century by German and American researchers, further enhanced the prestige of Maya civilization, considered by many students of that period as the crowning achievement of the prehispanic New World (Coe 1992; Houston et al. 2001; Stuart 1992).

Maudslay and other contemporary visitors acquired significant examples of prehispanic art for museums and collections in Europe and the United States, ranging from the carved wooden lintels of Tikal to the monumental sculptures of Cotzumalhuapa (Chinchilla Mazariegos 1996). In response, in 1893, the Guatemalan government first issued laws that entrusted the protection of archaeological remains to the government. A National Museum functioned precariously between 1866 and 1881, reopening in 1898, but little is known about its archaeological holdings (Luján

Muñoz 1973). Collections were also assembled in Guatemala, partly as a result of the growing coffee industry that intensified land use and made broad expanses of land accessible, especially on the Pacific Coast and in the northern highlands (figures 4.2–4.3; McCreery 1994; Wagner 2001).

Guatemalan institutions and intellectuals remained marginal to the growing international concern with Maya archaeology throughout the nineteenth century. Significant exceptions include Modesto Méndez (1955; Navarrete 1982), who first reported the site of Tikal in 1848, and Manuel García Elgueta, who conducted excavations at Chalchitán and other sites in the western highlands in the 1880s. The latter stands out among his contemporaries, who generally saw modern

Figure 4.3 A Maya woman surrounded by archaeological artifacts and modern handcrafts. Plate 2 from the book *Die Ethnologie der Indianerstamme von Guatemala* by the Swiss physician, linguist, and ethnographer Otto Stoll (1889).

indigenous peoples as an obstacle for the desired progress of modern Guatemala. García Elgueta studied the language and culture of the contemporary K'iche' and concluded that they were descendants of the builders of Tikal. Moreover, he believed that the material remains of their former grandeur could serve as examples to improve the modern K'iche' (Chinchilla Mazariegos 1999c). His excavations and the artifacts that he recovered gained some notoriety, but he did not succeed in gaining sustained attention from government officials or the public.

ARCHAEOLOGY IN THE BANANA REPUBLIC

During much of the twentieth century, archaeology in Guatemala was conducted almost exclusively by institutions and scholars from the United States. The initial impulse came from the Peabody Museum of Archaeology and Ethnology, Harvard University, which first organized systematic explorations at Maya sites in 1891, and it gradually developed academic programs dedicated to American archaeology (Hinsley 1984, 1985). At the same time, the growing ascendancy of American investments and political interests facilitated the work of American archaeologists in the country. While they collaborated with Guatemalan authorities and hired local personnel—notably artists who made important contributions as illustrators of archaeological finds—the aims, methods, and results of research were completely controlled by American researchers and institutions, making this a prime example of Trigger's imperialistic archaeology.

The Classic Maya site of Quirigua offers a clear example of the interplay between archaeology, politics, and foreign economic interests. This was the first site in Guatemala to become the focus of research-oriented archaeology, and it was also the first archaeological park in the country (figure 4.4). In 1910, the United Fruit Company—an American consortium that played a notorious role in Guatemala's politics and economy—set aside a seventy-five-hectare archaeological park at the ruins, which stood in the middle of an extensive banana plantation. The in situ preservation of the Quirigua stelae owes much to the company, which took care of the park for decades, while stimulating work by American archaeologists, beginning in 1912 (Morley 1935).

The Harvard-educated archaeologist Sylvanus G. Morley was a prominent participant in the first excavations at Quirigua. Morley founded and directed the Historical Division of the Carnegie Institution of Washington, which became the major driving force in Maya archaeology until the 1950s (Black 1990). Archaeologists at the Carnegie Institution carried out further research at Quirigua in the 1930s while also conducting a major project at Uaxactun. This project marked a departure from earlier work that focused on clearing major buildings, documenting the monuments, and recovering noteworthy artifacts. At Uaxactun, stratigraphic

studies and detailed ceramic analyses resulted in the formulation of a sound culture historical sequence for the Maya lowlands (Black 1990). Another focus of
attention was Kaminaljuyú, a major site in the Guatemala Valley, first noted by
Fuentes y Guzmán and later described by Maudslay. By the mid-twentieth century, the mounds of Kaminaljuyú were disappearing as a result of urban growth.
Multiple projects by Carnegie Institution archaeologists at this and other sites
produced a wealth of information for the culture history of the entire Maya area
(Kidder 1961).

Legislation and mild institutional development allowed Guatemalan authorities to stop the legitimate exportation of archaeological finds to foreign museums.
Beginning in 1930, the archaeological finds of American projects were housed in
the National Museum in Guatemala City. Following Mexico's example—where
a strong tradition of nationalist archaeology developed during this period—the
Guatemalan Instituto de Antropología e Historia (IDAEH) was created in 1946
in response to the nationalist policies of a newly elected government, after the
overthrow of Jorge Ubico's dictatorship in 1944 (Rubín de la Borbolla and Cerezo
Dardón 1953). For the first time, the country's archaeological sites were entrusted to
the care of a national institution that, despite its small size and limited resources,
promoted research and made important publications during its early years, in close
collaboration with American archaeologists working in the country.

The demise of the Carnegie Institution's Maya archaeology program coincided with the deterioration of Guatemalan-American relations during the early

Figure 4.4 The Guatemalan photographer Alberto Valdeavellano at work in the ruins
of Quirigua, ca. 1920. Postcard by Alberto Valdeavallano, collection of the Museo
Nacional de Historia, Guatemala.

1950s. Major American involvement in Guatemalan archaeology resumed after a coup d'état—arranged by the United States CIA—that overthrew the Guatemalan government in 1954 (Schlesinger et al. 1999). Beginning in 1956, the University of Pennsylvania Museum of Archaeology and Ethnology sponsored a long-term program of research at Tikal, which worked continuously until 1970. In many ways, this project marked a turning point in Guatemalan archaeology. From a scientific perspective, theoretical and methodological developments stimulated a gradual shift from culture history and monumental architecture to settlement patterns, subsistence, and the study of commoner residential areas. Equally important was the substantial investment made by the Guatemalan government, amounting to approximately half of the total budget of the Tikal Project (Coe 1982). Unlike earlier projects, where no effort was made to preserve the excavated buildings, work at Tikal involved the restoration of some of the largest buildings in the Maya area. As a result, Tikal became a prime tourist destination, making archaeological work relevant for the country's economy. Furthermore, the project provided training opportunities for Guatemalan personnel and students who subsequently played important roles in the development of professional archaeology in Guatemala.

ARCHAEOLOGY IN MODERN GUATEMALA

Professional training for archaeologists in Guatemala started belatedly in the mid-1970s. The creation of archaeology departments at the public Universidad de San Carlos and the private Universidad del Valle may find an explanation in the steady expansion of demand for higher education among an expanding urban middle-class (cf. Trigger 1989:14). The program at San Carlos was organized by the late Juan Pedro Laporte, an experienced archaeologist trained in Mexico, who conducted extensive research at Tikal and other sites in the Maya lowlands. The del Valle program was largely shaped by Marion Popenoe de Hatch, a graduate of the University of California, Berkeley, whose research concentrates on the highlands and Pacific coastal regions. Somewhat later, a third program was created at the University of San Carlos's campus in Santa Elena, Petén, in the heart of the lowland region where some of the largest Maya ruins are found. Once regarded as a remote wilderness, this region experienced a steady population growth in the previous decades, as a result of colonization programs sponsored by the Guatemalan government.

Professional archaeology has grown steadily, although a weak institutional development has severely limited the job market for Guatemalan archaeologists. To a large extent, Guatemalan archaeology remains strongly dependent on international collaboration. Research projects are still largely organized and directed by American archaeologists, joined in recent decades by researchers from other countries. Notably, French archaeologists have been active in Guatemala since the 1960s, producing important results for several regions of the country, while researchers from Spain, Japan, and other countries have also had a constant presence (Ichon 1996; Ciudad Ruiz 1984; Ohi 1994). Guatemalan archaeologists now form an important part of the staff of all research projects, although the collaboration is often unequal. While much of the fieldwork and artifact classification stages of every project are manned by Guatemalans, they rarely participate in the initial formulation of research, much less in the final stages of interpretation and publication of archaeological results at the international level. Language barriers, low incomes, and the marked weakness of libraries in the country make much of the resulting literature unavailable in the country. Yearly archaeological symposia, held at the National Museum of Archaeology and Ethnology since 1987, partly ameliorate these problems, while gradual improvements in training and expertise are turning Guatemalan researchers into active participants in current archaeological debates (see online memories of archaeology symposia on www. asociaciontikal.com).

Investment by the Guatemalan government in archaeology remains small, but research and restoration projects have been carried out at several sites, largely in hopes of promoting tourism. State-sponsored projects at major Maya sites, including Tikal, Uaxactun, Yaxha, Nakum, and Aguateca have been largely justified in terms of conservation and restoration for tourism, although they have also produced significant research results (e.g., Inomata et al. 2004; Laporte and Fialko 1995; Laporte and Valdés 1993; Orrego Corzo and Larios Villalta 1983; Quintana et al. 2001). Urged by the need to locate and record archaeological sites that are endangered by looting and development, the IDAEH also sponsors the Archaeological

Figure 4.5 A Maya tomb at the site of Chikin Tikal, during salvage work conducted by the archaeologist Miguel Orrego Corzo, in response to looting activities in the 1970s.

Atlas Project, a comprehensive effort to produce basic records of archaeological sites, whose coverage has grown steadily across the southern Maya lowlands (see reports on www.atlasarqueologico.com). Conservation problems are overwhelming, but there is a degree of protection at many archaeological sites in that region. By contrast, most sites in the highlands and Pacific coast remain unprotected. Exceptions include Mixco Viejo, Iximche, and Zaculeu in the highlands, while Tak'alik Ab'aj stands as the lone example of a long-running research and restoration project on the Pacific coast (Schieber de Lavarreda and Orrego Corzo 2010).

The international prestige of the ancient Maya was strengthened by the decipherment of hieroglyphic writing, pioneered in the 1950s by the Russian linguist Yurij Knorozov (Coe 1992; Stuart 1992). Moreover, the archaeological sites that were once buried in the jungle progressively became accessible to a growing tourist industry. Since the 1960s, an abrupt growth in the demand for ancient Maya artifacts in the international art market has spelled destruction by looting for many archaeological sites (figure 4.5). International treaties have limited the exportation of archaeological objects to some countries, but the efforts to quell looting activities and the illegal trade in antiquities have proved largely unsuccessful, due to acute problems of land tenure, low incomes in the countryside, political instability, and organized crime.

Accelerated development and urban growth are also taking a toll on the country's archaeological record. A large hydroelectric project in the Chixoy River prompted one of the few comprehensive programs of archaeological salvage, conducted in the 1970s by the French archaeologist Alain Ichon (1996). Responding to the urban growth of Guatemala City, multiple rescue projects have been carried out at Kaminaljuyú and other sites in the Guatemala valley. National legislation requiring archaeological rescue work has generated a contract archaeology sector in the country, but comprehensive programs of cultural-resources management are few, and the scientific results of many rescue projects remain dubious—a situation that parallels similar problems elsewhere in the modern world (Arroyo 2010).

Theoretical debates have played a partial role in Guatemalan archaeology. Like elsewhere in Latin America, the culture-historical approach remains strong, largely responding to local concerns about the history of the country and its modern inhabitants (Politis 2003). The Latin American social archaeology trend of the 1980s had a minor impact on the country (Oyuela Caycedo 1997; Patterson 1994). Currently, Guatemalan projects largely aim to document particular sites or regions, while the construction of local chronologies and the study of regional interaction remain strong. While a degree of technical sophistication has been achieved—often through collaboration with scholars from abroad—quantitative methods are rarely applied, and there are few attempts at theory building, cross-cultural comparison, modeling, or methodological development.

The early years of Guatemalan archaeology coincided with the height of the armed conflict between the state and guerrilla organizations that tore apart the country for several decades, reaching startling peaks of violence in the early 1980s. The Peace Agreements that ended this protracted conflict in 1996 resulted in renewed international cooperation and research. They also brought, for the first time in the country's history, an official recognition of the historical connections between modern Maya peoples and archaeological sites. However, this recognition acquired a distinctly religious overtone (Ivic de Monterroso 2004). The Peace Agreements labeled archaeological sites as "sacred places," emphasizing the state's obligation to secure access to such places for modern Maya spiritualists, an obligation that is now honored at every archaeological park in the country. More importantly, the end of the armed conflict resulted in rising levels of access to higher education for people of Maya ancestry. Archaeologists and other professionals that acknowledge a Maya ethnic identity are beginning to participate in archaeological research and archaeological site management in Guatemala. Furthermore, the expectations and decisions of both the Maya and non-Maya inhabitants of archaeological zones have become important factors in the planning and execution of research.

While Trigger's categories offer a useful comparative framework for the archaeological traditions of the modern world, their application to complex historical experiences, including Guatemala, is not easy. The archaeological concerns of Fuentes y Guzmán may be accurately termed colonialist, but the distinction between colonialist and nationalist archaeology became progressively blurred during the last two centuries. While only a few explicitly acknowledge a Maya ethnic identity, it would be grossly inaccurate to characterize the majority of Guatemalan archaeologists as having no connection with the archaeological past that they study, both in racial and cultural terms. Modern archaeology in Guatemala may still be considered imperialist in many ways, although legal procedures now regulate the activities of foreign researchers in the country, while their everyday collaborations with Guatemalan archaeologists have forged ties that significantly diminish the negative connotations of that term.

Guatemalan archaeology faces multiple challenges for the future. Yet, despite the problems and queries that have been described in this chapter, a vigorous tradition of research has gradually developed, producing significant contributions to ongoing debates about the country's ancient and modern history and society.

References

Anderson, Benedict. 1991. *Imagined Communities: Reflections on the Origin and Spread of Nationalism*. Verso, London.

Aguirre, Robert D. 2005. *Informal Empire: Mexico and Central America in Victorian Culture*. University of Minnesota Press, Minneapolis.

Arroyo, Bárbara, ed. 2010. *Entre cerros, cafetales y urbanismo en el valle de Guatemala: Proyecto de rescate Naranjo*. Academia de Geografía e Historia de Guatemala, Guatemala.

Black, Stephen L. 1990. The Carnegie Uaxactun Project and the Development of Maya Archaeology. *Ancient Mesoamerica* 1:257–276.

Brunhouse, Robert L. 1973. *In Search of the Maya: The First Archaeologists.* University of New Mexico Press, Albuquerque.

Brunhouse, Robert L. 1975. *Pursuit of the Maya: Some Archaeologists of Yesterday.* University of New Mexico Press, Albuquerque.

Castañeda Paganini, Ricardo. 1946. *Las ruinas de Palenque. Su descubrimiento y primeras exploraciones en el siglo XVIII.* Tipografía Nacional, Guatemala.

Chinchilla Mazariegos, Oswaldo. 1996. Peor es Nada: El origen de las esculturas de Cotzumalguapa en el Museum für Völkerkunde, Berlin. *Baessler-Archiv, Neue Folge* 44:295–357.

Chinchilla Mazariegos, Oswaldo. 1998. Archaeology and Nationalism in Guatemala at the Time of Independence. *Antiquity* 72:376–386.

Chinchilla Mazariegos, Oswaldo. 1999a. Francisco Antonio de Fuentes y Guzmán, precursor de la arqueología americana. *Anales de la Academia de Geografía e Historia de Guatemala* 74:39–69.

Chinchilla Mazariegos, Oswaldo. 1999b. Historia de la investigación arqueológica en Guatemala. In *Historia general de Guatemala*, edited by Jorge Luján Muñoz and Marion Popenoe de Hatch, vol. 1, pp. 99–118. Fundación para la Cultura y el Desarrollo, Guatemala.

Chinchilla Mazariegos, Oswaldo. 1999c. Historiografía de los Mayas de Guatemala: El pensamiento de Manuel García Elgueta. *Mesoamerica* 38:55–75.

Ciudad Ruiz, Andrés. 1984. *Arqueología de Agua Tibia, Totonicapán (Guatemala).* Cultura Hispánica, Madrid.

Coe, Michael D. 1992. *Breaking the Maya Code.* Thames and Hudson, London.

Coe, William R. 1982. *Introduction to the Archaeology of Tikal, Guatemala.* Tikal Report No. 12, University Museum Monograph 46. University of Pennsylvania, Philadelphia.

Fuentes y Guzmán, Francisco Antonio de. 1969–72. *Recordación Florida, discurso historial, natural, material, militar y político del reino de Guatemala.* Obras Históricas de Don Francisco Antonio de Fuentes y Guzmán, 3 vols. (edited by Carmelo Sáenz de Santa María). Biblioteca de Autores Españoles, vols. 230, 251, and 259. Ediciones Atlas, Madrid.

Graham, Ian. 2002. *Alfred Maudslay and the Maya: A Biography.* University of Oklahoma Press, Norman.

Hinsley, Curtis M. 1984. Wanted: One Good Man to Discover Central American Prehistory. *Harvard Magazine* 87(2):64A-64H.

Hinsley, Curtis M. 1985. From Shell-heaps to Stelae. Early Anthropology at the Peabody Museum. In *Objects and Others: Essays on Museums and Material Culture*, edited by George W. Stocking Jr., pp. 49–74. History of Anthropology, Vol. 3. University of Wisconsin Press, Madison.

Houston, Stephen D., Oswaldo Chinchilla Mazariegos, and David Stuart, eds. 2001. *The Decipherment of Ancient Maya Writing.* University of Oklahoma Press, Norman.

Huddleston, Lee Eldridge. 1967. *Origins of the American Indians. European Concepts, 1492–1729.* University of Texas Press, Austin.

Ichon, Alain. 1996. *La cuenca media del río Chixoy, Guatemala: Ocupación prehispánica y problemas actuales.* Centro Francés de Estudios Mexicanos y Centroamericanos, México/Guatemala.

Inomata, Takeshi, Erick Ponciano, Otto Román, Oswaldo Chinchilla, Véronique Breuil-Martínez, and Oscar Santos. 2004. An Unfinished Temple at the Classic Maya Centre of Aguateca, Guatemala. *Antiquity* 78:798–811.

Ivic de Monterroso, Matilde. 2004. The Sacred Place in the Development of Archaeology in Guatemala: An Analysis. In *Continuities and Changes in Maya Archaeology: Perspectives at the Millennium*, edited by Charles W. Golden and Greg Borgstede, pp. 295–307. Routledge, New York.

Kidder, Alfred V. 1961. Archaeological Investigations at Kaminaljuyu, Guatemala. *Proceedings of the American Philosophical Society* 105(6):559–570.

Laporte, Juan Pedro, and Vilma Fialko. 1995. Un reencuentro con Mundo Perdido, Tikal, Guatemala. *Ancient Mesoamerica* 6:41–94.

Laporte, Juan Pedro, and Juan Antonio Valdés. 1993. *Tikal y Uaxactún en el Preclásico*. Universidad Nacional Autónoma de México, México, D.F.

Luján Muñoz, Luis. 1972. Historia de la arqueología en Guatemala. *América Indígena* 32(2):353–376.

Luján Muñoz, Luis. 1973. El primer museo nacional de Guatemala (1866–1881). *Anales de la Sociedad de Geografía e Historia de Guatemala* 46:173–189.

Martínez Peláez, Severo. 2009. *La patria del criollo: An Interpretation of Colonial Guatemala*. Duke University Press, Durham.

Maudslay, Alfred P. 1889–1902. *Archaeology. Biologia Centrali-Americana*. 5 vols. R. H. Porter and Dualu & Co., London.

McCreery, David J. 1994. *Rural Guatemala 1760–1940*. Stanford University Press, Stanford, California.

Méndez, Modesto. 1955. Descubrimiento de las Ruinas de Tikal. *Antropología e historia de Guatemala* 7(1):3–7. [Originally published in 1848.]

Morley, Sylvanus G. 1935. *Guidebook to the Ruins of Quirigua*. Carnegie Institution, Washington, DC.

Navarrete, Carlos. 1982. Otra vez Modesto Méndez, Ambrosio Tut, y el moderno descubrimiento de Tikal. In *Historia y antropología de Guatemala. Ensayos en honor de J. Daniel Contreras R.*, edited by Jorge Luján Muñoz, 157–170. Facultad de Humanidades, Universidad de San Carlos, Guatemala.

Navarrete, Carlos. 2000. *Palenque, 1784: El inicio de la aventura arqueológica maya*. Universidad Nacional Autónoma de México, México, D.F.

Ohi, Kuniaki, ed. 1994. *Kaminaljuyú: 1991–1994*. 2 vols. Museo de Tabaco y Sal, Tokio.

Orrego Corzo, Miguel, and Rudy Larios Villalta. 1983. *Reporte de las Investigaciones Arqueológicas en el Grupo 5E-11, Tikal, Petén*. Instituto de Antropología e Historia, Guatemala.

Ortega y Medina, Juan A. 1953. Monroísmo arqueológico. *Cuadernos Americanos* 12(5):168–189 and 12(6):158–187.

Ortega y Medina, Juan A. 1990. La manipulación historiográfica estado unidense del pasado histórico y arqueológico latinoamericano. *Cuadernos Americanos, Nueva Época* 19:119–136.

Oyuela-Caycedo, Augusto, ed. 1994. *History of Latin American Archaeology*. Aldershot, England; Avebury, Brookfield, Vermont.

Oyuela-Caycedo, Augusto, ed. 1997. Social Archaeology in Latin America? Comments to T. C. Patterson. *American Antiquity* 62:365–374.

Patterson, T. C. 1994. Social Archaeology in Latin America: An Appreciation. *American Antiquity* 59:531–537.

Politis, Gustavo G. 2003. The Theoretical Landscape and the Methodological Development of Archaeology in Latin America. *American Antiquity* 68:245–272.

Preston, Richard. 1992. America's Egypt. John Lloyd Stephens and the Discovery of the Maya. *Princeton University Library Journal* 53(3):242–263.

Quintana, Oscar, Wolfgang W. Wurster, and Raúl Noriega. 2001. *Ciudades mayas del noreste del Petén, Guatemala: Un estudio urbanístico comparativo.* Verlag Phillip von Zabern, Mainz am Rhein.

Rubín de la Borbolla, Daniel F., and Hugo Cerezo Dardón. 1953. *Guatemala: Monumentos históricos y arqueológicos.* Instituto Panamericano de Antropología e Historia, Mexico.

Saint-Lu, André. 1978. *Condición colonial y consciencia criolla en Guatemala (1524–1821).* Primera edición, 1970. Editorial Universitaria, Guatemala.

Schieber de Lavarreda, Christa, and Miguel Orrego Corzo. 2010. Preclassic Olmec and Maya Monuments and Architecture at Takalik Abaj. In *The Place of Stone Monuments: Context, Use, and Meaning in Mesoamerica's Preclassic Transition*, pp. 177–205. Dumbarton Oaks, Washington, DC.

Schlesinger, Stephen, E., Stephen Kinzer, and John H. Coatsworth. 1999. *Bitter Fruit: The Story of the American Coup in Guatemala.* David Rockefeller Center for Latin American Studies, Harvard University, Cambridge, Massachusetts.

Stoll, Otto. 1889. *Die Ethnologie der Indianerstäme von Guatemala.* Verlag von P.W.M. Trap, Leiden.

Stuart, George E. 1992. Quest for Decipherment: A Historical and Biographical Survey of Maya Hieroglyphic Investigation. In *New Theories on the Ancient Maya*, edited by Elin C. Danien and Robert J. Sharer, pp. 1–65. University of Pennsylvania Museum, Philadelphia.

Trigger, Bruce. 1984. Alternative Archeologies: Nationalist, Colonialist, Imperialist. *Man* 19:355–370.

Trigger, Bruce. 1989. *A History of Archaeological Thought.* Cambridge University Press, Cambridge.

Wagner, Regina. 2001. *Historia del café en Guatemala.* Villegas Editores, Bogotá.

CHAPTER 5

THE ARCHAEOLOGY OF BELIZE IN THE TWENTY-FIRST CENTURY

JAIME J. AWE

LOCATED on the southeastern corner of the Yucatán Peninsula, Belize (Figure 5.1) is the second smallest country in Central America. In spite of its size, however, the country has an incredibly rich and diverse cultural heritage that includes the remains of pioneering preceramic cultures, numerous prehistoric cities that reflect the grandeur of Maya civilization, the ruins of several "Visita" churches that represent the failed efforts of sixteenth-century Spanish *entradas*, and various historic sites of the British colonial period. Today, management of this rich cultural resource is the responsibility of Belize's Institute of Archaeology, an institution that traces its origin to the late nineteenth century. This chapter provides a brief history of the management of archaeological resources in Belize, a summary of archaeological investigations during the last two hundred years, and the present direction of archaeological research in the country.

ARCHAEOLOGICAL-RESOURCE MANAGEMENT IN BELIZE

The management of archaeological resources in Belize has a long history. Indeed, the first antiquities legislation, The Ancient Monuments Protection Ordinance, was passed more than a century ago in 1894. The most important feature of this

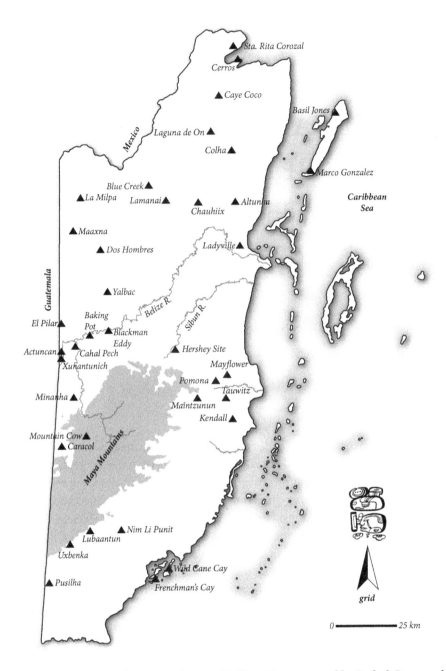

Figure 5.1 Selected archaeological sites of Belize. Map prepared by Rafael Guerra after Helmke (2003). Belize Institute of Archaeology, Belmopan.

legislation was that it provided recognition and protection for all monuments sited on land owned by the government. Thirty years later, in 1924, the passing of the Ancient Monument and Relics Ordinance established the first set of conditions for archaeological research in Belize. This was succeeded by the 1928 Antiquities

Ordinance, which provided legislation that addressed the acquisition of antiquities by the government and the forbiddance of exportation of antiquities without the consent of the Governor in Council.

In spite of these precocious pieces of legislation, however, there was still no government institution charged with the specific task of managing the country's archaeological resources in the first half of the twentieth century. This eventually changed in 1952 when Alexander Hamilton Anderson, an English colonial government officer, was appointed the first Assistant Secretary General with responsibility for archaeological activities in Belize. Although Anderson had no formal training in archaeology, he embraced his new position with considerable fervor and dedication, and it was largely as a result of his insight and perseverance that he subsequently convinced the colonial government to establish a Department of Archaeology in 1957 with him as the first Archaeological Commissioner. A year later, Anderson drafted amendments to the 1928 legislation, which, after their enactment, provided the fledgling department with greater legislative power to manage the country's archaeological resources. Throughout the next ten years, Anderson spent considerable effort recording sites across the country, and he also encouraged foreign archaeologists to come and conduct research in Belize (a tradition that continues today). Unfortunately, illness and the urgent need for medical attention forced Anderson to depart for England in 1967. In an effort to fill the void left by Anderson's premature departure, the Belize government convinced David Pendergast, a researcher from the Royal Ontario Museum (ROM), to serve, temporarily, as Acting Archaeological Commissioner. Less than a year later (1968), Peter Schmidt, a German national, was hired as Belize's second Commissioner of Archaeology. While credit must be given to Schmidt for continuing Anderson's pioneering work, his greatest contribution to the archaeology of Belize was his drafting of the Ancient Monuments and Antiquities Ordinance. Enacted in 1971, this comprehensive piece of legislation substantially improved the legal mandate of Belize's Department of Archaeology and served as the primary legal instrument for managing the country's archaeological heritage until 2003. The single most important contribution of this law is that it vested ownership of all monuments and antiquities, whether situated on land, below ground, or below water, to the people and government of Belize.

The year 1971 marked another important milestone in the history of Belizean archaeology; it witnessed the appointment of Joseph Palacio as the first native Belizean Archaeological Commissioner. Prior to taking over the helms of the department, Palacio had successfully pursued bachelor's and master's degrees in anthropology in Canada. In the early and mid-1970s, Palacio hired two other Belizean assistants, Harriot Topsey in 1973 and Jaime Awe in 1976. Topsey and Palacio subsequently left to continue studies in the United Kingdom and the United States, respectively, and Awe remained as Acting Head of the department until 1978 when he, too, left for studies abroad.

In the first two years (1978 to 1980) following Awe's departure, Elizabeth Graham, an American national, served as Archaeological Commissioner. Foremost among her accomplishments was the securing of funds to train several junior staff members in Canada, the United States, and the United Kingdom. After Graham's departure, the Belize Department of Archaeology continued to grow under the direction of several young Belizeans. In chronological order of service, these officers include the late Harriot Topsey and Winnel Branche, and Allan Moore, John Morris, Brian Woodye, and George Thompson.

The next, and perhaps most profound, change to the management of archaeology in Belize came in 2003 with the passing of the National Institute of Culture and History Act. This led to the creation of the National Institute of Culture and History (NICH), which brought together four previous departments of government (including the Department of Archaeology) that were historically responsible for the preservation and promotion of Belizean culture in all its manifestations. Today, the Institute of Archaeology continues to function under NICH, with a staff that is considerably larger and more professionally trained than it had been in 1971.

BELIZEAN ARCHAEOLOGY IN THE
LAST 200 YEARS

Three summaries of the development of archaeology in Belize have been published. In chronological order, these include articles by Heather McKillop and Jaime Awe (1983), by Norman Hammond (1983), and by David Pendergast (1993). Both the McKillop and Awe and Hammond articles subdivided the development of archaeology into four phases: the European period (1524–1840), the Exploratory period (1840–1925), the Institutional period (1925–1960), and the Problem-Oriented period (1960–1980s). In his more recent article, Pendergast subdivided the development into three major phases that roughly coincide with the last three phases discussed in the McKillop and Awe and Hammond articles. A summary of these phases follows.

Spanning from 1809 to 1925, Pendergast's phase 1 covers that period of time when all archaeologically related work was associated with the explorations of adventurers and archaeological aficionados. This phase was particularly dominated by the explorations of Thomas Gann, a British colonial medical doctor, who visited several Maya sites in the country. Many of Gann's early adventures are published in two major volumes (Gann 1925, 1926) that are now out of print. While limited in terms of their overall contribution to archaeological knowledge, both volumes provide useful ethnographic data, as well as unique information on Lubaantun and the mostly destroyed site of Santa Rita, Corozal.

The second phase (1925 to 1939) of investigations in Belize witnessed the introduction of the "first controlled archaeological research" (Pendergast 1993: 3), and the participation of several foreign institutions (Hammond 1983; McKillop and Awe 1983). The latter include Oliver Ricketson's (1931) Carnegie Institution of Washington's work at the Belize River valley site of Baking Pot, and the British Museum's investigations at Lubaantun in southern Belize (Joyce 1926, 1929; Joyce et al. 1927, 1928). George Mason's (1928) work at several cave sites in the Cayo District also pioneered cave research during this phase, but the single greatest contributor to the archaeology of Belize during this period was J. Eric S. Thompson. Following his brief collaboration with British colleagues at Lubaantun, Thompson (1931, 1939) subsequently investigated several sites in the southern Cayo District, followed by excavations at San Jose. The former work was conducted under the auspices of the Field Museum of Chicago, and the latter under the flag of the Carnegie Institution of Washington. As Pendergast (1993: 6) notes, Thompson's prominence as a leading Mayanist helped to bring Belizean archaeology to the attention of Mesoamericanists and also "served as the bridge between early and modern research in the country." In spite of these early achievements, however, the onset of the Second World War brought research to a close, and archaeological work in Belize became dormant for the greater part of the next decade.

The subsequent period of archaeological development in Belize, designated as the Problem-Oriented period by McKillop and Awe (1983) and Hammond (1983), is divided into three phases by Pendergast (1993). The latter's divisions include the Immediate Postwar period (1949–1960), the Beginning of Growth (1961–1970), and the Blossoming of Belize (1971–1990). Given the more recent temporal point of reference of this paper, I would extend the last subdivision to the year 2000, and a fourth subphase should be designated as the post-second millennia phase.

In the early years after the war, archaeological research was gradually resumed in Belize. These investigations included a short-lived project by William and Michael Coe (1956) at Nohoch Ek, Kidder and Ekholm's (1951) work at Pomona, Satterthwaite's (1951, 1954) explorations at Caracol, Meighan and Bennyhoff's (1951) survey of coastal sites, and Euan MacKie's (1985) Cambridge University expedition to Xunantunich. In spite of these limited efforts, it was actually during this early postwar period that Gordon Willey first introduced settlement-pattern research to Maya studies with his landmark investigations at Barton Ramie in the Belize Valley (Willey et al. 1965).

In the decade (1960–1970) following the postwar phase, archaeological work continued to be limited in Belize. Much of this work was also dominated by two projects conducted under the auspices of the Royal Ontario Museum (ROM), and Cambridge University. The ROM projects included William and Mary Bullard's (1965) excavations at Baking Pot and San Estevan (Bullard 1965), and David Pendergast's (1964, 1969, 1970, 1971, 1974) investigations of several cave sites and Altún Ha. Pendergast's (1979, 1982, 1990) investigations at Altún Ha are particularly noteworthy because, in addition to the wealth of information it produced on this coastal center, it represented the first long-term project conducted at a major site in Belize. The Cambridge University project (1969–1970), directed by Norman Hammond (1975a), produced important archaeological information on southern

Belize, and it was one of the first to apply a regional approach for understanding the political landscape of a lowland Maya subregion.

The 1970s to 1990s were referred to as "The Blossoming of Belize" by Pendergast (1993: 9). The reason for this label is most likely because these years witnessed a proliferation of foreign archaeological projects in the country. Many of the projects were also relatively smaller than those before, likely as a result of cutbacks in funding by the large institutions. Furthermore, in the 1970s and 1980s a large number of North American universities introduced Mesoamerican studies to their academic programs and this greatly increased the number of scholars interested in conducting research in this culture area. Given the large volume of scholarly work that was produced by so many archaeological projects, and the brevity of this chapter, only a few of these projects are described below.

In the 1970s, most archaeological investigations focused on northern Belize. Notable among these projects are Norman Hammond's (1973, 1975b) survey of the Corozal District; Dennis Puleston's (1977) and Billy Lee Turner and Peter Harrison's (1983) investigations of raised field systems; David Freidel's (1977, 1978) Southern Methodist University excavations at Cerros; Norman Hammond's (1991) investigations of Preclassic occupation at Cuello; the excavations of the chert manufacturing settlement at Colha by Tom Hester and Harry Shafer (1984; Hester et al. 1980, 1982); and David Pendergast's (1981) project at Lamanai, a settlement that was occupied from the Preclassic through the Spanish and British colonial periods. Significant research in other parts of the country included Elizabeth Graham's (1983, 1987) survey of coastal sites in the Stann Creek District, Heather McKillop's (1987) excavations at Moho Caye, Paul Healy's (Healy et al. 1983) work on agricultural terraces in the Maya Mountains, and Barbara MacLeod and Dorie Reents's (1980) investigations at Petroglyph Cave.

In the 1980s and 1990s, research projects continued to increase in number and diversity. In northern Belize, Diane Chase (1982) completed a project at the important Postclassic site of Santa Rita, and Richard MacNeish (1981, 1982; MacNeish et al. 1980) conducted the first reconnaissance of preceramic sites in Belize. Investigations by the University of Texas, Austin, at the location of Colha and its periphery also ended, and the results of much of this research are published in several volumes and dissertations (e.g., Buttles 2002; Valdez 1987). At Cob Swamp, just north of Colha, Mary Pohl and colleagues (1996) recovered important new data on early plant exploitation at the end of the Archaic period. Several new projects, such as Elizabeth Graham's Postclassic project at Lamanai (Graham et al. 1989), Adams and Valdez's work in the Three Rivers Region of Orange Walk (Scarborough et al. 2003), and Tom Guderjan's (2004) investigations at Blue Creek, were also started at this time.

After a relatively inactive 1970s, western and southern Belize witnessed a resurgence of archaeological activity in the 1980s and 1990s. In the south, Richard Leventhal (1990) expanded on the regional work previously conducted by Hammond in the seventies. In the west, Arlen and Diane Chase (1987, 1994) began their long-term research program at Caracol, and several new projects commenced investigations in the upper Belize River Valley. The latter included research at Tipu (Graham et al. 1985), Pacbitun (Healy 1990) Buena Vista (Ball and Taschek 1991, 2004), Cahal Pech (Awe 1992), Baking Pot (Audet and Awe 2004, 2005), Blackman Eddy (Brown 2003, Garber et al. 2004), Xunantunich (Leventhal and Ashmore 2004); and Minanha (Iannone 2005). A regional cave project by Awe (Awe, Griffith, and Gibbs 2005; Helmke 2009; Moyes 2006) investigated a number of subterranean sites in the Roaring Creek, Barton Creek, and Macal River valleys. The results of these numerous projects in the Belize Valley are available in various journals and in several volumes edited by James Garber (2004), Brady and Prufer (2005), LeCount and Yaeger (2010), and Prufer and Brady (2005), to name a few.

Important milestones for the national archaeology of Belize were the first major conservation efforts in the country, which were recorded in the early 1990s. The first of these projects was made possible by a grant from the United States Agency for International Development, and it resulted with limited preservation at Cahal Pech, Caracol, Xunantunich, Santa Rita, and Lamanai. A few years later, and with funding from the European Union, the Maya Archaeological Sites Development Program (MASDP) conserved a number of buildings in the site cores of Lubaantun and Nimli Punit. Of particular note is the fact the MASDP represents the first project of its kind to be directed by Belizean archaeologists. This tradition was continued in 2000–2004 when the Belize government launched the Tourism Development Project (TDP). The primary focus of the TDP was the excavation and conservation of several of Belize's major archaeological sites. Coordinated and directed by the Belizean archaeologists Jaime Awe and Allan Moore, the project not only produced a wealth of archaeological information, but also served to transform Caracol, Xunantunich, Cahal Pech, Altún Ha, Lamanai, and Lubaantun into major tourism destinations.

The single most important change of the new millennium, however, came in 2003 with the passing of the NICH Act and the establishment of the National Institute of Culture and History (NICH). Modeled along the lines of the Instituto Nacional de Antropología e Historia (INAH) in Mexico, this new statutory board incorporated several departments of government that were involved with cultural-resource management. With the stroke of a pen, the Department of Archaeology was dissolved and then transformed into the Institute of Archaeology (IOA). This transition gave the IOA greater freedom to pursue its initiatives and the opportunity to restructure the institution.

THE STRUCTURE, GOALS, AND DIRECTION OF THE IOA

The present IOA has some seventy officers: seventeen at its headquarters in the capital city, Belmopan, and a little more than fifty park managers and rangers that are stationed at fifteen parks countrywide. Today the Institute is also subdivided into four sections: Research, Education, Park Management, and Policy and Planning. The Research division is responsible for curating the national collection and for managing all fieldwork in the country, including the review of applications to conduct research and the oversight of archaeological projects. The Education division promotes and advances the knowledge, understanding, and appreciation of Belize's archaeological heritage. The Park Management division is responsible for the sustainable management of archaeological sites designated as tourism destinations, and it also ensures that the parks are maintained at international standards and that visitors have a high-quality experience. The Policy and Planning division concerns itself with developing policies and guidelines for the protection, preservation, and enhancement of cultural heritage. Collectively, these divisions of the IOA focus their energy on achieving the four major goals of the institution. These goals include the following:

1. To protect and preserve the archaeological heritage of Belize;
2. To encourage research in temporal, spatial, and topical areas where [the IOA believes] knowledge and scholarship for the country is lacking;
3. To disseminate knowledge of archaeological heritage to national and international communities; and
4. To integrate archaeology and tourism development in a sustainable manner.

Beginning in 2003, the IOA hosts an annual international symposium on Belizean archaeology and has successfully published the proceedings of these meetings in annual and internationally accredited, journal-style volumes (cf. Awe et al. 2004; Awe, Morris et al. 2005; Morris et al. 2006, 2007, 2008, 2009, 2010, 2011). In addition to these scholarly publications, the IOA produces a quarterly newsletter entitled "The Underground," and it conducts extensive outreach programs for primary, secondary, and tertiary institutions and for the general public.

In the area of research and conservation, Belize hosts, and supports, between fifteen and twenty annual foreign projects that are as diverse in their research focus as they are in their geographical distribution. The large quantity of data produced by these investigations ensures that Belizean content is present in almost all major publications focusing on Maya civilization. Encouragement of, and collaboration with, foreign researchers has also allowed Belize to be at the vanguard of Maya research. The latter is reflected by the fact that Belize was the first Mundo Maya country to apply light detection and ranging (LIDAR) technology to settlement research (Chase et al. 2011), and by its significant contribution of information on almost all topics and phases of lowland Maya development (Brown and Stanton 2003; Chase and Chase 1992; Chase et al. 1985; Graham et al. 1989; Hammond 1982; Helmke et al. 2003; Iannone and Connell 2003; Jones 1989; Lohse 2010; Lohse et al. 2005, 2006; Lucero 2006; Martin and Grube 2000; Mason 2000; McAnany 2004; McKillop 2002, 2005; Mock 1998; Rosenwig 2006; Scarborough 2003). Belize is also one of the only Mundo Maya countries that allow foreign field schools to work within its borders. This reflects the IOA's philosophical position on education and its commitment to participate in training the next generation of Mayanists.

Since the year 2000, the archaeology of Belize has certainly come of age. The Belize Institute of Archaeology has gained greater visibility and prestige as an institution. It supervises cutting-edge research, it maintains world-class management of its archaeological parks, it organizes an annual international symposium in archaeology, it encourages collaboration with foreign institutions, and it has been very successful in integrating archaeology and tourism development (Awe 2005). With its motto "Preserving the Past for the Future" and its missionary goals, Belize is certainly well positioned in the twenty-first century to continue contributing to knowledge of the Mesoamerican past.

REFERENCES

Audet, Carolyn M., and Jaime J. Awe. 2004. What's Cooking at Baking Pot: A Report of the 2001 to 2003 Seasons. *Research Reports in Belizean Archaeology* 1:49–59.

Audet, Carolyn M., and Jaime J. Awe. 2005. The Political Organization of the Belize Valley: Evidence from Baking Pot, Belize. *Research Reports in Belizean Archaeology* 2:357–364.

Awe, Jaime J. 1992. Dawn in the Land Between the Rivers: Formative Occupation at Cahal Pech, Belize and Its Implication for Preclassic Developments in the Maya Lowlands. PhD dissertation, Institute of Archaeology, University of London, England.

Awe, Jaime J. 2005. *Maya Cities and Sacred Caves: A Guide to the Archaeological Sites of Belize*. Cubola Books, Benque Viejo, Belize.

Awe, Jaime J., Cameron Griffith, and Sherry Gibbs. 2005. Cave Stelae and Megalithic Monuments in Western Belize, In *The Maw of the Earth Monster: Mesoamerican Ritual Cave Use*, edited by James E. Brady and Keith M. Prufer, pp. 223–249. University of Texas Press, Austin.

Awe, Jaime J., John M. Morris, and Sherilyne Jones, eds. 2004. *Research Reports in Belizean Archaeology*, Volume 1. Institute of Archaeology, Belize.

Awe, Jaime J., John M. Morris, Sherilyne Jones, and Christophe Helmke, eds. 2005. *Research Reports in Belizean Archaeology*, Volume 1. Institute of Archaeology, Belize.

Ball, Joseph W., and Jennifer T. Taschek. 1991. Late Classic Lowland Maya Political Organization and Central-Place Analysis. *Ancient Mesoamerica* 2(2):149–165.

Ball, Joseph W., and Jennifer T. Taschek. 2004. Buenavista del Cayo: A Short Outline of Occupational and Cultural History at an Upper Belize Valley Regal-Ritual Center. In *The Ancient Maya of the Belize Valley: Half a Century of Archaeological Research*, edited by James F. Garber, pp. 149–167. University Press of Florida, Gainesville.

Bullard, William R. 1965 *Stratigraphic Excavations at San Estevan, British Honduras*. Royal Ontario Museum, Art and Archaeology Occasional Papers 9, Royal Ontario Museum, Toronto.

Bullard, William R., and Mary R. Bullard. 1965. *Late Classic Finds at Baking Pot, British Honduras*. Royal Ontario Museum, Art and Archaeology Occasional Papers 8, Royal Ontario Museum, Toronto.

Brady James E., and Keith M. Prufer. 2005. *The Maw of the Earth Monster: Mesoamerican Ritual Cave Use*. University of Texas Press, Austin.

Brown, M. Kathryn. 2003. Emerging Complexity in the Maya Lowlands: A View from Blackman Eddy, Belize. PhD dissertation, Southern Methodist University.

Brown, M. Kathryn, and Travis W. Stanton, eds. 2003. *Ancient Mesoamerican Warfare*. Altamira Press, Walnut Creek, California.

Buttles, Palma J. 2002. Material and Meaning: A Contextual Examination of Select Portable Material Culture from Colha, Belize. PhD dissertation, University of Texas, Austin.

Chase, Arlen E., and Diane Z. Chase. 1987. *Investigations at the Classic Maya City of Caracol, Belize: 1985–1987*. Pre-Columbian Art Research Institute Monograph 3, San Francisco.

Chase, Arlen E., Diane Z. Chase, and Prudence M. Rice. 1985. *The Lowland Maya Postclassic*. University of Texas Press, Austin.

Chase, Arlen F., Diane Z. Chase, John F. Weishampel, Jason B. Drake, Ramesh L. Shrestha, K. Clint Slatton, Jaime J. Awe, and William E. Carter. 2011. Airborne LiDAR, Archaeology, and the Ancient Maya Landscape at Caracol, Belize. *Journal of Archaeological Science* 38(2):387–398.

Chase, Diane Z. 1982. Spatial and Temporal Variability in Postclassic Northern Belize. PhD dissertation, University of Pennsylvania, Philadelphia.

Chase, Diane Z., and Arlen E. Chase, eds. 1992. *Mesoamerican Elites: An Archaeological Assessment*. University of Oklahoma Press, Norman.

Chase, Diane Z., and Arlen E. Chase, eds. 1994. *Studies in the Archaeology of Caracol, Belize*. PARI, San Francisco.

Coe, William R., and Michael D. Coe. 1956. Excavations at Nohoch Ek, British Honduras. *American Antiquity* 21:370–382.

Freidel, David A. 1977 A Late Preclassic Monumental Mask at Cerros, Northern Belize. *Journal of Field Archaeology* 4:488–491.

Freidel, David A. 1978 Maritime Adaptations and the Rise of Maya Civilization: The View from Cerros, Belize. In *Prehistoric Coastal Adaptations: The Economy and Ecology of Maritime Middle America*, edited by Barbara L. Stark and Barbara Voorhies, pp. 239–265. Academic Press, New York.

Gann, Thomas A. 1925. *Mystery Cities: Explorations and Adventures in Lubaantun*. Duckworth, London.

Gann, Thomas A. 1926. *Ancient Cities and Modern Tribes: Exploration and Adventure in Maya Lands*. Duckworth, London.

Garber, James F., ed. 2004. *The Ancient Maya of the Belize Valley: Half a Century of Archaeological Research*. University Press of Florida, Gainesville.

Garber, James, M. Kathryn Brown, Jaime J. Awe, and Christopher J. Hartman. 2004. The Terminal Early Formative Kanocha Phase (1100–900 B.C.) at Blackman Eddy. *Research Reports in Belizean Archaeology* 1: 13–25.

Graham, Elizabeth. 1983. The Highlands of the Lowlands: Environment and Archaeology in the Stann Creek District, Belize, Central America. PhD dissertation, University of Cambridge, England.

Graham, Elizabeth. 1987. Resource Diversity in Belize and its Implications for Models of Lowland Trade. *American Antiquity* 52(4):753–767.

Graham, Elizabeth A., Grant D. Jones, and Robert R. Kautz. 1985. Archaeology and Ethnohistory on a Spanish Colonial Frontier: An Interim Report on the Macal-Tipu Project in Western Belize. In *The Lowland Maya Postclassic*, edited by Arlen F. Chase and Prudence M. Rice, pp. 206–214. University of Texas Press, Austin.

Graham, E., D. M. Pendergast, and G. D. Jones. 1989. On the Fringes of Conquest: Maya-Spanish Contact in Colonial Belize. *Science* 246: 1254–1259.

Guderjan, Thomas H. 2004. Public Architecture, Ritual and Temporal Dynamics at the Maya Center of Blue Creek, Belize. *Ancient Mesoamerica* 15:235–250.

Hammond, Norman. 1973. British Museum-Cambridge University Corozal Project 1973 Interim Report. Centre of Latin American Studies, Cambridge University, Cambridge.

Hammond, Norman. 1975a. *Lubaantun: A Classic Maya Realm*. Peabody Museum of Archaeology and Ethnology Monograph 2, Harvard University, Cambridge, Massachusetts.

Hammond, Norman. 1975b. Archaeology in Northern Belize: 1974–1975. Interim Report of the British Museum-Cambridge University Corozal Project, Centre of Latin American Studies, Cambridge University, Cambridge.

Hammond, Norman. 1982. The Prehistory of Belize. *Journal of Field Archaeology* 9:349–362.

Hammond, Norman. 1983. The Development of Belizean Archaeology. *Antiquity* 57:19–27.

Hammond, Norman, ed. 1991. *Cuello: An Early Maya Community in Belize*. Cambridge University Press, Cambridge.

Healy, Paul F. 1990. Excavations at Pacbitun, Belize: Preliminary Report on the 1986 and 1987 Investigations. *Journal of Field Archaeology* 17(3):247–262.

Healy, Paul F, John D. H. Lambert, J. T. Arnason, and R. J. Hebda. 1983. Caracol, Belize: Evidence of Ancient Maya Agricultural Terraces. *Journal of Field Archaeology* 10:397–410.

Helmke, Christophe. 2009. *Ancient Maya Cave Usage as Attested in the Glyphic Corpus of the Maya Lowlands and the Caves of the Roaring Creek Valley, Belize*. PhD dissertation, Institute of Archaeology, University of London.

Helmke, Christophe G. B.; Jaime J. Awe, and Cameron S. Griffith. 2003. "El Arte Rupestre de Belice" In *Arte Rupestre de México Oriental y Centro América*, edited by Martin Künne and Mattias Strecker, pp. 97–117. Gebr. Mann Verlag, Berlin.

Hester, T. R., and H. J. Shafer. 1984. Exploitation of Chert Resources by the Ancient Maya of Northern Belize, Central America. *World Archaeology* 16:157–173.

Hester, Thomas R., Jack D. Eaton, and Harry J. Shafer. 1980. *The Colha Project, Second Season, 1980 Interim Report*. University of Texas, San Antonio.

Hester, Thomas R., Harry J. Shafer, and Jack D. Eaton. 1982. *Archaeology at Colha, Belize: The 1981 Interim Report*. Center for Archaeological Research, the University of Texas at San Antonio and the Centro Studie Ricerche Ligabue, Venezia.

Iannone, Gyles. 2005. The Rise and Fall of an Ancient Maya Petty Royal Court. *Latin American Antiquity* 16(1):26–44.

Iannone, Gyles, and Samuel V. Connell, eds. 2003. *Perspectives on Ancient Maya Rural Complexity*. Monograph 49, Cotsen Institute of Archaeology, University of California, Los Angeles.

Jones, Grant, D. 1989. *Maya Resistance to Spanish Rule: Time and History on a Spanish Frontier*. University of New Mexico Press, Albuquerque.

Joyce, Thomas A. 1926. Report on the Investigations at Lubaantun, British Honduras. *Journal of Royal Anthropological Institute* 56:207–230.

Joyce, Thomas A. 1929. Report on the British Museum Expedition to British Honduras, 1929. *Journal of the Royal Anthropological Institute* 59:439–459.

Joyce, Thomas A., J. C. Clark, and J. Eric S. Thompson. 1927. Report on the British Museum Expedition to British Honduras, 1927. *Journal of Royal Anthropological Institute* 57:295–323.

Joyce, Thomas A., Thomas Gann, E. L. Gruning, and R. C. E. Long. 1928. Report
    on the British Museum Expedition to British Honduras, 1928. *Journal of Royal
    Anthropological Institute* 58:295–323.
Kidder, Alfred V., and Gordon F. Ekholm. 1951. Some Archaeological Specimens from
    Pomona, British Honduras. *Carnegie Institution of Washington Notes on Middle
    American Archaeology and Ethnology 102*. Carnegie Institution of Washington,
    Washington, DC.
LeCount, Lisa, and Jason Yaeger, eds. 2010. *Classic Maya Provincial Politics: Xunantunich
    and Its Hinterlands*. University of Arizona Press, Tucson.
Leventhal, Richard M. 1990. Southern Belize: An Ancient Maya Region. In *Vision and
    Revision in Maya Studies*, edited by Flora S. Clancy and Peter D. Harrison, pp.
    125–141. University of New Mexico Press, Albuquerque.
Leventhal, Richard M., and Wendy Ashmore. 2004. Xunantunich in a Belize Valley
    Context. In *The Ancient Maya of the Belize Valley: Half a Century of Archaeological
    Research*, edited by James F. Garber, pp. 168–179. University Press of Florida,
    Gainesville.
Lohse, Jon C. 2010. Archaic Origins of the Lowland Maya. *Latin American Antiquity*
    21(3):312–352.
Lohse, Jon C. Jaime J. Awe, Cameron Griffith, Robert Rosenswig, and Fred Valdez, Jr.
    2006. Preceramic Occupations In Belize: Updating the Paleoindian and Archaic
    Record. *Latin American Antiquity* 17(2):209–226.
Lohse, Jon C. and Fred Valdez, Jr., eds. 2004. *Ancient Maya Commoners*. University of
    Texas Press, Austin.
Lucero, Lisa J. 2006. *Water and Ritual: The Rise and Fall of Classic Maya Rulers*.
    University of Texas Press, Austin.
MacKie, Euan W. 1985. *Excavations at Xunantunich and Pomona in 1969–1950, Belize*.
    British Archaeological Reports (BAR) International Series.
MacNeish, R. S. 1981. *Second Annual Report of the Belize Archaic Archaeological
    Reconnaissance*. R. S. Peabody Foundation, Andover, Massachusetts.
MacNeish, R. S. 1982. *Third Annual Report of the Belize Archaic Archaeological
    Reconnaissance*. R. S. Peabody Foundation, Andover, Massachusetts.
MacNeish, R. S., S. J. K. Wilkerson, and A. Nelken-Terner. 1980. *First Annual Report
    of the Belize Archaic Archaeological Reconnaissance*. R. S. Peabody Foundation,
    Andover, Massachusetts.
Martin, Simon, and Nikolai Grube. 2000. *Chronicle of the Maya Kings and Queens:
    Deciphering the Dynasties of the Ancient Maya*. Thames and Hudson, London.
Mason, George. 1928. Pottery and Other Artifacts from Caves in British Honduras and
    Guatemala. *Museum of the American Indian, Heye Foundation, Indian Notes and
    Monographs 47*, Heye Foundation, New York.
Mason, Marilyn A. 2000. *In the Realm of Nachan Kan: Postclassic Maya Archaeology at
    Laguna de On, Belize*. University Press of Colorado, Boulder.
McAnany, Patricia A., ed. 2004. *K'axob: Ritual, Work, and Family in an Ancient Maya
    Village*. Monumenta Archaeologica 22, Cotsen Institute of Archaeology, University
    of California, Los Angeles.
McKillop, Heather. 1987. Wild Cane Caye, Belize: An Insular Classic Period to Post-
    Classic Period Maya Trading Station. PhD dissertation, University of California,
    Santa Barbara.
McKillop, Heather. 2002. *Salt, White Gold of the Ancient Maya*. University Press of
    Florida, Gainesville.

McKillop, Heather. 2005. *In Search of Maya Sea Traders.* Texas A&M University Press, College Station.

McKillop, Heather, and Jaime J. Awe. 1983. The History of Archaeological Research in Belize. *Belizean Studies* 11(2):1–9.

Meighan, Charles W., and J. A. Bennyhof. 1951. A Shell Snake Effigy from British Honduras. *American Antiquity* 16:352–353.

Mock, Shirley B., ed. 1998. *The Sowing and the Dawning: Termination, Dedication and Transformation in the Archaeological and Ethnographic Record of Mesoamerica.* University of New Mexico Press, Albuquerque.

Morris, John M., Sherilyne Jones, Jaime J. Awe, and Christophe Helmke, eds. 2006. *Research Reports in Belizean Archaeology*, Volume 3, Institute of Archaeology, Belize.

Morris, John M., Sherilyne Jones, Jaime J. Awe, and Christophe Helmke, eds. 2007. *Research Reports in Belizean Archaeology*, Volume 4, Institute of Archaeology, Belize.

Morris, John M., Sherilyne Jones, Jaime J. Awe, and Christophe Helmke, eds. 2008. *Research Reports in Belizean Archaeology*, Volume 5, Institute of Archaeology, Belize.

Morris, John M., Sherilyne Jones, Jaime J. Awe, George Thompson, and Christophe Helmke, eds. 2009. *Research Reports in Belizean Archaeology*, Volume 6, Institute of Archaeology, Belize.

Morris, John M., Sherilyne Jones, Jaime J. Awe, George Thompson, and Melissa Badillo, eds. 2010. *Research Reports in Belizean Archaeology*, Volume 7, Institute of Archaeology, Belize.

Morris, John M., Melissa Badillo, Jaime J. Awe and George Thompson, eds. 2011. *Research Reports in Belizean Archaeology*, Volume 8, Institute of Archaeology, Belize.

Moyes, Holley. 2006. The Sacred Landscape as a Political Resource: A Case Study of Ancient Maya Cave Use at Chechem Ha Cave, Belize, Central America. PhD Dissertation, Department of Anthropology, State University of New York at Buffalo.

Pendergast, David M. 1964. Excavations en la Cueva Eduardo Quiroz, Distrito Cayo, Honduras Britannica. *Estudios de Cultura Maya* 4: 119–139.

Pendergast, David M. 1969. The Prehistory of Actun Balam, British Honduras. *Art and Archaeology Occasional Paper* No. 16. Royal Ontario Museum, Toronto.

Pendergast, David M. 1970. A. H. Anderson's Excavations at Rio Frio Cave E. British Honduras (Belize). *Art and Archaeology Occasional Paper* No. 20. Royal Ontario Museum, Toronto.

Pendergast, David M. 1971. Excavations at Eduardo Quiroz Cave, British Honduras (Belize). *Art and Archaeology Occasional Paper* No. 21. Royal Ontario Museum, Toronto.

Pendergast, David M. 1974. Excavations at Actun Polbilche, Belize. *Royal Ontario Museum Monograph* 1. Toronto.

Pendergast, David M. 1979. *Excavations at Altun Ha, Belize, 1964–1970 Volume 1.* Royal Ontario Museum Publications in Archaeology, Toronto.

Pendergast, David M. 1981. Lamanai, Belize: Summary of Excavation Results, 1974–1980. *Journal of Field Archaeology* 8:29–53.

Pendergast, David M. 1982. *Excavations at Altun Ha, Belize, 1964–1970 Volume 2.* Royal Ontario Museum Publications in Archaeology, Toronto.

Pendergast, David M. 1990. *Excavations at Altun Ha, Belize, 1964–1970 Volume 3.* Royal Ontario Museum Publications in Archaeology, Toronto.

Pendergast, David M. 1993. The Center and the Edge: Archaeology in Belize, 1809–1992. *Journal of World Prehistory* 7(1): 1–33.

Pohl, Mary D., Kevin O. Pope, John G. Jones, John S. Jacob, Dolores R. Piperno, Susan deFrance, David L. Lentz, John A. Gifford, Marie E. Danforth, and J. Kathryn Josserand. 1996. Early Agriculture in the Maya Lowlands. *Latin American Antiquity* 7(4):355–372.

Prufer, Keith M., and James E. Brady. 2005. *Stone Houses and Earth Lords: Maya Religion in the Cave Context*. University Press of Colorado, Boulder.

Puleston, Dennis E. 1977. The Art and Archaeology of Hydraulic Agriculture in the Maya Lowlands. In *Social Process in Maya Prehistory: Studies in Honour of Sir Eric Thompson*, edited by Norman Hammond, pp. 449–467. Academic Press, London.

Reents, Doris J. 1980. The Prehistoric Pottery from Petroglyph Cabe, Caves Branch Valley, El Cayo District, Belize, Central America. M.A. thesis, University of Texas, Austin.

Ricketson, Oliver G., Jr. 1931. Baking Pot, British Honduras. *Carnegie Institution of Washington, Publication no. 403, Contributions to American Archaeology, no. 1*. Washington, DC.

Rosenswig, Robert M. 2006. Northern Belize and the Soconusco: A Comparison of the Late Archaic to Formative Transition. *Research Reports in Belizean Archaeology* 3:59–72.

Satterthwaite, L., Jr. 1951. Reconnaissance in British Honduras. *University Museum Bulletin* 16(1):21–36.

Satterthwaite, L., Jr. 1954. Sculptured Monuments from Caracol, British Honduras. *University Museum Bulletin* 18(1 & 2):3–45.

Scarborough, Vernon L. 2003 *The Flow of Power: Ancient Water Systems and Landscapes*. School of American Research Press, Santa Fe, New Mexico.

Scarborough, Vernon L., Fred Valdez Jr., and Nicholas Dunning, eds. 2003 *Heterarchy, Political Economy, and the Ancient Maya: The Three Rivers Region of the East-Central Yucatan Peninsula*. University of Arizona Press, Tucson.

Thompson, J. E. S. 1931. *Archaeological Investigations in the Southern Cayo District, British Honduras*. Field Museum of Natural History Anthropological Series, vol. 7, no. 3. Chicago.

Thompson, J. E. S. 1939. *Investigations at San Jose, British Honduras*. Carnegie Institution of Washington, Publication 506, Washington, DC.

Turner, Billy L. II, and Peter D. Harrison, eds. 1983. *Pulltrouser Swamp: Ancient Maya Habitat, Agriculture and Settlement in Northern Belize*. University of Texas Press, Austin.

Valdez, F., Jr. 1987. The Prehistoric Ceramics of Colha, Northern Belize. PhD dissertation, Department of Anthropology, Harvard University, Cambridge, Massachusetts.

Willey, Gordon R., William R. Bullard Jr., J. B. Glass, and James C. Gifford. 1965. *Prehistoric Maya Settlements in the Belize Valley*. Papers of the Peabody Museum of Archaeology and Ethnology, vol. 54. Harvard University, Cambridge, Massachusetts.

CHAPTER 6

ARCHAEOLOGY ON MESOAMERICA'S SOUTHERN FRONTIER

GEOFFREY MCCAFFERTY, FABIO
ESTEBAN AMADOR, SILVIA SALGADO
GONZÁLEZ, AND CARRIE DENNETT

THE southern frontier of Mesoamerica has fluctuated through time but has generally included portions of the Central American countries of El Salvador, Nicaragua, and Costa Rica (see also Henderson and Hudson in this volume). Tied into this liminal status, the history of archaeological research and the development of archaeological institutions in these countries have varied, sometimes emphasizing 'Mesoamerican-ness' and sometimes highlighting independent development. This essay presents the history of archaeological practice in El Salvador, Nicaragua, and Costa Rica; followed by a brief overview of the culture history of the region with particular emphasis on relations with Mesoamerican cultures.

One similarity shared by El Salvador and Nicaragua is the relative lack of archaeological research, with a greater emphasis on culture historical reconstructions grounded in ethnohistorical and linguistic evidence; Costa Rica is exceptional due to its longer tradition of locally trained archaeologists who, since 1970, have published their research in journals such as *Vínculos* out of the National Museum of Anthropology. When archaeological evidence *has* been applied to recent periods it has often been to supplement and confirm the historical accounts with minimal effort in critical evaluation (again, this criticism is less relevant in the case of Costa Rica). Consequently, investigations have tended to lag behind theoretical paradigms popularized in North American archaeologies. In part this is reasonable, owing to the existing gaps in fundamental knowledge such as site inventories and regional chronologies. With the recent expansion of archaeological programs in El Salvador, Nicaragua, and Costa Rica, and with young nationals entering the field with advanced professional degrees, we anticipate exciting developments in the upcoming decades that will greatly expand the archaeological dialogue to include more compelling social issues pertaining to the past.

ARCHAEOLOGY IN EL SALVADOR

El Salvador covers a relatively small region, about 20,000 square kilometers. Its landscape is diverse, containing active volcanoes, fertile valleys, rich coastal estuaries, and bountiful lakes and rivers. In the nineteenth century, interest in the past was the hobby of wealthy travelers and landowners (Peccorini 1913, 1926; Spinden 1915), and their early descriptions contributed to the creation of the first cultural histories for the region (Amador et al. 2007).

The second phase of investigations in El Salvador featured broad regional studies that were similar to those being conducted in many parts of Mesoamerica and Central America. The new approach incorporated survey, mapping, excavation, and ceramic analysis by professional archaeologists sponsored by renowned academic institutions (Boggs 1943a, 1943b, 1950; León Portilla and Longyear 1944; Lothrop 1926a; Ries 1940; Sol 1929). This phase represents the birth of scientific archaeology and served to establish the importance of ancient sites in the national identity.

The third phase of research began in the 1960s with excavations at large ceremonial centers, such as Tazumal (Sharer 1978), San Andrés (Boggs 1972), Cihuatán (Bruhns 1980; Fowler 1981, 1983, 1984; Kelley 1988), and Quelepa (Andrews 1976). There was also an increase in regional surveys and household archaeology (Casasola García 1974, 1975, 1978; Haberland 1960a, 1960b; Sheets 1976). This phase was grounded in a processualist theoretical perspective. Tazumal and Quelepa became the first sites that were subject to a new method of material analysis that focused on form and function, context, and provenience.

The late 1970s and early 1980s were times of political change in El Salvador, and popular revolution limited archaeological investigation. Nevertheless, important new sites such as Joya de Cerén (Sheets 1976, 1984b, 1989) were discovered, and surveys along the Lempa River and Zapotitan Valley revealed sites with unique cultural affinities (Fowler and Solís Angulo 1977). Most of the ongoing work was directed by Stanley Boggs from the David J. Guzmán National Museum and independent researchers (e.g., Amaroli 1986, 1988; Demarest 1981), and many of these works were published by CONCULTURA in the popular national journal *Tzumpame*.

The most recent phase of archaeological research in El Salvador is perhaps the most exciting, because for the first time the majority of work is being conducted by Salvadoran archaeologists. These new leaders include Herbert Erquicia, Marlon Escamilla, Roberto Gallardo, Federico Paredes, Claudia Ramírez, Fabricio Valdivieso, and Fabio Esteban Amador. Their combined efforts and expertise have expanded into underwater and nautical archaeology (Escamilla 2008), architectural conservation, cultural identity, rock art, and lithic and ceramic analysis. The past decade has also witnessed the first archaeology and anthropology programs offered at national universities. International congresses have been held at the new Museo Nacional de Antropología, and periodic seminars and workshops are held at the Casa Dueñas, home of the National Historical Academy. The current Department of Archaeology, under the Secretary of Culture, has been strengthened and expanded under the direction of Shione Shibata and his staff, incorporating a group of young archaeologists and students who are the future of the discipline in El Salvador. Finally, archaeological parks at sites such as Cihuatán and Joya de Cerén have been supported by the private organization Fundación Nacional de Arqueología de El Salvador (FUNDAR), which has also sponsored archaeological rescue projects and conservation at some of the principal sites.

Current research involves a combination of regional surveys and university-sponsored projects. For example, the Atlas Arqueológico de Oriente project represents the first archaeological study funded by the National University and is important because it incorporated university students from various departments in all activities related to the research. This represents a change in how research is conducted, and this directly benefits the development of archaeology in the country. The new atlas has produced an updated inventory of previously recorded and newly discovered sites of eastern El Salvador (east of the Lempa River), created a regional ceramic typology (Amador 2010) and established an online, searchable database for site management, research, and protection of national patrimony.

ARCHAEOLOGY IN NICARAGUA

As in other parts of Central America, the first "archaeologists" in Nicaragua were adventurers on other business. Ephraim Squier (1852, 1990 [1853]) collected information on Nicaraguan antiquities while investigating possible routes for a transoceanic canal. Carl Bovallius (1886) was a Swedish naturalist who mapped stone sculptures on the islands of Lake Nicaragua (Figure 6.1). Earl Flint, a medical doctor living in Granada, collected artifacts for the Smithsonian Institution and Harvard University in the late nineteenth century (Whisnant 1994), and was the first to identify human footprints in the volcanic ash at Acahualinca (Flint 1884). All of these scholars pursued the colonial pastime of archaeology with little concern for local scholarship. While their scientific interpretations often bordered on the fantastic, nevertheless they did serve to draw international attention to Central American antiquities.

Figure 6.1 Statue from Zapatera Island (Museo Ex-Convento de San Francisco, Granada) (photograph by Geoffrey McCafferty).

Archaeological interest in Nicaragua was sporadic during the twentieth century, in part due to political tensions, natural disasters, and ensuing economic woes, as well as the greater glamour of Mesoamerican and South American cultures. Samuel Lothrop (1926b) published a glossy, two-volume set on the ceramics of Nicaragua and Costa Rica that highlighted the beautiful iconography with symbolic associations with Mesoamerica. Another notable development was a brief project directed by Gordon Willey in the early 1960s in the Rivas region of southwest Nicaragua (Norweb 1964). This later became the substance of Paul Healy's PhD dissertation and subsequent monograph, *The Archaeology of the Rivas Region, Nicaragua* (1980), which remains a cornerstone of Nicaraguan archaeological literature. A German project directed by Wolfgang Haberland (1992) excavated the Los Angeles cemetery on Ometepe Island, recovering evidence for a long cultural sequence.

Nationalist archaeology during this period was largely in the hands of wealthy patrons of the prehispanic past who supported looting to amass large collections of artifacts and to display them in their homes and offices. Occasionally these collections were converted into small museums that were more akin to nineteenth-century "curiosity cabinets," including such things as rocks and minerals, stuffed animals, and historical objects. Archaeology was administered under the auspices of the Ministry of Culture but with minimal budget and staff. The exception was the National Museum, which housed archaeological collections and produced modest exhibitions under the direction of a professional staff.

A resurgence of scientific archaeology occurred in the 1990s, with several survey projects (Fletcher et al. 1994; Niemel 2003; Roman Lacayo n.d.; Salgado González 1996a) and rescue projects (Espinoza Pérez et al. 1999; Lange 1996). Frederick Lange played an important role in helping to develop Nicaraguan archaeology, including the organization of several symposia that focused on Central American archaeology, in general, and Pacific Nicaragua more specifically (e.g., Lange 1992; Lange et al. 1992). One important component of his work was an extensive compositional analysis of Greater Nicoya ceramics that employed the Smithsonian Institution's neutron activation laboratory (Bishop et al. 1988).

At this time the Universidad Nacional Autónoma de Nicaragua (UNAN) opened a specialized center for archaeological training and research: the Centro Arqueológico de Documentación e Investigación (CADI). This group was formed in collaboration with the University of Barcelona, and under the auspices of conducting several research and survey projects the CADI has trained a new generation of Nicaraguan archaeologists. Out of this program, Jorge Zambrana, Maria Lily Calero, Bosco Moroney, and Oscar Pavón have reached prominence in terms of their field expertise and positions in archaeological administration. Other former students are currently studying in international graduate programs, with the promise of a continued professionalization of the discipline.

The Office of Cultural Patrimony oversees archaeological permits and monitors development projects that would potentially impact cultural resources. In recent years this has included sending teams of Nicaraguan archaeologists (generally graduates of the CADI) to mitigate necessary impacts to important sites. The Office of Cultural Patrimony also sponsors an aggressive program designed to educate local officials on the importance of cultural resources and the legal issues surrounding looting and destruction of sites. This office administers the World Heritage site at León Viejo, an important colonial site that is the current focus of archaeotourism. There is also positive development in terms of regional museums, highlighted by the ex-convent of San Francisco and Mi Museo in Granada.

Beginning in 2000, Geoffrey McCafferty of the University of Calgary has directed several major projects in Pacific Nicaragua, especially at the sites of Santa Isabel, Tepetate, and El Rayo, with the goal of evaluating ethnohistorical accounts of ethnic migrations from central Mexico to Greater Nicoya during the Early Postclassic period (McCafferty 2011). Numerous graduate students have earned advanced degrees based on these projects (Debert 2005; Dennett n.d.; López-Forment 2007; Steinbrenner 2002, 2010), and a variety of specialized studies have been published (Debert and Sheriff 2007; Dennett et al. 2011; McCafferty 2008, 2010; McCafferty and McCafferty 2008, 2009, 2011; McCafferty and Steinbrenner 2005a, 2005b; Wilke et al. 2011).

A second international project is now underway, directed by Alex Geurds of Leiden University, investigating manufacturing areas for monumental sculpture on the eastern shore of Lake Nicaragua. With a very open attitude toward foreign scholars, Nicaragua offers excellent potential for collaborative projects involving an established cadre of experienced Nicaraguan archaeologists.

Archaeology in Costa Rica

In the sixteenth century, most of Costa Rica's territory was inhabited by Chibchan-speaking peoples, with the exception of the Mesoamerican Chorotega-Mangue speakers who occupied the northwest region. Recent linguistic and phylogenetic studies (Barrantes 1993; Barrantes et al. 1990; Constenla 1991) have demonstrated the long-term presence of Chibchan-speaking groups dating back at least to the Archaic period, with the border area between Costa Rica and Panama thought to be the heartland of the Chibchan languages. In addition, ethnohistoric and ethnographic research on Costa Rican indigenous peoples (Bozzoli de Wille 1984; Ibarra 1990) has shed light on cultural aspects such as cosmology and political and social structures. An interdisciplinary approach has renewed interest by archaeologists in questions of continuity and change in the culture history of indigenous people and opened a debate on a proposed Isthmo-Colombian region (Dennett 2008; Fonseca 1992; Fonseca and Cooke 1993; Hoopes and Fonseca 2003), which is seen by some as a culture area extending from northwest Colombia to eastern Honduras. Recent research, therefore, has focused on the culture history of Chibcha and their interaction with related people in Central and South America (Corrales 2000). However, the processes of social and cultural change resulting from the arrival of the Chorotega, as well as aspects of interaction with Mesoamerica, have also attracted some degree of continued attention (Carmack and Salgado González 2006; Ibarra and Salgado 2010).

Until the 1950s archaeological research was carried out mainly by aficionados and scientists other than archaeologists. Anastasio Alfaro (1892), the first director of the National Museum, dug at several cemeteries and, a few years later, Carl V. Hartman (1901, 1907) excavated funerary sites while following stratigraphic principles. The establishment of cultural sequences and their relation either to Mesoamerica or to South America dominated the agenda of archaeologists throughout the 1960s and 1970s (Baudez and Coe 1962; Haberland 1976; Lange 1976; Snarskis 1976), including Costa Rica's first professional archaeologist, Carlos Aguilar (1972, 1976). He was hired by the University of Costa Rica in 1962 and, in 1975, was instrumental in the establishment of an academic program that has trained dozens of Costa Rican archaeologists. At the same time the National Museum initiated a research program developed by the American archaeologists Michael J. Snarskis, Frederick W. Lange, and Robert Drolet—all of whom introduced theory and methods of cultural ecology, the "New Archaeology," and aided in training the first generation of archaeologists to graduate from the University of Costa Rica.

Over the last decades, questions of research have been driven mainly by tenets of cultural ecology (Drolet 1992; Lange 1984; Murillo 2010; Sheets 2003) and Marxist-based "Latinoamerican social archaeology" (Fonseca 1992), both sharing an interest in social change and the emergence of complexity but differing in the use of evolutionary or historical models, respectively. Recently, postprocessual theories and methods have been applied to study topics related to agency, meaning, and identity (Peytrequín 2008; Reyes 2009). Cristina Aguilar's ongoing M.A. research is the first centered on the reconstruction of gender roles.

In the Caribbean lowlands, current projects include investigation of the site of Las Mercedes by Ricardo Vázquez and Rob Rosenswig and of the site of Nuevo Corinto by Silvia Salgado Gonzáles, Mónica Aguilar, and John W. Hoopes. In addition, Ricardo Alarcón continues work at Guayabo de Turrialba in the Caribbean highlands. Francisco Corrales and Adrián Badilla are working in regional Pacific sites of the Diquís delta. Also important is the ongoing work of Patricia Fernández, of the Museo del Oro, who is utilizing compositional analysis of artifacts and metallurgical techniques to determine raw material sources, production centers, and exchange networks.

Contract archaeology has boomed in Costa Rica since the 1990s due to new legislation, and it employs most archaeologists. Unfortunately, few results are published, though the reports are available through the National Museum digital database known as *Orígenes*.

SHIFTING BOUNDARIES ON THE SOUTHERN FRONTIER

With consideration of these distinctive regional patterns for archaeological development in southern Central America, the evidence for Mesoamerican influence varies through time. What follows is a brief culture historical summary of some of the prominent discoveries connecting this peripheral region to the Mesoamerican heartland. Central America forms the isthmian land bridge by which Paleo-Indian and Archaic-period nomadic peoples migrated to South America, although little rigorous attention has been paid to these periods apart from the occasional discovery of early stone tools, with rare examples of Clovis, Folsom, and Fishtail points (Snarskis 1979). Lake sediments from Costa Rica's northwestern Cordillera (Sheets 1984a) have yielded pollen of maize and other grasses, declining percentages of tree pollen, and abundant charcoal, suggesting forest clearing and cultivation around 3550 BC and the spread of maize from Mesoamerica (Horn 2006), as has also been documented in Panama (Cooke 2005).

OLMEC INFLUENCES AND PRECLASSIC
INTERACTIONS 1500 BC-200 AD

The earliest occupation documented in western El Salvador is at the site of El Carmen. Although the pottery shares attributes with that of other sites along the Pacific coast of Mesoamerica, unique modal attributes—Bostan-phase ceramics first identified by Bárbara Arroyo with unique characteristics including white washes and slips as well as tear-shaped tecomates, which are limited to the El Carmen site—attest to a local style (Amador 2009; Arroyo 1991:205–206, 1995). During the Formative period, western El Salvador was clearly in contact with the Olmec, as demonstrated by monumental carvings from the site of Tazumal. Stronger contact between peoples in El Salvador and Pacific Guatemala is indicated by the shared occurrence of "pot belly" sculptures (McInnis Thompson and Valdez 2008). In the later Formative period, sites with monumental architecture and sculpture, dense settlements, organized labor, agriculture, and structured religious/political cults began to appear throughout the Mesoamerican southern frontier (Casasola 1974; Navarrete 1972; Sharer 1978). Usulutan-style pottery became a widely popular commodity often found in elite Maya centers in Guatemala, Honduras, and El Salvador (Andrews 1976).

There is also evidence for unique regional statuary traditions in western El Salvador (Demarest 1981; Paredes 2008) that are quite different from known traditions of the eastern region (Andrews 1976). These include stylized "jaguar heads" carved in stone, which have a limited distribution from the Rio Paz, bordering Guatemala, the Coast of Ahuachapan, and inland to Coatepeque Lake. Similarly, evidence from other regional studies suggests that there were also significant differences in pottery traditions between western and eastern El Salvador. Given stylistic differences between both statuary and pottery traditions it is possible that these societies, geographically divided by the Lempa River, were also culturally and ethnically differentiated (Amador 2010), with Mesoamerican groups inhabiting the western portion and, as historical documents indicate, Lenca-speaking groups in the eastern portion (Amador et al. 2007).

Usulután-style pottery is also present in Pacific Nicaragua, for example, at sites such as Villa Tiscapa, La Arenera, and Las Delicias in the Managua area. Petrographic analysis indicates that much of the Usulután-style pottery found in the region may be locally made (Lange et al. 2003; Dennett et al. 2011). Abundant obsidian recovered from these sites suggests exchange relations with Guatemala, probably through El Salvador. La Arenera was buried by a volcanic eruption, preserving intact house floors with crushed vessels abandoned in situ (McCafferty 2009; McCafferty and Salgado González 2000). Recent salvage excavation of the Las Delicias cemetery demonstrates the social complexity of a lakeside community dating to approximately 100–300 AD (Moroney Ubeda 2011; Pavón Sánchez 2010). Dispersed villages are common during this period, and although there is some indication of nucleated settlements, no detailed studies of community settlement patterns have been documented.

In Costa Rica, small villages became a common way of life in the Early Formative (Bradley 1994), with sophisticated pottery suggesting introduction from adjacent areas (Hoopes 1994; Snarskis 1984). By 500 BC most regions show an increase in the number and size of settlements, and regional differences are apparent. Greenstone production developed in northern Costa Rica at this time, where lapidaries utilized a wide variety of materials. Discernible differences in the distribution and quality of artifacts indicate that production likely occurred at the household level (Guerrero 1998). Davíd Mora-Marín (2002, 2005) has studied Mesoamerican jades from Costa Rica and argues for a direct and systematic exchange of greenstone between the Maya lowlands and Costa Rica beginning by at least the Late Formative (Figure 6.2). Recent research by Michael J. Snarskis and Juan Vicente Guerrero of the National Museum has uncovered the Lomas Corral cemetery, situated at the Bay of Culebra, which contains an abundance of jade artifacts and Usulutan-style pottery that provide additional support for Mora-Marín's arguments about dynamic exchange networks involving Mesoamerican and Chibchan-speaking (and perhaps Lenca-speaking) groups of lower Central America.

Maya Influences and Classic Interactions (200–800 ad)

The Classic period in western El Salvador can be characterized as an extension of the Maya world, with large sites featuring monumental architecture. The splendor of cultural development, however, was muted by a catastrophic volcanic eruption

Figure 6.2 Costa Rican jade with Olmec stylistic elements but Maya text.
(Photograph courtesy of the Museo del Jade, Costa Rica.)

during the fifth century AD (Dull et al. 2001), which affected the western and central regions (Sheets 1976, 1983). In contrast, eastern El Salvador went relatively unscathed and increased its ties with south-central Honduras and lower Central America (Amador 2010; Andrews 1976). The Middle Classic period does provide a glimpse of economic prosperity throughout El Salvador. Large centers such as Laguneta and Quelepa in eastern El Salvador actively constructed, modified, and enlarged formal architecture, while domestic and luxury goods were being produced, manufactured, and exchanged in long-distance trade networks. The Late and Terminal Classic periods demonstrate the most intense and abrupt cultural changes in the region.

Western El Salvador appears to have been affected by the political and economic collapse of the Maya southern lowlands as indicated by the apparent abandonment of some cities, lack of new constructions, and a focus on external influences that brought foreign ritual paraphernalia, as well as architectural and artistic canons, to the region (Amador 2010; Amaroli 1988; Andrews 1976; Boggs 1943a, 1943b; Longyear 1944; Sharer 1978; Sheets 1989, 1992). The blended culture of the Mesoamerican frontier is apparent at the site of Joya de Cerén, where a thick layer of volcanic ash preserved a small community with wattle-and-daub structures and even crops in the fields, including both maize and manioc (Sheets et al. 2011) (Figure 6.3). Although evidence of foreign intrusion has been documented in eastern El Salvador (Amador 2010; Andrews 1976), there is sufficient supporting evidence to suggest that this region continued to achieve economic and political

Figure 6.3 (a) Joya de Cerén structure against backdrop of layered volcanic ash; (b) insets of preserved wattle-and-daub architecture; and (c) cast of maize plant (photographs by Geoffrey McCafferty).

success independent of any major changes occurring to the west. In fact, the evidence suggests that at no time were the cultural, ethnic, stylistic, and perhaps linguistic differences more clear-cut than during the Late Classic period.

Relatively little archaeological evidence has been found for the Classic period in Nicaragua. Settlement pattern surveys in the Granada and Rivas regions indicate greater population densities and a more complex settlement hierarchy (Niemel 2003; Roman Lacayo n.d.; Salgado González 1996a). The site of Ayala, on the outskirts of modern Granada, is the most extensively investigated site, with pottery suggestive of limited contact with Honduras, El Salvador, and Costa Rica (Salgado González 1996b). Recent excavations at the site of El Rayo, on the Asese Peninsula south of Granada, have recovered rich deposits of residential debris associated with a possible terrace wall (McCafferty 2010; McCafferty et al. 2009). While there is some evidence for interaction with Mesoamerican regions, the great majority of the material culture implies independent local origins, probably representative of indigenous Chibchan cultural groups.

The emergence and consolidation of societies with institutionalized social hierarchies during the Classic period have recently become of increased interest to Costa Rican scholars (Hurtado de Mendoza and Troyo Vargas 2008). These societies are identified through the presence of complex architecture, elaborately carved stone sculptures, and fine and/or imported sumptuary goods. Guayabo de Turrialba is perhaps the largest regional center known to date, with architecture consisting of several round, earth-filled mounds with retaining walls of stone cobbles; open spaces, or *plazas*, delimited by stone walls; aqueducts; paved walkways connecting structures; and external causeways that facilitated the integration of other minor sites into Guayabo's political sphere. The largest of these causeways extends about 13 kilometers from the site to the Bonilla Lagoon. Similar sites are found in the Caribbean lowlands, the Central Highlands, and in the Diquís region of Costa Rica. These sociopolitical networks began in the early centuries AD and by the sixteenth century were documented in Spanish ethnohistorical accounts. Ibarra (1990) has amply discussed chiefdoms of the sixteenth century, focusing on how they were engaged—through trade and other mechanisms—in significant interactions among themselves and with other chiefdoms throughout Central America, Colombia, and even many of the Caribbean Islands.

MEXICAN INFLUENCES AND POSTCLASSIC INTERACTION (800–1530 AD)

The most widespread contacts with Mesoamerica occurred during the Postclassic period, as documented in ethnohistorical accounts and through historical linguistics (Fowler 1989; León Portilla 1972) when speakers of Nahuat and Oto-Manguean languages were found throughout western El Salvador, Pacific Nicaragua, and the Nicoya region of northwestern Costa Rica. Clarification of this relationship has often been a driving force in archaeological research, but this research has also provided a strong historical foundation for local cultural identity that has limited critical evaluation of the processes of foreign contact.

The eruption of the Loma Caldera around 600 AD once again buried the site of Joya de Cerén and produced far-reaching repercussions throughout El Salvador. When the region was reoccupied in the Early Postclassic period it was by a group with possible central Mexican affiliations relating to the so-called Pipil-Nicarao migrations (Fowler 1989, 1991). This relationship has long been argued to be characterized, and thus supported, by the spread of Mexican Gulf Coast–style stone yokes and *hachas*—equipment worn by players of the Mesoamerican ballgame (Jiménez Moreno 1966). Cihuatán in central El Salvador was built with a "Mexican-inspired" ceremonial center, including a ballcourt and large pyramid (Bruhns 1980; Kelley 1988) (Figure 6.4). Banderas Polychrome pottery features Mixteca-Puebla style iconography, and life-sized ceramic sculptures resemble those from the Gulf Coast (Bruhns and Amaroli 2009). Cihuatán was abandoned about 1100 AD, and little is known of the subsequent culture history of western El Salvador. When Alvarado's army reached the largest Nahua-Pipil city of Cuzcatlán in 1524, it marked the "beginning of the end" of a rich history of people, traditions, and culture. Recent research in the Izalcos region of western El Salvador by Kathryn Sampeck (2010) further clarifies Nahua-Pipil occupation and cultural traditions at Spanish contact. Insight into the early Colonial period has been recovered from the original, albeit short-lived, Spanish capital of Ciudad Vieja (Fowler 2006).

Eastern El Salvador was not subject to Mexican influence to the same degree as witnessed at Cihuatán; rather, the evidence suggests a continued southward-focused commercial network and, importantly, maintenance of its linguistic and probably ethnic independence despite the surrounding cultural, political, and economic influences (Amador 2010).

Figure 6.4 (a) Cihuatán ballcourt; (b) inset of life-size ceramic sculpture (photographs by Geoffrey McCafferty).

The same "Mexican" migrations influenced the Greater Nicoya region of Pacific Nicaragua and northwest Costa Rica (Carmack and Salgado González 2006). Beginning about 800 AD dramatic changes in settlement patterns and material culture indicate significant culture change, probably through the arrival of a migrant group. Ethnohistorical sources indicate that Oto-Manguean and Nahua languages were spoken in the region at the time of Spanish contact and that these groups migrated into Greater Nicoya during the Early Postclassic period. Sites such as Santa Isabel and El Rayo, on the shore of Lake Nicaragua, now provide excellent evidence of this transitional period (McCafferty 2008, 2011; McCafferty et al. 2009). Beautiful polychrome pottery bears notable similarities with Mixteca-Puebla polychromes from Cholula and the Gulf Coast, including the use of feathered serpent imagery (McCafferty and Steinbrenner 2005a) (Figure 6.5). Interestingly, however, the material culture from these sites also lacks important traits associated with Mesoamerican identity, including maize, incense burners, and ceremonial architecture.

While the dramatic break in the ceramic tradition at the Classic to Postclassic transition suggests population change, it is not yet clear where the new innovations originated. Investigation of social identities has been conducted by looking at objects of adornment, such as ear plugs and pendants, as well as figurines expressing emic concepts of "the body beautiful" (McCafferty and McCafferty 2009, 2011). The later Postclassic remains even more of a mystery as no sites securely dating between 1250 AD and Spanish contact have been extensively excavated, although Wolfgang Haberland (1963, 1992) did encounter late-period burials on Ometepe Island. The Colonial-period capital of León Viejo has been the site of extensive excavations, and the discovery of the skeleton of the conquistador Francisco Hernandez de Cordoba was instrumental in the site being declared a World Heritage site.

(a)    (b)

Figure 6.5 Vallejo Polychrome vessels with incised feather serpent iconography (photographs by Geoffrey McCafferty).

Research into the Postclassic period of Costa Rica has generally concentrated on possible Mesoamerican connections, especially in the northwest part of the country that is considered part of the Greater Nicoya subregion. Scholars such as Doris Stone (1982, 1984) and Jane Day (1994) demonstrated similarities between the Nicoya polychromes and the Mixteca-Puebla style from central Mexico. However, extensive research by Frederick Lange (1984) in the coastal sites of Guanacaste led him to conclude that evidence did not support either a significant presence of Mesoamericans or the incorporation of the region as part of Mesoamerica. Recent research, however, has reopened the debate on the significance of Mesoamerican groups in Guanacaste during the Postclassic. Large projects have excavated residential and cemetery areas, often in conjunction with tourism development. For example, at the site of Jícaro, located on the Bay of Culebra, Felipe Solís and Anayency Herrera (2008) have identified several individuals with cranial and dental modification coeval with the Early Postclassic, and they attribute this to the presence of Mesoamericans. However, a contemporary site located only a kilometer to the northwest has little evidence of such practices (Aguilar 2008). In the same region, the site of Papagayo shows architecture typified by circular mounds associated with Chibchan tradition (Baudez et al. 1992). The Guanacaste and Nicoya regions of northwest Costa Rica have seen extensive archaeological research, specifically addressing the question of Mesoamerican influence. It is notable that the results are so ambiguous, in keeping with the region's position on the Mesoamerican frontier.

FINAL THOUGHTS

The use and abuse of Mesoamerican models has been the subject of much discussion and debate (e.g., Coe 1962; Healy 1988; Lange 1993). Recently, John Hoopes and Oscar Fonseca (2003) have advocated greater emphasis on the indigenous Chibchan culture, a linguistic group that occupies territory from Honduras to Colombia, especially along the Atlantic watershed (Barrantes 1993; Barrantes et al. 1990). The choice to variably identify with Mesoamerican cultures has influenced the practice of archaeology in these Central American countries, with western El Salvador placing much more emphasis on "Mesoamerican-ness" in contrast to Nicaragua or Costa Rica, or even eastern El Salvador. The result is a complex cultural mosaic that deserves much more archaeological attention.

El Salvador, Nicaragua, and Costa Rica have long, if varied, archaeological traditions. While relatively undeveloped in comparison with greater Mesoamerica, they offer enormous research potential, and the open-mindedness of national patrimony offices makes future investigation very accessible. One important development of recent years has been the training of highly qualified local archaeologists.

Unfortunately, economic issues severely limit the scope of research, which is typically restricted to rescue projects in advance of development. This does open the door to collaborative projects with greater research orientation. The past decade has seen significant advances in archaeological involvement, in part due to political stability and economic development. We anticipate continued growth in terms of archaeological research programs, including greater integration of research agendas that cross national borders for more rigorous investigation of Mesoamerica's southern frontier.

References

Aguilar, Carlos. 1972. *Guayabo de Turrialba*. Editorial Costa Rica, San José.

Aguilar, Carlos. 1976. Relaciones de las culturas precolombinas en el intermontano central de Costa Rica. *Vínculos* 2:75–86.

Aguilar, Cristina. 2008. Informe final de la evaluación del sitio La Cascabel. Empresa consultora C.I.C.P.A.S.S.A. Unpublished manuscript on file, Archives of the National Museum, Costa Rica, and Península Papagayo S.A.

Alfaro, Anastasio. 1892. Arqueología costarricense. *El Centenario* 4:5–12. San José.

Amador, Fabio E. 2009. *La sociedad de El Carmen: Un análisis de la cultura material del período formativo temprano en la periferia sudeste de mesoamérica*. Papeles de arqueología—compilación de lecturas y documentos. Fundación CLIC: Arte y Nuevas Tecnologías, San Salvador.

Amador, Fabio E. 2010. *Atlas arqueológico de Oriente de El Salvador*. Manuscript on file, Universidad de El Salvador, San Salvador.

Amador, Fabio E., Rosa Maria Ramírez, and Paola Garnica. 2007. *La identidad cultural de la región Oriente de El Salvador en base a la evidencia arqueológica*. Papeles de Arqueología Salvadoreña. Fundación CLIC: Arte y Nuevas Tecnologías, San Salvador.

Amaroli, Paúl E. 1986. *Registro de sitios del departamento de Ahuachapán*. Manuscript on file, Museo David J. Guzmán, San Salvador, El Salvador.

Amaroli, Paúl E. 1988. *The Earliest Pipil: New Perspectives on "Toltec" Presence in Southern Mesoamerica*. Manuscript on file, Fundación Nacional de Arqueología de El Salvador, San Salvador.

Andrews V, E. Wyllys. 1976. *The Archaeology of Quelepa, El Salvador*. Middle American Research Institute, Publication No. 42. Tulane University, New Orleans.

Arroyo, Bárbara. 1991. El formativo temprano en Chiapas, Guatemala, y El Salvador. *Utz'ib* 1(1):7–14.

Arroyo, Bárbara. 1995. Early Ceramics from El Salvador: The El Carmen Site. In *The Emergence of Pottery: Technology and Innovation in Ancient Societies*, edited by William K. Barnett and John Arroyo, Barbara W. Hoopes, pp. 199–208. Smithsonian Institution Press, Washington, DC.

Barrantes, Ramiro. 1993. *Evolución en el trópico: Los amerindios de Costa Rica y Panamá*. Editorial Universidad de Costa Rica, San José.

Barrantes, Ramiro, Peter E. Smouse, Harvey W. Mohrenweiser, Henry Gershowitz, Jorge Azofeifa, Tomas D. Arias, and James V. Neel. 1990. Microevolution in Lower Central

America: Genetic Characterization of the Chibcha-Speaking Groups of Costa Rica and Panama, and a Consensus Taxonomy Based on Genetic and Linguistic Affinity. *American Journal of Human Genetics* 46:63–84.

Baudez, Claude F., Nathalie Borgnino, Sophie Laligat, and Valerie Lauthelin. 1992. *Papagayo: Un hameau Precolumbien du Costa Rica.* Éditions Recherche sur les Civilisations, Paris.

Baudez, Claude F., and Michael D. Coe. 1962. Archaeological Sequences in Northwestern Costa Rica. *Akten des 34 Internationalen Amerikanistenkongresses* 1:366–373. Verlag Ferdinand Berger, Hom, Wien.

Bishop, Ronald L., Frederick W. Lange, and Peter C. Lange. 1988. Ceramic Paste Compositional Patterns in Greater Nicoya Pottery. In *Costa Rican Art and Archaeology: Essays in Honor of Frederick R. Mayer,* edited by Frederick W. Lange, pp. 14–44. Univerversity of Colorado Press, Boulder.

Boggs, Stanley. 1943a. Notas sobre las excavaciones en la hacienda "San Andrés," Departamento de la Libertad. *Tzumpame* 3(1):104–126. Museo Nacional de El Salvador, San Salvador.

Boggs, Stanley. 1943b. Observaciones respecto a la importancia de Tazumal en la prehistoria Salvadoreña. *Tzumpame* 3(1):127–133. Museo Nacional de El Salvador, San Salvador.

Boggs, Stanley. 1950. "Olmec" Pictographs in the Las Victorias Group, Chalchuapa Archaeological Zone, El Salvador. *Notes on Middle American Archaeology and Ethnology* 4(99):85–92. Carnegie Institution of Washington, Washington, DC.

Boggs, Stanley. 1972. *Figurillas con ruedas de Cihuatán y el Oriente de El Salvador.* Revista Cultura del Ministerio de Educación, Colección de Antropología, No. 3. San Salvador.

Bovallius, Carl. 1886. *Nicaraguan Antiquities.* Swedish Society of Anthropology and Geography, Stockholm.

Bozzoli de Wille, María E. 1984. La posición social de los especialistas en medicina aborigen de Talamanca. *Revista de Ciencias Sociales* (Edición Especial) 1:9–21. Editorial de la Universidad de Costa Rica, San José.

Bradley, John E. 1994. Tronadora Vieja: An Archaic and Early Formative Site in the Arenal Region. In *Archaeology, Volcanism, and Remote Sensing in the Arenal Region, Costa Rica,* edited by Payson D. Sheets and Brian R. McKee, pp.73–86. University of Texas Press, Austin.

Bruhns, Karen Olsen. 1980. *Cihuatán: An Early Postclassic Town of El Salvador. The 1977-1978 Excavations.* University of Missouri Monographs in Anthropology, No. 5.Columbia.

Bruhns, Karen Olsen, and Paúl E. Amaroli. 2009. Yacatecuhtli in El Salvador. *Mexicon* 31(4):89–90.

Carmack, Robert M., and Silvia Salgado González. 2006. A World-Systems Perspective on the Archaeology and Ethnohistory of the Mesoamerican/Lower Central American Border. *Ancient Mesoamerica* 17:219–229.

Casasola García, Luis. 1974. Una figura Olmeca de Coatepeque, Santa Ana, El Salvador. *Notas Antropológicas* 1(18):139–146. Universidad Nacional Autónoma de México, Instituto de Investigaciones Antropológicas, Mexico City.

Casasola García, Luis. 1975. Dos figuras de Xipe Totec en El Salvador. In *Balance y Perspectivas de la Antropología de Mesoamérica y El Norte de México* 2:143–153. XIII Mesa Redonda de la Sociedad Mexicana de Antropología, Xalapa, México, 1973.

Casasola García, Luis. 1978. Notas sobre las relaciones prehispánicas entre El Salvador y la Costa de Veracruz. *Estudios de Cultura Maya* 10:115–138.

Coe, Michael D. 1962. Costa Rican Archaeology and Mesoamerica. *Southwestern Journal of Anthropology* 18:170–183.

Constenla, Adolfo. 1991. *Las lenguas del área intermedia: Un estudio areal.* Editorial de la Universidad de Costa Rica, San José.

Cooke, Richard G. 2005. Prehistory of Native Americans on the Central American Land Bridge: Colonization, Dispersal, and Divergence. *Journal of Archaeological Research* 13(2):129–187.

Corrales Ulloa, Francisco. 2000. An Evaluation of Long Term Cultural Change in Southern Central America: The Ceramic Record of the Diquis Archaeological Subregion, Southern Costa Rica. PhD dissertation, Department of Anthropology, University of Kansas, Lawrence.

Day, Jane Stevenson. 1994 Central Mexican Imagery in Greater Nicoya. In *Mixteca-Puebla: Discoveries and Research in Mesoamerican Art and Archaeology*, edited by H.B. Nicholson and Elinor Quiñones Keber, pp. 235–248. Labyrinthos Press, Culver City, California.

Debert, Jolene. 2005. Raspadita: A New Lithic Tool Type from Santa Isabel, Nicaragua. M.A. thesis, Department of Anthropology, University of Manitoba, Winnipeg, Manitoba.

Debert, Jolene, and Barbara L. Sheriff. 2007. Raspadita: A New Lithic Tool from the Isthmus of Rivas, Nicaragua. *Journal of Archaeological Science* 34:1889–1901.

Demarest, Arthur A. 1981. Santa Leticia and the Development of Complex Society in Southeastern Mesoamerica. PhD dissertation, Department of Anthropology, Harvard University, Cambridge.

Dennett, Carrie L. 2008. Río Claro: A Potential Ceramic Type-Site for Period VI Northeast Honduras. *Vínculos* 31:79–104.

Dennett, Carrie L. N.d. Ceramic Economy and Social Identity in Pre-Columbian Pacific Nicaragua. PhD dissertation, Department of Archaeology, University of Calgary, Calgary.

Dennett, Carrie L., Lorelei Platz, and Geoffrey McCafferty. 2011. Preliminary Ceramic Compositional Analysis from the La Arenera site, Pacific Nicaragua. *La Universidad* 14–15:373–397. Universidad de El Salvador.

Drolet, Robert P. 1992. The House and the Territory: The Organizational Structure for Chiefdom Art in the Diquís Subregion of Greater Chiriquí. In *Wealth and Hierarchy in the Intermediate Area*, edited by Frederick W. Lange, pp. 207–241. Dumbarton Oaks, Washington, DC.

Dull, Robert A., John R. Southon, and Payson D. Sheets. 2001. Volcanism, Ecology and Culture: A Reassessment of the Volcano Ilopango TBJ Eruption in the Southern Maya Realm. *Latin American Antiquity* 12:25–44.

Escamilla, Marlon. 2008. *Arqueología subacuática de El Salvador: Explorando el patrimonio cultural sumergido.* Papeles de Arqueología Salvadoreña. Fundación CLIC: Arte y Nuevas Tecnologías, San Salvador.

Espinoza Pérez, Edgar, Ramiro García V., and Fumiyo Suganuma. 1999. *Rescate arqueológico en el sitio San Pedro, Malacatoya, Granada, Nicaragua.* Instituto Nicaragüense de Cultura, Museo Nacional de Nicaragua, Managua, Nicaragua.

Fletcher, Laraine A., Ronaldo Salgado Galeano, and Edgar Espinoza Pérez. 1994. Gran Nicoya y el Norte de Nicaragua. *Vínculos* 18/19:173–189

Flint, Earl. 1884. Human footprints in Nicaragua. *American Antiquarian* 6:112–114.

Fonseca, Oscar M. 1992. *Historia antigua de Costa Rica: Surgimiento y caracterización de la primera civilización costarricense*. Editorial de la Universidad de Costa Rica, San José.

Fonseca, Oscar M., and Richard G. Cooke. 1993. El sur de la América Central: Contribución al estudio de la región histórica Chibcha. In *Historia Antigua*, edited by Robert M. Carmack, pp. 217–282. Historia general de Centroamérica, Vol. 1, Edelberto Torres-Rivas, general editor, FLACSO/Quinto Centenario España, Madrid.

Fowler, William R., Jr. 1981. The Pipil-Nicarao of Central America. PhD dissertation, Department of Archaeology, University of Calgary, Calgary.

Fowler, William R., Jr. 1983. La distribución prehistórica e histórica de los pipiles. *Mesoamérica* 6:348–372.

Fowler, William R., Jr. 1984. Late Preclassic Mortuary Patterns and Evidence for Human Sacrifice at Chalchuapa, El Salvador. *American Antiquity* 49:603–618.

Fowler, William R., Jr. 1989. *The Cultural Evolution of Ancient Nahua Civilizations: The Pipil-Nicarao of Central America*. University of Oklahoma Press, Norman.

Fowler, William R., Jr. 1991. The Formation of Complex Society among the Nahua Groups of Southeastern Mesoamerica: A Comparison of Two Approaches. In *The Formation of Complex Society in Southeastern Mesoamerica*, edited by William R. Fowler, Jr., pp. 193–214. CRC Press, Boca Raton.

Fowler, William R., Jr. 2006. *Arqueología histórica de la villa de San Salvador, El Salvador: Informe de las excavaciones (1996–2003)*. Historical Archaeology in Latin America, No. 17, Volumes in Historical Archeology XLIV, Stanley South, general editor, The South Carolina Institute of Archeology and Anthropology, University of South Carolina. Columbia.

Fowler, William R., Jr., and E. Margarita Solís Angulo. 1977. El mapa de Santa María: Un sitio posclásico de la región Cerrón Grande. *Anales del Museo Nacional "David J. Guzmán"* 50:13–20. San Salvador.

Guerrero, Juan Vicente. 1998. The Archaeological Context of Jade in Costa Rica. In *Jade in Ancient Costa Rica*, edited by Julie Jones, pp. 23–37. The Metropolitan Museum of Art, New York.

Haberland, Wolfgang. 1960a. A Pre-Classic Complex of Western El Salvador, C.A. *Anales Museo Nacional "David J. Guzman"* 8:29–32. San Salvador.

Haberland, Wolfgang. 1960b. Ceramic Sequences in El Salvador, C.A. *American Antiquity* 26:21–29.

Haberland, Wolfgang. 1963. Ometepe 1962–1963. *Archaeology* 16:287–289.

Haberland, Wolfgang. 1976. Gran Chiriquí. *Vínculos* 2:115–121.

Haberland, Wolfgang. 1992. The Cultural History of Ometepe Island: Preliminary Sketch (Survey and Excavation, 1962–1963). In *The Archaeology of Pacific Nicaragua*, edited by Frederick W. Lange, pp. 63–117. University of New Mexico Press, Albuquerque.

Hartman, Carl V. 1901. *Archaeological Researches in Costa Rica*. The Royal Ethnographic Museum, Stockholm.

Hartman, Carl V. 1907. *Archaeological Researches on the Pacific Coast of Costa Rica*. Memoirs of the Carnegie Museum of Natural History, Vol. 3, No.1. The Carnegie Museum of Natural History, Pittsburgh.

Healy, Paul F. 1980. Archaeology of the Rivas Region, Nicaragua. Wilfrid Laurier University Press, Waterloo, Ontario.

Healy, Paul F. 1988. Greater Nicoya and Mesoamerica: Analysis of Selected Ceramics. In *Costa Rican Art and Archaeology: Essays in Honor of Frederick R. Mayer*, edited by Frederick W. Lange, pp. 293–301. University of Colorado Press, Boulder.

Hoopes, John W. 1994. The Tronadora Complex: Early Formative Ceramics in Northwestern Costa Rica. *Latin American Antiquity* 5:3–30.

Hoopes, John W., and Oscar M. Fonseca. 2003. Goldwork and Chibchan Identity: Endogenous Change and Diffuse Unity in the Isthmo-Colombian Area. In *Gold and Power in Ancient Costa Rica, Panama, and Colombia,* edited by Jeffrey Quilter and John W. Hoopes, pp. 49–90. Dumbarton Oaks, Washington, DC.

Horn, Sally P. 2006. Pre-Columbian Maize Agriculture in Costa Rica: Pollen and Other Evidence from Lake and Swamp Sediments. In *Histories of Maize: Multidisciplinary Approaches to the Prehistory, Linguistics, Biogeography, Domestication, and Evolution of Maize,* edited by John E. Staller, Robert H. Tykot, and Bruce F. Benz, pp. 367–380. Elsevier Press, San Diego.

Hurtado de Mendoza, Luis, and Elena Troyo Vargas. 2008. Simbología de poder en Guayabo de Turrialba. *Cuadernos de Antropología* 17/18:23–65.

Ibarra, Eugenia. 1990. *Las sociedades cacicales de Costa Rica (siglo XVI)*. Editorial de la Universidad de Costa Rica, San José.

Ibarra, Eugenia, and Silvia Salgado. 2010. Áreas culturales, regiones históricas y la explicación de relaciones sociales de pueblos indígenas de nicaragua y costa rica, siglos XV y XVI. *Anuario Centroamericano de Estudios Sociales* 35–36. Editorial de la Universidad de Costa Rica, San José.

Jiménez Moreno, Wigberto. 1966. Mesoamerica before the Toltecs. Translated by M. Bullington and C.R. Wicke. In *Ancient Oaxaca: Discoveries in Mexican Archaeology and History,* edited by John Paddock, pp. 3–82. Stanford University Press, Stanford.

Kelley, Jane. 1988. Cihuatán, El Salvador: A Study in Intrasite Variability. Vanderbilt University Publications in Anthropology, No. 35. Vanderbilt University, Nashville.

Lange, Frederick W. 1976. Bahías y valles de la costa de Guanacaste. *Vínculos* 2:45–66.

Lange, Frederick W. 1984. The Greater Nicoya Archaeological Subarea. In *The Archaeology of Lower Central America*, edited by Frederick W. Lange and Doris Z. Stone, pp. 165–194. University of New Mexico Press, Albuquerque.

Lange, Frederick W. 1992. *Wealth and Hierarchy in the Intermediate Area*. Dumbarton Oaks, Washington, DC.

Lange, Frederick W. 1993. The Conceptual Structure of Lower Central American Studies: A Central American View. In *Reinterpreting Prehistory of Central America*, edited by Mark Miller Graham, pp. 277–324. University Press of Colorado, Niwot.

Lange, Frederick W. 1996. *Abundante cooperación vecinal: La segunda temporada del proyecto "arqueología de la zona metropolitana de Managua."* Alcaldía de Managua, Nicaragua.

Lange, Frederick W., Erin L. Sears, Ronald L. Bishop, and Silvia Salgado González. 2003. Local Production, Non-Local Production, and Distribution: Usulutan and Usulutan-Like Negative Painted Ceramics in Nicaragua. In *Patterns and Process: A Festschrift in Honor of Dr. Edward V. Sayre,* edited by Lambertus van Zelst, pp. 157–169. Smithsonian Institution Press, Washington, DC.

Lange, Frederick W., Payson D. Sheets, Anibal Martinez, and Suzanne Abel-Vidor. 1992. *The Archaeology of Pacific Nicaragua*. University of New Mexico Press, Albuquerque.

León Portilla, Miguel. 1972. *Religión de los Nicaraos: Análisis y Comparación de Tradiciones Culturales Nahuas.* Instituto de Investigaciones Historicas, Universidad Nacional Autonoma de México, Mexico, DF.

Longyear III, John M. 1944. *Archaeological Investigations in El Salvador.* Memoirs of the Peabody Museum of Archaeology and Ethnology, Vol. 9, No. 2. Harvard University, Cambridge.

López-Forment Vílla, Angélica. 2007. *Aprovechamiento cultural de los recursos faunísticos en el sitio de Santa Isabel, Nicaragua.* Manuscript on file, Escuela Nacional de Antropología e Historia, Mexico City.

Lothrop, Samuel K. 1926a. Lista de los sitios arqueológicos en El Salvador. *Revista de Etnología, Arqueología, y Lingüística* 1(5):19–23.

Lothrop, Samuel K. 1926b. *Pottery of Costa Rica and Nicaragua.* 2 vols. Museum of the American Indian, Memoir No. 8. Heye Foundation, New York.

McCafferty, Geoffrey G. 2008. Domestic Practice in Postclassic Santa Isabel, Nicaragua. *Latin American Antiquity* 19:64–82.

McCafferty, Geoffrey G. 2009. La Arenera, Nicaragua. Online resource, http://arky.ucalgary.ca/mccafferty/miscellaneous/la-arenera-nicaragua.

McCafferty, Geoffrey G. 2010. Diez años de arqueología en Nicaragua. *Mi Museo y Vos* 14:2–15.

McCafferty, Geoffrey G. 2011. Etnicidad chorotega en la frontera sur de Mesoamerica. *La Universidad* 14–15: 91–112. Universidad de El Salvador.

McCafferty, Geoffrey G., and Sharisse D. McCafferty. 2008. Spinning and Weaving Tools from Santa Isabel, Nicaragua. *Ancient Mesoamerica* 19:143–156.

McCafferty, Geoffrey G., and Sharisse D. McCafferty. 2009. Crafting the Body Beautiful: Performing Social Identity at Santa Isabel, Nicaragua. In *Mesoamerican Figurines: Small-Scale Indices of Large-Scale Social Phenomena*, edited by Christina T. Halperin, Katherine A. Faust, Rhonda Taube, and Aurore Giguet, pp. 183–204. University Press of Florida, Gainesville.

McCafferty, Geoffrey G., and Sharisse D. McCafferty. 2011. Bling Things: Ornamentation and Identity in Pacific Nicaragua. In *Identity Crisis: Approaches to the Archaeology of Identity*, edited by Lindsay Amundsen and Sean Pickering. Proceedings of the 40th Annual Chacmool Conference, Chacmool Archaeological Association of the University of Calgary, Calgary.

McCafferty, Geoffrey G., and Silvia Salgado González. 2000. Reporte preliminar de la evaluación del sitio La Arenera (N-MA-65) realizada del 4 al 8 de julio del 2000. Report submitted to Patrimonio Cultural, Instituto Nicaragüense de Cultura, Managua, Nicaragua.

McCafferty, Geoffrey G., Silvia Salgado González, and Carrie L. Dennett. 2009. *Cuando llegaron los Mexicanos? La transición entre los periodos Bagaces y Sapoa en Granada, Nicaragua.* Proceedings of the III Congreso Centroamericano de Arqueología en El Salvador. Digital version published by the Museo Nacional de Antropología, San Salvador, El Salvador.

McCafferty, Geoffrey G., and Larry L. Steinbrenner. 2005a. The Meaning of the Mixteca-Puebla Stylistic Tradition on the Southern Periphery of Mesoamerica: The View from Nicaragua. In *Art for Archaeology's Sake: Material Culture and Style across the Disciplines*, edited by Andrea Waters-Rist, Christine Cluny, Calla McNamee, and Larry Steinbrenner, pp.282–292. Proceedings of the 33rd Annual Chacmool Conference, Chacmool Archaeological Association of the University of Calgary, Calgary.

McCafferty, Geoffrey G., and Larry L. Steinbrenner. 2005b. Chronological Implications for Greater Nicoya from the Santa Isabel Project, Nicaragua. *Ancient Mesoamerica* 16:131–146.

McInnis Thompson, Lauri, and Fred Valdez Jr. 2008, Potbelly Sculpture: An Inventory and Analysis. *Ancient Mesoamerica* 19:13–27.

Mora-Marín, Davíd F. 2002. An Epi-Olmec Jade Pendant from Costa Rica. *Mexicon* 24:14–19.

Mora-Marín, Davíd F. 2005. The Jade-to-Gold Shift in Ancient Costa Rica: A World-Systems Perspective. Unpublished manuscript in possession of the author (Salgado González), San José, Costa Rica.

Moroney Ubeda, Bosco. 2011. Las Delicias: Poblado indígena mas antiguo de Managua. *Nuestra Identidad: Rescate Historico de Managua* 1(5):4–40. Alcaldía de Managua, Nicaragua.

Murillo, Mauricio. 2010. Diversidad sociopolítica en Costa Rica Precolombina: Implicaciones para la comprensión del cambio social. *International Journal of South American Archaeology* 6:16–34.

Navarrete, Carlos. 1972. El sitio arqueológico de San Nicolás, Municipio de Ahuachapan, El Salvador. *Estudios de Cultura Maya* 7:57–66.

Niemel, Karen. 2003. Social Change and Migration in the Rivas Region, Pacific Nicaragua (1000 BC–AD 1522). PhD dissertation, Department of Anthropology, State University of New York at Buffalo, New York.

Norweb, Albert H. 1964. Ceramic Stratigraphy in Southwestern Nicaragua. *Actas, 35th International Congress of Americanists* 1:551–561.

Paredes, Federico A. 2008. Early Local Identities in Western El Salvador. Paper presented at the 73rd annual meeting of the Society for American Archaeology, Vancouver.

Pavón Sánchez, Oscar. 2010. Descubrimientos en el sitio arqueológico Las Delicias, Nicaragua. *Mi Museo y Vos* 4(14):16–17. [http://www.granadacollection.org/Revista%20Mi%20MuseoNo14.pdf]

Peccorini, Atilio. 1913. Algunos datos sobre arqueología de la República del Salvador. *Journal de la Societé des Américanistes de Paris* 10:173–180.

Peccorini, Atilio. 1926. Ruinas de Quelepa. *Revista de Etnología, Arqueología y Lingüística* 1:249–250.

Peytrequín, Jeffrey. 2008. Los rituales funerarios: Un acercamiento teórico y metodológico al estudio de las prácticas mortuorias y sus significados durante la fase Curridabat (300–800 d.C.). *Cuadernos de Antropología* 17/18:11–21.

Reyes, Eduardo J. 2009. Unidad y heterogeneidad durante el período Formativo en Costa Rica (2000–300 a.C.): Una propuesta de interacción cultural. *Cuadernos de Antropología* 19:57–74.

Ries, Maurice. 1940. First Season's Archaeological Work at Campana San Andrés, El Salvador. *American Anthropologist* N.S. 42:712–713.

Roman Lacayo, Manuel A. N.d. Social and Environmental Risk and the Development of Social Complexity in Precolumbian Masaya, Nicaragua. PhD dissertation, Department of Anthropology, University of Pittsburgh, Pittsburgh.

Salgado González, Silvia. 1996a. Social Change in a Region of Granada, Pacific Nicaragua (1000 BC–AD 1522). PhD dissertation, Department of Anthropology, State University of New York, Albany.

Salgado González, Silvia. 1996b. The Ayala Site: A Bagaces Period Site Near Granada, Nicaragua. In *Paths to Central American Prehistory*, edited by Frederick W. Lange, pp.191–220. University Press of Colorado, Boulder.

Sampeck, Kathryn. 2010. Late Postclassic to Colonial Transformations of the Landscape in the Izalcos Region of Western El Salvador. *Ancient Mesoamerica* 21(2):261–282.

Sánchez, Luis Alberto. 2010. Las ocupaciones tempranas en Bahía Culebra: Tecnología, subsistencia y utilización del espacio por comunidades costeras de los periodos Orosí tardío y Tempisque (500 a.C. a 500 d.C.) en Manzanillo (G-430mz), Península de Nacascolo, Guanacaste. Unpublished manuscript on file, Archives of the National Museum, Costa Rica, and Península Papagayo S.A.

Sharer, Robert J. 1978. *The Prehistory of Chalchuapa, El Salvador*. 3 vols. University of
    Pennsylvania Press, Philadelphia.
Sheets, Payson D. 1976. *Ilopango Volcano and the Maya Protoclassic: A Report of the 1975
    Field Season of the Protoclassic Project in El Salvador*. University of Colorado Press,
    Boulder.
Sheets, Payson D. 1983. *Archaeology and Volcanism in Central America. The Zapotitan
    Valley of El Salvador*. University of Texas Press, Austin.
Sheets, Payson D. 1984a. Summary and Conclusions. In *Archaeology, Volcanism and
    Remote Sensing in the Arenal Region, Costa Rica*, edited by Payson D. Sheets and
    Brian R. McKee, pp. 312–325. University of Texas Press, Austin.
Sheets, Payson D. 1984b. The Prehistory of El Salvador: An Interpretive Summary. In
    The Archaeology of Lower Central America, edited by Frederick W. Lange and Doris
    Z. Stone, pp. 85–112. University of New Mexico Press, Albuquerque.
Sheets, Payson D. 1989. *Archaeological Investigations at the Cerén Site, El Salvador:
    A Preliminary Report*. Department of Anthropology, University of Colorado,
    Boulder.
Sheets, Payson D. 1992. *The Cerén Site: A Prehistoric Village Buried by Volcanic Ash in
    Central America*. Harcourt College, Orlando.
Sheets, Payson D. 2003. Summary and Conclusions: Proyecto Prehistórico Arenal.
    Vínculos 28:175–188.
Sheets, Payson D., Christine Dixon, Monica Guerra, and Adam Blanford. 2011. Manioc
    Cultivation at Cerén, El Salvador: Occasional Kitchen Garden Plant or Staple Crop?
    Ancient Mesoamerica 22(1):1–11.
Snarskis, Michael J. 1976. La vertiente Atlántica de Costa Rica. *Vínculos* 2:101–114.
Snarskis, Michael J. 1979. Turrialba: A Paleoindian Quarry and Workshop Site in Eastern
    Costa Rica. *American Antiquity* 44:125–138.
Snarskis, Michael J. 1984. Central America: The Lower Caribbean. In *The Archaeology
    of Lower Central America*, edited by Frederick W. Lange and Doris Z. Stone, pp.
    195–232. University of New Mexico Press, Albuquerque.
Sol, Antonio E. 1929. Informe sobre las ruinas de Cihuatán, Departamento de San
    Salvador. *Revista del Departamento de Historia* 1(1):19–23. San Salvador.
Solís, Felipe, and Anayensy Herrera. 2008. Informe final de campo: Sitio Jícaro.
    Unpublished manuscript on file, Archives of the National Museum, Costa Rica, and
    Península Papagayo, S.A.
Spinden, Herbert J. 1915. Notes on the Archeology of Salvador. *American Anthropologist*
    17:446–487.
Squier, Ephraim G. 1852. *Nicaragua: Its People, Scenery, Monuments and the Proposed
    Interoceanic Canal*. 2 vols. Appleton Co., New York.
Squier, Ephraim G. 1990 [1853]. *Observations on the Archaeology and Ethnology of
    Nicaragua*. Labyrinthos, Culver City, California.
Steinbrenner, Larry L. 2002. Ethnicity and Ceramics in Rivas, Nicaragua, AD 800–1550.
    MA thesis, Department of Archaeology, University of Calgary, Cal-1350gary.
Steinbrenner, Larry L. 2010. Potting Traditions and Cultural Continuity in Pacific
    Nicaragua, AD 800–1350. PhD dissertation, Department of Archaeology, University
    of Calgary, Calgary.
Stone, Doris Z. 1982. *Aspects of Mixteca-Puebla Style and Mixtec and Central Mexican
    Culture in Southern Mesoamerica*. Middle American Research Institute, Occasional
    Paper No. 4. Tulane University, New Orleans.

Stone, Doris Z. 1984. A History of Lower Central American Archaeology. In *The Archaeology of Lower Central America*, edited by Frederick W. Lange and Doris Z. Stone, pp. 13–32. University of New Mexico Press, Albuquerque.

Whisnant, David E. 1994. The Removal of Antiquities from Nicaragua in the Nineteenth Century: The Case of Earl Flint. Paper presented at the Latin American Studies Association, Atlanta, GA.

Wilke, Sacha, Geoffrey McCafferty, and Brett Watson. 2011. The Archaeology of Death on the Shore of Lake Nicaragua. In *Identity Crisis: Archaeological Perspectives on Social Identity*, edited by Lindsey Amundsen-Meyer, Nicole Engel, and Sean Pickering, pp. 178–188. Chacmool Archaeological Association, University of Calgary, Calgary.

CHAPTER 7

....

ARCHAEOLOGY AND INDIGENOUS PEOPLES

....

SHOSHAUNNA PARKS AND PATRICIA A. MCANANY

THROUGHOUT the Americas, the experience of European colonialism shaped the practice of archaeology and the relationship between indigenous peoples and their past. This situation is particularly acute in Mesoamerica—the nations of Mexico, Belize, Guatemala, Honduras, and El Salvador—in which tens of millions of indigenous peoples reside. Unlike in North America, where federal legislation yielded power over ancestral remains to native descendants (one example is the 1990s-era Native American Graves Protection and Repatriation Act in the United States), the nations of Mesoamerica have generally not recognized the rights of indigenous peoples to manage their archaeological heritage. In the interest of nation building, the national governments of Mesoamerican countries reserve the right to manage archaeological remains. Within the Maya region (the eastern portion of Mesoamerica), even the native status of indigenous peoples has been challenged (Adams 1994; Medina 1998; Stone 2000).

This chapter examines the present relationship between indigenous people and archaeology in Mesoamerica, with an emphasis on the Maya region. Here we provide a brief analysis of the historical and political conditions that have contributed to the disenfranchisement of indigenous peoples from the ancient past. We also look at recent interactions among stakeholders in the investigation, interpretation, and management of Mesoamerican archaeological heritage.

Indigenous communities within the Maya region have long Pre-Columbian histories (the Garifuna communities of coastal Honduras, Guatemala, and Belize, who trace their ancestry to both Africa and the Caribbean, are a notable exception)

but the region has also always been a "globalized" place of considerable population movement. Ethnohistoric sources that recount narratives of origins and
migrations—such as the *Codice de Calkiní* (Barrera Vasquez 1957)—provide evidence of how communities moved across the landscape in response to changing
political, economic, and environmental conditions. Movement quickened during
the Colonial period as indigenous peoples fled from the political control and economic demands of European colonizers (Farriss 1984). In the centuries following
the arrival of Spanish conquistadors, colonial officials attempted to break existing
indigenous political hierarchies and to remove communities from familiar landscapes by placing them in *congregaciones* (or *reducciones*) for easier monitoring
and control; those who escaped sought refuge in sparsely settled or relatively inac-
cessible regions (Jones 1989; Restall 1999). This pattern continued through the last
two centuries as many indigenous communities were forced to abandon native
lands and become political and economic refugees (Rugeley 1996; Wilk 1987, 1991),
the most brutal manifestation of which occurred in Guatemala during the 1970s
and 1980s (Carmack 1988; Jonas 1991; Manz 1988; Sanford 2003). Enmeshed within
violent clashes between the military and counterinsurgents, many indigenous
communities were forcibly resettled into "model villages" (Schirmer 2002; Stoll
1993), were internally displaced, or were granted amnesty in neighboring countries
or in North America (Loucky and Moors 2000). More recently, individuals from
indigenous communities throughout Mesoamerica, particularly men, have immigrated to Pacific coastal plantations or to North America in search of work (e.g.,
Cohen 2004; García 2006; Nolin 2006; Stephen 2007). The result of this turbulence
and movement is a landscape of indigenous communities that are disconnected
from place of origin, that are reduced in size, and that have experienced disruption
in traditional forms of governance and the communication of intangible cultural
heritage. These combined colonial and postcolonial forces of "heritage distancing"
have severely affected the valuation of archaeological heritage by indigenous communities (McAnany and Parks 2012).

This is not to say that indigenous communities in Mesoamerica do not place
importance on Pre-Columbian sites. From precolonial through modern times,
native people continuously engaged with ancient spaces—with both constructed
sites and natural features such as caves (e.g., Brown 2004, 2005; Bonfil Batalla 1996;
Fruhsorge 2007; MacKenzie 2009; Metz 2006; Wilson 1995). The spiritual energy
found in these places creates meaning and can be a significant factor in structuring the ways in which local people interact with their heritage. In communities that maintain ceremonial ties to ancient places, the appeasement of sources
of supernatural energy is often a priority for maintaining an ordered world. This
relationship can be profoundly altered by intrusive archaeological investigations
that disturb the source of such energy and disorder the relationships of reciprocity
that mark Mayan spirituality (Garcia 2003; Molesky-Poz 2006).

In Guatemala, the unique spiritual relationship between Maya peoples and
their cultural heritage is legally recognized (Ivic de Monterroso 2004). In 2002, the
Minister of Culture and Sports decreed that indigenous ritual specialists were free

to perform rituals at archaeological sites and ordered the construction of ceremonial spaces within them (Fruhsorge 2007: 43). The following year, the Commission
on Sacred Places was created as an advisory council within the Ministry of Culture
and Sports to coordinate spiritual efforts, foment tolerance for the practice of traditional Mayan spirituality, and ensure that Maya people have access to sites for
spiritual purposes.

These notable first steps within the Maya region take place against the backdrop of an intensely commodified landscape of archaeotourism that poses a hurdle
to opening archaeology and cultural-heritage management further to indigenous
peoples. Tourism is a major source of revenue throughout Mesoamerica, and
archaeological sites such as Teotihuacan, Chichén Itzá, and Tikal draw hundreds
of thousands of visitors each year. Although indigenous communities often are situated proximate to archaeological sites, they typically are not primary beneficiaries of archaeotourism (Breglia 2006; Castañeda 1996; McAnany 2007; Parks and
McAnany 2007; Parks 2010). Without the start-up capital and (often) the entrepreneurial skills required to establish a business, indigenous people tend to occupy
menial jobs with long hours and little pay (Chambers 2004; van der Berghe 1995).
Despite this reality, many towns and villages located near undeveloped sites are
enthusiastic about archaeological investigation because they associate the arrival
of archaeologists with the development of a local tourism industry. Unfortunately,
the increasingly saturated Mesoamerican archaeotourism market means that the
vast majority of developed archaeological sites will never draw sufficient visitors to
provide equitable, sustainable benefit to local communities.

There are other ways in which indigenous people have been distanced from
Maya cultural heritage. As Philip Kohl (1998; Kohl and Fawcett 1995) and others
have noted, archaeological interpretation can be manipulated by national governments as a means of legitimization. In Mexico, archaeological symbols and
interpretations have been co-opted as a tool to eradicate cultural difference and
create national identity via the process of *indigenismo* (Fowler 1987: 234; Lorenzo
1982, 1998; Patterson 1995). By drawing parallels between a burgeoning Mexican
nation and an ancient Aztec past, the Mexican government succeeded in foment-
ing solidarity among its people by designating indigenous symbols as "Mexican"
and expunging autonomous indigenous identity from the picture of a modern and
independent Mexico (King 1985; Watkins 2005: 436). More recently, the international community has influenced the relationship between indigenous peoples and
the ancient past through implementation of the World Heritage Convention 1975.
The redefinition of sites of Pre-Columbian Maya heritage—such as Tikal (listed in
1979), Copán (listed in 1980), and Joya de Cerén (listed in 1993)—as of "universal
value" to "mankind as a whole" overshadows the dynamic connections between
indigenous people and the past (Omland 2006: 248). Although enhanced site protection is a positive outcome of World Heritage status, assigning Maya heritage a
global position can disrupt traditional understandings of ancient places and relegate local, cultural, spiritual, and historical values to secondary status (Breglia
2006: 49).

Archaeologists who conduct field research in Mesoamerica grapple not only with the disenfranchisement of indigenous people from their precolonial past but also work amid current neocolonial economic and sociopolitical struggles in which indigenous communities are enmeshed (McGuire 2005, 2008). Following the passage of the International Labour Organization's Convention 169 in 1989, indigenous activism has increased. Although programs of activism are not cohesive across national, or even community, boundaries, native leaders work to protect and promote the rights of communities in matters of land, wealth distribution, and political access, as well as freedom of expression, spirituality, and culture (Fischer and Brown 1996; Jackson and Warren 2005; Montejo 2002; Munoz 2005; Warren 1998; Valdez 1998). For example, in Guatemala initial activism was aimed at reappropriating history and tradition from those who sought to destroy or otherwise usurp it (including state officials and "Mayanists," respectively; see Fischer 1996). As Maya activism progressed, however, the focus on ancestral pasts has declined (Demarest 2007). Even so, the struggle for indigenous rights has resulted in the use of archaeological heritage as sites and symbols of resistance. At Copán in western Honduras, the Ch'orti' have staged four takeovers of the archaeological park since 1998, the most memorable of which, in 2000, resulted in a violent clash between the Honduran National Police and Ch'orti' protestors (Joyce 2003; Mortensen 2006). Though the strikes were intended to call attention to violations of Convention 169 and to incite the restitution of land to the Ch'orti', leaders of the National Indigenous Council of the Maya-Ch'orti' of Honduras (CONIMCHH) also requested a portion of the revenue from entrance fees at the Copán archaeological park. Eventually, in 2005, the Honduran government agreed to discuss profit-sharing (Parks and McAnany 2007), although an arrangement has not been finalized.

In Mexico the authority of a local indigenous group over an archaeological site located on communal *ejido* land has been recognized by INAH. In 2003, when the Classic Maya site of Chacchoben in Quintana Roo, Mexico, was opened for tourism, guides bringing busloads of tourists from the "Costa Maya" agreed to contribute one dollar for each visitor to the local *ejido*. More commonly, however, power struggles between indigenous people and other stakeholders have significantly less sanguine results. In 2008, the takeover of the ancient Chiapan ceremonial site of Chinkultic by local Tzotzil and Tzeltal villagers came to an end when police attacked the protesters killing six and wounding or "disappearing" over two dozen. Less violent protests and other forms of resistance, such as the violation of carved monuments at Uxbenká, Belize, in the 1990s by the local Mopan community, have taken place at prehispanic sites throughout Mesoamerica (i.e., Breglia 2006; Parks 2010; Watkins 2005: 436). Despite these actions, the struggle for descendants' rights to prehispanic heritage in Mesoamerica is often secondary to struggles for land, education, and economic opportunity.

Another factor confounding the relationship between archaeology and indigenous peoples is a continued focus on monumental constructions of the past and the aristocracies that created them. This selective investigation of the past impacts interpretations of prehispanic Mesoamerica and conceals the past achievements of nonelites. By assigning archaeological value to particular ancient places, the archaeological community infringes on indigenous authority to define the places that represent *their* culture and heritage (see a general discussion in Hamilakis 2007: 28–30). For example, in the Yucatec region of Mexico, indigenous peoples rarely relate to Classic-period archaeological sites but do connect to places of more recent historical struggle created by the nineteenth-century Caste War (Rugeley 1996).

Archaeologists working in Mesoamerica are ever more cognizant of indigenous interests in securing rights to ancestral heritage. In the future, there is little doubt that the pursuit of indigenous rights will change the landscape of archaeological practice in the region. Some indigenous organizations—such as the Maya Leaders Alliance in Belize and Oxlaju Aj'pop in Guatemala—have already initiated conversations with archaeologists about their disenfranchisement from ancestral sites. Independently researchers at many archaeological projects throughout Mesoamerica have begun to consider the impact of their work on local and indigenous communities in places such as the Mixteca Alta (Geurds 2007) and the northern Mexican border community of Tohono O'odham (McGuire 2008).

Still, as the title of this chapter suggests, archaeology and indigenous people remain largely separate from each other in Mesoamerica. Although a number of archaeologists are working with local and indigenous communities to create a more inclusive archaeology, policy issues—such as the display of human remains and the repatriation of ceremonial objects to indigenous descendants—have not yet been addressed (Montejo 1999). The maintenance of Pre-Columbian sites and artifacts by Mesoamerican nation-states in trust for the national population arguably excludes indigenous communities that typically have little representation in national bodies of governance. Nevertheless, indigenous people are increasingly pursuing higher education, moving closer to representation in national political economies, and slowly entering the discipline of archaeology to emerge as scholars of their own past. Thus, while many aspects of archaeology and heritage management in Mesoamerica are far from inclusive, the greater participation of indigenous peoples in the processes of archaeological investigation, interpretation, and management is on the horizon.

References

Adams, Richard. 1994. A Report on the Political Status of the Guatemalan Maya. In *Indigenous Peoples and Democracy in Latin America*, edited by Van Cott and Donna Lee, pp. 155–186. St. Martin's, New York.

Barrera Vasquez, A., trans. 1957. *Codice de Calkiní*. Biblioteca Campechana 4, Campeche.

Bonfil Batalla, Guillermo. 1996. *México Profundo: Reclaiming a Civilization*. University of Texas Press, Austin.

Breglia, Lisa. 2006. *Monumental Ambivalene: The Politics of Heritage*. University of Texas Press, Austin, Texas.

Brown, Linda A. 2004. Dangerous Places and Wild Spaces: Creating Meaning with Materials and Space at Contemporary Maya Shrines on el Duende Mountain. *Journal of Archaeological Method and Theory* 11:31–58.

Brown, Linda A. 2005. Planting the Bones: Hunting Ceremonialism at Contemporary and Nineteenth-Century Shrines in the Guatemalan Highlands." *Latin American Antiquity* 16:131–146.

Carmack, Robert M., ed. 1988. *Harvest of Violence.* University of Oklahoma Press, Norman.

Castañeda, Quetzil E. 1996. *In the Museum of Maya Culture: Touring Chichen Itzá.* University of Minnesota Press, Minneapolis.

Chambers, Erve J. 2004. Epilogue: Archaeology, Heritage, and Public Endeavor. In *Places in Mind: Public Archaeology as Applied Anthropology,* edited by Paul A. Shackel and Erve J. Chambers, pp. 193–208. Routledge, New York.

Cohen, Jeffrey Harris. 2004. *The Culture of Migration in Southern Mexico.* University of Texas Press, Austin.

Demarest, Arthur A. 2007. Ethics and Ethnocentricity in Interpretation and Critique: Challenges to the Anthropology of Corporeality and Death. In *Warfare and Ritual Violence among the Indigenous Peoples of Latin America: Problems in Paradise,* edited by Richard Chacon and Ruben Mendoza, pp. 591–617. University of Arizona Press, Tucson.

Farriss, Nancy M. 1984. *Maya Society under Colonial Rule: The Collective Enterprise of Survival.* Princeton University Press, Princeton.

Fischer, Edward F. 1996. Induced Culture Change as a Strategy for Socioeconomic Development: The Pan-Maya Movement in Guatemala. In *Maya Cultural Activism in Guatemala,* edited by Edward F. Fischer and R. McKenna Brown, pp. 51–73. University of Texas Press, Austin.

Fischer, Edward F., and R. McKenna Brown, eds. 1996. *Maya Cultural Activism in Guatemala.* University of Texas Press, Austin.

Fowler, Don D. 1987. Use of the Past: Archaeology in the Service of the State. *American Antiquity* 52(2): 229–248.

Fruhsorge, Lars. 2007. Archaeological Heritage in Guatemala: Indigenous Perspectives on the Ruins of Iximche. *Archaeologies* 3(1): 39–58.

Garcia, David R. 2003. Vinculos espirituales y religion alrededor de Cancuen. In *XVI Simposio de Investigaciones Arqueologicas en Guatemala, 2002,* edited by Juan Pedro Laporte, Barbara Arroyo, Hector L. Escobedo, and Hector E. Mejia, pp. 11–16. Ministerio de Cultura y Deportes, Guatemala.

García, María Cristina. 2006. *Seeking Refuge: Central American Migration to Mexico, the United States, and Canada.* University of California Press, Berkeley.

Geurds, Alexander. 2007. *Grounding the Past: The Praxis of Participatory Archaeology in the Mixteca Alta, Oaxaca, Mexico.* CNWS Publications. Leiden, The Netherlands.

Hamilakis, Yannis. 2007. From Ethics to Politics. In *Archaeology and Capitalism: From Ethics to Politics,* edited by Yannis Hamilakis and Philip Duke, pp. 15–40. Left Coast Press, Walnut Creek, California.

Ivic de Monterroso, Matilde. 2004. The Sacred Place in the Development of Archaeology in Guatemala: An Analysis. In *Continuities and Changes in Maya Archaeology: Perspectives at the Millennium,* edited by Charles W. Golden and Greg Borgstede, pp. 295–308. Routledge, New York.

Jackson, Jean E., and Kay B. Warren. 2005. Indigenous Movements in Latin America, 1992–2004: Controversies, Ironies, New Directions. *Annual Review of Anthropology* 34: 549–573.

Jonas, Susanne. 1991. *The Battle for Guatemala: Rebels, Death Squads, and U.S. Power.* Westview Press, Boulder.

Jones, Grant D. 1989. *Maya Resistance to Spanish Rule: Time and History on a Colonial Frontier.* University of New Mexico Press, Albuquerque.

Joyce, Rosemary A. 2003. Archaeology and Nation Building: A View from Central
    America. *In The Politics of Archaeology and Identity in a Global Context*, edited
    by Susan Kane, pp. 79–100. Colloquia and Conference Papers 7, Archaeological
    Institute of America, Boston.
King, Jaime Litvak. 1985. Mesoamerica: Events and Processes, the Last 50 Years.
    American Antiquity 50:374–382.
Kohl, Phillip L. 1998. Nationalism and Archaeology: On the Constructions of Nations
    and the Reconstructions of the Remote Past. *Annual Review of Anthropology* 27: 223–246.
Kohl, Phillip L., and Clare Fawcett, eds. 1995. *Nationalism, Politics, and the Practice of
    Archaeology*. Cambridge University Press, Cambridge.
Lorenzo, José L. 1982. Archaeology South of the Rio Grande. *World Archaeology* 13(2):
    190–208.
Lorenzo, José L. 1998. La arqueología y México. Instituto Nacional de Antropología y
    Historia, Mexico City.
Loucky, James, and Marilyn M. Moors, eds. 2000. *The Maya Diaspora: Guatemalan
    Roots, New American Lives*. Temple University Press, Philadelphia.
MacKenzie, C. James. 2009. Judas off the Noose: Sacerdotes Mayas, Costumbristas, and
    the Politics of Purity in the Tradition of San Simón in Guatemala. *Journal of Latin
    American and Caribbean Anthropology* 14:355–381.
Manz, Beatriz. 1988. *Refugees of a Hidden War: The Aftermath of Counterinsurgency in
    Guatemala*. State University of New York Press, Albany.
McAnany, Patricia A. 2007. A View from Mesoamerica. *Cambridge Archaeological
    Journal* 17:19–22.
McAnany, Patricia A., and Shoshaunna Parks. 2012. Casualties of Heritage Distancing:
    Children, Ch'orti' Indigeneity, and the Copán Archaeoscape. *Current Anthropology*
    53(1):80-107.
McGuire, Randall H. 2005. *A Marxist Archaeology*. Percheron Press, Clinton Corners,
    New York.
McGuire, Randall H. 2008. *Archaeology as Political Action*. University of California
    Press, Berkeley.
Medina, Laurie Kroshus. 1998. History, Culture, and Place-Making: "Native"
    Status and Maya Identity in Belize. *Journal of Latin American Anthropology*
    4(1):134–165.
Metz, Brent E. 2006. *Ch'orti'-Maya Survival in Eastern Guatemala: Indigeneity in
    Transition*. University of New Mexico Press, Albuquerque.
Molesky-Poz, Jean. 2006. *Contemporary Maya Spirituality: The Ancient Ways Are Not
    Lost*. University of Texas Press, Austin.
Montejo, Victor D. 1999. The Year Bearer's People: Repatriation of Ethnographic and
    Sacred Knowledge to the Jakaltek Maya of Guatemala. *International Journal of
    Cultural Property* 8(1):151–166.
Montejo, Victor D. 2002. The Multiplicity of Mayan Voices: Mayan Leadership and the
    Politics of Self- Representation. In *Indigenous Movements, Self-Representation, and
    the State in Latin America*, edited by Kay B. Warren and Jean E. Jackson,
    pp. 123–148. University of Texas Press, Austin.
Mortensen, Lena. 2006. Experiencing Copán: The Authenticity of Stone. In
    Archaeological Site Museums in Latin America, edited by Helaine Silverman, pp.
    47–63. University of Florida Press, Gainesville.
Munoz, Alejandro Anaya. 2005. The Emergence and Development of the Politics of
    Recognition of Cultural Diversity and Indigenous Peoples' Rights in Mexico:

Chiapas and Oaxaca in Comparative Perspective. *Journal of Latin American Studies* 37(3):585–610.

Nolin, Catherine. 2006. *Transnational Ruptures: Gender and Forced Migration.* Ashgate Publishing Company, Burlington, Vermont.

Omland, Atle. 2006. The Ethics of the World Heritage Concept. In *Ethics of Archaeology: Philosophical Perspectives on Archaeological Practice*, edited by Chris Scarre and Geoffrey Scarre, pp. 242–259. Cambridge University Press, Cambridge.

Parks, Shoshaunna. 2010. The Collision of Heritage and Economy at Uxbenká, Belize. *International Journal of Heritage Studies* 16(6):434–448.

Parks, Shoshaunna, and Patricia A. McAnany. 2007. Reclaiming Maya Ancestry. In *Look Close, See Far: A Cultural Portrait of the Maya*, edited by Bruce T. Martin, pp. 13–22. George Brazilier, New York.

Patterson, Thomas C. 1995. Archaeology, History, *Indigenismo* and the State in Peru and Mexico. In *Making Alternative Histories: The Practice of Archaeology and History in Non-Western Societies*, edited by Peter R. Schmidt and Thomas C. Patterson, pp. 69–85. School of American Research Press, Santa Fe.

Restall, Matthew. 1999. *Maya Conquistador.* Beacon Press, Boston.

Rugeley, Terry. 1996. *Yucatan's Maya Peasantry and the Origins of the Caste War.* University of Texas Press, Austin.

Sanford, Victoria. 2003. *Buried Secrets: Truth and Human Rights in Guatemala.* Palgrave Macmillan, New York.

Schirmer, Jennifer. 2002. Appropriating the Indigenous, Creating Complicity: The Guatemalan Military and the Sanctioned Maya. In *The Politics of Ethnicity: Indigenous Peoples in Latin American States,* edited by David Maybury-Lewis, pp. 51–80. Harvard University Press, Cambridge.

Stephen, Lynn. 2007. *Transborder Lives: Indigenous Oaxacans in Mexico, California, and Oregon.* Duke University Press, Durham.

Stoll, David. 1993. *Between Two Armies in the Ixil Towns of Guatemala.* Columbia University Press, New York.

Stone, Michael. 2000. Becoming Belizean: Maya Identity and the Politics of a Nation. In *The Maya Diaspora: Guatemalan Roots, New American Lives,* edited by James Loucky and Marilyn M. Moors, pp. 119–140. Temple University Press, Philadelphia.

Valdez, Norberto. 1998. *Ethnicity, Class, and the Indigenous Struggle for Land in Guerrero, Mexico.* Garland, New York.

van der Berghe, Pierre L. 1995. Marketing Mayas: Ethnic Tourism Promotion in Mexico. *Annals of Tourism Research* 22(3):568–588.

Warren, Kay B. 1998. *Indigenous Movements and Their Critics: Pan-Maya Activism in Guatemala.* Princeton University Press, Princeton.

Watkins, Joe. 2005. Through Wary Eyes: Indigenous Perspectives on Archaeology. *Annual Review of Anthropology* 34:429–449.

Wilk, Richard R. 1987. The Kekchi and the Settlement of Toledo District. *Belizean Studies* 15(3):33–50.

Wilk, Richard R. 1991. *Household Ecology: Economic Change and Domestic Life among the Kekchi Maya of Belize.* Arizona Studies in Human Ecology. University of Arizona Press, Tucson.

Wilson, Richard. 1995. *Maya Resurgence in Guatemala: Q'eqchi' Experiences.* University of Oklahoma Press, Norman.

CHAPTER 8

TIME AND SPACE BOUNDARIES

CHRONOLOGIES AND REGIONS IN MESOAMERICA

SUSAN TOBY EVANS

To create the Mesoamerican world, its people, and the maize that they lived on, the gods sacrificed themselves. In gratitude for life and maize, the people in turn sacrificed themselves to nourish their gods. The pivotal role of maize in the Mesoamerican cosmos represents more general abundance, enough to support settled villages. There was enough abundance, ultimately, to support cities, states, and empires.

The following chapters look at Mesoamerica's regions and great cities in more detail, following in general a cultural evolutionary organizing framework, tracking the emergence of villages, cities, states, and empires. These community and organizational types represent important diagnostics in understanding any time period in the long history of the indigenous Mesoamerican culture area. This chapter describes in general terms the characteristics of major time periods, tracking the regions that directed or dominated events in each period. (Mesoamerican regions are presented in Figure 8.1.) (For general overviews of regions and chronology, see Evans 2013; Evans and Webster 2010; Kirchhoff 1981 [1943]; López Austin and López Luján 2005; Webster and Evans 2013; Willey 1966.)

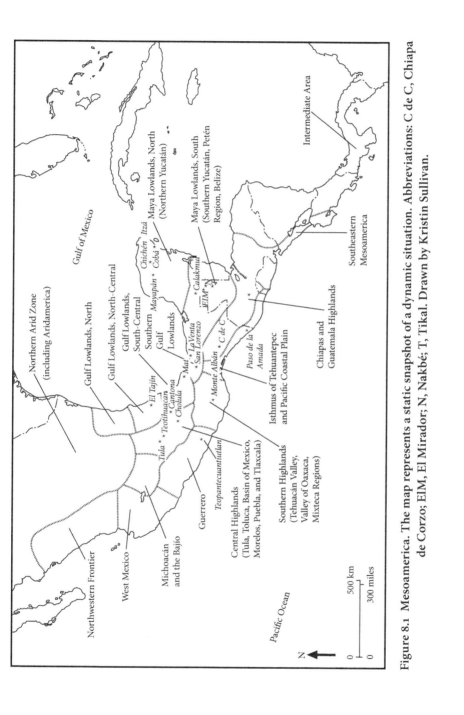

Figure 8.1 Mesoamerica. The map represents a static snapshot of a dynamic situation. Abbreviations: C de C, Chiapa de Corzo; ElM, El Mirador; N, Nakbé; T, Tikal. Drawn by Kristin Sullivan.

MESOAMERICA BEFORE MESOAMERICA: THE LATE ARCHAIC PERIOD (4000–2000 BC)

The outer boundaries of the culture area "Mesoamerica" correspond well with the outer limits of maize farming as it eventually became established in adjacent regions of a contiguous area. This culture area would eventually extend over a thousand miles from northwest to southeast, through the midsection of the Middle American subcontinent. It began to take substantial shape around 4,000 years ago, after several millennia of gestation.[1] Maize domestication, a seminal development, had occurred over 2,000 years before, and it had been one of many innovations that collectively tipped the scales of societal development toward village life, as more and more people gave up traditional, mobile hunter-forager lifeways and settled down.

Besides plant domestication, other successful Late Archaic innovations contributed to the establishment of village farming: durable buildings, intensive techniques of cultivation and resource exploitation, and whole new industries such as production of ceramics and of prismatic blades. These new traits represented energy invested in land and belongings, which are hallmarks of sedentism.

INITIAL FORMATIVE (PRECLASSIC) PERIOD (2000–1200 BCE): EARLY MESOAMERICA

Widespread evidence for sedentism marked the start of the Formative period 1000 BC-250 AD, and during the Initial Formative period, village farming provided a basis for the preconditions and prototypes of Mesoamerican civilization (Clark 2010). Surpluses produced within villages began to underwrite sophisticated features like ballcourts and elite architecture. Villagers held new spirits in reverence and expressed their beliefs as symbols in graphic and plastic forms.

---

[1] Climate change at the end of the Pleistocene slowly drove cultural evolution: see Hester 2010, MacNeish 2010, and Vivó Escoto 1964.

Mesoamerica's Outer Boundaries

Starting with the Initial Formative period, the Middle American subcontinent gave rise to three distinct culture areas: Mesoamerica's village farming distinguished it from its northern neighbor, Aridamerica, where traditional hunter-forager ways persisted. Mesoamerica's other outer border, to the southeast, was marked by sharp contrasts in important cultural traits such as linguistic affiliation. Adjacent to Mesoamerica was the Intermediate Area, where Chibchan speakers had strong ties with related cultures in South America. This was demonstrated near the end of the Late Archaic, in the Intermediate Area's pottery, the earliest in Middle America (ca. 3000–2500 BC), and an outgrowth of the already-established ceramic traditions of South America. However, maize was not in use in the southeast end of the Intermediate Area until 500 BC.

Even in the Initial Formative, Mesoamerica's boundary area with the Intermediate Area had the same general position as in the sixteenth century CE, around western Honduras's Ulúa and Cholulteca drainage systems. Mesoamerican traits, including language, marked cultures along the Pacific coastal plain of El Salvador, Nicaragua, and northwestern Costa Rica.

The boundary with Aridamerica was usually just above the Lerma River drainage zone, but it also shifted occasionally. Aridamerica's deserts and dry steppes extended north, reaching through the Great Basin of North America. Except for a few remarkable oases where permanent settlement was possible, this Gran Chichimeca region supported hunter-foragers throughout the entire Mesoamerican chronological sequence.

Within Mesoamerica, there were two Initial Formative adaptations. Initial Formative proto-Mesoamerican traits clustered in two adjacent regions: the humid tropical lowlands of the Isthmus of Tehuantepec (and adjacent coastal zones), and the temperate mountainous highlands to the west. Each had a particular form of village life. In the west, villages were increasing their commitment to maize. Sites are small, as evidenced by ceramics and occasional structural vestiges. Distributions of sites over regions do not suggest hierarchies, but nonlocal goods (including luxury goods like jade and shell) and designs (implying a widely shared ideology) reveal active interaction with other regions. Overall, however, the cultures of the highland regions had fairly simple goods.

In contrast, Isthmian adaptation sites and materials were more glamorous, and the culture was based on a more mixed economy with less commitment to maize farming. Wild food was abundant and the maize crop was probably reserved for brewing the beer that filled the Mokaya peoples' beautiful and sophisticated ceramic jars. Villages varied in size, suggesting the presence of a centralized authority and societal ranking. At Paso de la Amada, two important features of Mesoamerican civilization were in place by 1650 BC: the formal ballcourt and the elite residence. Further south and east, ceramics and settled life were evidenced in northern Honduras and southwestern Nicaragua.

EARLY FORMATIVE PERIOD
(CA. 1200-CA. 900 BC)
EARLY MESOAMERICAN *CIVILIZATION* BEGINS

The onset of the Early Formative period is marked by the first florescence of the Olmec cultural horizon, which was coming to maturity in the southern Gulf lowlands. San Lorenzo Tenochtitlan's sculpted and sculpture-rich plateau was a monumental center with masterful expressions of ideological principles and political rulership, including the earliest programmatic expression of some major traits of mature Mesoamerican civilization. In many other regions, cultures were on the verge of such monumental expression.

Throughout the Isthmus and regions east of it, the commitment to village farming gained strength. Sedentism was present at 1400 BC at Chiapa de Corzo in the western end of the Chiapas-Guatemala highlands, but several hundred years would pass before Maya village farming would be evident in the lowlands.

West of the Isthmus of Tehuantepec, in the Central Highlands and southern highlands, villages of 1,000 people indicated a scale of organization that commonly requires a ranked-society mode of rule. Beautiful objects in Olmec style were widely distributed, and some bear Olmec icons. In the eastern Balsas drainage of Guerrero, Teopantecuanitlan arose, a monumental site at the end of the Early Formative, bearing the earliest evidence of such traits as the elite residential arrangement of raised rooms around a central "sunken" patio and, even more important, the formal sweat bath. Sweat baths, like the ball game, are probably very ancient practices in Middle America, and they do not require formal structures. Elite versions of sweat baths and ballcourts were as impressive as palaces, showing that these practices had been invested with prestige and ideological meaning. Also in Guerrero, tombs featured corbelled vaults, an early expression of another trait that would gain wide usage.

MIDDLE FORMATIVE PERIOD (CA. 900–CA. 600 BC): MESOAMERICAN CIVILIZATION CONTINUES TO MATURE

Guerrero sites bridge the Early and Middle Formative periods, and they display early expressions of such essential Mesoamerican traits as bird-serpents and the association of rulership with bunches of *tule* reeds. Images on walls, monuments, and portable art link these concepts with the powerful political and spiritual associations of jades and jaguars, and these show them in Olmec art style. La Venta is the second and final great Olmec capital. La Venta's impressive pyramid, at 30 meters high, is traditionally thought to have dated from this period, and it resembled that of San Isidro, in the Chiapas plateau.

Our knowledge of the Isthmus during this period is hampered by incomplete evidence of sites and settlement patterns, but Mesoamerica shows a clear trend toward larger and more monumental sites and a more complex material culture repertoire, including, possibly, the integration of iconic symbols into a narrative notational system, perhaps the earliest known Mesoamerican writing system.

Were San Lorenzo and La Venta cities? Did the Olmecs have state-level political organization? The monumentality of these sites suggests a well-organized workforce directed by rulers whose positions of authority had become institutionalized. Did such rulers possess the right to use force against their own people (an important feature of the state)? Could the structures and art reflect, instead, effort expended out of a deep respect for a chief and a ranked rather than stratified society? Scholars debate about the timing of the emergence of Mesoamerican "cities" and "states," reflecting, of course, a range of opinions about how to define the operative terms and how to interpret the evidence.

Regardless of whether communities like La Venta were fully urbanized cities governed by the institutions of the state, we are now engaging these terms because at least some key diagnostic features are in place. Compared with Mesoamerica's later cities and states, the Isthmian manifestations are fairly modest. Compared with contemporaneous settlements beyond the Isthmus, they were monumental and assured in style. Elsewhere in Mesoamerica, communities continued to be relatively small, with steady expansions in size, numbers, and complexity. Intensification of cultivation also continued: extensive irrigation systems were being built in the Central Highlands (e.g., Coatitlan and Amalucan).

With the eclipse of Olmec culture in the southern Gulf lowlands, Mesoamerican civilization experienced its first rise-and-fall episode. The Early and Middle Formative heartland was virtually abandoned for a thousand years and never regained ascendancy. Mesoamerica's future lay in the highlands to the west and the Maya lowlands and highlands to the east.

MIDDLE TO LATE FORMATIVE PERIOD
(CA. 600–300 BC)

In the valleys of the highlands, distinctive regional styles in early statehood and urbanization were developing, using local economic surpluses created by the village farmers: food and labor. Monte Albán mushroomed in size, drawing in half the Oaxaca Valley's population. Little is known of the early site's layout, but building and provisioning this hilltop center required a substantial and well-organized labor force, subsidized by food surpluses. Oaxaca's earliest permanent irrigation system dates from this time.

Trading became more important. The long-distance movement of commodities is as old as the human occupation of Middle America, and itinerant trading probably grew strong with sedentism. Regularized marketplace activity has deep roots in these traditions, and its emergence coincided with the widespread use of plaza-centric community layout. This included the temple platform and the ruler's residence. Early Mesoamerican rulers may have controlled marketplaces and overseen transactions from the earliest times of town-centered exchange. For Aztec rulers, control of the marketplace was a dynastically held right, and this pattern might be an ancient one.

In this period, climate moderated along Mesoamerica's northern border, and this permitted farming in the Bajío region. During the Late Classic the border shifted south once more, prompting Epiclassic populations to migrate south (see below). At the southern end of Mesoamerica, Isthmian cultures of the Pacific coastal plain and adjacent uplands maintained well-settled systems of towns and villages that extended down into El Salvador. Maya sites grew in size and numbers over the lowlands of Yucatán, the Guatemala highlands, and the Petén.

LATE FORMATIVE PERIOD
(CA. 300 BC-1 AD)

The vibrant process of cultural evolution brought forth compelling examples of newborn states and cities in the Late Formative as complex societies in the tropical lowlands and more arid highlands expressed their growing wealth, influence, and social stratification. The Maya culture's first great monumental sites arose in the Petén region with Nakbé and El Mirador. A whole new grammar of civic and ceremonial architecture was created and would characterize major Maya sites for most of the coming millennium. Another important trend in the Maya area was stelae erection, documenting the rise of the practice of glorifying individual rulers to an extent unknown elsewhere in Mesoamerica. However, it drew upon the commonly held belief that rulers were more closely related to the gods than were commoners, and civic-ceremonial architecture in the tropics and in the western highlands bore ample evidence of the deity principles and mythic events that became part of Mesoamerica's shared ideology.

In the western highlands, Monte Albán's and Teotihuacan's populations increased; these quickly urbanizing communities showed distinctive traits such as social and ethnic diversity, occupational specialization, and the need for political administration more complex than kin-based solutions to problems. Monte Albán and Teotihuacan shared a pattern of demographic absorption from their surrounding hinterlands, though the stimuli were different. Monte Albán took advantage of the divided loyalties of communities in the three valleys branching out from its hilltop redoubt, and it became *the* regional central place—a "primate" center. Teotihuacan did this as well and had god(s) on its side: the city boomed in population as refugees from volcanic activity in the southern Basin of Mexico fled north. Both cities benefited from the influx of needy farmer artisans who could also, in the fallow season, serve in construction crews, helping to build these monumental sites.

TERMINAL FORMATIVE PERIOD
(CA. 1-250 AD)

The architectural programs of Teotihuacan, Monte Albán, and other cities demonstrate Mesoamericans' widespread reverence for a landscape animated by spiritual energy. Monte Albán's architectural layout replicated its position as a ridge within a larger valley system. It reinterpreted the plaza-based system, and its pyramid, palace complex, and other monuments formed a miniature version of the Valley of Oaxaca. Teotihuacan's planners warped the standard plaza into a restricted plaza at the north, extending south in a wide processional avenue, and lined it with some of Mesoamerica's largest pyramids, ever, whose forms echo those of the mountains around them. Cholulans began construction on their Great Pyramid, which would eventually be the largest structure in the ancient Americas.

In western Mexico, this period marked the greatest extent of the tradition of shaft tombs, and their association with early Teuchitlán sites and their circle-based layouts. The Teuchitlán tradition would peak in the mid-Classic period, but even at this early date, it was part of dynamic developments in this region. Mesoamerica's northern boundary was pushed north in the far west, with farming villages well north of the Lerma-Santiago River drainage. In the tropical lowlands, growth centered in the southern lowlands of Yucatán, where the emerging Maya monumental sites shared architectural patterns as well as subsistence practices, art styles, and deity principles.

EARLY CLASSIC PERIOD (CA. 250–600 AD)

In this age of mature states, this mode of political organization became common over Mesoamerica (Santley 2010). The Maya provide insight into how dynasties operated through their documents. These documents varied over the Maya area and over the six hundred years of their active use. They typically combined illustrations (often royal portraits) with one or more of several notational systems, narrative and numeric. The calendric system expressed in the texts is another cultural masterwork. Media to carry these messages included screen-fold books, sculpted panels, painted vases, and murals.

Notational systems were also in use in the Central Highlands, but these are less revealing than Mayan texts. Sophisticated art styles were prevalent at all major Early Classic sites, whether in the Central Highlands or Maya lowlands. Wealth differentials are striking, with a wide range in quality in a wide range of cultural materials, from houses to drinking cups. This is the material evidence of a complicated division of labor with refined grades of artisanship. Foreign motifs and materials also reflect well-developed systems of commodity transfers—generally in trade or as gifts. Kinship ties remained important regulating mechanisms at family and local levels in communities of all sizes, be they villages or the barrios of towns or cities.

In some regions, one city dominated the others. Were they empires? Taking empire to represent a complex political system dominated by one nation-state and integrating distinct nation-states, some of them foreign in culture,[2] then the existing evidence does not support the presence of empires at this time, despite claims of domination (e.g., Calakmul over Tikal) or the clear presence of far-ranging influence (e.g., of Teotihuacan on Kaminaljuyú, Matacapan, and Tikal).

LATE CLASSIC PERIOD (CA. 600–900 AD)

Teotihuacan's days of influence did not extend into the Late Classic, and the great city shrank in size and power. Maya centers in the southern lowlands entered their most vibrant stage, and the Maya dominate this period in any cultural narrative of Mesoamerica, in part because Mayanists are many and active researchers and also because Maya culture has beautiful and masterful monumental centers and fine arts, as well as accounts of dynastic interactions. The Maya were building impressive regal-ritual centers and maneuvering to control their hinterlands. The larger regal-ritual centers functioned as city-states, governing the smaller centers and outlying farming villages and hamlets.

Did the Maya have empires? Some centers of great size and complexity were vanquished by their neighbors and became vassals, but these political systems did not extend beyond the local region into territories controlled by non-Maya. The interdependence of southern lowland Maya states was constrained by the relative

---

[2] For example, the separate states in the British Isles that compose Great Britain were not the British Empire: the British Empire (technically, it began in 1859 when Queen Victoria became Empress of India) governed states and territories in Africa, Asia, and the Americas.

homogeneity of their humid tropical environment, which failed to foster economic interdependence, which can become a strong force for close relations (or conflicts) among states in a region. Such homogeneity also contributed to the fragility of this adaptation, as demonstrated by steep population declines over a relatively short period of time: the "Maya Collapse," beginning in the late 800s. Maya and Mixe-Zoque towns in the surrounding regions, the Chiapas and Guatemala highlands and Pacific coast, and northern Yucatán were smaller and simpler, and their development would mature in the Epiclassic period.

West of the Isthmus, the decline of Teotihuacan and Monte Albán created opportunities for rivals to grow strong. All over Mesoamerica, as the early great centers faded, new ones arose, each displaying a different expression of now well-established themes of rulership, trade, and warfare. The cult of the avian serpent grew powerful, with imagery found in sites hundreds of miles apart, and its greatest pilgrimage point was at Cholula. Across the Central Highlands and down to the Gulf of Mexico, the shared reverence for this deity/culture hero traced the great trading centers of these regions: merchants revered Quetzalcoatl/Ehecatl as their patron.

The Mesoamerican culture area gained ground in the north, encompassing the Northwestern Frontier and the northern Gulf lowlands. Settlements in the northwestern frontier had appeared in the early Classic and were sustained by farming and, in the case of Alta Vista, by mining and trading mined products, treasured by Teotihuacan elites. Sites in this region show early adoption of some traits that become standard across Mesoamerica, with renewed emphasis on human sacrifice in a new range of techniques and display. From the Late Classic until 1521, civic and ceremonial precincts all over Mesoamerica would feature the prominent display and artistic portrayal of skulls and bones in colonnaded rooms lined with banquettes, or along the walls of processional causeways and ballcourts.

Maguey farming was another innovation from the borderlands with Aridamerica. Maguey had been part of the diet in the highlands since the Archaic, but in the Classic period maguey farming was developed into an integrated household program to produce food, drink, and essential artisanal goods in habitats marginal for supporting farming. Thus maguey farming as a multifaceted household enterprise opened up a whole new range of habitats for settlement and allowed population densities to rise in the Central Highlands, making some centers rich in farmer-artisan labor and products.

Tula provides a good example of this. As Tula developed in the Late Classic, so did the terraced houselots of Coyotlatelco culture maguey farmers, spread over the waterless hill slopes around the site. This pattern would be repeated all over the Postclassic Central Highlands.

Another important Late Classic development was the introduction of metallurgy, starting in western Mexico. Mesoamerican metals would never be used to make cutting tools or (ultimately) machinery, as was the case in the Old World. They were valued for their brilliance and color and were reserved for the elite. Metalworking was a whole new industry that soon gave rise to specialized artisanship and production of refined symbols of wealth and authority. Another Late

Classic innovation was the wheel, but its use was limited to ritual figurines—more practical applications were never developed.

Epiclassic and Early Postclassic Periods (ca. 750–1200 AD)

The Epiclassic period, overlapping the last centuries of the Classic period and the early centuries of the Postclassic, is a useful chronological construct to highlight the vigorous cultures of this era, especially Tula, El Tajín, and Cantona in the west; in the Maya area, the Puuc sites, Cobá, and Chichén Itzá. Of these, Tula and Chichén dominate the scholarly literature because of the obvious stylistic parallels in site layouts and decorative motifs, indicating a shared taste in monumental central Mexican architecture and themes of militarism. There and elsewhere, motifs promote the power of eagles and jaguars, and the Postclassic documentation of formal military cadres of Eagle Knights and Jaguar Knights suggests that they may have roots in the Epiclassic or before.

Were Tula and Chichén the capitals of empires? Some scholars believe so. The cities certainly dominated their hinterlands, and they probably ruled over confederations of local states. Political organizations of this type would have built upon local alliances and previous examples of superstate administration and would set the stage for empire formation in the Late Postclassic. Tula and Chichén were both sliding toward ruin by the late twelfth century, but rising centers eagerly claimed to be their cultural heirs.

Middle Postclassic Period (ca. 1200–1400)

The rest of the Postclassic period—Middle and Late—tracks a booming Mesoamerica. The borders, north and south, experienced some losses to Aridamerica and the Intermediate Area, but elsewhere small states were found throughout the Postclassic and in all regions. Northern Yucatán lost its great capital, Chichén, and modest Mayapán failed to capture Chichén's prestige. By the 1500s northern Yucatán held a mosaic of over a dozen independent towns with allied hinterlands. The same was true in the Guatemala and Chiapas highlands and along the coast, extending north past the Isthmus of Tehuantepec and up to the mouth of the Balsas. Some of these local settlement systems were large and complicated enough to have urban and state-level characteristics.

In the highlands, Mixtec kingdoms ruled territories all over the Mixteca regions and also alongside Zapotec towns and territories in the Oaxaca Valley. Regional patterns of independent city-states were repeated across Mexico, from West Mexico to the Gulf of Mexico, and the development of city-state confederations in the fourteenth century is clearly demonstrated in several regions. Documents describing town politics in the Basin of Mexico and surrounding regions during this period (and written out much later) show that, centuries before the Aztecs took power (beginning ca. 1430), towns tried to bully their neighbors into tributary submission, and their dynastic histories record these squabbles, especially the successful ones.

LATE POSTCLASSIC PERIOD
(CA. 1400–1521 AD)

By about 1400, city-state confederations in the Basin of Mexico extended their territories into border zones with Tula and Toluca and northern Morelos. This supraregional approach was a step toward empire building as political confederations began to breach the nearest regional boundaries, creating a more international organization. Ethnic boundaries were vague in the borderlands, so the new overlords avoided the challenge of administering a population foreign in speech and habits.

City-state confederations can fall apart as some reclaim independence or fall prey to a more vigorous dynasty's ambitions. By the early 1430s, the Basin of Mexico's various independent towns and town confederations were drawn together into an alliance controlled by three of the basin's most powerful dynasties. Their earliest extra-basin conquests were south to Morelos and on to eastern Guerrero and the Balsas drainage. The lure of the tropical south may have been spurred by the need for chocolate and cotton, but most importantly, another set of towns some distance to the west (about 150 miles) was also expanding its scope toward the basin. The empire of the Aztecs was more extensive, in 1519, than that of the Tarascans, but after the Tarascans beat back the Aztecs to within about 50 miles of Tenochtitlan in the 1470s, they and the Aztecs secured a mutual north-to-south boundary with fortified sites on both sides, and the Tarascans ceased expansion of their domains along this frontier.

The dynamics of effective empire building are complicated, and when such programs create widespread ill-feeling on the part of the tributaries, the capital cannot expect voluntary support when another empire builder attempts a takeover. In effect, in 1521 the Aztec Empire created the Spanish empire, as it became the first truly foreign, complex multistate society to be brought under the control of the rather new Iberian confederation we know as Spain. That the colonial authorities left the Aztec power structure in place for many years after the conquest is a testimony to its organizational logic—and its usefulness to Spanish imperial authorities who had less practical experience in ruling an empire than did their new vassals.

REFERENCES

Clark, John E. 2010. Formative Period. In *Archaeology of Ancient Mexico and Central America: An Encyclopedia*, edited by Susan T. Evans and David L. Webster, pp. 278–283. Garland, New York.

Evans, Susan Toby. 2013. *Ancient Mexico and Central America: Archaeology and Culture History*. 3rd edition. Thames and Hudson, London.

Evans, Susan Toby, and David L. Webster, eds. 2010. *Archaeology of Ancient Mexico and Central America: An Encyclopedia*. Routledge, New York.

Hester, Thomas R. 2010. Paleoindian Period. In *Archaeology of Ancient Mexico and Central America*, edited by Susan T. Evans and David L. Webster, pp. 577–581. Garland, New York.

Kirchhoff, Paul. 1981 [1943]. Mesoamerica: Its Geographic Limits, Ethnic Composition and Cultural Characteristics. In *Ancient Mesoamerica*, edited by John Graham, pp. 1–10. (Reprinted from *Acta Americana* 1:92–107.) Peek Publications, Palo Alto, California.

López Austin, Alfredo, and Leonardo López Luján. 2005. *Mexico's Indigenous Past*. University of Oklahoma Press, Norman.

MacNeish, Richard S. 2010. Archaic Period. In *Archaeology of Ancient Mexico and Central America*, edited by Susan T. Evans and David L. Webster, pp. 30–33. Garland, New York.

Santley, Robert S. 2010. Classic Period. In *Archaeology of Ancient Mexico and Central America*, edited by Susan T. Evans and David L. Webster, pp. 147–152. Garland, New York.

Vivó Escoto, Jorge A. 1964. Weather and Climate of Mexico and Central America. In *Handbook of Middle American Indians*. Volume 1, edited by Robert C. West, pp. 187–215. University of Texas Press, Austin.

Webster, David L. and Susan Toby Evans. 2013. Mesoamerican Civilization. In *The Human Past*, edited by Chris Scarre (3rd ed., pp. 594–639). Thames and Hudson, New York and London.

Willey, Gordon R. 1966. *An Introduction to American Archaeology*, Volume 1: North and Middle America. Prentice-Hall, Englewood Cliffs, New Jersey.

PART II

HUNTER-GATHERERS
AND FIRST FARMERS

CHAPTER 9

....

ICE AGE HUNTER-GATHERERS AND THE COLONIZATION OF MESOAMERICA

....

GUILLERMO ACOSTA OCHOA

OVER the past century, diverse theories regarding the peopling of the New World have been presented. These models have examined northern Asia (Fladmark 1979; Dixon 1999), the southern Pacific (Rivet 1964), and even the Iberian Peninsula (Bradley and Stanford 2004) as the point of origin for the first Americans.

Data currently available indicate that the land bridge known as Beringia linked Asia with the Americas when the sea level dropped during the Pleistocene. To date, this appears to have been the most viable route for the first inhabitants of the New World, who may have followed game that migrated to the new continent. However, there is an ongoing debate regarding whether this migration occurred over land or along the coast and how early the process began.

One group of investigators argues that the initial peopling occurred at the end of the last glaciation (the Wisconsin Glacial Episode) and argues that it was not possible for migration to occur until the large glacial blocks that covered North America (the Laurentide and Cordilleran) melted between 11,000 and 12,000 BP. (All dates are in uncalibrated radiocarbon years (BP) before 1950 AD.) Known as *Clovis first*, this model posits that the first people were Clovis hunters who used fluted (Clovis) points and entered through the hypothetical "ice-free corridor," a narrow strip of exposed land between the glaciers that permitted passage through part of present-day Alberta in Canada (Fiedel 1996: 72).

The Clovis first model assumes an accelerated "migration wave" composed of groups hunting Pleistocene game. These groups would have rapidly populated the southern part of the continent and would have been responsible for the extinction of megafauna (Martin 1967). Unfortunately, there are some problems with this model. Paleoecological studies have indicated that the supposed corridor either was not open until very late in the Pleistocene, when the continent was already populated, or that it was uninhabitable for humans and other mammals (Jackson and Duk-Rodkin 1997: 6). The model also does not take into consideration the marked differences between the localized ecosystems of North and South America, and it does not explain the presence of widely accepted pre-Clovis sites like Monte Verde, Chile (Dillehay 2000).

Another argument regarding the peopling of the New World via Beringia, which would resolve the problems presented by the "ice-free corridor," is that the initial colonization occurred through coastal routes from the Pacific Northwest (Fladmark 1979). This model allows for the possibility that the first Americans gradually colonized coastal ice-free areas along the coast of Beringia and the Pacific Northwest via boats. The model is supported by studies that indicate that the coast of Beringia could have included ecosystems richer in resources than inland areas, suggesting a habitable migratory corridor along the continental landmass (Josenhans et al. 1997).

This second model also has its difficulties. The scarcity of sites dated prior to 11,500 BP and also the impossibility of evaluating evidence for early coastal sites lost to the rise in sea level at the end of the Pleistocene make it difficult to evaluate this proposal (Fiedel 2006). However, the coastal route model appears to be the most parsimonious theory for explaining the technological diversity observed toward the end of the Pleistocene, in both Middle America and the rest of the New World (Figure 9.1).

THE PROBLEM OF THE OLDEST SITES AND ARTIFACTS

Researchers have argued for human occupation of Mexico and Central America by 20,000 years ago, at sites including El Cedral, San Luis Potosí (Lorenzo and Mirambell 1986b); Tlapacoya, in the Basin of Mexico (Lorenzo and Mirambell 1986a); and El Bosque, Nicaragua (Page 1978). Unfortunately, these sites do not appear to meet the strict criteria necessary to consider them valid (Dixon 1999: 108) because the artifacts are either of dubious human manufacture or their dating is questionable, as discussed below.

Tlapacoya is located along the edge of the now-extinct Lake Chalco in the southeast portion of the Basin of Mexico. A total of eighteen areas were excavated

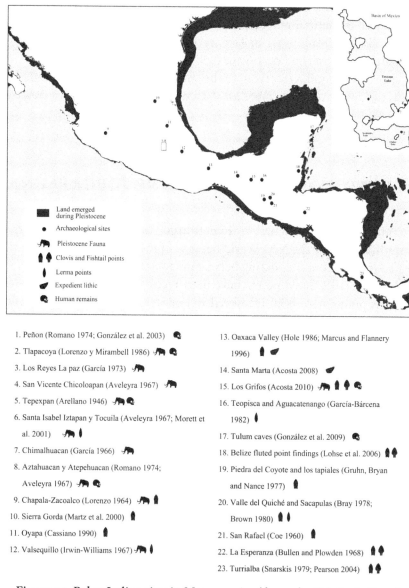

1. Peñon (Romano 1974; González et al. 2003)

2. Tlapacoya (Lorenzo y Mirambell 1986)

3. Los Reyes La paz (García 1973)

4. San Vicente Chicoloapan (Aveleyra 1967)

5. Tepexpan (Arellano 1946)

6. Santa Isabel Iztapan y Tocuila (Aveleyra 1967; Morett et al. 2001)

7. Chimalhuacan (García 1966)

8. Aztahuacan y Atepehuacan (Romano 1974; Aveleyra 1967)

9. Chapala-Zacoalco (Lorenzo 1964)

10. Sierra Gorda (Martz et al. 2000)

11. Oyapa (Cassiano 1990)

12. Valsequillo (Irwin-Williams 1967)

13. Oaxaca Valley (Hole 1986; Marcus and Flannery 1996)

14. Santa Marta (Acosta 2008)

15. Los Grifos (Acosta 2010)

16. Teopisca and Aguacatenango (García-Bárcena 1982)

17. Tulum caves (González et al. 2009)

18. Belize fluted point findings (Lohse et al. 2006)

19. Piedra del Coyote and los tapiales (Gruhn, Bryan and Nance 1977)

20. Valle del Quiché and Sacapulas (Bray 1978; Brown 1980)

21. San Rafael (Coe 1960)

22. La Esperanza (Bullen and Plowden 1968)

23. Turrialba (Snarskis 1979; Pearson 2004)

Figure 9.1 Paleo-Indian sites in Mesoamerica (drawn by Kristin Sullivan).

between 1965 and 1973 by the now-defunct Department of Prehistory of the National Anthropology and History Institute of Mexico (INAH, Instituto Nacional de Antropología e Historia). Two trenches were excavated to explore the oldest site, Tlapacoya I. The site is located on a Pleistocene beach composed of a bed of volcanic boulders and cobbles associated with a possible fire pit dating to 21,700±500 BP and two piles of Pleistocene animal bones, as well as another fire pit dated to 24,000±1000 BP and associated with possible flakes made of volcanic rock and an obsidian blade (Mirambell 1978; Lorenzo and Mirambell 1986a). However, other researchers have questioned whether the stone artifacts were made by humans, and some have argued that the concentrations of extinct fauna bones could have been produced by natural processes. Investigators have also pointed out that the prismatic obsidian blade was, in fact, recovered during the screening process rather than directly in situ (Waters 1985). Similar difficulties have been identified for the sites of Valsequillo reservoir, to the south of Puebla, where Cynthia Irwin-Williams (1967) recovered a scraper associated with a shell dated to ca. 20,000 BP.

Fluted-Point Hunters and Megafauna

As mentioned previously, many researchers argue that fluted-point hunters were the first inhabitants of the New World because of the abundance of Clovis points in North America from sites dating between 11,200 and 10,800 BP.

In Mexico, most fluted points have been recovered from northwest Mexico. Most Clovis points have been recovered in Sonora, all from the surface (Robles 1974; Montané 1988 : 96; Gaines et al. 2009).

To the south, fluted points have been recovered from the Sierra Gorda of Querétaro (Martz et al. 2000); Chapala, Jalisco (Lorenzo 1964); Metztitlán, Hidalgo (Casiano and Vázquez 1990); Oaxaca (Marcus and Flannery 2001); and Chiapas (Santamaría and García-Bárcena 1989; Acosta 2010). In Central America, fluted points have been identified in the Guatemala highlands (Coe 1960; Brown 1980), Belize (Kelly 1982: 93, Lohse et al. 2006), Honduras (Bullen and Plowden 1968), Costa Rica (Snarskis 1979; Pearson 2004), and Panama (Ranere and Cooke 1991).

The fluted points recovered from southern Mexico and Central America stand out because of their morphology, which is not "typically" Clovis. Rather, they have slightly concave lateral edges and are smaller in size (Snarskis 1979; García-Bárcena 1980). Thus, they are more similar to late Paleo-Indian fluted points from North America. They occasionally occur with "fishtail" points, as was the case at Los Grifos, Chiapas, and Belize (Lohse et al. 2006), and they generally are fluted (Cooke 1998). Points that Ranere and Cooke (1991) refer to as *waisted Clovis* appear to be a variant that falls somewhere between traditional Clovis points and fishtail points. As a result, some investigators (i.e., Santamaría and García-Bárcena 1989: 101) have argued that Central America was the point of contact between the two technologies originating in North (Clovis points) and South America (fishtail points).

The lithic toolkits associated with fluted points at sites like Los Tapiales, Los Grifos, and the Honduran highlands indicate that the subsistence system was highly dependent upon hunting, with specialized tools for defleshing game and preparing skin, like "slug-like" scrapers (*limace*), gravers, burins, and scrapers with lateral spurs. At Los Grifos, Chiapas (Acosta 2010), the faunal remains associated with the Clovis occupation are derived from medium-sized game like white-tail deer (*Odocoileus* sp.), peccary (*Tayassu* sp.), and Pleistocene horse (*Equus* sp.).

Some researchers argue that Clovis hunters were the first inhabitants of Central America (Morrow and Morrow 1999). However, associated dates are rare and relatively late compared with those associated with fluted points from the United States ("typical" Clovis points) and South America (fishtail points). In contrast, fluted points have not been recovered from the earliest sites in the region, including Santa Marta, Chiapas (Acosta 2008, 2010), and Alvina de Parita, Panama (Crusoe and Felton 1974). Moreover, the earliest dates from Los Tapiales, Guatemala (10,710±170 BP), are not clearly associated with Clovis materials, and the site also includes several dates from the Early Holocene (Gruhn et al. 1977).

In particular, dates from Los Grifos (9540±150 to 8800±100 BP) place the appearance of fluted points in Middle America very late in the Pleistocene and largely during the early Holocene (Santamaría 1981; Acosta 2010).

On the other hand, the association of Pleistocene fauna and lithic artifacts is particularly abundant in the Basin of Mexico. Unfortunately, the majority of these examples do not include diagnostic materials that could be used to associate them with a particular Pleistocene technology. The majority of the lithics associated with megafauna have been identified in contexts near lakeshores, indicating that the stalking, occasional hunting, and possibly scavenging were activities carried out by the occupants of the Basin between 11,000–9,000 BP.

Some of these sites, including Tepexpan (Arellano 1946), Acozac, Chimalhuacán, and Los Reyes La Paz (García 1966, 1973), have not been dated, as is also the case with the sites with retouched flakes associated with mammoth bones. Among the few sites that have been dated is Atepehuacan (9,670±400 BP), where remains from meat carving have been recovered in association with megafauna (Aveleyra 1967: 46). Another site with a possible modified bone industry is Tocuila, in the northern part of the Basin of Mexico. Here, flakes made of mammoth bone have been dated to 11,100±80 BP (Morett et al. 1998).

LERMA AND LEAF-SHAPED POINT (WILLOW-LEAF POINT) HUNTERS

Richard MacNeish (1958: 62) noted in his excavations in Tamaulipas that the deepest excavation levels included leaf-shaped points (*willow-leaf points*) associated with remains that suggest a mixed diet of small game, and there were points he identified as "Lerma points," dating the site to the end of the Pleistocene. However, the earliest radiocarbon date falls in the Early Holocene (9270±500 BP).

Among other sites in both northern and southern Mexico, Lerma points have been recovered from levels dating as early as the Pleistocene. Such points have been dated to 10,640±210 BP in La Calsada, Nuevo Leon, to the north (Nance 1992). The other site with dated Lerma points is Guilá Naquitz, Oaxaca, where Frank Hole

(1986: 116) identified an "unfinished Lerma" point below a level that was radiocarbon dated to 10,700±350 BP.

Interestingly, Santa Izabel Iztapan in the Basin of Mexico, one of the few sites with projectile points associated with Pleistocene fauna, includes a Lerma point (Aveleyra and Maldonado-Koerdell 1953). There, the remains of two *Mammuthus imperator* associated with three points (one Lerma, one Plainview, and one Angostura) were excavated in two distinct areas, along with other artifacts related to game processing (Aveleyra 1956). The stratum where the items were recovered was dated to 9,250±250 BP (Aveleyra 1967). Lerma points have also been recovered at Valsequillo, in the absence of clearly associated dates (Irwin-Williams 1967).

Lerma points have been reported on the surface in Chiapas and Guatemala, on the terraces of the Aguacatenango Lake, Chiapas (García-Bárcena 1982), and the Guatemala highlands (Brown 1980), but without associated dates.

BROAD-SPECTRUM GATHERERS AND EXPEDIENT TECHNOLOGY

Recently, it has been proposed that groups of hunters using expedient technology and nondiagnostic points composed one of several cultures in the Americas at the end of the Pleistocene. This is in contrast to arguments that such technology belonged to the Archaeolithic or "flake-and-core" culture prior to 13,000 BP (Lorenzo 1968). Such groups persisted in several regions of the New World until the beginning of the Holocene.

These groups, identified as having an "edge-trimmed tool tradition" or "flake industry" in South America (Dillehay 1999: 210), employed a broad-spectrum subsistence industry including nonspecialized prey and gathering freshwater snail inland and shellfish along the coast, using a poorly defined lithic technology composed principally of marginal retouch artifacts (Bate 1983). Until recently, these groups were not considered a Pleistocene culture of Middle America, although they are clearly present from the end of the Pleistocene in Brazil, Ecuador, and Colombia (Dillehay et al. 1992).

Coastal sites dating to the Late Pleistocene and Early Holocene with similar characteristics have been reported on the coast of northwestern Mexico, with occupations dating from 11,000 to 9,000 BP (Erlandson et al. 2008). The technology recovered from these sites tends to be flaked artifacts, including some bifaces, and a subsistence system focused on marine resources.

Unfortunately, in Mesoamerica long-term projects aimed at evaluating coastal settlements have not yet been carried out. Moreover, the available dates correspond to Archaic sites from the Middle and Late Holocene in Chiapas (Voorhies 2004).

However, the Santa Marta rockshelter in Chiapas is an inland Pleistocene site with expedient technology, a broad-spectrum subsistence pattern, and uncalibrated dates of 10,460±50 and 9800±50 BP (Acosta 2008: 132). Analysis of use wear and microresidue on the lithics (spokeshavers, scrapers, and marginal retouch flakes) and the chemical analysis of occupation surfaces indicate a marked emphasis on processing tropical vegetables and wood (Acosta 2010: 4).

In particular, the botanical remains from Santa Marta suggest that groups with considerable knowledge of the tropical resources in the area, including *Zea* (teosinte) and cacao (*Theobroma sp.*) pollen in Pleistocene levels (Layer XVII, dated between 10,460±50 and 10,050±90 BP), as well as ground stone tools in levels dating to 9,800±50 BP. This pattern of broad-spectrum gathering, associated with a growing dependence on plants, is not atypical of sites in southern Mexico and Central America. At Guilá Naquitz, Oaxaca, one of the principal sites for the study of early agriculture, ground stone tools were recovered in association with a primarily flake-based industry dating to 10,700±350 BP (Flannery 1986). These groups that relied on expedient technology had a considerable understanding of neotropical plants and animals. Thus, we would expect several generations of experimentation and the development of a cultural system adapted to this changing environment.

HUMAN REMAINS

Although rare, the osteological remains associated with preceramic occupation in Mexico offer the best direct evidence for human occupation in Mesoamerica at the end of the Pleistocene. Since the discovery of the Tepexpan "Man" by Helmut de Terra in the middle of the twentieth century (de Terra 1957), the number of human remains dating to the Pleistocene have increased as a result of fortuitous discoveries by systematic investigations, principally in central Mexico.

Among the sites at which human remains have been recovered as a result of these occasional finds are Tlapacoya I, Aztahuacán, and El Peñón. Tlapacoya I, with AMS (Accelerator Mass Spectrometry) dates of 10,200±65 BP (González et al. 2003: 385), was located accidentally in 1968 during highway construction (Lorenzo and Mirambell 1986a). At Aztahuacán, the excavation of a domestic well resulted in the recovery of three highly mineralized skeletons (Romano 1955) associated with an obsidian blade and charcoal dated to 9,640±400 BP (Romano 1974). A similar discovery occurred with the El Peñón Woman, recovered near the Mexico City airport, who was AMS dated to 10,755±75 BP (González et al. 2003: 381).

As a result of more formal projects like Tlapacoya XVIII, a Pleistocene beach along the banks of Lake Texcoco, lithics radiocarbon dated to 9,920±220 BP were recovered in association with a human skull (Lorenzo and Mirambell 1986a).

In southeastern Mexico, the only osteological remains dating to this period are a molar from Los Grifos associated with a stratum dated to ca. 9,500 BP (Pompa and Serrano 2001). However, in 2000, an underwater archaeological project identified human skeletal remains inside three submerged caves near Tulum (González et al. 2006). These skeletons, apparently deposited in the caves along with charcoal from fire pits, indicate human occupation of the caverns prior to the rise in sea level toward the end of the Pleistocene (ibid.: 78). The associated dates range from 8,050±130 BP for the Las Palmas cave skeleton to 11,670±60 BP for the Naharon skeleton, making the latter one of the few pre-Clovis remains in the New World (González et al. 2008).

TOWARD A MODEL FOR THE PEOPLING
OF MIDDLE AMERICA

The radiocarbon dates indicate an accelerated rate of colonization in the center of Mesoamerica at the end of the Pleistocene. The regular appearance of human remains during the *Younger Dryas* stadial (ca. 10,500–9,800 BP), a cold, dry period, could indicate accelerated demographic growth and not necessarily an initial period of colonization.

This idea is supported by the diversity of technological industries present in the New World during this period (Dixon 1999; Dillehay 1999). The period prior to 10,800 BP is represented by few sites and human remains, indicating a stage of slow demographic growth or of human groups confined to the coastal regions that were initially colonized and that are now underwater. The discovery of coastal pre-Clovis sites like Monte Verde in Chile, or of human remains with dates prior to the appearance of fluted points in submerged caves in Yucatán, suggests that the coastal areas were settled prior to 12,000 BP. However, further research is still required to confirm these possibilities.

We also have yet to identify the first people. If we accept that the groups using expedient or "flake-and-core" technology were part of these pioneering groups as proposed by authors like Krieger (1964) and Alan Bryan (1999), it is difficult to accept that this type of technology is nearly 40,000 years old, as argued for El Cedral (Lorenzo and Mirambell 1986b). On the other hand, we have yet to determine the origin of the Lerma points and their relationship to Jobo points from South America that have been radiocarbon dated to 12,000 (Dillehay 1999; Bryan et al. 1978).

What is certain is that fluted-point technology in Mesoamerica can be dated to the start of the Holocene, between 10,000 and 9,000 BP, when the region was already populated. This applies both to southeastern Mexico (Acosta 2010) and to the rest of Central America (Cooke 1998). Anthony Ranere (2006: 85) has suggested that fluted-point hunters may have moved from Central to South America when Clovis points were replaced by fishtail points.

Finally, we should clarify that the data that we have for groups of hunter-gatherers at the end of the Pleistocene and the beginning of the Holocene are very rare, particularly if we compare them with any other Mesoamerican period. Thus, the history of the early peopling of Middle America has yet to be written.

REFERENCES

Acosta, Guillermo. 2008. *La cueva de Santa Marta y los cazadores-recolectores del Pleistoceno final—Holoceno temprano en las regiones tropicales de México*, PhD thesis, Universidad Nacional Autónoma de México. Mexico, D.F.

Acosta, Guillermo. 2010. Late-Pleistocene/Early-Holocene Tropical Foragers of Chiapas, Mexico: Recent Studies. *Current Research in the Pleistocene* 27:3–5.

Arellano, Alberto. 1946. El elefante fósil de Tepexpan y el hombre primitivo. *Revista Mexicana de Estudios Antropológicos* 8:89–94.

Aveleyra, Luis. 1956. The Second Mammoth and Associated Artifacts at Santa Isabel Iztapan, México. *American Antiquity* 22(1):12–28.

Aveleyra, Luis. 1967. *Los cazadores primitivos de Mesoamérica*. Instituto de Investigaciones Históricas-UNAM, Mexico.

Aveleyra, Luis, and Manuel Maldonado-Koerdell. 1953. Association of Artifacts with Mammoth in the Valley of Mexico. *American Antiquity* 18(4):332–340.

Bate, Luis F. 1983. *Comunidades primitivas de cazadores recolectores en Sudamérica*. Historia General de Sudamérica, Vol. 2, Ediciones de la Presidencia de la república, Caracas.

Bradley, Bruce, and Dennis Stanford. 2004. The North Atlantic Ice-Edge Corridor: A Possible Paleolithic Route to the New World. *World Archaeology* 36:459–478.

Brown, Kenneth. 1980. A Brief Report on Paleoindian Archaic Occupation in the Quiche Basin, Guatemala. *American Antiquity* 45(2):313–324.

Bryan, Alan. 1999. El poblamiento originario. In *Historia General de America Latina*, Vol. 1, edited by Teresa Rojas and John Murra, pp. 41–68. UNESCO, New York.

Bryan, Alan, Roberto Casamiquela, Juan Cruxent, Ruth Gruhn, and Claudio Ochsenius. 1978. An El Jobo Mastodon Kill at Taima-Taima, Venezuela. *Science* 200:1275–1277.

Bullen, Robert, and William Plowden. 1968. Preceramic Archaic in the Highlands of Honduras. *American Antiquity* 28(2):382–385.

Casiano, Gianfranco, and Alberto Vázquez. 1990. Oyapa: Evidencias de poblamiento temprano. *Arqueología* 4:25–40.

Coe, Michael. 1960. A Fluted Point from Highland Guatemala. *American Antiquity* 25:412–413.

Crusoe, Daniel, and James Felton. 1974. La Alvina de Parita: A Paleoindian Camp in Panamá. *Florida Anthropologist* 27:145–148.

Cooke, Richard G. 1998. Human Settlement of Central America and Northernmost South America (14,000–8,000 BP). *Quaternary International* 49/50:177–190.

de Terra, Helmuth. 1957. *Man and Mammoth in Mexico*. Hutchinson, London.

Dillehay, Thomas. 1999. The Late Pleistocene Cultures of South America. *Evolutionary Anthropology* 7:206–217.

Dillehay, Thomas. 2000. *The Settlement of the Americas*. Basic Books, New York.

Dillehay, Thomas, Gustavo Politis, Gerardo Ardila, and Maria Beltrao. 1992. Earliest Hunters and Gatherers of South America. *Journal of World Prehistory* 6(2):145–204.

Dixon, E. James. 1999. *Bones, Boats and Bison. Archaeology and the First Colonization of Western North America*. University of New Mexico Press, Albuquerque.

Erlandson, Jon, Madonna Moss, and Matthew Des Lauriers. 2008. Life on the Edge: Early Maritime Cultures of the Pacific Coast of North America. *Quaternary Science Reviews* 27:2232–2245.

Fiedel, Stuart. 1996. *Prehistoria de América*. Editorial Crítica, Barcelona.

Fiedel, Stuart. 2006. Points in Time: Establishing a Precise Hemispheric Chronology for Paleoindian Migrations. In *Paleoindian Archaeology. A Hemispheric Perspective*, edited by Cristóbal Gnecco and Juliet Morrow, pp. 21–43. University Press of Florida, Gainesville.

Fladmark, Knut. 1979. Routes: Alternative Migration Corridors for Early Man in North America. *American Antiquity* 44:55–69.

Flannery, Kent. 1986. *Guilá Naquitz, Archaic Foraging and Early Agriculture in Oaxaca, México*. Academic Press, Orlando.

Gaines, Edmund, Guadalupe Sánchez, and Vance Holliday. 2009. Paleoindian Archaeology of Norhern and Central Sonora. *Kiva* 74(3):309–335.

García, Ángel. 1966. Excavación de un sitio pleistocénico en Chimalhuacán, Edo. de México, *Boletín INAH* 25:22–27.

García, Ángel. 1973. Dos artefactos de hueso en asociación con restos pleistocénicos en Los Reyes La Paz, México, *Anales 1972–1973*:237–250.

García-Bárcena, Joaquín. 1980. *Una punta acanalada de la Cueva de Los Grifos, Ocozocoautla, Chis*. Cuadernos de Trabajo 17, Instituto Nacional de Antropología e Historia, Mexico.

García-Bárcena, Joaquín. 1982. *El precerámico de Aguacatenango, Chiapas, México*. Colección Científica num. 11, Instituto Nacional de Antropología e Historia, Mexico.

González, Arturo, Alejandro Terrazas, Martha Benavente, and Wolfgang Stinnesbeck. 2006. Poblamiento temprano en la Península de Yucatán: Evidencias localizadas en cuevas sumergidas de Quintana Roo, México. In *2° Simposio Internacional Hombre Temprano en América*, edited by José Jiménez, Oscar Polaco, Gloria Martínez, and Rocío Hernandez, pp. 73–92, INAH, Mexico.

González, Arturo, Carmen Rojas, Alejandro Terrazas, Martha Benavente, Wolfgang Stinnesbeck, Jerónimo Aviles, Magdalena de los Ríos, and Eugenio Acevez. 2008. The Arrival of Humans on the Yucatan Peninsula: Evidence from Submerged Caves in the State of Quintana Roo, Mexico. *Current Research in the Pleistocene* 25:1–24.

González, Silvia, José Jiménez, Robert Hedges, David Huddart, James Ohman, Alan Turner, and José Antonio Pompa. 2003. Earliest Humans in the Americas: New Evidence from México. *Journal of Human Evolution* 44:379–387.

Gruhn, Ruth, Alain Bryan, and Roger Nance. 1977. "Los Tapiales: A Paleo-indian Campsite in the Guatemala Highlands." *Proceedings of the American Philosophical Society* 121:235–273.

Hole, Frank. 1986. Chipped-Stone Tools. In *Guilá Naquitz, Archaic Foraging and Early Agriculture in Oaxaca, México*, edited by Kent Flannery, pp. 97–140. Academic Press, Orlando.

Irwin-Williams, Cynthia. 1967. Association of Early Man with Horse, Camel and Mastodon at Hueyatlalco, Valsequillo (Puebla, México). In *Pleistocene Extinctions*, edited by Paul Martin, pp. 337–347. Yale University Press, New Haven.

Jackson, Lionel, and Alejandra Duk-Rodkin. 1996. Quaternary Geology of the Ice-
    free Corridor: Glacial Controls on the Peopling of the New World. In *Prehistoric
    Mongoloid Dispersals*, edited by Takeru Akazawa and Emoke Szathmáry, pp.
    214–227. Oxford University Press, New York.

Josenhans, Heiner, Daryl Fedje, Reinhard Pienitz, and John Southon. 1997. Early Humans
    and Rapidly Changing Holocene Sea Levels in the Queen Charlotte Islands-Hecate
    Strait, British Columbia, Canada. *Science* 277:71–74.

Kelly, Charles. 1982. Preceramic Projectile-point Typology in Belize. *Ancient
    Mesoamerica* 4:205–227.

Krieger, Alex D. 1964. Early Man in the New World. In *Prehistoric Man in the New World*,
    edited by John Jennings and Edward Norbeck, pp. 23–81. University of Chicago
    Press, Chicago.

Lohse, Jon, Jaime Awe, Cameron Griffith, Robert Rosenswig, and Fred Valdez. 2006.
    Preceramic Occupations in Belize: Updating the Paleoindian and Archaic Record.
    Latin American Antiquity 17(2):209–226.

Lorenzo, José Luis. 1964. Dos puntas acanaladas de la región de Chapala, México. *Boletín
    del INAH* 18:1–6.

Lorenzo, José Luis. 1968. *La etapa lítica en México*. Departamento de Prehistoria, Mexico.

Lorenzo, Jose Luis, and Lorena Mirambell, eds. 1986a. *Tlapacoya: 35.000 años de historia
    del Lago de Chalco*. INAH, colección Científica, Mexico.

Lorenzo, Jose Luis, and Lorena Mirambell, eds. 1986b. Preliminary Report on
    Archaeological and Paleoenvironmental Studies in the Area of El Cedral (San
    Luis Potosí), México, 1977–1980. In *New Evidence for the Pleistocene Peopling of
    the Americas*, edited by Alain Bryan, pp. 107–113. Center for the Study of the First
    Americans, University of Maine, Orono.

MacNeish, Richard. 1958. *A Preliminary Archaeological Investigation in the Sierra de
    Tamaulipas*. Transactions of the American Philosophical Society, Vol. 48, No. 6.
    Philadelphia.

Marcus, Joyce, and Kent Flannery. 2001. *La civilización Zapoteca*. Fondo de Cultura
    Económica, México.

Martin, Paul. 1967. Prehistoric Overkill. In *Pleistocene Extinctions: The Search for a
    Cause*, edited by Paul Martin and Henry Wright, pp. 75–120. Yale University Press,
    New Haven.

Martz, Hans, Miguel Pérez, Jorge Quiroz, and Alberto Herrera. 2000. Una punta
    acanalada en Jalpan de Serra, Querétaro, *Arqueología* 24:3–18.

Mirambell, Lorena. 1978. Tlapacoya: A Late Pleistocene Site in Central Mexico. In
    Early Man in America from a Circum-Pacific Perspective, edited by A. L. Bryan,
    pp. 221–230. Occasional Paper No 1, Department of Anthropology, University of
    Alberta, Ontario.

Montané, Luis. 1988. El Poblamiento temprano de Sonora. In *Orígenes del Hombre
    Americano*, edited by Alba González, pp. 83–116. Secretaría de Educación Pública,
    Mexico.

Morett, Luis, Joaquín Arroyo-Cabrales, and Oscar Polaco. 1998. Tocuila, a Remarkable
    Mammoth Site in the Basin of Mexico. *Current Research in the Pleistocene*
    15:118–120.

Morrow, Juliet, and Toby Morrow. 1999. Geographic Variation in Fluted Projectile Points:
    A Hemispheric Perspective. *American Antiquity* 64(2): 215–231.

Nance, Roger. 1992. *The Archaeology of La Calsada: A Rockshelter in the Sierra Madre
    Oriental, Mexico*. University of Texas, Austin.

Page, William. 1978. The Geology of the El Bosque Archaeological Site, Nicaragua. Early Man in America from a Circum-Pacific Perspective. In *New Evidence for the Pleistocene Peopling of the Americas*, edited by Alain Bryan, pp. 231–260. Center for the Study of the First Americans, University of Maine, Orono.

Pearson, Georges. 2004. Pan-American Paleoindian Dispersals and the Origins of Fishtail Proyectile Points as Seen through the Lithic Raw-Material Reduction Strategies and Tool-Manufacturing Techniques at the Guardiría Site, Turrialba Valley, Costa Rica. In *The Settlement of the American Continents*, edited by Michael Barton, Geoffrey Clark, David Yessner, and Georges Pearson, pp. 85–102. University of Arizona Press, Tucson.

Pompa, José Antonio, and Enrique Serrano. 2001. Los más antiguos americanos. *Arqueología Mexicana* 19 (52):36–41.

Ranere, Anthony. 2006. The Clovis Colonization of Central America. In *Paleoindian Archaeology. A Hemispheric Perspective*, edited by Juliet E. Morrow and Cristóbal Gnecco, pp. 69–85. University Press of Florida, Gainesville.

Ranere, Anthony, and Richard Cooke. 1991. Paleoindian Occupation in the Central American Tropics. In *Clovis: Origins and Adaptations*, edited by Bonnichsen Robson and Karen Turnmire, pp. 237–253. Center for the Study of the First Americans, Corvallis, Oregon.

Rivet, Paul. 1964. *Los orígenes del hombre americano*. Fondo de cultura, Mexico.

Robles, Manuel. 1974. Distribución de artefactos Clovis en Sonora. *Boletín del INAH* 2: 25–32.

Romano, Arturo. 1955. Nota preliminar sobre los restos humanos subfósiles de Santa María Aztahuacán, D.F. *Anales del INAH* 7:65–74.

Romano, Arturo. 1974. *Restos óseos humanos precerámicos de México*. Secretaría de Educación Pública-INAH, Mexico.

Santamaría, Diana. 1981. Preceramic Occupations at Los Grifos Rockshelter, Chiapas. In *Memorias X Congreso UISPP*, edited by Joaquín García-Bárcena and Francisco Sánchez, pp. 63–83. INAH, Mexico.

Santamaría, Diana, and Joaquín García-Bárcena. 1989. *Puntas de proyectil, cuchillos y otras herramientas sencillas de Los Grifos*, Instituto Nacional de Antropología e Historia, Mexico.

Snarskis, Michael. 1979. "Turrialba: A Paleoindian Quarry and Workshop Site in Eastern Costa Rica," *American Antiquity* 44:125–138.

Voorhies, Barbara. 2004. *Coastal Collectors in the Holocene: The Chantuto People of Southwest Mexico*. University Press of Florida, Gainesville.

Waters, Michael. 1985. Early Man in the New World: An Evaluation of the Radiocarbon-Dated Pre-Clovis Sites in the Americas. In *Environments and Extinctions: Man in the Late Glacial North America*, edited by Jim Mead and David Meltzer, pp. 25–143. Center for the Study of Early Man, University of Maine, Orono.

CHAPTER 10

....

ARCHAIC-PERIOD FORAGERS AND FARMERS IN MESOAMERICA

....

DOUGLAS J. KENNETT

THE Archaic period (~7000–2000 BC) in Mesoamerica is traditionally viewed as a long transitional interval between a poorly defined Paleo-Indian big-game hunting tradition and the rise and proliferation of agricultural villages. The absence of extinct Pleistocene animal remains and ceramics in archaeological sites of this age is the most salient defining characteristic of the interval, which is sometimes referred to as the preceramic. Archaeological sites dating to this long interval are rare, but rockshelter and open-air sites from various parts of Mesoamerica give us a glimpse as to how these peoples were organized socioeconomically and the strategies that were used to adapt to the region's diverse and changing environments. Two of Mesoamerica's key cultigens—maize and squash—were domesticated by Archaic-period hunter-gatherers (see Piperno and Smith, this volume). The use of cultigens is a defining characteristic of subsistence economies throughout the Archaic period (Smith 2001). However, the character of Archaic period adaptations differs regionally with some broader-scale differences evident between the semiarid highlands and the seasonally dry tropical lowlands. The archaeological and paleoecological datasets suggestive of these differences are explored below in greater detail (Figure 10.1).

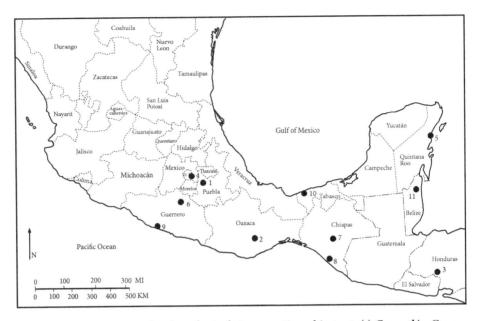

Figure 10.1 Locations of archaeological sites mentioned in text. (1) Coxcatlán Cave
and associated Tehuacán Valley sites; (2) Guilá Naquitz, Gheo-Shih, and associated
sites in the Valley of Oaxaca; (3) El Gigante Rockshelter; (4) La Playa; (5) Altún Ha
and Las Palmas; (6) Xihuatoxtla Cave; (7) Santa Marta Cave; (8) Cerro de las Conchas,
Tlacuachero, and other shell mounds; (9) Puerto Marquez; (10) San Andrés; (11)
Laguna de On, Caye Coco, Fred Smith, and San Estevan, and nearby sediment cores in
northern Belize. Drawn by Kristin Sullivan.

SEMIARID HIGHLANDS

The semiarid highlands of central Mexico have played a defining role in the characterization of the Mesoamerican Archaic due to the pioneering work of Richard
MacNeish in the Tehuacán Valley (MacNeish 1967). In the 1960s MacNeish surveyed different environmental zones in the valley, ranging from low elevation (1,500
meters above sea level [asl]) mesquite grasslands to high elevation (2,500 meters asl)
oak-pine forests, and then excavated nine sites with thirty-three Archaic-period
components. Several caves with long stratified sequences produced well-preserved plant and animal remains associated with chipped and ground-stone tool
assemblages. The deeply stratified deposits at Coxcatlán Cave produced fifteen of
these Archaic-period components and 75 percent of the stone tools (Zeitlin and
Zeitlin 2000: 75). MacNeish argued that people during the Archaic were seasonally
mobile and mapped onto the changing availability of resources in the valley. He
also defined three Archaic-period phases—El Riego (6500–5000 BC), Coxcatlán
(5000–3500 BC), and Abejas (3500–2300 BC)—and outlined a series of subsistence
and settlement changes during this 5,000-year period.

MacNeish argued that the building blocks of Archaic-period socioeconomic activity in the valley were *microbands*, each consisting of two to five individuals. Based on the variability in behavioral residues at different archaeological sites, he inferred that small groups capitalized on the availability of resources in different parts of the valley at different times of the year (e.g., high-elevation acorn harvesting in the fall). Periodically microbands would aggregate to form *macrobands* that each consisted of fifteen to twenty-five people; this occurred during the most salubrious times of the year when resources were more plentiful (e.g., the wet season). The earliest El Riego phase components were defined during the excavations of several caves: El Riego, Tecorral, Coxcatlán, and Purron. MacNeish argued that the Coxcatlán cave and terrace was a wet season macroband basecamp and the other caves were used as shorter-term microband encampments. This basic subsistence-settlement pattern is thought to have persisted throughout much of the Archaic followed by the possible establishment of more permanent settlements on river terraces during the Abejas phase (MacNeish 1967: 23).

Wild plants dominated the floral assemblage and a wide variety of species were harvested. Foxtail millet (*setaria*) was harvested and stored. Chewed maguey quids were identified, along with other edible pods and seeds from a range of trees. Animal bones included deer, cottontail rabbits, peccary, and a wide range of other species (Flannery 1967). Coxcatlán Cave also produced domesticated plants in components originally dated to between 5,000 and 3,400 BC (Coxcatlán Phase). These included small maize cobs and fragments of squash, chile, avocado, beans, and bottle gourd. However, there is now evidence for the downward movement of materials from rodent burrowing, insect activity or erosion, and later anthropogenic disturbances (Smith 2005). Maize cobs from these Middle Archaic components date to no earlier than the Late Archaic (2750 BC) with most dating even later in time (Benz and Long 2000). Direct Accelerator Mass Spectrometry (AMS) radiocarbon dates on the remains of squash also indicate vertical mixing, particularly on the western side of the cave, but the earliest dated domesticated squash remains (*C. Pepo*) fall between 5980–5880 BC (Smith 2001: 9441). This is not surprising given the early appearance of this and related domesticates (*C. argyrosperma*; Piperno et al. 2009) elsewhere in Mesoamerica (Smith 1997). At Coxcatlán Cave domesticated plants make up only 2 percent of the Archaic-period macrobotanical collection compared with 45 percent in the overlying ceramic-bearing levels dating after 2000 BC.

Questions regarding the stratigraphy and chronology of the Tehuacán Valley sites linger, given recent AMS radiocarbon-dating campaigns targeting the macrofossils of domesticated plants. However, Flannery's work in the Valley of Oaxaca largely supports the subsistence-settlement model proposed by MacNeish. He worked at four Archaic-period localities in the eastern (Tlacolula) branch of the valley: Guilá Naquitz, the Martínez rockshelter, Cueva Blanca, and Gheo-Shih. Gheo-Shih is an open-air site and the others are rockshelters and appear to have been locations visited periodically by small groups of people (*microbands*). Guilá Naquitz is the best documented and earliest occupied of these and it is positioned on the northern flanks of the valley (2,000 meters asl) near an ecotone between a thorn forest and a higher elevation oak-pine forest (Flannery 1986: 49). Six occupational horizons date to the Early Archaic (8900–6700 BC) and contain chipped and ground-stone tool assemblages comparable to the Tehuacán Valley materials. Preservation in the cave was excellent, and macrobotanical and faunal materials were plentiful. Acorns were by far the most abundant plant remains in the record, but other species recovered included maguey, mesquite (pods and seeds), prickly pear, runner beans, pine nuts, and a variety of other edible plants. Domesticated squash (*C. pepo*) remains were identified in the assemblage and were directly AMS radiocarbon dated to 8000 BC (Smith 1997). Domesticated maize was also recovered and directly dated to 4200 BC (Piperno and Flannery 2001). Animal remains in these deposits included deer, cottontail rabbits, turtles, collared peccaries, raccoons, and a variety of birds. Some evidence for acorn storage is evident, but Flannery interprets the overall assemblage as a temporary encampment used just six times by a small microband during the Early Archaic period. The earliest deposits at the El Gigante rockshelter (1,300 meters asl) in the highlands of Honduras also contain Early Archaic period deposits that are generally consistent with Flannery's observations at Guilá Naquitz (Scheffler 2008).

Flannery and his colleagues also conducted excavations at Gheo-Shih, a large (1.5 hectare) open-air site positioned on the Mitla River floodplains below the Guilá Naquitz rockshelter (Flannery and Spores 1983). Organic preservation in the site was poor, but the absence of ceramics places it in the Archaic period with diagnostic projectile points suggesting an age of 5000 to 4000 BC. Circular rock features may be the remains of houses, and artifact diversity is high, suggesting longer-term macrobands, perhaps during the wet season for mesquite harvesting or maize cultivation (Flannery and Spores 1983: 24). Ground-stone tools were concentrated in one part of the site and projectile points and associated butchering tools were found in another. There were also drilled-stone pendants recovered, suggesting the production of more specialized craft items. Two parallel lines of boulders 20 meters long and separated by 8 meters define a space that was purposely cleared. This was interpreted as some type of public space or possibly a "dance ground." The position of this larger settlement on prime farmland and the presence of *Zea* pollen are also suggestive of maize cultivation. Multiple studies now point to the domestication of maize in the lowlands of the Balsas River valley (see Piperno and Smith, this volume) and a small, carbonized maize cob (domesticated *Zea*) from Guilá Naquitz overlaps in age with the proposed age of Gheo-Shih (~4200 BC; Piperno and Flannery 2001). The more permanent lakeside settlement of La Playa in the Basin of Mexico appears to be contemporary with Gheo-Shih. It has a diverse artifact assemblage and the well-preserved plant remains recovered indicated a heavy reliance upon wild grasses (including the carbonized remains of *Zea mexicana*; Niederberger 1979). Work at Gheo-Shih and La Playa opens up questions of how important the cultivation of wild and domesticated plants was in the highlands during the Archaic period and how this compares with the development of swidden farming in the seasonally dry tropical lowlands described in the next section.

SEASONALLY DRY TROPICAL LOWLANDS

Early Archaic archaeological sites are particularly rare in the seasonally dry tropical lowlands of Mesoamerica. High sedimentation rates along the coasts and interior river basins obscure the record in this region along with thicker tropical vegetation cover. Many sites positioned immediately on the coast prior to ~5500 BC are now underwater or were obliterated by wave action as the sea level rose and stabilized between ~5500 and 4500 BC. Only the submerged cave sites of Aktun Ha and Las Palmas along the Yucatán Peninsula (Quintana Roo) provide tantalizing evidence for an early human presence along the Mesoamerican coast during the late Pleistocene and Early Holocene (~11,000–7000 BC; González González et al. 2008). These submerged caves contain human skeletons and what appear to be hearths and associated stone tools dating to the Early Archaic. The sea-level rise inundated the cave systems during the Early Holocene, but some materials were preserved in these protected environments. This study nicely demonstrates the challenges associated with identifying early coastal sites in other parts of Mesoamerica.

Some of the best Early Archaic records in the neotropical lowlands come from sites that are not directly on the coast. These include the Xihuatoxtla rockshelter, Guerrero (Piperno et al. 2009, Ranere et al. 2009) and Santa Marta Cave (Chiapas Central Depression; Acosta 2008; MacNeish and Peterson 1962). The Xihuatoxtla rockshelter is located on a tributary of the central Balsas River, the second largest river in Mexico flowing out of the central highlands to the Pacific coast. The large boulder that forms this natural shelter sits at 964 meters asl on the edge of a now seasonal stream and the flat river basin below. Excavations at the site exposed a 1-meter sequence with the earliest dated deposits between 6990 and 6610 BC. Late Archaic period materials (5590–5520 BC) also sit directly above these deposits along with two additional strata containing ceramics and dating to after ~1000 BC. A rich cultural deposit dating prior to 6990–6610 BC did not produce material for radiocarbon dating.

The deposits at Xihuatoxtla dating to between 6990 and 6610 BC contained 251 chipped-stone artifacts, including a concave scraper, five knives, and a biface fragment. Most of these were made from local materials (chalcedony, chert, quartz, etc.), but some obsidian from an unknown source was identified. A similar chipped-stone assemblage was found in the underlying stratum E, but the exact age of that deposit has not been determined. These earlier deposits also contained the base of a stemmed point, an indented base point, and a thick lanceolate point. Bifacial thinning flakes with ground platforms are considered to be characteristic of Paleo-Indian and Early Archaic period lithic technologies (Ranere et al. 2009: 5016). Unfortunately, faunal materials were not preserved in these sediments so the hunting strategies used by these early peoples cannot be determined. The presence of hand and milling stones were found in the two lower deposits and are indicative of plant processing and the dietary importance of carbohydrates.

Grinding stones also occur in the early deposits of Santa Marta Cave and in close association with *Zea* pollen (Acosta 2008). Maize starch grains were found on all of the ground-stone tools found in and below the stratum dating to 6990–6600 BC (Piperno et al. 2009). Maize and squash phytoliths were found in the surrounding sediments and support the early importance of this domesticate. These data are consistent with other molecular and biogeographical studies suggesting early domestication and use of maize in the Balsas River region (Piperno and Smith, this volume).

The earliest evidence for human occupation of the Pacific coastal plain comes from six shell-mound sites positioned on the landward edge of an extensive mangrove-estuary system that formed along much of coastal Chiapas, Mexico, as the sea level started to stabilize around 5500 BC (Voorhies et al. 2002). The shell mounds form artificial islands in these wetlands and range in size from 0.2 to 1.17 hectares and are between 3 and 11 meters above the water table at their centers (Voorhies 2004). All shell deposits at these locations were tested and extend well below the modern water table. The earliest of these sites, Cerro de las Conchas, has shell deposits dating to between 5500 and 3500 BC. It is situated on the inland margin of a large freshwater swamp, but the dominant mollusk species (*Polymesoda radiata*) indicates that a brackish-water estuary extended to this inland location at the time that the initial site was formed. The five additional shell mounds are located in the Acapetahua Estuary to the northwest of El Hueyate and date to between ~3500 and 2000 BC. Deposits of this age at all sites are dominated by the marsh clam *P. radiata*.

The shell mounds are generally characterized by alternating beds of well-preserved whole and burned fragmented marsh clam shell, which suggests periodic rather than continual use of these locations. This interpretation is bolstered by the general absence of house floors and formal hearths as well as a low diversity of tools and fauna (Voorhies 2004). Oxygen isotope seasonality studies indicate that, for much of the Archaic period, shellfish were harvested throughout the year with a greater emphasis on dry season exploitation (Kennett and Voorhies 1996). These aceramic deposits have traditionally been interpreted as locations where foragers, living elsewhere seasonally on the coastal plain, harvested shellfish and other estuarine resources (Voorhies 2004). However, an accumulation of paleoecological data from this region (Neff et al. 2006; Kennett et al. 2010) and elsewhere in the lowland neotropics of Mesoamerica, southern Central America, and South America (see Piperno and Smith, this volume) indicates that the Archaic-period populations in this area were more likely swidden farmers. This is consistent with evidence from Xihuatoxtla in the central Balsas for slash-and-burn farming and the cultivation of maize (Piperno 2007). The Late Archaic on the Pacific coast is characterized by an overall increase in the extraction of wild resources as indicated by the rapid accumulation of Late Archaic shell mounds on the Pacific coast of Chiapas (Tlacuachero, Kennett et al., 2011) and the targeting of schooling tunas and other fishes with boats and nets in coastal Guerrero (Puerto Marquez, Kennett et al. 2008).

Late Archaic-period sites are also known from the tropical Gulf Coast and Maya lowlands (Wilkerson 1975; Rosenswig 2004; Lohse 2010) and off-site paleo-ecological studies from these regions point to widespread forest clearing and the presence of charcoal and microfossils (pollen and phytoliths of domesticates) consistent with slash-and-burn farming extending back to ~5200 BC (San Andrés, Tabasco; Pope et al. 2001; Pohl et al. 2007) and 3500 BC (Belize; Jones 1994; Pohl et al. 1996), respectively. Late Archaic period deposits in northern Belize have been defined in a distinctive orange-soil horizon at Laguna de On, Caye Coco, Fred Smith, and San Estevan (Rosenswig and Masson 2001). Preservation is poor in these sites, but they contain a range of heavily patinated chert tools including a distinctive constricted unifacial tool with use wear consistent with cutting wood and digging earth (Rosenswig 2004). This all suggests a substantial commitment to swidden farming comparable to the Pacific lowlands (Kennett et al. 2010; Neff et al. 2006; Rosenswig 2006a). Ceramic technology arrived late in the Maya region and was most likely adopted *in situ* by Archaic period swidden farmers starting at around ~1000 BC (Lohse 2010).

CONCLUDING REMARKS

The Archaic-period archaeological record is incomplete and fragmentary, but work in the semiarid highlands and seasonally dry lowlands points to different adaptations and developmental trajectories. Hunting-and-gathering adaptations consistent with MacNeish's original model of seasonal aggregation and dispersal are most evident in the highlands during the earliest Archaic (8000–5000 BC). Wild plant and animal foods dominate these Early Archaic-period assemblages at Guilá Naquitz (Oaxaca; Flannery 1986) and El Gigante (Honduras; Scheffler 2008), but domesticated squash (*C. pepo*) is present early in these assemblages (Smith 1997). By the Middle Archaic there is some evidence for greater reliance upon domesticated plants. Gheo-Shih's position on prime agricultural land in the valley of Oaxaca coupled with the presence of *Zea* pollen is suggestive of a greater reliance on cultivation, at least during some parts of the year. The actual dietary importance of domesticated plants in the highlands during the earliest Archaic may be biased because most of the data come from caves that were far removed from the most suitable soils for farming. Settlements positioned on these soils are more likely to be deeply buried under alluvial sediments and difficult to detect archaeologically.

Genetic and biogeographical data indicate that maize was domesticated in the seasonally dry lowland environments of the Balsas River valley (Doebley 2004). Starch grains and phytoliths on tools from the site of Xihuatoxtla confirm the early domestication and economic importance of maize and squash during the

Early Archaic (Piperno et al. 2009). These data suggest that early populations in the lowlands relied more on these domesticates than on contemporary populations in the semiarid highlands. Paleoecological studies from the Gulf Coast and the Pacific Coast of Mexico now point to a substantial investment in slash-and-burn farming during the Middle Archaic (5500–3000 BC) that included maize. Other plants that are not as easily identifiable in microbotanical studies were probably cultivated with maize, given the large labor investments required to fell and burn tropical deciduous forest to prepare farming plots (Piperno and Pearsall 1998). Evidence for slash-and-burn farming is widespread in the lowlands during the Late Archaic period. There is also more evidence for the intensive extraction of wild resources (e.g., shellfish and schooling tunas). Future work will be required to improve the chronology of Tehuacán Valley sites, but some evidence points toward more permanent settlements on the alluvial bottomlands that would be consistent with farming activities in the highlands in the Late Archaic. This is prior to the widespread adoption of ceramics and a greater commitment to maize-based agriculture evident with the proliferation of early Formative-period villages across Mesoamerica (Clark and Cheetham 2002; Rosenswig 2006b). Although the Archaic period is traditionally viewed as an age of hunting and gathering it is becoming increasingly clear that farming economies were well established throughout much of Mesoamerica by the Late Archaic period and even earlier in the seasonally dry tropical lowlands.

REFERENCES

Acosta Ochoa, Guillermo. 2008. La cueva de Santa Marta: los cazadores-recolectores del Pleistoceno final—Holoceno temprano en las regiones tropicales de México. Two volumes. Unpublished PhD dissertation, Facultad de Filosofía y Letras, Instituto de Investigaciones Antropológicas, Universidad Nacional Autónoma de México.

Benz, Bruce F., and Austin Long. 2000. Prehistoric Maize Evolution in the Tehuacan Valley. *Current Anthropology* 41:459–465.

Clark, John E., and David Cheetham. 2002. Mesoamerica's Tribal Foundations. In *The Archaeology of Tribal Societies. International Monographs in Prehistory*, edited by William A. Parkinson, pp. 278–339. International Monographs in Prehistory, Ann Arbor, Michigan.

Doebley, John. 2004. The Genetics of Maize Evolution. *Annual Review of Genetics* 38:37–59.

Flannery, Kent V. 1967. Vertebrate Fauna and Hunting Patterns. In *The Prehistory of the Tehuacan Valley Volume 1. Environment and Subsistence,* edited by Douglas Byers, pp. 132–177. University of Texas Press, Austin.

Flannery, Kent V., ed. 1986. *Guilá Naquitz*. Academic Press, Orlando.

Flannery, Kent V., and Ronald Spores. 1983. Excavated Sites of the Oaxaca Preceramic. In *The Cloud People*, edited by Kent V. Flannery and Joyce Marcus, pp. 20–25. Academic Press, New York.

González González, Arturo H., Carmen Rojas Sandoval, Alejandro T. Mata, Martha B. Sanvicente, Wolfgang Stinnesbeck, Jeronimo Aviles O., Magdalena de los Ríos, and Eugenio Acevez. 2008. The Arrival of Humans on the Yucatan Peninsula: Evidence from Submerged Caves in the State of Quintana Roo, Mexico. *Current Research in the Pleistocene* 25:1–24.

Jones, John G. 1994. Pollen Evidence for Early Settlement and Agriculture in Northern Belize. *Palynology* 18:205–211.

Kennett, Douglas J., Brendan J. Culleton, Barbara Voorhies, and John R. Southon. 2011. Bayesian Analysis of High Precision AMS ¹⁴C Dates from a Prehistoric Mexican Shellmound. *Radiocarbon* 53:101–116.

Kennett, Douglas J., Dolores R. Piperno, John G. Jones, Hector Neff, Barbara Voorhies, Megan K. Walsh, and Brendan J. Culleton. 2010. Pre-Pottery Farmers on the Pacific Coast of Southern Mexico. *Journal of Archaeological Science* 37: 3401–3411. doi:10.1016/j.jas.2010.07.035

Kennett Douglas J., and Barbara Voorhies. 1996. Oxygen Isotopic Analysis of Archaeological Shells to Detect Seasonal Use of Wetlands on the Southern Pacific Coast of Mexico. *Journal of Archaeological Science* 23:689–704.

Kennett, Douglas J., Barbara Voorhies, Thomas Wake, and Natalia Martinez. 2008. Long-Term Effects of Human Predation on Marine Ecosystems in Guerrero, Mexico. In *Human Impacts on Marine Ecosystems in Guerrero, Mexico*, edited by T. Rick and J. Erlandson, pp. 103–136. University of California Press, Berkeley.

Lohse, Jon C. 2010. Archaic Origins of the Lowland Maya. *Latin American Antiquity* 21:312–352.

MacNeish, Richard. 1967. Introduction. In *The Prehistory of the Tehuacan Valley Volume 1. Environment and Subsistence*, edited by Douglas Byers, pp. 3–13. University of Texas Press, Austin.

MacNeish, Richard S., and Frederick A. Peterson. 1962. *The Santa Marta Rockshelter Ocozocoautla, Chiapas, Mexico*. Papers of the New World Archaeological Foundation No. 14, Brigham Young University, Provo, Utah.

Neff, Hector, Deborah M. Pearsall, John G. Jones, Bárbara Arroyo, Shawn K. Collins, and Dorothy E. Friedel. 2006. Early Maya Adaptive Patterns: Mid-late Holocene Paleoenvironmental Evidence from Pacific Guatemala. *Latin American Antiquity* 17: 287–315.

Niederberger, Christine. 1979. Early Sedentary Economy in the Basin of Mexico. *Science* 203:131–142.

Piperno, Dolores R., Jorge E. Moreno, Jose Iriarte, Irene Holst, Matthew Lachniet, John G. Jones, Anthony J. Ranere, and R. Castanzo. 2007. Late Pleistocene and Holocene Environmental History of the Iquala Valley, Central Balsas Watershed of Mexico. *Proceedings of the National Academy of Sciences USA* 104:11874–11881.

Piperno, Dolores R., and Kent V. Flannery. 2001. The Earliest Archaeological Maize (*Zea mays* L.) from Highland Mexico: New Accelerator Mass Spectrometry Dates and Their Implications. *Proceedings of the National Academy of Sciences USA* 98:2101–2103.

Piperno Dolores R., and Deborah M. Pearsall. 1998. *The Origins of Agriculture in the Lowland Neotropics*. Academic Press, San Diego.

Piperno, Dolores R., Anthony J. Ranere, Irene Holst, Jose Iriarte, and Ruth Dickau. 2009. Starch Grain and Phytolith Evidence for Early Ninth Millennium B.P. Maize from the Central Balsas River Valley, Mexico. *Proceedings of the National Academy of Sciences USA* 106:5019–5024.

Pohl, Mary E. D., Dolores R. Piperno, Kevin O. Pope, and John G. Jones. 2007.
    Microfossil Evidence for Pre-Columbian Maize Dispersals in the Neotropics from
    San Andrés, Tabasco, Mexico. *Proceedings of the National Academy of Sciences USA*
    104:6870–6875.
Pohl, Mary E. D., Kevin O. Pope, John G. Jones, John S. Jacob, Dolores R. Piperno, Susan
    D. de France, David L. Lentz, John A. Gifford, Marie E. Danforth, and J. Kathryn
    Josserand. 1996. Early Agriculture in the Maya Lowlands. *Latin American Antiquity*
    7:355–372.
Pope, Kevin O., Mary E. D. Pohl. John G. Jones, David L. Lentz, Christopher Von Nagy,
    Francisco J. Vega, and Irvy R. Quitmyer. 2001. Origin and Environmental Setting of
    Ancient Agriculture in the Lowlands of Mesoamerica. *Science* 292:1370–1373.
Ranere, Anthony J., Dolores R. Piperno, Irene Holst, Ruth Dickau, and Jose Iriarte.
    2009. The Cultural and Chronological Context of Early Holocene Maize and
    Squash Domestication in the Central Balsas River Valley, Mexico. *Proceedings of the
    National Academy of Sciences USA* 106:5014–5018.
Rosenswig, Robert M. 2004. The Late Archaic Occupation of Northern Belize: New
    Archaeological Excavation Data. *Research Reports in Belizean Archaeology*
    1:267–277.
Rosenswig, Robert M. 2006a. Northern Belize and the Soconusco: A Comparison of the
    Late Archaic to Formative Transition. *Research Reports in Belizean Archaeology*
    3:59–71.
Rosenswig, Robert M. 2006b. Sedentism and Food Production in Early Complex
    Societies of the Soconusco, Mexico. *World Archaeology* 38(2):329–354.
Rosenswig, Robert M., and Marilyn Masson. 2001. Seven New Preceramic Sites
    Documented in Northern Belize. *Mexicon XXIII*:138–140.
Scheffler, Timothy E. 2008. The El Gigante Rock Shelter, Honduras. PhD dissertation,
    Department of Anthropology, Pennsylvania State University, University Park.
Smith, Bruce D. 1997. The Initial Domestication of *Cucurbita pepo* in the Americas
    10,000 Years Ago. *Science* 276:865–996.
Smith, Bruce D. 2001. Low Level Food Production. *Journal of Archaeological Research*
    9:1–43.
Voorhies, Barbara. 2004. *Coastal Collectors in the Holocene: The Chantuto People of
    Southwest Mexico.* University of Florida, Gainesville.
Voorhies, Barbara, Douglas J. Kennett, John G. Jones, and Thomas A. Wake. 2002. A
    Middle Archaic Archaeological Site on the West Coast of Mexico. *Latin American
    Antiquity* 13:179–200.
Wilkerson, Samuel J. K. 1975. Pre-Agricultural Village Life: The Late Preceramic Period
    in Veracruz. *Contributions of the University of California Research Facility* 27:111–122.
Zeitlin, Robert N., and Judith Francis Zeitlin. 2000. The Paleoindian and Archaic
    Cultures of Mesoamerica. In *The Cambridge History of the Native Peoples of the
    Americas*, Vol. 2: Mesoamerica, Part 1, edited by R. E. W. Adams and M. J. MacLeod,
    pp. 45–121. Cambridge University Press, Cambridge.

CHAPTER 11

··

THE ORIGINS OF FOOD PRODUCTION IN MESOAMERICA

··

DOLORES R. PIPERNO AND

BRUCE D. SMITH

THE origins and dispersals of agricultural products have long been of great interest to scholars from a number of different disciplines, not least of which is archaeology. This profound transition in human lifeways from hunting and gathering to settled agriculture, occurred independently in at least seven to eight regions of the world during prehistory: namely, the eastern United States, Mesoamerica, South America, the Near East, China, New Guinea, probably mainland southeast Asia, and possibly India (see Barker 2006; Kennett and Winterhalder 2006; Zeder et al. 2006; Cohen 2009; and Price and Bar-Yosef 2011 for recent updates of the evidence). During the past ten to fifteen years, an enormous amount of new information has been published documenting the transition from foraging to food production in archaeological records worldwide. Moreover, a steady stream of paleoecological and molecular research has provided increasingly detailed information on the ecological contexts of food production origins, associated human modification of environments, ancestry of crop plants, and geography of agricultural origins (see Piperno 2006a, 2011, and in press for recent reviews of archaeological, paleoecological, and molecular data for Mesoamerica and Central and South America; see Smith 2006 for data for North America).

Mexico, along with the remainder of Mesoamerica in smaller part, formed one of the world's great centers for the independent development of agriculture. Dozens of crop plants were brought under cultivation and domesticated there in the prehistoric era. They include the most famous crop of the Americas, maize

(*Zea mays*); two species of squash (*Cucurbita pepo* and *C. argyrosperma*); the common bean and small-seeded (sieva) lima bean (*Phaseolus vulgaris* and *P. lunatus* [sieva type]); the pseudocereals *Amaranthus* and *Chenopodium*; avocados (*Persea americana*); at least one species of chile pepper (*Capsicum annuum*); and a number of important tree crops, including *Leucaena* spp. (the *guajes*) and *Spondias purpurea* (the hog plum). Two other premier plants, tomato (*Lycopersicum esculenta*) and cacao, or chocolate (*Theobroma cacao*), were native to South America but were probably domesticated in Mexico, based on current archaeological data and on the locations at which they were being cultivated when Europeans arrived. The early history of many of these plants is poorly understood and a few have not yet been found or recognized in archaeological records (Table 11.1).

Molecular research indicates that many species, including maize and *C. argyrosperma* squash, were domesticated once within a circumscribed region. Others, however, have been robustly shown by genetic and molecular data to have been domesticated two or more times either within Mesoamerica or in Mesoamerica, South America, and North America (e.g., *Chenopodium*, *Cucurbita pepo*, the common and lima bean, avocado, *Spondias purpurea*, and the turkey). A few domestications, such as in *Leucaena*, involved hybridizations between two different species that likely were facilitated by early human management in house gardens.

There is thus an increasingly rich and varied history of plant domestication and agriculture that has and will continue to provide a bounty of information for archaeologists, botanists, molecular biologists, and other scholars to explore. Table 11.1 lists the postulated geographic locales for the origins of Mesoamerican crops based on the present, combined evidence from molecular, archaeological, and botanical research. The table also provides a more complete, though still not exhaustive, list of crops known or thought to have been domesticated in Mesoamerica, along with the ages and areas of their early appearances. Mesoamerica is a region of great physical and ecological diversity; it has major mountain ranges and significant expanses of lowlands, with vegetation ranging from temperate and tropical forests of varying types to cactus/shrublands and deserts (Figure 11.1). Domestication and subsequent agricultural development occurred through a range of these ecological zones (Figure. 11.1; Table 11.1).

It is now clear that in both the highlands and tropical lowlands, plant cultivation and domestication emerged during the early Holocene period. This makes the chronology, if not the cultural and ecological contexts, of agricultural origins in both places similar to that in the Near East and China. It should be pointed out, however, that although our understanding of when and how Mesoamerican food production and agriculture emerged has become more clear recently, the evidence is still derived from relatively few lowland and highland sites, and mostly from cave and rock shelters that were sometimes occupied intermittently or ephemerally during the early and middle Holocene. Consequently, the sites probably provide incomplete information about the plants that were undergoing early cultivation and about the cultivated and domesticated crops that were available to human groups at various time periods for their subsistence economies. Moreover, even dry caves don't leave perfect records of prehistoric plant subsistence unbiased by preservation and sampling. The following sections discuss the available information in more detail.

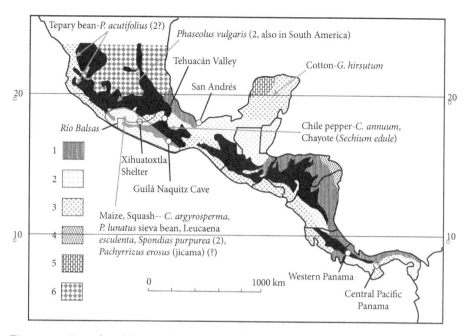

Figure 11.1 Postulated Domestication Areas for Various Crops in Mesoamerica. Open circles are archaeological and paleoecological sites in Mexico and Central America with early (10,000 BP–5000 BP) domesticated plant remains that include indigenous Mexican crops. The oval in Figure 11.1 designates an area where it appears that a number of important crops may have originated. Arrows designate approximate areas of origin. The numbers in parentheses after a taxon indicates that more than one independent domestication occurred. The possible area of origin for the sieva bean extends into the Pacific lowlands north of the oval area. See Pearsall and Piperno 1998 and Piperno 2011 and in press for more details and sources used in the figure. See also Motta-Aldana et al. in press; Matsuoka et al. 2002; Sanjur et al. 2002; Miller and Schaal 2005; Muñoz et al. 2006; Cross et al. 2006; Hughes et al. 2007; Chen et al. 2009; Kwak et al. 2009. Modern Vegetation Zone Guides for Figure 11.1. 1. Tropical evergreen forest, 2. Tropical semi-evergreen forest, 3. Tropical deciduous forest, 4. Savanna, 5. Low scrub/grass/desert. 6. Mostly cactus scrub and desert. Black areas indicate mountain zones greater than 1,500 meters above sea level. Drawn by Kristin S. Sullivan.

THE EMERGENCE OF LOWLAND FOOD PRODUCTION AND DOMESTICATION

The earliest evidence of food production in the lowlands presently comes from the Central Balsas region of southwestern Mexico, where the wild progenitors of maize and *C. argyrosperma* squash are members of the natural flora (e.g., Matsuoka et al.

Table 11.1 Cultivated and Domesticated Plants of Mesoamerica

Plant	Common Name	Date, and Place of Earliest Appearance; Probable Place of Domestication
Seed Crops and Vegetables		
Zea mays	Maize	8700 BP, Xihuatoxtla Shelter, Guerrero, Central Balsas region;[1] Central Balsas region of Guerrero/Michoacán
Cucurbita pepo	Pumpkin, zucchini	10,000 BP, Guilá Naquitz Cave, Oaxaca?;[2] wild ancestor unknown
Cucurbita argyrosperma	Silver-seeded squash	5085 BP, Romero's Cave, Tamaulipas[3] and possibly at 8700 BP at the Xihuatoxtla Shelter;[1] Central Balsas region
Phaseolus vulgaris	Common bean	2300 BP, Tehuacán Valley;[4] Lerma-Santiago Basin, Jalisco
Phaseolus lunatus	Sieva lima bean	?, NR?; humid lowlands of western Mexico
Phaseolus acutifolius	Tepary bean	2400 BP, Tehuacán Valley;[4] lowlands of Jalisco or Sinaloa
Phaseolus coccineus	Runner bean	500 BP, Tehuacán Valley;[4] cool, humid highlands of Mexico
Phaseolus dumosus	Year-long bean	?, NR; Guatemalan highlands?
Canavalia ensiformis	Swordbean	1600 BP, Oaxaca; Gulf region of Mexico?
Setaria macrostachya (D?)*	Foxtail millet	Between 6000 and 4400 BP (?), Ocampo caves, Tamaulipas; highland Mexico
Amaranthus cruentus		?, present in the Tehuacán sequence, chronology needs clarification; highland Mexico
Amaranthus hypochondriacus		?; highland Mexico
Chenopodium berlandieri		?, NR; southern Mexican highlands
Physalis philadelphica (C)	Ground cherry, green tomato	?, not certain if remains from Tehuacán are this species?
Sechium edule	*Chayote*	?, NR; humid forests of eastern highland Mexico
Tree Crops		
Crescentia cujete (C)	Tree gourd	By 3000 BP, Tehuacán Valley;[6] widely distributed in seasonal tropical forests of Mexico but it is unclear if the Tehuacán remains represent wild or cultivated plants
Persea americana	Avocado	By 3000 BP, Tehuacán Valley;[6] probably three separate domestications in the central and eastern highland forests of Mexico and lowland Guatemala
Leucaena esculenta	*Guaje colorado*	Sometime between 6000 (?) and 3000 BP, Tehuacán Valley;[6,7] lowland seasonal forests of southwestern Mexico—probably Balsas region

Table 11.1 (continued)

Plant	Common Name	Date, and Place of Earliest Appearance; Probable Place of Domestication
Leucaena leucocephala	*Guaje verde*	2300 BP, Tehuacán Valley;[6,7] lowland forests of central Veracruz?
Spondias purpurea	*Jocote*, hog plum	?, NR; seasonal tropical forests of western central Mexico and southern Mexico or Central America
Spondias mombin	*Ciruela*, hog plum	7000 BP (?), Tehuacán Valley;[6] lowland seasonal forest
Root Crops		
Pachyrrhizus erosus	*Jícama*	?, NR; lowland seasonal forest
Succulents		
Agave spp.	Maguey, century plant	?, it is uncertain if agave remains at Tehuacán[6] were cultivated
Opuntia ficus-indica	India fig, tuna cactus	?, NR; upland tropical habitats in central Mexico
Opuntia spp.	Prickly pears	?, it is uncertain if *Opuntia* remains at Tehuacán[6] were cultivated
Condiments and Beverages		
Theobroma cacao	Chocolate	3000 BP, Puerto Escondido site, Honduras;[8] wild ancestor native to tropical forests in Amazonia
Capsicum annuum	Chile pepper	Present throughout much of the Tehuacán Valley sequence,[6] chronology needs clarification; central Mexican highlands
Industrial Plants		
Gossypium hirsutum	Cotton	Present rarely throughout much of the Tehuacán sequence,[6] chronology needs clarification; Yucatán Peninsula

Notes: NR = Not presently recognized in the archaeological record; the plants were widely grown at European arrival. C = the plant was cultivated but does not exhibit phenotypic change distinguishing it from close wild relatives. *A seed-size increase interpreted as having resulted from artificial selection was described for these remains by Callen (1967), the original investigator.

Some crop plants that were once thought to be possibly native to Mesoamerica are now indicated to have their origins in South America. They include the domesticated squashes *C. moschata* and *C. ficifolia*, the root crop manioc (*Manihot esculenta*), and the food color/spice *Bixa orellana* (*achiote*). A large number of tree crops were cultivated or domesticated in Mesoamerica at European contact and the origins of some of them are still not determined.

A major root crop, sweet potato, has been thought by some scholars to be South American in origin. A Mexican origin was recently proposed again on the basis of the amount of genetic diversity in modern land races (Zhang et al. 2000). The presumed wild ancestor is *Ipomoea trifida*, a poorly demarcated taxon naturally distributed from Mexico through northern South America (Piperno and Pearsall 1998). Because modern centers of diversity can sometimes have little bearing on where something was originally domesticated, and the oldest evidence by far for the plant derives from western South America (Pearsall 2008), we suspect that the plant will be found to have a northern South American origin. Molecular work that focuses on a rigorous comparison of wild and domesticated sweet potatoes will help to resolve the issue.

Sources: (1) Ranere et al. 2009; Piperno et al. 2009; (2) Smith 1997a; (3) Smith 1997b; (4) Kaplan and Lynch 1999; (5) Callen 1967; Austin 2006; (6) C. E. Smith 1967; (7) Zárate 2000; (8) Henderson et al. 2007.

2002; Sanjur et al. 2002). At the Xihuatoxtla Shelter, in Guerrero state (Figure 11.1), starch grain and phytolith evidence indicates that maize and a squash (possibly but not conclusively *C. argyrosperma*) were domesticated by 8700 BP (all dates in this chapter are in calibrated ^{14}C years [BP]). Associated paleoecological evidence from lakes near the Xihuatoxtla Shelter within this region makes it clear that the ecological context of this development was a lowland, seasonally dry tropical forest (Piperno et al. 2007). Although agricultural developments in the Mesoamerican tropical lowlands were previously little studied and understood, especially when compared with research undertaken in the highlands, neither the age nor ecological setting of these domestication events is surprising for a number of reasons. For one thing, an abundance of microfossil data (phytoliths and starch grains) from archaeological sites indicates that maize had dispersed into tropical regions south of Mexico by 7600 BP (Piperno 2006b, 2011). Furthermore, the closest wild relatives of maize and *C. argyrosperma* are native to the Central Balsas region, and seasonal tropical forests elsewhere in the Americas were domestication hearths for a number of major seed, root, and tree crops (see Piperno and Pearsall 1998; Piperno 2006b, 2011 for discussions).

It is likely that the earliest kinds of food production now becoming evident in lowland tropical Mexico were versions of "dooryard horticulture." In other words, people created small plots adjacent or very close to their residential locations for planting a variety of species, including trees. After food production and domestication emerged and took hold, an important development related to the intensification of tropical agriculture was slash-and-burn cultivation, when more labor-intensive methods were used to clear larger tracts of land farther from residential areas. Paleoecological evidence from lakes in the Central Balsas region and from the Caribbean coast of Mexico indicate that by 7300 BP maize and likely other crops that aren't visible in the pollen and phytolith records were grown by using slash-and-burn methods of clearing forests and preparing fields (Pope et al. 2001; Pohl et al. 2007; Piperno et al. 2007). These systems of farming must have contributed significant amounts of food to diets. Evidence for the onset of slash-and-burn cultivation at 6500 BP is now available from the Soconusco region of Mexico (Kennett et al. 2010). It appears that the growth and intensification of food production along with the spread of domesticated species like maize and squashes out of their areas of origin were underway in a number of different regions of lowland Mexico during the eighth and seventh millennia BP.

Some information is available on the settlement patterns of these early farmers. In the Central Balsas region, pedestrian foot surveys combined with excavations of a number of archaeological sites indicate that early Archaic groups often lived in caves and rock shelters, engaged in a number of different subsistence pursuits that included hunting and plant collecting, and probably shifted their locations seasonally (Ranere et al. 2009). They utilized the productive resources of lakes, modifying the lakeside vegetation—including through fire—as early as the beginning of the Holocene (Piperno et al. 2007).

With particular regard to the early evolution of maize, macrofossils of this plant did not survive at the Xihuatoxtla site, located in the humid tropical Balsas region. Thus, the earliest macrofossil maize evidence is still represented by the 6,200-year-old cobs recovered from Guilá Naquitz Cave (Piperno and Flannery 2001), and we do not know what earlier maize looked like in ear morphology and other phenotypic characteristics. Some clues are provided by the phytolith evidence from Xihuatoxtla, which indicates that the genetic locus controlling the development of the hard cupulate fruitcase in teosinte, called *teosinte glume architecture 1*, was undergoing human manipulation at 8700 BP (Piperno et al. 2009).

OTHER INDIGENOUS LOWLAND CROPS

In our efforts to determine when and where maize and squash were domesticated and became important foods, we sometimes lose sight of the fact that a large number of other crops, including trees that are still commonly grown and eaten today, were domesticated in Mexico (Table 11.1 and Figure 11.1). It is likely that our existing archaeological records are poor representations of the mixtures of different plants that were being cultivated several thousand years ago. *Leucaena* and *Spondias,* for example, are two lowland tree genera that contributed important domesticated species. *Leucaena esculenta* is one of the most commonly cultivated food plants in house gardens in the Central Balsas region today, and *Leucaena leucocephala* is also frequently grown (Piperno, personal observation). Little is known about the early histories of these and other Mesoamerican plants; some are presently documented only in highland macrofossil records from the Tehuacán Valley outside their areas of origin and native ecological contexts (Table 11.1; Figure 11.1). As has been done with other crops present in the Tehuacán sequence (Smith 2005), direct dating efforts should be undertaken of these and other lowland tropical-forest plant specimens present at Tehuacán to firmly establish the chronology of their introductions there.

It will probably be difficult to empirically document some of these plants of lowland origins in their original homelands through microfossil records due to constraints related to production or taxonomic specificity of phytoliths and starch grains in their edible parts. Also many plants may not have been processed with stone tools before they were eaten, making their recovery from these artifacts unlikely. It is sometimes assumed that tree cropping followed the domestication of annual plants, but evidence from South America does not support this view (e.g., Piperno and Dillehay 2008; Piperno 2011). Clearly, more information is needed from archaeobotany on tree and other nonmaize, nonsquash cultivars (e.g., the yam bean and sieva bean) in order to better understand where, when, and how tropical-forest agriculture developed in Mesoamerica.

THE HIGHLANDS

The archaeological record for the transition to food production in the higher eleva-tion regions of Mesoamerica differs from that of the lowlands in several notable respects. In contrast to the evidence of early domesticates from lowland sites, which, due to preservation issues, consists primarily of "microbotanical" mate-rial (phytoliths and starch grains) and has been recovered from relatively recent excavations, the remains of early domesticates in highland sites are primarily "macrobotanical" (seeds, corn cobs, etc.) and come in large part from only five dry caves excavated between 1954 and 1966. Richard MacNeish excavated Romero's and Valenzuela's Caves near Ocampo in Tamaulipas (see Smith 1997b for refer-ences), as well as the Coxcatlán and San Marcos caves in Tehuacán, Puebla (Byers 1967), and Kent Flannery excavated Guilá Naquitz Cave in Oaxaca (Flannery 1986) (Figure 11.1).

The bottle gourd (*Lagenaria siceraria*) is one of the earliest domesticated plants to appear in the archaeological record of highland Mesoamerica as well as in other regions of the New World. Based on small-sample, accelerator mass spectrometry (AMS) radiocarbon dates obtained from morphologically diagnostic rind frag-ments recovered at Guilá Naquitz, domesticated *L. siceraria* was being cultivated in Mesoamerica by about 10,000 years ago (Erickson et al. 2005). Rather than being a food plant, the bottle gourd was a "container crop" grown for its lightweight hard-shelled fruits. Thought to have been initially domesticated from a wild pro-genitor somewhere in East Asia, *L. siceraria* was carried to the Americas either by the North Pacific Current, or more likely, by human colonists as they crossed Beringia at the end of the Pleistocene with another utilitarian domesticate, the dog (*Canis familiaris*) (Erickson et al. 2005).

Cucurbita pepo squash (the "jack-o-lantern" pumpkin) had also been domesti-cated in Mesoamerica by 10,000 BP, based on directly dated seeds and stems recov-ered from Guilá Naquitz (Smith 1997a, 2000). As yet, no extant populations of the wild progenitor of the Mexican lineage of domesticated *C. pepo* have been found.

Both bottle gourd and *C. pepo* squash subsequently show up in Coxcatlán Cave in Tehuacán by 7900–7200 BP, and they first appear farther north in the Ocampo caves by 5500 BP (Smith 1997b), reflecting a slow south to north diffusion for these early major crops. In contrast to maize and *C. pepo* squash, the common bean (*Phaseolus vulgaris*), a major protein source in Mesoamerica, is thought to have been initially domesticated not in southern Mexico but in Jalisco, western Mexico, based on genetic comparisons of modern domesticated beans with wild populations (Figure 11.1) (Chacón et al. 2004; Kwak et al. 2009). A western Mexico source for the domesticated common bean would account for its subsequent dif-fusion to the east and northeast and its roughly contemporaneous appearance in Oaxaca (2100 BP), Tehuacán (2300 BP), and Tamaulipas (1300 BP), more than 6,000 years after maize and squash first appear in the archaeological record (Kaplan and Lynch 1999; Smith 2001).

Interestingly, a second protein source—the South Mexican turkey (*Meleagris gallopavo gallopavo*)—also initially appears as a domesticate in the archaeological record of Mesoamerica at the same time as the common bean, perhaps reflecting a significant release from human reliance on wild animal protein sources linked to the initial establishment of larger, more sedentary farming villages (e.g., Flannery 2009). Genetic research encompassing both ancient and modern turkeys indicates that all modern domesticated stock derived from now-extinct South Mexican wild populations of *M.g. gallopavo* (Speller et al. 2010) and the earliest morphologically distinct domesticated turkeys are reported from ca. 2000 BP contexts in the Tehuacán Valley (Flannery 1967).

It is also possible, of course, that as additional early settlements are excavated across Mesoamerica, and as more specimens are directly dated, the temporal context of the initial domestication of beans and turkeys, along with many other domesticates, will change. Of the numerous species domesticated in Mesoamerica (Table 11.1), the initial appearance of only a small number can be confidently established. The domesticated chili peppers (*Capsicum annuum*) and amaranth (*Amaranthus cruentus*) from Coxcatlán Cave occupations thought to date to ca. 6000 BP (C. E. Smith 1967; Sauer 1967), for example, should be directly dated, given the potential for vertical displacement downward into earlier layers of plant material in cave deposits (Smith 2005). At the same time, domesticated chenopod (*Chenopodium berlandieri* ssp. *nuttallia*), which currently is only documented in very late Pre-Columbian contexts in Mesoamerica (McClung de Tapia and Rios-Fuentes 2006), may well be determined to have a deeper time depth. Similarly, while macrobotanical remains of *C. argyrosperma* have been directly dated to 4500 BP in the Ocampo caves, phytolith evidence indicates that this squash may well have been domesticated in the Balsas River Valley as early as 8700 BP.

DISCUSSION

The transition from a hunting-and-gathering way of life to agricultural economies in Mesoamerica was a long, complex, and regionally variable developmental process that spanned six millennia, with the first domesticated plants dating to about 10,000 BP, and the earliest "agricultural" villages not appearing until about 4000 BP (e.g., Pool 2006; Rosenswig 2006; Flannery 2009). As summarized in the brief overview provided here, the general spatial and temporal framework for this process is beginning to come into clearer focus in terms of where and when major crop plants were initially brought under domestication, along with their subsequent patterns of diffusion. Within this initial framework, future excavation across Mesoamerica and analysis are necessary in order to establish detailed, regional-scale developmental records that will both chart the early history of additional domesticates and will also document the long-term cultural developmental trajectories from initial domestication to agricultural economies.

Central Pacific Panama, northern Peru, and eastern North America, for example, have recently provided insights regarding the size and organization of small, sometimes sedentary communities cultivating multiple crops long before the emergence of sedentary village life and full-fledged agricultural economies. In the Zaña Valley in Peru, occupations between 10,000 BP and 7600 BP are small, circular houses located 200 to 400 meters apart with stone foundations and stone-lined storage pits. *C. moschata* squash has been found ca. 10,000 BP, followed by cultivated peanuts, *Phaseolus*, and *Inga feuillea* (a tree) at 9000 BP (Dillehay et al. 2007; Piperno and Dillehay 2008). In central Panama, small, probably season-ally occupied, settlements were growing a variety of plants, including *C. moschata* squash and root crops, ca. 9000 BP. At 7600 BP the food production system intensi-fied into slash-and-burn cultivation, and settlement sizes and organization appear to be characteristic of modern slash-and-burn farmers living in small hamlets and hamlet clusters (Ranere and Cooke 2003; Piperno and Pearsall 1998; Piperno 2011). In both Peru and Panama, nucleated and sedentary villages with all of their trap-pings did not emerge until after 5000–4000 BP. There are some obvious parallels here with the Mexican sequences described above. The Riverton site in Illinois—a small settlement of perhaps ten houses dating to 3800 BP (less than 1,200 years later than the earliest evidence for domesticates in eastern North America)—has yielded evidence of five domesticates (bottle gourd, sunflower, *C. pepo* squash, *Iva annua*, and two different varieties of *Chenopodium*) (Smith and Yarnell 2009). Similar settlements that document different points along the developmental trajectories of both lowland and highland regions of Mesoamerica remain to be discovered and excavated.

References

Austin, Daniel F. 2006. Fox-tail Millets (*Setaria*: Poaceae)—Abandoned Food in Two Hemispheres. *Economic Botany* 60:143–158.

Barker, Graeme. 2006. *The Agricultural Revolution in Prehistory: Why Did Foragers Become Farmers?* Oxford University Press, New York.

Byers, Douglas S., ed. 1967. *The Prehistory of the Tehuacán Valley Volume 1. Environment and Subsistence.* University of Texas Press, Austin.

Callen, Eric O. 1967. The First New World Cereal. *American Antiquity* 32:535–538.

Chacón, María I., Barbara Pickersgill, and Daniel G. Debouck. 2004. Domestication patterns in common bean (*Phaseolus vulgaris* L.) and the origin of the Mesoamerican and Andean cultivated races. *Theoretical and Applied Genetics* 110:432–444.

Chen, Hoafeng, Peter L. Morell, Vanessa E. T. M. Ashworth, Marlene de la Cruz, and Michael T. Clegg. 2009. Tracing the Geographic Origins of Major Avocado Cultivars. *Journal of Heredity* 100:56–65.

Cohen, Mark, ed. 2009. *Rethinking the Origins of Agriculture*. Special issue of *Current Anthropology*, volume 50.

Cross, Hugh, Rafael Lira Saade, and Timothy J. Motley. 2006. Origin and Diversification of Chayote. In *Darwin's Harvest*, edited by T. J. Motley, N. Zerega, and H. Cross, pp. 171–194. Columbia University Press, New York.

Dillehay, Tom D., Jack Rossen, Thomas C. Andres, and David E. Williams. 2007. Preceramic Adoption of Peanut, Squash, and Cotton in Northern Peru. *Science* 316:1890–1893.

Erickson, David L., Bruce D. Smith, Andrew C. Clarke, Daniel H. Sandweiss, and Noreen Tuross. 2005. An Asian Origin for a 10,000 Year-Old Domesticated Plant in the Americas. *Proceedings of the National Academy of Sciences USA* 102:18315–18320.

Flannery, Kent V. 1967. The Vertebrate Fauna and Hunting Patterns. In *The Prehistory of the Tehuacán Valley Volume 1. Environment and Subsistence,* edited by Douglas S. Byers, pp. 132–177. University of Texas Press, Austin.

Flannery, Kent V., ed. 1986. *Guilá Naquitz*. Academic Press, Orlando.

Flannery, Kent V, ed. 2009. *The Early Mesoamerican Village*. Left Coast Press, San Francisco.

Henderson, John S., Rosemary A. Joyce, Gretchen R. Hall, Jeffrey W. Hurst, and Patrick E. McGovern. 2007. Chemical and Archaeological Evidence for the Earliest Cacao Beverages. *Proceedings of the National Academy of Sciences USA* 104:18937–18940.

Hughes, Colin E., Rajanikanth Govindarajulu, Ashley Robertson, Denis L. Filer, Stephen A. Harris, and C. Donovan Bailey. 2007. Serendipitous Backyard Hybridization and the Origin of Crops. *Proceedings of the National Academy of Sciences USA* 104:14389–14394.

Kaplan, Lawrence, and Thomas F. Lynch. 1999. *Phaseolus* (Fabaceae) in Archaeology: AMS Radiocarbon Dates and Their Significance for Pre-Columbian Agriculture. *Economic Botany* 53:262–272.

Kennett, Douglas, Dolores R. Piperno, John G. Jones, Hector Neff, Barbara Voorhies, Megan Walsh, and Brendan J. Culleton. 2010. Pre-Pottery Farmers on the Pacific Coast of Southwest Mexico. *Journal of Archaeological Sciences* 37:3401–3411.

Kennett, Douglas J., and Bruce Winterhalder, eds. 2006. *Behavioral Ecology and the Transition to Agriculture*. University of California Press, Berkeley.

Kwak, Myounghai, James A. Kami, and Paul Gepts. 2009. The Putative Mesoamerican Domestication Center of *Phaseolus vulgaris* Is Located in the Lerma-Santiago Basin of Mexico. *Crop Science* 49:554–563.

Matsuoka, Yoshishiro, Yves Vigouroux, Major M. Goodman, Jesus Sanchez, Edward Buckler, and John Doebley. 2002. A Single Domestication for Maize Shown by Multilocus Microsatellite Genotyping. *Proceedings of the National Academy of Sciences USA* 99:6080–6084.

McClung de Tapia, Emily, and Joram Rios-Fuentes. 2006. Huauhtzontli (*Chenopodium berlandieri* ssp. *nuttalliae*) in Prehispanic Mesoamerica. Paper presented at the 71st annual meeting of the Society for American Archaeology. April 26, 2006. San Juan, Puerto Rico.

Miller, Allison, and Barbara Schaal. 2005. Domestication of Mesoamerican Cultivated Fruit Tree, *Spondias purpurea*. *Proceedings of the National Academy of Sciences USA* 102:12801–12806.

Motta-Aldana, Jenny R., Martha L. Serrano-Serrano, Jorge Hernández-Torres, Genis Castillo-Villamizar, Daniel G. Debouck, and Maria I. Chacón. In press. Domestication Patterns in Wild Lima Beans (*Phaseolus lunatus* L.) from the

Americas. In *Harlan II: Biodiversity in Agriculture: Domestication, Evolution, and Sustainability*, edited by A. Damania and P. Gepts.

Muñoz, L. Carmenza, Myriam C. Duque, Daniel G. Debouck, and Matthew W. Blair. 2006. Taxonomy of Tepary Bean and Wild Relatives as Determined by Amplified Fragment Length Polymorphism (AFLP) Markers. *Crop Science*: 46:1744–1754.

Pearsall, Deborah M. 2008. Plant Domestication and the Shift to Agriculture in the Andes. In *Handbook of South American Archaeology*, edited by H. Silverman and W. Isbell, pp. 105–130. Springer, New York.

Piperno, Dolores R. 2006a. A Behavioral Ecological Approach to the Origins of Plant Cultivation and Domestication in the Seasonal Tropical Forests of the New World. In *Foraging Theory and the Transition to Agriculture*, edited by D. Kennett and B. Winterhalder, pp. 137–166. University of California Press, Berkeley.

Piperno, Dolores R. 2006b. Quaternary Environmental History and Agricultural Impact on Vegetation in Central America. *Annals of the Missouri Botanical Garden* 93:274–296.

Piperno, Dolores R. 2011. The Origins of Plant Cultivation and Domestication in the New World Tropics: Patterns, Process, and New Developments. In *The Origins of Agriculture: New Data, New Ideas*, edited by T. Douglas Price and O. Bar-Yosef. *Current Anthropology* 52:S453–S470.

Piperno, Dolores R. In press. New Archaeobotanical Information on Early Cultivation and Plant Domestication Involving Microplant Remains. In *Harlan II: Biodiversity in Agriculture: Domestication, Evolution, and Sustainability*, edited by A. Damania and P. Gepts.

Piperno, Dolores R., and Tom D. Dillehay. 2008. Starch Grains on Human Teeth Reveal Early Broad Crop Diet in Northern Peru. *Proceedings of the National Academy of Sciences USA* 105:19622–19627.

Piperno, Dolores R., and Kent V. Flannery. 2001. The Earliest Archaeological Maize (*Zea mays* L.) from Highland Mexico: New Accelerator Mass Spectrometry Dates and Their Implications. *Proceedings of the National Academy of Sciences USA* 98:2101–2103.

Piperno, Dolores R., Javier E. Moreno, José Iriarte, Irene Holst, Matthew Lachniet, John G. Jones, Anthony J. Ranere, and R. Castanzo. 2007. Late Pleistocene and Holocene Environmental History of the Iguala Valley, Central Balsas Watershed of Mexico. *Proceedings of the National Academy of Sciences USA* 104:11874–11881.

Piperno, Dolores R., and Deborah M. Pearsall. 1998. *The Origins of Agriculture in the Lowland Neotropics*. Academic Press, San Diego.

Piperno, Dolores R., Anthony J. Ranere, Irene Holst, José Iriarte, and Ruth Dickau. 2009. Starch Grain and Phytolith Evidence for Early Ninth Millennium BP Maize from the Central Balsas River Valley, Mexico. *Proceedings of the National Academy of Sciences USA* 106:5019–5024.

Price, T. Douglas and Bar-Yosef, O., Eds. 2011. The Origins of Agriculture: New Data, New Ideas. *Current Anthropology*. The Wenner-Gren Symposium Series, Supplement 4, Volume 52.

Pohl, Mary E. D., Dolores R. Piperno, Kevin O. Pope, and John G. Jones. 2007. Microfossil Evidence for Pre-Columbian Maize Dispersals in the Neotropics from San Andrés, Tabasco, Mexico. *Proceedings of the National Academy of Sciences USA* 104:6870–6875.

Pool, Christopher A. 2006. Current Research on the Gulf Coast of Mexico. *Journal of Archaeological Research* 14:189–241.

Pope, Kevin O., Mary E. D. Pohl, John G. Jones, David L. Lentz, Christopher Von Nagy, Francisco J. Vega, and Irvy R. Quitmyer. 2001. Origin and Environmental Setting of Ancient Agriculture in the Lowlands of Mesoamerica. *Science* 292:1370–1373.

Ranere, Anthony J., and Richard G. Cooke. 2003. Late Glacial and Early Holocene Occupation of Central American Tropical forests. In *Under the Canopy: The Archaeology of Tropical Rain Forests*, edited by J. Mercader, pp. 219–248. Rutgers University Press, Piscataway, NJ.

Ranere, Anthony J., Dolores R. Piperno, Irene Holst, Ruth Dickau, and José Iriarte. 2009. Preceramic Human Occupation of the Central Balsas Valley, Mexico: Cultural Context of Early Domesticated Maize and Squash. *Proceedings of the National Academy of Sciences USA* 106:5014–5018.

Rosenswig, Robert M. 2006. Sedentism and Food Production in Early Complex Societies of Soconusco, Mexico. *World Archaeology* 38:330–355.

Sanjur, Oris, Dolores R. Piperno, Thomas C. Andres, and Linda Wessell-Beaver. 2002. Phylogenetic Relationships Among Domesticated and Wild Species of *Cucurbita* (Cucurbitaceae) Inferred from a Mitochondrial Gene: Implications for Crop Plant Evolution and Areas of Origin. *Proceedings of the National Academy of Sciences USA* 99:535–540.

Sauer, Jonathan D. 1967. The Grain Amaranths and Their Relatives: A Revised Taxonomic and Geographic Survey. *Annals of the Missouri Botanical Garden* 54:103–137.

Smith, Bruce D. 1997a. The Initial Domestication of *Cucurbita pepo* in the Americas 10,000 Years Ago. *Science* 276:865–996.

Smith, Bruce D. 1997b. Reconsidering the Ocampo Caves and the Era of Incipient Cultivation. *Latin American Archaeology* 7:1–43.

Smith, Bruce D. 2000. Guilá Naquitz Revisited: Agricultural Origins in Oaxaca, Mexico. In *Cultural Evolution: Contemporary Viewpoints*, edited by Gary Feinman and Linda Manzanilla, pp. 15–60. Kluwer Academic/Plenum, New York.

Smith, Bruce D. 2001. Documenting Plant Domestication: The Consilience of Biological and Archaeological Approaches. *Proceedings of the National Academy of Sciences USA* 98:1324–1326.

Smith, Bruce D. 2005. Reassessing Coxcatlan Cave and the Early History of Domesticated Plants in Mesoamerica. *Proceedings of the National Academy of Sciences USA* 102:9438–9445.

Smith, Bruce D. 2006. Eastern North America as an Independent Center of Plant Domestication. *Proceedings of the National Academy of Sciences USA* 103:12223–12228.

Smith, Bruce D., and Richard A. Yarnell. 2009. Initial Formation of an Indigenous Crop Complex in Eastern North America at 3800 BP. *Proceedings of the National Academy of Sciences USA* 106:6561–6566.

Smith, Claude E. 1967. Plant Remains. In *The Prehistory of the Tehuacán Valley, Volume 1, Environment and Subsistence*, edited by Douglas S. Byers, pp. 220–255. University of Texas Press, Austin.

Speller, Camilla F., Brian M. Kemp, Scott D. Wyatt, Cara Monroe, William D. Lipe, Ursula M. Arndt, and Dongya Yang. 2010. Ancient Mitochondrial DNA Analysis Reveals Complexity of Indigenous North American Turkey Domestication. *Proceedings of the National Academy of Sciences USA* 107:2807–2812.

Zárate, Sergio. 2000. The Archaeological Remains of *Leucaena* (Fabaceae) Revised. *Economic Botany* 54:477–499.

Zeder, Melinda, Daniel Bradley, Eve Emschwiller, and Bruce Smith, eds. 2006.
    Documenting Domestication: New Genetic and Archaeological Paradigms, University
    of California Press, Berkeley.
Zhang, Dapeng, Jim Cervantes, Zosimo Huamán, Edward Carey, and Marc Ghislain.
    2000. Assessing genetic diversity of sweet potato (*Ipomoea batatas* [L.] Lam.) Using
    Cultivars from Tropical America Using AFLP. *Genetic Resources and Crop Evolution*
    47:659–665.

PART III

VILLAGES, CITIES, STATES, AND EMPIRES

Formation of Early Complex Societies, Cities, and States

CHAPTER 12

THE FORMATION OF COMPLEX SOCIETIES IN MESOAMERICA

CHRISTOPHER A. POOL

THE story of the Formative (Preclassic) period in Mesoamerica is fundamentally one of sociopolitical origins. That is, anthropological interest in this time span revolves around the origins and early development of "complex" social institutions and the material conditions and ideological precepts that supported them. In this chapter I attempt to provide context for the regional syntheses that follow by broadly sketching issues surrounding the formation of complex societies and urban centers in early Mesoamerica, emphasizing regional variation and interregional interaction through the Middle Formative period.

COMPLEXIFICATION, URBANIZATION, AND STATE FORMATION

Much ink has been spilled in debates over whether this or that ancient society was complex—or urban—or a state (e.g., Clark 2007; Flannery 1998; Sanders and Price 1968; Spencer and Redmond 2004). Although they can be useful for organizing cross-cultural comparisons (e.g., Earle 1991), societal typologies have long been criticized for imposing arbitrary divisions on a continuum of variation, glossing over significant variation within categories, and promoting a transformational view of evolutionary change (e.g., Blanton et al. 1993:19, de Montmollin 1989: 12; Dunnell 1980; Easton 1959; Feinman and Neitzel 1984; Pauketat 2007; Smith 2003; Yoffee 1993, 2005).

Rapid organizational change surely occurred in the past, and at archaeological time scales such "flashpoints" (Carneiro 1998) may appear discontinuous. Human observers operating on the time scale of lived experience, however, are likely to see greater continuity. Thus, it may be more productive to focus on the historical processes of complexification, state formation, and urbanization than on pinpointing the thresholds, only definable in retrospect, at which any one society becomes complex, urban, or a state.

One way Mesoamericanists have tried to address the disadvantages of societal taxonomies is to characterize societies with respect to multiple dimensions of variability (or "bundled continua of variation" [de Montmollin 1989]). Blanton et al. (1993: 13–16) identify four "core features"—scale, integration, complexity, and boundedness—by which all societies may be compared. Scale here refers both to population and geographical extent; integration to the interdependence among social, political, and economic units; and boundedness to the degree to which a society restricts flows of materials, people, energy, or information with other societies. All are important and none is entirely independent of the others, but here I focus on the dimension of complexity.

Initially applied as an alternative to "civilization" (e.g., Mayer-Oakes 1963), "complex society" was soon extended to those societies commonly labeled as chiefdoms (Service 1962) and rank societies (Fried 1967). Consequently, the concept of social complexity is closely aligned in archaeological discourse with the emergence of social and political hierarchy. In the 1980s hunter-gatherer specialists began to unpack the notion of complexity, observing that it had most often been applied to sedentary agricultural societies (e.g., Price and Brown 1985), and today studies of hunter-gatherer complexity are commonplace. Such studies underscore the fact that most societies are complex in some respect, but they also point to a need for defining what is meant by complexity in any particular application of the term. For most archaeologists today, social complexity is a multidimensional phenomenon that includes functional differentiation among societal units, both horizontally through occupational specialization and vertically by rank (e.g., Blanton et al. 1993: 17), but also the integration of those units; the degree to which social groups hold and inherit differential access to prestige, wealth, and power, and the extent to which power is centralized in political hierarchies (Wenke and Osczewski 2007: 280; see also Feinman, this volume; Flannery 1972), Although they are interrelated, complexification along each of these dimensions does not proceed in lockstep, resulting in variant local trajectories and considerable organizational variability among complex societies.

THE INITIAL FORMATIVE TRANSITION

The domestication of plants and the development of sedentism were complex processes that took place over the course of several millennia beginning early in the
Archaic period (Kennett, this volume; Piperno and Smith, this volume). By the beginning of the Initial Formative period, around 2000 BC, maize, squash, and several
other food crops had been domesticated, and settled villages supported by varying
mixes of agricultural products and wild resources sprang up across Mesoamerica
over the next thousand years. The resulting ability to intensify and control access
to staples and ceremonial foods alike aided the subsequent development of social
inequalities and political hierarchies. Domesticated maize was an early and ultimately critical resource, but the intensity of its consumption varied considerably in
the first millennium of the Formative period (e.g., Blake et al. 1992; VanDerwarker
2006). Maize often may have been exploited for sugars and fermented beverages
more than as a grain (e.g., Clark and Blake 1994; Smalley and Blake 2002; Webster
2011). Paleoecological evidence likewise suggests that land clearance, presumably
from cultivation, expanded over different areas at highly variable rates, beginning
in the late Archaic period and extending through the Early Formative (Neff et al.
2006b; Pope et al. 2001). In favored estuarine, riverine, and lacustrine settings there
was a heavy reliance on aquatic resources (Blake et al. 1992; Kennett, this volume;
Wing 1980).

Other hallmarks of the Formative period likewise were adopted over a long
time span. Pottery appeared on the Pacific Coasts of Chiapas and Guatemala, the
Valley of Oaxaca, and the Tehuacán Valley in the 1900–1700 BC span, on the Gulf
Coast by 1550 BC, and in parts of Central Mexico after 1600 BC, but it was not wide-
spread until after 1400 BC and not ubiquitous in Mesoamerica until after 1000 BC
(Clark and Gosser 1995; Chase and Chase, this volume; Lesure et al. 2006; Rice, this
volume).[1] Patterns of residential mobility also varied considerably in the Initial and
Early Formative periods depending on the degree of reliance on storable domes-
tic crops and reliable aquatic resources versus seasonally restricted wild resources.
Settled villages appeared in the Soconusco before 1700 BC (Clark and Pye 2000),
and in the southern and Central Highlands of Mexico between 1650 and 1400 BC
(Cyphers Guillén and Grove 1987; Flannery and Marcus 1994; Niederberger 2000).
In southern Veracruz, sedentary villages appear in the Coatzacoalcos Valley before
1450 BC (Symonds et al. 2002) but not until about 1000 BC in the Tuxtla Mountains
(Arnold 1999, 2000; VanDerwarker 2006), and sedentary villages are only sparsely
documented in the Maya lowlands between 1400 and 1000 BC (see Chase and Chase,
this volume).

---

1. All dates in this chapter are in calendar years rather than uncalibrated
radiocarbon years.

EARLY COMPLEXIFICATION AND THE
EMERGENCE OF SOCIAL INEQUALITY

From this landscape of societies with varying degrees of commitment to agriculture and sedentism, the first vertically differentiated societies began to form in the Initial Formative period, with other societies joining their ranks in the Early Formative period, after about 1400 BC. Inequalities based on gender, age, experience, skill, and physical force exist in all societies, and they likely form the basis from which institutionalized inequalities emerge. In Mesoamerica, the first convincing examples of institutionalized inequalities appear in the Mazatán region of the Soconusco during the Locona phase (1700–1550 BC) (Figure 12.1). Paso de la Amada stood at the head of a two-tiered settlement hierarchy and contained a ballcourt and large buildings arranged around a plaza (Clark 2004; Hill et al. 1998). One of the large platforms has been argued to have supported a superimposed series of elite residences; successive rebuilding on the same spot suggests rank was passed on within households (Clark and Pye 2000; Lesure and Blake 2002). Clark and Blake (1994) convincingly argued that institutionalized social inequalities arose as the unintended consequence of competition among individuals to enhance their prestige and influence, particularly through the provision of feasts, beginning in the preceding Barra phase.

Similar development of sociopolitical hierarchy is not evident in other parts of Mesoamerica until later, but an elaboration of ceremonialism beginning around

Figure 12.1 Map of Initial and Early Formative sites and regions mentioned in the text.

1700 BC is indicated in the Coatzacoalcos basin of southern Veracruz by increasingly formalized offerings as at El Manatí, (Ortiz and Rodríguez 2000). By 1450 BC settlement hierarchies had developed in the Coatzacoalcos basin around a 20-hectare village at San Lorenzo and a settlement of 60 to 80 hectares at Estero Rabón (Borstein 2001: 151; Symonds et al. 2002: 44–45, 56).

Whatever competition for prestige existed in other Initial Formative societies, it seems not to have produced the kind of inherited social inequalities seen in the Mazatán area until later. In the Valley of Oaxaca, the Tierras Largas phase witnessed the establishment of permanent villages. The largest village, at San José Mogote, contained a few buildings with lime-plastered walls and floors, set on low platforms consistently oriented to eight degrees west of north, that likely were used as public structures for ceremonies (Flannery and Marcus 1994: 123–124; Marcus and Flannery 1996: 87).

ELABORATION AND INTENSIFIED INTERACTION: OLMEC CULTURE AND THE EARLY HORIZON

During the Early Formative period (ca. 1450–1000 BC), sociopolitical hierarchies emerged and expanded in the Soconusco and the southern Gulf lowlands, the Valley of Oaxaca, the Nochixtlán Valley, the southern Valley of Mexico, and the Balsas depression of Guerrero, creating "an archipelago of complexity" (Rosenswig 2010).

The most elaborate of these Early Formative societies was centered on the Olmec site of San Lorenzo in southern Veracruz. San Lorenzo is estimated to have covered 700 hectares (Cyphers and DiCastro 2009: 23; cf. Symonds et al. 2002). The summit of the plateau contained elite residences, caches of exotic materials (including six tons of perforated ilmenite cubes imported from Chiapas), basalt workshops, long drainlines that channeled water to the plateau's sides, and over one hundred stone monuments (Cyphers 1996; Coe and Diehl 1980a). The most impressive findings were ten colossal heads (Figure 12.2), usually interpreted as portraits of San Lorenzo's rulers, and tabletop altars/thrones (Cyphers 2004; Coe and Diehl 1980a; Gillespie 1999; Grove 1973; see also Pye, this volume, Figure 60.3). San Lorenzo occupied the apex of a three- to four-tiered settlement hierarchy in which secondary centers controlled key nodes in the surrounding channels of the Coatzacoalcos River and its tributaries (Clark 2007; Cyphers 1997; Symonds et al. 2002). Secondary centers of the Early Formative period here and elsewhere in the southern Gulf lowlands (or "Olman"), have yielded smaller altar/thrones and full-round sculptures of humans and mythological beings but no colossal heads, rein-

Figure 12.2 Olmec colossal head. San Lorenzo Monument 1 (Coe and Diehl 1980a,
Figure 423). Drawing by Felipe Dávalos. Courtesy of Michael D. Coe.

forcing the role of sculpture in Olmec expressions of political authority (Cyphers 2004: 34–35).[2]

San Lorenzo was the center of the largest, most socially stratified, and hierarchically differentiated polity in Early Formative Mesoamerica, but it is unlikely that it controlled all of Olman (Clark 2007: 15; Pool 2007: 124–132). At the same time, less hierarchical polities and autonomous villages were present in other areas of the Gulf Coast (e.g., Santley and Arnold 1996), and they participated in different, though overlapping, exchange networks; consequently, Arnold (this volume) calls for efforts to "build the Gulf Olmec from the ground up," with less emphasis on monumental sculpture as the hallmark of Olmec culture and greater examination of the different contexts in which the variant patterns within Olman emerged, persisted, and disappeared.

The precise mechanisms by which emerging elites in the Gulf lowlands attracted followers and consolidated power are still unclear. The evidence is weak that control over productive lands for maize agriculture was an important factor early in the Gulf lowlands, and the relatively open, poorly circumscribed social and environmental landscapes of the Early Formative would have made coercion of local populations difficult (Arnold, this volume; Stark 2000; cf. Coe and Diehl 1980b: 151–152). Cyphers (1996) and her colleagues (Ortiz Pérez and Cyphers 1997; Symonds et al. 2002) suggest control over the riverine transportation network gave emerging elites at San Lorenzo an advantage, while Grove (1994) points to the administration of exchanges between leaders occupying different resource

2. The anomalous colossal head from Cobata, Veracruz, is probably later than the Early Formative period and is not associated with a secondary center.

zones in Olman (cf. Rathje 1972). Clark and Blake's (1994) model of competitive generosity among early community leaders would seem to apply in the intensifiable contexts of the San Lorenzo and La Venta regions, but its assessment is hampered by a scarcity of excavated pre-Olmec contexts. Any evaluation of early social complexification in Olman must also take account of the increasingly formalized ceremonialism indicated by offerings of local and exotic goods at El Manatí and La Merced. By the time San Lorenzo emerged, it appears that control over ideological and economic sources of power (including long-distance exchange) were the principal underpinnings of elite authority (Pool 2007: 132–144).

As the chapters in this part describe, several other regions of Mesoamerica also saw manifestations of increasing social complexity in the Early Formative period. Surveys document the establishment of two-tiered settlement hierarchies in the Valley of Oaxaca (Kowalewski et al. 1989; Marcus and Flannery 1996); in the Nochixtlán Valley of the Mixteca Alta (Blomster 2004); in eastern Morelos (Hirth 1987; Grove 1996), and in the southern Valley of Mexico. Community labor was expended in the construction of platforms for public structures in the Valley of Oaxaca at San José Mogote (Marcus and Flannery 1996: 108–110), in Morelos at Chalcatzingo (Grove 1996: 108), and around the end of the period at Teopantecuanitlan in the Balsas depression of Guerrero (Niederberger 1996). In the Soconusco, Paso de la Amada was succeeded by regional centers, first at Cantón Corralito, then Ojo de Agua (Clark and Hodgson 2004; Clark and Pye 2000; Cheetham 2011).

Social roles were becoming more clearly differentiated as well. Horizontal differentiation can be seen in the establishment of craft specializations, probably part-time, manifested by uniformity and skillful execution within a variety of products, as well as distributions of manufacturing debris that suggest neighborhood or village specialization, as in the production of iron-ore mirrors in one area of San José Mogote (Marcus and Flannery 1996) or the manufacture of obsidian blades at Coapexco in the Valley of Mexico (Tolstoy 1989: 96). Increasing vertical differentiation appeared in many areas but this was to varying degrees and expressed in variant ways (Beekman, this volume; Blomster 2004: 74–75; Marcus and Flannery 1996: 96–106; Rosenswig 2000; Tolstoy 1989).

Regionally distinctive ceramic and figurine traditions proliferated in the Early Formative period (Arnold, this volume; Beekman, this volume; Elson, this volume; Grove 1996; Lesure 2000, 2011b; Lesure et al. 2006; Marcus 1999). None of these cultural traditions developed in complete isolation from one another, although the degree and form of interregional interaction varied considerably. Marine shell from both coasts, jade from Guatemala, and other greenstones from Guatemala and the southern Mexican highlands were widely distributed. Shaped and polished iron-ore artifacts from Oaxaca and Chiapas were traded to the Gulf lowlands and the Soconusco. Obsidian from central Mexico and Guatemala was exchanged widely, with the relative proportions of sources in different sites and regions reflecting participation in overlapping exchange systems (e.g., Cobean et al. 1991; Nelson and Clark 1998; Pool et al. 2010).

In addition to the regional developments emphasized above, the Early Formative saw the first widespread horizon style in Mesoamerica, identified by the presence of a distinctive, conventionalized set of symbols, usually carved and/or incised on black, black-and-white, and white or white-slipped vessels (Figure 12.3). Hollow, white-slipped figurines, in the form of chubby, sexless infants, are another widespread, though less frequent, hallmark (Blomster 2002; Reilly, this volume, Figure 57.1). Elements of the Early Horizon style are absent or rare in West Mexico (Beekman, this volume; cf. Mountjoy 1998) and in much of the Maya lowlands (Chase and Chase, this

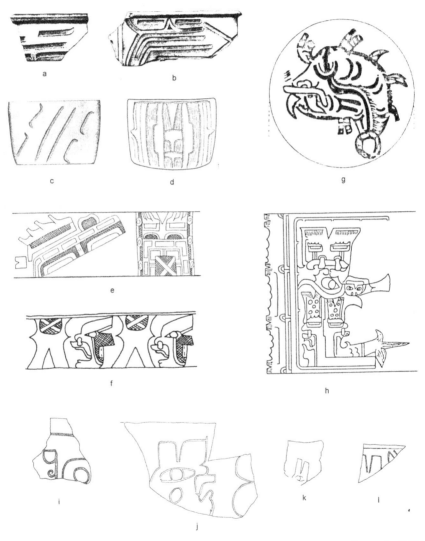

Figure 12.3 Early Horizon ceramic motifs (a-b) Olman, San Lorenzo phase; (c-d) Valley of Oaxaca, San José phase; (e-g) Basin of Mexico, Ayotla phase, (h) Basin of Mexico, Manantial phase; (i-l) Soconusco, Jocotal phase. (a-b from Coe 1981: Fig. 5-8; courtesy of Michael D. Coe) (c-d from Marcus and Flannery 199t: Fig. 86; courtesy of Joyce Marucs and Kent Flannery) (e-h redrawn from Niederberger 2000: Figs 8, 9, and 10) (i-l redrawn from Clark and Pye 2000: Fig. 32).

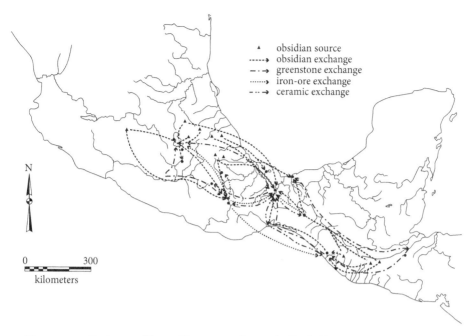

▲ obsidian source
·····→ obsidian exchange
—·→ greenstone exchange
·······→ iron-ore exchange
—··→ ceramic exchange

N

0 _____ 300
kilometers

Figure 12.4 Patterns of long-distance exchange in Early Formative Mesoamerica
(redrawn after Pool 2007: Figure 6.10).

volume; Stanton, this volume), although they are present in Early Preclassic contexts in
Copán and the Ulúa Valley of Honduras (Fash 1991; Joyce and Henderson 2001, 2010).
Elsewhere they are most prevalent in those areas and sites with evidence of greater
social differentiation, both horizontally and vertically (Flannery 1968; Grove 1993),
constituting Rosenswig's (2010) islands in his "archipelago of complexity." Different
sites and regions, however, differed in terms of the social contexts in which Early
Horizon motifs and artifacts were used (compare, e.g., Blomster 2004; Cheetham
2011; Coe and Diehl 1980a; Flannery and Marcus 1994; Joyce and Henderson 2010;
Reyes González et al. 2010; Rosenswig 2010; Tolstoy 1989; Wendt 2010).

Neutron activation analysis (NAA) has demonstrated that several areas
received pottery with Early Horizon motifs, whitewares, and figurines made at
San Lorenzo or elsewhere in the middle Coatzacoalcos Basin (Blomster et al. 2005;
Neff et al. 2006a). That study also showed that each of the areas investigated also
manufactured pottery with Early Horizon motifs, but it did not identify any examples that were traded between areas beyond the southern Gulf lowlands or from
those areas to San Lorenzo (cf. Flannery et al. 2005; Sharer et al. 2006; Stoltman
et al. 2005). Consequently, it seems likely that the export of ceramics from the
San Lorenzo polity played an important, though perhaps not exclusive, role in the
dissemination of significant elements of the Horizon style, including motifs as
well as the black-and-white ceramic technology. It also is likely that such vessels
were exchanged for the obsidian, serpentine, jade, iron-ore mirrors and cubes, and
other exotic artifacts that were imported from those regions—that is, the exchange
system was bidirectional with respect to San Lorenzo (or any other specific site),

and multidirectional in its overall character (Figure 12.4) (see Pool 2007: 217–216).[3] Moreover, the degree to which different areas in Mesoamerica modified, elaborated, and expanded the repertoire of Early Horizon symbols locally is remarkable (the degree to which Cantón Corralito replicates San Lorenzo style, form, and technology is exceptional [Cheetham 2010]).

Variant explanations for the Early Horizon phenomenon inspire strong disagreements about the character and causes of Early Formative complexification. These debates are encapsulated in the so-called Olmec Problem, which pits those who favor a single origin for Mesoamerican civilization in a Gulf Olmec "Mother Culture" against those who favor a multicentric origin in several "Sister Cultures" (e.g., Diehl and Coe 1995; Flannery and Marcus 2000; see discussion in Pool 2007: 15–17). Explanations of the Early Horizon style include imperial expansion by Gulf Coast Olmecs (Caso 1965; Bernal 1969), Gulf Olmec state hegemony [specifically for the Mazatán area] (Clark 1997, 2007), trade diaspora (Curtin 1984), and emulation and marriage alliances (e.g., Flannery 1968; Tolstoy 1989). Others downplay or question the extent of Gulf Olmec input (e.g., Flannery and Marcus 1994; Grove 1993).

The last decade has also seen calls to move beyond the polarizing Mother Culture debate (e.g., Lesure 2004; Pool 2007), and some novel explanations for the Early Horizon have been forthcoming (e.g., Blomster 2010; Rosenswig 2010). Ultimately, explanations for the development and wide distribution of the Early Horizon style will need to account for consistency in a set of standardized, abstract symbols and the media on which they were reproduced as well as elaboration in their form and their social contexts of use. The character of interactions varied from place to place, and the most productive lines of inquiry seem to be those that recognize the importance of exotic materials and products as resources for the construction of local power relations, although a coercive component to Olmec interactions with the Soconusco remains a possibility (Cheetham 2010). Recently, Blomster (2010) has suggested the Olmec style was the material expression of a religious cult spread from San Lorenzo, positing consistency in the meanings associated with core symbols while acknowledging their roles in local contestations of status and power. Rosenswig (2010) likens the exchange of symbolically charged articles by the Olmecs and their neighbors to the kula ring of the Trobriand Islanders and other nonmonetary political economies in which the possession of exotic and highly crafted objects manifested control over esoteric knowledge derived from distant times and places, and contributed to the power of emerging elites (see also Blomster 2010; Helms 1993; Stark 2000). All these models acknowledge that interregional interaction played a critical and early role in constructing social and political inequalities in Mesoamerica.

3. Much has been made of the "unidirectional" flow of Olmec-style pottery from San Lorenzo to other areas, because it tends to support the idea that other areas did not contribute to the development or elaboration of such motifs at San Lorenzo (Blomster et al. 2005). It is worth noting, however, that other materials did flow into San Lorenzo, quite possibly in direct exchange for pottery, and it is unlikely that other sites imported materials to which they had abundant local access. San José Mogote and El Mirador/Plumajillo did not import one another's iron ores; highland Guatemala sites did not import Mexican obsidian; Valley of Mexico sites did not import Guatemalan obsidian; and so on.

Regeneration, Complexification, and Urbanization in the Middle Formative Period

The material hallmarks of the Middle Formative period (1000–400 BC) include increasingly distinctive regional ceramic traditions, expanded trade in greenstone, a shift to stone as the principal medium for widely disseminated symbols, the proliferation and elaboration of public architecture, and the appearance of Olmec-style relief sculpture outside the Gulf lowlands, particularly along routes to greenstone and obsidian resource zones (Figures 12.5, 12.6). These developments suggest that elites in many societies were extending their control over ideological and material sources of power, with consequent changes in the forms of interactions among regions and communities (e.g., Grove 1993; Reilly 1995).

In the Gulf lowlands, the San Lorenzo polity collapsed, and populations fell in a swath from the Coatzacoalcos Basin through the southern foothills of the Tuxtla Mountains (Borstein 2001; Symonds et al. 2002; Killion and Urcíd 2001), while on the eastern and western margins of Olman, populations grew (Pool 2007: 151–154; Rust 2008; von Nagy 2003). Tres Zapotes emerged as a regional Olmec center (Pool and Ohnersorgen 2003), and La Venta expanded to become the most architecturally impressive of all Gulf Olmec capitals (González 1996). In the Soconusco, Ojo de Agua, which had replaced Cantón Corralito as the regional center when the former was buried under flood deposits, was itself replaced as a major center by La Blanca and then Uxujte (Love 1999). In contrast

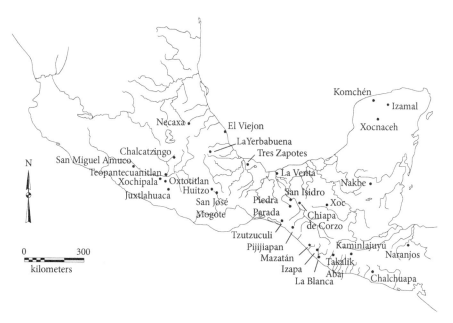

Figure 12.5 Map of Middle Formative sites and regions mentioned in the text.

Figure 12.6 Middle Formative Olmec-style relief sculptures: (a) San Miguel Amuco,
Guerrero; (b) Chalcatzingo, Morelos; (c) El Viejón, Veracruz; (d) La Venta, Tabasco;
(e) Tiltepec, Chiapas; (f) Tzutzuculi, Chiapas; (g) Padre Piedra, Chiapas; (h) Pijijiapan,
Chiapas; (i) Xoc, Chiapas; (j) La Unión, Chiapa; (k) Takalik Abaj, Guatemala; and
(l) Chalchuapa, El Salvador. After Clark and Pye 2000: Figure 228.

to such cycling, San José Mogote, Chalcatzingo, and Teopantecuanitlan continued to
grow and serve as the principal centers of their respective regions of highland Mexico.
Meanwhile, new centers proliferated at places such as Takalik Abaj in western Guatemala,
at Chiapa de Corzo in central Chiapas (Lowe 2001), at Kaminaljuyú and Naranjos in
highland Guatemala (Arroyo, this volume), at Nakbe in the Petén (Hansen 1998), and
at Komchén, Izamal, and other sites in the northern Yucatán Peninsula (Stanton, this
volume). Nevertheless, several regions, such as the northern Gulf lowlands, the Tuxtla
Mountains, much of the Maya lowlands, and the eastern Guatemala coast, seem to have
avoided regional political integration until the Late Formative period.

With some exceptions (see Love 2007; Symonds et al. 2002) regional populations generally increased through the Middle Formative (e.g., Blanton et al. 1993; Chase and Chase, this volume; Sanders et al. 1979; von Nagy 2003). Settlement hierarchies in most regions either maintained or increased the number of levels, regardless of whether they were administered by the same or new centers. Several of which expanded to cover areas well in excess of 100 hectares, a size that had been matched only by San Lorenzo in the preceding period.

Civic and ceremonial architecture expanded and proliferated to a remarkable degree, reflecting the centralization of political and religious institutions. La Blanca was an early and impressive example (Love, this volume), along with La Venta, which ultimately constructed a taller, stepped, pyramidal mound and expansive complexes of ceremonial and administrative architecture stretching a kilometer along a north-south axis, with impressive offerings of imported greenstone and other materials (González 1996). Some of these architectural and ceremonial patterns are prominently reflected in the Central Chiapas Depression at Chiapa de Corzo and San Isidro, supporting a historical connection among these centers (Bachand et al. 2009; Clark 2004; Lowe 1998). Despite an impressive degree of variation in architectural layouts and orientations, a number of features characteristic of later Mesoamerican cities can be identified in Middle Formative centers, including pyramidal platforms for religious and administrative structures arranged around large plazas, often oriented to cardinal directions or landscape features (e.g., Clark 2004).

The "true urban" status of Early and Middle Formative centers is a matter of debate (e.g., Niederberger 2000; González 1996; see also Blanton, this volume), but the processes of nucleation, expansion, and hierarchization of regional networks, as well as the centralization of administrative, redistributive, and religious functions at nodes within those networks, seem to have been well underway in many regions before the close of the Middle Formative. That does not mean that urbanization proceeded everywhere along a similar path or that "full urbanism" was an end state that all Middle Formative centers reached, much less aspired to, as Blanton's chapter and the regional syntheses in this volume attest. Understanding the causes of variation in different societal trajectories, and their concordance and discordance in adjacent regions, is one of the principal challenges that face Mesoamerican archaeologists in the future.

References

Arnold, Philip J. III. 1999. Tecomates, Residential Mobility, and Early Formative Occupation in Coastal Lowland Mesoamerica. In *Pottery and People*, edited by James M. Skibo and Gary M. Feinman, pp. 157–170. University of Utah Press, Salt Lake City.

Arnold, Philip J. III. 2000. Sociopolitical Complexity and the Gulf Olmecs: A View from the Tuxtla Mountains, Veracruz, Mexico. In *Olmec Art and Archaeology in Mesoamerica*, edited by John E. Clark and Mary E. Pye, pp. 117–135. National Gallery of Art, Washington, DC.

Bachand, Bruce, Lyneth S. Lowe, and Emiliano Gallaga. 2009. Chiapa de Corzo: nuevas evidencias del centro ceremonial. Paper presented at the 53rd International Congress of Americanists, Mexico City.

Bernal, Ignacio. 1969. *The Olmec World*. Translated by Doris Heyden and Fernando Horcasitas. University of California Press, Berkeley.

Blake, Michael, John E. Clark, Barbara Voorhies, Michael W. Love, and Brian S. Chisholm. 1992. Prehistoric Subsistence in the Soconusco Region. *Current Anthropology* 33:83–94.

Blanton, Richard, Gary M. Feinman, Stephen A. Kowalewski, and Laura M. Finsten. 1993. *Ancient Mesoamerica: A Comparison of Change in Three Regions*. Cambridge University Press, Cambridge.

Blomster, Jeffrey P. 2002. What and Where Is Olmec style? Regional Perspectives on Hollow Figurines in Early Formative Mesoamerica. *Ancient Mesoamerica* 13:171–195.

Blomster, Jeffrey P. 2004. *Etlatongo: Social Complexity, Interaction, and Village Life in the Mixteca Alta of Oaxaca, Mexico*. Case Studies in Archaeology. Thomson Wadsworth, Belmont, California.

Blomster, Jeffrey P. 2010. Complexity, Interaction, and Epistemology: Mixtecs, Zapotecs, and Olmecs in Early Formative Mesoamerica. *Ancient Mesoamerica* 21:135–149.

Blomster, Jeffrey P., Hector Neff, and Michael D. Glascock. 2005. Olmec Pottery Production and Export in Ancient Mexico Determined through Elemental Analysis. *Science* 307:1068–1072.

Borstein, Joshua P. 2001. Tripping over Colossal Heads: Settlement Patterns and Population Development in the Upland Olmec Heartland. PhD dissertation, Department of Anthropology, Pennsylvania State University, University Park.

Carneiro, Robert L. 1998. What Happened at the Flashpoint? Conjectures on Chiefdom Formation at the Very Moment of Conception. In *Chiefdoms and Chieftancy in the Americas*, edited by Elsa M. Redman, pp. 18–42. University Press of Florida, Gainesville.

Caso, Alfonso. 1965. Existió un imperio olmeca? *Memoria del Colegio Nacional* 5(3):30–52.

Cheetham, David. 2010. Cultural Imperatives in Clay: Early Olmec Carved Pottery From San Lorenzo and Cantón Corralito. *Ancient Mesoamerica* 21:165–185.

Cheetham, David. 2011. Americas' First Colony: Olmec Materiality and Ethnicity at Canton Corralito, Chiapas, Mexico. Unpublished PhD dissertation, Arizona State University, Tempe.

Clark, John E. 1997. The Arts of Government in Early Mesoamerica. *Annual Review of Anthropology* 26:211–234.

Clark, John E. 2004. Mesoamerica Goes Public: Early Ceremonial Centers, Leaders, and Communities. In *Mesoamerican Archaeology*, edited by Rosemary A. Joyce and Julia A. Hendon, pp. 43–72. Blackwell, Oxford.

Clark, John E. 2007. Mesoamerica's First State. In *The Political Economy of Ancient Mesoamerica*, edited by John E. Clark and Vernon L. Scarborough, pp. 11–46. University of New Mexico Press, Albuquerque.

Clark, John E., and Michael Blake. 1994. The Power of Prestige: Competitive Generosity and the Emergence of Rank in Lowland Mesoamerica. In *Factional Competition and Political Development in the New World*, edited by Elizabeth M. Brumfiel and John W. Fox, pp. 17–30. Cambridge University Press, Cambridge.

Clark, John E., and Dennis Gosser. 1995. Reinventing Mesoamerica's First Pottery. In *The Emergence of Pottery: Technology and Innovation in Ancient Societies*, edited by William K. Barnett and John W. Hoopes, pp. 209–221. Smithsonian Institution, Washington, DC.

Clark, John E., and John G. Hodgson. 2004. A Millennium of Wonders in Coastal Mesoamerica. Paper presented at the 103rd annual meeting of the American Anthropological Association, Atlanta, Georgia.

Clark, John E., and Mary E. Pye. 2000. The Pacific Coast and the Olmec Question. In *Olmec Art and Archaeology in Mesoamerica*, edited by John E. Clark and Mary E. Pye, pp. 217–251. National Gallery of Art, Washington, DC.

Cobean, Robert H., James R. Vogt, Michael D. Glascock, and Terrance L. Stocker. 1991. High-Precision Trace-Element Characterization of Major Mesoamerican Obsidian Sources and Further Analyses of Artifacts from San Lorenzo Tenochtitlan, Mexico. *Latin American Antiquity* 2:69–91.

Coe, Michael D., and Richard A. Diehl. 1980a. *In the Land of the Olmec, Vol. 1, The Archaeology of San Lorenzo Tenochtitlán*. University of Texas Press, Austin.

Coe, Michael D., and Richard A. Diehl. 1980b. *In the Land of the Olmec, Vol. 2, The People of the River*. University of Texas Press, Austin.

Curtin, Philip D. 1984. *Cross-Cultural Trade in World History*. Cambridge University Press, Cambridge.

Cyphers, Ann. 1996. Reconstructing Olmec Life at San Lorenzo. In *Olmec Art of Ancient Mexico*, edited by Elizabeth P. Benson and Beatríz de la Fuente, pp. 61–71. National Gallery of Art, Washington, DC.

Cyphers, Ann, ed. 1997. *Población, subsistencia y medio ambiente en San Lorenzo Tenochtitlán*. Universidad Nacional Autónoma de México, México City.

Cyphers, Ann. 2004. *Escultura Olmeca de San Lorenzo Tenochtitlán*. Universidad Nacional Autónoma de México, Mexico City.

Cyphers, Ann, and Anna DiCastro. 2009. Early Olmec Architecture and Imagery. In *The Art of Urbanism: How Mesoamerican Kingdoms Represented Themselves in Architecture and Imagery*, edited by William L. Fash and Leonardo López Luján, pp. 21–52. Dumbarton Oaks Research Library and Collections, Washington, DC.

Cyphers Guillén, Ann, and David C. Grove. 1987. Chronology and Cultural Phases at Chalcatzingo. In *Ancient Chalcatzingo*, edited by David C. Grove, pp. 56–62. University of Texas Press, Austin.

de Montmollin, Olivier. 1989. *The Archaeology of Political Structure: Settlement Analysis in a Classic Maya Polity*. Cambridge University Press, Cambridge.

Diehl, Richard A., and Michael D. Coe. 1995. Olmec Archaeology. In *The Olmec World: Ritual and Rulership*, edited by Jill Guthrie and Elizabeth P. Benson, pp. 11–25. The Art Museum, Princeton University, Princeton.

Dunnell, Robert Chester. 1980. Evolutionary Theory and Archaeology. *Advances in Archaeological Method and Theory* 3:38–99.

Earle, Timothy K. 1991. The Evolution of Chiefdoms. In *Chiefdoms: Power, Economy, and Ideology*, edited by Timothy K. Earle, pp. 1–15. Cambridge University Press, Cambridge.

Easton, David. 1959. Political Anthropology. *Biennial Review of Anthropology* 1959:210–262.

Fash, William L. 1991. *Scribes, Warriors and Kings*. Thames and Hudson, London.

Feinman, Gary M., and Jill Neitzel. 1984. Too Many Types: An Overview of Sedentary Prestate Societies in the Americas. In *Advances in Archaeological Method and Theory, Vol. 7*, edited by Michael J. Schiffer, pp. 39–102. Academic Press, New York.

Flannery, Kent V. 1968. The Olmec and the Valley of Oaxaca: A Model for Interregional Interaction in Formative Times. In *Dumbarton Oaks Conference on the Olmec*, edited by Elizabeth Polk Benson, pp. 79–110. Dumbarton Oaks, Washington, DC.

Flannery, Kent V. 1972. The Cultural Evolution of Civilizations. *Annual Review of Ecology and Systematics* 3:399–426.

Flannery, Kent V. 1998. The Ground Plans of Archaic States. In *Archaic States*, edited by
    Gary M. Feinman and Joyce Marcus, pp. 15–57. School of American Research Press,
    Santa Fe.
Flannery, Kent V., Andrew K. Balkansky, Gary M. Feinman, David C. Grove, Joyce Marcus,
    Elsa M. Redmond, Robert G. Reynolds, Robert J. Sharer, Charles S. Spencer, and Jason
    Yaeger. 2005. Implications of New Petrographic Analysis for the Olmec "Mother
    Culture" Model. *Proceedings of the National Academy of Sciences* 102:11219–11223.
Flannery, Kent V., and Joyce Marcus. 1994. *Early Formative Pottery of the Valley of
    Oaxaca, Mexico*. University of Michigan, Ann Arbor.
Flannery, Kent V., and Joyce Marcus. 2000. Formative Mexican Chiefdoms and the Myth
    of the "Mother Culture." *Journal of Anthropological Archaeology* 19:1–37.
Fried, Morton Herbert. 1967. *The Evolution of Political Society*. Colonial Press, Clinton,
    Massachusetts.
Gillespie, Susan D. 1999. Olmec Thrones as Ancestral Altars: The Two Sides of Power.
    In *Material Symbols: Culture and Economy in Prehistory*, edited by John E. Robb,
    pp. 224–253. Center for Archaeological Investigations, Occasional Paper No. 26.
    Southern Illinois University, Carbondale.
González Lauck, Rebecca. 1996. La Venta: An Olmec Capital. In *Olmec Art of Ancient
    Mexico*, edited by Elizabeth P. Benson and Beatríz de la Fuente, pp. 73–81. National
    Gallery of Art, Washington, DC.
Grove, David C. 1973. Olmec Altars and Myths. *Archaeology* 26:128–135.
Grove, David C. 1993. "Olmec" Horizons in Formative Period Mesoamerica: Diffusion
    or Social Evolution? In *Latin American Horizons*, edited by Don S. Rice, pp. 83–111.
    Dumbarton Oaks Research Library and Collections, Washington, DC.
Grove, David C. 1994. La Isla, Veracruz, 1991: A Preliminary Report, with Comments on
    the Olmec Uplands. *Ancient Mesoamerica* 5:223–230.
Grove, David C. 1996. Archaeological Contexts of Olmec Art Outside of the Gulf Coast.
    In *Olmec Art of Ancient Mexico*, edited by Elizabeth Polk Benson and Beatríz de la
    Fuente, pp. 105–117. National Gallery of Art, Washington, DC.
Hansen, Richard D. 1998. Continuity and Disjunction: The Pre-Classic Antecedents of
    Classic Maya Architecture. In *Function and Meaning in Classic Maya Architecture*,
    edited by Stephen D. Houston, pp. 49–122. Dumbarton Oaks Research Library and
    Collections, Washington, DC.
Helms, Mary W. 1993. *Craft and the Kingly Ideal*. University of Texas Press, Austin.
Hill, Warren D., Michael Blake, and John E. Clark. 1998. Ball Court Design Dates Back
    3,400 Years. *Nature* 392:878–879.
Hirth, Kenneth G. 1987. Formative Period Settlement Patterns in the Río Amatzinac
    Valley. In *Ancient Chalcatzingo*, edited by David C. Grove, pp. 343–367. University of
    Texas Press, Austin.
Joyce, Rosemary A., and John S. Henderson. 2001. Beginnings of Village Life in Eastern
    Mesoamerica. *Latin American Antiquity* 12:5–23.
Joyce, Rosemary A., and John S. Henderson. 2010. Being "Olmec" in Early Formative
    Period Honduras. *Ancient Mesoamerica* 21(1):187–200.
Killion, Thomas W., and Javier Urcíd. 2001. The Olmec Legacy: Cultural
    Continuity in Mexico's Southern Gulf Coast Lowlands. *Journal of Field
    Archaeology* 28:3–25.
Kowalewski, Stephen A., Gary M. Feinman, Laura Finsten, Richard Blanton, and Linda
    Nicholas. 1989. *Monte Albán's Hinterland, Part II: The Prehispanic Settlement
    Patterns in Tlacolula, Etla, and Ocotlán, the Valley of Oaxaca, Mexico*. Museum of
    Anthropology Memoir 23. University of Michigan, Ann Arbor.

Lesure, Richard G. 2000. Animal Imagery, Cultural Unities, and Ideologies of Inequality in Early Formative Mesoamerica. In *Olmec Art and Archaeology in Mesoamerica*, edited by John E. Clark and Mary E. Pye, pp. 193–215. National Gallery of Art, Washington, DC.

Lesure, Richard G. 2004. Shared Art Styles and Long-Distance Contact in Early Mesoamerica. In *Mesoamerican Archaeology*, edited by Rosemary A. Joyce and Julia A. Hendon, pp. 73–96. Blackwell, Oxford.

Lesure, Richard G. 2011. *Interpreting Ancient Figurines: Context, Comparison, and Prehistoric Art*. Cambridge University Press, Cambridge.

Lesure, Richard G., and Michael Blake. 2002. Interpretive Challenges in the Study of Early Complexity: Economy, Ritual, and Architecture at Paso de la Amada, Mexico. *Journal of Anthropological Archaeology* 21:1–24.

Lesure, Richard G., Aleksander Borejsza, Jennifer Carballo, Charles Frederick, Virginia Popper, and Thomas A. Wake. 2006. Chronology, Subsistence, and the Earliest Formative of Central Tlaxcala, Mexico. *Latin American Antiquity* 17:474–492.

Love, Michael W. 1999. Ideology, Material Culture, and Daily Practice in Pre-Classic Mesoamerica: A Pacific Coast Perspective. In *Social Patterns in Pre-Classic Mesoamerica*, edited by David C. Grove and Rosemary A. Joyce, pp. 127–153. Dumbarton Oaks, Washington, DC.

Love, Michael W. 2007. Recent Research in the Southern Highlands and Pacific Coast of Mesoamerica. *Journal of Archaeological Research* 15:275–328.

Lowe, Gareth W. 1998. *Los olmecas de San Isidro en Malpaso, Chiapas*. Serie Arqueología 371. Consejo Nacional para la Cultura y las Artes/Instituto Nacional de Antropología e Historia, Mexico City.

Lowe, Gareth W. 2001. Chiapa de Corzo (Chiapas, Mexico). In *Archaeology of Ancient Mexico and Central America: An Encyclopedia*, edited by Susan Toby Evans and David L. Webster, pp. 122–123. Garland, New York.

Marcus, Joyce. 1999. Men's and Women's Ritual in Formative Oaxaca. In *Social Patterns in Pre-Classic Mesoamerica*, edited by David Grove and Rosemary A. Joyce, pp. 67–96. Dumbarton Oaks, Washington, DC.

Marcus, Joyce, and Kent Flannery. 1996. *Zapotec Civilization: How Urban Society Evolved in Mexico's Oaxaca Valley*. Thames and Hudson, London.

Mayer-Oakes, William T. 1963. Complex Society Archaeology. *American Antiquity* 29:57–60.

Mountjoy, Joseph B. 1998. The Evolution of Complex Societies in West Mexico: A Comparative Perspective. In *Ancient West Mexico: Art and Archaeology of the Unknown Past*, edited by Richard Townsend, pp. 251–265. The Art Institute of Chicago, Chicago.

Neff, Hector, Jeffrey Blomster, Michael D. Glascock, Ronald L. Bishop, James M. Blackman, Michael D. Coe, George L. Cowgill, Ann Cyphers, Richard A. Diehl, Stephen Houston, Arthur A. Joyce, Carl P. Lipo, and Marcus Winter. 2006a. Smokescreens in the Provenance Investigation of Early Formative Mesoamerican Ceramics. *Latin American Antiquity* 17:104–118.

Neff, Hector, Deborah M. Pearsall, John G. Jones, Barbara Arroyo, Shawn K. Collins, and Dorothy E. Freidel. 2006b. Early Maya Adaptive Patterns: Mid- Late Holocene Paleoenvironmental Evidence from Pacific Guatemala. *Latin American Antiquity* 17:287–315.

Nelson, Fred W., and John E. Clark. 1998. Obsidian Production and Exchange in Eastern Mesoamerica. In *Rutas de intercambio en Mesoamérica*, edited by Evelyn Childs Rattray, pp. 277–333. III Coloquio Pedro Bosch Gimpera. Universidad Nacional Autónoma de México, Mexico City.

Niederberger, Christine. 1996. Olmec Horizon Guerrero. In *Olmec Art of Ancient Mexico*, edited by Elizabeth Polk Benson and Beatríz de la Fuente, pp. 95–103. National Gallery of Art, Washington, DC.

Niederberger, Christine. 2000. Ranked Societies, Iconographic Complexity, and Economic Wealth in the Basin of Mexico toward 1200 BC. In *Olmec Art and Archaeology in Mesoamerica*, edited by John E. Clark and Mary E. Pye, pp. 169–191. National Gallery of Art, Washington, DC.

Ortiz Ceballos, Ponciano, and Ma. del Carmen Rodríguez. 2000. The Sacred Hill of El Manatí: A Preliminary Discussion of the Site's Ritual Paraphernalia. In *Olmec Art and Archaeology in Mesoamerica*, edited by John E. Clark and Mary E. Pye, pp. 75–93. National Gallery of Art, Washington, DC.

Ortiz Pérez, Mario Arturo, and Ann Cyphers. 1997. La geomorfología y las evidencias arqueológicas en la región de San Lorenzo Tenochtitlán, Veracruz. In *Población, subsistencia y medio ambiente en San Lorenzo Tenochtitlán*, edited by Ann Cyphers, pp. 31–53. Universidad Nacional Autónoma de México, México City.

Pauketat, Timothy R. 2007. *Chiefdoms and other Archaeological Delusions*. Altamira, Lanham, Maryland.

Pool, Christopher A. 2007. *Olmec Archaeology and Early Mesoamerica*. Cambridge University Press, Cambridge.

Pool, Christopher A., and Michael Anthony Ohnersorgen. 2003. Archaeological Survey and Settlement at Tres Zapotes. In *Settlement Archaeology and Political Economy at Tres Zapotes, Veracruz, Mexico*, edited by Christopher A. Pool, pp. 7–31. Monograph 50. Cotsen Institute of Archaeology, University of California, Los Angeles.

Pool, Christopher A., Ponciano Ortiz Ceballos, María del Carmen Rodríguez, and Michael Loughlin. 2010. The Early Horizon at Tres Zapotes: Implications for Olmec Interaction. *Ancient Mesoamerica* 21:95–106.

Pope, Kevin O., Mary D. Pohl, John G. Jones, David L. Lentz, Christopher L. von Nagy, Francisco J. Vega, and Irvy R. Quitmyer. 2001. Origin and Environmental Setting of Ancient Agriculture in the Lowlands of Mesoamerica. *Science* 292:1370–1373.

Price, T. Douglas, and James A. Brown. 1985. *Prehistoric Hunter-Gatherers: The Emergence of Cultural Complexity*. Academic Press, New York.

Rathje, William L. 1972. Praise the Gods and Pass the Metates: A Hypothesis of the Development of Lowland Rainforest Civilizations in Mesoamerica. In *Contemporary Archaeology*, edited by M. Leone, pp. 365–392. Southern Illinois University Press, Carbondale.

Reilly, F. Kent III. 1995. Art, Ritual, and Rulership in the Olmec World. In *The Olmec World: Ritual and Rulership*, edited by Jill Guthrie and Elizabeth P. Benson, pp. 27–45. The Art Museum, Princeton University, Princeton.

Reyes González, Liliana Carla, and Marcus Winter. 2010. The Early Formative Period in the Southern Isthmus: Excavations at Barrio Tepalcate, Ixtepec, Oaxaca. *Ancient Mesoamerica* 21(1):151–163.

Rosenswig, Robert M. 2000. Some Political Processes of Ranked Societies. *Journal of Anthropological Archaeology* 19:413–460.

Rosenswig, Robert M. 2010. *The Beginnings of Mesoamerican Civilization: Inter-Regional Interaction and the Olmec*. Cambridge University Press, Cambridge.

Rust, William. 2008. A Settlement Survey of La Venta, Tabasco, Mexico. PhD dissertation, Department of Anthropology, University of Pittsburgh.

Sanders, William T., Jeffrey Parsons, and Robert S. Santley. 1979. *The Basin of Mexico: Ecological Processes in the Evolution of a Civilization*. Academic Press, New York.

Sanders, William T., and Barbara J. Price. 1968. *Mesoamerica: The Evolution of a Civilization*. Random House, New York.

Santley, Robert S., and Philip J. Arnold III. 1996. Prehispanic Settlement Patterns in the Tuxtla Mountains, Southern Veracruz, Mexico. *Journal of Field Archaeology* 23:225–249.

Service, Elman Rogers. 1962. *Primitive Social Organization: An Evolutionary Perspective*. Random House, New York.

Sharer, Robert J., Andrew K. Balkansky, James. Burton, Gary M. Feinman, Kent V. Flannery, David C. Grove, Joyce Marcus, Robert G. Moyle, T. Douglas Price, Elsa M. Redmond, Robert G. Reynolds, Prudence M. Rice, Charles S. Spencer, James B. Stoltman, and Jason Yaeger. 2006. On the Logic of Archaeological Inference: Early Formative Pottery and the Evolution of Mesoamerican Societies. *Latin American Antiquity* 17:90–103.

Smalley, John, and Michael Blake. 2002. Sweet Beginnings: Stalk Sugar and the Domestication of Maize. *Current Anthropology* 44:675–703.

Smith, Adam T. 2003. *The Political Landscape: Constellations of Authority in Early Complex Polities*. University of California Press, Berkeley.

Spencer, Charles S., and Elsa M. Redmond. 2004. Primary State Formation in Mesoamerica. *Annual Review of Anthropology* 33:173–199.

Stark, Barbara L. 2000. Framing the Gulf Olmecs. In *Olmec Art and Archaeology in Mesoamerica*, edited by John E. Clark and Mary E. Pye, pp. 31–53. National Gallery of Art, Washington, DC.

Stoltman, James B., Joyce Marcus, Kent V. Flannery, James H. Burton, and Robert G. Moyle. 2005. Petrographic Evidence Shows That Pottery Exchange between the Olmec and Their Neighbors Was Two-Way. *Proceedings of the National Academy of Sciences* 102:11213–11218.

Symonds, Stacey, Ann Cyphers, and Roberto Lunagómez. 2002. *Asentamiento prehispánico en San Lorenzo Tenochtitlán*. Universidad Nacional Autónoma de México, Mexico City.

Tolstoy, Paul. 1989. Coapexco and Tlatilco: Sites with Olmec Materials in the Basin of Mexico. In *Regional Perspectives on the Olmec*, edited by Robert J. Sharer and David C. Grove, pp. 85–121. Cambridge University Press, Cambridge.

VanDerwarker, Amber. 2006. *Farming, Hunting, and Fishing in the Olmec World*. University of Texas Press, Austin.

von Nagy, Christopher L. 2003. Of Meandering Rivers and Shifting Towns: Landscape Evolution and Community within the Grijalva Delta. PhD dissertation, Tulane University.

Webster, David L. 2011. Backward Bottlenecks: Ancient Teosinte/Maize Selection. *Current Anthropology* 52(1):77–104.

Wendt, Carl. 2010. A San Lorenzo Phase Household Assemblage from El Remolino, Veracruz. *Ancient Mesoamerica* 21:107–122.

Wenke, Robert J., and Deborah I. Olszewski. 2007. *Humankind's First Three Million Years*. 5th ed. Oxford University Press, Oxford.

Wing, Elizabeth S. 1980. Aquatic Fauna and Reptiles from the Atlantic and Pacific Sites. In *In the Land of the Olmec, Vol. 1, The Archaeology of San Lorenzo Tenochtitlán*, edited by Michael D. Coe and Richard A. Diehl, pp. 375–386. University of Texas Press, Austin.

Yoffee, Norman. 1993. Too Many Chiefs? (or Safe Texts for the '90s). In *Archaeological Theory: Who Sets the Agenda?* edited by Norman Yoffee and A. Sherrat, pp. 60–78. Cambridge University Press, Cambridge.

Yoffee, Norman. 2005. *Myths of the Archaic State*. Cambridge University Press, Cambridge.

CHAPTER 13

NOT CARVED IN STONE

BUILDING THE GULF OLMEC FROM THE BOTTOM UP

PHILIP J. ARNOLD III

Michelangelo was once asked how he had carved his marble masterpiece. The sculptor apocryphally responded that nothing could be simpler; all one needed was to remove everything that was not David. (Galison 1987:256)

IT seems only appropriate to begin a discussion of the Gulf Olmec with a reference to sculpture. And if published debates over Mother/Sister cultures, state/nonstate complexity, and export/import economies are any indication, then studies of the Gulf Olmec often take Michelangelo's riposte to heart.[1] Research conclusions have become fairly predictable; results are shaped as if simply revealing outcomes already foreseen within the data. Despite all that Gulf Olmec archaeologists have learned in the last twenty years (e.g., Pool 2009), the field currently offers far too few surprises.

Calls for redress encourage us to ask better questions and rethink old arguments (Diehl 2000; Pool 2009). But re-imagining possibilities is not enough; asking better questions also requires a critical examination of core concepts (e.g., González-Lauck 2008: 41). Pool (2009: 251) warns us not to treat Olmec as a "monolithic entity." The oblique reference to sculpture—intended or not—is certainly apropos.

---

1. There is no need to review the history of Gulf Olmec archaeology and the often tiresome debates about it. Several excellent overviews and syntheses summarize the current state of the field (see Diehl 2004; Pool 2007, 2009).

In contrast to *il metodo di Michelangelo*, I suggest that we build the Gulf Olmec from the bottom up. Rather than remove information considered extraneous and steer toward a particular result, we should combine different datasets and allow for unanticipated outcomes. Toward this end, the following discussion examines two concepts at the core of Gulf Olmec archaeology: (a) where they lived and (b) how they developed.

I begin with a Gulf Olmec précis that covers the space/time essentials. I then consider available data from the Gulf lowlands and argue for a more extensive "heartland" than is currently fashionable. Finally, I suggest that we reconsider the process of politico-economic development that has become the received wisdom of Gulf Olmec studies. Throughout the presentation I emphasize the value of allowing the data to take the lead, rather than shaping the information toward some pre-envisioned result.

GULF OLMEC

The Gulf Olmec name derives from an ethnohistoric culture called *Olmeca-Xicalanca*. Olmeca is actually a geocultural referent for the inhabitants of *Olman* (or *Ulman*), the "land of rubber." Despite this appellation, no one today would advocate a direct cultural connection between the ancient Gulf Olmec and the ethnohistoric Olmeca-Xicalanca. Thus, the archaeological identifier "Olmec" has long been recognized as problematic, but no alternative has garnered wide acceptance (see Pool 2007: 12–15).

Archaeological convention dictates that the Gulf Olmec region is bounded by the Gulf of Mexico to the north, the site of Las Limas to the south, and stretches from the Papaloapan Basin eastward to the Tonalá drainage. The area includes some of the most famous Gulf lowlands sites, including San Lorenzo, La Venta, and Tres Zapotes (Figure 13.1). The region also includes the Tuxtla Mountains, a resource-rich volcanic uplift that William Sanders (1952–1953: 66) once characterized as the crowning jewel of the southern Gulf lowlands environment.

Chronological treatments of the Gulf Olmec usually divide time into an Early Formative (ca. 1500–1000 BC) and a Middle Formative (ca. 1000–400 BC) sequence (e.g., Pool 2007: Figure 1.4). A Late Formative occupation (ca. 400 BC–100 AD) is frequently characterized as "Epi-Olmec" and falls outside the scope of the present discussion.

GULF OLMEC LOWLANDS

Prior to the 1960s, scholars recognized that Gulf Olmec occupation extended across considerable portions of the Gulf lowlands. While noting that southern Veracruz may have been a particular Olmec "stronghold" (Covarrubias 1957: 163), researchers

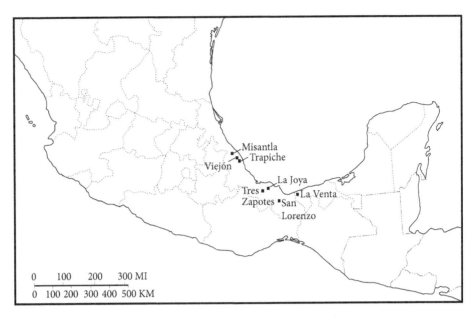

Figure 13.1 Gulf Olmec sites mentioned in the text.

observed that central and even northern Veracruz exhibited Formative-period materials with stylistic similarities to southern Veracruz and highland Mexico (e.g., Caso 1965: 14; Covarrubias 1957: 165; García Payón 1950). In fact, by the onset of the 1960s Medellín Zenil (1960: 8, Plano 3) identified four different zones of Formative occupation across central Veracruz.

Nonetheless, by the mid-1960s an emphasis on monumental sculpture focused research attention on sites in southern Veracruz and western Tabasco. Thus, it is no stretch to say that the distribution of megalithic artwork literally defined the Gulf Olmec region (e.g., Grove 1997: 53). The Olmec stronghold of Covarrubias (1957) became Michael Coe's (1965) "climax region," which morphed into the "metropolitan" area (Bernal 1969:13) and was then recast as the Olmec "heartland" (e.g., Coe 1989; Lowe 1989). More recent treatments have revisited Covarrubias (1946:82) and baptized the region "Olman" (Diehl 2000, 2004; Pool 2007).

Despite the "megalith curtain" that now delimits Olman, data from its western zone reveal a considerably more complicated Gulf Olmec landscape. Research in the Tuxtla Mountains (Arnold 2003, 2005a; Arnold and McCormack 2002; McCormack 2002) and at Tres Zapotes (Pool and Ortiz Ceballos 2008; Pool et al. 2010) has provided evidence for occupations that firmly date to the Early and Middle Formative periods. Artifacts recovered by these projects include traditional Gulf Olmec diagnostics such as pottery carved and incised with Olmec motifs (e.g., Joralemon 1971) and ilmenite perforated cubes (e.g., Lowe 1989: 53). Nonetheless, no sculpture from secure Early Formative contexts has been documented (Arnold and McCormack 2002; Diehl 2004: 19; Pool and Ortiz Ceballos 2008: 437).

Thus, this western portion of Olman is "Gulf Olmec" according to commonly accepted Early Formative diagnostics, save megalithic sculpture. At the same time, this region also reveals strong connections farther westward and northward along the coastal lowlands. These connections are displayed via figurine and obsidian assemblages. Moreover, pieces of Middle Formative sculpture occur within some of these same "extra-heartland" coastal contexts. Thus the material and temporal patterns evident at several of these sites closely correspond to artifact sequences within Olman.

According to published data from eastern Olman, Early Formative solid figurines rendered in the "traditional Olmec" style are characterized by "highly arched 'Oriental' eyebrows, thick, frowning lips, and triangular flat noses" (Coe and Diehl 1980a: 264; also Wendt 2010: 116; cf. Blomster 2002). In contrast, Early Formative figurines from western Olman are dominated by a style that exhibits eyes made from a single or double incision, an opened mouth created from a creased clay tab, and an appliqué, "hawkish" nose (Follensbee and Arnold 2001; Pool et al. 2010: 99; Vázquez Zárate 2007).

The western Olman figurine style also makes up the majority of figurines from the lowest levels of Trapiche in central Veracruz (García Payón 1966: Tabla XII; 1971: Figure 16a-e). Moreover, while not dated through radiometric means, the Trapiche figurines were associated with pottery types now commonly recognized as variants of Early Formative Gulf Olmec diagnostics (García Payón 1966: 75, Tabla X; also Coe and Diehl 1980a: 169). Also noteworthy is García Payón's (1942: 38) contention that the early Trapiche occupation was not intrusive but was instead an autochthonous coastal development (cf. Bernal 1969: 149–150). In recent years Trapiche-style figurines and additional Olmec diagnostics have been documented from a variety of deposits along the Gulf lowlands, ranging from the Sierra de Chiconquiaco south to the Sierra de los Tuxtlas (e.g., Pool et al. 2010: Figure 7; also see below). These artifacts constitute more than a few intrusive elements; rather, they reveal a Gulf Olmec presence that extends across considerable portions of the Gulf lowlands (Daneels 2010).

Obsidian distributions mirror the figurine data. From the Tuxtlas to the west and north, the Formative-period obsidian assemblage is dominated by material from the central Mexican highlands and occurs primarily as flakes and bipolar debitage. Two sources in particular provided the overwhelming majority of this obsidian: Guadalupe-Victoria and Pico de Orizaba (e.g., Cobean et al. 1991; Knight 2003; Pool et al. 2010; Santley et al. 2001; Stark et al. 1992). In contrast, obsidian from San Lorenzo (Coe and Diehl 1980a; Cobean et al. 1991), El Manatí (Ortíz Ceballos et al. 1997:90), and La Venta (Rojas Chávez 1990) includes material from Guatemalan sources (El Chayal, Ixtepeque); moreover, obsidian in these deposits occurs as both blades and flakes (Cobean et al. 1991:Table 5; Coe and Diehl 1980a: 247–248; Rojas Chávez 1990: 26). Thus, both the acquisition and consumption of obsidian affirm different but overlapping Gulf Olmec patterns.

Given these differences, some researchers prefer to excise portions of western Olman, such as the Tuxtla Mountains, from the "true Olmec core zone" (Diehl 2004: 18–19; also Cyphers and Zurita-Noguera 2006: Fig. 2.1). Not only unjustified, this reaction is ironic; olmequistas once identified the Tuxtla Mountains as the most likely candidate for the original Gulf Olmec homeland (e.g., Coe 1968: 89; Heizer 1968: 22; Saville 1929: 285, cited in Bernal 1969: 30). This identification was based, in part, on the San Martín Pajapan sculpture recovered from the eastern portion of the Tuxtlas (e.g., Blom and La Farge 1926: 45–46).

The traditional emphasis on sculpture is doubly ironic, given that it actually supports the more extensive Gulf Olmec presence proposed here. Despite the attention afforded southern Gulf lowland megaliths, such artwork also occurs in the central and north-central regions of Veracruz. For example, a large, three-dimensional sculpture from the vicinity of Misantla is rendered according to Gulf Olmec artistic canons (e.g., Bernal 1969: Plate 20; García Payón 1971: 529). From Viejón comes a somewhat later, but still Gulf Olmec style, stela (e.g., Bernal 1969: 149, Plate 70). Coe (1989: 69) refers to the Viejón monument as a geographically "unexplained outlier" relative to Olman.

The research conducted in the western portion of Olman suggests that the Misantla and Viejón sculptures are neither outliers nor inexplicable. Rather, multiple lines of evidence reveal a complicated Gulf Olmec presence throughout the Gulf lowlands. While the distribution of sculpture encapsulates broad areas of the Gulf lowlands, patterning in figurines and imported obsidian heralds multiple spheres of Gulf Olmec interactions. These patterns represent contingent, situational relationships that likely included a range of different settlement, subsistence, and social networks. Attempts to account for these patterns in terms of simple hierarchical complexity and geopolitical control are no longer tenable (e.g., Coe and Diehl 1980a: 391; Cyphers and Zurita-Noguera 2006: 48). It would be more constructive to approach this variability on its own terms, building the Gulf Olmec from the bottom up, and examining the different contexts in which these patterns emerged, endured, and disappeared.

GULF OLMEC DEVELOPMENT

The conventional story of Gulf Olmec development is one in which fertile agriculture levee-land constituted a localized resource, the control of which underwrote power differentials, the development of politico-economic complexity, and ultimately gave rise to civilization (e.g., Caso 1965; Coe and Diehl 1980b:150–152; Diehl 2004: 85; Evans 2004: 133). As used in the present discussion, agriculture (i.e., farming) refers to a commitment to and reliance on domesticated plants; in contrast, horticulture (i.e., gardening) denotes a minor investment in the production and consumption of cultigens. Gulf Olmec studies have not always made such a distinction, sometimes equating the simple presence of a domesticate, such as maize (*Zea mays*), with agriculture (e.g., Pope et al. 2001).

Fortunately, scholars have begun to move away from these simplistic scenarios. Evidence clearly shows that domesticated maize appeared along the Gulf lowlands by at least 5,000 years ago (e.g., Goman and Byrne 1998; Pohl et al. 2007; Sluyter and Dominguez 2006). Nonetheless, this evidence oscillated appreciably for several thousand years before significant politico-economic change was realized. Nor do currently published data support a prominent role for alternative cultigens, such as manioc (*Manihot* sp.) (Cyphers and Zurita-Noguera 2006: 39; Pope et al. 2001: 1373) or sunflower (*Helianthus annuus*) (Lentz et al. 2008; Smith 2006). Researchers now recognize that an array of wild resources, both faunal and floral, were basic to Gulf Olmec development (Arnold 2000, 2009; Pool 2009: 244–245; VanDerwarker 2006).

Settlement data from the southern Gulf lowlands raise additional questions about the impact of agriculture in Gulf Olmec development. Settlement patterns reflect the distribution of occupations and activities across the landscape; these differences are usually collapsed into hierarchical arrangements that represent social, economic, and political activities (e.g., Arnold and Stark 1997; Balkansky 2006). Settlement hierarchies, in turn, often serve as proxies for cultural complexity.

Settlement data have been used to argue for a multitiered, integrated political system in which certain Gulf Olmec sites controlled considerable portions of Olman (e.g., Cyphers and Zurita Noguera 2006; Grove 1997: 74–76; Pool 2007: 125–127; Symonds et al. 2002). Assumptions of agricultural production bolster many of these settlement-pattern models, particularly their hierarchical development. Nonetheless, a close reading of the available data undermines this interpretation. For example, Borstein (2001) undertook settlement-pattern studies to the west of San Lorenzo and noted a settlement shift into upland areas only toward the end of the Early Formative period, well after San Lorenzo became a regional center. According to Borstein (2001: 184), this settlement shift "represents a switch from a subsistence economy based largely on aquatic resources to one based primarily on agriculture." Similarly, Rust (2008) conducted extensive settlement research around La Venta in eastern Olman. Initial occupation within this area concentrated in wetland zones and "it appears unlikely [that] maize was a major factor in the subsistence diet of early settlements along the coastal rivers until after 1000 BC" (Rust 2008: 1413; also Seinfeld et al. 2009; von Nagy 2003: 1029). In fact, multiple settlement studies agree that Gulf Olmec sites were concentrated within wetland zones at the onset of the Early Formative period (Arnold 2009). These same studies indicate that it was not until after the emergence of Gulf Olmec politico-economic complexity that permanent settlements moved into the upland areas, which were more favorable to an agriculturally focused economy (Borstein 2001; Kruger 1996; Rust 2008; Symonds et al. 2002).

Gulf Olmec occupation within the Tuxtla Mountains offers a complementary case study. Here, the earliest settlements gravitated toward river valleys and only later adjusted their riparian focus (Santley and Arnold 1996; Santley et al. 1997). Excavation data from the Tuxtlas currently underwrite the most extensive, published treatment of Gulf Olmec subsistence (VanDerwarker 2006). These data (including artifacts, features, fauna, and flora) parallel the mounting evidence that maize agriculture was not a major factor in Gulf Olmec emergence (Arnold 2009). Cheetham and Blomster (2010: 92) recently affirm the meager evidence for Early Formative agriculture in the Tuxtlas, but they are simply wrong when they suggest that the Tuxtla pattern has been misapplied to other areas of Olman. As the above quotes by Borstein (2001) and Rust (2008) clearly show, there is a robust pattern of minimal agriculture prior to the emergence of Gulf Olmec politico-economic complexity across the southern Gulf lowlands.

Such uncritical adherence to "agricentrism" (Arnold 1996: 3–4) is interesting in light of the prior discussion regarding a critical examination of core concepts. Although the term "Olmec" is widely employed today, another name for this ethnohistoric group was *Uixtotín*, or "People of the Salt Water" (e.g., Sahagún 1938; Scholes and Warren 1965: 776). Moreover, according to the *Popol Vuh* the ancient ancestors from the east or the *"Tepeu Olomon"* ("sovereign Oloman") are also called the "Fish Keepers" (Tedlock 1985: 167–177, 189, 336, 361). In other words, the Olman cultural expression was tied as closely to an aquatic base as a terrestrial context. Thus, if archaeologists had initially emphasized the important role of wetland resources as a foundation for Gulf Olmec society, a very different perception of Gulf Olmec development and ideology may have come about (e.g., Arnold 2005b, 2009).[2]

Such an alternative perception would downplay the emphasis on hierarchical organization that frequently flavors discussions of Gulf Olmec society (e.g., Clark 2007; Cyphers and Zurita Noguera 2006). Unlike a prehispanic Athena, the Gulf Olmec did not spring fully developed from some *cabeza colosal*. In contrast to a predetermined, top-down model, researchers should consider more fluid political and economic relationships that shaped the development of ancient civilizations (e.g., Beekman and Baden 2005; Chapman 2003; Sassaman 2004).

Conclusion

Genius like Michelangelo's is hard to come by. Our attempts to follow his lead often seem to essentialize the data and move us toward some pre-envisioned past. To combat this tendency we must be willing to let the data take the lead, combine the information in creative ways, and build the Gulf Olmec from the bottom up.

2. Some may claim that wetland resources have always been emphasized as part of the Gulf Olmec adaptation. They would only be partly correct. While not negating the use of estuarine and riparian resources, models of Gulf Olmec development specifically removed such foodstuffs from the path to complexity: "If one is looking for entailable resources to explain the rise of the Gulf Olmec elite, fish and other aquatic resources can be excluded" (Coe and Diehl 1980b: 146).

We must also be willing to confront convention and critically examine long-standing, even cherished, core concepts. It is telling that one of the few recent surprises in Gulf Olmec archaeology speaks more to our ignorance than to our understanding. Wendt (2010) reports on his excavations at El Remolino, an Early Formative site only 5 kilometers from San Lorenzo. El Remolino has been characterized as a secondary center in the San Lorenzo political hierarchy, just below San Lorenzo itself (Symonds et al 2002: 38, 70, 72). Wendt's (2003, 2010) extensive analysis of the El Remolino data prompted the following observation:

> However, with its low quantity of San Lorenzo Horizon material culture
> markers, I believe that few Olmec specialists would identify [El Remolino] as
> San Lorenzo Olmec by examining its artifact assemblage alone.... Without
> a clearer idea of the variation of San Lorenzo Olmec (or for that matter,
> Gulf Olmec), how are we to identify and differentiate Olmec influence and
> migration? (Wendt 2010: 116–117).

The fact that an Early Formative secondary center adjacent to San Lorenzo cannot easily be identified as "San Lorenzo Olmec" is a sobering indictment of the current state of Gulf Olmec archaeology.

As argued above, Gulf Olmec archaeology needs more, not fewer, surprises. Cultural expression within the Olman region is neither internally homogeneous nor does it fully represent Gulf Olmec occupation along the Gulf lowlands. Similarly, the conventional, agricentric model of Gulf Olmec development is simply not justified. The typological and hierarchy-heavy approach that has characterized the field is becoming a monolithic impediment (Arnold 2005a; Pool 2009: 251). Michelangelo might be pleased that megalithic sculpture serves as the public face of the ancient Gulf Olmec. Researchers, in contrast, should remember that the practice of Gulf Olmec archaeology should never be carved in stone.

REFERENCES

Arnold, Jeanne E. 1996. Understanding the Evolution of Intermediate Societies. In
    Emergent Complexity: The Evolution of Intermediate Societies, edited by J. E.
    Arnold, pp. 1–12. International Monographs in Prehistory, Archaeological Series 9.
    International Monographs in Prehistory, Ann Arbor.
Arnold, Philip J., III. 2000. Sociopolitical Complexity and the Gulf Olmecs: A View
    from the Tuxtla Mountains, Veracruz, Mexico. In *Olmec Art and Archaeology in
    Mesoamerica*, edited by John E. Clark and Mary E. Pye, pp. 117–135. National Gallery
    of Art, Washington, DC.
Arnold, Philip J., III. 2003. Early Formative Pottery from the Tuxtla Mountains and
    Implications for Gulf Olmec Origins. *Latin American Antiquity* 14:29–46.
Arnold, Philip J., III. 2005a. Gulf Olmec Variation and Implications for Interaction. In
    New Perspectives on Formative Mesoamerican Cultures, edited by Terry G. Powis,
    pp. 73–84. BAR International Series 1377. Archaeopress, Oxford.

Arnold, Philip J., III. 2005b. The Shark-Monster in Olmec Iconography. *Mesoamerican Voices* 2:1–31.

Arnold, Philip J., III. 2009. Settlement and Subsistence among the Early Formative Gulf Olmec. *Journal of Anthropological Archaeology* 28:397–411.

Arnold, Philip J., III, and Valerie J. McCormack. 2002. En la sombra del San Martín: Final Field Report of the La Joya Archaeological Project. Report on file, Instituto Nacional de Antropología e Historia, Mexico.

Arnold, Philip J., III, and Barbara L. Stark. 1997. Gulf Lowland Settlement in Perspective. In *Olmec to Aztec: Settlement Patterns in the Ancient Gulf Lowlands*, edited by Barbara L. Stark and Philip J. Arnold III, pp. 310–329. University of Arizona Press, Tucson.

Balkansky, Andrew. 2006. Survey and Mesoamerican Archaeology: The Emerging Macroregional Paradigm. *Journal of Archaeological Research* 14:53–95.

Beekman, Christopher S., and William W. Baden, eds. 2005. *Non-linear Models for Archaeology and Anthropology: Continuing the Revolution*. Ashgate, Aldershot, UK.

Bernal, Ignacio. 1969. *The Olmec World*. University of California Press, Berkeley.

Blom, Frans, and Oliver La Farge. 1926. *Tribes and Temples: A Record of the Expedition to Middle America Conducted by the Tulane University of Louisiana in 1925*, vol. I. Middle American Research Institute, Tulane University, New Orleans.

Blomster, Jeffrey P. 2002. What and Where Is Olmec Style? Regional Perspectives on Hollow Figurines in Early Formative Mesoamerica. *Ancient Mesoamerica* 13:171–195.

Borstein, Joshua A. 2001. Tripping over Colossal Heads: Settlement Patterns and Population Development in the Upland Olmec Heartland. PhD dissertation, Department of Anthropology, Pennsylvania State University, University Park.

Caso, Alfonso. 1965. *¿Existió un Imperio Olmeca?* Memoria de El Colegio Nacional, tomo V, no. 3. México, D.F.

Chapman, Richard. 2003. *Archaeologies of Complexity*. Routledge, London.

Cheetham, David, and Jeffrey Blomster. 2010. Introduction. Special Section: Rethinking the Olmecs and Early Formative Mesoamerica. *Ancient Mesoamerica* 21:92–94.

Clark, John E. 2007. Mesoamerica's First State. In *The Political Economy of Ancient Mesoamerica: Transformations during the Formative and Classic Periods*, edited by Vernon L. Scarborough and John E. Clark, pp. 11–46. University of New Mexico Press, Albuquerque.

Cobean, Robert H., James, R. Vogt, Michael D. Glascock, and Terrance L. Stocker. 1991. High-Precision Trace-Element Characterization of Major Mesoamerican Obsidian Sources and Further Analyses of Artifacts from San Lorenzo Tenochtitlan, Mexico. *Latin American Antiquity* 2:69–91.

Coe, Michael D. 1965. The Olmec Style and Its Distribution. In *Archaeology of Southern Mesoamerica*, part 2, edited by Gordon R. Willey, pp. 739–775. *Handbook of Middle American Indians*, vol. 3. University of Texas Press, Austin.

Coe, Michael D. 1968. *America's First Civilization: Discovering the Olmec*. American Heritage, New York.

Coe, Michael D. 1989. The Olmec Heartland: Evolution of Ideology. In *Regional Perspectives on the Olmec*, edited by Robert J. Sharer and David C. Grove, pp. 68–82. Cambridge University Press, Cambridge.

Coe, Michael D., and Richard A. Diehl. 1980a. *In the Land of the Olmec, vol. 1: The Archaeology of San Lorenzo Tenochtitlán*. University of Texas Press, Austin.

Coe, Michael D., and Richard A. Diehl. 1980b. *In the Land of the Olmec, vol. 2: The People of the River*. University of Texas Press, Austin.

Covarrubias, Miguel. 1946. *Mexico South: The Isthmus of Tehuantepec*. Alfred A. Knopf, New York.

Covarrubias, Miguel. 1957. *Indian Art of Mexico and Central America*. Alfred A. Knopf, New York.

Cyphers, Ann, and Judith Zurita-Noguera. 2006. A Land That Tastes of Water. In *Precolumbian Water Management: Ideology, Ritual, and Power*, edited by Lisa J. Lucero and Barbara W. Fash, pp. 33–50. University of Arizona Press, Tucson.

Daneels, Annick. 2010. La presencia olmeca en el Centro-Sur de Veracruz y el origen de la cultura clásica del Centro de Veracruz. *Thule Rivista Italiana di studi americanistici* 22/23 (aprile-ottobre 2007) and 24/25 (aprile-ottobre 2008):317–341.

Diehl, Richard A. 2000. Olmec Archaeology after *Regional Perspectives*: An Assessment of Recent Research. In *Olmec Art and Archaeology in Mesoamerica*, edited by John E. Clark and Mary E. Pye, pp. 19–29. National Gallery of Art, Washington, DC.

Diehl, Richard A. 2004. *The Olmecs: America's First Civilization*. Thames and Hudson, London.

Evans, Susan Toby. 2004. *Ancient Mexico and Central America: Archaeology and Culture History*. Thames and Hudson, New York.

Follensbee, Billie, and Philip J Arnold III. 2001. Gulf Olmec Figurines from La Joya, Veracruz, Mexico. Presented at the 66th annual meeting of the Society for American Archaeology, New Orleans.

Galison, P. 1987. *How Experiments End*. University of Chicago Press, Chicago.

García Payón, José. 1942. Primer ensayo de interpretación de los restos de una cultura prehispánica encontrada en la región de Zempoala, Ver. Archivo Técnico del Consejo de Arqueología, Instituto Nacional de Antropología e Historia. Report on file in the Biblioteca García Payón, INAH Veracruz.

García Payón, José. 1950. Restos de una cultura Prehispánica encontrados en la región de Zempoala, Veracruz. *Uni-Ver*, año 2, vo. 2., no. 15. Universidad Veracruzana, Xalapa, Mexico.

García Payón, Jose. 1966. *Prehistoria de Mesomamérica: Excavaciones en Trapiche y Chalahuite, Veracruz, México 1942, 1951, y 1959*. Cuadernos 31, Universidad Veracruzana. Facultad de Filosofía, Letra, y Ciencias. Xalapa, Mexico.

García Payón, Jose. 1971. Archaeology of Central Veracruz. In *Archaeology of Northern Mesoamerica*, part 2, edited by Gordon F. Ekholm and Ignacio. Bernal, pp. 505–542. *Handbook of Middle American Indian*, vol. 11, University of Texas Press, Austin.

Goman, Michelle, and Roger Byrne. 1998. A 5,000-Year Record of Agriculture and Tropical Forest Clearance in the Tuxtlas, Veracruz, Mexico. *The Holocene* 8:83–89.

González-Lauck, Rebecca. 2008. La arqueología del mundo olmeca. In *Olmeca: Balance y perspectivas*, vol. II, edited by Maria T. Uriarte and Rebecca González-Lauck, pp. 397–410. UNAM, Instituto de Investigaciones Estéticas, México, D.F.

Grove, David C. 1997. Olmec Archaeology: A Half Century of Research and Its Accomplishments. *Journal of World Prehistory* 11:51–101.

Heizer, Robert F. 1968. New Observations on La Venta. In *Dumbarton Oaks Conference on the Olmec*, edited by Elizabeth P. Benson, pp. 9–36. Dumbarton Oaks, Washington, DC.

Joralemon, Peter D. 1971. *A Study of Olmec Iconography*. Studies in Pre-Columbian Art and Archaeology, no. 7. Dumbarton Oaks, Washington, DC.

Knight, Charles. 2003. Obsidian Production, Consumption, and Distribution at Tres Zapotes: Piecing Together Political Economy. In *Settlement Archaeology and Political Economy at Tres Zapotes, Veracruz, Mexico*, edited by Christopher. A. Pool, pp. 69–89. Monograph 50, Cotsen Institute of Archaeology, University of California at Los Angeles.

Kruger, Robert P. 1996. An Archaeological Survey in the Region of the Olmec, Veracruz, Mexico. PhD dissertation, Department of Anthropology, University of Pittsburgh.

Lentz, David L, Mary D. Pohl, José Luis Alvarado, Somayeh Tarighat, and Robert Bye. 2008. Sunflower (*Helianthus annuus* L.) as a Pre-Columbian Domesticate in Mexico. *Proceedings of the National Academy of Sciences USA* 105:6232–6237.

Lowe, Gareth W. 1989. The Heartland Olmec: Evolution of Material Culture. In *Regional Perspectives on the Olmec*, edited by Robert J. Sharer and David C. Grove, pp. 33–67. Cambridge University Press, Cambridge.

McCormack, Valerie J. 2002. Sedentism, Site Occupation, and Settlement Organization at La Joya, a Formative Village in the Sierra de los Tuxtlas, Veracruz, Mexico. PhD dissertation, Department of Anthropology, University of Pittsburgh.

Medellín Zenil, Alfonso. 1960. *Cerámicas del Totonacapan*. Universidad Veracruzana, Xalapa.

Ortiz Ceballos, Ponciano, Maria del Carmen Rodríguez M., and Afredo Delgado C. 1997. *Las investigaciones arqueológicas en el Cerro Sagrado Manatí*. Universidad Veracruzana, Xalapa, México.

Pohl, Mary E. D., Dolores R. Piperno, Kevin O. Pope, and John G. Jones. 2007. Microfossil Evidence for Pre-Columbian Maize Dispersals in the Neotropics from San Andrés, Tabasco, Mexico. *Proceedings of the National Academy of Sciences* 104:6870–6875.

Pool, Christopher A. 2007. *Olmec Archaeology and Early Mesoamerica*. Cambridge University Press, New York.

Pool, Christopher A. 2009. Asking More and Better Questions: Olmec Archeology for the Next *Katun*. *Ancient Mesoamerica* 20:241–252.

Pool, Christopher A., and Ponciano Ortiz Ceballos. 2008. Tres Zapotes como centro olmeca: nuevos datos. In *Olmeca: Balance y Perspectivas*, vol. II, edited by Maria T. Uriarte and Rebecca González-Lauck, pp. 425–443. UNAM, Instituto de Investigaciones Estéticas, México, D.F.

Pool, Christopher A., Ponciano Ortiz Ceballos, María del Carmen Rodríguez M., and Michael L. Loughlin. 2010. The Early Horizon at Tres Zapotes: Implications for Olmec Interaction. *Ancient Mesoamerica* 21:95–105.

Pope, Kevin O., Mary E. Pohl, John G. Jones, David L. Lentz, Christopher von Nagy, and Irvy Quitmyer. 2001. Early Agriculture in the Lowlands of Mesoamerica. *Science* 242:103–104.

Rojas Chávez, Juan Martín. 1990. Análisis preliminar de la industria de la lítica tallada de La Venta, Tabasco. *Arqueología* (enero-febrero) 3:25–32.

Rust, William F. 2008. A Settlement Survey of La Venta, Tabasco, Mexico. PhD dissertation, Department of Anthropology, University of Pennsylvania.

Sahagún, Fr. Bernardino de. 1938. *Historia general de las cosas de Nueva España*, Tomo III, Libros X y XI. Editorial Pedro Robredo, México, D.F.

Sanders, William T. 1952–1953. The Anthropogeography of Central Veracruz. In *Huastecos, Totonacos y sus vecinos*, edited by Ignacio Bernal, pp. 27–78. Revista Mexican de Estudios Antropológicos, Tomo XIII, 2 and 3. Sociedad Mexicana de Antropología, México, D.F.

Santley, Robert S., and Philip J. Arnold III. 1996. Prehispanic Settlement Patterns in the Tuxtla Mountains, Southern Veracruz, Mexico. *Journal of Field Archaeology* 23:225–249.

Santley, Robert S., Philip J. Arnold III, and Thomas P. Barrett.1997. Formative Period
    Settlement Patterns in the Tuxtla Mountains. In *Olmec to Aztec: Settlement Patterns
    in the Ancient Gulf Lowlands*, edited by Barbara L. Stark and Philip J. Arnold III, pp.
    174–205. University of Arizona Press, Tucson.
Santley, Robert S., Thomas P. Barrett, Michael D. Glascock, and Hector Neff. 2001.
    Pre-Hispanic Obsidian Procurement in the Tuxtla Mountains, Southern Veracruz,
    Mexico. *Ancient Mesoamerica* 12:49–63.
Sassaman, Kenneth E. 2004. Complex Hunter-Gatherers in Evolution and History:
    A North American Perspective. *Journal of Archaeological Research* 12:227–280.
Saville, Marshall H. 1929. Votive Axes from Ancient Mexico. *Indian Notes* VI:266–299,
    335–343. Museum of American Indian.
Scholes, France V., and Dave Warren. 1965. The Olmec Region at Spanish Contact. In
    Archaeology of Southern Mesoamerica, part 2, edited by Gordon R. Willey, pp.
    776–787. *Handbook of Middle American Indians*, volume 3, R. Wauchope, general
    editor. University of Texas Press, Austin.
Seinfeld, Daniel M., Christopher von Nagy, and Mary D. Pohl. 2009. Determining Olmec
    Maize Use through Bulk Stable Carbon Isotope Analysis. *Journal of Archaeological
    Science* 36:2560–2565.
Sluyter, Andrew, and Gabriela Dominguez. 2006. Early Maize (*Zea mays* L.) Cultivation
    in Mexico: Dating Sedimentary Pollen Record and Its Implications. *Proceedings of
    the National Academy of Science* 103:1147–1151.
Smith, Bruce D. 2006. Eastern North America as an Independent Center of Plant
    Domestication. *Proceedings of the National Academy of Science* 103:12223–12228.
Stark, Barbara L., Lynette Heller, Michael D. Glascock, J. Michael Elam, and Hector Neff.
    1992. Obsidian-Artifact Source Analysis for the Mixtequilla Region, South-Central
    Veracruz, Mexico. *Latin American Antiquity* 3:221–239.
Symonds, Stacey, Ann Cyphers, and Roberto Lunagómez. 2002. *Asentamiento
    prehispánico en San Lorenzo Tenochtitlán*. Universidad Nacional Autónoma de
    México, México, D.F.
Tedlock, Dennis, trans. 1985. *Popol Vuh: The Definitive Edition of the Mayan Book of the
    Dawn of Life and the Glories of Gods and Kings*. Simon and Schuster, New York.
VanDerwarker, Amber M. 2006. *Farming, Hunting, and Fishing in the Olmec World*.
    University of Texas Press, Austin.
Vázquez Zárate, Sergio R. 2007. *Las figurillas cerámicas del Horizonte Formativo en
    La Joya-Comoapan, región de Los Tuxtlas*. Tesis de Maestría, Escuela Nacional de
    Antropología e Historia, México, D.F.
von Nagy, Christopher. 2003. Of Meandering Rivers and Shifting Towns: Landscape
    Evolution and Community within the Grijalva Delta. PhD dissertation, Department
    of Anthropology, Tulane University, New Orleans.
Wendt, Carl J. 2003. Early Formative Domestic Organization and Community Patterning
    in the San Lorenzo Tenochtitlán region, Veracruz, Mexico. PhD dissertation,
    Department of Anthropology, Pennsylvania State University, University Park.
Wendt, Carl J. 2010. A San Lorenzo Phase Household Assemblage from El Remolino,
    Veracruz. *Ancient Mesoamerica* 21:107–122.

CHAPTER 14

THE DEVELOPMENT OF COMPLEX SOCIETIES IN FORMATIVE-PERIOD PACIFIC GUATEMALA AND CHIAPAS

MICHAEL LOVE

THE Pacific coastal plain stretching from Chiapas, Mexico, to El Salvador (Figure 14.1) has one of the richest Formative-period archaeological datasets in all of Mesoamerica. These data show that a trend of increasing complexity began soon at the end of the Archaic period and climaxed with the emergence of urbanism and early state societies during the Late Formative period. The long-term trajectory of increasing social complexity was not seamless, however, and there were significant disjunctions that suggest episodes of political cycling at various points within the sequence, manifested in the movement of political centers, economic reorganization, and changes in the ideological justifications of political power (Love 2002a).

Although bound together by geographical proximity and trade networks, the sites and districts of the coastal plain lacked unity in either political or cultural terms. Although frequently placed within the "Southern Maya Region," the coastal plain and piedmont was probably occupied by speakers of several languages during the Preclassic epoch (Josserand 2011). For many reasons, the coastal plain is

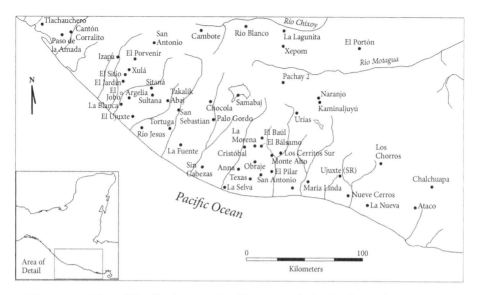

Figure 14.1 Map of Pacific Guatemala, Chiapas, and El Salvador with prominent
Formative-period sites.

best viewed as part of a multiethnic and multicultural interaction sphere that also
included the highlands of Chiapas and Guatemala.

THE ARCHAIC TO FORMATIVE TRANSITION

The emergence of social complexity in the Pacific coastal plain can be traced back
to changes in subsistence and economy that began in the Archaic period. The line
between the Archaic period and the earliest Formative is becoming increasingly
blurred as evidence shows that horticulture and partial sedentism emerged by the
Late Archaic, when cultivation supplemented the foraging economy. Large-scale
modification of the environment, especially the clearing and burning of forests,
accompanied the adoption of horticulture, according to data from pollen cores.

A series of cores found evidence of maize as well as other cultigens, including squash and arrowroot, prior to 3500 BC (Neff et al. 2006). The timing of forest clearance and initial cultivation is supported further by *Zea* phytoliths from a
clay floor dating to 3500 BC at the Tlacuachero shell mound (Jones and Voorhies
2004).Cores show significant increases in the levels of charcoal after 3500 BC, and
there were continued high levels through multiple episodes of forest burning up
to 2600 BC. Between 2500 BC and 2000 BC agricultural activity and forest disturbance declined, possibly in association with dessication. Many areas of the coast
show evidence of abandonment at around 2000 BC (Neff et al. 2006).

Although estuary shell middens are the most conspicuous Archaic sites on the coast, they were occupied only seasonally for the collection of specialized resources, while the cultivation of maize and other domesticates probably took place at permanent inland base camps such as Vuelta Limón (Voorhies 2004). If the evidence from Vuelta Limón can be generalized, the inland sites were central settlements that were occupied year-round but not for a great number of consecutive years.

THE EARLY FORMATIVE 1 (1900–1400 BC)

The beginnings of the Formative, marked by the first appearance of pottery, may bring about a greater visibility of archaeological sites but resulted in relatively few immediate changes in subsistence or patterns of mobility. The suggestion of Arnold (1999) that some early pottery users were still mobile and maintained many aspects of the Archaic period foraging strategy would explain the wide distribution and low concentration of early Formative ceramics.

The earliest ceramics on the coast are named the Barra and Madre Vieja complexes, dated to 1900–1600 BC. The two complexes are closely related and have complementary distributions, with Barra confined to coastal Chiapas and Madre Vieja to the central coast of Guatemala (Arroyo 2005; Clark and Cheetham 2005; Clark and Gosser 1995). The beauty and technological sophistication of this pottery has led some to deduce that the complexes represent a developed ceramic technology introduced from elsewhere (Coe 1961); others believe it is more likely that they represent the local adoption of ceramic technology rather than the emigration of potters (Clark and Gosser 1995). The equivocal evidence of drought and abandonment of the coast at the end of the Archaic leave open the possibility that the first Formative peoples were fresh emigrants who brought with them both pottery and a more stable horticultural adaptation.

Sedentism and an increasing reliance on cultivation of domesticates soon brought about an increase in population and the development of economic surpluses that enabled social inequality to be manifested as differences in wealth. By 1700 BC there are signs of differentiation among villages, with hierarchies defined by economics and religious ritual. The emergence of inequality and centralization is seen best in the Mazatán region of Chiapas, Mexico. Within that region several two-tiered settlement systems appeared by 1700 BC, suggesting a network of simple chiefdoms (Clark 2004). The early center of Paso de la Amada was laid out as a planned center, with buildings spaced along a central plaza and sharing the same orientation. Paso de la Amada was both a sacred place and a political center, possessing communal features that include an early ballcourt (Hill et al. 1998). A considerable amount of communal labor was used to construct that feature as well as other central buildings, which may be either elite residences or public buildings.

Paso de la Amada is for the moment the earliest known ceremonial center on the Pacific coastal plain and in Mesoamerica, but it is likely that other such settlements existed. Most important, however, the data from the Mazatán show the impact of the horticultural economy and sedentism on Formative-period societies. A course of increasing sociopolitical complexity had begun and the speed of change increased once again as the second half of the Early Formative began.

THE EARLY FORMATIVE 2 (1400–1000 BC)

The early Mazatán chiefdoms endured for several hundred years but an important disjunction occurred soon after 1400 BC, when new paramount settlements were established and new material cultural forms appeared. There are crucial data lacking for the latter part of the Early Formative period, but the major sites of Cantón Corralito and Ojo de Agua appear to represent successive capitals of a large regional polity.

Cantón Corralito became the Mazatán region's largest site after the decline of Paso de la Amada. Pottery and figurines indicate that Cantón Corralito had strong connections with San Lorenzo, Veracruz, and it has been suggested that it was a "colonial outpost" of the early Gulf Coast center (Cheetham 2006). It may be that people from San Lorenzo resided at Cantón Corralito, but undetermined is the nature of the colony, its size, and its relationship to the local population. At present we cannot determine whether the "Olmec" objects were used only by the elite or by wider sectors of the populace. If people from the Gulf Coast did reside at Cantón Corralito, it is unclear if they were elites or simply craftspeople contracted by local rulers. It is just as likely that any "colony" was established by groups fleeing San Lorenzo as it is that they represented it.

At about 1100 BC Cantón Corralito declined and was replaced by Ojo de Agua as the primary regional center of Mazatán. The extent of the site exceeded 100 hectares, although its precise boundaries have not been mapped. Tall mounds, prototypes of the pyramidal form common in Mesoamerica, surrounded a central plaza (Clark and Hodgson 2004). Sculptures from Ojo de Agua and the surrounding region form the only significant corpus of Olmec-style sculpture outside of the Gulf Coast for this time period.

THE MIDDLE FORMATIVE (1000–400 BC)

The Middle Formative period was a time of incipient urbanism throughout Mesoamerica. In the Pacific coast region, the period is marked by denser populations as well as larger overall settlement size, driven by a significant population boom in both the coast and the highlands (Love 2011). There were population losses in some areas at the end of the Early Formative, such as in the Mazatán region, but those losses reflect the political fortunes of specific sites and were highly localized. Even in regions lacking intensive surveys, such as the piedmont, the higher visibility of Middle Formative sites is notable.

In Middle Formative times many political systems straddled the classificatory divide between chiefdoms and states, if neoevolutionary categories are to be used. By most standards the largest polities would probably be called complex chiefdoms, but they have many attributes of states including incipient urbanism, administrative bureaucracies (reflected in more structured regional hierarchies), and rigid social stratification.

During the Middle Formative, major centers emerged along trade routes that included the Valley of Guatemala, coastal Escuintla, western Guatemala, and western El Salvador. Between these clusters, political centralization appears to have been absent or minimal. Beaudry-Corbett (2002) notes a lack of large centralized polities on the Guatemalan central coast, immediately west of the Escuintla region, during the Middle Formative, while intensive surveys on the Guatemalan eastern coast revealed only sparse occupation during that time (Estrada Belli 2002; Estrada Belli et al. 1996, 1998; Kaplan 2008; Kosakowsky et al. 2000). Excavations at the piedmont site of Chocolá have detected a Middle Formative occupation, but its extent is uncertain (Kaplan 2008; Kaplan and Valdés 2004; Valdés et al. 2004).

The Valley of Guatemala is discussed by Bárbara Arroyo elsewhere in this volume, so the present discussion is limited to the piedmont and Pacific coastal plain.

The Escuintla Region in the Middle Formative

A cluster of large settlements with public architecture developed in the Escuintla region during the Middle Formative. The sites of El Bálsamo, Monte Alto, Cristóbal, and La Morena (Bove 1989; Clewlow and Wells 1987; Shook and Hatch 1978) were all substantial settlements. Both El Bálsamo and Monte Alto have been intensively excavated, but final data have not been published. It is difficult to say more than that they appear to be centers of regional polities, although the centers and their polities were smaller than those of the Valley of Guatemala or the western Guatemala coast.

The Western Guatemalan Coast in the Middle Formative

Two major centers with large polities appear to have emerged in western Pacific Guatemala during the Middle Formative. In the piedmont zone, Takalik Abaj rose sui generis, while on the coastal plain, La Blanca developed as the heir to the earlier Mazatán political systems.

Takalik Abaj

The first substantial occupation of Takalik Abaj occurred in the Middle Formative, manifested in the Riachuelo ceramic complex, tentatively dated to 800-600 BC (Popenoe de Hatch et al. 2011). Excavations in the central zone of the site show that low platforms were built at this time, but the overall extent of the site has not been determined, and domestic structures have not been excavated. The most impressive manifestation of Middle Formative occupation at Takalik Abaj remains its corpus of sculpture (Graham et al. 1978; Schieber de Lavarreda and Orrego Corzo 2002, 2010). The corpus that can be stylistically dated to the Middle Formative includes petroglyphs (Monuments 1 and 64), heads (Monument 16/17), and sculpture in the round (Monument 55, 42). Less certain is the dating of other pieces such as Monuments 14, 15, and 23. Also difficult to place is Stela 50, which shows the Middle Formative niche-figure theme. Stela 50 bears a badly damaged initial series date whose ISIG shows the same curvilinear style as Tres Zapotes Stela C, suggesting that it dates to Baktun 7.

La Blanca

La Blanca developed following the collapse of the Ojo de Agua polity in Mazatán, at 1000 BC, and it appears to be in the line of polities that began with Paso de la Amada. It was the largest settlement of a complex regional system covering over 300 square kilometers and had incorporating at least eighty other settlements in a multitiered hierarchy (Love 2002b). The La Blanca polity may have extended west of the Río Suchiate and incorporated several small centers with low public mounds (Rosenswig 2005).

La Blanca's core was a 100-hectare area of terrain raised and leveled by over 2 meters of fill. A large acropolis west of the main plaza was raised an additional 2 meters and a smaller acropolis of elite residences was built east of the plaza. The main ceremonial buildings in the core shared a common orientation and the central axis of the site aligned with the tallest peak in Central America, the Tajumulco Volcano. The largest construction at the site, Mound 1, was over 25 meters in height, measuring 100 by 150 meters at its base. Constructed soon after 1000 BC, it was one of the earliest monumental temple pyramids in Mesoamerica. The total area of occupation at La Blanca covered at least 280 hectares, with dense occupation at the site core and more dispersed occupation at the outskirts. Few stone sculptures have been discovered at the site, but a unique earthen quatrefoil-shaped altar was discovered in association with an elite residence (Love and Guernsey 2007).

Economic Intensification and Exchange Systems of the Middle Formative

Economic intensification provided the material base for the expansion of elite power and the means to finance monumental public works during the Middle Formative. Data from La Blanca show that key elements of subsistence intensification were the increased consumption of maize and the use of the domesticated dog as a protein source (Love 1999).

The selection for increased cob size and number of rows was certainly part of the increased importance of maize to the Middle Formative economy. Improved maize provided the maximum return on labor, and the possibility of growing multiple crops each year further enhanced its productivity. The increased use of dogs, the only domesticated animal food source for the period, also reflects a maximizing strategy that minimized the amount of labor expended on food procurement. These two food sources helped support larger populations, and they also provided surpluses that financed public constructions and monumental art. Control of the subsistence surpluses also financed prestige goods consumption by the elite and stimulated interregional exchange.

Several authors have proposed that a reorganization of pan-Mesoamerican social and economic relationships took place at the beginning of the Middle Formative. David Grove (1989) proposed that increased trade in, and competition for, prestige goods resulted in formal alliances among centers. Arthur Demarest (1989) sees the Middle Formative as an era of greater interregional contact, reflected in the exchange of materials such as jade and obsidian, as well as in shared iconography.

One of the most significant aspects of the Middle Formative is that monumental sculpture in the Olmec style is found in large quantities outside the Gulf Coast. During the Middle Formative we find Olmec-style sculpture in the Central Highlands of Mexico and all along the Pacific coast as far south as El Salvador (Figure 14.2). Of particular interest is that while many of the Middle Formative sculptures in Pacific Guatemala resemble those of the Gulf Coast, they aren't simply copies. There is clearly a regional style and forms in region are not found elsewhere. This is true not only in the formal sense, but also in iconography, where we see symbols and meanings that are not found in the Gulf Coast sites. These regional manifestations indicate that people in Mesoamerica outside of the Gulf Coast were actively engaged in creating aspects of the Olmec style.

THE LATE FORMATIVE (400 BC–200 AD)

The trajectory of increasing urbanization and sociopolitical centralization climaxed in the Late Formative period with the development of fully urban states throughout much of the coastal plain as well as the highlands (Love 2011). Late Formative cities were both larger and more numerous than those of the Middle Formative, and they occurred over a larger area, stretching from the western boundaries of the Soconusco to El Salvador.

Figure 14.2 Middle Formative sculptures. (a) Shook Altar, from near San Antonio Suchitepequez, Guatemala; (b) Takalik Abaj Monument 42; (c) Takalik Abaj Monument 16/17; (d) Takalik Abaj Monument 55; (e) Takalik Abaj Monument 1; (f) Takalik Abaj Monument 14; (g) La Blanca Monument 1; (h) La Blanca Monument 3. Photograph "a" by Edwin M. Shook; photographs "b" and "f" courtesy of John A. Graham. All other photographs by the author.

During the Late Formative period the southern highlands and Pacific coast of Guatemala were filled by large settlements, the largest of which were urban and the capitals of small states. These city-states were linked by local and long-distance trade systems and had shared many elements of material culture. This region of interaction among emerging urban centers has been described as the Southern City-State Culture (Love 2011). The early states of the region (Kaminaljuyú, Takalik

Abaj, El Ujuxte, and Izapa, and possibly others such as Chalchuapa and Chocolá)
are best considered as city-states, or micro-states, with sustaining hinterlands generally under 1000 square kilometers.

Each of the major urban centers covered over 4 square kilometers and had a
ceremonial core of massive construction, generally exceeding 1 square kilometer.
Each had several large formal plazas within which public rituals might have been
staged. Sites such as Kaminaljuyú, Takalik, and Izapa have large and stylistically
heterogeneous bodies of sculpture that depict the actions of rulers and supernaturals (Guernsey 2006) (Figure 14.3).

Figure 14.3 Late Formative Stelae. (a) Takalik Abaj Stela 1; (b) Takalik Abaj Stela 4; (c)
Takalik Abaj Stela 5; (d) Takalik Abaj Stela 50; (e) Kaminaljuyú Stela 10; (f) Kaminaljuyú
Stela 11; (g) El Baul Stela 1; (h) Izapa Stela 1 with Altar 1. Photographs "c" and "g" cour-
tesy of John A. Graham; "h" courtesy of Julia Guernsey; all others by author.

The major urban centers each governed a polity having a well-defined hierarchy with at least four tiers, suggesting a complex governmental structure consistent with the definition of a state. The Izapa and Takalik Abaj polities each had at least four levels and covered over 400 square kilometers. The El Ujuxte polity covered over 600 square kilometers and encompassed at least five levels. Within the El Ujuxte polity the secondary centers each have small-scale copies of El Ujuxte's ceremonial core, while the third- and fourth-level sites have other forms of public architecture.

High Culture in the Late Formative Period

The Late Formative period is sometimes described as a time of increased regionalization but in southern Mesoamerica and particularly in the Pacific coast region, regional interaction and trade intensified. Interaction went well beyond trade, however, especially in the areas of high culture such as art, calendrics, writing, and political ideology.

While there are regional variations in forms and themes (Figure 14.4), stone sculpture on the Late Formative Pacific coast emphasizes a number of shared themes, especially the representation of myth, links between rulers and myths of creation, and the performance of ritual. Late Preclassic depictions of rulers share a distinctive visual system of communication that cuts across possible ethnic and linguistic boundaries (Guernsey 2011). Even in sites without large bodies of sculpture, similar ideologies were expressed through architecture, site layouts, and public ritual (Guernsey and Love 2005).

THE LATE PRECLASSIC COLLAPSE

The remarkable florescence of the Late Formative Southern City-State Culture ended abruptly during the second century CE. Although the Late Formative collapse affected much of southern Mesoamerica, as seen in the decline of lowland Maya centers such as El Mirador, Cival, and Cerros, the manifestation was particularly strong in the southern highlands and on the coastal plain. Unlike the cities of the Maya lowlands to the north, much of the south did not recover, as evidenced in how many areas of the Pacific coastal plain had lacked all trace of Early Classic occupation (Love 2007). Many of the major cities, such as Kaminaljuyú, Izapa, and Takalik Abaj survived into the Classic period but in different and perhaps diminished form from their Late Formative apogees. Others, such as El Ujuxte, were to lay abandoned for nearly five hundred years.

The available data suggest dessication and possible drought as the ultimate causes of the collapse. The pollen and phytolith data (Braswell and Robinson 2011;

Figure 14.4 (a) Potbelly (Monument 108) from Takalik Abaj; (b) Potbelly (Monument 41) from Takalik Abaj; (c) Potbelly (Monument 11) from Monte Alto; (d) Potbelly from Kaminaljuyú (Monument 8); (e) Pedestal sculpture (Monument 1 from La Argelia, Quetzaltenango); (f) Pedestal sculpture (from near Champerico, Retalhuleu); (g) Toad altar (Altar 1 from San Sebastian); (h) Altar with human image (Altar 1 from Las Conchitas, Quetzaltenango). All photographs by the author.

Neff et al. 2006; Popenoe de Hatch et al. 2002) are not completely convincing at the moment, but settlement data point strongly toward drought (Love 2007). The outer coastal plain, which has the lowest rainfall in the Pacific region, was abandoned rapidly at the end of the Formative period, while sites within the piedmont belt, which has much higher rainfall, survived. The abandonment of the coastal plain ultimately caused the collapse of the Late Preclassic trade networks that highland sites, including Kaminaljuyú, depended upon for their wealth.

REFERENCES

Arnold, Phillip J. 1999. Tecomates, Residential Mobility, and Early Formative Occupation in Coastal Lowland Mesoamerica. In *Pottery and People: A Dynamic Interaction*, edited by James M. Skibo and Gary M. Feinman, pp. 159–170. University of Utah Press, Salt Lake City.

Arroyo, Bárbara. 2005. Relaciones entre vecinos: El Formativo Temprano en el sureste de mesoamérica. In *Paper presented at the XIX Simposio de Investitaciones Arqueológicas en Guatemala, 2005*. Museo Nacional de Arqueología y Etnología, Guatemala.

Beaudry-Corbett, Marilyn. 2002. The Tiquisate Archaeological Zone: A Case of Delayed Societal Complexity? In *Incidents of Archaeology in Central America and Yucatán: Studies in Honor of Edwin M. Shook*, edited by Michael W. Love, Marion Popenoe de Hatch, and Héctor L. Escobedo, pp. 75–102. University Press of America, Lanham, Maryland.

Bove, Frederick J. 1989. *Formative Settlement Patterns on the Pacific Coast of Guatemala: A Spatial Analysis of Complex Societal Evolution*. BAR International Series Number 493. British Archaeological Reports, Oxford.

Braswell, Geoffrey E., and Eugenia J. Robinson. 2011. The Eastern Cakchiquel Highlands during the Preclassic Period: Interaction, Growth, and Depopulation. In *The Southern Maya in the Late Preclassic: The Rise and Fall of an Early Mesoamerican Civilization*, edited by Michael Love and Jonathan Kaplan, 287–315. University Press of Colorado, Boulder.

Cheetham, David. 2006. The America's First Colony? A Possible Olmec Outpost in Southern Mexico. *Archaeology* 59:42–45.

Clark, John E. 2004. Mesoamerica Goes Public: Early Ceremonial Centers, Leaders, and Communities. In *Mesoamerican Archaeology*, edited by Julia A. Hendon and Rosemary A. Joyce, pp. 43–72. Blackwell, Oxford.

Clark, John E., and David Cheetham. 2005. Cerámica formativa de Chiapas. In *La Producción alfarera en el México antiguo, Volume I*, edited by Beatrice L. Merion Carrión and Angel. García Cook, pp. 285–433. Colección Científica, no. 484. Instituto Nacional de Antropologia e Historia, México, D.F.

Clark, John E., and Dennis Gosser. 1995. Reinventing Mesoamerica's First Pottery. In *The Emergence of Pottery: Technology and Innovation in Ancient Societies*, edited by William. Barnett and John Hoopes, pp. 209–221. Smithsonian Institution Press, Washington, DC.

Clark, John E., and John G. Hodgson. 2004. A Millennium of Wonders in Coastal Mesoamerica. Paper presented at the annual meeting of the American Anthropological Association, Atlanta, Georgia.

Clewlow, C. William, and Helen F. Wells. 1987. El Balsamo: A Middle Preclassic Complex on the South Coast of Guatemala. In *The Periphery of the Southeastern Classic Maya Realm*, edited by Gary W. Pahl, pp. 27–40. UCLA Latin American Center Publications, Los Angeles.

Coe, Michael D. 1961. *La Victoria, An Early Site on the Pacific Coast of Guatemala*. Papers of the Peabody Museum of Archaeology and Ethnology LIII. Peabody Museum, Harvard University, Cambridge.

Demarest, Arthur A. 1989. The Olmec and the Rise of Civilization in Eastern Mesoamerica. In *Regional Perspectives on the Olmec*, edited by Robert. J. Sharer and David C. Grove, pp. 303–344. Cambridge University Press, Cambridge.

Estrada Belli, Francisco. 2002. Putting Santa Rosa on the Map: New Insights on the
    Cultural Development of the Pacific Coast of Southeastern Guatemala. In *Incidents
    of Archaeology in Central America and Yucatán: Studies in Honor of Edwin M.
    Shook*, edited by Michael W. Love, Marion Popenoe de Hatch, and Héctor L.
    Escobedo, pp. 103–128. University Press of America, Lanham, Maryland.

Estrada Belli, Francisco, Laura J. Kosakowsky, and Marc Wolf. 1998. El lugar de Santa
    Rosa en el mapa arqueológico de Guatemala: Desarrollo de sociedades complejas en
    la costa sureste de Guatemala. In *XI Simposio de Investigaciones Arqueológicas en
    Guatemala*, edited by Juan P. Laporte and Héctor L. Escobedo, pp. 319–338. vol. 1.
    Ministerio de Cultura y Deportes, Instituto de Antropología e Historia, Asociación
    Tikal, Guatemala.

Estrada Belli, Francisco, Laura J. Kosakowsky, Marc Wolf, and Damian Blank. 1996.
    Patrones de asentamiento y de uso de la tierra desde el Preclásico al Postclásico en
    la costa del Pacífico de Guatemala: La arqueología de Santa Rosa 1995. *Mexicon*
    XVIII(6):110–115.

Graham, John A., Robert F. Heizer, and Edwin M. Shook. 1978. Abaj Takalik 1976:
    Exploratory Investigations. *Contributions of the University of California
    Archaeological Research Facility* 36:85–113.

Grove, David C. 1989. Chalcatzingo and Its Olmec Connection. In *Regional Perspectives
    on the Olmec*, edited by Robert J. Sharer and David C. Grove, pp. 122–147.
    Cambridge University Press, New York.

Guernsey, Julia. 2006. *Ritual and Power in Stone: The Performance of Rulership in
    Mesoamerican Izapan-Style Art*. University of Texas Press, Austin.

Guernsey, Julia. 2011. Signifying Late Preclassic Rulership: Patterns of Continuity from
    the Southern Maya Zone. In *The Southern Maya in the Late Preclassic: The Rise and
    Fall of an Early Mesoamerican Civilization*, edited by Michael Love and Jonathan
    Kaplan, pp 115–138. University Press of Colorado, Boulder.

Guernsey, Julia, and Michael Love. 2005. Late Preclassic Expressions of Authority on the
    Pacific Slope. In *Lords of Creation: The Origins of Sacred Maya Kingship*, edited by
    Virginia M. Fields and Dorie Reents-Budet, pp. 37–43. Los Angeles County Museum
    of Art, Los Angeles.

Hill, Warren, Michael Blake, and John E. Clark. 1998. Ball Court Design Dates Back
    3,400 Years. *Nature* 302(6679):878–879.

Jones, John G., and Barbara Voorhies. 2004. Human and Plant Interactions. In *Coastal
    Collectors in the Holocene: The Chantuto People of Southwest Mexico*, edited by
    Barbara Voorhies, pp. 300–343. University of Florida Press, Gainesville.

Josserand, J. Kathryn. 2011. Languages of the Preclassic Period along the Pacific Coastal
    Plains of Southeastern Mesoamerica. In *The Southern Maya in the Late Preclassic*,
    edited by Michael Love and Jonathan Kaplan, pp. 141–174. University Press of
    Colorado, Boulder.

Kaplan, Jonathan. 2008. Hydraulics, Cacao and Complex Developments at Preclassic
    Chocolá, Guatemala: Evidence and Implications. *Latin American Antiquity*
    19:399–413.

Kaplan, Jonathan, and Juan Antonio Valdés. 2004. Chocolá, an Apparent Regional
    Capital in the Southern May Preclassic: Preliminary Findings from the Proyecto
    Arqueológico Chocolá (PACH). *Mexicon* XXVI(4):77–86.

Kosakowsky, Laura J., Francisco Estrada Belli, and Paul Pettitt. 2000. Preclassic through
    Postclassic: The Chronological History of the Southeastern Pacific Coast of
    Guatemala. *Ancient Mesoamerica* 11(2):1–17.

Love, Michael W. 1999. Economic Patterns in the Development of Complex Society in Pacific Guatemala. In *Pacific Latin America in Prehistory: The Evolution of Archaic and Formative Cultures*, edited by Michael Blake, pp. 89–100. Washington State University, Washington.

Love, Michael W. 2002a. Domination, Resistance and Political Cycling in Formative Period Pacific Guatemala. In *The Dynamics of Power*, edited by Maria O'Donovan, pp. 214–237. Occasional Paper No. 30. Center for Archaeological Investigations, Southern Illinois University, Carbondale.

Love, Michael W. 2002b. *Early Complex Society in Pacific Guatemala: Settlements and Chronology of the Río Naranjo, Guatemala*. Papers of the New World Archaeological Foundation 66. Brigham Young University, Provo.

Love, Michael W. 2007. Recent Research in the Southern Highlands and Pacific Coast of Mesoamerica. *Journal of Archaeological Research* 15:275–328.

Love, Michael W. 2011. Cities, States and City-State Culture in the Late Preclassic Southern Maya Region. In *The Southern Maya in the Late Preclassic: The Rise and Fall of an Early Mesoamerican Civilization*, edited by Michael Love and Jonathan Kaplan, pp. 47–75. University Press of Colorado, Boulder.

Love, Michael, and Julia Guernsey. 2007. Monument 3 from La Blanca, Guatemala: A Middle Preclassic Earthen Sculpture and Its Ritual Associations. *Antiquity* 81:920–932.

Neff, Hector, Deborah Pearsall, John G. Jones, Bárbara Arroyo, Shawn Collins, and Dorothy E. Freidel. 2006. Early Maya Adaptive Patterns: Mid-Late Holocene Paleoenvironmental Evidence from Pacific Guatemala. *Latin American Antiquity* 17(3):287–315.

Neff, Hector, Deborah M. Pearsall, John G. Jones, Bárbara Arroyo, and Dorothy E. Freidel. 2006. Climate Change and Population History in the Pacific Lowlands of Southern Mesoamerica. *Quarternary Research* 65:390–400.

Popenoe de Hatch, Marion, Erick M. Ponciano, Tomás Barrientos Q., Mark Brenner, and Charles Ortloff. 2002. Climate and Technological Innovation at Kaminaljuyu, Guatemala. *Ancient Mesoamerica* 13:103–114.

Popenoe de Hatch, Marion, Christa Schieber de Lavarreda, and Miguel Orrego Corzo. 2011. Late Preclassic Developments at Takalik Abaj, Department of Retalhuleu, Guatemala. In *The Southern Maya in the Late Preclassic: The Rise and Fall of an Early Mesoamerican Civilization*, edited by Michael Love and Jonathan Kaplan, pp. 203–236. University Press of Colorado, Boulder.

Rosenswig, Robert M. 2005. From the Land between Swamps: Cuauhtémoc in an Early Olmec World. PhD dissertation, Yale University, New Haven.

Schieber de Lavarreda, Christa, and Miguel Orrego Corzo. 2002. *Abaj Takalik*. Proyecto Nacional Abaj Takalik, Guatemala.

Schieber de Lavarreda, Christa, and Miguel Orrego Corzo. 2010. Preclassic Olmec and Maya Monuments and Architecture at Takalik Abaj. In *The Place of Stone Monuments: Context, Use and Meaning in Mesoamerica's Preclassic Transition*, edited by J. Guernsey, John E. Clark, and Bárbara Arroyo, pp. 177–205. Dumbarton Oaks Research Library and Collection, Washington, DC.

Shook, Edwin M., and Marion Popenoe de Hatch. 1978. The Ruins of El Balsamo. In *Journal of New World Archaeology*. vol. III. Institute of Archaeology, UCLA, Los Angeles.

Valdés, Juan Antonio, Jonathan Kaplan, Oscar Gutiérrez, Juan Pablo Herrera, and Frederico Paredes Umaña. 2004. Chocolá: Un centro intermedio entre la boca costa y el altiplano de Guatemala durante el Preclásico Tardío. In *XVII Simposio de Investigaciones Arqueológicas en Guatemala*, edited by Juan P. Laporte, Bárbara Arroyo, Héctor L. Escobedo, and Héctor E. Mejía, pp. 449–460. Ministerio de Cultura y Deportes, Instituto de Antropología e Historia, Asociación Tikal, Guatemala.

Voorhies, Barbara. 2004. *Coastal Collectors in the Holocene: The Chantuto People of Southwest Mexico*. University of Florida Press, Gainesville.

CHAPTER 15

IDEOLOGY, POLITY, AND SOCIAL HISTORY OF THE TEOTIHUACAN STATE

SABURO SUGIYAMA

THE development of early complex societies in the Central Mexican Highlands resulted in particular local traditions. The region twice served as the heartland for densely populated ancient cities—Teotihuacan and Tenochtitlan—the populations of which are estimated to have been between 100,000–150,000 and 150,000–200,000 people, respectively (Millon 1973; Sanders 1981). There seem to have been underlying local circumstances that favored the development of populous complex societies at an unprecedented scale in this region.

THE NATURAL AND SOCIAL ENVIRONMENT OF THE CENTRAL MEXICAN HIGHLANDS

The highlands, at an elevation of roughly 2,000 meters above sea level (asl), have a particularly rich natural environment characterized by alluvial plains and lakes surrounded by volcanic mountain ranges. The temperate climate and an average annual rainfall of 450–900 millimeters mean that the area is well suited for agriculture. The region's wide variety of plants and animals were intensively exploited by ancient people. The scheduling of gathering, hunting, and agricultural activities would have been determined by the highly contrasting rainy and dry seasons. Locally available materials like rocks and minerals (particularly obsidian), water from lakes, reeds, salt, wood, and cacti were used for construction, tools, ornamentation, food preparation, and rituals, enhancing the quality of everyday life.

Fundamental to social development were the abundant plants and animals exploited for food. The Central Mexican Highlands are particularly rich in living resources. A wide variety of plants were domesticated simultaneously at least since 5000 BC. During the Formative and Early Classic periods, advanced agricultural technologies, such as irrigation and terracing, were applied to consistently obtain sufficient amounts of a variety of foods—corn, beans, squash, tomato, amaranth, chili peppers, prickly pear cactus, and chia—to maintain populous communities (McClung de Tapia 1992). Raised agricultural fields, or chinampas, a unique and effective agricultural system developed to recover land from lakes or swamps in the Central Highlands, seem to have sustained increasing populations. It is often argued that only turkey and dogs were domesticated in Mesoamerica. However, widely diversified animals, including small game, were also abundant enough to be intensively exploited, including deer, peccaries, rabbits, and a variety of insects, frogs, freshwater fish, and waterfowl (Valadez 1999).

The long interaction process between particularly diversified natural resources and people in this lagoon region was fundamental to the development of early social organizations. The archaeological records suggest that the population and social complexity in the basin increased with the exploitation of resources and the development of other technological and organizational advances for ceramic production, obsidian, and other craft industries, as well as market economies (Clark and Parry 1991). Several populous villages were consequently established by the Middle Formative period (Sanders et al. 1979), when intra- and interregional relations also became critical to the development of complex societies. Large communities in the Central Highlands (Tlatilco, Las Bocas, Zohapilco, Chalcatzingo) exhibit features from distant Olmec centers on the Gulf Coast (Benson and Fuente 1996). By the Late Formative, Cuicuilco, Tlapacoya, and Cholula had become large nucleated villages or regional centers with monumental architecture.

Cuicuilco, on the southwestern lagoon plain in the Basin of Mexico, became the first urban center during the Late Formative period with 20,000 inhabitants. The site consists of a truncated, cone-shaped main monument (ca. 160-meter diameter) (Figure 15.1), smaller platforms of various shapes, houses, and plazas. The center functioned for centuries as a large ceremonial precinct until it was destroyed by lava from the Xitle volcano (Cummings 1933).

At present, 5 to 7 meters of lava cover most of the ancient city, making it nearly impossible to excavate and resulting in inconclusive interpretations regarding the center. The placement of the main monument suggests its solstitial significance (Sprajc 2001). Several dates have been proposed for the eruption of the Xitle

Figure 15.1 The main monument of Cuicuilco.

volcano, including 1 AD, 200 AD, and 400 AD. The eruption would not necessarily have caused the emergence of Teotihuacan as some have argued (Cordova et al. 1994; Heizer and Bennyhoff 1972; Pastrana 1997). If it erupted later, Cuicuilco coexisted with Teotihuacan for at least a few centuries, either as an allied or rival center. The eruption of the Popocatepetl volcano around the year 1 appears to have affected communities in the Valley of Mexico and Puebla, like Tetimpa (Plunket and Uruñuela 2006). The eruption also would have caused regionwide fires affecting the distribution of plants and animals, the relocation of people, and precipitating changes in worldview.

The Ancient City of Teotihuacan

Teotihuacan emerged as one of the most populous and stratified cities in the New World during the first two centuries AD (Millon et al. 1973). People living in the densely populated city for more than four centuries created a new religious ideology and political structure, invented new technologies, and developed social organizations that were larger and more complex than previous ones (Berlo 1992; Carrasco et al. 2000). In order to understand why and how the city developed in this particular area, at such an unprecedented scale, we must examine the specific components of its social and historical context.

Teotihuacan is well known for its monuments: the Sun Pyramid, the Moon Pyramid, and the Citadel's Feathered Serpent Pyramid (FSP) (Gamio 1922). They were apparently complementary elements of a planned city that harmoniously integrated other public buildings as well as numerous residential compounds along the Avenue of the Dead with the surrounding topography (Figure 15.2). More

Figure 15.2 The Sun Pyramid (right) and the Moon Pyramid (left, top) with the Avenue
of the Dead and "Cerro Gordo" mountain behind the Moon Pyramid.

than 2,000 apartment compounds were constructed, oriented to Teotihuacan
north. We have evidence for "barrios" occupied by people from distant areas like
Oaxaca, Veracruz, and northwestern Mexico, confirming the multiethnic nature
of the metropolis (Gómez 2002; Millon 1981; Spence 1992). Although a significant
number of buildings have been excavated, many themes require further investigation, including identification of the dominant ethnic groups, the language
spoken, conditions of urban life, the development of new sociopolitical organizations, the writing system, and state ideology (Pasztory 1997; Rattray 1992; Storey
1992; Taube 2001).

Recent excavations at the three major monuments provide new perspectives. Excavations at the Citadel and FSP revealed three construction stages:
pre-Citadel, Citadel-FSP, and semidetached platform (Cabrera et al.1991,
Gazzola 2009; Sugiyama 2005). At the Moon Pyramid, seven superimposed
structures have been documented inside the pyramid and designated Buildings
1–7, from the earliest to latest (Figure 15.3). In addition, five sacrificial burial
complexes with exceptionally rich offerings were discovered inside the pyramid
(Sugiyama and Cabrera 2007; Sugiyama and López 2007). New excavations at
the Sun Pyramid uncovered three construction stages: pre–Sun Pyramid, Sun
Pyramid Stage 1, and Sun Pyramid Stage 2 (Matos 1995; Sugiyama and Sarabia
2011). These modification processes reflect changing state politics, and the
contents of the associated burials or offerings represent state ideology and the
nature of the government.

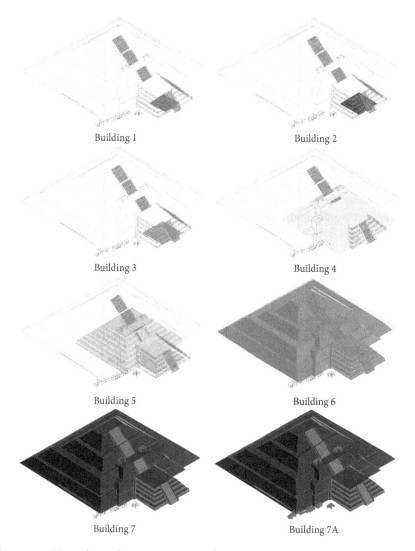

Figure 15.3 Hypothetical reconstruction of seven overlapping stages revealed at the Moon Pyramid.

THE BEGINNING OF TEOTIHUACAN

Based on the spatial distribution of early ceramics recovered from the surface, the population of the Teotihuacan Valley lived in small villages primarily on swampy lands near springs during the Cuanalan phase. The planned city of Teotihuacan seems to have developed rather quickly as a regional ritual center during the Patlachique phase. The area of greatest ceramic concentration shifted to the northern part of the city, and the area of the major monuments (Cowgill 1992).

Excavations at the Moon Pyramid revealed a pyramidal platform dated to the end of the Patlachique phase. Building 1 deviated about 4 degrees from the standard orientation followed throughout the city in later periods and likely predates the layout of the city as we see it today.

The remains of a large public structure predating the Sun Pyramid were identified during a recent exploration in 2010. The building consisted of a thick, long wall covered with plaster. Recent excavations in the Citadel have also revealed an architectural compound that existed prior to the construction of the Citadel and the FSP. These data indicate that the city began, under strong governmental control, as a public, ceremonial complex with a layout that was quite different from the one we see today. Most of these earlier structures were demolished when a grand-scale construction program began around 200 AD.

CITY LAYOUT AND THREE PRINCIPAL MONUMENTS

The Tzacualli and Miccaotli phases are notable for the large-scale changes in the layout of the city (Figure 15.4). By the end of the Tzacualli phase, which we now believe to have been around 200 AD based on radiocarbon dating, the urban area increased to approximately 20 square kilometers, with about 60,000 to 80,000 inhabitants living in the city (Millon 1981: 221). This unique citywide construction program could have been carried out to materialize a worldview that structured sacred urban space during the following centuries. The program integrated the three major monuments: the first stage of the Sun Pyramid, Building 4 of the Moon Pyramid, and the Citadel and FSP. Teotihuacan's leaders accomplished this citywide plan as a continuous or simultaneous event based on a master plan that started around 200 AD. However, the time span for this long-term construction program is still to be defined precisely, as the latest analyses of early ceramics and C14 samples suggest significantly varied absolute dates (Sugiyama et al. 2012).

The Teotihuacan grid system was rigorously set at 15.5 degrees east of astronomical north. Teotihuacan west follows a sight line to the setting of certain planets and stars on particular days, including the azimuth to the sunset at the western horizon on August 12 and April 29 (Aveni 1980, Dow 1967, Malmstrom 1978). The interval between these dates is 105 and 260 days, representing a complete cycle in the ritual calendar used throughout Mesoamerica. The setting sun on August 12 would also have commemorated the legendary date on which the present era began. The date coincides with the initial day of the Maya Long Count calendar, August 12, 3114 BC, the day when time and space were created (Drucker 1977). Thus, profound cosmogonic significance was explicitly and coherently incorporated into the city layout.

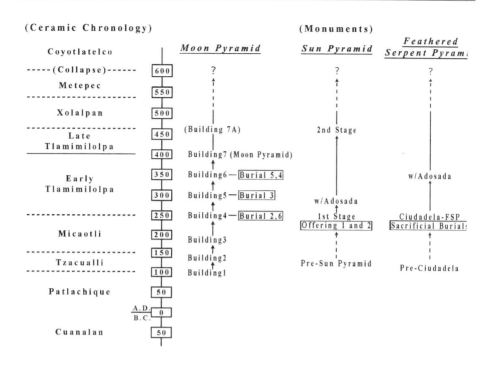

Figure 15.4 Chronology table of Teotihuacan with the modification process for three major monuments.

Analysis of the measurement unit used for Teotihuacan constructions indicates Teotihuacan's leaders were concerned with celestial bodies and the calendar system. Based on the city's spatial distribution, a basic measuring unit of 83 centimeters appears to have been used. The dimensions of monumental structures and the distances between them were determined based on specific multiples of this unit, in numbers important to the Mesoamerican worldview and calendar cycles (Sugiyama 1993, 2010) (Figure 15.5).

These two principles structuring urban planning, orientation, and the division of space, suggest the integrity and contemporaneity of the three monuments. However, this does not mean they were constructed simultaneously. Newly discovered dedication burials and offerings integrated into each monument simply support the idea of a complementary relation among them. The findings offer new perspectives regarding state ideology and polity.

The earthen nucleus of the Sun Pyramid shows two superimposed architectural stages: one square platform measuring roughly 215 meters per side and another almost completely covering the earlier one. The semidetached platform had at least four construction stages that corresponded to the first and second stages of the pyramid. The first stage of the Sun Pyramid was the central monument built around

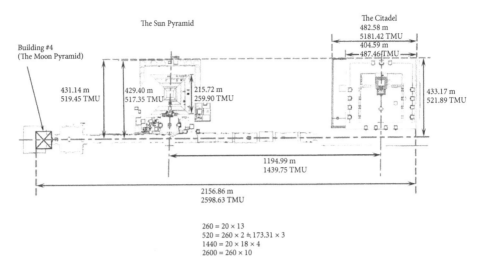

$260 = 20 \times 13$
$520 = 260 \times 2 \doteq 173.31 \times 3$
$1440 = 20 \times 18 \times 4$
$2600 = 260 \times 10$

Figure 15.5 City plan showing measurements in TMU that coincides to numbers significant in Mesoamerican worldview and calendar cycles, including 173.3 (eclipse cycle), 260, 365, 486 (number of days in which Venus was visible, according to the Mayan manuscripts), 520 (260 x 2 = 173.3 x 3), 584 (Venus cycle), 1,440 (20 x 18 x 4), and 2,600.

200 AD. During the following Miccaotli phase, the principal façade was partially covered by the semidetached platform with centrally located feline images (Millon 1973). The pyramid was enlarged during the Xolalpan phase. Although the data on ideological attributes or functions associated with the Sun Pyramid (2nd Stage) are still scarce, solid data regarding the polity and the presence of rulers are derived from inside the pyramid.

The entrance to a man-made tunnel was accidentally discovered at the foot of the main staircase of the semidetached platform in 1971. It descends 6.5 meters underneath the plaza floor and then continues horizontally toward the center of the pyramid, where four chamberlike rooms were uncovered. No mortuary materials were found inside. Therefore, the tunnel was erroneously interpreted as a natural formation and interpreted as the legendary place of human origin following later Aztec mythologies (Heyden 1975; Millon 1981). However, recent exploration clearly shows that it is a man-made tunnel excavated around the time the pyramid was erected (Manzanilla 1994; Sugiyama 2011). Its function could have been as a royal tomb, as suggested by the form of the "cave" with chambers and antechamber-like artificial space, evidence of exhaustive looting activities, and fragments found in the looters' deposits. The proposed royal tombs under the Sun Pyramid cannot be confirmed as the original context has been disturbed substantially. However, information recently recovered in a tunnel excavation inside the pyramid at plaza level supports the idea of conspicuously presented rulers, and this provides new perspectives on the city's divine authority.

One offering, corresponding to the first stage, was discovered in 2010 and includes the largest pyrite disk recovered to date at Teotihuacan (45-centimeter

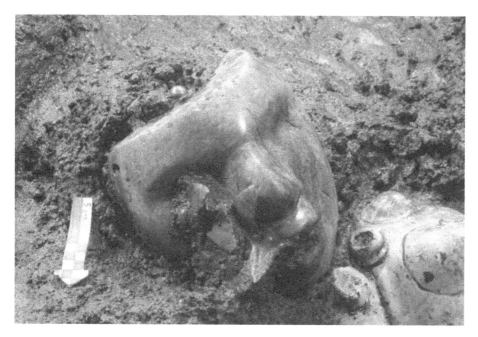

Figure 15.6 Greenstone mask found inside the Sun Pyramid with many other
symbolic objects.

diameter), an obsidian figurine, numerous projectile points, large obsidian bifacial
knives, and blades, worked shell objects, a greenstone mask and figurines (Figure
15.6), eleven Tlaloc jars, and animal bones, including the complete remains of a
sacrificed eagle. The set was found on the east-west axis of the pyramid, but not at
its center. They were carefully laid out approximately above the chambers of the
ancient tunnel mentioned above. Therefore, they may have been directly associated with whatever was buried in the tunnel. The inclusion of many war-related
objects suggests that the military institution was important to the city's early governance around 200 AD or earlier.

The construction of Building 4 of the Moon Pyramid explicitly represented
politico-religious messages at the time the city's layout was established around 200
AD (the Miccaotli phase). The monument was nine times the size of the previous one. Two sacrificial burials and offering complexes associated with Building 4
confirm unique traits of the powerful government and make up the richest dedication set recovered at Teotihuacan: thirteen sacrificial victims; numerous greenstone, obsidian, shell, and ceramic artifacts; various organic materials; and more
than fifty sacrificed animals, including eagles, jaguars, pumas, wolves, and rattle-
snakes. The inclusion of several martial objects confirm the importance of the
sacred warfare associated with the erection of the monument. Sacrificed animals
symbolized the sacred rulership and military institution, as proclaimed repeatedly
in ceramic or mural imagery from later periods (Berrin 1988; Berrin and Pasztory
1993; Langley 1986).

Figure 15.7 The main façade of the Feathered Serpent Pyramid in the ceremonial enclosure called Citadel.

The Citadel, which dates to the Miccaotli phase, was the largest ceremonial precinct in the southern portion of the city. It is a huge, nearly rectangular compound measuring about 400 meters on each side. Cowgill (1983) believes that the entire adult population of the city could have fit in the main plaza. The FSP, the most important structure in this precinct, was a unique monument in Mesoamerica at the time, the façades of which were completely covered with sculptures of the Feathered Serpent and an enigmatic sacred entity (Figure 15.7). Because the Feathered Serpent was a symbol of political authority until Aztec times, the monument and associated structures can be assumed to have been a politico-religious headquarters for the state.

One of the most significant discoveries was the more than 137 sacrificed individuals found with abundant symbolic offerings of exceptional quality in and around the pyramid. The distribution pattern of the graves clearly indicates a materialization of the Teotihuacan worldview and calendar systems. Sacrificial victims were buried in groups representing numbers important to Mesoamerican cosmology and calendric systems (Sugiyama 2005).

Most of the materials were symbolic items, insignia, or tools for warriors or priests: obsidian projectile points, slate disks, and human maxilla (real or shell imitations). The burial complex includes the mass sacrifice of warriors possibly brought to the city as captives and dressed as Teotihuacan warriors (White et al. 2007). Offerings include greenstone ornaments and a complete wood baton or scepter with the curved Feathered Serpent head, which may have symbolized individualistic political authority as it did among the Maya and Aztec.

Because they were buried anonymously, the sacrificial victims formed a uni-fied assemblage dedicated to the supreme deity worshipped at the monument. However, the recent discovery of a possible royal tomb under the FSP has pre-sented a new possibility. A large pit 14 meters deep was accidentally found in front of the semidetached platform. The pit continues horizontally as a tunnel about 100 meters toward the center of the FSP, similar to the tunnel under the Sun Pyramid. The tunnel has yet to be explored, but if the tunnel contained a royal grave, either to be found in intact condition or looted, the warriors could have served as retain-ers for the ruler buried directly under them and the FSP. They may have been sacred warriors whose function was to protect or accompany the dead ruler. The implication is that a powerful, charismatic ruler was conspicuously presented both symbolically and materially and that military institutions functioned in support of the state by 200 AD. Only the first 20 meters of the ancient tunnel have been explored as of early 2012; however, thousands of symbolic objects found in looters' disturbed layers strongly support the interpretation mentioned above.

EXPANSION OF THE STATE

The urban center seems to have entered a prosperous period during the Tlamimilolpa and Xolalpan phases. Ample data indicate that craft specialization and social stratifi-cation were well developed (Carballo 2011; Manzanilla 1993; Sempowski and Spence 1994). There was a notable period of enlargement or modification programs at the major monuments around 350 AD that suggests political and ideological expansion, consolidation, or transformation of the Teotihuacan state.

Building 6 of the Moon Pyramid represented another substantial enlargement of the monument during which it attained almost the same form and size as the building we see today. This monument was dedicated with two sacrificial burials. One consisted of seventeen severed human heads without any offerings. They seem to have been either war captives or victims brought from distant regions. Another burial was composed of three high-status individuals with Maya-style greenstone ornaments symbolizing rulership. They clearly indicate direct interaction with a Mayan dynasty around 350 AD.

The FSP's semidetached platform was the third construction phase at this pre-cinct and it almost covered the front façade of the main building around 350 AD (Sugiyama 1998). At the same time, some of the sacrificial burials mentioned above were looted, and sculptures were deliberately removed. The government might have experienced substantial change or ideological renovation, or suffered from internal or external threats.

Although the symbolism of the FSP was deemphasized, the Citadel continued functioning as a headquarters for the state. The production of ceramic censers with warrior symbolism and other ritual items found at an ancient workshop directly adjacent to the Citadel complex supports the idea that the state continuously expanded its influence with militaristic power after 350 AD.

During its heyday (the third through sixth centuries AD), Teotihuacan materials and ideology were exported widely (Aveni 1980: 226–229; Fash and Fash 2000). The Teotihuacan state controlled large areas well beyond the Basin of Mexico, and the city was likely affiliated with distant centers or it may have even conquered certain regions (Marcus 1983). Teotihuacan was a dominant locus of sociopolitical developments in Mesoamerica during the Late Preclassic to Early Classic periods.

COLLAPSE

The decline of the Teotihuacan state was rather quick. Evidence for possible threats has been recovered from the city's residences. Thick, high walls were integrated into architectural complexes: a wide, deep canal system and high platforms may have functioned as defensive facilities. Roughly made, unplastered stone walls blocked access to many residential complexes in the final architectural stage. The way in which the walls were constructed gives the impression that the inhabitants suddenly needed to strictly control access to residences.

The evidence of Teotihuacan's final destruction is unmistakable. Evidence of fires on the floors and walls of residences is conspicuous, and support for conflict increases as excavations progress (López et al. 2006). Temples and pyramids seem to have been burned (Millon 1988). It was a long-standing tradition in Mesoamerica to set fire to the temples of conquered areas. We still do not know exactly when this happened in absolute years, or who did it. However, we know that the disintegration of the state took place essentially as a consequence of political conflict and very probably involved the very military forces that Teotihuacan elites once used to establish their own political hegemonies.

REFERENCES

Aveni, Anthony F. 1980. *Skywatchers of Ancient Mexico*. University of Texas Press, Austin.

Benson, Elizabeth P., and Beatriz de la Fuente. 1996. *Olmec Art of Ancient Mexico*. National Gallery of Art, Washington, DC.

Berlo, Janet, ed. 1992. *Art, Ideology and the City of Teotihuacan*. Dumbarton Oaks, Washington, DC.

Berrin, Kathleen, ed. 1988. *Feathered Serpents and Flowering Trees: Reconstructing the Murals of Teotihuacan*. The Fine Arts Museums of San Francisco, and the University of Washington Press, Seattle.

Berrin, Kathleen, and Esther Pasztory, eds. 1993. *Teotihuacan: Art from the City of the Gods.* Thames and Hudson, and the Fine Arts Museums of San Francisco, New York.

Cabrera Castro, Rubén, Saburo Sugiyama, and George L. Cowgill. 1991. The Temple of Quetzalcoatl Project at Teotihuacan: A Preliminary Report. *Ancient Mesoamerica* 2:77–92.

Carballo, David M. 2011. *Obsidian and the Teotihuacan State: Weaponry and Ritual Production at the Moon Pyramid.* University of Pittsburgh, Pittsburgh.

Carrasco, Davíd, Lindsay Jones, and Scott Sessions, eds. 2000. *The Classic Heritage from Teotihuacan to Tenochtitan.* University of Colorado Press, Boulder.

Clark, John E., and William J. Parry. 1991. Craft Specialization and Cultural Complexity. *Research in Economic Anthropology* 12:289–346.

Cordova F. de A., Carlos, Ana L. Martin del Pozzo, and Javier López C. 1994. Palaeolandforms and Volcanic Impact on the Environment of Prehistoric Cuicuilco, Southern Mexico City. *Journal of Archaeological Science* 21:585–596.

Cowgill, George L. 1983. Rulership and the Ciudadela: Political Inferences from Teotihuacan Architecture. In *Civilization in the Ancient Americas: Essays in Honor of Gordon R. Willey,* edited by Richard M. Leventhal and Alan L. Kolata, pp. 313–343. University of New Mexico Press and Peabody Museum of Harvard University, Albuquerque.

Cowgill, George L. 1992. Toward a Political History of Teotihuacan. In *Ideology and Pre-Columbian Civilizations,* edited by Arthur A. Demarest and Geoffrey W. Conrad, pp. 87–114. School of American Research Press, Santa Fe.

Cummings, Byron. 1933. Cuicuilco and the Archaic Culture of Mexico. *Scientific Monthly* 23(4):289–304.

Dow, James W. 1967. Astronomical Orientations at Teotihuacan, a Case Study in Astro-Archaeology. *American Antiquity* 32:326–334.

Drucker, R. David. 1977. A Solar Orientation Framework for Teotihuacan. Paper presented at the XV Mesa Redonda of the Sociedad Mexicana de Antropología, Guanajuato.

Fash, William L., and Barbara W. Fash. 2000. Teotihuacan and the Maya: A Classic Heritage. In *The Classic Heritage from Teotihuacan to Tenochtitan,* edited by David Carrasco, Lindsay Jones, and Scott Sessions, pp. 433–464. University of Colorado Press, Boulder.

Gamio, Manuel. 1922. *La población del Valle de Teotihuacán.* 3 vols. Secretaria de Agricultura y Fomento, México, D.F. Republished in 1979. 5 vols. Instituto Nacional Indigenista, México, D.F.

Gazzola, Julie. 2009. Características arquitectónicas de algunas construcciones de fases tempranas de Teotihuacán. *Arqueología* segunda época: 42: 216–233.

Gómez, Sergio. 2002. Presencia del Occidente de México en Teotihuacan: Aproximaciones a la política exterior del Estado Teotihuacano. In *Ideología y política a través de materiales, imágenes y símbolos: Memoria de la primera mesa redonda de Teotihuacan,* edited by M. E. Ruiz G., pp. 563–625. Universidad Nacional Autónoma de México, and INAH, México, D.F.

Heizer, Robert, and James Bennyhoff. 1972. Archaeological Excavations at Cuicuilco, Mexico, 1957. *National Geographic Reports, 1955–1960:* 93–104.

Heyden, Doris. 1975. An Interpretation of the Cave Underneath the Pyramid of the Sun in Teotihuacán, Mexico. *American Antiquity* 40:131–147.

Langley, James C. 1986. *Symbolic Notation of Teotihuacan: Elements of Writing in a Mesoamerican Culture of the Classic Period.* BAR International Series 313, Oxford.

Leonardo López Luján, Laura Filloy Nadal, Barbara W. Fash, and William L. Fash. 2006. The Destruction of Images in Teotihuacan: Anthropomorphic Sculpture, Elite Cults, and the End of a Civilization. *RES: Anthropology and Aesthetics* 49/50:12–39.

Malmstrom, Vincent H. 1978. A Reconstruction of the Chronology of Mesoamerican Calendrical Systems. *Journal of the History of Astronomy* 9(2):105–116.

Manzanilla, Linda, ed. 1993. *Anatomía de un conjunto residencial teotihuacano en Oztoyahualco.* Two volumes. Universidad Nacional Autónoma de México, México, D.F.

Manzanilla, Linda, Luis Barba., René Chávez, Andrés Tejero, Gerardo Cifuentes, and Nayeli Peralta. 1994. Caves and Geophysics; an Approximation to the Underworld of Teotihuacan, Mexico. *Archaeometry* 36(1):141–157.

Marcus, Joyce. 1983. Stone Monuments and Tomb Murals of Monte Albán IIIa. In *The Cloud People: Divergent Evolution of the Zapotec and Mixtec Civilizations*, edited by Kent Flannery and Joyce Marcus, pp. 137–143. Academic Press, New York.

Matos Moctezuma, Eduardo. 1995. *La pirámide del sol, Teotihuacan.* Artes de México, Instituto Cultural Domecq, A.C., Mexico, D.F.

McClung de Tapia, Emily. 1992. The Origins of Agriculture in Mesoamerica and Central America. *The Origins of Agriculture: An International Perspective*, edited by C. Wesley Cowan and Patty Jo Watson, pp. 143–171. Smithsonian Institution Press, Washington, DC.

Millon, René. 1973. *Urbanization at Teotihuacan, Mexico: vol. 1: The Teotihuacan Map. Part One: Text.* University of Texas Press, Austin.

Millon, René. 1981. Teotihuacan: City, State, and Civilization. In *Supplement to the Handbook of Middle American Indians, Volume One: Archaeology*, edited by Jeremy Sabloff, pp. 198–243. University of Texas Press, Austin.

Millon, René. 1988. The Last Years of Teotihuacan Dominance. In *The Collapse of Ancient States and Civilizations*, edited by Norman Yoffee and George Cowgill, pp. 102–164. University of Arizona Press, Tucson.

Millon, René, Bruce Drewitt, and George L. Cowgill. 1973. *Urbanization at Teotihuacan, Mexico, Volume 1: The Teotihuacan Map. Part Two: Maps.* University of Texas Press, Austin.

Pastrana, Alejandro. 1997. Nuevos datos acerca de la estratigrafía de Cuicuilco. *Arqueología* 18:3–16.

Pasztory, Esther. 1997. *Teotihuacan: An Experiment in Living.* University of Oklahoma Press, Norman.

Plunket, Patricia, and Gabriela Uruñuela. 2006. Social and Cultural Consequences of a Late Holocene Eruption of Popocatépetl in Central Mexico. *Quaternary International* 151:19–28.

Rattray, Evelyn C. 1992. *The Teotihuacan Burials and Offerings: A Commentary and Inventory.* Vanderbilt University Publications in Anthropology No. 42, Nashville.

Sanders, William T. 1981. Ecological Adaptation in the Basin of Mexico: 23,000 BC to the Present. In *Supplement to the Handbook of Middle American Indians, Volume One: Archaeology*, edited by Victoria Bricker and Jeremy Sabloff, pp. 147–197. University of Texas Press, Austin.

Sanders, William T., Jeffrey R. Parsons, and Robert S. Santley. 1979. *The Basin of Mexico: Ecological Processes in the Evolution of a Civilization.* Academic Press, New York.

Sempowski, Martha L., and Michael W. Spence. 1994. *Mortuary Practices and Skeletal Remains at Teotihuacan.* University of Utah Press, Salt Lake City.

Spence, Michael W. 1992. Tlailotlacan, a Zapotec Enclave in Teotihuacan. In *Art, Ideology, and the City of Teotihuacan*, edited by Janet C. Berlo, pp.59–88. Dumbarton Oaks, Washington, DC.

Sprajc, Ivan. 2001. *Orientaciones astronómicas en la arquitectura prehispánica del centro de México.* Colección Científica 427, INAH, Mexico City.

Storey, Rebecca. 1992. *Life and Death in the Ancient City of Teotihuacan: A Modern Paleodemographic Synthesis.* University of Alabama Press, Tuscaloosa.

Sugiyama, Saburo. 1993. Worldview Materialized in Teotihuacan, Mexico. *Latin American Antiquity* 4(2):103–129.

Sugiyama, Saburo. 1998. Termination Programs and Prehispanic Looting at the Feathered Serpent Pyramid in Teotihuacan, Mexico. *The Sowing and the Dawning: Dedication and Termination Events in the Archaeological and Ethnographic Record of Mesoamerica*, edited by Shirley Mock, pp. 247–164. University of New Mexico Press, Albuquerque.

Sugiyama, Saburo. 2005. *Human Sacrifice, Warfare, and Rulership at Teotihuacan, Mexico: Materialization of State Ideology in the Feathered Serpent Pyramid.* Cambridge University Press, Cambridge.

Sugiyama, Saburo. 2010. Teotihuacan City Layout as a Cosmogram: Preliminary Results of the 2006 Measurement Unit Study. In *The Archaeology of Measurement: Comprehending Heaven, Earth and Time in Ancient Societies*, edited by Iain Morley and Colin Renfrew, pp. 130–149. Cambridge University Press, Cambridge.

Sugiyama, Saburo. 2011. Interactions between the Living and the Dead at Major Monuments in Teotihuacan. In *Between the Dead and the Living: Cross-Disciplinary and Diachronic Visions*, edited by James Fitzsimmons and Izumi Shimada, pp. 161–202" in Sugiyama 2011. University of Arizona Press, Tucson.

Sugiyama, Saburo, and Rubén Cabrera C. 2007. The Moon Pyramid Project and the Teotihuacan State Polity: A Brief Summary of the 1998–2004 Excavations. *Ancient Mesoamerica* 18(1):109–125.

Sugiyama, Saburo, and Leonardo López Luján. 2007. Dedicatory Burial/Offering Complexes at the Moon Pyramid, Teotihuacan: A Preliminary Report of 1998–2004 Explorations. *Ancient Mesoamerica* 18(1):127–146.

Sugiyama, Saburo, Enrique Pérez C., Nawa Sugiyama, and Alejandro Sarabia G. 2012. Exploración 2008–2011 en el interior de la Pirámide del Sol. In *Va mesa redonda de Teotihuacan: Investigaciones recientes. Centro y periféria.* INAH, Mexico City.

Sugiyama, Saburo, and Alejandro Sarabia G. 2011. Teotihuacan, la ciudad con una cosmovisión mesoamericana. *Arqueología Mexicana* 107: 39–45.

Taube, Karl. 2001. La Escritura Teotihuacana. *Arqueología Mexicana* 48:58–63.

Valadez A., Raúl. 1999. Los animales domésticos. *Arqueología Mexicana* 35:32–39.

White, Christine D., T. Douglas Price, and Fred J. Longstaffe. 2007. Residential Histories of the Human Sacrifices at the Moon Pyramid, Teotihuacan: Evidence from Oxygen and Strontium Isotopes. *Ancient Mesoamerica* 18(1):159–172.

CHAPTER 16

CULTURAL EVOLUTION IN THE SOUTHERN HIGHLANDS OF MEXICO

FROM THE EMERGENCE OF SOCIAL INEQUALITY AND URBAN SOCIETY TO THE DECLINE OF CLASSIC-PERIOD STATES

CHRISTINA ELSON

THE SOUTHERN HIGHLANDS AS A CULTURE ZONE

The modern state of Oaxaca is one of Mexico's most mountainous and ethnically diverse regions. Oaxaca formed the core of a distinct zone within Mesoamerica often called the southern highlands (Paddock 1966). Around half of Oaxaca's landscape is over 1,500 meters in elevation. Millennia ago, speakers of the Otomanguean family of languages settled in the valleys that break up this rugged expanse of terrain. Today the descendants of these people, including the Zapotec, Mixtec, Mixe, Mixe, Zoque, Chinantec, and Cuicatec, are the region's most prominent ethnic groups (Marcus 1983a).

Covering some 2,000 square kilometers, the Oaxaca Valley is the geographic center of and largest open area in the southern highlands. The valley is commonly divided into three subregions—Etla, Tlacolula, and the Valle Grande—that join to form a Y shape. At the valley's center sits Monte Albán, one of Mesoamerica's earliest urban settlements. Monte Albán was founded about 500 BC. North and west of the Oaxaca Valley lies the Mixteca Alta, a region dotted with numerous small valleys that measure in the low hundreds of square kilometers. One of the largest valleys in the Mixteca Alta is the Nochixtlan Valley, covering about 250 square kilometers. A third region of importance is Lower Río Verde. The Río Verde River valley on the Pacific Coast is created by the confluence of the Verde and Atoyac rivers that drain the Mixteca Alta and Oaxaca Valley.

This chapter will summarize research in these three regions and will describe the emergence of ranked societies and the formation of states (Figures 16.1 and 16.2). The southern highlands is a relatively well-studied area of Mesoamerica with a strong tradition of regional survey and site-focused archaeology complemented by ethnohistoric, ethnographic, and linguistic analyses (see Balkansky 2001; Flannery and Marcus 1983a; Joyce 2010: 10–17).

		MESOAMERICA	VALLEY OF OAXACA (traditional)	VALLEY OF OAXACA (revised)	MIXTECA ALTA	LOWER RIO VERDE
	800					
	700	Late Classic	Monte Albán IIIB	Xoo		Yuta Tiyoo
	600			Peche	Las Flores	
	500					
	400	Early Classic	Monte Albán IIIA	Pitao		Coyuche
	300			Tani		
	200					Chacahua
AD	100			Nisa		
BC	1	Terminal Formative	Monte Albán II		Late Ramos	Miniyua
	100					
	200	Late Formative	Late Monte Albán I	Pe	Early Ramos	Minizundo
	300					
	400		Early Monte Albán I	Danibaan		
	500	Middle Formative			Late Cruz	
	600		Rosario	Rosario		Charco
	700					

Figure 16.1 Chronology of the southern Mexican highlands (adapted from Markens 2008).

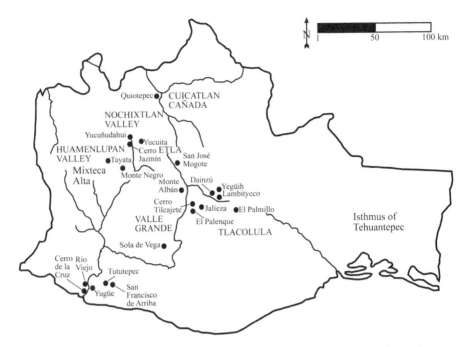

Figure 16.2 Southern Mexican highlands (drawn by Kristin Sullivan; from Blanton et al. 1999: Fig. 2.4).

THE ORIGINS OF RANKED SOCIETY

Many anthropologists are keenly interested in why hereditary inequality and ranking develop and how such an ideology becomes socially acceptable. The flash point may be when ambitious, socially prestigious leaders succeed in crafting a new explanation for their success: instead of claiming the *support* of supernatural forces, they advocate for *descent* from supernatural forces (Flannery 1999; Marcus and Flannery 1996).

Some researchers suggest that the southern highlands do not exhibit hereditary leadership until after 700 BC. Early Formative society (1200–700 BC) was egalitarian or organized into corporate groups led by nonhereditary leaders (Blanton et al. 1999; Blomster 2004; Blomster et al. 2005; Joyce 2010). Essentially, this view posits that chiefdoms arise first on the Gulf Coast at Olmec centers like San Lorenzo and that trade and exchange exposed Oaxaca to an ideology supporting ranked society. Proponents of this view argue that particular elements like monumental architecture (earthen mounds and buildings hypothesized to be "palaces"), sculpture (especially portraits of rulers carved from boulders), and motifs (such as "earth" and "sky") appear first on the Gulf Coast and are later adopted or copied in Oaxaca (see Joyce 2010: 114 for a summary).

To others, ranked society appears in the Oaxaca Valley by the close of the Early Formative (Flannery and Marcus 2000; Sharer 2007). Regional survey coverage and excavations at population centers like San José Mogote and smaller villages have produced data on a number of practices that, when viewed in isolation, can reflect either achieved or inherited status differences but, when viewed holistically, support a model suggesting "an extensive pattern of asymmetric relations in many aspects of society, including inequalities from birth." These traits are (1) a subset of males buried in a flexed position with more abundant offerings of pottery and jade; (2) ritually deposited scenes of figurines arrayed in positions of authority and obeisance; (3) the possible use of magnetite as a sumptuary good; (4) domestic excavations showing gradients in access to resources; (5) regional data placing San José Mogote at the center of a network of twelve to fourteen smaller communities; (6) the construction at San José Mogote of a range of public buildings placed on pyramidal platforms not found at smaller sites; (6) mortuary data linking particular individuals from birth with "earth" or "sky" motifs; and (7) the application of cranial deformation to some children (Marcus and Flannery 1996: 93–110).

The Early Formative is a time period when Mesoamerican regions entered into a pan-regional system of trade and exchange fueled in part by the desire of ambitious leaders to further their own aspirations in creating and maintaining social prestige. Each region developed locally relevant interpretations of elements, including burial practices, ceramic motifs, adobe architecture, lime plaster and stone masonry, and ritual buildings with solar or astral orientations. All contributed to an emerging Mesoamerican ideology that included the establishment of ranking and social inequality.

RANKED SOCIETIES AND THE ESCALATION OF WARFARE

During the Middle Formative (700-300 BC) chiefdoms in the southern lowlands likely varied greatly in population and in their degree of complexity.

In the Mixteca Alta, the site of Tayata in the Huamenlupan Valley is known from both survey and excavation. Tayata is first occupied in the Early Formative. Two burial contexts dating to around 1000 BC may suggest the emergence of ranking. Each contained an individual who had been cremated. The burials were associated with a high-status residence with evidence for feasting and craft production. The individuals were interred with figurines, shells, and dogs (possibly consumed during mortuary rituals). Ethnohistoric documents and pictorial codices record the cremation of nobles in the Mixteca region from about 1000 AD. The discovery of this very early context may indicate that cremation is specific elite cultural practice with a very deep history (Duncan et al. 2008). In the Middle Formative Tayata emerges as a regional center at the head of a two-tier settlement hierarchy. It is outfitted with public architecture including a large platform and a 90-meter-long plaza that could have accommodated 4,000 persons, likely the entire occupation of the valley (Balkansky 1998b).

In the Oaxaca Valley during the Rosario phase (700-500 BC) there is strong evidence for ranked societies that exhibit a hierarchy of three levels. Eventually chiefly centers appear in Etla (San José Mogote), Valle Grande (San Martín Tilcajete), and Tlacolula (Yegüih). Etla is the valley's demographic center, with eighteen to twenty-three out of seventy to eighty-five total villages. There is discussion about population estimates for Etla and for San José Mogote. Rosario phase population estimates are derived from counts of diagnostic sherds gathered in surface collections. Some consider that San José Mogote suffered a demographic decline in the Rosario period (Kowalewski et al. 1989: 72–77). Others point to an overreliance on elite wares in interpreting the Rosario population and suggest that when low-status households are proportionally represented the population does not decline and could be estimated at some 1,000 people (Marcus and Flannery 1996: 122–123).

The Middle Formative is notable for an escalation in competition and warfare among chiefly polities, suggesting the establishment of a pattern of raiding, temple burning, and capture for sacrifice. Regional evidence for conflict includes elevated counts in surface collections of burned clay daub from structures and the appearance of an uninhabited buffer zone at the center of the valley where the three branches meet (Flannery and Marcus 2003; Kowalewski et al. 1989: 70; Spencer 2003). Excavations at San José Mogote show the site was outfitted with a wattle-and-clay daub temple sitting on a lime-plastered platform. Over generations the temple was enlarged to reach 21.7 by 28.5 meters. At one point in its life span, the temple was burned in a fire so intense as to turn the clay daub into "masses of grayish, glassy cinders." A carved-stone monument dated to about 600 BC found near the temple shows a named person ("One Earthquake") who was a victim of heart sacrifice (Marcus and Flannery 1996: 124–130).

Scholars who posit that hereditary inequality emerged after 700 BC tie its development to a hypothesis suggesting political upheaval in the Oaxaca Valley resulting from a disruption of long-standing trade networks and interactions linking Mesoamerica. This view supports a demographic decline during the Rosario phase and the idea that San José Mogote lost population and influence to other chiefly centers in the valley. The town's burned temple represents a "stark demonstration of a profound political and religious crisis." In this environment, some elites gained control over sacred knowledge and authority, which facilitated the establishment of hereditary status distinctions (Joyce 2010: 121–124).

San José Mogote's burned temple was replaced by a stone masonry residence and tomb. The complement of goods recovered from the residence and tomb— serving bowls, anthropomorphic braziers, jade, whistles, and obsidian bloodletting tools and projectile points—shows the elites were well on their way to fulfilling roles as leaders in feasting, warfare, communicating with ancestors, and bloodletting ceremonies propitiating supernatural forces (Marcus 1989; Marcus and Flannery 1996: 131–134).

URBAN REVOLUTION AND STATE FORMATION

Between 500 and 100 BC sites in the Mixteca Alta and the Valley of Oaxaca developed into true urban centers, with state formation occurring by the end of the period (Marcus 2008).

Before examining the highlands, let us catch up with the Lower Río Verde. Until the Minizundo phase (400-150 BC) settlement here consisted of small communities of only a few hectares each. Studies of the ancient environment suggest a shift in the course of the Río Verde River, possibly due to anthropogenic erosion in the Mixteca Alta. As a result, the floodplain of the Río Verde expanded and agricultural production increased, although it is not clear if this in turn fostered demographic expansion (Joyce and Mueller 1997). Data on social organization and urbanization are available from work at Tututepec, San Francisco de Arriba, Cerro de la Cruz, Río Viejo, and Yugüe.

Burial data from excavations at Cerro de la Cruz and Yugüe lead some to posit that social organization was egalitarian until after 150 BC. In this view, burial rituals asserted a collective identity and masked social differences (Joyce 2010: 183). Two Cerro de la Cruz mortuary contexts date to the Minizundo phase. One context contained forty-eight adults buried without grave goods in a public area next to a residence. Nine individuals were discovered buried next to another structure and four of these contained grave goods (Joyce 1994, 2010). Excavations at a smaller site called Yugüe exposed a cemetery with a mortuary population of forty individuals, including neonates, children, and adults. A few individuals were placed with offerings (Barber 2005; Barber and Joyce 2007).

An alternative interpretation offered for the Cerro de la Cruz mortuary contexts is that these may be victims of violence who died during an attack against the site. Proponents of this view point to specific data including the interment of the larger group of forty-eight adults next to a structure with evidence for burning; the lack of a normal mortuary profile for this group; and the dense placement of bodies (Balkansky 2001; Redmond and Spencer 2006; Spencer 2007).

Urbanization may begin on the coast during the Minizundo phase, but it is not clear if this reflects increasing social hierarchy or an aggregation of population for defensive or ritual purposes. San Francisco de Arriba develops into a center of over 10,000 people and covers some 95 hectares of piedmont and hillsides; however, in the following Miniyua phase (150 BC–100 AD) it shrinks to about 34 hectares (Workinger 2002).

In the Miniyua phase the site of Río Viejo develops as a political center. It is outfitted with monumental architecture and a central acropolis. High-status residences incorporate burials accompanied by mortuary offerings. Smaller sites such as Yugüe also exhibit monumental architecture. Río Viejo may have suffered a violent collapse at 250 AD. One idea is that the region was invaded by Teotihuacan. Another is that elite demands for labor and services created tension and led commoners to revolt against local authority (Joyce 2003, 2010: 186–192).

In the Mixteca Alta, urbanization and the movement of populations from valley-floor settlements to terraced hilltops may be a reaction to Monte Albán's attempts at political expansion beyond the valley's borders. Tayata was abandoned about 400 BC, and its population, as well as that of nearby satellite centers, moved to a hilltop called Huamelulpan. Tayata's central precinct was rebuilt on Huamelulpan's highest point. Other prominent hilltop sites include Cerro Jazmín, Monte Negro, and Yucuita. Not all of these urban settlements were newly founded like Monte Albán. Huamelulpan and Monte Negro are new sites while Yucuita was an existing community that grew into a demographic center. Not all of these new urban centers flourished. Monte Negro and Cerro Jazmin were abandoned around 100 BC. Huamelulpan grew during the Late Ramos phase (100 BC–200 AD) to have a mean estimated population comparable to that of Monte Albán (about 12,500). While urbanized, Huamelulpan controlled only a small territory and developed into what can best be called a city-state, a pattern that continued in the Mixteca Alta until conquest (Balkansky 1998b; Kowalewski et al. 2009).

In the southern highlands, Monte Albán alone developed into an expansionistic state. The founding of Monte Albán is an event that has been described in detail from several perspectives (Blanton et al. 1999; Marcus and Flannery 1996; Flannery and Marcus 1983a; Joyce 2010). About 500 BC the population of San José Mogote and the Etla branch declined and a new settlement was built on a 1,400-meter-tall mountain at the juncture of the valley's three arms. Mesoamerican scholars recognize that mountaintop locations are defensive and also conceptualized as sacred places (Marcus and Flannery 1996: 139; Joyce 2010: 134).

For some, Monte Albán's founding can be likened to a process described for ancient Greece called *synoikism*, where multiple villages relocated to defensive locations to meet an external threat. In Oaxaca, ongoing warfare between chiefdoms in the valley's three branches and even external threats were a strong incentive for relocation (Marcus and Flannery 1996; Spencer and Redmond 2004). Others have posited that the need for defense alone could not have induced commoners to uproot and move to a barren mountaintop. In this view, emerging social stratification and social tensions between nobles and commoners fostered a social crisis. Monte Albán was a defensive location but, more important, it was a ceremonial venue built for the performance of politico-religious ceremonies (Joyce and Winter 2006; Joyce 2010: 131).

Monte Albán's initial population of some 5,000 more than tripled over the next four centuries. The city's earliest buildings, dating to Early Monte Albán I (500–300 BC), are poorly preserved due to overburdening from later constructions.

State architecture indicative of internal specialization—temples with two rooms and palace constructions—are not documented until the Monte Albán II (100 BC–200 AD) (Blanton 1978; Flannery and Marcus 1983b). However, excavations at competing centers in the Valle Grande branch called El Palenque that was occupied during Late Monte Albán I (300–100 BC) show that its ceremonial core was outfitted with these kinds of buildings. Thus, it is likely that similar constructions existed at Monte Albán during the Late I phase (Redmond and Spencer 2006).

The most striking Early Monte Albán I construction is a civic building called Building L, which was covered with hundreds of carved stones depicting nude individuals, often with closed eyes, headgear and jewelry, and evidence of genital mutilation. Stylistically the carvings show the continuation of an iconographic theme established at San José Mogote. Who these people are is disputed. There is general agreement that the carvings are meant to display the importance that the site's founders placed on sacrifice and warfare (Joyce 2010; Marcus 1992; Urcid 2011).

Scholars increasingly pinpoint state formation in the Oaxaca Valley to Late Monte Albán I (Balkansky 1998a; Marcus and Flannery 1996; Sherman et al. 2010; Spencer 2007; Spencer and Redmond 2001). Multiple lines of evidence support this hypothesis. One, cited above, is the appearance of building types associated with internal specialization. A second is Monte Albán's expansion into nearby valleys, including the Cuicatlán Cañada and Sola de Vega, in order to control trade routes and acquire nonlocal goods (Balkansky 2002; Spencer and Redmond 1997). Some assert raiding or political expansion all the way to the Pacific Coast, resulting in the possible violence suggested at Cerro de la Cruz (Sherman et al. 2010), a view contested by coastal researchers (Joyce et al. 2000). As noted, Monte Albán's expansionistic goals may have contributed to *synoikism* and state formation in the Mixteca Alta (Balkansky 1998b; Kowalewski et al. 2009). Expansion outside the valley happened before Monte Albán subjugated rival polities in the valley. Much of the Valle Grande was not incorporated until about 150 BC when El Palenque, the capital of a rival polity, was burned and abandoned and a smaller center demonstrating close ties with the capital established (Elson 2007; Spencer and Redmond 2004). The Ejutla Valley was not incorporated until around 200 AD (Feinman and Nicholas 1990).

Throughout the trajectory described above, culture areas of the southern highlands maintained regular interaction through many mechanisms, including raiding, trade, and the exchange of marriage partners. After 200 AD regions came to exhibit greater internal diversity, emerging as distinctly Mixtec, Zapotec, Chatino, and so on. However, these culture areas came to share (along with their Mesoamerican cousins) fundamental concepts including a core belief in the division of society into commoner and noble social strata. Commoner agriculturalists and craftspeople were the economic engines of Mesoamerican societies, and these individuals had their own ways of influencing politics and culture. As political leaders, nobles engaged in particular behaviors, including acting as intermediaries in rituals to communicate with ancestors and petition the supernatural, authorizing human sacrifice, and serving as military leaders. Social and cultural patterns that crystallize with urbanization and state formation have roots deep in the Formative and persist throughout the next centuries, outliving the expansion and contraction of southern highland political centers.

The Golden Age of Zapotec Civilization

For about five hundred years, beginning about 200 AD, the Zapotec experienced a "golden age" of civilization (Marcus and Flannery 1996: 208). Classic-period expressions of Zapotec art and architecture have their roots firmly planted in the Terminal Formative (100 BC–200 AD). Research at Monte Albán and valley sites, including San José Mogote, Cerro Tilcajete, Jalieza, and Dainzú, illuminates how political relationships between elites at the capital and at secondary centers developed during the life span of the Zapotec state. The Terminal Formative has been posited as a time when Monte Albán asserted political hegemony over the valley (Elson 2007; Marcus and Flannery 1996). Monte Albán's rulers integrated local elites through a number of mechanisms, including outfitting sites with standardized architecture used in state rituals (particularly temples with two rooms) and supplying them with elaborate ceramics, particularly footed bowls carrying lightning-*Cociyo* iconography that was made from a clay source controlled by the capital (Elson and Sherman 2007).

In the Early Classic, carved stone monuments, tomb murals, and decorated ceramics, particularly urns, show that elites are concerned with noble ancestors as well as associating themselves with jaguars, rain god deities, and militarism. Such iconography expresses the role nobles played in mediating nature, ensuring fertility, and acting as leaders in warfare (Marcus 1983c; Sellen 2002). Architecture and stylistic conventions seen at Monte Albán are mimicked at secondary centers, such as Jalieza, where local elites were managing growing populations and developing production networks extensive enough to allow them some leeway in negotiating peer-to-peer relationships with the capital (Casparis 2005).

Most of the restored architecture a visitor sees today at Monte Albán dates to the Late Classic. At its maximum extent, Monte Albán had a population of some 15,000 to 30,000, including settlement on two adjacent hills called Atzompa and Monte Albán Chico (Blanton 1983; Robles García and Cuautle 2011). The presence of spatially distinct mound groups surrounded by commoner residences suggests a degree of neighborhood organization: each mound group—a temple, public building, and palace complex—was the seat of a leading family charged with the neighborhood's administration (Blanton 1983: 129).

Many of Monte Albán's Late Classic palaces incorporate civic-ceremonial architecture such as temples and ballcourts. Some temples around the Central

Plaza develop into walled compounds. It has been hypothesized that Monte Albán's Main Plaza shifted from an accessible space surrounded by temples and public buildings to the core of a more restricted residential area, indicating that the city's nobility were more isolated from the general population than in previous time periods (Joyce 2010: 218–220). During the same time period, monumental carved stones and iconography linked with militaristic themes are replaced by small carved stones found in tombs at sites across the valley. These "genealogical registers," fabricated from about 600 to 900 AD, recorded birth, ancestry, origins, and the marriage of nobles and these may reflect a heightened effort by local families to establish royal dynasties independent of Monte Albán (Marcus 1983c).

MONTE ALBÁN, TEOTIHUACAN, AND SOUTHERN HIGHLAND POLITICS

The second-century AD rise of Teotihuacan, a military and commercial powerhouse, probably hampered the expansionistic designs of Monte Albán. After occupying the massive and intriguing fortress of Quiotepec (set at the northern end of the Cuicatlán Cañada) for several centuries, the Zapotec abandoned the site sometime in the Early Classic (Spencer and Redmond 1997). The relationship between Monte Albán and Teotihuacan has been evaluated in some detail (e.g., Flannery and Marcus 1983a). Scholars agree that the two empires maintained a special relationship that involved politics and diplomacy and not, as has been suggested for Maya sites such as Kaminaljuyú and Tikal, coercion or conquest (Marcus and Flannery 1996: 231–234). At Teotihuacan, a neighborhood occupied by Zapotec merchants or diplomats was founded by the Early Classic and occupied for several centuries (Paddock 1983).

Teotihuacan's long reach certainly extended into the Mixteca Alta and likely extended to the Pacific Coast, a primary source of luxury goods including feathers, jaguars, marine shell, cacao, and cotton. In the Lower Río Verde Valley, the site of Río Viejo emerged during the Terminal Formative as the capital of a relatively short-lived polity that collapsed about 250 AD. For the next 250 years the region maintained a decentralized political structure with some eight polities of roughly the same size competing for dominance (Barber and Joyce 2007). In the Late Classic, Río Viejo once again emerged as the capital of an independent regional state. Iconography on carved stones from elite contexts mirrors themes common in the highlands, including ancestors, jaguars, human sacrifice, and bloodletting (Joyce 2008).

In the Mixteca Alta, settlement patterns rooted in the Terminal Formative continued into the Classic period: sites occur on ridgetops and political centers continue to control small territories (Balkansky 1998b; Kowalewski et al. 2009).

Classic-period Mixteca Alta centers differ from Monte Albán in that they lack a central plaza. Instead, sites are built around a royal complex containing palaces, ballcourts, temples, and plazas. This complex is surrounded by lesser elite residences and, further downslope, commoner residences. One example of such a site is the Late Classic capital of Yucuñudahui (that takes over from Yucuita), which emerges as a fully planned urban center (Spores 1983a). Spores (1983b) points out that this pattern fits well with ethnohistoric documents describing the Postclassic organization of Mixtec capitals. Royal individuals were located at the center of the site and surrounded by loyal local nobility who maintained residences both at the capital and at their hometown, where they administered local production for the ruler. Finally, while it has been hypothesized that Mixteca Alta polities moved to hilltop centers for defense, there is no direct evidence that Monte Albán or Teotihuacan conquered any Mixtec polities, although the Mixtec may have engaged in warfare with both empires as well as with one another. The Mixtec also may have preferred hilltop locations for more esoteric reasons related to royal ideology (Spores 1983c).

Teotihuacan's collapse at ca. 600 AD (Cowgill 2008) certainly impacted the balance of power in Mesoamerica. Mixteca Alta settlement patterns become more hierarchical with well-defined social stratification (Spores 1983c). In contrast, the state capitals of Río Viejo and Monte Albán decline. The Río Viejo state collapsed by 800 AD and abandonment of the capital was accompanied by the denigration of physical spaces and artifacts associated with rulership (Joyce 2008). For some time it has been understood that the collapse of Monte Albán, traditionally set at about 700 AD, was a process lasting for several centuries. Beginning around the seventh century, the capital's power and influence waned and populations drifted away from the city to other urban centers where nobles were seeking to establish royal lineages independent of the capital. Many expressions of elite iconography—carved stones, urns, and writing—disappear from the archaeological record. New research is illuminating power and economy at valley centers including Lambityeco, Jalieza, and El Palmillo during the Classic-to-Postclassic transition (Blomster 2008; Elson 2011; Feinman et al., 2008; Lind and Urcid 2009; Markens 2008).

REFERENCES

Balkansky, Andrew K. 1998a. Origin and Collapse of Complex Societies in Oaxaca (Mexico): Evaluating the Era from 1965 to the Present. *Journal of World Prehistory* 12:451–493.

Balkansky, Andrew K. 1998b. Urbanism and Early State Formation in the Huamelulpan Valley of Southern Mexico. *Latin American Antiquity* 9:37–67.

Balkansky, Andrew K. 2001. On Emerging Patterns in Oaxaca Archaeology. *Current Anthropology* 42:559–561.

Balkansky, Andrew K. 2002. *The Sola Valley and the Monte Albán State: A Study of Zapotec Imperial Expansion.* Museum of Anthropology, University of Michigan, Memoirs 36, Ann Arbor.

Barber, Sarah B. 2005. Heterogeneity, Identity, and Complexity: Negotiating Status and Authority in Terminal Formative Coastal Oaxaca. PhD dissertation, University of Colorado at Boulder.

Barber, Sarah B., and Arthur A. Joyce. 2007. Polity Produced and Community Consumed: Negotiating Political Centralization through Ritual in the Lower Río Verde Valley, Oaxaca. In *Mesoamerican Ritual Economy: Archaeological and Ethnological Perspectives,* edited by E. Christin Wells, and Karla L. Davis-Salazar, pp. 211–255. University of Colorado Press, Boulder.

Blanton, Richard E. 1978. *Monte Alban: Settlement Patterns at the Ancient Zapotec Capital.* Academic Press, New York.

Blanton, Richard E. 1983. Urban Monte Albán during Period III. In *The Cloud People: Divergent Evolution of the Zapotec and Mixtec Civilizations,* edited by Kent V. Flannery and Joyce Marcus, pp. 128–131. Academic Press, New York.

Blanton, Richard E., Gary M. Feinman, Stephen A. Kowalewski, and Linda M. Nicholas. 1999. *Ancient Oaxaca: The Monte Albán State.* Cambridge University Press, Cambridge.

Blomster, Jeffrey P. 2004. *Etlatongo: Social Complexity, Interaction, and Village Life in the Mixteca Alta of Oaxaca, Mexico.* Wadsworth, Belmont, California.

Blomster, Jeffrey P., ed. 2008. *After Monte Albán: Transformation and Negotiation in Oaxaca, Mexico.* University of Colorado Press, Boulder.

Blomster, Jeffrey P., Hector Neff, and Michael D. Galscock. 2005. Olmec Pottery Production and Export in Ancient Mexico Determined through Elemental Analysis. *Science* 307:1068–1072.

Casparis, Luca. 2005. Early Classic Jalieza and the Monte Alban State. Unpublished PhD dissertation, University of Geneva.

Cowgill, George. 2008. An Update on Teotihuacan. *Antiquity* 82:962–975.

Duncan, William N., Andrew K. Balkansky, Kimberly Crawford, Heather A. Lapham, and Nathan J. Meissner. 2008. Human Cremation in Mexico 3,000 Years Ago. *Proceedings of the National Academy of Sciences* 105:5315–5320.

Elson, Christina M. 2007. *Excavations at Cerro Tilcajete: A Monte Albán II Administrative Center in the Valley of Oaxaca.* Memoir 42, Museum of Anthropology, University of Michigan, Ann Arbor.

Elson, Christina M. 2011. Jalieza: Su transición de un centro secundario a un cacicazgo en la época Clásica tardía? In *Memoria de la quinta mesa redonda de Monte Albán,* edited by N. M. Robles García and A. I. Riviera Guzmán. Instituto Nacional de Antropología e Historia, Mexico, D.F.

Elson, Christina M., and R. Jason Sherman. 2007. Serving Wares and Social Integration: A Study of Pottery from ca. 100 BC–AD 200 in the Oaxaca Valley (Mexico). *Journal of Field Archaeology* 32(3):265–282.

Feinman, Gary M., and Linda M. Nicholas. 1990. At the Margins of the Monte Albán State: Settlement Patterns in the Ejutla Valley, Oaxaca, Mexico. *Latin American Antiquity* 1:216–246.

Feinman, Gary M., Linda M. Nicholas, and Edward F. Maher. 2008. Domestic Offerings at El Palmillo: Implications for Community Organization. *Ancient Mesoamerica* 19(2):175–194.

Flannery, Kent V. 1999. Process and Agency in Early State Formation. *Cambridge Archaeological Journal* 9:3–21.

Flannery, Kent V., and Joyce Marcus, eds. 1983a. *The Cloud People: Divergent Evolution of the Zapotec and Mixtec Civilizations.* Academic Press, New York.

Flannery, Kent V., and Joyce Marcus. 1983b. The Earliest Public Buildings, Tombs, and Monuments at Monte Albán, with Notes on the Internal Chronology of Period. In *The Cloud People: Divergent Evolution of the Zapotec and Mixtec Civilizations,* edited by Kent V. Flannery and Joyce Marcus, pp. 87–91. New York, Academic Press.

Flannery, Kent V., and Joyce Marcus. 2000. Formative Mexican Chiefdoms and the Myth of the "Mother Culture." *Journal of Anthropological Archaeology* 19:1–37.

Flannery, Kent V., and Joyce Marcus. 2003. The Origin of War: New 14C Dates from Ancient Mexico. *Proceedings of the National Academy of Sciences of the USA* 100:11801–11805.

Joyce, Arthur A. 1994. Late Formative Community Organization and Social Complexity on the Oaxaca Coast. *Journal of Field Archaeology* 21:147–168.

Joyce, Arthur A. 2003. Imperialism in Pre-Aztec Mesoamerica: Monte Albán, Teotihuacan, and the Lower Río Verde Valley. In *Ancient Mesoamerican Warfare,* edited by M. Kathryn Brown and Travis W. Stanton, pp. 49–72. Altamira, Walnut Creek, California.

Joyce, Arthur A. 2008. Domination, Negotiation, Collapse. In *After Monte Albán: Transformation and Negotiation in Oaxaca, Mexico,* edited by Jeffery Blomster, pp. 219–254. University of Colorado Press, Boulder.

Joyce, Arthur A. 2010. *Mixtecs, Zapotecs, and Chatinos: Ancient Peoples of Southern Mexico.* Wiley-Blackwell, Oxford.

Joyce, Arthur A., and Raymond G. Mueller. 1997. Prehispanic Human Ecology and the Río Verde Drainage Basin. *World Archaeology* 29(1):75–94.

Joyce, Arthur A., Robert N. Zeitlin, Judith F. Zeitlin, and Javier Urcid. 2000. On Oaxaca Coast Archaeology: Setting the Record Straight. *Current Anthropology* 41:623–625.

Joyce, Arthur A., and Marcus Winter. 2006. Ideology, Power, and Urban Society in Pre-Hispanic Oaxaca. *Current Anthropology* 37:33–47.

Kowalewski, Stephen A., Andrew L. Balkansky, Laura R. Stiver Walsh, Thomas J. Pluckhahn, John F. Chamblee, Veronica Pérez Rodríguez, Vernice Y. Heredia Espinoza, and Charlotte A. Smith. 2009. *Origins of the Ñuu: Archaeology in the Mixteca Alta.* Mexico. University Press of Colorado, Boulder.

Kowalewski, Stephen A., Gary M. Feinman, Larua Finsten, Richard E. Blanton, and Linda M. Nicholas. 1989. *Monte Alban's Hinterland, Part II: Prehispanic Settlement Patterns in Tlacolula, Etla, and Ocotlán, the Valley of Oaxaca, Mexico.* Museum of Anthropology, University of Michigan, Memoirs 23, Ann Arbor.

Lind, Michael, and Javier Urcid. 2009. *The Lords of Lambityeco: Political Evolution in the Valley of Oaxaca during the Xoo Phase.* University Press of Colorado, Boulder.

Marcus, Joyce. 1983a. The Genetic Model and the Linguistic Divergence of the Otomangueans. In *The Cloud People: Divergent Evolution of the Zapotec and Mixtec Civilizations,* edited by Kent V. Flannery and Joyce Marcus, pp. 4–13. Academic Press, New York.

Marcus, Joyce. 1983b. Stone Monuments and Tomb Murals of Monte Albán IIIa. In *The Cloud People: Divergent Evolution of the Zapotec and Mixtec Civilizations,* edited by Kent V. Flannery and Joyce Marcus, pp. 137–144. Academic Press, New York.

Marcus, Joyce. 1983c. Changing Patterns of Stone Monuments after the Fall of Monte Albán AD 600–900. In *The Cloud People: Divergent Evolution of the Zapotec and Mixtec Civilizations,* edited by Kent V. Flannery and Joyce Marcus, pp. 191–197. Academic Press, New York.

Marcus, Joyce. 1989. Zapotec Chiefdoms and the Nature of Formative Religions. In *Regional Perspectives on the Olmec,* edited by Robert Sharer and David. Grove, pp. 148–197. Cambridge University Press, Cambridge.

Marcus, Joyce. 1992. *Mesoamerican Writing Systems: Propaganda, Myth, and History in Four Ancient Civilizations.* Princeton University Press, Princeton.

Marcus, Joyce. 2008. The Archaeological Evidence for Social Evolution. *Annual Review of Anthropology* 37:251–266.

Marcus, Joyce, and Kent V. Flannery. 1996. *Zapotec Civilization: How Urban Society Evolved in Mexico's Oaxaca Valley.* Thames and Hudson, London.

Markens, Robert. 2008. Advances in Defining the Classic-Postclassic Portion of the Valley of Oaxaca Ceramic Assemblage, In *After Monte Albán: Transformation and Negotiation in Oaxaca, Mexico,* edited by Jeffery Blomster, pp. 59–94. University of Colorado Press, Boulder.

Paddock, John. 1966. Oaxaca in Ancient Mesoamerica. In *Ancient Oaxaca: Discoveries in Mexican Archaeology and History,* edited by John Paddock, pp. 83–242. Stanford University Press, Stanford.

Paddock, John. 1983. The Oaxaca Barrio at Teotihuacan. In *The Cloud People: Divergent Evolution of the Zapotec and Mixtec Civilizations,* edited by Kent V. Flannery and Joyce Marcus, pp. 170–175. Academic Press, New York.

Redmond, Elsa M., and Charles S. Spencer. 2006. From Raiding to Conquest: Warfare Strategies and Early State Development in Oaxaca, Mexico. In *The Archaeology of Warfare: Prehistories of Raiding and Conquest,* edited by Elizabeth N. Arkush and Mark W. Allen, pp. 336–393. University of Florida Press, Gainesville.

Robles García, Nelly M., and Agustín E. Andrade Cuautle. 2011. El proyecto arqueológico del conjunto monumental de Atzompa. In *Memoria de la quinta mesa redonda de Monte Albán,* edited by N. M. Robles García and A. I. Riviera Guzmán, Instituto Nacional de Antropología e Historia, Mexico, D.F.

Sellen, Adam. 2002. Storm God Impersonators from Ancient Oaxaca. *Ancient Mesoamerica* 13(1):2–19.

Sharer, Robert J. 2007. Early Formative Pottery Trade and the Evolution of Mesoamerican Civilization. *Antiquity* 81:201–203.

Sherman, Jason, Andrew K. Balkansky, Charles S. Spencer, and Brian D. Nicholls. 2010. Expansionary Dynamics of the Nascent Monte Albán State. *Journal of Anthropological Archaeology.* doi:10.1016/j.jaa.2010.04.001.

Spencer, Charles S. 2003. War and Early State Formation in Oaxaca, Mexico. *Proceedings of the National Academy of Sciences of the USA* 100:11185–11187.

Spencer, Charles S. 2007. Territorial Expansion and Primary State Formation in Oaxaca, Mexico. In *Latin American Indigenous Warfare and Ritual Violence,* edited by Richard Chacon and Ruben Mendoza, pp. 55–72. University of Arizona Press, Tucson.

Spencer, Charles S., and Elsa M. Redmond. 1997. *Archaeology of the Cañada de Cuicatlán, Oaxaca.* Anthropological Paper 80, American Museum of Natural History, New York.

Spencer, Charles S., and Elsa M. Redmond. 2001. Multilevel Selection and Political Evolution in the Valley of Oaxaca, 500–100 BC. *Journal of Anthropological Archaeology* 20:195–229.

Spencer, Charles S., and Elsa M. Redmond. 2004. A Late Monte Albán I phase (300–100 BC) Palace in the Valley of Oaxaca. *Latin American Antiquity* 15:441–455.

Spores, Ronald. 1983a. Las Flores Phase Settlement Patterns in the Nochixtlan Valley.
    In *The Cloud People: Divergent Evolution of the Zapotec and Mixtec Civilizations*,
    edited by Kent V. Flannery and Joyce Marcus, pp. 152–155. Academic Press, New
    York.
Spores, Ronald. 1983b. Yucuñudahui. In *The Cloud People: Divergent Evolution of the
    Zapotec and Mixtec Civilizations*, edited by Kent V. Flannery and Joyce Marcus,
    pp. 155–158. Academic Press, New York.
Spores, Ronald. 1983c. Postclassic Mixtec Kingdoms: Ethnohistoric and Archaeological
    Evidence. In *The Cloud People: Divergent Evolution of the Zapotec and Mixtec
    Civilizations*, edited by Kent V. Flannery and Joyce Marcus, pp. 255–260. Academic
    Press, New York.
Urcid Serrano, Javier. 2011. Los oráculos y la guerra: el papel de las narrativas pictóricas
    en el desarrollo temprano de Monte Albán (500 a.C.-200 d.C.). In *V mesa redonda
    de Monte Alban*, edited by Ivan Rivera and Nelly Robles, pp. 163–237. Instituto
    Nacional de Antropología e Historia, Oaxaca City.
Workinger, Andrew G. 2002. Coastal/Highland Interaction in Prehispanic Oaxaca,
    Mexico: The Perspective from San Francisco de Arriba. PhD dissertation,
    Vanderbilt University.

CHAPTER 17

ARCHAEOLOGY OF THE MAYA HIGHLANDS

BÁRBARA ARROYO

THE Guatemala highlands is an area of contrasting climate, topography, and agricultural potential. High basins and fertile valleys are situated among a series of mountain ranges from the Pacific Coastal volcanic chains to the massive uplifts to the northeast, offering several advantages that facilitate human settlement. Some areas are surrounded by large ravines that impede large settlements (Borhegyi 1965). The Central Highlands are home to important natural routes, including the Motagua River, which drains into the Atlantic Ocean and separates a series of these mountain ranges crisscrossing Guatemala from east to west. To the north, tributaries of the Chixoy River irrigate the Central Highlands.

There is still much to learn about the Guatemala highlands. Excavations have been carried out at some sites, as well as a few regional surveys (Smith 1955; Robinson 1994; Robinson et al. 2002); however, the majority of these projects took place in the 1940s and 1950s. Recently, there has been a resurgence of work in the region with many projects now entering the final phases of analysis and publication, as is the case with Xacbal and El Soch in Quiché.

In this chapter, I focus on the Central Highlands, and in particular on the primary site of Kaminaljuyú, which can be used as a proxy to better understand developments throughout the region.

THE CENTRAL HIGHLANDS

The Central Highlands are composed of the Departments of Guatemala, Sacatepéquez, and Chimaltenango. The region is mountainous and volcanic, with some fertile valleys. The highlands are bounded by the Motagua River to the north, the Los Platanos River and the Las Nubes Mountains to the east, Lake Atitlán to the west, and the piedmont to the south (Figure 17.1).

Prehispanic occupation in the area dates to the Preclassic period, around 1000 BC, and it continued through the Postclassic. Developmental dynamics in the region varied, as can be observed in changes in the size and importance of Kaminaljuyú over time. This site was located in the Valley of Guatemala and included more than

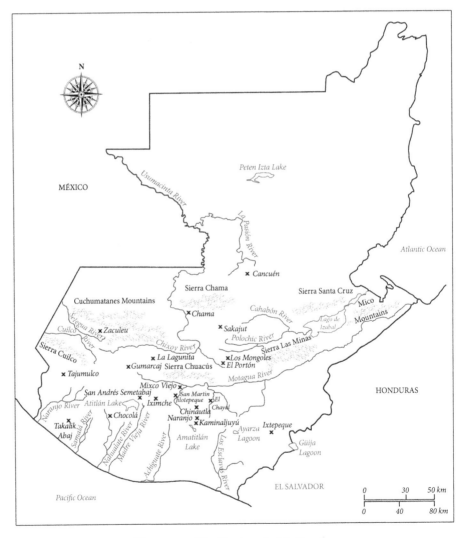

Figure 17.1 The Guatemala highlands.

two hundred structures (Kidder 1961). These constructions consisted of earthen or rubble-filled platforms, the surfaces of which were covered with a layer of clay. In the central valley, Shook (1952) reported interconnected settlements, although none rivaled the size of Kaminaljuyú. Given its geographically strategic location, Kaminaljuyú could control the exchange of goods like obsidian, cacao, jade, and cotton. This control afforded Kaminaljuyú its role as protagonist throughout the prehispanic history of the region.

More complex developments are observed in the Middle Preclassic period. During this period (800-400 BC), several structures were erected around the Miraflores Lake. This area was extremely important because control of the lake allowed prehispanic rulers to control the flow of water used to irrigate fields, starting as early as 500 BC (Barrientos 1997). Social differentiation can be identified in burials with particularly rich offerings in the central part of the site, offering a stark contrast with those in lower-class residential areas. Recent research has revealed a contemporary ceremonial center at Naranjo (800-400 BC), 3 kilometers north of Kaminaljuyú (Arroyo 2010). Most of the plain monuments in the Maya area are from this site, which has a total of thirty-five monuments. Shook (1952) identified thirteen other sites in the Central Highlands with plain stelae; however, the majority had just two or three examples. Thus, Naranjo is assumed to have been of greater importance, making it the regional center during this period.

Researchers from Pennsylvania State University (Michels 1979) have proposed the presence of five dominant lineages, each controlling particular parts of the Central Highlands. This proposal was later investigated through large-scale surveys (Murdy 1984). Nonetheless, Kaminaljuyú seems to have been the most important center, and Love (2008) has suggested that the site was a state, rather than a complex chiefdom, beginning as early as the Middle Preclassic. In the Late Preclassic, the social organization of the site became more complex given that 70 percent of the visible structures were built during this period and then later remodeled. This era of florescence was one in which Kaminaljuyú exercised commercial control throughout the highlands and southern coast, promoting cultural contact with important centers in the neighboring region of Chalchuapa to the east and sites in the Department of Escuintla to the south. The Central Highlands were linked with the northern highlands throughout the Preclassic period.

THE NORTHERN HIGHLANDS

The northern highlands include the Departments of Alta Verapaz, Baja Verapaz, and Quiché. This region is bordered by the Motagua River to the south; the Chamá Mountain Range to the north; the Polochic River Basin to the east; and the Ixcán, Negro, and Chixoy Rivers and their tributaries to the west (see Figure 17.1). There were significant settlements in Baja and Alta Verapaz. Work by Sharer and Sedat (1987) has revealed settlement in the Salamá Valley beginning in the Preclassic period, around 1200 BC. The French Archaeological Mission in Guatemala documented the sites of Sakajut in Alta Verapaz, El Portón in Baja Verapaz, and Río Blanco in Quiché (Ichon and Arnauld 1985).

Population increased from the Middle to Late Preclassic, with the greatest concentration located in the Salamá Valley (Sharer and Sedat 1987). Social classes are demonstrated by the presence of individuals buried with special offerings, human crania that were likely included as trophies, and twelve bodies buried outside of a crypt in Los Mangales, Verapaz. This group likely originated in the southern highlands or the Pacific piedmont and surrounding lowlands. The site of Los Mangales was located along a natural route from the northeast, offering particular commercial advantages.

El Portón, in the Salamá Valley, appears to have been founded as a political center for the entire region with the residences of the nobility located at the neighboring site of Las Tunas. The Salamá Valley is also home to sculpted monuments that included very ancient hieroglyphic texts, generally contemporaneous with the first texts from Kaminaljuyú. These monuments are carved in a very particular style linked to sites to the Central Highlands (Fahsen 2010).

Surveys and other projects in the northern highlands have identified two population groups during the Preclassic: one to the west near the middle course of the Chixoy River and in adjacent Quiché, and one to the east in Baja and Alta Verapaz. Evidence suggests links between the Central Guatemala Valley, the Pacific Coast, and the Maya lowlands to the north, particularly the area near the Pasión River.

Notably, none of the sites mentioned reached the size of centrally located Kaminaljuyú. This fact contributes to the notion that Kaminaljuyú achieved its enormous economic power through control of the exchange in obsidian, jade, cacao, and other important perishable items. Its strategic location along a natural trade route favored an unprecedented development of social complexity at the site during the Late Preclassic.

Toward the end of the Preclassic, an important change has been observed. Popenoe de Hatch (2003) has proposed that this change was brought about by the intrusion of groups from the western highlands, possibly from near La Lagunita in Quiché. This change, and the potential conflict associated with it, is evidenced by the destruction of monuments representing important rulers and community leaders. However, it is possible that intruding groups were not the only cause.

Paleoenvironmental records have documented that around 200 AD an environmental shift with considerable ecological impact affected many centers, particularly Kaminaljuyú. Similar records from the extinct Miraflores Lake reveal its desiccation and the abandonment of its canals around 250 AD (Popenoe de Hatch 2003). The environmental changes appear to have affected other places as well. In neighboring Sacatepéquez, evidence from the Quilisimate Lagoon indicates a drought occurred around 260 AD (Robinson et al. 2002). Paleoenvironmental research on the Pacific Coast also demonstrates that this region suffered a drought at the end of the Late Preclassic, around 200 AD (Neff et al. 2006). Based on recent research by Lozano-García and colleagues (2010) at Verde Lake in the Tuxtlas Mountain range, this event had an impact far beyond the Maya highlands and the southern coast.

If Kaminaljuyú maintained a strong relationship with several great Mesoamerican centers, as well as other sites of lesser importance in the hierarchy, the drought must have affected the social organization. The result could have been rebellions, and external groups taking advantage of the opportunity of weakened political control to confront and possibly subjugate the Preclassic population of this important center.

Climactic conditions stabilized during the Classic period, as observed in the decline in forested areas and the increase in plant species that thrive in open areas (Neff et al. 2006). This situation favored population expansion, and, through alliances, may have resulted in a group of highland Maya wielding considerable economic and social power. Beginning around 400 AD, Kaminaljuyú extended its exchange networks to the Central Mexican Highlands, as seen in the site's architecture and rich tombs suggesting strong ties with Teotihuacan (Kidder, Jennings, and Shook 1946; Sanders and Michels 1977). Nevertheless, recent osteological analyses indicate that Kaminaljuyú had ties with both Teotihuacan and the Maya lowlands (Wright et al. 2010). Kaminaljuyú continued to be an important center with a political system distinct from that of the Preclassic, distinguishing and formalizing itself as the center of power by controlling several important trade routes. These routes were controlled by this new group, which Hatch refers to as a Mexicanized group (Popenoe de Hatch 2003), who entered the valley at the end of the Preclassic and took over control of Kaminaljuyú.

The social complexity achieved by the population of the neighboring region of Salamá at the end of the Preclassic and beginning of the Classic is exemplified by the burial of a leader or shaman at the site of La Lagunita (Ichon 1985). During this period (100–600 AD), impressive cultural developments are seen in the largest ceremonial group (Group A) of La Lagunita with pyramids 10 meters tall and a cruciform spatial layout. The axes of the site included offerings of thirteen statuettes in front of the entrance to an artificial cave in the center of the plaza. Inside of the man-made cave, large stone slabs were found on the floor along with multiple objects, including three hundred ceramic vessels. The cave was sealed sometime between 350 and 400 AD.

Interestingly, Arnauld (2003) has identified linguistic differences among the groups that inhabited the northern highlands, possibly reflecting sociopolitical or ethnic/cultural fragmentation in the region at the beginning of the Classic period (100–400 AD). This same pattern may have also prevailed during the Epiclassic (900–1100 AD) when instability arose among the groups in the Verapaz regions following the demographic growth of the Late Classic period (600–900 AD).

In the Late Classic, there was a short hiatus in occupation although the ceramic materials indicate continuity in populations. Remarkably, ballcourts and the sculptures that served as field markers have been reported from several sites dating to this period (Shook 1952). Late Classic sites are located in the valleys and on slopes of the Central Highlands. The administration of these sites appears to have become less centralized during this period, and ties with the Pacific Coast were strengthened (Popenoe de Hatch and Shook 1999).

Site density increased in the northern highlands (Figure 17.1), with site organization and orientation dictated by the terrain. Topography had the greatest impact on the spatial organization of these centers. During the Protohistoric period, ballcourts are found with patios or plazas, and defensive sites were located in the high mountains or on peninsulas of land surrounded by ravines.

The northern highlands may have had contact with sites in Chiapas and the Maya lowlands as early as the Preclassic, certainly by the Early Classic. These contacts continued into the Protohistoric period. The region appears to have entered into conflict during the Postclassic period because defensive locations and settlements surrounded by walls and terraces became the norm (Smith and Kidder 1951; Woodbury and Trik 1953).

Recently, several projects have focused on the northern highlands, examining sites such as Xacbal (Velásquez, personal communication, 2010) and El Soch. These studies have offered a general view of the highlands, indicating a social organization more closely resembling that of chiefdoms with commercial economies, veneration of cave systems, and less investment in art.

One of the most important sites in the region is Cancuén in Alta Verapaz. Recent research at the site indicates that it was a- key commercial center during the Classic period, enjoying strong ties with the Maya lowlands to the north. The discovery of a jade workshop at the site suggests it was an important area for the production of jade objects traded with distant areas to the north (Kovacevich 2006). The site's architecture follows the highland pattern of using stone slabs, although some sections of the site, like the palace, more closely resemble the lowland style. This has led Demarest (Demarest and Martinez 2010) to suggest that the site had an international style and functioned as a critical commercial center. Demarest argues that toward the end of the Classic, Cancuén was a hegemonic state with specialized exchange, production of jade and other items for export, control of a long-distance exchange network, and a subdivided political structure (Demarest and Martinez 2010).

The highlands suffered a drastic drop in population at the beginning of the Postclassic period (1000-1200 AD). Centers changed in size and function, and it seems that the population was now concentrated in nucleated villages. Some of the sites in the central valley include Kaminaljuyú, Taltic, San Antonio Frutal, and Solano. The sites in Chimaltenango include La Merced, Chuabaj, Saquitacaj-Chibalo, and Tzabalaj-Comalapa. Some of these sites have stone sculptures.

In contrast to the Early Postclassic, the latter half of this period (1200-1524 AD) saw a substantial increase in the population at most of the sites in Chimaltenango and the Departments of Sacatepéquez and Guatemala. This may have been related to migrations from outside the region. Kaminaljuyú became a dispersed village, while a large, regional center was located at either Chinautla or Beleh. The latter site was characterized by a natural defensive system, a feature it shared with contemporary settlements in other regions where conflict between social groups had increased.

Investigation of the Postclassic period in the northern highlands has focused on sites in the Chixoy River Basin, with Cauinal and Cahyup being the most important sites at this time. Cahyup, to the north of Rabinal in Baja Verapaz, was founded in the twelfth century by the Pokomames, who were later conquered by the Agaabes, a Quiché group. Cauinal, which was flooded by the Chixoy reservoir, is located in the valley of the same name.

THE WESTERN HIGHLANDS

Few studies have been conducted in the western highlands but the area was occupied during the Preclassic and Classic periods. Sites here include Semetabaj and Chukumuk near Lake Atitlán, although both also have Classic-period occupations (Shook, Popenoe de Hatch, and Donaldson 1979). At neighboring Huehuetenango, Cambote (Clark et al. 2001) was important, with pottery similar to that found in the central and western highlands, including figures and vessels very similar to those from Kaminaljuyú that demonstrates contact between these regions as early as 800 BC.

The site of Zaculeu was the capital of a Mam kingdom and had significant occupation during the Early Classic and Postclassic periods. It is surrounded by drainages that afforded a defensive position (Woodbury and Trik 1953). Zaculeu was the most important site during the Classic period. Rich tombs dating to 400 AD have been uncovered, as well as evidence of important texts during the Late Classic (Woodbury and Trik 1953). Surveys in the Huehuetenango area have documented a population increase in the valley during the Late Classic and Early Postclassic. Other sites in the region also show indications of multicultural change (Iglesias Ponce de León and Ciudad 1999). The site of Gumarcaaj and its Quiché inhabitants conquered lands to the north, south, east, and west of the highlands. They dominated critical commercial routes like those between the highlands and the Pacific Coast and thus maintained control of the region and defended it against the Mam.

The neighboring Chiapas highlands, particularly the Grijalva Basin, offer information comparable to studies in the Guatemala highlands. During the Late Preclassic (400 BC–100 AD), some sites in the western Guatemala highlands (e.g., Cambote) had ties with the Chiapas highlands through the transport and distribution of obsidian. The largest population occurs during the latter part of the Late Preclassic and the early part of the Classic period, with ties to the site of Kaminaljuyú. In particular, Ojo de Agua, Chiapas, is an important Early

Classic-period site, and it is possible that subsequent population density in Grijalva Basin settlements during the Classic period have buried evidence of earlier occupations. Examples of Late Classic-period sites include Lagartero, Tenam Rosario, Ojo de Agua, and Guajilar (Bryant, Clark, and Cheetham 2005). The Postclassic has not been well studied; still, we know that Canajasté (Blake 2010) was significant, as were Guajilar and Los Encuentros (Bryant, Clark, and Cheetham 2005).

FINAL COMMENTS

Kaminaljuyú was the key site in the region from its beginnings in the Classic period when it enjoyed decentralized power, although the settlement became more dispersed toward the end of that period. Contacts maintained throughout the site's history extended to the Pacific Coast, eastern Guatemala, the Petén lowlands, and southeastern Mesoamerica. Due to its location in the valley occupied by Guatemala City, considerable information has been lost to modern settlements. However, this has not obscured Kaminaljuyú's importance in the region.

The Guatemala highlands offer several research opportunities for furthering our understanding of prehispanic Mesoamerica. There are sites throughout the highlands that have never been investigated and would considerably increase our understanding and improve the archaeological record of the area. More work is needed to truly understand the nature of the region and to be able to compare it with better-known regions. The region has enjoyed a dynamic history with various groups taking advantage of this strategic location to control critical resources and trade routes and maintain power throughout history.

REFERENCES

Arnauld, Marie Charlotte. 2003. ¿El fin del mundo? La Lagunita (El Quiché)? In *Misceláneas en honor a Alain Ichon*, edited by M. Ch. Arnauld, A. Breton, M. F. Fauvet-Berthelot, and J. A. Valdés, pp. 37–48. CEMCA and Asociación Tikal, Guatemala.

Arroyo, Bárbara. 2010. *Entre cerros, cafetales y urbanismo en el Valle de Guatemala: Proyecto de Rescate Naranjo*. Publicación Especial No. 47 de la Academia de Geografía e Historia de Guatemala.

Barrientos, Tomás. 1997. Desarrollo evolutivo del sistema de canals hdiráulicos en Kaminaljuyú. B.A. thesis, Universidad del Valle de Guatemala.

Blake, Michael. 2010. Colonization, Warfare and Exchange at the Postclassic Maya Site of Canajaste, Chiapas, Mexico. *Papers of the New World Archaeological Foundation* No. 70, Brigham Young University, Provo, Utah.

Borhegyi, Stephan F. de. 1965. Archaeological Synthesis of the Guatemalan Highlands. *Handbook of Middle American Indians*, vol. 1, edited by G. R. Willey, pp. 3–50. University of Texas Press, Austin.

Bryant, Douglas Donne, John E. Clark, and David Cheetham. 2005. Ceramic Sequence of the Upper Grijalva Region, Chiapas, Mexico. *Papers of the New World Archaeological Foundation,* No. 67, Brigham Young University, Provo, Utah.

Clark, John E., M. Tejada, D. Castillo, D. Cheetham, D. Nuttall, and B. Balcárcel. 2001. Prospección arqueológica de la cuenca superior del Río Grijalva en Huehuetenango, Guatemala. Reporte Final de la Temporada 1999. Manuscript submitted to the Instituto de Antropología e Historia de Guatemala.

Demarest, Arthur A., and H. Martinez. 2010. El intento infructuoso a una transición Clásico Postclásico en Cancuen. En *XXIII Simposio de Investigaciones Arqueológicas en Guatemala*, edited by Bárbara Arroyo, Adriana Linares, and Lorena Paiz, pp. 609–620. Museo Nacional de Arqueología y Etnología y Asociación Tikal.

Fahsen, Federico. 2010. *The Place of Stone Monuments, Context, Use and Meaning in Mesoamerica's Preclassic Transition*, edited by Julia Guernsey, John E. Clark and Bárbara Arroyo, pp. 231–258. Dumbarton Oaks, Washington, DC.

Ichon, Alain. 1985. La fouille du groupe a de La Lagunita (periode protoclassique). In *Le Protoclassique a La Lagunita, El Quiché, Guatemala*, edited by Alain Ichon and M. Ch. Arnauls, pp. 11–102. CNRS, Institut dÉthnologie, Paris.

Ichon, Alain, and M. Ch. Arnauld. 1985. *Le Protoclassique a La Lagunita, El Quiché, Guatemala.* CNRS, Institut dÉthnologie, Paris.

Iglesias Ponce de León, María Josefa, and A. Ciudad Ruiz. 1999. El Altiplano Occidental. In *Historia General de Guatemala*, Volume I, Época Precolombina, edited by Marion Poponoe de Hatch, pp. 265–288. Asociación de Amigos del País, Guatemala.

Kidder, Alfred V. 1961. Archaeological Investigations at Kamianl Juyu, Guatemala. *American Philosophical Society* 105(6):559–570.

Kidder, Alfred V., J. Jennings, and E. M. Shook. 1946. *Excavations at Kamianljuyu, Guatemala.* Pennsylvania State University, University Park.

Kovacevich, Brigitte. 2006. Reconstruction of Classic Maya Economic Systems: Production and Exchange at Cancuen, Guatemala. PhD dissertation, Department of Anthropology, Vanderbilt University, Nashville, Tennessee.

Love, Michael. 2008. Early States in the Southern Maya Region. Paper presented at the Early Maya States conference organized by Robert Sharer and Loa Traxler at the University Pennsylvania Museum, Philadelphia.

Lozano García, Socorro, Margarita Caballero, Beatriz Ortega, Susana Sosa, Alejandro Rodríguez, and Peter Schaaf. 2010. Late Holocene Paleoecology of Lago Verde: Evidence of Human Impact and Climate Change in the Northern Limit of the Neotropics during the Late Formative and Classic Periods. *Vegetation History Archaeobotany*19:177–190.

Michels, Joseph. 1979. *The Kaminaljuyú Chiefdom.* Pennsylvania State University, University Park.

Murdy, Carson. 1984. Prehistoric Man-Land Relationships through Time in the Valley of Guatemala. PhD dissertation. Pennsylvania State University, University Park.

Neff, Hector, D. Pearsall, J. Jones, B. Arroyo, and D. Freidel. 2006. Climate Change and Population History in the Pacific Lowlands of Southern Mesoamerica. *Quaternary Research* 65:390–400.

Popenoe de Hatch, Marion. 2003. La ceramic del Altiplano Noroccidental de Guatemala, La Lagunita y la Tradición cerámica Solano: Algunas comparaciones. In

Misceláneas en honor a Alain Ichon, edited by Charlotte M. Arnauld, Alain Breton, Marie-Francis,Fauvet-Berthelot, and Juan Antonio Valdés, pp. 49–64. CEMCA and Asociación Tikal, Guatemala.

Popenoe de Hatch, Marion, and E. M. Shook. 1999. *La arqueología de la Costa Sur*. In *Historia general de Guatemala*, Volume I, Época Precolombina, edited by Marion Popenoe de Hatch, pp. 171–190. Asociación de Amigos del País, Guatemala.

Robinson, Eugenia. 1994. Reporte preliminar del Proyecto Kaqchikel: Area de las faldas del Volcán de Agua entre Ciudad Vieja y San Miguel Escobar. Report submitted to the Instituto de Antropología e Historia de Guatemala.

Robinson, Eugenia, Pat M. Farrell, Kitty F. Emery, Dorothy E. Freidel, and Geoffrey E. Braswell. 2002. Preclassic Settlements and Geomorphology in the Highlands of Guatemala: Excavations at Urías, Valley of Guatemala. In *Incidents of Archaeology in Central America and Yucatán, Essays in Honor of Edwin M. Shook*, edited by Michael Love, Marion Popenoe de Hatch, and Héctor Escobedo, pp. 251–276. University Press of America, Oxford.

Sanders, William T., and J. W. Michels. 1977. *Teotihuacan and Kaminaljuyu: A Study in Prehistoric Culture Contact*. Pennsylvania State University, University Park.

Sharer, Robert J., and D. W. Sedat. 1987. *Archaeological Investigations in the Northern Maya Highlands, Guatemala: Interaction and the Development of Maya Civilization*. The University Museum Monograph 59, University of Pennsylvania, Philadelphia.

Shook, Edwin. 1952. Lugares arqueológicos del Altiplano meridional central de Guatemala. *Antropología e Historia de Guatemala* 4(2):3–40.

Shook, Edwin M., Marion P. de Hatch, and Jamie Donaldson. 1979. *Ruins of Semetabaj, Department of Solola, Guatemala*. University of California, Berkeley.

Smith, A. Ledyard 1955. *Archaeological Reconnaissance in Central Guatemala*. 608 Carnegie Institution of Washington, Washington, DC.

Smith, A. Ledyard, and A. V. Kidder. 1951. *Excavations at Nebaj, Guatemala*. 594 Carnegie Institution of Washington, Washington, DC.

Woodbury, Richard B., and A. S. Trik. 1953. *The Ruins of Zaculeu, Guatemala*, 2 volumes. William Byrd Press, United Fruit Company, Richmond.

Wright, Lori, Juan A. Valdés, James H. Burton, T. Douglas Price, and Henry P. Schwarcz. 2010. The Children of Kaminaljuyú: Isotopic Insight into Diet and Long-Distance Interaction in Mesoamerica. *Journal of Anthropological Archaeology*, 29:155–178.

CHAPTER 18

COMPLEX SOCIETIES IN THE SOUTHERN MAYA LOWLANDS

THEIR DEVELOPMENT AND FLORESCENCE IN THE ARCHAEOLOGICAL RECORD

ARLEN F. CHASE AND

DIANE Z. CHASE

THE evolution of sociopolitical complexity in the southern Maya lowlands is much discussed but as yet is incompletely resolved. Considerations are hampered by the fact that most early archaeological materials lie deeply buried beneath later human construction activity, making it difficult to locate remains that are directly relevant to questions bearing on the rise of complexity. Even should such remains be located, the overlying constructions usually make areal exposure of the earlier materials difficult. Nevertheless, sufficient evidence exists to posit a trajectory of complexity developing from Preclassic villages to Early Classic states to Late Classic attempts at creating hegemonic empires.

DIVERSE EARLY POPULATIONS

While there is some evidence for Archaic hunters in the coastal lowlands of Belize as early as 3400 BC, based primarily on archaeologically recovered lithic points (Lohse et al. 2006), the remains relevant to the earliest sedentary Maya appear in the southern lowlands (Figure 18.1) some three millennia ago at the onset of the Early Preclassic period (1200–900 BC). When encountered, these materials represent fully formed village societies. These early populations were familiar with raised-platform architecture and participated in broader Mesoamerican networks. Each of these early developments is associated with regional ceramic styles that are largely distinct. While the earliest dates may vary slightly from site to site, shortly after 900 BC complex regional developments can be found in the archaeological record of the southern Maya lowlands for northern Belize (Swasey), for west-central Belize (Cunil), for the central Petén (Eb), and for the Usumacinta area (Xe). Interments were simple compared to the later Classic period, but nevertheless they regularly contained pottery vessels and, in some cases, imported shell or jadeite adornments. No solid archaeological evidence has yet been encountered for in situ developmental precedents for these village groups, causing some researchers to argue for an influx of other Mesoamerican

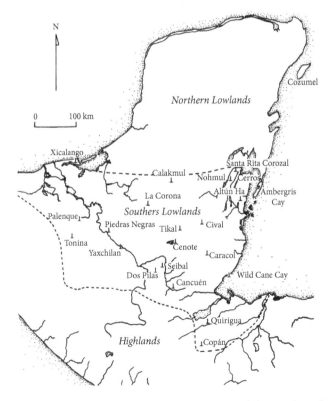

Figure 18.1 Map of the Maya area, showing the location of the southern lowlands and the major sites mentioned in the text.

populations, such as the Mixe-Zoque from Veracruz and Chiapas, into the Maya area at this early date (Ball and Taschek 2003). Whatever the case, a series of diverse village communities dotted the landscape of the Maya southern lowlands in the first half of the first millennium BC. Sometime after 600 BC, the cultural remains associated with these communities became more standardized, especially in terms of ceramics and architecture, becoming readily identifiable as "Maya."

EARLY IDEOLOGY AND A PAN-MESOAMERICAN CONNECTION

Most researchers do not see any direct linkage between the contemporary Olmec ceramic complexes recovered at San Lorenzo and La Venta, Mexico, and those found in the Maya southern lowlands (Andrews V 1987). However, it is possible that both the Maya and the Olmec used the same conceptual base for their earliest public plazas, generally referred to either as "Astronomical Commemorative Assemblages" or as "E Groups" (A. Chase and D. Chase 2006). The importance of ideology to the founding of Maya sites may also be found in early deposits deeply buried in the sacred locations around which Maya sites were centered. Such deposits are difficult to find because early Maya earth-moving efforts resulted in the construction of massive horizontal platforms (Joyce 2004). While interments with offerings are found by at least 900 BC, the earliest elaborate Maya caches appear to date several hundred years later, dating to between 700 to 600 BC. Among the earliest of these ritual deposits to be found associated with monumental architecture are two cruciform cache pits, both associated with jadeite celts (Estrada-Belli 2006). One cache derives from Seibal, Guatemala, and the other is from Cival, Guatemala. Other early deposits of jadeite celts, horizontally arranged in rows, have been recovered more recently deep beneath the Seibal plazas. The material similarities in content between these Maya caches and those known from the Olmec area raise questions of interconnections between these two cultures, further suggesting that, even though ceramic complexes differ, ritual components of early Maya ideology may share some material aspects with those known from the Olmec area.

E-GROUP CRYSTALLIZATION

The Maya of the southern lowlands adopted the E Group configuration (consisting of a western pyramid and an eastern platform supporting three structures) as the basic plan for the public architecture of almost all major centers (Figure 18.2). This

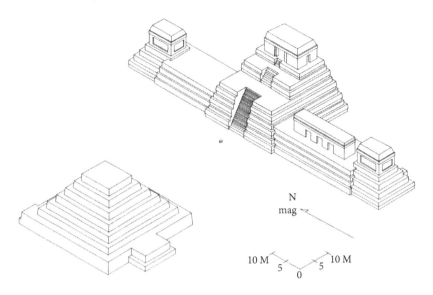

Figure 18.2 Isometric reconstruction of the Cenote E Group (after A. Chase and
D. Chase 1995).

architectural complex differentiates the early Maya of the southern lowlands from
their neighbors elsewhere in Mesoamerica (A. Chase and D. Chase 1995). E Groups
have commonly been assumed to function as observatories useful for defining
astronomical events such as solstices and equinoxes; however, the variation in
their formal structural alignments (e.g. Aimers and Rice 2006) suggests that this
was likely not the case. The architectural buildings that make up the grouping
are more probably associated with a series of deities important to the founding of
Maya social order. The western pyramid in the E Group has been correlated with
maize iconography (Estrada-Belli 2006). Rather than representing the transition
of the sun over the course of a year, the three buildings situated upon the eastern
platforms in the various E Groups may represent the "triad"—sacred deities noted
in epigraphic texts that were important in the formal founding of each Maya center
(A. Chase and D. Chase 2006).

     By 300 BC, many sites also exhibited large vertical architectural complexes—
distinct from the original E Groups—that consisted of three pyramidal structures
set atop a tall raised platform. In concert with the E Groups, these triadic platforms
formed part of the architectural charter that provided legitimization for elite rule.
The murals from San Bartolo, Guatemala, reflect this cosmological charter and
explicitly show how Maya rulership was centered—in terms of five world trees or
directions and based on an explicit association with the maize god; the human
ruler was viewed as a representative of this deity (Saturno et al. 2005). This ideology and the triadic architectural complexes came into general use in the southern
Maya lowlands during the Late Preclassic period (300 BC to 250 AD). The widespread popularity of this architectural charter is echoed in the ceramic uniformity that characterized the Maya lowlands at this time. The Maya may have been

the source of inspiration for both triadic groups and an E Group found in central Teotihuacan, Mexico (LaPorte and Fialko 1995), a suggestion consistent with the widespread economic and multidirectional sociopolitical interaction that characterized early Mesoamerica.

DIFFERENTIATION

For almost four hundred years of the Late Preclassic period (300 BC–250 AD), similar material culture characterized much of the Maya lowlands. Sometime around 100 AD, however, segments of the material culture began to change. After a long period that focused on the use of monochrome red slip in Maya ceramics, polychromy was introduced, as were new pottery forms that were reminiscent of other parts of Mesoamerica. The intensification of agriculture also increased the economic output for the Maya and provided the necessary resources for the elaboration of Maya society. During the Late Preclassic period, agricultural intensification was focused on raised-field architecture (Turner and Harrison 1981); in the Classic period (250–800 AD), agricultural intensification in several lowland areas focused on extensively terracing the landscape.

A florescence of Maya society occurred in the Late Preclassic in the northern Petén lowlands—as represented by the sites of Mirador and Nakbe (Hansen 2005). During this era, the inhabitants of Mirador constructed some of the largest pyramidal structures seen in the southern Maya lowlands. It has also been suggested that an elaborate causeway system tied together the first regional state to arise in the Maya area. Yet the archaeological remains have yet to confirm that Maya elites had fully differentiated themselves from other members of society.

Major changes occurred in the Maya area at the end of the Late Preclassic period, with some of the more precocious sites, like Mirador, being largely abandoned until the Late Classic period. During this same time frame (ca. 100 AD), however, some of the earliest archaeologically excavated Maya elite tombs were situated within public architecture (Coe 1990). The appearance of these tombs can be linked to the celebration of specific human ancestors who were beginning to change the ideological charter for rule away from the deity-based E Group complexes. By 250 AD—at the onset of the Early Classic period—both elite tombs and carved stone monuments with hieroglyphic texts became conjoined with E Groups, signifying that elite families were claiming specific ritual locations and control over established communities. Various aspects of this conjunction can be seen in the archaeology of the central Petén of Guatemala at the sites of Cenote, Tikal, and Cival. Once cosmologically centered and hieroglyphically sanctioned, however, Maya rulership became expressed and accessorized in different ways at the various sites of the southern lowlands.

Architectural complexes, referred to colloquially as "palaces" (Inomata and Houston 2001), became widespread throughout the lowlands and were paired with a concomitant florescence of the stela-altar cult (in which vertical stones portraying ruling individuals and containing hieroglyphic texts were paired with horizontal carved or plain altars). The written hieroglyphic records on these stone monuments served to position Maya leaders within cosmological time and to foster their political competitiveness. Many Maya centers used these texts to establish founding dates for their political dynasties, the bulk of which fell within the Early Classic time frame: 100 AD for Tikal; 320 AD for Yaxchilán; 331 AD for Caracol; and 426 AD for Copán. Other sites, however, like Naranjo and Palenque, claimed foundings in earlier mythological time.

It is clear from the burial data that minimally rank, and in some places stratified, societies were in place throughout the Maya lowlands at the beginning of the Early Classic period (250–550 AD) and that rulership was a prerogative of a small elite group at each site. This group differentiated itself in death through an ostentatious display of wealth (Figure 18.3). With this differentiation, the sites of the southern lowlands followed varied paths after 500 AD. Ostentatious display by the Maya elites continued at some sites, like Tikal, into the Late Classic period. At other sites, like Caracol, the elites utilized a different strategy for governing.

The Early Classic period (250–550 AD) in the southern Maya lowlands was characterized by the emergence of several primary centers—and presumably states—in the southern lowlands; these included Palenque to the west, Caracol to

Figure 18.3 Photograph of an elaborate Early Classic tomb from Santa Rita Corozal, Belize. Along with eight pottery vessels, the tomb contained a carved stone bowl, jadeite and pyrite earrings, a blue-jadeite pendant a chert ceremonial bar, three chert spearpoints, three jadeite tinklers, three large seashells, three turtle shells, stuccoed artifacts, and a host of other artifactual remains (see D. Chase and A. Chase 2005).

the east, Copán to the southeast, Piedras Negras on the Usumacinta River, El Perú and Tikal in the central Petén, and Calakmul in south-central Yucatán. The elites at most of these sites coveted Teotihuacan-style material culture, which was originally utilized to emphasize their higher status. A rich cremation from Caracol suggests that at least one Teotihuacano may have married into that site's elite prior to 350 AD (A. Chase and D. Chase 2011). While some epigraphers suggest that actual Teotihuacanos controlled the political scene in the Maya lowlands during the Early Classic and were responsible for the Tikal dynasty, the archaeological data suggest otherwise (Braswell 2003). Stable isotope analyses show that only local inhabitants were present in the "Teotihuacanoid" elite tombs of Tikal, consistent with similar data from the Guatemalan highland site of Kaminaljuyú (Wright 2005).

The majority of these polities were relatively small city-states, whose interactions with neighboring groups are documented in hieroglyphic texts. However, Tikal emerged as the preeminent site of the Early Classic period and may have formed the first—although fleeting—hegemonic Maya empire.

The Interpretive Politics
of the Late Classic Maya

The Late Classic period was characterized by a series of competing states. While Maya epigraphers have constructed a story of the Late Classic period as being characterized by conflict between two large hegemonic centers—Calakmul and Tikal (Martin and Grube 2000)—both the epigraphy and the archaeology can be interpreted as revealing something far more complicated. Hieroglyphic texts don't tell the whole story; they need to be contextualized. Besides political matters, these writings also deal extensively with cosmology (Stuart 2005). In some cases, multiple ideological interpretations can be generated from the same texts and, in other cases, the political texts themselves don't match the archaeological reality.

One key to our epigraphic understanding of the Late Classic period are widespread hieroglyphic references to the "snake emblem," also referred to as "Site Q," which is thought to be a prime mover and potential "super-state" (Martin and Grube 2000). Researchers have tended to assign Site Q to the center of Calakmul, largely because of that site's size and extensive stela count. However, contrary to the established epigraphic paradigm, the location of Site Q and the function of the emblem glyph itself remain open to interpretation. The emblem may be an arbitrarily grouped cacophony of animal heads (Harrison 2008), and textual reference to the enigmatic Site Q emblem may refer to ideology and cosmology rather than to political matters (A. Chase et al. 2009).

The Late Classic period (550–800 AD) in the southern lowlands represented the height of Maya artistic expression, particularly with regard to polychrome figure vases and carved-stone monuments (Figure 18.4). This was also the time of the greatest population density in the southern lowlands; almost every residential group excavated there contains evidence of habitation during this time span (Culbert and Rice 1990). A multitude of sites flourished, and the evidence for extensive agricultural intensification in the form of terracing during the Early and Late Classic periods in the Maya Mountains of Belize and the southern Yucatán Peninsula has long been recognized (Donkin 1979). Although such agricultural intensification cannot be readily identified everywhere in the southern lowlands, it likely existed given the evidence for substantial population numbers.

Our view of Classic Maya society is currently in flux. In the past it has been characterized on the basis of limited sampling, both of mapped areas of sites and of

Figure 18.4 The back of Late Classic Caracol Stela 6, portraying a deceased ruler (after Beetz and Satterthwaite 1981).

excavation of architectural groups. Because of the limited nature of the data classes that were collected, contrasting models of ancient Maya society have arisen (e.g., Fox et al. 1996). However, new technologies, such as Light Detection And Ranging (LIDAR), are in the process of redefining how Maya landscape studies can be done (A. Chase et al. 2010). These technologies reveal that the Late Classic Maya lived in a heavily modified anthropogenic environment; they show that sites once considered to be discrete units are actually part of a unified whole; and, they suggest that the Maya were far more complex than some researchers believed.

Maya cities also gained their greatest areal extent in the Late Classic; some, like Caracol (Figure 18.5) and Tikal, had each occupied and completely utilized a landscape on the order of 200 square kilometers in size and contained upwards of 100,000 occupants. These Maya low-density cities are consistent with other tropical expressions of urbanism noted for Southeast Asia and Africa (Fletcher 2009). Many ancient Maya cities contain spatially distinct areas of public architecture separated by several kilometers. In some cases, these architectural complexes were linked together into a cohesive system through the use of causeways (Shaw 2008) and continuous residential settlements. The integrated siting of large plazas through a Maya landscape, conjoined with the widespread distribution of commodities and exotics like pottery and obsidian, suggest that the Late Classic Maya participated in a market economy (A. Chase and D. Chase 2007).

Figure 18.5 Photograph of Caracol's central architectural complex, "Caana." Rising 43.5 meters above its frontal plaza, this unique construction serves as the Late Classic palace for a 200-square-kilometer metropolis. It mimics triadic complexes of a much earlier era.

LATE CLASSIC MAYA CITIES, STATES, AND EMPIRES

As seen through archaeological evidence for the existence of stratification, the Maya surely achieved state-level societies by the beginning of the Early Classic period, if not before (A. Chase et al. 2009). In contrast to Early Classic states that were generally centered around one primary city, Late Classic states often incorporated other smaller centers into broader polities. In some cases, other larger centers were brought under direct political control for an extended period of time, forming what might be referred to as an "empire." An example is Caracol, which appears to have controlled Naranjo, some 42 kilometers away, for approximately fifty years. In other cases, loose alliances were formed in which one center is viewed as having the upper hand, forming what have been termed as "hegemonic empires" in Mesoamerica; both Tikal and Calakmul are referred to in these terms.

Much of our interpretation about Maya states is predicated on the hieroglyphic inscriptions of the various rulers who occupied the cities of the southern lowlands. Without hieroglyphic texts (or with badly eroded records), sites like Altún Ha in Belize and Xultun in Guatemala tend to be excluded from political reconstructions even though they have evidence for extensive settlements and substantial external trade. Because the hieroglyphic texts focus on the individual within the institution of rulership, Maya states have often been framed as being controlled by "divine kings" (Freidel 2008). These divine kings are believed to have been situated in the main palaces of certain Maya cities (Inomata and Houston 2001)—but many Maya cities supported more than one palace, implying that others qualified for these quarters.

During the Late Classic period, there was further differentiation of political structures among sites. The spatial extent, population numbers, and public works present at many Maya cities and polities are apparent and must have required some sort administrative bureaucracy that would have functioned as a secondary elite. At sites like Caracol, administrative bureaucracy moved to the forefront and divine kingship moved to the background (D. Chase and A. Chase 2008). At Caracol, the attempt to return to divine kingship in the Terminal Classic period (800–900 AD) provides a key impetus to the collapse in providing an ill-advised dynastic intervention that broke with long-established economic patterns. While Maya states may have been fairly uniform in the Early Classic period, over the course of the Classic period different Maya polities came to focus on distinct governing strategies that helped to create very diverse Late Classic polities. These differences determined the varied and protracted nature of the Maya collapse.

By the end of the Late Classic there were multiple kinds of states in existence in the southern lowlands. Some focused on divine kingship, but others had moved to more complex political orders. The largest Maya states were characterized by huge populations—between 50,000 and 115,000 people in the main center and between 300,000 to 600,000 people in the regional state. The various polities in the Maya southern lowlands used diverse strategies to manage their inhabitants. Some states managed huge regional areas and effectively regulated their landscapes, while others may have been more cavalier in their treatment of the environment. Thus, a complicated set of polities existed throughout the southern lowlands at the end of the Late Classic period. While some, like Dos Pilas, Guatemala, were destroyed by war shortly after 760 AD (O'Mansky and Dunning 2004), other states continued to prosper for another 140 years before succumbing to the complex events that eventually caused Classic Maya civilization in the southern lowlands to essentially disappear shortly after 900 AD (D. Chase and A. Chase 2006).

CONCLUSION

While the archaeological data for the development of Maya civilization in the southern lowlands are difficult to synthesize, investigations over the last century have revealed a civilization with great complexity. The Maya filled the southern lowlands with people and created complex political systems, grounded in ancient cosmology, to manage their populations. Like peoples throughout the world, Maya elites fought and schemed to gain social and economic control not only of their own populations but also of their neighbors' societies. The Maya contribution to a general understanding of complex societies is only now coming to fruition as we gain better archaeological samples. Much of the current research is resulting in a completely new understanding of the place of the ancient Maya among the world's past civilizations.

REFERENCES

Aimers, James J., and Prudence M. Rice. 2006. Astronomy, Ritual, and the Interpretation of Maya "E-Group" Architectural Assemblages, *Ancient Mesoamerica* 17:79–96.

Andrews V, E. Wyllys. 1990. Early Ceramic History of the Lowland Maya. In *Vision and Revision in Maya Studies*, edited by F. Clancy and P. D. Harrison, pp. 1–19. University of New Mexico Press, Albuquerque.

Ball, Joseph W., and Jennifer T. Taschek. 2003. Reconsidering the Belize Valley Preclassic: A Case for Multiethnic Interactions in the Development of a Regional Culture Tradition. *Ancient Mesoamerica* 14:179–217.

Beetz, Carl P., and Linton Satterthwaite. 1981. *The Monuments and Inscriptions of Caracol, Belize.* Monograph 45, University of Pennsylvania Museum, Philadelphia.

Braswell, Geoffrey E. 2003. *The Maya and Teotihuacan: Reinterpreting Early Classic Interaction.* University of Texas Press, Austin.

Chase, Arlen F., and Diane Z. Chase. 1995. External Impetus, Internal Synthesis, and Standardization: E Group Assemblages and the Crystallization of Classic Maya Society in the Southern Lowlands. *Acta Mesoamericana* 8:87–101.

Chase, Arlen F., and Diane Z. Chase. 2006. En medio de la nada, en el centro del universo: Perspectivas sobre el desarrollo de las ciudades mayas. In *Nuevas ciudades, nuevas patrias: Fundacion y relocalizacion de ciudades en Mesoamerica y el Mediterraneo Antiguo*, edited by Mª Josefa Iglesias Ponce de Leon, Rogelio Valencia Rivera, and Andrés Ciudad Ruiz, pp. 39–64. S.E.E.M., Madrid.

Chase, Arlen F., and Diane Z. Chase. 2007. Ancient Maya Urban Development: Insights from the Archaeology of Caracol, Belize. *Belizean Studies* 29(2):60–72.

Chase, Arlen F. and Diane Z. Chase. 2011. Status and Power: Caracol, Teotihuacan, and the Early Classic Maya World. *Research Reports in Belizean Archaeology* 8:3–18.

Chase, Arlen F., Diane Z. Chase, and John F. Weishampel. 2010. Lasers in the Jungle: Airborne Sensors Reveal a Vast Maya Landscape. *Archaeology* 63(4):29–31.

Chase, Arlen F., Diane Z. Chase, and Michael E. Smith. 2009. States and Empires in Ancient Mesomaerica. *Ancient Mesoamerica* 20:175–182.

Chase, Diane Z., and Arlen F. Chase. 2005. The Early Classic Period at Santa Rita Corozal: Issues of Hierarchy, Heterarchy, and Stratification in Northern Belize. *Research Reports in Belizean Archaeology* 2:111–129.

Chase, Diane Z., and Arlen F. Chase. 2006. Framing the Maya Collapse: Continuity, Discontinuity, Method, and Practice in the Classic to Postclassic Southern Maya Lowlands. In *After Collapse: The Regeneration of Complex Societies*, edited by Glenn Schwartz and John Nichols, pp. 168–187. University of Arizona Press, Tucson.

Chase, Diane Z., and Arlen F. Chase. 2008. Que no nos cuentan los jeroglificos? Arqueología e historia en Caracol, Belice. *Mayab* 20:93–108.

Coe, William R. 1990. *Excavations in the Great Plaza, North Terrace, and North Acropolis of Tikal*. Tikal Report 4, University Museum, University of Pennsylvania, Philadelphia.

Culbert, T. Patrick, and Don S. Rice. 1990. *Precolumbian Population History in the Maya Lowlands*. University of New Mexico Press, Albuquerque.

Donkin, R. A. 1979. *Agricultural Terracing in the Aboriginal New World*. University of Arizona Press, Tucson.

Estrada-Belli, Francisco. 2006. Lightning Sky, Rain, and the Maize God: The Ideology of Preclassic Maya Rulers at Cival, Peten, Guatemala. *Ancient Mesoamerica* 17:57–78.

Fletcher, Roland. 2009. Low-Density, Agrarian-Based Urbanism: A Comparative View. *Insights* 2:2–19.

Fox, John, Scott Cook, Arlen F. Chase, and Diane Z. Chase. 1996. Questions of Political and Economic Integration: Segmentary versus Centralized States among the Ancient Maya. *Current Anthropology* 37:795–801.

Freidel, David. 2008. Maya Divine Kinship. In *Religion and Power: Divine Kingship in the Archaeological World and Beyond*, edited by Nicole Brisch, pp. 91–206. University of Chicago, Chicago.

Hansen, Richard D. 2005. Perspectives on Olmec-Maya Interaction in the Middle Formative Period. In *New Perspectives on Formative Mesoamerican Cultures*, edited by Terry G. Powis, pp. 51–72. BAR International Series 1377, Archaeopress, Oxford.

Harrison, Peter D. 2008. Animales como nombres de familias reales en Tikal y algunas consideraciones sobre Calakmul. *Mayab* 20:109–124.

Inomata, Takeshi, and Stephen D. Houston. 2001. *Royal Courts of the Ancient Maya*. Westview Press, Boulder, Colorado.

Joyce, Rosemary A. 2004. Unintended Consequences? Monumentality as a Novel Experience in Formative Mesoamerica. *Journal of Archaeological Method and Theory* 11(1):5–21.

Laporte, Juan Pedro, and Vilma Fialko. 1995. Un reencuentro con Mundo Perdido, Tikal, Guatemala. *Ancient Mesoamerica* 6:41–94.

Lohse, Jon C., Jaime Awe, Cameron Griffith, Robert M. Rosenswig, and Fred Valdez Jr. 2006. Preceramic Occupations in Belize: Updating the Paleoindian and Archaic Record. *Latin American Antiquity* 17:209–226.

Martin, Simon, and Nikolai Grube. 2000. *Chronicle of the Maya Kings and Queens: Deciphering the Dynasties of the Ancient Maya*. Thames and Hudson, New York.

O'Mansky, Matt, and Nicholas P. Dunning. 2004. Settlement and Late Classic Political Disintegration in the Petexbatun Region, Guatemala. In *The Terminal Classic in the Maya Lowlands*, edited by Arthur A. Demarest, Prudence M. Rice, and Don S. Rice, pp. 83–101. University of Colorado Press, Boulder.

Saturno, William A., Karl A. Taube, David Stuart, and Heather Hurst. 2005. The Murals of San Bartolo, El Peten, Guatemala: Part 1: The North Wall. *Ancient Mesoamerica* 7, Center for Ancient American Studies, Barnardsville, North Carolina.

Shaw, Justine M. 2008. *White Roads of the Yucatan: Changing Social Landscapes of the Yucatec Maya*. University of Arizona Press, Tucson.

Stuart, David. 2005. *The Inscriptions from Temple XIX at Palenque: A Commentary*. Pre-Columbian Art Research Institute, San Francisco.

Turner, Billie L., and Peter D. Harrison. 1981. Prehistoric Raised-Field Agriculture in the Maya Lowlands. *Science* 213:399–405.

Wright, Lori E. 2005. Identifying Immigrants to Tikal, Guatemala: Defining Local Variability in Strontium Isotope Ratios of Human Tooth Enamel. *Journal of Archaeological Science* 32:555–566.

CHAPTER 19

THE RISE OF FORMATIVE-PERIOD COMPLEX SOCIETIES IN THE NORTHERN MAYA LOWLANDS

TRAVIS W. STANTON

WHILE the study of the rise and development of early complex societies in the southern Maya lowlands has a long history of scholarship (e.g., Freidel and Robertson 1986; Hammond 1991; Ricketson and Ricketson 1937), our knowledge of how Formative-period communities developed in the northern lowlands (Figure 19.1) has expanded only in the last few decades, with investigations intensifying over the past fifteen years. Archaeologists who worked for Carnegie Institution projects in the first half of the twentieth century had identified a Late Formative component to the ceramic sequence at northern sites like Yaxuná and Acanceh (Brainerd 1958; Smith 1971; Thompson 1954), but little concerted work was undertaken to comprehend what early sites were like. Formative-period occupation was generally ignored, given the wealth of better-preserved and more "spectacular" Classic cities.

This lack of systematic work on early sites began to change with the groundbreaking research at Dzibilchaltún during the 1960s (Andrews and Andrews 1980). Unfortunately, the first Middle to Late Formative ceramic sequence developed at Dzibilchaltún by Joesink-Mandeville (1970) has proved incompatible with the

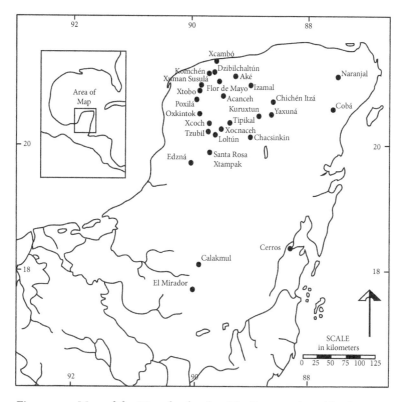

Figure 19.1 Map of the Maya lowlands with sites mentioned in the text.

accepted type-variety system first implemented by Smith (1971) and used by all subsequent researchers. Ball (1978a, 1978b) began to rectify this work, adapting Smith's classificatory system to early ceramic sequences in the northern lowlands, but it was not until Andrews (1988) published the outline of the Komchen sequence that a workable ceramic chronology was in place and the first steps to actually understanding early northern lowland societies were undertaken.

Migrations Versus In Situ Development

Archaeologists have known for some time that the northern part of the Yucatán Peninsula was inhabited by Paleo-Indian peoples. Discoveries in caves like those reported at Loltún, and more recently cenotes, have revealed megalithic fauna (possibly in association with cultural material) and the actual human remains of these early populations (Mercer 1896; Velázquez Valadez 1980). Very little, unfortunately, has been published on these finds. What should be the subsequent Archaic period is even less understood. In fact, there are neither published arti- facts that look Archaic nor absolute dates that indicate occupation at this time. In northern Belize, Lohse (1995, 2010) has reported an Archaic component to the archaeological sequence, which suggests that if more systematic research were undertaken in caves and cenotes in the northern lowlands some evidence of this occupation might be revealed. Yet the possibility remains that the northern low- lands were generally unoccupied at this time, possibly due to climatic factors.

The inability to understand the Archaic in the northern lowlands frustrates our attempts to understand the remains of the earliest identifiable Maya communities. E. W. Andrews (1990; see also Bey 2006: 21–22) proposed that modal ties between ceramics in Yucatán and southwest Petén/Chiapas during the Middle Formative indicate that the northern lowlands were settled rapidly by early Maya sedentary farmers, maybe as early as 800 BC. The earliest pollen evidence (from lake coring) for forest clearing around the site of Cobá, however, has been dated to 1650 BC and the first maize pollen to 850 BC (Leyden et al. 1998). These data appear to confirm the suspicions of many archaeologists working in the northern lowlands that an undocumented Early Formative occupation of the peninsula exists, yet it has not been identified due to current research strategies focused on later contexts and the fact that early deposits are often deeply buried. Therefore, we are unclear as to how much of the Middle Formative occupation now documented was a result of in situ development out of an unknown Archaic/Early Formative period (with maintained contact with the southern lowland Maya explaining cultural similari- ties) or how much was the result of population replacement through migrations out of the southern lowlands (Stanton 2000; Stanton and Ardren 2005). We know that migrations were frequent in the Maya area during the Postclassic (Rice and Rice 2009), and we suspect it occurred at earlier times. Yet without stable isotope analyses on human bone samples, the reconstruction of possible migrations based on stylistic similarities in ceramics remains problematic. What we can say is that the northern lowland Maya of the Middle Formative shared many cultural traits with their southern neighbors, while at the same time expressing important differ- ences. For the time being, the origin of the Maya in the northern lowlands remains a mystery.

THE MIDDLE FORMATIVE

Ball's (1977, 1978a) characterization of the Formative-period Maya as being orga- nized in "chiefdoms" helps us, in part, to understand why E. W. Andrews (1990) argues for migrations. The first known archaeological remains of the Maya in the northern lowlands date to the Early Nabanché (equivalent to the late Middle

Formative or Mamom horizon), which we could arguably place between 800 and 400 or 300 BC with the few radiocarbon samples dating to this span of time (Glover and Stanton 2010). Sites from this period exhibit a range of characteristics indicating prestate complexity that can only be explained by external influence (including, but not limited to migration) and the existence of an undocumented Early Formative.

One of the most compelling traits demonstrating prestate complexity during the Early Nabanché is the variability in the sizes of sites and public architecture. Andrews and Robles Castellanos (2004; see also Anderson 2005) have conducted one of only two thorough surveys of Formative-period sites in the northern lowlands in the region to the northwest of Mérida; Glover (2006) has also conducted a survey in northern Quintana Roo, but few Middle Formative materials were reported. While excavation data are understandably minimal, given the size of the survey region that was explored, Andrews and Robles Castellanos report a large number of sites with Formative-period materials on the surface. Given the lack of comprehensive excavations, however, it is difficult to correlate site size by period to formulate settlement hierarchies. Yet at sites like Poxilá and Xtobo sizable public architecture and settlement indicate that settlement hierarchies were in place during the Early Nabanché in this region. Anderson (2010) calculates that Xtobo, a site boasting pyramidal structures, a plaza, causeways, and a ballcourt, had a population of around 1,500 people at its apex, probably at the Middle to Late Formative transition. In fact, more than twenty ballcourts have been found in this region, many of them dating to the Middle or Late Formative (Medina Castillo and Lawton 2002). These data indicate that fairly complex sociopolitical organizations were in place not only to organize labor, but also to plan and implement strategies (e.g., rituals and games) to integrate sizable communities.

Fairly large Middle Formative public architecture and extensive settlements have been reported in other parts of the northern lowlands, among others at the sites of Izamal (Quiñones Cetina 2003, 2006), Komchén (Andrews and Ringle 1992; Andrews et al. 1984; Ringle 1985, 1999; Ringle and Andrews 1988, 1990), Xcoch (Smyth and Ortegón 2008; Smyth et al. n.d.), Xocnaceh (Stanton and Gallareta 2002), and Yaxuná (Stanton and Ardren 2005; Stanton and Freidel 2005; Suhler 1996). Specifically, Izamal is a site that calls the attention of archaeologists because it boasts the largest pyramid north of the Mirador Basin in Guatemala. This site, however, has substantial Protoclassic, Terminal Classic, Postclassic, colonial, and modern occupations, resulting in a mass of architectural overburden that has obscured the potentially very sizable Middle Formative occupation.

Both Xocnaceh and Yaxuná exhibit large pyramidal structures and platforms dating to the Middle Formative. These sites have substantial Late Formative occupations, however. Therefore, the Middle Formative building phases have been gleaned only though deep test pits and trenches. At Yaxuná, Str. 5E-19 has a Middle Formative substructure at a height of 11 meters above the surrounding ground surface. Yet given that there are Late Formative buildings up to 22 meters in height that have not been deeply probed at Yaxuná, it is possible that even larger structures exist. In the Puuc region, where Xocnaceh and Xcoch are located, a Middle Formative ballcourt at Paso del Macho has been reported, and at Yaxuná a Middle Formative causeway has been published (Stanton 2005a; Stanton and Freidel 2005; Stanton et al. 2010). These data indicate that while not many ball-courts or causeways have been securely dated to the Middle Formative outside of the northwest part of the peninsula, the patterns reported by Andrews and Robles Castellanos (2004; see also Anderson 2010) are more widespread.

Archaeologists have also recently discovered that the northern lowland Maya were active participants in long-distance exchange relationships at this early date. Andrews (1986, 1987) was the first to report the presence of Olmec-style green-stones from a looted context at Chacsinkin, located in south-central Yucatán. Since this time, Middle Formative Olmec-style jades have been reported from the small site of Tipikal (Peraza Lope et al. 2002) and Yaxuná (Suhler 1996), among others. Andrews (1986, 1987) also identified ceramics from the northern Maya lowlands at La Venta, Tabasco, indicating a Gulf Coast exchange network that may have included important perishable goods such as salt, found in abundance along the coast of Yucatán. Yet exchange networks appear to have extended beyond the Gulf Coast as Central Mexican ceramics, classified by Mayanists in the El Llanto group, have been reported at Edzná and Yaxuná (Stanton and Ardren 2005).

The greenstone and ceramic data indicate ties between the Gulf Coast Olmec and the Yucatec Maya during the Middle Formative, but it is the architectural evidence that suggests that the northern lowland Maya were participating in ideology that was widespread throughout Mesoamerica at this time. We are starting to understand that one of the principal types of public architecture in the northern lowlands is the in-line triadic structure; a long building with three superstructures, the middle one being the tallest, flanked by two symmetrical buildings (Figure

Figure 19.2 An example of in-line triad architecture at Poxilá, Yucatán.

Figure 19.3 Middle Formative cache vessel at Yaxuná, Yucatán.

19.2). Triadic architecture, in different forms, was widespread in different areas
of Mesoamerica during the Formative. The in-line triadic form is found across
southeast Mesoamerica and may be an ancestor to the early E-Group form concentrated in the southern lowlands, discussed in more detail by Chase and Chase
in Chapter 18. Only one E-Group, found at Yaxuná, has been identified with cer-
tainty in the northern lowlands. Another may be located at Santa Rosa Xtampak.
Yet the in-line triadic form has now been reported at a number of sites across the
northern plains.

A pair of dance platforms, also reported at Yaxuná (Stanton and Freidel 2005;
Suhler 1996; Suhler et al. 1998), indicates that "Olmec" ideological concepts made
their way into the northern Maya lowlands. Both platforms were performance stages
with internal corridors that snaked around each structure in the form of the Kan
Cross, most famously depicted in Olmec iconography on Chalcatzingo Monument
9, where it represents the mouth of the cave of the underworld. Staircases led up
from the corridors to the platforms' stages, allowing participants to appear from
the underworld and perform for a large public. In the center of each platform the
corridors led to a central sanctuary where in one case a Middle Formative vessel
with four colors present on its surface (not to be confused with later Protoclassic
and Classic polychromes) was found with an Olmec-style greenstone (Figure 19.3).
At the end of the Middle Formative the structures were burned and abandoned.
Radiocarbon assays have been performed on two burned wood samples recovered
from above the floor of Str. 6E-120 but sealed within and sealed by the building's
roof collapse. The first sample dates this event to 2250+/-40 BP (Beta-265025) with
an intercept of 370 BC (calibrated). The second sample returned a date of 2360+/-40
BP (Beta-265026) with an intercept of BC 400 (calibrated). Both dates mark the
abandonment of the building.

On a final note, there is growing evidence that the northern lowland Maya
were using caves as early as the Middle Formative, with early ceramics being
reported from Loltún (Robles Castellanos 1997), Kuruxtun (Donald Slater, personal

communication, 2009), and numerous caves in the Yalahau region of Quintana Roo (Rissolo 2003; Rissolo et al. 2005). While the use of caves for ritual purposes has a long history in Mesoamerica, given the lack of surface water in the northern lowlands many of these caves may have been used for water sources as well.

THE LATE FORMATIVE

While there is growing evidence for a substantial population in the northern lowlands during the Middle Formative, it is during the Late Formative that regions of Yucatán and Quintana Roo reached high demographic levels (Glover 2006; Glover et al. 2005; Quintal Suaste 1993, 1995; Stanton 2000). Just as the cities of the southern Maya lowlands increased the size of their populations and monumental centers (e.g., Hansen 1998; Hansen et al. 2008), Late Formative northern lowland sites grew exponentially. Places like Xcoch, Xocnaceh, and Yaxuná (Smyth et al. n.d.; Stanton 2000; Stanton and Gallareta 2002) experienced vigorous building episodes with some of the largest structures at these sites erected during this period; however, none reached the size of structures like those found at El Mirador or Calakmul in the southern lowlands. Both research and salvage projects across the northern plains demonstrate that even rural areas were being filled in by smaller towns and homesteads (e.g., Andrews and Robles Castellanos 2004; Glover 2006; Hernández Hernández 2005; Hernández Hernández and Arias 2003; Hernández Hernández and Viana Camps 2006; Peniche May et al. 2009). The Late Formative rivals the Late-Terminal Classic in terms of reaching the greatest demographic levels during Pre-Columbian times. Again, apart from the surveys conducted by Andrews and Robles Castellanos (2004) and Glover (2006), no systematic data have been collected to understand settlement hierarchies specifically for the Late Formative. Yet it is clear that polity development reached a sufficient complexity to indicate the existence of great towns and possibly cities, which controlled a sizable area of their hinterlands.

Given the size of sites in the north and the fact that some southern lowland Maya sites were employing iconography directly related to kingship we suspect that a similar institution was in place in the northern lowlands by the Late Formative. We know that kings existed at some sites during the Classic period, given glyphic texts and iconography on stone monuments. Yet even during this period, there are few sites that really display these trappings of kingship so common in the southern lowlands, suggesting that political organization and the use of political propaganda could have varied somewhat between the northern and southern lowlands for quite some time. In any event, we know that there is at least one Late Formative image of a Maya king at Loltún cave in the Puuc region of western Yucatán (Freidel and Andrews n.d.). Further, a thronelike feature in what has been interpreted as a small Late Formative palace structure has been reported from the site of Xaman Susulá near Mérida (Peniche May et al. 2009). Yet until royal tombs, stelae, and glyphs are introduced during the Early Classic period there are few other pieces of data to suggest kings were present. This mirrors the low occurrence of clear symbols of kingship in the southern lowlands during the Late Formative.

Contact between the northern and southern lowlands during the Late Formative seems to have been prevalent, as is amply demonstrated by ceramic studies that show less variation in ceramic modes from region to region during the Chicanel Horizon (e.g., Smith 1971). Shared ideological expressions also appear in the large stucco masks found at Acanceh (Quintal Suaste 1999), similar to masks on temple façades at sites in the south like Cerros, Belize (Freidel and Robertson 1986). The tendency toward homogeneity in ceramics at this time suggests increased contact among potting communities across the lowlands, implying more widespread social and perhaps political ties. At some sites in the northern lowlands like Xocnaceh and Yaxuná, visual analysis of paste and surface treatments strongly suggests that southern lowland ceramics were being imported, possibly as containers for other products.

At Yaxuná specifically, a large quantity of Petén-looking ceramics in Late Formative assemblages raises questions concerning the origins of the E-Group at the site. In the first half of the twentieth century Brainerd (1958) excavated some trenches into this structure and the associated Central Acropolis. While the data are not clear for the E-Group, he reported that the Central Acropolis is Late Formative in date, suggesting that the E-Group also has a Late Formative component. During the Early Classic, Yaxuná continued to have high amounts of southern lowland ceramics, specifically polychromes, indicating that it may have been located on an overland trade route between the southern lowland kingdoms and the north coast of Yucatán. In fact, later Classic-period polities appeared to have vied to control this trade route. During the Late Classic, the site of Cobá was at its apex, controlling the coastal trade in the northern Caribbean area. At this time, the longest causeway ever constructed in Mesoamerica, Sacbé 1, was extended for 100 kilometers between Yaxuná and Cobá, effectively incorporating Yaxuná into the Cobá polity. Shortly thereafter, Chichén Itzá was founded a mere 18 kilometers to the north of Yaxuná, cutting off access to the north coast. During the Formative period there are only small sites reported along the coast of Yucatán (Eaton 1978). Coastal trade appears to really begin to develop during the Early Classic at sites like Xcambó (Sierra Sosa 1999). The presence of clearly southern-looking ceramics and architecture at Yaxuná during the Late Formative may indicate that southern lowland peoples were involved in establishing and maintaining this inland trade route during the Formative. Later on, Yaxuná and its location on this trade route would have presented a problem for communities like Cobá and Chichén Itzá, intent on controlling trade along the coast (A. Andrews 1990). The placement of Chichén Itzá just to the north of Yaxuná in the Terminal Classic brought an end to occupation at Yaxuná (Suhler 1996) and cut off an important direct route that the southern lowland kingdoms had to the salt flats of Yucatán.

The Late Preclassic Maya Collapse
and the Protoclassic Transformation

At the end of the Formative period, lowland Maya civilization underwent a drastic transformation. A massive depopulation has been recorded in many areas of the Maya lowlands (Glover and Stanton 2010) as well as in other parts of Mesoamerica. Preliminary data suggest that a drought event, coupled with high population density and environmental degradation, could have contributed to this collapse (Hansen et al. 2002). In the northern Maya lowlands, we can note the sharp drop in population levels from the Late Formative to the Early Classic. Many sites like Xocnaceh and Xcoch in the Puuc region were abandoned, most likely in the first centuries AD. A limited number of centers survived, and some even thrived during this period. Izamal appears to have experienced unprecedented monumental construction during this period of time (Quiñones Cetina 2003), and it may have developed into a regional state based on the fact that a series of causeways connected important sites sharing a similar architectural style (Figure 19.4) in the north-central region of Yucatán (see Covarrubias Reyna and Burgos Villanueva n.d.; Maldonado Cárdenas 1979).

How the expansion of a possible regional state in the northern lowlands may have been affected by the collapse of places like the Mirador Basin in the south is uncertain. There is evidence to suggest that many Classic-period dynasties traced their origins to El Mirador (Hansen et al. 2008), giving the impression that local political developments in many regions of the Maya lowlands were integrally tied to the fall of this Formative center. To be sure, there are dynasties established in the northern lowlands by at least the fourth century AD at sites like Oxkintok. There is, however, no glyphic evidence to suggest that the explosion of construction at

Figure 19.4 Example of the Megalithic architectural style at Aké, Yucatán.

Izamal or the settlement and architectural patterns in its surrounding region (which suggest state development) was somehow related to events in the southern lowlands. In any event, the first suggestive evidence of state formation in the northern lowlands appears during a time of stress and social reorganization.

THE EARLY CLASSIC RISE OF DYNASTIES

The Early Classic marks the slow resurgence of Maya polities in the wake of the Late Formative collapse. While sites such as Izamal, Aké, and Yaxuná appear to have weathered the collapse and even flourished during the Protoclassic, there is notably less occupation during the Early Classic across the northern lowlands. Several new centers with scant evidence of previous occupation, however, were founded during the early part of the Classic period. One of these centers is Oxkintok, where a rich tradition of carved stelae highlights the development of a royal dynasty. Early Classic royal tombs have been reported at both Yaxuná and Oxkintok, and this indicates that at least some northern lowland Maya paralleled their southern neighbors in the early development of regional royal lineages.

One issue that inevitably comes to mind when discussing the Early Classic is the central Mexican city of Teotihuacan. Despite claims that people from Teotihuacan were living in Yucatán during the Early Classic (Smyth 2006), there is relatively little evidence of any direct contact (Stanton 2005b). Talud-tablero architecture and tripod cylinder vases reported at sites such as Chunchucmil, Dzibilchaltún, Oxkintok, and Yaxuná are dated to the period 550–700 AD, after the fall of Teotihuacan and centuries after their appearance at sites in the southern lowlands (Varela Torrecilla and Braswell 2003). There are a few artifacts dating from 250–600 AD that look to have a central Mexican influence in Yucatán (e.g., Suhler 1996), but they are isolated finds that do not shed much light on any possible contact between people from central Mexico and people in the northern Maya lowlands. Why the "trappings" of Teotihuacan culture appear so late in the sequence is unclear. Yet as population levels began to rise again toward the end of the Early Classic, these symbols become prominent tools in the ideological toolkit of northern Maya dynasts.

CONCLUSIONS

The study of the origins of complex societies in the northern lowlands has increased exponentially over the past few decades, giving us a better understanding not only of the early archaeological sequence, but also of the questions that need to be researched. While the scarce data from Paleo-Indian contexts are tantalizing, very little systematic work has been done to investigate the apparent plentiful data in caves and cenotes. Further, we really have no understanding of the Archaic period and how it may have transitioned to the Formative. The earliest data we have for a Maya occupation of the northern lowlands indicate a fairly complex society with strong, but distinct, cultural ties to their neighbors to the south. These data have spawned speculations that the northern lowlands were populated by Maya migrating out of the south, but to this date, the evidence is ambiguous. We also now know that large sites existed in the Late Formative and that the Maya of the northern lowlands experienced a similar collapse as that documented for the southern lowlands. The pace and pattern of this development, collapse, and transition to the Classic, however, have yet to be teased out of the archaeological data, making the early archaeological sequence of the northern lowlands an exciting topic of research. Finally, while there is solid evidence that the northern lowland Maya developed the institution of divine kingship in the Early Classic, there is scant evidence of Teotihuacan "influence" among the northern kingdoms. While continued research may change this view, it appears that the north was impacted by Teotihuacan to a lesser extent than their southern neighbors had been.

REFERENCES

Anderson, David. 2005. Preclassic Settlement Patterns in Northwest Yucatán. *Mono y Conejo* 3:13–22.

Anderson, David. 2010. Xtobo, Yucatan, Mexico: The Study of a Preclassic Community. Unpublished PhD dissertation, Department of Anthropology, Tulane University, New Orleans.

Andrews, Anthony P. 1990. The Role of Trading Ports in Maya Civilization. In *Vision and Revision in Maya Studies*, edited by Flora S. Clancy and Peter D. Harrison, pp. 159–167. University of New Mexico Press, Albuquerque.

Andrews, Anthony P., and Fernando Robles Castellanos. 2004. An Archaeological Survey of Northwest Yucatan, Mexico. *Mexicon* 25:7–14.

Andrews, E. Wyllys, IV, and E. Wyllys Andrews V. 1980. *Excavations at Dzibilchaltun, Yucatan, Mexico*. Middle American Research Institute, Pub. 48. Tulane University, New Orleans.

Andrews, E. Wyllys, V. 1986. Olmec Jades from Chacsinkin, Yucatan, and Maya Ceramics from La Venta, Tabasco. In *Research and Reflections in Archaeology and History: Essays in Honor of Doris Stone*, edited by E. Wyllys Andrews V, pp. 11–49. Middle American Research Institute, Pub 57. Tulane University, New Orleans.

Andrews, E. Wyllys, V. 1987. A Cache of Early Jades from Chacsinkin, Yucatan. *Mexicon* 9:78–85.

Andrews, E. Wyllys, V. 1988. Ceramic Units from Komchen, Yucatan, Mexico. *Ceramica de Cultura Maya* 15:51–64.

Andrews, E. Wyllys, V. 1990. The Early Ceramic History of the Lowland Maya. In *Vision and Revision in Maya Studies*, edited by Flora S. Clancy and Peter D. Harrison, pp. 1–19. University of New Mexico Press, Albuquerque.

Andrews, E. Wyllys, V, and William M. Ringle. 1992. Los mayas tempranos en Yucatán: investigaciones arqueológicas en Komchen. *Mayab* 8:5–17.

Andrews, E. Wyllys, V, William M. Ringle, Philip J. Barnes, Alfredo Barrera Rubio, and Tomás Gallareta Negrón. 1984. Komchen: An Early Maya Community in Northwest Yucatán. In *Investigaciones recientes en el área maya: XVII Mesa Redonda, Sociedad Mexicana de Antropología, Sn. Cristóbal de Las Casas, Chiapas, 21–27 junio 1981, Tomo I*, pp. 73–92. Sociedad Mexicana de Antropología, Chiapas.

Ball, Joseph W. 1977. The Rise of the Northern Maya Chiefdoms: A Socioprocessual Analysis. In *The Origins of Maya Civilization*, edited by Richard E. W. Adams, pp. 101–132. University of New Mexico Press, Albuquerque.

Ball, Joseph W. 1978a. The Rise of the Northern Maya Chiefdoms: A Socioprocessual Analysis. *Estudios de Cultura Maya* 10:209–222.

Ball, Joseph W. 1978b. *Archaeological Pottery of the Yucatan-Campeche Coast*. Middle American Research Institute, Pub. 46. Tulane University, New Orleans.

Bey, George J., III. 2006. Changing Archaeological Perspectives on the Northern Maya Lowlands. In *Lifeways in the Northern Maya Lowlands: New Approaches to Archaeology in the Yucatán Peninsula*, edited by Jennifer P. Mathews and Bethany A. Morrison, pp. 13–37. University of Arizona Press, Tucson.

Brainerd, George W. 1958. *The Archaeological Ceramics of Yucatan*. Anthropological Records, Volume 19. University of California, Berkeley.

Covarrubias Reyna, Miguel, and Rafael Burgos Villanueva. N.d. Investigaciones arqueológicas en la región centro-norte del estado de Yucatán. In *The Archaeology of Yucatán: New Directions and Data*, edited by Travis W. Stanton. BAR International Series. Archaeopress, Oxford.

Eaton, Jack D. 1978. *Studies in the Archaeology of Coastal Yucatan and Campeche, Mexico: Archaeological Survey of the Yucatan-Campeche Coast*. Middle American Research Institute, Pub. 41. Tulane University, New Orleans.

Freidel, David A., and Anthony P. Andrews. N.d. The Loltun Bas-Relief and the Origins of Maya Kingship. Manuscript in possession of the author.

Freidel, David A., and Robin A. Robertson. 1986. *Archaeology at Cerros Belize, Central America, Volume I: An Interim Report*. Southern Methodist University Press, Dallas.

Glover, Jeffrey B. 2006. The Yalahau Regional Settlement Pattern Survey: A Study of Ancient Maya Social Organization in Northern Quintana Roo, Mexico. Unpublished PhD dissertation, Department of Anthropology, University of California, Riverside.

Glover, Jeffrey B., Dominique Rissolo, and Fabio Esteban Amador. 2005. The Yalahau Preclassic: Reflections on Initial Survey and Ceramic Data. *Mono y Conejo* 3:23–31.

Glover, Jeffrey B., and Travis W. Stanton. 2010. Assessing the Role of Preclassic Traditions in the Formation of Early Classic Yucatec Cultures. *Journal of Field Archaeology* 35:58–77.

Hammond, Norman, ed. 1991. *Cuello: An Early Maya Community in Belize*. Cambridge University Press, Cambridge.

Hansen, Richard D. 1998. Continuity and Disjunction: The Pre-Classic Antecedents of Classic Maya Architecture. In *Function and Meaning in Classic Maya Architecture*, edited by Stephen D. Houston, pp. 49–122. Dumbarton Oaks Research Library and Collection, Washington, DC.

Hansen, Richard D., Steven Bozarth, John Jacob, David Wahl, and Thomas Schreiner. 2002. Climatic and Environmental Variability in the Rise of Maya Civilization: A Preliminary Perspective from Northern Peten. *Ancient Mesoamerica* 13:273–295.

Hansen, Richard D., Wayne K. Howell, and Stanley P. Guenter. 2008. Forgotten Structures, Haunted Houses, and Occupied Hearts: Ancient Perspectives and Contemporary Interpretations of Abandoned Sites and Buildings in the Mirador Basin, Guatemala. In *Ruins of the Past: The Use and Perception of Abandoned Structures in the Maya Lowlands*, edited by Travis W. Stanton and Aline Magnoni, pp. 25–64. University Press of Colorado, Boulder.

Hernández Hernández, Concepción. 2005. La cerámica del periodo preclásico tardío (300 a.C.–350 d.C.) en el norte de la península de Yucatán. In *La producción alfarera en el México antiguo I*, edited by Beatriz L. Merino Carrión and Ángel García Cook, pp. 753–779. Instituto Nacional de Antropología e Historia, Mexico, D.F.

Hernández Hernández, Concepción, and José Manuel Arias López. 2003. Los entierros del conjunto habitacional de Ni'Chac: un sitio del preclásico tardío en el norte de Yucatán. In *Los investigadores de la cultura maya 11*, pp. 279–301. Universidad Autónoma de Campeche, Campeche.

Hernández Hernández, Concepción, and Leonid Viana Camps. 2006. El sitio "Flor de Mayo": aportaciones para la arqueología del Norte de Yucatán. In *Los mayas de ayer y hoy: memorias del Primer Congreso Internacional de Cultura Maya, Tomo I*, edited by Alfredo Barrera Rubio and Ruth Gubler, pp. 104–131. Eugenia Montalván Proyectos Culturales S.C.P., Mérida.

Joesink-Mandeville, LeRoy V. 1970. The Comparative Cultural Stratigraphy of Formative Complexes in the Maya Area: A Reappraisal in Light of New Evidence from Dzibilchaltun, Yucatan. Unpublished PhD dissertation, Department of Anthropology, Tulane University, New Orleans.

Leyden, Barbara W., Mark Brenner, and Bruce H. Dahlin. 1998. Cultural and Climatic History of Coba, a Lowland Maya City in Quintana Roo, Mexico. *Quaternary Research* 49:111–122.

Lohse, Jon. 1995. The Archaic of Northern Belize: A Reconsideration of the Functionality of Constricted Unifaces. In *Memorias del Segundo Congreso Internacional de Mayistas, Tomo I*, pp. 181–194. Universidad Nacional Autónoma de México, D.F.

Lohse, Jon. 2010. Archaic Origins of the Lowland Maya. *Latin American Antiquity* 21:312–352.

Maldonado Cárdenas, Rubén. 1979. Los sacbeob de Izamal-Aké y Uci-Cansahcab en el noroeste de Yucatán. *Antropología e Historia* 27:23–29.

Medina Castillo, Edgar, and Crorey Lawton. 2002. El juego de pelota: nuevos hallazgos en el noreste de Yucatán. In *Investigadores de la cultura maya 10*, pp. 278–285. Universidad Autónoma de Campeche, Campeche.

Mercer, Henry C. 1896. *The Hill-Caves of Yucatan: A Search for Evidence of Man's Antiquity in the Caverns of Central America*. Lippincott, Philadelphia.

Peniche May, Nancy, Mónica E. Rodríguez Pérez, and Teresa N. Ceballos Gallareta. 2009. La función de un edificio del periodo preclásico: la Estructura 1714 de Xaman Susulá. *In Los investigadores de la cultura maya 17, tomo II*, pp. 253–264. Universidad Autónoma de Campeche, Campeche.

Peraza Lope, Carlos, Pedro Delgado Kú, and Bárbara Escamilla Ojeda. 2002. Intervenciones en un edificio del preclásico medio en Tipikal, Yucatán. *In Los investigadores de la cultura maya 10*, pp. 262–276. Universidad Autónoma de Campeche, Campeche.

Quiñones Cetina, Lucía G. 2003. Del preclásico medio al clásico temprano: una propuesta de fechamiento para el área nuclear de Izamal, Yucatán. Tesis Profesional, Licenciado en Ciencias Antropológicas en la Especialidad de Arqueología, Universidad Autónoma de Yucatán, Mérida.

Quiñones Cetina, Lucía G. 2006. Del Preclásico Medio al Clásico Temprano: una propuesta de fechamiento para el área nuclear de Izamal, Yucatán. *Estudios de Cultura Maya* 28:51–66.

Quintal Suaste, Alicia Beatriz. 1993. Los asentamientos arqueológicos de Aké, Yucatán: una aproximación a su organización social. Tesis Profesional, Licenciado en Ciencias Antropológicas en la Especialidad de Arqueología, Universidad Autónoma de Yucatán, Mérida.

Quintal Suaste, Alicia Beatriz. 1995. Patrón de asentamiento de Aké, Yucatán. In *Memorias del Segundo Congreso Internacional de Mayistas, Tomo I*, pp. 505–514. Universidad Nacional Autónoma de México, D.F.

Quintal Suaste, Alicia Beatriz. 1999. Los mascarones de Acanceh. *Arqueología Mexicana* 37:14–17.

Rice, Prudence M., and Don S. Rice, eds. 2009. *The Kowoj: Identity, Migrations, and Geopolitics in Late Postclassic Petén, Guatemala.* University Press of Colorado, Boulder.

Ricketson, Oliver G., and Edith B. Ricketson. 1937. *Uaxactun, Guatemala, Group E.* Carnegie Institution of Washington, Pub. 447. Carnegie Institution of Washington, Washington, DC.

Ringle, William M. 1985. The Settlement Patterns of Komchen, Yucatán, Mexico. Unpublished PhD dissertation, Department of Anthropology, Tulane University, New Orleans.

Ringle, William M. 1999. Pre-Classic Cityscapes: Ritual Politics among the Early Lowland Maya. In *Social Patterns in Pre-Classic Mesoamerica*, edited by David C. Grove and Rosemary A. Joyce, pp. 183–223. Dumbarton Oaks Research Library and Collection, Washington, DC.

Ringle, William M., and E. Wyllys Andrews V. 1988. Formative Residences at Komchen, Yucatan, Mexico. In *Household and Community in the Mesoamerican Past,* edited by Richard R. Wilk and Wendy Ashmore, pp. 171–197. University of New Mexico Press, Albuquerque.

Ringle, William M., and E. Wyllys Andrews V. 1990. The Demography of Komchen, Yucatan, Mexico. In *Precolumbian Population History in the Maya Lowlands,* edited by T. Patrick Culbert and Don S. Rice, pp. 215–244. University of New Mexico Press, Albuquerque.

Rissolo, Dominique A. 2003. *Ancient Maya Cave Use in the Yalahau Region, Northern Quintana Roo, Mexico.* Bulletin Number 12. Association for Mexican Cave Studies, Austin.

Rissolo, Dominique A., José Manuel Ochoa Rodríguez, and Joseph W. Ball. 2005. A Reassessment of the Middle Preclassic in Northern Quintana Roo. In *Quintana Roo Archaeology*, edited by Justine M. Shaw and Jennifer P. Mathews, pp. 66–76. University of Arizona Press, Tucson.

Robles Castellanos, Fernando. 1997. Tipología de la cerámica de la Gruta Loltún, Yucatán, qué se encuentra en el Museo Peabody de la Universidad de Harvard. In *Homenaje al Profesor César A. Sáenz*, edited by Ángel García Cook, Alba Guadalupe Mastache, Leonor Merino, and Sonia Rivero Torres, pp. 143–158. Serie Arqueología. Instituto Nacional de Antropología e Historia, Mexico, D.F.

Sierra Sosa, Thelma N. 1999. Xcambó: Codiciado enclave económico del Clásico Maya. *Arqueología* 7(37):40–47.

Smith, Robert E. 1971. *The Pottery of Mayapan*. Papers of the Peabody Museum of Archaeology and Ethnology, Vol. 66. Harvard University, Cambridge.

Smyth, Michael P. 2006. Architecture, Caching, and Foreign Contacts at Chac (II), Yucatán, Mexico. *Latin American Antiquity* 17:123–149.

Smyth, Michael P., and David Ortegón Zapata. 2008. A Preclassic Center in the Puuc Region: A Report on Xcoch, Yucatan, Mexico. *Mexicon* 30:63–68.

Smyth, Michael P., David Ortegón Zapata, Nicholas P. Dunning, and Eric Weaver. N.d. Settlement Dynamics, Climate Change, and Human Response at Xcoch in the Puuc Region of Yucatan, Mexico. In *The Archaeology of Yucatán: New Directions and Data*, edited by Travis W. Stanton. BAR International Series. Archaeopress, Oxford.

Stanton, Travis W. 2000. Heterarchy, Hierarchy, and the Emergence of the Northern Lowland Maya: A Study of Complexity at Yaxuna, Yucatan, Mexico (400 BC–AD 600). Unpublished PhD dissertation, Department of Anthropology, Southern Methodist University, Dallas.

Stanton, Travis W. 2005a. Formative Maya Causeways: Incipient Internal Site Design at Yaxuná, Yucatán, Mexico. *Mono y Conejo* 3:32–34.

Stanton, Travis W. 2005b. Taluds, Tripods, and Teotihuacanos: A Critique of Central Mexican Influence in Classic Period Yucatán. *Mayab* 18:17–35.

Stanton, Travis W., and Traci Ardren. 2005. The Middle Formative of Yucatán in Context: The View from Yaxuná. *Ancient Mesoamerica* 16:213–228.

Stanton, Travis W., and David A. Freidel. 2005. Placing the Centre, Centring the Place: The Influence of Formative Sacbeob in Classic Site Design at Yaxuná, Yucatán. *Cambridge Archaeological Journal* 15:225–249.

Stanton, Travis W., David A. Freidel, Charles K. Suhler, Traci Ardren, James N. Ambrosino, Justine M. Shaw, and Sharon Bennett. 2010. *Excavations at Yaxuná, 1986–1996: Results of the Selz Foundation Yaxuná Project*. BAR International Series 2056. Archaeopress, Oxford.

Stanton, Travis W., and Tomás Gallareta Negrón. 2002. *Proyecto Xocnaceh: 1ª. temporada de campo marzo-julio 2002*. Technical report submitted to the Consejo de Arqueología del Instituto Nacional de Antropología e Historia, Mexico, D.F.

Suhler, Charles K. 1996. Excavations at the North Acropolis, Yaxuna, Yucatan, Mexico. Unpublished PhD dissertation, Department of Anthropology, Southern Methodist University, Dallas.

Suhler, Charles K., David A. Freidel, and Traci Ardren. 1998. Northern Maya Architecture, Ritual, and Cosmology. In *Anatomía de una civilización: aproximaciones interdisciplinarias a la cultura maya*, edited by Andrés Ciudad Ruiz, Yolanda Fernández Marquínez, José Miguel García Campillo, María Josefa Iglesias Ponce de León, Alfonso Lacadena García-Gallo, and Luis T. Sanz Castro, pp. 253–273. Sociedad Española de Estudios Mayas, Madrid.

Thompson, J. Eric S. 1954. *The Rise and Fall of Maya Civilization*. University of Oklahoma Press, Norman.

Varela Torrecilla, Carmen, and Geoffrey E. Braswell. 2003. Teotihuacan and Oxkintok: New Perspectives from Yucatán. In *The Maya and Teotihuacan: Reinterpreting Early Classic Interaction*, edited by G. E. Braswell, pp. 249–271. University of Texas Press, Austin.

Velázquez Valadéz, Ricardo. 1980. Recent Discoveries in the Caves of Loltun, Yucatan, Mexico. *Mexicon* 2:53–55.

....

CHAPTER 20

INTERACTION AMONG THE COMPLEX SOCIETIES OF CLASSIC-PERIOD MESOAMERICA

....

SERGIO GÓMEZ CHÁVEZ AND MICHAEL W. SPENCE

In the third century AD a number of Formative-period centers continued to grow: Lamanai, Altún Ha, Nakbé, Tikal, Caracol, Kaminaljuyú, Monte Albán, Cholula, Teotihuacan, and others. The states that arose with these first class societies, generally associated with high demographic indices and complex urban developments and cultural manifestations, expanded and consolidated their networks, positioning themselves at the center of their systems. The implementation of various strategies generated benefits for the more connected and better-adapted sites, as well as for the local elites who consolidated their positions in the power structures of their communities. Major centers in western Mesoamerica tended to be widely dispersed, at least in the Early Classic (250–600 AD), while the Maya lowlands of eastern Mesoamerica presented a more politically crowded landscape, with a number of centers alternating between cooperation and conflict. Teotihuacan played a major role in Mesoamerica at this time and is considered by some to have briefly been the seat of a hegemonic empire, based primarily in the Basin of Mexico and adjacent areas but with a significant political presence in some select areas beyond that (Smith and Montiel 2001; Chase et al. 2009: 177–178).

All of the Classic-period (250–900 AD) societies of Mesoamerica carried on trade and diplomatic exchanges with their neighbors, but some were also involved in direct contacts over much greater distances. Long-distance exchange was structured to a considerable degree by the diversity of natural environments and the variety of ecological niches existing in Mesoamerica, particularly the contrast between highlands and lowlands (Miller 1983; Joyce 1993). Cotton, cacao, rubber, salt, marine shell, and copal sap were desirable lowland and coastal products, while obsidian, nopal and maguey products, basalt, jadeite, and various semiprecious stones were primarily highland items. Other goods (e.g., decorated ceramics) acquired their value from the input of highly skilled labor. In many cases the goods and routes of these exchange systems had developed much earlier, for example, the movement of highland Guatemalan obsidian throughout the Maya region (Nelson and Clark 1998). In the Early Classic they expand and intensify. This may reflect growing formal relationships among the rulers and nobles of the various states— alliances sustained by intermarriage, reciprocal visits, frequent gift exchanges, and perhaps tribute.

MODELS

Attempts to analyze these complex systems have drawn upon world systems, core-periphery, and central place models (e.g., Santley 1983; Price 1986; Santley and Alexander 1992). Most such models position central Mexico as the core and place more distant regions in subordinate roles. They also involve the troubling assumption that the political and economic spheres were inextricably linked (Stein 1998). However, these models are presently giving way to more balanced network models (Santley and Alexander 1996; Spence 2000).

Demarest and Foias (1993; Demarest 2003) suggest a multidirectional network in which no one site dominated interaction. Also, Renfrew's (1986) peer-polity interaction model with its concept of symbolic entrainment has been adopted by some (Stark and Curet 1994; Jiménez Betts and Darling 2000). These have the advantage of not assuming that any one society exerted political or economic domination over the others or was capable of altering the trajectory of their development. However, they may be a little too even-handed.

In complex systems the structure of certain kinds of networks, called scale-free, shows that the degree of interconnection is not the same for each node that forms part of the network. On the contrary, there is a preference for already existing nodes with a larger number of connections, with no limit on their continuing to expand their links (Barabási and Bonabeau 2003). These highly connected nodes (hubs), which constitute centers or nuclei of the network, are not necessarily the oldest but rather those that develop better strategies or are better adapted to obtain more links. It is important to point out not only that material goods circulated through these complex networks, but also that a large amount of information and ideas were transferred.

In a scale-free network Teotihuacan would have been a hub. The disappearance of Cuicuilco with the eruption of the volcano Xitle was a catastrophe that acted to Teotihuacan's advantage, as it positioned itself as the central node of a network that gradually expanded to establish links with other systems. It became the most important and highly developed state in central Mexico during the Classic period. Over several centuries it maintained absolute hegemony over all of the Basin of Mexico, dominating numerous communities that provisioned the city with the resources needed by a population that at some point in its history might have reached 150,000 people (Millon 1976, 1981). As early as 150 AD the urban settlement extended over an area of 20 square kilometers. By 300 AD the metropolis was formed of more than 2,000 apartment compounds.

Beyond that, there is reason to believe that Teotihuacan aggressively promoted its interests abroad. The sacrificial burials of the Feathered Serpent Pyramid indicate a military large enough to absorb the sacrifice of over one hundred of its soldiers (Sugiyama 2005). Oxygen isotope data show that soldiers were recruited from a broad region and fought battles far beyond the city (White et al. 2002; Spence, White, Longstaffe, and Law 2004). At the same time Teotihuacan was exporting its founding myth that it was Tollan, the place where time began and the universe was created (Millon 1992, 1993). Much of the Mesoamerican world apparently accepted this conceit (Stuart 2000; Fash 2002).

WESTERN MESOAMERICA

Teotihuacan's relationship with Michoacán was direct and possibly political. Some of the Michoacán Early Classic public structures had talud-tablero façades and some Michoacanos settled in Teotihuacan (Pollard 2000; Gómez Chávez 2002; Gómez Chávez and Gazzola 2007; Filini and Cárdenas García 2007). However, this network did not reach western Michoacán. From there through Jalisco and beyond, the Teuchitlán Tradition was dominant (Weigand 2008). It is characterized by a form of circular architecture, often of monumental proportions, quite unlike anything else in Mesoamerica. Teotihuacan is represented there by very few artifacts (Weigand 1992). A series of fortified sites at points of access into the core area suggests that the Teuchitlán people actively resisted overtures from the east (Beekman 1996).

The Zapotec state centered at Monte Albán had stronger relations with Teotihuacan than with other major Mesoamerican polities (Marcus and Flannery

1996: 231; Cabrera Castro 1998: 59–66). Millon (1981) and Marcus (1983) have characterized this relationship as amicable, but Winter et al. (2002) suggest that Teotihuacan forces conquered and occupied Monte Albán. Although the evidence for this is weak, there was evidently some sort of Teotihuacan representation on the North Platform, the probable location of the ruler's palace (Martínez López 1994; Winter 1998; Winter et al. 2002). The large deposits of mica there are chemically related to those found in the Viking Group and Xalla, both important public areas of the Teotihuacan state (Rosales 2004; Manzanilla et al. 2005).

There are numerous Teotihuacan-related artifacts in Gulf Coast sites, but few believe that Teotihuacan intruded politically in the region (Stark and Curet 1994; Daneels 2002; Stark 2008: 103–104). Arnold and Santley (2008) suggest that Teotihuacanos settled in Matacapan and introduced several Teotihuacan features in the region. Some of this has been disputed (Yarborough 1992; Spence 1996a: 343–345; Daneels 2002). Of particular importance is Daneels's (2002:665) suggestion that the talud-tablero façades in Matacapan may actually be Late Classic. The Cerro de las Navajas obsidian there, which would be the only material actually imported from Teotihuacan, is sparsely represented and many of the blade platforms are ground, a trait not seen in central Mexico until the Epiclassic (Santley 1989; Arnold and Santley 2008; Hirth et al. 2003: 182).

Eastern Mesoamerica

The major Early Classic Maya sites interacted frequently with each other, creating alliances, intermarrying, exchanging gifts, and sometimes going to war (Schele and Freidel 1990). There was a regular flow of goods between the lowlands and the Guatemalan highlands and, to judge by isotopic data, some movement of people as well (Nelson and Clark 1998; White et al. 2000; Valdés and Wright 2004). Beyond the Maya region, Teotihuacan figured most prominently in external relations. A recent volume edited by Geoffrey Braswell (2003) offers a comprehensive analysis of Maya-Teotihuacan relations. The authors run the gamut of opinion, some arguing that the city had a major impact (e.g., Bove and Medrano, Borowicz) while others minimize its involvement (e.g., Pendergast, Laporte, Iglesias, Marcus). Cowgill (2003) provides a balanced assessment.

Talud-tablero façades and related architectural elements have been considered indicators of strong Teotihuacan influence (Sanders and Price 1968). However, Laporte (2003) rejects this interpretation, pointing out that they were present at Tikal before the main appearance of Teotihuacan influence, were widespread in the region, and continued after Teotihuacan's collapse. He notes that the talud-tablero appeared in the Puebla-Tlaxcala region before Teotihuacan (García Cook 1981; Plunket and Uruñuela 2002).

Nevertheless, we maintain that talud-tablero façades in the Maya region are generally direct political references to Teotihuacan, where they occurred on the Feathered Serpent Pyramid and the Adosada of the Sun Pyramid, both constructed about 200 AD (Sugiyama 2005: 54). In the Classic period they graced the façade of virtually every public structure in the city. They are also depicted on Tikal's Problematical Deposit 50 vessel (Marcus 2003: 339–342, fig. 13.1), where they are associated with people in Teotihuacan dress. Those who commissioned, decorated, and received this vessel must have understood the identification of the talud-tablero façade with Teotihuacan. The installation of the façade on Maya structures, then, was a proclamation of Teotihuacan's importance in the political life of the community. The Late Classic survival of the talud-tablero was probably due to the enduring political value of the concept of Tollan and its appropriation by local rulers (Stone 1989).

There have also been suggestions that Teotihuacan-style apartment compounds were present at some sites: Matacapan (Arnold and Santley 2008; but see Daneels 2002), Montana (Bove and Medrano Busto 2003: 63), Tikal (Becker 2009; but see Laporte 2003: 207–208), and Chac II (Smyth 2009). However, these may just be elite residences, which tend to be larger and more complex than commoner residences.

The nature of Teotihuacan's role in Maya public life is revealed to some degree in textual evidence and public art (Stuart 2000, 2004; Borowicz 2003; Sharer 2003). Rulers appear to be claiming Teotihuacan affiliation and sometimes military support for their reign. Some prominent figures—Yax Nuun Ayiin at Tikal and K'inich Yaax K'uk' Mo' at Copán—are even said to be foreigners from the west, presumably Teotihuacan. Other rulers or nobles thought to possibly be Teotihuacanos are the principal individuals in the tombs of Kaminaljuyú Mounds A and B (Kidder et al. 1946; Sanders and Michels 1977) and the occupant of Tomb F-8/1 in Altún Ha (Pendergast 1971, 2003). In the latter case, a large and complex offering of Cerro de las Navajas obsidian artifacts is much like offerings from early Teotihuacan state contexts (Spence 1996b: 29–30), suggesting that the person in the tomb was closely affiliated with the Teotihuacan state.

In recent years notable advances involving stable isotope analysis have been made in determining the geographic identity of an individual or group and the movements that occurred over the course of their lives, to help us better understand interaction between sites or regions (White et al. 1998; Price et al. 2000). Oxygen and strontium isotope analyses have now established that none of these putative Teotihuacanos was born in Teotihuacan (White et al. 2000, 2001; Buikstra et al. 2004; Valdéz and Wright 2004; Wright 2005a), although some were outsiders to the areas where they were buried. Perhaps the inscriptions and iconography were recording claims to Teotihuacan affiliation but not specifically birth. Such claims could not have been made lightly, given the likely presence of rivals quick to challenge them and of Teotihuacan representatives monitoring local affairs. The display of Teotihuacan materials would have exhibited their ties with the metropolis, gaining them greater legitimacy for their exercise of power.

There may have been a more substantial Teotihuacan presence in the Guatemalan piedmont (Berlo 1984; Bove 1993; Bove and Medrano Busto 2003). As early as 200–250 AD, caches at the Balberta site included Cerro de las Navajas obsidian, Thin Orange sherds, and ceramic effigies of cacao beans, indicating a flow of cacao and Teotihuacan goods between the two regions (Bove and Medrano Busto 2003: 50–51). The possible presence of Teotihuacanos in Balberta and the later Montana site is strongly supported, though not established, by oxygen-isotope data (Christine White, personal communication, 2010).

The presence of Teotihuacanos in the Maya region is echoed by the probable presence of Maya in Teotihuacan. Clara Millon (1973) and Taube (2003) discuss elements in Tetitla's art that indicate the presence of Maya artists. Some Maya probably also lived in the Merchants' Barrio (Rattray 2004). Some of the sacrificed individuals in the central features of the Feathered Serpent Pyramid, dated about 200 AD, may have been Maya (White et al. 2002: 232–234). The three sacrificed individuals in Burial 5 of the Moon Pyramid, ca. 350 AD, were Maya nobles of very high rank (Sugiyama and López Luján 2007; White et al. 2007). The sacrifice of Maya lords indicates a considerable imbalance in some Maya-Teotihuacan relationships.

LATE CLASSIC

The period following the collapse of Teotihuacan (ca. 600 AD) is referred to as the Epiclassic in western Mesoamerica but the Late Classic in eastern Mesoamerica, where the term Epiclassic is reserved for the last century. In the west, Cholula and Monte Albán continued and many new regional centers appeared: El Tajín, Cantona, Cacaxtla-Xochitécatl, Xochicalco, Teotenango, Tingambato, La Quemada, and Alta Vista. The numerous Maya centers continued. Interaction was multidirectional, with no one state dominant. The public art of several Maya sites and of Cacaxtla-Xochitécatl and Xochicalco (which have strong Maya influences in their art) celebrates war and conquest. Much of it incorporates military themes and iconography derived from Teotihuacan (Stone 1989; Nagao 1989; Hirth 1989, 2000).

Blanton et al. (1996) suggest that Late Classic rulers practiced a network strategy, solidifying their positions through a combination of warfare and widespread alliances. The circulation of goods and ideas that this encouraged led to an "international style" in prestige goods and iconographic elements. Turquoise from the American Southwest and copper goods from western Mexico now entered the system but remained scarce until the Postclassic period (Weigand and Harbottle 1992).

Exotic goods like jadeite and marine shell may have become scarcer or more restricted in distribution in some societies, such as Cacaxtla-Xochitécatl (Nagao 1989), La Quemada (Nelson 2008: 529), and Monte Albán (González Licón 2009). Nevertheless, in the Copán region these prestige goods appear even in some small rural sites (Hendon 2009: 114). Other goods, like obsidian, still moved in quantity over long distances and across class lines (Nelson and Clark 1998).

ALTERNATIVE NETWORKS

Sempowski (1994: 264, 268–272) notes that marine shell, mica, and jadeite were more widespread in Teotihuacan during its earlier phases, and González Licón (2009) found a similar trend in Monte Albán. Cerro de las Navajas obsidian occurred in a variety of social contexts at Tikal (Moholy-Nagy 1999). Some of this may have been a trickle-down effect, as members of the upper class exchanged their wealth in markets or passed it as gifts or reimbursement to their social inferiors. Elite largesse, however, cannot explain all of it. The working of precious and semiprecious stones, marine shell, and a variety of other exotic materials in workshops in the La Ventilla barrio was probably controlled by the elite (Gazzola 2005), but similar production on the northeast edge of Teotihuacan (Turner 1992) was not under state control (Gazzola 2005: 844). Obsidian specialists in Xochicalco managed their own raw material procurement (Hirth 2009: 55). Apparently there were networks for exotic goods that did not involve the state or elites.

Much of this independent economic activity was probably conducted by individuals or families. In some cases, though, more formal organizations were involved. The communities of foreigners resident in Teotihuacan preserved and reproduced for centuries some of the most important traditions of their places of origin, including their languages. This would have allowed the cohesion of the group and would have ensured control over certain resources. A principal economic activity of these foreigners may have been the trade of raw materials and products from the regions from which they had emigrated or from related diaspora communities. Their knowledge of the language, roads, and territories would have given them an advantage in carrying out this activity, which also maintained their links with their homelands.

The network of Zapotec enclaves in several central Mexico areas is a case in point (Hirth and Swezey 1976; Spence 2005). Oxygen isotope analysis of the Tlailotlacan skeletons shows that women as well as men had significant mobility. Also, it is possible that the children of the Zapotec women in this barrio were taken for some time to other Zapotec diaspora settlements, where they acquired some form of social acknowledgment before returning to Teotihuacan (White, Spence et al. 2004). Mica in Tlailotlacan is from the same source as the large deposits in Monte Albán's North Platform and Teotihuacan's Viking Group and Xalla, but it is of poorer quality and is more crudely cut (Rosales 2004). This indicates that the Tlailotlacanos obtained mica from connections independent of the state-level system. Probably other goods like obsidian, lime for plaster, and Thin Orange ware also circulated through this diaspora network (Spence 2005).

The Merchants' Barrio, with connections to the Gulf Coast and Maya lowlands, may have been part of another independent network, bringing lowland and coastal products into Teotihuacan (Rattray 2004; Spence, White, Longstaffe, Rattray, and Law 2004). The skeletons of the Merchants' Barrio indicate that the men were foreigners and throughout their lives had much mobility. On the other hand the barrio women were natives or long-term residents of Teotihuacan and probably moved little or not at all during their lives. The basic ethnic identities of the barrio residents thus had at least three regions of origin.

There were also at least one settlement (perhaps two) of Michoacanos in Teotihuacan (Gómez Chávez 1998, 2002; Gómez Chávez and Gazzola 2007). Isotopic data confirm that they maintained relations with communities in the region of Pátzcuaro. It appears that some of the individuals were born in Teotihuacan but remained away for long periods of time, returning shortly before their deaths, although it is also possible that their remains had been carried back to Teotihuacan only to be buried.

These nonstate networks and institutions require more investigation. An important tool for this is stable isotope analysis. Isotopic studies have shown that a surprisingly high proportion of Teotihuacanos and Tikaleños had foreign origins (White, Storey et al. 2004; Wright 2005b). As more isotopes (e.g., lead, sulfur) are included, we may be able to identify the homelands of these travelers with considerable accuracy (Spence and White 2009: 237–239). There should also be more detailed analyses of the consumption of foreign goods. We need to know how their distributions were correlated with class and other boundaries, as well as what social mechanisms were responsible for their procurement and circulation. It may be that a considerable proportion of the interaction among these early class societies was conducted outside the formal institutions of the state.

REFERENCES

Arnold, Philip J., III, and Robert S. Santley. 2008. Classic Currents in the West-Central Tuxtlas. In *Classic Period Cultural Currents in Southern and Central Veracruz*, edited by Philip J. Arnold III and Christopher A. Pool, pp. 293–321. Dumbarton Oaks Research Library and Collections, Washington, DC.

Barabási, Albert-Láslő, and Eric Bonabeau. 2003. Scale-Free Networks. *Scientific American* 288:60–69.

Becker, Marshall Joseph. 2009. Tikal: Evidence for Ethnic Diversity in a Prehispanic Lowland Maya State. In *Domestic Life in Prehispanic Capitals: A Study of Specialization, Hierarchy, and Ethnicity*, edited by Linda R. Manzanilla and Claude Chapdelaine, pp. 89–104. Memoir 46, Museum of Anthropology, University of Michigan, Ann Arbor.

Beekman, Christopher. 1996. Political Boundaries and Political Structure: The Limits of the Teuchitlán Tradition. *Ancient Mesoamerica* 7:135–147.

Berlo, Janet. 1984. *Teotihuacan Art Abroad: A Study of Metropolitan Style and Provincial Transformation in Incensario Workshops*. BAR International Series 180. British Archaeological Reports, Oxford.

Blanton, Richard, Gary Feinman, Stephen Kowalewski, and Peter Peregrine. 1996. A Dual-Processual Theory for the Evolution of Mesoamerican Civilization. *Current Anthropology* 37:1–14.

Borowicz, James. 2003. Images of Power and the Power of Images: Early Classic Iconographic Programs of the Carved Monuments of Tikal. In *The Maya and Teotihuacan: Reinterpreting Early Classic Interaction*, edited by Geoffrey E. Braswell, pp. 217–234. University of Texas Press, Austin.

Bove, Frederick J. 1993. The Terminal Formative-Early Classic Transition. In *The Balberta Project: The Terminal Formative-Early Classic Transition on the Pacific Coast of Guatemala*, edited by Frederick Bove, Sonia Medrano Busto, Brenda Lou, and Barbara Arroyo, pp. 177–194. Memoirs in Latin American Archaeology no.6, University of Pittsburgh, Pittsburgh.

Bove, Frederick J., and Sonia Medrano Busto. 2003. Teotihuacan, Militarism, and Pacific Guatemala. In *The Maya and Teotihuacan: Reinterpreting Early Classic Interaction*, edited by Geoffrey E. Braswell, pp. 45–79. University of Texas Press, Austin.

Braswell, Geoffrey E., ed. 2003. *The Maya and Teotihuacan: Reinterpreting Early Classic Interaction*. University of Texas Press, Austin.

Buikstra, Jane E., T. Douglas Price, Lori E. Wright, and James H. Burton. 2004. Tombs from the Copán Acropolis: A Life History Approach. In *Understanding Early Classic Copán*, edited by Ellen Bell, Marcello Canuto and Robert Sharer, pp.185–205. University of Pennsylvania Museum, Philadelphia.

Cabrera Castro, Rubén. 1998. Teotihuacan. Nuevos Datos para el Estudio de las Rutas de Comunicación. In *Rutas de intercambio en Mesoamérica: III Coloquio Pedro Bosch Gimpera*, edited by Evelyn Rattray, pp. 57–75. Universidad Nacional Autónoma de México, Mexico, D.F.

Chase, Arlen, Diane Chase, and Michael Smith. 2009. States and Empires in Ancient Mesoamérica. *Ancient Mesoamerica* 20:175–182.

Cowgill, George L. 2003. Teotihuacan and Early Classic Interaction: A Perspective from Outside the Maya Region. In *The Maya and Teotihuacan: Reinterpreting Early Classic Interaction*, edited by Geoffrey E. Braswell, pp. 315–335. University of Texas Press, Austin.

Daneels, Annick. 2002. Presencia de Teotihuacan en el Centro y Sur de Veracruz. In *Ideología y política a través de materiales, imágenes y símbolos: Memoria de la primera mesa redonda de Teotihuacan*, edited by María Elena Ruiz Gallut, pp. 655–683. Instituto Nacional de Antropología e Historia, Mexico, D.F.

Demarest, Arthur. 2003. Foreword. In *The Maya and Teotihuacan: Reinterpreting Early Classic Interaction*, edited by Geoffrey E. Braswell, pp. xiii–xvi. University of Texas Press, Austin.

Demarest, Arthur, and Antonia Foias. 1993. Mesoamerican Horizons and the Cultural Transformations of Maya Civilization. In *Latin American Horizons*, edited by Don Rice, pp. 147–191. Dumbarton Oaks Research Library and Collection, Washington, DC.

Fash, William. 2002. El Legado de Teotihuacan en la Ciudad Maya de Copán, Honduras. In *Ideología y política a través de materiales, imágenes y símbolos: Memoria de la primera mesa redonda de Teotihuacan*, edited by María Elena Ruiz Gallut, pp. 715–729. Instituto Nacional de Antropología e Historia, Mexico, D.F.

Filini, Agapi, and Efraín Cárdenas García. 2007. El Bajío, la cuenca de Cuitzeo y el estado teotihuacano. Un estudio de relaciones y antagonismos. In *Dinámicas culturales*

entre el Occidente, el Centro-Norte y la cuenca de México, del Preclásico al Epiclásico,
edited by Brigitte Faugère, pp. 137–154. El Colegio de Michoacán, Zamora.

García Cook, Ángel. 1981. The Historical Importance of Tlaxcala in the Cultural
Development of the Central Highlands. In *Archaeology*, edited by Jeremy Sabloff,
pp. 244–276. Handbook of Middle American Indians, Supplement 1. University of
Texas Press, Austin.

Gazzola, Julie. 2005. La producción lapidaria en Teotihuacan. Estudio de las actividades
productivas en los talleres de un conjunto habitacional. In *Arquitectura y urbanismo:
Pasado y presente de los espacios en Teotihuacan. Memoria de la tercera mesa
redonda de Teotihuacan*, edited by María Elena Ruiz Gallut and Jesús Torres Peralta,
pp. 841–878. Instituto Nacional de Antropología e Historia, Mexico, D.F.

Gómez Chávez, Sergio. 1998. Nuevos datos sobre la relación de Teotihuacán y el
Occidente de México. In *Antropología e historia del Occidente de México: XXIV
mesa redonda de la Sociedad Mexicana de Antropología III*, pp.1461–1493. Sociedad
Mexicana de Antropología, México, D.F.

Gómez Chávez, Sergio. 2002. Presencia del Occidente de México en Teotihuacan.
Aproximaciones a la política exterior del estado teotihuacano. In *Ideología y política
a través de materiales, imágenes y símbolos: Memoria de la primera mesa redonda de
Teotihuacan*, edited by María Elena Ruiz Gallut, pp. 563–625. Instituto Nacional de
Antropología e Historia, Mexico, D.F.

Gómez Chávez, Sergio, and Julie Gazzola. 2007. Análisis de las relaciones entre
Teotihuacán y el Occidente de México. In *Dinámicas culturales entre el Occidente,
el Centro-Norte y la cuenca de México, del Preclásico al Epiclásico*, edited by Brigitte
Faugère, pp. 113–135. El Colegio de Michoacán, Zamora.

González Licón, Ernesto. 2009. Ritual and Social Stratification at Monte Albán, Oaxaca:
Strategies from a Household Perspective. In *Domestic Life in Prehispanic Capitals: A
Study of Specialization, Hierarchy, and Ethnicity*, edited by Linda R. Manzanilla and
Claude Chapdelaine, pp. 7–20. Memoir 46, Museum of Anthropology, University of
Michigan, Ann Arbor.

Hendon, Julia. 2009. Maya Home Life: Daily Practice, Politics, and Society in Copan,
Honduras. In *Domestic Life in Prehispanic Capitals: A Study of Specialization,
Hierarchy, and Ethnicity*, edited by Linda R. Manzanilla and Claude Chapdelaine,
pp. 105–129. Memoir 46, Museum of Anthropology, University of Michigan, Ann
Arbor.

Hirth, Kenneth. 1989. Militarism and Social Organization at Xochicalco, Morelos. In
Mesoamerica after the Decline of Teotihuacan AD 700–900, edited by Richard Diehl
and Janet Berlo, pp. 69–81. Dumbarton Oaks Research Library and Collection,
Washington, DC.

Hirth, Kenneth, ed. 2000. *Archaeological Research at Xochicalco*. University of Utah
Press, Salt Lake City.

Hirth, Kenneth. 2009. Household, Workshop, Guild, and Barrio: The Organization
of Obsidian Craft Production in a Prehispanic Urban Center. In *Domestic Life in
Prehispanic Capitals: A Study of Specialization, Hierarchy, and Ethnicity*, edited by
Linda R. Manzanilla and Claude Chapdelaine, pp. 43–65. Memoir 46, Museum of
Anthropology, University of Michigan, Ann Arbor.

Hirth, Kenneth, Bradford Andrews, and J. Jeffrey Flenniken. 2003. The Xochicalco Production
Sequence for Obsidian Prismatic Blades: Technological Analysis and Experimental
Inferences. In *Mesoamerican Lithic Technology: Experimentation and Interpretation*,
edited by Kenneth Hirth, pp. 182–196. University of Utah Press, Salt Lake City.

Hirth, Kenneth, and W. Swezey. 1976. The Changing Nature of the Teotihuacan Classic: A Regional Perspective from Manzanilla, Puebla. In *Las fronteras de Mesoamérica: XIV mesa redonda de la Sociedad Mexicana de Antropología*, pp.12–23. Sociedad Mexicana de Antropología, Mexico, D.F.

Jiménez Betts, Peter, and J. Andrew Darling. 2000. Archaeology of Southern Zacatecas: The Malpaso, Juchipila, and Valparaiso- Bolaños Valleys. In *Greater Mesoamerica: The Archaeology of West and Northwest Mexico*, edited by Michael Foster and Shirley Gorenstein, pp.155–180. University of Utah Press, Salt Lake City.

Joyce, Arthur. 1993. Interregional Interaction and Social Development on the Oaxaca Coast. *Ancient Mesoamerica* 4:67–84.

Kidder, Alfred V., Jesse Jennings, and Edwin Shook. 1946. *Excavations at Kaminaljuyu, Guatemala*. Carnegie Institution of Washington Publication No.561, Washington, DC.

Laporte, Juan Pedro. 2003. Architectural Aspects of Interaction between Tikal and Teotihuacan in the Early Classic Period. In *The Maya and Teotihuacan: Reinterpreting Early Classic Interaction*, edited by Geoffrey E. Braswell, pp. 199–216. University of Texas Press, Austin.

Manzanilla, Linda, Leonardo López Luján, and William Fash. 2005. Cómo definir un palacio en Teotihuacan. In *Arquitectura y urbanismo: Pasado y presente de los espacios en Teotihuacan. Memoria de la tercera mesa redonda de Teotihuacan*, edited by María Elena Ruiz Gallut and Jesús Torres Peralta, pp. 185–209. Instituto Nacional de Antropología e Historia, Mexico D.F.

Marcus, Joyce. 1983. Teotihuacán Visitors on Monte Albán Monuments and Murals. In *The Cloud People: Divergent Evolution of the Zapotec and Mixtec Civilizations*, edited by Kent Flannery and Joyce Marcus, pp. 175–181. School of American Research, Santa Fe.

Marcus, Joyce. 2003. The Maya and Teotihuacan. In *The Maya and Teotihuacan: Reinterpreting Early Classic Interaction*, edited by Geoffrey E. Braswell, pp. 337–356. University of Texas Press, Austin.

Marcus, Joyce, and Kent Flannery. 1996. *Zapotec Civilization: How Urban Society Evolved in Mexico's Oaxaca Valley*. Thames and Hudson, London.

Martínez López, Cira. 1994. La cerámica de estilo teotihuacano en Monte Albán. In *Monte Albán: Estudios recientes*, edited by Marcus Winter, pp. 25–54. Contribution no. 2, Proyecto Especial Monte Albán 1992–1994, Oaxaca.

Miller, Arthur, ed. 1983. *Highland-Lowland Interaction in Mesoamerica: Interdisciplinary Approaches*. Dumbarton Oaks Research Library and Collection, Washington, DC.

Millon, Clara. 1973. Painting, Writing and Polity in Teotihuacan, Mexico. *American Antiquity* 38:294–314.

Millon, René. 1976. Social Relations in Ancient Teotihuacan. In *The Valley of Mexico: Studies in Pre-Hispanic Ecology and Society*, edited by Eric Wolf, pp.205–248. The School of American Research, Santa Fe.

Millon, René. 1981. Teotihuacan: City, State, and Civilization. In *Archaeology*, edited by Jeremy Sabloff, pp. 198–243. Handbook of Middle American Indians, Supplement 1. University of Texas Press, Austin.

Millon, René. 1992. Teotihuacan Studies: From 1950 to 1990 and Beyond. In *Art, Ideology, and the City of Teotihuacan*, edited by Janet Berlo, pp. 339–419. Dumbarton Oaks Research Library and Collection, Washington, D..

Millon, René. 1993. The Place Where Time Began: An Archaeologist's Interpretation of What Happened in Teotihuacan History. In *Teotihuacan: Art from the City of the Gods*, edited by Kathleen Berrin and Esther Pasztory, pp. 16–43. Thames and Hudson, London.

Moholy-Nagy, Hattula. 1999. Mexican Obsidian at Tikal, Guatemala. *Latin American Antiquity* 10:300–313.

Nagao, Debra. 1989. Public Proclamation in the Art of Cacaxtla and Xochicalco. In *Mesoamerica after the Decline of Teotihuacan AD 700-900*, edited by Richard Diehl and Janet Berlo, pp. 83–104. Dumbarton Oaks Research Library and Collection, Washington, DC.

Nelson, Ben. 2008. Urbanism beyond the City: La Quemada, Zacatecas. In *Urbanism in Mesoamerica, Vol. II*, edited by Alba Guadalupe Mastache, Robert H. Cobean, Ángel García Cook, and Kenneth G. Hirth, pp. 501–537. Pennsylvania State University Press, University Park.

Nelson, Fred W., and John E. Clark. 1998. Obsidian Production and Exchange in Eastern Mesoamerica. In *Rutas de intercambio en Mesoamérica: III coloquio Pedro Bosch Gimpera*, edited by Evelyn Rattray, pp. 277–333. Universidad Nacional Autónoma de México, Mexico, D.F.

Pendergast, David. 1971. Evidence of Early Teotihuacan-Lowland Maya Contact at Altun Ha. *American Antiquity* 36:455–460.

Pendergast, David. 2003. Teotihuacan at Altun Ha: Did it Make a Difference? In *The Maya and Teotihuacan: Reinterpreting Early Classic Interaction*, edited by Geoffrey E. Braswell, pp. 235–247. University of Texas Press, Austin.

Plunket, Patricia, and Gabriela Uruñuela. 2002. Antecedentes conceptuales de los conjuntos de tres templos. In *Ideología y política a través de materiales, imágenes y símbolos: Memoria de la primera mesa redonda de Teotihuacan*, edited by María Elena Ruiz Gallut, pp. 529–546. Instituto Nacional de Antropología e Historia, Mexico, D.F.

Pollard, Helen. 2000. Tarascans and Their Ancestors: Prehistory of Michoacán. In *Greater Mesoamerica: The Archaeology of West and Northwest Mexico*, edited by Michael Foster and Shirley Gorenstein, pp.59–70. University of Utah Press, Salt Lake City.

Price, Barbara. 1986. Teotihuacan as World System: Concerning the Applicability of Wallerstein's Model. In *Origen y formación del estado en Mesoamérica*, edited by A. Medina, Alfredo López Austin, and Mari Carmen Serra Puche, pp. 169–194. Universidad Nacional Autónoma de México, Mexico, D.F.

Price, T. Douglas, Linda Manzanilla, and William Middleton. 2000. Immigration and the Ancient City of Teotihuacan in Mexico: A Study Using Strontium Isotope Ratios in Human Bone and Teeth. *Journal of Archaeological Science* 27:903–913.

Rattray, Evelyn. 2004. Etnicidad en el barrio de los comerciantes, Teotihuacan, y sus relaciones con Veracruz. In *La Costa del Golfo en tiempos teotihuacanos: Propuestas y perspectivas. Memoria de la segunda mesa redonda de teotihuacan*, edited by María Elena Ruiz Gallut and Arturo Pascual Soto, pp.493–512. Instituto Nacional de Antropología e Historia, Mexico, D.F.

Renfrew, Colin. 1986. Introduction. In *Peer Polity Interaction and Socio-Political Change*, edited by Colin Renfrew and John Cherry, pp. 109–116. Cambridge University Press, Cambridge.

Rosales, Edgar. 2004. Usos, manufactura y distribución de la mica en Teotihuacan. Unpublished thesis, Escuela Nacional de Antropología e Historia, Mexico D.F.

Sanders, William T., and Joseph Michels, eds. 1977. *Teotihuacan and Kaminaljuyu: A Study in Prehistoric Culture Contact*. Pennsylvania State University Press, University Park.

Sanders, William T., and Barbara Price. 1968. *Mesoamerica: The Evolution of a Civilization*. Random House, New York.

Santley, Robert S. 1983. Obsidian Trade and Teotihuacan Influence in Mesoamerica. In *Highland- Lowland Interaction in Mesoamerica: Interdisciplinary Approaches*, edited by Arthur Miller, pp. 69–124. Dumbarton Oaks Research Library and Collection, Washington, DC.

Santley, Robert S. 1989. Obsidian Working, Long-Distance Exchange, and the Teotihuacan Presence on the South Gulf Coast. In *Mesoamerica after the Decline of Teotihuacan AD 700-900*, edited by Richard Diehl and Janet Berlo, pp. 131–151. Dumbarton Oaks Research Library and Collection, Washington, DC.

Santley, Robert S., and Rani T. Alexander. 1992. The Political Economy of Core-Periphery Systems. In *Resources, Power, and Interregional Interaction*, edited by Edward Schortman and Patricia Urban, pp. 23–49. Plenum Press, New York.

Santley, Robert S., and Rani T. Alexander. 1996. Teotihuacan and Middle Classic Mesoamerica: A Precolumbian World System? In *Arqueología Mesoamericana: Homenaje a William T. Sanders*, edited by Alba Guadalupe Mastache, Jeffrey R. Parsons, Robert S. Santley, and Mari Carmen Serra Puche, pp. 173–194. Instituto Nacional de Antropología e Historia, Mexico, D.F.

Schele, Linda, and David Freidel. 1990. *A Forest of Kings: The Untold Story of the Ancient Maya*. William Morrow, New York.

Sempowski, Martha. 1994. Mortuary Practices at Teotihuacan. In *Mortuary Practices and Skeletal Remains at Teotihuacan*, edited by René Millon, pp. 1–311. Urbanization at Teotihuacan, Mexico, Vol. 3. University of Utah Press, Salt Lake City.

Sharer, Robert. 2003. Founding Events and Teotihuacan Connections at Copán, Honduras. In *The Maya and Teotihuacan: Reinterpreting Early Classic Interaction*, edited by Geoffrey E. Braswell, pp. 143–165. University of Texas Press, Austin.

Smith, Michael E., and Lisa Montiel. 2001. The Archaeological Study of Empires and Imperialism in Prehispanic Central Mexico. *Journal of Anthropological Archaeology* 20:245–284.

Smyth, Michael 2009. Beyond Capitals and Kings: Domestic Organization and Ethnic Dynamics at Chac-Sayil, Yucatan. In *Domestic Life in Prehispanic Capitals: A Study of Specialization, Hierarchy, and Ethnicity*, edited by Linda R. Manzanilla and Claude Chapdelaine, pp. 131–149. Memoir 46, Museum of Anthropology, University of Michigan, Ann Arbor.

Spence, Michael W. 1996a. A Comparative Analysis of Ethnic Enclaves. In *Arqueología Mesoamericana: Homenaje a William T. Sanders*, edited by Alba Guadalupe Mastache, Jeffrey R. Parsons, Robert S. Santley, and Mari Carmen Serra Puche, pp. 333–353. Instituto Nacional de Antropología e Historia, Mexico, D.F.

Spence, Michael W. 1996b. Commodity or Gift: Teotihuacan Obsidian in the Maya Region. *Latin American Antiquity* 7:21–39.

Spence, Michael W. 2000. From Tzintzuntzan to Paquimé: Peers or Peripheries in Greater Mesoamerica? In *Greater Mesoamerica: The Archaeology of West and Northwest Mexico*, edited by Michael Foster and Shirley Gorenstein, pp.255–261. University of Utah Press, Salt Lake City.

Spence, Michael W. 2005. A Zapotec Diaspora Network in Classic-Period Central Mexico. In *The Archaeology of Colonial Encounters: Comparative Perspectives*, edited by Gil J. Stein, pp.173–205. School of American Research Press, Santa Fe.

Spence, Michael W., and Christine D. White. 2009. Mesoamerican Bioarchaeology: Past and Future. *Ancient Mesoamerica* 20:233–240.

Spence, Michael W., Christine D. White, Fred J. Longstaffe, and Kimberley R. Law. 2004.
    Victims of the Victims: Human Trophies Worn by Sacrificed Soldiers from the
    Feathered Serpent Pyramid, Teotihuacan. *Ancient Mesoamerica* 15:1–15.
Spence, Michael W., Christine D. White, Fred J. Longstaffe, Evelyn C. Rattray, and
    Kimberley R. Law. 2004. Un análisis de las proporciones de los isótopos del oxígeno
    en los entierros del Barrio de los Comerciantes. In *La Costa del Golfo en tiempos
    teotihuacanos: Propuestas y perspectivas. Memoria de la segunda mesa redonda de
    teotihuacan*, edited by María Elena Ruiz Gallut and Arturo Pascual Soto,
    pp. 469–492. Instituto Nacional de Antropología e Historia, Mexico D.F.
Stark, Barbara. 2008. Polity and Economy in the Western Lower Papaloapan Basin.
    In *Classic Period Cultural Currents in Southern and Central Veracruz*, edited by
    Philip J. Arnold III and Christopher A. Pool, pp. 85–119. Dumbarton Oaks Research
    Library and Collections, Washington, D.C.
Stark, Barbara, and Antonio Curet. 1994. The Development of Classic-Period Mixtequilla
    in South Central Veracruz, Mexico. *Ancient Mesoamerica* 5:267–287.
Stein, Gil. 1998. World Systems Theory and Alternative Modes of Interaction in the
    Archaeology of Culture Contact. In *Studies in Culture Contact: Interaction, Culture
    Change and Archaeology*, edited by J. Cusick, pp. 220–255. Occasional Paper 25,
    Center for Archaeological Investigations, Southern Illinois University, Carbondale.
Stone, Andrea. 1989. Disconnection, Foreign Insignia, and Political Expansion:
    Teotihuacan and the Warrior Stelae of Piedras Negras. In *Mesoamerica after the
    Decline of Teotihuacan AD 700-900*, edited by Richard Diehl and Janet Berlo,
    pp. 153–172. Dumbarton Oaks Research Library and Collection, Washington, DC.
Stuart, David. 2000. "The Arrival of Strangers": Teotihuacan and Tollan in Classic Maya
    History. In *Mesoamerica's Classic Heritage: From Teotihuacan to the Aztecs*, edited
    by Davíd Carrasco, Lindsay Jones, and Scott Sessions, pp. 465–513. University Press
    of Colorado, Boulder.
Stuart, David. 2004. The Beginnings of the Copan Dynasty: A Review of the
    Hieroglyphic and Historical Evidence. In *Understanding Early Classic Copán*,
    edited by Ellen Bell, Marcello Canuto and Robert Sharer, pp. 215–247. University of
    Pennsylvania Museum, Philadelphia.
Sugiyama, Saburo. 2005. *Human Sacrifice, Militarism, and Rulership: Materialization of
    State Ideology at the Feathered Serpent Pyramid, Teotihuacan*. Cambridge University
    Press, Cambridge.
Sugiyama, Saburo, and Leonardo López Lújan. 2007. Dedicatory Burial/Offering
    Complexes at the Moon Pyramid, Teotihuacan: A Preliminary Report of 1998–2004
    Explorations. *Ancient Mesoamerica* 18:127–146.
Taube, Karl. 2003. Tetitla and the Maya Presence at Teotihuacan. In *The Maya and
    Teotihuacan: Reinterpreting Early Classic Interaction*, edited by Geoffrey E. Braswell,
    pp. 273–314. University of Texas Press, Austin.
Turner, Margaret. 1992. Style in Lapidary Technology: Identifying the Teotihuacan
    Lapidary Industry. In *Art, Ideology, and the City of Teotihuacan*, edited by Janet Berlo,
    pp. 89–112. Dumbarton Oaks Research Library and Collection, Washington, DC.
Valdés, Juan Antonio, and Lori E. Wright. 2004. The Early Classic and Its Antecedents at
    Kaminaljuyu: A Complex Society with Complex Problems. In *Understanding Early
    Classic Copán*, edited by Ellen Bell, Marcello Canuto and Robert Sharer, pp. 337–355.
    University of Pennsylvania Museum, Philadelphia.
Weigand, Phil C. 1992. Central Mexico's Influences in Jalisco and Nayarit during the
    Classic Period. In *Resources, Power, and Interregional Interaction*, edited by Edward
    Schortman and Patricia Urban, pp. 221–232. Plenum Press, New York.

Weigand, Phil C. 2008. The Teuchitlán Tradition and the Excavations at the
    Guachimontones de Teuchitlán, Jalisco. In *Urbanism in Mesoamerica, Vol. II*, edited
    by Alba Guadalupe Mastache, Robert H. Cobean, Ángel García Cook, and Kenneth
    G. Hirth, pp. 557–592. Pennsylvania State University Press, University Park.

Weigand, Phil C., and Gar Harbottle. 1992. The Role of Turquoises in the Ancient
    Mesoamerican Trade Structure. In *The American Southwest and Mesoamerica:
    Systems of Prehistoric Exchange*, edited by T. Baugh and J. Ericson, pp. 159–177.
    Plenum Press, New York.

White, Christine D., Fred Longstaffe, and Kimberley Law. 2001. Revisiting the
    Teotihuacan Connection at Altun Ha: Oxygen-Isotope Analysis of Tomb F-8/1.
    Ancient Mesoamerica 12:65–72.

White, Christine D., T. Douglas Price, and Fred J. Longstaffe. 2007. Residential Histories
    of the Human Sacrifices at the Moon Pyramid, Teotihuacan: Evidence from Oxygen
    and Strontium Isotopes. *Ancient Mesoamerica* 18:159–172.

White, Christine D., Michael W. Spence, Fred J. Longstaffe, and Kimberley Law. 2004.
    Demography and Ethnic Continuity in the Tlailotlacan Enclave of Teotihuacan:
    The Evidence from Stable Oxygen Isotopes. *Journal of Anthropological Archaeology*
    23:385–403.

White, Christine D., Michael W. Spence, Fred J. Longstaffe, and Kimberley R. Law. 2000.
    Testing the Nature of Teotihuacán Imperialism at Kaminaljuyú Using Phosphate
    Oxygen-Isotope Ratios. *Journal of Anthropological Research* 56:535–558.

White, Christine D., Michael W. Spence, Fred J. Longstaffe, Hilary Stuart-Williams,
    and Kimberley R. Law. 2002. Geographic Identities of the Sacrificial Victims from
    the Feathered Serpent Pyramid, Teotihuacan: Implications for the Nature of State
    Power. *Latin American Antiquity* 13:217–236.

White, Christine D., Michael W. Spence, Hilary Stuart-Williams, and Henry P. Schwarcz.
    1998. Oxygen Isotopes and the Identification of Geographical Origins: The Valley of
    Oaxaca versus the Valley of Mexico. *Journal of Archaeological Science* 25:643–655.

White, Christine D., Rebecca Storey, Fred J Longstaffe, and Michael W. Spence. 2004.
    Immigration, Assimilation and Status in the Ancient City of Teotihuacan: Isotopic
    Evidence from Tlajinga33. *Latin American Antiquity* 15:176–198.

Winter, Marcus. 1998. Monte Albán and Teotihuacan. In *Rutas de intercambio en
    Mesoamérica: III coloquio Pedro Bosch Gimpera*, edited by Evelyn Rattray, pp.
    153–184. Universidad Nacional Autónoma de México, Mexico, D.F.

Winter, Marcus, Cira Martínez López, and Alicia Herrera Muzgo T. 2002. Monte Albán
    y Teotihuacan: Política e ideología. In *Ideología y política a través de materiales,
    imágenes y símbolos: Memoria de la primera mesa redonda de Teotihuacan*, edited
    by María Elena Ruiz Gallut, pp. 627–644. Instituto Nacional de Antropología e
    Historia, Mexico, D.F.

Wright, Lori E. 2005a. In Search of Yax Nuun Ayiin I: Revisiting the Tikal Project's
    Burial 10. *Ancient Mesoamerica* 16:89–100.

Wright, Lori E. 2005b. Identifying Immigrants to Tikal, Guatemala: Defining Local
    Variability in Strontium Isotope Ratios of Human Tooth Enamel. *Journal of
    Archaeological Science* 32:555–566.

Yarborough, Clare. 1992. Teotihuacan and the Gulf Coast: Ceramic Evidence for Contact
    and Interactional Relationships. Unpublished PhD dissertation, University of
    Arizona, Tucson.

Developmental Cycles:
Collapse and Regeneration

CHAPTER 21

CONCEPTS OF COLLAPSE AND REGENERATION IN HUMAN HISTORY

GEORGE L. COWGILL

IT is impossible to discuss concepts of collapse and regeneration without taking into account recent heated debates between Jared Diamond (2005) and his critics, notably in the book edited by Patricia McAnany and Norman Yoffee (2010). Diamond tends to explain collapses by societal choices that were environmentally unwise; his critics often deny or underplay the reality of collapses. On all sides, there is room for improvement. One thing at issue is the potential impact of these books on correcting or perpetuating popular misconceptions. That is important, but here I will concentrate on concepts employed by Mesoamericanists.

WHAT IS COLLAPSING OR REGENERATING?

Much mischief is caused by ambiguities about what it is that is supposed to be collapsing or regenerating. Most often, what is at issue is either the fragmentation of a large polity or the termination of a major cultural tradition. To be sure, support by a large and powerful polity that has many material resources at its disposal is conducive to the persistence and elaboration of cultural traditions, but polities and traditions are not the same thing. I tried to make this clear some time ago (Cowgill 1988: 255–257) but with little success. In ancient Egypt, Mesopotamia, and China, for example, there were alternating episodes of political centralization and fragmentation. In Egypt periods of centralization tended to be long and episodes of fragmentation relatively brief, while the opposite was more typical in Mesopotamia. China was probably somewhere in between. In all three cases, cultural traditions underwent changes over time but were far more enduring.

Mesoamericanists have not always clearly distinguished the fragmentation of polities from the termination of major cultural traditions. The very concept of "Mesoamerica" is based on a broad cultural tradition that goes back to at least 1500 BC (this is not the place to debate whether any single society formulated a "Mother" culture) and that tradition changed somewhat over time and diverged into regional variants but survived many vicissitudes, even the shock of European conquest. In discussing collapses and regenerations in Mesoamerica, it seems best to focus on political alternations, although migrations, demographic changes, and alterations of ethnic identities must also be considered. Scholars can, and will, also discuss the fates of cultural traditions, but they should make themselves clear on the distinction between that and the histories of polities.

THE CASE OF ROME

For the Roman Empire, Peter Brown (1971), looking at it from a cultural and religious standpoint, argued persuasively that, during the so-called Dark Ages, Roman civilization underwent many changes but clearly survived. I add that less than a century ago no one of European culture could claim to be really well educated if he or she was not well versed in a number of "classics" in the original Latin (and, at least to some extent, Greek). In that sense we may only now be witnessing the real end, or at least a major decline, in that tradition.

Politically and economically, it was far otherwise for Rome. By the 300s AD, for practical purposes the empire had split into western and eastern segments, and archaeological and other evidence shows that by the 400s at least the western part was in serious economic decline (Ward-Perkins 2005). In studies that are very rich in data from both written and archaeological sources, Peter Heather (2006, 2009) argues persuasively that the famous annihilation of three entire legions by Germanic tribesmen in 7 AD was an anomaly and not a significant deterrent to Roman expansion east of the Rhine (perhaps a bit like the annihilation by Native Americans of a much smaller force under Custer in 1876). Instead, Heather argues, the real reason is that, with Gaul and many other provinces well under control, the small and weak polities of central Europe had little to offer Roman imperialists. In the subsequent centuries he does not see any significant increase in elite

Roman factionalism (always present), decline in environmental conditions, problems because barbarians were enlisted in Roman armies, or problems introduced by the adoption of Christianity as the state religion. Instead, he sees the invasions of the 400s by newly powerful Germanic polities (Ostrogoths, Visigoths, Franks, Vandals, and others) as partly spurred by pressures of the Asiatic Huns upon them but especially because the numerous small polities of the first century had grown into a few large kingdoms with powerful and wealthy rulers who could mobilize large armies. The rise of these ambitious and powerful rulers was, in turn, made possible by wealth flowing to them over the centuries from Rome, in exchange for various products, notably slaves. In this unexpected way, Rome's external relations created the new polities that could effectively deprive them of their provinces and bring the Roman state to ruin. Especially damaging were the Vandals, whose takeover of most of the western part of Mediterranean North Africa deprived Rome of a major source of grain and of tax revenues.

None of these successor kingdoms had either the geographic scope or the political institutions to make possible anything like reconstitution of the Roman Empire in Europe, in spite of the famous efforts of Frankish Charlemagne and his successors to do so in the late 700s and after, and the limited success of the Christian church in trying to make itself a universal institution. Rome is thus a notable case where political regeneration has never happened. Even today, the European Union, with its (mostly) wealthy and contentious independent states, is at most a weak confederacy, rather than even a pale reflection of imperial Rome. The eastern (Byzantine) part of the Roman Empire survived as a political as well as a cultural entity for another millennium, into the 1400s, but on a reduced scale (Heather 2009).

Heather's explanation for the fragmentation of the Roman polity is new to me, and I know of no effort to examine its possible applications in Mesoamerica. Perhaps it has little applicability to Mesoamerican cases, but I wonder. It is certainly something to think about.

A NULL HYPOTHESIS

Relatively large and wealthy polities have rarely been created that have lasted more than a few centuries before they fragmented into units that were smaller and had fewer resources at their disposal. Often, but not always, relatively large polities were again created from these smaller polities in the same region. It could be argued that that is really all there is to it and that all arguments for cycling or patterning are simply founded on the human proclivity to see patterning in random or chaotic data—the "inkblot" effect. I do not believe this, but I think it is useful heuristically to set it up as a sort of null hypothesis against which to test data. Rather than asking "What are the patterns?" (assuming there must be patterns of some sort), we must ask "What patterns are there?" Rather than assuming that cycles somehow have a life of their own (as may be the case with many animal populations), we should be asking (1) "What sorts of things favor long or short duration of large polities?" and (2) "What impact, if any, does the previous existence of a large polity in a region of small polities have on the creation of new large polities?" Note that I say "creation" rather than "rise" or "emergence" of polities: human intentions are always involved, even if outcomes are not the ones intended. Are some regions simply more conducive to the creation of large polities than other regions are, or are the fragmented polities that succeed them somehow systematically different from the kinds of polities that preceded them?

Regeneration, Cumulative Change, and the Concepts of "Resilience" and "Cycling"

In an article that is now dated in many ways but was seminal at the time, Julian Steward (1949) included the concept of an era of cyclical conquests, in which ancient empires grew by conquest, suffered rebellions, and fragmented into local states until new conquests initiated another cycle. Joyce Marcus (1998), using far better data, has updated and refined this model. I am very skeptical of her notion that four or five archaeologically recognizable features are secure diagnostics of polities that qualify as archaic states rather than as chiefdoms, but otherwise her review and comparison of data from a variety of cases in both hemispheres is valuable and thought-provoking. However, I wonder if alternating episodes of large territorial polities and fragmentation into smaller autonomous units are best described as "cyclic." That term suggests some uniform rhythmic process whereas, as Marcus makes clear, intervals of unity and disunity are quite variable both within and between regions. The concept of "episodes" of centralization and decentralization seems better.

Others (e.g., McAnany and Yoffee 2010) occasionally use the term "resilience" to refer to the continuation of cultural traditions or the reappearance of large regional polities after an episode of fragmentation. But, to me, "resilience" should refer to the ability to maintain, or quickly restore, in the face of a challenge, conditions considered highly desirable. This might apply, for example, to continuation of the Teotihuacan state after whatever episode of turmoil is marked by desecratory destruction of the Feathered Serpent Pyramid ca. 300 AD (Sugiyama 2005). But episodes of political fragmentation lasting more than a few years strike me as failures of resilience. Why is eventual reconstitution of a large polity somehow an example of "resilience" when the first large polity in a region or tradition was not?

The concept of "secondary" states implies some sort of cumulative change. Cumulative developments in technology are often recognizable archaeologically, but cumulations in statecraft and in economic institutions are harder to discern. Are small polities that preceded the first big one necessarily different from those that followed a big one? Are any lessons learned from the past, especially in statecraft? The sheer knowledge that it was done before may encourage ambitious leaders to try to do it again. To what extent is the recurrence of large polities in some regions simply because of the continuation of environmental circumstances that favored generation of a large polity in the first place, as proposed by William Sanders (1956) for Central Mexico?

The Central Mexican Case

I sketch my current views on central Mexico. For a more detailed account, including references, see Cowgill (2013). I differ somewhat from Jeffrey Parsons and Yoko Sugiura in this volume, who are more skeptical than I am of large migrations and more accepting of claims of considerable derivation from Teotihuacan antecedents. They ignore nonceramic evidence for migrations, such as lithics and linguistics. As to Teotihuacan antecedents, they apparently accept some problematic claims. For example, Margarita Gaxiola González (2006: 45, Figure 6) describes a vessel in which I can see no Teotihuacan features at all as a Teotihuacan-Coyotlatelco "hybrid."

The immense city of Teotihuacan did not develop suddenly from nothing but was preceded in the Basin of Mexico by a large urban center called Cuicuilco, which developed around 400 to 300 BC. Cuicuilco was eventually covered by volcanic lava, but this probably occurred only after it had been vanquished by rapidly growing Teotihuacan, probably around 1 AD. The spatial extent of Teotihuacan's direct political control is unknown, but for several centuries it was the most influential polity in Mesoamerica. Then, perhaps around 500–550 AD, there are signs of decline, though no clear evidence of environmental problems. Internal sociopolitical stresses were very likely important, but I now wonder whether the rise of some other central Mexican cities, such as Xochicalco in the nearby state of Morelos, could possibly have been favored by its relations with Teotihuacan. Marcus (1998) suggests that expansionist states often peak early and then decline at least partly because provinces tend to break free. This is somewhat along the lines that Heather proposes for Rome, except that in that case it was the growing power of polities outside the empire. Unfortunately, limitations of chronological and other data make it difficult to test this conjecture about Teotihuacan at the present, but it should be considered in future research.

At roughly the same time, there are multiple lines of evidence, again hampered by chronological imprecision, strongly suggestive of sizable migrations from in or near the modern state of Guanajuato, in western Mexico. Around 600–650 AD, major Teotihuacan civic ceremonial structures were desecrated and burned, at least some residential structures throughout the city were rapidly abandoned and left unoccupied for a while, and the Teotihuacan state collapsed. The in-migrants may have been a major factor in this collapse or they may have arrived a little later to take advantage of it. In any case, their interactions with surviving Teotihuacanos were complex, and material culture, in both ceramics and lithics, changed drastically. Teotihuacan survivors, who may or may not have been active participants in the city's destruction, probably very soon abandoned their Teotihuacano identities, making them untraceable in the archaeological record, except possibly through genetic markers. As pointed out by Berdan et al. (2008) and many others, identities need not persist but instead are quite malleable in response to changing conditions.

The immediate outcome was a return to tiny independent polities. Before long, the polity centered on the city of Tula expanded to become a sizable regional state. Neither the city nor its influence grew as large as Teotihuacan had been, though it was somewhat larger than proposed by Smith and Montiel (2001). It likely included the northern part of the Basin of Mexico while the southern basin was more likely under the sway of a competing state whose capital was Cholula in the state of Puebla (Crider et al. 2007; Crider 2013). Collapse of the Tula state led to another episode of political fragmentation into competing small polities and, after 1428, creation of the Aztec Empire, which far exceeded the Teotihuacan state in the number of people it controlled and very likely in the sophistication of its economic and administrative institutions. There were cumulative advances in high-temperature technology in metals and ceramics and in large-scale water management.

DEMOGRAPHY AND THE LOWLAND MAYA CASE

Perhaps because lowland Maya cultural achievements were so brilliant and most of their polities so small, Mayanists seem especially prone to emphasize the continuity of cultural traditions more than the volatility of their polities. What is often ignored, or at most barely acknowledged, is the massive demographic collapse in the central Petén district of the southern lowlands during the Terminal Classic period, in the 800s AD. For example, after well-taken corrections of popular misconceptions about the Maya and a skeptical review of proposed reasons for Terminal Classic "collapse" in the southern lowlands, Patricia McAnany and Tomás Gallareta Negrón (2010: 159) only fleetingly acknowledge "a draw down of population in the southern part of the lowlands." David Webster (this volume) gives a far better and more balanced account of the complexity and regional variability of events in the Maya lowlands during this period. It is not just that civic-ceremonial centers were abandoned or that settlement patterns shifted: large areas of the Petén were almost completely depopulated.

This demographic collapse is unlike anything in central Mexico where populations declined at times but never to nearly such an extent. It is a gigantic fact, and nothing about the vicissitudes of Maya culture can be understood if it is not acknowledged. The mere absence of people was enough to cause a major cultural discontinuity in the central Petén, whatever else may (or may not) have been involved.

References

Berdan, Frances F., John K. Chance, Alan R. Sandstrom, Barbara L. Stark, James M. Taggart, and Emily Umberger. 2008. *Ethnic Identity in Nahua Mesoamerica: The View from Archaeology, Art History, Ethnohistory, and Contemporary Ethnography.* University of Utah Press, Salt Lake City.

Brown, Peter R. L. 1971. *The World of Late Antiquity.* Thames and Hudson, London.

Cowgill, George L. 1988. Onward and Upward with Collapse. In *The Collapse of Ancient States and Civilizations*, edited by Norman Yoffee and George L. Cowgill, pp. 244–276. University of Arizona Press, Tucson.

Cowgill, George L. 2013. Migrations, Disruptions, and Identities in the Central Mexican Epiclassic. *Ancient Mesoamerica*, in press.

Crider, Destiny. 2013. Shifting Alliances: Epiclassic and Early Postclassic Interactions at Cerro Portezuelo. *Ancient Mesoamerica* in press.

Crider, Destiny, Deborah L. Nichols, Hector Neff, and Michael D. Glascock. 2007. In the Aftermath of Teotihuacan: Epiclassic Pottery Production and Distribution in the Teotihuacan Valley, Mexico. *Latin American Antiquity* 18(2):123–143.

Diamond, Jared. 2005. *Collapse: How Societies Choose to Fail or Succeed.* Viking, New York.

Gaxiola González, Margarita. 2006. Tradición y estilo en el estudio de la variabilidad cerámica del Epiclásico en el centro de México. In *El fenómeno Coyotlatelco en el centro de México: Tiempo, espacio, y significado*, edited by Laura Solar Valverde, pp. 31–54. Instituto Nacional de Antropología e Historia, Mexico City.

Heather, Peter. 2006. *The Fall of the Roman Empire: A New History of Rome and the Barbarians.* Oxford University Press, Oxford.

Heather, Peter. 2009. *Empires and Barbarians: The Fall of Rome and the Birth of Europe.* Oxford University Press, Oxford.

Marcus, Joyce. 1998. The Peaks and Valleys of Ancient States: An Extension of the Dynamic Model. In *Archaic States*, edited by Gary M. Feinman and Joyce Marcus, pp. 59–94. School of American Research Press, Santa Fe.

McAnany, Patricia A., and Tomás Gallareta Negrón. 2010. Bellicose Rulers and Climatological Peril? Retrofitting Twenty-First-Century Woes on Eighth-Century Maya Society. In *Questioning Collapse: Human Resilience, Ecological Vulnerability, and the Aftermath of Empire*, edited by Patricia McAnany and Norman Yoffee, pp. 142–175. Cambridge University Press, Cambridge.

McAnany, Patricia A., and Norman Yoffee, eds. 2010. *Questioning Collapse: Human Resilience, Ecological Vulnerability, and the Aftermath of Empire*. Cambridge University Press, Cambridge.

Sanders, William T. 1956. The Central Mexican Symbiotic Region. In *Prehistoric Settlement in the New World*, edited by Gordon R. Willey, pp. 115–127. Viking Fund Publications in Anthropology 23. Wenner Gren Foundation, New York.

Smith, Michael E., and Lisa Montiel. 2001. The Archaeological Study of Empires and Imperialism in Prehispanic Central Mexico. *Journal of Anthropological Archaeology* 20:245–284.

Steward, Julian H. 1949. Cultural Causality and Law: A Trial Formulation of the Development of Early Civilizations. *American Anthropologist* 51:1–27.

Sugiyama, Saburo. 2005. *Human Sacrifice, Militarism, and Rulership: The Symbolism of the Feathered Serpent Pyramid at Teotihuacan, Mexico*. Cambridge University Press, Cambridge.

Ward-Perkins, Brian. 2005. *The Fall of Rome and the End of Civilization*. Oxford University Press, Oxford.

CHAPTER 22

TEOTIHUACAN AND THE EPICLASSIC IN CENTRAL MEXICO

JEFFREY R. PARSONS AND YOKO SUGIURA Y.

THE collapse of Teotihuacan as a major center in the seventh century AD was part of a widespread series of changes that occurred throughout Mesoamerica at that time. The nature and causes of these changes and of the polities and economies that developed in the subsequent centuries of the Epiclassic (ca. 600-900 AD) (Table 22.1) have been studied by many archaeologists working in central Mexico over the past four decades (e.g., Acosta 1972; Dumond and Muller 1972; Sanders et al. 1979; Diehl and Berlo 1989; García 1995; Rattray 1996; Sugiura 1996; Manzanilla 2005; Solar 2006; Dumond 1972; García Cook and Merino 1990; Hicks and Nicholson 1964; Rattray 1972; Sanders 1989; Santana 1990; Sugiura 2001). In this chapter we discuss the highlights of these and other studies and offer an assessment of our current understandings.

CHANGING URBAN AND REGIONAL SETTLEMENT PATTERNS

Settlement-pattern data have illuminated the collapse of Teotihuacan and its aftermath in central Mexico. In this section we consider the implications of these data from the Teotihuacan heartland in the Basin of Mexico and bordering regions (Figures 23.1 and 23.2).

Table 22.1 Basin of Mexico ceramic phases.

Period	Date (AD)	Phase
	1520	Aztec IV
		Aztec III
Postclassic		Aztec II
	900	Mazapan/Aztec I
Epiclassic		Coyotlatelco
	600	Metepec/Oxtotipac(?)
		Xolalpan
Classic Teotihuacan		Tlamimilolpa
		Miccaotli
	100	
Terminal Formative		Tzacualli

THE BASIN OF MEXICO

By the Metepec phase, ca. 600 AD, Teotihuacan had begun its long and irreversible decline. Archaeologists continue to debate the rapidity and completeness of this decline, and what part the emergent new centers outside the Basin of Mexico and

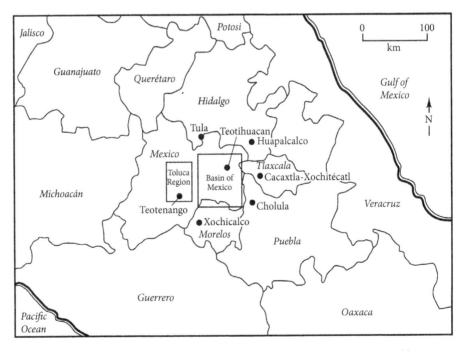

Figure 22.1 Central Mexico, with principal Epiclassic sites. Prepared by
Larry Gorenflo.

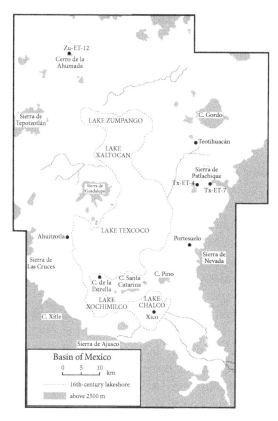

Figure 22.2 The Basin of Mexico, with principal Epiclassic sites.

new immigrants into the basin may have played in the ensuing changes. As the old
Classic center lost population and influence, several large Epiclassic sites developed throughout the basin and in neighboring regions in areas previously characterized by modest levels of population and urbanization. Rapid population loss at
Teotihuacan and rapid population buildup at these new centers indicate a significant movement of people away from the old Classic city. Around the peripheries of
the basin important new centers developed at Huapalcalco and Tula (Tula Chico)
in southern Hidalgo, Teotenango, in the southwestern State of Mexico, Xochicalco
in western Morelos, and Cacaxtla-Xochitécatl in Tlaxcala. In the Basin of Mexico,
most of these major Epiclassic centers had previously been small Classic-period
sites, and many of them continued to be occupied on a more modest scale into the
subsequent Early Postclassic.

Archaeologists disagree about the nature of the Teotihuacan center itself during
the Epiclassic. There are two main views: (1) the "large-site" crowd, which argues
that Teotihuacan continued to be the largest and most important Epiclassic center
in the Basin of Mexico, with a surface area of roughly 10 square kilometers and a
population estimated at about 35,000 people (or possibly much higher in the early
Epiclassic) (e.g., Sanders et al. 1979; Diehl 1989; Gorenflo and Sanders 2007); and (2)

the "small-site" crowd, which argues that Teotihuacan degenerated into a cluster of dispersed villages and hamlets whose few thousand inhabitants—including recent immigrants from north and west of the Basin of Mexico who brought with them new ceramic traditions, most particularly Coyotlatelco Red/Buff pottery—settled at Teotihuacan after it had been virtually abandoned for perhaps a half century (e.g., Rattray 1996, 2006; Gómez and Cabrera 2006).

These contrasting views derive from differing interpretations of the same archaeological data. There are two main, and still unresolved, issues:

(1) The continuing uncertainty about ceramic chronology: it remains difficult to define the key transitional Oxtotipac phase to everyone's satisfaction and to separate it from the antecedent Metepec and succeeding Coyotlatelco phases. Those who partially conflate Metepec and Oxtotipac phases see more long-term occupational continuity (e.g., Sanders 2006), while those who prefer a finer degree of separation between these phases see major abandonment and partial resettlement (e.g., Rattray 2006).

(2) Disagreement about how to interpret the widespread distribution of Epiclassic (Coyotlatelco phase) surface pottery at Teotihuacan. This material extends in variable concentration over an area of ca. 10 square kilometers, about half the surface area of the florescent Classic city (Millon 1966). The large-site crowd regards this area as a good approximation of the overall size of the Epiclassic center, just as the distribution of Classic surface pottery is for estimating the surface area of the antecedent Classic city. The small-site crowd, pointing to the results of several recent excavations that reveal dispersed Epiclassic settlements in shoddily built structures in abandoned Classic buildings, feels that the overall distribution of Epiclassic surface does not adequately reflect subsurface reality.

THE TULA REGION

During the Classic period, most settlements were situated in the eastern sector of this region, an area of low limestone hills and irrigable alluvial valley floor, with two small local centers and numerous small villages and hamlets, all with clear architectural and ceramic links to Teotihuacan. The subsequent early Epiclassic witnessed a dramatic shift of occupation into the western sector of the region, with the rapid settlement at seven high-hilltop centers and in numerous small, low-lying sites. In central Mexico these seemingly autonomous hilltop centers with Coyotlatelco ceramics are unique to the Tula region and neighboring areas to the west and south, and they shared a common material culture characterized by the distinctive architectural and ceramic styles that may have been partly rooted in the Bajío region to the northwest (Braniff 1972; Mastache and Cobean 1989; Mastache et al. 2002). By contrast, the coeval small, low-lying early Epiclassic settlements in the Tula region are characterized by pottery showing greater continuity with the Teotihuacan Metepec-phase ceramic tradition (this early Epiclassic ceramic continuity is also seen in the nearby Toluca region, see below). This contrast may indicate that the hilltop sites were settled by immigrant groups who for a time lived in defensible hilltop settlements apart from the indigenous population who occupied the low-lying sites.

Recent excavations have revealed that these hilltop centers in the Tula region were abandoned after only two or three generations. Later in the Epiclassic they were replaced by a single new regional center at Tula Chico, a large, strategically situated settlement that administered a regional polity that subsequently developed into the Early Postclassic Toltec state centered at Tula, a major urban community that expanded from its original core at Tula Chico.

Puebla-Tlaxcala

The Epiclassic witnessed a major decline of Cholula, the principal Classic regional center with close architectural and ceramic links to Teotihuacan, and a rapid growth of a new regional center at Cacaxtla-Xochitécatl, a strategically situated hilltop settlement that had been important during Terminal Formative times but that had been abandoned for several centuries during Teotihuacan's Classic florescence (Serra and Lazcano 1997). New architectural and ceramic styles, and a near absence of Coyotlatelco ceramics, suggest that this development at Cacaxtla-Xochitécatl was not directly linked in the same way that the Tula and Toluca regions, where Coyotlatelco pottery is abundant, were connected to events in the Basin of Mexico. Similarly, the absence of Coyotlatelco ceramics at the large Huapalcalco site in southeastern Hidalgo north of Cacaxtla-Xochitécatl suggests a comparable absence of strong cultural links with the Basin of Mexico along that section of its northeastern periphery (Gaxiola 1999). However, in the intervening area of northwestern Tlaxcala, between Cacaxtla-Xochitécatl and Huapalcalco, within the old "Teotihuacan Corridor" along which contacts between the Classic center and the Gulf Coast had been concentrated during the period of Teotihuacan's florescence, continuing close ceramic and architectural links with the Basin of Mexico persisted in a region characterized by numerous small Epiclassic polities (Salomon 2006).

The Cacaxtla-Xochitécatl center declined rapidly after the early tenth century. This decline replicated coeval declines at many other Epiclassic centers around the peripheries of the Basin of Mexico, but in this case it may also have been related to volcanic-ash depositions that would have destroyed much of the local agricultural infrastructure (Siebe et al. 1996).

MORELOS

During the Epiclassic an important new hilltop center developed in southwestern Morelos at the site of Xochicalco (Hirth 2000). There had been only limited antecedent Classic occupations in this part of Morelos, an agriculturally more marginal region relative to the productive irrigable floodplains of eastern Morelos that were of greater interest to Teotihuacan-linked groups (Hirth 1974, 1978; Angulo and Hirth 1981).

The rapid development of Xochicalco was part of notable settlement-pattern changes in Morelos during the seventh century. As in nearby Puebla-Tlaxcala, the near absence of Coyotlatelco ceramics at Xochicalco and throughout Morelos suggests a regional polity and economy that operated largely independently of what was going on in the Basin of Mexico during the Epiclassic (Cyphers 2000; Canto 2006). The defensible hilltop locale of Xochicalco (Hirth 1989)—a topographic setting it shared with numerous Epiclassic centers around the peripheries of the Basin of Mexico—is notable. The rapid decline and dispersal of the population at Xochicalco after the early tenth century (Smith 2000) also characterize most other hilltop Epiclassic centers in central Mexico—whatever the defense-related attraction of these hilltop locations were, they did not prove to be adaptive in the long term when more secure conditions apparently prevailed (Kabata 2010).

THE TOLUCA REGION

This region shows an accelerated population increase during the final stage of Classic Teotihuacan with an increasing tendency to occupy the most fertile zone in the southern portion of the region. A subsequent Epiclassic population increase was accompanied by the development of a more complex settlement pattern with clear hierarchical differences evidenced by new small regional centers and a doubling of the number of rural sites. It was during the Epiclassic that the Toluca region attained its first cultural florescence.

Contrary to some neighboring regions, site distribution in the Toluca region did not show strong discontinuity from Classic to Epiclassic. Nearly one third of the Classic sites, including those of a short transitional phase (corresponding to the Oxtotipac phase in the Basin of Mexico), continued to be occupied during the Epiclassic, and some regional Classic centers subsequently became larger and

more complex. The sudden population increase can best be explained by substantial immigration from the adjacent western Basin of Mexico during the collapse
of Teotihuacan in the seventh century. This population movement and the high
degree of settlement continuity may have been due to a shared Otomian ethnic
identity between the new immigrants and the original inhabitants of the Toluca
region. Newly developed regional centers on hilltops and other places of difficult
access from the passes that link the western Basin of Mexico to the Toluca region
are also evidence for this connection. The later Epiclassic is distinguished by the
development of regional centers, such as Teotenango; some of these sites continued
as regional centers during the subsequent Early Postclassic.

EPICLASSIC CERAMICS IN CENTRAL MEXICO

Much of the effort to understand Epiclassic society at Teotihuacan and throughout central Mexico has focused on the distinctive Coyotlatelco Red/Buff pottery
first formally defined in excavations at Ahuitzotla and nearby Cerro Tenayo in the
western Basin of Mexico (Tozzer 1921; Rattray 1966). Coyotlatelco Red/Buff pottery
has come to be the main archaeological hallmark of the Epiclassic in the Basin of
Mexico and around its northern and western peripheries. Virtually all the major
Epiclassic centers in the Basin of Mexico, including Teotihuacan itself, share this
assemblage of decorated pottery featuring a complex series of geometric and curvilinear red designs painted in zoned panels around the walls of simple bowls and
other vessel forms (Figure 22.3).

Dumond and Muller (1972) identified the main issues involving the interpretation of Epiclassic ceramics that still confront archaeologists today. They distinguished two categories of Red/Buff ceramics and two "complexes" of Epiclassic
pottery: (1) a narrowly defined category of Red/Buff pottery (included in their
"Complex B"), which corresponds to Coyotlatelco Red/Buff as previously defined
by Tozzer (1921) and Rattray (1966), which occurs throughout the Basin of Mexico,
the Toluca and Tula regions, and northwestern Tlaxcala, and which lacks clear stylistic links to antecedent Classic ceramics at Teotihuacan; and (2) a more generalized Red/Buff category (included in their "Complex A"), which occurs throughout
much of central Mexico—including Teotihuacan itself, the Basin of Mexico, and
all the bordering regions considered in this paper—and which has stylistic linkages to Classic Teotihuacan-related pottery in and around the Basin of Mexico.

The importance of this distinction between Complexes A and B has been
emphasized by several recent archaeologists (e.g., Gaxiola 1999; Cyphers 2000),
who have argued that because an overly broad definition of Coyotlatelco Red/
Buff in recent decades has conflated much of Complex A and B, several essential lines of interpretation have been neglected or obscured. By returning to the

Figure 22.3 Examples of Coyotlatelco Red/Buff ceramics from the Toluca region.

key distinctions made by Dumond and Muller, and considering the refinements of recent years (e.g., Solar 2006), we can recognize that although there are several categories of Epiclassic ceramic decoration and vessel form at Teotihuacan that lack local Classic antecedents, at the same time there are many continuities between Classic and Epiclassic ceramics at Teotihuacan and elsewhere (Table 23.2).

This view of ceramic variability makes it possible to accommodate the idea of importation of new styles and perhaps some immigration of new peoples into

Table 22.2 Some continuities and innovations in Epiclassic ceramics at Teotihuacan and in central Mexico. (Compiled from Cyphers 2000; Gaxiola 1999; Dumond and Muller 1972; Sanders 1986; Rattray 1966, 1987; Crider 2002; Sugiura 2005b, 2010; Solar 2006)

Continuities	Innovations
Stick-polished brown vessels	High-walled comals
Brown vessels with stamped decoration	Spindle whorls (in the Basin of Mexico)
Paste, firing, and finishing techniques	Handled censers (sahumeros)
Utilitarian pottery—forms and paste	Ladles
"Simple" Red/Buff decoration (part of Complex A)	Coyotlatelco Red/Buff decoration (part of Complex B)
Figurine styles	Ollas with "double handles"
Braseros	Tripod plates

Epiclassic Teotihuacan and other parts of central Mexico, while at the same time maintaining a significant degree of demographic and cultural continuity with the antecedent period of Teotihuacan's Classic development. Indeed, Teotihuacan had long been a magnet for people, products, and ideas from all over Mesoamerica during its long Classic florescence, and it is not surprising that these interregional relationships should have continued to some degree, however truncated, into the Epiclassic. This reasoning is consistent with the results of recent analyses of strontium isotope ratios and DNA from bone and teeth in burials from several Classic and Epiclassic contexts at Teotihuacan, which suggest the presence of some immigrant people who died there but who were born elsewhere (Price et al. 2000; Manzanilla 2005). Discoveries of Epiclassic workshops at Teotihuacan that produced Coyotlatelco Red/Buff indicate that, whatever its ultimate origins, some Coyotlatelco pottery was produced at and distributed from Teotihuacan during the Epiclassic (Rattray 1981).

Looking more broadly at central Mexico, Gaxiola (1999) has noted that there are three major Epiclassic ceramic traditions that intersect roughly at the northeastern corner of the Basin of Mexico to the northeast of Teotihuacan: (1) the Coyotlatelco tradition, extending to the west and southwest; (2) the Gulf Coast Orange Ware tradition, extending to the east and northeast; and (3) a Gray Ware tradition, extending to the south and southeast. Although the borders and content of these traditions, and the relationships between the groups that used these ceramics remain to be more precisely defined, these distributions undoubtedly reflect the complex new regional sociopolitical configurations and exchange networks that developed after the collapse of Classic Teotihuacan.

Part of the problem with interpreting Coyotlatelco pottery involves the still-controversial Oxtotipac phase (Obermayer 1963; Millon 1966; Sanders 1986), often viewed as transitional at Teotihuacan between the Metepec and Coyotlatelco phases. The Oxtotipac phase appears to have been less than a century in length, and its short duration has undoubtedly contributed to the difficulty archaeologists have had in dealing with it. However, its reality and significance are supported by the findings of several other investigators who have recently defined what appear to be comparably very short Early Epiclassic ceramic phases in the Toluca region (Sugiura 2005a, 2005b, 2010), at Xochitécatl in Tlaxcala (Serra et al. 2004), and in the Tula region (Mastache and Cobean 1989). The collapse of Classic Teotihuacan and the early development of its Epiclassic successors throughout central Mexico may well have occurred in short stages, each of which produced a characteristic ceramic "signature" recognizable only with especially fine-scale analysis.

In the Toluca region, a transitional phase equivalent to Oxtotipac is clearly identifiable. At many sites, it overlaps with Terminal Classic occupations and shares both Metepec and Coyotlatelco attributes. Coyotlatelco Red/Buff is distributed throughout the entire Toluca region. Relative to most of the Basin of Mexico, Coyotlatelco pottery from the Toluca region exhibits a much higher technical quality of decoration and greater variation in decorative motifs. The close relationship between the Coyotlatelco materials from the Toluca region and those of the western Basin of

Mexico is seen by an almost identical range of vessel forms and decorative motifs. This indicates that the west-central Basin of Mexico had stronger ties with the neighboring Toluca region than it did with the rest of the basin during the Epiclassic, as this region developed its own well-defined regional style. Other utilitarian vessel forms—as well as some used for ritual practices, such as *braseros* with Teotihuacan-derived motifs and figurines—are associated with the Coyotlatelco Red/Buff, suggesting an additional degree of cultural continuity between the Classic and the Epiclassic. The ladle censer, for example, is extremely abundant in the Toluca region and the Basin of Mexico—another sign of shared ritual practices during the Epiclassic.

The proliferation of Coyotlatelco ceramics in the Toluca region coincided with changes in long-distance exchange systems evidenced by the intensification of the Zinapécuaro-Ucareo obsidian network and by the new pottery procurement system with the south of the present State of Mexico (Kabata 2009).

The End of the Epiclassic, ca. 900 AD

Archaeologists have generally paid less attention to the end of the Epiclassic at Teotihuacan and throughout central Mexico than to its beginnings. By the early tenth century both Tula and Cholula were emerging as the dominant centers in central Mexico. As these two urban communities expanded, the Basin of Mexico apparently became a sort of buffer zone between these two emergent Early Postclassic centers, a region characterized by declining population and overall ruralization, processes that prevailed in much of the basin until the subsequent Middle Postclassic. Early Postclassic Teotihuacan remains understudied, but apparently population declined significantly there as well, as it did at most former Epiclassic centers in central Mexico.

In the Toluca region population increased from the Epiclassic to the Postclassic, and the latter was a time when the ethnic Matlatzinca played a preponderant role both politically and culturally. Increasing sociopolitical stability in the Toluca region at the end of the Epiclassic is suggested by population saturation in the fertile south and southwestern zone of the valley where the main Matlazinca centers are located (Sugiura 2005a, 2005b).

Summary and Conclusions

We have considered five major, interrelated points:

(1) Epiclassic Teotihuacan must be comprehended in both site-specific and
    regional terms. The transition from Classic to Epiclassic at Teotihuacan
    and throughout central Mexico is defined by major changes in urban and

rural settlement patterns and in material culture: archaeologically observable changes that reflect significant changes in polity, economy, daily lifeways, and even ideology. The precise nature of these changes often continues to elude us, although it seems clear that there were major shifts of people within and outside the Basin of Mexico during the transitional seventh century AD.

(2) The physical and organizational character of Epiclassic Teotihuacan remains unclear. Contradictory views have been persuasively argued, largely on different interpretations of the same archaeological data. Clearly, there is a great need for new studies that refine our understanding of ceramic chronology, residential patterns, production, consumption, exchange, administration, and ritual practices.

(3) The size and internal organization of the several Epiclassic polities that succeeded Teotihuacan throughout central Mexico remain imperfectly understood. There is a clear distinction between the relatively short-lived Epiclassic hilltop centers in most regions bordering the Basin of Mexico and with the low-lying major settlements within and around the basin that proved to be more enduring in the long term. New archaeological studies are needed to resolve these questions.

(4) Immigrants from outside the Basin of Mexico in the seventh century may have played a role both in terms of the observed changes in ceramic decoration and in larger organizational changes we can detect in polity and economy at Teotihuacan and in the Basin of Mexico during the Epiclassic. Similarly, a strong case can be made for the importance of immigrants into the Toluca region from the western Basin of Mexico during the early Epiclassic. In addition to additional chemical isotope and DNA studies on well-provenienced human bones, finer chronological phasing and stylistic definition of early Epiclassic ceramic assemblages, most particularly further clarification of the elusive Oxtotipac and its equivalent phases in adjacent regions, will be needed in order to resolve the roles of such population movements. In particular, further attention needs to be focused on the cultural mechanisms, in addition to immigration of new people, that may have introduced new kinds of material culture: examples would include changing trade networks, new kinds of elite alliances, and changing domestic and political economies. These and other mechanisms remain understudied and underconceptualized.

(5) The Epiclassic-to-Early Postclassic transition at ca. 900 AD remains understudied at Teotihuacan and in central Mexico generally, especially outside the Tula region.

The ongoing and accelerating destruction of the archaeological record in central Mexico means that archaeologists must undertake this recommended new work in a timely and prioritized manner, in both the field at surviving archaeological sites and in the laboratory with re-analyses of existing collections that often remain precariously housed.

REFERENCES

Acosta, Jorge. 1972. El epilogo de Teotihuacán. *Teotihuacán XI mesa redonda*, 1:149–156.
    Sociedad Mexicana de Antropología, Instituto Nacional de Antropología e História,
    México, D.F.

Angulo, Jorge, and Kenneth Hirth. 1981. Presencia Teotihuacana en Morelos. In
    Interacción cultural en México central, edited by E. Rattray, J. Litvak, and C. Diaz,
    pp. 81–97. Instituto de Investigaciones Antropológicas, Universidad Nacional
    Autónoma de México, México, D.F.

Braniff, Beatriz. 1972. Secuencias arqueológicas en Guanajuato y la Cuenca de
    México: Intento de correlación. *Teotihuacán XI mesa redonda*, 2:273–323. Sociedad
    Mexicana de Antropología, Instituto Nacional de Antropología e História,
    México, D.F.

Canto, Giselle. 2006. La cerámica del Epiclásico en Morelos. In *El fenomeno Coyotlatelco
    en el Centro de México: Tiempo, espacio, y significado*, edited by L. Solar, pp. 361–374.
    Instituto Nacional de Antropología e História, México, D.F.

Crider, Destiny. 2002. Interaction among Coyotlatelco Phase Communities at
    Teotihuacan. Paper present in a Symposium "Alternative Visions, Alternative
    Worlds: Teotihucan's Demise and the Beginnings of the Epiclassic," 67th Annual
    Meeting, Society for American Archaeology, Denver, March 20–24, 2002.

Cyphers, Ann. 2000. Cultural Identity and Interregional Interaction during the
    Gobernador Phase: A Ceramic Perspective. In *Archaeological Research at
    Xochicalco*, edited by K. Hirth, 2:102–135. University of Utah Press, Salt
    Lake City.

Diehl, Richard. 1989. A Shadow of Its Former Self: Teotihuacan during the Coyotlatelco
    Period. In *Mesoamerica After the Decline of Teotihuacan, AD 700–900*, edited by R.
    Diehl and J. Berlo, pp. 9–18. Dumbarton Oaks, Washington, DC.

Diehl, Richard, and Janet Berlo, eds. 1989. *Mesoamerica after the Decline of Teotihuacan,
    AD 700–900*. Dumbarton Oaks, Washington, DC.

Dumond, Don. 1972. Demographic Aspects of the Classic Period in Puebla-Tlaxcala.
    Southwestern Journal of Anthropology 28:101–130.

Dumond, Don, and Florencia Muller. 1972. Classic to Postclassic in Highland Central
    Mexico. *Science* 175:1208–1215.

García Chávez, Raúl, 1995. *Variabilidad cerámica en la cuenca de Mexico durante
    el Epiclásico*. Tesis de Maestro en Arqueología, Escuela Nacional de
    Antropología e História, Instituto Nacional de Antropología e História,
    México, D.F.

García Cook, Angel, and Beatriz Merino. 1990. El Epiclásico en la región Poblano-
    Tlaxcalteca. In *Mesoamérica y Norte de México, Siglo IX-XII*, edited by F. Sodi,
    1:257–280. Instituto Nacional de Antropología e História, México, D.F.

Gaxiola, Margarita. 1999. Huapalcalco y las tradiciones alfareras del Epiclásico.
    Arqueología 21:45–72.

Gomez, Sergio, and Ruben Cabrera. 2006. Contextos de la ocupación Coyotlatelca en
    Teotihuacan. In *El fenomeno Coyotlatelco en el Centro de México: Tiempo, espacio,
    y significado*, edited by L. Solar, pp. 231–256. Instituto Nacional de Antropología e
    História, México, D.F.

Gorenflo, Larry, and William Sanders. 2007. *Archaeological Settlement Pattern Data from
    the Cuautitlan, Temascalapa, and Teotihuacan Regions, Mexico*. Occasional Papers

in Anthropology No. 30, Dept. of Anthropology, Pennsylvania State University, University Park.

Hicks, Fred, and Henry Nicholson. 1964. The Transition from Classic to Postclassic at Cerro Portesuelo, Valley of Mexico. *Actas del XXXV Congreso Internacional de Americanistas* 1:493–506. México, D.F.

Hirth, Kenneth. 1974. Precolumbian Population Development along the Rio Amatzinac: The Formative through Classic Periods in Eastern Morelos. PhD dissertation, University of Wisconsin at Milwaukee.

Hirth, Kenneth. 1978. Teotihuacan Regional Population Administration in Eastern Morelos. *World Archaeology* 9:320–333.

Hirth, Kenneth. 1989. Militarism and Social Organization at Xochicalco. In *Mesoamerica After the Decline of Teotihuacan, AD 700–900*, edited by R. Diehl and J. Berlo, pp. 78–90. Dumbarton Oaks, Washington, DC.

Hirth, Kenneth, ed. 2000. Archaeological Research at Xochicalco. 2 volumes. University of Utah Press, Salt Lake City.

Kabata, Shigeru. 2009. La indústria obsidiana y su abastecimiento a Santa Cruz Atizapan. In *La gente de la Ciénega en tiempos antiguos: La história de Santa Cruz Atizapan*, edited by Yoko Sugiura, pp. 243–260. El Colegio Mexiquense, Universidad Nacional Autónoma de México, México, D.F.

Kabata, Shigeru. 2010. *La Dinámica regional entre el Valle de Toluca y las áreas circundantes: Intercambio antes y después de la caída de Teotihuacan*. Tesis doctorado, Universidad Nacional Autónoma de México, México, D.F.

Manzanilla, Linda. 2005. Migrantes Epiclásicos en Teotihuacan: Propuesta metodológica para el análisis de migrantes del Clásico al Posclásico. In *Reacomodos Demográficos del Clásico al Posclásico en el Centro de México*, edited by L. Manzanilla, pp. 261–273. Instituto de Investigaciones Antropológicas, Univeresidad Nacional Autónoma de México, México, D.F.

Mastache, Alba Guadalupe, and Robert Cobean. 1989. The Coyotlatelco Culture and the Origins of the Toltec State. In *Mesoamerica after the Decline of Teotihuacan, AD 700–900*, edited by R. Diehl and J. Berlo, pp. 49–68. Dumbarton Oaks, Washington, DC.

Mastache, Alba Guadalupe, Robert Cobean, and Dan Healan. 2002. *Ancient Tollan: Tula and the Toltec Heartland*. University Press of Colorado, Boulder.

Millon, René. 1966. Extensión y población de la ciudad de Teotihuacán en sus diferentes períodos: un cálculo provisional. In *Teotihuacan, Onceava Mesa Redonda*, pp. 57–78. Sociedad Mexicana de Antropología, INAH, México, D.F.

Obermayer, Gerald. 1963. A Stratigraphic Trench and Settlement Pattern Survey at Oxtotipac, Mexico. MA thesis, Department of Anthropology and Sociology, Pennsylvania State University, University Park.

Price, Douglas, Linda Manzanilla, and William Middleton. 2000. Immigration and the Ancient City of Teotihuacan in Mexico: A Study Using Strontium Isotope Ratios in Human Bone and Teeth. *Journal of Archaeological Science* 27:903–913.

Rattray, Evelyn. 1966. An Archaeological and Stylistic Study of Coyotlatelco Pottery. *Mesoamerican Notes* 7–8:87–193, Universidad de las Américas, Mexico, D.F.

Rattray, Evelyn. 1972. El complejo cultural Coyotlatelco. *Teotihuacan XI Mesa Redonda* 2:201–210. Sociedad Mexicana de Antropología, Instituto Nacional de Antropología e História, México, D.F.

Rattray, Evelyn. 1981. La industria de obsidiana durante el periodo Coyotlatelco. *Revista Mexicana de Estudios Antropológicos* 27(2):213–223.

Rattray, Evelyn. 1996. A Regional Perspectiva on the Epiclassic Period in Central Mexico.
    In *Arqueología Mesoamericana: Homenaje a William T. Sanders*, edited by Alba
    Guadalupe Mastache, Jeffrey Parsons, Robert Santley, and Mari Carmen Serra,
    1:213–231. Instituto Nacional de Antropología e História, México, D.F.

Rattray, Evelyn. 2006. El Epiclásico de Teotihuacan y Azcapotzalco. In *El fenómeno
    Coyotlatelco en el centro de México: Tiempo, espacio, y significado*, edited by Laura
    Solar, pp. 201–214. Instituto Nacional de Antropología e História, México, D.F.

Salomon, María. 2006. Cerámicas del Epiclásico en el Valle de Puebla-Tlaxcala:
    Reflexiones desde el Cerro Zapotecas. In *El fenómeno Coyotlatelco en el centro de
    México: Tiempo, espacio, y significado*, edited by Laura Solar, pp. 345–360. Instituto
    Nacional de Antropología e História, México, D.F.

Sanders, William. 1989. The Epiclassic as a Stage in Mesoamerican Prehistory. In
    Mesoamerica after the Decline of Teotihuacan, AD 700–900, edited by Richard Diehl
    and Janet Berlo,, pp. 211–218. Dumbarton Oaks, Washington, DC.

Sanders, William. 2006. Late Xolalpan-Metepec/Oxtotipac-Coyotlatelco: Ethnic
    Succession or Changing Patterns of Political Economy. In *El fenómeno Coyotlatelco
    en el centro de México: Tiempo, espacio, y significado*, edited by Laura Solar,
    pp. 183–200. Instituto Nacional de Antropología e História, México, D.F.

Sanders, William, ed. 1986. *The Teotihuacan Valley Project, Final Report Volume 4: The
    Toltec Period Occupation of the Valley, Part 1: Excavations and Ceramics*. Occasional
    Papers in Anthropology No. 13, Department of Anthropology, Pennsylvania State
    University, University Park.

Sanders, William, Jeffrey Parsons, and Robert Santley. 1979. *The Basin of Mexico:
    Ecological Processes in the Evolution of a Civilization*. Academic Press, New York.

Santana, Ana. 1990. Cacaxtla durante la transición del periodo Clásico al Postclásico. In
    Mesoamérica y norte de México, Siglo IX-XII, edited by F. Sodi, 1:281–288. Instituto
    Nacional de Antropología e História, México, D.F.

Serra, Mari Carmen, and Carlos Lazcano. 1997. Xochitecatl-Cacaxtla en el periodo
    Epiclásico (650–950 d.C.) *Arqueología* 18:85–102.

Serra, Mari Carmen, Carlos Lazcano, and Manuel Torres. 2004. *Cerámica de Xochitecatl*.
    Instituto de Investigaciones Antropológicas, Universidad Nacional Autónoma de
    México, México, D.F.

Siebe, Claus, Michael Abrams, José Marias, and Johannes Obenholzner. 1996. Repeated
    Volcanic Disasters in Prehispanic Time at Popocatepetl, Central Mexico: Past Key to
    the Future! *Geology* 24.399–402.

Smith, Michael. 2000. Postclassic Developments at Xochicalco. In *Archaeological Research
    at Xochicalco*, edited by K. Hirth, 2:167–183. University of Utah Press, Salt Lake City

Solar, Laura, ed. 2006. *El fenómeno Coyotlatelco en el centro de México: Tiempo, espacio, y
    significado*. Instituto Nacional de Antropología e História, México, D.F.

Sugiura, Yoko. 1996. El Epiclásico y el problema del Coyotlatelco vistos desde el valle de
    Toluca. In *Arqueología Mesoamericana: Homenaje a William T. Sanders, I.* edited by
    Alba Guadalupe Mastache, Jeffrey Parsons, Robert Santley, and Mari Carmen Serra,
    pp. 233–257. Instituto Nacional de Antropología e História, México, D.F.

Sugiura, Yoko. 2001. La zona del altiplano central en el Epiclásico. In *El Horizonte
    Clásico. História antiga de México*, edited by Linda Manzanilla 2:347–390. Instituto
    Nacional de Antropología e História, México, D.F.

Sugiura, Yoko. 2005a. *Yatrás quedó la ciudad de los dioses: História de los asentamientos
    en el Valle de Toluca*. Instituto de Investigaciones Antropológicas, Universidad
    Nacional Autónoma de México, México, D.F.

Sugiura, Yoko. 2005b. Reacomodo demográfico y conformación multiétnica en el valle de Toluca durante el Posclásico: una propuesta desde la arqueología. In *Reacomodos demográficos del Clásico al Posclásico en el centro de México*, edited by L.Manzanilla, pp. 175–202, UNAM, México, D.F.

Sugiura, Yoko. 2010. Reflexiones en torno a los problemas del Epiclásico y el Coyotlatelco. In *La cerámica del Bajío y regiones aledañas en el Epiclásico: cronología e interacciones,* edited by Gregory Pereira. CEMCA-INAH-El Colegio Michoacán, México, D.F.

Tozzer, Alfred. 1921. *Excavations at a Site at Santiago Ahuitzotla, D. F., Mexico.* Bureau of American Ethnology, Bulletin No. 74. Washington, DC.

CHAPTER 23

....

THE CLASSIC MAYA COLLAPSE

....

DAVID WEBSTER

THE Classic Maya (250-900 AD) of southern and eastern Mesoamerica have long been famous for the purported catastrophic collapse of their civilization and the abrupt disappearance of their population. By the mid-nineteenth century ancient ruins and inscribed monuments were known from Copán on the southeast all the way to northwestern Yucatán. Although there were still plenty of Maya people in the northern part of the Yucatán Peninsula, the whole southern Maya lowlands (an area of about 60,000 square miles) was practically deserted (Figure 23.1). Hernán Cortés and his small army, who in 1524-1525 were the first Europeans to traverse this territory, could not imagine that eight hundred years earlier it had supported numerous kingdoms, that it contained millions of people, and that the tropical forest was once cleared away for agriculture. The abandonment of this landscape was the first big "fact" known about the ancient Maya—a colossal failure since enshrined in the literature as the "Classic Maya Collapse" (Webster 2002).

At first the most compelling evidence was the ruins themselves. By the early twentieth century, scholars also understood the calendrical inscriptions on Maya monuments. Principal dates usually refer to specific period-endings in the Long Count calendar—especially intervals of about twenty years called *katuns* (the larger implications of these endings were then unknown). Early dated monuments appeared shortly before 300 AD, rose in frequency for the next four hundred years, and then peaked in about 770-800 AD. Thereafter dates tailed off rapidly until the early decades of the tenth century. The interval between 250 and 900 AD was accordingly labeled the Classic Maya period (also the "Old Empire" in pre-World War II parlance), and the late eighth century was widely acknowledged as the mature phase of Classic Maya civilization. Early impressions of the collapse

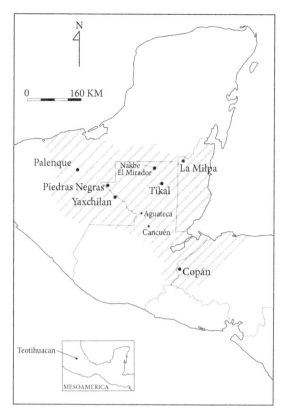

Figure 23.1 Approximate area of the Classic Maya collapse, with sites mentioned in the text.

process thus were derived from monuments erected by Maya kings and other elites, although this was not clear until well into the 1960s. In any case, the collapse seemed abrupt and catastrophic, and the Maya tradition of the southern lowlands was seen as essentially played out by 900 AD. In northern Yucatán archaeologists labeled a supposedly later and derived cultural tradition the "New Empire," heavily influenced by Mexicans, which thrived until the arrival of the Spaniards. Because the northern Maya recorded few Long Count dates, it was difficult to correlate their chronology with that of the south.

WHAT COLLAPSED?

These early conceptions of the collapse developed long before anyone had a good grasp of what Classic Maya society was like and before radiocarbon dating provided an independent chronology in the 1960s. Archaeologists knew something about the chronological and spatial patterning of the collapse but comparatively little about *what* had failed so spectacularly. Partly because the inscriptions resisted decipherment, during the 1930s and 1940s many archaeologists and the public subscribed to a mystique that characterized the Maya as unique among ancient civilizations, a perspective that inhibited understanding of what happened to them while reinforcing the myth of a mysterious demise (Webster 2006). Central components of this mystique were that centers were vacant ceremonial places, that the Maya lacked dynasties of rulers, and that there was no serious warfare. That the Maya mysteriously disappeared contributed heavily to the mystique. Although these ideas have been long discredited, a more general conception of Maya exceptionalism is very tenacious.

We now know that there were forty to fifty Classic Maya polities (and hundreds of large sites) closely packed into a landscape about the size of Colorado. Mayanists argue heatedly about demographic reconstructions, but most would agree that there were minimally several million people in this region by the late eighth century. Many local populations experienced very rapid growth beginning around 550-600 AD, a phenomenon yet to be explained. Most polities were distinguished by an emblem glyph, which was a sign associated with a particular royal capital, kingdom, or dynasty that is always appended to the names and titles of rulers. Dates and other inscriptions feature kings, who usually inherited their offices through dynastic lines that sometimes stretched back for centuries (queens and other elite people are also portrayed; see Martin and Grube 2008). Kings emphasized their close relationships with gods and ancestors, and they styled themselves as guarantors of cosmic order and prosperity. Beginning in the fourth century some dynasties, especially Tikal's, were heavily influenced by Teotihuacan.

Settlement surveys, along with inscriptions, show that by the eighth century a powerful Maya "overking" such as the Tikal ruler might have directly controlled 50,000-60,000 people in his royal capital and its immediate hinterland, and he had indirect influence over thousands of others, whose lesser kings were "possessed" by him. More modest rulers had 10,000 subjects or even fewer. Some kingdoms were a millennium old by the eighth century, while others were much more recent. Some had long histories while others grew and declined rapidly. Many royal capitals—essentially great court centers dominated by temples and palaces—were less than a day's walk apart. Kings and other elites were linked through marriage and alliance, a necessity in an increasingly cutthroat political environment. Large or small, old or new, Maya kingdoms waged fierce wars on each other, although seldom with lasting sociopolitical effects. There was never any kind of Maya "empire," although some Maya rulers after about 450 AD sported the grandiose title *kalo'mte'*, which has the sense of a militant overlord who dominated other kingdoms. (Some archaeologists champion the idea of a "Teotihuacan-Maya" empire during the fifth century. While Teotihuacan symbolism and other influences are widespread, the idea of a Teotihuacan-dominated imperial system is not widely accepted.) The northern Maya tradition, far from being a late offshoot of the southern collapse, turns out to have its own deep roots in Classic and Preclassic times.

Ninety percent or more of the population of any kingdom consisted of farmers or other people who extracted a living from the landscape. Sometimes, as at Tikal, commoner households were quite scattered, decreasing in numbers at greater distances from the royal center. At Palenque, Piedras Negras, and Copán, most people instead lived within a few hundred meters of the palaces of their kings, so the royal courts immediately overlooked the demographic mass of the polity. The nature of the Maya agrarian economy is a matter of great debate, stimulated in part by disagreements about population size and density. Some archaeologists think that upland rainfall agriculture (swidden) supplemented by wetland cultivation and terracing were the main agricultural strategies. Others believe that various forms of intensive agriculture and arboriculture were dominant by Late Classic times and that the eighth-century Maya were canny managers of their tropical ecosystems. Everywhere, maize was the most important staple. Its ideological value to the Maya cannot be overstated—maize was central to conceptions about the origins of the world and of humans and also to Maya kingship.

Early impressions of Classic civilization derived from a few major sites or regions, such as Tikal and Copán. It is now clear that kingdoms varied greatly, not only in their specific culture histories and scales, but also in their adaptations to local ecological niches that were by no means as uniform as the early archaeological literature sometimes asserted. Another revelation is the degree to which the defining characteristics of Classic society, such as calendars, writing, royal dynasties, worldview, and architecture, all emerged during Middle to Late Preclassic times. Relatively unchanged, however, are the implications of the dated inscriptions. Many more are now known, but they retain the same overall chronological implication recognized a century ago—a rapid decline between roughly 800–900 AD. Measured simply by this old method, the Classic collapse was not a sudden event but a long process lasting from about 760 to 909 AD, or 150 years.

Although we now possess a much better understanding of what Maya society was like during the late eighth century, six issues remain unknown or controversial:

1. The size and density of Late Classic Maya populations;
2. The mix of agricultural strategies that supported them;
3. How Maya farmers "mapped onto" their agricultural landscapes (i.e., in terms of some sort of rights to cultivate land and to transfer or inherit them) and how they were attached to the political superstructures of their polities;
4. The degree to which kings or other elites managed agrarian affairs;
5. Whether Maya farmers effectively managed their tropical forest environments or instead created serious anthropogenic degradation; and
6. The degree to which Maya economies were predominantly local or instead were characterized by complex and essential systems of exchange.

Opinions concerning the Classic collapse vary according to one's attitudes concerning these issues.

MULTIPLE COLLAPSES

Native Maya historiography (as mainly seen in codices and ethnohistoric documents from northern Yucatán) is notably gloomy. Wars, invasions, droughts, and famines endlessly afflict people. Rulers are oppressive, nobles feud with one another, and powerful centers rise and fall. Migrants seek new places to settle, and the great calendrical cycles and prophets promise no end to these travails. That the Maya should be so pessimistic is understandable. We now know that there was not one collapse but many throughout their culture history. An early one occurred in the Mirador Basin of northern Guatemala, where huge capitals such as Nakbe and El Mirador—almost certainly ruled by early kings—emerged during Middle and Late Preclassic times. By 150–250 AD these centers were abandoned, and most of the basin's population permanently disappeared. A more episodic pattern characterizes the Petexbatún region, which was heavily occupied during the Late Preclassic, largely abandoned during the Early Classic, and then reoccupied. Some Classic centers such as La Milpa in northern Belize appeared suddenly, thrived for a century or so, and then were abandoned. Judging from the epigraphic record many kingdoms seem to have endured a time of troubles in the late sixth and seventh centuries (Guentner 2002). Seen against this backdrop, the "big collapse" seems less exceptional, although certainly unprecedented in scale.

EXPLAINING THE COLLAPSE

Because the Classic Maya were never politically unified, the proper way to analyze the collapse is on a site-by-site and region-by-region basis, an impossible task for this chapter (see Demarest, Rice, and Rice 2004 for this perspective). Traditionally the emphasis has been on the larger, collective decline, in part because comparable data from any particular set of sites or regions are so spotty or even nonexistent. Archaeologists now commonly recognize that there are several dimensions to this general collapse:

1. The disappearance of royal dynasties and their ideological underpinnings;
2. The dissolution of larger sociopolitical patterns, most importantly the disappearance of nonroyal elites; and
3. A demographic collapse that greatly reduced populations or eliminated them altogether.

All these things were once commonly assumed to be closely linked, but it is increasingly evident that we must treat each one independently. Dynastic collapse has long been the linchpin of our perspective and is best documented, given the penchant of Maya archaeologists to work in royal centers. Internal political dissolution of entire polities is becoming clearer as work on subroyal elites progresses. Data for overall demographic collapse are by far the most difficult to acquire, and this dimension remains contentious. With regard to the latter process, the really big puzzle is why there was never any appreciable demographic recovery in the southern Maya lowlands.

Archaeologists agree that, whatever else it was, the "big" collapse represented the failure of an ancient tradition of kingship and its attendant ideologies and rituals, as recorded in the monument dates (although many centers lack inscriptions or have only illegible ones). It seems to have begun when the Petexbatún kingdom in the western lowlands fragmented beginning about 761 AD. Syndromes of royal presentation (inscriptions, depictions of kings, royal architectural complexes, and representational polychrome pottery) faltered at many other centers between 800 and 830 AD, then sporadically disappeared during the following three generations. Despite some fitful efforts the old royal ways were never successfully reconstituted in the southern lowlands and were largely avoided by the northern Maya. Royal authority appears to have been undermined by the inability of kings to deliver order and prosperity. An early explanation of the collapse envisioned "peasant revolts" that eliminated oppressive priest-rulers (e.g., Thompson 1954). A modern (and increasingly likely) refinement of this internal conflict hypothesis holds that subroyal nobles sometimes overthrew their dynastic overlords and survived them for some time. Neither explanation, however, accounts for the eventual disappearance of whole populations.

Other forms of "ideological" failure have been championed by some archaeologists (e.g., Puleston 1979; P. Rice 2004), particularly because the Maya preoccupation with cycles of time might have heavily influenced their worldview and behavior. Such explanations are still present in various forms, but none of these are generally accepted.

Another form of conflict—intense warfare—was present throughout Maya culture history and peaked during the Late Classic. Warfare is implicated in the early downfall of some regional polities, most conspicuously in the western lowlands at Piedras Negras, Yaxchilán, Palenque, Bonampak, Dos Pilas, Aguateca, and Cancuén. Invading foreigners were once thought responsible for some of this mayhem, but such incursions, at least on any scale, now seem unlikely. Some centers have conspicuous records of warfare, while at others, like Copán, such evidence is much more muted. Few centers anywhere show signs of violent and widespread destruction, whether from warfare or from natural causes such as earthquakes, volcanic eruptions, or hurricanes. Warfare undoubtedly caused severe stresses in Late Classic society, but cannot by itself explain the overall disintegration of Maya polities and the disappearance of their populations.

A prominent explanation for the collapse was (and for some still is) the disruption of trade. At one time the Classic Maya were envisioned as participants in pan-Mesoamerican trade networks heavily dominated by Teotihuacan, whose purported demise in the eighth century conveniently paralleled troubles in the Maya lowlands. It now appears that Teotihuacan declined as a major power at about 550 AD, two centuries before the collapse began. There is plenty of evidence for exchanges of many elite materials and objects among Late Classic Maya polities, along with such mundane commodities as obsidian and salt. Whether trade disruption is a plausible cause of the collapse depends on whether one envisions interpolity exchanges as central to Maya economies or instead that such economies were highly localized in terms of essential raw or finished materials. No archaeologist has presented a convincing argument about how disruption of trade or other forms of exchange could by itself have caused the known patterns of the collapse.

The Black Death in fourteenth-century Europe and the impact of Old World diseases on Mesoamerican populations in the sixteenth century show that epidemic diseases can cause rapid and immense mortality and severe social disruption. No diseases of this kind, however, are known for Mesoamerica before Spanish contact—smallpox, typhus, influenza, and cholera all appear to be European introductions. The protracted 150-year collapse is not what we would expect of a pandemic. Populations typically rebound from pandemics over fairly short intervals, but the Maya did not. That the whole southern lowlands remained sparsely populated for more than a millennium might be explained by the presence of endemic diseases such as malaria or yellow fever, but these, too, seem to be imported from the Old World. In the early sixteenth century Cortes encountered the thriving Itzá kingdom in the heart of the abandoned region, and its people were not afflicted by such diseases (Jones 1998). Where large Late Classic skeletal samples have been studied, as at Copán (Storey 1999), there is convincing evidence for high infant and juvenile mortality, along with widespread infections and other conditions consistent with poor diet and high physical stress.

Central to many explanations is just how fast regional populations declined. This issue is hotly debated, in part because it is much more difficult to detect and date the disappearance of farmers than that of kings and nobles. Most archaeologists think that the demographic decline closely followed dynastic collapse and that supporting populations were gone by about 900-950 AD. Controversial demographic reconstructions at Copán show that some elites had hung on until about 950-1000 AD and that a protracted overall demographic decline had lasted another century or two (Webster, Freter, and Gonlin 2000).

Betty Meggers (1954) imagined that the Maya lowlands were an inhospitable environment for the emergence and maintenance of complex culture. Her hypothesis—that Maya civilization was introduced from elsewhere and doomed to failure—has long been discredited. Nevertheless, imbalances (whether of natural or anthropogenic origin) between Maya populations and their agrarian resources have long been the most popular and durable explanations for the collapse for three reasons. First, disruption of the agricultural systems of premodern agrarian civilizations can have severe political, social, and demographic consequences. Second, reconstructed Maya population densities are sufficiently large to suggest human alteration of the landscape (Culbert and Rice 1990). Third, agrarian crises can subsume many of the other causes discussed above: loss of confidence in leaders, ideological fatigue, increased warfare, social unrest, famine, endemic disease, and even the many "mini-collapses" that characterized Maya culture history.

Considerable evidence exists for two anthropogenic transformations of the agricultural landscape—deforestation and soil erosion, although the data are by no means uniform (D. Rice 1993; Beach et al. 2009). Archaeologists have long assumed that such disturbance was most intense during the Late Classic. It now appears that some regions were affected by the end of the Preclassic, so many Late Classic Maya people inherited ecological niches that were already degraded. Most archaeologists agree that large populations during the seventh through the ninth centuries exacerbated environmental deterioration. There is definite (if spotty) evidence for terracing, wetland modifications, and other forms of agricultural intensification at that time. Those who champion the Maya as being expert tropical ecologists interpret such features as signs of resilience and effective landscape management. Others see them as efforts, ultimately unsuccessful, to cope with human-induced environmental deterioration.

Since 1995 the favorite ecological cause is a series of intense droughts identified by paleoclimatologists for the interval between about 770 and 1100 AD (Hodell et al. 1995; Haug et al. 2003; Hodell et al. 2005). Temporal propinquity with the collapse interval apart, the major appeal of the drought hypothesis is that it helps explain demographic collapse. It also diminishes the role of anthropogenic change, thus gratifying those who see the Maya as canny ecosystem managers. Some archaeologists asserted that drought was the "prime mover" of the collapse—Gill (2000) imagined Maya populations dying of thirst. Problems with this extreme view were apparent from the outset. Many major polities were located near river systems or lakes that never dried up. Analysis of sediment cores did not produce the drought signature everywhere, and the collapse paradoxically occurred in the southern, wettest parts of the Maya lowlands, while populations and polities in the drier north continued to thrive. A more recent and measured view is that the effects of droughts must be assessed on a site-by-site and region-to-region basis and that the "prime mover" interpretation is much overstated. While droughts did occur, their effects were probably exacerbated by the demands of dense Late Classic populations on agrarian niches that had been increasingly degraded for centuries.

Fascination with what happened to the Maya is currently exemplified by debate centered on two books, Jared Diamond's (2005) *Collapse: How Societies Choose to Fail or Succeed*, and *Questioning Collapse*, edited by Patricia McAnany and Norman Yoffee (2008). The debate opposes those who believe that humans sometimes create (or are affected by) conditions that trigger dramatic failure (Diamond) and those who believe that our perceptions of historic failure are distortions of the predominant human capacity for resilience (McAnany and Yoffee). Contributors to the latter book, especially in McAnany and Negron's Maya chapter, make several critical points:

1. There were thriving Maya kingdoms in the northern Yucatán and the highlands of Mexico and Guatemala when the Spaniards arrived, and there are still seven million Maya speakers in Mesoamerica. To speak of general cultural collapse is thus inappropriate.

2. Interpretations of environmental degradation are based on very frag-
    mentary evidence and probably mask the presence of intricately managed
    landscapes created by clever and resilient Maya populations in the face of
    droughts or bad decisions made by their leaders.
3. In the modern, postcolonial world the narrative of the Classic collapse
    demeans the proud cultural tradition of living Maya people.

I believe this debate is framed in very dubious ways. On the one hand,
"societies" usually do not make choices at all. Choices are made by human individuals or small groups (albeit often in thrall to customary or other prescribed
behavior, or environmental factors). Some societies are sufficiently centralized or
ideologically constrained so that leaders and other individuals can make bad decisions that have wide implications. Whether this was true of the Maya is a matter of
debate. Sometimes societies fail despite human decisions or intentions. My position
is that the decisions of countless Maya people, from commoners to kings, resulted
in unsustainable systems that were vulnerable to both anthropogenic change and
broader environmental stresses, including drought. Here I use the word system
carefully, to refer to more or less well-integrated sets of populations, landscapes,
institutions, agricultural strategies, and ideologies, which is what Classic Maya
polities or kingdoms were for a long time. What failed was not "Maya culture"
or "Maya civilization" in some grandiose conception of those terms but rather
many such local systems (admittedly linked to one another in important ways).
Archaeologists and historians do not deny that vigorous variants of the wider
Maya tradition thrived, and continue to do so, after the Classic Maya demise. The
concept of collapse pertains *strictly to the southern Maya lowlands* where just such
integrated systems unraveled dramatically, however long it took, and where almost
all the people disappeared (and most of them did not vote with their feet to move
elsewhere, as happens when rural communities in the United States are abandoned
for greater opportunities in other places). My own work at Copán has championed
the idea that Maya populations and even elites were more resilient than we usually
imagine, and I suspect that this was true elsewhere as well.

Nevertheless, large-scale, well-managed landscapes lurking behind our reconstructions of ancient Maya environmental change seems very unlikely. That only a
handful of people lived in the southern Maya lowlands in Cortés's time implies to
me that, for whatever set of reasons, resilience—whether human or environmental—had reached some sort of limit. One may call this long process whatever one
chooses, but "collapse" seems as good a term as any. Saying that we should not use
words like "collapse" or "failure" because they demean living people seems profoundly patronizing to me. Modern "Maya" cultures and communities have complex and disparate origins, and Maya people are perfectly able to contemplate their
own histories, warts and all, just like the rest of us (or to ignore them, as humans
of all stripes usually do).

Ultimately the current debate juxtaposes those who take a hopeful long-
term view of the human condition and those who do not. Regardless of one's

predispositions along these lines, no single cause or "prime mover" will ever explain the protracted and complex unraveling of Classic Maya civilization. Site-by-site and region-by region research has revealed so much variety that some archaeologists now prefer not to use the term "collapse." But no matter what we call it, and however variable the fates of individual kingdoms, something dramatic undermined one of the most deeply rooted and flamboyant Mesoamerican traditions of complex culture, eliminated most of its population, and suppressed its resilience for centuries.

REFERENCES

Beach, Timothy, Sheryl Luzzaddar-Beach, Nicholas Dunning, John Jones, Jon Lohse, Tom Guderjan, Steve Bozarth, Sara Millspaugh, and Tripti Bhattacharya. 2009. A Review of Human and Natural Changes in Maya Lowlands Wetlands over the Holocene. *Quaternary Science Reviews* 28:1710–1724.

Culbert, T. Patrick, and Don Rice, eds. 1990. *Precolumbian Population History in the Maya Lowlands*. University of New Mexico Press, Albuquerque.

Demarest, Arthur, Prudence Rice, and Don Rice, eds. 2004. *The Terminal Classic in the Maya Lowlands*. University of Colorado Press, Boulder.

Diamond, Jared. 2005. *Collapse: Why Societies Choose to Fail or Succeed*. Viking, New York.

Geunter, Stanley. 2002. Under a Falling Star: The Hiatus at Tikal. Unpublished MA thesis, La Trobe University, Victoria, Australia.

Gill, Richardson. 2000. *The Great Maya Droughts*. University of New Mexico Press, Albuquerque.

Haug, Gerald, Detlef Gunther, Larry Peterson, Daniel Sigman, Konrad Hughen, and Beat Aeschliman. 2003. Climate and the Collapse of Maya Civilization. *Science* 299:1731–1735.

Hodell, David, Mark Brenner, and Jason Curtis. 2005. Terminal Classic Drought in the Northern Maya Lowlands Inferred from Multiple Sediment Cores in Lake Chichancanab (Mexico). *Quaternary Science Reviews* 24:1413–1427.

Hodell, David, Jason Curtis, and Mark Brenner. 1995. Possible Role of Climate in the Collapse of Classic Maya Civilization. *Nature* 375:391–394.

Jones, Grant. 1998. *The Conquest of the Itzá Kingdom*. Stanford University Press, Stanford.

Martin, Simon, and Nikolai Grube. 2008. *Chronicle of the Maya Kings and Queens: Deciphering the Dynasties of the Ancient Maya*. Thames and Hudson, London.

McAnany, Patricia, and Tomas Gallareta Negron. 2008. Bellicose Rulers and Climatological Peril? In *Questioning Collapse*, edited by Patricia McAnany and Norman Yoffee, pp. 143–170. Cambridge University Press, Cambridge.

McAnany, Patricia, and Norman Yoffee, eds. 2008. *Questioning Collapse: Human Resilience, Ecological Vulnerability, and the Aftermath of Empire*. Cambridge University Press, Cambridge.

Meggers, Betty. 1954. Environmental Limitation on the Development of Culture. *American Anthropologist* 56:801–824.

Puleston, Dennis E. 1979. An Epistemological Pathology and the Collapse, or Why the Maya Kept the Short Count. In *Maya Archaeology and Ethnohistory*, edited by Norman Hammond and Gordon Willey, pp. 63–71. University of Texas Press, Austin.

Rice, Don. 1993. Eighth-Century Physical Geography, Environment, and Natural Resources in the Maya Lowlands. In *Lowland Maya Civilization in the Eighth Century AD*, edited by Jeremy Sabloff and John Henderson, pp. 11–64. Dumbarton Oaks, Washington DC.

Rice, Prudence. 2004. *Maya Political Science: Time, Astronomy, and the Cosmos*. University of Texas Press, Austin.

Storey, Rebecca. 1999. Late Classic Nutrition and Skeletal Indicators at Copan, Honduras. In *Reconstructing Ancient Maya Diet*, edited by Christine White, pp. 169–182. University of Utah Press, Salt Lake City.

Thompson, J. Eric S. 1954. *The Rise and Fall of Maya Civilization*. University of Oklahoma Press, Norman.

Webster, David. 2002. *The Fall of the Ancient Maya*. Thames and Hudson, London.

Webster, David. 2006. The Mystique of the Ancient Maya. In *Archaeological Fantasies: How Pseudoarchaeology Misrepresents the Past and Misleads the Public*, edited by Garrett Fagan, pp. 129–153. Routledge, New York.

Webster, David, AnnCorinne Freter, and Nancy Gonlin. 2000. *Copan: The Rise and Fall of an Ancient Maya Kingdom*. Harcourt, New York.

CHAPTER 24

SEARCHING FOR TOLLAN

AUTHORITY AND URBANISM IN OAXACA AFTER MONTE ALBÁN

JEFFREY P. BLOMSTER

THE Late Classic period ended in 800 AD with the demise of the largest state, Monte Albán, in prehispanic Oaxaca, Mexico. The Postclassic (Early, 800–1200; Late, 1200–1521) period features dramatic transformations in politics and urban society. *Cacicazgos* (an Arawakan term that the Spanish applied to Mixtec city-states and remains used by scholars for Postclassic kingdoms in Oaxaca [Lind 1979; Spores 1967]), already extant and perhaps implicated in Monte Albán's demise as competitors, flourished throughout Late Postclassic Oaxaca. What collapsed was not society but political systems and elite classes that mismanaged factional competition and were no longer supported by commoners as they engaged in increasingly exclusionary strategies (see Blomster 2008a; Joyce et al. 2001). As Monte Albán and major cities throughout Mesoamerica collapsed, Classic elite paraphernalia and administrative tools also disappeared. A renewed class of leaders and elites, who reestablished authority and legitimacy in ways that resonated with other groups within society, ruled thriving Late Postclassic urban centers. In the shadow of the collapse of Classic states throughout Oaxaca, elites reinstituted a covenant with commoners that reasserted their privileged position and reordered society in a way that is compatible with smaller urban centers—what I refer to as searching for Tollan. Both translated and represented graphically as "Place of the Reeds," the concept of Tollan is best known from ethnohistoric documents associated with the Aztecs, who idealized the site of Tula (in the modern state of Hidalgo) as the epitome of crafting and legitimacy.

I distinguish between the more generic "Tollan," which can refer to numerous real and imagined places, and Tula, Hidalgo—the Aztecs' Tollan and an important Early Postclassic state. I use "Toltec" to refer to people (or their descendants) from Tula or to people who claimed to be descended from a Tula-related lineage. Associated with civilization and legitimacy, Tollan signified a new suite of alliances, paraphernalia, and even identity as Postclassic leaders established themselves as part of heroic narratives and new alliance corridors. Ruling dynasties throughout Oaxaca tapped into these new networks, genealogies, and retooled ideologies. Authority was constantly challenged and negotiated with internal factions and external competitors; the Postclassic is one of the most dynamic eras in Oaxaca, not simply the decadent aftermath of Monte Albán's collapse.

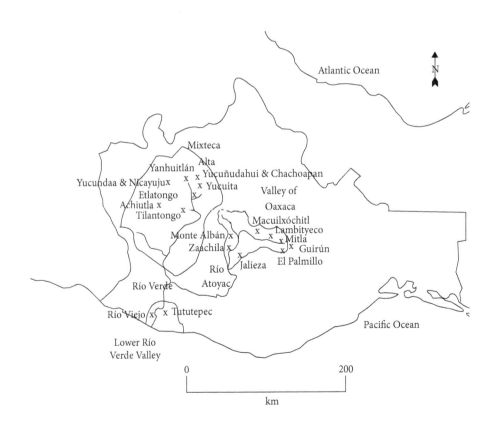

Figure 24.1 A map of Late Classic to Postclassic Oaxaca, showing select sites.

REGIONS AND SITES IN POSTCLASSIC OAXACA

I focus on three ethnolinguistic groups in Oaxaca for which substantial excavation data and intensive site surveys are available (see Figure 24.1): the Valley of Oaxaca Zapotecs, the Mixtecs of the Mixteca Alta, and the Chatinos and Mixtecs of the Coast/Lower Verde Valley. Through the pioneering efforts of Alfonso Caso and his successors, research in the Valley of Oaxaca has focused on the rise and collapse of Monte Albán, situated at the center of the three subvalleys that compose it (Caso et al. 1967). Critical studies also exist for several important Late Postclassic centers, such as Mitla, Yagul, and Zaachila (Bernal and Gamio 1974; Gallegos Ruiz 1978; Robles García and Moreira Quirós 1990). Recently, there has been sustained research on Late Classic or Postclassic occupations of centers such as El Palmillo, Guirún, Jalieza, Lambityeco, Macuilxóchitl, and Xaagá (Feinman and Nicholas 2004; Finsten 1995; Lind 2008; Markens et al. 2008).

The various Mixtec regions extend over 50,000 square kilometers of rugged mountainous terrain. I focus here on only Postclassic occupations in the largest of these regions, the Mixteca Alta, specifically the valleys of Nochixtlán and Teposcolula: Chachoapan, Etlatongo, Nicayuju, Tilantongo, Yucuita, and Yucundaa, the "old city" of Teposcolula (Caso 1938; Blomster 2004, 2008b; Byland and Pohl 1994; Lind 1979; Pérez Rodríguez 2006; Spores and Robles García 2007). While this list sounds extensive, most of the excavations have been restricted to Postclassic finds in test units or the excavation of several houses; only at Yucundaa has there been large-scale exposure of numerous kinds of architecture and features. The relative lack of large Postclassic archaeological research is partly due to the presence of indigenous Mixtec codices that represent an incredibly rich source of information (Jansen and Pérez Jiménez 2007; Pohl 1994) but are uneven and biased, as codices narrate the heroic history of particular cities and dynasty/elite families. For example, no extant codex focuses on Etlatongo, although colonial documents refer to it as one of the major Nochixtlán Valley kingdoms, and excavation and intensive site surveys show it covered at least 208 hectares (Blomster 2008b). Archaeology, in addition to indigenous and colonial documents, is necessary to provide a more holistic account of Postclassic politics and urbanism.

Since the late 1980s, a long-term research project in the Lower Río Verde Valley, a hot, coastal plain, has provided data that are crucial for understanding Late Classic to Postclassic dynamics. According to ethnohistoric records, this region was probably occupied by Chatinos until they were displaced by Mixtecs in the twelfth century (Joyce et al. 2004). I focus on two major Postclassic centers: Río Viejo and Tututepec (King 2008; Levine 2007). One problem is while the ceramic chronologies of the Lower Verde Valley and Valley of Oaxaca have become more refined (see Joyce 2008; Markens 2008), the Mixteca Alta still suffers from an overly long (700-year) Postclassic phase, hindering regional surveys and resultant interpretations (Kowalewski et al. 2009).

COLLAPSES AND CONTINUITIES

Rather than viewing Monte Albán's collapse as the end of a great cycle (Marcus and Flannery 1996), there were numerous declines and collapses that occurred around 800 AD throughout Oaxaca. In the Valley of Oaxaca, impacted sites include Cerro de la Campana, Cuilapan, El Palmillo, Jalieza, Lambityeco, Macuilxóchitl, Monte Albán, Santa Ana del Valle, Xoxocotlán, and Yagul. In the southern Mixteca Alta, codices suggest the Late Classic/Postclassic transition took at least 140 years, with some Classic centers, such as Achiutla, surviving into the Postclassic (Byland 2008). In the lower Verde Valley, regional settlements declined and shifted back to the piedmont (Joyce 2008). Prior to their collapse, cities such as Monte Albán and Río Viejo evince increasingly exclusionary practices, with monumental art and ritual more restricted and elite residences enclosed and removed from the majority of the population. A combination of factors specific to each region, from political to environmental, contributed to the collapse of Classic states; due to the links between cities, the collapse of dynastic allies undoubtedly impacted this process (Blomster 2008a; Joyce 2008; Winter 2008).

The impact of these collapses was most pronounced on the elite. In the Valley of Oaxaca, Zapotec writing and grayware effigy urns disappear after 800 AD, and extravagant tombs are absent in the Early Postclassic (to be revived in the Late Postclassic at centers such as Zaachila). Such changes highlight the depth of the political crisis that leaders faced. Indeed, Mixtec codices may show that their creators viewed what archaeologists refer to as the "Late Classic/Postclassic transition" as a major rupture, perhaps associated with an event known at the "War that came from Heaven," with Late Classic centers (shown in Mixtec codices as platforms without temples—ruins) conceptualized as part of a previous creation and vanished social order (Hamann 2002). Archaeological manifestations of the demise of Late Classic models of authority come from Río Viejo, where the acropolis was reoccupied by Early Postclassic commoners, with no hiatus from its elite and ritual Late Classic use (Joyce et al. 2001). As further evidence of symbolic denigration, a Late Classic stela fragment from Río Viejo, with a noble's or ruler's image, was reused as a metate in the Early Postclassic (Joyce 2008). In the Valley of Oaxaca, Lambityeco was at its maximum size (64 hectares) during the Late Classic with its own aggrandizing nobles who commissioned innovative sculptural friezes depicting male ancestors of the noble lineage, each holding a human femur. In the Early Postclassic, Lambityeco declined to nearly half its former size, with architecture and artifacts interpreted as evincing a focus on salt production (Lind 2008). In this case, the destruction of Lambityeco's noble lineage around 700 AD may have been one of the last gasps of Monte Albán's authority, which probably reorganized the site to control salt production more efficiently, making it no longer an individual household activity; residents responded by largely abandoning the site.

As suggested by the Lambityeco and Río Viejo examples, the roles of nonelites were crucial in the transformations that emerged in the Postclassic. Contra to the political chaos, commoner lifeways exhibit continuity and economic enrichment in the Postclassic. Quotidian objects, such as ceramics, demonstrate great continuity, as do burial patterns and houses. The typical Late Classic house layout was a patio surrounded by rooms, a pattern that continued into the Postclassic, with elite palaces at Yagul and Mitla being larger and more complex and featuring more patios and restricted access (Figure 24.2).

At Macuilxóchitl, the community was reoccupied in the Late Postclassic after being virtually abandoned during the Early Postclassic; a Late Postclassic house demonstrates surprising continuity in terms of both architectural layout and household activities with the Late Classic house atop of which it was built (Markens et al. 2008). Based on data from Tututepec and Río Viejo, commoners thrived during this transition, engaging in a more diverse domestic economy and with more access to imported prestige goods (such as copper axes and polychrome pottery). They retained more control over important productive efforts, such as cotton textiles (Levine 2007). Excavations at Río Viejo suggest little variation in

Figure 24.2 Restricted interior patio, northernmost court of the Hall of the Columns, Mitla. Ethnohistoric sources describe this as the residence of Mitla's powerful oracular priest. Mosaic fretwork on the walls is made of volcanic tuff.

wealth and power during the Early Postclassic. Residents participated in markets and were well connected to multiple exchange networks and, based on its high density, enjoyed ready access to imported obsidian (King 2008). At Postclassic Nicayuju, commoner households also had some autonomy from the state in their economic pursuits, as seen by agricultural intensification and the construction and maintenance of *lama-bordo* terraces (Pérez Rodríguez 2006). While such houses had access to luxury goods, they had only a small fraction of fancy ceramics compared to contemporaneous elite Mixtec houses at Yucuita and Chachoapan (Lind 1979). Unlike the Río Viejo houses, the Nicayuju houses had only limited access to obsidian.

RENEWAL: POSTCLASSIC URBANISM AND POLITICS

The Postclassic features major changes in urbanism, elite ideology, and paraphernalia. A city-state, generally with less economic control over populations (especially those not in the center), exhibits an identity defined by affiliation with a ruler rather than a territory (Smith 2003: 36). In Oaxaca, a royal family ruled a cacicazgo, with close kinsmen as noble administrators; each had a capital center (*cabecera*) and surrounding subject communities that provided labor and support (Spores 1967). In the Mixteca Alta, a cacicazgo was called a *yuhuitayu*, combining the Mixtec words for reed mat and pair/couple; it is literally the seat of rulership for a married couple (Terraciano 2001). In the Nochixtlán Valley, an average cacicazgo contained a population of 2,000 to 10,000 people (Winter 1994). In the Valley of Oaxaca, some thirteen cacicazgos (*queche* in Zapotec) displayed great variability in size and influence. For example, Zaachila had extensive political control, receiving tribute from cities scattered throughout the region, while Mitla had overarching religious import, similar to the renown of select Mixtec cities—Achiutla and Chalcatongo—as oracular centers.

Each queche was headed by a hereditary ruler (*coqui*), who resided in a palace at the cabecera and appointed other nobles to rule subject communities. As with the Mixtecs, ethnohistoric documents show the coqui with his principal wife, suggesting similar ideas about gender complementarity and what was considered a legitimate city-state as well as the importance of appropriate descent and birth order (Oudijk 2002). There is less emphasis on the ultimate power of the ruler than in the Classic; other stakeholders appear crucial, such as the priestly hierarchy who controlled access to sacred bundles symbolic of the city and played important roles in enthronement ceremonies (Pohl 1994).

In both the Mixteca Alta and Valley of Oaxaca, Postclassic cities came down from Classic hilltops and lay near the valley bottomland, often located near valley floor sites that had Late Classic components and continued to grow in the Postclassic, such as Cuilapan, Mitla, and Zaachila. In some cases, such as Etlatongo, Postclassic sites simply expanded down from a still-occupied Classic hilltop site. Guirún, an important Late Classic hilltop terrace center, expanded to 120 hectares during the Postclassic; this defensive site encompassed a stone quarry, public architecture, and cruciform tombs with stone mosaics (Feinman and Nicholas 2004). Zapotec cities (such as Yagul and Mitla) were often associated with a fortified palace on a nearby ridge for times of conflict. Some large Classic cities, such as Río Viejo, continued as first-order centers but at a reduced size in the Postclassic. Tututepec, founded by the famed Mixtec ruler Lord 8 Deer "Jaguar Claw," became a massive Late Postclassic city focused on a hill and covered 2,185 hectares, although with a dispersed population estimated at 16,388. Featuring a complex internal organization and larger than any other cacicazgo in Oaxaca, the Tututepec state was spatially larger than central Mexican cities (Joyce et al. 2004: 293).

Cities varied greatly in architectural layout, with distinct regional features. Yucundaa exhibits elite architecture composed of alternating vertical stone slabs and fine mosaic panels, as well as a major roadway encircling the site (Spores and Robles García 2007)—a probable processional feature that has roots in the Mixteca nearly 1,500 years earlier at Monte Negro. Postclassic cities feature a reduced amount of monumental construction and a change in the nature of monumental art. With Late Classic precedents (such as Lambityeco), Postclassic palaces combined elite living, ritual, and administration; at Mitla, palaces were covered with intricate stone mosaics (Figure 24.2), perhaps indicative of different lineages involved in its administration rather than featuring images of aggrandizing leaders (in contrast to Classic Monte Albán). At Río Viejo, Late Classic sculptures of elaborately costumed rulers were replaced by images of personages who lack glyphs and regalia and may represent deities (Joyce 2008). As the seat of power of Lord 8 Deer, who through conquest and alliance controlled much of the Mixteca, Tilantongo represents an exception to Postclassic patterns of less monumental architecture, with the massive Temple of Heaven placed atop a huge Classic platform, which was symbolic of Lord 8 Deer's aspirations (Figure 24.3).

SEARCHING FOR TOLLAN: AUTHORITY AND LEGITIMACY REDEFINED

In the wake of the collapse of many forms of their power, elites searched for new strategies and initiated a new covenant with commoners, which reemphasized elites' roles in providing Earth and Rain with sacrifices as their ancestors were present at the First Sunrise—the creation of the current era (Hamann 2008; Monaghan 1995). Individuals who figure as powerful ancestors in the heroic histories of

Figure 24.3 Looking north from the summit of Tilantongo's Temple of Heaven, which
is approximately 25 meters per side (John Pohl, 2010, personal communication).

Postclassic dynasties come from distant places, such as the idealized center encapsulated by the concept of "Tollan." Founding ancestors are consistently shown as coming from a sacred origin place outside of the community, which was often a tree, hill, or river; the founder of Macuilxóchitl's genealogy came from a "Lagoon of Primordial Blood," while some Mixtec ancestors come from a tree at Apoala or Achiutla (Byland 2008; Oudijk 2008). These founders are often explicitly linked with foreign Nahua groups, such as the connection between Atonal, who established the ruling dynasty of Coixtlahuaca, and Lord 4 Jaguar (also an ally of Lord 8 Deer), who clearly comes from a Tollan (Byland and Pohl 1994). The specific location of this Tollan cannot be ascertained nor was that the point; the concept referred to a sacred "civilized" place of legitimating power, a superordinate center (Blomster 2008a; Helms 1993). Important Postclassic Tollans include Cholula, Tula, Chichén Itzá, and Tenochtitlan; Classic Teotihuacan may have been the first Tollan (Ringle 2004). Within the Mixteca, Cholula—due to its geographical proximity and its role as the center of the Postclassic Quetzalcoatl cult—may have been the most salient Tollan, although perhaps Coixtlahuaca itself became one, and undoubtedly Tilantongo, under Lord 8 Deer, aspired to be one. The Tollan concept is visually expressed by reeds growing out of water, such as in Cholula's 1581 *Relación geográfica*, where the reeds are combined with red scrolls symbolizing blood. This associates Tollan with both of these primordial fluids and also links Macuilxóchitl's "blood lagoon" with Tollan (Oudijk 2008).

Figure 24.4 Tututepec Monument 6. Late Postclassic "Toltec" sculpture, with
details of face and front body.

The Oaxacan focus on Tollan appears visually expressed mostly after the collapse of Tula (Figure 24.4). The impact of Tula on Early Postclassic Mesoamerica
remains debated (Cobos 2006), with some scholars focusing on the shared visual
imagery related to Toltec art as expressing elite interaction rather than conquest
(Ringle 2004). Evidence for Tollan's ideological importance abounds in imagery,
such as Mitla's painted murals and the Mixtec codices. In *Codex Bodley*, the Toltec
Lord 4 Jaguar pierces the nose of Lord 8 Deer (probably in 1097), who then wears
a nose ornament as a badge of office and membership in the Toltec royal house.
Lord 8 Deer, whose birth (his parents were unrelated to the ruling dynasty; see
Joyce et al. 2004) made him ineligible for the Tilantongo throne via inheritance,
thus innovated new strategies to ultimately accede as ruler. In addition to founding a new polity, Tututepec, to control this rich coastal region, Lord 8 Deer is the
first Mixtec ruler shown engaging in the decidedly non-Mixtec nose-piercing ceremony, inevitably shown as being administered by Toltecs and associated with a
title granted to Tolteca-Chichimeca noblemen of the Pueblan-Tlaxcalan city-states
(Pohl 1994: 89–90).

The Oaxacan focus on Tollan appears visually expressed mostly after the col-
Archaeological evidence of Toltec exchange and interaction in Mesoamerica
traditionally focuses on Tohil Plumbate pottery, a distinctive ware with a lustrous
surface made in coastal Guatemala but associated with Tula's trade routes (Neff
1989). Few examples of Tohil Plumbate have been found in Oaxaca, with two vessels
in late Monte Albán tombs, one from Mitla, and a fuller assemblage of Plumbate
pottery excavated at Paso Aguascalientes on the isthmus (Caso and Bernal 1952:
Fig. 424; Markens 2008; Winter 2008). These ceramics were the medium for a set
of common symbols that spread along trade routes and connected allies and may
be linked with the diffusion of a new international religion and series of rituals.

This Early Postclassic symbol set may be a precursor to the Mixteca-Puebla style that characterizes Late Postclassic interaction.

As with Aztec archaizing of Toltec-inspired imagery, related sculpture in Oaxaca comes from later in the Postclassic. Tututepec Monument 6 (Figure 24.4) resembles the colossal atlantid warriors from Tula, but it represents a female and the sculpture itself is Late Postclassic (Pohl 1999). At Etlatongo, a carved stone (Figure 24.5) depicting what is probably a striding warrior or lord, is comparable to one from Tilantongo and has been interpreted as coming from a stone bench or banquette (Blomster 2008b). The hypothesized bench would have been similar to those created by the Aztecs for the House of the Eagles in Tenochtitlan, the inspiration of which can be traced back to benches at Tula. Indeed, the largely unidentified cross-hatched object held diagonally by the Etlatongo figure is similar to objects held higher by figures in a codex-like mural from the Eagle House, identified there as pairs of blue maguey spines (López Luján 2006: Fig. 212a). As a way of legitimizing their new authority, Etlatongo elites materialized this Tollan reference to promote the heroic history of the ruling dynasty over internal factions and external competitors. Associations with both temporally distant ancestors and

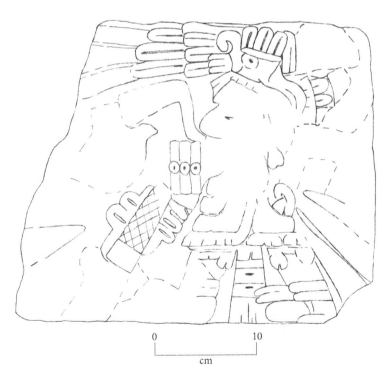

Figure 24.5 Drawing of Late Postclassic carved stone from Etlatongo, interpreted as part of a banquette. Only visible features have been drawn, with dashed lines indicating eroded areas. Drawn by the author with the scale corrected from Blomster (2008b: Fig. 9.6).

contemporaneous allies and other elite dynasties were also embedded in Mixteca-Puebla polychrome pottery, found in various quantities throughout Oaxaca.

Association with Toltec-derived ideology began in the Early Postclassic, and this formed part of a new ensemble that became an important legitimizing narrative for elite authority that reordered the elites' covenant with society. These new alliances and ideologies proved crucial in the success of Late Postclassic city-states and provided models for indigenous leaders in the early colonial era when they reoriented their efforts and used elements of Catholicism and the Spanish legal system that enhanced their local authority and provided tools in ongoing competitions among cacicazgos.

REFERENCES

Bernal, Ignacio, and Lorenzo Gamio. 1974. *Yagul: El palacio de los seis patios*. Instituto de Investigaciones Antropológicas, Universidad Nacional Autónoma de México, Mexico City.

Blomster, Jeffrey P. 2004. *Etlatongo: Social Complexity, Interaction, and Village Life in the Mixteca Alta of Oaxaca, Mexico*. Wadsworth, Belmont, California.

Blomster, Jeffrey P. 2008a. Changing Cloud Formations: The Sociopolitics of Oaxaca in Late Classic/Postclassic Mesoamerica. In *After Monte Albán: Transformation and Negotiation in Oaxaca, Mexico*, edited by Jeffrey P. Blomster, pp. 3–46. University Press of Colorado, Boulder.

Blomster, Jeffrey P. 2008b. Legitimization, Negotiation, and Appropriation in Postclassic Oaxaca: Mixtec Stone Codices. In *After Monte Albán: Transformation and Negotiation in Oaxaca, Mexico*, edited by Jeffrey P. Blomster, pp. 295–330. University Press of Colorado, Boulder.

Byland, Bruce E. 2008. Tree Birth, the Solar Oracle, and Achiutla: Mixtec Sacred History and the Classic to Postclassic Transition. In *After Monte Albán: Transformation and Negotiation in Oaxaca, Mexico*, edited by Jeffrey P. Blomster, pp. 331–364. University Press of Colorado, Boulder.

Byland, Bruce E., and John M. D. Pohl. 1994. *In the Realm of 8 Deer: The Archaeology of the Mixtec Codices*. University of Oklahoma Press, Norman.

Caso, Alfonso. 1938. *Exploraciones en Oaxaca: Quinta y sexta temporadas 1936–1937*. Publicación No. 34. Instituto Panamericano de Geografía e Historia, Mexico City.

Caso, Alfonso, and Ignacio Bernal. 1952. *Urnas de Oaxaca*. Memorias del Instituto Nacional de Antropología e Historia, No. II. INAH, Mexico City.

Caso, Alfonso, Ignacio Bernal, and Jorge R. Acosta. 1967. *La cerámica de Monte Albán*. Memorias del Instituto Nacional de Antropología e Historia, No. XIII. INAH, Mexico City.

Cobos, Rafael. 2006. The Relationship between Tula and Chichén Itzá: Influences or Interactions? In *Lifeways in the Northern Maya Lowlands: New Approaches to Archaeology in the Yucatán Peninsula*, edited by Jennifer P. Matthews and Bethany A. Morrison, pp. 173–183. University of Arizona Press, Tucson.

Feinman, Gary M., and Linda M. Nicholas. 2004. *Hilltop Terrace Sites of Oaxaca, Mexico: Intensive Surface Survey at Guirún, El Palmillo, and the Mitla Fortress*. Fieldiana No. 37. Field Museum of Natural History, Chicago.

Finsten, Laura. 1995. *Jalieza, Oaxaca: Activity Specialization at a Hilltop Center.* Vanderbilt University Publications in Anthropology No. 48. Nashville, Tennessee.

Gallegos Ruiz, Roberto. 1978. *El Señor 9 Flor en Zaachila.* Universidad Nacional Autónoma de México, Mexico City.

Hamann, Byron. 2002. The Social Life of Pre-Sunrise Things. *Current Anthropology* 43(3):351–382.

Hamann, Byron. 2008. Heirlooms and Ruins: High Culture, Mesoamerican Civilization, and the Postclassic Oaxacan Tradition. In *After Monte Albán: Transformation and Negotiation in Oaxaca, Mexico,* edited by Jeffrey P. Blomster, pp. 119–168. University Press of Colorado, Boulder.

Helms, Mary W. 1993. *Craft and the Kingly Ideal: Art, Trade, and Power.* University of Texas Press, Austin.

Jansen, Maarten, and Gabina Aurora Pérez Jiménez. 2007. *Encounter with the Plumbed Serpent: Drama and Power in the Heart of Mesoamerica.* University Press of Colorado, Boulder.

Joyce, Arthur A. 2008. Domination, Negotiation, and Collapse: A History of Centralized Authority on the Oaxaca Coast before the Late Postclassic. In *After Monte Albán: Transformation and Negotiation in Oaxaca, Mexico,* edited by Jeffrey P. Blomster, pp. 219–254. University Press of Colorado, Boulder.

Joyce, Arthur A., Laura Arnaud Bustamante, and Marc N. Levine. 2001. Commoner Power: A Case Study from the Classic Period Collapse on the Coast of Oaxaca. *Journal of Archaeological Method and Theory* 8(4):343–385.

Joyce, Arthur A., Andrew G. Workinger, Byron Hamann, Peter Kroefges, Maxine Oland, and Stacie M. King. 2004. Lord 8 Deer "Jaguar Claw" and the Land of the Sky: The Archaeology and History of Tututepec. *Latin American Antiquity* 15(3):273–297.

King, Stacie M. 2008. Interregional Networks of the Oaxacan Early Postclassic: Connecting the Coast and the Highlands. In *After Monte Albán: Transformation and Negotiation in Oaxaca, Mexico,* edited by Jeffrey P. Blomster, pp. 255–291. University Press of Colorado, Boulder.

Kowalewski, Stephen A., Andrew K. Balkansky, Laura R. Stiver Walsh, Thomas J. Pluckhahn, John F. Chamblee, Verónica Pérez Rodríguez, Verenice Y. Heredia Espinoza, and Charlotte A. Smith. 2009. *Origins of the Ñuu: Archaeology in the Mixteca Alta, Mexico.* University Press of Colorado, Boulder.

Levine, Marc N. 2007. Linking Household and Polity at Late Postclassic Period Yucu Dzaa (Tututepec), a Mixtec Capital on the Coast of Oaxaca, Mexico. Unpublished PhD dissertation, Department of Anthropology, University of Colorado at Boulder.

Lind, Michael D. 1979. *Postclassic and Early Colonial Mixtec Houses in the Nochixtlán Valley, Oaxaca.* Vanderbilt University Publications in Anthropology No. 23. Nashville, Tennessee.

Lind, Michael D. 2008. The Classic to Postclassic at Lambityeco. In *After Monte Albán: Transformation and Negotiation in Oaxaca, Mexico,* edited by Jeffrey P. Blomster, pp. 171–192. University Press of Colorado, Boulder.

López Luján, Leonardo. 2006. *La Casa de las Águilas: un ejemplo de la arquitectura religiosa de Tenochtilan.* 2 volumes. Instituto Nacional de Antropología e Historia, Mexico City.

Marcus, Joyce, and Kent V. Flannery. 1996. *Zapotec Civilization: How Urban Society Evolved in Mexico's Oaxaca Valley.* Thames and Hudson, New York.

Markens, Robert. 2008. Advances in Defining the Classic-Postclassic Portion of the Valley of Oaxaca Ceramic Chronology. In *After Monte Albán: Transformation and*

Negotiation in Oaxaca, Mexico, edited by Jeffrey P. Blomster, pp. 49–94. University Press of Colorado, Boulder.

Markens, Robert, Marcus Winter, and Cira Martínez López. 2008. Ethnohistory, Oral History, and Archaeology at Macuilxóchitl: Perspectives on the Postclassic Period (800–1521 CE) in the Valley of Oaxaca. In *After Monte Albán: Transformation and Negotiation in Oaxaca, Mexico*, edited by Jeffrey P. Blomster, pp. 193–215. University Press of Colorado, Boulder.

Monaghan, John. 1995. *The Covenants with Earth and Rain: Exchange, Sacrifice, and Revelation in Mixtec Sociality*. University of Oklahoma Press, Norman.

Neff, Hector. 1989. Origins of Plumbate Pottery Production. In *Economies of the Soconusco Region of Mesoamerica*, edited by Barbara Voorhies, pp. 175–193. University of Utah Press, Salt Lake City.

Oudijk, Michel R. 2002. The Zapotec City-State. In *A Comparative Study of Six City-State Cultures: An Investigation Conducted by the Copenhagen Polis Centre*, edited by Mogens Herman Hansen, pp. 73–90. The Royal Danish Academy of Sciences and Letters, Copenhagen.

Oudijk, Michel R. 2008. The Postclassic Period in the Valley of Oaxaca: The Archaeological and Ethnohistorical Records. In *After Monte Albán: Transformation and Negotiation in Oaxaca, Mexico*, edited by Jeffrey P. Blomster, pp. 95–118. University Press of Colorado, Boulder.

Pérez Rodríguez, Verónica. 2006. States and Households: The Social Organization of Terrace Agriculture in Postclassic Mixteca Alta, Oaxaca, Mexico. *Latin American Antiquity* 17(1):3–22.

Pohl, John M. D. 1994. *The Politics of Symbolism in the Mixtec Codices*. Vanderbilt University Publications in Anthropology No. 46. Nashville, Tennessee.

Pohl, John M. D. 1999. The Lintel Paintings of Mitla and the Function of the Mitla Palaces. In *Mesoamerican Architecture as a Cultural Symbol*, edited by J. Kowalski, pp. 176–197. Oxford University Press, New York.

Ringle, William M. 2004. On the Political Organization of Chichen Itza. *Ancient Mesoamerica* 15(2):167–218.

Robles García, Nelly M., and Alfredo J. Moreira. 1990. *Proyecto Mitla: Restauración de la zona arqueológica en sus contexto urbano*. Colección Científica No. 193. Instituto Nacional de Antropología e Historia, Mexico City.

Smith, Michael E. 2003. Small Polities in Postclassic Mesoamerica. In *The Postclassic Mesoamerican World*, edited by Michael E. Smith and Frances Berdan, pp. 35–39. University of Utah Press, Salt Lake City.

Spores, Ronald A. 1967. *The Mixtec Kings and Their People*. University of Oklahoma Press, Norman.

Spores, Ronald A., and Nelly M. Robles García. 2007. A Prehispanic (Postclassic) Capital Center in Colonial Transition: Excavations at Yucundaa Pueblo Viejo de Teposcolula, Oaxaca, Mexico. *Latin American Antiquity* 18(3):333–353.

Terraciano, Kevin. 2001. *The Mixtecs of Colonial Oaxaca: Ñudzahui History, Sixteenth through Eighteenth Centuries*. Stanford University Press, Stanford, California.

Winter, Marcus. 1994. The Mixteca Prior to the Late Postclassic. In *Mixteca-Puebla: Discoveries and Research in Mesoamerican Art and Archaeology*, edited by H. B. Nicholson and Eloise Quiñones Keber, pp. 201–221. Labyrinthos, Culver City, California.

Winter, Marcus. 2008. Classic to Postclassic in Four Oaxaca Regions. In *After Monte Albán: Transformation and Negotiation in Oaxaca, Mexico*, edited by Jeffrey P. Blomster, pp. 393–426. University Press of Colorado, Boulder.

CHAPTER 25

··

DEVELOPMENTAL CYCLES IN THE GULF LOWLANDS

ANNICK DANEELS

LITTLE is known even among Mesoamerican researchers about Classic and Postclassic Gulf Coast archaeology: the small sizes of Gulf Coast sites in comparison to the major contemporary sites of the Central Highlands and Maya area is certainly one of the reasons for this. But recent studies have shown that a smaller size should not be confused with a lack of complexity or transcendence (Arnold and Pool 2008; Pool 2006; Ruiz Gallut and Pascual Soto 2004; Stark and Arnold 1997; Zaragoza Ocaña 2009). After all, the Gulf produced cultures whose impact can only be compared to Teotihuacan; after the Olmecs of the southern Gulf, the Classic Central Veracruz culture's volute styles and polished-stone sculptures known as *yugos*, *hachas*, and *palmas* range throughout Mesoamerica, and the Postclassic Huastec culture is considered the cradle of many gods of the pantheon.

Though geographically the Gulf Coast goes from Florida to the tip of the Yucatán, culturally it is limited to the modern state of Veracruz and parts of Tamaulipas, Puebla, and Tabasco. It is a relatively narrow coastal area with mostly deep soils and abundant rains, bounded between the Gulf of Mexico and the Sierra Madre Oriental, cut in two by the Sierra de Chiconquiaco (Figure 25.1). To the north are rolling hills, while to the south, but for the Tuxtlas Mountains, huge floodplains are crossed by three of the major Mesoamerican rivers—Papaloapan, Coatzacoalcos, and Grijalva—and bordered to the southeast by the karstic limestone from the Yucatán Peninsula. Though piedmont and mountain slopes provide a variety of climates and biodiversity at short distances, the largest archaeological settlements of the Gulf seem to be located in the hot and humid lowlands, a natural

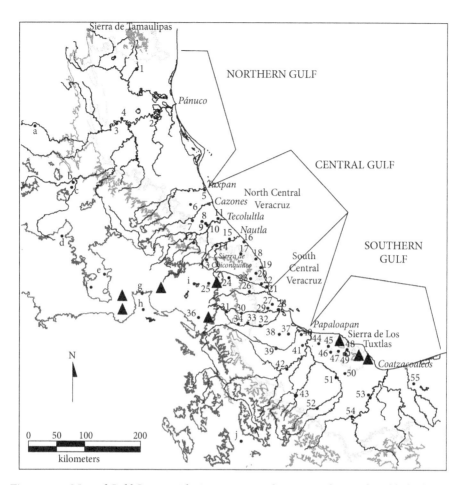

Figure 25.1 Map of Gulf Coast, with sites mentioned in text and/or with published references available (F is Formative, PC is Protoclassic, C is Classic, P is Postclassic), and major geographical references. Drawn by Annick Daneels and Kristin Sullivan. Map contour lines designed by Gerardo Jimenez-Delgado, Mapoteca IIA-UNAM, from the elevation contours of Mexico's INEGI website (www.inegi.org.mx).

1. San Antonio Nogalar (C); 2. Pánuco (F, C, P); 3. Tantok (C, P); 4. Tamuin (P); 5. Tabuco (P); 6. Castillo de Teayo (P); 7. Coralillos (C); 8. Tajín (C); 9. Morgadal (C); 10. Cerro Grande (C); 11. Santa Luisa (F, C); 12. Yohualichan (C); 13. Xiutetelco (C); 14. Cuajilotes (C) and Vega de la Peña (P); 15. Pital (PC, C); 16. Higueras (F, C); 17. Paxil (P); 18. Viejón (F, PC, C); 19. Quiahuistlan (P); 20. Mozomboa (P); 21. Chachalacas (C, P); 22. Chalahuite (F, PC), Zempoala (P); 23. Ranchito de las Ánimas (C) and Cerro Montoso (P); 24. Macuiltepetl (PC); 25. Napatecuhtlan (C); 26. Carrizal (PC, C); 27. Loma Iguana (C); 28. La Joya (F, PC, C); 29. Remojadas (C); 30. Ameyal (C); 31. Yerbabuena (F, PC, C, P); 32. Cotaxtla (P); 33. Quauhtochco (P); 34. Toro Prieto (C); 35. Maltrata (F, C, P); 36. Aljojuca (C); 37. Cerro de las Mesas (F, PC, C); Zapotal (C), and El Sauce (P); 38. Callejón del Horno (P); 39. Nopiloa (C); 40. Patarata (C); 41. La Mojarra (PC, C); 42. Tuxtepec (P); 43. Playa Vicente (C,P); 44. El Mesón (F, PC, C); 45. Tres Zapotes (F, PC, C); 46. Totogal (P); 47. Matacapan (C); 48. Teotepec (PC, C); 49. Agaltepec (P); 50. Laguna de los Cerros (C); 51. El Marquesillo (C); 52. Jonotal (C); 53. Ahuatepec (C); 54. Las Limas (F, C); 55. La Venta (F, C); a. Río Verde (San Luís Potosí) (C); b. Ranas (Sierra Gorda) (C); c. Toluquilla (Sierra Gorda) (C); d. Tula (P); e. Teotihuacan (C); f. Tenochtitlan (P); g. Cacaxtla (F, C); h. Cholula (C, P); i. Cantona (PC, C); j. Monte Albán (C).

home to major Mesoamerican cash crops like cotton, cacao, and rubber. Here, the major risk factors are floods and volcanic eruptions.

Culturally the Gulf is arranged in three sections: the north, from the Sierra de Tamaulipas to the Tuxpan or the Cazones River; the center, from the Cazones to the Papaloapan; and the south until the Tonalá (a former Grijalva affluent). As we will see, these borders shift through time, but the main geographical blocks seem to correspond to the major areas and subareas of the Gulf cultures (Wilkerson 1972; Pool 2006). Interaction throughout the region was continuous with a major isthmian lowland corridor stretching from the Pacific coast of Central America to the coast of Tamaulipas, and highland contacts were intense along, though not restricted to, the major river courses, which connect the Gulf to northern Mesoamerica, the central plateau, and the Oaxaca-Guerrero valleys (Daneels 2001, 2002; Parsons 1978).

The focus here is on the developments during the first and early second millennium AD (Figure 25.2). The Classic period civilizations seem to have risen progressively from a Preclassic background, a product of mainly isthmian interaction, but ceramics and lithics show a development up to some point parallel to the central plateau, a possible result of the highlands' interest in coastal resources and styles. The Gulf Coast way of life, as represented in settlement patterns and architecture, on the other hand, is clearly a tropical lowland adaptation, with a dispersed population subsisting on a combination of agriculture, horticulture, forest husbandry, and extensive exploitation of sylvan and aquatic resources. In contrast, the Postclassic witnesses major changes, as in most of Mesoamerica. The new cultures, while respecting the boundaries of the Classic period areas, appear to be the result of major foreign migrations. Particularly in the last two decades, investigation has focused on the theme of political entities, their urban centers, internal organization, and forms of interaction, a focus that this chapter will reflect. Another recurrent theme, ethnic identity, is a topic of long standing but in which little consensus has yet been reached.

THE CLASSIC CENTRAL VERACRUZ CULTURE

The Classic Central Veracruz culture, bracketed between the Cazones and the Papaloapan rivers, extends on the Central Highlands along the Sierra Madre Oriental's western piedmont. As a culture area it has been defined since the nineteenth century through its distinctive volute style, its portable stone sculptures (known as yokes, *hachas*, and *palmas*), and its variety in ceramic figurines like smiling faces and monumental figures (Strebel 1885). Beginning in the 1940s, the early modern archaeological work by García Payón and Medellín Zenil coincided

	NORTHERN GULF			NORTH-CENTRAL GULF		
	SIERRA	PÁNUCO	TAMIAHUA	TECOLUTLA TAJIN	NAUTLA BASIN	ACTOPAN BASIN
1500		PÁNUCO VI	Castillo de			ZEMPOALA IV
		TAMUIN	Teayo			
1400	LOS ANGELES			CABEZAS	Vega de la Peña	ZEMPOALA III
1300				--------------		ZEMPOALA II
						Mozomboa
1200	--------------	--------------	Tabuco	CRISTO		ZEMPOALA I
		PÁNUCO V				Quiahuistlan
1100		TAMUL		--------------		Isla de Sacrificios
		LAS FLORES				Cerro Montoso
1000		--------------	-----?---------	ISLA B	HIGUERAS	ZEMPOALA
					Xiutetelco	TEMPRANO
900	--------------	TANQUIL		--------------	Cuajilotes	
		PÁNUCO IV		Tajin		
800		Zaquil		Coralillos		La Gloria
						SAN CARLOS
700		--------------	PEÑON	ISLA A	ACACALCO	
		LATE COY			Higueras	
600	LA SALTA	PÁNUCO IV		--------------		
						CHACHALACAS
500	--------	--------------	--------------	CACAHUATAL		
	--------			Morgadal		
400	San Antonio	EARLY COY		Cerro Grande		Ranchito
	Nogalar	PÁNUCO III	PITHAYA			de las Ánimas
300	ESLABONES	El Lomerío		--------------		

200	-------	--------------				
				TECOLUTLA		
100		TANTOAN III				
		Altamirano				
0	--------------			--------------		Chalahuite
					Pital	
100		--------------	-----?------		VEGA	
				ARROYO		
200	LAGUNA	TANTOAN II	TANCOL	GRANDE		
		EL PRISCO				
300		--------------	--------------	--------------		
400						Trapiche
		TANTOAN I		ESTEROS B	BARRETA 2	
500		CHILA				
600		--------------		--------------		
700					Viejón	
		TAMPAON				
800		AGUILAR		ESTEROS A	BARRETA 1	
				Santa Luisa		
900		--------------				
1000		CHACAS		--------------		
		PONCE		OJITE	ESTERO	
1100		--------------		--------------		
1200						
		PUJAL		MONTE		
1300		PAVÓN		GORDO		

1400		--------------		ALMERIA		

1500	--------------			RAUDAL		
	ALMAGRES	CHAJIL				
	McNeish 1958	Ekholm 1944	Sanders	Wilkerson 1972,	Wilkerson 1994	García Payón
	Stresser Péan	McNeish 1954	1978	1981	Lagunes 1995	1951, 1966, 1971
	1977	Merino and		Brüggemann	Castillo 1997	
		García Cook		1992, 1995	Arellanos 2006	
		1987, 1997		Pascual 2006		
		García and				
		Merino 2004				

Figure 25.2 Chronological chart for the Gulf lowlands. Uppercase: phase names, lowercase: principal archaeological sites of the period. No limits are indicated when the sequence lacks radiocarbon dates. Dates are in uncorrected radiocarbon years.

SOUTH-CENTRAL GULF			
COTAXTLA BASIN			MIXTEQUILLA
REMOJADAS	CORDOBA	MALTRATA	
Cotaxtla, Quauhtochco			
LATE POSTCLASSIC 8° ASSEMBLAGE	Itzteyocan	Rincón Brujo	LATE POSTCLASSIC
			MIDDLE POSTCLASSIC
----		....	....
EARLY POSTCLASSIC 7° ASSEMBLAGE	PARAJE -------	Tetel del Calvano	
....	-------		-------
----		....	-------
LATE CLASSIC 6° ASSEMBLAGE		La Mesita	LATE
Loma Iguana	TORO PRIETO III	EPICLÁSICO	CLASSIC Zapotal
....		....	-------
----			-------
MIDDLE CLASSIC II 5° ASSEMBLAGE	....	Rincón de Aquila	------
....	TORO PRIETO II		EARLY CLASSIC
MIDDLE CLASSIC II 4° ASSEMBLAGE	....	....	
	TORO PRIETO I	Tepeyacatitla	....
....	....		TRANSITION TERM.PC./E.C.
EARLY CLASSIC 3° ASSEMBLAGE	CUEVAS	....	TERMINAL PRECLASSIC
....			
PROTOCLASSIC REMOJADAS INFERIOR 2° ASSEMBLAGE (LATE)			Cerro de las Mesas
----			....
....			POZAS PHASE ¿LATE FACET?
LATE PRECLASSIC 2° ASSEMBLAGE (EARLY)	Yerbabuena AMATLÁN	Rincón de Aquila	LATE PRECLASSIC
....	....		-- -- -- ? -- -- --
	MIDDLE PRECLASSIC		
MIDDLE PRECLASSIC 1° ASSEMBLAGE		Barriales de las Besanas	POZAS PHASE EARLY FACET
			MIDDLE PRECLASSIC
....		Tetel de Rancho Verde	....
EARLY PRECLASSIC			EARLY PRECLASSIC
			....
-----?-----			
		crude figurines	
Medellín 1960	Miranda and	Lira 2004	Stark 1989, 1994
Daneels 1988, 1997,	Daneels 1998		2001; 105-106,
2002, 2005, 2009	Cobean 2003		140-141.
	Pastrana 1994		

Left vertical labels: REM. SUP. II ; REMOJADAS SUPERIOR I

Figure 25.2 (*continued*)

PAPALOAPAN PATARATA	WESTERN TUXTLAS TRES ZAPOTES	SOUTHERN GULF TOTOGAL/PICAYO	CENTRAL TUXTLAS	COATZA-COALCOS	
Palmira				Villa del Espíritu	1500
PALANTLA		LATE POSTCLASSIC	Agaltepec	Santo	
----		TOTOGAL			1400
----					1300
GUACAMAYA		----	POSTCLASSIC		1200
----	SONCUAUTLA EARLY POSTCLASSIC	VIGÍA			1100
----	----	EARLY POSTCLASSIC	LATE CLASSIC CLÁSICO TARDÍO	----	1000
-------		LATE LATE CLASSIC	El Salado, Teotepec	LATE	900
SAN CRISTOBAL	QUEMADO	CLASSIC	Ranchoapan	VILLA ALTA	
LIMÓN	----	----	-- -- -- -- -- --	----	800
La Campana	LATE CLASSIC	CHANEQUE	LATE CLASSIC	EARLY VILLA ALTA	
----		----	MATACAPAN F	----	700
	----	SANTIAGO B	----	ORTICES	
CAMARÓN 3		------	MATACAPAN E	----	600
----	RANCHITO	-----	MIDDLE CLASSIC MATACAPAN D	MIDDLE CLASSIC	500
CAMARÓN 2	EARLY CLASSIC	------	MATACAPAN C	EARLY CLASSIC	400
----	----	SANTIAGO A	Chuniapan, Matacapan		
CAMARÓN I	----	----	----		300
----	NEXTEPETL			----	200
	TERMINAL FORMATIVE or PROTOCLASSIC		LATE BEZUAPAN		
La Mojarra			----		100
----					0
	HUEYAPAN B		LATE FORMATIVE	----?----	100
----	--- LATE --- FORMATIVE		EARLY BEZUAPAN	REMPLAS	200
	HUEYAPAN A		MATACAPAN B	----?----	300
LA BOCA	----		----	----?----	400
----	TRES ZAPOTES			PALANGANA	500
	MIDDLE FORMATIVE		GORDITA MIDDLE	----?----	600
			MIDDLE FORMATIVE	----	700
				NACASTE	800
			---- COYAME B EARLY FORMATIVE	----	900
----			----	SAN LORENZO B	1000
	ARROYO		COYAME A EARLY FORMATIVE	SAN LORENZO A MACAYAL	1100
----			TULIPAN (E. FORM.) MATACAPAN A	CHICHARRAS ----?----	1200
	....		----	BAJÍO ----?----	1300
	"OCOS"			OJOCHI	1400
				MANATI A Manati	1500

Stark 1977	Ortiz 1975	Ortiz 1975	Santley & Lunagó-mez 1991	Coe Diehl 1980
Stark&Curet 1994	Pool 2003	Venter 2008	Pool 1995	Rodríguez and Ortiz 1997
Delgado 1966	Pool 2008		Santley & Arnold 1996	Pool 1995
Jiménez 2001			Pool & Britt 2000	Symonds, Cyphers and Luna-gómez 2002
Aguilar 2008			Arnold 2003, 2009	Arellanos and Beauregard 2001

Figure 25.2 (*continued*)

in considering the Classic period development as strong and as an influence on Teotihuacan (García 1971; Medellín 1960). Sometimes referred to as Totonacapan, there now seems to exist a consensus that such a term would be valid only for the Postclassic North Central Veracruz area (until the Antigua River after 1000-1100 AD). Due to the presence of volute styles in both Tajín stone reliefs and the ceramics of Totonac sites, Krickeberg (1933), following Seler, considered them as part of the same Totonac culture; he was probably the main inspiration for Medellín (1960) to consider all of Central Veracruz as of Totonac stock. Wilkerson's (1972) work on Huastec and Totonac ethnogenesis, following García Payón's pioneering work, rejects this interpretation, because archaeological and historical evidence places the Totonac on the Gulf Coast no earlier than the Postclassic, and never south of the Antigua river, a view also supported by Pascual Soto's recent DNA analysis (2009: 22, 121–122, 142–143). Other terms applied are the Tajín culture and Remojadas culture, but these also apply only to specific areas and periods (Brüggemann 2004; Coe 1965). The different applications of the term "Remojadas" have created confusion; consequently, most researchers now avoid it or recommend a more restricted use (León 1995; Daneels 2005).

The small sizes of the Gulf sites and their dispersed settlement pattern led Sanders (1953, 1971) to develop his cultural ecological model of the rise of state, which still looms large in Mesoamerican research (Webster and Sanders 2001). He reasoned that, historically, tropical lowlands relied on slash-and-burn agriculture, a technique that requires fallow cycles that promote dispersed settlement, which would not allow the demographic growth and concentration necessary to reach the threshold of urbanism and statehood. Thus, major sites in the tropical lowlands are regal-ritual centers with low resident populations; not until the Postclassic, with evidence of agricultural intensification, do real states arise. And yet, since the 1980s and 1990s, detailed settlement patterns have shown that high population densities and agricultural intensification developed during the Classic period in Central Veracruz, including thousands of hectares for intensive cotton growing and of raised field systems for maize, along with four-tiered settlement systems, palace architecture, writing, and rulers' stelae, which are recognized hallmarks of states.[1]

The rise of the Classic Central Veracruz culture is interesting in that it incorporates two contiguous areas that were separate in the Preclassic period. South Central Veracruz's material assemblage virtually parallels that of Southern Veracruz, though poorer (lack of major stone sculpture, poorer ceramic and

1. Recent studies on settlement patterns and agricultural production are listed and reviewed in Pool 2006. See also Pascual 2006, Lira 2010, Siemens, this volume. On palace architecture, see Daneels 2008a; on writing and ruler's stelae, see Justeson, this volume. Major published sites in north central Veracruz are Tajín (Brüggemann 1992; Ladrón 2010; Pascual Soto 2006, 2009), Cuajilotes (Filobobos) (Cortés Hernández 1994), Pital (Wilkerson 1994), Higueras (Arellanos Melgarejo 2006). In South Central Veracruz are Cerro de las Mesas, Nopiloa, and Azuzules (Stark 1999, 2003), Zapotal (Torres Guzmán 2004), and La Joya (Daneels 2008a).

lithic assemblage), and is therefore closely related to the Olmec. North Central Veracruz presents a mixed assemblage of a local tradition related to the North Gulf (where ceramic grinding bowls are present with the very first ceramics), and the Central Highlands' red-on-cream jars tradition, in which early Chiapas's ceramics and Olmec materials are only minor, foreign elements (Wilkerson 1981). As a culture, Classic Central Veracruz culture is characterized by a shared ballgame ritual, including iconography of decapitation scenes and volutes, paraphernalia of yokes and *hachas*, and a complex settlement pattern where high-ranking sites have ballcourts as part of the main architectural compound (Daneels 2008b). Its earliest evidence is found in Protoclassic South Central Veracruz at Cerro de las Mesas (Stark 2007). During the Classic, this "symbolic package" is adopted in North Central Veracruz and possibly in part of the northern Gulf. The ceramic assemblages, while not identical, are dominated by convex bowls with orange-on-cream double-slip, fine-walled globular jars, no grinding bowls, and, at the end of the period, relief-molded bowls (Daneels 2006). The whole central and southern region participates in the obsidian trade for prismatic cores from the Zaragoza-Oyameles sources, controlled by Cantona (Arnold and Santley 2008; Daneels and Miranda Flores 1999; Knight and Glascock 2009; Pascual Soto 2009; Pool 2006: 205–206; Stoner 2011). This highland site has twenty-five ballcourts whose layouts are similar both to those of South Central Veracruz (the Standard Plan, with the ballcourt facing the main pyramid across the plaza) and North Central Veracruz (with the court on the side of the main plaza or on the side of the main pyramid) (García Cook 2003).

Settlement during the Classic shows a steady increase through much of the first millennium that reached an all-time high in the Late Classic period, particularly in the Tajín area, the Mixtequilla, and the Córdoba valley. Thus, surveys do not reflect a major impact of Teotihuacan's rise or collapse on the Classic Central Veracruz, suggesting that Teotihuacan's contact in South Central Veracruz was indirect, perhaps prompted by its interests in Gulf Coast resources such as cotton and cacao (Daneels 2002; Miranda and Daneels 1998; Stark and Johns 2004). In North Central Veracruz interaction has been interpreted as more intense, possibly represented by major Nahua population movements toward El Pital (Pascual Soto 2006; Wilkerson 1994).

Evidence of a settlement hierarchy is both quantitative and qualitative: in absolute size and volume, as well as in the size of major pyramids, there is a three-tiered distribution of sites with formal architectural compounds (few are large, more are medium, many of them are small) that stand out against a multitude of low mounds and surface ceramic scatter that reflect the residences of a dispersed population. When taken with functional diversity, the ranks become better defined. Capital sites are large, multifunctional centers: main plazas are associated to major pyramids (10 to 25 meters high) and ballcourts, reflecting ritual use; monumental platforms that have mounds and sometimes pyramids on top are palatial residences; secondary plazas, of smaller size, may be used for other political, administrative, or mercantile purposes. Some form of barrier, long mounds or artificial water ponds, delimits the major architectural groups from the residential wards. At the same time, these sites present a higher population density than subordinate settlements, running into 1,200 persons per square kilometer. Second-rank sites present the same nuclear layout as the capital, reflecting a multifunctional purpose (a main plaza with pyramid and ballcourt; a monumental platform as elite residence; a secondary plaza and architectural barriers), but they are smaller in size and volume and lack high-population density. Third-rank sites have a wide range of variation in size, with the largest of them surpassing smaller, second-rank centers, but they are unifunctional. Either they are plaza groups, dominated by a larger pyramidal mound but without a ballcourt, or they are represented by a major platform. The presence of a plaza in the first suggests events of assembly, and thus an organization on the basis of consensus, while its absence in elite residence centers suggests a control by a local governor or nobility, an organizing principle more suggestive of coercion (Daneels 2008b).

Most political entities defined are small, ranging from less than 100 square kilometers to a few hundred (Daneels 2008b; Stark 2008). Distance between high-ranking sites seems to increase in inverse proportion with the quality of the soils. In first-class soils with high productivity, major sites can be as close to each other as 6 or 10 kilometers. In areas of lesser productivity, or where large tracts of land are unusable for long periods of time (flooded or too dry), the major sites seem to be more widely spaced. Also initial surveys of the piedmont in Central Veracruz fail to reveal major sites in terms of size and volume, compared to those on alluvial terraces of the coastal plains, though the same architectural layout with the ballcourt in the same axis as the pyramid (the Standard Plan) remains characteristic of the upper-tier sites. It is still not clear whether major sites will be found or if there is a progressive scaling down of architectural sizes of the sites, as population density does not appear to be noticeably inferior. In all, the entities would rank among microstates, or city-states; thus, small polities seem to have been the norm not only for Postclassic Mesoamerica but also for the preceding centuries.[2] The internal organization of these entities seems to have been varied: in the fertile alluvial soils of the Cotaxtla and the Mixtequilla, settled since the Preclassic, authority was centralized at the major sites. In the lesser fertile hills, colonization was a Classic phenomenon and gave rise to larger entities with the major sites surrounded by a set of second-rank centers, themselves closely surrounded by third-rank centers, home to potentially strong landed elites, in a pattern similar to segmentary states (Daneels 2008b; Stark 2003). Tajín, the best-known site of Central Veracruz, seems, according to this pattern, to have been the head of a segmentary state as major sites

2. For the central Gulf, Daneels (2008b) speaks of microstates. Also Stark (2008) views dynastic centralized leadership increasingly challenged by powerful landed elites, reducing territories from 1,700 square kilometers to 400 to 500 square kilometers. Wilkerson (1994) uses the term city-state to speak of Pital. Compare with Chase and Chase, Smith and Sergheraert, Beekman, and Scarborough, this volume.

including ballcourts as well as sculpture, like Morgadal and Cerro Grande, are located at a very short distance.

Tajín is famous for its niches and cornice architecture and rich decoration in interlaced volute styles. The central ballcourt relief panels are crucial in interpreting the role of the ballgame in Central Veracruz society. While the major apogee of the site is at the end of the Classic period, evidence shows it is the result of a long local trajectory and part of a Central Veracruz urban tradition (García Payón 1971; Wilkerson 1972; Pascual Soto 2006, 2009; Ladrón de Guevara 2010). This opposes Brüggemann's model of urbanism as a Postclassic phenomenon, based principally on extensive excavations of the site's last period buildings and one radiocarbon date (Brüggemann 1995; for a contrary opinion, see Daneels 2009). In the absence of a larger-scale settlement pattern, the size of the Tajín entity is still a matter of conjecture. It may have been small, restricted to the Tlahuanapa-lower Tecolutla drainage, if Coralillos turns out to be a rival site in the adjoining Cazones basin (Vásquez Zárate 1997). On the other hand, architectural similarity with sites like Yohualichan has prompted the proposal that Tajín governed most of North Central Veracruz. This may have been a late scenario, as suggested by the war-and-conquest iconography of the palace of 13 Rabbit, who was probably Tajín's last king (Agüero Reyes and Daneels 2009; Koontz, this volume; Pascual Soto 2009).

THE NORTHERN AND SOUTHERN GULF IN THE CLASSIC PERIOD

The cultural sequence in both these areas also indicates a progressive development from the Preclassic period cultures, reaching a peak in the Protoclassic period: the epi-Olmec apogee of Tres Zapotes in the Tuxtlas area of Southern Veracruz, and the stage called Tantuan II-III in Northern Veracruz. But in contrast to Central Veracruz, there seems to be a slump during the Early and Middle Classic, a phenomenon also observed in other parts of Mesoamerica (e.g., Tlaxcala, Michoacán, Guerrero, and northern Petén). Settlements pick up rapidly again in the Late Classic, but in both cases it is not completely clear whether the Late Classic sites relate to the Protoclassic ones: are they the same people, or is there an influx of population from the outside? The chronological coincidence with the rise of Teotihuacan has often been cited as a possible reason for the apparent depopulation due to massive emigration toward the highlands, with groups returning to their homeland after the decline of the metropolis (García Payón 1971, Medellín Zenil 1960). Nevertheless, the lack of clear connections to Teotihuacan material culture from the "returning" populations does not support the claim (Ruiz Gallut and Pascual Soto 2004).

In the northern Gulf, the architecture, ceramics, and figurines of the Coy phase (ca. 200–700 AD) seem to denote continuity in the cultural development, with a more pronounced change in architectural layouts during the following Late Classic Tanquil (ca. 700–1000 AD), characterized by the dominance of rectangular buildings over circular ones, ballcourts, and the presence of yokes. This phenomenon seems to expand toward the Sierra Gorda and the Río Verde Valley in San Luis Potosí, a development that may be linked to the apogee of Tajín (Daneels 2006; Ekholm 1944; Merino Carrión and García Cook 1987; Michelet 1996; Mejía Pérez-Campos 2009; Muñoz Espinoza 2007).

In Southern Veracruz there seems to be a marked contrast between the lowlands, where Early and Middle Classic settlements seem to be virtually absent, and the Tuxtlas Mountains and piedmont, where a thriving population exists throughout the Classic (Symonds et al. 2002; Borstein 2005; Pool 2006). Much of the Classic-period Tuxtlas research centers on Matacapan, a site first revealed in the 1930s by Valenzuela (1945) as having Teotihuacan talud-tablero architecture and ceramics. This sparked a long-term project headed by Santley in 1979, who, after the Basin of Mexico project, went on to identify Matacapan as a Teotihuacan enclave on the southern Mesoamerica route (Santley 2007). Intensive surface surveys proved that while the architecture at Matacapan shows a special connection to the metropolis, the Teotihuacan-style ceramics (candeleros, cylindrical tripods with slab supports, and mold-made figurines) are locally made copies that represent only a very small fraction of the regional production; besides, they have a quite large distribution across the Tuxtlas region, which weakens the enclave hypothesis because it is not restricted to one site. An alternative view is furthered by Arnold, who considers that the Teotihuacanos present at Matacapan may represent a small dissident group, rather than the result of an imperial strategy (Arnold and Santley 2008; Daneels 2002). A better candidate for a Veracruz enclave might be in the Maltrata Valley, at the foot of the Pico de Orizaba volcano (Lira López 2004, 2010).

The Late Classic represents a period of intense construction, with hundreds of sites of different sizes appearing in the lowlands (above the flood level). The architectural layout is recurrent: a rectangular plaza limited by long platforms on both sides, with a high conical mound on a short side (up to 30–36 meters in height) and a low mound on the opposite end. These are variously called and occur in a very large area (13,000 square kilometers), including the coastal area east of the Tuxtlas.[3] Many also have large platforms (palaces?), secondary plazas, and water ponds, just as in Central Veracruz, but structures interpreted as ballcourts (unconfirmed as none have been as yet excavated) seem to have only a secondary role, as they are placed on the outside of the main plaza or at the periphery of the site. They differ from the Central Veracruz layouts where square

---

3. Grupo arquitectónico A (Symonds et al. 2002), Villa Alta Quadripartite Arrangement or VAQA (Borstein 2005), Long-Plaza groups (Urcid and Killion 2008), or when the layout is repeated along an axis: COPLA or Conjunto Plazas Adjuntas (Heredia 2008).

plazas dominate, but they bear some resemblance to Chontal Late Classic to Postclassic sites of Tabasco, a similarity also reflected in the ceramic complex characterized by fine orange and fine graywares; thus, a possible Maya Chontal component in the Late Classic Southern Veracruz lowlands is certainly a possibility (Borstein 2005; Daneels 2006). But what is their relationship to the local population, the Olmecs and their descendants who apparently remained in the Tuxtlas? Interestingly, central Tuxtlas shows a mix of site layouts, including rectangular plazas, Standard Plans, and Tres Zapotes Plaza Groups (TZPG), sometimes within the same site (Stoner 2011).

The chronological span of the long plaza layouts is actually thought to be of Late Classic to maybe Early Postclassic date (Symonds et al. 2002), but two arguments could point to a longer chronology: on the one hand, the long-plaza layout seems to be attested in Middle Preclassic La Venta (Stark 2007) and in Tabasco until the end of the Postclassic period (Berlin 1956). On the other hand, the diagnostic Villa Alta ceramic wares of fine orange and fine gray continue both in the Coatzacoalcos drainage and in Tabasco until the end of the Postclassic (Arellanos Melgarejo and Beauregard García 2001).

The political organization of Southern Veracruz during the Classic period shows some variation also. Pool (2006) considers that the fourfold repetition of a plaza layout (Tres Zapotes Plaza Group) during Tres Zapotes' apogee could represent a corporate strategy of four factions or wards within the site, with the institution of an assembly form of government (similar to what Manzanilla proposes for Teotihuacan). Among the long plaza groups in the lowlands, the wider spacing of the major sites suggests larger territories that would closely match Renfrew's Early State Module (Renfrew and Cherry 1986), possibly organized in a segmentary system (Borstein 2005). Reevaluations of the actual sizes of the territories will be necessary, as large sites are being defined through extensive surveys (Heredia 2008). A major site like Marquesillo (Doering 2007, see location in Figure 25.1), not taken into account by Borstein (2005) or Urcid and Killion (2008), rivals Laguna de los Cerros and would thus modify the currently proposed territory reconstructions.

POSTCLASSIC

The Postclassic dynamics differ again within the Gulf lowlands: while the northern and central parts witnessed major changes that seem to be attributable at least in part to migration, the south seems to keep on its course in close affinity to the Maya Chontal lowlands, a trajectory apparently initiated in the Late Classic. In general, the chronology of this approximately five-hundred-year period preceding the Conquest is badly understood in all three Gulf subareas. Though most researchers agree in the existence of an early and a late facet, the limit between them ranges from 1200 AD (i.e., just after the fall of Tula), 1300 AD, or 1350 AD (i.e., the beginning of the Aztec interaction). Mainly, the problem seems to be defining the material traits diagnostic for each facet, as the material culture, once established, shows a rather great homogeneity. In general, Postclassic centers throughout the Gulf are smaller in size and volume, and they also lack the standardized architectural layouts at different scales typical of their Classic counterparts. Also, they are more likely to be organized along a *barrio* system, with several major architectural compounds in the sites. This reflects profound changes in the ways societies were thinking and acting. This observation is not restricted to the Gulf but could be applied to much of Postclassic Mesoamerica, where it has been attributed to the secularization and militarization of society from an evolutionist perspective (Piña Chán 1976).

NORTHERN GULF

In the northern Gulf area, the so-called Huastec culture diagnostic ceramics of Black-on-White and Black-and-Red-on-White appear without clear reference to earlier traditions. Where kaolin is available, these types are made of it, which presupposes the introduction of a specialized firing technique (Daneels 2006). The large stone sculptures, like the *adolescente* and the *apoteososis,* as well as the large openwork conch pectorals, also seem to be new artistic expressions. While conforming to a stylistically distinctive and easily recognizable assemblage, local variations have been shown to exist from south to north (Ekholm 1944; Gutiérrez Mendoza and Ochoa Salas 2009; Ochoa Salas 2001; Zaragoza Ocaña 2009). On the other hand, several traits show great temporal depth: ceramic grinding bowls with deep incisions on the bottom (*molcajetes*), ceramic ladles, long-legged Barbie-like figurines, and rounded architecture remain frequent, but rectangular structures, sometimes with rounded corners, are probably as frequent; ballcourts continue to be built. Thus, some degree of continuity with both the Preclassic and Classic traditions seems supported. Other materials show awareness of more international styles, such as the so-called Mixteca-Puebla codex style in mural painting (Zaragoza Ocaña 2003) and Maya Terminal Classic and Postclassic ceramic forms (Daneels 2006; Zaragoza Ocaña 2009), while others (metallurgy, tobacco pipes) represent possible evidence of occasional long-distance trade with the Mississippi Valley (Dávila 2009).

Archaeologically, sites such as Castillo de Teayo, where architecture and sculpture follow Central Highland (Nahua) prototypes, indicate the presence of non-Huastecs (Solís 1981). A multiethnic configuration with groups that speak Nahua, Otomí, Pame, Tepehua, and Totonac and intermingle with Teenek

(Huastec) speakers, as well as Aztec conquest wars, are historically documented and may explain the little-understood mix of continuity and innovation that characterizes the northern Gulf (Stresser Péan 1998, Faust and Richter eds. 2015). The political organization of Postclassic entities has been interpreted as *altepeme* (city-states), mainly based on contact-period Spanish sources, although the volume and size of sites vary and are generally modest (Ochoa Salas 2001: 49).

CENTRAL VERACRUZ

What used to be the Central Veracruz Classic culture area is split again in two during the Postclassic period. The north, from between the Tuxpan and the Cazones rivers to the Antigua River, was settled by Totonac groups, according to historical sources (Acuña 1985; Díaz del Castillo 1976; Torquemada 1975). They originated from the northern Puebla highlands and Sierra, possibly displaced by large population movements from north to south that intensify during the eleventh century. Apparently they appropriated a series of traits from the Late Classic Tajín Culture: architecture using taluds and cornices (and sometimes niches and step-fret decoration), ballcourts (with the new addition of goal rings, or *tlachtemalacatl*), volutes (though these are now expressed in painting on ceramic vessels of Isla de Sacrificios type), and a preference for red/orange combinations on fancy ceramics, though vessel form and decorative motives change, with an obvious relation to the Mixteca-Puebla codex style. These loans seem to be a way to legitimize the Totonac groups' claim to the possession of the region. Major sites include Paxil, Vega de la Peña, Quiahuistlan, Isla de Sacrificios, and Zempoala, though many more are known from older surveys (Arellanos Melgarejo 1997; Brüggemann 1991; García Payón 1971; Medellín Zenil 1955; Ruiz Gordillo 1989, 1999; Strebel 1885). A series of sites between the Chiconquiaco range and the Antigua River (Zempoala, Quiahuistlan, and Oceloapan) shows a change to altiplano-style architecture and ceramics in their last stages, lending credence to the historic sources citing "Chichimec" coming to power in Totonac centers. Differences in ware proportions and ceramic decoration suggest that these Nahua, though closely related, were not the same as those settled in the Cotaxtla drainage (see below).

In the southern part of Central Veracruz, the tradition that had evolved locally since 1000 BC was suddenly replaced by a completely new assemblage, with clear ties to the Mixteca-Puebla assemblage of the Central Highlands, though its specific point of origin is as yet undefined. Settlement patterns show a preference for high grounds along main rivers, meaning three-fourths of the Classic-period territory is abandoned. And yet these provinces paid a heavy cotton tribute at the time of the Conquest. Sites are smaller in size and volume, lack ballcourts, but show instead double-pyramid mounds, encircling walls or *coatepantlis*, and many small mounds that seem to be altars (Daneels 1997). When in stone, the buildings have the almost vertical talud walls and dadoed balustrade tops typical of altiplano architecture (Daneels 2010). Ceramic pastes, forms, decoration, color combination, and manufacturing techniques change, along with ways of eating and preparing food (new are tortilla griddles, grinding chile in terracotta *molcajetes* with relief-molded bottoms, grinding corn on footed *metates*) (Daneels 1997; Stark and Chance 2008; Skoglund et al. 2006). Sitting positions change, with raised knees instead of the cross-legged position that dominated in Classic Mesoamerica. Religion changes with the altiplano-style gods Tlaloc, Xilonen, and Quetzalcoatl, in stone and large and small ceramic figurines (Daneels 1997; Stark and Chance 2008). Obsidian procurement shifted: Zaragoza-Oyameles is abandoned in favor of high-quality Pico de Orizaba obsidian obtained through deep-shaft mining, a technique previously unknown on the Gulf, and cores now consistently have ground platforms, untrimmed from the blades, together with a low proportion of green Sierra de Navajas blades (Daneels and Miranda Flores 1999).

These changes are clearly evident in the Cotaxtla drainage and in the Mixtequilla, which later became the Aztec tributary provinces of Quauhtochco and Cotaxtla. As clear Early Postclassic materials seemed to be lacking, it was first thought that these groups entered a region that had been severely depopulated. Actually, with evidence of the persistence of the Late Classic assemblage until at least 1000 AD, and an earlier inception date of some of the Postclassic wares (the *guinda complex* of the highlands), it is highly probable the migrating groups actually absorbed, conquered, or eradicated local inhabitants (Daneels 1997; Stark and Chance 2008).

SOUTHERN GULF

The Postclassic in the southern Gulf was long a paradox: historic sources attested to a dense population, but archaeologically it was invisible (Venter 2008). Being part of the Aztec Empire (as a province of Tuxtepec), it seemed logical to expect ceramics similar to those of the Cotaxtla and Quauhtochco provinces of neighboring Central Veracruz, but these are absent from the region. Late Postclassic ceramics now have been found in the Lower Coatzacoalcos drainage, at Villa del Espíritu Santo (Arellanos Melgarejo and Beauregard García 2001) and in the Tuxtlas at Agaltepec (Arnold 2003) and Totogal (Venter 2008), showing the persistence of most Classic-period wares, with fine orange and fine gray accounting for almost half of the assemblage, along with very scarce, probably imported, Aztec (Texcoco Molded censers) and Totonac types (Tres Picos). Wares show clear parallels to Tabasco's Cintla Horizon (Berlin 1956). Rather than ceramics, obsidian may prove to be a more reliable chronological indicator, because a shift from black or dark gray-banded blades from Zaragoza-Oyameles to Pico de Orizaba clear gray and

Pachuca green blades with ground platforms is general in the central and southern Gulf and reflects the demise of Cantona as a producer. At Agaltepec (Arnold 2003), the one-to-nine proportion of green and light gray obsidian closely parallels the changes observed in the Cotaxtla Basin (Daneels and Miranda Flores 1999). In contrast, the dominance of green obsidian at Callejón del Horno in the Mixtequilla, Totogal, Villa del Espíritu Santo, and all the way to Tabasco (Venter 2008) may be a late phenomenon. Systematic research is only beginning, but rapid advances are to be expected, which will provide a better understanding of Postclassic assemblages and settlement history. Thus, some of the hundreds of sites attributed to the Villa Alta phase may date to the Postclassic period.

CONCLUSION

The Classic and Postclassic periods in the Gulf reveal a mosaic of cultures, each with their own particular trajectories that varied even within the same cultural areas and periods. Much information is as yet unpublished or available only through very specialized channels, making it difficult for nonspecialists to appreciate the complexity of these cultures. To understand how Gulf cultures interacted with the other major Mesoamerican civilizations it is necessary to define with which part of the Gulf and in which period these interactions took place. The archaeological evidence shows the existence of a very large number of small, independent, state-level political entities, organized according to a variety of political systems ranging from centralized to segmentary (without necessarily passing through cycles of centralization and balkanization as anticipated by Marcus 1998), with power groups within them developing both corporate and network strategies to further their positions. These entities share, at a gradually increasing scale, domestic cults, ceramic assemblages, state religion, and long-distance networks for the procurement of basalt and obsidian. At the political level, however, they remained quite autonomous in their decision making. The enormous potential of the Gulf lowlands to produce cash crops such as cotton, cacao, and rubber; their strategic location on major Mesoamerican commerce routes; and the regional variation in risk factors due to floods and volcanic eruptions have certainly been factors that promoted such varied trajectories.

References

Acuña, René, ed. 1985. *Relaciones geográficas del Siglo XVI: Tlaxcala Tomo 2*. Instituto de
    Investigaciones Antropológicas, Serie Antropología 59, Universidad Nacional Autónoma
    de México, Mexico DF.
Agüero Reyes, Adriana, and Annick Daneels. 2009. Playing Ball. Competition as a
    Political Tool. In *Blood and Beauty: Organized Violence in the Art and Archaeology of
    Mesoamerica and Central America*, edited by Heather Orr and Rex Koontz,
    pp. 117–138. Series Ideas, Debates, and Perspectives 4, Cotsen Institute of Archaeology
    Press, University of California, Los Angeles.
Aguilar Pérez, María Antonia. 2008. El Tesechoacán y Los Tuxtlas. In *Arqueología, Paisaje y
    cosmovisión en los Tuxtlas*, edited by Lourdes Budar and Sara Ladrón de Guevara, pp.
    91–103. Universidad Veracruzana, Xalapa.
Arellanos Melgarejo, Ramón. 1997. *La arquitectura monumental postclásica de Quiahuiztlan*.
    Universidad Veracruzana. Xalapa.
Arellanos Melgarejo, Ramón. 2006. *Las Higueras (Acacalco). Dinámica Cultural*. Serie
    Biblioteca, Universidad Veracruzana, Xalapa.
Arellanos Melgarejo Ramón, and Lourdes Beauregard García. 2001. *La Villa del Espíritu
    Santo y sus materiales culturales*. Ediciones Cultura de Veracruz Xalapa.
Arnold, Philip J.III. 2003. *Isla Agaltepec: Postclassic Occupation in the Tuxtla Mountains,
    Mexico*. Foundation for the Advancement of Mesoamerican Studies, Crystal River
    http://www.famsi.org/reports/00046, accessed August 1, 2010.
Arnold, Philip J.III. 2009. Settlement and Subsistence among the Early Formative Gulf
    Olmec. *Journal of Anthropological Archaeology* 28: 397–411.
Arnold, Philip J. III, and Christopher A. Pool, eds. 2008. *Classic-Period Cultural
    Currents in Southern and Central Veracruz*. Dumbarton Oaks Research
    Library and Collections. Precolumbian Studies. Harvard University Press,
    Washington, DC.
Arnold, Philip J. III and Robert S. Santley. 2008. Classic Currents in the West-Central Tuxtlas.
    In *Classic-Period Cultural Currents in Southern and Central Veracruz*, edited by Philip
    J. Arnold III and Christopher A. Pool, pp. 293–321. Dumbarton Oaks Research Library
    and Collections, Precolumbian Studies, Harvard University Press, Washington, DC.
Berlin, Heinrich. 1956. *Late Pottery Horizons of Tabasco, Mexico*. Contributions to American
    Anthropology and History, Vol XII, No. 59, Washington, DC.
Borstein, Joshua A. 2005. Epiclassic Political Organization in Southern Veracruz, Mexico:
    Segmentary versus Centralized Integration. *Ancient Mesoamerica* 16(1):11–21.
Brüggemann, Jürgen Kurt. 1992. La ciudad y la sociedad. In *Tajín*, by Jürgen Kurt
    Brüggemann, Álvaro Brizuela Absalón, Sara Ladrón de Guevara, Patricia Castillo,
    Mario Navarrete, and René Ortega, pp. 47–78. Veracruz en la Cultura, Encuentros y
    Ritmos, Gobierno del Estado de Veracruz—PEMEX—Taller Artes Gráficas Panorama
    SA de CV, Mexico DF.
Brüggemann, Jürgen Kurt. 1995. La zona del Golfo en el Clásico. In *Historia
    antigua de México, Volume II: El horizonte Clásico*, edited by Linda Manzanilla and
    Leonardo López Luján, pp. 11–40. CONACULTA/Instituto Nacional de Antropología
    e Historia, UNAM-Coordinación de Humanidades/Instituto de Investigaciones
    Antropológicas, Grupo Editorial Miguel Ángel Porrúa,
    Mexico DF.

Brüggemann, Jürgen Kurt. 2004. ¿Dónde está la presencia teotihuacana en El Tajín?. In *La costa del Golfo en tiempos teotihuacanos: propuestas y perspectivas. Memoria de la segunda mesa redonda de Teotihuacan*, edited by María Elena Ruiz Gallut and Arturo Pascual Soto, pp. 349–368. Instituto Nacional de Antropología e Historia, Mexico DF.

Brüggemann, Jürgen Kurt, ed. 1991. *Zempoala: el estudio de una ciudad prehispánica*. Colección Científica, Serie Arqueología no. 232, Instituto Nacional de Antropología e Historia, Mexico DF.

Castillo Peña, Patricia, 1997. Tipología Preliminar para el sitio de Cuajilote, dentro del Proyecto Arqueológico Filobobos. In *Memoria del coloquio Arqueología del centro y sur de Veracruz*, edited by Sara Ladrón de Guevara and Sergio Vásquez Zárate, pp. 35–43. Universidad Veracruzana, Xalapa.

Cobean, Robert H. 2003. *La Yerbabuena, Veracruz: A Salvage Investigation of an Olmec Regional Center near Pico de Orizaba Volcano*. Foundation for the Advancement of Mesoamerican Studies, Crystal River. http://www.famsi.org/reports/97012. Accessed February 1, 2012.

Coe, Michael D. 1965. Archaeological Synthesis of Southern Veracruz and Tabasco. In *Archaeology of Southern Mesoamerica*, edited by Gordon R. Willey, pp. 679–715. Handbook of Middle American Indians, vol. 3, part 2, University of Texas Press, Austin.

Coe, Michael D. and Richard A. Diehl, 1980. *In the Land of the Olmec. Volume I: The Archaeology of San Lorenzo Tenochtitlan*. University of Texas Press, Austin and London.

Cortés Hernández, Jaime. 1994. *Filobobos*. Guía. Salvat/Instituto Nacional de Antropología e Historia, Mexico DF.

Daneels, Annick, 1988. La cerámica de Plaza de Toros y Colonia Ejidal. Informe sobre las excavaciones realizadas en 1984 en el marco del proyecto "Exploraciones en el Centro de Veracruz". Archivo Técnico de la Coordinación de Arqueología, Instituto Nacional de Antropología e Historia. Mexico DF.

Daneels, Annick. 1997. Settlement History in the Lower Cotaxtla Basin. In *Olmec to Aztec Settlement Patterns in the Ancient Gulf Lowlands*, edited by Barbara L. Stark and Philip J. Arnold III, pp. 279–309. University of Arizona Press, Tucson.

Daneels, Annick. 2001. La relación entre la costa del Golfo y la Costa Pacífica de Centroamérica, vista desde Veracruz. In *XIV Simposio de Investigaciones Arqueológicas en Guatemala, 2000*, edited by Juan Pedro Laporte, Ana Claudia de Suásnavar, and Bárbara Arroyo, pp. 1174–1190. Museo Nacional de Arqueología y Etnología, Guatemala City.

Daneels, Annick. 2002. Presencia de Teotihuacan en el centro y sur de Veracruz. In *Ideología y política a través de materiales, imágenes y símbolos. Memoria de la primera mesa redonda de Teotihuacan*, edited by María Elena Ruiz Gallut, pp. 655–683. Universidad Nacional Autónoma de México, Instituto de Investigaciones Antropológicas e Instituto de Investigaciones Estéticas—Instituto Nacional de Antropología e Historia, Mexico DF.

Daneels, Annick. 2005. El Protoclásico en el centro de Veracruz. Una perspectiva desde la cuenca baja del Cotaxtla. In *Arqueología Mexicana. IV Coloquio Pedro Bosch Gimpera, Volume II: Veracruz, Oaxaca y mayas*, edited by Ernesto Vargas Pacheco, pp. 453–488. Universidad Nacional Autónoma de México, Instituto de Investigaciones Antropológicas, Mexico DF.

Daneels, Annick. 2006. La cerámica del Clásico en Veracruz, 0–1000 d.Cr. In *La producción alfarera en el México antiguo, Volume II; La Alfarería durante el Clásico 100–700 d.Cr.*, edited by Beatriz Leonor Merino Carrión and Ángel García Cook, pp. 393–504. Colección Científica, Serie Arqueología, no. 495, Instituto Nacional de Antropología e Historia, Mexico DF.

Daneels, Annick. 2008a. *Monumental Earthen Architecture at La Joya, Veracruz,*
    Mexico. Foundation for the Advancement of Mesoamerican Studies, Crystal River
    http://www.famsi.org/reports/07021. Accessed August 1, 2010.

Daneels, Annick. 2008b. Ballcourts and Politics in the Lower Cotaxtla Valley: A Model to
    Understand Classic Central Veracruz? In *Classic-Period Cultural Currents in Southern*
    and Central Veracruz, edited by Philip J. Arnold III and Christopher A. Pool, pp.
    197–223. Dumbarton Oaks Research Library and Collections, Precolumbian Studies,
    Harvard University Press, Washington, DC.

Daneels, Annick. 2009. Algunos problemas en la cronología del Golfo Veracruzano.
    In *Quinto Coloquio Pedro Bosch Gimpera. Cronología y periodización de Mesoamérica*
    y el Norte de México, edited by Annick Daneels, pp. 263–292. Universidad Nacional
    Autónoma de México: Instituto de Investigaciones Antropológicas, Mexico DF.

Daneels, Annick. 2010. Central Veracruz. In *Precolumbian Architecture in Mesoamerica,*
    edited by María Teresa Uriarte, pp. 157–178. Abbeville Press,
    New York.

Daneels, Annick, Emilio Ibarra, Fabio Flores, and Manuel Zolá. 2005. Paleoagriculture on the
    Gulf Coast: Two Possible Cases of the Classic Period, Central Veracruz, Mexico. In *Gulf*
    Coast Archaeology. The Southeastern United States and Mexico, edited by Nancy Marie
    White, pp. 205–222. University Press of Florida, Gainesville.

Daneels, Annick, and Fernando A. Miranda Flores. 1999. La industria prehispánica de
    la obsidiana en la región de Orizaba. In *El valle de Orizaba. Textos de historia y*
    antropología, edited by Carlos Serrano Sánchez and Agustín García Márquez,
    pp. 27–60. Cuadernos de divulgación 3. Universidad Nacional Autónoma de México,
    Museo de Antropología de la Universidad Veracruzana, H. Ayuntamiento de Orizaba,
    Mexico DF.

Dávila, Patricio. 2009. La Huasteca: problemática y nexos culturales. In *Memoria del taller*
    arqueología de la Huasteca. Homenaje a Leonor Merino Carrión., edited by Diana
    Zaragoza Ocaña, pp. 33–48. Colección Científica, Serie Arqueología, no. 541. Instituto
    Nacional de Antropología e Historia, Mexico DF.

Delgado, Agustín. 1966. Arqueología de la Chinantla, N.E. de Oaxaca, México. In *Summa*
    Anthropologica. Homenaje a Roberto J. Weitlaner, edited by Antonio Pompa y Pompa:
    81–90. Instituto Nacional de Antropología e Historia, Mexico DF.

Díaz del Castillo, Bernal. 1976. *Historia verdadera de la conquista de la Nueva España.* Porrúa,
    Mexico DF.

Doering, Travis F. 2007. An Unexplored Realm in the Heartland of the South Gulf Olmec:
    Investigations at El Marquesillo, Veracruz, Mexico. PhD dissertation, Department of
    Anthropology, University of South Florida, Tampa.

Ekholm, Gordon F. 1944. *Excavations at Tampico y Pánuco in the Huasteca, Mexico.*
    Anthropological Papers 38 (Part 5): 321–509. American Museum of Natural History,
    New York.

Faust, Katherine A., and Kim N. Richter, eds. 2015. *The Huasteca Culture, History, and*
    Interregional Exchange. University of Oklahoma Press, Norman.

García Cook, Ángel. 2003. Cantona: The City. In *El Urbanismo en Mesoamerica/Urbanism in*
    Mesoamerica, Vol. 1, edited by Guadalupe Mastache and William T. Sanders, pp. 311–343.
    Instituto Nacional de Antropología e Historia and The Pennsylvania State University,
    University Park.

García Cook, Ángel, and Leonor Merino Carrión. 2004. Secuencia cultural para el Formativo
    en la Cuenca baja del río Pánuco. *Arqueología* 32: 5–27.

García Payón, José. 1951. *Breves Apuntes sobre la Arqueología de Chachalacas.* Universidad
    Veracruzana, Xalapa.

García Payón, José. 1966. *Prehistoria de Mesoamérica. Excavaciones en Trapiche y Chalahuite, Veracruz, México, 1942, 1951 y 1959.* Cuadernos de la Facultad de Filosofía, Letras y Ciencias No. 31. Universidad Veracruzana, Xalapa.

García Payón, José. 1971. Archaeology of Central Veracruz. In *Archaeology of Northern Mesoamerica*, edited by Gordon F. Ekholm and Ignacio Bernal, pp. 505–542. Handbook of Middle American Indians, Vol. 11, Part 2, University of Texas Press, Austin.

Gutiérrez Mendoza, Gerardo, and Lorenzo Ochoa Salas. 2009. Los límites culturales de la región Huasteca. In *Memoria del taller arqueología de la Huasteca*, edited by Diana Zaragoza, pp. 77–92. Colección Científica, Serie Arqueología, no. 541. Instituto Nacional de Antropología e Historia, Mexico DF.

Heredia Barrera, Luis. 2008. Conjuntos plaza durante el clásico tardío en el sur de Veracruz. *Revista Ollin Centro INAH Veracruz* 5:44–59.

Jiménez Lara. Pedro. 2001. La arqueología en la Cuenca Baja del Río Papaloapan, Veracruz, México (primeros resultados). *Actas Latinoamericanas de Varsovia* 24: 11–32.

Knight, Charles L. F., and Michael D. Glascock. 2009. The Terminal Formative to Classic Period Obsidian Assemblage at Palo Errado, Veracruz, Mexico. *Latin American Antiquity* 20(4):507–524.

Krickeberg, Walter. 1933. *Los Totonaca. Contribución a la etnografía histórica de la América Central.* Talleres Gráficos del Museo Nacional de Arqueología, Historia y Etnografía, Secretaría de Educación Pública, Mexico DF.

Ladrón de Guevara, Sara. 2010. *El Tajín. La urbe que representa el orbe.* Sección de obras de historia, Fideicomiso Historia de las Américas, Fondo de Cultura Económica-Colegio de México, Mexico DF.

Lagunes Gushiken, Concepción. 1995. La cerámica arqueológica de Vega de la Peña. *Arqueología* 13–14: 79–84.

León Pérez, Ignacio. 1995. *Remojadas, una regionalidad cultural.* Instituto Veracruzano de la Cultura e Instituto Nacional de Antropología e Historia, Veracruz.

Lira López, Yamile. 2004. Presencia Teotihuacana en el Valle de Maltrata, Veracruz. In *La costa del Golfo en tiempos teotihuacanos: propuestas y perspectivas. Memoria de la segunda mesa redonda de Teotihuacan*, edited by María Elena Ruiz Gallut and Arturo Pascual Soto, pp. 5–22. Instituto Nacional de Antropología e Historia, Mexico DF.

Lira López, Yamile. 2010. *Tradición y cambio en las culturas Prehispánicas del Valle de Maltrata, Veracruz.* Universidad Veracruzana, Instituto de Antropología/Universidad Nacional Autónoma de México, and S y G Editores, Mexico DF.

Marcus, Joyce. 1998. The Peaks and Valley of Ancient States: An Extension of the Dynamic Model. In *Archaic States*, edited by Gary Feinman and Joyce Marcus, pp. 59–94. University of New Mexico Press, Santa Fe.

MacNeish, Richard S. 1954. *An Early Archaeological Site near Pánuco, Veracruz.* Transactions 44 (5), American Philosophical Society, Philadelphia.

MacNeish, Richard S. 1958. *Preliminary Archaeological Investigations in the Sierra de Tamaulipas, Mexico.* Transactions 48 (6), American Philosophical Society, Philadelphia.

Medellín Zenil, Alfonso. 1955. *Exploraciones en la Isla de Sacrificios. Informe.* Gobierno del Estado de Veracruz, Dirección General de Educación, Departamento de Antropología, Mexico DF.

Medellín Zenil, Alfonso. 1960. *Cerámicas del Totonacapan. Exploraciones arqueológicas en el Centro de Veracruz.* Instituto de Antropología, Universidad Veracruzana, Xalapa.

Mejía Pérez-Campos, Elizabeth. 2009. Interpretación preliminar respecto a la temporalidad de Toluquilla, Querétaro. In *Quinto Coloquio Pedro Bosch Gimpera. Cronología y periodización de Mesoamérica y el Norte de México*, edited by Annick Daneels, pp. 209–231. Instituto de Investigaciones Antropológicas, Universidad Nacional Autónoma de México, Mexico DF.

Merino Carrión, B. Leonor, and Ángel García Cook. 1987. Proyecto Arqueológico Huasteca. *Arqueología* 1:31–88.

Merino Carrión, B. Leonor, and Ángel García Cook. 1997. Los enterramientos del Formativo en el noroeste de México. In *Homenaje al Profesor César A. Sáenz*, edited by Ángel García Cook, Alba González Jácome, Leonor Merino and Sonia Rivero Torres, pp. 319–366. Instituto Nacional de Antropología e Historia, Mexico DF.

Michelet, Dominique. 1996. *Río Verde, San Luís Potosí.* Instituto de la Cultura de San Luís Potosí, Lascasiana S.A. de C.V., Centre d´Etudes Mésoaméricaines et Centraméricaines, Mexico DF.

Miranda Flores, Fernando A., and Annick Daneels. 1998. Regionalismo cultural en el valle del río Atoyac. In *Contribuciones a la historia prehispánica de la región Orizaba-Córdoba*, edited by Carlos Serrano Sánchez, pp. 53–72. Cuadernos de divulgación 2, UNAM Instituto de Investigaciones Antropológicas, and H. Ayuntamiento de Orizaba, Mexico DF.

Muñoz Espinoza, María Teresa. 2007. *Cultura e historia de la Sierra Gorda de Querétaro: presente y pasado.* CONACYT and Plaza y Valdés, Mexico DF.

Ochoa Salas, Lorenzo. 2001. *Historia antigua de México, Volume III: El horizonte Postclásico*, edited by Linda Manzanilla and Leonardo López Luján, pp. 13–56. 2nd edition. CONACULTA/INAH, UNAM-Coordinación de Humanidades/Instituto de Investigaciones Antropológicas, Grupo Editorial Miguel Ángel Porrúa, Mexico DF.

Ortiz Ceballos, Ponciano. 1975. La cerámica de Los Tuxtlas. Tesis de Maestría. Facultad de Antropología de la Universidad Veracruzana, Xalapa.

Parsons, Lee A. 1978. The Peripheral Coastal Lowlands and the Middle Classic Period. In *Middle Classic Mesoamerica, AD 400-700*, edited by Esther Pazstory, pp. 25–34. Columbia University Press, New York.

Pascual Soto, Arturo. 2006. *El Tajín: en busca de los orígenes de una civilización.* Instituto de Investigaciones Estéticas de la Universidad Nacional Autónoma de México and Instituto Nacional de Antropología e Historia, Mexico DF.

Pascual Soto, Arturo. 2009. *El Tajín. Arte y poder.* Instituto Nacional de Antropología e Historia—Consejo Nacional para la Cultura y las Artes, and Instituto de Investigaciones Estéticas de la Universidad Nacional Autónoma de México, Mexico DF.

Pastrana, Alejandro. 1994. Estrategia militar de la Triple Alianza y el control de la obsidiana: el caso de Izteyocan. *Trace* 25:74–80.

Piña Chán, Román, ed. 1976. *Los señoríos y estados militaristas.* Instituto Nacional de Antropología e Historia, Mexico DF.

Pool, Christopher A. 1995. Cerámica del Clásico Tardío y el Postclásico en la sierra de los Tuxtlas. *Arqueología* 13–14: 35–48.

Pool, Christopher A. ed. 2003. *Settlement Archaeology and Political Economy at Tres Zapotes, Veracruz, Mexico.* Monograph 50, Cotsen Institute of Archaeology, University of California, Los Angeles.

Pool, Christopher A. 2006. Current Research on the Gulf Coast of Mexico. *Journal of Archaeological Research* 14:189–241.

Pool, Christopher A. 2008. Architectural Plans, Factionalism, and the Proto-Classic-Classic Transition at Tres Zapotes. In *Classic-Period Cultural Currents in Southern and Central Veracruz*, edited by Philip J. Arnold III and Christopher A. Pool, pp. 121–157. Dumbarton Oaks Research Library and Collections, Precolumbian Studies, Harvard University Press. Washington, DC.

Pool, Christopher A. and Georgia Mud Britt. 2000. A Ceramic Perspective on the Formative to Classic Transition in Southern Veracruz, Mexico. *Latin American Antiquity* 11(2):139–161.

Renfrew, Colin, and John F. Cherry, eds. 1986. *Peer Polity Interaction and Socio-Political Change*. Cambridge University Press, New York.

Rodríguez, María del Carmen and Ponciano Ortiz Ceballos, 1997. Olmec Ritual and Sacred Geography at Manatí. In *Olmec to Aztec. Settlement Patterns in the Ancient Gulf Lowlands*, edited by Barbara L. Stark and Philip J. Arnold III, pp. 68–95. University of Arizona Press, Tucson.

Ruiz Gallut, María Elena, and Arturo Pascual Soto, eds. 2004. *La costa del Golfo en tiempos teotihuacanos: propuestas y perspectivas. Memoria de la segunda mesa redonda de Teotihuacan*. Instituto Nacional de Antropología e Historia, Mexico DF.

Ruiz Gordillo, Omar. 1989. *Oceloapan: Apuntes para la historia de un sitio arqueológico en Veracruz*. Cuadernos de Trabajo, Instituto Nacional de Antropología e Historia, Mexico DF.

Ruiz Gordillo, Omar. 1999. *Paxil: La conservación en una zona arqueológica en la región de Misantla, Veracruz*. Colección Textos Básicos y Manuales, Serie Conservación, Instituto Nacional de Antropología e Historia, Mexico DF.

Sanders, William T. 1953. The Anthropogeography of Central Veracruz. *Revista Mexicana de Estudios Antropológicos* XIII:27–78.

Sanders, William T. 1971. Cultural Ecology and Settlement Patterns of the Gulf Coast. In *Archaeology of Northern Mesoamerica*, edited by Gordon F. Ekholm and Ignacio Bernal, pp. 543–557. Handbook of Middle American Indians Volume 11, Part 2, University of Texas Press, Austin.

Sanders, William T. 1978. *The Lowland Huasteca Archaeological Survey and Excavation, 1957 Field Season*. Monographs in Anthropology, University of Missouri,Columbia.

Santley, Robert S. 2007. *The Prehistory of the Tuxtlas*. University of New Mexico Press, Albuquerque.

Santley, Robert S., and Philip J. Arnold III. 1996. Prehispanic Settlement Patterns in the Tuxtlas Mountains, Southern Veracruz, Mexico. *Journal of Field Archaeology* 23(2):225–249.

Santley, Robert S., and Roberto Lunagómez Reyes. 1991. Informe final de campo: proyecto "Reconocimiento arqueológico de los Tuxtlas"; Temporada 1991. Archivo Técnico de la Coordinación Nacional de Arqueología. Instituto Nacional de Antropología e Historia, Mexico DF.

Skoglund, Thanet, Barbara L. Stark, Hector Neff, and Michael D. Glascock. 2006. Compositional and Stylistic Analysis of Aztec Era Ceramics: Provincial Strategies at the Edge of Empire, South-central Veracruz, Mexico. *Latin American Antiquity* 17(4):451–559.

Solís, Felipe. 1981. *El catálogo de las esculturas en Castillo de Teayo, Veracruz*. UNAM, Mexico DF.

Stark, Barbara L. 1977. *Prehistoric Ecology at Patarata 52, Veracruz, Mexico: Adaptation to the Mangrove Swamp*. Publications in Anthropology No. 18, Vanderbilt University, Nashville.

Stark, Barbara L. 1989. *Patarata Pottery. Classic Period Ceramics of the South-Central Coast, Veracruz, Mexico*. Anthropological Papers No. 51, University of Arizona Press, Tucson.

Stark, Barbara L. 1999. Formal Architectural Complexes in South-Central Veracruz, Mexico: A Capital Zone? *Journal of Field Archaeology* 26(2):197–225.

Stark, Barbara L., ed. 2001. *Classic Period Mixtequilla, Veracruz, Mexico. Diachronic Inferences from Residential Investigations*. Monograph 12, Institute for Mesoamerican Studies. University at Albany, New York.

Stark, Barbara L. 2003. Cerro de las Mesas: Social and Economic Perspectives on a Gulf
     Center. In *El Urbanismo en Mesoamerica/Urbanism in Mesoamerica*, Vol. 1, edited
     by Guadalupe Mastache and William T. Sanders, pp. 391–422. Instituto Nacional de
     Antropología e Historia and Pennsylvania State University, University Park.

Stark, Barbara L. 2007. Out of Olmec. In *The Political Economy of Ancient Mesoamerica:
     Transformations during the Formative and Classic Periods*, edited by Vernon
     L. Scarborough and John E. Clark, pp. 47–63. University of New Mexico Press,
     Albuquerque.

Stark, Barbara L. 2008. Polity and Economy in the Western Lower Papaloapan Basin. In
     Classic-Period Cultural Currents in Southern and Central Veracruz, edited by Philip J.
     Arnold III and Christopher A. Pool, pp. 86–119. Dumbarton Oaks Research Library and
     Collections, Precolumbian Studies, Harvard University Press, Washington, DC.

Stark, Barbara L., and Philip J. Arnold III, eds. 1997. *Olmec to Aztec Settlement Patterns in the
     Ancient Gulf Lowlands*. University of Arizona Press, Tucson.

Stark, Barbara L., and John Chance. 2008. Diachronic and Multidisciplinary Perspectives
     on Mesoamerican Ethnicity. In *Ethnic Identity in Nahua Mesoamerica: The View from
     Archaeology, Art History, Ethnohistory, and Contemporaneous Ethnography*, edited by
     Frances F. Berdan, John K. Chance, Alan Sandstrom, Barbara L.
     Stark, James Taggart, and Emily Umberger, pp. 1–37. University of Utah Press, Salt Lake
     City.

Stark, Barbara L., and L. Antonio Curet. 1994. The Development of Classic-Period
     Mixtequilla in South Central Veracruz, Mexico. *Ancient Mesoamerica* 5 (2):
     267–287.

Stark, Barbara L., and Kevin Johns. 2004. Veracruz sur-central en tiempos teotihuacanos. In
     *La Costa del Golfo en tiempos Teotihuacanos: Propuestas y perspectivas, memoria de la
     segunda mesa redonda de Teotihuacan*, edited by María Elena Ruiz Gallut and Arturo
     Pascual Soto, pp. 307–328. Instituto Nacional de Antropología e Historia, Mexico DF.

Stoner, Wesley D. 2011. Disjuncture among Classic Period Cultural Landscapes in the Tuxtla
     Mountains, Southern Veracruz, Mexico. Unpublished PhD dissertation, University of
     Kentucky, Lexington.

Strebel, Hermann. 1885. *Alt-Mexiko. Archäologische Beiträge zur Kulturgeschichte seiner
     Bewohner.* Leopold Voss Verlag, Hamburg-Leipzig.

Stresser Péan, Guy.1977. *San Antonio Nogalar.* Centre d'Etudes Mésoméricaines et
     Centreaméricaines, Mexico DF.

Stresser Péan, Guy. 1998. *Los Lienzos de Acaxochitlán (Hidalgo). Su importancia en la historia
     del poblamiento de la Sierra Norte de Puebla y zonas vecinas.* Gobierno del Estado de
     Hidalgo, Instituto Hidalguense de Educación Media Superior y Superior, Consejo
     Estatal para la Cultura y las Artes de Hidalgo, Centre d'Etudes Mésoméricaines et
     Centreaméricaines, Mexico DF.

Symonds, Stacey, Ann Cyphers, and Roberto Lunagómez. 2002. *Asentamiento Prehispánico
     en San Lorenzo Tenochtitlan.* Serie San Lorenzo, edited by Ann Cyphers, volume
     2. Instituto de Investigaciones Antropológicas y Dirección General de Asuntos del
     Personal Académico, Universidad Nacional Autónoma de México, Mexico DF.

Torquemada, Fray Juan de. 1975 [1615]. *De los veynte y un libros rituales y Monarquía Yndiana,
     con el origen y guerras de los Yndios Occidentales, De sus Poblazones, descubrimiento,
     conquista, conversión y otras cosas maravillosas de la mesma tierra, distribuydo en tres
     tomos.* Tercera edición, Instituto de Investigaciones Históricas, Universidad Nacional
     Autónoma de México, Mexico DF.

Torres Guzmán, Manuel. 2004. Los entierros múltiples en la zona arqueológica de El Zapotal, Veracruz. In *Prácticas funerarias en la Costa del Golfo de México*, edited by Yamile Lira López and Carlos Serrano Sánchez, pp. 203–212. Instituto de Antropología de la Universidad Veracruzana, Instituto de Investigaciones Antropológicas de la Universidad Nacional Autónoma de México, Asociación Mexicana de Antropología Biológica, Mexico DF.

Urcid, Javier, and Thomas W. Killion. 2008. Social Landscapes and Political Dynamics in the Southern Gulf-Coast Lowlands (AD 500-1000). In *Classic-Period Cultural Currents in Southern and Central Veracruz*, edited by Philip J. Arnold III and Christopher A. Pool, pp. 259–291. Dumbarton Oaks Research Library and Collections, Precolumbian Studies, Harvard University Press, Washington, DC.

Valenzuela, Juan. 1945. Las exploraciones efectuadas en los Tuxtlas, Veracruz. *Anales del Museo Nacional de Arqueología, Historia y Etnografía* Tomo III:83–108.

Vásquez Zárate, Sergio. 1997. Investigaciones arqueológicas en Zacate Colorado y Corallillos, Ver. In *Memoria del V Foro Anual "Docencia, Investigación, Extensión y Difusión de la Facultad de Antropología,"* edited by Sergio Vásquez Zárate, pp. 25–29. Fondo para el Fomento de las Actividades de la Universidad Veracruzana, Xalapa.

Venter, Marcie L. 2008. Community Strategies in the Aztec Imperial Frontier: Perspectives from Totogal, Veracruz, Mexico. PhD dissertation, University of Kentucky, Lexington.

Webster, David, and William T. Sanders. 2001. La antigua ciudad mesoamericana. Teoría y concepto. In *Reconstruyendo la ciudad maya: el urbanismo en las sociedades antiguas*, edited by Andrés Ciudad Ruiz, María Josefa Ponce de León, and María del Carmen Martínez Martínez, pp. 43–64. Sociedad Española de Estudios Mayas, Publicación No. 6, Madrid.

Wilkerson, S. Jeffrey K. 1972. Ethnogenesis of the Huastecs and Totonacs. Early Cultures of North-Central Veracruz at Santa Luisa, Mexico. PhD dissertation, Tulane University, New Orleans.

Wilkerson S. Jeffrey K. 1981. The Northern Olmec and Pre-Olmec Frontier on the Gulf Coast, *The Olmec and Their Neighbors. Essays in Memory of Matthew W. Stirling*, edited by Elisabeth P. Benson, pp. 181–194. Dumbarton Oaks Research Library and Collections, Washington, DC.

Wilkerson, S. Jeffrey K. 1994. The Garden City of El Pital: The Genesis of Classic Civilization in Eastern Mesoamerica. *National Geographic Research and Exploration* 10(1):56–71.

Zaragoza Ocaña, Diana. 2003. *Tamohi: su pintura mural*. Serie Museo de la Cultura Huasteca. Gobierno del Estado de Tamaulipas, Secretaría de Educación, Cultura y Deporte, Instituto Tamaulipeco para la Cultura y las Artes, Gobierno Municipal, CONACULTA/ Instituto Nacional de Antropología e Historia, Mexico DF.

Zaragoza Ocaña, Diana. 2009. La Huasteca, una propuesta de definición: siglos XV y XVI. In *Memoria del Taller Arqueología de la Huasteca*, edited by Diana Zaragoza, pp. 219–236. Colección Científica, Serie Arqueología, no. 541, Instituto Nacional de Antropología e Historia, Mexico DF.

Zaragoza Ocaña, Diana, ed. 2009. *Memoria del taller arqueología de la Huasteca. Homenaje a Leonor Merino Carrión*. Colección Científica, Serie Arqueología, no. 541, Instituto Nacional de Antropología e Historia, Mexico DF.

CHAPTER 26

TULA AND THE TOLTECS

DAN M. HEALAN AND ROBERT H. COBEAN

TULA, Hidalgo, was one of several sites that rose to prominence during the Epiclassic period (Figure 26.1) after the demise of Teotihuacan, and during the Early Postclassic period was probably the largest and most influential center in central Mexico. For over a century various scholars have argued that Tula was the legendary *Tollan* ("place of reeds"), which, according to Aztec and other indigenous sources, was the capital of the Toltec civilization that dominated central Mexico prior to the arrival of the Aztecs (Jimenez Moreno 1941). For this reason the site, its inhabitants, and its material culture are often referred to as Toltec, although there is evidence that "Tollan" and "Toltec" are pan-Mesoamerican concepts whose origins may go back at least as far as Teotihuacan, if not earlier (Stuart 2000).

Tula is located around 80 kilometers northwest of modern Mexico City on the edge of a large alluvial plain (Figure 26.2). Although earliest explorations date from the nineteenth century, the first systematic excavations of Tula were conducted by Acosta (1956–1957) beginning in 1940, who restored many of the buildings in Tula's principal monumental precinct known as "Tula Grande" (Figure 26.3). Acosta's twenty-year program of investigation was followed by other projects that explored the larger city and its hinterland.

EARLY HISTORY

Intensive regional surveys (Mastache et al. 2002) indicate that the first substantial occupation of the region occurred during the Classic-period Chingú

	AD	
	1600	TESORO
LATE POSTCLASSIC	1500	
	1400	PALACIO
MIDDLE POSTCLASSIC	1300	FUEGO
	1200	
EARLY POSTCLASSIC	1100	LATE TOLLAN
	1000	EARLY TOLLAN
	900	TERMINAL CORRAL
EPICLASSIC	800	CORRAL
	700	PRADO
	600	LAMESA

Figure 26.1 Ceramic chronology for Tula and the Tula region (Source: Cobean 1990; Mastache et al. 2002).

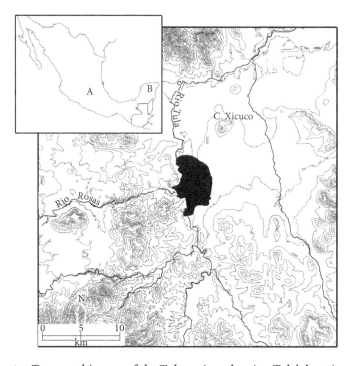

Figure 26.2 Topographic map of the Tula region, showing Tula's location and its approximate limits during its apogee (black).

phase, with numerous settlements associated with pottery from Teotihuacan's Tlamimilolpa, Xolalpan, and Metepec phases. These include several large, nucleated sites, the largest of which (Chingú) covers more than 2.5 square kilometers and appears to be a regional center that mimics Teotihuacan in its layout and principal structures. Chingú phase settlements appear to represent the outright colonization of the region by Teotihuacan, possibly for exploitation of its lime and agricultural resources. There is no evidence that Tula itself was occupied at this time.

Tula was settled during the Epiclassic period as one of a number of sites in the region associated with Coyotlatelco red on brown ceramics, including at least ten nucleated hilltop sites situated along the periphery of the alluvial plain. These settlements constitute an intrusive complex whose earliest components may overlap with the Chingú phase settlements. Coyotlatelco ceramics are also characteristic of Epiclassic sites in the neighboring Basin of Mexico, and there is ongoing debate regarding where, when, and how this complex originated. Some trace Coyotlatelco to ceramic traditions to the north and west, as far away as the Chalchihuites region of Zacatecas and Jalisco or as near as the Bajío region of southern Guanajuato and Queretaro, while others favor a local origin. There appears to be an emerging middle ground (e.g., Manzanilla 2005; Solar Valverde 2006) that sees Coyotlatelco as a fusion of the preexisting Teotihuacan ceramic tradition with a nonlocal tradition possibly introduced by migrating populations, although more indirect forms of interaction could also have been responsible. As many of these authors note, the Bajío seems the most likely region of origin, given its proximity and a vibrant red on buff tradition that goes back to Late Formative (Chupícuaro) times. Moreover, Coyotlatelco site lithic assemblages are commonly dominated by obsidian from the Ucareo obsidian source in the eastern Bajío. The proximity of the Bajío, particularly to the Tula region, would facilitate regular interaction with minimal movement by populations who were probably familiar with the region.

Tula seemingly arose as the center of a regional state that consolidated various Coyotlatelco polities and perhaps the remnants of the Chingú phase settlement system. The earliest (Prado/Corral phase) settlement at Tula was centered around a monumental precinct known as "Tula Chico," whose similar layout suggests it was the prototype for Tula Grande, some 1.5 kilometers to the south (Figure 26.3). At this time Tula is estimated as being between 3 and 6 square kilometers in size.

Around the end of the Epiclassic period Tula witnessed the burning and abandonment of Tula Chico, followed by the construction of Tula Grande and urban growth that reached its apogee in the Early Postclassic Tollan phase. That Tula Chico remained in ruins even after it was surrounded by the Tollan phase city, somewhat like the Acropolis in modern Athens, is one of the most enigmatic aspects of Tula's history.

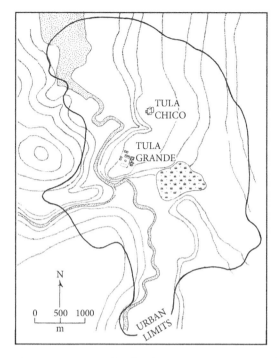

Figure 26.3 Planimetric map of Tula, showing its monumental precincts.

TULA GRANDE AND THE TOLLAN
PHASE CITY

Acosta's extensive excavations at Tula Grande (Figure 26.4) produced many architectural and sculptural examples (Jimenez Garcia 1998) commonly referred to as
"Toltec." Distinctive elements include the use of columns inside buildings and in
colonnades. Examples of the former include three prominent buildings (Buildings
1, 3, 4; see Figure 26.4) containing two or more grand rooms or halls supported
by columns that were initially interpreted as palaces, although at least Buildings
1 and 3 appear to have been designed for more public functions. Other forms
include anthropomorphic and zoomorphic columns, including the 4.6-meter-
tall "Atlantean" warrior figures atop Pyramid B: these figures are among the
best-known prehispanic sculptures in Mesoamerica. Other well-known sculptures
include *chacmool* figures and bas relief carvings that include "warrior columns"
and processional scenes of human, animal, and supernatural subjects. Yet another
distinctive form includes panels of elaborately attired individuals in a reclining or
supine pose that apparently lined the atria of several columned halls. One complete
and one partial panel of essentially identical reclining personages were encountered in recent excavations at Tula Chico (Mastache et al. 2009).

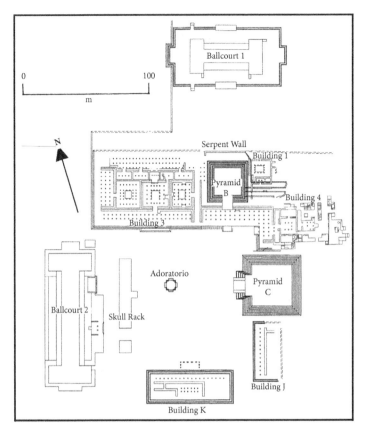

Figure 26.4 Plan of Tula Grande, Tula's principal monumental precinct.

Tula Grande also contains two large pyramids and several smaller platformed structures, ballcourts, and a skull rack (*tzompantli*). With one possible exception,[1] no palaces have been clearly identified at Tula Grande, although probable elite residences were excavated by Acosta and Charnay in the surrounding area.

Surface surveys indicate Tollan-phase Tula covered an area of about 16 square kilometers, encompassing a remarkably diverse landscape of hills, plains, alluvial valleys, and brackish marsh (Figure 26.3), with a population estimated at around 60,000. Residential structures were encountered in excavation in at least twenty-two different localities within the ancient city (Healan n.d., 2009; Paredes Gudiño 1990), most of which appear to be multifamily compounds. Two areas of the city contained neighborhoods whose households engaged in the specialized production of ceramics and obsidian core/blade artifacts, respectively (Healan n.d.). Evidence of other possible household craft activities include the manufacture of ceramic

---

[1] Baez Urincho (2007) and Cobean believe that the recently excavated Building 4 (Figure 26.4) was a royal palace.

Figure 26.5 Distribution of Tollan phase sites in the Tula region (after
Mastache et al. 2002).

figurines, travertine (*tecali*) vessels, and cloth. It does not appear, however, that
craft production was a major source of wealth for the city.

The Tollan phase witnessed an equally dramatic growth of settlements in
the surrounding region, extending into peripheral areas with little or no previous occupation. A multitiered settlement hierarchy is evident, with the largest
rural sites situated along the periphery of the region while smaller sites occupy
the interior (Figure 26.5). Tula's immediate hinterland population is estimated at
between 30,000 and 50,000 (Mastache et al. 2002). Site surveys and excavation
show the rural population generally enjoyed access to the same ceramic production and marketing systems as the city did (Bey 1986; Cobean and Mastache 1999).
This is also true for obsidian, with both rural and urban lithic assemblages showing a predominance of prismatic blades and green (Pachuca) obsidian. Cultivated
food remains from rural households include maize, amaranth, and maguey, whose
sugary sap is today consumed fresh or fermented (*pulque*), and its roasted leaf
and trunk are eaten as well. Several authors have suggested that the production
of maguey sap was a major activity in Tula's hinterland, based in part upon rather
high proportions of Blanco Levantado, a distinctive olla, in essence a "New World
amphora," that may have been used to store, transport, and perhaps collect and
serve it (Bey 2007). Blanco Levantado production loci were encountered at several
hinterland sites.

The importance of maize, amaranth, and maguey in Tula's subsistence base supports recent arguments that the expansion of Mesoamerican civilization into the dry highland regions of northern central Mexico was made possible by "the integration of seed-based cultivation and specialized maguey production" (Parsons and Darling 2000: 82). Critical aspects of this strategy include not only the high caloric and nutritional levels of maguey sap and flesh but also the adaptability of maguey cultivation to marginal soils and climates and its year-round availability, which makes it a near-perfect complement to seed-based cultivation.

Tula's hinterland almost certainly extended beyond the 17-kilometer radius covered in the intensive regional survey. A buildup of settlement associated with Tollan-phase ceramics in the north and north-central portions of the neighboring Basin of Mexico is believed to reflect their incorporation into Tula's hinterland (Parsons 2008), and Tollan-phase ceramics are an integral component of Cerro Portezuelo farther to the south (Crider n.d.). Ceramic evidence suggests that Tula's hinterland extended for about 125-150 kilometers in a north-south direction, with Tula near the middle, while its east-west extent, which probably included the Pachuca obsidian source area to the east and Jilotepec to the west, is estimated at about 135 kilometers.

Despite Aztec accounts that Tollan controlled a large empire purported to cover much of western Mesoamerica, there is little supporting archaeological evidence for this. There is, however, evidence that Tula's hegemony extended well beyond its hinterland to the north and west. This includes three sites around the modern city of Queretaro, 135 kilometers to the northwest, that contain Tula-like ceramics and other features, including portions of a *chacmool* and an Atlantean-style "colossal" sculpture. Still farther to the north are several sites in northern Guanajuato and southern San Luis Potosí, as much as 250 kilometers away, whose ceramic assemblages likewise contain substantial proportions of Tollan-phase types. The extension of settlements with a strong Tula affiliation across the eastern Bajío and into the arid interior of north-central Mexico as far as San Luis Potosí recalls earlier arguments (Armillas 1969) of a "northern-oriented Toltec state," and in fact, colonnades, columned halls, and skull racks occur at several sites in northern Mexico that appear to be at least as old as Tula (Hers 1989).

There is also evidence that Tula interacted regularly with eastern and southern Mesoamerica, most notably the ubiquity of Tohil plumbate from Soconusco, comprising nearly 2 percent of identifiable Tollan-phase pottery from surface surveys at Tula (Healan 1989). In turn, the abundant "Mexican" elements in Central America attributed to Pipil migrations from central Mexico during the Early Postclassic period include ceramics, sculpture, and architecture with close ties to those of Tula (Fowler 1989, 2001).

Clearly the most striking evidence of interaction involves Tula and Chichén Itzá in northern Yucatán, whose countless detailed correspondences in architecture, sculpture, and iconography argue strongly for a common origin. Ethnohistorical accounts of invasion, conquest, and colonization of Chichén Itzá by Tollan were initially assumed to explain these similarities but have since been rejected by many if not most scholars on several grounds, including the distance between the two sites (ca. 1,100 kilometers), which strains the credibility of a military campaign. Other evidence of interaction between the two sites include an overwhelming predominance of obsidian from the same two principal central Mexican sources (Ucareo and Pachuca) at both sites (Healan 2007) and the recent discovery of what appear to be local imitations of Tula-style domestic pottery at Chichén Itzá (Sylviane Boucher, personal communication, 1994). It seems likely that the two functioned as peer polities that shared many aspects of their respective political, ideological, and symbolic systems, but how and why this occurred between two sites so widely separated geographically remains one of the most challenging interpretive problems in Mesoamerican archaeology (Kowalski and Kristan-Graham 2007).

Tula during the Aztec Period

The succeeding Fuego phase is marked by apparent depopulation and, in some cases, destruction of the Tollan-phase city. This includes the reoccupation and subsequent burning of several structures at Tula Grande that is associated with Aztec II ceramics, which are rather scarce in other parts of the city and hinterlands. A similar paucity of Aztec II settlements in the northern Basin of Mexico is presumed to reflect depopulation following Tula's demise (Parsons and Gorenflo n.d.). The ca. 1150–1200 AD dating of the end of the Tollan phase, based initially on the dating of Aztec II ceramics in the Basin of Mexico, is supported by some forty-seven published radiocarbon dates from Tollan-phase contexts, whose two-sigma ranges consistently fall short of or do not extend significantly beyond 1150 AD (Healan n.d.; Paredes Gudiño 2005).

There seems to be little doubt that Tula Grande was destroyed and that this occurred at the hands of Fuego-phase peoples whose ceramics bracket the destruction horizon. While it may seem logical to assume that this destruction was part of a conquest of the larger city, there is no reason to assume that the end of the Tollan phase and the beginning of the Fuego phase were coterminous. Tula Grande could have already been abandoned when Fuego-phase peoples occupied and burned its buildings.

The subsequent Palacio and Tesoro phases are local manifestations of the Aztec III and IV ceramic complexes of the Basin of Mexico, a time of considerable population expansion that reached its climax in the era of the Triple Alliance. There likewise appears to have been substantial settlements in Tula's hinterland region at this time, although apparently not as great as in the preceding Tollan phase. At Tula itself, surveys and excavation indicate that the Aztec-period settlements were far less dense than the Tollan-phase settlements and probably not urban in character.

Aztec-period construction at Tula Grande is a collection of insubstantial platforms and other ill-defined structures erected above earlier Tollan-phase structures. There are also numerous intrusive excavations associated with the burial of Aztec objects as well as the apparent exhumation of objects, recalling ethnohistorical accounts of the Aztecs' systematic removal of relics from Tollan's ruins. This agrees with the recent recovery of a *chacmool* at Tenochtitlan that appears to be from Tula, which, along with numerous seemingly deliberate imitations of Tula's architecture and sculpture, may reflect a belief that these objects were imbued with the power of gods who once dwelled in what the Aztecs considered Tollan, as well as an attempt to legitimize their claim to being Tollan's rightful heirs (López Luján and Lopez Austin 2009). This may explain Aztec burials encountered in two other localities at Tula with otherwise little evidence of Aztec occupation, which may have been brought to Tula specifically for interment in its ruins.

CONCLUDING REMARKS

Tula has always been somewhat of an enigma, including its location in the semiarid northern reaches of central Mexico, and until relatively recently virtually all archaeological knowledge of Tula came from Acosta's twenty years of investigation at Tula Grande that, for better or worse, came to embody the entire site. One of the most significant discoveries in the post-Acosta era was Tula's large size and its dense, urban character, which are not obvious given the widespread use of adobe walls and mud-mortared stone in domestic architecture that left few visible remains. Nevertheless, Tula's "adobe city" is among the largest and densest Mesoamerican cities. Another major discovery was its large, rather dense hinterland that, along with Tula, appears to reflect a highly successful mode of adaptation involving integrated seed and maguey cultivation, in light of which its location in the semiarid northern reaches of central Mexico is no longer an enigma.

Tula's domination of its hinterland while depending on it for food and other revenue are defining characteristics of *administrative cities* in Fox's (1977) five-part urban typology. Tula Grande is distinctive in containing several buildings with large columned halls that may have been venues for libation, feasting, and other group activities, given the surrounding benches embellished with procession scenes and in situ ollas and stacked ritual and serving vessels and tobacco pipes in Buildings 4 and 3, respectively. Their prominence at Tula Grande may indicate a pattern of group leadership typical of corporate political strategies in which power is shared by different groups or sectors of society (Blanton et al. 1996). That Tula's origins may lie in the consolidation of various regional polities suggests that a corporate power strategy may have been in place from the very beginning.

One of the most striking aspects of the pre-Aztec archaeological record at Tula is the pervasive pattern of continuity that is particularly evident in its ceramic sequence. Even the destruction of Tula Chico occurs within an uninterrupted succession of waxing and waning ceramic types, suggesting that wholly internal processes, perhaps of a nonbellicose nature, were involved. Continuity is also seen in other aspects of Tula's material culture, including the sculpture recently unearthed at Tula Chico, which indicates at least some elements of Tula Grande's distinctive corpus of "Toltec"-style sculpture go back as far as the Prado/Corral-phase settlement. The events surrounding the end of Tollan-phase Tula and the subsequent Aztec occupation are unclear, as is their timing. Surveys and excavation indicate that the Aztec-period occupation was oddly limited and selective, often interacting with the ruins of the Tollan-phase city rather than supplanting them. In this regard, the archaeological record supports ethnohistorical and other archaeological evidence of an Aztec preoccupation with Tula's ruins and suggests it was almost certainly the place the Aztecs were referring to when they spoke of Tollan.

REFERENCES

Acosta, Jorge R. 1956–1957. Interpretacion de algunos datos obtenidos en Tula relativos a la Epoca Tolteca. *Revista mexicana de estudios antropologicos* 14:75–110.

Armillas, Pedro. 1969. The Arid Frontier of Mexican Civilization. *Transactions of the New York Academy of Sciences*, Series II 31:697–704.

Baez Urincho, Fernando. 2007. El Edificio 4: Palacio del Rey Tolteca. *Arqueologia Mexicana* 15:51–54.

Bey, George J., III. 1986. A Regional Analysis of Toltec Ceramics, Tula, Hidalgo, Mexico. PhD dissertation, Tulane University.

Bey, George J., III. 2007. Blanco Levantado: A New World Amphora. In *Pottery Economics in Mesoamerica*, edited by Chris A. Pool and George J. Bey, pp. 114–146. University of Arizona Press, Tucson.

Blanton, Robert E., Gary M. Feinman, Stephen A. Kowalewski, and Peter N. Peregrine. 1996. A Dual-Processual Theory for the Evolution of Mesoamerican Civilization. *Current Anthropology* 37:1–14.

Cobean, Robert H. 1990. *La ceramica de Tula, Hidalgo*. Colección Cientifica, Instituto Nacional de Antropologia e Historia, Mexico City.

Cobean, Robert H., and Alba G. Mastache, eds. 1999. *Tepetitlan: A Rural Household in the Toltec Heartland*. University of Pittsburgh, Pittsburgh.

Crider, Destiny. N.d. Shifting Alliances: Epiclassic and Early Postclassic Interactions at Cerro Portezuelo. *Ancient Mesoamerica*.

Fox, Richard G. 1977. *Urban Anthropology*. Prentice-Hall, Englewood Cliffs, New Jersey.

Fowler, William R. 1989. *The Cultural Evolution of Ancient Nahua Civilizations: The Pipil-Nicarao of Central America*. University of Oklahoma Press, Norman.

Fowler, William R. 2001. Cihuatan and Santa Maria (San Salvador, El Salvador). In *Archaeology of Ancient Mexico and Central America: An Encyclopedia*, edited by Susan T. Evans and David L. Webster, pp. 143–145. Garland, New York.

Healan, Dan M., ed. 1989. *Tula of the Toltecs Excavations and Survey*. University of Iowa Press, Iowa City.

Healan, Dan M. 2007. New Perspectives on Tula's Obsidian Industry and Its Relationship to Chichén Itzá. In *Twin Tollans: Chichén Itzá, Tula, and the Epiclassic to Early Postclassic Mesoamerican World*, edited by Jeff K. Kowalski and Cynthia Graham, pp. 429–447. Harvard University Press, Washington, DC.

Healan, Dan M. 2009. Household, Neighborhood, and Urban Structure in an "Adobe City": Tula, Hidalgo, Mexico. In *Domestic Life in Prehispanic Capitals: A Study of Specialization, Hierarchy, and Ethnicity*, edited by Linda Manzanilla and Claude Chapdelaine, pp. 67–88. University of Michigan, Museum of Anthropology, Ann Arbor.

Healan, Dan M. N.d. The Archaeology of Tula, Hidalgo, Mexico. *Journal of Archaeological Research*.

Hers, Marie-Areti. 1989. *Los Toltecas en tierras chichimecas*. Universidad Nacional Autonoma de Mexico, Mexico City.

Jimenez Garcia, Elizabeth. 1998. *Iconografia de Tula: El caso de la escultura*. Instituto Nacional de Antropología e Historia, Mexico City.

Jimenez Moreno, Wigberto. 1941. Tula y los Toltecas segun las Fuentes historicas. *Revista mexicana de estudios antropologicos* 5:79–83.

Kowalski, Jeff K., and Cynthia Kristan-Graham, eds. 2007. *Twin Tollans: Chichen Itza, Tula, and the Epiclassic to Early Postclassic Mesoamerican World*. Dumbarton Oaks, Washington, DC.

López Luján, Leonardo, and Alfredo Lopez Austin. 2009. The Mexica in Tula and Tula in Mexico-Tenochtitlan. In *The Art of Urbanism: How Mesoamerican Kingdoms Represented Themselves in Architecture and Imagery*, edited by William L. Fash and Leonardo López Luján, pp. 384–422. Dumbarton Oaks, Washington, DC.

Manzanilla, Linda, ed. 2005. *Reacomodos Demograficos del Clasico al Postclasico en el Centro de Mexico*. Universidad Nacional Autónoma de México, Mexico City.

Mastache, Alba Guadalupe, Robert H. Cobean, and Dan M. Healan. 2002. *Ancient Tollan: Tula and the Toltec Heartland*. University Press of Colorado, Boulder.

Mastache, Alba Guadalupe, Robert H. Cobean, and Dan M. Healan. 2009. Four Hundred Years of Settlement and Cultural Continuity in Epiclassic and Early Postclassic Tula. In *The Art of Urbanism: How Mesoamerican Kingdoms Represented Themselves in Architecture and Imagery*, edited by William L. Fash and Leonardo López Luján, pp. 290–328. Dumbarton Oaks, Washington, DC.

Paredes Gudiño, Blanca Luz. 1990. *Unidades habitacionales en Tula, Hidalgo*, Colección Cientifica no. 210. Instituto Nacional de Antropologia e Historia, Mexico City.

Paredes Gudiño, Blanca Luz. 2005. Análisis de flujos migratorios y composición multiétnica de la población de Tula, Hgo. In *Reacomodos demográficos del Clásico al Posclasico en el centro de México*, edited by Linda Manzanilla, pp. 203–225. Instituto de Investigaciones Antropológicas, UNAM.

Parsons, Jeffrey R. 2008. *Prehispanic Settlement Patterns in the Northwestern Valley of Mexico, The Zumpango Region*. Memoirs No. 45. Museum of Anthropology, University of Michigan, Ann Arbor.

Parsons, Jeffrey R., and J. Andrew Darling. 2000. Utilization in Mesoamerican Civilization: A Case for Precolumbian "Pastoralism." *Boletín de la Sociedad Botánica de México* 66:81–91.

Parsons, Jeffrey R., and L. Gorenflo. N.d. Why Is Aztec II Black/Orange So Scarce in
    the Zumpango Region? A Regional Perspective from the Basin of Mexico on Tula's
    Collapse and Its Aftermath. Manuscript in possession of author.
Solar Valverde, Laura, ed. 2006. *El fenómeno Coyotlatelco en el centro de México: tiempo,
    espacio y significado*. Instituto Nacional de Antropologia e Historia, Mexico City.
Stuart, David. 2000. The Arrival of Strangers: Teotihuacan and Tollan in Classic Maya
    History. In *Mesoamerica's Classic Heritage: From Teotihuacan to the Aztecs*, edited
    by David Carrasco, Lindsay Jones, and Scott Sessions, pp. 465–514. University Press
    of Colorado, Boulder.

OTHER RECOMMENDED READING

Braniff, Beatriz, and Marie-Areti Hers. 1998. Herencias Chichimecas. *Arqueologia*
    19:55–80.
Charnay, Desire. 1887. *Ancient Cities of the New World*. Chapman and Hall, London.
Cobean, Robert H., and Luis M. Gamboa Cabezas. 2007. Investigaciones recientes en la
    Zona Monumental de Tula (2002–2006). *Arqueologia Mexicana* 15:36–41.
Cobean, Robert H., and Alba Guadalupe Mastache. 2003. Turquoise and Shell Offerings
    in the Palacio Quemado of Tula, Hidalgo, Mexico. In *Colecciones Latinoamericanas/
    Latin American Collections: Essays in Honour of Ted J. J. Leyenaar*, edited by Dorus
    Kop Jansen and Edward K. de Bock, pp. 51–66. Tetl, Leiden.
Davies, Nigel. 1977. *The Toltecs until the Fall of Tula*. University of Oklahoma Press,
    Norman.
Diehl, Richard A. 1983. *Tula: The Toltec Capital of Ancient Mexico*. Thames and Hudson,
    London.
Fournier Garcia, Patricia. 2007. *Los Hñahñu: del Valle del Mezquital: Maguey, Pulque y
    Alfareria*. Instituto Nacional de Antropologia e Historia, Mexico City.
Gamboa Cabezas, Luis M. 2007. El Palacio Quemado, Tula: Seis decadas de
    investigaciones. *Arqueología Mexicana* 15:42–47.
Getino, Fernando. 2000. El edificio K de Tula, Hidalgo. Licenciatura thesis, Escuela
    Nacional de Antropologia e Historia.
Healan, Dan M. 1993. Urbanism at Tula from the Perspective of Residential Archaeology.
    In *Prehispanic Domestic Units in Western Mesoamerica*, edited by Robert S. Santley
    and Kenneth G. Hirth, pp. 105–120. CRC Press, Boca Raton, Florida.
Healan, Dan M., ed. 1989. *Tula of the Toltecs: Excavations and Survey*. University of Iowa,
    Iowa City.
Healan, Dan M., and Robert H. Cobean. 2009. La interaccion cultural entre el centro y el
    Occidente de Mexico vista desde la Region de Tula. In *Las sociedades complejas del
    Occidente de Mexico en el mundo Mesoamericano: Homenaje al Dr. Phil C. Weigand*,
    edited by Eduardo Williams, Lorenza Lopez Mestas, and Rodrigo Esparza, pp.
    327–347.
Healan, Dan M., Janet M. Kerley, and George J. Bey III. 1983. Excavation and Preliminary
    Analysis of an Obsidian Workshop in Tula, Hidalgo. *Journal of Field Archaeology*
    10:127–145.
Kirchhoff, Paul, ed. 1976. *Historia tolteca chichimeca*. Instituto Nacional de Antropologia
    e Historia, Mexico City.

Kristan-Graham, Cynthia. 1989. Art, Rulership and the Mesoamerican Body Politic at
     Tula and Chichen Itza. PhD dissertation, University of California, Los Angeles.
Kubler, George. 1961. Chichen-Itza y Tula. *Estudios de Cultura Maya* 1:47–80.
López Aguilar, Fernando, Laura Solar Valverde, and Rodrigo Vilanova de Allende. 1996.
     El Valle del Mezquital: Encrucijadas en la historia de los asentamientos humanos en
     un espacio discontinuo. *Arqueologia* 20:21–40.
López Austin, Alfredo, and Leonardo López Luján. 1999. *Mito y realidad de Zuyua.*
     Fideicomiso Historia de las Americas, Mexico City.
Martinez Landa, Blanca Estela. 2009. La ceramica arqueologia de La Mesa, Hidalgo.
     Licenciatura thesis, Escuela Nacional de Antropologia e Historia.
Matos Moctezuma, Eduardo, ed. 1974. *Proyecto Tula: Primera parte.* Colección Cientifica
     Arqueología no. 33. Instituto Nacional de Antropologia e Historia, Mexico City.
Merino Carrion, Beatriz Leonor, and Angel Garcia Cook, eds. 2005. *La producción
     alfarera en el Mexico antiquo.* Instituto Nacional de Antropologia e Historia, Mexico
     City.
Nicholson, Henry B. 1971. Major Sculpture in Pre-Hispanic Central Mexico. In *The
     Handbook of Middle American Indians*, edited by Robert Wauchope, Gordon F.
     Ekholm, and Ignacio Bernal, vol. 10, pp. 92–134. University of Texas Press, Austin.
Nicholson, Henry B. 2001. *Topilzin Quetzalcoatl: The Once and Future Lord of the Toltecs.*
     University of Colorado Press, Boulder.
Parsons, Jeffrey R. 2008. *Prehispanic Settlement Patterns in the Northwestern Valley of
     Mexico: The Zumpango Region.* Museum of Anthropology, University of Michigan,
     Ann Arbor.
Sanders, William T., Jeffrey R. Parsons, and Robert S. Santley. 1979. *The Basin of Mexico:
     Ecological Processes in the Evolution of a Civilization.* Academic Press, New York.
Schmidt, Peter J. 2006. Nuevos hallazgos en Chichen Itza. *Arqueología Mexicana*
     13:48–57.
Sterpone Canuto, Osvaldo. 2006. Tula-Mazapa entre Coyotlatelco y Tollan. *Cuicuilco.
     Nueva Epoca.* 13:71–96.
Suarez Cortes, Maria Elena, Dan M. Healan, and Robert H. Cobean. 2007. Los origenes
     de la dinastía real de Tula: Excavaciones recientes en Tula Chico. *Arqueología
     Mexicana* 15:48–50.
Taube, Karl. 1994. The Iconography of Toltec Period Chichen Itza. In *Hidden among the
     Hills: Maya Archaeology of the Northwest Yucatan Peninsula*, edited by Hanns J.
     Prem, 212–246. Anton Saurwein, Mockmuhl, Germany.
Yadeun Angulo, Juan. 1975. *El estado y la ciudad: El caso de Tula, Hgo.* Instituto Nacional
     de Antropologia e Historia, Mexico City.

CHAPTER 27

THE LATE CLASSIC TO POSTCLASSIC TRANSITION AMONG THE MAYA OF NORTHERN YUCATÁN

WILLIAM M. RINGLE AND
GEORGE J. BEY III

LATE Classic Maya civilization of northern Yucatán grew from vigorous Formative and Early Classic antecedents (see Chapter 19) to include sites of a size and density every bit as impressive as those of the southern lowlands (Figure 27.1). A recent compendium (Brown and Witschey 2010) registers over 2,400 sites north of the 19th parallel, impressive despite the lack of intensive survey in the central and eastern portions of the peninsula. The region includes such giants as Izamal, estimated at over 50 square kilometers (Burgos Villanueva et al. 2004) and Cobá at 65–70 square kilometers (Folan et al. 1983: 50), as well as several others between 10–30 square kilometers. Where not impacted by modern settlement, household density is also elevated, even in many smaller communities.

The northern end of the Yucatán Peninsula consists of an expansive Pleistocene and Tertiary limestone shelf with very little relief. A precipitation gradient runs from east to northwest, from subhumid to dry, with the area north of Merida barely receiving enough rain for maize cultivation. Soils vary along this same gradient, with those within the state of Yucatán being thin and often rocky. As a consequence,

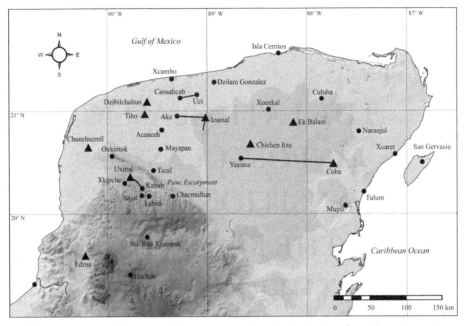

Figure 27.1. Late Classic and Postclassic archaeological sites of northern Yucatán.

intensive agricultural practices such as have been reported for the south were never practicable on the northern plains. Rivers, streams, and lakes are rare, except for the wetlands along the Holbox fracture zone and the lake district around Cobá. Elsewhere, solution features such as *cenotes* allowed access to the water table. Nearer the coastline, wells could be chipped through the bedrock; further inland, wells occasionally perforated the base of deep but dry sinkholes (*rejolladas*).

The northern plains were delimited to the south by a long escarpment running southeast-northwest across the western half of the peninsula. The uplifted area behind this escarpment is known as the Puuc Hills and was home to the Puuc and Chenes subcultures, although the latter also settled in areas to the west of the hill district. Settlers in this area had no access to the aquifer and relied almost completely on artificial water storage devices such as household cisterns (*chultuns*). (In a few favored cases, perched ponds [*aguadas*] could be utilized, although some of these may also be artificial.) Despite this drawback, soils between hills were deeper than on the northern plains, and during the Late-to-Terminal Classic period this region experienced explosive population growth, only to be almost completely abandoned during the Postclassic period. To date, no evidence for intensive practices such as terracing has been reported, however. In contrast, western Campeche around the site of Edzná includes extensive "flats" of deep fertile soils. Extensive hydraulic channelization has been detected around that site (Matheny et al. 1983) but it is unclear the extent to which this was practiced elsewhere. The central and eastern portions of the peninsula remain poorly known.

NORTHERN POLITIES

During the Late Classic period, a series of large centers, among them Chunchucmil, Dzibilchaltún,[1] Izamal, Chichén Itzá, Ek Balam, and Cobá, were spaced at intervals of around 50–60 kilometers. To the southwest, Edzná may have been the major regional center of western Campeche. It is probably wrong to identify polities only with these larger sites, however, because lesser sites were often extensive. Where we have information, there is little to suggest well-defined territorial borders. Rather, centers were probably enmeshed in a shifting set of political alliances, with smaller sites perhaps beholden to multiple overlords.

Settlement patterns in the Puuc Hills differed somewhat. Population rose explosively during the Late Classic period, resulting in a densely packed landscape of small to medium-sized sites, except in the Valle de Santa Elena, where the less rugged topography permitted large sites such as Uxmal, Kabáh, and Nohpát to thrive. The degree of fealty paid to Uxmal by other Puuc sites continues to be a matter of debate: some see Uxmal as the regional capital, others see the Puuc as a landscape of independent city-states (e.g., Dunning and Kowalski 1994). A middle ground argues for indirect hegemonic control, perhaps through tribute and central confirmation of officeholders.

Puuc architecture (Figures 27.2, 27.3) is characterized by the use of fine veneer-over-rubble construction, upper wall zones decorated with colonnettes, and later the use of cut stone-mosaic ornamentation, including "Chak" masks. This style, sometimes referred to as Pure Florescent architecture, widely influenced construction in the northern plains at least as far east as Culubá but, interestingly, never reached Cobá. Chichén Itzá was particularly affected, but it is almost certain that Puuc architecture originated in the hill district because the very plain Early Puuc style is only evident there. The Puuc style in turn was probably influenced by decorative styles to the south, but again the Early Puuc style seems to be of local origin.

Writing came late to Yucatán and was utilized for reasons somewhat different than those of the southern lowlands (Grube 2003). The earliest long count date is 9.2.0.0.0 (475 AD) on Oxkintok Lintel 1, but very few others can be placed in the Early Classic period. Long count dates are rare, with most dates instead being recorded in the short count, which repeats every 256 years (Thompson 1937). Records of births, deaths, accessions, marriages, and wars were seemingly of little interest to northern rulers; only Edzná (Pallán Gayol n.d.), Ek Balam (Lacadena García-Gallo 2004), and probably Cobá (Gronemeyer 2004) have anything resembling a dynastic history, although the stelae of Cobá are in very poor condition. Instead, *tun* and *k'atun* commemorations and building dedications seem to be the favored topics. A continuing debate is the language of the inscriptions; perhaps the most favored position is that texts record a version of Classic Maya (a relative

---

1. One caveat for all of Yucatán concerns the size of settlements destroyed by modern towns and cities. This is especially true for Merida, because ethnohistorical accounts indicate its prehispanic importance, and salvage operations indicate its large size during the Formative period.

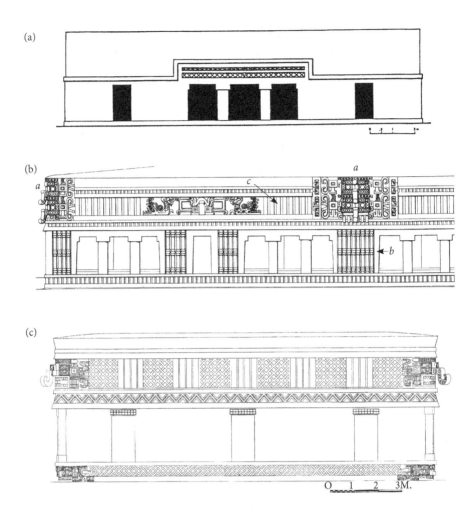

Figure 27.2. Examples of Pure Florescent architecture. (a) The Early Puuc style: Kiuic
Str. N1025E1160 (Andrews 1995: Figure 29); (b) The Mosaic style: Sayil Str. 2B1,
second level (detail of Pollock 1980: Figure 178); (c) The House of the Three Lintels
(7B3), Chichén Itzá (Ruppert 1957: Figure 108).

of Ch' olti'), but with an admixture of Yucatec Maya, almost certainly the spoken
vernacular of the region.

A case can be made that the latter half of the eighth century experienced a set
of changes that were perhaps related. One was the more widespread use of writing.
Texts from several sites record rule by a *kaloomte'*, a supreme title of rulership almost
certainly derived from the southern lowlands. At Ek Balam, the ruling family in fact
claimed that an individual with this title arrived from elsewhere to help found its
dynasty (Lacadena García-Gallo 2004). Another was the reintroduction of the ballgame after centuries of neglect. Puuc architecture also spread to the northern plains
at about this time, as did new forms of civic architecture, such as elongated halls with
multiple doorways placed on large platforms. Overall population swelled dramatically, as did the number of elites, judging from the increase in masonry buildings.

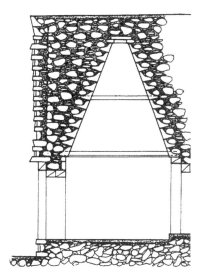

Figure 27.3. Comparative masonry techniques. Left: Early Puuc construction employing slab vaulting, Str. 3C5, Oxkintok (Andrews 1995: Figure 9); Right: Uxmal, east building of the Nunnery: Pure Florescent veneer construction using specialized "boot stones" for vaulting (Andrews 1995: Figure 40).

Production and Exchange

Despite commonalities in other areas, Late Classic ceramic production in the north decisively diverged from the southern lowlands as sites from coast to coast shifted to production of so-called slatewares. The Cehpech ceramic sphere, broadly defined, was dominated by well-made unslipped and monochrome wares, with decoration confined largely to plastic modifications of the surface and occasional painted designs, almost always of a single color and casually applied. Save for imports, the tradition of elaborate, inscribed polychrome beakers was largely absent, the nearest counterpart being the restricted use of Chochola vessels, which are carved rather than painted. This suggests that the commensal drinking of cacao, which was so important to southern elites, was less important or was practiced in other ways in the northern lowlands.

The remarkably wide distribution of slatewares has recently been divided into approximately seven subspheres by Robles Castellanos (2006).[2] (It should be noted that although the ceramics of Chichén Itzá are often assigned to a separate Sotuta sphere, most ceramicists consider them as but a variant of the Cehpech tradition.) Interestingly, most of these subspheres are dominated by a single large center, suggesting a correlation between production, distribution, and political influence. Lithics are generally scarce and of poor quality. Obsidian is also infrequent at most sites except for Chichén Itzá and other sites within the Itzá trade network. Means of production are also obscure. Usable chert deposits have been found in some

2. Robles Castellanos does not include areas south and west of the Puuc in his analysis.

areas, such as the *akalche* zone of the southern Puuc, but little investigation has been carried out with regard to production centers.

Yucatán presumably produced several perishable commodities, such as cotton, wax, honey, and salt. A lively coastal trade linked sites on islands, barrier beaches, and coasts all the way around the peninsula. Probably the best studied of these are Xcambo, located near the edge of the coast estuaries above present-day Motul (Sierra Sosa 1999), and Isla Cerritos, a Terminal Classic–Early Postclassic site thought to be the port of Chichén Itzá (Gallareta Negrón 1998). Xcambo was active until the advent of the Terminal Classic period, and it had clear contacts with Campeche and the Petén, while Isla Cerritos drew on goods from much greater distances, including highland Guatemala, central Mexico, and Veracruz. Isla Cerritos continued functioning well into the Postclassic period.

CHICHÉN ITZÁ

Beginning in the ninth century, if not earlier, the art and architecture of certain cities of northern Yucatán, especially Chichén Itzá and Uxmal, increasingly reflected strong influences from Mesoamerican high cultures west of the Isthmus of Tehuantepec. Such influences are customarily referred to as "Mexican" or "Toltec," though the former is anachronistic and imprecise, while the latter presumes an exclusive historical relationship between Chichén Itzá and the capital of the Toltecs, Tula Xicocotitlan in the modern state of Hidalgo. Although strong resemblances between the two sites are undeniable (Kowalski 2007; Kowalski and Kristan-Graham 2007; Taube 1994), Chichén Itzá also shared traits with Epiclassic sites such as El Tajín, Xochicalco, and Cacaxtla, suggestive of a broader and perhaps earlier "Toltec" sphere (López Austin and López Luján 2000; Ringle, Gallareta Negrón, and Bey 1998). Understanding the motivations behind this new mode of political and religious discourse has engaged scholars for more than a century, but it clearly signaled a more direct engagement with the greater Mesoamerican world, because later sites such as Mayapán and Tulum also display strong ties with non-Maya visual systems. During the Postclassic period, this system is called the Mixteca-Puebla style or, less restrictively, the International Style, and its roots can likely be traced to the earlier Terminal Classic wave of non-Maya symbolism.

Chichén Itzá is located at the center of the northern peninsula of Yucatán, but it seems to have been favored by no particular environmental factors except that, like Ek Balam, it lies in a dense zone of *rejolladas* that have slightly higher soil humidity and are today favored by farmers for specialty crops. (Ethnohistoric documents indicate cacao was cultivated locally.) Chichén Itzá may also have controlled the rich salt beds along the coast to the north and benefited also from the associated coastal trade network through trading ports such as Isla Cerritos (Andrews et al. 1988).

In contrast to most other Maya cities, Chichén Itzá never entirely passed from memory. Fragments of historical events concerning Chichén Itzá are mentioned in native colonial chronicles, and it continued to be venerated as a place of ancestry and pilgrimage from the Postclassic period onward. It was also visited by some of the earliest Spanish observers. Bishop Landa described several features of Chichén Itzá and repeated the story that it had been founded by a great lord from the west named K'uk'ulkan, who after his return to "Mexico" was known as Quetzalcoatl, the famous feathered serpent (Tozzer 1941). Landa relates that he was also responsible for the founding of Mayapán, Cozumel, and Champotón; the latter is a site on the west coast of Campeche.

Three centuries after Landa, the French archaeologist Désiré Charnay identified Tula, Hidalgo, as the home of (Topiltzin) Quetzalcoatl and noted many archaeological similarities between it and Chichén Itzá. The first notable excavation finds came from Edward Thompson's dredging of the Great Cenote in the early years of the twentieth century, a strategy later pursed by Piña Chan (Coggins and Shane 1992; Piña Chan 1970; Proskouriakoff 1974; Ringle and Bey 2009). In 1913, Sylvanus Morley convinced the Carnegie Institution to begin fieldwork at Chichén Itzá, although the beginning of the project was delayed until 1924. From then until the early 1930s, and then sporadically thereafter, the site was mapped, and several major structures were excavated and reported, though no comprehensive overview ever appeared. Shortly after initiation of the Carnegie project, the Mexican government also began large-scale excavation and restoration of the Castillo, the Great Ballcourt, and several smaller structures of the Great Terrace (Maldonado Cárdenas 1997).

Unfortunately, no ceramic analysis of the material recovered by either project was ever conducted until long afterward, by which time the provenience for these objects had been lost for a substantial proportion of the lots (Brainerd 1958; Smith 1971). Thus, the chronology developed for Chichén Itzá depended primarily on ethnohistorical accounts of its founding and abandonment, as well as on stylistic comparisons with Tula and elsewhere. Alfred Tozzer (1957) posited an early ethnically Maya settlement that was supplanted by a Toltec migration from the north. The majority of the Sotuta complex ceramics were assumed to belong to these Toltec migrants and to follow Cehpech ceramics, the sphere shared by most other Terminal Classic sites of northern Yucatán, but very little stratigraphic information could be marshaled in support of this chronology.

This two-stage chronology was reflected in the division of Chichén Itzá into "Old" and "New" sectors. Old Chichén refers to the structures to the south of the Great Terrace built in a variant of the Pure Florescent style, including Las Monjas, La Iglesia, the House of the Deer, and others, as well as outlying groups such as the Temple of the Initial Series and the Temple of the Four Lintels, all of which were presumed to be the result of an earlier, more purely Maya population resident between 800–1000 AD. Virtually all Maya hieroglyphic inscriptions found at Chichén Itzá appear in this area; except for a few outliers, their dates cluster between 860–890 AD (Boot 2005; Grube and Krochock 2007).

(a)   (b)

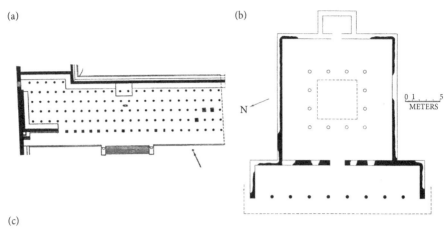

(c)

Figure 27.4. Modified Florescent architecture from Chichén Itzá. (a) Colonnaded hall
2D10 (Ruppert 1957: Figure 17); (b) Gallery-patio structure 3B8 (Ruppert 1957: Figure 22);
(c) Upper Temple of the Jaguars 2D1 (Andrews 1995: Figure 43). Characteristic features
include battered lower wall zone, prowling animal frieze, serpent columns, and
"hombre-pajaro-serpiente" sculptures on balustrades.

New Chichén, presumed to have been built by the Toltec occupiers, refers to
those buildings occupying the Great Terrace, a vast artificial platform supporting some of the most famous structures, such as the Castillo, the Great Ballcourt,
the Temple of the Warriors, and the Group of the Columns, all built in what is
termed the Modified Florescent style (Figure 27.4). Hieroglyphic writing is absent
for the most[3] part with only a few central Mexican–style name glyphs accompanying sculptures. A causeway leads from the Great Terrace north to the Great Cenote,

3. The exceptions are a column of the Osario, whose date may be 995 AD, and a large
stone hat, possibly from the Great Ballcourt. The outlying Modified Florescent structure
5B18 also has hieroglyphic texts.

while the Osario (the High Priest's Grave) and several other smaller temples were built on an extension of the Great Terrace to the south. Together with the nearby Cenote Xtoloc, they form a miniature version of the Castillo and its associated temples. In the traditional view, New Chichén flourished between 1000–1200 AD, according to some chronological reconstructions of the central Mexican chronicles concerning Quetzalcoatl and to the archaeological chronology of Tula itself.

Problems with this neat division were recognized from the beginning, because "Maya" and "Toltec" traits did not segregate neatly. Several structures of "Old" Chichén bear "Toltec" traits, such as the famous Caracol, while "Maya" traits such as "Chak" masks are abundant on "Toltec" buildings of New Chichén. Virtually no evidence demonstrated Sotuta ceramics were stratified over Cehpech deposits (the latter were in any case present in only minor amounts) or that they bore any resemblance to the ceramics of Tula. Thus, by the late 1970s and early 1980s, some degree of overlap between "Toltec" Chichén and the rest of the peninsula was being considered (Lincoln 1986; Andrews and Sabloff 1986).

Today, many argue for the onset of Sotuta ceramics by the beginning of the ninth century, if not earlier. At the other extreme, some contend that monumental construction ceased by ca. 1050 AD, though the site was probably never completely abandoned. The net result is to call into question Chichén Itzá's derivation from Tollan-phase Tula (900–1200 AD), although excavations at the latter are also moving its Toltec occupation back in time. No broad changes in ethnicity have been identified, though small groups of foreigners may well have played significant roles in the city.

In recent years, a long-term project directed by Peter Schmidt (2007) has provided much new information on the Temple of the Big Tables and the Osario Group in New Chichén and on the Group of the Initial Series, a southern outlier of Old Chichén. Work at the Group of the Initial Series has charted the transformation of a typical elite residential complex, whose origins apparently predate Sotuta ceramics, through Pure Florescent and Modified Florescent additions and renovations, all within the Sotuta phase. In association with this project, Rafael Cobos Palma (2003) resurveyed the area covered by the Carnegie map, and he greatly extended coverage to the northwest and east as part of a study of the sacbe system of Chichén Itzá. New excavations of the Great Terrace, directed by Cobos Palma, promise to finally resolve many of the ambiguities surrounding the relative construction sequence of the Pure and Modified Florescent structures on it.

Architecture

The basic techniques of Pure Florescent construction at Chichén Itzá are shared with and almost certainly derived from the Puuc centers of northwest Yucatán, including the use of fine stone veneer over a concrete-and-rubble core, wedge- or boot-shaped vault stones, mosaic decoration, and mosaic façade masks (Andrews 1995; Ruppert 1952). Distinguishing features of Modified Florescent architecture include the use of beam-and-mortar roofs supported by extensive colonnades, serpent columns, sloping (battered) lower wall zones, chacmool and atlantean statues, and decorative motifs such as friezes of felines or canids. Within the Maya area, certain building forms are unique to Chichén Itzá, such as gallery-patio structures[4] and serpent-column temples, while others, such as ballcourts, have traits distinguishing them from non-Itzá counterparts. With regard to the latter, Chichén Itzá has both the largest and most numerous collection of ballcourts (ten) in northern Yucatán. Indeed, the Great Ballcourt is the largest known in Mesoamerica. Round structures such as the Casa Redonda are distributed more widely in the Maya area and have been taken by some to be markers of Itzá expansionism, though some examples elsewhere may antedate those from Chichén Itzá. Traits such as round temples, gallery-patio structures, colonnaded halls, and serpent-column temples are present at Tula, but also elsewhere in western Mesoamerica, suggesting a widespread network of Epiclassic and Early Postclassic Tollans.

The urban organization of Chichén Itzá clearly owes much more to the practices of northern Yucatán than to central Mexico. At Tula, household compounds were surrounded by walls and densely arranged along a gridlike pattern of streets, whereas Chichén Itzá, like many of its neighbors, is a haphazard and rather low-density scatter of masonry platforms (Cobos Palma 2003; Ruppert 1952). Like most houses in northern Yucatán, those at Chichén Itzá are typically arranged around an open central patio and consist of a single row (occasionally two) of rooms, each opening to the exterior, while the few well-surveyed houses from Tula show a much more complex set of internal divisions about one or more interior courtyards. At Chichén, platforms were often surrounded by ample open areas that could have served as work areas or kitchen gardens. Cobos Palma's survey has shown that elite platforms usually support a complex of Modified Florescent structures consisting of a small temple, an altar, a gallery-patio structure, and often a colonnaded hall and a ballcourt, in some cases added to existing Pure Florescent structures.

Surveys by Kilmartin (in Ruppert 1952), Lincoln (1990), and Cobos Palma (Cobos Palma and Winemiller 2001) have identified a complex web of internal causeways (*sacbeob*) connecting major groupings of elite architecture. The sacbeob are a common feature of northern Maya urban centers altogether lacking at Tula. Some seventy of these sacbeob have been identified, the longest stretching for 6 kilometers to Cumtun. With the possible exception of this last and a shorter one to Poxila, none were truly intersite roads, such as the Yaxuná-Cobá or Ucí-Kansacab causeways. Cobos Palma estimates that Chichén at its apogee extended over approximately 16 square kilometers, making it one of the larger, but by no means the largest, urban centers of northern Yucatán.

Production and Exchange

Apart from ceramic trade wares (mainly Fine Orange and Plumbate), Sotuta pottery differs only in minor respects from the domestic Cehpech types produced

4. Nohmul Structure 20 (Chase and Chase 1983) is a possible patio structure, but it lacks a gallery.

elsewhere on the peninsula, and hence this is a further indication of the indigenous roots of the city (Smith 1971). Although present in only modest amounts at most other northern sites, a corridor of sites with some Sotuta pottery extends to the salt beds and trade routes of the northern Gulf Coast. Some argue that international trade, particularly in salt, was the engine fueling Chichén Itzá's rise to prominence, perhaps as part of a prehispanic "world system" (Kepecs 2007). This may be so, but the extensive household excavations necessary to support such an argument are yet to be carried out. Present evidence shows little variation in household inventories and certainly nowhere near the variety of ceramics reported from households in Tula or other highland communities (Bey and Ringle 2007).

Chichén Itzá does seem to have enjoyed privileged access to certain trade goods such as obsidian from west of the Isthmus of Tehuantepec, as well as X Fine Orange and Plumbate pottery. However, very little if any pottery bears similarities to that produced in Tula. Other imports include turquoise, copper, and gold, none of which have been found at other sites of the inland northern peninsula in amounts indicating sustained exchange. Thus, with the exception of obsidian and perhaps Fine Orange pottery, Chichén Itzá seems to have been more a point of consumption than of redistribution in the international trade in exotics.

A substantial fraction of the obsidian at Chichén Itzá was from outside the Maya area and seems to have been imported as preprepared blades or blanks (Braswell and Glascock 2002; Healan 2007). The Zinapecuaro-Ucareo source was most represented, with Pachuca green obsidian about 60 percent as frequent. This correlates with the sources used at Tula during the Late Corral–Early Tollan phase, prior to the construction of most of the classic Toltec structures there (Bey and Ringle 2007; Ringle et al. 1998). Turquoise is another exotic commodity distinguishing Chichén Itzá. Turquoise-mosaic mirrors, one from a dedicatory cache beneath the stairs of the Castillo and another placed upon a jaguar throne from the Castillo-sub, indicate the presence of turquoise when Modified Florescent structures began to be built, possibly prior to 900 AD. Sourcing of the turquoise is necessary to determine whether it derived from the higher quality sources from the Southwest United States, which on present evidence seem to have flourished only after 1000 AD, or whether it came from lesser quality sources in northern Mexico.

Political Structure and Influence

Relief sculptures and murals indicate Chichén possessed a highly organized military with numerous insignias marking rank or sodality. The composition of the controlling political structure is still a matter of controversy (Boot 2005; Cobos Palma 2007; Ringle 2004). Whether a single paramount, a pair of rulers, or perhaps a supreme council directed the government continues to be debated, but clearly councils were operative at several levels of the hierarchy. In several cases a military council seems to have complemented a council of nobles. It is likely that during the latter part of its occupation, outlying elite platforms were the places where individual warrior sodalities met and conducted political rituals, perhaps in gallery-patio structures. It is clear that these, and those of the center, bear strong similarities to the political theater of Late Postclassic Mixteca-Puebla and Nahua groups.

Yet material or iconographic evidence supporting the contention that Chichén Itzá ruled supreme over a northern Maya conquest state is slight. The most cohesive manifestation of "Toltec" traits outside of Chichén Itzá is to be found in certain late structures of the great Puuc site of Uxmal, principally the House of the Governor, the Ballcourt, and the Nunnery, all probably built within a decade or so of 900 AD and otherwise examples of the high Puuc style of architecture (Kowalski 1987; Ringle 2012). Opinion is divided over whether these traits represent conquest by Chichén Itzá, some form of fealty to that site, or their independent adoption by local elites (Kowalski 2003; Ringle 2004; Stanton and Gallareta Negrón 2001). As the manner in which these external traits were incorporated differs considerably from Chichén Itzá, local initiative in joining the Epiclassic Toltec symbolic sphere is indicated, though various forms of political alliance with other such sites are not improbable.

MAYAPÁN

During the Late Postclassic period, Yucatecan political authority seems to have been concentrated at the site of Mayapán, at least for the western half of the peninsula. Mayapán also lies well inland on the northern plains, but farther to the west and closer to the Puuc Hills than does Chichén Itzá. Nevertheless, Mayapán's cultural debt to that site is evident. Chronicles record the flight of the Cocom family from Chichén Itzá (where the name appears in hieroglyphic texts) to the province of Sotuta in central Yucatán, and from there to lordship over Mayapán (Roys, in Pollock et al. 1962). The Xiu family, who traced their origins to Uxmal, was also prominent and at times held rulership of the city. The location of Mayapán may reflect political compromise between these two dominant factions.

Very little is known about Postclassic settlement elsewhere in the interior, though clearly nothing rivaled Mayapán (see, however, Kepecs 2003). A string of coastal communities indicates the continued importance of water-borne trade, especially along the Caribbean. These communities, like Mayapán, reflect strong influence from central Mexico, now expressed through International Style painting[5] and sculpture and by the depiction of central Mexican deities, the most important of which remained the Feathered Serpent (see essays in Vail and Hernández 2010). As with Chichén Itzá, outside influence by no means obscured the presence of traditional Maya forms and deities; the whole was rather a syncretic blend of the

---

5. Some argue that sculpture and mural painting more closely resemble Aztec artwork, though clearly Mayapán flourished before the rise of Tenochtitlan.

two great culture areas. This is evident in the formal similarities between Mayapán stelae and the few hieroglyphic codices that have survived. The Madrid, Paris, and Dresden codices also exemplify the International Style and, together with some poorly preserved monuments from Mayapán and elsewhere, they demonstrate that Maya hieroglyphic writing had not been altogether abandoned.

Mayapán became the last major Maya excavation sponsored by the Carnegie Institution. The site was mapped and extensively excavated between 1949 and 1956 under the direction of H. E. D. Pollock (Pollock et al. 1962). More recently, major field projects directed by Carlos Peraza Lope and Marilyn Masson, working separately and jointly (Masson 2010; Masson et al. 2006; Peraza Lope et al. 2006), have extended mapping of the site and conducted excavations directed at understanding Mayapán's economy and chronology. Susan Milbrath and Carlos Peraza Lope (2003, 2009) have also directed renewed attention to the iconographic and sculptural record of the city. As a result, it is the best understood community of the Late Postclassic Maya.

According to native histories recorded in the books of Chilam Balam, Mayapán was set up as a seating place in *k'atun* 13 Ajaw (probably 1263–1283 AD), while Landa speaks of a second coming of K'uk'ulkan in the *k'atun* ending in either 984 or 1244 (Roys, in Pollock et al. 1962). This agrees reasonably well with the more than thirty-eight radiocarbon dates reported from Mayapán, because only nine are statistically earlier than 1250 AD. Of these last, three are from sealed contexts late in the eleventh or early twelfth centuries, including an early stage of the main pyramid. Thus, the ethnohistorical seating event, if it actually occurred, probably postdates significant construction activity by at least 150 years.

How long this postdates the collapse of Chichén Itzá is unknown. Chilam Balam texts suggest the latter resulted from the treachery of the Mayapán leader Hunac Ceel in *k'atun* 8 Ajaw (1185–1204 AD) or the succeeding *k'atun* 6 Ajaw (1204–1224 AD). Neither date is particularly believable, nor is their placement one cycle (256 years) earlier, and archaeological evidence is still sparse. Possibly the span from 1050–1250 AD was a "dark age" during which Mayapán struggled to establish itself while Chichén Itzá slowly declined (Andrews et al. 2003), but the interval may have been much briefer, perhaps only fifty years. The gap is probably associated with the advent of Hocaba ceramics, which at Chichén are mixed with Sotuta ceramics and associated with crude postmonumental renovations and additions, and at Mayapán with initial construction levels, but there mixed with ceramics of the Postclassic Tases complex.

Settlement, Architecture, and Social Organization

In contrast to Chichén Itzá, the majority of households at Mayapán were densely concentrated within an area of 4.2 square kilometers bounded by a wall some 9 kilometers in circumference. Recent survey has demonstrated that this core was surrounded by a wide fringe of less intense settlement, indicating the site may have covered a total of 8.8 square kilometers, with an estimated total population of 17,000 (Russell 2008). Most houses were also surrounded by rough houselot walls, and for the most part, sacbeob were replaced by narrow, winding paths. Each Mayapán house usually had a front and rear room connected by a doorway, a form rare or absent at Chichén Itzá and Uxmal. Only 2.5 percent of Mayapán houses had more than two rooms, suggesting a more limited nobility and a fundamentally different form of social organization that emphasized the delimitation of houselots and deemphasized the residential propinquity of nonelites and their masters.

In contrast to these differences, several of the principal public buildings are clear derivatives of prototypes at Chichén Itzá (Aveni et al. 2004). The Castillo, like its namesake at Chichén Itzá, is a stepped radial pyramid with serpent balustrades, supporting a serpent-column temple at its summit. The round structure Q-152 is usually viewed as a smaller replica of the Caracol from Chichén Itzá. The absence of ballcourts, skull racks (*tzompantlis*), and gallery-patio structures indicates that Mayapán was not simply a replica of the earlier site, however.

Politically, early sources depict the city as the capital of a confederacy of the major families of western Yucatán, each of whom presided over a particular province. Debate has raged over whether a paramount presided over these elites or whether ultimate power was vested in a council (so-called *multepal* rule, which has also been suggested for Chichén Itzá) (Cobos Palma 2007, Ringle and Bey 2001). Whatever the case, each of the major families may have had a seat in one of the thirteen or so colonnaded halls that constitute much of the remainder of the central sector, as well as the outlying elite group of Itzmal Ch'en (Proskouriakoff, in Pollock et al. 1962). The colonnaded hall usually occurs with an oratory and a shrine, and often with temples, in which case they are referred to as "temple assemblages." Prokouriakoff (1962) suggested each was associated with one of the major factions comprising the city. Some of the temples have serpent columns, suggesting an affiliation with the Cocom faction, while some of the halls incorporate reutilized Puuc mosaic masks, perhaps indicating Xiu affiliation. Similar complexes are prominent at contemporary sites in highland Guatemala, whose residents also claimed Toltec ancestry, and in the central Petén, where ties with both Chichén Itzá and Mayapán were claimed.

Exchange

Extensive excavations have yielded surprisingly limited evidence of foreign exchange, especially from beyond the Isthmus of Tehuantepec (Masson 2010; Robles Castellanos 2010). Obsidian importation shifts from the substantial reliance on central Mexican sources evident at Chichén Itzá to the Ixtepeque source in Guatemala. Mayapán parallels Chichén Itzá in that Fine Orange ware was its primary ceramic import, but Postclassic Matillas Fine Orange probably originated no farther away than the Xicalango province. Central Mexican pottery is almost nonexistent. Jade is present in very low frequencies and turquoise is absent. Although the scarcity of foreign trade goods may be explained in part by their perishability, the absence of durable raw materials and goods directly attributable to non-Maya producers is striking.

Mayapán may have profited indirectly from long-distance exchange, through control of ports of trade or through tribute, or its source of power may have lain elsewhere.

The Collapse of Mayapán

Although the foundation date of Mayapán is as yet unclear, we are on firmer ground with respect to its abandonment, which ethnohistorical sources attribute to an internal revolt in *k'atun* 8 Ajaw (1441–1461 AD). Radiocarbon dates are consistent with this, as those falling after this *k'atun* were either clearly contaminated or do not pertain to construction. Dates from the late thirteenth or fourteenth century for two mass graves from the main plaza and the Itzmal Chen group hint at earlier episodes of unrest, however (Serafin and Peraza Lope 2008).

Following its collapse, the major families either returned to rule their home provinces or founded new ones, as in the case of the Pech family. That said, the archaeology of the Mayapán diaspora is almost wholly unknown. A possible exception is the Kowojs, a family who claimed an origin in Mayapán before leaving to settle along the shore of Lake Petén Itzá, a region recently subjected to intensive archaeological study. There they led one of the important factions of this last independent Maya realm (Jones 1998, 2009; Rice and Rice 2009).

CONCLUSIONS

One way of understanding the connections between Chichén Itzá, Mayapán, and Uxmal, as well as the exaggerated territories claimed for each, is to see them as regional Tollans, active in legitimizing the rulers and high elites of a wide network of client communities (Ringle 2004; Wren and Schmidt 1991). As with Tula, the Feathered Serpent served as the paramount political symbol, but active political control may have been exerted over a fairly limited area, with only indirect influence beyond that. Later mention of these three as constituting the "League of Mayapán" may have resulted from the historical conflation of three sites similar in kind, though of different periods. If true, this may explain the presence of foreign influence (mostly imitated) as the local emulation and expression of a political ideology based in western Mesoamerica. It would also explain some of the historical dynamics, because Chichén Itzá and Uxmal would in this view have served the eastern and western halves of the peninsula during the Terminal Classic, only to have their descendants unite in the governance of Mayapán. This desire to maintain both the general forms of Toltec symbolism together with the specific prestige of an earlier Tollan would also account for the close similarities between the architecture of Chichén Itzá and Mayapán. Concentration of power at the latter ultimately failed, however, resulting in a fragmentation of authority that the Spaniards were able to exploit a century later.

References

....

Andrews, Anthony P., Tomás Gallareta Negrón, Fernando Robles Castellanos, Rafael
    Cobos Palma, and Pura Cervera Rivera. 1988. Isla Cerritos: An Itza Trading Port on
    the North Coast of Yucatan, Mexico. *National Geographic Research* 4:196–207.

Andrews, Anthony P., E. Wyllys Andrews, and Fernando Robles Castellanos. 2003. The
    Northern Maya Collapse and Its Aftermath. *Ancient Mesoamerica* 14(1):151–156.

Andrews, George F. 1995. *Pyramids and Palaces, Monsters and Masks: The Golden Age of
    Maya Architecture. Vol. 1: Architecture of the Puuc Region and the Northern Plains.*
    Labyrinthos, Lancaster, Calif.

Andrews V, E. Wyllys, and Jeremy A. Sabloff. 1986. Classic to Postclassic: A Summary
    Discussion. In *Late Lowland Maya Civilization*, edited by Jeremy A. Sabloff and E.
    Wyllys V. Andrews, pp. 433–456. School of American Research/University of New
    Mexico Press, Albuquerque.

Aveni, Anthony F.; Susan Milbrath, and Carlos Peraza Lope. 2004. Chichen Itza's Legacy
    in the Astronomically Oriented Architecture of Mayapan. *Res: Anthropology and
    Aesthetics* 45:123–144.

Bey, George J., III, and William M. Ringle. 2007. From the Bottom Up: The Timing and
    Nature of the Tula-Chichén Itzá Exchange. In *Twin Tollans: Chichén Itzá, Tula and
    the Epiclassic to Early Postclassic Mesoamerican World*, edited by Jeff K. Kowalski
    and Cynthia Kristan-Graham, pp. 377–427. Dumbarton Oaks, Washington, DC.

Boot, Erik. 2005. *Continuity and Change in Text and Image at Chichen Itza, Yucatan,
    Mexico: A Study of the Inscriptions, Iconography, and Architecture at a Late Classic to
    Early Postclassic Maya Site.* CNWS Publications, Leiden.

Brainerd, George W. 1958. *The Archaeological Ceramics of Yucatan.* Anthropological
    Records, Vol. 19. University of California Press, Berkeley.

Brown, Clifford T., and Walter W. Witschey. 2010. *The Electronic Atlas of Ancient Maya
    Sites: A Geographic Information System (GIS).* Electronic document, http://mayagis.
    smv.org/ (accessed 25 October 2011).

Braswell, Geoff, and Michael D. Glascock. 2002. The Emergence of Market Economies in
    the Ancient Maya World; Obsidian Exchange in Terminal Classic Yucatan, Mexico.
    In *Geochemical Evidence for Long-distance Exchange*, edited by Michael D. Glascock,
    pp. 33–52. Bergen & Garvey, Westport, CT.

Burgos Villanueva, Rafael, Miguel Covarrubias, and José Estrada Faisal. 2004. Estudios
    sobre la periferia de Izamal, Yucatán. *Los investigadores de la cultura maya*
    12(1):248–257.

Chase, Arlen F., and Diane Z. Chase. 1983. Archaeological Investigations at Nohmul and
    Santa Rita: 1979–1980. *Belizean Studies* 11(5):23–27.

Cobos Palma, Rafael. 2003. Ancient Community Form and Social Complexity at Chichen
    Itza, Yucatan. In *El urbanismo en Mesoamérica; Urbanism in Mesoamerica*, vol. 1,
    edited by William T. Sanders, Alba G. Mastache, and Robert H. Cobean,
    pp. 451–472. Instituto Nacional de Antropología e Historia/Pennsylvania State
    University, México, D.F.

Cobos Palma, Rafael. 2007. Multepal or Centralized Kingship? New Evidence on
    Governmental Organization at Chichén Itzá. In *Twin Tollans: Chichén Itzá,
    Tula and the Epiclassic to Early Postclassic Mesoamerican World*, edited by Jeff
    K. Kowalski and Cynthia Kristan-Graham, pp. 315–343. Dumbarton Oaks,
    Washington, DC.

Cobos Palma, Rafael, and Terance L. Winemiller. 2001. Late and Terminal Classic-Period Causeway Systems of Chichen Itza, Yucatan, Mexico. *Ancient Mesoamerica* 12:283–291.

Coggins, Clemency C., and Orrin C. Shane III, eds. 1992. *Artifacts from the Cenote of Sacrifice, Chichen Itza, Yucatan*. Memoirs of the Peabody Museum of Archaeology and Ethnology, vol. 10, no. 3. Harvard University, Cambridge.

Dunning, Nicholas P., and Jeff K. Kowalski. 1994. Lord of the Hills: Classic Maya Settlement Patterns and Political Iconography in the Puuc Region, Mexico. *Ancient Mesoamerica* 5:63–95.

Folan, William J., Ellen R. Kintz, and Laraine A. Fletcher. 1983. *Coba: A Classic Maya Metropolis*. Academic Press, New York.

Gallareta Negrón, Tomás. 1998. Isla Cerritos, Yucatan. *Arqueología mexicana* 6 (33): 24–31.

Gronemeyer, Sven. 2004 A Preliminary Ruling Sequence of Cobá, Quintana Roo. *Wayeb Notes* 14. Electronic document, http://www.wayeb.org/notes/wayeb_notes0014.pdf (accessed April 10, 2012).

Grube, Nikolai. 2003. Hieroglyphic Inscriptions from Northwest Yucatán: An Update of Recent Research. In *Escondido en la selva*, edited by Hanns J. Prem, pp. 339–370. Universidad de Bonn/Instituto Nacional de Antropología e Historia, Bonn/México, D.F.

Grube, Nikolai, and Ruth J. Krochock. 2007. Reading between the Lines: Hieroglyphic Texts from Chichén Itzá and Its Neighbors. In *Twin Tollans: Chichén Itzá, Tula and the Epiclassic to Early Postclassic Mesoamerican World*, edited by Jeff K. Kowalski and Cynthia Kristan-Graham, pp. 205–249. Dumbarton Oaks, Washington, DC.

Healan, Dan M. 2007. New Perspectives on Tula's Obsidian Industry and Its Relationship to Chichen Itza. In *Twin Tollans: Chichén Itzá, Tula and the Epiclassic to Early Postclassic Mesoamerican World*, edited by Jeff K. Kowalski and Cynthia Kristan-Graham, pp. 429–447. Dumbarton Oaks, Washington, DC.

Jones, Grant D. 1998. *The Conquest of the Last Maya Kingdom*. Stanford University Press, Stanford.

Jones, Grant D. 2009. The Kowoj in Ethnohistorical Perspective. In *The Kowoj: Identity, Migration, and Politics in Late Postclassic Petén, Guatemala*, edited by Prudence M. Rice and Don S. Rice, pp. 55–69. University Press of Colorado, Boulder.

Kepecs, Susan M. 2003. Chikinchel. In *The Postclassic Mesoamerican World*, edited by Michael E. Smith and Frances F. Berdan, pp. 259–268. University of Utah Press, Salt Lake City.

Kepecs, Susan M. 2007. Chichén Itzá, Tula, and the Epiclassic: Early Postclassic Mesoamerican World Systems. In *Twin Tollans: Chichén Itzá, Tula and the Epiclassic to Early Postclassic Mesoamerican World*, edited by Jeff K. Kowalski and Cynthia Kristan-Graham, pp. 129–149. Dumbarton Oaks, Washington, DC.

Kowalski, Jeff K. 1987. *The House of the Governor*. University of Oklahoma Press, Norman.

Kowalski, Jeff K. 2003. Collaboration and Conflict: An Interpretation of the Relationship between Uxmal and Chichén ltzá during the Terminal Classic/Early Postclassic Periods. In *Escondido en la selva*, edited by Hanns J. Prem, pp. 235–272. Universidad de Bonn/Instituto Nacional de Antropología e Historia, Bonn/México, D.F.

Kowalski, Jeff K. 2007. What's "Toltec" at Uxmal and Chichén Itzá? Merging Maya and Mesoamerican Worldviews and World Systems in Terminal Classic to Early Postclassic Yucatán. In *Twin Tollans: Chichén Itzá, Tula and the Epiclassic to Early*

Postclassic Mesoamerican World, edited by Jeff K. Kowalski and Cynthia Kristan-Graham, pp. 250–313. Dumbarton Oaks, Washington, DC.

Kowalski, Jeff K., and Cynthia Kristan-Graham, eds. 2007. *Twin Tollans: Chichén Itzá, Tula and the Epiclassic to Early Postclassic Mesoamerican World*. Dumbarton Oaks, Washington, DC.

Lacadena García-Gallo, Alfonso. 2004. *The Glyphic Corpus from Ek' Balam, Yucatán, México*. Electronic document, Foundation for the Advancement of Mesoamerican Studies, http://www.famsi.org/reports/01057/index.html (accessed 30 October 2011).

Lincoln, Charles E. 1986. The Chronology of Chichen Itza: A Review of the Literature. In *Late Lowland Maya Civilization*, edited by Jeremy A. Sabloff and V. Andrews, pp. 141–198. School of American Research/University of New Mexico Press, Albuquerque.

Lincoln, Charles E. 1990. Ethnicity and Social Organization at Chichen Itza, Yucatan, Mexico. Unpublished PhD dissertation, Department of Anthropology, Harvard University.

López Austin, Alfredo, and Leonardo López Luján. 2000. The Myth and Reality of Zuyua: The Feathered Serpent and Mesoamerican Transformations from the Classic to the Postclassic. In *Mesoamerica's Classic Heritage: From Teotihuacan to the Aztecs*, edited by Davíd Carrasco, Lindsay Jones, and Scott Sessions, pp. 21–84. University Press of Colorado, Boulder.

Maldonado Cárdenas, Rubén. 1997. Las intervenciones de restauración arqueológica en Chichén Itzá (1926–1980). In *Homenaje al profesor César A. Sáenz*, edited by Angel García Cook, Alba G. Mastache, Leonor Merino, and Sonia Rivero Torres, pp. 103–131. Instituto Nacional de Antropología e Historia, México, D.F.

Masson, Marilyn A. 2010. Evidence for Maya-Mexican Interaction in the Archaeological Record of Mayapan. In *Astronomers, Scribes, and Priests*, edited by Gabrielle Vail and Christine Hernández, pp. 77–113. Dumbarton Oaks, Washington, DC.

Masson, Marilyn A., Timothy S. Hare, and Carlos Peraza Lope. 2006. Postclassic Maya Society Regenerated at Mayapan. In *After Collapse: The Regeneration of Complex Societies*, edited by Glenn M. Schwartz and John J. Nichols, pp. 188–207. University of Arizona Press, Tucson.

Matheny, Ray T., Deanne L. Gurr, Donald W. Forsyth, and F. Richard Hauck. 1983. *Investigations at Edzná, Campeche, Mexico: 1(1). The Hydraulic System*. Papers of the New World Archaeological Foundation 46. Brigham Young University, Provo.

Milbrath, Susan, and Carlos Peraza Lope. 2003. Revisiting Mayapan: Mexico's Last Maya Capital. *Ancient Mesoamerica* 14:1–46.

Milbrath, Susan, and Carlos Peraza Lope. 2009. Survival and Revival of Terminal Classic Traditions at Postclassic Mayapan. *Latin American Antiquity* 20:581–606.

Pallán Gayol, Carlos. N.d. *Secuencia dinástica, glifos-emblema y topónimos en las inscripciones jeroglíficas de Edzná, Campeche (600–900 D.C.): Implicaciones históricas*. Tesis de maestreria en Estudios Mesoamericanos, Universidad Autonoma, México, D.F.

Peraza Lope, Carlos, Marilyn A. Masson, Timothy S. Hare, and Pedro Candelario Delgado Ku. 2006. The Chronology of Mayapan: New Radiocarbon Evidence. *Ancient Mesoamerica* 17:153–176.

Piña Chan, Román. 1970. *Informe preliminar de la reciente exploración del cenote sagrado de Chichén Itzá*. Investigaciones 24. Instituto Nacional de Antropología e Historia, México, D.F.

Pollock, H. E. D. 1980. *The Puuc*. Memoirs of the Peabody Museum Vol. 19, Peabody
    Museum of Archaeology and Ethnology, Harvard University, Cambridge.
Pollock, H. E. D., Ralph L. Roys, Tatiana Prokouriakoff, and A. Ledyard Smith. 1962.
    Mayapan, Yucatan, Mexico. Carnegie Institution of Washington, Pub. 619. Carnegie
    Institution of Washington, Washington, DC.
Proskouriakoff, Tatiana A. 1962. Civic and Religious Structures of Mayapan. In
    Mayapan, Yucatan, Mexico, edited by H. E. D. Pollock, Ralph L. Roys, Tatiana
    Proskouriakoff, and A. L. Smith, pp. 86–163. Carnegie Institution of Washington,
    Washington, D.C.
Proskouriakoff, Tatiana. 1974. *Jades from the Cenote of Sacrifice, Chichen Itza, Yucatan*.
    Memoirs of the Peabody Museum of Archaeology and Ethnology, vol. 10, no. 1.
    Harvard University, Cambridge.
Rice, Prudence M., and Don S. Rice, eds. 2009. *The Kowoj: Identity, Migration, and
    Politics in Late Postclassic Petén, Guatemala*. University Press of Colorado, Boulder.
Ringle, William M. 2004. On the Political Organization of Chichen Itza. *Ancient
    Mesoamerica* 15(2):167–218.
Ringle, William M. 2009. The Art of War: Imagery of the Upper Temple of the Jaguars,
    Chichen Itza. *Ancient Mesoamerica* 20:15–44.
Ringle, William M. 2012. The Nunnery Quadrangle of Uxmal. In *The Ancient Maya of
    Mexico: Reinterpreting the Past of the Northern Maya Lowlands*, edited by Geoff
    Braswell, pp. 189–226. Equinox Press, London.
Ringle, William M., and George J. Bey III. 2001. Post-Classic and Terminal Classic
    Courts of the Northern Maya Lowlands. In *Royal Courts of the Ancient Maya.
    Volume 2: Data and Case Studies*, edited by Takeshi Inomata and Stephen D.
    Houston, pp. 266–307. Westview Press, Boulder.
Ringle, William M., and George J. Bey III. 2009. The Face of the Itzas. In *The Art of
    Urbanism: How Mesoamerican Kingdoms Represented Themselves in Architecture
    and Imagery*, edited by William L. Fash and Leondardo López Luján, pp. 329–383.
    Dumbarton Oaks Research Library and Collection, Washington, DC.
Ringle, William M., Tomás Gallareta Negrón, and George J. Bey III. 1998. The Return
    of Quetzalcoatl: Evidence for the Spread of a World Religion during the Epiclassic
    Period. *Ancient Mesoamerica* 9:183–232.
Robles Castellanos, Fernando. 2006. Las esferas cerámicas de Cehpech y Sotuta
    del apogeo del Claásico tardío (730–900 D.C.) en el norte de la península.
    In *La producción alfarera en el México antiguo III*, edited by Beatriz Leonor
    Merino Carrión and Ángel García Cook, pp. 281–343. Conaculta/I.N.A.H.,
    México, D.F.
Robles Castellanos, Fernando. 2010. Interaction between Central and Eastern
    Mesoamerica before and during the Culhua Mexica Expansion. In *Astronomers,
    Scribes, and Priests*, edited by Gabrielle Vail and Christine Hernández, pp. 37–76.
    Dumbarton Oaks, Washington, DC.
Ruppert, Karl. 1952. *Chichen Itza: Architectural Notes and Plans*. Carnegie Institution of
    Washington, Pub. 595. Carnegie Institution of Washington, Washington, DC.
Russell, Bradley W. 2008. Postclassic Maya Settlement on the Rural-Urban Fringe
    of Mayapán, Yucatán, Mexico. Unpublished PhD dissertation, Department of
    Anthropology, State University of New York at Albany.
Schmidt, Peter J. 2007. Birds, Ceramics, and Cacao: New Excavations at Chichén Itzá,
    Yucatan. In *Twin Tollans: Chichén Itzá, Tula and the Epiclassic to Early Postclassic*

Mesoamerican World, edited by Jeff K. Kowalski and Cynthia Kristan-Graham, pp. 151–203. Dumbarton Oaks, Washington, DC.

Serafin, Stanley, and Carlos Peraza Lope. 2008. Human Sacrificial Rites among the Maya of Mayapán: A Bioarchaeological Perspective. In *New Perspectives on Human Sacrifice and Ritual Body Treatments in Ancient Maya Society*, edited by Vera Tiesler and Andrea Cucina, pp. 232–250. Springer, New York.

Sierra Sosa, Thelma N. 1999. Xcambó: codiciado enclave económico del Clásico maya *Arqueología mexicana* 7(37):40–47.

Smith, J. Gregory. 2001. Preliminary Report of the Chichen Itza-Ek Balam Transect Project. *Mexicon* 23(2):30–35.

Smith, Robert E. 1971. *The Pottery of Mayapan*. Papers of the Peabody Museum of Archaeology and Ethnology, Vol. 66. Harvard University, Cambridge.

Stanton, Travis W., and Tomás Gallareta Negrón. 2001. Warfare, Ceramic Economy, and the Itza: A Reconsideration of the Itza Polity in Ancient Yucatan. *Ancient Mesoamerica* 12:229–245.

Taube, Karl A. 1994. The Iconography of Toltec Period Chichen Itza. In *Hidden among the Hills*, edited by Hanns J. Prem, pp. 212–246. Acta Mesoamericana, Vol. 7. Verlag Von Flemming, Möckmühl.

Thompson, J. Eric. 1937. A New Method of Deciphering Yucatecan Dates with Special Reference to Chichen Itza. *Contributions to American Archaeology* No. 22, Carnegie Institution, Washington, DC.

Tozzer, Alfred M., ed. and trans. 1941. *Landa's relación de las cosas de Yucatán*. Papers of the Peabody Museum of American Archaeology and Ethnology, Vol. XVIII. Harvard University, Cambridge.

Tozzer, Alfred M., ed. and trans. 1957. *Chichen Itza and Its Cenote of Sacrifice: A Comparative Study of Contemporaneous Maya and Toltec*. Memoirs of the Peabody Museum of Archaeology and Ethnology, vols. 11, 12. Harvard University, Cambridge.

Vail, Gabrielle, and Christine Hernández, eds. 2010 *Astronomers, Scribes, and Priests*. Dumbarton Oaks, Washington, D.C.

Wren, Linnea H., and Peter Schmidt. 1991. Elite Interaction during the Terminal Classic Period: New Evidence from Chichen Itza. In *Classic Maya Political History: Hieroglyphic and Archaeological Evidence*, edited by T. P. Culbert, pp. 199–225. S.A.R./Cambridge University Press, Cambridge.

CHAPTER 28

THE ARCHAEOLOGY OF THE LATE POSTCLASSIC MAYA HIGHLANDS

GREG BORGSTEDE AND EUGENIA ROBINSON

THE Maya highlands region runs west to east from central Chiapas, Mexico (near Chiapa de Corzo), to central Guatemala (near Guatemala City) and north to south from the southern Maya lowlands to the Pacific coastal piedmont (Figure 28.1). The Maya highlands is a convenient heuristic label for a geographic space of about 35,000 square miles; "Maya" refers to the predominant cultural-linguistic groups present in the area at the time of Spanish conquest in the 1520s, and "highlands" contrasts the region with the lowlands of the Petén and Yucatán. The label has been in place for archaeological research purposes since at least the 1940s (Kidder 1940; Thompson 1943); even though it provides a useful analytic framework for defining research agendas—peripheries/boundaries, interregional trade, and migration— its utility as a monolithic culture area during the Late Postclassic period (1200 to 1524 AD) is open for debate.

Scientific research up to the 1960s provided initial understandings of the region's archaeology and resulted in the delineation of subregions based primarily on topography and modern political units. Borhegyi (1965: 3–4) limited the highlands to "geographical and cultural units" located at least 2,000 feet above sea level. Along with Lowe and Mason (1965: Fig. 2), Borhegyi (1965: Fig. 1) defined the

Figure 28.1 Regional map of the Late Postclassic Maya highlands, showing the sites mentioned in the text.

subdivisions currently in use: (1) the central Chiapas/Chiapas plateau (the Chiapas highlands); (2) the valley of the Grijalva River; (3) Sierra Madre (in Chiapas and Guatemala); (4) the western Guatemalan highlands; (5) the central Guatemalan highlands; and (6) hilly middle country (or the northern Maya highlands—Alta and Baja Verapaz and northern El Quiché). Recent research has highlighted developments within smaller geographic units, such as the Cuchumatan Mountains (Borgstede and Romero 2004) or the middle Chixoy River drainage (Ichon 1996). As Love (2007: 276–277) points out, the high degree of cultural diversity means that the region should not be treated as a monolithic whole but needs to be understood in more culturally and geographically refined terms.

The constitution of the geographical subdivisions frames archaeological research and other lines of historic evidence. Because the subdivisions are based on topography—river valleys, mountain massifs, and so on—archaeologists utilize them to define areas of research and, by implication, research topics. For example, research in the northern Maya highlands has tended to focus on relations— trade and culture—with the neighboring lowlands (Sharer and Sedat 1987), while research in the Grijalva depression has focused on ethnic relations between Maya and Mixe-Zoque who had been occupying the lower valley (Lowe 1983). In addition, researchers have stressed the interpretive ties between archaeological and ethnohistoric evidence, which is labeled the "conjunctive approach" (Carmack and Weeks 1981). The geographic subdivisions, however, may serve to mask broader cultural developments, and ethnohistorians (e.g., Hill 1984) and anthropologists (e.g., Tax 1937) continue to seek emic organizing units, particularly for the Late Postclassic period. Much uncertainty remains in determining the relationships between archaeological units that are based primarily on topography, and cultural units that are based primarily on ethnohistory and a direct historical approach.

Arguably more archaeological research has been conducted on the Late Postclassic period in the Maya highlands than on any of the other Pre-Columbian periods. The Late Postclassic, as the terminal prehispanic phase, has been of particular interest to archaeologists, ethnohistorians, and anthropologists because of the existence of native chronicles documenting the Late Postclassic, such as the *Popol Vuh* (Tedlock 1996) and the Annals of the Kaqchikels (Maxwell and Hill 2006); the Spanish accounts of encounters with Late Postclassic groups (Recinos 1952); the widespread visibility of Late Postclassic archaeological sites on the highland landscape and the occupation of major sites—Utatlan, Iximche, Zaculeu, Mixco Viejo—at the time of Spanish contact; and, lastly, the perceived continuity between Late Postclassic sociocultural formations and the modern Maya (Borgstede and Yaeger 2008).

Dating of the Late Postclassic has traditionally relied on historic documents. Although European impact preceded (via disease and trade) the Spanish physical presence, the end of the period is typically placed at 1524 AD when Pedro de Alvarado invaded the Maya highlands from central Mexico to begin the conquest of the extant Quiché, Kaqchikel, and Tzutujil Maya states. The beginning of the period is more difficult to assign a date to, however. Typically 1200 AD is used (see Borhegyi 1965: table 1; Smith 1955: 3), a date that has been proposed as the founding for the Quiché Maya capital of Utatlan (Wauchope 1947: 64). The period's beginning is often assumed to be the point at which native documents begin to chronicle "historical" events (as opposed to "mythical" events, such as the travails of the hero twins in the *Popol Vuh*); significantly, these documents focus on the central Guatemalan highlands, such as the founding of Utatlan (see Carmack 1981: 127–130). Native documents provide a nonarchaeological "window" on the period, to the point that it has been termed the "protohistoric" (Smith 1955: 69; Wauchope 1970: 99; see also Fox 1980: 48). Overall, researchers typically frame the period as 1200 to 1524 AD.

For this time period, archaeologists have long recognized central Mexican influence on the region. The influence has been glossed as the "Mexicanization" of the Maya highlands (see Navarrete 1996) or "Nahualization" (see Braswell 2001b). Purported "foreign" traits, particularly in architecture and ceramics, incorporated into highland Maya cultural formations during the Postclassic are of "unmistakable Mexican influence" (Fox 1980: 45); Thompson (1943) and subsequent researchers have attributed these similarities to the theory that Mexican peoples had migrated into the Maya highlands. Fox (1980: 45–47) suggested that Mexicanization occurred from 800 to 1200 AD and listed Mexican influence in the categories of architecture (long houses, round temples, colonnaded buildings, and I-shaped enclosed ballcourts); ceramics (fine-paste ceramics, animal effigy vessels, and step-fret designs); sculpture (esp. the feathered serpent); and site layout (a radial pyramid centered in a plaza with a ballcourt and long structure). Carmack

(1968: 62–63) highlighted the Postclassic Mexican (or "Toltec") features of a defensive location, twin-temple pyramids, sloping walls, cremation burials, and specific ceramic types (i.e., Fortress White-on-Red and Chinautla Polychrome). Recently added to this list is the sculptured skull platform (Smith 2003: 185). Anthropologists have suggested other Mexican traits: Nahuat loan words appeared in highland Maya languages during this period (Campbell 1977); toponyms may be interpreted as central Mexican (Fox 1987: 2–3); and some social forms, such as military "battle units," appear to have central Mexican similarities (Carmack 1968: 80–81).

In addition, Mexicanization of the Maya highlands has been approached through Pre-Columbian art. Mural paintings depict warriors, deities, and mythological figures in a subset of the Southwestern Postclassic international style (Boone and Smith 2003) at the capitals of Utatlan (Carmack 1981: 295–299; Fox et al. 1992: 176–178) and Iximche (Guillemin 1977: Fig. 2). Rock art located in a central, public area at La Casa de Las Golondrinas (Robinson 2008) in the Antigua Valley displays an elite Late Postclassic Mexican symbol set (Boone and Smith 2003; Smith 2003), including symbols of warfare, such as the fireserpent/Xiuhcoatl, Huitzilopochtli's fire weapon, and a bloody flint, as well as solar imagery such as rayed motifs (Figure 28.2). Also, Mexican dates and iconography appear in rock art at Piedra de Ayarza in the central Guatemalan highlands (Stone and Ericastilla 1998) and date important political events of the mythohistorical traditions that established political legitimacy (Stone 1999: 4).

Assuming that central Mexico and the Maya highlands can be treated as unified "culture areas" exhibiting distinct sets of traits—a problematic assumption at best—the complex of Mexican traits strongly suggests some form of interaction. Two key issues remain unresolved: the process and the timing of the interaction(s).

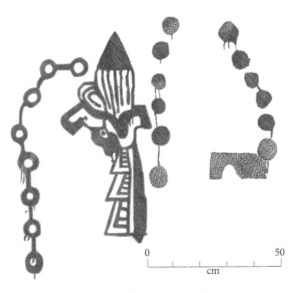

0   50
cm

Figure 28.2 The Late Postclassic Xiucoatl and Flint Glyphs, Painting B1,
La Casa de las Golondrinas, Guatemala.

Explanations for the process—or how central Mexican culture infiltrated the Maya highlands—oscillate between two extremes: (1) in-migration of Mexican groups (or "Mexicanized" groups, such as the Gulf Coast Putun/Chontal Maya [Thompson 1970; Fox 1989: 672]) and (2) cultural "borrowing" of traits by autochthonous groups (Popenoe de Hatch 1999: 504; see also Brown 1982). Some interpretations incorporate both: Fox (1987), for example, argues for a period of in-migration from the Gulf Coast, followed by a period of more gradual adoption of cultural traits. The polar positions, however, derive from theoretical predispositions. Proponents of in-migration explain introduced traits as the result of population movement into a new culture area—discrete, bounded areas displaying a suite of traits that can be tracked over time and space (e.g., Kroeber 1931; Wissler 1927). Autochthonous development, on the other hand, views culture and society in a more fluid manner, eschewing "trait" list descriptions of culture as overly reductive and also suggesting that constantly changing cultural configurations would be manifested in different ways, most probably as expressions of elites and the consolidation of political power (see Smith 2003: 185).

For the Maya highlands, positions on these issues tend to align with empirical datasets that vary across the subdivisions of the highlands. Overarching models of in-migration and cultural adoption that may apply for the central Guatemalan highlands (Fox 1987), for example, may not fit data for the Chiapas Plateau, which exhibits "little evidence of Mexican influence...in contradistinction to much of the neighboring highland region of Guatemala" (Lowe and Mason 1965: 234; see also Adams 1961: 357–358). Even relatively small subareas have produced highly localized explanations: Ichon (1993: 117) argued that the western portion of middle Chixoy River drainage saw in-migration while Arnauld (1993: 49) argued that the eastern portion did not. Similarly, Iglesias and Ciudad (1984: 30) argue that Mexicanization did not occur at all in the Samalá Valley near Quetzaltenango.

Understanding how the Mexicanization process worked is inextricably linked to knowing when it happened. The process of in-migration would presumably be shorter than gradual adoption. In addition to the length of timing is the issue of assigning specific dates or periods in the prehispanic sequence to the process, however it is understood. This is not straightforward, with Mexicanization variously being assigned to the Epiclassic (Fox 1980: 45), the Early Postclassic (Carmack 1968: 60), and the Late Postclassic (see Braswell 2001b), or some combination of these, basically a period from 800 to 1540 AD. As with the process, much interpretation for timing has been based on data from the central Guatemalan highlands at the expense of other subdivisions. In those subdivisions where further research suggests that Mexicanization did indeed take place, such as in the Grijalva depression and Sierra Madre de Chiapas (Lowe and Mason 1965: 230; Navarrete 1966), the picture is not of a clearly timed event, but of change at different points in highly localized sequences. As a process, therefore, the specifics of the timing of Mexicanization will depend on close examination of small, discrete areas within the broader Maya highlands sphere. In one sense, the Mexicanization of the Maya highlands can be viewed as analogous to the Classic "collapse" in the Maya lowlands (Demarest et al. 2004)—highly localized manifestations of a general trend that varies in time and execution.

The issue of Mexicanization is fundamental to understanding the Late Postclassic period because scholars argue that it underlies the origin and development of the dominant social formations of the period: the Quiché and Kaqchikel Maya polities. In a series of influential publications, John Fox (1980, 1987) has argued for two periods of in-migration of Mexicanized groups from the Gulf Coast, the first related to the Toltecs and establishing new, distinct centers, and the second involving smaller groups that intermixed with autochthonous Maya groups and legitimized their rule through claims of Mexican ancestry from Tollan and the earlier Toltec migrants. According to Fox, the second group, once established in the central Guatemalan highlands, began to slowly expand political control over much of highland Guatemala (Fox 1978, 1981) and ultimately developed the Quiché Maya state, a "militaristic" or "expansionist" polity centered at greater Utatlan (Carmack 1981; Wallace 1977; Weeks 1983). Basing his argument on ethnohistoric narratives and interpretations of the archaeological record—associating specific site plans with ethnic groups, for example—Fox argued that the Quiché state, organized by lineages into a "segmentary state" (Fox 1989; but see Chase and Chase 1996; Fox et al. 1996; Gillespie 2000), eventually atomized and led to the development of rival polities, such as the Kaqchikel, centered at Iximche, (Guillemin 1977; Nance et al. 2003) and the Tzutujil, centered at Chuitinamit, (Orellana 1973, 1984). Other Maya groups also challenged the Quiché, such as the Mam at Zaculeu (Woodbury and Trik 1953) and the Pokoman at Mixco Viejo (Miles 1957; Navarrete 1962). Fox's model neatly correlates numerous lines of evidence to interpret the history broadly of the Postclassic Maya highlands. For the middle Chixoy River drainage, for example, Ichon (1996: 171) argues that the carbon dates from early levels at Cawinal support the idea of an in-migration; he (Ichon 1993: 117) states that there was a clear Postclassic "rupture" with strong outside influence.

However, researchers have challenged this model based on alternate explanations of the material and ethnohistoric records. For example, Akkeren (2000: 28) proposes that the ethnohistoric evidence indicates that the Late Postclassic Quiché were descendants of allied Pacific Coast (Toltec-derived Mayanized lineages), Yucatecan, and Mexican lineages. The Late Postclassic Quiché claims to Toltec ancestry were part of their mythohistorical traditions. Akkeren also reinterprets the ethnohistoric record on a number of different topics, including challenging the assignation of certain Quiché ethnohistoric toponyms to specific archaeological sites (Akkeren 2002). Concurrently, Braswell (2001a: 316) argues that Fox's interpretation of site plans is conjectural, and site organization cannot be correlated with ethnic groups and their expansion, a fundamental element of Fox's model. Looking at ceramics, Popenoe de Hatch (1999) argues for much greater cultural continuity in the central and western Guatemalan highlands, effectively ruling out the in-migrations proposed by Fox. The ethnohistoric evidence has also been variously interpreted, and Hill (1996, 1998) has challenged Fox's model for the Kaqchikel area, arguing for more localized development. He suggests that ethnohistoric references to Mexican elements, especially Tollan, reflect a claim of Toltec ancestry by the Chajoma Kaqchikel as a "propaganda tactic to legitimize [their] rise to power" (Hill 1996: 65), rather than a strict interpretation of long-distance migration.

As with any scientific endeavor, continuing research continues to modify and expand existing interpretations. The Quiché and Kaqchikel dominated the central Guatemalan highlands during the period of Spanish conquest and figure prominently in Spanish historic documents. As researchers continue to explore and examine both the archaeological and ethnohistorical records of highland subdivisions outside of central Guatemala, and even reinterpret data recovered decades ago (see Nance et al. 2003), overarching models of general development for the Late Postclassic appear premature. This is not to say that Fox's model will not ultimately prove accurate in certain aspects, only that the Maya highlands cannot be treated as a monolithic culture area; locally focused research is undermining the grand narrative.

The highly localized nature of Late Postclassic developments has also been highlighted in recent settlement-pattern studies across the region. Researchers looking at the Cuchumatan Mountains (Borgstede 2004), the Antigua Valley (Robinson 1997), around San Martín Jilotepeque (Braswell 1996), Alta Verapaz (Arnauld 1986), and the upper tributaries of the Grijalva River (Bryant et al. 2005) are considering new swaths of the region long untouched by research. These studies show that the region was a complex mosaic of small and large polities, trade interactions, and relations among ethnic groups. In fact, many of the Maya linguistic groups extant at Spanish conquest and mentioned in historic documents—Mam, Pokoman, Acahal, Tzeltal, Tzotzil, Chuj, Jacaltec, Kekchi, Coxoh, and others— have unique Pre-Columbian histories that are just beginning to emerge from the shadow of the long-standing questions on the Quiché and Kaqchikel polities. Recently uncovered evidence shows a highly variable Late Postclassic settlement pattern across the highlands. For example, there is strong evidence for population and material culture continuity from the Early Postclassic to the Late Postclassic in the Alta Verapaz (e.g., Arnauld 1986, 1993), while in other areas there is a marked disjunction between the periods, manifesting itself in the founding of new sites with new organizing principles (Ichon 1993).

A hallmark of Postclassic settlement patterns has long been understood to be the transition to more "defensive" locations from the preceding Late Classic period (Smith 1955: 69, 77; Borhegyi 1965: 42), suggesting a "warlike" culture in the Postclassic (Smith 1955: 77). Recent studies suggest, however, that increasing defensiveness (from Late Classic to Postclassic) is overstated for some areas of the Maya highlands, such as the Cuchumatan Mountains (Borgstede and Mathieu 2007) or parts of the middle Chixoy River drainage (Ichon 1996: 170); the "defensive" center of Zaculeu was occupied since at least the Early Classic (Dimick 1955). The long-standing interpretation of increased defensiveness was built upon, and may be attributed primarily to, sites in the central Guatemalan highlands (see Smith 1955; Fox 1978: 295–297). Finally, settlement-pattern studies have clarified the complexity of site hierarchies—three- or four-tier hierarchies, organized in different ways, have been uncovered in previously unstudied areas, such as in Alta Verapaz (Arnauld 1986). Overall, the settlement-pattern results mirror other research, demonstrating the localized nature of highland development rather than the overarching control and influence of dominant states. Research in other relatively understudied regions—the Tzutujil polity (Orellana 1984), the Mam polity (Woodbury and Trik 1953), the Grijalva Depression (Blake 2010), the Chiapas Plateau (Culbert 1965), and parts of the Sierra Madre (Navarette 1978), in particular—would expect to uncover a similarly complicated mosaic of local developments tied to but not defined by region- and Mesoamerica-wide processes.

Simultaneously, research on the major Postclassic states is clarifying and altering understandings of their boundaries, structure, and operation. For example, the core of the Quiché polity has long been understood to be a central zone of multiple sites: greater Utatlan incorporated sites such as Chisalin, Ismachi, Pakaman, and so on (Carmack 1981; Carmack et al. 1975; Wallace 1977; Weeks 1983; see also Macario et al. 2007). Outside of the core zone, however, material correlates of the Quiché polity are less clear and are tied to ceramics (i.e., Fortress White on Red; Fox 1978: 282), site layouts (Fox 1978, 1987), or ethnohistoric ascriptions of place (Fox 1978). As research in the middle Chixoy River drainage has shown (e.g., Ichon 1996), all of these ascriptions can be contested, as in ceramics (Ichon 1987), site layouts (Arnauld 1993: 49, 96), and toponymics (Akerren 2002).

Similarly, the organization and operation of the Kaqchikel polity also remain in question. While the polity has long been assumed to be centralized under the control of two rulers from Iximche (Guillemin 1977), recent research has suggested a more divided and politicized landscape with the domain of the Chajoma Kaqchikel (Hill 1996) separate from the Iximche Kaqchikel. The evaluation of ceramic, lithic, and osteological evidence from Iximche itself has resulted in a reassessment of artifactual and architectural correlations (Nance 2003: 305) as well as reformulating external ties and relations (Nance et al. 2003). Additionally, the structure of the Iximiche polity has been reconceptualized, with arguments for a three-tier hierarchy containing defensive sites at the upper tier. One of these, Chitaqtz'aq, was a walled regional center (Robinson 1997, 1998) located in a non-defensive location on a plain but well located for holding the border between the Iximche and Chajoma polities.

In conclusion, the Late Postclassic period in the Maya highlands has long been one of the most-studied phases in Pre-Columbian Mesoamerican development with a rich corpus of archaeological and historic material. Importantly, holistic research issues have resonance with modern, descendant populations living in the Maya highlands. While cultural continuity remains an anthropological topic of study (Borgstede and Yaeger 2008), the modern Maya have begun to present claims on interpretations of the past and its material manifestations, primarily through concepts of sacredness in the landscape (Ivic de Monterroso 2004; Fruhsorge 2007). Clearly, however, the debate about Mexicanization, in-migration, and autochthonous development has relevance to modern political claims of indigenous control over and rights to land and sites. The highland Maya have long been used as analogues for understanding the ancient Maya (Deal 1998; Hayden and Cannon 1984;

Vogt 1983), but modern indigenous social movements are increasingly questioning the use of living peoples as sources of objective anthropological data divorced from political, economic, and sociocultural impact (Montejo 2005).

The Maya highlands as a region contains a diverse and complex geography, a diversity that is represented in the material record. While archaeological and ethnohistoric evidence from the central Guatemalan highlands has long dominated discussion of the Late Postclassic period, research has shown that developments outside of this subregion were extremely variable and localized. A focus on the Quiché and Kaqchikel states has resulted in an important and rich body of evidence that has undeniable importance to Maya and Mesoamerica studies, as well as modern Maya peoples. Concurrent analyses of areas beyond this core zone are uncovering equally important developments that are challenging long-held interpretations; the Late Postclassic period across the entire Maya highlands still promises much fruitful research in the future.

References

Adams, Robert McC. 1961. Changing Patterns of Territorial Organization in the Central Highlands of Chiapas, Mexico. *American Antiquity* 26:341–360.

Akkeren, Ruud van. 2000. *Place of the Lord's Daughter: Rab'inal, Its History, Its Dance-Drama*. CNWS Publications, Vol. 91, Leiden University, Leiden.

Akkeren, Ruud van. 2002. El lugar en donde salió el primer sol para los K'ich'e; Jakawits, su nueva ubicación. In *XV simposio de investigaciones arqueológicas en Guatemala, 2001*, edited by Juan Pedro Laporte, Hector Escobedo, and Bárbara Arroyo, pp. 1–12. Museo Nacional de Arqueología y Etnología, Guatemala.

Arnauld, Marie Charlotte. 1986. *Archelogie de l'habitat en Alta Verapaz, Guatemala*. Collection Etudes Mesoamericaines 10, Centre d'Etudes Mexicaines et Centramericaines, Mexico City.

Arnauld, Marie Charlotte. 1993. Los territorios politicos de las cuencas de Salamá, Rabinal, y Cubulco en el Postclasico. In *Representaciones del espacio político en las tierras altas de Guatemala*, edited by Alain Breton, pp. 43–110. Cuadernos de estudios guatemaltecos 2, Piedra Santa, Guatemala.

Blake, Michael. 2010. *Colonization, Warfare and Exchange at the Postclassic Maya Site of Canajasté, Chiapas, Mexico*. New World Archaeological Foundation, Provo, Utah.

Boone, Elizabeth, and Michael Smith. 2003. Postclassic International Styles and Symbol Sets. In *The Postclassic Mesoamerican World*, edited by Michael Smith and Frances Berdan, pp. 186–193. University of Utah Press, Salt Lake City, Utah.

Borgstede, Greg. 2004. Ethnicity and Archaeology in the Western Maya Highlands, Guatemala. Unpublished PhD dissertation, Department of Anthropology, University of Pennsylvania, Philadelphia.

Borgstede, Greg, and James Mathieu. 2007. Defensibility and Settlement Patterns in the Guatemalan Maya Highlands. *Latin American Antiquity* 18(2):191–211.

Borgstede, Greg, and Luis A. Romero. 2004. Patrones de asentamiento y variación en las tierras altas occidentales, Guatemala. *Estudios: Revista de Antropología, Arqueología, e Historia* 2004:68–110.

Borgstede, Gregory J., and Jason Yaeger. 2008. Notions of Cultural Continuity and Disjunction in Maya Social Movements and Maya Archaeology. In *Archaeology and the Postcolonial Critique*, edited by Uzma Z. Rizvi and Matthew Liebmann, pp. 91–108. Altamira, Lanham, Maryland.

Borhegyi, Stephan F. de. 1965. Archaeological Synthesis of the Guatemalan Highlands. In *Handbook of Middle American Indians, Volume Two: Archaeology of Southern Mesoamerica, Part One*, edited by Gordon R. Willey, pp. 3–58. University of Texas Press, Austin.

Braswell, Geoffrey E. 1996. A Maya Obsidian Source: The Geoarchaeology, Settlement History, and Ancient Economy of San Martin Jilotepeque. Unpublished PhD dissertation, Department of Anthropology, Tulane University, New Orleans, Louisiana.

Braswell, Geoffrey E. 2001a. Post-Classic Maya Courts of the Guatemalan Highlands. In *Royal Courts of the Ancient Maya: Data and Case Studies*, edited by Takeshi Inomata and Stephen D. Houston, pp. 308–334. Westview Press, Boulder, Colorado.

Braswell, Geoffrey E. 2001b. Cultural Emulation, Ethnogenesis, and Survival: The "Nahualization" of the Highland Maya in the Fifteenth and Sixteenth Centuries. In *Maya Survivalism*, edited by U. Hostettler and Matthew Restall, pp. 51–58. Acta Mesoamericana 12, Verlag Anton, Markt Swaben, Germany.

Brown, Kenneth L. 1982. Prehistoric Demography within the Central Quiché Area. In *Historical Demography of Highland Guatemala*, edited by Robert Carmack, J. Early, and Christopher Lutz, pp. 35–48. Institute for Mesoamerican Studies, Publication No. 6, State University of New York, Albany.

Bryant, Douglas D., John E. Clark, and D. Cheetham, eds. 2005. *Ceramic Sequence of the Upper Grijalva Region, Chiapas, Mexico*. New World Archaeological Foundation, Brigham Young University, Papers No. 67, Provo, Utah.

Campbell, Lyle. 1977. *Quichean Linguistic Prehistory*. University of California Press, Berkeley.

Carmack, Robert. 1968. *Toltec Influence on the Postclassic Culture History of Highland Guatemala*. Middle American Research Institute Publications, no. 26, Tulane University, Middle American Research Institute, New Orleans, Louisiana.

Carmack, Robert. 1981. *The Quiché Mayas of Utatlan: The Evolution of a Highland Guatemala Kingdom*. University of Oklahoma Press, Norman.

Carmack, Robert, John Fox, and Russell E. Stewart. 1975. *La formación del reino Quiché*. Instituto de Antropología e Historia de Guatemala, Guatemala City.

Carmack, Robert, and John M. Weeks. 1981. The Archaeology and Ethnohistory of Utatlan: A Conjunctive Approach. *American Antiquity* 46:323–341.

Chase, Arlen F., and Diane Z. Chase. 1996. More Than Kin and King: Centralized Political Organization among the Late Classic Maya. *Current Anthropology* 37(5):803–810.

Culbert, T. Patrick. 1965. *The Ceramic History of the Central Highlands of Chiapas, Mexico*. Papers of the New World Archaeological Foundation No. 14, Brigham Young University, Provo, Utah.

Deal, Michael. 1998. *Pottery Ethnoarchaeology in the Central Maya Highlands*. University of Utah Press, Salt Lake City.

Demarest, Arthur A., Prudence M. Rice, and Don S. Rice. 2004. The Terminal Classic in the Maya Lowlands: Assessing Collapses, Terminations, and Transformations. In *The Terminal Classic in the Maya Lowlands*, edited by Arthur A. Demarest, Prudence M. Rice, and Don S. Rice, pp. 545–572. University of Colorado Press, Boulder.

Dimick, John. 1955. La antiguedad de Zaculeu. *Antropologia e Historia de Guatemala* 7:19–23.

Fox, John W. 1978. *Quiché Conquest: Centralism and Regionalism in Highland Guatemalan State Development.* University of New Mexico Press, Albuquerque.

Fox, John W. 1980. Lowland to Highland Mexicanization Processes in Southern Mesoamerica. *American Antiquity* 45:43–54.

Fox, John W. 1981. The Late Postclassic Eastern Frontier of Mesoamerica: Cultural Innovation along the Periphery. *Current Anthropology* 22(4):321–346.

Fox, John W. 1987. *Maya Postclassic State Formation: Segmentary Lineage Migration in Advancing Frontiers.* Cambridge University Press, Cambridge.

Fox, John W. 1989. On the Rise and Fall of Tulans and Maya Segmentary States. *American Anthropologist* 91(3):656–681.

Fox, John W., Garrett W. Cook, Arlen F. Chase, and Diane Z. Chase. 1996. Questions of Political and Economic Integration: Segmentary vs. Centralized States among the Ancient Maya. *Current Anthropology* 37(5):795–801.

Fox, John W., Dwight T. Wallace, and Kenneth L. Brown. 1992. The Emergence of the Quiché Elites: The Putun-Palenque Connection. In *Mesoamerican Elites*, edited by Diane Z. Chase and Arlen F. Chase, pp. 169–190. University of Oklahoma Press, Norman.

Fruhsorge, Lars. 2007. Archaeological Heritage in Guatemala: Indigenous Perspectives on the Ruins of Iximche. *Archaeologies* 3(1):39–58.

Gillespie, Susan D. 2000. Rethinking Ancient Maya Social Organization: Replacing "Lineage" with "House." *American Anthropologist* 102(3) 467–484.

Guillemin, George F. 1977. Urbanism and Hierarchy at Iximche. In *Social Process in Maya Prehistory: Studies in Honour of Sir Eric Thompson*, edited by Norman Hammond, pp. 227–264. Academic Press, New York.

Hayden, Brian, and Aurbrey Cannon. 1984. *The Structure of Material Systems: Ethnoarchaeology in the Maya Highlands.* Papers of the Society for American Archaeology 3, Society for American Archaeology, Washington, DC.

Hill, Robert M. 1984. Chinamit and Molab: Late Postclassic Highland Maya Precursors of Closed Corporate Community. *Estudios de Cultura Maya* 15:301–327.

Hill, Robert M. 1996. Eastern Chajoma Political Geography: Ethnohistorical and Archaeological Contributions to the Study of a Late Postclassic Maya Polity. *Ancient Mesoamerica* 7:63–87.

Hill, Robert M. 1998. Los otros kaqchikeles: los chajoma vinak. *Mesoamerica* 35:229–254.

Ichon, Alain. 1987. Regional Ceramic Development in El Quiché and Baja Verapaz, Guatemala. In *Maya Ceramics*, edited by Prudence Rice and Robert Sharer, pp. 277–306. BAR International Series 345, Oxford, United Kingdom.

Ichon, Alain. 1993. Los sitios postclasicos de la cuenca de San Andres Sajacaba. In *Representaciones del espacio politico en las tierras altas de Guatemala*, edited by Alain Breton, pp. 111–162. Cuadernos de estudios guatemaltecos 2, Piedra Santa, Guatemala.

Ichon, Alain. 1996. El poblamiento prehispanico. In *La cuenca media del Rio Chixoy*, pp. 43–198. Cuadernos de estudios guatemaltecos 3, Caudal, Guatemala City.

Iglesias Ponce de Leon, M. Josefa, and Andres Ciudad Ruiz. 1984. Exploraciones arqueológicas en la cuenca alta del río Samalá, Guatemala. *Revista Española de Antrolopogía Americana* 14:9–32.

Ivic de Monterroso, Matilde. 2004. The Sacred Place in the Development of Archaeology in Guatemala: An Analysis. In *Continuities and Change in Maya Archaeology:*

Perspectives at the Millennium, edited by Charles Golden and Greg Borgstede, pp. 295–307. Routledge, New York.

Kidder, Alfred V. 1940. Archaeological Problems of the Highland Maya. In *The Maya and Their Neighbors*, edited by Clarence Hay, pp. 117–125. D. Appleton Century, New York.

Kroeber, Alfred L. 1931. The Culture-Area and Age-Area Concepts of Clark Wissler. In *Methods in Social Science, A Case Book*, edited by S. Rice, pp. 248–265. University of Chicago Press, Chicago.

Love, Michael. 2007. Recent Research in the Southern Highlands and Pacific Coast of Mesoamerica. *Journal of Archaeological Research* 15:275–328.

Lowe, Gareth W. 1983. Los olmecas, mayas, y mixe-zoques. In *Antropologia e historia de los Mixe-Zoques y Mayas*, edited by L. Ochoa and Thomas A. Lee, pp. 125–130. Universidad Nacional Autonoma de Mexico.

Lowe, Gareth W., and J. Alden Mason. 1965. Archaeological Survey of the Chiapas Coast, Highlands, and Upper Grijalva Basin. In *Handbook of Middle American Indians, Volume Two: Archaeology of Southern Mesoamerica, Part One*, edited by Gordon R. Willey, pp. 195–235. University of Texas Press, Austin.

Macario C., M. Raquel, et al. 2007. Proyecto etnoarqueologico Q'umarkaj, Quiché, Guatemala, 2003–2006. In *XX simposio de investigaciones arqueológicas en Guatemala, 2006*, edited by Juan Pedro Laporte, Bárbara Arroyo, and Hector Mejía, pp. 971–986. Museo Nacional de Arqueología y Etnología, Guatemala.

Maxwell, Judith M., and Robert M. Hill II. 2006. *Kaqchikel Chronicles*. University of Texas Press, Austin.

Miles, Susan W. 1957. The Sixteenth-Century Pokom-Maya: A Documentary Analysis of Social Structure and Archaeological Setting. *Transactions of the American Philosophical Society* 47:731–781.

Montejo, Victor D. 2005. *Maya Intellectual Renaissance: Identity, Representation, and Leadership*. University of Texas Press, Austin.

Nance, C. Roger. 2003. Settlement Plan and Architecture. In *Archaeology and Ethnohistory of Iximche*, edited by C. Roger Nance, Stephen L. Whittington, and Barbara E. Borg, pp. 305–320. University Press of Florida, Gainesville.

Nance, C. Roger, Stephen L. Whittington, and Barbara E. Borg. 2003. Conclusion. In *Archaeology and Ethnohistory of Iximche*, edited by C. Roger Nance, Stephen L. Whittington, and Barbara E. Borg, pp. 321–335. University Press of Florida, Gainesville.

Navarrete, Carlos. 1962. *La cerámica de Mixco Viejo*. Cuadernos de Antropologia No. 1, Universidad de San Carlos de Guatemala, Guatemala.

Navarrete, Carlos. 1966. *The Chiapanec, History and Culture*. New World Archaeological Foundation Papers 21, Brigham Young University, Provo, Utah.

Navarrete, Carlos. 1978. *Un reconocimiento de la sierra madre de Chiapas*. Universidad Autónoma de Mexico, Mexico City.

Navarrete, Carlos. 1996. Elementos arqueologicos de mexicanizacion en las tierras altas mayas. In *Temas mesoamericanos*, edited by S. Lombardo and E. Nalda, pp. 309–356. Instituto Nacional de Antropología e Historia, Mexico City.

Orellana, Sandra L. 1973. Ethnohistorical and Archaeological Boundaries of the Tzutujil Maya. *Ethnohistory* 20:125–142.

Orellana, Sandra L. 1984. *The Tzutujil Maya: Continuity and Change, 1250–1630*. University of Oklahoma Press, Norman.

Popenoe de Hatch, Marion. 1999. El desarrollo en el Noroccidente de Guatemala desde el Preclásico hasta el Posclásico. In *XII simposio de investigaciones arqueológicas en Guatemala, 1998*, edited by Juan Pedro Laporte and Hector L. Escobedo, pp. 497–508. Museo Nacional de Arqueología y Etnología, Guatemala City.

Recinos, Adrian. 1952. *Pedro de Alvarado, conquistador de Mexico y Guatemala*. Fondo de Cultura Economica, Mexico City.

Robinson, Eugenia J. 1997. The Prehistoric to Colonial Settlement Transition in Antigua, Guatemala. In *Historical Archaeology in Middle and South America*, edited by Janice Gasco and Greg Smith, pp. 59–70. Institute of Archaeology, University of California, Los Angeles.

Robinson, Eugenia J. 1998. Organizacion del estado Kaqchikel: El centro regional de Chitak Tzak. In *Estudios Kaqchikeles: en memorium William R. Swezey*, edited by Eugenia J. Robinson and Robert M. Hill, pp. 217–228. Centro de Investigaciones Regionales de Mesoamerica, Antigua, Guatemala.

Robinson, Eugenia J. 2008. Memoried Sacredness and International Elite Identities: The Late Postclassic at La Casa de las Golondrinas, Guatemala. In *Archaeologies of Art: Time, Place and Identity*, edited by Inés Domingo Sanz, Dánae Fiore, and Sally K. May, pp. 131–150. Left Coast Press, Walnut Creek, California.

Sharer, Robert J., and David W. Sedat. 1987. *Archaeological Investigations in the Northern Maya Highlands, Guatemala: Interaction and the Development of Maya Civilization*. The University Museum, University of Pennsylvania, Philadelphia.

Smith, A. Ledyard. 1955. *Archaeological Reconnaissance in Central Guatemala*. Carnegie Institute of Washington Publication 608, Carnegie Institute of Washington, Washington, DC.

Smith, Michael. 2003. Information Networks in Postclassic Mesoamerica. In *The Postclassic Mesoamerican World*, edited by Michael Smith and Frances Berdan, pp. 181–185. University of Utah Press, Salt Lake City.

Stone, Andrea. 1999. Postclassic Rock Art in Historical Context. Paper presented at the International Rock Art Congress, Ripon, Wisconsin.

Stone, Andrea, and S. Ericastilla Godoy. 1998. Registro de arte ruprestre en las tierras altas de Guatemala: Resultados del reconocimiento de 1997. In *XII simposio de investigaciones arqueologicas en Guatemala, 1997*, edited by Juan Pedro Laporte, Hector Escobedo, and A. Monzón de Suasnávar, pp. 775–783. Ministerio de Cultura y Deportes, Instituto de Antropologia e Historia, and Asociacion Tikal, Guatemala City.

Tax, Sol. 1937. The Municipios of the Midwestern Highlands of Guatemala. *American Anthropologist* 39:423–444.

Tedlock, Dennis. 1996. *Popol Vuh*. Simon and Schuster, New York.

Thompson, J. Eric S. 1943. A Trial Survey of the Southern Maya Area. *American Antiquity* 9:106–134.

Thompson, J. Eric S. 1970. Putun (Chontal Maya) Expansion in Yucatan and the Pasión Drainage. In *Maya History and Religion*, by J. Eric S. Thompson, pp. 3–47. University of Oklahoma Press, Norman.

Vogt, Evon Z. 1983. Ancient and Contemporary Maya Settlement Patterns: A New Look from the Chiapas Highlands. In *Prehistoric Settlement Patterns in the New World*, edited by Gordon Willey, pp. 89–114. University of New Mexico Press, Albuquerque.

Wallace, Dwight. 1977. An Intra-Site Analysis of Utatlan: The Structure of an Urban Site. In *Archaeology and Ethnohistory of the Central Quiché*, edited by Dwight

Wallace and Robert Carmack, pp. 20–54. Institute for Mesoamerican Studies, State
    University of New York, Albany.
Wauchope, Robert. 1947. An Approach to the Maya Correlation Problem through
    Guatemala Highland Archaeology and Native Annals. *American Antiquity* 13:59–66.
Wauchope, Robert. 1970. Protohistoric Pottery of the Guatemala Highlands. In
    Monographs and Papers in Maya Archaeology, edited by William Bullard, pp.
    89–243. Papers of the Peabody Museum of Archaeology and Ethnology Vol. 61,
    Harvard University, Cambridge, Massachusetts.
Weeks, John. 1983. *Chisalin: A Late Postclassic Maya Settlement in Highland Guatemala.*
    BAR International Series 169, Oxford, United Kingdom.
Wissler, Clark. 1927. The Culture Area Concept in Social Anthropology. *American
    Journal of Sociology* 32:881–891.
Woodbury, Richard B., and Aubrey S. Trik. 1953. *The Ruins of Zaculeu.* United Fruit,
    Richmond, Virginia.

CHAPTER 29

THE SOUTHERN PACIFIC COASTAL REGION OF MESOAMERICA

A CORRIDOR OF INTERACTION FROM OLMEC TO AZTEC TIMES

ROBERT M. ROSENSWIG

THE Pacific coast of Mesoamerica has always been a well-traveled corridor (Figure 29.1). This is in part due to geography: if you wish to journey from central Mexico south to Central America, virtually all lowland travel will follow the Pacific coast. Three decades ago, Parsons and Price (1971: 170), with very broad brushstrokes, divided Mesoamerica into highland and lowland zones as well as "a third perhaps equally important one, a transition area called the 'peripheral coastal lowlands.' ... Included in this long continuous region is the Gulf Coast of Mexico and the southern Pacific Coast of Chiapas-Guatemala-El Salvador; the Isthmus of Tehuantepec is the geographic link between these two coastal plains." My focus here is the southern portion of this "peripheral coastal lowlands," what Demarest (2004: 67) refers to as the "southern 'corridor' of interaction" and Love (2007: 277), in a comprehensive recent review of the area, calls the "southern Pacific region." Here I refer to a loosely defined Southern Pacific Coastal Region (SPCR) that minimally encompasses the Pacific side of Chiapas, Guatemala, and El Salvador.

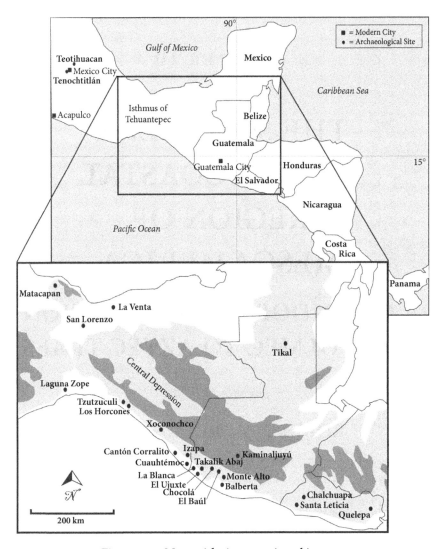

Figure 29.1 Map, with sites mentioned in text.

I engage this macro-region with equally large temporal brushstrokes and
note that the Olmec, Teotihuacan, and Aztec systems of interregional interaction
each extended over a surprisingly similar geographic area that encompassed the
SPCR, Mexico's Gulf Coast, and the Central Highlands. I consider this the core
communication corridor of Mesoamerica and the SPCR to be the southern half
of this core area. In this chapter, I review archaeological evidence of the Olmec,
Teotihuacan, and Aztec horizons in the SPCR. I also present what is known of a
system of emergent urban centers and "Izapan-style" iconography that unite the
SPCR as a discrete region in its own right during the Late Formative period.

Adopting macro-temporal and macro-spatial frameworks is consistent with
a world-systems perspective (Blanton and Feinman 1984; Schortman and Urban
1992; Smith and Berdan 2003). Such an approach allows for synthetic treatment

of geographically dispersed peoples sharing elements of symbolic culture and exchanging goods (Frank 1990, 1993). Philip Kohl (1987: 18) provides a practical definition of Bronze Age West Asia that "can be considered at some level as a unit, that formed some form of complex, multicentered world system(s)." He noted that the geographic extents of the Bronze Age world system parallel the initial spread of Islam in later times and proposes that a similarly distributed interaction network persisted for a very long time (Kohl 1987: 28). Such Old World connections were strongly influenced by physical geography in the same way that the medieval spice routes funneled water travel through the straits of Hormuz and Malacca, replicating modern shipping patterns; these connections and routes are also similar to the earlier spread of Islam (Bernstein 2008). Physical geography matters and forms the basis for trade routes and the resulting social relations required to keep goods flowing and symbolic information passing from one region to the next.

In both West Asia and Mesoamerica, similar exchange routes appear to have persisted for millennia and resulted in cyclical remaking of interaction systems over similar areal extents. In West Asia, "The original Bronze Age world systems did not simply collapse but left a complex, weblike legacy of political, economic, and, in the broad sense, cultural interconnections that in turn were acted upon and influenced later historical developments" (Kohl 1987: 28). In Mesoamerica, the Olmec, Teotihuacan, and Aztec horizons each minimally encompassed portions of the Mexican Central Highlands and Gulf Coast as well as the Pacific coasts of Chiapas and Guatemala, with some evidence of influence extending further south. So for example, the southern extent of known Olmec-style artifacts recovered from lower Central America parallels that of historically known migrations from Central Mexico of Nawa- and Chorotegan-speaking peoples as far south as Nicaragua (Carmack and Salgado 2006: Figure 1; Fowler 1989; McCafferty and Steinbrenner 2005). This is unlikely to have been simple coincidence.

TRAVEL ALONG THE PACIFIC COAST

Perhaps the best-known region on Mesoamerica's Pacific Coast is the Soconusco, which was an important Spanish colonial territory, which the Aztec and Quiché had both previously conquered (Navarrete 1970; Voorhies and Gasco 2004: 3–9). During Postclassic and early colonial times it was primarily cacao that brought successive waves of invaders to the area (Gasco 2006). The desirability of the Soconusco lies largely in the local environmental richness but equally important is its strategic location along a natural transportation corridor.

Most land travel during colonial times was along the edge of the Sierra Madre piedmont. This was the Colonial-period *camino real* that the principal modern highway still follows. Early colonial accounts of this route are provided by both

Fray Alonso Ponce from his 1574 journey to Guatemala City (Coe 1961) and by Pedro de Alvarado on his way to conquer Utatlán in 1524 (Navarrete 1978: 76). Both men followed the coastal route to get from Mexico City to the Guatemalan highlands. A series of eighteenth-century accounts describe basically the same travel conditions (Orellana 1995: 13).

Another method of travel along the Pacific Coast was by canoe through a system of estuary canals. These canals are formed when the coastal rivers are blocked by sandbars formed by discharge of the silt load they carry (Navarrete 1978: 80–81). An anonymous, late eighteenth-century account states: "The products of this Province can be carried by the estuaries on the one hand to the Alcaldía Mayor of Escuintla, that is near Goatemala [i.e., modern city of Antigua], and on the other hand to Teguantepeque [i.e., Oaxaca]" (Navarrete 1978: 80). Archaeological data indicate that the estuary travel route was also important during the Postclassic period (Gasco 2003). In 1965, Carlos Navarrete began to collect accounts of this estuary canal route that was used up to the 1908 inauguration of the coastal railway line. Old merchants told him that before the railways were built, convoys of up to forty canoes would make journeys up and down the coast primarily to transport cacao (but also crocodile hides, dried shrimp, fish, and iguanas) out of the Soconusco and to import ceramics from Guatemala and Oaxaca. During the nineteenth century, travel along these estuary canal systems extended as far south as El Salvador. Shrimp continued to be transported along the Chiapas coast through this route into the 1960s (Paillés 1980: 11). Such accounts provide a guide as to the ease of such travel, which helps explain why, during successive epochs, the SPCR had such extensive contact from Chiapas to El Salvador, and beyond to both north and south.

Pacific Coast Archaeology

Early and Middle Formative Olmec Horizons

There is considerable debate over what the distribution of Early Formative Olmec-style objects means in cultural terms (e.g., Blomster et al. 2005; Flannery et al. 2005). However, it is clear that some form of interaction was responsible for such far-flung shared aesthetic standards. The strongest arguments for another area having been integrated into the San Lorenzo political dominion comes from the Mazatán zone of the Soconusco (Clark 1997; Clark and Pye 2000). While this interpretation is hotly contested (Flannery and Marcus 2000), detailed studies of figurines and carved pottery from Cantón Corralito do indicate that this was some sort of an outpost or enclave with close ties to San Lorenzo (Cheetham 2009, 2010; Cheetham et al. 2009).

Regardless of the nature of interaction that accounts for the spread of the early Olmec style, the area over which these objects were used is clear. On the Pacific coast, early Olmec-style objects are known from both sides of the Soconusco: north as far as Laguna Zope (Zeitlin 1978: 193) and Barrio Tepalcate (Winter 2007) as well as south along the coast of Guatemala (Arroyo 2003). White-rimmed black-ware serving vessels, figurines with infantile facial characteristics (Figure 29.2), and Mesoamerica's first abstract iconography were employed by inhabitants across Parson and Price's entire "peripheral coast lowlands" as well as the Basin of Mexico and neighboring areas of the central Mexican highlands (Rosenswig 2010: 57–59). In other words, the early Olmec horizon covers roughly the same extents at the Aztec Empire. Equally significant is where both early Olmec and Aztec horizons are not found: the Maya lowlands of modern day Petén, Belize, and Yucatán.

The following Middle Formative period, beginning at cal. 1000 BC, marks a time of major economic intensification based on increased maize use as well as greater reliance on dog and deer meat (Blake et al. 1992; Chisholm and Blake 2006; Love 2002a; Rosenswig 2006, 2007; Wake and Harrington 2002). The site of La Blanca, measuring 300 hectares with a central mound rising 25 meters, emerged at this time as the center of a multitiered settlement system with an unprecedented level of social stratification (Love 2002a; Love and Guernsey 2011; Rosenswig 2007, 2008). Increased population density around La Blanca, and the abandonment of surrounding areas, formed a nucleated island of cultural complexity that had no counterpart anywhere on the Pacific Coast of Mesoamerica at this time (Rosenswig 2011).

The La Blanca polity lasted a century or two and collapsed as a series of centers emerged along the Pacific piedmont by 700–500 cal. BC: Tzutzuculi (McDonald 1983), Izapa (Lowe et al. 1982), Takalik Abaj (Schieber de Lavarreda 1994), Monte Alto (Bove

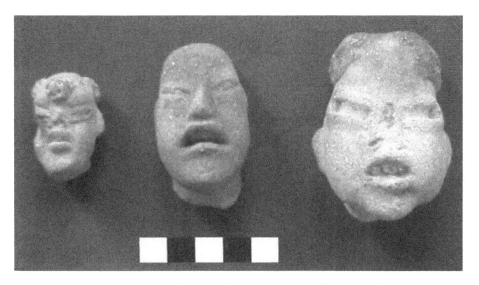

Figure 29.2 Early Formative Olmec-style figurines from the Cuauhtémoc site in the Suchiate zone of the Soconusco.

1989), and Chocolá (Kaplan 2008), among others. These centers developed during the second part of the Middle Formative at the same time as La Venta was established on the Gulf Coast (Rosenswig 2010: 71–74). Details of the founding of these SPCR sites (and their initial layout) are poorly understood as most subsequently developed into the large Late Formative urban centers, for which the region is best known.

Late Formative Horizon

The Late Formative was a time of strong local traditions across Mesoamerica (e.g., Chicanel, Monte Albán) when urban states emerge. The SPCR was a discrete culture area at this time and a series of such urban centers were established during the three centuries before the common era (see Love 2007: 291–296). Despite the early work done at Izapa (Lowe et al. 1982), and the well-known and distinctive local art style dubbed "Izapan" (Figure 29.3) (Guernsey 2006), the Late Formative period remains poorly understood in the Soconusco. Major Late Formative settlements are better known from the Guatemalan piedmont at sites such as Takalik Abaj, Monte Alto, and Chocolá (Bove 1989; Kaplan 2008; Miles 1965; Schieber de Laverrada 1998; Parsons 1986) as well as sites further south such as Santa Rosa

Figure 29.3 Late Formative Stela 21 from Izapa (drawn by Ayax Moreno, courtesy of the New World Archaeological Foundation).

(Estrada Belli 2002). While many large centers are known from the piedmont, the site of El Ujuxte (Love 2002b) was an important site on Guatemala's coastal plain. Adjacent areas of Guatemalan highlands such as Kaminaljuyú were also linked to this Pacific piedmont phenomenon (Popenoe de Hatch 2002).

Early urban centers sharing a related artistic aesthetic extended down the Pacific side of El Salvador at Chalchuapa (Sharer 1978), Santa Leticia (Demarest 1986), and Quelepa (Andrews 1976). While there are Maya-influenced stelae at sites such as Takalik Abaj (Love 2007: 293), equally significant was that lower Central American influences moved north through the SPCR. Such influence was especially evident in the distinctive Usulután ceramics and potbelly sculpture both known from all along the Pacific coast of Guatemala and the Soconusco (e.g., Coe 1961; Guernsey 2011; Kosakowsky et al. 2000: 380–381; Parsons 1986: Plates 89–123; Thompson and Valdez 2008). Usulután ceramics originate in western El Salvador (Demarest and Sharer 1982) and/or eastern Guatemala (Neff et al. 1999) but they are also documented as far south as the Pacific coast of Nicaragua (e.g., Healy 1980: 239–242) and Costa Rica (Creamer 1987: 52) as well as in the Maya area in low frequencies. These sculptures and ceramics often co-occur and it is significant that when potbelly sculptures are found at Maya sites such as Tikal, there are also Usulután ceramic wares (Culbert 1993: Figures 4–13). Potbellies are found all along the SPCR (Thompson and Valdez 2008: Figure 17) and may derive from appropriating Middle Formative-period ceramic figurine forms from the Soconusco into the public sphere (Guernsey 2011; Guernsey and Love 2008). However, low relief boulder carvings are common along the Pacific coasts of Nicaragua and Costa Rica, making this another possible source of inspiration. The SPCR hangs together at this time as a distinct culture area with stronger ties to lower Central America (Creamer 1987: 45–47) and the Maya area (Love 2007: 296–297) than the Gulf Coast or Mexican highlands.

Early Classic Teotihuacan Horizon

Ties between Teotihuacan and the Gulf Coast at Matacapan and Kaminaljuyú in the Guatemalan highlands during the Early Classic period have long been proposed on the basis of talud tublero architecture, ceramic vessel forms and style, common iconographic conventions, as well as green Pachuca obsidian from 200–600 cal. AD (Cowgill 2008). Centers such as Izapa and Takalik Abaj continued to be occupied during the Early Classic period but new ceremonial architecture was not erected (Lowe et al. 1982; Popenoe de Hatch 2002). However, El Ujuxte was abandoned at the end of the Late Formative and "no substantial Early Classic occupation" was documented around this site (Love 2007: 298) nor in the area directly across the Mexican border between Izapa and the coast (Rosenswig 2008). The Early Classic was a period of major political change in the SPCR.

Two large Early Classic centers are known from the SPCR with ties to the expanding Teotihuacan Empire. First, on the central coast of Chiapas, Garcia-Des Laurier (2007) provides detailed evidence from Los Horcones, including Teotihuacan-style stelae (Figure 29.4), site layouts, obsidian, mold-made figurines, and ceramic vessels. The area surrounding Los Horcones was most densely occupied during the Early Classic period (Voorhies 1989: Figure 5.12). Second, on the central Guatemalan coast Bove and Medrano (2003: 76) interpret data from the sites of Balberta and Montana as evidence of a Teotihuacan invasion. Balberta was the largest Early Classic site on the coast of Guatemala and demonstrates population nucleation and political centralization (Love 2007: 299). The earlier Olmec core area seems to have been recreated during the Early Classic period with central Mexican and Gulf Coast links to the SPCR (Cowgill 2008: 970). Cultural connections over this area during the Early Classic period are consistent with Kaufman and Justeson's (2007) reconstruction that peoples in each of these areas spoke Mije-Soquean languages.

Late Classic and Early Postclassic Balkanization

The Late Classic and Early Postclassic were periods of renewed balkanization across Mesoamerica. The SPCR has long been known from these times as the source of Plumbate pottery, which are found in elite contexts across most areas

Figure 29.4 Early Classic Los Horcones Stela 3 (courtesy of Claudia Garcia-Des Laurier).

of Mesoamerica (Shepard 1948). Chemical sourcing data have located the production of Plumbate to the Pacific Coast on both sides of the Mexican-Guatemalan border (Neff 2002), the time when this area also reached its densest prehispanic occupation (Love 2007: 301; Rosenswig 2008). Previously central to long-distance exchange routes, peoples in the SPCR likely maintained the contacts required to distribute the distinctive and beautiful Plumbate wares. In the Soconusco, the site core of Izapa shifted at this time and Group F built north of the earlier plaza groups (Lowe et al. 1982). On the central Guatemalan coast, the Cotzumalhuapa culture, best known from the site of El Baúl, seems to have been a separate phenomenon (Love 2007: 301–302) with links to coastal Guerrero (Pye and Gutiérrez 2007: 240–242).

Late Postclassic Aztec Horizon

From the Late Postclassic period, we know that the Soconusco was prized for its cacao production: the Aztec Empire collected tribute from eight named towns that were supervised by two named tax collectors (Gasco 2003; Voorhies and Gasco 2004: 3–5). Voorhies and Gasco (2004) have documented Xoconochco, the largest of the Aztec tributaries and the one that gave its name to the entire region, where an Aztec garrison was supposedly stationed (Carrasco 1999). The Soconusco region was briefly conquered by the Quiché Maya (Carmack 1981), so keeping the SPCR open to Aztec trade may have been one reason why the Soconusco province was established at such a distance from Tenochtitlan. Numerous Aztec-period sites are identified along the coast by the presence of distinctive zoomorphic tripod vessel supports (Figure 29.5) and central Mexican obsidian. Related Late Postclassic remains are documented along the Guatemalan coast (Bove et al. 2006) and as far south as Nicaragua (Carmack and Salgado 2006: Figure 3b). As previously noted, Nawa speakers are known all along the Pacific Coast as far south as Nicaragua— the Nawa-speaking Nicarao being those who gave the modern country its name (Fowler 1989; Orellana 1995). Nawa occupation of the Gulf Coast is well known ethnohistorically (Berdan 1994) as well as archaeologically (Garraty and Stark 2002; Ohnersorgen 2006), and so the central Mexican highland-Gulf Coast-SPCR cultural connection in the decades preceding the Spanish arrival is again well documented.

Conclusion

This brief review of the SPCR provides macro-temporal and macro-spatial patterns. Incongruous with micro-scale perspectives that prioritize events, agents, and actors, a world-systems perspective guides my distillation of 3,500 years of history

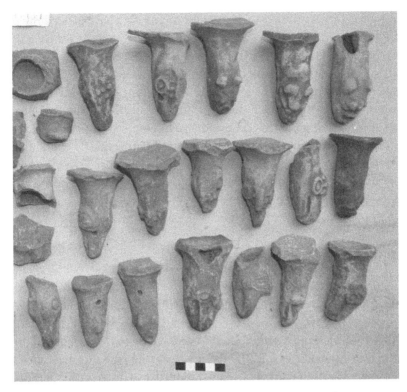

Figure 29.5 Zoomorphic supports (mostly avian) from Late Postclassic Aztec-style tripod vessels, from the Gonzalo Hernandez site in the Suchiate zone of the Soconusco.

over thousands of square kilometers into this brief chapter. The SPCR forms a natural corridor of interaction that saw multiple cycles of collapse and regeneration. That the extents of interaction were repeatedly reestablished over similar (but certainly not exactly the same) areas attests to the influence of physical geography on travel patterns and resulting trade networks. I argue that the core of Mesoamerica linked the central Mexican highlands, the Gulf Coast, and the SPCR during the Early Formative Olmec period, the Early Classic Teotihuacan period, as well as the Late Postclassic Aztec horizon. An explanation for close Gulf Coast–SPCR cultural connections was undoubtedly that the Isthmus of Tehuantepec was the only break in the Sierra Madre that allowed relatively easy intercoastal travel and trade. Travel along the Pacific Coast was then facilitated by the inland canal system that allowed efficient travel from the south side of the isthmus down to El Salvador and Nicaragua. The SPCR of Chiapas, Guatemala, and El Salvador can be productively considered a discrete culture area (Love 2007: 277)—one whose character was shaped by physical geography to form a natural corridor of interaction linking peoples in a similar manner over many millennia.

REFERENCES

Andrews V, E. W. 1976. *The Archaeology of Quelepa, El Salvador*. Middle American Research Institute Publication 42, Tulane University, New Orleans.

Arroyo, Bárbara. 2003. Los Últimos 25 años en la arqueología de la Costa Sur de Guatemala. *Anales de la Academia de Geografía e Historia de Guatemala* LXXVIII:23–48.

Berdan, Francis F. 1994. Economic Alternatives under Imperial Rule: The Eastern Aztec Empire. In *Economies and Polities in the Aztec Realm*, edited by Mary G. Hodge and Michael E. Smith, pp. 291–312. Institute of Mesoamerican Studies, Studies in Culture and Society 6, University at Albany, Albany.

Bernstein, William J. 2008. *A Splendid Exchange: How Trade Shaped the World*. Grove Press, New York.

Bove, Frederick J. 1989. *Formative Settlement Patterns on the Pacific Coast of Guatemala: A Spatial Analysis of Complex Societal Evolution*, BAR International Series No. 493, British Archaeological Reports, Oxford.

Bove, F. J., Genovez, J. V., and Batres, C. 2006. Migration and Ethnicity: The Archaeology of the Nahua/Pipil of Postclassic Pacific Guatemala. In *Olmec, Maya, Aztec: Contributions Honoring H. B. Nicholson*, edited by Mary P. Beaudry-Corbett. Cotsen Institute of Archaeology, University of California, Los Angeles.

Bove, Frederick J., and Sonia Medrano Busto. 2003. Teotihuacan, Militarism, and Pacific Guatemala. In *The Maya and Teotihuacan: Reinterpreting Early Classic Interaction*, edited by Geoffrey E. Braswell, pp. 46–79. University of Texas Press, Austin.

Blake, Michael, B. S. Chisholm, John E. Clark, Barbara Voorhies, and Michael W. Love. 1992. Prehistoric Subsistence in the Soconusco Region. *Current Anthropology* 33:83–94.

Blanton, Richard, and Gary Feinman. 1984. The Mesoamerican World System. *American Anthropologist* 86:673–682.

Blomster, Jeffrey P., Hector Neff, and Michael D. Glascock. 2005. Olmec Pottery Production and Export in Ancient Mexico Determined through Elemental Analysis. *Science* 307:1068–1072.

Carmack, Robert M. 1981. *The Quiché Maya of Utatlán*. University of Oklahoma Press, Norman.

Carmack, Robert M., and Silvia Salgado González. 2006. A World-Systems Perspective on the Archaeology and Ethnohistory of the Mesoamerican/Lower Central American Border. *Ancient Mesoamerica* 17:219–229.

Carrasco, Pedro. 1999. *The Tenochca Empire of Ancient Mexico*. University of Oklahoma Press, Norman.

Cheetham, David. 2009. Early Olmec Figurines from Two Regions: Style as Cultural Imperative. In *Mesoamerican Figurines: Small-Scale Indices of Large-Scale Social Phenomena*, edited by Cristina T. Halperin, Katherine A. Faust, Rhonda Taube, and Aurore Giheut, pp. 149–179. University Press of Florida, Gainesville.

Cheetham, David. 2010. Cultural Imperatives in Clay: Early Olmec Carved Pottery from San Lorenzo and Cantón Corralito. *Ancient Mesoamerica* 21: 165–185.

Cheetham, David, Susana E. Gonzáles, Richard J. Behl, Michael D. Coe, Richard A. Diehl, and Hector Neff. 2009. Petrographic Analyses of Early Formative Olmec Carved Pottery. *Mexicon* 31:69–72.

Chisholm, Brian, and Blake, Michael. 2006. Diet in Prehistoric Soconusco. In *Histories of Maize: Multidisciplinary Approaches to the Prehistory, Linguistics, Biogeography, Domestication, and Evolution of Maize*, edited by John Stoller, Robert H. Tykot, and Bruce F. Benz, pp. 161–172. Elsevier/Academic Press, New York.

Clark, John E. 1997. The Arts of Government in Early Mesoamerica. *Annual Review of Anthropology* 26:211–234.

Clark, John E., and Mary E. Pye. 2000. The Pacific Coast and the Olmec Question. In *Olmec Art and Archaeology in Mesoamerica*, edited by John E. Clark and Mary E. Pye, pp. 217–251. National Gallery of Art, Washington, DC.

Coe, Michael D. 1961. *La Victoria: An Early Site on the Pacific Coast of Guatemala*. Papers of the Peabody Museum of Archaeology and Ethnology Vol. 53, Peabody Museum, Cambridge, Massachusetts.

Cowgill, George L. 2008. An Update on Teotihuacan. *Antiquity* 82:962–975.

Creamer, Winifred. 1987. Mesoamerica as a Concept: An Archaeological View from Central America. *Latin American Research Review* 22:35–62.

Culbert, T. Patrick. 1993. *The Ceramics of Tikal*. Tikal Report 25, University of Pennsylvania, Philadelphia.

Demarest, Artur A. 1986. *The Archaeology of Santa Leticia and the Rise of Maya Civilization*. Middle American Research Institute Publication 52, Tulane University, New Orleans.

Demarest, Artur A. 2004. *Ancient Maya: The Rise and Fall of a Rainforest Civilization*. Cambridge University Press, Cambridge.

Demarest, Arthur A., and Robert J. Sharer. 1982. The Origins and Evolution of Usulutan Ceramics. *American Antiquity* 47:810–822.

Estrada Belli, Francisco. 2002. Putting Santa Rosa on the Map: New Insights on the Cultural Development of the Pacific Coast of Southeastern Guatemala. In *Incidents of Archaeology in Central America and Yucatan: Studies in Honor of Edwin M. Shook*, edited by Michael W. Love, Marion Popenoe de Hatch, and Héctor L. Escobedo, pp. 103–128. University Press of America, Lanham, Maryland.

Flannery, K. V., A. K. Balkansky, G. M. Feinman, D. C. Grove, J. Marcus, E. M. Redmond, R. G. Reynolds, R. J. Sharer, C. S. Spencer, and J. Yaeger. 2005. Implications of New Petrographic Analysis for the Olmec "Mother Culture" Model. *Proceedings of the National Academy of Science* 102:11219–11223.

Flannery, Kent V., and Joyce Marcus. 2000. Formative Mesoamerican Chiefdoms and the Myth of the "Mother Culture." *Journal of Anthropological Archaeology* 19:1–37.

Fowler, William R. Jr. 1989. *The Cultural Evolution of Ancient Nahua Civilization: The Pipil-Nicarao of Central America*. Civilization of the American Indian Series Vol. 194, University of Oklahoma Press, Norman.

Frank, André G. 1990. A Theoretical Introduction to 5,000 Years of World Systems History. *Review* 12:155–248.

Frank, André G. 1993. Bronze Age World System Cycles. *Current Anthropology* 34:383–430.

Garcia-Des Lauriers, Claudia. 2007. Proyecto Arqueologico Los Horcones Investigating the Teotihuacan Presence on the Pacific Coast of Chiapas, Mexico. Unpublished PhD dissertation, University of California, Riverside.

Garraty, Christopher P., and Barbara L. Stark. 2002. Imperial and Social Relations in Postclassic South-Central Veracruz, Mexico. *Latin American Antiquity* 13:3–33.

Gasco, Janine. 2003. Polities of the Soconusco. In *The Postclassic Mesoamerican World*, edited by M. E. Smith and F. F. Berdan, pp. 50–54. University of Utah Press, Salt Lake City.

Gasco, Janine. 2006. Soconusco Cacao Farmers Past and Present: Continuity and Change in an Ancient Way of Life. In *Chocolate in Mesoamerica: A Cultural History of Cacao*, edited by C. McNeil, pp. 322–337. University Press of Florida, Gainesville.

Guernsey, Julia. 2006. *Ritual and Power in Stone: The Performance of Rulership in Mesoamerican Izapan-Style Art*. University of Texas Press, Austin.

Guernsey, Julia. 2011. Rulers, Gods, and Potbellies: A Consideration of Sculptural Forms and Themes from the Preclassic Pacific Coast and Piedmont of Mesoamerica. In *The Place of Stone Monuments in Mesoamerica's Preclassic Transition: Context, Use, and Meaning*, edited by J. Guernsey, J. E. Clark, and B. Arroyo, pp. 207–230. Dumbarton Oaks, Washington, DC.

Guernsey Julia, and Michael Love. 2008. Cerámica y piedra: relaciones entre alfarería, figurillas y escultura en el Preclásico de la Costa Sur. In *XXI simposio de investigaciones arqueológicas en Guatemala*, 2007, edited by Juan P. Laporte and Bárbara Arroyo, pp. 1167–1192. Ministerio de Cultura y Deportes, Instituto de Antropología e Historia, and the Asociación Tikal, Guatemala City.

Healy, Paul F. 1980. *Archaeology of the Rivas Region, Nicaragua*. Wilfrid Laurier University Press, Waterloo.

Kaplan, Jonathan. 2008. Hydraulics, Cacao, and Complex Developments at Preclassic Chocolá, Guatemala: Evidence and Implications. *Latin American Antiquity* 19:399–413.

Kaufman, Terence, and John Justeson. 2007. The History of the Word for Cacao in Ancient Mesoamerica. *Ancient Mesoamerica* 18:193–237.

Kohl, Philip L. 1987. The Use and Abuse of World Systems Theory: The Case of the Pristine West Asian State. *Advances in Archaeological Method and Theory* 11:1–35.

Kosakowsky, Laura J., Francisco Estrada Belli, and Paul Petit. 2000. Preclassic through Postclassic: The Chronological History of the Southeastern Pacific Coast of Guatemala. *Ancient Mesoamerica* 11:1–17.

Love, Michael W. 2002a. *Early Complex Society in Pacific Guatemala: Settlements and Chronology of the Río Naranjo, Guatemala*. New World Archaeological Foundation 66, Brigham Young University, Provo, Utah.

Love, Michael W. 2002b. Ceramic Chronology of Preclassic Period Western Pacific Guatemala and Its Relationship to Other Regions. In *Incidents of Archaeology in Central America and Yucatán: Essays in Honor of Edwin M. Shook*, edited by Michael W. Love, Marion Popenoe de Hatch, and Héctor L. Escobedo, pp. 51–73. University Press of America, Lanham, Maryland.

Love, Michael W. 2007. Recent Research in the Southern Highlands and Pacific Coast of Mesoamerica. *Journal of Archaeological Research* 15:275–328.

Love, Michael W., and Julia Guernsey. 2011. La Blanca and the Soconusco Middle Formative Period, 900–600 BC. In *Sociopolitical Transformation in Early Mesoamerica: Archaic to Formative in the Soconusco Region*, edited by Richard Lesure, pp. 207–230. University of California Press, Berkeley.

Lowe, Gareth W., Thomas A. Lee Jr., and E. M. Espinoza. 1982. *Izapa: An Introduction to the Ruins and Monuments*. Papers of the New World Archaeological Foundation 31, Brigham Young University, Provo, Utah.

McCafferty, Geoffrey G., and Larry Steinbrenner. 2005. Chronological Implications for Greater Nicoya from the Santa Isabel Project, Nicaragua. *Ancient Mesoamerica* 16:131–146.

McDonald, Andrew. 1983. *Tzutzuculi: A Middle-Preclassic Site on the Pacific Coast of Chiapas, Mexico*. Papers of the New World Archaeological Foundation 47, Brigham Young University, Provo, Utah.

Miles, Suzanne W. 1965. Sculpture of the Guatemalan-Chiapas Highlands and Pacific
    Slopes and Associated Hieroglyphs. In *Archaeology of Southern Mesoamerica*, edited
    by Gordon R. Willey, pp. 237–275. Handbook of Middle American Indians Vol. 2,
    University of Texas Press, Austin.
Navarrete, Carlos. 1970. Evidencias de la lengua Quiché en el Soconusco. *Boletín Escritura
    Maya* 11(2):32–33.
Navarrete, Carlos. 1978. The Prehispanic System of Communication between Chiapas
    and Tabasco. In *Mesoamerican Communication Routes and Cultural Contacts*,
    edited by Thomas. A. Lee Jr. and Carlos Navarrete, pp. 75–106. Papers of the New
    World Archaeological Foundation 40, Provo, Utah.
Neff, Hector. 2002. Sources of Raw Material Used in Plumbate Pottery. In *Incidents of
    Archaeology in Central America and Yucatán: Essays in Honor of Edwin M. Shook*,
    edited by Michael W. Love, Marion Popenoe de Hatch, and Hectór L. Escobedo,
    pp. 217–231.University Press of America, Lanham, Maryland.
Neff, Hector, James W. Cogswell, Laura Kosakowsky, Fransisco Estrada Belli, and
    Frederick J. Bove. 1999. A New Perspective on the Relationships among Cream
    Paste Ceramic Traditions of Southeastern Mesoamerica. *Latin American Antiquity*
    10:281–299.
Ohnersorgen, Michael A. 2006. Aztec Provincial Administration at Cuetlaxtlan,
    Veracruz. *Journal of Anthropological Archaeology* 25:1–32.
Orellana, Sandra L. 1995. *Ethnohistory of the Pacific Coast*. Labyrinthos, Lancaster.
Paillés, Maricruz H. 1980. *Pampa El Pajón, An Early Estuarine Site, Chiapas, Mexico*.
    Papers of the New World Archaeological Foundation 44, Brigham Young University,
    Provo, Utah.
Parsons, Lee A. 1986. *The Origins of Maya Art: A Study of the Monumental Sculpture
    of Kaminaljuyu, Guatemala and the Southern Pacific Coast*. Dumbarton Oaks,
    Washington, DC.
Parsons, Lee A., and Barbara J. Price. 1971. Mesoamerican Trade and Its Role in the
    Emergence of Civilization. In *Observations on the Emergence of Civilization
    in Mesoamerica*, edited by Robert F. Heizer and John A. Graham, pp. 169–195.
    Contributions of the University of California Research Facility No 11, University of
    California, Berkeley.
Popenoe de Hatch, Marion. 2002. New Perspectives on Kaminaljuyu, Guatemala:
    Regional Interaction during the Preclassic and Classic Periods. In *Incidents of
    Archaeology in Central America and Yucatan: Studies in Honor of Edwin M. Shook*,
    edited by Michael W. Love, Marion Popenoe de Hatch, and Hectór L. Escobedo,
    pp. 277–296. University Press of America, Lanham, Maryland.
Pye, Mary E., and Gerardo Gutiérrez. 2007. The Pacific Coast Trade Route of Mesoamerica:
    Iconographic Connections between Guatemala and Guerrero. In *Archaeology, Art,
    and Ethnogenesis on Mesoamerican Prehistory: Papers in Honor of Gareth W. Lowe*,
    edited by Lynneth S. Lowe and Mary E. Pye, pp. 229–246. Papers of the New World
    Archaeological Foundation 68, Brigham Young University, Provo, Utah.
Rosenswig, Robert M. 2006. Sedentism and Food Production in Early Complex Societies
    of the Soconusco, Mexico. *World Archaeology* 38:329–354.
Rosenswig, Robert M. 2007. Beyond Identifying Elites: Feasting as a Means to
    Understand Early Middle Formative Society on the Pacific Coast of Mexico. *Journal
    of Anthropological Archaeology* 26:1–27.
Rosenswig, Robert M. 2008. Prehispanic Settlement in the Cuauhtémoc Region of the
    Soconusco, Chiapas, Mexico. *Journal of Field Archaeology* 33:389–411.

Rosenswig, Robert M. 2010. *The Beginnings of Mesoamerican Civilization: Inter-Regional Interaction and the Olmec.* Cambridge University Press, New York.

Rosenswig, Robert M. 2011. An Early Mesoamerican Archipelago of Complexity. In *Sociopolitical Transformation in Early Mesoamerica: Archaic to Formative in the Soconusco Region,* edited by Richard Lesure, pp. 242–271. University of California Press, Berkeley.

Schieber de Lavarreda, Christina. 1994. A Middle Preclassic Ballcourt at Abaj Takalik. *Mexicon* 16:77–84.

Schieber de Lavarreda, Christina. 1998. *Taller arqueología de la región de la Costa Sur de Guatemala.* Ministerio de Cultura y Deportes, Guatemala.

Schortman, Edward M., and Patricia A. Urban. 1992. *Resources, Power and Inter-regional Interaction.* Plenum, New York.

Sharer, Robert J. 1978. *Pottery and Conclusions, The Prehistory of Chalchuapa. El Salvador, Vol. 3.* University of Pennsylvania Press, Philadelphia.

Shepard, Anna O. 1948. *Plumbate: A Mesoamerican Tradeware.* Publication No. 528, Carnegie Institution of Washington, Washington, DC.

Smith, Michael E., and Francis F. Berdan, eds. 2003. *The Postclassic World.* University of Utah Press, Salt Lake City.

Thompson, Lauri McInnis, and Fred Valdez Jr. 2008. Potbelly Sculpture: An Inventory and Analysis. *Ancient Mesoamerica* 19:13–27.

Voorhies, Barbara. 1989. Settlement Patterns in the Western Soconusco: Methods of Site Recovery and Dating Results. In *New Frontiers in the Archaeology of the Pacific Coast of Southern Mesoamerica,* edited by Frederick Bove and Lynette Heller, pp. 103–124. Anthropological Research Papers No. 39, Arizona State University, Tempe.

Voorhies, Barbara, and Janine Gasco. 2004. *Postclassic Soconusco Society: The Late Prehistory of the Coast of Chiapas, Mexico.* Monograph, Institute of Mesoamerican Studies 14, University at Albany, Albany.

Wake, T. A., and L. R. Harrington. 2002. Appendix II: Vertebrate Faunal Remains from La Blanca, Guatemala. In *Early Complex Society in Pacific Guatemala: Settlements and Chronology of the Rio Naranjo, Guatemala,* edited by M. W. Love, pp. 237–252. Papers of the New World Archaeological Foundation 66, Brigham Young University, Provo, Utah.

Winter, Marcus. 2007. Recent Archaeological Investigations of Preclassic Occupation in the Southern Isthmus of Tehuantepec. In *Archaeology, Art, and Ethnogenesis on Mesoamerican Prehistory: Papers in Honor of Gareth W. Lowe,* edited by Lynneth S. Lowe and Mary E. Pye, pp. 193–207. Papers of the New World Archaeological Foundation 68, Brigham Young University, Provo, Utah.

Zeitlin, Robert N. 1978. Long-Distance Exchange and the Growth of a Regional Center: An Example from the Southern Isthmus of Tehuantepec, Mexico. In *Prehistoric Coastal Adaptations,* edited by Barbara L. Stark and Barbara Voorhies, pp. 183–210. Academic Press, New York.

....

CHAPTER 30

THE TARASCAN EMPIRE

POSTCLASSIC SOCIAL COMPLEXITY IN WESTERN MEXICO

....

HELEN PERLSTEIN POLLARD

In the vast region of western Mexico, social complexity first emerged during the Late Preclassic and Classic periods in the Teuchitlán cultural tradition of Jalisco (see Beekman, this volume; Beekman 2010; Pollard 1997; Weigand 2007). But it was during the Postclassic period that unequivocal states and a powerful empire appeared; this was the Tarascan Empire (Figure 30.1), the most complex polity known to us from western Mexico and a significant enemy of the contemporaneous Aztec Empire (see Smith and Sergharaert, this volume).

While the Teuchitlán cultural tradition, best known for its circular monumental architecture and shaft-tomb mortuary complex, developed from the earlier Preclassic regional cultures of Jalisco, Nayarit, and Colima (see Chapter 35), the Tarascan Empire had its roots in the cultural traditions of the Bajío and Michoacán. During the Late Postclassic period the Tarascan Empire was the second largest in Mesoamerica (more than 75,000 square kilometers) and was ethnically dominated by a population the Spaniards called Tarascos, who spoke a language known as Tarasco, or *Purépecha*. But while the empire only emerged in the two centuries before the Europeans' arrival, Purépecha culture can be identified at least two millennia earlier. The massive transformations this cultural tradition underwent with

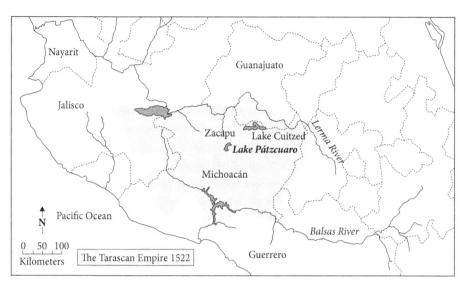

Figure 30.1 The Tarascan Empire.

the emergence of a centralized state and an expansionist empire have dominated the archaeology and ethnohistory of this region for the last century (Beekman 2010; Carot 2004; Michelet 1995; Pollard 1997; Williams 1993).

TARASCAN ARCHAEOLOGY AND ETHNOHISTORY

Interest in this region dates to the late nineteenth century (e.g., León 1888), but with the founding of modern Mexican archaeology the first systematic excavations took place in the late 1930s and 1940s (e.g., Acosta 1939; Kelly 1947; Porter Weaver 1969). With few exceptions, this first burst of research was followed by little new field or archival work until the 1980s (Beltrán 1994; Castro Leal 1986; Pollard 1993; Williams 1993). The past three decades have seen the establishment of major archaeology programs, resulting in the first chronometrically dated and stratigraphically defined sequences of occupation from several of the lake basins of central and northern Michoacán, regional surveys in these same lake basins and large portions of the Lerma Valley, and targeted surveys and excavations (Arnauld et al. 1993; Darras and Faugère 2005; Fernández-V. Medina 2004; Gorenstein 1985; Healan 1997; Macías Goytia 1989, 1990; Manzanilla López 1988; Michelet 1992; Michelet et al. 1989; Pereira et al. 2005; Pollard 1995, 2005; Pulido Méndez 2003, 2006; Silverstein 2000; Valdez and Liot 1994). Scholars have transcribed and analyzed sixteenth- and seventeenth-century documents in Spanish and Purépecha;

have published new print and online editions of the *Relación de Michoacán* (RM [1980, 2000, 2001, 2009]), the primary extant document describing the Tarascan Empire; and have published modern critical analyses of the RM and other ethno-historic documents (e.g., Aguilar González 2005; Beltrán 1994; Castro Gutiérrez and Monzón García 2008; Espejel Carbajal 2008; Haskell 2008; Martínez Baracs 2005; Monzón 2003; Monzón et al. 2009; Roskamp 1999; Roskamp and César Villa 2003; Stone 2004; Warren 1985).

Cultural Roots of the Tarascan Empire

The Purépecha heartland was located in central and northern Michoacán, especially in the Zacapu, Cuitzeo, and Pátzcuaro lake basins. The available evidence confirms the presence of a distinguishable Purépecha cultural tradition in the Pátzcuaro Basin by the Late Preclassic period and the emergence of a politically centralized and socially stratified state during the Middle Postclassic period. Based on maize pollen from sediment cores dating to 1500 BC, the Pátzcuaro Basin probably was first inhabited by sedentary or semisedentary agriculturalists during the Early-Middle Preclassic period (Table 30.1). Evidence from the Bajío and Cuitzeo basin suggests that it is likely that these populations were culturally part of the Chupícuaro tradition (Darras 2006; Darras and Faugère 2005, 2007; Porter Weaver 1969).

The following Loma Alta phase represents a period of transition between the earlier Chupícuaro phases and the societies of the Classic and Postclassic from which Purépecha culture developed. Loma Alta occupation has been found in the Pátzcuaro Basin, the Zacapu Basin, and at several sites in the Cuitzeo Basin

Table 30.1 **Tarascan Cultural Chronology.**

Period	Local Phases
Late Postclassic	Tariacuri (1350–1525 AD)
Middle Postclassic	Late Urichu (1000/1100–1350 AD)
Early Postclassic	Early Urichu (900–1000/1100 AD)
Epiclassic	Lupe (600/700–900 AD)
Middle Classic	Jarácuaro (550–600/700 AD)
Early Classic	Loma Alta 3 (AD 350–550)
Late/Terminal Preclassic	Loma Alta 1 and 2 (150 BC–350 AD)
Middle Preclassic	Chupícuaro (≥ 500–150 BC)

(Arnauld et al. 1993; Carot 2001; Filini 2004; Manzanilla López 1988; Michelet et al. 1989; Pollard 2005, 2008), and this occupation is closely related to the Mixtlán phase of the Bajío in the Lerma Basin in Guanajuato (Cárdenas García 1999b; Fernández-V. Medina 2004; Pereira et al. 2005). Loma Alta populations inhabited both lacustrine and nonlacustrine settlements, and they practiced canal irrigation with intensified agricultural production dominated by maize. The Pátzcuaro Basin site at Erongarícuaro covered at least 20 hectares, including stone architecture, and at the type-site in the Zacapu Basin, the appearance of sunken plaza/platform architecture in the Loma Alta 2b phase (250-350 AD) with a central altar, walls of worked stone, and stairways (Carot et al. 1998) is associated with construction materials of basalt and clay brought from almost 10 kilometers away and a new burial tradition in which richness of interment is directly related to proximity to platform centrality (Pereira 1996). These burial deposits are currently the best evidence for the timing of the emergence of social ranking, documenting the existence of small-scale, socially ranked agrarian societies. Long-distance exchange is documented from obsidian tools from northeastern Michoacán (Ucareo) and central Mexico (Pachuca), and from Thin Orange pottery from central Mexico and which suggests indirect linkages to Teotihuacan (Cárdenas García 1999a; Gómez Chávez 1998; Filini 2004; Filini and Cárdenas García 2007).

During the Epiclassic Lupe phase there was an increase in the number of settlements and larger populations in the Pátzcuaro Basin (Pollard 1995, 2008; Pollard et al. 2001). In the adjacent Zacapu Basin some of these communities had plazas and ballcourts at the same time that a major expansion of obsidian mining took place at the Zináparo complex (Darras 1999; Michelet 1992).

There is evidence of Epiclassic-period elites at Urichu and Erongarícuaro in the Pátzcuaro Basin (Pollard 1995; Pollard et al. 2001), Tingambato (Lagunas Rodríguez 1987; Piña Chan and Oí 1982), Guadalupe in the Zacapu Basin (Arnauld et al. 1993; Michelet 1992; Michelet et al. 1989; Pereira 1999), and Tres Cerritos in the Lake Cuitzeo Basin (Macías Goytia 1989). Their broadly shared heritage from the Chupícuaro and Loma Alta societies is reflected in the ceramic tradition and many aspects of mortuary behavior (Porter Weaver 1969). The elites were buried in group tombs that were similar to each other in their methods of construction and their uses over multiple generations (Pollard and Cahue 1999), although only some families have formal tombs. Grave goods included precious goods imported from other regions of Mesoamerica, which, along with cranial deformation and dental mutilation, distinguished these families from the rest of the population. They not only reveal their role as intermediaries with distant powers to the east and west but also self-define the males as warriors, with projectile points, atlatls, maces, and the costumes of warriors (Pereira 1999).

During the Early Urichu phase (900 to 1100 AD) the number of sites increased and the number of hectares that was occupied almost doubled the settlement pattern of the Pátzcuaro Basin. The lake level began to drop during this phase, and in the southwestern portion of the basin, lacustrine settlements moved to the new lake margins. By the end of this phase the lake was at its lowest level in the last two millennia (Fisher et al. 2003). Some small settlements were now located on newly exposed islands and in marsh zones while many other communities occupied the *malpaís* zones with terraces, mounds, and retaining walls similar to those in the Zacapu Basin. This phase marked the last use of the excavated tomb at Urichu and the end of multiple-use tombs in Michoacán. The last three burials in the tomb at Urichu are the richest, with objects imported from central Mexico, some of which may be ritual paraphernalia imported from Tula or in Toltec style (flutes, censer). These cultural links to the east also were reflected in trade networks that moved Ucareo obsidian to the urban center of Tula (Hernández and Healan 2008; Paredes Gudiño 2004; Pereira 1999).

The Middle Postclassic or Late Urichu phase (1100–1300 AD) includes the two centuries during which the Tarascan state formed and to which the legendary accounts of state emergence and ethnic affiliation pertain. Archaeological evidence comes from the Pátzcuaro Basin, with some comparative data from the Zacapu and Cuitzeo basins, although the phase has not been chronometrically isolated in these regions. In these centuries the sites in the Pátzcuaro Basin increased and the area of occupation again doubled. As in the Early Urichu phase, settlement expanded onto islands as the lake level remained low, but it also markedly expanded in upland zones and on to the malpaís in defensible locations. As the shifts in lacustrine resources were due to climate fluctuations of the Medieval Climate Anomaly, they were felt throughout the Tarascan heartland. Nevertheless, basic resources such as obsidian, basalt, and pottery were being produced, distributed, and consumed in patterns unchanged since the Loma Alta phase. In the last decades of this phase, the lake level rose again, reaching its contact-period level of 2,041 meters above sea level (O'Hara 1993). This resulted in the abandonment of low-lying communities and agricultural land, as well as the relocation of marsh production zones. Given the size of the population in the region, and the existence of sociopolitical elites in the larger communities, competition over expanding, diminishing, and shifting resources must have become fierce. For example, in the Zacapu Basin the Postclassic was marked by a 50 percent increase in the number of sites (Arnauld and Faugère-Kalfon 1998) and a shift to the malpaís above Zacapu, where up to 20,000 people inhabited thirteen sites covering 5 square kilometers (Michelet 2008; Migeon 1998). In addition, obsidian production from the Zináparo zone was reorganized, and prismatic blade technology was introduced (Darras 2008).

Thus, during the Early and Middle Postclassic periods the Purépecha cultural heartland came to be composed of several competing chiefly/small-state societies. This was a transition period when settlements shifted and elite mortuary patterns changed. Both the archaeological and ethnohistoric records suggest that patterns of leadership and control were in flux. While the legendary histories record several episodes of migration of non-Purépecha populations into the region from the Bajío, these population movements are not visible in the archaeological record (Michelet et al. 2005).

THE TARASCAN STATE AND EMPIRE

During the Late Postclassic or Tariacuri phase, after low-lying sites were flooded, settlements shifted to the new lakeshore and upland areas of high agricultural fertility. Tzintzuntzan was the largest of some ninety-plus Tarascan settlements located around Lake Pátzcuaro (Figure 30.2). Of the basin's estimated total population of 80,000 in 1522 (Gorenstein and Pollard 1983), Tzintzuntzan had about 35,000 (Pollard 1977, 2003), with several secondary and tertiary administrative centers, each with 5,000 to 15,000 people (Pollard 1980, 1995, 2003). Tzintzuntzan was a regional primate center on the basis not only of its population size, but also because of its control of the administrative, tributary, market, religious, and social hierarchies. Throughout the Tarascan heartland, population density reached its zenith and the largest and most populous settlements within any single region, whether ceremonial centers or cities, also date to the Late Postclassic (Macías Goytia 1990; Michelet 2008; Pollard 2003; Pulido Méndez 2003).

The denser occupations occurred during a time when previously irrigable lands were flooded, and this meant that new economic mechanisms were required to support local populations. The core of the Tarascan state in the Pátzcuaro Basin was not viable economically on purely local terms, and it thrived only by the exchange of goods and services through local and regional markets and various

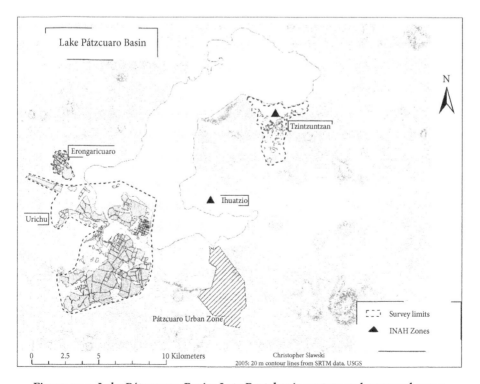

Figure 30.2 Lake Pátzcuaro Basin: Late Postclassic centers and surveyed areas.

state institutions (Pollard 1993). While documents indicate the existence and location of markets, the tributary relationships of many communities, and the nature
of goods acquired by state long-distance merchants, detailed sourcing analyses of
archaeological collections are clarifying the complex nature of the production, distribution, and consumption patterns of obsidian, pottery, shell, and metal objects
(see Darras 2008; Esparza López and Tenorio 2004; Hirshman 2008; Hosler 1994;
Hosler and Macfarlane 1996; Maldonado and Rehren 2009; Pollard 2003; Pollard et
al. 2001). Recent research indicates that unlike most of the empire, in the Pátzcuaro
Basin the tribute collectors (*ocámbecha*) were probably organizers of tribute-in-
labor, not goods (Aguilar González 2005), and the identities of some long-distance
merchants were ethnic *nahuas*, who assisted a Tarascan king in repressing an
insurrection in Tzintzuntzan in the mid-fifteenth century and were granted noble
status and permission to live in the capital (Monzón et al. 2009).

The royal dynasty officially allocated all access to land, water, forests, and
Analyses of obsidian artifacts, for example, suggest that while Zináparo obsidian production was widely dispersed and exchanged in local and regional markets
(Darras 2008), much of the production or distribution of prismatic blades from
the Ucareo sources was under state control (Pollard 2008). Metal objects of gold,
silver, copper, and bronze alloys were produced within the empire and used for
ritual, status, and utilitarian purposes (see Chapter 45; Hosler 1994; Pollard 1993;
Roskamp 1999). Some of the mining, smelting, and production of objects was carried out by full-time craft specialists and tenants under the direct control of the
state (*Minas de Cobre* [1533] in Warren 1968). The production of ingots took place
at smelting centers in the Balsas River drainage, and some of the crafting of objects
took place in the Tarascan capital, possibly within the king's palace. Other metals
or smelted ingots were obtained through tribute, particularly for gold and silver,
especially from the frontier zones of the southeast and the west where there is some
evidence of independent production and distribution in local or regional markets.
They were associated with elite administrators' residences, probably reflecting the
redistribution of state goods to officeholders. Limited metal sourcing suggests that
artifacts were produced from ores mined in the Balsas Basin and adjacent Jalisco
(Hosler and Macfarlane 1996).

The royal dynasty officially allocated all access to land, water, forests, and
mineral resources, although, in practice, access to land was distributed within
communities by traditional kin ties and land was acquired by kings for the support of state administrators (*angámecha*) and state temples. In addition, there were
state copper mines, obsidian mines, forests, fisheries, and craft workshops. The
documents are unclear about the degree to which they were seen as resources traditionally held by specific communities or resources to which communities were
allowed access by the king. Sixteenth-century documents suggest the latter, but,
if so, this was a change in the ideology of resource ownership that would only
have emerged with the unification of the state in the Middle Postclassic period.
The royal dynasty did claim large landholdings in the southeast portion of the
basin and smaller parcels in many other communities (e.g., Beltrán 1994; Martínez
Baracs 2005; Warren 1985).

According to the *Relación de Michoacán*, the division between noble and commoner was absolute, as lineages did not cross class boundaries and marriages were within one's class. Among the nobility, a distinction was made among the royal dynasty, the upper nobility, and the lower nobility; commoners varied by ethnicity (although overwhelmingly Purépecha), occupation, and whether they were slaves (generally war captives). The royal dynasty was located in the capital (Tzintzuntzan) and at the sacred religious center of Ihuatzio; members of the upper and lower nobility were found in at least eleven settlements in the Pátzcuaro Basin. Elites and commoners who were located in secondary and tertiary centers of the Tarascan heartland consumed the same goods as did the residents in the capital, and they all shared Tarascan elite/commoner identity and participated in a single social system (Pollard and Cahue 1999; Stawski 2008).

The creation of the Tarascan state was accompanied by the establishment of a new ideology that made the Pátzcuaro Basin the center of cosmic power (Espejel Carbajal 2008; Monzón 2003; Pollard 1993, 2008; *Relación de Michoacán* 1541 [1980]). The patron gods of the now-dominant ethnic elite were elevated to celestial power, while various regional deities and worldviews—themselves products of generations of change—were elevated, incorporated, or marginalized. The clearest evidence of this process involves the joining of the ethnic Chichimec or *uacúsecha* deity, Curicaueri, with the ethnic "islander" or Purépecha goddess, Xarátanga. In the prophetic language of a great epic, "Curicaueri will conquer this land, and you for your part will stand with one foot on the land and one on the water…and we shall become one people" (*Relación de Michoacán* 1980, 40). Taríacuri's prophetic dream of a unified state mandated by his god is interpreted in the following decades as the "event" that delegitimizes all previous and competing claims to authority. This union of deities can also be seen in Tarascan ritual architecture. A specialized pyramid form, the *yácata*, consisting of a keyhole shape, was constructed at major religious centers associated with the Tarascan sun god Curicaueri. The greatest number (five) were located in Tzintzuntzan, but at Ihuatzio there were not only three yácatas but also two rectangular pyramids associated with Xarátanga, adjacent to a ballcourt. Stone *chacmool* sculptures, associated with human sacrifice, were placed in front of the yácatas at Tzintzuntzan and Ihuatzio, scenes of major ceremonies celebrating the state and cosmic order.

The transformation associated with, first, the emergence of a politically unified Pátzcuaro Basin and, second, its expansion throughout and then beyond the Tarascan heartland, involved a shift in elite identity from one primarily associated with imported finished goods from distant powerful centers and control of prestige goods networks to an identity primarily associated with locally produced, distinctively Tarascan, goods and control of tributary, military, political, and ideological networks (e.g., Pollard and Cahue 1999). Thus, the emergence of a new political economy was also associated with a new state religion and a new regional elite identity. The political structure of the state, and the empire that expanded between AD 1350 and 1500, is primarily known from documents and limited archaeological research and includes studies of the nature of Tarascan warfare, frontier fortresses, and the Tarascan-Aztec conflicts (Beltrán 1994; Gorenstein 1985; Pollard 1993; Silverstein 2000, 2001; Valdez and Liot 1994). While these sources present a picture of a highly centralized, hierarchical polity, Purépecha-language documents and more nuanced analyses of the *Relación de Michoacán* (1541) raise important questions about *how* this new state, identity, and system of authority emerged and the degree to which the centralized model was a product of power struggles following the Spanish Conquest (Castro Gutiérrez and Monzón García 2008; Espejel Carbajal 2008; Haskell 2008; Martínez Baracs 2005; Monzón et al. 2009; Stone 2004).

For the Purépecha (commoners) of central and northern Michoacán, this new society was a major transformation on the macro-level but it also permitted continuities on the household and village scale. The social continuity represented by the long cultural tradition from the Preclassic to the Postclassic is visible in ceramic technology, ceramic designs, the use of negative (resist) on polychrome pottery, the types of figurines, mortuary patterns, basic technology, diet, and household organization of labor. They emphasize the degree of continuity at the level of the household, despite major changes in the political economies that took place during those 2,000 years. Nevertheless, the emergence of this new empire was a product of local, regional, and macro-regional scale interaction that provides us with knowledge of yet another variant of Mesoamerican civilization.

REFERENCES

Acosta, Jorge. 1939. Exploraciones arqueológicas realizadas en el estado de Michoacán durante los años de 1937 y 1938. *Revista Mexicana de Estudios Antropológicos* 3(2):85–99.

Aguilar González, José Ricardo. 2005. Tzintzuntzan Irechequa. Política y sociedad en el Estado tarasco. Unpublished licenciatura thesis, Facultad de Historia, Universidad Michoacana, Morelia.

Arnauld, Marie Charlotte, Patricia Carot, and Marie-France Fauvet-Berthelot. 1993. *Arqueología de las Lomas en la cuenca lacustre de Zacapu, Michoacán, México.* Cuadernos de Estudios Michoacanos 5, Centre d'Etudes Mexicaines et Centraméricaines, México, D.F.

Arnauld, Charlotte, and Brigitte Faugère-Kalfon. 1998. Evolución de la ocupación humana en el Centro-Norte de Michoacán (Proyecto Michoacán, CEMCA) y la emergencia del Estado Tarasco. In *Génesis, culturas y espacios en Michoacán*, edited by Véronique Darras, pp. 13–34. CEMCA, México, D.F.

Beekman, Christopher S. 2010. Recent Research in Western Mexican Archaeology. *Journal of Archaeological Research* 18(1):41–109.

Beltrán, Ulises. 1994. Estado y sociedad Tarascos en la epoca Prehispánica. In *El Michoacán antiguo*, edited by Brigitte Boehm de Lameiras, pp. 31–163. El Colegio de Michoacán y Gobierno del Estado de Michoacán, Zamora, México.

Cárdenas García, Efraín. 1999a. Santa María, Morelia: Un desarrollo cultural local con notables influencias externas. In *Arqueología y etnohistoria. La región del Lerma,* edited by E. Williams and P. C. Weigand, pp. 213–244. El Colegio de Michoacán, Zamora, Zamora, Michoacán.

Cárdenas García, Efaín. 1999b. *El bajío en el Clásico*. El Colegio de Michoacán, Zamora, Zamora, Mexico.

Carot, Patricia. 2001. *Le site de Loma Alta, Lac de Zacapu, Michoacan, Mexique*. Paris Monographs in American Archaeology 9, British Archaeological Reports International Series no. 920, Archaeopress, Oxford.

Carot, Patricia. 2004. Arqueología de Michoacán: nuevas aportaciones a la historia purhépecha. In *Introducción a la arqueología del Occidente de México*, edited by Beatriz Braniff Cornejo, pp. 443–474. Universidad de Colima and Instituto Nacional de Antropología e Historia, México, D.F.

Carot, Patricia, Marie-France Fauvet Berthelot, Luis Barba, Karl Link, Agustín Ortiz, and Albert Hesse. 1998. La arquitectura de Loma Alta, Zacapu, Michoacán. In *El occidente de México: arqueología, historia y medio ambiente. Perspectivas regionales*, edited by Ricardo Avila, Jean P. Emphoux, Luis G. Gastélum, Susana Ramírez, Otto Schondube, and Francisco Valdez, pp. 345–361. Universidad de Guadalajara and Orstom, Guadalajara, México.

Castro Gutiérrez, F., and Cristina Monzón García. 2008. El lenguaje del poder: Conceptos tarascos en torno a la autoridad. In *Símbolos de poder en Mesoamérica*, edited by Guilhem Oliver, pp. 31–46. Universidad Nacional Autónoma de México, México, D.F.

Castro Leal, Marcia. 1986. Tzintzuntzan, capital de los tarascos. Gobierno del Estado de Michoacán, Morelia.

Darras, Véronique. 1999. *Tecnologías prehispánicas de la obsidiana: Los centros de producción de la región de Zináparo-Prieto, Michoacán*. Cuadernos de Estudios Michoacanos 9, Centre Français d'Etudes Mexicaines et Centraméricaines, México, D.F.

Darras, Véronique. 2006. Las relaciones entre Chupícuaro y el centro de México durante el preclásico reciente. Una crítica de las interpretaciones arqueológicas. *Journal de la Société des Américanistes* 92:69–110.

Darras, Véronique. 2008. Estrategias para la producción de navajas de obsidiana en la región de Zacapu y la vertiente del Lerma (Michoacan, México) entre el Epiclásico y el Posclásico Tardío. *Ancient Mesoamerica* 19(2):243–264.

Darras, Véronique, and Brigitte Faugère. 2005. Cronología de la cultura Chupícuaro. Estudio del sitio La Tronera, Puruagüita, Guanajuato. In *El antiguo occidente de México. Nuevas perspectivas sobre el pasado prehispánico*, edited by Eduardo Williams, Phil C. Weigand, Lorenza López Mestas, and David Grove, pp. 255–281. El Colegio de Michoacán-Instituto Nacional de Antropología e Historia, Guadalajara, México.

Darras, Véronique, and Brigitte Faugère. 2007. Chupícuaro, entre el Occidente y el Altiplano central. Un balance de los conocimientos y las nuevas apotaciones. In *Dinámicas culturales entre el Occidente, el Centro-Norte y la cuenca de México, del Preclásico al Epiclásico*, edited by B. Faugère, pp. 51–83. El Colegio de Michoacán and Centro Francés de Estudios Mexicanos y Centroamericanos (CEMCA), Zamora, Michoacán.

Esparza López, Rodrigo, and Dolores Tenorio. 2004. Las redes de intercambio de la obsidiana en la tierra caliente de Michoacán durante los periodos epiclásico y postclásico. In *Bienes estratégicos del antiguo occidente de México*, edited by Eduardo Williams, pp. 77–112. El Colegio de Michoacán, Zamora.

Espejel Carbajal, Claudia. 2008. La justicia y el fuego. Dos claves para leer la Relación de
    Michoacán. Vols. 1 and 2. El Colegio de Michoacán, Zamora, Michoacán.
Fernández-V. Medina, Eugenia. 2004. Evidencias de una tradición mesoamericana en
    Zaragoza. In *Las tradiciones arqueológicas del Occidente de México*, edited by Efraín
    Cárdenas García, pp. 291–305. El Colegio de Michoacán, Zamora, México.
Filini, Agapi. 2004. *The Presence of Teotihuacan in the Cuitzeo Basin, Michoacán, Mexico.*
    British Archaeological Reports International Series 1279, Archaeopress, Oxford.
Filini, Agapi, and Efraín Cárdenas García. 2007. El Bajío, la cuenca de Cuitzeo y el Estado
    teotihuacano. Un estudio de relaciones y antagonismos. In *Dinámicas culturales
    entre el Occidente, el Centro-Norte y la Cuenca de México, del Preclásico al Epiclásico*,
    edited by B. Faugère, pp. 137–154. El Colegio de Michoacán and Centro Francés de
    Estudios Mexicanos y Centroamericanos (CEMCA), Zamora, Michoacán.
Fisher, Christopher T., Helen P. Pollard, Isabel Israde, Victor Hugo Garduno, and Subir
    K. Banerjee. 2003. A Reexamination of Human-Induced Environmental Change
    within the Lake Pátzcuaro Basin, Michoacán, Mexico. *Proceedings of the National
    Academy of Sciences* 100(8): 4957–4962, supplementary tables online.
Gómez Chávez, Sergio. 1998. Nuevos datos sobre la relación de Teotihuacán y el
    Occidente de México. *Antropología e Historia del Occidente de México*. Tomo III,
    pp. 1461–1493. XXIV Mesa Redonda de la Sociedad Mexicana de Antropología,
    UNAM, México, D.F.
Gorenstein, Shirley .1985. *Acambaro: Frontier Settlement on the Tarascan-Aztec Border.*
    Vanderbilt University Publications in Anthropology 32, Nashville.
Gorenstein Shirley, and Helen Perlstein Pollard. 1983. *The Tarascan Civilization: A Late
    Prehispanic Cultural System*. Vanderbilt University Publications in Anthropology
    28, Nashville.
Haskell, David L. 2008. The Cultural Logic of Hierarchy in the Tarascan State. *Ancient
    Mesoamerica* 19(2):231–241.
Healan, Dan M. 1997. Pre-Hispanic Quarrying in the Ucareo-Zinapecuaro Obsidian
    Source Area. *Ancient Mesoamerica* 8:77–100.
Hernández, Christine L., and Dan M. Healan. 2008. The Role of Late Pre-contact
    Colonial Enclaves in the Development of the Postclassic Ucareo Valley, Michoacan,
    Mexico. *Ancient Mesoamerica* 19(2):265–282.
Hirshman, Amy J. 2008. Tarascan Ceramic Production and Implications for Ceramic
    Distribution. *Ancient Mesoamerica* 19:299–310.
Hosler, Dorothy. 1994. *The Sounds and Colors of Power, the Sacred Metallurgical
    Technology of Ancient West Mexico*. MIT Press, Cambridge.
Hosler, Dorothy, and Andrew Macfarlane. 1996. Copper Sources, Metal Production, and
    Metals Trade in Late Postclassic Mesoamerica. *Science* 273:1819–1824.
Kelly, Isabel T. 1947. Excavations at Apatzingan, Michoacan. Viking Fund Publications in
    Anthropology 7. Viking Fund, New York.
Lagunas Rodríguez, Zaid. 1987. Análisis de los restos óseos humanos procedentes de la
    tumba núm. 1 de Tinganio, Tingambato, Michoacán. *Avances en antropología física.
    Tomo III*. Cuaderno de Trabajo 4, pp. 7–72. Instituto Nacional de Antropología e
    Historia, México, D.F.
León, Nicolás. 1888. Las Yacatas de Tzintzuntzan. *Anales del museo Michoacano*, Morelia
    1:65–70.
Macías Goytia, Angelina. 1989. Los entierros de un centro ceremonial tarasco. *Estudios
    de antropología biológica*, serie antropológica 100, pp. 531–559. Universidad Nacional
    Autónoma de México, México, D.F.

Macías Goytia, Angelina. 1990. *Huandacareo: Lugar de juicios, tribunal.* INAH, Colección Científica, No. 222, México, D.F.

Maldonado, Blanca, and Thilo Rehren. 2009. Early Copper Smelting at Itziparátzico, Mexico. *Journal of Archaeological Science* 36:1998–2006.

Manzanilla López, Rubén. 1988. Salvamento arqueológico en Loma Santa María, Michoacán. In *Primera reunión sobre las sociedades prehispánicas en el centro-occidente de México.* Cuaderno de Trabajo 1, pp. 151–160. Centro Regional de Querétaro, Instituto Nacional de Antropología e Historia, México, D.F.

Martínez Baracs, Rodrigo. 2005. *Convivencia y utopía. El gobierno indio y español de la "ciudad de Mechuacan," 1521–1580.* Fondo de Cultura Económico-Instituto Nacional de Antropología e Historia (INAH), México, México, D.F.

Michelet, Dominique, ed. 1992. *El proyecto Michoacán 1983–1987. Medio ambiente e introducción a los trabajos arqueológicos.* Collection Etudes Mésoaméricains II-12, Cuadernos de Estudios Michoacanos 4, Centre Français d'Etudes Mexicaines et Centraméricaines, México, D.F.

Michelet, Dominique. 1995. La zona occidental en el Posclásico. In *Historia antigua de México,* Vol. III, el horizonte Posclásico y algunos aspectos intelectuales de las culturas mesoamericanas, edited by Linda Manzanilla and Leonardo López Luján, pp. 153–188. INAH, UNAM, and Grupo Editorial Miguel Angel Porrúa, México, D.F.

Michelet, Dominique. 2008. Living Differently. The Sites of the Milpillas Phase (1250–1450 AD) in the Malpaís de Zacapu (Michoacán). In *Urbanism in Mesoamerica. El urbanismo en Mesoamérica,* edited by A. G. Mastache, R. H. Cobean, A. García Cook, and K. G. Hirth, pp. 593–620. Vol. 2. Pennsylvania University Press, Instituto Nacional de Antropología e Historia, Mexico, University Park; México, D.F.

Michelet, Dominique, Marie Charlotte Arnauld, and Marie-France Fauvet Berthelot. 1989. El proyecto del CEMCA en Michoacán. Etapa I: Un balance. *Trace* 16:70–87. Centre Français d'Etudes Mexicaines et Centraméricaines, México, D.F.

Michelet, Dominique, Grégory Pereira, and Gérald Migeon. 2005. La llegada de los Uacúsechas a la región de Zacapu, Michoacán: datos arqueológicos y discusión. In *Reacomodos demográficos del Clásico al Posclásico en el centro de México,* edited by Linda Manzanilla, pp. 137–153. Instituto de Investigaciones Antropológicas, Universidad Nacional Autónoma de México, México, D.F.

Migeon, Gérald. 1998. El poblamiento del Malpaís de Zacapu y de sus Alrededores, del Clásico al Posclásico. In *Génesis, culturas y espacios en Michoacán,* edited by Véronique Darras, pp. 35–45. Centre Français d'Etudes Mexicaines et Centraméricaines, México, D.F.

Monzón, Cristina. 2003. Los principales dioses tarascos: un ensayo de análisis etimológico en la cosmología tarasca. In *Entre tradición e innovación: cinco siglos de literatura amerindia,* edited by Jean Philippe Husson, pp. 137–168. Fondo editorial de la Pontífica Universidad Católica del Perú.

Monzón, Cristina, Hans Roskamp, and Benedict Warren. 2009. La memoria de don Melchor Caltzin (1543): historia y legitimación en Tzintzuntzan, Michoacán. *Estudios de Historia Novohispana, México.* Universidad Nacional Autónoma de México 40:21–55.

O'Hara, Sarah. 1993. Historical Evidence of Fluctuations in the Level of Lake Pátzcuaro, Michoacán, México over the Last 600 Years. *The Geographical Journal* 159(1):51–62.

Paredes Gudiño, Blanca. 2004. El Occidente de México en la conformación de la sociedad
    tolteca. In *Las tradiciones arqueológicas del Occidente de México*, edited by Efraín
    Cárdenas García, pp. 329–343. El Colegio de Michoacán, Zamora, Mexico.

Pereira, Gregory. 1996. Nuevos hallazgos funerarios en Loma Alta, Zacapu, Michoacán.
    In *Las cuencas del occidente de México. Época prehispánica*, edited by Eduardo
    Williams and Phil C. Weigand, pp. 105–129. Centre Français d'Études Mexicaines
    et Centraméricaines-Instituto de Investgación Científica para el Desarrollo en
    Cooperación-El Colegio de Michoacán, Mexico.

Pereira, Gregory. 1999. *Potrero de Guadalupe. Anthropologie funéraire d'une communauté
    pré-tarasque du nord du Michoacán, Mexique*. British Archaeological Reports
    International Series 816, Archaeopress, England.

Pereira, Gregory, Gerald Migeon, and Dominique Michelet. 2005. Transformaciones
    demográficas y culturales en el centro-norte de México en vísperas del Posclásico:
    los sitios del Cerro Barajas (suroeste de Guanajuato). In *Reacomodos demográficos
    del Clásico al Posclásico en el centro de México*, edited by L. Manzanilla, pp. 123–136.
    Instituto de Investigaciones Antropológicas, Universidad Nacional Autónoma de
    México, Mexico, D.F.

Piña Chan, Román, and Kuniaki Oí. 1982. *Exploraciones arqueológicas en Tingambato,
    Michoacán*. Instituto Nacional de Antropología e Historia, México, D.F.

Pollard, Helen Perlstein. 1977. An Analysis of Urban Zoning and Planning in Prehispanic
    Tzintzuntzan. *Proceedings: American Philosophical Society* 121:46–69.

Pollard, Helen Perlstein. 1980. Central Places and Cities: A Consideration of the
    Protohistoric Tarascan State. *American Antiquity* 45:677–696.

Pollard, Helen Perlstein. 1993. *Tariacuri's Legacy: The Prehispanic State*. University of
    Oklahoma Press, Norman.

Pollard, Helen Perlstein. 1995. Estudio del surgimiento del estado tarasco: Investigaciones
    recientes. In *Arqueología del Occidente y Norte de México*, edited by Eduardo
    Williams and Phil C. Weigand, pp. 29–63. El Colegio de Michoacán, Zamora,
    México.

Pollard, Helen Perlstein. 1997. Recent Research in West Mexican Archaeology. *Journal of
    Archaeological Research* 5:345–384.

Pollard, Helen Perlstein. 2003. Central Places and Cities in the Core of the Tarascan
    State. In *Urbanization in Mesoamerica*, edited by William T. Sanders and Alba
    Guadalupe Mastache, pp. 345–390. INAH and Pennsylvania University Press,
    University Park.

Pollard, Helen Perlstein. 2005. Michoacán en el mundo mesoamericano prehispánico:
    Erongarícuaro, Michoacán y los estados teotihuacano y tarasco. In *El antiguo
    occidente de México. Nuevas perspectivas sobre el pasado prehispánico*, edited by
    Eduardo Williams, Phil C. Weigand, Lorenza López Mestas, and David Grove, pp.
    283–303. El Colegio de Michoacán-INAH, Guadalajara.

Pollard, Helen Perlstein. 2008. A Model of the Emergence of the Tarascan State. *Ancient
    Mesoamerica* 19(2):217–230.

Pollard, Helen Perlstein, and Laura Cahue. 1999. Mortuary Patterns of Regional Elites in
    the Lake Patzcuaro Basin of Western Mexico. *Latin American Antiquity* 10:259–280.

Pollard, Helen Perlstein, Amy Hirshman, Hector Neff, and Michael Glascock. 2001. Las
    elites, el intercambio de bienes y el surgimiento del area nuclear tarasca: analisis
    de la ceramica de la cuenca de patzcuaro. In *Estudios ceramicos en el occidente y
    norte de Mexico*, edited by Eduardo Williams and Phil C. Weigand, pp. 289–309. El
    Colegio de Michoacán, Zamora, México.

Porter Weaver, Murial Noe. 1969. A Reappraisal of Chupícuaro. In *The Natalie Wood Collection of Pre-Columbian Ceramics from Chupícuaro, Guanajuato, Mexico*, edited by Jay R. Frierman, pp. 81–92. University of California, Los Angeles.

Pulido Méndez, Salvador. 2003. Salvamento arqueológico en dos carreteras de Michoacán. Resultados de las investigaciones. *Arqueología* 29:45–62.

Pulido Méndez, Salvador. 2006. Los tarascos y los tarascos-uacúsecha: diferencias sociales y arqueológicas en un grupo. Colección Divulgación. Instituto Nacional de Antropología e Historia, Mexico, Mexico, D.F.

Relación de Michoacán. (1541) (RM) 1980. *La relación de Michoacán*. Versión Paleográfica, Separación de Textos, Ordenación Coloquil, Estudio Preliminar Y Notas de F. Miranda. Estudios Michoacanos V. Fimax, Morelia, Michoacán, México.

Relación de Michoacán. (1541) (RM) 2000. *Relación de la ceremonias y rictos y población y gobernación de los indios de la provincia de Michoacán*. Moisés Franco Mendoza (coordinador de edición y estudios), El Colegio de Michoacán, Gobierno del Estado de Michoacán, Zamora.

Relación de Michoacán. (1541) (RM) 2001. *Relación de Michoacán*. Armando Mauricio Escobar Olmedo (coordinador general de la obra), Patrimonio Nacional, H. Ayuntamiento de Morelia, Testimonio Compañía Editorial, Madrid.

Relación de Michoacán. (1541) (RM) 2009. *Relación de Michoacán, instrumentos de consulta*. Searchable online edition edited by C. Espejel Carbajal at http://etzakutarakua.colmich.edu.mx/proyectos/relaciondemichoacan/default.asp

Roskamp, Hans. 1999. La historiografía indígena de Michoacán: El lienzo de jucutácato y los títulos de Carapan. Research School CNWS, Leiden University, CNWS Publications, Leiden.

Roskamp, Hans, and Guadalupe César Villa. 2003. Iconografía de un pleito: El Lienzo de Aranza y la conflictividad política en la sierra tarasca, siglo XVII. In *Autoridad y gobierno indígena en Michoacán*. Vol. 1. El Colegio de Michoacán, edited by Marta Tarán and Carlos Paredes, pp. 217–239. CIESAS, INAH-Dirección de Estudios Históricos, UMSNH-Instituto de Investigaciones Históricas, Zamora, Michoacán.

Silverstein, Jay E. 2000. A Study of the Late Postclassic Aztec-Tarascan Frontier in Northern Guerrero, Mexico: The Oztuma-Cutzamala Project. Unpublished PhD dissertation, Department of Anthropology, Pennsylvania State University, University Park.

Silverstein, Jay E. 2001. Aztec Imperialism at Oztuma, Guerrero: Aztec-Chontal Relations during the Late Postclassic and Early Colonial Periods. *Ancient Mesoamerica* 12:1–30.

Stawski, Christopher James. 2008. Residential Zoning at Prehispanic Tzintzuntzan, Mexico Revisited: A Quantitative Analysis. Unpublished MA thesis, Department of Anthropology, Michigan State University, East Lansing.

Stone, Cynthia L. 2004. *In Place of Gods and Kings. Authorship and Identity in the Relación de Michoacán*. University of Oklahoma Press, Norman.

Valdez, Francisco, and Catherine Liot. 1994. La cuenca de Sayula: yacimientos de sal en la frontera oeste del estado tarasco. In *El Michoacán antiguo*, edited by Brigitte Boehm de Lameiras, pp. 285–305. El Colegio de Michoacán and El Gobierno del Estado de Michoacán, Zamora.

Warren, J. Benedict. 1968. Minas de Cobre de Michoacan, 1533. *Anales del Museo Michoacano* 6:35–52.

Warren, J. Benedict. 1985. *The Conquest of Michoacan*. University of Oklahoma Press, Norman.

Weigand, P. C. 2007. States in Prehispanic Western Mesoamerica. In *The Political Economy of Ancient Mesoamerica: Transformations during the Formative and Classic Periods*, edited by V. L. Scarborough and J. E. Clark, pp. 101–113. University of New Mexico Press, Albuquerque.

Williams, Eduardo. 1993. Historia de la arqueología en Michoacán. In *II coloquio Pedro Bosch-Gimpera*, edited by María Teresa Cabrero G., pp. 195–236. Instituto de Investigaciones Antropológicas, UNAM, México.

CHAPTER 31

....

THE AZTEC EMPIRE

....

MICHAEL E. SMITH AND
MAËLLE SERGHERAERT

THE Aztec Empire expanded through conquest to cover much of northern Mesoamerica in the decades before the arrival of Hernando Cortés in 1519. It is the most extensively documented polity of ancient Mesoamerica; Spanish soldiers described its armies and cities, and Colonial-period friars wrote lengthy descriptions of its history and organization. Native books and paintings provide insight into the nature and organization of the empire, and in recent decades archaeological excavations have contributed new insights into the processes of imperial expansion.

The Aztec Empire was created within a setting of competing city-states (*altepetl*) that covered the landscape of central Mexico starting around 1100 AD. These small polities, ruled by kings (*tlatoani*) and a council of nobles, consisted of a modest urban center and the surrounding farmland (Smith 2008). In a dynamic political setting, *tlatoque* (plural of tlatoani) sought to expand their areas of control, and by 1400 AD several small empires had been formed through conquest. The largest of these were the domains of Texcoco, capital of the Acholhua region in the eastern Basin of Mexico, and the more powerful Azcapotzalco, capital of the Tepanec domain in the western part of the basin. In the Tepanec War of 1428 AD the armies of Azcapotzalco were attacked by an alliance of Texcoco, Tenochtitlan (capital of the Mexica domain), and several other cities. Upon the defeat of Azcapotzalco, Texcoco, and Tenochtitlan joined with Tlacopan (a dissident Tepanec altepetl) to form the "Triple Alliance." These three cities agreed to begin a program of expansion and share the resulting tribute and tax payments. By the time Cortés arrived in Tenochtitlan in 1519, the empire covered much of northern Mesoamerica (Figure 31.1). Although it officially remained an "alliance" until the end, in fact the power and influence of Tenochtitlan grew steadily over the decades to the point where the tlatoque of this city could be

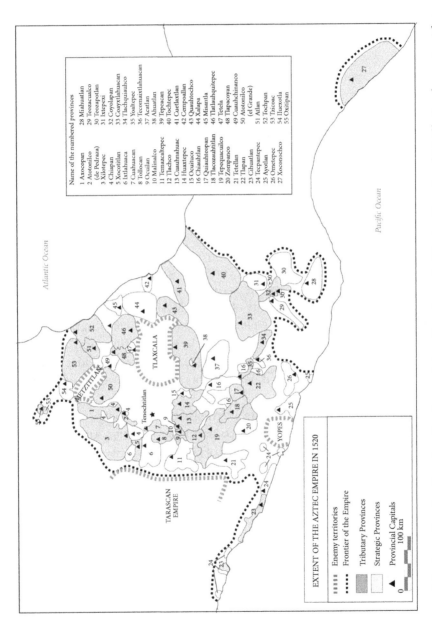

Name of the numbered provinces

1 Axocopan	28 Miahuatlan
2 Atotonilco	29 Teozacualco
(de Pedraza)	30 Teozapotlan
3 Xilotepec	31 Ixtepexi
4 Chiapan	32 Coyolapan
5 Xocotitlan	33 Coayxtlahuacan
6 Ixtlahuaca	34 Tlachquiauhco
7 Cuahuacan	35 Yoaltepec
8 Tollocan	36 Tecomaixtlahuacan
9 Ocuilan	37 Acatlan
10 Malinalco	38 Ahuatlan
11 Temazcaltepec	39 Tepeacan
12 Tlachco	40 Tochtepec
13 Cuauhnahuac	41 Cuetlaxtlan
14 Huaxtepec	42 Cempoallan
15 Ocuituco	43 Quauhtochco
16 Chiauhtlan	44 Xalapa
17 Quiauhteopan	45 Misantla
18 Tlacozauhtitlan	46 Tlatlauhquitepec
19 Tepequacuilco	47 Tetela
20 Zompanco	48 Tlapacoyan
21 Tetellan	49 Quauhchinanco
22 Tlapan	50 Atotonilco
23 Cihuatlan	(el Grande)
24 Tecpantepec	51 Atlan
25 Ayotlan	52 Tochpan
26 Ometepec	53 Tzicoac
27 Xoconochco	54 Iluexolla
	55 Oxitipan

EXTENT OF THE AZTEC EMPIRE IN 1520

- Enemy territories
- Frontier of the Empire
- Tributary Provinces
- Strategic Provinces
- ▲ Provincial Capitals

0   100 km

Atlantic Ocean

Pacific Ocean

TARASCAN EMPIRE

METZTITLAN

TLAXCALA

YOPES

Tenochtitlan

Figure 31.1 Map of the Aztec Empire. Based on Berdan et al. (1996); redrawn by Marion Forest and Maëlle Sergheraert, with permission of Frances Berdan.

considered the rulers of the empire; indeed, they assumed the title *huey tlatoani* ("high king") (Carrasco 1999; Rojas and Smith 2007).

TENOCHTITLAN, THE IMPERIAL CAPITAL

When Cortés and his soldiers crossed the causeway and entered Tenochtitlan for the first time, they were overwhelmed by the size and opulence of the city and the hustle and bustle of its streets and markets. With over 200,000 inhabitants, this was the largest city ever to flourish in the Pre-Columbian Americas. The size and wealth of the city were direct consequences of its role as capital of the Aztec Empire. Goods flowed into Tenochtitlan from all over Mesoamerica. They included items of money (cotton textiles and cacao beans), exotic animal products (colorful tropical bird feathers, jaguar skins), luxury goods (jewelry of gold and greenstone), utilitarian goods (pottery, wax), and grains and other food. Many of these were offered for sale in the huge marketplace of Tenochtitlan's sister city Tlatelolco, where tens of thousands of people gathered daily. Some luxury goods were used as adornments by nobles, and others were destined for use in religious rituals (Smith 2012).

At the heart of the city of Tenochtitlan was the sacred precinct, a large walled compound with many temples, shrines, and other features. Numerous ceremonies took place here, ranging from large public spectacles to secluded rites of the priests. Exotic goods and ritual items were buried in offerings at the central temple, where archaeologists have now excavated them (Matos 1988). The wealth and cosmopolitan influences of the empire stimulated the production of fine art in Tenochtitlan and nearby cities. New forms of pictorial codices were devised, and stone sculpture reached its greatest level of technical and aesthetic development in ancient Mesoamerica. The production of jewelry, ritual ceramic vessels, and other luxury objects increased greatly.

Much of the artistic production in Tenochtitlan was sponsored by the Mexica tlatoque, who commissioned monuments, codices, and other items that celebrated their conquests and proclaimed the cosmic destiny of the empire. Myths were rewritten in the service of imperial ideology and were illustrated in codices and sculptures (Umberger, this volume).

When foreign tlatoque and nobles visited Tenochtitlan they were shown massive imperial sculptures and treated to elaborate feasts and ceremonies where human sacrifices were featured. The Mexica account of their reaction was recorded by the Spanish friar Diego Durán:

> They saw that [the Mexica] were masters of the world, their empire so wide and abundant that they had conquered all the nations and that all were their vassals. The guests, seeing such wealth and opulence and such authority and power, were filled with terror (1994: 336)

It is important to recognize that this statement describes the official imperial perspective; it is not an objective description of the foreigners' reactions. As such it is one of many examples of imperial propaganda, designed to influence other tlatoque and nobles to cooperate with the empire. Furthermore, in the period after the Spanish conquest, such propaganda also served to celebrate the ancient glories of the Aztec Empire after it had come crashing down by sword and microbe in 1521.

THE DYNAMICS OF IMPERIAL EXPANSION

Between 1430 to 1520 AD, the Aztecs extended their domination over a large part of northern Mesoamerica (Berdan et al. 1966). How did they conquer such a large area in only ninety years? The Triple Alliance counted on strong military forces and most of the new territories were subjected during military campaigns. All men received military training during their youth, whether they were nobles or not, and they could be required to participate in military activities at any time. The army was composed of professional warriors (including the famous Eagle and Jaguar warriors) and common people (*macehuales*), who rose in the military hierarchy based upon the number of enemies they captured. Contributions of supplies and warriors were demanded of altepetl previously conquered by the Triple Alliance. These practices allowed imperial forces to become almost invincible (Hassig 1988).

Spanish chronicles detail the process of military campaigns. First, the Aztecs looked for a legitimate reason to launch a new expedition (e.g., the murder of long-distance merchants, the absence of a tlatoani invited to attend an imperial ceremony, refusal to provide supplies or warriors to Aztec armies when they passed by). In such cases, they dispatched emissaries to ask the tlatoani if he were going to surrender without any resistance—a proposition that was always rejected. Then, Aztec leaders reassembled their military forces and sent them to the battlefield. Typical warrior equipment consisted of a padded cotton armor named *ichcahuipilli*, a wooden shield to prevent injuries and different kind of weapons; a *macuahuitl* (sword whose edges were composed of rows of razor-sharp obsidian blades); an *atlatl* (spear thrower), and bows and arrows. High-level warriors also wore sandals, jewels, specific headgear, and back devices.

The battle began with the sound of drums and shell trumpets. The battlefield objective was not to kill the enemy—even if some actually died—but to capture enemy soldiers to sacrifice to their gods back to the capital. When the enemy finally surrendered, battle ceased and winners imposed tax payments.

Figure 31.2 Conquest of Cuetlaxtlan by Tenochtitlan. Codex Teleriano-Remensis, folio 37r; redrawn by Maëlle Sergheraert.

In their campaigns of expansion, the Aztecs concentrated on conquering the major cities. When an altepetl capital was subdued, imperial rule was initiated over the entire area of the altepetl and all of its population, not just the individual city that was defeated. This principle is illustrated in many of the depictions of conquest found in Aztec pictorial histories, where the name of the defeated city is tied to the symbol for "altepetl." Figure 31.2 shows the conquest of Cuetlaxtlan in the year 10 reed, or 1475 (Cuetlaxtlan is province no. 41 in Figure 31.1).

The Mexica warrior is on the right, linked to the glyph for Tenochtitlan (a cactus growing out of a rock). He defeats a warrior whose domain is the entire altepetl (the hill emblem, *tepetl*) of Cuetlaxtlan (the tied cord element). The shield and arrows under the hill are symbols of military defeat. By employing this strategy of conquest, the Aztecs did not have to conquer all of the towns and villages, only the most important towns in each province (Sergheraert 2009).

The Aztec Empire did not cover a single contiguous range of territory; the map of the empire (Figure 31.1) shows many blank areas. This configuration is partly a consequence of the practice of targeting only specific key towns for conquest. Another reason for this pattern lies in basic Mesoamerican patterns of political control. The extent of a polity was defined not in terms of a border surrounding an area of territory, but rather as the area in which the people subject to the king lived. This principle operated at both the altepetl level and the imperial level. The areas included in the provinces in Figure 31.1 add up to 135,000 square kilometers (Berdan et al. 1996).

INCOME FROM THE EMPIRE

Many scholars agree that the main motivation for Aztec imperial expansion was economic. This does not mean that religious and social motives were unimportant to the soldiers and officials who created and ran the empire. There was an elaborate mythological justification for warfare and imperial expansion, and soldiers gained status for themselves and their families by performing well in battle. But tlatoque, nobles, and commoners all benefited greatly from the growing quantities of goods moving from the provinces into the imperial capitals. These goods arrived through three main channels: commerce, gifts, and taxes.

1. *Commerce.* Professional merchants (*pochteca*) from the Basin of Mexico traded widely both within and outside of the provinces. These long-distance merchants worked together with imperial officials to the benefit of each. Imperial armies conquered and protected key provincial market towns, and merchants gathered information on resources and defenses in external areas.
2. *Gifts.* Tlatoque and nobles throughout northern Mesoamerica gave each other expensive gifts as part of the process of diplomacy. Provincial notables sent expensive gifts to the emperor, and in the case of some border states these gifts were sent in place of taxes.
3. *Taxes.* The tax system was the most important mechanism by which the imperial capitals obtained resources from the provinces. Although Mesoamericanists have traditionally used the term "tribute" for these payments, they in fact correspond more closely to the definition of taxes in economic history: payments were regularly scheduled, recorded in official documents, and collected by teams of professional tax collectors. "Tribute," from a comparative perspective, refers to single lump-sum payments made by subject polities to their conquerors or overlords. Aztec tax obligations were assessed by province and recorded in pictorial documents.

The *Matrícula de Tributos* is a surviving pre-Spanish tax record, and its early colonial copy, the *Codex Mendoza*, is the clearest and most heavily studied tax roll (Berdan and Anawalt 1992). The taxes for each tributary province in the Codex Mendoza (Figure 31.1) are listed in these documents. The page for the province of Huaxtepec (Figure 31.3) shows how the taxes were recorded. The towns that made up this province are listed down the left side and bottom of the page, starting with the provincial capital, Huaxtepec. At the top are images of ten cotton textiles, each with a feather that indicates 400 items. These were paid twice a year, for an annual total of 8,000 textiles. Then come 46 warrior costumes with shields; two large bins of grain; and finally 2,000 gourd bowls and 8,000 pieces of bark paper (for painting codices). When the annual income in the Codex Mendoza is added up, the totals are impressive.

Taxes were collected by a battery of officials called *calpixque*. There were several types of calpixque, from low-level officials who ran errands and organized

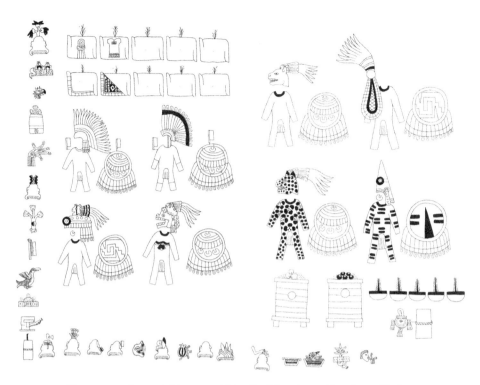

Figure 31.3 Imperial taxes paid by the Huaxtepec Province. Codex
Mendoza, folio 24v–25r; from Berdan and Anawalt (1992: vol. 4, pp. 54–55). Reproduced
with permission.

labor on public works for local tlatoque to the heads of the imperial tax system. Tax
records like the Matrícula de Tributos were kept by the highest level of calpixque
in Tenochtitlan. Each province had two high-level calpixque, one in Tenochtitlan
and one in the provincial capital, who was aided by a series of lower-ranking tax
collectors (Smith 2012).

Maintaining Control

Although scholars have traditionally emphasized the indirect nature of control
of the provinces, recent research suggests that the empire may have wielded more
power in provincial areas than has been thought. The nature of imperial control
varied considerably throughout the Empire, but three major categories, based on
location and context, can be identified.

1. *The Central Provinces.* Provinces closest to Tenochtitlan were strongly
   controlled. The Aztecs reorganized the preexisting local hierarchy (unlike

what they did in the outer provinces) by appointing new faithful governors, as well as judges, tax collectors, and other administrators in most
altepetl. Some local tlatoque were also asked to live in Tenochtitlan an
important part of the year and their sons were educated in the capital. The
Aztecs ensured themselves the support of these new authorities by various
means: marriage alliances, gift giving and reciprocal exchange of luxury
goods, attendance at political rituals, participation in military campaigns,
and tax redistribution in case of victory, labor, and materials for building
public work (Berdan et al. 1996).

2. *The Outer Provinces.* The Aztecs controlled the outer provinces through
   both direct and indirect methods. In many areas, local tlatoque and
   nobles were invited to ceremonies in Tenochtitlan and in some cases
   marriage alliances were established with important provincial dynasties. Unlike some ancient empires, the Triple Alliance did not invest in
   the construction of roads, cities, or other infrastructure in provincial
   areas. But the indirect forms of control should not obscure the presence
   of more direct channels of administration and the role of military threat.
   Many examples of imperial-style objects and carvings have been found
   in provincial areas, and one notable feature of these is the prominence of
   military and imperial symbols and themes (Figure 31.4).

   Detailed comparisons of written, pictographic, and archaeological data
reveal the specific ways in which the Aztecs targeted the most important

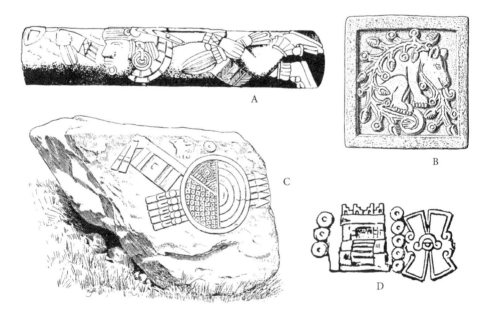

Figure 31.4 Aztec-style reliefs from provincial contexts in the state of Morelos.
(A) wood drum from Tepoztlan; (B) stone relief from Tepoztlan; (C) stone relief from
Cuernavaca; (D) stone relief from Huaxtepec. Adapted from Smith (2010).

altepetl in each region in order to achieve strong control with a minimum of effort. In this strategy, Aztec administrative governors were sent to rule directly the principal altepetl of the outer provinces (often the provincial capital). They were typically accompanied by military forces, settlers, or tax collectors to reinforce Aztec presence. When available, archaeological data attest to this strong presence, with significant concentrations of Aztec artifacts in the capitals of the major altepetl: temples and palaces were often redecorated with Aztec architectural ornaments; Aztec sculptures were displayed in visible areas; and imported Aztec censers, temple models, and other ritual paraphernalia were used in religious ceremonies.

In dealing with important but less powerful altepetl, the Aztecs tended to establish good relationships with local authorities (e.g., gift giving, attendance at imperial celebrations) and to encourage their cooperation with a slighter Aztec presence (perhaps a tax collector or small garrison). Finally, they did not engage themselves in the smallest altepetl: it was not necessary because they were already controlled by bigger altepetl. This mechanism allowed the Aztecs to maintain a firm control of the outer territory at a minimal expense. Imperial impact on the local area was low, but control was maintained (Sergheraert 2009).

3. *Frontier Provinces.* The Aztecs entertained special relationships of mutual benefits with tlatoque in the frontier provinces; these helped to defend the imperial borders in exchange for being protected against external enemies. They served as strategic buffer zones between the inner empire and its frontiers, in a role similar to the client kings of the eastern Roman Empire. In Figure 31.1, these areas are called "strategic provinces." These altepetl did not pay imperial taxes (they are not included in the tax records), but their tlatoque did give "gifts" of soldiers and luxury goods to the Aztec huey tlatoque (Berdan et al. 1996).

Conclusions

In ninety years, the Aztecs built an extensive empire through the strategic use of existing political organizations in each altepetl, both for expanding their territories and maintaining control. As the empire grew, it was progressively organized in order to ensure various incomes to the imperial capital. Imperial strategy generated the cohesion of the empire, even if the Aztecs did not have total control over their territories. Rebellions happened each time a subjected people had the feeling that the empire was weakened (e.g., at times of tlatoque succession). But the Aztecs were fast to respond and always put down these rebellions. The arrival of the Spaniards in 1519 presented a new occasion for some of the subjected people to rebel against the Aztecs, uniting themselves with the Spanish forces, and this time, they were stronger. The Aztec Empire fell at the hands of its Spanish and native enemies on August 13, 1521.

REFERENCES

Berdan, Frances F., and Patricia R. Anawalt, eds. 1992. *The Codex Mendoza.* 4 volumes. University of California Press, Berkeley.

Berdan, Frances F., Richard E. Blanton, Elizabeth H. Boone, Mary G. Hodge, Michael E. Smith, and Emily Umberger. 1996. *Aztec Imperial Strategies.* Dumbarton Oaks, Washington, DC.

Carrasco, Pedro. 1999. *The Tenochca Empire of Ancient Mexico: The Triple Alliance of Tenochtitlan, Tetzcoco, and Tlacopan.* University of Oklahoma Press, Norman.

Durán, Fray Diego. 1994. *The History of the Indies of New Spain,* translated by Doris Heyden. University of Oklahoma Press, Norman.

Hassig, Ross. 1988. *Aztec Warfare: Imperial Expansion and Political Control.* University of Oklahoma Press, Norman.

Matos Moctezuma, Eduardo. 1988. *The Great Temple of the Aztecs.* Thames and Hudson, New York.

Rojas, José Luis de, and Michael E. Smith. 2007. El imperio de la triple alianza (Tenochtitlan, Texcoco y Tlacopan) en el siglo XXI. *Revista Española de Antropología Americana* 37:81–97.

Sergheraert, Maëlle. 2009. L'expansion mexica (1430–1520 après J.-C.): La question du contrôle impérial dans les provinces extérieures de l'Empire. PhD dissertation, Department of Archaeology, Université Paris 1, Panthéon-Sorbonne.

Smith, Michael E. 2008. *Aztec City-State Capitals.* University Press of Florida, Gainesville.

Smith, Michael E. 2010. La época posclásica en Morelos: surgimiento de los Tlahuica y Xochimilca. In *La arqueología en Morelos: Dinámicas sociales sobre las construcciones de la cultura material,* edited by Sandra López Varela., pp. 131–156. Universidad Autónoma del Estado de Morelos, Ayuntamiento de Cuernavaca, Instituto de Cultura de Morelos, Cuernavaca.

Smith, Michael E. 2012. *The Aztecs.* 3rd ed. Blackwell, Oxford.

CHAPTER 32

THE CONQUEST OF MEXICO

MICHEL R. OUDIJK

The Spanish Conquest of Mexico

While the encounter of the Old and the New Worlds, embodied by Christopher Columbus setting foot on American soil, may be considered one of the most determining moments in history, those who lived it at the time were not as enthusiastic about it after the initial excitement died down. The Antillian Islands were a far cry from the dream of "El Dorado" that would be created fifty years later. Soon enough this became clear as no great sources of riches were found, causing interest to dwindle.

Everything changed after 1519 when Hernán Cortés set foot on what was to be called New Spain. It was not so much the event itself that changed European perception of the New World, but rather the letters that Cortés wrote and sent back to the king, Charles V. Cortés's undertaking was actually illegal because his permission to explore was revoked by Governor Diego Velázquez de Cuéllar shortly before he set sail. So as soon as Cortés settled on the mainland, he founded the town of Vera Cruz and started writing letters to the king in order to gain his support. It is, thus, no wonder that Cortés beautifully described the Mesoamerican world in great detail with all its wonders and riches, only to make more glorious his feat of claiming this land in the name of the king.

While Cortés's first letter was lost, the second, written on October 30, 1520, arrived in Spain and was published in 1522. A year later a French version came out, followed by Latin and Dutch translations in 1524. Cortés's story thus became somewhat of a best-seller in early sixteenth-century Europe and it still is today all over the world. Some thirty years later in 1552, Francisco López de Gómara (1987), chaplain of Cortés, published the *Conquest of Mexico*. This story is basically the same as that told by Cortés, but this time it is primarily focused on him with very little attention for the other conquistadors or the indigenous allies. Cortés rises as an omnipresent hero, who controlled every bit of the conquest. By the end of the century his narrative had been published in twenty-nine editions in Spanish, French, Italian, and English, and it had firmly established the history of the Spanish conquest.

Obviously, to this string of publications one has to add the *True History of the Conquest of New Spain* written by Bernal Díaz del Castillo (1992) in 1568 in response to López de Gómara's story. Díaz del Castillo was so angry about López's decision to leave out the feats of the other conquistadors that he decided to set the record straight. In a long detailed history, Díaz del Castillo tells of his own experiences and of those of the other conquistadors. No doubt much of the latter came from stories that were told to him by his brothers in arms. Even though it is a much more personal story than those of Cortés and López de Gómara, it is hardly different in the actual events. It was written in 1568 but only published in 1632 and probably again before 1665, long after the history of the Spanish conquest was set. It was only in the nineteenth century, when it was published several times into Spanish, English, German, French, and Hungarian, that the *True History* became a major source for scholars and laymen.

These are the three main sources that have been used to describe the conquest. Later "official" histories (Solís de Ribadeneyra 1684; Prescott 1843; Thomas 1993) have basically followed the same structure and story line as the accounts of the conquerors, although they applied the methodological instruments of their time. Of course, there are many more scholars who have written about the conquest (León-Portilla 1959; Todorov 1984; Clendinnen 1987; Restall 1998, 2003; Brienen and Jackson 2008) and although very different in focus, all have something in common. From Solís in 1684 until today, historians all have continuously asked the same question: How was it possible for five hundred Spaniards to conquer a Mexican empire? A small group arrived in Veracruz, walked through Mexico to Tenochtitlan and took the emperor Moctezuma prisoner, battled against thousands of Indians, and destroyed their temples....How was that possible? For more than three hundred years, historians have looked for an explanation and have proposed many. The military genius of Cortés, divine intervention, the superiority of European arms, the structural weakness of Mesoamerican empires, and its internal cultural diversity, the idea of the return of Quetzalcoatl: all these reasons, and more, have been suggested but none has completely convinced the laymen or the academic public.

In trying to resolve the question, historians have applied all kinds of methodological instruments but particularly have critically analyzed the sources. All have recognized the obvious subjectivity of the main sources of Cortés, López de Gómara, and Díaz del Castillo. The response has been either to verify the information given by these authors with that of archival documents and other accounts by Spanish conquerors, or to confront the Spanish sources with indigenous ones. These have been very useful methods that have clarified many of the doubts and mistakes represented in the main sources, but they have always confirmed the main story line of the Spanish conquest of Mexico.

THE INDIGENOUS CONQUEST
OF MEXICO

A chance encounter with a sixteenth-century document made clear why the explanations by so many historians had had no satisfying response to the main question about the Spanish conquest. In 1564 a large group of Indians from central and southern Mexico claimed in 848 pages that they were indigenous conquistadors (Archivo General de Indias, Seville, Justicia 291, Exp. 1). Reading through this thick file, witness after witness tells how they, with thousands of indigenous warriors and a few Spaniards, came south to conquer Chiapas, Guatemala, Honduras, and El Salvador. If Spaniards are mentioned at all, it is normally to refer to them as nuisances in battle who continuously had to be rescued, be taken care of, and be carried around. Reading through the document one becomes perplexed by disbelief. This is not the history of the conquest that we know, which is taught in school or is written up in so many history books and Spanish sources.

The "official" account of the conquest is so entrenched in our minds after almost five hundred years of repetition, that the first reaction is that this document must be a setup. This must have been organized by some indigenous leaders to mislead the colonial authorities and obtain certain privileges and exemptions from tribute. But soon enough more documents were found that confirmed the claims by these indigenous conquistadors in Guatemala. Letters of merit, reports about indigenous participations in military campaigns, petitions with long accounts of indigenous campaigns in the name of the king, and representations in pictographic documents, coats of arms, and grants all talk about the same thing: the conquest of Mesoamerica may have been sparked by the arrival of the Spaniards, but it certainly was not a Spanish undertaking alone. The Spanish also did not control it and at times they did not even take part in it (See Matthew and Oudijk [2007] for an extensive discussion of the indigenous participation in the conquest of Mesoamerica.)

INDIGENOUS ARGUMENTATION

The arguments put forth by these indigenous conquistadors are based on two particular aspects: (1) they became allies of the Spaniards right from the start and therefore joined the military conquest of Mesoamerica or parts of it, and (2) shortly after they became allies they were baptized and had been faithful Christians ever since. As such, these arguments are not very different from those of the Spanish conquistadors, although these did not need to prove their Christianity. Shortly after the fall of Tenochtitlan and continuously for the next fifty years, numerous letters of merit were written by Spanish conquistadors or their descendants and sent to the king to ask for *encomiendas*, coats of arms, and other privileges. Similarly, but beginning slightly later, the indigenous allies wrote petitions to the king too.

It is particularly striking that the indigenous petitions came from all over New Spain, indicating that it was not just Nahua-speaking groups from central Mexico who participated. Instead, any indigenous group from anywhere could have allied themselves. A good example comes from Pedro de Alvarado's 1523 campaign to Guatemala. According to Díaz del Castillo the army consisted of Spaniards, Tlaxcalteca, Cholulteca, and Mexicanos (probably from Tenochtitlan and Tlatelolco). However, indigenous sources add that thousands of warriors joined underway like those from Tlaxcala, Huexotzinco, Tepeaca, Cuilapan, Oaxaca, Tehuantepec, and finally Kaqchikeles in Guatemala.[1] Similarly, in 1576 indigenous survivors of the conquests of Yucatán filed a complaint about their impoverished condition, which, they claimed, they did not deserve because they were conquistadors. Only fifty-six of them were left at the time, but they came from several central Mexican towns like Azcapotzalco, Huexotzingo, Texcoco, and Xochimilco. There were furthermore Chontal, Popoluca, and Zoque Indians from Tabasco, and Lenca and Jicaque from Honduras.[2] In northern New Spain, Mexica, Tarascans, Otomí, and "pacified" Chichimecs were used as *flecheros*, a military force against the Chichimecs, who threatened the silver mines of Zacatecas, as well as the trade routes connecting these mines with central Mexico.[3]

Many historians, fueled by Cortés's letters, have marveled at his incredible capacity to use the tensions that existed between the many ethnic groups and city-states that made up the Mesoamerican political landscape. While this may be true to a certain extent, from an indigenous point of view making alliances was the most normal thing in the world, something that was also applied to the newcomers from overseas. Postclassic Mesoamerica was made up of various city-state cultures (Hansen 2000, 2002), which constituted highly complex political constructs of autonomous entities that were interconnected through many sociopolitical relationships, one of which was that of alliances (Lind 2000; Smith 2000; Oudijk 2002). The Mixtec and Zapotec genealogical codices are, rather, registers of inter-city-state relationships, which continued in the Colonial-period alphabetic documents (Terraciano 2001: 171–179; Chance 2008). Similarly, the famed Triple Alliance

---

1. See Matthew (2007) for an account of the conquest of Guatemala, and see Asselbergs (2004, 2007) for a discussion on how historical events are represented in the Lienzo de Quauhquechollan, a pictorial from central Mexico.

2. See Chuchiak (2007) for an in-depth analysis of the indigenous conquest of Yucatán.

3. See Blosser (2007) for a description of the *flecheros* in New Galicia.

between Tenochtitlan, Texcoco, and Tlacopan was a continuation of another Triple Alliance between Azcapotzalco, Culhuacan, and Coatlinchan, which was preceded by one made up of Culhuacan, Tula, and Otumba (Chimalpahin 1991: Chapters 7, 15). Such prehispanic alliances did not share "a common ethnic identity" and functioned as "special purpose institutions, arising from perceived needs and persisting as long as needs were satisfied" (Hassig 1988: 23). Therefore, the multiple examples in the Spanish conquest literature about alliances with indigenous lords and rulers can be regarded as evidence of Cortés's political shrewdness, but at the same time they serve as evidence of a continuing Mesoamerican practice by these very indigenous lords and rulers.

Contrary to what the Spanish sources and letters of merit suggest, from the indigenous petitions it becomes clear that the allies, or *indios amigos*, normally outnumbered the Spanish troops and sometimes actually conquered without any Spaniards present. Although the numbers are confusing, New Galicia was conquered by an army of anywhere between 10,000 and 20,000 indigenous soldiers, accompanied by 150 Spanish horsemen and another 150 soldiers on foot.[4] According to Díaz del Castillo and Cortés, four hundred Spaniards and three hundred Tlaxcalteca, Cholulteca, and Mexica participated in the above-described campaign to Guatemala. However, indigenous sources tell us there were only two hundred Spaniards and in Oaxaca some three thousand Indians from Tlaxcala, Huexotzingo, and Tepeaca joined the army. This practice continued until the army was a tremendous force of six thousand men when it arrived in Guatemala. Such a practice was taken to its extreme in the case of the conquest of southern Puebla and northern Oaxaca (Oudijk and Restall 2008). Here, shortly after the *noche triste*, or the Spanish defeat in Tenochtitlan, Cortés met with the local cacique of Tepexi de la Seda, Don Gonzalo Mazatzin Moctezuma, with whom an agreement was reached: Cortés would return to Tenochtitlan while Don Gonzalo, in the name of the king of Spain, would take care of Puebla and Oaxaca. The Spanish conquistador, who does not make any notice of this meeting in his letters, claims to have aborted his military campaign to the south and to have marched on Tenochtitlan due to his need for revenge (Cortés 1992: 2nd letter). In the meantime, Don Gonzalo indeed conquered the southern Puebla and northern Oaxacan regions with an army of his indigenous allies in which no Spaniard participated. It is very difficult to call this victory part of the Spanish conquest.

For any army to be able to march and fight, be it a Spanish or indigenous one, it is of the utmost importance to be well fed and have moments of safety in between battles. Before Cortés found an ally in the so-called Fat Cacique of Zempoala, he, and Díaz del Castillo confirms this, continuously mentioned that they were suffering from hunger and thirst as the indigenous towns that they encountered either were battlegrounds or were left empty upon their arrival. This dramatically changed after the first alliance with the Fat Cacique, who ensured that the allied army was fed on its way to Tenochtitlan by friendly communities and allies of his

---

4. Altman (2007) gives an exhaustive account of this conquest.

town. This became even better after the Tlaxcaltec lordships joined the alliance and with them all their allies. At the same time the indigenous allies provided the armies with spies and guides. It would have simply been impossible for the Spaniards to cross the Mesoamerican landscape toward Tenochtitlan, or any other place for that matter, without the guidance of local people. Without knowledge of the language, landscape, and war tactics, the Spaniards would have perished shortly after leaving the coast; this aspect is mentioned over and over again by the indigenous conquistadors.

As the allied armies were guided by indigenous guides and by existing relationships between city-states, the routes of conquest followed existing commercial routes. This becomes particularly clear if the routes of conquest are projected over a map that shows the prehispanic production and resource-extraction zones (Figure 32.1). A strong relationship between these aspects emerges from this map, as all conquest routes go to or go through these prehispanic zones and therewith follow old trade routes. Although very little is known about why the allied armies went to these particular regions, the sources do contain indications. In just about all the early military campaigns Cortés justified them by saying that these regions had rebelled or were harming friendly or allied provinces. Only in two cases does he mention economic reasons: Tehuantepec and Chiapas, and Oaxaca, the latter for being en route to the Southern Sea. However, in the beginning of his fourth letter Cortés also relates that he always made the efforts to inform himself about the "secrets of these parts," no doubt referring to such aspects as military strength, political organization, and economic wealth (Cortés 1992: 175). In fact, very early on in his stay in Tenochtitlan, Cortés had asked Moctezuma where he got his gold (Cortés 1992: 56). So, it being clear that the Spaniards were after riches, it is no surprise the indigenous guides took them along the Mesoamerican routes to the zones of extraction.

This brings us to the motives and objectives for the indigenous rulers to ally themselves to the armies. This was briefly touched upon above, but it deserves more attention. Whereas Cortés was desperately looking for strongholds on the mainland, the Fat Cacique thought the five hundred Spanish conquistadors were good allies for his own objectives. These objectives became immediately clear once they crossed the border to the next town where Cortés did not find a garrison of Moctezuma, but rather a town that had been fighting against Zempoala for years. While this might confirm that Cortés was using Mesoamerican internal divisions, these same indigenous alliances made the military campaign to Tlaxcala and Tenochtitlan possible. Too often, the main motive suggested by historians for the indigenous alliance with the Spaniards has been that the indigenous city-states wanted to liberate themselves from the Mexica imperial tribute state. Although that may have been true in part, other motives were clearly at work. If not, how would one explain that after the fall of Tenochtitlan indigenous groups continued to become part of the allied forces even though the Mexica empire no longer existed? In the above-mentioned alliance with Don Gonzalo Mazatzin, it was this Tepexi lord who shrewdly managed the new political situation. He took over part of the most important trade routes that

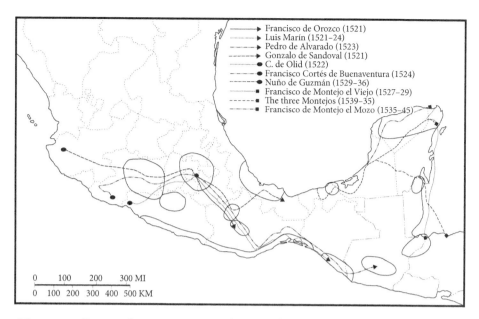

Figure 32.1 Routes of conquest projected over prehispanic production and resource-extraction zones.

connected central Mexico with its southern parts, and he sent Cortés's army back to Tenochtitlan where it had received a serious defeat a couple of months earlier. Don Gonzalo's strategy was clear: if a second defeat would follow, he would control these trade routes, but if Tenochtitlan would be defeated he would be a powerful ally of the new lord and, following prehispanic practice, he would receive important privileges and rights to land and tribute (Oudijk and Restall 2008). So each city-state had its own objectives in making an alliance; some of these we know due to documents left to us, others we can guess at, but most we will never know. No doubt, often Cortés was left in the same dark.

CONCLUSIONS

The objective of bringing forth indigenous documents about the conquest of Mesoamerica is not to discredit the Spanish sources. Rather, it is important to reflect on the meaning of all sources, evaluate them, apply a historical critique, and reconsider the historical version of the conquest as we know it. That is, we must consider indigenous sources as equal to Hispanic ones. Although this process has begun relatively recently, its consequences for our perception of the events of the conquest are dramatic. Whereas it has always been described as a Spanish undertaking, it now seems to have been much more influenced by existing Mesoamerican patterns.

Mesoamerican people, arms, food, and knowledge made the conquest possible, as
well as Mesoamerican ideas of conquest and alliance. From the very start the encounter between the Old and New Worlds produced a syncretic history with the process
of the "double mistaken identity" fully at work (Lockhart 1985). Where Spanish conquistadors reported on how they won the Spanish conquest, their indigenous brothers
in arms fought an indigenous conquest right by their side. Sadly, the latter's part has
since been largely ignored. Still a lot needs to be done to put the balance back.

REFERENCES

Altman, Ida. 2007. Conquest, Coercion, and Collaboration: Indian Allies and the
    Campaigns in Nueva Galicia. In *Indian Conquistadors: Indigenous Allies in the
    Conquest of Mesoamerica*, edited by Laura Matthew and Michel R. Oudijk,
    pp. 145–174. University of Oklahoma Press, Norman.
Archivo General de Indias, Sevilla, Justicia 291. 1564. Exp. 1, El fiscal con los yndios
    mexicanos, tlascaltecas y çapotecas del Reyno de Guatemala sobre pago de tributos,
Asselbergs, Florine G. L. 2004. *Conquered Conquistadors. The Lienzo de
    Quauhquechollan: A Nahua Vision of the Conquest of Guatemala*. Research School
    CNWS, Leiden.
Asselbergs, Florine G. L. 2007. The Conquest in Images: Stories of Tlaxcalteca and
    Quauhquecholteca Conquistadors. In *Indian Conquistadors: Indigenous Allies in the
    Conquest of Mesoamerica*, edited by Laura Matthew and Michel R. Oudijk,
    pp. 65–101. University of Oklahoma Press, Norman.
Blosser, Bret. 2007. "By the Force of Their Lives and the Spilling of Blood": Flechero
    Service and Political Leverage on a Nueva Galicia Frontier. In *Indian Conquistadors:
    Indigenous Allies in the Conquest of Mesoamerica*, edited by Laura Matthew and
    Michel R. Oudijk, pp. 289–316. University of Oklahoma Press, Norman.
Brienen, Rebecca P., and Margaret A. Jackson, eds. 2008. *Invasion and Transformation.
    Interdisciplinary Perspectives on the Conquest of Mexico*. University Press of
    Colorado, Boulder.
Chance, John K. 2008. Alianzas matrimoniales coloniales entre caciques mixtecos: El
    caso de Acatlan-Petlalcingo. *Anuario de Estudios Americanos* 65:71–86.
Chimalpahin Quauhtlehuanitzin, Domingo de San Anton Muñon. 1991. *Memorial breve
    acerca de la fundación de la ciudad de Culhuacan*. Translated by Victor M. Castillo
    Farreras. Universidad Nacional Autónoma de México, Mexico City.
Chuchiak IV, John F. 2007. Forgotten Allies: The Origins and Roles of Native
    Mesoamerican Auxiliaries and Indios Conquistadores in the Conquest of
    Yucatan, 1526–1550. In *Indian Conquistadors: Indigenous Allies in the Conquest
    of Mesoamerica*, edited by Laura Matthew and Michel R. Oudijk, pp. 175–226.
    University of Oklahoma Press, Norman.
Clendinnen, Inga. 1998 [1987]. *Ambivalent Conquests: Maya and Spaniard in Yucatan,
    1517–1570*. Cambridge University Press, Cambridge.
Cortés, Hernán. 1992. *Cartas de relación*. Sepán cuantos... No. 7, Editorial Porrúa,
    Mexico City.

Díaz del Castillo, Bernal. 1992. *Historia verdadera de la conquista de la Nueva España.* Sepán cuantos...No. 5, Editorial Porrúa, Mexico City.

Hansen, Mogens Herman, ed. 2000. *A Comparative Study of Thirty City-State Cultures.* C.A. Reitzels Forlag, Copenhagen.

Hansen, Mogens Herman, ed. 2002. *Seven Studies of City-State Cultures.* C.A. Reitzels Forlag, Copenhagen.

Hassig, Ross. 1988. *Aztec Warfare: Imperial Expansion and Political Contact.* University of Oklahoma Press, Norman.

León-Portilla, Miguel. 1992 [1959]. *La visión de los vencidos. Relaciones indígenas de la Conquista.* Universidad Nacional Autónoma de México, Mexico City.

Lind, Michael D. 2000. Mixtec City-States and Mixtec City-State Culture. In *A Comparative Study of Thirty City-State Cultures*, edited by Mogens Herman Hansen, pp. 567–580. C.A. Reitzels Forlag, Copenhagen.

Lockhart, James. 1985. Some Nahua Concepts of Postconquest Guise. In *History of European Ideas*, Vol. 6, pp. 465–482. [This article was published again in *Of Things of the Indies: Essays Old and New in Early Latin American History*. Stanford University Press, Stanford, 1999, pp. 98–119.]

López de Gómara, Francisco. 1987. *La conquista de México.* Historia 16, Madrid.

Matthew, Laura. 2007. Whose Conquest? Nahua, Zapoteca, and Mixteca Allies in the Conquest of Central America. In *Indian Conquistadors: Indigenous Allies in the Conquest of Mesoamerica*, edited by Laura Matthew and Michel R. Oudijk, pp. 102–126. University of Oklahoma Press, Norman.

Matthew, Laura, and Michel R. Oudijk, eds. 2007. *Indian Conquistadors: Indigenous Allies in the Conquest of Mesoamerica.* University of Oklahoma Press, Norman.

Oudijk, Michel R. 2002. The Zapotec City-State. In *Seven Studies of City-State Cultures*, edited by Mogens Herman Hansen, pp. 73–90. C.A. Reitzels Forlag, Copenhagen.

Oudijk, Michel R., and Matthew Restall. 2008. *La conquista indígena de Mesoamérica: El caso de Don Gonzalo Mazatzin Moctezuma.* Secretaria de Cultura del Estado de Puebla/Universidad de las Américas Puebla/Instituto Nacional de Antropología e Historia, Puebla.

Prescott, W. H. 1914 [1843]. *The Conquest of Mexico.* 2 volumes. J. M. Dent and Sons, London.

Restall, Matthew. 1998. *Maya Conquistador.* Beacon, Boston.

Restall, Matthew. 2003. *Seven Myths of the Spanish Conquest.* Oxford University Press, Oxford.

Smith, Michael E. 2000. Aztec City-States. In *A Comparative Study of Thirty City-State Cultures*, edited by Mogens Herman Hansen, pp. 581–596. C.A. Reitzels Forlag, Copenhagen.

Solís de Ribadeneyra, Antonio de. 1947 [1684]. *Historia de la conquista de Méjico.* Espasa-Calpe, Buenos Aires.

Terraciano, Kevin. 2001. *The Mixtecs of Colonial Oaxaca: Ñudzahui History, Sixteenth through Eighteenth Centuries.* Stanford University Press, Stanford.

Thomas, Hugh. 1994 [1993]. *La conquista de México.* Planeta, Madrid.

Todorov, Tzvetan. 1984. *The Conquest of America. The Question of the Other.* Harper Perennial, New York.

Peripheries and Frontiers

....

CHAPTER 33

NETWORKS, CORES, AND PERIPHERIES

NEW FRONTIERS IN INTERACTION STUDIES

....

EDWARD SCHORTMAN AND

PATRICIA URBAN

THE terms "core," "periphery," and "frontier" conjure up spatial distinctions correlated with divisions among societies based on size, economic organization, and power. Leaders of core states are generally presumed to dominate developments within the smaller, poorer, less powerful societies arrayed around them (Stein 2002). Territorial distinctions thus have important behavioral consequences. How those outcomes are understood depends heavily on the theoretical framework in which cores, frontiers, and peripheries are modeled. We will review the most prominent of these conceptual structures and the mechanisms of intersocietal interaction that they highlight (diffusion, trade, exploitation, and hybridity). The essay concludes with a call for a new approach to the study of cores, peripheries, and frontiers that does not presuppose the existence of these entities and the nature of interregional interactions generally.

DIFFUSION

....

Most archaeological research through the 1950s in Mesoamerica was devoted to identifying culture areas understood as zones of more or less homogeneous behaviors and beliefs, each with its own distinct history (Kroeber 1939). These units were largely defined archaeologically by the spatial distribution of material traits, such as pottery styles and architectural forms, that were seen as emblematic of distinct sociolinguistic groups. Changes in such diagnostic features were usually ascribed to the movement of cultural forms from innovating centers within each area and across their borders either alone (diffusion) or in association with migrating populations (Dixon 1928). Culture areas were thus crucial units of analysis and the means for organizing information about the past in publications and museum displays. At a higher level of synthesis, Mesoamerica was defined as a distinct zone of closely interrelated culture areas of which the Valleys of Mexico and Oaxaca and the Maya lowlands were thought to have been the most prominent (Kirchoff 1966). It was residents of these core zones who played the greatest roles in shaping Mesoamerican prehistory.

In the course of pursuing such culture-historical studies, boundaries were drawn, denoting fixed limits across which interchanges were restricted, if not precluded (De Atley and Findlow 1984). Research then concentrated on charting developments within and diffusion of traits among, innovating cores while people living beyond these borders were mostly ignored. Few, if any, archaeologists still subscribe to these simplistic premises. The basic distinction between active, innovative culture cores and the passive, culturally conservative societies arrayed on their margins, however, persists as a guiding principle of investigation just as culture areas defined in the early twentieth century continue to structure research specialties, publications, and the arrangement of museum cases.

TRADE

Increased interest, by the 1960s, in societies situated on Mesoamerica's borders was motivated in part by changing theoretical perspectives. The advent of processualism, with its initial focus on the causal primacy of adaptive processes in determining culture form and change, did not immediately lead to new research here. Major questions concerning such developments as the shift to domestication and the appearance of states focused on studying human-land relations within traditional Mesoamerican cores where, it was argued, these processes must have originated and reached their fullest expressions (Sanders and Price 1968).

There was, however, a growing recognition that sustaining local populations, especially those organized within large, complex core states, required inputs from beyond their borders (Adams 1974; Earle and Ericson 1977; Sabloff and Lamberg-Karlovsky 1975). The major adaptive processes thought to spur economic, social, and political change were increasingly seen as occurring within webs of interregional interaction that incorporated societies of varying sizes and levels of complexity (Price 1977; Rathje 1971; Sanders 1962). Intersocietal trade was, therefore, imagined as potentially fueling core growth and as a mechanism by which core innovations spread to, and evoked emulation among, those living on their margins (cf. Renfrew and Cherry 1986). What had been boundaries delimiting cultures were transformed under the aegis of trade into porous peripheries across which goods and influences of all kinds traveled. These movements were, however, largely attributed to the initiatives of core rulers and primarily benefited those magnates. Influence coursed "downhill," from "high" to "low" cultures yielding in peripheries pale reflections of the economic, social, political, and ideological forms seen in cores (Dietler 1998). Nevertheless, systematic investigations were initiated throughout Mesoamerica's peripheries by the 1960s and have intensified ever since. Not necessarily seen at first as important in their own rights, research in peripheral societies could at least enrich explanations of cultural shifts within cores.

EXPLOITATION

Trade research initially described interaction networks by using an ever-increasing number of analytical techniques (e.g., Tite 1972) and explained the developmental impact of these transactions in relation to how they met the basic subsistence or social needs of interaction partners. Whereas the descriptive procedures have proliferated, trade as a process was reconceived by some researchers, beginning in the late 1960s, less as a way to survive and more as a means to power. Investigators pursuing this line of inquiry have generally subscribed to some versions of world systems (WST) and prestige goods theory (PGT).

Wallerstein originally developed WST to account for the impact of capitalist expansion out of western Europe on populations around the globe since the fifteenth century (1974, 1981; cf. Wolf 1982). The dynamic of this spread was and is characterized by a stark division in the organization of labor and power between cores and peripheries (their relations often mediated by residents of semiperipheries). Those living in peripheries provide labor and raw materials at low costs to core enterprises that convert these commodities into expensive finished goods. The latter items are then shipped from cores to peripheries, the resulting trade imbalance yielding the systematic impoverishment of peripheries and the enrichment of core leaders. Global capitalism is thus predicated on the development of underdevelopment in peripheries (Frank 1971).

Applying WST to prehistoric cases required redefining basic terms and reimagining processes of exploitation operating on interregional scales (Algaze 1993; Blanton and Feinman 1984; Chase-Dunn and Hall 1995; Kohl 1987; Stein 1998). While researchers approached these problems in diverse ways, there was a growing consensus in the 1980s about several key issues. First, most of what was exchanged among prehistoric societies consisted of high-value, low-bulk items that could be transported relatively easily over long distances (Schneider 1977). This was especially the case in Mesoamerica where, lacking beasts of burden, much trade was conducted by human carriers. The developmental significance of these "luxuries," though discounted by Wallerstein, was attributed to their importance in initiating and instantiating crucial social relations within and across polities. Researchers working from the PGT perspective focused on this aspect of interregional exchanges. They generally posited that those who monopolized the importation, production, or local distribution of social valuables were well positioned to convert equals into dependents who surrendered labor and loyalty for items essential to defining their social personas and relations with others (Ekholm 1972; Friedman and Rowlands 1977; Helms 1993). Social valuables were, therefore, central to the functioning of multiple, interdependent political economies and underwrote sociopolitical hierarchies and power centralization in numerous societies.

Second, it was stressed that no society existed in isolation. Developments in one realm were affected by events occurring in others with which its members were directly or indirectly in contact. The nature of these interactions was characterized by some level of inequality with large, militarily powerful, economically productive, and politically complex core states exercising varying levels of control over their smaller, weaker, less productive interaction partners in the peripheries (Stein 1999). In extreme cases, political and economic disparities between cores and peripheries were so great that elites in the former could systematically drain resources from the latter. Such unequal flows of goods impoverished peripheries while contributing to the growth of core industries and elite power and wealth. This outcome generally resembles the processes of interregional exploitation that Wallerstein outlined for Europe's rapacious relations with the rest of the world from the mid-fifteenth century onward. More commonly, core rulers of noncapitalist states did not dictate the terms of exchange to their interaction partners because they could not sustain viable military threats against distant realms and could not monopolize the transportation technologies and vital goods desired by all interactors (Kohl 1987; Schortman and Urban 1994). Consequently, the developmental significance of core/periphery relations varied considerably. Where core dominance was muted, peripheral elites could translate their favored relations with core states into power at home by monopolizing the local distribution of valued items secured from their powerful partners (Stein 1999). Much work conducted under the aegis of PGT has been devoted to studying just these sorts of relations.

PGT and WST have the salutary effect of tying dealings among members of different societies explicitly to the operation of local political economies. They also stress that developments in peripheries are not of secondary interest to those occurring in cores. Both demand detailed examination in part because the ways in which interaction partners in all societies take advantage of opportunities for advancement offered by intersocietal contacts can affect not only local events but the very structure of the interaction web and the flow of politically crucial resources through it.

Nevertheless, legacies of earlier core-periphery models permeate these approaches. Many using PGT and WST still attribute disproportionate amounts of causal significance to the actions of core rulers who are generally seen as providing blueprints for sociopolitical change and the means, in the form of high-prestige exports, to achieve those transformations within peripheral realms. As in the past, ideas and goods do not flow from peripheries and impact developments in cores. Rather the reverse is thought to be true. Core elites may not control directly the actions of their peripheral counterparts but they do play outsized roles in firing and enabling the political aspirations of those living on their margins.

HYBRIDITY

By the 1990s a number of scholars grew dissatisfied with the causal weight attributed in WST to core elites and economic processes of exploitation in shaping peripheries. Inspired, in part, by postcolonial and globalization theory (e.g., Bhabha 1996; el-Ojeili and Hayden 2006), some researchers argued that borders are and were innovative locales where people from diverse backgrounds forge new identities and cultural forms in the process of daily interactions (Lightfoot and Martinez 1995; Naum 2010). Rather than searching for broad commonalities in the nature of cross-border dealings, as was generally the case with WST applications, investigations of borderlands highlight their volatile, historically contingent, and culturally fragmented nature. The hybrid cultures crafted by diverse agents drawing on the conceptual structures and goods of diverse origins available to them are conditioned by shifting political, economic, and ideological relations that are rarely stable and whose outcomes are largely unpredictable. Patterned behaviors at any one moment are, therefore, seen less as determined by such macro-regional processes as intersocietal exploitation than by the reflexive actions of individuals and factions who maneuver within these broad structural constraints to create their own unique histories.

Borderland studies successfully counter the traditional notion of passive peripheries. The "third space" (Bhabha 1996, 2004) created at the junction of two or more cultures is reimagined as a venue for the exercise of, if not unbridled, at least significant, agency. Further, the cultural translations, misinterpretations, and syntheses that characterize cross-border dealings are seen as operating among agents from societies of varying sizes, thus avoiding the traditional emphasis on the one-way flow of innovations from core states. As important and exciting as such analyses are, however, they still presuppose the existence of identifiable and bounded cultures and polities. Traditional interests in cores and their borders thus continue to structure research, albeit in new ways, as do entrenched core/periphery distinctions. It may well be that boundaries are fertile zones of cultural innovation, but are such clearly drawn limits the products of centralized control associated with the creation of nation-states over the last several centuries? As with WST, we may be in danger here of projecting recent, if now pervasive, understandings of intersocietal dealings on what is likely to have been a far more diverse array of past interaction processes.

NETWORKS

In reimagining intersocietal relations it might be best to ask what we are trying to accomplish. One important goal is to understand how processes operating on multiple spatial and temporal scales are interwoven in trajectories of change through the actions of different agents residing in diverse locales. Seeing as the transformations of greatest current concern deal with the ability of actors to exercise power over others or to protect their own autonomy (Wolf 1990), we might narrow the question to "How were interactions that took place over various territorial extents implicated in processes of political centralization and hierarchy building that operated at different levels of spatial inclusiveness?" In some instances, established perspectives, such as WST, will provide the best framework for answering this query. The particular modes of inequality implied in that approach, however, do not define the totality of structures in which interactions transpiring over different distances and periods occur (Schortman and Urban 1998; Stein 1999). Rather than trying to map a wide array of interaction processes within the narrow confines of those that presuppose cores, peripheries, and borders, it might be more profitable to develop a conceptual scheme that encourages consideration of how transactions transpiring at all scales and locales were related to political processes occurring within specific cultural and historical circumstances (Schortman and Urban 2011; Stein 2002).

An approach that employs social networks as basic units of analysis could help accomplish this goal (Campbell 2009). Social networks refer here to groups of people who regularly marshal conceptual and tangible resources, of local or foreign derivation, in pursuit of common political objectives. These goals may include concentrating power and institutionalizing invidious distinctions by maintaining exclusive local membership in networks through which essential goods and ideas are acquired, along the lines laid out in PGT. Alternatively, those resisting such efforts could maneuver to preserve some measure of autonomy by producing or securing critical assets within nets of their own creation. Successful pursuit of these and other political aims requires allying with some to obtain needed resources, often in competition with others organized along similar lines for comparable purposes (Giddens 1984; Mann 1986; Ortner 1995: 187, 191; Preucel 2000: 59–61). Social networks are thus the means by which diverse agents—acting in contexts from households to empires, in cities, villages, and along borders—contest for symbols and goods central to establishing, defending, and challenging claims to power (Mauss 2007; Stein 1998: 6).

We are all born into networks not of our creation. The frameworks composed of these nets, operating over differing territorial extents, determine the distribution of assets and, hence, what political projects are feasible. They do not, however, define which of that range of options will be acted upon at any time (Bourdieu 1977; Giddens 1984; Wolf 1990). It is the manners in which available resources are marshaled by those cooperating within webs that transform this set of possible structural configurations into the one that is enacted in a specific period and place.

Collaborating with others in social nets is strengthened when members of a web share a distinct identity performed through displays of material symbols (Barth 1969; Bentley 1987: 27, 429-30; Stein 2002: 905; Wells 1998; Wobst 1977, 1999). The more intense the competition for resources, the more often network membership is stressed in daily interactions, the more prominent and frequent the markers of membership are likely to be (Hodder 1979; Schortman 1989; Worsley 1984: 240–251). It is important to bear in mind, however, that no matter how much specific webs vary in their salience, people commonly subscribe to multiple networks at any time and may well change affiliations throughout their lives. Such memberships can be actualized situationally, stressing certain criteria of belonging while downplaying others that are more relevant in other circumstances (Alcock 2005; Goffman 1997: 23; Schortman et al. 2001). Such shifting allegiances add an air of tension to many interpersonal dealings, especially in cases where assets used to support the political projects of one web are re-channeled to subsidize those pursued by participants in another. Nonetheless, we hypothesize that it is through these complexly overlapping networks of networks that resources move with variable ease among interactors and from which the structure channeling their dealings is in a constant process of emerging (Smith 2005). This overarching framework is never more than provisional. Any shifts in allegiances that affect the flow of crucial resources can have wide-ranging implications for all who operate within these interconnected webs.

In sum, we propose that traditional research foci such as households, societies, polities, and empires might be profitably viewed as contingent, temporary outcomes of dynamic interactions channeled through nets that fragment them internally even as they transcend their boundaries. Thus, participants in a household may be divided by religious affiliations that link them differentially to others living at variable distances even as they regularly enact membership in the same domestic unit. Grasping the behavioral implications of such complex arrangements at all scales may be advanced by subscribing to the following premises: the principles underlying sociopolitical structures significantly affect interpersonal dealings when they are performed; these enactments of power and hierarchy are funded by tangible and intangible resources secured through alliances organized within webs; the resulting political formations, operating at an array of spatial scales, are composed of networks of networks that variably unite and divide people living in different locales; these formations change as crucial resources are rechanneled by diverse actors working within multiple, shifting coalitions.

Unlike core-periphery models, a network approach focuses on how people live their lives and compete for crucial resources close to the ground. As such, it does not assume the existence of such structural features as the inequality of cores and peripheries, but it concentrates on how those grand frameworks emerge from the dealings of all interaction partners. Political structures come alive, and are susceptible to change, through the transactions they channel. Drawing inspiration from borderland studies, a network approach highlights in detail how local and interregional political processes are interwoven through the initiatives of goal-driven agents. Such agency, however, does not depend on the existence of bounded cultural and political entities. In fact, barring major physical obstacles to contact, the existence of borders that curtail the free operation of social webs is not taken as a given but as a process that demands explanation. By using networks as basic analytical units we can, thus, get beyond simplified divisions between external and local processes and deeply engrained emphases on territorially delimited social groups. In doing so we hope to grasp how the political structures channeling interpersonal dealings at all scales and locations arose from the initiatives of people operating in variably enduring groups over variable distances.

The implications of such a perspective for archaeological research include: treating the nested sets of territorially bounded units that traditionally structure research as the volatile outcomes of power contests waged within social nets that variably divided and transcended such entities; understanding these processes using a multiscalar approach that examines how assets drawn from varying sources were combined in political strategies by agents organized within networks of networks; and allowing for the active participation of elites and nonelites in such developments (Stein 2002: 907). Achieving the above goals requires: identification of ancient networks through the patterned distribution of their distinctive membership symbols (Earle 1997; Jeske 1999); specification of how their participants manipulated the production, exchange, and consumption of goods and ideas in pursuit of political goals by identifying the ways in which these processes figured in efforts to centralize power and construct hierarchies (Dietler 1998; Smith 1998; Stein 2002: 906; Wells 1980); and evaluating the success of these endeavors as measured by such factors as differential control over labor and valuables. Essentially, this is a call to analyze the operation of political economies as they functioned simultaneously over different spatial extents (Schortman and Urban 2011).

We do not claim that a network approach is the only fruitful perspective on intersocietal interactions. It does, we argue, offer a way of understanding how micro- and macro-regional processes of various sorts were enacted within, and challenged, political structures functioning over differing distances without presupposing the existence of cores, peripheries, or borders. In this way we might capture something of the volatility that characterizes a great many human interactions at all spatial scales in all times and places. At least we hope that such analyses will help us see Mesoamerica's peripheries as homes to agents who were as active in the creation of their own lives as those who resided in the better-known, larger societies that have heretofore dominated scholarly and public attention.

REFERENCES

Adams, Robert McC. 1974. Anthropological Perspectives on Ancient Trade. *Current Anthropologist* 15:239–258.

Alcock, Susan. 2005. Roman Colonies in the Eastern Empire: A Tale of Four Cities. In *The Archaeology of Colonial Encounters: Comparative Perspectives*, edited by Gil Stein, pp. 297–329. School of American Research, Santa Fe.

Algaze, Guillermo. 1993. *The Uruk World System*. University of Chicago Press, Chicago.

Barth, Frederick. 1969. Introduction. In *Ethnic Groups and Boundaries: The Social Organization of Culture Difference*, edited by Frederick Barth, pp. 9–38. Little Brown, Boston.

Bentley, G. Carter. 1987. Ethnicity and Practice. *Comparative Studies in Society and History* 29:24–55.

Bhabha, Homi. 1996. Culture's In-Between. In *Questions of Cultural Identity*, edited by Stuart Hall and Paul Du Gay, pp. 53–60. London, Sage.

Bhabha, Homi. 2004. *The Location of Culture*. Routledge, London.

Blanton, Richard, and Gary Feinman. 1984. The Mesoamerican World System. *American Anthropologist* 86:673–682.

Bourdieu, Pierre. 1977. *Outline of a Theory of Practice*. Translated by Richard Nice. Cambridge University Press, Cambridge.

Campbell, R. 2009. Toward a Networks and Boundaries Approach to Early Complex Polities. *Current Anthropology* 50:821–848.

Chase-Dunn, Christopher, and Thomas Hall. 1995. Cross-World-Systems Comparisons: Similarities and Differences. In *Civilizations and World Systems: Studying World-Historical Change*, edited by Stephen Anderson, pp. 109–135. Altamira Press, Walnut Creek, California.

De Atley, Suzanne, and Frank J. Findlow, eds. 1984. *Exploring the Limits: Frontiers and Boundaries in Prehistory*. British Archaeological Reports Series No. 223, Oxford.

Dietler, Michael. 1998. Consumption, Agency, and Cultural Entanglement: Theoretical Implications of a Mediterranean Cultural Encounter. In *Studies in Culture Contact: Interaction, Culture Change, and Archaeology*, edited by John Cusick, pp. 288–315. Center for Archaeological Investigations, Occasional Papers 25, Southern Illinois University, Carbondale.

Dixon, R. 1928. *The Building of Cultures*. Charles Scribner's Sons, New York.

Earle, Timothy. 1997. *How Chiefs Come to Power*. Stanford University Press, Stanford.

Earle, Timothy, and Jonathon Ericson, eds. 1977. *Exchange Systems in Prehistory*. Academic Press, New York.

Ekholm, Kasje. 1972. *Power and Prestige: The Rise and Fall of the Kongo Kingdom*. SKRIV Service AB, Uppsala.

Frank, Andre. 1971. Development of Underdevelopment. In *Imperialism and Underdevelopment: A Reader*, edited by Robert Rhodes, pp. 4–17. Monthly Review Press, New York.

Friedman, Jonathan, and Michael Rowlands. 1977. Notes Towards an Epigenetic Model of the Evolution of Civilization. In *The Evolution of Social Systems*, edited by Jonathan Friedman and Michael Rowlands, pp. 201–276. University of Pittsburgh Press, Pittsburgh.

Giddens, Anthony. 1984. *The Constitution of Society: Outline of the Theory of Structuration*. University of California Press, Berkeley.

Goffman, Erving. 1997. *The Goffman Reader.* Edited by Charles Lemert and Ann
     Branaman. Blackwell, Oxford.
Helms, Mary. 1993. *Craft and the Kingly Ideal.* University of Texas Press, Austin.
Hodder, Ian. 1979. Economic and Social Stress and Material Culture Patterning.
     American Antiquity 44:446–454.
Jeske, Robert. 1999. World Systems Theory, Core-Periphery Interactions, and Elite
     Economic Exchanges in Mississippian Societies. In *World Systems Theory in
     Practice: Leadership, Production, and Exchange,* edited by P. Nick Kardulias,
     pp. 203–221. Rowman and Littlefield, Lanham, Maryland.
Kirchoff, Paul. 1966. Mesoamerica: Its Geographic Limits, Ethnic Composition and
     Cultural Characteristics. In *Ancient Mesoamerica: Selected Readings,* edited by John
     Graham, pp. 1–14. Peek Publications, Palo Alto, California.
Kohl, Phillip. 1987. The Use and Abuse of World Systems Theory: The Case of the
     Pristine West Asian State. *Advances in Archaeological Method and Theory* 11:1–35.
Kroeber, Alfred. 1939. *Cultural and Natural Areas of Native North America.* University of
     California Publications in American Archaeology and Ethnology 38:1–242.
Lightfoot, Kent, and Antoinette Martinez. 1995. Frontiers and Boundaries in
     Archaeological Perspective. *Annual Review of Anthropology* 24:471–492.
Mann, Michael. 1986. *The Sources of Social Power, Volume 1: A History of Power from the
     Beginning to AD 1760.* Cambridge University Press, Cambridge.
Mauss, Marcel. 2007. *Manual of Ethnography.* Translated by Dominique Lussier. Edited
     by N. J. Allen. Durkheim Press/Berghahn Books, New York.
Naum, Magdalena. 2010. Re-Emerging Frontier: Postcolonial Theory and Historical
     Archaeology of the Borderlands. *Journal of Archaeological Method and Theory*
     17:101–131.
El-Ojeili, Chamsy, and Patrick Hayden. 2006. *Critical Theories of Globalization.* Palgrave,
     New York.
Ortner, Sherry. 1995. Resistance and the Problem of Ethnographic Refusal. *Comparative
     Studies in Society and History* 37:173–193.
Preucel, Robert. 2000. Making Pueblo Communities: Architectural Discourse at Kotyiti,
     New Mexico. In *The Archaeology of Communities: A New World Perspective,* edited
     by Marcello Canuto and Jason Yaeger, pp. 58–77. Routledge, New York.
Price, Barbara. 1977. Shifts in Production and Organization: A Cluster-Interaction
     Model. *Current Anthropology* 18:209–233.
Rathje, William. 1971. The Origin and Development of Lowland Classic Maya
     Civilization. *American Antiquity* 36:275–285.
Renfrew, Colin, and John Cherry, eds. 1986. *Peer Polity Interaction and Socio-Political
     Change.* Cambridge University Press, Cambridge.
Sabloff, Jeremy, and C. C. Lamberg-Karlovsky, eds. 1975. *Ancient Civilization and Trade.*
     University of New Mexico Press, Albuquerque.
Sanders, William. 1962. Cultural Ecology of Nuclear America. *American Anthropologist*
     64:34–44.
Sanders, William, and Barbara Price. 1968. *Mesoamerica: The Evolution of a Civilization.*
     Random House, New York.
Schneider, Jane. 1977. Was There a Pre-Capitalist World System? *Peasant Studies* 6:20–29.
Schortman, Edward. 1989. Interregional Interaction in Prehistory: The Need for a New
     Perspective. *American Antiquity* 54:52–65.
Schortman, Edward, and Patricia Urban. 1994. Living on the Edge: Core/Periphery
     Relations in Ancient Southeastern Mesoamerica. *Current Anthropology* 35:401–430.

Schortman, Edward, and Patricia Urban. 1998. Culture Contact Structure and Process. In *Studies in Culture Contact: Interaction, Culture Change, and Archaeology*, edited by John Cusick, pp. 102–125. Center for Archaeological Investigations, Occasional Papers 25, Southern Illinois University, Carbondale.

Schortman, Edward, and Patricia Urban. 2011. *Networks of Power: Political Relations in the Late Postclassic Naco Valley, Honduras*. University of Colorado Press, Boulder.

Schortman, Edward, Patricia Urban, and Marne Ausec. 2001. Politics with Style: Identity Formation in Prehispanic Southeastern Mesoamerica. *American Anthropologist* 103:1–19.

Smith, Monica. 2005. Networks, Territories, and the Cartography of Ancient States. *Annals of the Association of American Geographers* 95:832–849.

Smith, Stuart. 1998. Nubia and Egypt: Interaction, Acculturation, and Secondary State Formation from the Third to First Millennium BC. In *Studies in Culture Contact: Interaction, Culture Change, and Archaeology*, edited by John Cusick, pp. 256–287. Center for Archaeological Investigations, Occasional Papers 25, Southern Illinois University, Carbondale.

Stein, Gil. 1998. Heterogeneity, Power, and Political Economy: Some Current Research Issues in the Archaeology of Old World Complex Societies. *Journal of Archaeological Research* 6:1–44.

Stein, Gil. 1999. *Rethinking World Systems: Diasporas, Colonies, and Interactions in Uruk Mesopotamia*. University of Arizona Press, Tucson.

Stein, Gil. 2002. From Passive Periphery to Active Agents: Emerging Perspectives in the Archaeology of Interregional Interaction. *American Anthropologist* 104:903–916.

Tite, Michael. 1972. *Methods of Physical Examination in Archaeology*. Academic Press, London.

Wallerstein, Immanuel. 1974. *The Modern World System I*. Academic Press, New York.

Wallerstein, Immanuel. 1981. *The Modern World System II*. Academic Press, New York.

Wells, Peter. 1980. *Culture Contact and Culture Change*. Cambridge University Press, Cambridge.

Wells, Peter. 1998. Culture Contact, Identity, and Change in the European Provinces of the Roman Empire. In *Studies in Culture Contact: Interaction, Culture Change, and Archaeology*, edited by John Cusick, pp. 316–334. Center for Archaeological Investigations, Occasional Paper 25, Southern Illinois University, Carbondale.

Wobst, H. Martin. 1977. Stylistic Behavior and Information Exchange. In *For the Director: Research Essays in Honor of James B. Griffin*, edited by Charles Cleland, pp. 317–342. University of Michigan, Anthropological Papers No. 61, Ann Arbor.

Wobst, H. Martin. 1999. Style in Archaeology or Archaeologists in Style. In *Material Meanings: Critical Approaches to the Interpretation of Material Culture*, edited by Elizabeth Chilton, pp. 118–132. University of Utah Press, Salt Lake City.

Wolf, Eric. 1982. *Europe and the People without History*. University of California Press, Berkeley.

Wolf, Eric. 1990. Distinguished Lecture: Facing Power—Old Insights, New Questions. *American Anthropologist* 92:586–596.

Worsley, Peter. 1984. *The Three Worlds*. University of Chicago Press, Chicago.

CHAPTER 34

THE SOUTHEASTERN FRINGE OF MESOAMERICA

JOHN S. HENDERSON AND KATHRYN M. HUDSON

THE southeastern fringe (or frontier or periphery, though these are sometimes distinguished) of Mesoamerica is usually taken to be the area in which features that typify Mesoamerican societies blend with and eventually give way to cultural and behavioral patterns that characterize non-Mesoamerican societies of Central America. Because scholarly opinion as to the features essential to a Mesoamerican way of life varies, even specifying the geographic extent of the fringe is problematic. It is usually conceived—imprecisely, to say the least—as beginning east of the area in which the key features—most often Maya hieroglyphic texts, Maya iconography, or Mayan speech—were common, extending south and east to some point at which the frequency of recognizably Mesoamerican traits is sufficiently low to be accounted for as a result of "Mesoamerican influence." Moreover, the distribution of such features was not static, so the geography of the periphery shifts through time. Not surprisingly, notions of the location of the fringe zone have varied wildly. A zone stretching from west-central Honduras and El Salvador east through the mountainous zones of east-central Honduras and north-central Nicaragua, and south through Pacific Nicaragua to the Nicoya region of northwestern Costa Rica (Figure 34.1) can serve as a rough initial approximation of the zone occupied by relevant societies. It is more productive, however, to think in terms of intersecting webs of interaction than in terms of trait lists or language distributions.

Approaches to the Southeastern Fringe in Historical Perspective

Characterizing a fringe zone where material remains did not quite match patterns thought to be typical of Maya regions was a salient issue long before Mesoamerican archaeology crystallized as a distinct field. When the political situation in Honduras interrupted investigations at the quintessentially Maya city of Copán in 1896, George Byron Gordon temporarily shifted his focus to the lower Ulúa Valley to the east. He quickly formed the view that "if not a branch of the Mayas, the people, with whose remains on the Ulúa River we are now brought in contact, were in close relations with some portion of that race, whose customs they adopted and by whose culture they were enriched." Gordon concluded that "they were, in fact, subject to the Maya civilization" and he resumed work at Copán as soon as it was practicable (Gordon 1898: 38–39). Generations of Mesoamericanists after him came to hold essentially the same views: areas east of the part of the Maya world with spectacular architecture and sculpture were occupied by societies whose cultures were derivative. The important issues were how far proper Maya culture extended and how much influence it exerted on other groups. Lothrop (1939: 52) summed up the situation this way: "Eastward of the typical Mayan sites, occasional trade pieces of polychrome Mayan pottery have been found, but only in association with objects which are not Mayan.... These and similar finds show not an extension of the Mayan area but dispersion by trade of Mayan artifacts."

In the 1960s, the Instituto Hondureño de Antropología e Historia (IHAH) began to take an active role in field research as well in shaping the trajectories of collaborative work with foreign institutions (Véliz 1983). Investigations at Copán resumed after a hiatus that began with World War II and interest in the southeast fringe of Mesoamerica simultaneously intensified. Copán, by far the best-known site in Honduras, embodies archaeology and the Maya-ness of Honduran prehistory in the public imagination, and it has continued to be the focus of research organized and sponsored by such national agencies as the Asociación Copán as well as international institutions. IHAH has always had to divide its efforts between coordinating and supervising work at Copán—the focus of Honduran tourism and the source of a significant portion of IHAH's budget—and fostering investigations elsewhere in the country.

Relationships with the Maya world continued to be a key theme in research along Mesoamerica's southeast fringe. Core-periphery models—especially world systems theory, developed by the historian Immanuel Wallerstein (1974)—became a popular framework for understanding interaction in the fringe area (e.g., Robinson 1987; Schortman and Urban 1987, 1994a, 1999) and Copán was (implicitly) taken to be a Maya core influencing a non-Maya periphery. Classic core-periphery perspectives have not been very helpful in this precapitalist, noncolonial context, where its assumptions—especially that peripheries are simpler in all ways than cores and dependent on them for inspiration and innovation—are hard to justify (e.g., Stein 1999). Modified world-systems analysis perspectives with fewer problematic assumptions continue to inform discussion of Mesoamerica and its southeast fringe (Carmack and Salgado González 2006; Kardulias and Hall 2008; Smith and Berdan 2003).

Identity is another rubric that has enjoyed increasing attention from interpreters of the southeast fringe (Henderson 1992a; Schortman et al. 2001). This perspective has been most useful when focused on local social identities (e.g., Stockett 2007). By contrast, attempts to recognize higher-level identities of very broad applicability—Maya, Lenca, non-Maya, for example (e.g., Gerstle 1987)—have been far less enlightening. The problem stems in part from uncertainty about what kinds of material remains might reflect identities of such broad reach, but also founder in confusion about the nature of and bases for archaeological, linguistic, and emic categories. The notion of a homogeneous Maya identity is particularly problematic.

One might have expected that the southeast fringe would have been viewed as part of the Maya world on grounds of similarity in craft styles, persistent exchange relationships, and the presence of features like ballcourts. Despite increased attention to the specifics of regional prehistory and recognition that developmental trajectories are very similar to those of eastern Mesoamerica proper, orthodoxy has power: the idea that the southeast fringe is impoverished in comparison with the Maya world, from which its societies received influence, perseveres.

Figure 34.1 Geographic features in the southeast fringe of Mesoamerica.

Prehistory of the Southeastern Fringe

The archaeological record of the southeastern fringe is spotty. Generalizations about developmental trajectories and cultural relationships necessarily gloss over regional variability, relying heavily on a few regions (Figure 34.1) with relatively fuller documentation:

- The lower Ulúa valley, northwestern Honduras (Gordon 1898; Henderson 1984, 1992b; Henderson and Beaudry-Corbett 1993; Henderson and Joyce 2004; Henderson et al. 2007; Joyce 1991, 1993; Joyce and Henderson 2001; Luke 2002; Luke and Tykot 2007; Stone 1941; Strong et al. 1938; Wonderley 1985, 1991)
- Los Naranjos, northwestern Honduras (Baudez and Becquelin 1973; Joyce and Henderson 2002; Strong et al. 1938)
- The Naco valley, northwestern Honduras (Henderson 1977; Henderson et al. 1979; Schortman and Urban 1994a, 1994b; Wonderley 1981)
- The middle Ulúa valley, northwestern Honduras (Schortman et al. 1986)
- The Comayagua valley, central Honduras (Canby 1949; Dixon 1987, 1989, 1992; Dixon et al. 1994; Stone 1957)
- The El Cajón region, Sulaco and Humuya valleys, central Honduras (Hirth et al. 1989)
- Northeastern Honduras (Cuddy 2007; Healy 1974, 1978a, 1978b; Strong 1934, 1935)
- Chalchuapa, western El Salvador (Sharer 1974, 1978)
- The Zapotitlán and Paraíso valleys, central El Salvador (Bruhns 1980; Bruhns and Amaroli 2009; Fowler 1989; Kelley 1988; Sheets 1983, 1992)
- Quelepa, eastern El Salvador (Andrews 1976)
- Greater Nicoya, Pacific Nicaragua and Nicoya Peninsula, Costa Rica (Carmack and Salgado González 2006; Day 1984; Healy 1980; Lange and Guerrero 2001; Salgado González 1996)

The following schematic summary of prehistoric developments in the southeast fringe will emphasize the lower Ulúa Valley, which, for many, is the embodiment of a peripheral region that was influenced by Maya cities but not part of the Maya world.

Early village life in the region is best documented at Puerto Escondido in the lower Ulúa Valley (Figure 34.2) (Joyce and Henderson 2001; Henderson and Joyce 2004; Henderson et al. 2007). Pottery made by the earliest villagers between 1600 and 1100 BC closely resembles contemporary ceramics found on the Pacific Coast, as far west as Soconusco. By 1100 BC Puerto Escondido was clearly part of the Olmec world; after 900 BC that affiliation is reflected at Playa de los Muertos as well. At Los Naranjos (on the shore of Lake Yojoa) and Chalchuapa, monumental platform construction and stone sculptures in the Olmec style testify to the developing complexity and social differentiation that suggest incipient elites (Baudez and Becquelin 1973; Joyce and Henderson 2002; Sharer 1974, 1978). From the beginning of settled life in the region, relationships with Mesoamerican societies to the west are unmistakable.

By approximately 600 BC the Olmec world had disintegrated, but the development of complexity continued during the late first millennium BC and early first millennium AD. Platforms for public buildings were built in the Naco Valley, at Río Pelo in the lower Ulúa Valley (Wonderley 1991), at Yarumela in the Comayagua Valley (Dixon et al. 1994), at San Andres in the Zapotitlán Valley (Sheets 1983), and at Quelepa (Andrews 1976), where an altar with relief carving echoes sculptural styles of highland Guatemala. At Chalchuapa (Sharer 1974, 1978), where construction was truly massive, relief sculpture includes a stela with a hieroglyphic text. Distinctive, resist-decorated Usulután pottery probably developed first in El Salvador late in the first millennium BC, spread quickly to Pacific Nicaragua, central Honduras, northwestern Honduras, western El Salvador, and beyond into the Maya world (Demarest and Sharer 1982). The techniques by which the resist decoration was produced are not obvious, so the broad distribution of Usulután pottery indicates that interaction among communities was sustained. Communities in eastern Honduras were not yet tied into this network, at least not at the same level of intensity: Usulután pottery is rare in the region at this time, and monumental construction activity is not documented before about 250 AD (Begley 1999). The third century AD eruption of Ilopango covered western El Salvador and adjacent areas in volcanic ash, sending the region into a long period of decline.

Most regions of the southeastern fringe prospered during the period from ca. 300 to 1000 AD, corresponding to the Classic period in eastern Mesoamerica. Populations grew; communities proliferated and increased in scale and complexity. In the lower Ulúa Valley, a multitiered settlement hierarchy developed (Henderson 1992b; Joyce 1991; Stone 1941). By the eighth century AD, Travesía was easily the largest town in the valley, but there is no evidence that it maintained centralized political control. Comparable towns developed in much of the fringe: at Los Naranjos (Baudez and Becquelin 1973), La Sierra in the Naco Valley (Henderson et al. 1979; Schortman and Urban 1994b), Gualoquito in the middle Ulúa Valley (Schortman et al. 1986), Salitrón Viejo in the Cajón (Hirth et al. 1989), Marañones in the Culmí Valley (Begley 1999), Wankibila in the Patuca Valley (Cuddy 2007), Chalchuapa (the part of the site zone known as Tazumal) (Sharer 1974, 1978), San Andres in the Zapotitlán Valley (Sheets 1983), and Quelepa (Andrews 1976) farther to the east. Each town held considerable economic and political sway in its region but—in sharp contrast with areas to the west—increasing social stratification and political centralization did not result in centralized states. Developments were not uniform across the region. Ballcourts are documented throughout the western and central sectors of the southeast fringe, but they are rare in the northeast and currently unattested in Greater Nicoya. Volcanic activity continued to disrupt life in El Salvador, though the effects were less sweeping than those of the earlier Ilopango event. One of these localized eruptions in the Zapotitlán Valley in the seventh century resulted in the rapid burial of the farming village of Cerén and material traces of many aspects of daily life not normally preserved in the archaeological record (Sheets 1983, 1992).

In crafts, painted pottery was produced in great variety; styles of polychrome painting and their complex imagery are particularly helpful in mapping relationships across the area. The lower Ulúa Valley, Lake Yojoa Basin, Cajón region, and Comayagua Valley made up the core of a region in which related styles of polychrome painting, usually grouped together as Ulúa Polychrome, were the preferred decoration for fine serving vessels (Henderson and Beaudry-Corbett 1993; Joyce 1993). Ulúa Polychromes were also used, with less frequency, alongside vessels decorated in regional polychrome styles in the Naco and middle Ulúa valleys, El Salvador, Greater Nicoya, and northeastern Honduras. Elements of Ulúa Polychrome vessel form, style, and iconography strongly resemble those in various parts of the Maya world. Distinctive and elaborately carved Ulúa marble vessels were distributed from the lower Ulúa Valley in very small quantities during the seventh and eighth centuries AD (Luke 2002; Luke and Tykot 2007). Their presence in the Maya world to the north, the Naco and Comayagua valleys, Olancho, and Greater Nicoya probably reflects ties among elite families. While Ulúa marbles have not been found in the northeast, very similar ceramic vessels were produced there.

At Quelepa, carved stone yokes, palmas, and hachas, along with wheeled ceramic figurines, indicate a strong new connection with the Gulf Coast of Mexico. Fine paste pottery without local antecedents may reflect the same relationship

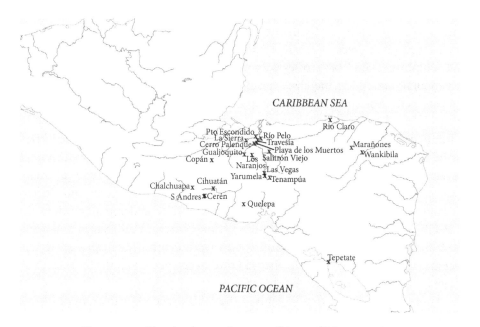

Figure 34.2 Sites in the southeastern fringe of Mesoamerica.

(Andrews 1976: 184–186). New connections with the west appeared also in Greater Nicoya, where imagery on polychrome pottery began to incorporate elements with strong resemblances to central Mexican styles.

During the ninth and tenth centuries, the southeast fringe experienced political and economic changes related to those that transformed the Maya world (Henderson 1992b; Henderson and Beaudry-Corbett 1993): old centers were abandoned and new ones emerged, often in different kinds of locations; settlement hierarchies were simplified; the existence of fewer and smaller communities suggested demographic decline. New styles of serving vessels replaced long-established fashions. The intensity of these changes varied, but the processes affected every region to some degree. Many communities in the lower Ulúa Valley were abandoned, and Cerro Palenque, a highly defensible hilltop town, appears to have been dominant (Joyce 1991). Ulúa Polychromes gave way to new polychrome styles and fine paste wares, as in the Maya world to the north and west. Tenampúa, the largest town in Comayagua, was situated on the edge of a steep escarpment overlooking the valley with a defensive wall blocking the gentler approaches (Dixon 1987, 1989, 1992).

By the eleventh century AD, the lower Ulúa Valley contained only villages, as did the Naco and middle Ulúa valleys (Schortman et al. 1986); the Cajón region may have been abandoned (Hirth et al. 1989). Los Naranjos (Baudez and Becquelin 1973) was greatly reduced in size, and the modest town of Las Vegas was the largest in the Comayagua Valley (Dixon 1989, 1992; Stone 1957). Settlement systems contracted in northeast Honduras, indicating population decline, but these changes were less striking (Cuddy 2007). Styles of pottery decoration—most notably Bay Island Polychrome—increasingly resembled those of Greater Nicoya. By the time of the Spanish invasion a few communities, including Río Claro in the lower Aguán Valley (Healy 1978a), had grown into large towns. At Chalchuapa, the Tazumal group continued to function as a regional center (Sharer 1978); it appears to have had no appreciable decline until the thirteenth century AD. Architecture and sculpture—talud-tablero terraces, a round platform, carved-stone reclining chacmool figures, and a life-size ceramic figure resembling the Aztec deity Xipe— indicate new western connections that extended to central Mexico (Sharer 1974: 172–173). San Andres declined, perhaps in part as the result of another localized volcanic eruption (Sheets 1983). Cihuatán, in the Paraíso Basin, emerged briefly as the largest town in central El Salvador prior to its destruction by fire in the eleventh century; it, too, has a round platform (Bruhns 1980; Bruhns and Amaroli 2009; Fowler 1989; Kelley 1988). In Greater Nicoya, Tepetate grew into the largest community in a three-tiered settlement hierarchy and remained dominant in Pacific Nicaragua until the Spanish invasion (Carmack and Salgado González 2006; Salgado González 1996). Motifs with close central Mexican counterparts became even more prominent in Nicoya Polychrome pottery in the fourteenth and fifteenth centuries (Day 1984; Healy 1980).

After 1200 AD, Naco developed into the most prosperous town in northwestern Honduras (Wonderley 1981, 1985); its economic sphere probably extended beyond the Naco Valley to include the lower Ulúa. Naco's long-distance exchange relationships extended north and west to the Gulf Coast of Mexico as well as east and south. Its fame as a trading center made it a focus of the Spanish invasion: Cortés's desire to check on his subordinates there was the motivation for his famous march to Honduras after the conquest of central Mexico.

Historical Linguistics

The distribution of languages along the southeast fringe of Mesoamerica at the time of the Spanish invasion (Figure 34.3) provides an interesting complement to the archaeological record (Campbell 1997). Speakers of Pipil, a language belonging to the Nahua family spoken mainly in central and northern Mexico, occupied much of central and western El Salvador (Fowler 1989). Lenca, of uncertain affiliation, was spoken from eastern El Salvador, through central Honduras, probably extending north to the lower Ulúa Valley. Speakers of Tol (Jicaque), whose taxonomic relationships are also problematic, had a much more limited distribution in central Honduras. To the east was a block of Chibchan languages: Sumu in the north (Miskito may not yet have separated from its Misumalpan relatives),

Figure 34.3 Language distributions in the southeastern fringe of Mesoamerica.

Pech (Paya), and Matagalpa in the south. The languages of Greater Nicoya—
Nicarao, Chorotega, and Subtiaba—are all related to languages far to the west in
Mesoamerica. Nicarao, like Pipil, is a Nahua language; Chorotega and Subtiaba are
part of the Otomanguean family. Chorotega is related to Chiapanec, and Tlapanec,
spoken in Guerrero, is the closest relative of Subtiaba. Campbell (1997: 159) posits
that Chorotega speakers migrated from Chiapas to Nicaragua during the second
half of the first millennium AD and that Subtiaba speakers arrived from Guerrero
somewhat later, likely a few centuries before the Spanish invasion.

The presence in the southeast fringe of languages whose closest relatives are far
to the west in Mesoamerica, along with ethnohistorical accounts of migration legends, suggest that the distribution of central Mexican material traits noted above
reflects not only interaction between communities in the southeast fringe and
their contemporaries in Mesoamerica but population movements as well. There is
no doubt that these migrations are reflected in material remains, but how the two
datasets should be correlated is still a matter of considerable debate.

COMMENTS

The lower Ulúa Valley, the Lake Yojoa Basin, the Cajón, and the Comayagua Valley
exhibit a persistent pattern of close linkages and can be considered to constitute a
stable Ulúa subarea of the southeast fringe. Communities in the Naco Valley, the
middle Ulúa Valley, and western-central El Salvador seem to have interacted less
intensively; they show more indications of episodes of intense connection with
the Maya world, particularly Copán, and with areas of Mesoamerica farther west.
Communities east and south of Comayagua, through eastern El Salvador and
Greater Nicoya, appear to have had similarly loose affiliations. The fewest indications of interaction with Mesoamerica and most of the other southeastern regions
are found in northeastern and eastern Honduras; in part this reflects the reality
that these are the least well-documented regions of the southeastern fringe. Greater
Nicoya forms another coherent subarea of the southeast fringe. Societies farther
east and south, beyond the Greater Nicoya region, participated in a distinctly different set of interaction spheres and show many fewer indications of interaction
with Mesoamerica (Hoopes and Fonseca 2003).

Communities in all regions of the southeast fringe interacted—in different
ways and with different degrees of intensity through time—with contemporaries
to the west in Mesoamerica. The classificatory status of southeast fringe societies
as part of the Maya world and Mesoamerica is much less the issue than the fact
that they form an essential part of the context for understanding those areas. It
is considerably more productive to think in terms of intersecting webs of interaction than in terms of trait lists. What is—or should be—of greatest interest is the

story the material remains have to tell about the societies of their makers and their relationships with communities to the north and west in Mesoamerica and with Central American societies to the south and east.

REFERENCES

Andrews, E. Wyllys. 1976. *The Archaeology of Quelepa, El Salvador.* Middle American Research Institute, Publication 42, Tulane University, New Orleans.

Baudez, Claude F., and Pierre Becquelin. 1973. *Archéologie de Los Naranjos, Honduras.* Mission Archéologique et Ethnologique Française au Méxique, Mexico.

Begley, Christopher T. 1999. Elite Power Strategies and External Connections in Ancient Eastern Honduras. Unpublished PhD dissertation, Department of Anthropology, University of Chicago, Chicago.

Bruhns, Karen O. 1980. *Cihuatan: An Early Postclassic Town of El Salvador: The 1977-1978 Excavations.* Monographs in Anthropology, No. 5, Museum of Anthropology, University of Missouri, Columbia.

Bruhns, Karen Olsen, and Paúl E. Amaroli Bertolucci. 2009. An Early Postclassic Round Structure at Cihuatán, El Salvador. *Arqueologia Iberoamericana* 2:35–45.

Campbell, Lyle R. 1997. *American Indian Languages: The Historical Linguistics of Native America.* Oxford University Press, New York.

Canby, Joel. 1949. Excavations at Yarumela, Spanish Honduras. Unpublished PhD dissertation, Department of Anthropology, Harvard University.

Carmack, Robert M., and Silvia Salgado González. 2006. A World-Systems Perspective on the Archaeology and Ethnohistory of the Mesoamerican/Lower Central American Border. *Ancient Mesoamerica* 17:219–229.

Cuddy, Thomas W. 2007. *Political Identity and Archaeology in Northeast Honduras.* University Press of Colorado, Boulder.

Day, Jane S. 1984. New Approaches in Stylistic Analysis: The Late Polychrome Period Ceramics from Hacienda Tempisque, Guanacaste Province, Costa Rica. Unpublished doctoral dissertation, Department of Anthropology, University of Colorado, Boulder.

Demarest, Arthur, and Robert J. Sharer. 1982. The Origins and Evolution of the Usulutan Ceramic Style. *American Antiquity* 47:810–822.

Dixon, Boyd. 1987. Conflict along the Southeast Mesoamerican Periphery: A Defensive Wall System at the Site of Tenampua. In *Interaction on the Southeast Mesoamerican Frontier: Prehistoric and Historic Honduras and El Salvador,* edited by Eugenia J. Robinson, pp. 142–153. BAR International Series 327, British Archaeological Reports, Oxford.

Dixon, Boyd. 1989. A Preliminary Settlement Pattern Study of a Prehistoric Cultural Corridor: The Comayagua Valley, Honduras. *Journal of Field Archaeology* 16:257–272.

Dixon, Boyd. 1992. Prehistoric Political Change on the Southeast Mesoamerican Periphery. *Ancient Mesoamerica* 3:11–25.

Dixon, Boyd, Leroy V. Joesink-Mandeville, Nobukatsu Hasebe, Michael Mucio, William Vincent, David James, and Kenneth Petersen. 1994. Formative-Period Architecture at the Site of Yarumela, Central Honduras. *Latin American Antiquity* 5:70–87.

Fowler, William R. 1989. *The Cultural Evolution of Ancient Nahua Civilization: The Pipil-Nicarao of Central America*. University of Oklahoma Press, Norman.

Gerstle, Andrea. 1987. Ethnic Diversity and Interaction at Copan, Honduras. In *Interaction on the Southeast Mesoamerican Frontier: Prehistoric and Historic Honduras and El Salvador*, edited by Eugenia J. Robinson, pp. 328–356. BAR International Series 327, British Archaeological Reports, Oxford.

Gordon, George Byron. 1898. *Researches in the Uloa Valley, Honduras*. Memoirs of the Peabody Museum of American Archaeology and Ethnology, Vol. 1, No. 4, Harvard University, Cambridge.

Healy, Paul F. 1974. The Cuyamel Caves: Preclassic Sites in Northeast Honduras. *American Antiquity* 39:433–437.

Healy, Paul F. 1978a. Excavations at Rio Claro (H-CN-12), Northeast Honduras: Preliminary Report. *Journal of Field Archaeology* 5:15–28.

Healy, Paul F. 1978b. Excavations at Selin Farm (H-CN-5), Colon, Northeast Honduras. *Vinculos* 4:57–79.

Healy, Paul F. 1980. *Archaeology of the Rivas Region, Nicaragua*. Wilfred Laurier University Press, Waterloo, Ontario.

Henderson, John S. 1977. The Valle de Naco: Ethnohistory and Archaeology in Northwestern Honduras. *Ethnohistory* 24:363–377.

Henderson, John S. 1992a. Elites and Ethnicity along the Southeastern Fringe of Mesoamerica. In *Mesoamerican Elites: An Archaeological Assessment*, edited by Diane Z. Chase and Arlen F. Chase, pp. 157–168. University of Oklahoma Press, Norman.

Henderson, John S. 1992b. Variations on a Theme: A Frontier View of Maya Civilization. In *New Theories on the Ancient Maya*, edited by Elin C. Danien and Robert J. Sharer, pp. 161–171. University Museum, Philadelphia.

Henderson, John S., ed. 1984. *Archaeology in Northwestern Honduras: Interim Reports of the Proyecto Arqueológico Sula*. Latin American Studies Program, Cornell University, Ithaca.

Henderson, John S., and Rosemary A. Joyce. 2004. Puerto Escondido: exploraciones preliminares del Formativo Temprano. In *VII Seminaro de Antropología de Honduras "Dr. George Hasemann,"* pp. 93–113. Instituto Hondureño de Antropología e Historia, Tegucigalpa.

Henderson, John S., and Marilyn P. Beaudry-Corbett, eds. 1993. *Pottery of Prehistoric Honduras: Regional Classification and Analysis*. Institute of Archaeology Monograph 35, University of California, Los Angeles.

Henderson, John S., Rosemary A. Joyce, Gretchen R. Hall, W. Jeffrey Hurst, and Patrick E. McGovern. 2007. Chemical and Archaeological Evidence for the Earliest Cacao Beverages. *Proceedings of the National Academy of Sciences (USA)* 104:18937–18940.

Henderson, John S., Ilene S. Wallace, Anthony Wonderley, and Patricia A. Urban. 1979. Archaeological Investigations in the Valle de Naco, Northwestern Honduras: A Preliminary Report. *Journal of Field Archaeology* 6:169–192.

Hirth, Kenneth G., Gloria Lara Pinto, and George Hasemann. 1989. *Archaeological Research in the El Cajon Region. 1: Prehistoric Cultural Ecology*. Memoirs in Latin American Archaeology, Department of Anthropology, University of Pittsburgh, Pittsburgh.

Hoopes, John W., and Oscar Fonseca Z. 2003. Goldwork and Chibchan Identity: Endogenous Change and Diffuse Unity in the Isthmo-Colombian Area. In *Gold and Power in Ancient Costa Rica, Panama, and Colombia*, edited by Jeffrey Quilter and John W. Hoopes, pp. 49–89. Dumbarton Oaks, Washington, DC.

Joyce, Rosemary A. 1991. *Cerro Palenque: Power and Identity on the Maya Periphery.* University of Texas Press, Austin.

Joyce, Rosemary A. 1993. The Construction of the Maya Periphery and the Mayoid Image of Honduran Polychromes. In *Reinterpreting Prehistory of Central America*, edited by Mark Miller Graham, pp. 51–101. University Press of Colorado, Niwot.

Joyce, Rosemary A., and John S. Henderson. 2001. Beginnings of Village Life in Eastern Mesoamerica. *Latin American Antiquity* 12:5–23.

Joyce, Rosemary A., and John S. Henderson. 2002. La arqueología del periodo Formativo en Honduras: nuevos datos sobre el "estilo olmeca" en la zona maya. *Mayab* 15:5–17.

Kardulias, P. Nick, and Thomas D. Hall. 2008. Archaeology and World-Systems Analysis. *World Archaeology* 40:572–583.

Kelley, Jane H. 1988. *Cihuatán, El Salvador: A Study in Intrasite Variability.* Publications in Anthropology No 35, Vanderbilt University, Nashville.

Lange, Frederick W., and Juan V. Guerrero. 2001. Nicoya, Greater and Guanacaste Region. In *Archaeology of Ancient Mexico and Central America: An Encyclopedia*, edited by Susan T. Evans and David L. Webster, pp. 517–522. Garland, New York.

Lothrop, Samuel K. 1939. The Southeastern Frontier of the Maya. *American Anthropologist* 41:42–54.

Luke, Christina M. 2002. Ulúa Style Marble Vases. Unpublished PhD dissertation, Department of Anthropology, Cornell University, Ithaca.

Luke, Christina M., and Robert H. Tykot. 2007. Celebrating Place through Luxury Craft Production. *Ancient Mesoamerica* 18:315–328.

Robinson, Eugenia J., ed. 1987. *Interaction on the Southeast Mesoamerican Frontier: Prehistoric and Historic Honduras and El Salvador.* BAR International Series 327, British Archaeological Reports, Oxford.

Salgado González, Silvia. 1996. Social Change in a Region of Granada, Pacific Nicaragua (1000 BC—1522 AD). Unpublished PhD dissertation, Department of Anthropology, State University of New York, Albany.

Schortman, Edward M., and Patricia A. Urban 1987. Modeling Interregional Interaction in Prehistory. In *Advances in Archaeological Method and Theory,* Vol. 11, edited by Michael B. Schiffer, pp. 37–95. Academic Press, San Diego.

Schortman, Edward M., and Patricia A. Urban. 1994a. Living on the Edge: Core/Periphery Relations in Ancient Southeastern Mesoamerica. *Current Anthropology* 35:401–430.

Schortman, Edward M., and Patricia A. Urban, eds. 1994b. *Sociopolitical Hierarchy and Craft Production: The Economic Bases of Elite Power in a Late Classic Southeastern Polity 3: The 1992 Naco Valley Season.* Instituto Hondureño de Antropología e Historia, Tegucigalpa. Copies available from Kenyon College, Gambier.

Schortman, Edward M., and Patricia A. Urban. 1999. Thoughts on the Periphery: The Ideological Consequences of Core/Periphery Relations. In *World-Systems Theory in Practice: Leadership, Production, and Exchange*, edited by P. Nick Kardulias, pp. 125–152. Rowman and Littlefield, Lanham, Maryland.

Schortman, Edward M., Patricia A. Urban, Wendy Ashmore, and Julie Benyo. 1986. Interregional Interaction in the Southeast Maya Periphery: The Santa Barbara Archaeological Project 1983–1984 Seasons. *Journal of Field Archaeology* 13:259–272.

Schortman, Edward M., Patricia A. Urban, and Marne Ausec. 2001. Politics with Style: Identity Formation in Prehispanic Southeastern Mesoamerica. *American Anthropologist* 103:312–330.

Sharer, Robert J. 1974. The Prehistory of the Southeastern Maya Periphery. *Current Anthropology* 15:165–187.

Sharer, Robert J. 1978 *The Prehistory of Chalchuapa, El Salvador*. 3 volumes. University of Pennsylvania Press, Philadelphia.

Sheets, Payson D. 1983. *Archaeology and Volcanism in Central America: The Zapotitlan Valley of El Salvador*. University of Texas Press, Austin.

Sheets, Payson D. 1992. *The Ceren Site: A Prehistoric Village Buried by Volcanic Ash in Central America*. Harcourt Brace Jovanovich, New York.

Smith, Michael E., and Frances F. Berdan, eds. 2003. *The Postclassic Mesoamerican World*. University of Utah Press, Salt Lake City.

Stein, Gil J. 1999. *Rethinking World-Systems: Diasporas, Colonies, and Interaction in Uruk Mesopotamia*. University of Arizona Press, Tucson.

Stockett, Miranda K. 2007. Performing Power: Identity, Ritual, and Materiality in a Late Classic Southeast Mesoamerican Crafting Community. *Ancient Mesoamerica* 18:91–105.

Stone, Doris Z. 1941. *Archaeology of the North Coast of Honduras*. Memoirs of the Peabody Museum of Archaeology and Ethnology, Vol. 9, No. 1, Harvard University, Cambridge.

Stone, Doris Z. 1957. *The Archaeology of Central and Southern Honduras*. Papers of the Peabody Museum of Archaeology and Ethnology, Vol. 49, No. 3, Harvard University, Cambridge.

Strong, William D. 1934. Hunting Ancient Ruins in Northeastern Honduras. In *Explorations and Fieldwork of the Smithsonian Institution in 1933*, pp. 44–48, 51–57. Smithsonian Institution, Washington, DC.

Strong, William D. 1935 *Archaeological Investigations in the Bay Islands, Spanish Honduras*. Smithsonian Miscellaneous Collections Vol. 92, No. 14, Smithsonian Institution, Washington, DC.

Strong, William Duncan, Alfred V. Kidder, and A. J. Drexel Paul. 1938. *Preliminary Report on the Smithsonian Institution-Harvard University Archeological Expedition to Northwestern Honduras, 1936*. Smithsonian Miscellaneous Collections Vol. 97, No. 1. Smithsonian Institution, Washington, DC.

Véliz R., Vito. 1983. Síntesis histórica de la arqueología en Honduras. *Yaxkin* 6(1–2):1–8.

Wallerstein, Immanuel. 1974. *The Modern World System I*. Academic Press, New York.

Wonderley, Anthony W. 1981. Late Postclassic Excavations at Naco, Honduras. Unpublished PhD dissertation, Department of Anthropology, Cornell University, Ithaca.

Wonderley, Anthony W. 1985. The Land of Ulua: Research in the Naco and Sula Valleys, Honduras. In *The Lowland Maya Postclassic*, edited by A. F. Chase and Prudence M. Rice, pp. 245–269. University of Texas Press, Austin.

Wonderley, Anthony W. 1991. The Late Preclassic Sula Plain, Honduras: Regional Antecedents to Social Complexity and Interregional Convergence in Ceramic Style. In *The Formation of Complex Society in Southeastern Mesoamerica*, edited by William R. Fowler, pp. 143–169. CRC Press, Boca Raton.

CHAPTER 35

CURRENT VIEWS ON POWER, ECONOMICS, AND SUBSISTENCE IN ANCIENT WESTERN MEXICO

CHRISTOPHER S. BEEKMAN

FAR western Mexico has occupied an ambiguous position within Mesoamerican research, as the region both displays continuity with Mesoamerican culture and provides informative differences. The region is loosely defined by that segment of the highland Neovolcanic Belt which lies between the Lerma and Balsas rivers and the adjoining Pacific coastal plain. This corresponds generally to the states of Jalisco, Nayarit, Colima, and western Michoacán (Figure 35.1). The area has been an integral part of the societal networks that criss-cross Mesoamerica, and I aim to demonstrate this through four major transitions over the Pre-Columbian period.

THE ORIGINS OF AGRICULTURAL AND MARITIME ADAPTATIONS (7000–2000 BC)

Theoretical research into the origins of plant domestication and early agricultural practices would do well to incorporate the western Mexican prehistoric record. The region is not marginal to the rest of highland Mesoamerica in any climatic

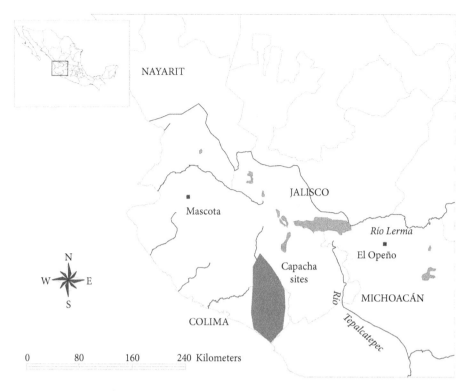

Figure 35.1 Map of western Mexico, showing modern states and sites from the Early
and Middle Formative periods (2000–300 BC).

sense, and the quantity and timing of precipitation is comparable to central or
southern Mexico. Evidence for early human occupation is both sparse and widely
distributed prior to the Formative period (Aliphat Fernández 1988; Benz 2000;
Hardy 1994; Irish et al. 2000). Recent excavations at Xihuatoxtla, Guerrero, have
identified squash and the earliest maize evidence dating to 6700 BC (Piperno
et al. 2009; Ranere et al. 2009). The site lies at the far eastern end of the Balsas
Depression, long considered the most likely area for the domestication of maize,
while the far western end extends into southern Jalisco along the Río Tepalcatepec.
Zizumbo-Villarreal and Colunga-García Marín (2010) observe that early domesticated crops diffused through Mexico along river valleys such as this one and that
genetic analyses have located the closest surviving wild ancestors to domesticated
maize, beans, and squash within or near far western Mexico (Doebley et al. 1990;
Sanjur et al. 2002; Zizumbo-Villarreal et al. 2009). They propose that the inter-
cropped milpa complex of maize, beans, and squash first came together in the state
of Jalisco.

The western Mexican coast shows an altogether different pattern, with a consistent focus on maritime resources. To date this is most clearly represented by
shell collection, as at the Matanchén site on the Nayarit coast ca. 2850-2200 BC
(Mountjoy 1970, 2000; Mountjoy and Claassen 2005). A closely contemporary

pyramidal mound of unopened clam shells at Cerro el Calón on the border with Sinaloa (Scott and Foster 2000) may be a ritualization of this subsistence adaptation, much as maize later took on a central role in Mesoamerican religion and cosmology. The similarities with remains much further down the Pacific Coast are increasingly evident (Voorhies 1996).

THE INDEPENDENT EMERGENCE OF INEQUALITIES (2000–300 BC)

Early Formative-period communities strongly marked the landscape with family tombs and cemeteries. This pattern is largely known from the El Opeño-style family tombs and the Capacha cemeteries (Figure 35.1). The former are subterranean family tombs accessed by a stairway, and they are known primarily from a single cemetery in the Jacona-Zamora Valley of northwestern Michoacán (Noguera 1942; Oliveros Morales 2004, 2006; Weigand 1985). At lower elevations in Colima and Jalisco, there are small cemeteries designated Capacha for their deeply engraved/punctated or zone-painted ceramic offerings (Kelly 1980; López Mestas and Ramos de la Vega 2005; Mountjoy 1989) and late examples have recently been excavated in Mascota (Mountjoy 2006). Still later in the Middle Formative, the curation of the remains of the dead occurred in an increasingly diverse array of tombs, cysts, and burial mounds throughout the lake basins of central Jalisco (Liot et al. 2006a; Weigand 1985: 60–63). I have argued previously (Beekman 2008, 2010) that the preference for repeated use of the same burial locale over time implies attachments to place and to ancestors that are found among other early sedentary populations (e.g., Buikstra and Charles 1999).

The social importance of mortuary practices is less evident on the coast. Populations were concentrated along the narrow strip of Jalisco and Colima but extended up into the broader plains of Nayarit as well. Settlement, perhaps year-round, dates from ca. 900 BC and is defined by habitation terraces and pottery similar to that of Capacha. Research has described a mixed subsistence strategy that combined modest farming with the intensive exploitation of marine resources. People clearly had access to watercraft, as the remains of larger deepwater marine animals such as dolphins show up alongside shellfish harvested from shallow tide-pools (Mountjoy 1970, 1982, 1989, 1993, 2000; Mountjoy and Claassen 2005). Boats may have been used in other activities as well, such as exchange down the coast.

The El Opeño tombs are dated to 1400–1000 BC, and the primary Mascota cemetery to 1000–800 BC. They are therefore contemporaneous with the early (San Lorenzo) and later (La Venta) Gulf Coast Olmec, yet there is almost nothing in either local or imported material culture that would suggest Gulf Coast stylistic influence (Niederberger 1987; Oliveros Morales 2004; Tolstoy 1971). Imagery took the form of hollow animal and human figures that clearly presage the later empha-sis on portable artwork, but half-human jaguars and other hallmarks of Gulf Coast religious art are absent.

Oliveros Morales (2004, 2006) has nonetheless pointed to the evidence at El Opeño for underworld symbolism and figurines depicting a version of the rubber ballgame, all widespread practices of Mesoamerican society and religion. Furthermore, varying tomb sizes and degrees of wealth among the El Opeño lineage tombs suggest vari-ability in social status among families, likely in relation to the abundant evidence for trade. Jade from the Motagua Valley of Guatemala, marine shell from both coasts, iron pyrite mirrors like those documented for Oaxaca (Pires-Ferreira 1975: 37–55), and green obsidian from Pachuca in central Mexico testify to deeply intertwined networks that transferred wealth across great distances (Oliveros Morales 2004; Robles and Oliveros Morales 2005). Inequalities are less evident at Capacha sites, but Mountjoy (2006) has reported jade and iron pyrite from these more modest burials as well.

Highland western Mexico in the Early and Middle Formative therefore shared in certain general Mesoamerican practices and beliefs, participated in exchange networks, and showed signs of emerging inequalities. These developments show no dependence upon the people of Olman, and on the contrary demonstrate the limits of specifically Gulf Coast involvement in the genesis of the Mesoamerican world. Whatever precocity and influence Gulf Coast societies may have exhib-ited among their neighbors, they were not the sole template for social complexity among those societies sharing underlying Mesoamerican practices.

POLITICS AND POWER SHARING AMONG LINEAGES (300 BC–500/600 AD)

The distinctive shaft tombs and circular temples known as *guachimontones* that appeared during this short span of eight-hundred-plus years have come to epito-mize western Mexico for many, yet these exotic remains have tended to obscure characteristics of more theoretical interest. The greatest evidence of social com-plexity in the form of these temples and tombs occurred in the lake basins and val-leys surrounding the Tequila volcano. Residential settlement is poorly dated, but literally thousands of household groups practicing infield agriculture cut a con-tinuous swath across the southern valleys (Ohnersorgen and Varien 1996; Weigand 1993, 2000) and with lesser densities in the northern valleys (Heredia Espinoza 2008). Situated throughout this residential zone are several dozen ceremonial centers defined by the presence of one or more guachimontones and ballcourts (Weigand 1991). These settlements were dubbed the Teuchitlán tradition (Weigand 1985, 1996, 1999), but the label increasingly obscures rather than highlights relevant spatial and temporal variations.

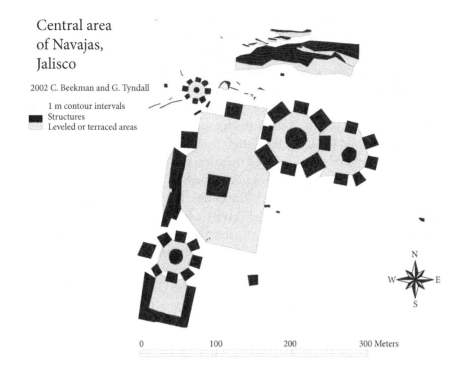

Central area
of Navajas,
Jalisco

2002 C. Beekman and G. Tyndall

1 m contour intervals
Structures
Leveled or terraced areas

0   100   200   300 Meters

Figure 35.2 Central area of the site of Navajas, Jalisco. Several guachimontón temple complexes are visible. Courtesy Tequila Valley Regional Archaeological Project, directed by Christopher Beekman.

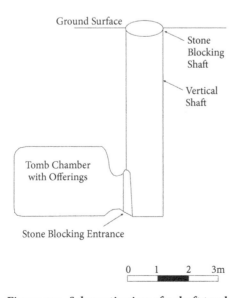

Ground Surface

Stone Blocking Shaft

Vertical Shaft

Tomb Chamber with Offerings

Stone Blocking Entrance

0   1   2   3m

Figure 35.3 Schematic view of a shaft tomb.

The guachimontones are composed of a central circular pyramid or altar surrounded by usually eight evenly spaced temple platforms that were likely developed from earlier burial mounds (Figure 35.2). The apparent surface symmetry is less obvious upon excavation, as each platform was constructed by different work groups using their own methods and materials (Beekman 2008). Elaborate lineage-based shaft and chamber tombs are sometimes beneath the temple platforms (Corona Nuñez 1955; Long 1966; Ramos de la Vega and López 1996). Each platform was built and maintained by a separate lineage, whose high status was evident in both the location and wealth of their shaft tombs (Figure 35.3). Cemeteries of simpler shaft tombs and pit burials served the rural population (Galván Villegas 1991). Shaft tombs are known for offerings in the form of elaborate jewelry and hollow ceramic figures (Von Winning 1969). The tombs clearly developed from the earlier El Opeño style and were adopted selectively across the highlands and coasts of western Mexico, though invariably smaller than the contemporary examples in central Jalisco (Corona Nuñez 1955; Gifford 1950; Jarquín Pacheco and Martínez Vargas 2004; Kelly 1978; Schöndube 1980; Valdez et al. 2006) and encompassing a diversity of mortuary practices (compare Cabrero García and López Cruz 2002; Mountjoy 1993; Mountjoy and Sandford 2006).

The usual eight lineages associated with a guachimontón displayed and justified their status through multiple layers of religious symbolism. The architectural layout of the guachimontón itself replicates a cross-section of eight-rowed maize, a more productive group of varieties that emerged in far western Mexico by the Late Formative period (Beekman 2003a). Unique ceramic models found within some shaft tombs depict a pole-climbing ritual within the guachimontón patio that most closely resembles the green maize harvest ceremony of the later Mesoamerican calendar (Beekman 2003b). The guachimontón temples therefore embody the multileveled universe of Mesoamerican cosmology through the burials beneath and the pole reaching to the heavens above (Beekman 2003a; Kelley 1974; Witmore 1998). The symbolism inherent in the architecture and in shell and jade jewelry (López Mestas 2004, 2005) associated elites with maize and fertility and with the cosmos, a frequent linkage in Mesoamerican ideology that usually supported political systems empowering a cosmic ruler with the ability to bring about agricultural prosperity. Here, however, power was shared across eight elite families, none of whom could monopolize power (Beekman 2008).

How these local social dynamics translated into regional-level political organization remains unexplored, and we are better off focusing on what elites actually did. Besides agricultural ritual, elites were probably involved in the material aspects of intensive farming, seen in extensive and organized tracts of raised fields and canal systems in the western part of the Tequila valleys (Stuart 2005). Obsidian sources are plentiful within the valleys (Esparza López 2003; Weigand et al. 2004), and while major workshops are known from the larger centers (Soto de Arechavaleta 1990), attempts to control the ubiquitous resource appear limited to specialized jewelry (e.g. Beekman and Weigand 2008: 314). Finally, fortified or strategic centers oversaw several passes into the Tequila valleys, and the primary center of Los Guachimontones may have succeeded in territorially unifying the central valleys (Beekman 1996a).

The political and/or religious prominence of the Tequila valley polity shifted with the transition to the Classic period (Beekman and Weigand 2008). Newly built circles are smaller in size, and there was a decline in the importance of corporate groups as seen in the reduced size of the shaft tombs. Regardless, farmers still used the raised fields and elaborated the hydraulic system (Stuart 2005). Local elites in neighboring states adopted the guachimontón's symbolic design and probably its agricultural ritual (Beekman 2000; Cabrero García 1989, 1993, 2005; Cabrero García and López Cruz 1997, 2002; Crespo Oviedo 1993; Mountjoy 2000; Mountjoy et al. 2003; Sánchez Correa and Marmolejo Morales 1990; Weigand et al. 1999). Explanations for the diaspora of guachimontones have focused on negotiating with cooperating elites along routes toward rare resources (Beekman 2000; Cabrero García 1989; Weigand 2000). But today I suspect that the increasing aridity of the Classic period (Metcalfe and Davies 2007) would have made the agricultural ritual of the guachimontones attractive to populations across the region (Figure 35.4).

Once again, the coast was a world apart. Mountjoy's (2000) quantification of maritime resources and agricultural production suggests that agriculture may have become more important but it remained part of a diverse subsistence strategy. He relates the relocation of settlements farther inland to the growing importance

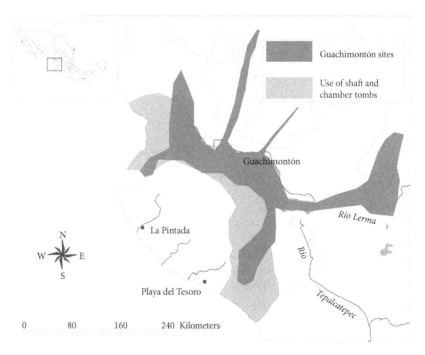

Figure 35.4 Map of western Mexico in the Late Formative to Classic periods (300 BC–500/600 AD), showing the distribution of shaft tombs and guachimontón architecture centered on central Jalisco.

of floodplain farming (Beltrán Medina 1994; López Mestas and Ramos de la Vega 2005; Mountjoy 1970, 1989). This may also relate to the trend toward aridity—shifting locations closer to where the rivers exit the narrow canyons would have given more sure access to fresh water. Population grew notably during this period, and sites like La Pintada (Tomatlán Valley, Jalisco) reach populations of over 1,000 people with mound groups and open plazas that show little resemblance to those of the highlands. La Pintada and Playa del Tesoro (Colima) show evidence for extensive shell workshops, which were evidently producing for interior markets (Beltrán Medina 1994, 2001; Mountjoy 1982, 1989, 2000). Beltrán Medina (1994) has argued that the coastal sites were producing for Teotihuacan, which is quite possible. Sites on the Colima coast consistently display different pathways of interaction during the Formative, Classic, and Postclassic (Matos and Kelly 1974; Olay Barrientos 2004; Paradis 1974) than elsewhere on the coast.

Western Mexico interacted broadly with the rest of Mesoamerica during this period, but this has been obscured by the claims of exoticism for the circular architecture (Weigand 1996) or for South American origins of the shaft tombs (e.g., Anawalt 1998). But the tombs exhibit an aggrandizement of lineage ancestors reminiscent of that at Teotihuacan (Headrick 1999), and the guachimontones illustrate the Mesoamerican worldview in the temple architecture. Pan-Mesoamerican religious beliefs relating maize and cosmology to earthly rulers made their first clear appearance in the western highlands in the Late Formative, accompanying what may have been a greater reliance upon maize agriculture. Individuals thus expressed familiar ideas in often unfamiliar ways. There is no uniform interpretation of Mesoamerican beliefs and practices, nor a single wellspring from which all Mesoamerican beliefs radiate, but these pernicious assumptions continue to impact modern interpretation.

EPICLASSIC REORGANIZATION AND THE POSTCLASSIC EXPANSION OF TRADE NETWORKS (500/600–1520 AD)

Paleoclimatic data across the central Mexican highlands indicate that the progressive trend toward aridity reached its culmination in the period 700–1200 AD (Metcalfe and Davies 2007). Debates over the significance of this climatological trend have been voiced primarily in the high precipitation zones of the Maya lowlands (Gill 2001; Hodell et al. 1995), yet Mesoamericanists should give greater consideration to the better evidenced regions of highland Mexico that lie perilously close to the precipitation minima for maize agriculture.

Artifactual and settlement changes along the northern frontier indicate major alterations to society during the Epiclassic (Beekman 1996b; Jiménez Betts

1988, 1992), and the period has long been associated with the end of the older Mesoamerican political order. López Austin and López Luján (1999) have argued that the Epiclassic transformation reflected the expansion of a new world religion based on the feathered serpent. Jiménez Betts (2006, 2007) interprets the changes in macro-economic terms, as older networks were broken down and reorganized—the introduction of metallurgy from South America (Hosler 1994: 44–85) or the intensified production of salt (Liot 1998) could be interpreted within this framework as well. Other researchers agree (Beekman and Christensen 2003, 2011) but add that this reorganization was in response to climatic stresses that ultimately led to the near depopulation of Guanajuato, Querétaro, Zacatecas, and northeastern Jalisco by 900 AD (originally posited by Armillas 1969). Population movements provoked by these changes brought the Nahuatl language into central Mexico (older variations on this idea originate with Braniff 1972 and Mastache and Cobean 1989).

New communities in far western Mexico were founded that incorporated novel forms of public architecture such as large rectangular platforms (Ixtépete, La Higuerita—Galván Villegas 1975; López Mestas and Montejano Esquivias 2003), or U-shaped complexes composed of a pyramid and two flanking platforms (Santa Cruz de Bárcenas, El Grillo, Oconahua—Galván Villegas and Beekman 2001; Weigand 1990; Weigand et al. 2005). There were no longer discrete spaces for lineages in the new organization of sacred and social space. Lineages had already been in decline since the beginning of the Classic, and the last of the shaft tombs that were so closely associated with repeated family use were replaced by small box tombs designed for individual burials (Schöndube and Galván Villegas 1978).

The settlement shifts of the Epiclassic led ultimately to the abandonment of the central part of the northern frontier, and the Pacific Coast became a major artery for trade in the Early Postclassic (Liot et al. 2006b; Ramírez Urrea 2006; Ramírez Urrea et al. 2005; Weigand and García de Weigand 2001) (Figure 35.5). The Aztatlán complex uniting coastal cultures was defined on the basis of ceramic similarities (Sauer and Brand 1932) that continue inland to the Laguna Chapala (Lister 1949; Meighan and Foote 1968) and beyond, as many have related the elaborate Aztatlán iconography to the Mixteca-Puebla art style of the Central Highlands (Ekholm 1942; Smith and Heath-Smith 1980). The major ceremonial center of El Chanal in the interior of Colima had quite different connections, with architecture, ceramics, and religious iconography much more reminiscent of Tula (Kelly 1980; Olay Barrientos 1998, 2004).

Today the Aztatlán complex is defined as a socioeconomic phenomenon (Beltrán Medina 2004): the previously modest coastal communities grew in size around ceremonial architecture such as pyramids and ballcourts. Every major river valley along the coast held a primary center that sat directly on the river and close to the coast. Examples include Nahuapa, Ixtapa, Chacalilla (Mountjoy 1970, 1993; Mountjoy et al. 2003), Amapa (Meighan 1976), and smaller centers farther up the coast (Ekholm 1942; Kelly 1938, 1945). Coastal researchers (Bordaz 1964; Meighan 1976; Mountjoy 2000; Scott and Foster 2000) have drawn upon a variety of archaeological and ethnohistoric data to reconstruct specialized production and exploitation of ceramics, copper, shell jewelry, cotton, cacao, tobacco, and oysters.

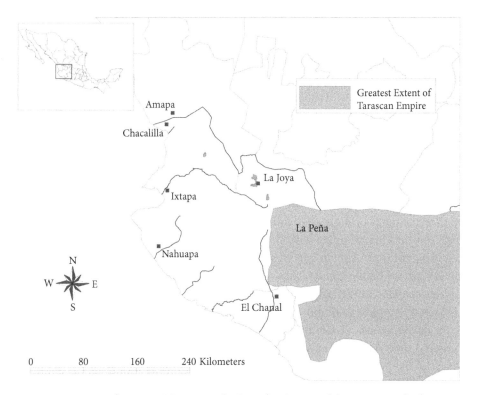

Figure 35.5 Map of western Mexico in the Postclassic period (900–1520 AD), showing
the distribution of sites participating in the Aztatlán complex and those highland sites
that demonstrate specialized production.

Intensive production in the highlands, such as at the obsidian source of La Joya,
funneled products down to the coast (Mountjoy 2000; Spence et al. 2002), creating
a network of interlocking specialized economies. While some areas of the highlands came under pressure from the Tarascan Empire (Acosta Nieva and Uruñuela
Ladrón de Guevara 1997), the coast remained apart and continued its intensive
trading activities through the Postclassic.

CONCLUSION

Research in far western Mexico can contribute and has contributed to numerous
theoretical problems of broad relevance to archaeology. I have singled out a few
examples for consideration here: the Archaic emergence of subsistence practices,
Formative social ranking in the absence of Gulf Coast influence, power-sharing
forms of governance in the Late Formative-Classic, and the fragility of settlement
and trade networks in the face of Epiclassic climate change. For future research on

these topics to thrive, scholars will need to incorporate the insights to be found in the archaeology of far western Mexico.

References

Acosta Nieva, Rosario, and Gabriela Uruñuela Ladrón de Guevara. 1997. Patrones de enterramiento en la cuenca de Sayula: la fase Amacueca en Atoyac. In *El cuerpo humano y su tratamiento mortuorio*, edited by Elsa Malvido, Gregory Pereira, and Vera Tiesler, pp. 179–191. Instituto Nacional de Antropología e Historia, México, D.F.

Aliphat Fernández, Mario M. 1988. La cuenca Zacoalco-Sayula: ocupación humana durante el Pleistocene final en el occidente de México. In *Orígenes del hombre Americano (seminario)*, edited by Alba González Jácome, pp. 145–176. Secretaría de Educación Pública, México, D.F.

Anawalt, Patricia R. 1998. They Came to Trade Exquisite Things: Ancient West Mexican-Ecuadorian Contacts. In *Ancient West Mexico: Art and Archaeology of the Unknown Past,* edited by Richard F. Townsend, pp. 233–250. Art Institute of Chicago, Chicago.

Armillas, Pedro. 1969. The Arid Frontier of Mexican Civilization. *Transactions of the New York Academy of Sciences* 31:697–704.

Beekman, Christopher S. 1996a. Political Boundaries and Political Structure: The Limits of the Teuchitlan Tradition. *Ancient Mesoamerica* 7:135–147.

Beekman, Christopher S. 1996b. El complejo El Grillo del centro de Jalisco: una revisión de su cronología y significado. In *Las cuencas del occidente de México: época prehispánica*, edited by Eduardo Williams and Phil C. Weigand, pp. 247–291. Colegio de Michoacán, Zamora.

Beekman, Christopher S. 2000. The Correspondence of Regional Patterns and Local Strategies in Formative to Classic Period West Mexico. *Journal of Anthropological Archaeology* 19:385–412.

Beekman, Christopher S. 2003a. Fruitful Symmetry: Corn and Cosmology in the Public Architecture of Late Formative and Early Classic Jalisco. *Mesoamerican Voices* 1:5–22.

Beekman, Christopher S. 2003b. Agricultural Pole Rituals and Rulership in Late Formative Central Jalisco. *Ancient Mesoamerica* 14:299–318.

Beekman, Christopher S. 2008. Corporate Power Strategies in the Late Formative to Early Classic Tequila Valleys of Central Jalisco. *Latin American Antiquity* 19:414–434.

Beekman, Christopher S. 2010. Recent Research in Western Mexican Archaeology. *Journal of Archaeological Research* 18(1):41–109.

Beekman, Christopher S., and Alexander F. Christensen. 2003. Controlling for Doubt and Uncertainty through Multiple Lines of Evidence: A New Look at the Mesoamerican Nahua Migrations. *Journal of Archaeological Method and Theory* 10:111–164.

Beekman, Christopher S., and Alexander F. Christensen. 2011. Power, Agency, and Identity: Migration and Aftermath in the Mezquital Area of North-Central Mexico. In *Current Developments in the Anthropological Study of Past Human Migration*, edited by Graciela Cabana and Jeffrey Clark. University Press of Florida, Gainesville.

Beekman, Christopher S., and P. C. Weigand. 2008. Conclusiones, cronología, y un intento a síntesis. In *La tradición Teuchitlán,* edited by Phil C. Weigand, Christopher S. Beekman, and Rodrigo Esparza, pp. 303–337. Colegio de Michoacán, Zamora.

Beltrán Medina, José C. 1994. Una visión arqueológica de las bahías de Manzanillo a través del puerto de Salagua. *Anales del Museo Michoacano* 5:14–44.

Beltrán Medina, José C. 2001. *La explotación de la costa en el occidente de Mesoamérica y los contactos con Sudamérica y con otras regiones culturales.* Universidad Autónoma de Nayarit, Tepic, Mexico.

Beltrán Medina, José C. 2004. Los concheros y el desarrollo cultural en Nayarit, la tradición Aztatlán. In *Introducción a la arqueología del occidente de México,* edited by Beatriz Braniff C., pp. 397–410. Instituto Nacional de Antropología e Historia, México, D.F.

Benz, Bruce F. 2000. The Origins of Mesoamerican Agriculture: Reconnaissance and Testing in the Sayula-Zacoalco Lake Basin. Report submitted to the Foundation for Ancient Mesoamerican Studies, Inc., http://www.famsi.org/reports/99074/, accessed April 5, 2010.

Bordaz, Jacques. 1964. Pre-Columbian Ceramic Kilns at Peñitas, a Post-classic Site in Coastal Nayarit, Mexico. Unpublished PhD dissertation, Faculty of Political Science, Columbia University, New York.

Braniff C., Beatriz. 1972. Secuencias arqueológicas en Guanajuato y la cuenca de México: intento de correlación. In *Teotihuacan: XI mesa redonda,* pp. 273–323. Sociedad Mexicana de Antropología, México, D.F.

Buikstra, Jane E., and Douglas K. Charles. 1999. Centering the Ancestors: Cemeteries, Mounds and Sacred Landscapes of the Ancient North American Midcontinent. In *Archaeologies of Landscape. Contemporary Perspectives,* edited by Wendy Ashmore and A. Bernard Knapp, pp. 201–228. Blackwell, Oxford.

Cabrero García, María T. 1989. *Civilización en el norte de México: arqueología de la cañada del Río Bolaños (Zacatecas y Jalisco).* Universidad Nacional Autónoma de México, México, D.F.

Cabrero García, María T. 1993. Hallazgos recientes en el Cañón de Bolaños, Jalisco. *Anales de Antropología* 30:47–72.

Cabrero García, María T. 2005. Bolaños Canyon and the West Mexican Shaft Tomb Tradition. In *Archaeology without Limits, Papers in Honor of Clement W. Meighan,* edited by Brian D. Dillon and Matthew A. Boxt, pp. 283–293. Labyrinthos, Lancaster.

Cabrero García, María T., and Carlos López Cruz. 1997. *Catálogo de piezas de las tumbas de tiro del cañón de Bolaños.* Instituto de Investigaciones Antropológicos, Universidad Nacional Autónoma de México, México, D.F.

Cabrero García, María T., and Carlos López Cruz. 2002. *Civilización en el norte de México, volumen II.* Instituto de Investigaciones Antropológicas, Universidad Nacional Autónoma de México, México, D.F.

Corona Nuñez, José. 1955. *Tumba de El Arenal, Etzatlán, Jalisco.* Instituto Nacional de Antropología e Historia, México, D.F.

Crespo Oviedo, Ana María. 1993. Estructuras de planta circular en el Bajío. *Cuadernos de Arquitectura Mesoamerica* 25:79–87.

Doebley, John, Adrian Stec, Jonathan Wendel, and Marlin Edwards. 1990. Genetic and Morphological Analysis of a Maize-Teosinte F2 Population: Implications for the Origin of Maize. *Proceedings of the National Academy of Sciences* 87:9888–9892.

Ekholm, Gordon F. 1942. *Excavations at Guasave, Sinaloa, Mexico.* Anthropology Papers No. 38(4), American Museum of Natural History, New York.

Esparza López, Rodrigo. 2003. La obsidiana en el contexto arqueológico de Los Guachimontones: un recurso estratégico en el desarrollo de sociedades estatales. *Revista del Seminario de Historia Mexicana* IV:73–95.

Galván Villegas, Luís J. 1975. Informe preliminar de las exploraciones efectuadas en la zona arqueológica de 'El Ixtépete', Jalisco, durante el mes de mayo de 1973. In *Balance y perspectiva. XIII mesa redonda, vol. 1*, pp. 395–410. Sociedad Mexicana de Antropología, México, D.F.

Galván Villegas, Luís J. 1991. *Las tumbas de tiro del valle de Atemajac.* Instituto Nacional de Antropología e Historia, México, D.F.

Galván Villegas, Luís J., and Christopher S. Beekman. 2001. El Grillo. In *The Archaeology of Ancient Mexico and Central America: An Encyclopedia*, edited by Susan T. Evans and David L. Webster, pp. 299–300. Garland, New York.

Gifford, Edward W. 1950. *Surface Archaeology of Ixtlán del Rio, Nayarit.* University of California Press, Berkeley.

Gill, Richardson. 2001. *The Great Maya Droughts: Water, Life, and Death.* University of New Mexico Press, Albuquerque.

Hardy, Karen. 1994. Colecciones líticas de superficie del occidente de México. In *Arqueología del occidente de México: nuevas aportaciones*, edited by Eduardo Williams and Roberto Novella, pp. 123–138. Colegio de Michoacán, Zamora.

Headrick, Annabeth. 1999. The Street of the Dead, It Really Was: Mortuary Bundles at Teotihuacan. *Ancient Mesoamerica* 10:69–85.

Heredia Espinoza, Verenice Y. 2008. The Agave Landscape and Its Archaeological Context in the Tequila Volcano Area. Report submitted to the Foundation for Ancient Mesoamerican Studies, Inc., http://www.famsi.org/reports/07012/, accessed March 5, 2010.

Hodell, David A., Jason Curtis, and Mark Brenner. 1995. Possible Role of Climate in the Collapse of Classic Maya Civilisation. *Nature* 375:391–394.

Hosler, Dorothy. 1994. *The Sounds and Colors of Power: The Sacred Metallurgical Technology of Ancient West Mexico.* Massachusetts Institute of Technology Press, Cambridge.

Irish, Joel D., Stanley Davis, John Lobdell, and Frederico A. Solórzano Barreto. 2000. Prehistoric Human Skeletal Remains from Jalisco, Mexico. *Current Research in the Pleistocene* 17:95–97.

Jarquín Pacheco, Ana M., and Enrique Martínez Vargas. 2004. Ritos y mitos prehispánicos nahuas en dos tumbas de La Campana, Colima. *Estudios de Cultura Náhuatl* 35:75–94.

Jiménez Betts, Peter. 1988. Ciertas inferencias de la arqueología del sur de Zacatecas. In *Primera reunión sobre las sociedades prehispánicas en el centro occidente de México*, pp. 39–50. Centro Regional de Querétaro, Instituto Nacional de Antropología e Historia, México.

Jiménez Betts, Peter. 1992. Una red de interacción del noroeste de Mesoamérica: una interpretación. In *Origen y desarrollo de civilización en el occidente de México*, edited by Brigitte Boehm de Lameiras, and Phil C. Weigand, pp. 177–204. Colegio de Michoacán, Zamora.

Jiménez Betts, Peter. 2006. La problemática de Coyotlatelco vista desde el noroccidente de Mesoamérica. In *El fenómeno Coyotlatelco en el centro de México: tiempo, espacio y significado*, edited by Laura Solar V., pp. 375–392. Instituto Nacional de Antropología e Historia, México, D.F.

Jiménez Betts, Peter. 2007. Alcances de la interacción entre el occidente y el noroeste de Mesoamérica en el epiclásico. In *Dinámicas culturales entre el occidente, el centro-*

norte y la Cuenca de México, del Preclásico al Epiclásico, edited by Brigitte Faugère, pp. 157–164. Colegio de Michoacán, Zamora.

Kelley, J. Charles 1974. Speculations on the Culture History of Northwestern Mesoamerica. In *The Archaeology of West Mexico*, edited by Betty Bell, pp. 19–39. Sociedad de Estudios Avanzados del Occidente de México, Ajijic.

Kelly, Isabel T. 1938. *Excavations at Chametla, Sinaloa*. University of California Press, Berkeley.

Kelly, Isabel T. 1945. *Excavations at Culiacán, Sinaloa*. University of California Press, Berkeley.

Kelly, Isabel T. 1978. Seven Colima Tombs: An Interpretation of Ceramic Content. *Contributions of the University of California Archaeological Research Facility* 36:1–36.

Kelly, Isabel T. 1980. *Ceramic Sequence in Colima: Capacha, an Early Phase*. University of Arizona Press, Tucson.

Liot, Catherine. 1998. La sal de Sayula: cronología y papel en la organización del poblamiento prehispánico. In *El occidente de México: arqueología, historia y medio ambiente: perspectivas regionales: actas del IV coloquio internacional de occidentalistas*, edited by Ricardo Ávila, Jean P. Emphoux, Luís Gómez Gastélum, Susana Ramírez, Otto Schöndube, and Fred Valdez, pp. 135–156. Universidad de Guadalajara, Guadalajara.

Liot, Catherine, Javier Reveles, and Rosario Acosta Nieva. 2006a. Grupo A-área III: inhumaciones del preclásico medio. In *Transformaciones socioculturales y tecnológicas en el sitio de La Peña, Cuenca de Sayula, Jalisco*, edited by Catherine Liot, Susana Ramírez Urrea, Javier Reveles, and Otto Schöndube, pp. 265–289. Universidad de Guadalajara, Guadalajara.

Liot, Catherine, Susana Ramírez Urrea, Javier Reveles, and Otto Schöndube, eds. 2006b. *Transformaciones socioculturales y tecnológicas en el sitio de La Peña, Cuenca de Sayula, Jalisco*. Universidad de Guadalajara, Guadalajara.

Lister, Robert H. 1949. *Excavations at Cojumatlán, Michoacán, Mexico*. Publications in Anthropology No. 5, University of New Mexico, Albuquerque.

Long, Stanley V. 1966. Archaeology of the Municipio de Etzatlán, Jalisco. Unpublished PhD dissertation, Department of Anthropology, University of California, Los Angeles.

López Austin, Alfredo, and Leonardo López Luján. 1999. *Mito y realidad de Zuyuá*. El Colegio de México, México, D.F.

López Mestas, Lorenza. 2004. El intercambio de concha en el occidente de México durante el Preclásico Tardío y el Clásico Temprano. In *Bienes estratégicos del antiguo occidente de México: producción e intercambio*, edited by Eduardo Williams, pp. 183–206. Colegio de Michoacán, Zamora.

López Mestas, Lorenza. 2005. Producción especializada y representación ideología en los albores de la tradición Teuchitlán. In *El antiguo occidente de México: nuevas perspectivas sobre el pasado prehispánico*, edited by Eduardo Williams, Phil C. Weigand, Lorenza López Mestas, and David C. Grove, pp. 233–254. Colegio de Michoacán, Zamora.

López Mestas, Lorenza, and Marisol Montejano Esquivias. 2003. Investigaciones arqueológicas en la Higuerita, Tala. *Revista del Seminario de Historia Mexicana* IV:11–34.

López Mestas, Lorenza, and Jorge Ramos de la Vega. 2005. Explotación de recursos marino-litorales en sitios costeros: proyecto Colimilla-Barra de Navidad. In *IV coloquio Pedro Bosch Gimpera, el occidente y centro de México*, edited by Ernesto Vargas Pacheco, pp. 75–98. Instituto de Investigaciones Antropológicas, Universidad Nacional Autónoma de México, México, D.F.

Mastache, A. Guadalupe, and Robert H. Cobean. 1989. The Coyotlatelco Culture and the Origins of the Toltec State. In *Mesoamerica after the Decline of Teotihuacan AD 700–900*, edited by Richard A. Diehl and Janet C. Berlo, pp. 49–67. Dumbarton Oaks, Washington, DC.

Matos, Eduardo, and Isabel T. Kelly. 1974. Una vasija que sugiere relaciones entre Teotihuacan y Colima. In *The Archaeology of West Mexico,* edited by Betty Bell, pp. 202–205. Sociedad de Estudios Avanzados del Occidente de México, Ajijic.

Meighan, Clement. 1976. *The Archaeology of Amapa, Nayarit*. Institute of Archaeology, University of California, Los Angeles.

Meighan, Clement W., and Leonard J. Foote. 1968. *Excavations at Tizapan el Alto, Jalisco*. University of California Press, Los Angeles.

Metcalfe, Sarah E., and Sarah J. Davies. 2007. Deciphering Recent Climate Change in Central Mexican Lake Records. *Climatic Change* 83:169–186.

Mountjoy, Joseph B. 1970. Prehispanic Culture History and Cultural Contact on the Southern Coast of Nayarit, Mexico. Unpublished PhD dissertation, Department of Anthropology, Southern Illinois University, Carbondale.

Mountjoy, Joseph B. 1982. *Proyecto Tomatlán de salvamento arqueológico: fondo etnohistórico y arqueológico, desarrollo del proyecto, estudios de la superficie.* Instituto Nacional de Antropología e Historia, México, D.F.

Mountjoy, Joseph B. 1989. Algunas observaciones sobre el desarrollo del Preclásico en la llanura costera del occidente. In *El Preclásico o Formativo: avances y perspectivas*, edited by Martha Carmona Macías, pp. 11–26. Instituto Nacional de Antropología e Historia, México, D.F.

Mountjoy, Joseph B. 1993. El pasado prehispánico del municipio de Puerto Vallarta. In *Una aproximación a Puerto Vallarta*, edited by Jaime Olveda, pp. 23–40. Colegio de Jalisco, Zapopan.

Mountjoy, Joseph B. 2000. Prehispanic Cultural Development along the Southern Coast of West Mexico. In *Greater Mesoamerica: The Archaeology of West and Northwest Mexico*, edited by Michael S. Foster and Shirley Gorenstein, pp. 81–106. University of Utah Press, Salt Lake City.

Mountjoy, Joseph B. 2006. Excavaciones de dos panteones del Formativo Medio en el Valle de Mascota, Jalisco, México. Report submitted to the Foundation for Ancient Mesoamerican Studies, Inc., http://www.famsi.org/reports/03009es/, accessed May 15, 2010.

Mountjoy, Joseph B., and Cheryl P. Claassen. 2005. Middle Formative Diet and Seasonality on the Central Coast of Nayarit, Mexico. In *Archaeology without Limits: Papers in Honor of Clement W. Meighan*, edited by Brian D. Dillon and Matthew A. Boxt, pp. 267–282. Labyrinthos, Lancaster.

Mountjoy, Joseph B., and Mary K. Sandford. 2006. Burial Practices during the Late Formative/Early Classic in the Banderas Valley Area of Coastal West Mexico. *Ancient Mesoamerica* 17:313–327.

Mountjoy, Joseph B., Tammy C. Smith, Ryun Papson, Debbie Guida, John Pleasants, Chris Witmore, and Cheryl Cross. 2003. Arqueología del municipio de Puerto Vallarta. http://www.uncg.edu/arc/Vallarta/, accessed April 25, 2010.

Niederberger, Christine B. 1987. *Paleopaysages et archeologie pre-urbaine du bassin de Mexico*. Centre d'Etudes Mexicaines et Centramericaines, México, D.F.

Noguera, Eduardo. 1942. Exploraciones en El Opeño, Michoacán. In *XXVII Congreso Internacional de Americanistas (1939), Vol. 1*, pp. 574–586. México, D.F.

Ohnersorgen, Michael A., and Mark Varien. 1996. Formal Architecture and Settlement Organization in Ancient West Mexico. *Ancient Mesoamerica* 7:103–120.

Olay Barrientos, María. 1998. Divinos relieves, el grabado en piedra de El Chanal, Colima. In *Antropología e historia del occidente de México, XXIV mesa redonda, sociedad Mexicana de antropología, tomo II*, edited by R. Brambila Paz, pp. 753–778. Universidad Nacional Autónoma de México, México, D.F.

Olay Barrientos, María. 2004. *El Chanal, Colima: lugar que habitan los custodios del agua*. Instituto Nacional de Antropología e Historia, México, D.F.

Oliveros Morales, J. Arturo. 2004. *Hacedores de tumbas en El Opeño, Michoacán*. Colegio de Michoacán, Zamora.

Oliveros Morales, J. Arturo. 2006. *El espacio de la muerte: recreado a partir del occidente prehispánico*. Colegio de Michoacán, Zamora.

Paradis, Louise I. 1974. The Tierra Caliente of Guerrero, Mexico: An Archaeological and Ecological Study. Unpublished PhD dissertation, Department of Anthropology, Yale University, New Haven.

Piperno, Dolores R., Anthony J. Ranere, Irene Holst, José Iriarte, and Ruth Dickau. 2009. Starch Grain and Phytolith Evidence for Early Ninth Millennium BP Maize from the Central Balsas River Valley, Mexico. *Proceedings of the National Academy of Sciences* 106:5019–5024.

Pires-Ferreira, Jane W. 1975. *Formative Mesoamerican Exchange Networks with Special Reference to the Valley of Oaxaca*. Memoirs No. 7, Museum of Anthropology, University of Michigan, Ann Arbor.

Ramírez Urrea, Susana. 2006. Relaciones interregionales en la tradición Aztatlán (Postclásico Temprano y Medio). In *Transformaciones socioculturales y tecnológicas en el sitio de La Peña, cuenca de Sayula, Jalisco*, edited by Catherine Liot, Susana Ramírez Urrea, Javier Reveles, and Otto Schöndube, pp. 435–444. Universidad de Guadalajara, Guadalajara.

Ramírez Urrea, Susana, Catherine Liot, Javier Reveles, Otto Schondube, Cinthya Cárdenas, Franca Mata, Carmen Melgarejo, Leonardo Santoyo, and Victoria Bojórquez. 2005. La Peña: un sitio de transición entre el Epiclásico y el Posclásico temprano en la cuenca de Sayula, Jalisco. In *El antiguo occidente de México: nuevas perspectivas sobre el pasado prehispánico*, edited by Eduardo Williams, Phil C. Weigand, Lorenza López Mestas, and David C. Grove, pp. 305–330. Colegio de Michoacán, Zamora.

Ramos de la Vega, Jorge, and Lorenza López Mestas. 1996. Datos preliminares sobre el descubrimiento de una tumba de tiro en el sitio de Huitzilapa, Jalisco. *Ancient Mesoamerica* 7:121–134.

Ranere, Anthony J., Dolores R. Piperno, Irene Holst, Ruth Dickau, and José Iriarte. 2009. The Cultural and Chronological Context of Early Holocene Maize and Squash Domestication in the Central Balsas River Valley, Mexico. *Proceedings of the National Academy of Sciences* 106:5014–4018.

Robles C., Jacinto, and J. Arturo Oliveros Morales. 2005. Estudio mineralógico en lapidaria prehispánica de El Opeño, Michoacán: evidencias de organización social hacia el formativo medio en el occidente de México. *Arqueología* 35:5–22.

Sánchez Correa, Sergio A., and Emma G. Marmolejo Morales. 1990. Algunas apreciaciones sobre el 'Clásico' en el Bajío central, Guanajuato. In *La época Clásica: nuevos hallazgos, nuevas ideas*, edited by Amalia Cardos de Méndez, pp. 267–278. Instituto Nacional de Antropología e Historia, México, D.F.

Sanjur, Oris I., Dolores R. Piperno, Thomas C. Andres, and Linda Wessel-Beaver. 2002. Phylogenetic Relationships among Domesticated and Wild Species of Cucurbita (Cucurbitaceae) Inferred from a Mitochondrial Gene: Implications for Crop Plan Evolution and Areas of Origin. *Proceedings of the National Academy of Sciences* 99:535–540.

Sauer, Carl O., and Donald Brand. 1932. *Aztatlán: Prehistoric Mexican Frontier on the Pacific Coast.* Ibero-Americana 1, University of California Press, Berkeley.

Schöndube, Otto. 1980. Capitulos V–XI. In *Historia de Jalisco, tomo I,* edited by José Maria Muría, pp. 111–258. Gobierno de Estado de Jalisco, Guadalajara.

Schöndube, Otto, and Luís J. Galván Villegas. 1978. Salvage Archaeology at El Grillo-Tabachines, Zapopan, Jalisco, Mexico. In *Across the Chichimec Sea: Papers in Honor of J. Charles Kelley,* edited by Carroll L. Riley and Basil C. Hedrick, pp. 144–164. Southern Illinois University Press, Carbondale.

Scott, Scott D., and Michael S. Foster. 2000. The Prehistory of Mexico's Northwest Coast: A View from the Marismas Nacionales of Sinaloa and Nayarit. In *Greater Mesoamerica: The Archaeology of West and Northwest Mexico,* edited by Michael S. Foster and Shirley Gorenstein, pp. 107–135. University of Utah Press, Salt Lake City.

Smith, Michael E., and Cynthia Heath Smith. 1980. Waves of Influence in Postclassic Mesoamerica? A Critique of the Mixteca-Puebla Concept. *Anthropology* 42:15–50.

Soto de Arechavaleta, Dolores. 1990. Areas de actividad en un taller de manufactura de implementos de piedra tallada. In *Nuevos enfoques en el estudio de la lítica,* edited by Dolores Soto de Arechavaleta, pp. 215–242. Universidad Nacional Autónoma de México, México, D.F.

Spence, Michael W., Phil C. Weigand, and Dolores Soto de Arechavaleta. 2002. Production and Distribution of Obsidian Artifacts in Western Mexico. In *Pathways to Prismatic Blades: A Study in Mesoamerican Obsidian Core Blade Technology,* edited by Kenneth Hirth and Bradford Andrews, pp. 61–79. Monograph #45, Cotsen Institute of Archaeology, University of California, Los Angeles.

Stuart, Glenn. 2005. Agricultura de tierras húmedas en el núcleo de la tradición teuchitlán. In *El antiguo occidente de México: nuevas perspectivas sobre el pasado prehispánico,* edited by Eduardo Williams, Phil C. Weigand, Lorenza López Mestas, and David C. Grove, pp. 185–210. Colegio de Michoacán, Zamora.

Tolstoy, Paul. 1971. Recent Research into the Early Preclassic of the Central Highlands. *Contributions of the University of California Archaeological Research Facility* 11:25–48.

Valdez, Francisco, Jean P. Emphoux, Rosario Acosta, Susana Ramírez, Javier Reveles, and Otto Schöndube. 2006. Late Formative Archaeology in the Sayula Basin of Southern Jalisco. *Ancient Mesoamerica* 17:297–311.

Von Winning, Hasso. 1969. *Pre-Columbian Art of Mexico and Central America.* Thames and Hudson, London.

Voorhies, Barbara. 1996. The Transformation from Foraging to Farming in Lowland Mesoamerica. In *The Managed Mosaic: Ancient Maya Agriculture and Resource Use,* edited by Scott Fedick, pp. 17–29. University of Utah Press, Salt Lake City.

Weigand, Phil C. 1985. Evidence for Complex Societies during the Western Mesoamerican Classic Period. In *The Archaeology of West and Northwest Mesoamerica,* edited by Michael S. Foster and Phil C. Weigand, pp. 47–91. Westview Press, Boulder.

Weigand, Phil C. 1990. Discontinuity: The Collapse of the Teuchitlán Tradition and the Early Postclassic Cultures of Western Mesoamerica. In *Mesoamérica y norte de*

México, siglo IX–XII, Vol. 1, edited by Federico Sodi Miranda, pp. 215–222. Instituto Nacional de Antropología e Historia, México, D.F.

Weigand, Phil C. 1991. The Western Mesoamerican Tlachco: A Two-Thousand-Year Perspective. In *The Mesoamerican Ballgame*, edited by Vernon L. Scarborough and David R. Wilcox, pp. 73–86. University of Arizona Press, Tucson.

Weigand, Phil C. 1993. Large-Scale Irrigation Works in Prehispanic Western Mesoamerica. In *Economic Aspects of Water Management in the Prehispanic New World*, edited by Vernon L. Scarborough and Barry Isaac, pp. 223–262. JAI Press, Greenwich.

Weigand, Phil C. 1996. The Architecture of the Teuchitlan Tradition of the Occidente of Mesoamerica. *Ancient Mesoamerica* 7:91–101.

Weigand, Phil C. 1999. The Architecture of the Teuchitlán Tradition of Mexico's Occidente. In *Mesoamerican Architecture as a Cultural Symbol*, edited by Jeff Kowalski, pp. 30–47. Oxford University Press, New York.

Weigand, Phil C. 2000. The Evolution and Decline of a Core of Civilization: The Teuchitlán Tradition and the Archaeology of Jalisco. In *Greater Mesoamerica. The Archaeology of West and Northwest Mexico*, edited by Michael S. Foster and Shirley Gorenstein, pp. 43–58. University of Utah Press, Salt Lake City.

Weigand, Phil C., and Acelia García de Weigand. 2001. A Macroeconomic Study of the Relationships between the Ancient Cultures of the American Southwest and Mesoamerica. In *The Road to Aztlan: Art from a Mythic Homeland*, edited by Virginia M. Fields and Victor Zamudio Taylor, pp. 184–196. Los Angeles County Museum of Art, Los Angeles.

Weigand, Phil C., Acelia García de Weigand, and Eric Cach. 2005. *El palacio de Ocomo: tecpan monumental en el occidente de México*. Antropologia en Jalisco, una vision actual 13, Secretaría de Cultura del Gobierno de Jalisco, Guadalajara.

Weigand, Phil C., Acelia García de Weigand, and J. Andrew Darling. 1999. El sitio arqueológico: 'Cerro de Tepecuazco' (Jalapa, Zacatecas), y sus relaciones con la tradición Teuchitlán (Jalisco). In *Tercer simposium: los altos de Jalisco a fin de siglo*, edited by Cándido González Pérez, pp. 241–274. Universidad de Guadalajara, Guadalajara.

Weigand, Phil C., Acelia García de Weigand, and Michael D. Glascock. 2004. La explotación de los yacimientos de obsidiana del centro-oeste de Jalisco. In *Bienes estratégicos del antiguo occidente de México: producción e intercambio*, edited by Eduardo Williams, pp. 113–135. Colegio de Michoacán, Zamora.

Witmore, Christopher. 1998. Sacred Sun Centers. In *Ancient West Mexico: Art and Archaeology of the Unknown Past*, edited by Richard F. Townsend, pp. 137–150. Art Institute of Chicago, Chicago.

Zizumbo-Villarreal, Daniel, and Patricia Colunga-García Marín. 2010. Origin of Agriculture and Plant Domestication in West Mesoamerica. *Genetic Resources and Crop Evolution*, doi: 10.1007/s10722-009-9521-4

Zizumbo-Villarreal, Daniel, Roberto Papa, Matthew Hufford, Shelby Repinski, and Paul Gepts. 2009. Identification of New Wild Populations of *Phaseolus Vulgaris* in Western Jalisco, Mexico, Near the Mesoamerican Domestication Center of Common Bean. *Annual Report of the Bean Improvement Cooperative* 52:24–25.

CHAPTER 36

....

MESOAMERICA AND THE SOUTHWEST/ NORTHWEST

....

RANDALL MCGUIRE

IN 1581, Spanish soldiers and Franciscan friars journeyed north from Chihuahua to investigate claims of another Mexico. After a fifty-day trek across the lands of the Chichimecas, they came to a pueblo of forty-five houses set amidst fields of corn, beans, and squash (Hammond and Rey 1966: 141). They named this land *Nuevo México*. Here as in the *Mēxihco* of the Aztecs, people lived in fixed towns of rectangular houses, intensively farmed well-established fields, and made fine cotton clothing and pottery. Like the Spanish friars had done, twentieth-century ethnographers also observed numerous parallels between the southwest of the United States and the northwest of Mexico (the Southwest/Northwest) and Mesoamerica (Broda 2004).

Parallels occur in cosmology, iconography, metaphor, and ritual (Parson 1939: 1016–1025; Schaafsma 1999; Hays-Gilpin and Hill 2000; Taube 2001). In both regions, cosmologies include the belief in a multitiered cosmos with a watery underworld, cyclic destruction and rebirth of the world, migration histories that begin with emergence from a previous world, the flower world, and the young sun god. Iconographies include color-directional symbolism, warrior twins associated with the planet Venus, and feathered or horned serpents related to fertility, floods, and earthquakes. Shared metaphors would include serpent mouths standing in for cave openings, with water issuing from them; clouds signifying ancestors; cruciforms denoting the planet Venus and warfare; flowers, butterflies, and parrots representing the flower world; mountains associated with the watery underworld; wind as the source of rain and equation of wind and breath; and water jars representing rain. In both regions, rituals were performed to control the cycles of the world and to stave off destruction. Common rituals included the new fire ceremony, the swallowing of sticks and handling of snakes, pole climbing, contests, racing and ballgames, blessings with corn meal and water, prayer offerings (sticks, feathers, and gum paper), clowns or jesters, and masked dances to bring rain. Human sacrifice occurred commonly in Mesoamerica but was primarily mythic and symbolic in the Southwest/Northwest.

Some contemporary scholars link these parallels to the worship of Tlaloc and Quetzalcoatl, the feathered serpent (Schaafsma 2001; Taube 2001; Philips et al. 2006). They argue that the Mesoamerican rain god Tlaloc manifests itself in the Pueblo Katsina religion and that Katsinas reflect Mesoamerican concepts that transform ancestors into rainmakers. The Mesoamerican feathered serpent Quetzalcoatl sustained fertility and regeneration; legitimated political power; controlled underworld waters, the earth, and the sky; symbolized militarism associated with the planet Venus; demanded human sacrifice; and controlled water-bearing winds. In the Southwest/Northwest, native peoples associate feathered and horned serpents with the unity of the earth and sky, as manifest in floods, rain, earthquakes, and landslides. Especially in the Rio Grande, Pueblos associated horned serpents with Venus and warfare. Human sacrifice occurs in Pueblo and O'odham myths, where priests kill twin children to appease the feathered serpent.

The similarities between Southwest/Northwest religions and Mesoamerican religions, however, existed in very dissimilar social contexts. The scale of Southwestern/Northwestern societies, with communities of up to a few thousand people, pales in comparison with even minor Mesoamerican cities with monumental architecture and populations in the tens of thousands. In the Southwest/Northwest all households farmed while Mesoamerican peasants specialized in agriculture, artisans in crafts, merchants in trade, and warriors in conflict. Noble elites ruled Mesoamerican cities sustained by castes of priests, merchants, and warriors. Nobles lived in palaces and used the force of arms to control resources and people. In the Southwest/Northwest, by contrast, everyone lived in similar houses and elite power rested in esoteric ritual knowledge. Unlike an overt Mesoamerica hierarchy, Pueblo communal societies maintained a constant tension between egalitarianism and ranking (McGuire and Saitta 1996).

The regions actualized shared rituals and metaphors in very different ways. Both peoples performed ceremonies to maintain the cycle of the world, but the rituals took dynamically different forms. Postclassic Mesoamerican kings and high priests performed rituals, including the sacrifices of war captives, atop temple pyramids. Pueblo Katsinas danced in plazas, everyone participated in the Katsina religion, and most people were initiated into the Katsina sodality. In Mesoamerican cities, by contrast, elites maintained the cults of the state, while the common people had their own rituals (Gonlin and Lohse 2007). In both places, priests controlled esoteric ritual and cosmological knowledge, but in the Southwest/Northwest people expected elites to be humble and generous. Postclassic Mesoamerican priests formed one of three or four elite classes living in opulence, and the common people gave them great deference. The Postclassic Quetzalcoatl cult legitimated elite power, while the rituals of the Katsina religion redistributed food and sacred clowns ridiculed hubris.

We thus have a paradox. We can identify a profound degree of shared cosmology, iconography, metaphor, and ritual between the two regions, yet the societies of the two regions remain qualitatively different. Resolving this paradox begins by realizing that the parallels between the two areas have different histories and origins. Some of them transcend both regions (Wilcox 2008). Across North America, indigenous religions share a wide range of iconographies, rituals, and beliefs. Serpent and color-directional symbolism appears throughout the continent. The twins of Mesoamerica and the Southwest/Northwest appear among the Iroquois in New York, and many North American indigenous peoples believe that their ancestors emerged from a previous world. Other parallels came with the Spanish, including Catholicism and the Matachine Dance. Mesoamerican Indians who came with the Spaniards probably inspired some Pueblo rituals such as pole climbing. But even if we put aside these parallels, many others resulted from a complex aboriginal history.

History of the Mesoamerican Connection

For more than a millennium, the social relations that defined the Southwest/ Northwest and Mesoamerica ebbed and flowed over the landscape. The boundary between the two regions was always fuzzy, ever changing, and sometimes absent. The most dynamic spaces in this process were west and northwest Mexico.

Formative Beginnings

It is only several hundred years after a full Formative pattern appears that it is possible to distinguish a Southwest/Northwest from developments in northwestern and West Mexico. Several authors link the expansion of agriculture and a shared cosmology, symbols, and rituals with the spread of the Uto-Aztecan language family from the Valley of Mexico to Utah (Hays-Gilpin and Hill 2000; LeBlanc 2008; Mabry et al. 2008).

In the north and west of Mesoamerica, the Formative begins by 250 BC with the advent of the Chupícuaro Tradition. A continuum of ceramics styles appears from Zacatecas, to Durango, to Chihuahua, and to New Mexico. Parallels include red-on-brown decoration, similar vessel forms, and quartered designs with bilateral symmetry (Braniff 1974). In West Mexico, the development of early village life, pottery making, and agriculture look much like the Pioneer-period Hohokam.

The Classic Period and the Hohokam, Mogollon, and Ancestral Pueblo

During the Classic period, West Mexico had its own trajectory of stylistic, social, political, and economic development distinct from the rest of Mesoamerica (Weigand 2007). In Durango, Zacatecas, and Jalisco, the beginnings of the Chalchihuites culture appear between 300 to 500 AD with villages and towns, red-on-buff pottery, and red-on-brown pottery.

Hohokam aesthetics, with their use of anthropomorphic and zoomorphic figures on ceramics and shell, differed markedly from other areas of the southwestern United States. Both the iconography and style of these images as well as Hohokam ceramic figurines greatly resemble the iconography and style of West Mexico and Chalchihuites art. Shell jewelry manufacture (especially shell bracelets), use of ballcourts, red-on-buff pottery, and effigy vessels also connect the Hohokam with West Mexico (McGuire and Villalpando 2007).

The absence of these parallels from pre-900 AD Mogollon and Ancestral Pueblo traditions suggests that the Hohokam related to West Mexico in ways the other "Southwestern Traditions" did not. Southwestern scholars usually see the Hohokam as an island of Mesoamerican influence, but from a Mesoamerican perspective they become the tip of a peninsula. In Sonora, recent research has documented Trincheras and Huatabampo traditions linking the Hohokam to West Mexico. Few if any of the things that make the Hohokam part of West Mexico (iconography, ballcourts, shell bracelets, etc.) ended up in the Pueblo World. The linkages that bring Mesoamerican materials to the rest of the Southwest did not appear until the Mesoamerican Postclassic period.

The Epiclassic, the Postclassic, and the Hohokam, Mimbres, and Chaco Canyon

The Epiclassic of Mesoamerica spanned the time between the fall of Teotihuacan around 600-700 AD and the beginnings of the Postclassic ca. 900 AD (Smith and Berdan 2003; Kowalski and Kristan-Graham 2007). During the Epiclassic, Mesoamerica expanded and became more economically interconnected, more politically divided, and more cosmologically uniform. The Chalchihuites centers of La Quemada and Alta Vista in Zacatecas were the northernmost point of this expansion. Toward the conclusion of this period, the growth of the Aztatlán tradition drew West Mexico more firmly into the Mesoamerican economic, religious, and political orbit. The Aztatlán tradition signaled the emergence of a reorganized Mesoamerica in the Postclassic period. By the end of this period, Mesoamerican elements began to show up in Chaco Canyon, the Mimbres, and the Sedentary-period Hohokam.

In the Epiclassic, trade became decentralized, and it thrived in the peripheries. In the Mesoamerican core, exchange developed into commercialized marketplace trade directed by a merchant class. The volume of trade increased with a greater diversity of trade goods that included more bulk commodities. Late in the Epiclassic, copper objects (mainly bells) from West Mexico entered the trade networks of Mesoamerica and the Southwest/Northwest (Vargas 1995). Turquoise from the Chalchihuites region and the Southwest/Northwest also became a major commodity, reaching all the way to the Maya lowlands (Weigand 2008).

Epiclassic polities and city-states were diverse with ethnically defined classes of rulers, merchants, priests, warriors, and commoners. Movement of goods and artisans helped to produce a uniform set of prestige goods and symbols that identified and legitimized the elite. Nomadic peoples and agriculturalists from the north, the famed Chichimecs, entered core Mesoamerica. Increased levels of violence, warfare, and human sacrifice accompanied Epiclassic political instability and change.

Epiclassic elites legitimated their position, power, and conquests by identifying themselves with Quetzalcoatl (Sugiyama 2005). Quetzalcoatl conveyed leaders from the underworld to positions of power in this world. Across Mesoamerica, elites mobilized the Quetzalcoatl cult to provide mythological charters for the new political order. These elites used war, trade, and migrations to spread the cult, and they adorned their cities with Quetzalcoatl shrines to establish pilgrimage routes (Ringle 2004).

The Epiclassic, from 600 to 900 AD, witnessed the massive expansion and growth of the Chalchihuites centers of Alta Vista and La Quemada in Zacatecas (Nelson 1997; Hers 2001). Agriculturalists abandoning the region around 900 AD may have traveled south as invading Chichimecs. Clear evidence exists connecting the Chalchihuites regional centers with Mesoamerica, West Mexico, and the Southwest/Northwest. The icon of the humped-back flute player originated in the southwest United States and spread to the Chalchihuites. Southwest turquoise occurred in Chalchihuites along with West Mexican copper bells and scarlet macaws.

The West Mexican regional manifestation of the Mixteca-Puebla Horizon, the Aztatlán Tradition, appears in the transition between the Epiclassic to Postclassic period (ca. 900 AD). The Mixteca-Puebla Horizon has a distinct iconography and style (Smith 2007). Iconography refers to symbols or icons while style references how craftspeople produced that iconography. The early iconography of the Mixteca-Puebla Horizon occurs principally on polychrome ceramics exchanged in regional trade. After the thirteenth century, a new iconography appeared with calendric and codex symbols. Mesoamerican artisans executed both of these symbol sets in the same style.

Many archaeologists interpret the appearance of the Aztatlán Tradition as the Mesoamericanization of West Mexico (Carpenter 2008). It persisted in northern Sinaloa until the abandonment of Gusave in 1350 AD. Polychrome ceramics decorated with early Mixteca-Puebla iconography and executed in a Mesoamerican style marked the appearance of the Aztatlán Tradition. West Mexican artisans used the pseudo-cloisonné technique during this period on pottery and on sandstone backs for iron-pyrite mirrors. The Aztatlán Tradition did not spread into the Sonoran Desert, leaving what had been the West Mexican Huatabampo, Trincheras, and Hohokam traditions un-Mesoamericanized. These Sonoran traditions became more integrated into networks of cultural and economic relations extending north and west to the Pueblos and Casas Grandes.

The iconography and cosmology of the Mesoamerican Epiclassic reached the Southwest/Northwest by the end of the AD 900s. With it came scarlet macaws, copper bells, pseudo-cloisonné mirror backs, and cocoa from a Mesoamericanized West Mexico. Scarlet macaws live in the Gulf Coast lowlands of Mexico but small populations survive today in West Mexico (Wilcox 2008). The iconography and objects appeared most clearly among the Phoenix Basin Hohokam in the Mimbres and at Chaco Canyon.

The Hohokam remained linked to West Mexico at the end of the tenth century. During the Santa Cruz Phase (550-900 AD) the Hohokam looked like a West Mexican tradition with red-on-buff pottery, shell jewelry (especially bracelets), ballcourts, platform mounds, bird and snake motifs, humped-back flute players, and thick-billed parrots. A Santa Cruz red-on-buff sherd from Snaketown has the earliest representation of a horned or feathered serpent in the Southwest/Northwest (Haury 1976: 235). The Sacaton Phase (900-1100 AD) continued this culture pattern with the addition of items from the now-Mesoamericanized West Mexico, including copper bells, iron-pyrite mirror backs, ceramic vessels, and dozens of scarlet macaws. Despite the spread of Aztatlán iconography, the Hohokam style remained similar to pre-Aztatlán West Mexico and the Chalchihuites; it did not reflect a Mesoamerican style.

By 900 AD, people in Mimbres, New Mexico, were building pueblos with open plazas and hundreds of rooms. Evidence for Epiclassic Mesoamerican iconography comes from Mimbres Classic ceramics (1000-1150 AD). These vessels displayed the first solid evidence for feathered serpents and masked dancers in the Southwest/Northwest. They also exhibited macaws or parrots, possible human sacrifice, twins, Tlálocs, and other icons that may reference Mesoamerica. The presence of shell bracelets and fish imagery suggests that Mimbres people actually visited the west coast of Mexico.

Most Mesoamerican elements at Chaco Canyon, including shell bracelets, roads, colonnades, and copper bells, originate from West Mexico or Chalchihuites (Nelson 2006). Residue analysis indicates that Chacoan cylinder vessels contained cacao (Crown and Hurst 2009). This cacao probably came from Colima and Nayarit in West Mexico. Archaeologists cannot trace any of these things to specific Mesoamerican empires or capitals. But the presence of these Mesoamerican items suggests that Chacoan notions of power and legitimacy may have been cloaked in references to distant places, landscapes, and celestial phenomena.

By 1000 AD, some elements of early Mixteca-Puebla iconography, specifically the feathered serpent, appear in the Southwest/Northwest. We do not, however, see a Mesoamerican style. Hohokam style most closely resembles pre-Aztatlán West Mexico and the Chalchihuites, and the same might be said for the iconographic painting on Mimbres Classic pottery. Copper bells, pseudo-cloisonné mirror backs, parrots, and possibly bracelets indicate trade with West Mexico. Scarlet macaws and cocoa may demonstrate connections reaching directly or indirectly to core Mesoamerica, but these things also occurred in West Mexico. It might be tempting to propose that these developments represent Chalchihuites rulers, priests, and artisans migrating to the Southwest/Northwest, even as some of their Chichimec brethren descend upon core Mesoamerica. There is little proof of this. In each case, we have evidence of in situ development and no evidence of foreign intruders, and the parallels seem too generalized to result from a wholesale importation of cosmology, aesthetics, and artesian skills. Most noteworthy is the absence of a Mesoamerican style. It seems more likely that emergent Southwestern/Northwestern elites exploited already existing connections to West Mexico to draw on goods, beliefs, iconographies, and rituals that would legitimate their status.

POLYCHROMES, ELITES, MIGRANTS, AND CULTS IN THE SOUTHWEST/NORTHWEST

By the early 1300s, the regional centers of the Hohokam, Mimbres, and Chaco Canyon had declined or had been deserted (Wilcox 2008). Over the next fifty to one hundred years, Southwest/Northwest societies reorganized in ways that erased the Hohokam, Mogollon, and Ancestral Pueblo and established new webs of social relations. Archaeologists struggled for years to understand these new relations as cultures including Salado, Casas Grandes, Western Pueblo, or Pueblo IV, but these new networks resist such categorization.

In the late Prehispanic period, several polychrome ceramic wares developed that crosscut the black-on-white, red-on-brown, and red-on-buff traditions that had defined the Ancestral Pueblos, Mogollon, and Hohokam. These wares included Chihuahuan Polychromes in Chihuahua, Salado Polychromes in southeastern Arizona and southwestern New Mexico, White Mountain Red Ware along the Mogollon Rim, Jeddito Yellow Wares in northeast Arizona, and Glaze ware traditions at Zuni and along the Rio Grande in New Mexico.

Numerous authors link the polychrome traditions to new religions (Di Peso 1974; Adams 1991; Crown 1995; Van Pool and Van Pool 2007; Mathiowetz 2009). Minimally these religions would include one centered on Casas Grandes, a Salado religion linked to Salado Polychrome and the Katsina religion that originated along the upper Little Colorado River and then spread to the Rio Grande. All of the new wares include Mixteca-Puebla iconography replete with parrots and other birds, horned serpents, water imagery, butterflies, flowers, the sun, stars, and masked dancers, but none are executed in a Mesoamerican style. The iconography does not, however, reveal the wholesale adoption of the Postclassic Quetzalcoatl cult.

Rather, it exhibits a convergence of select elements from Quetzalcoatl from older Mesoamerican beliefs such as Tlaloc from earlier Southwest/Northwest beliefs and probably from West Méxican cosmologies as well.

Several common factors mark the reorganization of the Southwest/Northwest at the beginning of the fourteenth century. Trade expanded with a shared set of prestige goods that included turquoise on shell mosaic, conch trumpets, parrots and macaws and their feathers, and copper bells. Whole communities migrated and merged with others to form multiethnic towns that then would break apart and lead to more migrations. Pueblo peoples describe this time in their stories of emergence and the migrations they undertook to find the center place. There is evidence for increased violence and warfare, including the marks on human bones, fortified communities, vacant buffer zones, and icons of warriors and cruciforms representing Venus.

The Mesoamerican elements of post-thirteenth-century Southwest/Northwest religions arrived via many routes, from many sources and over more than a millennium. Archaeologists see this movement in the Mesoamerican objects traded north such as copper bells, iron-pyrite mirrors and macaws, and in the turquoise traded south. People seldom trade for goods based solely on their rarity or aesthetic appeal. They develop ritual contexts for the display of these goods and apply formal mechanisms for absorbing new symbols. Southwestern peoples used these things to create new religions. They did not, however, simply import a Mesoamerican religion but instead created creeds unique to the Southwest/Northwest. For example, no ethnographic evidence exists for a Katsina-like religion between the Valley of Mexico and the Pueblos (Beals 1944: 248).

Making Sense of the Mesoamerican Connection and Regional Transformations

Southwest/Northwest archaeologists have tried to explain the changes of the late thirteenth century in terms of migrations, elite interactions, the spread of cults, or intrusions from Mesoamerica. It is striking how much these changes resemble the transformations in Mesoamerica from the Classic to the Postclassic. Before the change, cultural developments centered on large regional centers (in the southwest these include Chaco, Hohokam, and Mimbres; in Classic-period Mesoamerica, they include Teotihuacan and Monte Albán). A period of dislocation, transformation, and shifting boundaries followed, which reorganized social networks. New polities and elites used prestige goods and cults to link and legitimate themselves and thus produced greater uniformity across the culture area (Glowacki and Van

Keuren 2011). This process in Mesoamerica arose from relations *among* migrations, commerce, conquest, religion, and elites through time and across space.

Mesoamerican-derived rituals, cosmologies, and iconographies provided common threads that ran through the Casas Grandes religion, the Salado religion, and the Katsina religion. The three movements, however, wove these threads into different designs and patterns that varied in how much they resembled the patterns of Mesoamerica. They also differed in how these threads wove together other aspects of society and culture. As a result, the lived experience of these religions varied from the lived experiences of Mesoamericans and from each other.

Casas Grandes (1250–1450 AD) is the most Mesoamerican of all of the archaeological sites in the Southwest/Northwest (Di Peso 1974). The community included effigy mounds, elaborate elite burials, two I-shaped ballcourts, and many other Mesoamerican architectural features. The ceramics exhibit a rich and complex iconography that includes many early Mixteca-Puebla elements. Moreover, more Mesoamerican objects including copper bells, macaws, shells, and ceramics have been found here than anywhere else in the cultural area along with evidence of human sacrifice and the ritual use of human bone. In the Southwest/Northwest, Casas Grandes most closely resembled the Mesoamerican Postclassic Quetzalcoatl cult.

Kayenta migrants living in settlements along the Mogollon Rim apparently created the Salado Polychromes in the 1270s (Clark et al. 2008: 3–4). The ceramic ware and Kayenta migrants spread from this area to much of southern Arizona, including the Phoenix and Tonto basins, and to southwest New Mexico. Salado Polychromes incorporate symbols from early Mixteca-Puebla iconography including horned serpents, the sun and stars, and parrots or macaws. Many designs represent masked dancers. The religion resembled the Mesoamerican Postclassic Quetzalcoatl cult and the Katsina religion as it sought to ensure fertility and to control the weather.

The Salado and their religion look a lot like the Mesoamerican Epiclassic. A large area became more economically interconnected, more politically divided, more ethnically diverse, and more cosmologically uniform. Elites in platform-mound communities used a common set of objects/symbols (including conch trumpets, turquoise on shell mosaic, copper bells, and macaws) to legitimize their power. Trade became more decentralized, and the volume of goods increased. Artisans moved from community to community in order to set up separate villages or barrios to practice their craft. In Epiclassic Mesoamerica, the movement of goods and artisans produced a uniform set of prestige goods and symbols that identified and legitimated the elite. Similarly the Salado religion provided a shared ideology that both unified diversity and legitimized social differentiation and inequality. This cult incorporated many Mesoamerican elements but lacked others such as Mesoamerican style, extensive human sacrifice, and the common ritual use of human bone.

The Pueblo IV Katsina religion developed on the margins of the Mesoamerican connection to the late Prehispanic Southwest/Northwest (Adams 1991). Salado and Casas Grandes sites with their compounds, platform mounds, elite residences, and elite tombs are more similar to Mesoamerican communities than are Pueblo IV and Late Mogollon pueblos, and they contain more Mesoamerican goods than the pueblos had. The Mesoamerican components that were key to the religion existed first among the Hohokam and the Mimbres, and the earliest representations of masks occurs with Jornada Mogollon rock art in southeast New Mexico. The ethnographically known Katsina religion probably also incorporated Mesoamerican features via Casas Grandes.

The Katsina religion incorporated many aspects of Mesoamerican cosmology, belief, and metaphor. However, the practice of this religion in its ritual, its proscriptions for daily behavior, and its role in social relations differed from Mesoamerica in significant and important ways. This means that Pueblo priests may have been able to argue theology with Aztec priests but that the lived experience of their religions would have been profoundly different for them and their peoples. A Pueblo man dancing in the plaza as the masked embodiment of a Katsina experiences his religion in a very different way than an Aztec war captive draped over a stone waiting for his heart to be cut out. By the same token, the experience of the Pueblo priest laying corn pollen blessings on the masked dancer is very different than that of the Aztec priest who wielded the obsidian blade.

REFERENCES

Adams, E. Charles 1991. *The Origin and Development of the Pueblo Katsina Cult.* University of Arizona Press, Tucson.

Beals, Ralph. 1944. Relations between Mesoamerica and the Southwest. In *El Norte de México y el sur de Estados Unidos,* pp. 245–252. Sociedad Mexicana de Antropología, Mexico City.

Braniff, Beatriz. 1974. Sequencias arqueológicas en Guanajuato y la cuenca de México: Intento de correlación. In *Teotihuacan: XI mesa redonda,* pp. 273–323. Sociedad Mexicana de Antropología, Mexico City.

Broda, Johanna Prucha. 2004. Paisajes rituales entre los Indios Pueblo y Mexica: Una comparación. In *Desierto y fronteras: El Norte de México y otros contextos,* edited by H. Salas and R. Pérez, pp. 265–295. Plaza y Valdes, Mexico, D.F.

Carpenter, John P. 2008. El conjunto mortuorio de el Ombligo: Su análisis e interpretación. In *Excavaciones en Gusave, Sinaloa,* by Gordon F. Ekholm, pp. 149–181. Siglio XXI Editores, México.

Clark, Jeffery, Patrick D. Lyons, J. Brett Hill, Anna A. Neuzil, and William H. Doelle. 2008. Immigrants and Population Collapse in the Southern Southwest. *Archaeology Southwest* 22(4):1–4.

Crown, Patricia L. 1995. *Ceramics and Ideology: Salado Polychrome Pottery.* University of New Mexico Press, Albuquerque.

Crown, Patricia L., and W. Jeffery Hurst. 2009. Evidence of Cacao Use in the Prehispanic American Southwest. *Proceedings of the National Academy of Sciences* 106(7):2110–2113.

Di Peso, Charles C. 1974. *Casas Grandes: A Fallen Trade Center of the Gran Chichimeca.* Vols. 1–3, Northland Press, Flagstaff, Arizona.

Glowacki, Donna M., and Scott Van Keuren. 2011. *Religious Transformations in the Late Pre-Hispanic Pueblo World.* University of Arizona Press, Tucson.

Gonlin, Nancy, and John C. Lohse, eds. 2007. *Commoner Ritual and Ideology in Ancient Mesoamerica.* University of Colorado Press, Boulder.

Hammond, George P., and Agapito Rey. 1966. *The Rediscovery of New Mexico, 1580–1594.* University of New Mexico Press, Albuquerque.

Haury, Emil W. 1976. *The Hohokam: Desert Farmers and Craftsmen.* University of Arizona Press, Tucson.

Hays-Gilpin, Kelley, and Jane Hill. 2000. The Flower World in Prehistoric Southwest Material Culture. In *The Archaeology of Regional Interaction*, edited by Michelle Hegmon, pp. 411–429. University of Colorado Press, Boulder.

Hers, Marie-Areti. 2001. Zacatecas y Durango, Los confines Tolteca-Chichimecas. In *La gran Chichimeca: El lugar de las rocas secas*, edited by Beatriz Braniff C., pp. 113–154. Jaca Books, Milán.

Kowalski, Jeff Karl, and Cynthia Kristan-Graham, eds. 2007. *Twin Tollans: Chichén Itzá and the Epiclassic to Early Post Classic Mesoamerican World.* Harvard University Press, Cambridge.

LeBlanc, Steven A. 2008. The Case for Early Farmer Migration into the Greater American Southwest. In *Archaeology without Borders: Contact, Commerce, and Change in the U.S. Southwest and Northwestern Mexico*, edited by Laurie D. Webster and Maxine E. McBrinn, pp. 107–144. University of Colorado Press, Boulder.

Mabry, Jonathan B., John P. Carpenter, and Guadalupe Sanchez. 2008. Archaeological Models of Early Uto-Aztecan Prehistory in the Arizona-Sonora Borderland. In *Archaeology without Borders: Contact, Commerce, and Change in the U.S. Southwest and Northwestern Mexico*, edited by Laurie D. Webster and Maxine E. McBrinn, pp. 155–184. University of Colorado Press, Boulder.

Mathiowetz, Michael. 2009. The Mountain of Dawn: Sacred Landscape and Political Power at Paquimé, Chihuahua, Mexico. Paper presented at the 53rd meeting of the International Congress of Americanists, Mexico City.

McGuire, Randall H., and Dean Saitta. 1996. Although They Have Petty Captains, They Obey Them Badly: The Dialectics of Prehispanic Western Pueblo Social Organization. *American Antiquity* 61(2):197–216.

McGuire, Randall H., and Elisa Villalpando C. 2007. The Hohokam and Mesoamerica. In *The Hohokam Millennium*, edited by Suzanne K. Fish and Paul R. Fish, pp. 57–64. School for Advanced Research Press, Santa Fe.

Nelson, Ben. 1997. Chronology and Stratigraphy at La Quemada, Zacatecas, Mexico. *Journal of Field Archaeology* 24(1):85–109.

Nelson, Ben. 2006. Mesoamerican Objects and Symbols in Chaco Canyon Contexts. In *The Archaeology of Chaco Canyon: An Eleventh Century Pueblo Regional Center*, edited by Stephen H. Lekson, pp. 339–421. SAR Press, Santa Fe.

Parsons, Elsie Clews. 1939. *Pueblo Indian Religion.* University of Chicago Press, Chicago.

Philips, David, A. Christine S. Van Pool, and Todd L. Van Pool. 2006. The Horned Serpent Tradition in the North American Southwest. In *Religion in the Prehispanic Southwest*, edited by Christine Pool Todd. L. Van Pool, and David A. Philips, pp. 17–29. Altamira, London.

Ringle, William M. 2004. On the Political Organization of Chichen Itza. *Ancient Mesoamerica* (15):167–218.

Schaafsma, Polly. 1999. Tlalocs, Kachinas, Sacred Bundles and Related Symbolism in
    the Southwest and Mesoamerica. In *The Casas Grandes World*, edited by Curtis F.
    Schaafsma, pp.164–192. University of Utah Press, Provo.

Schaafsma, Polly. 2001. Quetzalcoatl and the Horned and Feathered Serpent of the
    Southwest. In *The Road to Aztatlan: Art from a Mythic Homeland*, edited by
    Virginia M. Fields and Victor Zamudio-Taylor, pp. 138–149. Los Angeles County
    Museum of Art, Los Angeles.

Smith, Michael E. 2007. Tula and Chichén Itzá: Are We Asking the Right Questions?
    In *Twin Tollans: Chichén Itzá, Tula, and the Epiclassic to Early Postclassic
    Mesoamerican World*, edited by Jeff Karl Kowalski and Cynthia Kristan-Graham,
    pp. 579–617. Dumbarton Oaks, Washington, DC.

Smith, Michael E., and Francis F. Berdan, eds. 2003. *The Postclassic Mesoamerican
    World*. University of Utah Press, Provo.

Sugiyama, Saburo. 2005. *Human Sacrifice, Militarism, and Rulership: Materialization of
    State Ideology at the Feathered Serpent Pyramid, Teotihuacan*. Cambridge University
    Press, Cambridge.

Taube, Karl. 2001. The Breath of Life: The Symbolism of Wind in Mesoamerica and the
    American Southwest. In *The Road to Aztatlan: Art from a Mythic Homeland*, edited
    by Virginia M. Fields and Victor Zamudio-Taylor, pp. 102–123. Los Angeles County
    Museum of Art, Los Angeles.

Van Pool, Christine, and Todd Van Pool. 2007. *Signs of the Casas Grandes Shamans*.
    University of Utah Press, Provo.

Vargas, Victoria D. 1995. Copper Bell Trade Patterns in the Prehispanic U.S. Southwest
    and Northwest Mexico. *Arizona State Museum Archaeological Series 187*, Tucson.

Weigand, Philip C. 2007. States in Prehispanic Western Mesoamerica. In *The Political
    Economy of Ancient Mesoamerica: Transformations during the Formative and Classic
    Periods*, edited by Vernon Scarborough and John Clark, pp. 101–113. University of
    New Mexico Press, Albuquerque.

Weigand, Philip C. 2008. Turquoise: Formal Economic Interrelationships between
    Mesoamerica and the North American Southwest. In *Archaeology without Borders:
    Contact, Commerce, and Change in the U.S. Southwest and Northwestern Mexico*,
    edited by Laurie D. Webster and Maxine E. McBrinn, pp. 343–354. University of
    Colorado Press, Boulder.

Wilcox, David R. 2008. Ancient Cultural Interplay of the American Southwest and the
    Mexican Northwest. *Journal of the Southwest* 50(12):103–135.

CHAPTER 37

AZTEC BOUNDARY INTERACTIONS

MICHAEL A. OHNERSORGEN AND MARCIE L. VENTER

BERDAN (2003: 73) recently outlined a framework for conceptualizing relationships at the boundaries of the Aztec Empire, characterizing them as tenuous, permeable, discontinuous (cf. Barlow 1949), and multidimensional. Interactions at the margins of imperial expansion were also multidirectional, with polities and groups in such areas able to differentially influence the success of imperial strategies. As such, a process of negotiation characterized boundary regions; they were often contested, requiring regular maintenance by imperial administrators and local groups.

Berdan's (2003) description of imperial margins includes seemingly interchangeable concepts of boundaries, borders, and borderlands. We prefer Parker's (2002, 2006) terminology that defines boundaries as general delimiters of sets of geographical and cultural phenomena defined by distinct groups and across which multidimensional interactions (e.g., political, economic, etc.) fall at different points along a continuum of permeability. At one end of this continuum are formal borders—closed, impermeable dividing lines, sometimes reinforced, that often mark political or territorial boundaries and restrict interactions. At the other end are frontiers, which are open, fluid, unrestricted, and capable of fostering exchanges (see also Weber and Rausch 1994). Interactions at the Aztec imperial edges varied considerably, with some marked by a general congruence of political, economic, and symbolic domains, suggesting that borderlike conditions shaped interactions, while other boundary areas were more permeable frontiers where cultural domains overlapped and were interconnected, but differently bounded (Berdan 2003; Stark 1990).

The complexity and diversity of Aztec boundary relationships resulted in a mosaic of imperial control, sometimes direct and imposing (Ohnersorgen 2001, 2006), and sometimes indirect and reliant on local populations for access to tribute products, trade thoroughfares, and administrative support (Berdan 2003; Carrasco 1999; Smith 1996; Venter 2008). Such variability stemmed from a range of factors including the preexisting organizational complexity in boundary areas, distance from the imperial capital, the demand for and location of strategic resources, proximity to enemy states, the ethnicity or language of groups involved, and local responses to Aztec incursions (Berdan 2003; Garraty and Ohnersorgen 2009; Hassig 1985; Ohnersorgen 2006; Schreiber 1992).

Because Aztec strategies of alliance building frequently targeted elites at the top tier of regional-settlement hierarchies (Smith and Montiel 2001), boundary interactions often were nodal. When no clear hierarchy existed, and polities were organized more heterarchically, particular centers or factions might have been pitched against others, and intraregional tensions exploited (Hicks 1994). From the reverse standpoint, political tensions within boundary regions may have led some factions to bolster their local authority by associating with the empire (e.g., Skoglund et al. 2006). At the same time, some boundary groups strongly resisted Aztec political domination but remained receptive to interregional trade, creating complex frontiers.

The resulting archaeological expression of Aztec suzerainty yielded a provincial pattern that largely appears directed at particular settlements but ultimately depended on a complex set of factors (Berdan 1996; Berdan and Anawalt 1992). For example, a provincial tributary capital would have more direct interactions with the empire than its hinterland villages and hamlets (Venter 2008; Venter and Stoner 2009). The uneven burden of tribute payments, however, would have indirectly involved such smaller settlements (Berdan 2003: 76; Smith 1992; Venter 2008). As a result, different strategies of interaction may have been employed throughout local settlement hierarchies, with some factions adopting strategies of cooperation or emulation, and competing factions attempting strategies of resistance or exodus (e.g., Carrasco 1999; Pollard and Smith 1993; Skoglund et al. 2006; see also Lightfoot and Martinez 1995). The widespread but uneven adoption of Texcoco molded censers throughout the Tochtepec tributary, Toztlan, may represent an example of this phenomenon (Venter and Stoner 2009).

The tenuous character of boundary interactions meant that Aztec-local relationships were dynamic over time. Important contingencies entered negotiations at imperial boundaries that were affected by local actors' willingness or reluctance to cooperate with imperial representatives (Garraty and Ohnersorgen 2009; Venter 2008). Perceived benefits of imperial association certainly influenced some boundary communities to cooperate or to seek or change alliances. Where resistance was encountered, the desirability of a boundary region—its strategic location or tributary potential—may have determined the empire's willingness to tolerate prolonged negotiations versus outright conquest.

Most previous characterizations of Aztec boundary interactions come from sixteenth-century Basin of Mexico documents or late sixteenth-century *Relaciones*

Geográficas (Paso y Troncoso 1905; see also Gerhard 1993). Data from recent archaeological projects complement the rich ethnohistorical record, and several of these studies explicitly frame Aztec provincial relationships as a dynamic process of negotiation. Summaries of this information are presented for the western, southern, and eastern margins of the Aztec Empire.

INTERACTIONS AT THE WESTERN AND SOUTHERN AZTEC BOUNDARIES

The western Aztec boundary was fairly well defined, located roughly along the modern Michoacán-Mexico border between the Lerma and Balsas rivers. This boundary simultaneously formed the eastern limit of the enemy Tarascan Empire. South of the Balsas River, the Aztecs expanded west to subdue much of the Pacific coast of Guerrero, although control of this coast was discontinuous, interrupted by the small enemy state of Yopitzinco. The southern Aztec imperial boundary was also discontinuous and relatively unstable, but it included conquered provinces in northern and central Oaxaca, where the Postclassic Mixtec and Zapotec kingdoms were located. Beyond Oaxaca, the Aztecs conquered the single distant province of Soconusco on the Pacific coast of Chiapas. In these areas, a range of responses from diverse ethnic and political groups shaped Aztec political and economic relationships.

Interactions were most restricted along boundaries abutting enemy states, where the most formalized borders were manifested. The clearest expression of such a boundary was along the shared edges of the Aztec and Tarascan empires, where fierce conflicts characterized interactions as each empire sought to control access to strategic resources (Carrasco 1999; Pollard 2000; Pollard and Smith 2003; Williams 2003). Aztec forces took control of the Toluca Valley, but efforts to expand further west were unsuccessful. Ultimately, a series of parallel fortifications was established between the Lerma and Balsas rivers, marking Aztec-Tarascan territorial boundaries (Hassig 1985; Hernández Rivero 1994; Pollard 1993, 2000; Pollard and Smith 2003). The Tarascan fortress of Acámbaro and Aztec Oztoma are the best known of these archaeologically (Gorenstein 1985; Armillas 1944, 1948; Silverstein 2001). The Aztecs eventually penetrated to the Pacific coast south of Tarascan territory, establishing control as far north as Zacatula, a key trading port at the mouth of the Balsas.

Aztec-Tarascan political tensions greatly restricted interaction, resulting in essentially a "closed border," across which movement was limited, especially for ethnic Aztecs or Tarascans (Pollard and Smith 2003: 88). Few Aztecs or Tarascans actually occupied the border zone, where local ethnic groups retained a primary presence, falling on both sides of the imperial borders as a result of conquest, exodus, and resettlement. Local groups could move more fluidly across imperial borders than Aztecs or Tarascans, and they were occasionally employed as imperial messengers, spies, and translators (Carrasco 1999; Pollard and Smith 2003). Aztec colonists and officials were sent to settle in rebellious provinces, and a large colony of Aztecs helped fortify Oztoma and its neighbors. In general, however, the provinces were governed indirectly, with cooperative local elites left in charge. Subjects typically paid tribute in the form of military service, labor to construct fortifications, or surplus food for the military (Berdan 1996; Carrasco 1999: 270–271). Local populations also provisioned Aztec settlers, and this, coupled with the indirect administrative presence, resulted in few imperial-style material remains (see Umberger [1996] and Umberger and Klein [1993] for summaries). Aztec III Black-on-Orange pottery has been reported from surveys in the Toluca and Balsas River Valleys but not in high frequencies. The garrison of Oztoma is an exception, where Aztec pottery types make up 6 percent of the pottery assemblage (Silverstein 2001). Aztec-style architecture has been identified at two fortresses: Oztoma and Cerro San Gaspar (Hernández Rivero 1994).

Despite the formal political-territorial border at the Aztec-Tarascan boundary, it was not entirely closed to economic interactions. Official state merchants could travel to the imperial borders to exchange goods, and some border towns (e.g., Taximoroa) served as official ports of trade (Pollard 2000; Relación de Michoacán 1980). Local groups probably served as third parties to facilitate Aztec-Tarascan exchanges or acted as independent merchants to move goods across the border, if not overtly, then operating as a "black market" (Carrasco 1999; Pollard and Smith 2003: 90). Archaeological evidence suggests that obsidian, metal, and occasionally ceramics moved across the imperial boundaries, although other goods likely did also (e.g., marine products, wood, cotton, greenstone, food) (Carrasco 1999; Pollard 2000; Pollard and Smith 2003). Styles closely associated with either empire were more restricted and probably only crossed the border under special circumstances. Only a few Aztec pottery sherds have been found in Tarascan territory, recovered from contexts associated with diplomatic missions (Pollard 1993, 2003: 85), and only a single Tarascan-elite polychrome vessel was found at Aztec Oztoma (Silverstein 2001). Similar interactions likely characterized Aztec boundaries alongside other enemy states, such as Yopitzinco on the Guerrero coast, and Tlaxcala and Metztitlan in the eastern and northeastern areas of the empire. These enemy states were each surrounded by Aztec-controlled provinces, some with military garrisons, suggesting similar tensions governing interactions.

Aztec relationships in the Oaxaca region are less well understood, especially in terms of their archaeological manifestations. The Aztecs established provinces in the northern Mixteca Alta, including a garrison at Zozollan that helped them secure access to the Pacific Coast through Guerrero. In central Oaxaca, the Aztecs established the tributary province of Coyolapan. In both areas, local Mixtec and Zapotec rulers largely maintained their authority, although Aztec officials were stationed in some key towns. Following a rebellion, Huaxyacac (Oaxaca) was resettled with Aztecs from the Basin of Mexico and a garrison was established (Carrasco 1999). Tribute from these provinces mainly included gold, cloaks, feathers, precious stones, food, and cochineal, although Carrasco (1999: 304) observes that in the Mixteca Alta such items were often "gifts" rather than tribute, suggesting strategic Mixtec-Aztec political relationships more than economic ties (cf. Smith 1996), perhaps for mutual assistance fighting other Mixteca Alta groups (Carrasco 1999). Marriage alliances also were used strategically, and a royal marriage helped cement Aztec-Zapotec relations and secure imperial access to the Isthmus of Tehuantepec (Marcus 1983). Subject towns throughout Oaxaca were ethnically diverse, and allegiances were typically oriented toward local elites, not to the Aztecs (Carrasco 1999). Tribute was paid grudgingly, and Aztec control over many towns remained unsettled up to Spanish contact.

Despite persistent efforts, the Aztecs never effectively integrated the Oaxaca provinces. Local alliances shifted frequently, contributing to political unrest and resulting in a boundary that fluctuated over time. It was not as formal or restrictive as the Tarascan border, however, politically or economically. Some tribute items from these provinces were secured through long-distance trade, extending economic interactions beyond political domains (Carrasco 1999). Given the documented record of Aztec activity in Oaxaca, there is remarkably little archaeological evidence of their presence. Surveys in the Mixteca Alta and the Valley of Oaxaca have yielded very little Aztec pottery, even at key provincial centers (Blanton 1983; Spores 1984: 63). Umberger (1996) attributes this scarcity to the provisioning of Aztecs by local groups, but it may also reflect the Aztecs' indirect administrative strategies, as well as a largely resistant local population. In contrast, the Mixtecs had a profound influence on Aztec art, and Mixtec crafts were highly prized in Tenochtitlan, indicating again that political boundaries did not impede economic or stylistic exchanges and that such interactions can be multidirectional.

INTERACTIONS WITHIN THE EASTERN AZTEC BOUNDARY

Berdan has recently written about the eastern Aztec boundary, so to avoid confusion we employ her admittedly arbitrary definition of that region here. The eastern Aztec boundary extended discontinuously from the northernmost Oxitipan Province in the interior Huasteca, to the southern edge of Tochtepec Province in the eastern Papaloapan Basin (Berdan 2003: 74). This region, which included much of the modern state of Veracruz and accounted for most of the Veracruz Affluent Production Zone (Smith and Berdan 2003), encompassed environmentally diverse mountain, alluvial, and coastal habitats that teamed with abundant and varied luxury natural resources that were coveted by Aztec elites (Berdan 2003; Medel y Alvarado 1993; Stark 1978; Venter 2008). Some of these rich resource zones were also important for their convenient locations along natural transportation arteries that connected the highlands to the Gulf Coast and international trade centers. Others were situated at intersections of overland trade corridors (Gasco and Berdan 2003; Carrasco 1999).

Many areas near the eastern Aztec boundary had seen a series of complex polities thrive and transform from Preclassic times onward. Like many parts of Mesoamerica, what we know about the period before Aztec expansion suggests that several small and competing polities dotted the landscape of the Early and Middle Postclassic periods (e.g., Arnold and Venter 2004; Daneels 1997; Garraty and Stark 2002; Stark 2008; Venter and Stoner 2009). These centers were rarely built on the ruins of Classic-period ones; most often, they represented new or previously inconsequential settlements that arose out of the vacuums left by the decline of Late and Epiclassic cities (e.g., El Zapotal, Totocapan).

Several Postclassic settlements that later formed part of the eastern imperial boundary had hosted waves of Nahuat-speaking immigrants that settled alongside native Chinantec, Huastec, Totonac, and Sierra Popoluca (Berdan 2003; Kauffman 2001; Umberger 1996). Some of the newcomers probably immigrated during the Early to Middle Postclassic periods, and others may have arrived during the Late Postclassic (Kauffman 2001; Ohnersorgen 2006; Stark 2008; Umberger 1996; Venter 2010). The latter groups included imperial administrators and support personnel that oversaw military garrisons and fortresses, as well as calpixque (imperial tribute collectors) who collected tribute. Most of the provinces located along the eastern boundary had imperial garrisons, while those with fortresses were concentrated in the area east of enemy Tlaxcala (i.e., Cuetlaxtlan, Quauhtochco, and Cempoallan) (Smith 1996: Figure 6–1; see also Carrasco 1999). Calpixque were stationed at key collection points throughout this expansive boundary (e.g., Tochpan, Tlacotalpan, and Toztlan [Berdan 1996: Table 5–5]).

Because of the complexities described above, the interactions that characterized the eastern Aztec boundary were varied. The differently construed character of interactions in particular locations meant that their material patterning was equally variable. Archaeological and art historical evidence, tallied by Umberger (1996; see also Curet et al. 1994; Ohnersorgen 2006; Umberger and Klein 1993), suggests what material assemblages at sites may include when imperial interactions occurred. Material components included Aztec styles in architecture, sculpture, pottery (Aztec III Black-on-Orange-style vessels and Texcoco molded-style censers), cookie-cutter figurines, and temple models. Sites containing all or most of these elements have been interpreted as having frequent and direct (asymmetrical and imposing) interactions with the empire; the presence of figurines has been inferred to reflect the presence of Aztec colonists (Ohnersorgen 2006). The extent to which new residents were involved in conquests of communities (e.g., at Cuetlaxtlan) is uncertain (Durán 1967; Ohnersorgen 2006).

Sites in the Mixtequilla (Garraty and Stark 2002; Skoglund et al. 2006) and in the Tuxtlas (Arnold and Venter 2004; Venter 2008; Venter and Stoner 2009) that contained only ceramic components of this material style set have been differently interpreted. For these parts of the south-central and southern Gulf lowlands, a variety of interaction options have been described—ones that introduce a greater degree of boundary group agency (Skoglund et al. 2006; Stark 1990; Venter 2008). The selective incorporation of Aztec-style materials was perhaps related to the frequency and intensity of interactions within this distant corner of the empire, but it also may represent more specific attempts by local elites or others to bolster or somehow negotiate their own status, to minimize the effects of imperial overtures, and to reject a large-scale Aztec presence (i.e., public architectural footprints).

For example, Skoglund et al. (2006: 557) suggest that the emulation of imperial-style Aztec III Black-on-Orange pottery and Texcoco molded ritual censers may represent efforts by local elites and others to engage in the widespread Mesoamerican practice of foreigner "quotation," whereby groups in the Mixtequilla region attempted to convey an aura of prestige by association. Perhaps because of local demand, imperial-style ceramics were market-distributed throughout that region and adopted by elites and nonelites alike.

At Totogal, located in the western Tuxtla Mountains (i.e., Toztlan [Gerhard 1993]), elites attempted to negotiate measured capitulation that would allow them to maintain favorable status at home and to comply with some of the empire's demands (Venter 2008), especially the tributary payment of cotton clothing (Berdan 1996: Table 5–6). Archaeological evidence at Totogal suggests that one of the ways the site's elites generated conformance between imperial and local nonelite interests was public ceremony that involved feasting. The reliance on sponsored ceremonies and feasts is suggested by the larger sizes of plates in contexts with civic-ceremonial or elite architecture, the higher frequency of serving vessels with elaborate decoration in and near these same contexts, and the more frequent (but not exclusive) use of Texcoco molded censers and green obsidian in these same core areas. While improved access to green obsidian may have been a benefit of stronger imperial ties, it was not directly related to a community's location within the empire as high proportions are reported for Villa Espíritú Santo in autonomous Coatzacoalcos (Arellanos and Beauregard 2001).

The approval of and engagement by some nonelite segments of the population in elite strategies is suggested by the presence of all of the above items in domestic contexts beyond the site's center and other nearby settlements. If increases in tribute payments were passed on to those living outside of Totogal's immediate hinterland near the best cotton-producing fields of the coastal plain, resulting resentments may explain the dearth of Texcoco molded ceramics in those areas (Loughlin 2012; Venter 2008). The distribution of Texcoco molded censers was relatively wide within Totogal and other mountainous parts of Toztlan (Arnold and Venter 2004; Kruszczynski 2001; Venter and Stoner 2009). Conflict between Toztlan and autonomous Coatzacoalcos (Paso y Troncoso 1905; Medel y Alvarado 1993) adds another layer of complexity to the character of imperial-local interactions that may have inspired the cooperation suggested for Toztlan.

CONCLUSION

Realization of Aztec expansion was the result of multiple factors that were directly impacted by the character of interactions and negotiations occurring at the margins of empire. It is important to consider how local conditions influenced the success of Aztec imperialism in a particular area, as well as the efforts and challenges faced in negotiations among Aztecs and local groups. Documentary sources underscore the difficulty in characterizing Aztec boundary areas uniformly. By nature, imperial expansion seeks to integrate diverse subjects, and as a result the boundaries are complex and dynamic zones of cultural intersections. At the margins of the Aztec Empire, such areas were ethnically and linguistically diverse, political alliances formed and shifted at various levels (often cross-cutting ethnic boundaries), and a suite of individual motivations and interests affected action and response at every location with which the Aztecs came into contact. Boundaries with enemy states were probably the most formalized and restrictive, whereas boundaries with other regions were more flexible and permeable. Interestingly, even where political-territorial boundaries were the most restrictive, the Aztecs and their Mesoamerican neighbors maintained some degree of economic interaction, with economic ties often extending well beyond political boundaries.

Documenting the imperial boundaries archaeologically remains a challenge, and more fieldwork is certainly needed to understand imperial strategies and interactions at the margins of the empire. The selective use of Aztec ceramic styles, accompanied by the differential distribution of larger infrastructural investments, demonstrates that avenues existed for boundary-residing groups to affect the outcomes of imperial expansion, thus contributing to the mosaic of control that has been described for the Aztec Empire (Berdan 2003; Ohnersorgen 2006; Stark 1990).

REFERENCES

Arellanos Melgarejo, R., and L. Beauregard García. 2001. *La Villa del Espiritu Santo y sus materiales culturales*. Ediciones Cultura de Veracruz, Mexico City.

Armillas, Pedro. 1944. Oztuma, Gro., fortaleza de los mexicanos en la frontera de Michoacan. *Revista Mexicana de Estudios Antropologicos* 6:165–175.

Armillas, Pedro. 1948. Fortalezas mexicanos. *Cuadernos Americanos* 7(5):143–163.

Arnold, Philip J. III, and Marcie L. Venter. 2004. Postclassic Occupation at Isla Agaltepec, Southern Veracruz, Mexico. *Mexicon* 16(6):121–126.

Barlow, Robert H. 1949. *The Extent of the Empire of the Culhua-Mexica*. University of California Press, Berkeley.

Berdan, Frances F. 1996. The Tributary Provinces. In *Aztec Imperial Strategies*, by Frances F. Berdan, Richard E. Blanton, Elizabeth H. Boone, Mary G. Hodge, Michael E. Smith, and Emily Umberger, pp. 115–136. Dumbarton Oaks Research Library and Collections, Washington, DC.

Berdan, Frances F. 2003. Borders in the Eastern Aztec Empire. In *The Postclassic Mesoamerican World*, edited by Michael E. Smith and Frances F. Berdan, pp. 73–77. University of Utah Press, Salt Lake City.

Berdan, Frances F., and Patricia Anawalt. 1992. *The Codex Mendoza*. University of California Press, Berkeley.

Blanton, Richard E. 1983. The Aztec Garrison of "Acatepec." In *The Cloud People: Divergent Evolution of the Zapotec and Mixtec Civilizations*, edited by Kent V. Flannery and Joyce Marcus, p. 318. Academic Press, New York.

Carrasco, Pedro. 1999. *The Tenochca Empire of Ancient Mexico: The Triple Alliance of Tenochtitlan, Tetzcoco, and Tlacopan*. University of Oklahoma Press, Norman.

Curet, L. Antonio., Barbara L. Stark, and Sergio Vásquez Z. 1994. Postclassic Changes in Veracruz, Mexico. *Ancient Mesoamerica* 5:13–32.

Daneels, Annick. 1997. Settlement History in the Lower Cotaxtla Basin. In *Olmec to Aztec: Settlement Patterns in the Ancient Gulf Lowlands*, edited by Barbara L. Stark and Philip J. Arnold III, pp. 206–252. University of Arizona Press, Tucson.

Durán, Fray Diego. 1967. *Historia de las Indias de Nueva España e islas de la tierra firma*. Translated by Angel Garabay. L. Editorial Porrua, Mexico.

Garraty, Christopher P., and Michael A. Ohnersorgen. 2009. Negotiating the Aztec Landscape: The Geopolitics of Aztec Control in the Outer Provinces of the Empire. In *The Archaeology of Meaningful Places*, edited by Brenda J. Bowser and María Nieves Zedeño, pp. 107–131. University of Utah Press, Salt Lake City.

Garraty, Christopher P., and Stark, Barbara L. 2002. Imperial and Social Relations in Postclassic South-Central Veracruz, Mexico. *Latin American Antiquity* 13:3–33.

Gasco, Janine, and Francis F. Berdan. 2003. International Trade Centers. In *The Postclassic Mesoamerican World*, edited by Michael E. Smith and Frances F. Berdan, pp. 109–116. University of Utah Press, Salt Lake City.

Gerhard, Peter. 1993. *A Guide to the Historical Geography of New Spain*. Revised edition. University of Oklahoma Press, Norman.

Gorenstein, Shirley. 1985. *Acámbaro: Frontier Settlement on the Tarascan-Aztec Border*. Publications in Anthropology 32, Vanderbilt University, Nashville.

Hassig, Ross. 1985. *Trade, Tribute, and Transportation: The Sixteenth Century Political Economy of the Valley of Mexico*. University of Oklahoma Press, Norman.

Hernández Rivero, José. 1994. La arqueología de la frontera Tarasco-Mexica: Arquitectura bélica. In *Contribuciones a la arqueología y etnohistoria del Occidente de México*, edited by Eduardo Williams, pp. 115–155. El Colegio de Michoacan, Zamora.

Hicks, Frederick. 1994. Alliance and Intervention in Aztec Imperial Expansion. In *Factional Competition and Political Development in the New World*, edited by Elizabeth M. Brumfiel and John W. Fox, pp. 111–117. Cambridge University Press, Cambridge.

Kauffman, Terrence. 2001. The History of the Nawa Language Group from the Earliest Times to the Sixteenth Century: Some Preliminary Results. Online document: http://www.albany.edu/pdlma/Nawa.pdf.

Kruszczynski, Mark. 2001. Prehistoric Basalt Exploitation and Core-Periphery Relations Observed from the Cerro el Vigía Hinterland of Tres Zapotes, Veracruz, Mexico. Unpublished PhD dissertation, Department of Anthropology, University of Pittsburgh, Pittsburgh.

Lightfoot, Kent, and Antoinette Martinez. 1995. Frontiers and Boundaries in Archaeological Perspective. *Annual Review of Anthropology* 24:471–492.

Loughlin, Michael L. 2012. *El Mesón Regional Survey: Settlement Patterns and Political Economy in the Eastern Lower Papaloapan Basin, Veracruz, Mexico.* PhD Dissertation, Department of Anthropology, University of Kentucky, Lexington, KY.

Marcus, Joyce. 1983. Aztec Military Campaigns against the Zapotecs: The Documentary Evidence. In *The Cloud People: Divergent Evolution of the Zapotec and Mixtec Civilizations*, edited by Kent V. Flannery and Joyce Marcus, pp. 314–318. Academic Press, New York.

Medel y Alvarado, Lorenzo. 1993. *Historia de San Andres Tuxtla (1525–1975).* Fascimile of 1963 edition. Estado de Veracruz.

Ohnersorgen, Michael A. 2001. Social and Economic Organization of Cotaxtla in the Postclassic Gulf Lowlands. PhD dissertation, Department of Anthropology, Arizona State University, Tempe. UMI, Ann Arbor, MI.

Ohnersorgen, Michael A. 2006. Aztec Provincial Organization at Cuetlaxtlan, Veracruz. *Journal of Anthropological Archaeology* 25:1–32.

Parker, Bradley J. 2002. At the Edge of Empire: Conceptualizing Assyria's Anatolian Frontier ca. 700 BC. *Journal of Anthropological Archaeology* 21(3):371–395.

Parker, Bradley J. 2006. Toward an Understanding of Borderland Processes. *American Antiquity* 71(1):77–100.

Paso y Troncoso, Francisco. 1905. *Papeles de Nueva España.* 2nd series, 7 vols. Suc. de Rivadeneyra, Madrid.

Pollard, Helen P. 1993. *Tariacuri's Legacy: The Prehispanic Tarascan State.* University of Oklahoma Press, Norman.

Pollard, Helen P. 2000. Tarascan External Relationships. In *Greater Mesoamerica*, edited by Michael S. Foster and Shirley Gorenstein, pp. 71–80. University of Utah Press, Salt Lake City.

Pollard, Helen P., and Michael E. Smith. 2003. The Aztec/Tarascan Border. In *The Postclassic Mesoamerican World*, edited by Michael E. Smith and Frances F. Berdan, pp. 87–90. University of Utah Press, Salt Lake City.

Relación de Michoacán. 1980. *Relación de Michoacán: Versión paleográfica, separación de textos, ordenación coloquial, estudio preliminar y notas de F. Miranda.* Estudios Michoacanos, vol. 5. Fimax, Morelia.

Schreiber, Katharina. 1992. *Wari Imperialism in Middle Horizon Peru.* Anthropological Paper 87, Museum of Anthropology, University of Michigan, Ann Arbor.

Silverstein, Jay E. 2001. Aztec Imperialism at Oztuma, Guerrero: Aztec-Chontal Relations during the Late Postclassic and Early Colonial Periods. *Ancient Mesoamerica* 12:31–48.

Skoglund, Thanet, Barbara L. Stark, Hector Neff, and Michael Glascock. 2006. Compositional and Stylistic Analysis of Aztec-Era Ceramics: Provincial Strategies at the Edge of Empire, South-Central Veracruz, Mexico. *Latin American Antiquity* 17(4):542–559.

Smith, Michael E. 1992. *Archaeological Research at Aztec-Period Rural Sites in Morelos, Mexico.* University of Pittsburgh Memoirs in Latin American Archaeology, number 41, Pittsburgh.

Smith, Michael E. 1996. The Strategic Provinces. In *Aztec Imperial Strategies*, edited by Frances F. Berdan, Richard Blanton, Elizabeth Hill Boone, Mary G. Hodge, Michael E. Smith, and Emily Umberger. Dumbarton Oaks Research Library and Collection, Washington, DC.

Smith, Michael E., and Francis F. Berdan. 2003. Spatial Structure in the Mesoamerican World System. In *The Postclassic Mesoamerican World*, edited by Michael E. Smith and Frances F. Berdan, pp. 21–31. University of Utah Press, Salt Lake City.

Smith, M. E., and Lisa Montiel. 2001. The Archaeological Study of Empires and
    Imperialism in Pre-Hispanic Central Mexico. *Journal of Anthropological
    Archaeology* 20:245–284.
Spores, Ronald. 1984. *The Mixtecs in Ancient and Colonial Times*. University of
    Oklahoma Press, Norman.
Stark, Barbara L. 1978. Ethnohistoric Model for Native Economy and Settlement Patterns
    in Southern Veracruz, Mexico. In *Prehistoric Coastal Adaptations: The Economy
    and Ecology of Maritime Middle America*, edited by Barbara L. Stark and Barbara
    Voorhies, pp. 211–238. Academic Press, New York.
Stark, Barbara L. 1990. The Gulf Coast and the Central Highlands of Mexico: Alternative
    Models for Interaction. *Research in Economic Anthropology* 12:243–285.
Stark, Barbara L. 2008. Archaeology and Ethnicity in Postclassic Mesoamerica. In *Ethnic
    Identity in Nahua Mesoamerica*, by Francis Berdan, John Chance, Alan Sandstrom,
    Barbara Stark, James Taggert, and Emily Umberger, pp. 38–63. University of Utah
    Press, Salt Lake City.
Umberger, Emily. 1996. Aztec Presence and Material Remains in the Outer Provinces.
    In *Aztec Imperial Strategies*, by Frances F. Berdan, Richard E. Blanton, Elizabeth
    H. Boone, Mary G. Hodge, Michael E. Smith, and Emily Umberger, pp. 151–180.
    Dumbarton Oaks, Washington, DC.
Umberger, Emily, and Cecilia Klein. 1993. Aztec Art and Imperial Expansion. In
    Latin American Horizons, edited by Don S. Rice, pp. 295–336. Dumbarton Oaks,
    Washington, DC.
Venter, Marcie L. 2008. Community Strategies in the Aztec Imperial Frontier:
    Perspectives from Totogal, Veracruz, Mexico. PhD Dissertation, Department of
    Anthropology, University of Kentucky, Lexington.
Venter, Marcie L. 2010. Innovations in Cooking Technology: The Implications of Comal
    Use in the Late Postclassic Tuxtla Mountains. Paper presented at the 75th annual
    meeting of the Society for American Archaeology, St. Louis, Missouri.
Venter, Marcie L., and Wesley D. Stoner. 2009. Classic to Postclassic Changes in the
    Tepango Valley of Southern Veracruz, Mexico. Poster presented at the 74th annual
    meeting of the Society for American Archaeology, Atlanta, Georgia.
Weber, David J., and Jane M. Rausch. 1994. Introduction. In *Where Cultures Meet:
    Frontiers in Latin American History*, edited by David J. Weber and Jane M. Rausch,
    pp. xiii–xli. Scholarly Resources, Wilmington, Delaware.
Williams, Eduardo. 2003. *La sal de la tierra*. El Colegio de Michoacán and Secretaría de
    Cultura del Estado de Jalisco, Zamora, Michoacán, and Guadalajara, Jalisco.

PART IV

INSTITUTIONS,
BELIEFS, AND
PRACTICES: TOPICAL
AND COMPARATIVE
PERSPECTIVES

Economies and Economic Relations

CHAPTER 38

AGRICULTURAL LAND USE AND INTENSIFICATION

VERNON L. SCARBOROUGH

MESOAMERICA remains one of the most diverse cultural and geographical areas of the world; as a consequence of the varied environments and the societies that evolved on those landscapes, it reveals a cultivated set of highly complex land-and-water-use strategies over an extended time. With the advent of sedentism and a commitment to generational place, these ancient societies significantly altered their surroundings, frequently in an image of their own cultural signature. Although we generally associate such material cultural differences with kinds of architecture or ceramic types, an engineered landscape footprint can also broadly distinguish a group's identity.

At the outset, agricultural intensification is the process whereby land-use activity is heightened through an increase in production on a plot (cf. Morrison 1994; cf. Brookfield 1984). Production can be stimulated by an increase in the amount or kind of labor invested, the incorporation of crops that yield more food or fiber, or the use of a novel technology. In Mesoamerica, few "technological breakthroughs" precipitated change, rather the developmental trajectory for intensification was based on labor allocation and slow advances in the amount of food potentially harvested by an evolving process of plant domestication—principally maize (Kirkby 1973).

The triggering mechanisms for agricultural intensification are as complicated and nonlinear as the implicated processes. The most touted, single-cause explanation continues to be population pressure (Boserup 1965), a significant factor but seldom culturally explained by way of social organizational constraints or institutional traditions that underpin all societal decision making. Of more telling import is the kind and amount of consumption that a group deems necessary—beyond simple survival—and how this relates to demographic structure. As is apparent today, how a society organizes its work routines (scheduling) and the degrees to which it technologically buffers itself from its biophysical environment markedly influences its consumption practices or economy (Scarborough 2003a). What is considered overpopulated versus underpopulated on a landscape is a function of the social system operating within a particular human ecological system, inclusive of the kinds of crops grown (e.g., paddy rice to milpa maize [Scarborough 2003b]). Nevertheless, population figures—though subject to debate—are accessible in the archaeological record, while consumption practices are much more conjectural. Generally speaking, population estimates represent a highly useful index of social complexity and significantly aid in evaluative judgments concerning intensification.

Another factor in the causal intensification literature is on-site invention or the subsequent adoption of an innovative technology from elsewhere. As with the population pressure trigger, the acceptance of the device is seldom discussed in the context of the societal organizational parameters identified—or by way of that "other" society that might lack the invention (Scarborough 2003a). Why was the wheel not developed as a technological breakthrough in the New World—or herd animals not somewhere domesticated or why weren't metals annealed for cutting? Elsewhere I have suggested that the constraining scale of the biophysical settings—semitropical swamps juxtaposed with towering mountain chains—that defined Mesoamerica countered the attraction (Scarborough 2000). Human labor pools were always elevated in the New World (Scarborough and Burnside 2010a; Trigger 2003)—providing the "work" required to build ancient cities and farm a hinterland—and if coupled with conservative social values and mores, then technological acceptances would have been less attractive to maintain. I suppose the adage "if it ain't broke, then why fix it" comes to mind (Scarborough 2005).

Yet a third catalyst for intensification that is now receiving considerable global attention is climate change. Several authors (Allen 2012; Bawden and Reycraft 2000; Vita-Finzi and Giegengack 2010; Williams 2006) have suggested that periods of long-term drought fluctuation induce degrees of intensification in an attempt to maintain an earlier recognizable level of production, or, during truly severe climatic deterioration, to extract minimal amounts of food and water from a shrinking human-made and formerly productive environment. Under these conditions, societies may reduce the land area exploited and can invest in new ways to harvest and direct water—the latter is the principal variable in climate-change modeling. If conditions persist or degrade further, outmigration or abandonment are clear options. In Mesoamerica less attention has been devoted to the impact of climatic oscillations (relative to Peru), except for a growing recent literature from the Maya lowlands (Gill 2000; cf. Gunn et al. 1995; Haug et al. 2003; Hodell et al. 1995; Hodell and Guilderson 2001; contra Yaeger and Hodell 2008). (Do note the causal confusion associated with a lack of temporal control in several climatic modeling efforts [Scarborough and Burnside 2010b].)

Although many zones throughout Mesoamerica were significant loci for agricultural intensification, only four will be reviewed here. They reflect a diverse set of environments and the cultures that occupied them. Unlike conventional definitions of intensification in the ancient archaeological record of the Old World, Peru, or the U.S. Southwest, sophisticated canalization schemes are poorly identified in Mesoamerica. Lake shores and related wetland settings are the principal environmental backdrop (Scarborough 2006, 2007) with the only known canalization "system" of significant spatial scale found in the Tehuacán Valley, Puebla (Neely 2001; Woodbury and Neely 1972).

WEST MEXICO

Recent work by Fisher and his colleagues (2003) clearly demonstrate that portions of the greater Tarascan region were highly engineered and productive for centuries (see also Weigand 1993, 2007). Both terraced slopes and raised and ditched fields at lake margins provided a built environment capable of supporting thousands. During the Postclassic period, the Tarascans produced one of the most formidable complex societies of Mesoamerica. By way of assessing the processes that established and subsequently diminished their power and influence, Fisher and colleagues indicate the role played by the Spanish conquest. During the "encounter," Tarascan society collapsed, with conventional wisdom arguing that their engineered landscape adaptations—lake-margin fields and extensive terracing—were a simplistic set of land-use adjustments that reflect a crude understanding of their environment and a clear case of a native population overshooting its resource base and leading to elevated erosional rates and degradation of field systems (Butzer 1993; O'Hara 1993). However, more focused assessments now suggest that the engineered landscape was actually elaborately constructed, the landscape providing cultural insights into the sophistication of their land-use activities *prior* to the Spanish arrivals. Evidence suggests that the Tarascans carefully assessed their environmental constraints and parameters in producing a harvestable terrain by way of significantly altering their agricultural surfaces. Fisher and company maintain that this was a sustainable landscape before the Spanish arrived.

Of special interest here is the disrupting influence of a western European group highly dependent on tractable animals, wheeled vehicles (and the pulley), and the highly efficient cutting edge of metal tools. These technological breakthroughs, when coupled with a very different definition of cultural mores and rules, especially those reflective of labor allocations and community interdependencies, resulted in indigenous institutional collapse. When European disease and military sophistication were added, a near complete socioeconomic and sociopolitical breakdown was predictable (Dobyns 1966, 1983; Scarborough 2010).

The example demonstrates the primary role of social organization and institutional identity that maintained and sustained the vibrancy of a great ancient Mesoamerican state. The Tarascan demise shows that the pivotal role of labor tasking (Scarborough 2003a; Scarborough and Burnside 2010a)—or the set of generational skills and work routines associated with an accretional modification of the landscape in improving intensification potential—was well established prior to the colonial embrace. As a consequence of marked depopulation due to European distress on indigenous peoples, coupled with the radical changes associated with societal traditions and values, labor routines were severely disrupted—even truncated. The highly engineered landscapes required extended hours of intense care and maintenance that were never again reestablished or reenergized, which only further tripped a cascading set of social and environmental erosional processes. The example from western Mexico permits a degree of clarity in the contrasting definitions of agricultural intensification perhaps dichotomized by a New World versus Old World before the encounter. Intensification in the New World was sustainable and could be expansive without major technological innovation— and dependent on well-coordinated, though very large, populations of workers. I would suggest much of the success of these indigenous systems was grounded on ideological worldviews that incrementally developed—self-organized—in the context of deep generational roots to a place.

CENTRAL HIGHLAND MEXICO

A tremendous amount of work has been conducted by archaeologists, geographers, and cultural historians in the Central Valley of highland Mexico. Intensification was initially argued to be a causal result of Wittfogel's hydraulic hypothesis (Sanders and Price 1968), but that position was subsequently replaced by a demographic trigger (Sanders, Parson, and Santley 1979) arguing the estimated half-a-million people in the Basin of Mexico precipitated the Aztec state and its complexity. That school strongly suggests that it was this Postclassic threshold of population that precipitated the need for extensive raised-field systems or chinampas throughout the interconnected five-lake depression identifying the basin (cf. Nichols 1987). Although there is little doubt that a spike in built environmental activity occurred at this time, sizable populations inhabited the valley from the Late Formative and raised or ditch fields at the lake margins extend back to about that time (Armillas 1971).

Drawing on Fisher's insights for intensification, it is apparent that the relatively short-lived Aztec presence was preceded by sizable populations and intensive agricultural landscape investments. The incentive for intensification was likely not either population pressure or water management control, but rather a slow incremental adaptation to the landscape that over centuries accommodated growing consumption demands. There is no doubt that an increasing population requires more food and related resources derived from the landscape, but surplus is always a necessary end, given the lag in crop fruition from its initial sowing, how much it will actually produce, and the seasonal conditions under which a crop is grown—to say nothing about disease vectors and capricious climatic conditions. Once harvested, however, it is consumed, stored, or traded. Several thinkers propose that a state is a necessary prerequisite for developing a significant surplus, and certainly in the two examples proposed thus far the state affects outcomes of some facet of surplus. Regarding the Aztec case, and perhaps to a lesser extent in western Mexico, the controlling role of the state in regulating water levels into chinampa fields was likely a function only it could assume. The artificial lake embayment within Lake Texcoco (the largest of the basin lakes)—cordoned off by the construction of the Netzahualcoyotl Dike and replenished by freshwater springs conveyed by aqueducts from the mainland to the island capital of Tenochtitlan— reveals a kind of planning and corporate sophistication well beyond individual community coordination. Salinization concerns within any closed-basin lake system associated with a truly urbanscape was a condition with which only a state might manage.

Nevertheless, it is not at all clear that the state is either the cause or the effect of agricultural intensification in most cases. Erickson (2012) has articulated significant levels of social complexity unassociated with the state from Amazonia, illustrating that the highly patterned raised-field system over contiguous regions covering hundreds of square kilometers is a consequence of intensive agricultural production operating at the small-scale intercommunity level. Although highly interconnected, the extensive swamplike settings lend themselves to this kind of self-organization of the landscape. A similar type of (re)examination of the lake district in the Basin of Mexico would seem appropriate not only for pre-Aztec periods but also for the Aztec themselves.

THE VALLEY OF OAXACA

The ancient occupants of the Valley of Oaxaca have received considerable attention regarding aspects of intensification over their prehispanic landscapes (Blanton et al. 1999; Kowalewski 2003). Like much of semiarid Mesoamerica, this area is identified by few prominent perennial streams, but unlike the previous two regional examples lake access is absent. Again, the state has played a prominent role in how, when, and where populations were positioned through deep time across the agriculturally modified landscape—a top-down assessment of a highly rigid,

hierarchically demanding state at times followed by a weak state apparatus inca-
pable of these controls, with a period in which empirelike expansion permitted a
more "laissez-faire" association with the state and its immediate sustaining population (Blanton et. al 1999). A recent set of articles by Feinman (2006) and his
teams (Feinman and Nicholas 2007) suggests that conventional maize yields may
not have always been the primary crop. Especially during the Postclassic period
and some distance from the nexus center site of Monte Alban of the Classic period,
Feinman shows that maguey and related succulents may have been the more attractive crops. From the terraced surfaces, many positioned within the sizable town of
El Palmillo, highly water-resistant plants were deliberately cultivated and in excess
of anything akin to immediate local demand. It remains difficult to discern if a
statelike institution is really involved, but it seems unlikely. In this extremely arid
eastern arm of the valley, a surplus was created and exchanged for foodstuff of
greater nutrient richness. Climatic conditions are implicated in this kind of intensification adaptation.

MAYA LOWLANDS

In the Maya lowlands the environment differs substantially from that noted in
the examples above. The landscape was highly intensified but modified over
time in a relatively accretional manner. Although rainfall is considerable in these
semitropical climes, it is highly seasonal. Furthermore, the karstic setting pre-
vents truly significant riverine development in most regions. Unlike their Gulf
Coast Olmec precursors occupying perennially swampy, yet drained settings, and
accommodating levee margin "islotes" or sizable tract-raised fields (Cyphers and
Zurita-Noguera 2006), the Maya had to deal with severe annual drought. During
the Late Preclassic period, several communities constructed "concave microwatersheds" in which they positioned their dispersed settlement towns and cities
(Scarborough 1983, 1993, 1998, 2003a). These naturally shallow basins were further quarried in building temples, ballcourts, and housemounds, and in so doing
excavating tanks or reservoirs to contain an otherwise vertically percolating water
source. By carefully plastering all relevant civic surfaces and directing runoff into
deliberately modified depressions, the Maya produced a water-catchment system
capable of sustaining them through the lengthy dry season. Some form of "pot
irrigation"—not unlike that proposed for the much more arid environs of Oaxaca
(Flannery et al. 1967)—was incorporated in proximity to these tanks as well as
the use of a highly focused type of slash-and-burn agriculture. Although considerable support for the difficulties associated with cutting down even a small
plot of forest with stone axes is demonstrated in both Amazonia (Denevan 1992a,
1992b, 2001) and the eastern woodlands of North America (Doolittle 2000: 190),

Late Preclassic sedentists did accelerate soil erosional rates more extreme than apparent from any other period in Maya prehistory (Scarborough and Burnside 2010a).

This kind of intensification proved exceptionally costly, likely further exacerbated by a droughtlike period at the end of the Late Preclassic. The Early Classic-period Maya resiliently adapted by relocating their largest towns and urbanlike communities to the summits of ridges and hillock above the natural and previously altered Late Preclassic concave microwatersheds. These "convex microwatersheds" of the Classic period were planned by way of sizable quarrying efforts to build the largest pyramids and related structures, with the now-elevated quarry scars converted into large reservoirs providing the potable sources for supporting the large populations in proximity (Scarborough 1993, 1998, 2003b; Scarborough and Gallopin 1991). During the rainy season, water was more than abundant with the large elevated tanks filling to capacity. During the extended dry season, water was now released by gravity, making the water-management system a much more controllable one. Here, something akin to centralized control is suggested with a state decision-making apparatus at work.

Raised or drained fields were extended over the landscape by at least the Middle Preclassic and terracing is conservatively identified by the Late Preclassic period (Scarborough 2007). These forms of intensification continued into the Terminal Classic as well. Significant and lengthy drought conditions are now understood to have influenced the Maya collapse or "great fragmentation" (see above). The significant role of slash-and-burn agriculture remains enigmatic, given the difficulties associated with its incorporation into Native American subsistence strategies. When utilized it may well have required the most labor and "intensification" to implement, given the absence of steel until the appearance of Europeans (Denevan 1992a, 1992b).

Agricultural intensification is a key factor in understanding social complexity. In Mesoamerica, skilled labor and its allocation was the focus of its trajectory through time. Landscapes were altered and sustained for extended periods based on local ecological knowledge and generational memory of place, though sometimes accented by state intervention.

REFERENCES

Allen, Susan. 2012. Water Management in Ancient Greece and the Mediterranean. *Water and Humanity: A Historical Overview* (*History of Water and Civilization Book Series, Volume VII*), edited by Vernon L. Scarborough. UNESCO, Paris.

Armillas, Pedro. 1971. Gardens on Swamps. *Science* 174:653–61.

Bawden, Garth, and Rick Reycraft, eds. 2000. *Natural Disaster and the Archaeology of Human Response*. Maxwell Museum of Anthropology and the University of New Mexico Press, Albuquerque.

Blanton, Richard E., Gary M. Feinman, Stephen A. Kowalewski, and Linda M. Nicholas. 1999. *Ancient Oaxaca: The Monte Alban State*. Cambridge University Press, Cambridge.

Boserup, Ester. 1965. *The Conditions of Agricultural Growth*. Aldine, Chicago.

Brookfield, Harold C. 1984. Intensification Revisited. *Pacific Viewpoint* 25:15–44.

Butzer, Karl W. 1993. No Eden in the New World. *Nature* 362:15–17.

Cyphers, Ann, and Judith Zurita-Noguera. 2006. A Land That Tastes like Water. In *Precolumbian Water Management: Ideology, Ritual, and Power*, edited by Lisa J. Lucero and Barbara W. Fash, pp. 35–50. University of Arizona Press, Tucson.

Denevan, William M. 1992a. The Pristine Myth: The Landscapes of the Americas in 1942. *Annals of the Association of American Geographers* 82:369–385.

Denevan, William M. 1992b. Stone vs. Metal Axes: The Ambiguity of Shifting Cultivation in Prehistoric Amazonia. *Journal of the Steward Anthropological Society* 20:153–165.

Denevan, William M. 2001. *Cultivated Landscapes of the Native Amazonia and the Andes*. Oxford University Press, Oxford.

Dobyns, Henry F. 1966. Estimating Aboriginal American Populations: An Appraisal of Techniques with a New Hemispheric Estimate. *Current Anthropology* 7:395–416.

Dobyns, Henry F. 1983. *Their Number Become Thinned: Native American Population Dynamics in Eastern North America*. University of Tennessee Press, Knoxville.

Doolittle, William. 2000. *Cultivated Landscapes of Native North America*. Oxford University Press, Oxford.

Erickson, Clark L. 2012. Pre-Columbian Water Management in Lowland South America. In *Water and Humanity: A Historical Overview (History of Water and Civilization Book Series, Volume VII)*, edited by Vernon L. Scarborough. UNESCO, Paris.

Feinman, Gary M. 2006. The Economic Underpinnings of Prehispanic Zapotec Civilization: Small-Scale Production, Economic Interdependence, and Market Exchange. In *Agricultural Strategies*, edited by Joyce Marcus and Charles Stanish, pp. 255–280. Cotsen Institute of Archaeology, University of California, Los Angeles.

Feinman, Gary M., and Linda M. Nicholas. 2007. The Socioeconomic Organization of the Classic Period Zapotec State: A Bottom-Up Perspective from El Palmillo. In *The Political Economy of Ancient Mesoamerica: Transformations during the Formative and Classic Periods*, edited by Vernon L. Scarborough and John Clark, pp. 135–148. University of New Mexico Press, Albuquerque.

Fisher, C. T., Helen P. Pollard, Isabel Israde- Alcantara, Victor H. Garduno-Monroy, and Subir K. Banerjee. 2003. A Reexamination of Human-Induced Environmental Change within the Lake Patzcuaro Basin, Michoacan, Mexico. *Proceedings of the National Academy of Sciences* 100(8):4957–4962.

Flannery, Kent V., Anne V. T. Kirkby, Michael J. Kirkby, and Aubtry Williams Jr. 1967. Farming Systems and Political Growth in Ancient Oaxaca. *Science* 158:445–454.

Gill, R. B. 2000. *The Great Maya Drought*. University of New Mexico Press, Albuquerque.

Gunn, Joel, William J. Folan, and Hubert R. Robichaux. 1995. A Landscape Analysis of the Candelaria Watershed in Mexico: Insights into Paleoclimates Affecting Upland Horticulture in the Southern Yucatan Peninsular Semi-Karst. *Geoarchaeology* 10:3–42.

Haug, Gerald H., Detlef Gunther, Larry C. Peterson, Daniel M. Sigman, Konrad A. Hughen, and Beat Aeschlimann. 2003. Climate and the Collapse of Maya Civilization. *Science* 299:1731–1735.

Hodell, David A., Jason H. Curtis, and Mark Brenner. 1995. Possible Role of Climate in the Collapse of Classic Maya Civilization. *Nature* 375:391–394.

Hodell, David A., and Thomas Guilderson. 2001. Solar Forcing of Drought Frequency in the Maya Lowlands. *Science* 292:1367–1370.

Kirkby, Anne V. T. 1973. *The Use of Land and Water Resources in the Past and Present Valley of Oaxaca, Mexico.* Museum of Anthropology Memoir 5, University of Michigan, Ann Arbor.

Kowalewski, Stephen A. 2003. Scale and Explanation of Demographic Change: 3,500 Years in the Valley of Oaxaca. *American Anthropologist* 105:313–325.

Morrison, Kathleen D. 1994. The Intensification of Production: Archaeological Approaches. *Journal of Archaeological Method and Theory* 1(2):111–159.

Neely, James. 2001. A Contextual Study of the "Fossilized" Prehispanic Canal Systems of the Tehuacan Valley, Puebla, Mexico. *Antiquity* 75:505–506.

Nichols, Deborah L. 1987. Risk and Agricultural Intensification during the Formative Period in the Northern Basin of Mexico. *American Anthropologist* 89:596–616.

O'Hara, Sarah L., F. Alayne Street- Perrott, and Timothy P. Burt. 1993. Accelerated Soil Erosion around a Mexican Highland Lake Caused by Prehispanic Agriculture. *Nature* 362:48–51.

Sanders, William T., Jeffrey R. Parsons, and Robert S. Santley. 1979. *The Basin of Mexico: Ecological Processes in the Evolution of a Civilization.* Academic Press, New York.

Sanders, William T., and Barbara J. Price. 1968. *Mesoamerica: The Evolution of a Civilization.* Random House, New York.

Scarborough, Vernon L. 1983. A Preclassic Water System. *American Antiquity* 48(4):719–744.

Scarborough, Vernon L. 1993. Water Management in the Southern Maya Lowlands: An Accretive Model for the Engineered Landscape. In *Economic Aspects of Water Management in Prehispanic New World*, edited by V. L. Scarborough and B. L. Isaac, pp. 17–69. Research in Economic Anthropology, Supplement 7, JAI Press, Greenwich, Connecticut.

Scarborough, Vernon L. 1998. Ecology and Ritual: Water Management and the Maya. *Latin American Antiquity* 8(2):135–159.

Scarborough, Vernon L. 2000. Resilience, Resource Use, and Socioeconomic Organization: A Mesoamerican Pathway. In *Natural Disaster and the Archaeology of Human Response*, edited by Garth Bawden and Rick Reycraft, pp. 195–212. Maxwell Museum of Anthropology and the University of New Mexico Press, Albuquerque.

Scarborough, Vernon L. 2003a. *The Flow of Power: Ancient Water Systems and Landscapes.* School of American Research Press, Santa Fe.

Scarborough, Vernon L. 2003b. How to Interpret an Ancient Landscape. *Proceedings of the National Academy of Sciences* 100:4366–4368.

Scarborough, Vernon L. 2005. Landscapes of Power. In *A Catalyst for Ideas: Anthropological Archaeology and the Legacy of Douglas W. Schwartz*, edited by Vernon L. Scarborough, pp. 209–228. School of American Research Press, Santa Fe.

Scarborough, Vernon L. 2006. An Overview of Mesoamerican Water Systems. In *Precolumbian Water Management: Ideology, Ritual and Power*, edited by Barbara L. Fash and Lisa J. Lucero, pp. 223–236. University of Arizona Press, Tucson.

Scarborough, Vernon L. 2007. Colonizing a Landscape: Water and Wetlands in Ancient Mesoamerica. In *The Political Economy of Ancient Mesoamerica: Transformations during the Formative and Classic Periods*, edited by Vernon

L. Scarborough and John Clark, pp. 163–174. University of New Mexico Press, Albuquerque.

Scarborough, Vernon L. 2010. The Archaeology of Sustainability: Mesoamerica. *Ancient Mesoamerica* 20(2):197–203.

Scarborough, Vernon L., and William R. Burnside. 2010a. Complexity and Sustainability: Perspectives from the Ancient Maya and the Modern Balinese. *American Antiquity* 75(2):327–363.

Scarborough, Vernon L., and William R. Burnside. 2010b. Global Change: Mapping Culture onto Climate. In *Climate Crises in the Human Past*, edited by Claudio Vita-Finzi and Robert Giegengack, pp. 175–187. Transactions of the American Philosophical Society and Lightning Rod Press, volume 6.

Scarborough, Vernon L., and Gary Gallopin. 1991. A Water Storage Adaptation in the Maya Lowlands. *Science* 251:658–662.

Trigger, Bruce G. 2003. *Understanding Early Civilization: A Comparative Study.* Cambridge University Press, Cambridge.

Vita-Finzi, Claudio, and Robert Giegengack, eds. 2010. *Climate Crises in the Human Past.* Transactions of the American Philosophical Society and Lightning Rod Press, volume 6.

Weigand, Phil C. 1993. Large-Scale Hydraulic Works in Prehistoric Western Mesoamerica. In *Economic Aspects of Water Management in the Prehispanic New World*, edited by Vernon L. Scarborough, and Barry L. Isaac, pp. 223–262. Research in Economic Anthropology, Supplement 7, JAI Press, Greenwich, Connecticut.

Weigand, Phil C. 2007. States in Prehispanic Western Mesoamerica. In *The Political Economy of Ancient Mesoamerica: Transformations during the Formative and Classic Periods*, edited by Vernon L. Scarborough, and John Clark, pp. 101–114. University of New Mexico Press, Albuquerque.

Williams, Patrick Ryan. 2006. Agricultural Involution, Intensification, and Sociopolitical Development: The Case of Highland Irrigation Agriculture on the Pacific Ocean Watersheds. In *Agricultural Strategies*, edited by Joyce Marcus and Charles Stanish, pp. 309–333. Cotsen Institute of Archaeology, University of California, Los Angeles.

Woodbury, Richard B., and James A. Neely. 1972. Water Control Systems of the Tehuacan Valley. In *The Prehistory of the Tehuacán Valley, Vol. 4: Chronology and Irrigation*, edited by Frederick Johnson, pp. 81–154. University of Texas Press, Austin.

Yaeger, Jason, and David A. Hodell. 2008. The Collapse of Maya Civilization: Assessing the Interaction of Culture, Climate, and Environment. In *El Niño, Catastrophism, and Culture Change in Ancient America,* edited by Dan H. Sandweiss and Jeffery Quilter, pp. 187–242. Harvard University Press, Cambridge.

FURTHER READING

Erickson, Clark L. 2006. Intensification, Political Economy, and the Farming Community: In Defense of a Bottom-Up Perspective of the Past. In *Agricultural Strategies*, edited by J. Marcus and C. Stanish, pp. 334–363. Cotsen Institute of Archaeology, University of California, Los Angeles.

Fisher, Christopher T., J. Brett Hill, and Gary M. Feinman, eds. 2009. *The Archaeology of Environmental Change: Socionatural Legacies of Degradation and Resilience.* University of Arizona Press, Tucson.

Lucero, Lisa J., and Barbara W. Fash, eds. 2006. *Precolumbian Water Management: Ideology, Ritual and Power.* University of Arizona Press, Tucson.

Marcus, Joyce, and Charles Stanish, eds. 2006. *Agricultural Strategies.* Cotsen Institute of Archaeology, University of California, Los Angeles.

Netting, Robert. 1993. *Smallholders, Householder: Farm Families and the Ecology of Intensive Sustainable Agriculture.* Stanford University Press, Palo Alto, California.

Scarborough, Vernon L., ed. 2012. *Water and Humanity: A Historical Overview (History of Water and Civilization Book Series, Volume VII).* UNESCO, Paris.

Scarborough, Vernon L., and Barry L. Isaac, eds. 1993. Economic Aspects of Water Management in Prehispanic New World. Research in Economic Anthropology, Supplement 7, JAI Press, Greenwich, Connecticut.

Thurston, Tina L., and Christopher T. Fisher, eds. 2007. *Seeking a Richer Harvest: The Archaeology of Subsistence Intensification, Innovation and Change.* Springer, New York.

Whitmore, Thomas M., and B. L. Turner II. 2001. *Cultivated Landscapes of Middle America on the Eve of the Conquest.* Oxford University Press, Oxford.

CHAPTER 39

SEARCHING OUT PREHISPANIC LANDSCAPES IN MESOAMERICA BY MEANS OF AERIAL RECONNAISSANCE

ALFRED H. SIEMENS

AERIAL imagery in its various forms is prime material for the location and contextualization of ancient remains; it also contributes to an ample appreciation of the significance of *landscape*. It has been used in the investigation of many long-occupied Mesoamerican places, but not always systematically or explicitly. This chapter considers some lessons and possibilities but focuses on a disciplined application of aerial reconnaissance and the use of oblique air photos.

Small-plane reconnaissance was initially developed for military purposes. It was already used in World War I and then applied with striking results after World War II in the searching out of ancient landscapes in the British Isles (e.g., Frere and St. Joseph 1983). In 1929 Oliver Ricketson Jr. and A. V. Kidder of the Carnegie Institution undertook an extensive aerial search for ancient sites in the Maya region, piloted by none other than Charles A. Lindbergh (Ricketson and Kidder 1930). Their observations on optimal altitudes and light direction, on search techniques, particularly the selection of likely ecological niches, as well as the great

Figure 39.1 Comparison of vertical and oblique air photography.

potential of this way of seeing, are still quite plausible, and their oblique air photos are impressive. This discipline was not applied again in the region until the 1960s. There may well have been fortuitous sightings from the air, but deliberate reconnaissance is not apparent in the literature.

Vertical, as distinct from oblique, air photo coverage (Figure 39.1) was commercially available for considerable portions of Mesoamerican countries by the mid-1950s (Stone 1959). Vertical air photo coverage has been an ancillary resource in many archaeological investigations in subsequent decades: sometimes it is specified and sometimes only indicated. The images seem to serve mostly as surrogates or bases for maps. Good-quality vertical imagery from the Compañia Mexicana de Aerofoto, a highly appreciated repository until late in the 1980s, provided striking evidence for extensive prehispanic wetland agriculture in the Valley of Mexico (Armillas 1971). Vertical and oblique images from the same source contributed very effectively to the elucidation of ecological processes and the portrayal of the dramatic landscapes of the Basin of Mexico (Sanders et al. 1979). Aerial imagery contributed to the mapping of ancient occupation at Tres Zapotes (Pool and Ohnersorgen 2003: 7) and the Tuxtlas (Santley 2007: 5).

In recent years satellite imagery, which is mostly vertical, has provided highly useful small-scale imagery, using various wavelengths, for regional environmental contextualization of ancient landscapes and the detection of linear anthropogenic features (e.g., Sever and Irwin 2003). High-resolution IKONOS imagery is especially promising for archaeological research. And who can resist the access to satellite photography provided by Google Earth for entertainment or research planning?

We have long wished there were some way to penetrate forest cover by means of remote sensing. The work of Arlen and Diane Chase in Belize indicates that this is now possible by means of LIDAR (Light Detection and Ranging, i.e., imagery produced by a reflected laser beam; Wilford 2010). Sadly, forest cover is no longer the issue it once was in tropical areas; the grassland that has succeeded it over vast areas can be highly revealing under direct visual scrutiny.

OBJECTIVE

My purpose here is to outline procedures and constraints in the search for evidence of ancient landscapes in Mesoamerica by means of light plane reconnaissance at 1,000 to 3,000 feet above the surface by using the visible segment of the electromagnetic spectrum for the production of oblique photographs. Aerial photo reconnaissance along these lines complements controlled vertical air photography and remote sensing; it facilitates exploration, it can initiate or contextualize investigations, and it can suggest hypotheses. It often delivers surprises.

THE DISCIPLINE

It is important to distinguish the nature and yield of oblique versus vertical air imagery. The first of the three images compared in Figure 39.1 is a vertical air photograph with a scale of about 1:60,000 taken in 1976 over the town of Catemaco in Los Tuxtlas. The second is an oblique air photograph taken of the same town in 2002, showing not only a different kind of image but also the changes that occurred over time. The third shows the portion of the first that is included in the second. The vertical image is taken with a fixed camera in the fuselage of a plane and a perspective perpendicular to the landscape. Its scale is roughly the same overall, facilitating measurement and cartography. Direction and altitude are controlled as well as possible and the photos are taken at regular intervals with an overlap of something like 30 percent. These overlapping portions allow stereoscopy; the photos must be in hard copy and kept loose, to allow proper placement below the lenses in order to achieve an exaggerated third dimension, which is always instructive. This remains the basic resource for the preparation of flights of reconnaissance and the subsequent location of the oblique images obtained.

Oblique air photography during reconnaissance allows for an infinity of perspectives: the scale in the resulting images varies continuously from the bottom of the photograph to the top. They thus do not allow measurement or cartography directly; however, since the perspective is merely an exaggeration of the bipedal human view of surroundings they are more or less readable at first glance. The vertical photograph, in contrast, represents a fundamentally unfamiliar perspective and needs symbology, usually elaborate guides that indicate, for example, the normal meaning of particular tones.

The oblique image documents exploration: it is primary evidence that can place archaeological, historical, and paleoecological features in their natural and cultural landscapes. The manual transfer of data from oblique images to topographic coverage facilitates measurement and the making of analytical maps and landscape models.

Mosaics of black-and-white vertical air photography that have been reconciled to latitude and longitude are also available from agencies such as the Mexican Instituto Nacional de Estadística y Geografía (INEGI). They are useful for the location of features already georeferenced during reconnaissance by an onboard GPS.

The investigator, ideally seated at an open door, must control the whole process closely by radio headset; that is, he or she must signal the course and altitude and attitude as well as scan the landscape and do the photography—all of which makes for some intensive hours. It is most important to have a very competent pilot who understands the project and is willing to maneuver.

Climatically, flights during the dry season (i.e., from October to May) are optimal. At this time of year differences in vegetation due to variations in residual soil humidity obtrude; this facilitates, for example, the search for built-up and dried-out remains of ancient agricultural features in wetlands. One hopes to arrive between *nortes*, the periodic southward incursions of cold-air masses from North America during the dry season that bring wind and rain all around the Gulf of Mexico. The interstices are likely to have the clearest skies. One must not wait too long, however, because widespread burning starts just before the usual time of the onset of rains and shrouds the landscapes in gray. One may be able to take advantage of gaps in the rainy season, but on most days during this time, the skies become clouded and turbulent by midday.

Daily atmospheric variations must be taken into account. Flying between 10:00 AM and 2:00 PM will minimize shadows, but even under clear skies the colors are likely to be quite dull. Later in the afternoon colors become richer. It is useful to fly in circular patterns, searching for a perspective more or less against low incoming light, which maximizes shadows. At that moment even the slightest mounds become apparent. Such reconnaissance is likely to yield at an altitude around 1,000 feet above the surface of the landscape: at this height one can resolve detail quite well, penetrate the usual haze, and still freeze the landscape with a high shutter speed. The lower one flies the faster the landscape seems to move. Once the detail of a landscape has proved interesting at an altitude of about 1,000 feet it is useful to fly it all again at something like 3,000 feet, including the horizon and prominent features in the surroundings in order to aid the subsequent location of the close-ups. Repeated flights over a given area are advisable; what is obscured by the vagaries of natural vegetation or land use on one pass may well be revealed in the next.

Basic to any air reconnaissance, as Ricketson, Kidder, and Lindbergh soon found, is the selection of likely landscapes over which to concentrate the search. They were impeded by dense forest cover over most of the peninsula; they paid particular attention to the margins of bodies of water as likely locations of prominent ruins. We found that the upper slopes of the piedmont on the seaward margins of the Tuxtla Mountains yielded evidence of dozens of previously undetected ceremonial centers. The margins of many riverine wetlands in the lowlands that surround the Gulf of Mexico turned out to be patterned with the remains of raised fields. All this begs some issues regarding the concept of *landscape* that should be touched on before some yields of aerial searches are presented.

REGARDING *LANDSCAPE*

This word has various meanings. It can be taken to denote simply a material assemblage of physiographic features, including landforms, water bodies, and vegetation, as well as settlements, production facilities, and transportation infrastructure. These can be mapped, measured, subdivided, and indeed coded, as is common in landscape ecology, and thus made to serve land-use planning. Conditions such as overuse and processes such as erosion may be identified. Sustainable systems are likely to be the objective and reforestation will be one of the recommendations. This is decidedly not the way in which *landscape* is used here.

Human geographers tend to be less categorical and more flexible as to scale and demarcation. From a viewpoint or the open door of a light plane they are likely to view the material assemblage for signs of the passage of time, of cultural imprinting, of human versus natural agency. All this is affected by particular interests and sensibilities, as well as by the objectives of a given study. Such a view of landscape is obviously contingent and subjective, and the results may be considered as constructs. It is one thing to proceed thus with the landscape immediately in view: it is a challenge to tease similar nuances out of underlying landscapes suggested by remains.

Various metaphors can enrich a discussion of landscape and change. Investigations by whatever means may be seen in total as an excavation, which penetrates a stratigraphy, through one landscape into what lies beneath. The past is likely to be seen through the present, the logic of past and present landscapes is inevitably compared, and interrelationships may well become apparent. One may invoke the botanical metaphor of *succession*, which emphasizes the growth of one landscape out of another. The whole view out of the open door of a plane may be thought of as a text, written and overwritten, freighted with symbols by a succession of occupants (Barnes and Duncan 1992). Air photo interpretation, oblique or vertical, is indeed a *reading* of the landscape.

Broad currents have flowed back and forth in landscape interpretation. Human geographers used to distinguish quite clearly between natural and cultural landscapes: the untouched versus the imprinted. Then it became apparent that most landscapes were in fact anthropogenic to one degree or another: they were cultural landscapes; even the tropical forest was an artifact. Subsequent reflection and new data have led to the affirmation that there really are few pristine landscapes, which has strongly affected the interpretation of landscapes in the Americas before and after the coming of the Europeans (Denevan 1992).

The study of landscape change often takes place now within the convergence called *environmental history*—one or another of its synonyms serve equally well. There are numerous formulations of its basic imperative: to clarify the diachrony of the interplay between natural conditions and human agency, the study of "people and the land through time" (Russell 1997). It may well be, to follow one of its most influential practitioners, that the most important insight of environmental history has been the reappreciation of physical limitations, of ecological constraints (Worster 1998).

Much of all this has ethical roots and devolves on the causes of and responsibilities for dire conditions. In botanical literature on the Tuxtlas, for example, the
inhabitants are largely seen as disturbers or destroyers, the forest is being cut back,
species are disappearing, biodiversity is severely menaced: all ominous enough, of
course (González Soriano et al. 1997). It also remains true that traditional agriculturalists must make a living and that cattlemen will continue to try to accumulate
capital, as most of us strive to do as well. It may be preferable, therefore, to reconsider such a negative view of human agency and to speak of change rather than
destruction and thus maintain an equable discussion. It also helps to keep in mind
that in tropical lowlands at least deforestation has taken place more than once
before, with intervening reforestations.

It was encouraging to read in the introduction to a collection of essays, mostly
by archaeologists, that

> studies of ancient landscapes have matured into well-rounded inquiries
> regarding humanity's engagement with the environment. Whereas many
> remain centered on topics such as the distribution of settlements through a
> region, the modification of the environment for agricultural purposes, and
> large-scale water management projects, they are complemented by an array of
> newer studies focussed on ... "socio-symbolic aspects of human environment
> interaction." What unites these seemingly disparate perspectives is the concept
> that landscapes are formed by collective human activity and, as such, are
> culturally constructed. (Koontz et al. 2001, p. xxiii)

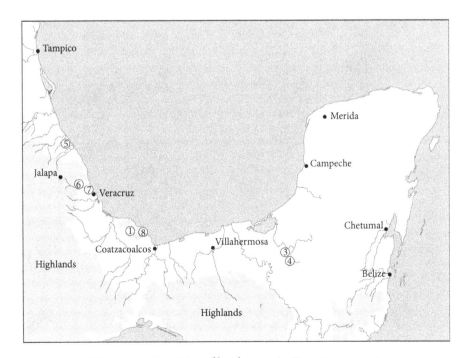

Figure 39.2 Location of landscapes in Figures 39.1–39.8.

CANDELARIA RIVER BASIN

My pursuit of prehistoric anthropogenic landscapes by means of aerial recon-naissance and its various related research methods began in the late 1960s along the Candelaria River of Campeche (e.g., Siemens and Puleston 1972; Siemens 1989). There had been predictions that evidence for intensive agriculture, per-haps something like the *chinampas* of central Mexico, would soon be found in the Maya lowlands. During air reconnaissance in 1968 rectilinear remains of what came to be called raised fields were recognized, together with webs of other lines, the remains of canals: these were all regular features among amorphous vegetation (Figure 39.3). The discussion of subsistence systems in the Maya region and other Mesoamerican lowlands could now be enlarged, as it was in a moveable feast of symposia at various academic meetings during the following years. The other lines (Figure 39.4) became controversial; from their geographical logic, from excavations and from historical documents it was apparent that some were prehistoric, others historic. Problems arose between commentators making blanket judgments and others attempting to make dis-tinctions. In any case, a vast waterborne transportation infrastructure became apparent.

Figure 39.3 Remains of raised fields in the Candelaria River basin: key evidence for
imputation of intensive agriculture to the ancient Maya.

Figure 39.4 A segment of the network of canal lines in the basin.

ESTERO DE TRES BOCAS

The clearest example of landscape superimposition or succession in my archive of
oblique air photographs comes from along the Estero de Tres Bocas, north of the city
of Veracruz (Figure 39.5; Siemens 1989). It is one of numerous such assemblages found
during reconnaissance over lowland northern Veracruz in the 1970s, few of which
have been studied in any detail. The mounds of the site of Santa Elena are visible
just in from the river and large complexes of canals and planting platforms, or raised
fields, presumably are associated with them. Over the site are now the facilities, pastures, and orchards of a sizable rancho, a landscape readable in contemporary terms.
Showing through from below is a landscape with another, but perhaps not such a different, logic. The first can be modeled as on the inset within Figure 39.5: (a) a zone on
the top of the levee, which is fairly secure except during catastrophic flooding, and is
suitable for building and horticulture; (b) the downslope of the levee, with remains
of canalization, possibly to accelerate drainage and provide early access to agricultural land in the interstices; (c) a cross-canalized margin of the wetland, subject to
benign yearly flooding, to be considered as an area of raised fields; and (d) a swamp
in which water is close to the surface even in the dry season, draining eventually into
the main stream near its mouth. It can be hypothesized on the basis of a great deal
of evidence out of wetlands throughout Mesoamerica that in the course of a year
agriculture would migrate downslope as the waters receded and back up again with
the coming of the rains. It has proved sensible to consider raised-field agriculture in
the Gulf lowlands as largely an adaptation for the use of wetland margins subject to
annual flooding and to model the nature and use of this niche in those terms. There

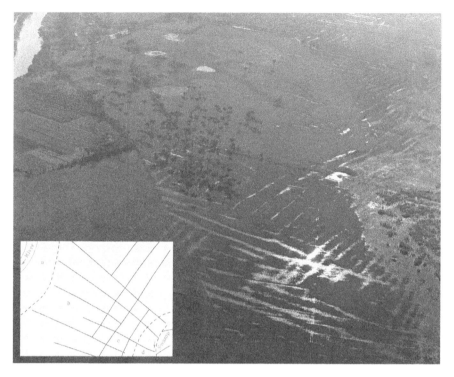

Figure 39.5 A contemporary ranching landscape in Northern Veracruz with the prehispanic site of Santa Elena and profuse canalization showing through it. The inset provides a heuristic model of linked microenvironments and land use.

are also indications that over longer periods the entire system moved downslope with intensification of use consequent on drying (Siemens 2004).

The modern inhabitants seek the highest ground for their dwellings, horticulture, and ranch installations. Pasturage moves downslope with the recession of the water and then move back up again with the *cresciente*, the seasonal flood in the vernacular of the region. The fences seen in the image seem to allow sequential access. A seasonal movement of cattle up and down slope has historically been a standard feature of extensive ranching in coastal Veracruz (Siemens 1998). The rancher responds to the rhythm of the landscape as did the ancient agriculturalist.

STONE LINES OR TERRACES, OR *METLEPANTLI*, ON GENTLY SLOPING PIEDMONT

An observer's readiness for signs of the prehistoric, even over areas that are not the immediate objective, can pay off remarkably. On the way between an airport and a wetland on one occasion, patterning became apparent on the gently sloping piedmont

Figure 39.6 Windows on a distant past.

just northwest of the city of Veracruz. It was toward the end of the dry season, and some rain had fallen, darkening the soil: farmers had begun to cultivate with the heavy tractor-drawn ploughs common to this region of stony soils (Figure 39.6). Unknowingly they had opened windows onto a distant past (Sluyter and Siemens 1992).

Ground reconnaissance and test excavations indicated that what showed light on a dark background were concentrations of stones in lines and rounded mounds, the latter with some ceramics interspersed. We were able to find numerous instances over hundreds of square kilometers over an area of semiarid piedmont with generally stony soils. In some cases numerous house mounds and lines among them that appeared to be boundary markers or walkways revealed whole communities—these are good beginnings on site maps should anyone be interested. More important to us, as it happens, were the webs of lines generally perpendicular to slopes; they could be deduced to have served soil and moisture conservation. We have since found freshly built stone lines for similar purposes in upland Mexico; they have been called metlepantli and in some locations have been found to date well back into prehispanic times (West 1970). Moreover, such complexes of stone lines, perhaps to be thought of as terrace retaining walls, were shown to be in close proximity to canalization in aid of raised fields in wetland margins. The first would be a means of dealing with land dependent on seasonal rains; the stones in the soil themselves would help to conserve moisture and the stone lines would be a means of harvesting rainfall, thus facilitating cultivation during the wetter part of the year. The second would allow cultivation of land subject to seasonal inundation and exposed during the dry season. The two were apparently very advantageously interdigitated elements in regional land-management strategies of prehistoric inhabitants. Aerial reconnaissance allowed the apprehension of fleeting evidence, which nevertheless suggested a robust hypothesis.

A Benign Flood

In July 1993, after the beginning of a wet season, it was possible to view the San Juan/La Antigua river basin in central Veracruz from the air during a seasonal flood (Figure 39.7; Siemens 1998). Flooding is part of the region's annual environmental rhythm; it is not terribly destructive, and moreover it brings various benefits to the land such as the elimination of weeds and pests and the introduction of films of new sediments. A seasonal flood is in fact a short fallow.

For just a few days a lake that is a shrunken affair at the bottom of the basin during the height of the dry season reasserted itself. Numerous extensive complexes of raised fields had already been found and mapped in the basin; a major portion of the remains were flooded, indicating that this will probably have been a hazard or a benefit that needed to be figured into any reconstruction of the function of that earlier intensive agriculture and related settlement. Currently such floods do not last more than a few days; cattlemen have cut many drainage canals in order to bring down the water level as soon as possible and thus hasten the entry of their animals into the reinvigorated pastures. It may be deduced that the canalization in aid of raised fields would have served a similar purpose, particularly as in segment b of the model shown in Figure 39.5.

The Mexican governmental agency in charge of river-basin development, Recursos Hidraulicos, intervened in this area in the late 1940s and early 1950s to straighten and deepen the San Juan/La Antigua river and thus drain this whole wetland and secure the land for commercial agriculture and modernized ranching. The canalized course

Figure 39.7 Flooding in the San Juan/La Antigua river basin in 1993, illustrating various aspects of the seasonal rhythm of this landscape and allowing deductions about ancient land use.

intended for the river now threads through the landscape as a great embarrassing ruin. It never achieved its purpose; the proposed outlet to the sea turned out not to be deep enough and many other aspects of the project were ill-considered as well.

Fingers of sedimentary formations reach down into the basin from the west, on the left of the photograph. Their outliers form "islands" within the flooded lowlands, which are places of refuge for cattle. In the corrals one can find numerous ceramics underfoot, an indication of a similar function for human occupants in the distant past. Interrelationships between successive or superimposed landscapes help in the interpretations of what appears before the open door of a light plane on a given day.

An Archaeological "Empty Quarter"

Early in a collaborative investigation of the Tuxtlas at the Institute of Ecology in Xalapa, several intriguing mound groups were noted in pastures on the coastal piedmont, an area that had been of little interest to archaeologists

Figure 39.8 One of the many largely unstudied ceremonial centers on the coastal piedmont of the Los Tuxtlas mountains. The inset shows the typical location in relation to topography, stream network, and the coast.

(Figure 39.8; Siemens 2002). The piedmont was largely forested until the mid-
twentieth century and then there were new settlers in various legal contexts.
Landscapes of pasturage replaced the forest, which is worrisome ecologically, of course. I decided to take the deforestation as a given and concentrate
on what was apparent of earlier landscapes once this carpet was lifted. On
repeated flights, with many circular searches, it was possible to hone the discipline and identify numerous ceremonial centers, most of which have not
been studied. (The term "ceremonial center" is used tentatively here, without
prejudgment as to other functions that these concentrations of monumental
structures may have had.)

    Careful analysis of vertical air photo coverage and 1:50,000 topographic map
coverage, before and after each flight, together with onboard GPS, allowed the
preparation of the map shown in Figure 39.9. A landscape model was generated,
and hypotheses are currently under consideration regarding site morphology. A
string of wetlands just behind the coast were also included in our purview, some
of which show hints of patterning and canalization. All of this suggests research
possibilities and promises to add a good deal to the prehistory of the region; the
"empty quarter" is not as empty as it had seemed.

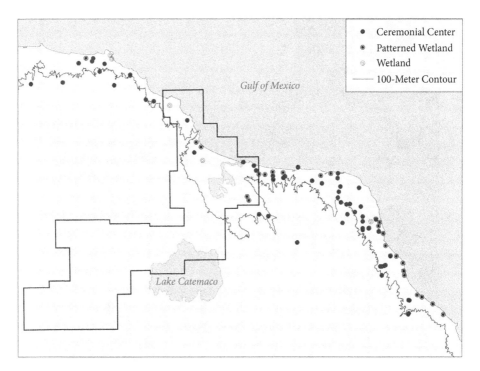

Figure 39.9 Georeferenced remains found during our reconnaissance and the study
area on which Santley based *The Prehistory of the Tuxtlas* (2007).

SUMMARY

An ample range of aerial imagery is now available for the investigation of ancient anthropogenic landscapes, including vertical air photo coverage at various scales and small-scale satellite imagery, especially the high-resolution IKONOS and the vegetation-penetrating LIDAR. The objective here has been to outline a way of taking full advantage of the straightforwardly visible portion of the spectrum through aerial reconnaissance and large-scale oblique photography. Such reconnaissance is not a "point-and-shoot" exercise but rather a discipline that requires extensive preparation, including the analysis of vertical air and topographic coverage, attention to atmospheric conditions, close onboard control of the parameters of flight, and also a readiness to improvise on the basis of in-flight realizations, as well as georeferencing before, during, and after flight. The higher the quality of photographic equipment and the simpler the in-cabin procedure, the better, of course, the research results will be. Meanwhile, it helps to think of the landscape below not only as an intriguing array of physical and cultural features but as a product of the interaction of "people and the land through time" (Russell 1997). Aerial reconnaissance uniquely facilitates exploration; it has initiated a series of investigations in Mesoamerica and can provide convincing illustrations.

ACKNOWLEDGMENTS

My deep appreciation goes to the many pilots who have flown for me over the years, particularly the pilots of LIGHTHAWK, a voluntary American organization of pilots who fly single-engine wing-overhead planes, such as the Cessna 206, in aid of ecological projects. My sincere thanks must go to the Institute of Ecology in Jalapa, Veracruz, especially to its ex-director, Dr. Sergio Guevara Sada, for the invitation to participate in a multidisciplinary collaborative study of the volcanic "island" of the Tuxtlas, and in particular to pursue the environmental history of this region by means of aerial reconnaissance (Siemens 2010).

REFERENCES

Armillas, Pedro. 1971. Gardens on Swamps. *Science* 174 (4010):653–661.
Barnes, Trevor J., and James S. Duncan, eds. 1992. *Writing Worlds*. Routledge, London.
Denevan, William M. 1992. The Pristine Myth: The Landscape of the Americas in 1492. *Annals of the Association of American Geographers* 82:369–385.
Frere, S. S., and J. K. S. St. Joseph. 1983. *Roman Britain from the Air*. Cambridge University Press, Cambridge.

González Soriano, Enrique, Rodolfo Dirzo, and Richard C. Vogt. 1997. *Historia natural de Los Tuxtlas*. Universidad Nacional Autónoma de México, México, D.F.

Koontz, Rex, Kathryn Reese-Taylor, and Annabeth Headrick. 2001. *Landscape and Power in Ancient Mesoamerica*. Westview, Boulder.

Pool, Christopher A., and Michael A. Ohnersorgen. 2003. Archaeological Survey and Settlement at Tres Zapotes. In *Settlement Archaeology and Political Economy at Tres Zapotes*, edited by Christopher A. Pool, pp. 7–31. Cotsen Institute of Archaeology Monograph 50, University of California, Los Angeles.

Ricketson Jr., Oliver, and A. V. Kidder. 1930. An Archaeological Reconnaissance by Air in Central America. *Geographical Review* XX(2):177–206.

Russell, Emily W. B. 1997. *People and the Land through Time: Linking Ecology and History*. Yale University Press, New Haven.

Sanders, William T., Jeffrey R. Parsons, and Robert S. Santley. 1979. *The Basin of Mexico: Ecological Processes in the Evolution of a Civilization*. Academic Press, New York.

Santley, Robert S. 2007. *The Prehistory of the Tuxtlas*. University of New Mexico Press, Albuquerque.

Sever, Thomas L. and Daniel E. Erwin. 2003. Landscape Archaeology: Remote Sensing Investigation of the Ancient Maya in the Peten Rainforest of Northern Guatemala. *Ancient Mesoamerica*, 14:113–122.

Siemens, Alfred H. 1989. *Tierra configurada*. Consejo Nacional para la Cultura y las Artes, México, D.F.

Siemens, Alfred H. 1998. *A Favored Place: San Juan River Wetlands, Central Veracruz, AD 500 to the Present*. University of Texas Press, Austin.

Siemens, Alfred H. 2002. El "Rub al-Kahli" prehispánico de Los Tuxtlas: Una interpretacón del paisaje. In *Estudios sobre historia y ambiente en América II*, edited by Bernardo García Martínez and María del Rosario Prieto, pp. 161–202. El Colégio de México, México, D.F.

Siemens, Alfred H. 2004. Modelling the Tropical Wetland Landscape and Adaptations. *Agriculture and Human Values* 21:243–253.

Siemens, Alfred H. 2010. *Una manera de ver: Los Tuxtlas*. CONABIO, México, D.F.

Siemens, Alfred H. and Dennis E. Puleston. 1972. Ridged Fields and Associated Features in Southern Campeche: New Perspectives on the Lowland Maya. *American Antiquity* 37:228–239.

Sluyter, Andrew, and Alfred H. Siemens. 1992. Vestiges of Prehispanic, Sloping-Field Terraces on the Piedmont of Central Veracruz, Mexico. *Latin American Antiquity* 3:148–160.

Stone, Kirk H. 1959. World Air Photo Coverage. *Professional Geographer* 11:2–6.

West, Robert C. 1970. Population Densities and Agricultural Practices in Pre-Columbian Mexico, with Emphasis on Semi-Terracing. *Proceedings of the XXXVIII International Congress of Americanists* 2:361–369.

Wilford, John Noble. 2010. Mapping Ancient Civilization, in a Matter of Days. *New York Times*, May 10.

Worster, Donald, ed. 1988. *The Ends of the Earth*. Cambridge University Press, Cambridge.

CHAPTER 40

....

ECOLOGICAL APPROACHES TO ARCHAEOLOGICAL RESEARCH IN CENTRAL MEXICO

NEW DIRECTIONS

....

EMILY MCCLUNG DE TAPIA

ECOLOGICAL thinking applied to archaeological problems has evolved considerably over the past two decades, and this contribution seeks to examine some of the perspectives that have developed in Mesoamerican archaeology and what the future may hold. Ecological approaches to the study of prehispanic cultural evolution in this region are most frequently associated with the "cultural ecological" concepts developed largely by W. T. Sanders's (1965; Sanders and Price 1968), colleagues and students. Much of this research focused on agricultural systems and their potential productivity, often relying on modern environmental characteristics and production regimes to envision prehispanic conditions (e.g., Sanders et al. 1970, 1979). Other approaches carried out under the direction of MacNeish (1967, 1972) and Flannery (1986), in the Tehuacán Valley, Puebla, and the central valleys of Oaxaca looked more explicitly at the natural environment and the potential resources available, particularly but not exclusively to archaic and early Formative communities, considering wild and cultivated plant resources together with fauna preserved in the archaeological record, and the potential spatial distribution and availability of these resources in the surrounding landscape. Lorenzo (1968; Lorenzo and Mirambell 1986) gave some attention to paleoenvironmental conditions, particularly related to the movement of human populations into North America following the Late Glacial Maximum, from the end of the Pleistocene and transition to the Holocene, in relation to evidence for early human occupations in central Mexico.

While it is beyond the scope of this discussion to refer to the numerous frameworks within which human cultural evolution has been examined through the lens of environmental adaptation, it is apparent that the literature reflects a relative lack of interest on the part of Mexican scholars in general. In contrast, North American colleagues have dominated this line of research. The reasons for this tendency are strongly related to the history of archaeology as a discipline in both North America and Mexico, and the outright rejection of environmental research as deterministic (Lorenzo 1988, 1991) has had an impact as well.

Much of the archaeological investigation during the second half of the twentieth century by research groups under North American leadership placed varying degrees of emphasis on the environment itself or on human exploitation of specific resources within an implicit ecosystemic or equilibrium-based conceptual model (e.g., Flannery 1968, 1972). Mexican archaeologists were more influenced by a prehistory approach in which generalized paleoenvironmental conditions, territorial expansion, and toolkits were emphasized with little concern for the organization of human groups. Niederberger's work in the southeastern Basin of Mexico (1976, 1979), which bridged the prehistory emphasis with an anthropological view of human cultural evolution, is an important exception to this tendency. Sugiura's (2005) archaeological survey of the Upper Lerma Basin (Toluca Valley) together with her recent emphasis on lacustrine habitats in the region were strongly influenced by Sanders's and Parsons's experiences in the Basin of Mexico (Sugiura 2009). However, in this case paleoenvironmental analyses were systematically incorporated into the research (Caballero-Miranda et al. 2002), together with historical information and ethnoarchaeological studies of contemporary regional adaptations to the lake system, providing elements for the integration of the archaeological record with local environmental and cultural processes.

Two significant developments have emerged in recent decades in response to many of the difficulties associated with ecologically oriented research problems, whether they are placed in a framework of cultural ecology (Sanders 1965, 1981; Sanders and Price 1968; Sanders et al. 1979), ecosystemic approaches (Moran 2000, 2010), human ecology, or other schemes. One reflects a movement away from equilibrium models in ecology toward nonlinear dynamic models of systems and interactions among variables within the system (Pickett et al. 1994; Scoones 1999; Zimmerer 1994). The other refers to the various ways in which this paradigm shift has played out in anthropology and archaeology. New approaches to the study of human-natural relations include the emphasis on complex adaptive systems within the framework of resilience theory (Fisher 2005; Levin 1998; Redman and Kinzig 2003) and what has been called historical ecology (Crumley 1994, 2007; Balée 2006), which also incorporates some of the fundamental concepts associated with dynamic systems in ecology. Neither of these perspectives has had a significant impact in Mesoamerican archaeology as yet. However, they provide useful tools for visualizing complex relationships in historical perspective, based on local and regional developments. Other areas that have contributed to a better understanding of the complex relationships among human groups and their environments include environmental history (Endfield 2007) and landscape history (Crumley 1994). World-systems approaches (Hornberg and Crumley 2007) have also developed in an attempt to bridge the divide between scientific disciplines to develop a true interdisciplinary approach to contemporary human-environmental problems.

A major difficulty for anthropological and, particularly, archaeological research is sorting out the overlapping tendencies shared by many of these approaches, and recognizing important differences. On occasion, the tendency toward overstatement by some practitioners is even belligerent and leaves scholars floundering for the correct path in the maze of differing perspectives. Bennett (1976) discussed this problem decades ago, but, if anything, the problem has intensified. The proliferation of terms is confusing and counterproductive for the most part. I suspect that some degree of convergence is in the air, at least insofar as world-systems and resilience-theory approaches are concerned, and these perspectives have the potential to offer important tools for Mesoamerican archaeology.

Looking at prehispanic cultural development in the Central Highlands of Mexico in terms of the operation of complex adaptive systems and the concept of resilience, applied to both societies and the natural environment, offers a fresh perspective, while at the same time providing a useful framework within which to develop a clearer understanding of the interactions among human communities and the landscape. The traditional ecosystemic approach (cf. McClung de Tapia 2005) generally stagnates at the stage of a functionalist description of the interactions among several measurable or at least observable variables. McGlade (1995) criticized the mechanical causality of ecological approaches in archaeology based on traditional systems theory, in which the assumption of a fundamental difference between human and ecological spheres led to the view that humans were somehow placed onto the natural environment and that their activities inevitably provoked a disturbance of the equilibrium that was assumed to have existed prior to their presence. This ultimately led to the perception that any modification of the equilibrium provoked by disturbance (such as deforestation, for example) was considered pathological. He proposed instead that environments modified by human action were the result of coevolutionary processes characterized by a complex series of social and cultural interdependencies operating within a dynamic self-organizing system—what Walker et al. (2004) term a socioecological system. Additional considerations by McGlade in his critique of environmental approaches in archaeology included the dependence on natural science models, resulting in the

acquisition of knowledge through fragmented observations by different specialists
to be compiled later into a synthetic reconstruction; the emphasis on equilibrium
and its implications; and the emphasis on rational human behavior at the expense
of perception, cognition, and action.

Resilience is commonly viewed as the capacity of a system to continue operating in the face of stress and to recuperate following perturbation. Continuing
along this line, Walker and colleagues (2004) proposed that the dynamic processes
through which human groups interact with the environment emerge through the
attributes of *resilience, adaptability*, and *transformability*. Assuming that a system
exhibits multiple stable states rather than a single optimal equilibrium, resilience
refers to the capacity of the system to absorb perturbations and reorganize as it
experiments change. Its components include *latitude*, the degree of change a system
can sustain before losing the capacity to recover; *resistance*, the degree of difficulty
or facility with which the system may change; and *precariousness*, or the degree
of proximity to the threshold, or limit before the system will change. Adaptability
refers to the capacity of actors within the system to influence or manipulate resilience, whereas transformability indicates the capacity to create a fundamentally
new system when changes in ecological, social, or economic structures render
the system unviable. The true challenge is to identify real transformations from
what are essentially new situations within the range of configurations a system
can manifest. One might question how such frameworks offer new or different
perspectives beyond the neofunctionalist approach offered by earlier attempts to
understand the interaction between interrelated variables and their relationship to
cultural complexity (McClung de Tapia 1984). Adaptation and adaptability (Kirch
1980) take on new significance in this framework; it is possible to go beyond the
simplistic appraisal that survival and continued sociocultural evolution of human
communities imply that they are adapted to their environmental conditions,
whereas their demise somehow implies "unadaptedness." Adaptability thus refers
to a range of potential responses that may be invoked in the face of internal and
external stressors. The emphasis then is placed on ranges of variability and flexibility of responses.

In Mesoamerican archaeology, studies of cultural adaptation to environmental conditions have largely dealt with the development and intensification of agricultural systems (e.g., Sanders et al. 1979) and the observed limitations imposed
by local environmental conditions such as temperature and precipitation regimes,
available hydrological resources, soil quality, and various kinds of risks (frequency
of frosts, drought, atypical precipitation, for example). However, much of this
research depended on detailed ethnographic knowledge of modern or fairly recent
conditions and technologies practiced in the specific region of interest, projected
into the past with the help of historical documents that relate broadly similar practices employed in prior times. The archaeological record rarely documents specific agricultural practices further back in the past than a few centuries before
the early sixteenth-century conquest; direct evidence from earlier periods is frequently altered beyond recognition by more recent practices. Considerable effort

has been invested in calculating agricultural potential or the carrying capacity of specific regions, based on essentially modern productivity, and much of this effort has been directed toward exploring how a preindustrial city the size and density of Teotihuacan (1–650 D.C.) could have sustained an urban population of approximately 100,000 or more inhabitants, not to mention those residents in surrounding rural communities. Recent research in the Teotihuacan Valley (McClung de Tapia et al. 2005), the Texcoco region (Córdova 1997; Córdova and Parsons 1997), and the southeastern Basin of Mexico (Frederick 1997; Hodge et al. 1996) indicates that modern landscapes in these regions are significantly different from their predecessors, as a consequence of the interplay between natural phenomena and the impact of prehispanic as well as colonial and modern land use. The presence of buried soils associated with prehispanic occupations, for example, in the Teotihuacan region (Rivera et al. 2007; Solleiro et al. 2010), indicates that different agricultural conditions were available for earlier populations in at least some areas. The evidence for settlements and architectural remains that is buried under several meters of redeposited sediments detected in some parts of the Basin of Mexico (Córdova 1997; Cabrera Castro 2005) point to the need for more sophisticated methodological and technical approaches toward the understanding of prehispanic adaptation in many sectors of the region. And yet, in spite of potentially more productive soils in part of the Teotihuacan region, urban expansion in the second and third centuries AD led to the removal of at least some irrigated lands from agricultural production (Nichols 1987; Nichols et al. 1991). Furthermore, archaeological evidence suggests that the high-water-table area southwest of the prehispanic city may not have been intensively developed as a productive agricultural area until at least the Late Postclassic and, probably, the Colonial period (Gonzalez-Quintero and Sánchez-Sánchez 1991; Gazzola 2009). Thus, a reevaluation of environmental conditions, agricultural practices, and human adaptation in this area, which has already been the subject of decades of research, is in order. Recent evidence contests the view that Teotihuacan could have sustained its maximum population based on intensive exploitation of a relatively circumscribed adjacent area (Sanders et al. 1976, 1979), while at the same time it suggests that some sectors of the region may have been considerably more productive than the modern soils on which the carrying capacity figures are based (cf. Charlton 1970; Lorenzo 1968).

It is not clear that estimates of the carrying capacity of agricultural systems offer a meaningful way to understand how prehispanic populations adapted to changing environmental conditions. New evidence suggests that human modification of the environment together with the impact of occasional natural disasters (such as floods, tectonic events, volcanic eruptions, and droughts) necessitated more flexible, variable adaptive options on the part of local populations.

Mesoamerican archaeologists generally view prehispanic state-based societies as tightly structured with hierarchical class-based social organization locked into a rigid top-down system. However, outside of scant documentary evidence for a limited number of cases in the pre-conquest/Colonial transition period, we really know little about earlier Mesoamerican social and political organization in the

Central Highlands and how it operated at different levels. While the most com-monly cited examples of societies thought to have overreached the carrying capac-ity of their sustaining areas usually emphasize the Maya lowlands, the collapse of the Teotihuacan state has also been associated with environmental degrada-tion (Sanders 1981). However, Tainter (2006) argued that none of the most recur-rently cited examples of overshoot (of carrying-capacity overload), including the Maya lowlands, really represent an overextension of the landscape's capacity to sustain human population as a consequence of population growth, but rather were affected by external pressures such as drought, for example, that exacerbated sys-tems in a precarious state. Similarly, although Manzanilla (1997) suggested that Teotihuacan may have been affected by drought at the time of its collapse, there is no clear evidence in the regional archaeological or paleoenvironmental record at this time. Caballero and colleagues (2002) found indications for decreased humid-ity in the Upper Lerma Basin that corresponded to the seventh and eighth centu-ries. Lachniet and colleagues (2012) report similar conditions from the Juxtlahuaca cave in Guerrero during the seventh and eighth centuries as well, and the droughts cited in southeast Mexico (Hodell et al. 2005) are associated with the eighth cen-tury. While available evidence currently does not support the hypothesis that urban centers in the Basin of Mexico, such as Teotihuacan, experienced overshoot, much research remains to be directed to these problems of correlation and causa-tion (e.g., Sandweiss and Quilter 2008).

CONCLUSION

As Redman and colleagues (2009) have emphasized, once the "balance of nature" concept is rejected, ecologists are inclined to view ecosystem stability and change as the consequence of the intersection between persistent ecological processes and contingent historical events, which can include human action. The relationships of dynamic human components of ecosystems to the environmental components are recursive. However, evidence increasingly demonstrates that humans altered and, occasionally, degraded their environments over millennia (Redman 1999), and a number of Mesoamerican archaeologists now reject the notion that indigenous peoples always lived in harmony with nature. However, this perspective has yet to take root among others. While human modification of the environment may stabilize the ecosystems affected, when social or economic structures that sustain them collapse, drastic consequences ensue for both humans and the ecosystems in question.

Recent developments in ecology and the study of socionatural systems offer new perspectives for archaeological research. For example, looking rather at demise and adaptation instead of what is traditionally viewed as collapse and abandonment allows archaeologists to consider how human populations have confronted changing circumstances. From the perspective of the landscape, how does this play out in terms of variability in disturbance regimes? In the study of socioecological systems, it necessarily represents a qualitative approach in which the components and scales of complex adaptive systems can be identified and conceptualized and their interactions delineated (Walker et al. 2004).

Recognition of the relevance of archaeology for the current and future understanding of environmental and climate change impacts, the adaptability of human groups, and the adaptability of human-natural landscapes is emerging. Redman (2005) and Redman and Kinzig (2003) stress the significant role of archaeology, which offers a unique long-term historical perspective (*longue durée*) of human cultural development and responses to diverse stressors. Considering human societies as socioecological systems also facilitates the integration of paleoethnobotanical and faunal studies as well as evidence for past soils, all of which provide evidence for the relationship between human communities and their environments. The knowledge of biological resources available to past societies also contributes to conservation and restoration efforts in the present (Hayashida 2005).

However, there are important limitations in operationalizing this view. The archaeological record is partial and archaeologists' ability to interpret such evidence requires constant refinements in theoretical, methodological, and technical skills as well as interdisciplinary collaboration. Qualitative interpretations are often necessary because the resolution of the archaeological record is inadequate for meaningful quantitative approaches to certain questions.

Dearing and colleagues (2006; Dearing 2007) argue for the need to treat humans in past natural systems explicitly as actors, rather than as stressors. This focus requires a more ambitious integration to reconstruct what these researchers have called "parallel histories." They propose an emphasis on narratives, scenarios, and parallel histories because quantitative analytical methods are not always applicable in historical contexts, especially prehistoric contexts. The upshot of this perspective is the use of dynamic simulations of human-environmental interactions to detect emergent phenomena arising from microscale interactions. At the same time, Oldfield (2007) has emphasized the need for cultural and social scientists to place their work into a firm theoretical framework.

Two perspectives should be considered. The first is the role of human actors as agents (historical ecology) and the second is the view of the landscape as an ecological/natural system (landscape history). While it is clear that landscapes are perceived and used differently in historical time, I would argue that they can be viewed as systems in which human actors are (1) a biological species that interacts with others and with the abiotic components of ecosystems, and (2) bearers of cultural knowledge, values, and goals that drive their behavior. Thus the ecological components of the landscape are themselves variables in dynamic relationships with each other at different scales, subject to various degrees of disturbance.

Focusing on how human societies reorganized to adapt to changing environmental circumstances, rather than emphasizing system collapse and abandonment, represents a positive approach in which emergent behaviors can be examined. However, caution is in order because, in its extreme form, this view runs the risk of ignoring the evidence for overexploitation and poor or inadequate management of resources when it did occur.

What do world-systems and resilience approaches and other recent ecological orientations have in common? They converge in the concept of complex adaptive systems based on a modern-systems framework in which nonlinearity of processes, multiple stable states (nonequilibrium conditions), self-organization, and unpredictability (surprise) are the norms rather than a linear succession leading to an optimal climax or stable state. Initial conditions are of fundamental importance because the legacy of past changes will influence the direction that new processes and developments have taken or can take in the future (Dearing et al. 2006: 116).

REFERENCES

Balée, William. 2006. The Research Program of Historical Ecology. *Annual Review of Anthropology* 35:75–98.

Bennett, John W. 1976. *The Ecological Transition: Cultural Anthropology and Human Adaptation.* Pergamon, New York.

Caballero-Miranda, M. E., B. Ortega, F. Valadez, S. Metcalfe, J. L. Macías, and Y. Sugiura. 2002. Sta Cruz Atizapan: A 22 ka Lake Level Record and Climatic Applications for the Late Holocene Human Occupation in the Upper Lerma Basin, Central Mexico. *Palaeogeography, Palaeoclimatology, Palaeoecology* 186:217–235.

Cabrera-Castro, Ruben. 2005. Nuevas evidencias arqueológicas del manejo de agua en Teotihuacan. El Campo y la Ciudad. In *Arquitectura y Urbanismo: Pasado y Presente de los Espacios en Teotihuacan. Memoria de la Tercera Mesa Redonda de Teotihuacan*, edited by Maria Elena Ruiz-Gallut and Jesús Torres-Peralta, pp. 121–161. Instituto Nacional de Antropologia e Historia, Mexico.

Charlton, Thomas H. 1970. Contemporary Agriculture of the Valley. In *The Natural Environment, Contemporary Occupation and 16th Century Population of the Valley. The Teotihuacan Valley Project. Final Report. Volume 1*, edited by William T. Sanders, Anton Kovar, Thomas Charlton, and Richard A. Diehl, pp. 253–384. Occasional Papers in Anthropology. No. 3, Department of Anthropology, Pennsylvania State University, University Park.

Córdova, Carlos E. 1997. Landscape Transformation in Aztec and Spanish Colonial Texcoco, Mexico. PhD dissertation, Department of Geography, University of Texas, Austin.

Córdova, Carlos E., and Jeffrey R. Parsons. 1997. Geoarchaeology of an Aztec Dispersed Village on the Texcoco Piedmont of Central Mexico. *Geoarchaeology* 12(3):177–210.

Crumley, Carole L., ed. 1994. *Historical Ecology: Cultural Knowledge and Changing Landscapes.* School of American Research, Santa Fe.

Crumley, Carole L. 2007. Historical Ecology: Integrated Thinking at Multiple Temporal and Spatial Scales. In *The World System and the Earth System*, edited by Alf

Hornborg and Carole L. Crumley, pp. 15–28. Left Coast Press, Walnut Creek, California.

Dearing, John A. 2007. Integration of World and Earth Systems: Heritage and Foresight. In *The World System and the Earth System,* edited by Alf Hornborg and C. L. Carol Crumley, pp. 38–55. Left Coast Press, Walnut Creek, California.

Dearing, John A., Richard W. Battarbee, Ruth Dickau, Isabelle Larocque, and Frank Oldfield. 2006. Human-Environment Interactions: Towards Synthesis and Simulation. *Journal of Regional Environmental Change* 6:115–123.

Endfield, Georgina H. 2007. Archival Explorations of Climate Variability and Social Vulnerability in Colonial Mexico. *Climatic Change* 83:9–38.

Fisher, Christopher T. 2005. Demographic and Landscape Change in the Lake Patzcuaro Basin, Mexico: Abandoning the Garden. *American Anthropologist* 107:87–95.

Flannery, Kent V. 1968. Archaeological Systems Theory and Early Mesoamerica. In *Anthropological Archaeology in the Americas,* edited by B. J. Meggers, pp. 196–222. Anthropological Society of Washington, Washington, DC.

Flannery, Kent V. 1972. The Cultural Evolution of Civilization, *Annual Review of Ecology and Systematics* 3:339–426.

Flannery, Kent V. 1986. Empirical Determination of Site Catchments in Oaxaca and Tehuacán. In *The Early Mesoamerican Village,* edited by K. V. Flannery, pp. 103–117. Academic Press, New York.

Frederick, Charles D. 1997. Landscape Change and Human Settlement in the Southeastern Basin of Mexico. Manuscript on file, Department of Archaeology and Prehistory, University of Sheffield, Sheffield, United Kingdom.

Gazzola, Julie. 2009. Una propuesta sobre el proceso, factores y condiciones del colapso de Teotihuacan. *Revista Dimensión Antropológica,* Instituto Nacional de Antropología e Historia, http://www.dimensionantropologica.inah.gob.mx/?p=794 (accessed March 30, 2010).

González-Quintero, Lauro, and Jesús Evaristo Sánchez-Sánchez. 1991. Sobre la existencia de chinampas y el manejo del recurso agrícola-hidraúlico, In *Teotihuacan 1980–1982. Nuevas Interpretaciones,* edited by R. Cabrera-Castro, I. Rodríguez-García, and N. Morelos-García, pp. 345–375. Instituto Nacional de Antropología e Historia, Mexico, D.F.

Hayashida, Frances M. 2005. Archaeology, Ecological History and Conservation. *Annual Review of Anthropology* 34:43–65.

Hodell, David A., Mark Brenner, and Jason H. Curtis. 2005. Terminal Classic Drought in the Northern Maya Lowlands Inferred from Multiple Sediment Cores in Lake Chichancanab (Mexico). *Quaternary Science Reviews* 25:1413–1427.

Hodge, Mary G., Carlos E. Cordova, and Charles D. Frederick. 1996. Los asentamientos prehispánicos y el medio cambiante del sureste de la cuenca de México. In *Tierra, agua y bosque. Historia y medio ambiente en el México central,* edited by A. Tortolero-Villaseñor, pp. 49–68. Centre Français d'Études Mexicaines et Centraméricaines, Instituto de Investigaciones, Universidad de Guadalajara, Mexico.

Hornborg, Alf, and Carole Crumley, eds. 2007. *The World System and the Earth System.* Left Coast Press, Walnut Creek, California.

Kirch, Patrick V. 1980. The Archaeological Study of Adaptation: Theoretical and Methodological Issues. *Advances in Archaeological Method and Theory* 3:101–148.

Lachniet, Matthew S., Juan Pablo Bernal, Yemane Asmerom, Victor Polyak, and Dolores Piperno. 2012. A 2400-yr Mesoamerican Rainfall Reconstruction Links Climate and Cultural Change. *Geology.* doi: 10.1130/G32471.1

Levin, Simon A. 1998. Ecosystems and the Biosphere as Complex Adaptive Systems. *Ecosystems* 1:431–436.

Lorenzo, José L. 1968. Clima y agricultura en Teotihuacan. In *Materiales para la arqueología de Teotihuacan*, edited by J. L. Lorenzo, pp. 53–72. Instituto Nacional de Antropología e Historia, Mexico.

Lorenzo, José L. 1988. El hombre y su ambiente. In *La antropología en México: Panorama histórico. 3. Las cuestiones medulares (antropología física, lingüística, arqueología y etnohistoria)*, edited by C. García Mora, pp. 431–449. Colección Biblioteca del INAH, Instituto Nacional de Antropología e Historia, Mexico.

Lorenzo, José L. 1991. La arqueología Mexicana y los arqueólogos Norteamericanos. In *Prehistoria y arqueología*, edited by L. Mirambell-Silva and J. A. Pérez-Gollán, pp. 371–389. Instituto Nacional de Antropología e Historia, Mexico.

Lorenzo, José L., and Lorena Mirambell, eds. 1986. *Tlapacoya: 35 000 años de historia del Lago de Chalco*. Instituto Nacional de Antropología e Historia, Mexico.

MacNeish, Richard S. 1967. A Summary of the Subsistence. In *The Prehistory of the Tehuacan Valley. Vol. 1. Environment and Subsistence*, edited by Douglas S. Byers, pp. 290–309. University of Texas Press, Austin.

MacNeish, Richard S. 1972. The Evolution of Community Patterns in Tehuacán Valley of Mexico and Speculations about the Cultural Processes. In *Man, Settlement and Urbanism*, edited by Peter J. Ucko, Ruth Tringham, and George W. Dimbleby, pp. 67–93, Schenkman, Cambridge, Massachusetts.

Manzanilla, Linda. 1997. The Impact of Climate Change on Past Civilizations: A Revisionist Agenda for Future Research. *Quaternary International* 43/44:153–159.

McClung de Tapia, Emily. 1984. *Ecología y cultura en Mesoamérica*. 2nd ed. Instituto de Investigaciones Antropológicas, Universidad Nacional Autonóma de México, México, D.F.

McClung de Tapia, Emily. 2005. Enfoque ecológico en la arqueología de Teotihuacan y la cuenca de México. *IV Coloquio Bosch Gimpera*, tomo 1, pp. 253–272. Instituto de Investigaciones Antropológicas, Universidad Nacional Autónoma de México, Mexico.

McClung de Tapia, Emily, Irma Domínguez-Rubio, Elizabeth Solleiro-Rebolledo, Jorge Gama-Castro, and Sergey Sedov. 2005. Radiocarbon Dates from Soil Profiles in the Teotihuacan Valley, Mexico: Indicators of Geomorphological Processes. *Radiocarbon* 47(1):159–175.

McGlade, James. 1995. Archaeology and the Ecodynamics of Human-Modified Landscapes. *Antiquity* 69:113–132.

Moran, Emilio F. 2000. *Human Adaptability: An Introduction to Ecological Anthropology*. 2nd ed. Westview Press, Boulder.

Moran, Emilio F. 2010. *Environmental Social Science*. Wiley-Blackwell, United Kingdom.

Nichols, Deborah L. 1987. Prehispanic Irrigation at Teotihuacan, New Evidence: The Tlajinga Canals. In *Teotihuacan. Nuevos datos, nuevas síntesis, nuevos problemas*, edited by E. McClung de Tapia and E. C. Rattray, pp. 133–160. Instituto de Investigaciones Antropológicas, Universidad Nacional Autónoma de México, Mexico.

Nichols, Deborah L., Michael W. Spence, and Mark D. Borland. 1991. Watering the Fields of Teotihuacan: Early Irrigation at the Ancient City. *Ancient Mesoamerica* 2:119–129.

Niederberger, Christine. 1976. *Zohapilco. Cinco milenios de ocupación humana en un sitio lacustre de la cuenca de México*. Colección Científica 30, Instituto Nacional de Antropología e Historia, México.

Niederberger, Christine. 1979. Early Sedentary Economy in the Basin of Mexico. *Science* 203:131–142.

Oldfield, Frank. 2007. Toward Developing Synergistic Linkages between the Biophysical and the Cultural: A Paleoenvironmental Perspective. In *The World System and the Earth System*, edited by Alf Hornborg and Carole L. Crumley, pp. 29–37. Left Coast Press, Walnut Creek, California.

Pickett, Steward T. A., Jurek Kolasa, and Clive G. Jones. 1994. *Ecological Understanding: The Nature of Theory and the Theory of Nature*. Academic Press, San Diego.

Redman, Charles L. 1999. *Human Impact on Ancient Environments*. University of Arizona Press, Tucson.

Redman, Charles L. 2005. Resilience Theory in Archaeology. *American Anthropologist* 107(1):70–77.

Redman, Charles L., and Ann P. Kinzig. 2003. Resilience of Past Landscapes: Resilience Theory, Society and the *Longue Durée*. *Conservation Ecology* 7(1):14, http://www.consecol.org/vol7/iss1/art14 (accessed April 4, 2004).

Redman, Charles L., Margaret C. Nelson, and Ann P. Kinzig. 2009. The Resilience of Socioecological Landscapes. Lessons from the Hohokam. In *The Archaeology of Environmental Change*, edited by Christopher T. Fisher, J. Brett Hill, and Gary M. Feinman, pp. 15–39. University of Arizona Press, Tucson.

Rivera-Uria, María, Yazmin, Sergey Sedov, Elizabeth Solleiro-Rebolledo, Julia Pérez-Pérez, Emily McClung, Alfredo González, and Jorge Gama-Castro. 2007. Degradación ambiental en el valle Teotihuacan: Evidencias geológicas y paleopedológicas, *Boletín de la Sociedad Geológica Mexicana* 59(2):203–217.

Sanders, William T. 1965. The Cultural Ecology of the Teotihuacan Valley. Preliminary Report of the Teotihuacan Valley Project. Department of Sociology and Anthropology, Pennsylvania State University. University Park.

Sanders, William T. 1981. Ecological Adaptation in the Basin of Mexico: 23,000 BC to the Present. In *Handbook of Middle American Research. Supplement 1. Archaeology*. University of Texas Press, Austin.

Sanders, William T., Anton Kovar, Thomas Charlton, and Richard A. Diehl. 1970. The Natural Environment, Contemporary Occupation and 16th Century Population of the Valley. The Teotihuacan Valley Project. Final Report-Volume 1. Occasional Papers in Anthropology, Department of Anthropology, Pennsylvania State University, University Park.

Sanders, William T., Jeffrey R. Parsons, and Michael H. Logan. 1976. Summary and Conclusions. In *The Valley of Mexico. Studies in Pre-Hispanic Ecology and Society*, edited by Eric R. Wolf, pp. 161–178. University of New Mexico Press, Albuquerque.

Sanders, William T., Jeffrey R. Parsons, and Robert S. Santley. 1979. *The Basin of Mexico: Ecological Processes in the Evolution of a Civilization*. Academic Press, New York.

Sanders, William T., and Barbara J. Price. 1968. *Mesoamerica: The Evolution of a Civilization*. Random House, New York.

Sandweiss, Daniel H., and Jeffrey Quilter. 2008. Climate, Catastrophe and Culture in the Ancient Americas. In *El Niño, Catastrophism and Culture Change in Ancient America*, edited by Daniel H. Sandweiss and Jeffrey Quilter, pp. 1–11. Dumbarton Oaks Research Library and Collection, Washington, DC.

Scoones, Ian. 1999. New Ecology and the Social Sciences: What Prospects for a Fruitful Engagement? *Annual Review of Anthropology* 28:479–507.

Solleiro-Rebolledo, Elizabeth, S. Sycheva, Sergey Sedov, Emily McClung de Tapia, Yazmin Rivera-Uria, César Salcido-Berkovich, and A. Kuznetsova. 2010. Fluvial Processes and Paleopedogenesis in the Teotihuacan Valley, Mexico: Responses to Late Quaternary Environment Changes. *Quaternary International*, doi:10.1016/j.quaint.2010.08.005 (accessed September 20, 2010).

Sugiura Yamamoto, Yoko. 2005. Y atrás quedó la ciudad de los dioses. Historia de los asentamientos en el valle de Toluca. Instituto de Investigaciones Antropológicas, Universidad Nacional Autónoma de México.

Sugiura Yamamoto, Yoko, ed. 2009. *La gente de la Ciénaga en tiempos antiguos. La historia de Santa Cruz Atizapan*. El Colegio Mexiquense, A.C./Instituto de Investigaciones Antropológicas, UNAM/Dirección General de Asuntos del Personal Académico, México.

Tainter, Joseph A. 2006. Archaeology of Overshoot and Collapse. *Annual Review of Anthropology* 35:59–74.

Walker, Brian, C. S. Holling, Stephen R. Carpenter, and Ann Kinzig. 2004. Resilience, Adaptability and Transformability in Social-Ecological Systems. *Ecology and Society* 9(2):5, http://www.ecologyandsociety.org/vol9/iss2/art5 (accessed July 5, 2005).

Zimmerer, Karl S. 1994. Human Geography and the "New Ecology": The Prospect and Promise of Integration. *Annals of the Association of American Geographers* 84(1):108–125.

CHAPTER 41

··

SOURCES AND
SOURCING

··

RONALD L. BISHOP

Archaeologists require information about the production and distribution of artifacts to better understand the complexity of human interactions. Frequently carried out as an investigation of trade and exchange, these studies attempt to form groups of compositionally similar artifacts. These groups are then attributed to variously defined "sources" of the materials from which they were made as a step in determining the direction of movement from the area of extraction to the location of artifact recovery.

Sourcing investigations rely on the "characterization" of some culturally used material, whether naturally occurring or slightly altered (e.g., obsidian, basalt, jade, chert, turquoise, amber) or culturally constituted (e.g., pottery). All culturally used materials obtained from natural resources are made up of multiple components, varying in composition and texture. Even obsidian, a naturally formed, relatively homogeneous glassy material, may exhibit variation in mineral crystallization. For example, jade is a rock often made up of several minerals, of which jadeite or jadeitite is a major constituent. It is formed from preexisting rocks during fluid transport and recrystallization, thus introducing mineralogical and chemical variation (Bishop, Sayre, and Mishara 1993; Harlow 1993). Turquoise is composed of a group of minerals, varying in structure and chemistry and frequently incorporating streaks of matrix impurities. Marble is a metamorphic rock formed from dolomite or limestone, both of which are often embedded with mineralogical impurities. Pottery, as the product of naturally variable raw materials (clays, silts, sands [quartz and volcanic], crushed pottery, dung, etc.), is highly complex, combining the inherent natural variation with introduced variation from cultural practices. Attempts to characterize these materials involve collaboration of archaeologists with natural and physical scientists, and usually involve the use of sophisticated instrumentation. An underlying expectation is that variation among possible sources of raw materials will exceed the variation found within the sources. Further, if one uses a sufficiently sensitive and precise analytical technique, it may be possible to determine a suite of objective parameters to identify objects made from those resources and to differentiate other similarly considered objects made from different sources or formed using different practices.

The scientific analysis of artifacts has a long history, with early work depending on tedious wet-chemical analysis of only a few specimens (Harbottle 1982). Finding this analysis to be far too slow, Anna Shepard chose instead to use techniques of the mineralogical sciences. From the 1930s through the 1960s she made extensive use of low-power microscopy and petrographic examinations for mineralogical identifications of tempers in pottery from sites in Mexico, Guatemala, and British Honduras (Belize). She also produced a seminal publication on the technologically sophisticated Plumbate pottery, which she identified as having been made along the Pacific slope of southern Mexico (Shepard 1948). While Shepard was busy with ceramics and petrography, German scientists were aggressively amassing chemical data on archaeological materials through the instrumental use of optical emission spectroscopy. A spark source was used to volatilize a sample, causing it to emit light, which would be captured on a photographic plate. Recorded lines represented characteristic wavelengths for elemental identification, with relative densities indicating abundance. Although highly sensitive for the detection of elements present, analytical complexities and an "artful" reading of line densities resulted in poor reproducibility of concentration data.

Following World War II, new uses for controlled nuclear fission were of interest to the U.S. government. At Brookhaven National Laboratory (BNL), Edward Sayre undertook the first application of neutron activation analysis in the early 1950s for the study of pottery from Greek and Maya civilizations. During the next decade and a half, instrumentation evolved rapidly, protocols improved, and Mesoamerica became a major focus of research, especially for ceramics and jade. Other nuclear research facilities became involved in the study of archaeological materials from Mesoamerica, most notably the Missouri University research reactor (MURR), which, in 1979, began a massive program involving the characterization of obsidian (e.g., Braswell and Glascock 2010; Cobean 2002; Glascock, Braswell, and Cobean 1998; Vogt et al. 1989). Although other laboratories had more limited involvement, BNL and MURR emerged as the leading suppliers of neutron activation data from Mesoamerican materials. Later, as archaeologically oriented projects ceased at BNL, the Mesoamerican emphasis was transferred to the Smithsonian Institution's collaborative program with the National Institute of Standards and Technology (Beaudry 1991).

INAA offered low sample-preparation time, simultaneous multielemental determinations that were free of matrix problems, high sensitivity, good analytical precision, and a reasonably high throughput of samples. The sensitivity of the technique to detect elemental concentrations in minute abundance with high precision offered the opportunity to objectively differentiate among "sources" within a small geographical area. Good reproducibility combined the comparative use of certified reference materials of known concentration and permitted the data to feed into growing databases and even be shared among laboratories that used similar standards (Harbottle 1976; Glascock 1992, 2002; Minc et al. 2007; Neff 2000, 2002). Additionally, the quantified data, involving several elemental determinations, were amenable to statistical analysis involving the procedures of numerical taxonomy, especially those that considered not only absolute abundances but also incorporated the patterns of interelemental covariation (Bishop and Neff 1989; Harbottle 1976; Neff 2000, 2002). For almost four decades INAA has been the established technique to generate elemental data for archaeological source determination and is the de facto standard against which other techniques are evaluated.

Although petrographic examination remains indispensable for the identification and quantification of mineralogical constituents in pottery (Cecil 2007; Levan 2006; Rands and Bishop 2003; Shepard 1960; Stoltman 1989; Varela Torrecilla 1999), and the relation of temper to the geological environment, the majority of sourcing studies rests heavily upon precise chemical data obtained by instrumental analysis. INAA certainly is not the only instrumental technique that has been applied successfully and useful reviews are provided by Pollard and Heron (2008) and Tykot (2004). Many of the techniques may be classified according to those that yield information from bulk chemical analysis (like INAA), with samples taken from throughout a specimen, and those that produce data from the surface or near the surface of an artifact. This distinction is not absolute but it is useful in choosing a technique that is more likely to provide the type and quality of information sought from an analysis. Each application is experimental and the number of elements that are well quantified will vary by technique and by material. The detection limits given by distributors are ideal situations unlikely to be achieved in practice. Such considerations aside, however, it appears that selection among techniques is more influenced by instrumental availability, cost, presence of an interested analyst, and is susceptible to the old designer's adage: good, fast, cheap—pick any two.

Here I comment briefly on some of the more popular techniques being applied. The references provided are highly selective and not all variants are mentioned in any detail. One of the older instrumental approaches is X-ray fluorescence (XRF), which uses X-ray beams directed onto the surface of a sample, causing it to emit wavelengths of light that can be used to determine elemental constituents. Similar to the developments of instrumentation in INAA, techniques using X-rays have improved greatly with variants of the application in wavelength-dispersive X-ray fluorescence (WDXRF), energy-dispersive XRF (EDXRF), and total reflection XRF (TXRF). An alternative to the use of X-ray is found in particle-induced X-ray emission (PIXE), which involves the use of an accelerator and a focused beam of protons onto an externally placed specimen (Gazzola et al. 2009; Ruvalcaba-Sil et al. 1999, 2008). This produces a much lower background than XRF and increases the detection level. These techniques do not require that a sample be taken. That advantage, however, is offset by being limited to surface analysis and to lowered precision caused by irregularities in surface textures. Not surprisingly, XRF and PIXE have been highly successful for the analysis of relatively homogeneous obsidian but less so for other materials unless a large sample is extracted, ground, and pressed into a flat pellet.

Improvements of detectors and miniaturized X-ray tubes have resulted in portable, suitcase-sized XRF instruments that permit analyses in the field. Such portability has strong appeal and there has been a relative rush to acquire the even more compact handheld XRF analyzers (PXRF). These instruments are a marvel of technology. They have been demonstrated to differentiate obsidian successfully from among well-separated sources (El Chayal, Ixtepeque, and Pachuca); however, comparability with data from other handheld analyzers remains problematic (Nazaroff, Prufer, and Drake 2010). Rigorous testing of the validity and utility of the technique for other classes of archaeological materials, especially those that are heterogeneous or exhibit textural irregularities, has not yet been carried out. Interestingly, a recent paper emphasizes the need to improve the levels of detection but does not address the more important need for precision (Caneva and Ferretti 2010).

A bright spot on the horizon involves increasing facilities for precise, multielemental analysis by inductively coupled plasma mass spectroscopy (ICP-MS). Fully dissolved samples are atomized in very hot plasma, forming ions. The ions are separated by a mass spectrometer that generates signals that are proportional to abundance, and quantification is achieved through the use of appropriate standards. The technique is extremely sensitive, even three orders of magnitude more sensitive than XRF or PIXE, and able to yield high-precision data for many elements, even when they occur in low concentrations. Limitations include the need to use hazardous acids to put the entire sample into solution, and interferences caused by high matrix concentrations. Problems associated with sample preparation might explain its limited use for archaeological sourcing in Mesoamerica. Instrumental enhancement combines ICP-MS with laser ablation (LA-ICP-MS), which permits elemental analysis without needing to remove a sample (depending on the size of the object) (Iñañez et al. 2010; Kovacevich, Neff, and Bishop 2005; Resano, García-Ruiz, and Vanhaecke 2010; Tabares et al. 2005). Both sensitivity and precision, however, may be impacted by incomplete atomization, elemental fractionation, and differences in the matrices of standards and unknowns. Heterogeneous materials pose significant difficulties (Dussubieux et al. 2008). While these problems currently preclude the technique for achieving an established status for archaeology, with the increasing loss of INAA facilities it seems likely that LA-ICP-MS and ICP-MS eventually will become major generators of compositional data for sourcing (Robertson, Neff, and Higgins 2002; Speakman and Neff 2005). Additionally, a new generation of "multicollectors" (MC-ICP-MS) has improved accuracy and precision, especially for the source-sensitive rare earths, isotope ratios, including lead that can be used to trace metal objects to ore sources or to seek differences in lead glazes (Luke, Tykot, and Scott 2006; Iñañez et al. 2010). These are "big ticket" instruments and not yet heavily engaged in archaeological applications—however, perhaps they will be used in the next decade.

Many of the analytical techniques applied to archaeology share one thing in common: they produce a variably precise and accurate quantification of chemical abundance for each sample analyzed. At that point, the scientific application has ended. These data remain to be mined for patterns that may lend themselves to a meaningful archaeological interpretation. Several considerations are involved with this endeavor.

Sourcing Considerations

At one level of consideration, all sourcing studies, whether carried out at the site or subregional level, are spatial in nature (Bishop and Blackman 2002). It comes down to what is similar, what is different, and how sharp the boundaries are among differences in composition. One might be able to locate the source in terms of geographical coordinates (Neff and Glowacki 2002). However, attribution may be limited to a particular lithology, river, river valley, or, if lucky when working with pottery, a workshop of unknown location in a variably designated subregion. What is meant by a "source" depends on how one formulates the initial questions or summarizes the data once they are in hand. Since there is unlikely to be advanced knowledge of the number or makeup of "natural" groups in a dataset, extensive sampling is required.

Because many variables are quantified for many samples, mathematical and statistical procedures become necessary as the data matrix must be reduced to a lower dimensional form that permits internal patterning to be seen. One approach involves the selection of some measure of intersample similarity that can be used to group together those samples that are deemed "sufficiently" close to one another in the multivariate space. If a "sufficient" number of group members are present, a probability of group membership, for those samples in the group or for comparative purposes, can be calculated. Such probabilities are largely advisory as few of the statistical assumptions are met for rigorous testing. Nonetheless, these compositional groups represent a center of mass within the elemental data assembled for a particular study. Data with low tendencies to form "tight" groups nonetheless may be shown to have directional trends in the compositional variation.

Groups are assembled according to different procedures and measures for different purposes (Neff 1998). Groups that are formed to demonstrate separation from some other group may not have sufficient internal homogeneity to be credibly used to assess the likelihood that an external, comparative sample might be an acceptable member of the group. Use of an overly inclusive group, although separable from others, can result in distortive or erroneous conclusions. In presentation of group data, therefore, it is imperative to provide information concerning the relative homogeneity of the reference group, commonly by presenting measures of central tendency and coefficients of variation. In most applications, statistics may mean less than the strength of covariation with multiple, nonchemical datasets (e.g., Culbert and Rands 2007).

ATTRIBUTION

Ideally, groups of artifacts or raw materials that are formed on the basis of similar composition could be attributed to a specific or generalized source area through correspondence with the analysis of raw material (e.g., obsidian, jade, clay) from known locations, or, in the case of pottery, to the similarly textured and tempered, abundantly available pottery from regional sites. The use of an analytical technique *does not* identify a source from which raw materials were extracted; it merely provides objective data that can be used to inferentially attribute an artifact or groups of artifacts to a likely source or source area.

A usefully accurate compositional attribution of archaeological materials to a source area depends on several factors: the relative mineralogical and chemical distinctiveness of regional resources; a level of social complexity so that the repetitive exercise of extractive or manufacturing practices resulted in products that were sufficiently similar and abundant so that they might be picked up in sampling; and an appropriate technique. Adequacy of sampling is always a concern, and individual sites are frequently used to proxy for larger subregional sources of production. A reality is that compositional approaches to issues of production and distribution, trade and exchange, are based on the opportunistic sampling of collections that vary in the representativeness of time and space.

At present, archaeologists clamor for objectively derived data to feed into their theoretical models of trade and exchange. What is more likely to occur is the documentation of material movement. If expensive data are going to be maximized, greater attention will need to be given to issues of geology and geochemistry, limitations of sampling, and the structure-imposing nature of data analysis as well as to the archaeological context. It is an inherently interdisciplinary endeavor (De Atley and Bishop 1991) and it should be approached as such.

REFERENCES

Beaudry, Marilyn P. 1991. New World Paste Compositional Investigations. In *The Ceramic Legacy of Anna O. Shepard*, edited by Ronald L. Bishop and Frederick W. Lange, pp. 224–256. University Press of Colorado, Niwot.

Bishop, Ronald L., and M. James Blackman. 2002. Instrumental Neutron Activation
    Analysis of Archaeological Ceramics: Scale and Interpretation. *Accounts of
    Chemical Research* 35:603–610.

Bishop, Ronald L., and Hector Neff. 1989. Compositional Data Analysis in Archaeology.
    In *Archaeological Chemistry IV*, edited by Ralph O. Allen, pp. 576–586. Advances in
    Chemistry Series 220, American Chemical Society, Washington, DC.

Bishop, Ronald L., Edward V. Sayre, and Joan Mishara. 1993. Compositional and
    Structural Characterization of Maya and Costa Rican Jadeitites. In *Precolumbian
    Jade: New Geological and Cultural Interpretations*, edited by Frederick W. Lange,
    pp. 30–60. University of Utah Press, Salt Lake City.

Braswell, Geoffrey E., and Michael D. Glascock. 2010. Procurement and Production of
    Obsidian Artifacts at Calakmul. In *The Technology of Maya Civilization: Political
    Economy and Beyond Lithic* Studies, edited by Zachary X. Hruby, Geoffrey E.
    Braswell, and Oswaldo Chinchilla Mazariegos, pp. 232–256. Equinox Press, London.

Caneva, Claudio, and Marco Ferretti. 2010. XRF Spectrometers for Non-Destructive
    Investigations in Art and Archaeology: The Cost of Portability. Proceedings, 15th
    World Conference on Non-Destructive Testing, October 15–21, 2000, in Rome.
    http://www.ndt.net/article/wcndt00/papers/idn680/idn680.htm.

Cecil, Leslie G. 2007. Postclassic Maya Ceramic Advances: Conjoining Stylistic,
    Technological and Chemical Compositional Data. In *Developments in Ceramic
    Materials Research*, edited by Dena Rosslere, pp. 1–34. Nova Science, Hauppauge,
    New York.

Cobean, Robert H. 2002. *Un mundo de obsidian: mineria y comercio de un vidrio volcanic
    en el Mexico antiguo.* [*A World of Obsidian: The Mining and Trade of a Volcanic
    Glass in Ancient Mexico*]. Instituto Nacional de Antropología e Historia (Mexico)
    and the Department of Anthropology, University of Pittsburgh.

Culbert, T. Patrick, and Robert L. Rands. 2007. Multiple Classifications: An Alternative
    Approach to the Investigation of Maya Ceramics. *Latin American Antiquity*
    18:181–190.

De Atley, Susanne P., and Ronald L. Bishop. 1991. Toward an Integrated Interface for
    Archaeology and Archaeometry. In *Anna O. Shepard: A Ceramic Legacy*, edited by
    Ronald L. Bishop and Frederick W. Lange, pp. 358–382. University Press of Colorado,
    Niwot.

Dussubieux, Laure, Aurelie Deraisme, Gérard Frot, Christopher Stevenson, Amy Creech,
    and Yves Bienvenu. 2008. LA-ICP-MS, SEM-EDS and EPMA Analysis of Eastern
    North American Copper-Based Artifacts: Impact of Corrosion and Heterogeneity on
    the Reliability of the LA-ICP-MS Compositional Results. *Archaeometry* 50:643–657.

Gazzola, Julie, Manuel Sánchez del Río, Corína Solís, and Thomas Calligaro. 2009.
    Particle-Induced X-Ray Emission (PIXE) Analysis of Obsidian from Teotihuacan.
    Archaeometry 52:343–354.

Glascock, Michael D. 1992. Characterization of Archaeological Ceramics at MURR
    by Neutron Activation Analysis and Multivariate Statistics, In *Chemical
    Characterization of Ceramic Pastes in Archaeology,* edited by Hector Neff, pp. 11–30.
    Monographs in World Archaeology No. 7, Prehistory Press, Madison, Wisconsin.

Glascock, Michael D. 2002. Obsidian Provenance Research in the Americas. *Accounts of
    Chemical Research* 35:611–617.

Glascock, Michael D., Geoffrey E. Braswell, and Robert H. Cobean. 1998. A Systematic
    Approach to Obsidian Source Characterization. In *Archaeological Obsidian Studies:
    Method and Theory*, edited by M. Steven Shackley, pp. 15–66. Plenum, New York.

Harbottle, Garman. 1976. Activation Analysis in Archaeology. *Radiochemistry* 3:33–72.

Harbottle, Garman. 1982. Chemical Characterization in Archaeology. In *Contexts for Prehistoric Exchange*, edited by Jonathan E. Ericson and Timothy K. Earle, pp. 13–51. Academic Press, New York.

Harlow, George E. 1993. Middle American Jade: Geologic and Petrologic Perspectives on Variability and Source. In *Precolumbian Jade. New Geological and Cultural Interpretations*, edited by Frederick W. Lange, pp. 7–29. University of Utah Press, Salt Lake City.

Iñañez, Javier G., Jeremy J. Bellucci, Enrique Rodríguez-Alegría, Richard Ash, William McDonough, and Robert J. Speakman. 2010. Romita Pottery Revisited: A Reassessment of the Provenance of Ceramics from Colonial Mexico by LA-ICP-MS. *Journal of Archaeological Science* 37:2698-2704.

Kovacevich, Brigitte, Hector Neff, and Ronald Bishop. 2005. Laser Ablation-ICP-MS Chemical Characterization of Jade from a Jade Workshop in Cancuen, Guatemala. In *Laser Ablation ICP-MS in Archaeology*, edited by Robert J. Speakman and Hector Neff, pp. 39–58. University of New Mexico Press, Albuquerque.

Levan, Larry. 2006. Interaction at the Sites of El Paraíso and El Cafétal, Honduras during the Late Classic Period. Master's thesis in Archaeological Studies, Yale University.

Luke, Christina, Robert H. Tykot, and Robert W. Scott. 2006. Petrographic and Stable Isotope Analyses of Late Classic Ulua Marble Vases and Potential Sources. *Archaeometry* 48:13–29.

Minc, Lea D., R. Jason Sherman, Christina Elson, Charles S. Spencer, and Elsa M. Redmond. 2007. "M Glow Blue": Archaeometric Research at Michigan's Ford Nuclear Reactors. *Archaeometry* 49:215–228.

Nazaroff, Adam J., Keith M. Prufer, and Brandon L. Drake. 2010. Assessing the Applicability of Portable X-Ray Fluorescence Spectrometry for Obsidian Provenance Research in the Maya Lowlands. *Journal of Archaeological Science* 32:885–895.

Neff, Hector. 1998. Units in Chemistry-Based Ceramic Provenance Investigations. In *Unit Issues in Archaeology: Measuring Time, Space, and Material*, edited by Ann F. Ramenofsky and Anastasia Steffen, pp. 115–127. University of Utah Press, Provo.

Neff, Hector. 2000. Neutron Activation Analysis for Provenance Determination in Archaeology. In *Modern Analytical Methods in Art and Archaeology*, edited by Enrico Ciliberto and Giuseppe Spoto, pp. 81–134. John Wiley and Sons, New York.

Neff, Hector. 2002. Quantitative Techniques for Analyzing Ceramic Compositional Data. In *Ceramic Production and Circulation in the Greater Southwest: Source Determination by INAA and Complementary Mineralogical Investigations*, edited by Donna M. Glowacki and Hector Neff, pp. 15–37. Cotsen Institute of Archaeology, Monograph 44, University of California, Los Angeles.

Neff, Hector, and Donna M. Glowacki. 2002. Ceramic Source Determination by Instrumental Neutron Activation Analysis in the American Southwest. In *Ceramic Production and Circulation in the Greater Southwest. Source Determination by INAA and Complementary Mineralogical Investigations*, edited by Donna M. Glowacki and Hector Neff, pp. 1–14. Monograph 44, Cotsen Institute of Archaeology, University of California, Los Angeles.

Pollard, A. Mark, and Carl Heron. 2008. *Archaeological Chemistry*. The Royal Society of Chemistry, Cambridge, United Kingdom.

Rands, Robert L., and Ronald L. Bishop. 2003. The Dish-Plate Tradition at Palenque: Continuity and Change. In *Patterns and Processes: A Festschrift in Honor of*

Dr. Edward V. Sayre, edited by L. van Zelst, pp. 109–134. Smithsonian Center for Materials Research and Education, Washington, DC.

Resano, Martín, Esperanza García-Ruiz, and Frank Vanhaecke. 2010. Laser Ablation-Inductively Coupled Plasma Mass Spectrometry in Archaeometric Research. *Mass Spectrometry Reviews* 29:55–78.

Robertson, J. David, Hector Neff, and Barry Higgins. 2002. Microanalysis of Ceramics with PIXE and LA-ICP-MS. *Nuclear Instruments and Methods in Physics Research, Section B: Beam Interactions with Materials and Atoms* 189:378–381.

Ruvalcaba-Sil, J. L., Linda Manzanilla, E. Melgar, and R. Lozano Santa Cruz. 2008. PIXE and Ionoluminescence for Mesoamerican Jadeite Characterization. *X-Ray Spectrometry* 37(2):96–99.

Ruvalcaba-Sil, José Luis, Maria Angeles Ontalba Salamanca, Linda Manzanilla, Javier Miranda, Jaqueline Cañetas Ortega, and C. López. 1999. Characterization of Pre-Hispanic Pottery from Teotihuacan, Mexico, by a Combined PIXE-RBS and XRD Analysis. *Nuclear Instruments and Methods in Physics Research Section B: Beam Interactions with Materials and Atoms* 150:591–596.

Shepard, Anna O. 1948. *Plumbate: A Mesoamerican Tradeware*. Publication 473, Carnegie Institution of Washington, Washington, DC.

Shepard, Anna O. 1960. *Ceramics for the Archaeologist*. Publication 509, Carnegie Institution of Washington, Washington, DC.

Speakman, Robert J., and Hector Neff. 2005. The Application of Laser Ablation ICP-MS to the Study of Archaeological Materials—An Introduction. In *Laser Ablation-ICP-MS in Archaeological Research*, edited by Robert J. Speakman and Hector Neff, pp. 1–16. University of New Mexico Press, Albuquerque.

Stoltman, James B. 1989. A Quantitative Approach to the Petrographic Analysis of Ceramic Thin-Sections. *American Antiquity* 54(1):147–160.

Tabares, A. Natasha, Michael Love, Robert J. Speakman, Michael D. Glascock, and Hector Neff. 2005. Straight from the Source: Obsidian Prismatic Blades at El Ujuxte, Guatemala. In *Laser Ablation ICP-MS in Archaeology*, edited by Robert J. Speakman and Hector Neff, pp. 17–29. University of New Mexico Press, Albuquerque.

Tykot, Robert H. 2004. Scientific Methods and Applications to Archaeological Provenance Studies. In *Proceedings of the International School of Physics "Enrico Fermi" Course CLIV. Physics Methods in Archaeometry*, edited by Marco Martini, Mario Milazzo, and Mario Piacentini, pp. 407–432. IOS Press, Amsterdam.

Verela Torrecilla, Carmen. 1999. Enigmas cerámicos: análisis petrográfico de la cerámica pizarra de Oxkintok, Yucatán, México. *Revista Española de Antropología Americana* 29:101–129.

Vogt, James R., C. C. Graham, Michael D. Glascock, and Robert H. Cobean. 1989. Determinación de elementos traza de yacimientos de obsidiana en Mesoamérica por análisis de activación neutrónica. In *La obsidiana en Mesoamérica*, edited by M. Gaxiola and John E. Clark, pp. 27–37. Instituto Nacional de Antropología e Historia. México, D.F.

....

CHAPTER 42

CRAFTING AND MANUFACTURING IN MESOAMERICA

CRITICAL ENGAGEMENTS WITH THEORY AND METHOD

....

E. CHRISTIAN WELLS

PRODUCTION systems have long been an important subject of archaeological research in Mesoamerica. Studying how and why people formed particular groups and how those groups allocated labor and resources helps us to identify the social, economic, cultural, political, and even cosmological constraints and pressures that motivate people to make things. Examining and comparing changes in production systems over time and space also allows us to consider how and why social groups become more or less organized politically and economically. Mesoamerica has been (and continues to be) an ideal testing ground for understanding the causes and consequences of various kinds of production industries, because the area encompasses a very broad time scale of human occupation (on the order of thousands of years) and includes societies representing the full spectrum of human organizations—from hunter-gatherer economies, to small-scale and middle-range societies, to regionally expansive states and empires.

Driven, in part, by object-hungry museum directors in the nineteenth and early twentieth centuries, early excavations in Mesoamerica often focused almost exclusively on recovering and analyzing only the most exquisite and intricately fashioned goods—"luxury items" or "prestige goods." But by the mid-twentieth century, thanks to the pioneering efforts of Gordon Willey and others, the zeal to acquire and study luxury items was matched by comparable efforts to collect and consider quotidian or utilitarian materials, which revealed a great deal of detail about the daily lives of ancient Mesoamericans. Recent work on both kinds of goods published over the last few decades has made important contributions to understanding how production is organized and for what ends. In this chapter, I provide a selective and critical review of this literature, summarizing important findings and suggesting future directions. Notably, three important edited volumes have emerged recently from the Archeological Papers of the American Anthropological Association (Costin and Wright 1998; Hruby and Flad 2007; Hirth 2009a), which critically engage the theory and method of craft production. I draw heavily on these works, and I also include a few outstanding papers from other sources.

Crafting and Manufacturing

I follow Mary Helms's (1993: 14–18) useful distinction between objects that are skillfully crafted and those that are simply manufactured. According to Helms (1993: 16–17), skilled crafting "is political and ideological rather than economic in nature.... It is oriented toward elucidating, via the tangible qualities of things produced, the intangible qualities of individuals or of interpersonal, inter-group, or inter-realm associations." In contrast, "manufacturing is materialistic, technical, routine, impersonal, and oriented toward the continuous production, in series, of goods as end; in a word, it is economic" (Helms 1993: 16). I choose to work with these concepts as opposed to the more commonly used "wealth goods" and "subsistence goods" (Brumfiel and Earle 1987: 4), because crafting and manufacturing foreground the agentive properties of productive labor rather than the products of labor. This perspective is becoming more common in studies of Mesoamerican economies (Wells 2006: 279–282). While Helms's simple dichotomy certainly does not apply broadly to the production of all classes of materials in Mesoamerica, it allows me to organize the recent literature into meaningful groups for synthesis and discussion, much the same way ideas about exchange value and use value have been constructive for organizing conversations about what people do with these sorts of objects once produced. This distinction has the further advantage of allowing me to dodge a thorny issue in recent studies of craft production, namely the ambiguity of the phenomenon labeled "crafts" (as opposed to the transitive verb "crafting"), which is increasingly seen as a problematic term in negotiating between native categories and archaeologists' analytical categories (Clark and Houston 1998: 37–39; Costin 2007: 146–147; Hendon 2006: 355; Rice 2009: 125–126).

Whether (or when) someone is crafting or manufacturing, she or he is engaged in the practice of creation or, more specifically, the transformation of raw materials or existing artifacts into cultural products. The ways in which archaeologists identify and study production have been the subject of intense debate (Clark 1995; Costin 2005; Schortman and Urban 2004). Twenty years ago, Cathy Costin (1991) advanced how archaeologists can operationalize production theories in the material record by analyzing and critiquing the growing number of typologies and terminologies for specialization. Costin suggested a multidimensional or "characterizational" (Pool 1992) framework with four independent dimensions of craft production (context, concentration, scale, and intensity) to identify different production arrangements (see also Costin 2001, 2005), which subsequently has been evaluated systematically with hard data from Mesoamerica and beyond (e.g., Hendon 1996; Smith 2004). Recent interrogation of this and other frameworks (e.g., Clark and Parry 1990; Rice 2009) once again wrestles with this challenging topic, questioning, for example, the analytical utility of distinguishing between specialized and nonspecialized production (Menon 2008) and even the usefulness of studying production as a specific category of human behavior (Clark 2007). Suffice it to say, Mesoamerican archaeologists are increasingly exploring alternative ideas about production and its social and cultural (as well as political and economic) contexts to consider notions of agency and materiality at the expense of social evolution (e.g., McAnany 2010; Wells and Davis-Salazar 2007). Below I highlight some of the contributions that Mesoamerican archaeologists have made to engage critically Costin's original multidimensional model. While this model continues to provide useful analytical vocabulary, its ability to account for cultural and historical variation in Mesoamerican societies of different scales and scopes, especially in household contexts, is being challenged in interesting and intellectually healthy ways.

CONTEXT

The nature of control over crafting and manufacturing processes is one dimension along which production arrangements vary. At one end of the continuum is independent production, where the sociopolitical context of production is muted and has little or no influence on crafting and manufacturing. Independent producers are free to determine what they produce, how they produce it, when and where production takes place, and so on. Of course, this is an idealized characterization; no producer is completely independent of social and political forces (although they may *think* they are). At the other end of the continuum are "attached" or "sponsored" artisans, whose productive capacity is entirely determined by an elite or governmental sponsor. Again, since this is a behavioral model, it is more likely the case that no artisan (except perhaps enslaved individuals) is ever completely embedded in sociopolitical contexts. Further, as Elizabeth Brumfiel (1991) has shown for Aztec women's production through weaving and cooking in highland central Mexico, the extent to which a craft producer's work is tied to social and political (as well as economic and religious) forces can vary over time, even within a single year or season. In other words, there is a great deal of fluidity in the degree to which Mesoamerican craft producers worked independently of elite and governing agencies.

At the Classic (ca. 250-900 AD) lowland Maya settlement of Aguateca in the southwestern Petén region of Guatemala, Takeshi Inomata (2001, 2007) and colleagues (Inomata and Triadan 2010; Inomata et al. 2002) have unearthed evidence that elite families participated directly in crafting, particularly of socially valued goods, including jade ornaments, pyrite mosaic mirrors, and other objects critical to social and political reproduction. Inomata (2001) argues that this finding challenges the evolutionary model wherein attached production emerges in societies to fuel the material demands of an elite class. Instead, he suggests that elites can and did participate in the production of skillfully crafted items and that such engagement with these materials—and the specialized knowledge and technological skills required to produce them—were intimately tied to their social status as elites. Moreover, the fact that elite artisans undertook demanding physical labor suggests a commitment to the aesthetic and moral values associated with artistic production (Inomata 2007). In other words, the Aguateca elites were active cultural agents who manufactured, to some extent, their own status as elites, or at least the materials used to ideologically support and justify that status.

CONCENTRATION

The geographic organization of production and the regional concentration of production facilities constitute other important parameters of crafting and manufacturing. Producers can be dispersed or aggregated on the landscape, depending on the location of the consumers they serve, the nature of the surrounding terrain, and the spatial distribution of raw materials. Transportation of the finished products becomes important if production arrangements are nucleated. Production activities that are regionally concentrated, for instance, are often located alongside marketplaces, where transportation costs for the producers are negligible. Deborah Nichols and colleagues (2002; Crider et al. 2007), for example, have documented the emergence of nucleated production in step with market exchange in the Basin of Mexico from the eighth to seventeenth centuries AD. They show that the manufacture of Epiclassic serving wares was highly localized (conforming to a solar market model) and increased over time in terms of regionalism alongside political alliance networks to more efficiently serve marketplaces. Similarly, Barbara

Stark and Christopher Garraty (Garraty and Stark 2002; Stark and Garraty 2004) show how production nucleation is a dynamic and diachronic property of manufacturing by documenting how production centers aggregated and dispersed between the Late Classic and Late Postclassic (600–1521 AD) in the Gulf lowlands of southern Veracruz. Such changes appear to have been in response to shifts in the regional political economy, especially those in sync with the development of market exchange and marketplaces (Stark and Ossa 2010).

Another study, however, challenges the idea that production nucleation is necessarily linked to market exchange. In the Naco Valley in southeastern Mesoamerica, Edward Schortman and Patricia Urban (1994; Schortman et al. 2001) have shown that the manufacturing activities of several craft industries were colocated at the regional political capital, La Sierra, during the Late Classic period (ca. 600–800 AD). Schortman and Urban found facilities and implements for the production of kiln-fired pottery and figurines, prismatic obsidian blades, textiles, shell ornaments, and ground stone, where each industry appears to have been uniquely associated with a different residential compound. They also found that many of the products created at La Sierra ended up at other households elsewhere in the valley where there is scant evidence for crafting or manufacturing of any kind. While the specific distribution mechanisms are still unclear, the spatial distance between producers and consumers was noteworthy. And although there appears to have been a significant clay source at La Sierra, the potters used that source only for certain vessels, preferring other clay types located much farther away for figurines and specialty pots (Connell 2002; Urban et al. 1997). Schortman and Urban's findings suggest that the concentration of production does not necessarily correspond to distribution mechanisms, production efficiency, the location of consumers, or the proximity of raw materials.

SCALE

The third dimension identified in Costin's (1991) framework concerns the scale of the production units in terms of size (the number of individuals in the production unit) and social composition (how the individuals are biologically related). Production units vary from small, kin-based enterprises to larger-scale workshops or factories where labor is contracted in some way. Labor recruitment is the defining factor, where small-scale production involves the immediate family in contrast to large-scale production that invites labor from those who are not related. Kenneth Hirth and colleagues (Hirth 2006b), for example, identify a range of production scales for chipped-stone industries at Epiclassic (ca. 650–900 AD) Xochicalco in highland central Mexico, from household production and domestic workshops to marketplace production and precinct workshops. While household manufacturing of obsidian tools relied on the productive labor of family members (probably adult males), Hirth (2006a: 201) believes that marketplace production would have allowed for individuals from different families and perhaps even from those living outside of Xochicalco (as itinerant artisans) to participate in production, although no more than three to five artisans would have engaged in marketplace manufacturing at any one time, given the estimated population of the site.

While scale can be used to characterize the size and organization of the labor pool, Mesoamerican archaeologists have demonstrated that scale should not be confused with intensity. As Gary Feinman and Linda Nicholas (Feinman 1999; Feinman and Nicholas 2000) have shown for the Classic period (ca. 200–800 AD) Ejutla Valley in southern Oaxaca, some households appear to have been engaged in the high-intensity production of marine-shell ornaments. In Ejutla, more than 20,000 pieces of cut, abraded, and modified pieces of marine shell were excavated from middens and other deposits associated with a single house structure. Of these materials, only a tiny proportion (less than 1 percent) made up finished ornaments, indicating that the inhabitants were producing for nonresident clients, some of whom likely occupied Monte Albán (Feinman 1999: 87). When combined with evidence for other production activities in the household, including pottery and figurine making, cooking, spinning (fiber), weaving, and agriculture, Feinman (1999: 95–96) argues that crafting and manufacturing were high-intensity industries in the household. This work demonstrates that, even though it is a small-scale enterprise, household production does not necessarily equal a part-time, low-intensity industry. Instead, small-scale production units can engage in high-intensity production.

INTENSITY

The final parameter for describing production organization is the intensity at which the activity occurs. Intensity is often characterized in terms of the amount of time spent on the activity, for instance, part- or full-time. According to Costin (1991), efficiency (routinized production), risk (dependence on others for one's subsistence), and scheduling (balancing subsistence demands) determine intensity. Among the Aztec, for example, Brumfiel (1987) shows how rural landholding craft specialists tended to operate at part-time intensity, balancing their manufacturing with agricultural pursuits. In urban centers, however, craft specialists practiced their trades on a full-time basis, partly because they often produced for nobles and partly because their subsistence needs could be met by local marketplaces. The different levels of intensity held important consequences for the artisans' social identities and their access to political and economic capital (Brumfiel 1998).

Some Mesoamerican archaeologists, however, have found that characterizing crafting and manufacturing in terms of intensity is not always useful. For example, Julia Hendon (2006: 368) notes that, despite a continuous and high demand for textiles in Aztec and Maya societies, there is no indication that weavers were ever organized as a specific occupational specialization. Textile production was embedded in the household, such that its practice was intermittent, integrated with other domestic tasks, and often reliant on the assistance of multiple family members. Mesoamerican archaeologists are coming to the same conclusion for other crafting and manufacturing activities as well (e.g., Aoyama 2009; McAnany 2010). In the case of textile production, to characterize it in terms of intensity would create a false dichotomy and miss the point that manufacturing textiles was also very much about manufacturing identity and personhood (Hendon 1997, 1999). Moreover, while intensity describes how much time is spent on a given activity, it does not reveal the value or meaning of that activity to the producer. Recently, Hirth (2009b) advocates for the exploration of two alternative concepts: "intermittent crafting" (periodic crafting and manufacturing) and "multicrafting" (pursuing multiple production activities in a single household). He argues that these concepts are useful for understanding how craft production is often integrated with other household activities, subsistence work, labor scheduling, and the like. This notion promises to open archaeological inquiry into the meaning and value of productive activities apart from the amount of time investment in any one craft (e.g., Shimada 2007).

CONCLUSION

As Brumfiel and Nichols (2009: 246) observe, Mesoamerican archaeologists' ideas about the organization of prehispanic crafting and manufacturing have tended, until recently, to be biased by a few detailed cases that have surfaced from contact-period Mexico and the Classic Maya world. As archaeologists continue to document and grapple with unexpected diversity and complexity in production systems both large and small, we are forced to revisit, revise, and rethink our conceptual frameworks. The recent work emerging from the Mesoamerican cases discussed here emphasizes alternative ways of arriving at social and behavioral explanations that are not overly burdened by formalist economic assumptions or the logic of modern capitalism. And such successful work will only be sustained if we continue to document crafting and manufacturing in empirical detail, not allowing our ideas to outpace our data.

REFERENCES

Aoyama, Kazuo. 2009. *Elite Craft Producers, Artists, and Warriors at Aguateca: Lithic Analysis*. University of Utah Press, Salt Lake City.

Brumfiel, Elizabeth M. 1987. Elite and Utilitarian Crafts in the Aztec State. In *Specialization, Exchange, and Complex Societies*, edited by Elizabeth M. Brumfiel and Timothy K. Earle, pp. 102–118. Cambridge University Press, Cambridge.

Brumfiel, Elizabeth M. 1991. Weaving and Cooking: Women's Production in Aztec Mexico. In *Engendering Archaeology: Women and Prehistory*, edited by Joan M. Gero and Margaret W. Conkey, pp. 224–253. Blackwell, Oxford.

Brumfiel, Elizabeth M. 1998. The Multiple Identities of Aztec Craft Specialists. In *Craft and Social Identity*, edited by Cathy Lynne Costin and Rita P. Wright, pp. 145–152. Archeological Papers No. 8, American Anthropological Association, Arlington, Virginia.

Brumfiel, Elizabeth M., and Timothy K. Earle. 1987. Specialization, Exchange, and Complex Societies: An Introduction. In *Specialization, Exchange, and Complex Societies*, edited by Elizabeth M. Brumfiel and Timothy K. Earle, pp. 1–9. Cambridge University Press, Cambridge.

Brumfiel, Elizabeth M., and Deborah L. Nichols. 2009. Bitumen, Blades, and Beads: Prehispanic Craft Production and the Domestic Economy. In *Housework: Craft Production and Domestic Economy in Ancient Mesoamerica*, edited by Kenneth G. Hirth, pp. 239–251. Archeological Papers of the American Anthropological Association, No. 19, Wiley-Blackwell, New York.

Clark, John E. 1995. Craft Specialization as an Archaeological Category. *Research in Economic Anthropology* 16:267–294.

Clark, John E. 2007. In Craft Specialization's Penumbra: Things, Persons, Action, Value, and Surplus. In *Rethinking Craft Specialization in Complex Societies: Archaeological Analyses of the Social Meaning of Production*, edited by Zachary X. Hruby and Rowan K. Flad, pp. 20–35. Archeological Papers No. 17, American Anthropological Association, Arlington, Virginia.

Clark, John E., and Stephen D. Houston. 1998. Craft Specialization, Gender, and Personhood among the Postconquest Maya of Yucatan, Mexico. In *Craft and Social Identity*, edited by Cathy Lynne Costin and Rita P. Wright, pp. 31–46. Archeological Papers No. 8, American Anthropological Association, Arlington, Virginia.

Clark, John E., and William J. Parry. 1990. Craft Specialization and Cultural Complexity. *Research in Economic Anthropology* 12:289–346.

Connell, Samuel V. 2002. Getting Closer to the Source: Using Ethnoarchaeology to Find Ancient Pottery Making in the Naco Valley, Honduras. *Latin American Antiquity* 13:401–417.

Costin, Cathy L. 1991. Craft Specialization: Issues in Defining, Documenting, and Explaining the Organization of Craft Production. In *Archaeological Method and Theory*, Vol. 3, edited by Michael B. Schiffer, pp. 1–56. University of Arizona Press, Tucson.

Costin, Cathy L. 2001. Craft Production Systems. In *Archaeology at the Millennium: A Sourcebook*, edited by Gary M. Feinman and T. Douglas Price, pp. 273–327. Kluwer Academic/Plenum, New York.

Costin, Cathy L. 2005. Craft Production. In *Handbook of Archaeological Methods*, edited by Herbert D. G. Maschner, pp. 1034–1107. Altamira, Walnut Creek, California.

Costin, Cathy L. 2007. Thinking about Production: Phenomenological Classification and Lexical Semantics. In *Rethinking Craft Specialization in Complex Societies: Archaeological Analyses of the Social Meaning of Production*, edited by Zachary X. Hruby and Rowan K. Flad, pp. 143–162. Archeological Papers No. 17, American Anthropological Association, Arlington, Virginia.

Costin, Cathy Lynne, and Rita P. Wright, eds. 1998. *Craft and Social Identity.*
    Archeological Papers No. 8, American Anthropological Association, Arlington,
    Virginia.
Crider, Destiny, Deborah L. Nichols, Hector Neff, and Michael D. Glascock. 2007. In the
    Aftermath of Teotihuacan: Epiclassic Pottery Production and Distribution in the
    Teotihuacan Valley, Mexico. *Latin American Antiquity* 18:123–143.
Feinman, Gary M. 1999. Rethinking Our Assumptions: Economic Specialization at
    the Household Scale in Ancient Ejutla, Oaxaca, Mexico. In *Pottery and People: A
    Dynamic Interaction*, edited by James M. Skibo and Gary M. Feinman, pp. 81–98.
    University of Utah Press, Salt Lake City.
Feinman, Gary M., and Linda M. Nicholas. 2000. High-Intensity Household-Scale
    Production in Ancient Mesoamerica: A Perspective from Ejutla, Oaxaca. In *Cultural
    Evolution: Contemporary Viewpoints*, edited by Gary M. Feinman and Linda
    Manzanilla, pp. 119–142. Kluwer Academic/Plenum, New York.
Garraty, Christopher P., and Barbara L. Stark. 2002. Imperial and Social Relations in
    Postclassic South-Central Veracruz, Mexico. *Latin American Antiquity* 13:3–33.
Helms, Mary W. 1993. *Craft and the Kingly Ideal: Art, Trade, and Power.* University of
    Texas Press, Austin.
Hendon, Julia A. 1996. Archaeological Approaches to the Organization of Domestic
    Labor: Household Practice and Domestic Relations. *Annual Review of Anthropology*
    25:45–61.
Hendon, Julia A. 1997. Women's Work, Women's Space, and Women's Status among the
    Classic Period Maya Elite of the Copan Valley, Honduras. In *Women in Prehistory:
    North America and Mesoamerica*, edited by Cheryl Claassen and Rosemary A. Joyce,
    pp. 33–46. University of Pennsylvania Press, Philadelphia.
Hendon, Julia A. 1999. Spinning and Weaving in Pre-Hispanic Mesoamerica: The
    Technology and Social Relations of Textile Production. In *Mayan Clothing
    and Weaving through the Ages*, edited by Barbara Knoke de Arathoon, Nacie
    L. Gonzalez, and John M. Willemsen Devlin, pp. 7–16. Museo Ixchel del Traje
    Indígena, Guatemala City.
Hendon, Julia A. 2006. Textile Production as Craft in Mesoamerica: Time, Labor, and
    Knowledge. *Journal of Social Archaeology* 6:354–378.
Hirth, Kenneth G. 2006a. Market Forces or State Control: The Organization of Obsidian
    Craft Production in a Civic-Ceremonial Context. In *Obsidian Craft Production in
    Ancient Central Mexico*, edited by Kenneth G. Hirth, pp. 179–201. University of Utah
    Press, Salt Lake City.
Hirth, Kenneth G., ed. 2006b. *Obsidian Craft Production in Ancient Central Mexico.*
    University of Utah Press, Salt Lake City.
Hirth, Kenneth G., ed. 2009a. *Housework: Craft Production and Domestic Economy
    in Ancient Mesoamerica.* Archeological Papers of the American Anthropological
    Association, No. 19, Wiley-Blackwell, New York.
Hirth, Kenneth G. 2009b. Housework and Domestic Craft Production: An Introduction.
    In *Housework: Craft Production and Domestic Economy in Ancient Mesoamerica*,
    edited by Kenneth G. Hirth, pp. 1–12. Archeological Papers of the American
    Anthropological Association, No. 19, Wiley-Blackwell, New York.
Hruby, Zachary X., and Rowan K. Flad, eds. 2007. *Rethinking Craft Specialization in
    Complex Societies: Archaeological Analyses of the Social Meaning of Production.*
    Archeological Papers No. 17, American Anthropological Association, Arlington,
    Virginia.

Inomata, Takeshi. 2001. The Power and Ideology of Artistic Creation: Elite Craft
    Specialists in Classic Maya Society. *Current Anthropology* 42:321–350.
Inomata, Takeshi. 2007. Knowledge and Belief in Artistic Production by Classic Maya
    Elites. In *Rethinking Craft Specialization in Complex Societies: Archaeological
    Analyses of the Social Meaning of Production*, edited by Zachary X. Hruby and
    Rowan K. Flad, pp. 129–141. Archeological Papers No. 17, American Anthropological
    Association, Arlington, Virginia.
Inomata, Takeshi, and Daniela Triadan, eds. 2010. *Burned Palaces and Elite Residences of
    Aguateca: Excavations and Ceramics*. University of Utah Press, Salt Lake City.
Inomata, Takeshi, Daniela Triadan, Erick Ponciano, Estela Pinto, Richard E. Terry,
    and Markus Eberl. 2002. Domestic and Political Lives of Classic Maya Elites:
    The Excavation of Rapidly Abandoned Structures at Aguateca, Guatemala. *Latin
    American Antiquity* 13:305–330.
McAnany, Patricia A. 2010. *Ancestral Maya Economies in Archaeological Perspective*.
    Cambridge University Press, Cambridge.
Menon, Jaya. 2008. Archaeological Problems with Specialization. *Studies in History*
    24:137–157.
Nichols, Deborah L., Elizabeth M. Brumfiel, Hector Neff, Mary Hodge, Thomas H.
    Charlton, and Michael D. Glascock. 2002. Neutrons, Markets, Cities, and Empires:
    A 1,000-Year Perspective on Ceramic Production and Distribution in the Postclassic
    Basin of Mexico. *Journal of Anthropological Archaeology* 21:25–82.
Pool, Christopher A. 1992. Integrating Ceramic Production and Distribution. In *Ceramic
    Production and Distribution: An Integrated Approach*, edited by George J. Bey III
    and Christopher A. Pool, pp. 275–313. Westview Press, Boulder, Colorado.
Rice, Prudence M. 2009. Late Classic Maya Pottery Production: Review and Synthesis.
    Journal of Archaeological Method and Theory 16:117–156.
Schortman, Edward M., and Patricia A. Urban. 1994. Living on the Edge: Core/
    Periphery Relations in Ancient Southeastern Mesoamerica. *Current Anthropology*
    35:401–430.
Schortman, Edward M., and Patricia A. Urban. 2004. Modeling the Roles of Craft
    Production in Ancient Political Economies. *Journal of Archaeological Research*
    12:185–226.
Schortman, Edward M., Patricia A. Urban, and Marne T. Ausec. 2001. Politics with
    Style: Identity Formation in Prehispanic Southeastern Mesoamerica. *American
    Anthropologist* 103:312–330.
Shimada, Izumi, ed. 2007. *Craft Production in Complex Societies: Multicraft and Producer
    Perspectives*. University of Utah Press, Salt Lake City.
Smith, Michael E. 2004. The Archaeology of Ancient State Economies. *Annual Review of
    Anthropology* 33:73–102.
Stark, Barbara L., and Christopher P. Garraty. 2004. Evaluation of Systematic Surface
    Evidence for Pottery Production in Veracruz, Mexico. *Latin American Antiquity*
    15:123–143.
Stark, Barbara L., and Alana Ossa. 2010. Origins and Development of Mesoamerican
    Marketplaces: Evidence from South-Central Veracruz. In *Archaeological Approaches
    to Market Exchange in Ancient Societies*, edited by Christopher P. Garraty and
    Barbara L. Stark, pp. 99–126. University Press of Colorado, Boulder.
Urban, Patricia A., E. Christian Wells, and Marne T. Ausec. 1997. The Fires Without and
    the Fires Within: Evidence for Ceramic Production Facilities at the Late Classic
    Site of La Sierra, Naco Valley, Northwestern Honduras, and in Its Environs. In *The*

Prehistory and History of Ceramic Kilns, edited by Prudence M. Rice, pp. 173–194. American Ceramic Society, Westerville, Ohio.

Wells, E. Christian. 2006. Recent Trends in Theorizing Prehispanic Mesoamerican Economies. *Journal of Archaeological Research* 14:265–312.

Wells, E. Christian, and Karla L. Davis-Salazar, eds. 2007. *Mesoamerican Ritual Economy: Archaeological and Ethnological Perspectives*. University Press of Colorado, Boulder.

CHAPTER 43

THE DOMESTICATION OF STONE IN MESOAMERICA

JOHN CLARK

MESOAMERICA presents challenges to universal explanations of civilization, a primary one being the absence there of practical metallurgy. Mesoamerican peoples were on the verge of a Bronze Age at the time they were subjugated by Spanish adventurers in the early 1500s. For the Aztecs, metallurgy was largely confined to the production of gold trinkets. In standard accounts, lust for soft, precious metals drew the Spanish into Mexico, and hammered Toledo steel swords and a bit of gunpowder allowed these few hundred Europeans to conquer the Aztec Empire, by all accounts the bloodiest in the Americas. Explained from the native point of view, the Aztecs' reliance on obsidian and flint edges for their wooden spears and swords sealed their doom. The technological disparity between Old and New World peoples portrayed in accounts of the conquest makes one wonder how civilization ever arose among benighted peoples dependent on rocks rather than on iron. The question entails its answer. Mesoamericans mastered stone and made cutting, killing, and pounding tools capable of accomplishing all the tasks performed by hard metals in other preindustrial civilizations.

There are only a limited number of ways of producing useful objects and products from stone, and these depend on the innate properties of different stones. For the Aztecs, shells were also considered stones. Techniques for breaking down stone and shell in Mesoamerica (fracturing, cutting, pulverizing, drilling, abrading, burning) were employed by most neolithic peoples, so Mesoamerican stone technologies present few novelties for world prehistory. As with their nascent metallurgy, the most complex stone-working techniques in Mesoamerica were reserved for fabricating beads, earspools, and other jewelry (Melgar Tísoc and Solís Ciriaco 2009, 2010; Sahagún 1959). Making things to beautify elites was an important pursuit for all Mesoamerican civilizations. Their bauble obsession inspired innovations in their stone science. Mesoamericans also had their more practical side. They relied on locally available resources to fulfill most basic tool needs for processing food and harvesting wood. Tools that required special, nonubiquitous stone (e.g., obsidian, jade, basalt) unavailable in most regions had to be imported, so geological realities played a role in the geopolitics of tool production and exchange and in the fortunes of particular peoples and civilizations. Obsidian and jade have received disproportionate scholarly attention because they were the stones most widely exchanged, and they represent possible controllable resources, technologies, and products. Both types of stone were used to make utilitarian tools before they were co-opted by jewelry makers. It has gone largely unremarked that the most frequent bulk use of stone, and the energetically most expensive for most Mesoamericans, was for constructing buildings and sculptures.

The portion of Middle America that became Mesoamerica was extensive and geologically complex, so most rock, stone, and mineral resources useful to humans were available within it. Arcs of active volcanoes with their fresh igneous rocks defined early Mesoamerica's northern and southern boundaries, and there were mountains of older volcanic, metamorphic, and sedimentary rocks nearly everywhere else, except for the large limestone shelf that is the Yucatán Peninsula. As recorded by Diego de Landa, an early Spanish priest, the rock-rich but iron-poor Yucatán was blessed with an abundance of flint that provided ironlike utilitarian tools. Stones as different as limestone, flint, and obsidian had to be worked in different ways. The general evolution of stone use in Middle America conforms to the worldwide progression from paleolithic technologies of chipped flint and quartzite implements to neolithic technologies of ground and polished tools. This technological shift corresponded to the invention of new tool types (axes, adzes) made of different kinds of stone not easily or effectively worked by simple fracture, so the new stone-working techniques effectively expanded the universe of useful rocks and their availability. Of course, some rocks could be used without modification.

UNMODIFIED STONE

The domestication of stone in Mesoamerica required thorough knowledge of the physical properties of different kinds of stones, how to find and/or extract them, and how to process them. Even for unmodified stones, their effective use depended on proper selection. Not just any rock would do for a given task. Using a rock to smash something is about the simplest use imaginable, but even a stone hammer must have properties suitable to the task. Hammerstones of different hardnesses, densities, textures, shapes, and sizes were needed to flake obsidian, flint, basalt, and jade. In Mesoamerica, hammerstones were selected and transported—especially to the obsidian quarries, but no adequate study has yet been done of them. Modern knappers would sooner part with several hundred pounds of knapping stone than a favorite hammerstone, a sentiment perhaps shared with ancient artisans. Stream beds and alluvial tills are good places to find rounded cobbles suitable for pounders and pebbles for missiles to throw or to sling. Small pebbles (usually of quartzite) were widely used in Mesoamerica as stone polishers for burnishing ceramic vessels. Small smooth stones were even used by Aztec goldsmiths to smooth and polish sheets of gold. Other exceptional stones, such as quartz crystals, were collected and appear to have had nonutilitarian uses in rituals and shaman bundles. River cobbles were used for cooking and also for grinding seeds, at least in the beginning days of this subsistence pursuit. The most frequent use of natural stone, however, was for building, either as construction fill or façades. Before the dawn of Mesoamerica around 1500 BC, most needed stones were picked up during a group's seasonal round. With the advent of civilization, there was an increase in the volume and kinds of stones and rocks used and in their specialized extraction, production, and transport. Some stone had to be broken from outcrops or extracted from mines. Some of these operations may have required the use of fire to spall off rock. The use of cobbles and pebbles as hammers, punches, pounders, abraders, grinders, polishers, cooking stones, or even missiles is well known. Other natural lithic products escape notice. A famous Aztec war with a southern province was over access to emery sand needed by the lapidaries of Tenochtitlan. The working of hard stones required graded sets of abrasives. Some had to be sorted in much the same way that placer gold was separated from river sand; other abrasives and polishing powders had to be manufactured by crushing rocks and sorting their dust.

CHIPPED STONE

The most fearful Aztec weapons the Spanish faced were wooden swords edged with obsidian blades. These swords were sharper than their steel Iberian counterparts but not as durable or versatile. Obsidian blades were the most evolved form of chipped stone tools in Mesoamerica and were made by controlled knapping (Figure 43.1). Only hard stones that fracture conchoidally, such as volcanic glass (obsidian, ignimbrite) and stones with a microcrystalline structure (flint, chert, quartzite, rhyolite, some basalt), are suitable for knapping (Hirth 2003; Kidder 1947). Different products represented varying levels of production difficulty. The

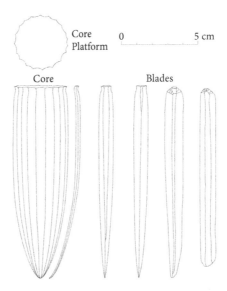

Figure 43.1 Drawings of fine obsidian blades and the core from which they came
(redrawn from Kidder et al. 1946: 137, Fig. 55).

simplest technique (direct percussion) was to hit one stone with another to break off a piece. Given their hard glassy texture, flakes removed from obsidian cobbles had razor-sharp edges and could be used without further modification as knives or scrapers. For more formal tools, smaller flakes were removed from original large flakes to give them the proper three-dimensional shape. This process involved direct percussion with hammerstones or tools made from antler, bone, or wood (Clark 1988). Arrowheads and spearheads known the world over were shaped this way. Because these tools have two flat faces shaped by the removal of small flakes, they are known as "bifaces." The large flint knives used by the Aztecs in human heart sacrifice were elaborate forms of bifaces (Figure 43.2a). For some chipped tools, greater precision was achieved by applying force to a stone directly or indirectly. For instance, when an artisan holds a bone tool in one hand and places its tip on a work stone and slowly applies pressure to force small chips off the stone, this is a pressure technique. If the bone is used instead as a chisel and struck with a hammerstone or mallet, this is indirect percussion. The flint eccentrics found in the Maya region were made largely with indirect percussion by mallets and small antler punches (Figure 43.2b). Mesoamericans made flakes, blades, bifaces, and some nonutilitarian objects with these techniques. Blades were long, thin, parallel-sided forms that reminded the Spaniards of their steel razors, and blades were sometimes used for this purpose (Figure 43.1). Obsidian blade production required the special shaping of long cores by percussion and then the removal of blades by the application of pressure with a large wooden tool. Blade making and other difficult techniques were performed by specialists.

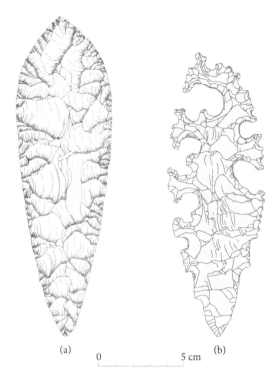

(a)

0   5 cm

(b)

Figure 43.2 Drawings of flint bifaces. (a) Aztec-style sacrificial knife from Izapa,
Mexico; (b) flint eccentric from northern Guatemala (author drawings).

GROUND STONE

Some useful stones lack the fracture properties of flint and cannot be effectively
sculpted by chipping. They were shaped by tediously pecking away minute portions until a desired form was achieved. This gave a pocked texture to their dressed
surfaces. Tools made with this technique are called "ground stone," a misnomer
in terms of production technique but an apt functional label for its most famous
products: milling stones. Mesoamerican stone sculptures and shaped building
stones were produced by this technique. For most Mesoamerican households, the
mano and metate for grinding corn were the most expensive items in the house.
These heavy tools were widely traded, with the preferred stone being vesicular
basalt because of its hardness, natural voids, and rough texture—all of which combined to make an ideal surface for shearing soaked corn and grinding it into a pal-
atable paste. The earliest grinding stones in Middle America were selected cobbles
used without modification, but later grinding stones were sculpted to standard
sizes and shapes (Clark 1988). The later metates in Mesoamerica were carved with
short legs that built the proper working angle into the implement. These specialized, primary tools are still being made and used today.

The pecking technique for sculpting metates is not significantly different from direct percussion; both require the direct application of force by swinging a hammerstone to break off pieces from the stone being worked. Some hammerstones used in these techniques could be similar, but for most pecking work, a sharp rather than a rounded hammerstone was used. These look like crude, hand-size chopping tools. With use, the sharp edges of these tools become blunted. For most sculpting, the artisan used a glancing blow to avoid breaking the work piece. Most of the sculptures for which Mesoamerica is famous, especially those of the hardest stone, were fashioned by pecking. It is not known whether artisans used hammerstones directly in the hand or attached them to handles to increase the force and accuracy of their blows. Chisels may have been used in carving limestone monuments in the Maya lowlands. Blunted jade chisels have been found, and some of the carved backgrounds of low-relief sculptures appear to have chisel marks. Maya depictions show the use of hafted peccary tusks for carving. Finer details were incised with stone flakes. Tool marks at limestone quarries show that some large slabs used for sculptures and building blocks were chopped out of bedrock using hafted chert axes.

POLISHED STONE

The same process of chipping and pulverizing away stone to make manos and metates was used as the preliminary step for shaping objects such as jade axes. Axe production required additional steps of grinding away surface irregularities and polishing. This required a suite of coarse-to-fine abrasives. For the Aztecs, the final polish for jade items was obtained by rubbing them with pieces of cane. Hard gemstones and shells were worked by lapidary specialists with the same techniques. The pieces that were worked were sometimes shattered from stones, but chipping and pecking were not prominent steps in the manufacture of small polished objects. Abrasive stones such as basalt and sandstone were sometimes used for grinding, but most of the steps of the process depended on loose abrasives and devices that allowed their application. Large jade boulders on display in the National Museum in Guatemala City show that sheets of jade were cut and broken from them. Thin saws of stiff material rather than strings were used to forcefully apply the cutting abrasives. Evidence of string sawing is apparent on other pieces. Removed jade slabs were further cut into shape with saws (likely of wood or cane with embedded abrasives) and drills (solid and hollow). The detailed workmanship of some jade plaques and sculptures in Mesoamerica rivals that of Chinese jades, and all without the benefit of metal tools. The precise details of how objects were stabilized, drilled, and polished over concave and convex surfaces need to be determined through technical and experimental studies. Polished items in Mesoamerica included beads, earspools, pendants, plaques, mirrors, mosaics, idols, and vases made from a range of materials, from shell and alabaster to pyrite and quartz crystal (Melgar Tísoc and Solís Ciriaco 2009, 2010). The earliest polished hard-stone items known for the Americas are small animal-shaped beads that date to Late Archaic times. With the Olmec emphasis on iron-ore mirrors and jade jewelry at about 1400 BC, the lapidary arts came into ascendancy in Mesoamerica.

BURNED STONE

Surveys of Mesoamerican stone technology generally end with polished stone, but there is much more to learn. In terms of processing stone to make useful products, one of the major stone industries was the production of lime. Much ado has been made over Teotihuacan's obsidian industries, but these pale beside its cement consumption. The production of cement required several hundred times the work force and energy that was expended in making obsidian spearheads and knives (Barba and Córdova 2010). Also, in the Maya lowlands there are many plaster-coated pyramids and stucco sculptures. Stucco production involved reduction of limestone by fire, a process fundamental to metallurgy and ceramic production. Similar processes may have been employed to manufacture some pigments. In some regions of the world, flint was baked to improve its flakeability. For the moment, there is no clear evidence of this technique in Mesoamerica. Most thermally altered flint artifacts there were burned (probably ritually) after they were made rather than being chipped from heat-treated stone.

Stone-working techniques are commonly characterized as reductive technologies compared to additive ceramic technology. This characterization holds for most stone processing in Mesoamerica, but the production of lime was clearly a first step for a complex of additive technologies. There is also Postclassic evidence for the production of fake greenstone. Veneers of synthetic greenstone were applied to carved alabaster skeletal cores to make small idols that looked like jade objects. Manufacture of this liquid rock would have required dust from pulverized gemstones as well as a bonding agent to hold the dust together and affix it to the alabaster core. Conceptually this was similar to affixing stucco to stone armatures to make stone sculptures. Little information is available for ancient glues and adhesives, but these were important in lapidary and feather work and widely used to put together other products, such as obsidian-edged swords. Whether glues were integral to some production techniques remains to be discovered.

REFERENCES

Barba, Luis, and José Luis Córdova. 2010. *Materiales y energía en la arquitectura de Teotihuacan*. IIA-UNAM, Mexico.

Clark, John E. 1988. *The Lithic Artifacts of La Libertad, Chiapas, Mexico*. Papers of the New World Archaeological Foundation, No. 52, Brigham Young University, Provo.

Hirth, Kenneth G., ed. 2003. *Mesoamerican Lithic Technology: Experimentation and Interpretation.* University of Utah Press, Salt Lake City.

Kidder, Alfred V. 1947. *The Artifacts of Uaxactun, Guatemala.* Carnegie Institution of Washington, Publication 576, Washington, DC.

Kidder, Alfred V., Jesse D. Jennings, and Edwin M. Shook. 1946. *Excavations at Kaminaljuyu.* Carnegie Institution of Washington, Publication 561, Washington, DC.

Melgar Tísoc, Emiliano Ricardo, and Reyna Beatriz Solís Ciriaco. 2009. Caracterización de huellas de manufactura en objetos lapidarios de obsidiana del Templo Mayor de Tenochtitlan. *Arqueologia* 42:118–134.

Melgar Tísoc, Emiliano Ricardo, and Reyna Beatriz Solís Ciriaco. 2010. Manufacturing Techniques of the Turquoise Mosaics from the Great Temple of Tenochtitlan, Mexico. In *2nd Latin-American Symposium on Physical and Chemical Methods in Archaeology, Art and Cultural Heritage Conservation: Symposium on Archaeological and Art Issues in Materials Science, IMRC 2009*, edited by J. L. Ruvalcaba Sil, J. R. Trujeque, and A. Velázquez, pp. 119–124. Sociedad Mexicana de Materiales, A.C., INAH-UNAM-UAC, Mexico City.

Sahagún, Fray Bernadino de. 1959. *Florentine Codex: General History of the Things of New Spain. Book 9—the Merchants.* Translated by C. E. Dibble and A. J. O. Anderson. University of Utah Press, Salt Lake City.

CHAPTER 44

....

CERAMIC
TECHNOLOGY AND
PRODUCTION

....

PRUDENCE M. RICE

SOME of the most beautiful art objects of the ancient Western Hemisphere were created by Mesoamerican potters. Meticulously painted in multiple colors ("polychrome"), sometimes with delicately rendered, lifelike human figures, this pottery was nonetheless produced by simple technologies. Prehispanic Mesoamerican ceramics are best described as terra cotta or earthenware: generally low-fired and porous, unvitrified, and unglazed. Potters formed vessels without the use of a wheel and fired them, for the most part, in the absence of formal kiln structures.

ORIGINS

....

There is little to suggest an independent invention of pottery making in Mesoamerica. Instead, the technology for making ceramics was likely introduced from outside the region, perhaps into southern Mesoamerica from Central America in the third millennium BC (Clark and Gosser 1995; Flannery and Marcus 1994). This pottery typically mimicked the shapes of squashes and gourds (Joesink-Mandeville 1973), replacing the latter as food containers.

TECHNOLOGY OF MANUFACTURE

Mesoamerican ceramics were produced by relatively simple technologies of form-ing, decorating, and firing. Few actual workshops have been located and exca-vated to provide definitive evidence of physical infrastructure, and the potter's toolkit does not appear to have been elaborate. Ethnographic studies of modern Mesoamerican potters (e.g., Reina 1966) suggest that ancient potters would have had big open tubs for holding raw clay and water, smaller bowls or cups to hold pigments, and a variety of ad hoc tools—made of wood, plant materials, broken pottery, stone, and cloth—for scraping and smoothing the interior and exterior. Pots were not formed on a wheel, but rather on a mat or board. In several areas of Mesoamerica, twentieth-century potters used small devices of wood or pot-tery—the *kabal* in Yucatán (Brainerd 1958); the *molde* in central Mexico (Foster 1959)—which could be rotated with their feet while their hands worked the clay. It is not known if such devices were used in ancient times or if they were innovations adapted from the pottery wheel (which was introduced by the Spanish).

Production began with the selection of raw materials: clays, tempers, and pig-ments. Ethnographic studies suggest that clays are generally obtained close to a potter's community, whereas other ingredients, such as temper and pigments, used in smaller quantities, may be obtained at greater distances and perhaps through trade (Arnold 1985). Varied clays were used in making ancient pottery, reflecting the broad geological variation of Mesoamerica. As in other areas of the world, white or light-firing clays, lacking iron impurities and other colorants, seem to have been particularly valued.

Some clays exhibit ideal characteristics for making pottery. These include optimal proportions of different sizes and shapes of particles naturally present in the clay that confer desirable "working properties," such as plasticity, without being too sticky or too stiff. Other clays need modification of these properties for general workability and for the vessels' intended uses, and so the potter may com-bine them with other ingredients. These ingredients, commonly called "temper," are typically crushed local rock or sand or, especially in Mesoamerica, volcanic ash, although a great range of materials, including other clays, crushed shell, plant fibers, and even liquids, may have been used at different times and places. Still other clays may have too much coarse material present naturally, and these might have been crushed and sieved or left to soak in water for a time (levigated), in order to separate the coarse and fine fractions.

The most common technique for forming a pottery vessel appears to have been hand building by coiling, although "drawing" (thinning and pulling upward a large lump of clay) was used in the Guatemala highlands in modern times (Reina and Hill 1978). Sometimes several techniques were combined: for example, a base was formed in a preformed saucer or broken pot, and then coils were added and smoothed to build up the body. Molding does not appear to have been widely used to form whole vessels, although molds were common for making other items of clay. For example, jars and dishes were often modified for use by the addition of handles, supports, spouts, and flanges, and these components were sometimes formed in molds. In general, because the final steps of finishing vessel surfaces— careful scraping, smoothing, and burnishing or polishing—eliminate traces of forming, it is difficult to know what construction methods were used in prehispanic times.

DECORATION

Perhaps the most striking characteristic of Mesoamerican pottery is its decoration. Highly visible pottery used in serving food or for other purposes, whether domestic or ritual, was often extravagantly embellished, and such embellishment, while largely "decorative," also conveyed information about the status, identity, and beliefs of the owners and users. Decoration can be described in terms of the addition of coloration and plastic manipulation.

The simplest surface coloration is by means of a "slip": a suspension of fine clay, usually colored or with the addition of colorants, in water. Applied to a vessel before firing, a slip is typically polished to create an attractive luster and to help it adhere to the clay body. Slips applied to Mesoamerican pottery were most commonly red, orange, black, gray, and white-cream. Different colored slips might be applied to interior and exterior surfaces. Some very elaborate Late Classic Maya painted wares had a whitish slip under the paint and a semitranslucent coating over all or part of it. True vitrified glazes were not used until Spanish times, but Plumbate pottery from the Chiapas/Guatemala border area had a shiny sintered surface that resulted from the unique properties of the slip clay (Neff 2003).

More complex decoration was created by multicolored painting, best known from the Classic period in the Maya lowlands (Figure 44.1) and from the Early Postclassic period (Mixteca-Puebla style; Nicholson and Quiñones Keber 1994) in central Mexico. Prefiring colors included the common red, orange, cream-to-white, and black, but also pink, dark purplish-red, yellow, and gray; greens and blues ("Maya Blue") were sometimes added after firing. These pigments were used to paint a seemingly limitless range of images, from simple geometric motifs to glyphic texts, plants and animals, gods and symbols, mythical figures, court scenes, and so on. Rollout photographs of Classic lowland Maya polychromes taken by Justin Kerr are available on the website of the Foundation for the Advancement of Mesoamerican Studies (Kerr n.d.; also Reents-Budet 1994).

Plastic decoration involves manipulation of the vessel surface by any number of techniques including incising, excising, punctating, carving, gadrooning, fluting, impressing, stamping, combing or striating, and molding or modeling. Other techniques include applying (appliqué) small modeled or molded elements.

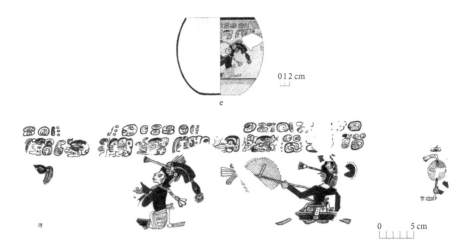

Figure 44.1 Rollout drawing of a partially reconstructed early Late Classic Saxche Polychrome (red and black on orange) bowl, dating approximately to 550–600 AD, recovered from building fill in Caracol Structure I2 (courtesy of A. and D. Chase, www.caracol.org, 2007 Field Report: Fig. 20e).

Well-known examples of elaborate plastic decoration include Formative/Preclassic vessels carved and gadrooned into squashlike shapes, Late Classic and Early Postclassic Plumbate vessels with modeled faces on them, and the molded-carved scenes on Fine Orange pottery from the western Maya lowlands.

Utilitarian domestic pottery, used in a variety of food-preparation tasks, typically exhibited little surface elaboration and finishing might have been intended to enhance the object's functions. Large water-storage jars were often striated on the exterior, sometimes in decorative patterns, presumably to enhance evaporative cooling of the water. Shallow footed bowls for grating chili peppers and other substances exhibited deep and often patterned incising or stamping to roughen the interior (Figure 44.2). In general, however, embellishment on such vessels was little more than altering the shape of the lip, or adding a painted stripe or impressions of fingers, hollow reeds, or a die, and the like.

The firing of these vessels is perplexing, because prehispanic pottery kilns have been identified by archaeologists in only a few areas of Mesoamerica. This suggests that archaeologists do not recognize firing structures or do not know where to look for them. Also, it could mean that most of the pottery made and used in this large area for three thousand years was fired without benefit of the protection and temperature control offered by the enclosed chamber of a kiln.

Nonkiln firing is typically called "open" or "bonfire" firing. As described by ethnographers, this method typically involves carefully arranging single or multiple tiers of pottery on a layer of coarse fuel (typically wood), covering them with finer fuel (e.g., dried grasses, palm thatch),sometimes with large fragments placed over the pots to protect them, and then setting the pile on fire. The fire burns

Figure 44.2 A (modern) grater bowl or *molcajete* from Mexico, showing an incised interior. The interior and upper rim are covered with a thin, clear, lead glaze (author's personal collection).

rapidly at first and may briefly attain temperatures as high as 900°C or more, after which the fire begins to cool as the larger pieces of fuel under the pottery burn more slowly. Because open firings do not fully protect vessels from contact with fuel, other pots, or gusts of wind, pottery fired in bonfires typically have blotchy colors ("fireclouds") that demonstrate variable degrees of oxidation of the pigments (especially iron) in the clay or slip.

The elaborate polychrome vases and dishes characteristic of many areas and periods of Mesoamerica generally lack fireclouds, suggesting that they were fired more carefully. These may have been fired by placing them inside large pots that acted as protective saggars, with the fire built around the outside of the container and not touching the vessel being fired.

Bonfire firings may have taken place in the patios of potters' residential compounds or in areas away from settlements where the smoke would not be noxious. Locating these firing areas is often serendipitous, but they can be identified by several indicators: burned surface soils or limestone, layers of ash, charcoal fragments, and wasters, pots, or fragments that show evidence of cracking, warping, overfiring, or other misfiring (Stark 1985).

Kilns for firing pottery are primarily known from Mexico. Pottery might have been fired in "pit kilns," such as those discovered at Classic-period Ejutla, in Oaxaca (Feinman and Balkansky 1997). Measuring about 2–4 meters across and excavated about 40–70 centimeters deep into soft bedrock (Figure 44.3), these pits would have offered some protection from winds during firing. Formally constructed kiln structures are known from Matacapan, in southern Veracruz, Mexico. There, the remains of about forty Classic-period kilns have been found, primarily south of the

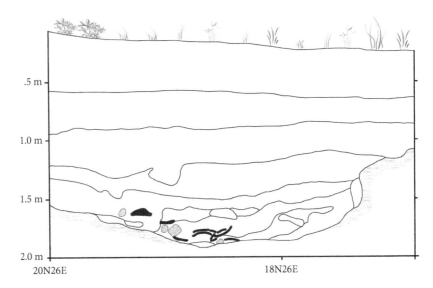

.5 m

1.0 m

1.5 m

2.0 m

20N26E   18N26E

Figure 44.3 Profile drawing of a pit kiln excavated at Ejutla, Oaxaca, Mexico. The firing pit had been excavated roughly 60 centimeters into bedrock, and it held layers of ash and charcoal plus large ceramic sherds and rock. Above the pit were midden materials in clay-loam soil, with the plow zone uppermost (redrawn after Feinman and Balkansky 1997: Fig. 4).

civic-ceremonial center (Pool 1997). These kilns, built of fiber-tempered clay and stones, are small, circular, updraft, double-chambered (the fire pit excavated into the ground), and open-topped. They appear to have been used to fire four types of pottery known as Fine Gray, Fine Orange, Coarse Orange, and Coarse Brown.

FORMS

Mesoamerican pottery was made in many forms, which can be broadly categorized as containers and noncontainers, all in varied sizes and with uses ranging from domestic through ritual.

Ceramic containers include vessels for domestic food preparation, cooking, and storage, plus those for eating and serving. Preparation, cooking, and storage containers are typically simple globular vessels, with or without necks or collars, and with mouths that range from wide to narrow depending on their use in carrying liquids or solids. A common cooking vessel is the open-mouthed globular *olla*; jars for carrying water or for storage of various items often have narrow necks and mouths, and sometimes handles.

Several items of the early Mesoamerican kitchen can be linked to the role of maize and chili peppers in the diet. For example, a ceramic colander was used to soak and drain shelled, dried maize in a solution of lime water before grinding it into a flour. A griddle, or *comal*, for toasting tortillas of maize continues to be used today, although modern *comales* are often made of metal. One of the earliest ceramic forms is the *tecomate*, a medium-sized, neckless, globular jar with a restricted orifice, associated with keeping (and probably serving) tortillas. A fourth form is the incised *molcajete*, or grater bowl.

Pots for cooking and storage were typically coarse-textured, with relatively greater amounts of temper in larger sizes. For cooking wares, the porosity conferred by such tempering agents accommodated the stresses of repeated heating and cooling; in storage jars, particularly those for water storage, the porosity allowed for evaporative cooling.

The most common serving vessels can be described as bowls, plates, and cups, but they appear with varied elaborations and in a range of sizes, from individual dishes through large open platters for serving foods like tamales or meats in larger feasts. Numerous other vessel forms are distinctive of particular times, places, and cultures: small spouted "chocolate pots" appear in the Preclassic Maya lowlands; variably proportioned cylindrical vessels with three feet, or supports ("cylinder tripods"), are common in Teotihuacan and in the Guatemala highlands; cylindrical vases are characteristic of the Late Classic Maya lowlands.

The production of serving wares was more labor-intensive than that for cooking wares, and vessels may be elaborated with handles, spouts, and supports. The paste or fabric of the pottery is often more finely textured; some vessels (e.g., Fine Orange) appear to lack temper. In others, the temper chosen was not local in origin: some Late Classic lowland Maya pottery was made with volcanic ash from the highlands. These vessels are generally highly decorated. Some of the most elaborate of them were likely restricted to the highest of elite households, but otherwise they appear to have circulated among households representing a wide range of social statuses. These vessels also commonly accompany burials, and their quantities vary with the status of the deceased.

A specialized but ubiquitous category of pottery throughout Mesoamerica is the incense burner (*incensario*; *sahumador*) for burning aromatic resins during various rituals. These take many forms—cups, bowls, vases—and exhibit assorted embellishments. The simplest may have incising or appliqué decoration, whereas the most complex vessels or their cylindrical stands (e.g., those from Palenque: Cuevas García 2000) are adorned with effigies of deities and related symbols. Other elaborate incense burners include "theater" censers from Classic Teotihuacan and the Guatemala highlands (Figure 44.4; Berlo 1982), Postclassic incensarios with deity effigies on the lids in Oaxaca (Caso and Bernal 1952), and lowland Maya Postclassic vase censers with effigy figures attached to the front.

Noncontainer ceramics include many different forms that occur throughout Mesoamerica from Formative through conquest-period times. Figurines, for example, may be solid or hollow or modeled or mold-made. The western Mexican states of Jalisco, Nayarit, and Colima had a lively Preclassic tradition of producing modeled and painted figurines of humans and dogs, as well as three-dimensional

Figure 44.4 A stylized Classic Teotihuacan incense burner, showing the massively decorated lid over the small receptacle for the incense. Multiple small molded components were added to flat plaques, which were then attached to a framework. A tall narrow chimney behind the decorative plaques carries the smoke as the incense is burned (redrawn after Berlo 1982: Fig. 5).

scenes of daily life that depicted people and homes (Bell 1971). These were typically deposited in tombs. Musical instruments, such as drums, whistles, and flutes, may be made of pottery. Other items include braziers, stamps and seals, candeleros, beads, and various items that may be specially formed or made from broken fragments of pottery, such as net sinkers, spindle whorls, lids, and gaming pieces.

REFERENCES

Arnold, Dean E. 1985. *Ceramic Theory and Cultural Process*. Cambridge University Press, Cambridge.

Bell, Betty. 1971. Archaeology of Nayarit, Jalisco, and Colima. In *Archaeology of Northern Mesoamerica*, edited by Gordon F. Ekholm and Ignacio Bernal, pp. 694–753. University of Texas Press, Austin.

Berlo, Janet Catherine. 1982. Artistic Specialization at Teotihuacan: The Ceramic Incense Burner. In *Pre-Columbian Art History: Selected Readings*, edited by Alana Cordy-Collins, pp. 83–100. Peek Publications, Palo Alto, California.

Brainerd, George W. 1958. The Archaeological Ceramics of Yucatán. *Anthropological Records*, vol. 19. University of California Press, Berkeley.

Caso, Alfonso, and Ignacio Bernal. 1952. *Urnas de Oaxaca*. Memorias 2, Instituto Nacional de Antropología e Historia, Mexico City.

Clark, John E., and D. Gosser. 1995. Reinventing Mesoamerica's First Pottery. In *The Emergence of Pottery. Technology and Innovation in Ancient Societies*, edited by William K. Barnett and John W. Hoopes, pp. 209–221. Smithsonian Institution Press, Washington, DC.

Cuevas García, Martha. 2000. Los incensarios del Grupo de las Cruces, Palenque. *Arqueología Mexicana* 82(45):54–61.

Feinman, Gary M., and Andrew Balkansky. 1997. Ceramic Firing in Ancient and Modern Oaxaca. In *The Prehistory and History of Ceramic Kilns*, edited by Prudence M. Rice, pp. 129–147. American Ceramic Society, Columbus, Ohio.

Flannery, Kent V., and Joyce Marcus. 1994. Early Formative Pottery of the Valley of Oaxaca, Mexico. Prehistory and Human Ecology of the Valley of Oaxaca, vol. 10. *Memoirs of the Museum of Anthropology* 27, University of Michigan, Ann Arbor.

Foster, George M. 1959. The Coyotepec Molde and Some Associated Problems of the Potter's Wheel. *Southwestern Journal of Anthropology* 15:53–63.

Joesink-Mandeville, Leroy. 1973. The Importance of Gourd Prototypes in the Analysis of Mesoamerican Ceramics. *Katunob* 8:47–53.

Kerr, Justin. N.d. The Kerr Collections. Maya Vase Data Base. An Archive of Rollout Photographs Created by Justin Kerr. http://www.famsi.org/research/kerr/index.html.

Neff, Hector. 2003. Analysis of Mesoamerican Plumbate Pottery Surfaces by Laser Ablation–Inductively Coupled Plasma-Mass Spectrometry (LA-ICP-MS). *Journal of Archaeological Science* 30(1):21–35.

Nicholson, H. B., and Eloise Quiñones Keber, eds. 1994. *Mixteca-Puebla. Discoveries and Research in Mesoamerican Art and Archaeology*. Labyrinthos, Culver City, California.

Pool, Christopher A. 1997. Prehispanic Kilns at Matacapan, Veracruz, Mexico. In *The Prehistory and History of Ceramic Kilns*, edited by Prudence M. Rice, pp. 149–171. American Ceramic Society, Columbus, Ohio.

Reents-Budet, Dorie, ed. 1994. *Painting the Maya Universe: Royal Ceramics of the Classic Period*. Duke University Press, Durham, North Carolina.

Reina, Ruben A. 1966. *The Law of the Saints: A Pokomam Pueblo and Its Community Culture*. Bobbs-Merrill, New York.

Reina, Ruben A., and Robert M. Hill III. 1978. *The Traditional Pottery of Guatemala*. University of Texas Press, Austin.

Stark, Barbara L. 1985. Archaeological Identification of Pottery-Production Locations: Ethnoarchaeological and Archaeological Data in Mesoamerica. In *Decoding Prehistoric Ceramics*, edited by Ben A. Nelson, pp. 158–194. Southern Illinois University Press, Carbondale.

CHAPTER 45

MESOAMERICAN METALLURGICAL TECHNOLOGY AND PRODUCTION

BLANCA MALDONADO

THE development of metallurgy as a craft occurred gradually over a long period. The time span between the use of metals such as silver, gold, and copper in their native state, and the process of roasting and smelting ores of these minerals was extensive. The earliest reported evidence of smelted copper in the Old World dates to the fifth or sixth millennium BC (see, e.g., Betancourt 2006). In the Pre-Columbian Americas it came much later. New World metallurgy emerged in the Andean region of South America between 1800 and 200 BC (Lechtman 1980). Metallurgical knowledge seems to have spread toward the north, as far as Mesoamerica. Archaeological evidence indicates that mining practices were rudimentary, while metallurgical techniques were complex and advanced. Copper, gold, silver, and their alloys were fashioned mainly as ornaments used in religious ceremonies and for the enhancement of elite cultural status; the manufacture of metal tools and weapons was secondary and occurred relatively late.

By the time of the Spanish conquest, three main centers of metallurgical production coexisted in the New World: the Peruvian area, the Colombian-Lower Central American region, and the Tarascan-West Mexican zone (Hosler 1994; West 1994). Native American metal craftsmen from these centers rivaled their European counterparts in the sophistication of their technical skills, but the ideological and social constructs in which they worked were very different. The Spanish were caught up in the early stages of modern capitalism. Conversely, for Native Americans metals were of great value, but they were not a commodity, in the sense that they were not produced for the purpose of market trade. Gold, for some Pre-Columbian peoples, was considered the "feces of the gods" (e.g., Sahagún 1969–1982, book 11: 233), valuable to humans but, ultimately, the "waste products of greater truth and beauty" (Quilter 1998: 1058).

THE DEVELOPMENT OF MINING AND METALLURGY IN MESOAMERICA

The earliest known locus of metallurgy and metalworking in Mesoamerica is western Mexico (Figure 45.1). The craft appeared suddenly in this region between 600 and 700 AD (Hosler 1994, 2009). The relatively late date of its appearance and the similarity of the techniques employed by the native metalsmiths to those developed in South America have led many scholars to suggest that metallurgy was introduced into western Mexico from Peru and Ecuador, by traders using watercraft capable of long-distance voyages along the Pacific coast of South and Central America (Edwards 1969; Meighan 1969; Montjoy 1969; Hosler 1994). Hosler (1994) and others (e.g., Arsandaux and Rivet 1921) have extensively discussed the technological relationships between western Mexican and South American metallurgies. Like the Andean region, Mesoamerican metallurgy and metalworking were based mainly on copper, often alloyed with tin, lead, silver, and gold. Although some utilitarian implements such as needles and fishhooks were made, most metal objects were considered to be sacred and were used for adornment in religious ceremonies and to enhance the social and political status of the elites (Hosler 1994; Pollard 1987). Current archaeological evidence for mining and extractive metallurgy is sparse. Nevertheless, the use of multiple lines of investigation, including ethnohistorical and geological information, may provide a basis for minimizing the data gaps in the *chaîne opératoire* of western Mexican metallurgy.

MINERAL RESOURCES AND MINING

The extraction of ores from mineral deposits is the first step in producing metals. Not coincidentally, most of the western Mexican territory lies within a rich metalliferous belt, and the variety of metal ores available in this zone is relatively abundant (Hosler 1994; Ostroumov and Corona-Chávez 2000). Apart from references

Figure 45.1 Western Mexico archaeological sites (modified from Solís 1999). Drawn by
Kristin Sullivan.

to several mines in Spanish colonial sources, little is known about metal mining
in Mesoamerica. During the 1940s Hendrichs (1940, 1943–44) located a number
of open-pit mines in western Guerrero, consisting essentially of large holes dug
into hillsides to follow oxidized veins of copper. Evidence indicates that the tools
used to excavate the mines and extract the ores were stone hammers, made of
dense lithic materials such as diorite and andesite and probably hafted with wood.
A stone hammer apparently used for copper processing is reported from Moho
Cay, on the coast of Belize (Bruhns and Hammond 1983). Hendrichs (1940) also
reported the presence of large stone mortars, either portable or fixed on the walls
of the mines. Other tools include bone scrapers and digging sticks, ceramic ladles,
obsidian blades, and wooden wedges. Remains of *ocote* torches and vegetal fibers
impregnated with resin, baskets, ropes, and ceramics pots have also been recorded.
Unfortunately, no recent systematic investigations of these features have been carried out in Guerrero.

Grinberg (1995), based on her interpretations of indigenous accounts in the
Legajo 1204 (an important sixteenth-century manuscript), conducted explorations
north of the El Infiernillo dam in Michoacán, and she confirmed the existence
of prehispanic copper mines on the Mayapito hill near the town of Churumuco
(Figure 45.2). These mines were open-pit operations that seem to have been

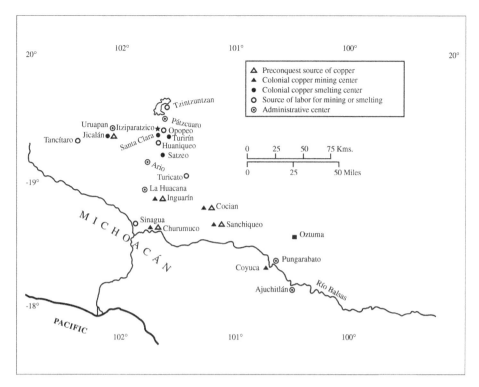

Figure 45.2 Prehispanic and colonial mining centers in the Central Balsas Basin
(adapted from Barrett 1987: Map 2). Drawn by Kristin Sullivan.

excavated with wooden or antler tools. The *Legajo* states that the indigenous people
collected greenstones and extracted copper from the mines. This suggests that the
mineral exploited was malachite. The recovery of this mineral on the surface supports this idea. Other prehispanic mines were found in the same district, including
a very deep open-pit mine (now partially collapsed) that was located between two
hills (Cerro Camacho and Cerro del Huaco) near the coast.

Various scientific methods have been employed to determine the nature of the
ores mined in western Mexico. Grinberg (1989) performed absorption analysis of
copper ore from two mines in Michoacán, La Verde, and Churumuco (see Figure
45.2). The results suggest that the ore processed at the former was probably chalcopyrite or bornite, while that at the latter appears to be either malachite or chalcocite
(see Hosler 1994: 27). Hosler and Macfarlane (1996) carried out lead isotope studies of
copper ores from several deposits in western Mexico, Oaxaca, and Veracruz, as well
as a representative sample of copper artifacts recovered from excavations at a number of sites in western Mexico and other areas in Mesoamerica. Their initial results
seemed to indicate that only a few western Mexican mining zones—Inguarán and
Bastan in Michoacán, and the regions of Ayutla and Autlán in Jalisco—provided
copper metal for a number of sites in western Mexico and beyond. Subsequent data,
however, revealed that the lead isotope ratios of copper ores from Guerrero's *tierra
caliente* coincide with those of Michoacán and Jalisco (Lopez et al. 1999).

THE PREHISPANIC COPPER-SMELTING PROCESS

The earliest metals collected by western Mexicans were probably native metals (copper, gold, and silver), which occur naturally and could be processed into objects by techniques of hammering, tempering, cutting, and grinding. The exploitation of mineral ores, however, implies a major change in metallurgical methods, including the reduction of ores and the creation of alloys. Although the types of metal artifacts and the manufacturing methods and materials (pure metals and alloys) employed in their fabrication have been relatively well established (e.g., Grinberg 1990, 2004; Hosler 1994; Pendergast 1962; Rubín de la Borbolla 1944), the technological processes used for the extraction of metal from ore remain poorly documented for most parts of the New World.

One of the major challenges in the development of metallurgy in the Americas was the attainment of sufficiently high temperatures to smelt metals from ores. In the ancient Old World, metalsmiths often attained high temperatures in small furnaces with the aid of hand-operated bellows to supply a blast of air and to increase the amount of oxygen into a mixture of ore and burning charcoal. Air bellows, however, were likely unknown in the Americas prior to the arrival of the Europeans. Andean smiths in Pre-Columbian Peru developed the blow tube, which was made of a hollowed stem of cane through which a worker would blast air toward the

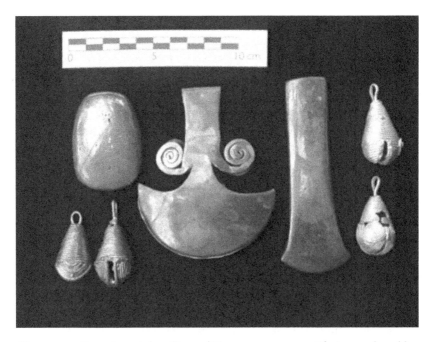

Figure 45.3 Experimental replicas of Tarascan copper artifacts, produced by
B. Maldonado (2002). Photo by F. Hayashida.

burning coals within a clay furnace. A ceramic nozzle, or *tuyère*, was placed on the furnace end of the tube to protect it from the coals. The temperature achieved in this process was high enough to smelt ore. Scores of broken nozzles have been found by Shimada and his colleagues (Shimada et al. 1983; Shimada and Merkel 1991) from the important metallurgical site of Batán Grande in northern Peru.

Ethnohistorical evidence reveals that a similar form of blowpipe was used by Mesoamerican smiths. The *Lienzo de Jicalán*, a pictographic document dating from the second half of the sixteenth century, illustrates metalworkers from Michoacán crouching in front of a brazier or crucible, melting metal by blowing through pipes (Roskamp 2001, 2004) (Figure 45.3). Similar representations are shown in other documents such as the *Relación de Michoacán* (Alcalá 2000: Lám. XIX) and the Codex Mendoza (Berdan and Anawalt 1992: 70r). These illustrations might represent melting of metal ingots for final processing, rather than smelting of ores. The right oxygen-starved conditions for smelting would be difficult to achieve using small open crucibles and lung-powered blowpipes (see Rehder 1994). According to early accounts by Spaniards, the actual extractive operations were carried out by heating small quantities in shallow earthen pits, lined with a mixture of clay and ash, intensifying the heat by blowing through cane tubes (Barrett 1987; Warren 1968). Documentary sources say that, when using this method, it was necessary to heat the ore two or three times to produce any metal of useful quality.

Hosler (2009) has reported evidence of copper-smelting activities involving the processing of malachite and cuprite at three sites in the *tierra caliente* of Guerrero: La Barranca de las Fundiciones de El Manchón, Cerro del Chivo, and Agua Fría. The analysis of slag samples from these sites indicates a smelting temperature no higher than 1150°C (Hosler 2009). Grinberg (1996) had previously examined slag from various Tarascan sites and found evidence of the smelting of sulfidic ores. Slag samples from the archaeological zone of Itziparátzico, Michoacán, have been analyzed for microstructure and compositional properties and the processed ore has been shown to also be a sulfidic ore, chalcopyrite. These slags were recovered from excavated contexts associated with the Late Postclassic period (1350–1520 AD). The most outstanding feature of Itziparátzico is its location about 125 kilometers away from the mines themselves. The data indicate that copper ore was brought a considerable distance to this locality for smelting (Maldonado 2009; Maldonado et al. 2005, Maldonado and Rehren 2009).

Analyses of slag samples from Itziparátzico indicate a consistent smelting temperature of around 1200°C, under strongly reducing conditions. These indicators provide compelling evidence for a specialized furnace technology, although the furnaces themselves might have been only semipermanent structures, most likely left to decay in situ once copper production at the site had ceased. This, and the general fragility of furnace-wall fragments in the archaeological record, might explain the absence of recognizable furnace-wall material at the site. These data present something of a dilemma, in that their implications do not fit preconceived notions of Mesoamerican metallurgy. In essence, the epitome of prehispanic smelting is embodied in the crucible-bound and mouth-blown model. Scientific studies contradict the accepted wisdom, pointing toward other technological possibilities.

Both the absence of hand-worked bellows in prehispanic Mesoamerica, and the exposed position to prevailing strong winds in the Itziparátzico area, have led us to consider that a naturally wind-aided processing may have taken place at the site. Nevertheless, further investigations will be required before an acceptable set of indicators for this type of metallurgical technology can be developed.

Itziparátzico might not represent an isolated occurrence. Large deposits of slag in (presumably) prehispanic contexts have been recorded at Jicalán El Viejo, a site that occupied a strategic position on the frontier between the Tierra Caliente and the Sierra Tarasca in Michoacán (Roskamp et al. 2003). Slag samples from Jicalán were subjected to the same analyses as the samples from Itziparátzico, producing similar results: evidence of a smelting technology that used sulfidic ores and very efficient furnaces. Jicalán is also located in an area where wind-powered pyro-metallurgy seems feasible (Roskamp, personal communication). Metallurgical findings from other sites in Michoacán (Grinberg 1996)—El Manchón, Guerrero (Hosler 2009), and more remote locations in the Maya area (e.g., Simmons et al. 2009)—suggest a new set of analytical data may soon be available for further comparison.

Alloy Technology and Fabrication
of Artifacts

In Mesoamerica, copper was not only the predominant metal, but it was the most extensively used base material. Between ca. 650–1200/1300 AD, western Mexican metalsmiths appear to have worked almost exclusively with native copper and eas-ily smelted oxidized copper ores. But from 1300 to the Spanish conquest in 1521 metalworkers in Michoacán, Jalisco, Colima, northwest Guerrero, and the south-ern parts of the state of Mexico produced an assortment of copper-based alloys, including binary alloys such as copper-silver, copper-gold, copper-arsenic, and copper-tin, and ternaries like copper-silver-gold, copper-silver-arsenic, copper-arsenic-antimony, and copper-arsenic-tin (Hosler 1994, 2009). Recent data from the Sayula Basin in Jalisco suggest an even earlier development of copper-tin and copper-arsenic bronzes. Metal objects recovered mainly from burials at the sites of Tasajillo, Caseta, and Atoyac date to 1040–1300 AD (García 2007). Copper-silver alloys were derived mainly by smelting copper ores and silver ores separately, and then melting the two metals together. This combination is unmistakably inten-tional because there are no ores that contain both copper and silver in concentra-tions high enough to produce such compositions.

During the early stages of development, western Mexican metalsmiths fash-ioned copper objects by cold-working them from a cast blank. Although most worked artifacts were ritual and status items, tools were also produced. When metalworkers began to experiment with copper alloys, the enhanced physical and mechanical properties of these new materials allowed them to elaborate, refine, and in some cases redesign the same object types that they had been crafting in copper (Hosler 1994). Changing the elements and the concentrations present in an alloy leads to stronger, more flexible materials (Charles 1967; Lechtman 1996; Ryndina 2009). The main classes of Mesoamerican artifacts produced by working metal to shape include open rings, tweezers, axes, needles, awls, and sheet-metal ornaments. These were fashioned from a cast ingot (or blank) usually by cold-working the material with intermittent rounds of annealing. Nonetheless, if the material processed was an alloy with a concentration of tin or arsenic high enough to cause brittleness, hot-working or forging was employed (Hosler 1994). The *Relación de Michoacán* (1540–1541) describes and illustrates goods made of copper alloys of gold or silver and copper-tin and copper-arsenic bronzes (Alcalá 2000: 65, 203, 211) (see also Figure 45.4).

Cast bells were among the most distinctive metal objects produced in Mesoamerica, and they are frequently found in funerary and ritual contexts. The primary technique to produce them was lost-wax casting, which possibly originated in lower Central America and Colombia around 100 AD, and along with goldsmithing, it entered Mesoamerica through systems of overland trade during

Figure 45.4 Mesoamerican crucible and blow-pipes (from the Lienzo de Jicalán, in Roskam 2004: Fig. 6).

the Classic period (Hosler 1994; Smith 2003). In several documents written around the time of the Spanish conquest (e.g., the Florentine Codex), bells are represented as being attached to the garments of elites and deities and to musical instruments. In the early stages of metallurgy, most of these bells were cast in copper. Later, tin-bronze was widely used for their manufacture. Bells represent about 60 percent of the artifacts in western Mexican collections, which suggests that they were produced in larger quantities than any other prehispanic metal objects (Hosler 1994). During the Late Postclassic period, the most important center of production and use of bells was the Tarascan Empire in the Pátzcuaro Basin, Michoacán (Hosler 1994; Pollard 1987). Evidence of the production of copper and copper-alloyed bells has, however, been reported from other regions in Mesoamerica, including central Mexico (see Schulze 2007) and the Maya area (e.g., Paris 2008).

While copper and bronze metallurgy was most heavily concentrated in western Mexico, the late Postclassic Mixtec of Oaxaca were renowned as skilled goldsmiths. Some of the finest prehispanic gold objects ever found come from Mixtec tombs in the Valley of Oaxaca (Smith 2003; Ortiz Díaz 2002). Goldworking had also developed into an important luxury craft in the Valley of Mexico. It is known that a number of Mixtec artisans lived in Tenochtitlan, although it is unclear from the sources whether Aztec gold jewelry was made by resident Mixtecs, native Aztecs, or both (Smith 2003). The Florentine Codex contains a chapter on goldworking and goldsmiths, including a detailed description of lost-wax casting. This was the primary technique for manufacturing lip plugs, bells, pendants, and other items of gold jewelry in Late Postclassic Mesoamerica.

CONCLUDING THOUGHTS

This chapter has attempted to link multiple lines of evidence to produce as complete a picture as possible of the chaîne opératoire of prehispanic metal production in Mesoamerica. The technological choices made throughout metallurgical production reflect economic and environmental factors, dimensions of the social sphere, and the values and ideologies embedded in the culture in which they are made. In this case, like in other contexts of production and consumption of craft products, individuals and groups are linked in intricate webs of interdependence and interaction. Metal production involved social groups of various sizes. Producers also interacted with those who acquired and used their products (i.e., elite patrons). The nature of these interrelationships may have also varied over time and place.

Although the precise timing of these technological events and the historical circumstances surrounding them are poorly known, a hypothetical reconstruction is possible through the use of archaeological research, ethnohistorical evidence, and scientific and technological analyses. The operational sequence of producing metal artifacts from copper ore and the interplay between technology and organizational forms can be observed from the moment the raw material (e.g., copper) was procured to the achievement of the final result: the metal object. As Hosler (1994) has noted, while the technology of Mesoamerican metallurgy underwent major changes in materials and methods during its nine hundred years of development, its main focus on the value of metals as adornments and objects of high status and symbolic significance remained almost unaltered.

REFERENCES

Alcalá, Jerónimo de, Fray. 2000. *Relación de las ceremonias y rictos y población y gobernación de los Indios de la provincia de Mechuacan.* El Colegio de Michoacán, Zamora.

Arsandaux, Henry, and Paul Rivet.1921. Contribution à l'etude de la métallurgie Mexicaine. *Journal de la Société des Américanistes de Paris* 13:261–280.

Barrett, Elinore M. 1987. *The Mexican Colonial Copper Industry.* University of New Mexico Press, Albuquerque.

Berdan, Frances F., and Patricia R. Anawalt. 1992. *The Codex Mendoza.* University of California Press, Berkeley.

Betancourt, Philip P. 2006. *The Chrysokamino Metallurgy Workshop and Its Territory.* Hesperia Supplement 36, ASCSA Publications, Princeton.

Bruhns, Karen Olsen, and Norman Hammond. 1983. The Moho Cay Hammer: A Revised Opinion. *Antiquity* 57:136–137.

Charles, James A. 1967. Early Arsenical Bronzes: A Metallurgical View. *American Journal of Archaeology* 71:21–26.

Edwards, Clinton R. 1969. Possibilities of Pre-Columbian Maritime Contacts among New World Civilizations. In *Precolumbian Contact within Nuclear America,* Mesoamerican Studies vol. 4, edited by J. Charles Kelley and Carroll L. Riley, pp. 3–10. Southern Illinois University Press, Carbondale.

Garcia, J. 2007. Arqueometalurgia del occidente de Mexico: la Cuenca de Sayula, Jalisco como punto de conjuncion de tradiciones metalurgicas precolombinas. Tesis de Licenciatura en Arqueologia Escuela de Literatura, Lenguas y Antropologia, UAG, Mexico.

Grinberg, Dora M. K. de. 1989. Tecnologías metalúrgicas Tarascas. *Ciencia y Desarrollo* 15(89):37–52.

Grinberg, Dora M. K. de. 1990. *Los señores del metal. Minería y metalurgia en Mesoamérica.* Dirección General de Publicaciones del CNCA/Pangea, Mexico.

Grinberg, Dora M. K. de. 1995. El legajo 1204 del archivo general de Indias, el lienzo de jucutacato y las minas prehispánicas de cobre del ario, Michoacán. In *Arqueología del Norte y Occidente de Mexico,* edited by Barbo Dahlgren and Ma. Dolores Soto de Arechavaleta, pp. 211–265. UNAM, Instituto de Investigaciones Antropológicas, Mexico.

Grinberg, Dora M. K. de. 1996. Técnicas minero-metalúrgicas en Mesoamérica. In *Mesoamérica y los Andes,* edited by Mayán Cervantes, pp. 427–471. Centro de Investigaciones y Estudios Superiores de Antropología Social, Mexico.

Grinberg, Dora M. K. de. 2004. ¿Qué sabían de fundición los antiguos habitantes de Mesoamérica? *Ingenierías* VII(22):64–70.

Hendrichs, Pedro. 1940. Datos sobre la técnica minera prehispánica. *Mexico Antiguo* 5:148–160, 179–194, 311–238.

Hendrichs, Pedro. 1943-1944. *Por tierras ignotas: Viajes y observaciones en la región del Río de las Balsas.* 2 vols. Editorial Cultura, Mexico.

Hosler, Dorothy. 1994. *The Sounds and Colors of Power.* MIT Press, Cambridge.

Hosler, Dorothy. 2009. West Mexican Metallurgy: Revisited and Revised. *Journal of World Prehistory* 22:185–212.

Hosler, Dorothy, and Andrew Macfarlane. 1996. Copper Sources, Metal Production, and Metals Trade in Late Postclassic Mesoamerica. *Science* 273(5283):1819–1824.

Lechtman, Heather N. 1980. The Central Andes: Metallurgy without Iron. In *The Coming of the Age of Iron*, edited by Theodore A. Wertime and James D. Muhly, pp. 267–334. Yale University Press, New Haven.

Lechtman, Heather N. 1996. Arsenic Bronze: Dirty Copper or Chosen Alloy? A View from the Americas. *Journal of Field Archaeology* 23:477–515.

Lopez, R., Hosler, D., Pantoja, J., Martini, B., Morales, J. J., Solis-Picharo, G., et al. 1999. Coastal and Inland Pb Isotope Groups of Paleocene Cu Ores from the Rio Balsas Basin, Guerrero State, Mexico. Geophysical Union Annual Meeting, San Francisco.

Maldonado, Blanca, 2002. Modern Metallurgy, Prehispanic Roots: Coppersmithing in México. Paper presented at the SAA meetings, Denver, Colorado. Unpublished manuscript.

Maldonado, Blanca. 2009. Metal for the Commoners: Tarascan Metallurgical Production in Domestic Contexts. In *Housework: Specialization, Household Economy and Domestic Craft Production in Mesoamerica*, edited by Kenneth G. Hirth. Archaeological Papers of the American Anthropological Association 19(1):225–238. American Anthropological Association, Washington, DC.

Maldonado, Blanca, and Thilo Rehren. 2009. Early Copper Smelting at Itziparátzico, Mexico. *Journal of Archaeological Science* 36(9):1998–2006.

Maldonado, Blanca, Thilo Rehren, and Paul R. Howell. 2005. Archaeological Copper Smelting at Itziparátzico, Michoacan, Mexico. *Materials Issues in Art and Archaeology VII*, edited by Pamela B. Vandiver, Jennifer L. Mass, Alison Murray, pp. 231–240. MRS Proceedings Volume 852, Warrendale, Pennsylvania.

Meighan, Clement W. 1969. Cultural Similarities between Western Mexico and Andean Regions. In *Precolumbian Contact within Nuclear America*, Mesoamerican Studies vol. 4, edited by J. Charles Kelley and Carroll L. Riley, pp. 11–25. Southern Illinois University Press, Carbondale.

Mountjoy, Joseph B. 1969. On the Origin of West Mexican Metallurgy. In *Precolumbian Contact within Nuclear America*, Mesoamerican Studies vol. 4, edited by J. Charles Kelley and Carroll L. Riley, pp. 26–42. Southern Illinois University Press, Carbondale.

Ortiz Díaz, Edith. 2002. Los Zapotecos de la Sierra de Juárez: ¿Antiguos Orfebres? *Anales del Instituto de Investigaciones Estéticas* XXIV(81):141–149.

Ostroumov, Mikhail, and Pedro Corona-Chávez. 2000. Yacimientos minerales en Michoacán: Aspectos geológicos y metalogenéticos. *Revista Ciencia Nicolaita* 23:7–22.

Paris, Elizabeth H. 2008. Metallurgy, Mayapan, and the Postclassic Mesoamerican World System. *Ancient Mesoamerica* 19:43–66.

Pendergast, David M. 1962. Metal Artifacts in Prehispanic Mesoamerica. *American Antiquity* 27(4):520–545.

Pollard, Helen P. 1987. The Political Economy of Prehispanic Tarascan Metallurgy. *American Antiquity* 52(4):741–752.

Quilter, Jeffrey. 1998. Metallic Reflections. *Science* 282(5391):1058–1059.

Rehder, John E. 1994. Blowpipes versus Bellows in Ancient Metallurgy. *Journal of Field Archaeology* 21:345–350.

Roskamp, Hans. 2001. Historia, mito y legitimación: El lienzo de Jicalán. In *La Tierra Caliente de Michoacán*, edited by Eduardo Zárate Hernández, pp. 119–151. El Colegio de Michoacán/Gobierno del Estado de Michoacán, Zamora.

Roskamp, Hans. 2004. Los caciques indígenas de Xiuhquilan y la defensa del las minas en el siglo XVI: El lienzo de Jicalán. In *Ritmo del fuego: El arte y los artesanos de Santa Clara del Cobre, Michoacán, Mexico*, edited by Michele Feder-Nadoff, pp. 186–197. Fundación Cuentos, Chicago.

Roskamp, Hans, Mario Retiz, Anyul Cuellar, and Efraín Cárdenas. 2003. Pre-Hispanic and Colonial Metallurgy in Jicalán, Michoacán, Mexico: An Archaeological Survey. Reports submitted to FAMSI, http://www.famsi.org/reports/02011/index.html.

Rubín de la Borbolla, Daniel F. 1944. Orfebrería Tarasca. *Cuadernos Americanos* 3:125–138.

Ryndina, Natalia. 2009. The Potential of Metallography in Investigations of Early Objects Made of Copper and Copper-Based Alloys. *Journal of the Historical Metallurgy Society* 43:1–18.

Sahagún, Fray Bernardino de. 1969-1982. *Florentine Codex: General History of the Things of New Spain, 1590.* 12 books. Translated and edited by Arthur J. O. Anderson and Charles E. Dibble. School of American Research and the University of Utah Press, Santa Fe and Salt Lake City.

Schulze, Niklas. 2007. "For Whom the Bell Tolls" Mexican Copper Bells from the Templo Mayor Offerings: Analysis of the Production Process and Its Cultural Context. In *Materials Issues in Art and Archaeology VIII*, vol. 1047, edited by Pamela B. Vandiver, Blythe McCarthy, Robert H. Tykot, Jose Luis Ruvalcaba-Sil, and Francesca Casadio, 1047-Y02-02. Materials Research Society Proceedings, Warrendale, Pennsylvania.

Shimada, Izumi, Stephen M. Epstein, and Alan K. Craig. 1983. The Metallurgical Process in Ancient North Peru. *Archaeology* 35(5):38–45.

Shimada, Izumi, and John F. Merkel. 1991. Copper-Alloy Metallurgy in Ancient Peru. *Scientific American* 265(1):80–86.

Simmons, Scott E., David M. Pendergast, and Elizabeth Graham. 2009. The Context and Significance of Copper Artifacts in Postclassic and Early Historic Lamanai, Belize. *Journal of Field Archaeology* 34(1):57–75.

Solís O., Felipe R., 1999. Arte Funerario en el Occidente de México durante la Época Prehispánica. Correo del Maestro 42: http://www.correodelmaestro.com/multimedia/multimedia.htm

Smith, Michael E. 2003. *The Aztecs*. 2nd ed. Blackwell, Malden, Massachusetts.

Warren, J. Benedict. 1968. Minas de cobre de Michoacán, 1533. *Anales del Museo Michoacano* 6:35–52.

West, Robert C. 1994. Aboriginal Metallurgy and Metalworking in Spanish America. In *Quest of Mineral Wealth: Aboriginal and Colonial Mining and Metallurgy in Spanish America*, edited by Alan K. Craig and Robert C. West, pp 5–20. Louisiana State University, Baton Rouge.

....

CHAPTER 46

AS THE WHORL TURNS

FUNCTION AND MEANING IN MESOAMERICAN TEXTILE PRODUCTION

....

GEOFFREY McCAFFERTY AND SHARISSE McCAFFERTY

WOVEN textiles were highly prized commodities in Pre-Columbian Mesoamerica, to the extent that they were commonly used as tribute items and even as a standard of value in commercial exchange (Berdan 1987; Hicks 1994). The Codex Mendoza (1992) provides unique insights into textile exchange during the contact period with details on both raw materials and finished products. Beautiful textiles are depicted in various artistic representations, including murals, sculptures, and pictorial manuscripts. Unfortunately, due to the poor preservation of cloth in the region, archaeological textiles are rare. Instead, archaeological correlates of textile production, particularly in the form of spindle whorls, provide some of the best evidence for these perishable items. This chapter will discuss ways that textile production has been approached archaeologically in terms of both its function and cultural meanings.

Ethnographic textiles from traditional societies throughout Mesoamerica have been collected and studied for over a century (e.g., Cordry and Cordry 1968; Foxx et al. 1997). Anthropologists and art historians have documented different costume styles as they relate to regional identities, as well as the symbolic meanings attached to particular design elements. These studies provide a glimpse of the possible levels of meaning that may have existed in Pre-Columbian textiles.

Building on this potential, Patricia Anawalt published a comprehensive study of Pre-Columbian costume in her *Indian Clothing before Cortes* (1981) in which she documented different clothing styles for Aztec, Mixtec, Maya, and Tarascan groups using (primarily) pictorial manuscripts. As noted, relatively few pre-Columbian textiles have been recovered; a notable exception was from the La Garrafa cave in Chiapas (Landa et al. 1988), where polychrome garments were decorated with Mixteca-Puebla codex-style figures (Figure 46.1). Other textile fragments have been found in caches at the Aztec Templo Mayor. Most costume analysis, however, has been based on pictorial representations, where it has been used to consider gender and status identities. For example, Karen Olsen Bruhns (1988) discussed the elaborate dress of Maya noble-women in one of the earliest articles on prehispanic gender. We used a detailed costume analysis of the Cacaxtla Battle murals to argue that the two central individuals of the defeated "bird"- army were portrayed in female dress, and we thereby concluded that the scene represented the capture of the founding queen of a new dynasty (McCafferty and McCafferty 1994a). Anawalt (1990) has also considered a particular style of tie-dye decoration in Aztec imagery as a symbolic referent to the Toltec past and therefore as an act of legitimation.

Weaving in ancient Mesoamerica was done with a backstrap loom (Figure 46.2), and additional decoration was created with colored threads, dying, and

Figure 46.1 Prehispanic textile with polychrome decoration from La Garrafa cave, Chiapas (from Landa et al. 1988).

Figure 46.2 Woman using backstrap loom (after Sahagún 1950–1982).

embroidery. This technique is still used by indigenous women today, providing insights into both the practice and ideology associated with the process (Schaeffer 1989). Again, because of generally poor preservation, little archaeological evidence for weaving technology has been recovered. Irmegard Johnson de Weitlaner (1971) described a loom kit from a dry cave in the Tehuacán Valley, including a wooden batten with seeds embedded to create a rattling noise when used (similar to a "rain stick"). At Santa Isabel in Pacific Nicaragua, on the southern frontier of Mesoamerica, we have recovered a wide range of bone tools, including needles, awls, picks, and battens (McCafferty and McCafferty 2008). These were clustered at Mound 6, suggesting a possible specialized production area.

By far the most abundant artifact class relating to textile production is the spindle whorl, or *malacate* (Figure 46.3). Spindle whorls function as flywheels on long wooden spindle shafts to maintain inertia while raw fiber is twisted into thread. Whorls can be made of a variety of materials, but the most common in archaeological contexts are of baked clay. Some are simply made of re-worked potsherds ground into a round disk and perforated in the center. More complex whorls are modeled or mold-made (Figure 46.4). These can be decorated with incisions, slip, and paint; mold-made whorls often included elaborate mold-impressed designs.

Mary Parsons (1972) was the first scholar to make the connection between whorl sizes and their possible functional variation. Based on a large assemblage of spindle whorls collected from the Teotihuacan and Texcoco valley surveys, Parsons identified three whorl types, with Types 1 and 2 relatively larger in diameter, height, and weight than the smaller Type 3. Parsons inferred that the smaller Type 3 whorls would have been used for cotton fiber, whereas the larger Type 1 and 2 whorls would have been used for coarser maguey fibers. Because maguey grows abundantly in the Basin of Mexico while cotton does not grow at the high elevation, Parsons used the functional properties of whorl size and weight to infer trade patterns for Postclassic Mexico.

Other scholars working in and around the Basin of Mexico have expanded on Parsons's interpretations. Michael Smith and Kenneth Hirth (1988) analyzed spindle

Figure 46.3 Woman spinning cotton in a bowl (from Charnay 1887).

whorls from Morelos, a cotton-producing area south of the Basin of Mexico, and found a relatively higher frequency of the smaller "cotton" whorls. Smith and Hirth also identified a large number of small bowls that they interpreted as "spinning bowls" for supported spinning. Elizabeth Brumfiel (1991) interpreted diachronic

Figure 46.4 Ceramic spindle whorls from Pacific Nicaragua.

changes in relative frequencies of spindle whorls from surface collections from the southern Basin of Mexico as an indication of intensification of production with the rise of the Aztec state, especially as seen in the allocation of women's labor (following ethnohistorical evidence that spinning and weaving were stereotypically female tasks). In a later study, Brumfiel (1996) considered changes in whorl size as evidence of reaction to Aztec and colonial tribute demands. At Otumba, in the northern Basin of Mexico, high concentrations of larger whorls were interpreted as evidence of household workshops where specialized maguey processing occurred (Nichols et al. 2000). Stacie King (2011) has recently evaluated different ways of reporting whorl densities as they relate to intensity of production.

Textile production was also an important activity in the religious and economic center of Cholula, located in the adjacent Puebla Valley. Based on a large assemblage of spindle whorls from excavated domestic and ceremonial contexts, we developed a multi-variant classification system for generating distinctive whorl types (McCafferty and McCafferty 2000: Table 6). The incentive for this new methodology was based on ethnohistorical and ethnographic evidence for the variety of fibers used, as well as varying techniques (including both supported- and drop spinning) and the desired quality of the finished thread. For example, Sahagún (1950–1982: Book 8:49) described "feather whorls" as being both wide and shallow, and these likely correspond to the Type D whorls found at Cholula. A whorl with a large diameter but low height would produce a relatively slow rotation, resulting in a loosely spun thread. A taller whorl relative to its diameter would produce a faster rotation, resulting in a tighter twist and a finer thread. Following these considerations we consider the "shape" measurement, being the ratio of height to diameter, to be an important means of inferring whorl function. This more complex method for characterizing whorl function has now been used in other parts of Mesoamerica, including El Salvador and Nicaragua, and even in northern Africa.

One generalization about spindle whorl use in central Mexico is that whorls seem to have been introduced during the Classic to Postclassic transition, with no whorls dating to earlier periods. This does not imply that fiber spinning was not practiced, only that permanent whorls were not used. Perishable whorls could have been made from organic materials or, as is common now in coastal Oaxaca, from sun-baked clay. Thus, the absence of evidence is not necessarily evidence of absence. A clue to why more permanent whorls may have been adopted is found in Barbara Hall's study (1997) of whorls from the Mixtequilla region of central Veracruz. There, baked ceramic whorls were only associated with high-status houses near the site center, suggesting a degree of elite ideology associated with the more permanent whorls. Commoner houses lacked permanent whorls, but commoners still may have processed fiber into thread by using perishable whorls.

Spindle whorls *were* common in Classic Maya contexts, as has been demonstrated in several projects over the past decade. The first major study of Maya archaeological textile production was by Julia Hendon (1997), for the site of Copán. Analyses of spindle whorls as well as other weaving tools (and other domestic objects) produced information on domestic practices, especially "women's work" at the Maya center. Recent studies by Christina Halperin (2008) and by Arlen and Diane Chase (and colleagues; 2008) have expanded these inferences for Motul de San José and Caracol, respectively. As more scholars provide detailed studies of spindle whorls from different regions of Mesoamerica, a greater understanding of the political economy of textiles will be possible.

SYMBOLIC SIGNIFICANCE

While much of the archaeological attention to ancient textile production has focused on the material culture, especially spindle whorls, ethnohistorical sources also indicate that spinning and weaving had deep symbolic significance in ancient Mesoamerican societies. These tasks were closely linked to female identity and to ideologies associated with prominent female deities. One of the first to recognize this was Thelma Sullivan (1982) in her article on the central Mexican goddess Tlazolteotl-Ixcuina. Associated with a range of female qualities, including sexuality, childbirth, duality, and curing, Tlazolteotl-Ixcuina was also the patroness of spinning and weaving. In fact, spinning and weaving were used as metaphors for coitus and pregnancy, as seen in the Aztec riddle "What is it that they make pregnant, that they make big with child in the dancing place?" The answer was "spindles," which grew around the middle as fiber was spun into thread and wrapped around the spindle (Sahagún 1950–1982, Book 6: 240.

The association between textile production and female deities was widespread throughout Mesoamerica. For example, goddesses in the Pre-Columbian codices were often associated with spinning and weaving tools. Cihuacóatl is represented in the Codex Magliabechiano (1983: 45) holding a weaving batten, as is Lady 13 Flower in the Mixtec Codex Nuttall (1975: 19). Tlazolteotl wears spindles with whorls in her headdress in numerous representations, especially in the Codex Borgia (1963), and goddesses are depicted with spindles and whorls in Mixtec and Maya representations. In the Codex Cospi (1988: 25), Xochiquetzal holds a spearthrower, but in place of a lance is a spindle with whorl (Figure 46.5). In fact, spindles, battens, and whorls were metaphorically linked to male weapons; for example, battens are still known as "*machetes*" throughout Mexico, and spindle whorls were often decorated with shield patterns and were known as "*tehuehuelli*," or "little shields" (McCafferty and McCafferty 1991).

Mortal women are often depicted with spinning and weaving tools in non-textile production contexts. For example, in the Codex Nuttall (1975: female descendants of lineage founders from Zaachila in the Valley of Oaxaca were represented with spinning and weaving objects, as well as costume elements linking

(a)   (b)

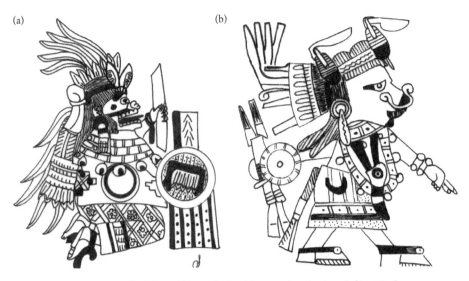

Figure 46.5 Goddess Cihuacóatl with weaving batten (after Codex
Magliabechiano1983); (b) Goddess Tlazolteotl with spindle whorls (after Codex
Borgia 1963).

them to female deities (Hamann 1997; McCafferty and McCafferty 2003). Female
war chiefs from the southern Basin of Mexico carried battens in place of masculine weapons in representations on the Tizoc and Cuauhxicalli Stones. It is probably this linkage between spinning and weaving tools with female power through
various goddess cults that explains the presence of material objects in ceremonial contexts. The most spectacular example was the discovery of thirty-four bone
weaving tools, especially miniature battens, in Tomb 7 at Monte Albán (Caso 1969;
McCafferty and McCafferty 1994b, 2003). Battens, spindle whorls, spinning bowls,
and a carved-bone weaving comb were all found with Individual 1, the focus of a
burial shrine dedicated to a goddess of the earth/fertility cult related to the Mixtec
goddess 9 Grass or the Aztec Cihuacóatl. A glimpse at the possible time-depth of
the symbolic nature of weaving tools is presented by Billie Follensbee (2008) in
her analysis of Olmec carved greenstone "spoons," which she infers to be weaving
picks. Other greenstone, and therefore probably effigy, weaving tools are known
from Nicaragua and Costa Rica (McCafferty and McCafferty 2008).

As spindle whorls are the most abundant material object relating to textile
production, they provide the best evidence for symbolic content. Whorls are often
decorated with incising, paint, and mold impressions (Figure 46.3). Jorge Enciso
(1971) compiled a catalogue of beautiful and diverse spindle-whorl designs from
central Mexico. We have argued that with the strong association of textile production and female gender identity, whorl decoration should correspond to female
symbolic discourse (McCafferty and McCafferty 1991) (Figures 46.4 and 46.5).
Using a large corpus of decorated whorls from Postclassic Cholula, we have identified designs consistent with iconography of the female deity complex, using
shields depicted with female deities in Sahagún's (1993) *Primeros Memoriales* for

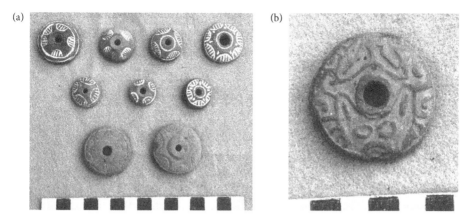

Figure 46.6 Decorated spindle whorls from Cholula.

comparison (Figure 46.6). Vegetal and especially floral motifs are also common, and they may be particularly related to the goddess Xochiquetzal. These motifs seem to have been locally significant, however, since Elizabeth Brumfiel (2007) has found solar symbolism on whorls from the Basin of Mexico, which she interprets as evidence of a solar cult.

CONCLUSION

Textile production was important both functionally and symbolically. Major female deities from throughout Mesoamerica were closely associated with this important aspect of domestic production, which was also linked metaphorically with sexual reproduction. Ethnographic research indicates that this aspect of female ideology continues (Schaefer 1989). In fact, Cecelia Klein (1982) inferred a weaving paradigm for the Mesoamerican cosmos in her article "Woven Heaven, Tangled Earth." We interpret similar evidence in the use of textile symbolism in Mixtec codices to denote architectural and natural spaces, as a metaphor for the acculturation of the landscape (McCafferty and McCafferty 2006).

Studies of the material evidence for textile production have also advanced beyond simply using whorls to identify possible fibers. Julia Hendon (2006) recently wrote about textile production as craft, with implications of how labor was organized and knowledge was communicated. Nichols and colleagues (2000) considered the organization of production at Otumba, and we have discussed cottage industries for textile production at both Cholula (Puebla) and Santa Isabel (Nicaragua) (McCafferty and McCafferty 2000, 2008). With more studies such as these, textile production will continue to develop as an important avenue for interpreting ancient political economy, while also providing unique insights into gender ideologies and female participation in Mesoamerican culture.

REFERENCES

Anawalt, Patricia R. 1981. *Indian Clothing before Cortes: Mesoamerican Costumes from the Codices.* University of Oklahoma Press, Norman.

Anawalt, Patricia R. 1990. The Emperor's Cloak: Aztec Pomp, Toltec Circumstance. *American Antiquity* 55:291–307.

Berdan, Frances Frei. 1987. Cotton in Aztec Mexico: Production, Distribution and Uses. *Mexican Studies/Estudios Mexicanos* 3(2):235–262.

Bruhns, Karen O. 1988. Yesterday the Queen Wore…an Analysis of Women and Costume in Public Art of the Late Classic Maya. In *The Role of Gender in Pre-Columbian Art and Architecture*, edited by Virginia E. Miller, pp. 105–134. University Press of America, Lanham, Maryland.

Brumfiel, Elizabeth. 1991. Weaving and Cooking: Women's Production in Aztec Mexico. In *Engendering Archaeology: Women and Prehistory*, edited by Joan M. Gero and Margaret W. Conkey, pp. 224–251. Basil Blackwell, Oxford.

Brumfiel, Elizabeth. 1996. The Quality of Tribute Cloth: The Place of Evidence in Archaeological Argument. *American Antiquity* 61: 453–462.

Brumfiel, Elizabeth. 2007. Solar Disks and Solar Cycles: Spindle Whorls and the Dawn of Solar Art in Postclassic Mexico. *Treballs d'Arqueologia* 13:91–113.

Caso, Alfonso. 1969. *El tesoro de Monte Albán.* Memorias del INAH III, Instituto Nacional de Antropología e Historia, Mexico, D.F.

Charnay, Desire. 1887. The Ancient Cities of the New World: Being Voyages and Explorations in Mexico and Central America from 1857–1882 (translated by J. Gonino and H. S. Conant). NY: Harper.

Chase, Arlen F., Diane Z. Chase, Elayne Zorn, and Wendy Teeter. 2008. Textiles and the Maya Archaeological Record. *Ancient Mesoamerica* 19:127–142.

Codex Borgia. 1963. *Codice Borgia* (facsimile). Fondo de Cultura Económica. Mexico, D.F.

Codex Cospi. 1988. *Codice Cospi: Calendario messicano 4093, Biblioteca Universitaria de Bolonia* (with commentary by C. Aguilera). Centro Regional de Puebla, INAH, SEP. Puebla, Mexico.

Codex Magliabechiano. 1983. *The Book of the Life of the Ancient Mexicans Containing an Account of Their Rites and Superstitions.* Translated and with commentary by Zelia Nuttall. University of California Press, Berkeley. [Reprint of the 1903 edition]

Codex Mendoza. 1992. *The Codex Mendoza.* 4 vols. Edited by Frances F. Berdan and Patricia R. Anawalt. University of California Press, Berkeley.

Codex Nuttall. 1975. *The Codex Nuttall. A Picture Manuscript from Ancient Mexico. The Peabody Museum Facsimile.* Edited by Zelia Nuttall with an introduction by A. G. Miller). Dover, New York.

Cordry, Donald, and Dorothy Cordry. 1968. *Mexican Indian Costumes.* University of Texas Press, Austin.

Enciso, Jorge. 1971. *Designs from Pre-Columbian Mexico.* Dover, New York.

Follensbee, Billie J. 2008. Fiber Technology and Weaving in Formative-Period Gulf Coast Cultures. *Ancient Mesoamerica* 19:87–110.

Foxx, Jeffrey Jay, Margot B. Schevill, Linda Schele, and Linda De Barrios. 1997. *Maya Textile Tradition*. Harry N. Abrams, New York.

Hall, Barbara A. 1997. Spindle Whorls and Cotton Production at Middle Classic Matacapan and in the Gulf Lowlands. In *Olmec to Aztec: Settlement Patterns in the Ancient Gulf Lowlands*, edited by Barbara L. Stark and Philip J. Arnold, pp. 115–136. University of Arizona Press, Tucson.

Halperin, Christina T. 2008. Classic Maya Textile Production: Insights from Motul de San José, Peten, Guatemala. *Ancient Mesoamerica* 19:111–125.

Hamann, Byron. 1997. Weaving and the Iconography of Prestige: The Royal Gender Symbolism of Lord 5 Flower's/Lady 4 Rabbit's Family. In *Women in Prehistory: North America and Mesoamerica*, edited by Cheryl Claassen and Rosemary A. Joyce, pp. 153–172. University of Pennsylvania Press, Philadelphia.

Hendon, Julia A. 1997. Women's Work, Women's Space, and Women's Status among the Classic-Period Maya Elite of the Copan Valley, Honduras. In *Women in Prehistory: North America and Mesoamerica*, edited by Cheryl Claassen and Rosemary A. Joyce, pp. 33–46. University of Pennsylvania Press, Philadelphia.

Hendon, Julia A. 2006. Textile Production as Craft in Mesoamerica: Time, Labor, and Knowledge. *Journal of Social Archaeology* 6:354–378.

Hicks, Frederick. 1994. Cloth in the Political Economy of the Aztec State. In *Economies and Polities in the Aztec Realm*, edited by Mary Hodge and Michael E. Smith, pp. 89–112. Institute for Mesoamerican Studies, Albany

Johnson de Weitlaner, Irmegard. 1971. Basketry and Textiles. In *Handbook of Middle American Indians, Vol. 10: Archaeology of Northern Mesoamerica, Part 1*, edited by Robert Wauchope, Gordon F. Ekholm, and Ignacio Bernal, pp. 297–321. University of Texas Press, Austin.

Klein, Cecilia F. 1982. Woven Heaven, Tangled Earth: A Weaver's Paradigm of the Mesoamerican Cosmos. In *Ethnoastronomy and Archaeoastronomy in the American Tropics*, vol. 385, edited by Anthony F. Aveni and Gary Urton. pp. 1–35. Annals of the New York Academy of Sciences.

Landa A., Maria Elena, Eduardo Pareyon M., Alejandro Huerta C., Emma E. Herrera G., Rosa Lorena Román T., Martha Guajardo P., Josefina Cruz R., Sara Altamirano R., and Eva Rodriguez C. 1988. *La Garrafa. Cuevas de La Garrafa, Chiapas. Estudio y conservación de algunos objetos arqueológicos*. Centro Regional de Puebla. Instituto Nacional de Antropología e Historia, Mexico, D.F.

McCafferty, Geoffrey G., and Sharisse D. McCafferty. 2003. Questioning a Queen? A Gender-Informed Evaluation of Monte Alban's Tomb 7. In *Ancient Queens: Archaeological Explorations*, edited by Sarah Nelson, pp. 41–58. Altamira, Walnut Creek, California.

McCafferty, Sharisse D., and Geoffrey G. McCafferty. 1991. Spinning and Weaving as Female Gender Identity in Post-Classic Central Mexico. In *Textile Traditions of Mesoamerica and the Andes: An Anthology*, edited by Margot Schevill, Janet C. Berlo, and Edward Dwyer, pp. 19–44. Garland, New York.

McCafferty, Sharisse D., and Geoffrey G. McCafferty. 1994a. The Conquered Women of Cacaxtla: Gender Identity or Gender Ideology? *Ancient Mesoamerica* 5(2):159–172.

McCafferty, Sharisse D., and Geoffrey G. McCafferty. 1994b. Engendering Tomb 7 at Monte Albán, Oaxaca: Respinning an Old Yarn. *Current Anthropology* 35(2):143–166.

McCafferty, Sharisse D., and Geoffrey G. McCafferty. 2000. Textile Production in Postclassic Cholula, Mexico. *Ancient Mesoamerica* 11:39–54.

McCafferty, Sharisse D., and Geoffrey G. McCafferty. 2006. Weaving Space: Textile Imagery and Landscape in the Mixtec Codice. In *Space and Spatial Analysis in Archaeology*, edited by Elizabeth C. Robertson, Jeffrey D. Seibert, Deepika C. Fernandez, and Marc U. Zender. University of Calgary Press, Calgary.

McCafferty, Sharisse D., and Geoffrey G. McCafferty. 2008. Spinning and Weaving Tools from Santa Isabel, Nicaragua. *Ancient Mesoamerica* 19:43–156.

Nichols, Deborah L., Mary Jane McLaughlin, and Maura Benton. 2000. Production Intensification and Regional Specialization. *Ancient Mesoamerica* 11:267–291.

Parsons, Mary H. 1972. Spindle Whorls from the Teotihuacan Valley, Mexico. In *Miscellaneous Studies in Mexican Prehistory*, by Jeffrey R. Parsons, Michael W. Spence, and Mary H. Parsons, pp. 45–80. Anthropological Papers of the Museum of Anthropology No. 45, University of Michigan, Ann Arbor.

Sahagún, Bernadino de. 1950–1982 [1547–85]. *Florentine Codex: General History of the Things of New Spain*. Edited and translated by Arthur J. D. Anderson and Charles E. Dibble, 13 volumes. University of Utah Press and School of American Research, Salt Lake City and Santa Fe.

Sahagún, Bernadino de. 1993. *Primeros Memoriales*. Civilizations of the American Indian Series, 100, University of Oklahoma Press, Norman.

Schaefer, Stacy B. 1989. Loom and Time in the Huichol World. *Journal of Latin American Lore* 15(2):179–194.

Smith, Michael E., and Kenneth G. Hirth. 1988. The Development of Cotton Spinning Technology in Postclassic Morelos, Mexico. *Journal of Field Archaeology* 15:349–358.

Sullivan, Thelma. 1982. Tlazolteotl-Ixcuina: The Great Spinner and Weaver. In *The Art and Iconography of Late Post-Classic Central Mexico*, edited by Elizabeth H. Boone, pp. 7–36. Dumbarton Oaks, Washington, DC.

CHAPTER 47

....

MARKETS, MERCHANTS, AND SYSTEMS OF EXCHANGE

....

KENNETH HIRTH

THE production and exchange of goods and services is a fundamental feature of all human societies, and this certainly was the case in ancient Mesoamerica. Complex forms of exchange linked every level of Pre-Columbian society from simple households to the king's palace. Trade was important for two reasons: meeting the needs that people had for specific goods and reducing subsistence risk and resource shortages. While anthropologists believe that households had self-sufficiency as their economic ideal, archaeological data indicate that self-sufficiency was rarely, if ever, achieved. Exchange was common in Mesoamerica and the marketplace was at the heart of its economy. While the marketplace varied in importance from region to region, it was the primary way that households obtained the goods that they did not produce themselves.

That Mesoamerica had an active exchange economy is interesting given the fact that Mesoamerica had the worst transportation system in the ancient world. It lacked the wheel, beasts of burden, and active maritime commerce. Under these conditions the movements of goods were limited by what human porters could carry (Hassig 1985). This clearly restricted long-distance trade and reduced how far bulk goods could be moved. Despite these limitations, exchange flourished and merchant groups appeared that specialized in transporting goods over space (Acosta Saignes 1945; Bittman and Sullivan 1978) and marketplaces developed

(Berdan 1989; Blanton 1996; Hirth 1998; Smith 1979). These merchants and marketplaces connected regions in a series of transportation relays that helped move a wide range of commodities, including bulk staple goods.

This chapter examines systems of exchange within Mesoamerica's dual economy. The structure of the economy is discussed along with the role of the marketplace in Mesoamerican exchange systems and how resources were exchanged through both professional and nonprofessional commercial networks.

MESOAMERICA'S DUAL ECONOMY

The economy is frequently defined in terms of the production, distribution, and consumption of goods and resources (Nash 1964). This is a good functionalist view of an economy. It defines an economy in terms of the activities that individuals engage in to support themselves socially and to reproduce themselves biologically. While this approach defines a domain of "economic" behavior, it is not particularly useful for identifying "how" economic activities were organized. I use a structural model to address this issue that groups production and distribution activities by their two primary goal-oriented units of consumption: the domestic and institutional economies.

All complex societies have a two-part dual economy (Hirth 2013). One component is the *domestic economy*: the way that households access resources either individually or communally to meet their social and biological needs. The domestic economy has always been the backbone of ancient societies. Moreover, the history of emerging sociopolitical complexity is one of how household labor and the resources produced in the domestic sector were mobilized by elites for the purposes of political gain (Johnson and Earle 1987). The second part of the dual economy is the *institutional economy*: the way that social activities above the household level are organized, funded, and carried out. Socioeconomic, political, and religious institutions provide the integrative synergy that allows societies to grow in size and avoid the conflicts that lead to fission and breakup. Together the domestic and institutional economies provide the framework in which production, distribution, and consumption activities take place.

The domestic economy consists of the array of production and distribution activities that households engage in to provision themselves with the resources needed for subsistence and social reproduction (Hirth 2009). The domestic economy enables a society's population to grow and reproduce. By necessity, households in Mesoamerica were auto-sufficient and in business for themselves. They were responsible for their own survival and failure to produce or obtain the resources they required could result in the starvation and death of household members. This is important for two reasons. First, from an organizational perspective, it means that households will be entrepreneurial in their endeavors to support themselves. Because social networks are not designed to support unproductive individuals, households had to engage in productive subsistence pursuits to make ends meet or perish. Second, because of the need to be self-reliant, households will not willingly relinquish control over the resources critical for their survival; instead they will fight to maintain access to *all* critical resources. The domestic economy is the engine behind cultural expansion. Households produce and distribute the bulk of the resources produced in society. The fact that these resources are consumed at home makes them invisible compared to resources consumed in institutional settings.

The institutional economy refers to the production and mobilization of resources needed to support and fund the institutions that provide social integration above the individual household. It includes all of the social, political, religious, and economic institutions that promote cohesion at the community and regional levels. There were several important components of the institutional economy in Mesoamerica. Local and state-level political activities were supported through tribute and taxation obligations discussed by Berdan elsewhere in this volume. Religious and military organizations were supported through the cultivation of specific lands by using corvée (unpaid) labor. The most important economic institution in prehispanic society was the marketplace, and it is described here because it was where households and other important institutions intersected within society.

THE MESOAMERICAN MARKETPLACE

The marketplace served a number of important functions within societies. First and foremost, it was a special place of economic interaction. It was where people came to buy and sell goods and interact with one another for a range of socioeconomic reasons. This may seem natural to us, but in highly stratified societies it was not. The reason is that in stratified societies people do not interact as equals but as representatives of their higher or lower socioeconomic classes. A marketplace is unusual in that it temporarily erases these differences and allows individuals to interact as equals and haggle over prices to establish equivalent value (Plattner 1989a, 1989b). This was an unnatural situation in ancient societies and explains why marketplaces were established as special places under the auspices and supervision of local rulers. While this was the principle of the marketplace, it probably was rare that high-status people actually haggled over prices with low-status producers. Instead, high-status individuals probably sent their servants to the marketplace, thereby escaping the specter of equality that marketplace interactions established (Figure 47.1).

Figure 47.1 A Tarascan lord overlooking the marketplace at Asaveto, Michoacán
(modified from Crain and Reindorp 1970: Plate 29).

Marketplaces were also vital places of resource mobilization. Centralized marketplaces made it easy to find needed goods. Sellers transported goods to the market venue, where they were available for everyone who wanted them. The Spanish
conquistadors marveled at both the quantity and diversity of goods available in
the main marketplaces. As Díaz del Castillo (1956: 215–216) stated in his visit to the
Tlatelolco marketplace, he was "astonished at the number of people and the quality
of merchandise that it contained... one could see every sort of merchandise that is
to be found in the whole of New Spain." This type of mobilization made it easier
for households to allocate their time efficiently; instead of trying to raise small
amounts of produce in the exact quantities that they could use, households would
focus on what they could grow best, exchanging it in the marketplace for what they
could not.

Another important feature of marketplaces is how they enabled other forms of
economic development. The assembly of large numbers of potential buyers made
it possible for entrepreneurial households to grow crops specifically for sale in
the marketplace. This included raising fruit, vegetables, and specialty items like
flowers and tobacco. It also allowed specialized forms of production that included
selling prepared food, manufacturing craft goods, or collecting and processing
natural resources for resale (see below). The market enabled households to engage
in a degree of economic diversification that provided important supplements to
household income.

Finally, and perhaps most importantly, the marketplace was the primary location for resource conversion. It was where the domestic and the institutional economies met and goods were sold by households for use in different institutional
settings (Carrasco 1978). It was also where commercial behavior reached its most
advanced form in the Pre-Columbian world. Commodity money, in the form of

cacao beans and cotton textiles, was used to purchase items and to accumulate readily negotiable wealth (Coe and Coe 2007; Katz 1966; Millon 1955). The use of commodity money made it possible to calculate relative value and to avoid the bottlenecks associated with direct barter. It is within the marketplace that we see a highly textured commercial landscape involving a diversity of practitioners that included producer-vendors, wholesalers, retailers, long-distance elite merchants, commercial agents, peddlers, and money changers (Sahagún 1961). The marketplace was where economic and noneconomic forces met in one of the most vibrant commercial exchange systems of the ancient world.

In structural terms the marketplace was part of the institutional economy. As an institution it was designed to facilitate provisioning and the conversion of resources between all sectors of the society. Unfortunately, the marketplace was also a place where fraud could be perpetrated: for this reason, it needed administrative oversight. Among the Aztec, marketplaces were policed and supervised, volumetric measures were standardized, and disputes over economic transactions were adjudicated quickly by a panel of judges. These expenses as well as the cost of cleaning the marketplace were covered by a small market tax levied on individuals who sold their goods there. For these reasons, marketplaces were held under the auspices of city rulers who guaranteed fair dealing to all marketgoers irrespective of their wealth, ethnicity, or social class.

PRODUCTION AND EXCHANGE
IN THE DOMESTIC ECONOMY

The domestic economy supported the majority of a society's population, and it accounted for the bulk of the goods produced and circulated within it. Most households were engaged in agriculture and they produced the bulk of the maize, beans, and chile that its members consumed. While auto-sufficiency was a household goal, this virtually was never achieved. Instead, households exchanged the products that they produced for the ones that they did not, procuring goods in the marketplace or through informal systems of household-to-household exchange. One salient feature of highland Mesoamerica was the sharp juxtaposition of ecological zones caused by elevation changes that affected local temperature-rainfall gradients. This created regional variation in growing cycles and provided a time frame for when orchard and agricultural products could be harvested and consumed. Seasonal variation for when agricultural products or wild resources were available led to a considerable degree of commercial activity by individual households.

The forces of domestic exchange were at their strongest when households came to sell their goods in the marketplace. The best information on household

Table 47.1. Types of Producer-Vendors Found in Central Mexico Marketplaces.

Types of Producer-Vendors	Number	Percentage
Food Producers	16	14.3
Food Vendors	15	13.4
Foragers and Collectors	16	14.3
Craft Producers	54	48
Service Providers	11	10
Total Producer Vendors	112	100

involvement in the marketplace is provided by Sahagún (1961), who described the Tlatelolco marketplace. This information was supplied by native Tlatelolco informants who probably were members of the *pochteca* professional-merchant class. What is important about Sahagún's account is the overwhelming involvement of commoners who were producer-vendors in the commercial life of the marketplace (Rojas 1995; Sahagún 1961). Examination of the sources reveals 112 producer-vendors selling goods in the marketplace; these goods were grown, collected, processed, or manufactured in their homes (Table 47.1). Producer-vendors from commoner households represent approximately 75 percent of all the vendors listed in the marketplace. They were the primary individuals selling staples like grain, meat, vegetables, and craft goods, and they almost certainly were involved in moving the greatest volume of goods through the marketplace (Figure 47.2). It is clear from Sahagún's account and from other scattered market documents (Anderson et al. 1976; Carrasco and Monjarás-Ruiz 1978: 188–195) that the commoner household was the lifeblood of the marketplace.

Commoner households did not sell just small amounts of surpluses in the marketplace; they also used the marketplace to improve their overall economic

Figure 47.2 The frijole seller (modified from Sahagún 1961: Plate 122).

Figure 47.3 Weaving in the domestic setting (from Sahagún 1961: Plate 58).

well-being in an entrepreneurial sense. Most craft production in Mesoamerica took place in commoner households (Feinman 1999; Hirth 2009). Elites sponsored some craft production but much of this was for elite goods that did not circulate to the wider population through the marketplace. All textiles, household goods, and tools were manufactured by craft specialists in their households. Sahagún mentions fifty-four craft producers at the Tlatelolco marketplace (Table 47.1). The majority of their production was intermittent in nature, with craft producers

Figure 47.4 The carpenter (modified from Sahagún 1961: Plate 135).

combining part-time crafting with agriculture and other domestic subsistence activities. While small in scale, intermittent crafting was an important source of auxiliary income for households that engaged in it. This was possible because the marketplace brought together a large number of potential buyers to which part-time producers could offer their wares.

When we look at Mesoamerican commercial systems, the professional pochteca merchants stand out. These merchants were transportation specialists. They worked full-time in the procurement and the exchange of goods for profit (Figures 47.3 and 47.4). According to Sahagún (1961: 59), the pochteca merchant was "a vendor, a seller, a practiser of commerce . . . a maker of profits." The pochteca operated as individuals in their economic dealings, but they worked and traveled together as members of an integrated trade association (Figures 47.5 and 47.6). The pochteca have been characterized as a trade guild, but it is unclear whether they had the same form of organization as craft and professional guilds found in other regions throughout the world (Curtin 1984).

The pochteca were an upwardly mobile commoner class made wealthy by involvement in long-distance trade that was important for Aztec society. They engaged in dangerous, long-distance trading ventures for wealth goods and served as emissaries and spies outside the empire. These activities made them wealthy and targets of envy among the established agrarian elite. But the pochteca also oversaw the operation of the marketplace, evaluated fair trade practices within it, served as economic agents for the elites, and operated as retailers, wholesalers, bankers, and money changers within the marketplace (Berdan 1978). While the pochteca provided important functions for the institutional economy (see below), they operated primarily for their commercial advantage. As such, they are a good example of how the Mesoamerican commercial system permitted the accumulation of wealth at the individual and household levels.

Figure 47.5 Two pochteca on the road, carrying cargo (from Sahagún 1959: Plate 13).

Figure 47.6 Pochteca merchants and the range of goods that they offered for sale
(modified from Sahagún 1959: Plate 14).

An important question, of course, is how far goods actually moved under poor transportation conditions when most goods were moved by human porters (Figure 47.3). We know that lightweight, high-value goods, including feathers, gold, jade, cacao, and textiles, were traded by pochteca over distances as far as 1,000 kilometers. But what about staple goods that commoner households consumed or wanted to sell as part of their normal subsistence routine? Here, contact-period sources are disturbingly silent and while archaeological research is helpful in this regard, it has not provided a framework large enough to trace the volume and movement of goods like ceramics and lithic items. This is an important question because it addresses the extent that commoner households participated in regional and interregional exchange systems.

Fortunately, some information exists in the *Relaciones Geográficas* (Acuña 1982–1988; de la Garza et al. 1983), a royal cartographic survey requested by Phillip II in 1577–1581. The responses to the survey contain excellent information on a variety of staple goods that indian populations either procured from neighboring areas or took to sell in regional marketplaces. These data reveal that commoner households traveled 40–100 kilometers to buy maize when they needed it and 20–50 kilometers to sell fruit. Other food products such as beans, chile, squash, tomatoes, fish, turkeys, and honey moved from 10–100 kilometers, depending on local conditions, with 50–70 kilometers being the norm. Bulk goods like lime, wooden beams, planks, and firewood normally moved short distances of 10–30 kilometers, while lighter goods including ceramics, gourd containers, baskets, cordage, mats, tar, and amole soap moved much farther (20–90 kilometers). Good information exists for the salt trade, which, at the time of the survey, was still manufactured at the household level. Salt was an important component of indigenous diets and was sold by producer-vendors and itinerant merchants over fairly wide areas of 70–150 kilometers.

The information suggests that commoner households were actively involved in the production, movement, and sale of staple goods over intermediate-scale distances across Mesoamerica. A day's walk was somewhere between 21–30 kilometers, depending on the terrain, the hours traveled, the pace maintained, and the load carried. Most of the distribution ranges for staple goods in the *Relaciones Geográficas* exceed that of a normal day's walk. Nevertheless, products brought for sale were sold in the marketplace. Heavy products like lime and wooden beams were brought from within a day's walk, while fruit, food, crafts, and salt moved in a broader circuit of 1 to 5 days of travel from home. What this implies is that a broad cross-section of commoner households could engage in intermediate-scale trade if they chose to do so. Like their involvement in the Tlatelolco marketplace (Sahagún 1961), it is likely that commoner households were active participants in intermediate-scale exchange networks.

EXCHANGE IN THE INSTITUTIONAL ECONOMY

The marketplace was the primary area for exchange within the institutional economy. The other political, religious, and social institutions were supported and financed by production and mobilization strategies and not by exchange (see Berdan, this volume). Strategies based primarily on production employed rotational labor on prebendal estates or lands set aside for special use (Hirth 1996). This production was part of the broad system of *tequitl* (service) obligations that commoners paid for societal purposes, which also included the transportation of goods (Carrasco 1978; Sluyter 1993). Nevertheless, there were two areas where exchange was important for the institutional economy even if it was supplementary to other forms of resource procurement.

The first of these was the role that pochteca merchants played in procuring resources used by the state to finance institutional activities. First among these was their involvement in obtaining precious raw materials like gold, jade, turquoise, and quetzal, spoonbill, and cotinga feathers. These raw materials were used by craft producers to make wealth goods used in high-status elite lifestyles. They also traded for fine cotton textiles, jade necklaces, gold ear plugs, lip ornaments, and cacao (Sahagún 1959: 1–2). Likewise, merchants served as economic agents for the king (Berdan 1978, 1982; Katz 1966).

Figure 47.7 Pochteca merchants receiving goods from Ahuitzotl for trade as agents in
his name (modified from Sahagún 1959: Plate 12).

In a widely cited instance (Sahagún 1959: 7–8) the Aztec king Ahuitzotl gave
pochteca merchants 1,600 cotton capes as capital to trade, which the pochteca converted into "ruler's capes" and other speciality trade goods on his behalf (Figure
47.7).1 Finally, merchants also traded high-value goods that were included in the
tribute levies of conquered provinces. Some of these provinces had to supply gold,
jade, and other resources that they did not have access to. Several scholars (Berdan
1982; Katz 1966) have argued that this was an intentional dimension of Aztec tribute planning, designed to enrich merchants and/or the king whom they represented. Whether intentional or not, merchants certainly played a role supplying
conquered provinces with nonlocal wealth required as tribute.

The second role of exchange in the institutional economy takes us back to the
marketplace. No tribute system, no matter how well designed, can anticipate all of
the resource needs of its political institutions. It is through the marketplace that those
needs were fulfilled and where it served as a clearinghouse to convert surplus grain

---

¹ Barry Isaac (1986) feels that this was not a typical practice because it is mentioned
only in regard to dealings with Ahuitzotl. I disagree and feel it was a normal relationship,
because some trade appears to have been carried out through a political alliance and the
use of economic agents was a regular part of pochteca operations (Sahagún 1961; Berdan
1982).

from elite estates into durable goods, or tribute goods from state storehouses into food for periodic public festivals. The marketplace lay at the intersection of domestic, merchant, state, and elite economic interests, and it served to mobilize, convert, and transfer resources from one economic sector to the other as needs arose.

CONCLUSION

Mesoamerica had a dual economy. One component encompassed the domestic economy, which included all the multifaceted strategies that households used to meet their normal subsistence needs. It is here that exchange played an important role in the lives of commoner households, whether farmer-craft producers or full-time professional merchants. Both were involved in the production, movement, and sale of goods in regional marketplaces. While they differed in the types and quantity of goods sold, professional merchants and commoner households actively pursued their livelihoods, carrying surplus goods to local, intermediate, and distant marketplaces. The second component of Mesoamerica's dual economy consisted of the mechanisms by which its primary institutions were supported and provisioned with key resources. While the domestic economy operated along the normal principles of commercial pricing, the institutional economy was structured on the basis of "command and deliver." Here, exchange was less important because resource flows were either one-sided or because goods were produced for institutional consumption by using corvée labor and forms of assigned production.

REFERENCES

Acosta Saignes, Miguel. 1945. *Los pochteca. Ubicación de los mercaderes en la estructura social Tenochca*. Acta Anthropologica 1(7). Mexico, D.F.

Acuña, René. 1982-1988. *Relaciones geográficas del siglo XVI*. Serie Antropológica, 10 volumes. Instituto de Investigaciones Antropológicas, UNAM, Mexico City.

Anderson, Arthur, Frances Berdan, and James Lockhart. 1976. *Beyond the Codices*. University of California Press, Berkeley.

Berdan, Frances. 1978. Tres formas de intercambio en la economía Azteca. In *Economía política e ideología en el México prehispánico*, edited by Pedro Carrasco and JoAnna Broda, pp. 75–94. Editorial Nueva Imagen, Mexico.

Berdan, Frances. 1982. *The Aztecs of Central Mexico. An Imperial Society*. Holt, Rinehart and Winston, New York.

Berdan, Frances. 1989. Trade and Markets in Precapitalist States. In *Economic Anthropology*, edited by Stuart Plattner, pp. 78–107. Stanford University Press, Stanford.

Bittman, Bente, and Thelma Sullivan. 1978. The Pochteca. In *Mesoamerican Communication Routes and Culture Contacts*, edited by Thomas Lee and Carols Navarrete, pp. 211–218. Papers of the New World Archaeological Foundation no. 40.

Blanton, Richard. 1996. Basin of Mexico Market System and the Growth of Empire. In *Aztec Imperial Strategies,* edited by Frances F. Berdan, Richard Blanton, Elizabeth Hill Boone, Mary Hodge, Michael Smith, and Emily Umberger, pp. 47–84. Dumbarton Oaks Research Library and Collection, Washington, DC.

Carrasco, Pedro. 1978. La economía del México prehispánico. In *Economía política e ideología en el México prehispánico*, edited by Pedro Carrasco and Johanna Broda, pp. 13–74. Editorial Nueva Imagen, México.

Carrasco, Pedro, and Jesús Monjarás-Ruiz. 1978. *Colección de documentos sobre Coyoacan (volumen segundo)*. Colección Científica 65, INAH, Mexico City.

Coe, Sophie, and Michael Coe. 2007. *The True History of Chocolate*. Thames and Hudson, New York.

Crain, Eugene R., and Reginald Carl Riendorp. 1970. *The Chronicles of Michoacán*. University of Oklahoma Press, Norman,

Curtin, Philip. 1984. *Cross-Cultural Trade in World History*. Cambridge University Press, Cambridge.

de la Garza, Mercedes, Ana Luisa Izquierdo, and Maria del Carmen León y Tolita Figueroa. 1983. *Relaciones histórico-geográficas de la gobernación de Yucatán (Mérida, Valladolid y Tabasco)*. 2 vols. UNAM, Mexico City.

Díaz del Castillo, Bernal. 1956. *The Discovery and Conquest of Mexico 1517–1521*. Farrar, Straus and Cudahy, New York.

Feinman, Gary M. 1999. Rethinking Our Assumptions: Economic Specialization at the Household Scale in Ancient Ejutla, Oaxaca, Mexico. In *Pottery and People*, edited by James Skibo and Gary M. Feinman, pp. 81–98. University of Utah Press, Salt Lake City.

Hassig, Ross. 1985. *Trade, Tribute and Transportation. The Sixteenth-Century Political Economy of the Valley of Mexico*. University of Oklahoma Press, Norman.

Hirth, Kenneth. 1996. Political Economy and Archaeology: Perspectives on Exchange and Production, *Journal of Archaeological Research* 4:203–239.

Hirth, Kenneth. 1998. The Distributional Approach: A New Way to Identify Market Behavior Using Archaeological Data. *Current Anthropology* 39:451–476.

Hirth, Kenneth. 2009. Craft Production, Household Diversification, and Domestic Economy in Prehispanic Mesoamerica, In *Housework: Craft Production and Domestic Economy in Ancient Mesoamerica*, edited by K. Hirth, pp. 13–32. Archaeological Publications of the American Anthropological Society No 19.

Hirth, Kenneth. 2013. The Merchant's World: Commercial Diversity and the Economics of Interregional Exchange in Highland Mesoamerica. In *Merchants, Trade and Exchange in the Pre-Columbian World*, edited by Kenneth Hirth. Dumbarton Oaks Research Library and Collection, Washington, DC.

Isaac, Barry. 1986. Notes on Obsidian, the Pochteca, and the Position of Tlatelolco in the Aztec Empire. In *Research in Economic Anthropology, Supplement No. 2. Economic Aspects of Prehispanic Highland Mexico*, edited by Barry Isaac, pp. 1–19. JAI Press, Greenwich, Connecticut.

Johnson, Allen, and Timothy Earle. 1987. *The Evolution of Human Societies*. Stanford University Press, Stanford.

Katz, Friedrich. 1966. *Situación social y económica de los Aztecas durante los siglos XV y XVI*. Instituto de Investigaciones Históricas, UNAM, Mexico City.

Millon, René. 1955. When Money Grows on Trees: A Study of Cacao in Ancient
    Mesoamerica. PhD dissertation, Department of Anthropology, Columbia
    University, New York.
Nash, Manning. 1964. The Organization of Economic Life. In *Horizons of Anthropology*,
    edited by Sol Tax, pp. 171–180. Aldine, Chicago.
Plattner, Stuart. 1989a. Economic Behavior in Markets. In *Economic Anthropology*, edited
    by Stuart Plattner, pp. 209–221. Stanford University Press, Stanford.
Plattner, Stuart. 1989b. Markets and Marketplaces. In *Economic Anthropology*, edited by
    Stuart Plattner, pp. 171–208. Stanford University Press, Stanford.
Rojas, José Luis de. 1995. *México Tenochtitlan. Economía y sociedad en el siglo XVI*. Fondo
    de Cultura Económica, Mexico City.
Sahagún, Fray Bernardino de. 1959. *Florentine Codex. General History of the Things
    of New Spain, Book 9, the Merchants*. Translated by Arthur J.O. Anderson.
    Monographs of the School of American Research, No. 14, Part 10, Santa Fe.
Sahagún, Fray Bernardino de. 1961. *Florentine Codex. General History of the Things of
    New Spain, Book 10, the People*. Translated by Arthur J. O. Anderson and Charles
    Dibble. Monographs of the School of American Research and the University of
    Utah, No. 14, Part 11, Santa Fe.
Sluyter, Andrew. 1993. Long-Distance Staple Transport in Western Mesoamerica: Insights
    through Quantitative Modeling. *Ancient Mesoamerica* 4:193–199.
Smith, Michael. 1979. The Aztec Marketing System and Settlement Pattern in the Valley
    of Mexico: A Central-Place Analysis. *American Antiquity* 44:110–125.

CHAPTER 48

CENTRAL MEXICAN STATES AND IMPERIAL TRIBUTE SYSTEMS

FRANCES F. BERDAN

TRIBUTE in central Mexican prehistory consisted of one-way movements of goods and labor from conquered polities to their conquerors. Military conquests were frequent, especially during the Postclassic period, and repeated aggressive excursions often resulted in conquest states or, more extensively, in empires. A common goal of conquest was control over economic resources and production, and this goal was achieved through the imposition of tribute demands on conquered peoples.

TRIBUTE AND TAXES

Recent discussions of central Mexican (especially Aztec) tribute have focused on terminologies and categories, particularly the distinction between tribute and taxes. Both "types" involve the movements of economic resources (including labor) to some centralized authority; in other words, these payments occur within hierarchical political and social systems. One distinction made between tribute and taxes focuses on the relationships between payer and recipient: taxes are paid by a citizenry to its own polity while tribute involves payments demanded beyond one's own polity, customarily on a collectivity by a conquering polity (Mair 1977:

98; Berdan 2001: 262). Alternatively, Daniel Tarschys (1988) suggests that the term "tribute" should be reserved for relatively irregular and unpredictable payments levied on collectives and involving "more personal and emotional ties" (3), while "taxes" would more appropriately refer to regularized payments "based on the calendar, not on particular events or on the arrival of certain commodities" (7). In other words, he makes a distinction between "largely unpredictable tributes" and "the imposition of more predictable tax payments" (20). His primary criterion is scheduling, whether regular and predictable (taxes) or more irregular and discretionary (tribute).

In the case of central Mexico, these approaches are not exactly compatible. In particular, regularly scheduled, calendar-based payments were made by Aztec imperial subjects to their overlords (Berdan and Anawalt 1992). Are these tributes or taxes? Michael Smith (2010) prefers the "taxation terminology, finding it useful in comparisons with other state systems." While this is a valuable approach, I prefer here to emphasize political relationships rather than scheduling. These same imperial subjects also rendered payments in labor and goods on a more sporadic or opportunistic basis to their same overlords, and I find it useful to encompass all of these obligations under a single broad umbrella. An important advantage of this approach is that it addresses the dual nature of tribute, as payment and as symbol. It highlights its institutional one-way and asymmetrical nature along with the symbolic reaffirmation of a dominant-subordinate relationship.

For present purposes, then, I consider tribute to encompass those obligatory economic demands, in goods or services, placed on the people of a subject polity by a dominant polity. In central Mexico, these polities were most commonly city-states.

MATTERS OF SCALE

The most abundant information on tribute in central Mexico applies to the Aztec Empire (1428–1521 AD), and I focus on that largest of Mesoamerican empires. The Aztec Empire was constructed from the conquest of numerous city-states and conquest states throughout central Mexico. Political bureaucracies and elite lifestyles were supported at all of these levels by the efforts of commoners. Within city-states, commoners supported their local nobles with palatial household services (especially textile weaving and maize grinding), construction and maintenance of nobles' houses, and provision of goods, including foodstuffs, cotton cloaks and raw cotton, rabbit-fur cloaks, sandals, birds, feathers, and weapons (Berdan et al. 1996: 230, 231, 232, 239–240; Smith 1994). Some of these and other goods (such as cacao beans and turkeys) worked their way up to the city-state rulers (*tlatoque*), paid by the city-state's local nobles. Tlatoque are also recorded as receiving gold,

gold dust, jewelry, cotton cloaks, feathers, honey, chiles, personal services, and aid in time of war from their subjects (Berdan et al. 1996: 230, 280, 281, 283).

In some cases a city-state was conquered by another, creating a conquest state; the vanquished city-state *tlatoani* (ruler) was required to pay tributes to his new overlord. While these demands were apparently assessed collectively on the conquered city-state and its tlatoani, the commoner population bore the brunt of the tribute obligations. As with most information on tribute demands, data on this level of tribute payments are derived from relevant colonial assessments. Nonetheless, many of these levies included indigenous goods that most likely reflect prehispanic patterns: cotton textiles, cacao, gold ornaments, tropical feathers, pottery, foodstuffs, firewood, and slaves (Smith 1994: 334–335).

Historically, conquest states preceded the growth of the Aztec Empire, and that empire built on the political and economic institutions already established in conquest states of the Basin of Mexico (such as Azcapotzalco) and neighboring valleys (such as Quauhnahuac). At its apex, the Aztec Empire was a triple alliance of the three powerful city-states of Tenochtitlan, Texcoco, and Tlacopan. Each of these three powers also constituted a conquest state, expanding and retaining its own control over external areas (Carrasco 1999), as well as operating as a larger imperial coalition.

Types of Tribute

Tribute as used here embraces a wide array of types of payments: calendrically scheduled levies of specific goods, situational levies to support special events or to satisfy immediate imperial needs (such as a royal funeral or ritual event, or special materials for a construction project), service in the imperial palace by conquered nobles, and military service to the empire. Again, focus is on the richly documented Aztecs, because they exercised their power to harness the resources and energy of conquered peoples for these several purposes.

The imperial capitals of the triple alliance levied specific material tribute demands on conquered populations, as recorded in the pictorial *Matrícula de Tributos* (1980) and in the Codex Mendoza (Berdan and Anawalt 1992). These payments were normally negotiated between a conqueror and the conquered immediately after conquest, with the victor also carrying home enemy warriors (for sacrifice) and a certain amount of booty and luxurious gifts obtained on the spot. The negotiated payments were expected to arrive predictably in the triple alliance capitals (especially Tenochtitlan) annually, semiannually, or every eighty days. Failure to meet that schedule was tantamount to rebellion and resulted in renewed imperial military incursions. Payments included staple foodstuffs, large quantities of cotton clothing, feathered warrior costumes and shields, woods, dyes, animal pelts, copal incense, rubber, shells, cacao, precious stones, feathers, and metals (see also Smith, this volume). At the time of the Spanish conquest (1521 AD), the Aztec Empire extracted such tribute from 371 city-states, which were grouped into 38 tributary provinces. Several city-states not listed in the Codex Mendoza also paid tribute in utilitarian and luxury goods, although the scheduling of these payments is not known (Berdan 1996). These tributes were collected by imperial tribute collectors (*calpixque*) stationed in the provinces, by imposed imperial governors, or by local rulers.

In a variation of these demands, the Aztecs established "client" relations with 80 (and perhaps as many as 134; see Smith 1996: 137) city-states in strategically advantageous relations to the empire: along hostile borders, near critical resources, or astride important trade and transport routes. These city-states were not listed on the scheduled tribute tallies (such as the Codex Mendoza). Imperial-client relations favored the empire, although clients sometimes provided gifts rather than tribute "out of friendship" and "on request to the imperial powers" (Berdan et al. 1996: 276, 280, 281, 283, 284). These presents appear to be more symbolic than material in value.

In addition to the regularly scheduled levies on tributary provinces, subject peoples were also called upon to pay up on special occasions such as specific ceremonial festivals, the dedication of a temple, or a ruler's coronation or funeral. Some of these were also scheduled. For instance, rich clothing, fine jewelry and feathers, warriors' costumes, and slaves were delivered by conquered peoples for the celebration of five major Aztec ceremonies (Scholes and Adams 1957). Other duties included the provision of materials for other specific rituals, work and maintenance on specific temples, and the offering of slaves for ceremonial sacrifices (Berdan et al. 1996: 231, 269; Berdan and Anawalt 1992: vol. 3, folio 19r; Durán 1994: 329–331). These historically recorded levies were only part of the story: many (if not most) of the materials and objects deposited in the more than 140 excavated caches around Tenochtitlan's Templo Mayor may have derived from these and perhaps more spontaneous ritual assessments. According to López Luján (2005), the vast majority of the artifacts in these offerings hailed from beyond the Basin of Mexico. Special-purpose tributes also were levied on conquered peoples at the coronation or funeral of a ruler. At such events, allied and conquered peoples delivered vast quantities of goods to their overlord's city; this was done with great pomp and ceremony as the subjects publicly displayed their subservience (e.g., Durán 1994, 291–298, 302–303, 383–385). Other tributes paid in service included periodic obligations by conquered rulers to personally serve their imperial overlord in his palace. Thus, not only commoners but also nobles were subject to tribute payments.

Some tribute demands were satisfied through military service. This ranged from direct participation on the battlefield to service as porters and obligations to supply Aztec troops on the march. Some provinces and clients situated along hostile borderlands engaged in low-grade, persistent battles with nonimperial neighbors, supplying the imperial rulers with enemy prisoners. Other conquered city-states contributed to the daily maintenance of nearby imperial garrisons and fortresses (Berdan et al. 1996: 236, 237, 267, 272, 275–284, 290, 292).

USES OF TRIBUTE

At all levels, tribute payments required expanded economic efforts on the part of the vanquished while at the same time they provided material revenue for the victors. Tribute was used to maintain rulers' palatial households, support an increasingly complex bureaucracy, finance military campaigns, reward accomplished warriors, reimburse state and royal workers whether they be masons or jewelers, and provide stores against possible famine or other emergency. Rulers also drew on their tribute storehouses to establish and maintain politically advantageous relations with external polities, whether through reciprocal gifts at special events or through promoting foreign trade (Durán 1994: 333, 402–408; Sahagún 1950–1982: Book 9; Berdan 2005: 44–46).

Tribute also had its uses on the symbolic level. A properly humbled and contrite population "promised perpetual subjection and servitude, as well as rich tribute…to their conquerors" (Durán 1994: 165). Other pointed phrases that dot the documents are "subservience," "humiliation," and "disgrace." While displaying these attitudes, the vanquished ruler and his attendant nobles vowed from fear to serve the Aztecs as their vassals…to the death, if necessary (e.g., Durán 1994: 83, 85, 101, 102, 110).

PATTERNS AND QUESTIONS

Studies of central Mexican (notably Aztec) tribute systems reveal several intriguing patterns. In the first place, tribute payments consisted of both raw materials and manufactured goods, with an emphasis on manufactured items. For instance, there were enormous quantities of cotton clothing and smaller amounts of raw cotton. Warrior costumes fashioned of fine feathers were abundant, compared with smaller quantities of raw feathers. One suggestion here is that tribute demands stimulated craft production in the conquered provinces, giving correspondingly less support to the urban artisans of the triple alliance.

A second pattern is that the conquerors demanded materials and items that were readily available to the conquered people. This does not mean that they were necessarily produced locally, because many materials (such as precious stones, amber, cacao, and fine feathers for warrior costumes) were not suited to local ecologies, and they must have habitually arrived in the province through long-standing trading and market networks (some from outside the imperial net). Therefore, the tribute system to some extent depended on these pre-imperial networks, and the economic thrall of the empire in some cases extended beyond its actual conquests.

Third, as the empire expanded geographically, more and more luxuries were demanded in tribute. This was no coincidence. Preciosities such as feathers and fine stones for mosaics were highly valued and relatively light items; they were more readily transportable from long distances (than, say, bulky foodstuffs), where all transport was on foot or by canoe. They also tended to be found in regions far distant from the Aztec capitals. As time passed during Aztec imperial expansion, the ranks of the nobility grew, as did their exorbitant lifestyle full of pomp and display. More and more exquisite luxuries were needed by the imperial lords, and they were provided from tribute levies on rich, distant provinces.

Recognizing these patterns, a number of questions persist. The first involves the impact of tribute imposition on the vanquished individuals, households, communities, and city-states. How onerous were the demands? Did the levies require changes in their economic, social, and political relationships and lives? Looking at the matter differently, what did the conquered people get in return for their payments? For instance, warriors in provinces close to the imperial capitals joined in military campaigns and received appropriate rewards for their achievements; more distant provinces received promises of protection from enemy groups. To what extent did these strategies serve to integrate (or not) conquered peoples into imperial goals and enterprises?

A second and perpetually nagging question concerns the extent to which tribute contributed to changing royal, state, and imperial needs. In particular, to what degree did tribute underwrite the state bureaucracy and finance imperial expansion? To what extent did prior conquests contribute to future ones?

Finally, how representative or unique is the Aztec case, through space and time?

While all of these questions are likely to persist for some time, they nonetheless offer a guide for future archaeological and ethnohistorical research on the role of tribute in expanding empires.

REFERENCES

Berdan, Frances F. 1996. The Tributary Provinces. In *Aztec Imperial Strategies*, edited by Frances F. Berdan et al., pp. 115–135. Dumbarton Oaks Research Library and Collection, Washington, DC.

Berdan, Frances F. 2001. Tribute. In *The Oxford Encyclopedia of Mesoamerican Cultures, Volume 3*, edited by David Carrasco, pp. 262–264. Oxford University Press, Oxford.

Berdan, Frances F. 2005. *The Aztecs of Central Mexico: An Imperial Society*. 2nd edition. Wadsworth, Belmont, California.

Berdan, Frances F., and Patricia Rieff Anawalt. 1992. *The Codex Mendoza*. 4 vols. University of California Press, Berkeley.

Berdan, Frances F., Richard E. Blanton, Elizabeth Hill Boone, Mary G. Hodge, Michael E. Smith, and Emily Umberger. 1996. *Aztec Imperial Strategies*. Dumbarton Oaks Research Library and Collections, Washington, DC.

Carrasco, Pedro. 1999. *The Tenochca Empire of Ancient Mexico: The Triple Alliance of Tenochtitlan, Tetzcoco, and Tlacopan*. University of Oklahoma Press, Norman.

Durán, Diego. 1994. *The History of the Indies of New Spain*. University of Oklahoma Press, Norman.

López Luján, Leonardo. 2005. *The Offerings of the Templo Mayor of Tenochtitlan*. University of New Mexico Press, Albuquerque.

Mair, Lucy. 1977. *African Kingdoms*. Oxford University Press, Oxford.

Matrícula de Tributos. 1980. *Matrícula de tributos, Museo de Antropología, Mexico (Col. 35–52)*. Akademische Druck-u Verlagsanstalt, Graz, Austria.

Sahagún, Bernardino de. 1950–1982. *Florentine Codex: General History of the Things of New Spain*, edited by Arthur J. O. Anderson and Charles E. Dibble. 12 vols. University of Utah Press, Salt Lake City.

Scholes, France V., and Eleanor B. Adams. 1957. *Información sobre los tributos que los Indios pagaban a Motezuma, año de 1554*. Documentos para la Historia del Mexico Colonial, vol. 4. Mexico.

Smith, Michael E. 1994. Economies and Polities in Aztec-Period Morelos: Ethnohistoric Overview. In *Economies and Polities in the Aztec Realm*, edited by Mary G. Hodge and Michael E. Smith, pp. 313–348. Institute for Mesoamerican Studies, Albany, New York.

Smith, Michael E. 1996. The Strategic Provinces. In *Aztec Imperial Strategies*, edited by Frances F. Berdan, Richard Blanton, Elizabeth Hill Boone, Mary G. Hodge, Michael Smith, and Emily Umberger, pp. 137–150. Dumbarton Oaks Research Library and Collection, Washington, DC.

Smith, Michael E. 2010. Aztec Taxation at the City-State and Imperial Levels. Paper presented at a conference on fiscal regimes and the political economy of early states, May 2010, Stanford, California.

Tarschys, Daniel. 1988. Tributes, Tariffs, Taxes and Trade: The Changing Sources of Government Revenue. *British Journal of Political Science* 18(1):1–20.

Social and Political Relations

CHAPTER 49

....

ARCHAEOLOGY
OF GENDER IN
MESOAMERICAN
SOCIETIES

....

ROSEMARY A. JOYCE

THE first Spanish accounts of a Mesoamerican society, the Mexica, written in the sixteenth century, recorded how children were socialized to become adults by their compliance with the expectations elders and the state had for good men and women. These accounts describe a range of ways adult men and women actually lived and even rebelled against normative expectations.

Research on archaeological materials has provided similarly rich understandings of what it was like to be men and women in Mesoamerica (Ardren 2002; Ardren and Hutson 2006; Gustafson and Trevelyan 2002; Joyce 2001b; Miller 1988; Robin and Brumfiel 2008). Critical advances in the archaeology of gender in Mesoamerica include explorations of how status and age differences intersected with gender to affect the lives of men and women; increased understandings of how women in different societies and of different ranks were able to exercise power; and understandings of different experiences of sexuality.

Sex cannot be treated as providing a natural basis on which cultural gender develops as a secondary phenomenon, because all cultural life, including the identification of biological sex, is experienced through patterns of thought, experience, and speech. Gender is thus better understood as a persistent way of acting as an embodied person, aware of socially sanctioned precedents for how to be a person with affective, sexual, and potentially reproductive relations (Butler 1993). Whether and how formal gender categories are defined becomes a subject for empirical examination. Biological sex itself is not dual, and many societies recognize more than two biological sexes.

Mesoamerican peoples are arguably among those who recognize sex as more than a simple duality. Klein (2001) has argued in analyses of Mexica sculptures of earth deities that supernatural beings with both male and female aspects were part of some Mesoamerican cosmologies. This led Joyce (2000a) to propose that Mexica practices for the shaping of gender presupposed that infants were born of undefined gender and that adult gender was a product of practices to which children were repeatedly subjected. Yet the same Mexica sources have been used to argue that children occupied polar male and female genders from birth. Mesoamerican gender ideologies are consequently characterized by different scholars either as dichotomous or as forming a continuum of multiple ways to enact gender.

Scholars agree that being male or female in sixteenth-century Mesoamerica was signified by distinctive clothing and by distinct participation in labor. Literature and visual culture have presented the stereotypical work of Mexica women as textile production and that of Mexica men as warfare (McCafferty and McCafferty 1991). But there were many domains in which men and women both participated, including religion, craft production, and trade (Kellogg 1995; McCafferty and McCafferty 1988). Sixteenth-century legal documents demonstrate that women could make bequests and inherit property (Kellogg 1986). Mexica documentary history has been interpreted as exemplifying gender parallelism, rather than a hierarchy in which men dominated women (Kellogg 1995).

Archaeologists have extended the association of women with textile production to visual culture from Classic and Postclassic Oaxacan and Maya archaeological sites. Figurines portray images of women or goddesses weaving, women or goddesses with spinning tools, and cloth as a political valuable (Hamann 1997; Hendon 1999b). Where visual or literary warrants exist, textile production tools have been used to explore women's experiences in Classic and Postclassic Mesoamerica.

Brumfiel (1991, 1996) demonstrated that the composition of assemblages of spindle whorls in settlements absorbed into the Aztec Empire changed in ways indicative of the reorganization of labor, particularly women's labor. Building on ethnographic studies showing that spindle diameter and weight vary with the fiber being spun, she inferred that demands for tribute cloth produced changes in spindle whorl sizes. She also showed that cooking methods changed, an outcome she explained as due to the need to redirect women's efforts to the added production of tribute cloth. While Brumfiel's work was based on surface-collected samples, other scholars of Aztec society have explored the spatial associations of artifacts associated with gendered activities in locations such as small town palaces (Evans 1998).

Repeated associations of textile production with residences of ruling or noble families have been taken as indicating the significance of women's labor in the Classic Maya political economy (Ardren et al. 2010; Chase et al. 2008; Hendon 1999b). Hendon (1999a) argued that household production formed a basis for women to assert their own power, through their economic contributions to the formation of social relations and political alliances, a point echoed by others (Chase et al. 2008). Monumental inscriptions indicate that some Classic Maya women acted as regents or ruled in their own right (Josserand 2002). Some Maya noble-women claimed military titles and perhaps roles (Ayala Falcón 2002) or the title of scribe (Closs 1992). Joyce (1996) argued that Classic Maya women of the highest social rank were represented in monumental art as collaborators in political ceremonies and rituals, consistent with ethnographic accounts from contemporary Maya communities that stress the complementarity of men and women in ritual action.

Other scholars have proposed that Classic Maya society was patriarchal, with the products of women's labor being appropriated by men who monopolized political power (McAnany and Plank 2001). While paleopathology suggests that women at some sites suffered from poor health (Storey 1998), an overview of analyses of diet and sex found that social rank accounted for more variation than did distinctions between men and women (White 2005). Analyses of artifacts associated with women's assumed roles in textile production, food preparation, and craft production from households of commoners suggest that women were important social actors there as well, especially in the context of status competition between households (Fung 1995; Lopiparo 2006; Morehart and Helmke 2008; Robin 2002; Sweely 1999).

The variability of evidence supports the proposition that gender was not always the most salient social structure governing experiences in Classic Maya society. A similar argument has been made for Teotihuacan, the largest city in Classic-period Mesoamerica (de Lucia 2008). There, identity with a residential group was arguably more significant than gender identification in determining variation in postmortem treatment. Sex difference may have been deliberately deemphasized in visual culture. There is no clear evidence for gendered activities in visual culture or in patterns of spatial segregation.

The distribution of spinning and weaving tools in burials in the Classic Maya area (Chase et al. 2008) supports the close association of these activities with high-status women, also as suggested by visual culture. Studies in other parts of Mesoamerica have assumed women were textile producers (Stark et al. 1998), but sometimes the individuals buried with these implements were biologically male (McCafferty and McCafferty 1994, 2000). In certain times and places, intensification of textile production may have allowed or required recruitment of people who would not stereotypically be expected to participate in these activities. Alternatively, the suggestion that some individuals identified as biologically male, buried with textile tools, such as the principal individual in Tomb 7 from Monte Albán, formed a third gender, although greeted with deeply polarized responses, needs to be seriously considered (McCafferty and McCafferty 1994).

Arguments for Mesoamerican third- and fourth-gender persons (biological males who share some aspects of gender performance with women, and biological females who share some aspects of gender performance with men), while always contested, have accumulated (Joyce 2001b; Looper 2002). A person in one tomb of the ruling dynasty of Copán has even been described as probably intersexed (Storey 2005). Intersex refers to someone whose expressed biological sex is affected by a chromosomal makeup that is neither normative male (XY) or normative female (XX). The proposed intersexed individual from Copán was buried in the manner of a royal woman but had a parry fracture typical of participants in warfare and was accompanied by trophy skulls.

While additional genders should not automatically be taken as evidence of homosexuality, the spectrum of sexual practices in Mesoamerica clearly extended beyond heterosexuality. The existence of same-sex sexual relations by men and women, stigmatized as abnormal in surviving texts that represent state perspectives, is well demonstrated for the Mexica (Sigal 2007). At least transitory sexual activity between young men in some Classic Maya sites, where visual culture celebrates male homosociality, has also been suggested (Joyce 2000b). Maya cave paintings depict male masturbation and a man engaged in a sex act with a second male in women's clothing (Stone 1988). This Classic and Postclassic male homosociality has been related to the formation of a masculinity linked closely to the recruitment of boys as warriors and their segregation in same-sex quarters. Monumental phallic sculptures (Ardren and Hixson 2006; Joyce 2000b) visually express this exaggerated masculinity.

Classic and Postclassic gender studies analyze stratified states, and most concern noble strata. Less common are examinations of gender among commoners in Classic and Postclassic villages (Fung 1995; Lopiparo 2006; Morehart and Helmke 2008; Pankonian 2008; Robin 2002; Sweely 1999). Research on the Formative period provides more examples from settlements with less pronounced social and economic inequality, or where stratification developed over time (Tejeda 2008).

Formative visual culture presents a diversity of stereotypes of gender. Cyphers Guillén (1993) has proposed that Chalcatzingo's figurines reflect stages in the developmental biology of maturing and pregnant women, which she related to their use in household settings that she saw as women's spaces. Marcus (1998) went further, associating the household with women, and she identified figurines at San José Mogote as representations of women's ancestors. She contrasted the household with separate buildings she identified as men's houses, proposing strong gender segregation already existed.

Chalcatzingo and San José Mogote are both regional centers. Other analyses of figurines and gender come from villages where rank differences may not have been as pronounced. Joyce (2003) argues that the predominant female subjects in figurines from the Ulúa Valley are represented at times of life-course rituals, rather than strictly biological events, and suggests that these were moments for relatively public celebrations in village communities. Lesure (1997, 1999) suggests that young females at Paso de la Amada are shown as marriageable dependents whose futures were negotiated by elders, both male and female, represented in the assemblage by figurines of seated and masked men and women. These two interpretations are united by an understanding that, in village societies, social life was dominated by the relations formed between families through marriage and the birth of children. Sexuality and reproductive potential would thus be sites for elaboration of distinct gendered experiences and ideologies.

Discussions of gender based on monumental sculptures are more contentious. Some scholars conservatively identify only individuals shown with an apparent adult breast as female. Others use criteria that were formalized by Follensbee (2009), which take the waist-to-hip ratio as key to recognizing female figures, especially those who may not be shown with developed breasts. What is at issue in these debates is not simply which images represent women: it is different understandings of whether women in political roles are unusual or unremarkable during the Formative period. Scholarly consensus agrees that Chalcatzingo Monument 21 depicts a standing woman. Cyphers Guillén (1984) suggested she played a role in the transaction of a political alliance through marriage. More contested is the proposal that a seated figure in a cave on Chalcatzingo Monument 1 from which issues rainclouds was female. Where the figure on Monument 21 has a clearly depicted breast in profile view, the seated figure on Monument 1 holds a bundle that obscures the chest. Identification of this figure as a possible woman rests on identifying the garment covering the thighs as a skirt, assumed to contrast with loincloths as markers of female and male sex in Formative-period visual culture.

Follensbee (2009) developed her analysis of diagnostic features for recognizing male and female genders in a study of Gulf Coast Olmec figurines, assuming that the makers of these images would have been consciously or unconsciously concerned to reflect a relatively naturalistic body type. Her analysis showed that the vast majority of Gulf Coast figurines depicted likely female subjects, with smaller numbers of males. Based on her analyses, she identified a short skirt or a pubic apron as female items of dress, contrasting with a loincloth for male figures.

Follensbee then applied the same criteria to monumental sculptures. She observed that monumental heads do not include sex-specific characteristics, arguing that they should not be assumed to be males. She noted that a larger proportion of monumental heads than figurines are shown with signs of age. Her argument echoed the proposal by Joyce (2001b), based on analyses of burials and figurines, that in Formative-period Mesoamerica age may have been a more significant dimension of status difference than sex. At sites like Tlatilco, women's burials incorporated large numbers of objects, including the most exclusive materials, such as iron-ore mirrors, and variability was most closely tied to age and local clusters corresponding to different residences (Joyce 2001a).

While there are likely tools for textile production in the Formative period, there is no visual culture associating textile production with only one gender. Analysis of the distribution of textile-related objects in burials at Tlatilco found no statistically significant correlation with sex (Joyce 2001a). Nor is there an obvious visual culture that might associate masculinity with warfare until late in the Formative period. Gendered labor may be a product of intensification and reorganization of household production in some Formative-period societies (Tejeda 2008).

Studies of gender in Mesoamerican societies document great complexity, with little evidence for simple gender hierarchies and ample evidence for change over time and variation across social ranks. If we compare the sixteenth-century Mexica to their Formative predecessors with an interest in creating histories of gender relations, we can develop models for how, in some times and places, gender hierarchies developed and were fostered both as state ideologies and as personal sexual identities (Joyce 2001b). Greater social stratification might be linked to increased disadvantage for women by state interests in controlling the products of women's labor and alienating them from credit for their work, or by increasing importance of military power projected as inherently masculine, supporting a polarization of masculinity and femininity. But such relations must be demonstrated, not assumed (Pyburn 2004).

An excellent example of historicizing gender relations is Robin's (2006) discussion of changes in labor organization in Maya agriculture. Her results exemplify a somewhat counterintuitive but repeated outcome of gender research: this has complicated what once was understood to be a simple association of gender and activity. It can be argued that this shows that studies of gender in Mesoamerican archaeology have progressed from what Wylie (1991) identified as a first step of finding women in the past, to the stage of critically examining underlying assumptions and categories previously taken for granted. Now that analyses of variation between males and females have become an integrated part of Mesoamerican archaeology, we have every reason to expect the continued expansion of the understanding of long-term historical development of gender relations and of local variability in gendered divisions of labor, access to power, and gender ideologies.

REFERENCES

Ardren, Traci, ed. 2002. *Ancient Maya Women*. Altamira, Walnut Creek, California.
Ardren, Traci, and David Hixson. 2006. The Unusual Sculptures of Telantunich, Yucatan: Phalli and the Concept of Masculinity among the Ancient Maya. *Cambridge Archaeological Journal* 16:7–25.
Ardren, Traci, and Scott Hutson, eds. 2006. *The Social Experience of Childhood in Ancient Mesoamerica*. University Press of Colorado, Boulder.
Ardren, Traci, T. Kam Manahan, Julie K. Wesp, and Alejandra Alonso. 2010. Cloth Production and Economic Intensification in the Area Surrounding Chichen Itza. *Latin American Antiquity* 21:274–289.
Ayala Falcón, Maricela. 2002. Lady K'awil, Goddess O, and Maya Warfare. In *Ancient Maya Women*, edited by Traci Ardren, pp. 105–113. Altamira, Walnut Creek, California.
Brumfiel, Elizabeth M. 1991. Weaving and Cooking: Women's Production in Aztec Mexico. In *Engendering Archaeology: Women and Prehistory*, edited by Joan Gero and Margaret Conkey, pp. 224–251. Basil Blackwell, Oxford.
Brumfiel, Elizabeth M. 1996. Quality of Tribute Cloth: The Place of Evidence in Archaeological Argument. *American Antiquity* 61:453–462.

Butler, Judith. 1993. *Bodies That Matter: On the Discursive Limits of "Sex."* Routledge, New York.

Chase, Arlen, Diane Chase, Elayne Zorn, and Wendy Teeter. 2008. Textiles and the Maya Archaeological Record: Gender, Power, and Status in Classic Period Caracol, Belize. *Ancient Mesoamerica* 19:127–142.

Closs, Michael P. 1992. "I am a Kahal; My Parents were Scribes"/Soy un Kahal; mis padres fueron escribas. *Research Reports on Ancient Maya Writing* 39. Center for Maya Research and Instituto Nacional de Antropología e Historia, Washington, DC and Mexico D.F.

Cyphers Guillén, Ann. 1984. Possible Role of a Woman in Formative Exchange. In *Trade and Exchange in Early Mesoamerica*, edited by Kenneth G. Hirth, pp. 115–123. University of New Mexico Press, Albuquerque.

Cyphers Guillén, Ann. 1993. Women, Rituals, and Social Dynamics at Ancient Chalcatzingo. *Latin American Antiquity* 4:209–224.

de Lucia, Kristin. 2008. Looking beyond Gender Hierarchy: Rethinking Gender at Teotihuacan, Mexico. In *Gender, Households, and Society: Unraveling the Threads of the Past and the Present*, edited by Cynthia Robin and Elizabeth Brumfiel, pp. 17–36. Archaeological Papers of the American Anthropological Association No. 18, American Anthropological Association, Arlington, Virginia.

Evans, Susan Toby. 1998. Sexual Politics in the Aztec Palace: Public, Private, and Profane. *Res* 33:166–183.

Follensbee, Billie J. 2009. Formative Period Gulf Coast Ceramic Figurines: The Key to Identifying Sex, Gender, and Age Groups in Gulf Coast Olmec Imagery. In *Mesoamerican Figurines*, edited by Christina Halperin, Katherine Faust, Rhonda Taube, and Aurore Giguet, pp. 77–118. University Press of Florida, Gainesville.

Fung, Christopher. 1995. Domestic Labor, Gender and Power on the Mesoamerican Frontier. In *Debating Complexity: Proceedings of the 26th Annual Chac Mool Conference*, edited by Daniel A. Meyer, Peter C. Dawson, and Donald T. Hanna, pp. 65–75. Archaeology Association, University of Calgary, Calgary.

Gustafson, Lowell, and Amy Trevelyan, eds. 2002. *Ancient Maya Gender Identity and Relations*. Greenwood, Westport, Connecticut.

Hamann, Byron. 1997. Weaving and the Iconography of Prestige: The Royal Gender Symbolism of Lord 5 Flower's/Lady 4 Rabbit's Family. In *Women in Prehistory: North America and Mesoamerica*, edited by Cheryl Claassen and Rosemary A. Joyce, pp. 153–172. University of Pennsylvania Press, Philadelphia.

Hendon, Julia A. 1999a. Multiple Sources of Prestige and the Social Evaluation of Women in Prehispanic Mesoamerica. In *Material Symbols: Culture and Economy in Prehistory*, edited by John Robb, pp. 257–276. Center for Archaeological Investigations, Occasional Paper No. 26, Southern Illinois University, Carbondale.

Hendon, Julia A. 1999b. Spinning and Weaving in Pre-Hispanic Mesoamerica: The Technology and Social Relations of Textile Production. In *Mayan Clothing and Weaving through the Ages*, edited by Barbara Knoke de Arathoon, Nancie L. Gonzalez, and John M. Willemsen Devlin, pp. 7–16. Museo Ixchel del Traje Indígena, Guatemala City.

Josserand, J. Kathryn. 2002. Women in Classic Maya Hieroglyphic Texts. In *Ancient Maya Women*, edited by Traci Ardren, pp. 114–151. Altamira, Walnut Creek, California.

Joyce, Rosemary A. 1996. The Construction of Gender in Classic Maya Monuments. In *Gender in Archaeology: Essays in Research and Practice*, edited by Rita Wright, pp. 167–195. University of Pennsylvania Press, Philadelphia.

Joyce, Rosemary A. 2000a. Girling the Girl and Boying the Boy: The Production of Adulthood in Ancient Mesoamerica. *World Archaeology* 31:473–483.

Joyce, Rosemary A. 2000b. A Precolumbian Gaze: Male Sexuality among the Ancient Maya. In *Archaeologies of Sexuality*, edited by Barbara Voss and Robert Schmidt, pp. 263–283. Routledge, London.

Joyce, Rosemary A. 2001a. Burying the Dead at Tlatilco: Social Memory and Social Identities. In *New Perspectives on Mortuary Analysis*, edited by Meredith Chesson, pp. 12–26. Archaeological Papers of the American Anthropological Association No. 10, American Anthropological Association, Arlington, Virginia.

Joyce, Rosemary A. 2001b. *Gender and Power in Prehispanic Mesoamerica*. University of Texas Press, Austin.

Joyce, Rosemary A. 2003. Making Something of Herself: Embodiment in Life and Death at Playa de los Muertos, Honduras. *Cambridge Archaeological Journal* 13:248–261.

Kellogg, Susan. 1986. Aztec Inheritance in Sixteenth-Century Mexico City: Colonial Patterns, Prehispanic Influences. *Ethnohistory* 33:313–330.

Kellogg, Susan. 1995. Woman's Room: Some Aspects of Gender Relations in Tenochtitlan in the Late Pre-Hispanic Period. *Ethnohistory* 42:563–576.

Klein, Cecelia F. 2001. None of the Above: Gender Ambiguity in Nahua Ideology. In *Gender in Pre-Hispanic America*, edited by Cecelia Klein, pp. 183–253. Dumbarton Oaks, Washington, DC.

Lesure, Richard G. 1997. Figurines and Social Identities in Early Sedentary Societies of Coastal Chiapas, Mexico, 1550-800 BC. In *Women in Prehistory: North America and Mesoamerica*, edited by Cheryl Claassen and Rosemary A. Joyce, pp. 227–248. University of Pennsylvania Press, Philadelphia.

Lesure, Richard G. 1999. Figurines as Representations and Products at Paso de la Armada, Mexico. *Cambridge Archaeological Journal* 9:209–20.

Looper, Matthew G. 2002. Women-Men (and Men-Women): Classic Maya Rulers and the Third Gender. In *Ancient Maya Women*, edited by Traci Ardren, pp. 171–202. Altamira, Walnut Creek, California.

Lopiparo, Jeanne. 2006. Crafting Children: Materiality, Social Memory, and the Reproduction of Terminal Classic House Societies in the Ulúa Valley, Honduras. In *The Social Experience of Childhood in Ancient Mesoamerica*, edited by Traci Ardren and Scott Hutson, pp. 133–168. University Press of Colorado, Boulder.

Marcus, Joyce. 1998. *Women's Ritual in Formative Oaxaca: Figurine-Making, Divination, Death and the Ancestors*. University of Michigan Museum of Anthropology Memoirs 33, University of Michigan Museum of Anthropology, Ann Arbor.

McAnany, Patricia A., and Shannon Plank. 2001. Perspectives on Actors, Gender Roles, and Architecture at Classic Maya Courts and Households. In *Royal Courts of the Ancient Maya, Vol. 1: Theory, Comparison, and Synthesis*, edited by Takeshi Inomata and Stephen D. Houston, pp. 84–129. Westview Press, Boulder, Colorado.

McCafferty, Sharisse D., and Geoffrey G. McCafferty. 1988. Powerful Women and the Myth of Male Dominance in Aztec Society. *Archaeological Review from Cambridge* 7:45–59.

McCafferty, Sharisse D., and Geoffrey G. McCafferty. 1991. Spinning and Weaving as Female Gender Identity in Post-Classic Mexico. In *Textile Traditions of Mesoamerica and the Andes: An Anthology*, edited by Janet C. Berlo, Margot Schevill, and Edward B. Dwyer, pp. 19–44. Garland, New York.

McCafferty, Sharisse D., and Geoffrey G. McCafferty. 1994. Engendering Tomb 7 at Monte Alban: Respinning an Old Yarn. *Current Anthropology* 35:143–166.

McCafferty, Sharisse D., and Geoffrey G. McCafferty. 2000. Textile Production in Postclassic Cholula, Mexico. *Ancient Mesoamerica* 11:39–54.

Miller, Virginia, ed. 1988. *The Role of Gender in Precolumbian Art and Architecture*. University Press of America, Lanham, Maryland.

Morehart, Christopher, and Christophe Helmke. 2008. Situating Power and Locating Knowledge: A Palaeoethnobotanical Perspective on Late Classic Maya Gender and Social Relations. In *Gender, Households, and Society: Unraveling the Threads of the Past and the Present*, edited by Cynthia Robin and Elizabeth Brumfiel, pp. 60–75. Archaeological Papers of the American Anthropological Association No. 18, American Anthropological Association, Arlington, Virginia.

Pankonien, Dawn. 2008. She Sells Seashells: Women and Mollusks in Huatulco, Oaxaca, Mexico. In *Gender, Households, and Society: Unraveling the Threads of the Past and the Present*, edited by Cynthia Robin and Elizabeth Brumfiel, pp. 102–114. Archaeological Papers of the American Anthropological Association No. 18, American Anthropological Association, Arlington, Virginia.

Pyburn, K. Anne. 2004. Introduction: Rethinking Complex Society. In *Ungendering Civilization*, edited by K. Anne Pyburn, pp. 1–46. Routledge, London.

Robin, Cynthia. 2002. Outside of Houses: The Practices of Everyday Life at Chan Noohol, Belize. *Journal of Social Archaeology* 2:245–268.

Robin, Cynthia. 2006. Gender, Farming, and Long-Term Change: Maya Historical and Archaeological Perspectives. *Current Anthropology* 47:409–434.

Robin, Cynthia, and Elizabeth M. Brumfiel, eds. 2008. *Gender, Households, and Society: Unraveling the Threads of the Past and the Present*. Archaeological Papers of the American Anthropological Association No. 18, American Anthropological Association, Arlington, Virginia.

Sigal, Pete. 2007. Queer Nahuatls: Sahagun's Faggots and Sodomites, Lesbians and Hermaphrodites. *Ethnohistory* 54:9–34.

Stark, Barbara, Lynette Heller, and Michael Ohnersorgen. 1998. People with Cloth: Mesoamerican Economic Change from the Perspective of Cotton in South-Central Veracruz. *Latin American Antiquity* 9:7–36.

Stone, Andrea J. 1988. Sacrifice and Sexuality: Some Structural Relationships in Classic Maya Art. In *The Role of Gender in Precolumbian Art and Architecture*, edited by Virginia Miller, pp. 75–103. University Press of America, Lanham, Maryland.

Storey, Rebecca. 1998. Mothers and Daughters of a Patrilineal Civilization: The Health of Females among the Late Classic Maya of Copán, Honduras. In *Sex and Gender in Paleopathological Perspective*, edited by Anne L. Grauer and Patricia Stuart-Macadam, pp. 133–148. Cambridge University Press, Cambridge.

Storey, Rebecca. 2005. Health and Lifestyle (before and after Death) among the Copán Elite. In *Copán: The History of an Ancient Maya Kingdom*, edited by E. Wyllys Andrews and William L. Fash, pp. 315–344. School of American Research Press, Santa Fe.

Sweely, Tracy L. 1999. Gender, Space, People and Power at Ceren, El Salvador. In *Manifesting Power: Gender and the Interpretation of Power in Archaeology*, edited by Tracy Sweely, pp. 155–171. Routledge, London.

Tejeda, Ana. 2008. Rethinking Polity Formation: A Gendered Perspective on Formative Period Household Development in the Pacific Coast Region of Guatemala. In *Gender, Households, and Society: Unraveling the Threads of the Past and the Present*, edited by Cynthia Robin and Elizabeth Brumfiel, pp. 87–101. Archaeological Papers

of the American Anthropological Association No. 18, American Anthropological
    Association, Arlington, Virginia.
White, Christine D. 2005. Gendered Food Behaviour among the Maya: Time, Place,
    Status and Ritual. *Journal of Social Archaeology* 5:356–382.
Wylie, Alison. 1991. Gender Theory and the Archaeological Record: Why Is There No
    Archaeology of Gender? In *Engendering Archaeology*, edited by Margaret W. Conkey
    and Joan Gero, pp. 31–54. Basil Blackwell, Oxford.

CHAPTER 50

....

CLASS AND ETHNICITY IN ANCIENT MESOAMERICA

....

ELIZABETH M. BRUMFIEL AND CYNTHIA ROBIN

THE term "class" has both broad and narrow definitions. Speaking in broad terms, class refers to individuals who share a similar social standing within a nonegalitarian, stratified society. In this context, class is primarily a descriptive term that asks how the members of each class differ from the members of other classes in terms of their access to status, wealth, and power. Alternatively, class can be used in a narrow Marxist sense, to refer to individuals who share a distinctive relationship to the means of production. This definition attempts to isolate the causative factors in class formation by asking how the members of each class gain access to essential economic resources and how their differential access is perpetuated across generations.

In the neoevolutionary typologies of mid-twentieth-century anthropology, class stratification was contrasted with systems of rank (Fried 1960; Sanders and Price 1968; Service 1958). Both stratification and rank were defined as systems of hereditary inequality. Class-stratified societies were characterized as having sharply discrete classes of rulers and the ruled, with ruling-class dominance supported by the payment of tribute or taxes, the coercive power of the state institutions, and a range of ideological mechanisms to win the consent of the governed.

In contrast, rank societies were defined as having a continuous gradient of status, wealth, and power based on genealogy. In rank societies, all members of the social group were linked by ties of common descent, but individuals with the most genealogical seniority ranked highest on the social scale and members of cadet lineages ranked lower. In neoevolutionary models of ancient civilizations, rank societies were regarded as a simple, early stage of social inequality, and class-stratified states were regarded as a later, more complex form of social inequality (Yoffee 1993). Thus, much of the debate over rank versus class in ancient Mesoamerica reflected disagreement about the structure and sophistication of various prehispanic Mesoamerican cultures.

Documents from sixteenth-century Mesoamerica describe indigenous social systems in terms that suggest the existence of classes in the late prehispanic era. The terms *pilli* in Nahua and *almenhen* in Maya, both commonly translated as "noble," denoted individuals who were supported by tribute paid in labor and goods. The terms *macehualli* in Nahua and *yalba uinic* in Maya, both translated as "commoner," referred to individuals who supplied tribute and labor to their overlords. Sixteenth-century documents suggest that noble and commoner groups were largely endogamous, that they differed in their kinship reckoning (descent was important in determining social standing for nobles but not for commoners), that they exercised differential claims to agricultural land, and that they were marked by sumptuary distinctions. The two groups also assumed different social roles in native society, with elites monopolizing high offices in government, religion, and the military, and commoners practicing agriculture, a range of extractive and craft activities, and some services such as midwifery and divination. In some regions, nobles monopolized elite crafts and long-distance trade (Carrasco 1976; Farriss 1984; Hicks 1986; Lockhart 1992; Marcus 1992; Martinez Hernández 1929; Restall 1997; Spores 1974).

However, many archaeologists question whether this model of class stratification, so clearly described in the documents, accurately portrays ancient Mesoamerica or whether it constitutes a misreading of Mesoamerican society. Misunderstanding might be due to Spanish observers who imposed their own medieval European understanding of social structure on their newly conquered subjects, or due to archaeologists who have imposed inappropriate models based upon twentieth-century ethnography in other regions of the world. When archaeologists have examined material remains for evidence of social inequality in ancient Mesoamerica, the seemingly clear case for the existence of two distinct classes becomes less certain.

Archaeologists have looked for class stratification in three bodies of data: (1) the location, size, and elaboration of domestic architecture in ancient Mesoamerica; (2) the distribution of highly crafted and imported goods across households; and (3) the size and richness of burials and other ritual deposits. Two-tiered class stratification should be evident in a bimodal pattern of architecture, household goods, and ritual deposits within a single site or region, one mode representing the practices of nobles and the other the practices of commoners. But when archaeologists examine the material record, the variation seems to be distributed along a continuum of quantity and quality, suggesting the existence of a continuum of social differentiation in ancient Mesoamerica rather than segmentation into discrete classes. Moreover, the various dimensions of the evidence (architecture, consumer goods, and rituals) often do not coincide to yield consistent rankings of residences or individuals. Even within a single domain of evidence, such as domestic architecture or burials, the various attributes that might indicate social differentiation do not coincide. For example, large elaborate residences are frequently located in sparsely occupied site peripheries instead of being centrally located within a high-status civic-ceremonial complex. Graves with the greatest number of items do not necessarily contain the most elaborate craft goods, and so on (Chase and Chase 1992). Even the humblest households had access to a range of valuable goods (Brumfiel and Rodríguez-Alegría 2010; De Lucia 2010; Garraty 2000; Sheets 2002; Smith and Heath-Smith 1994; Robin 2003).

The continuum of social differentiation implied by material culture appears to be grounded in several factors. First, a system of continuous rank operated within the noble class. For the Nahua, ruling offices were passed from a father to an eldest son, or from an elder brother to a younger brother, with siblings ranked according to both their birth order and the social standing of their mothers (rulers tended to be polygamous, so half-siblings were ranked according to their mothers' status). For the Maya, rules for accession to kingship within noble families were highly flexible (Robin 2001; Sharer 1993). Noble descent was reckoned through both the maternal and paternal lines, as the Yucatec Maya term for "noble," almehen, refers to the child of a woman (al) and a man (mehen) (Restall 1997).

Second, kingdoms were composite units made up of many subgroups (teccalli in Nahuatl), each with its own ruling lineage, its own agricultural lands, and its own population of tribute-paying commoners (Carrasco 1976). Because noble houses differed in size, wealth, and status, according to their histories of service to the ruler, the standing of any noble within a kingdom depended on the status of his or her subgroup vis-à-vis other subgroups and his or her personal rank within the subgroup as determined by birth order and maternal status. A noble's standing might be further modified by personal qualities such as military prowess, commercial success, moral education, an unblemished private life, and advantageous marriage. With these multiple determinants of wealth, power, and status, it is not surprising that nobles failed to constitute a homogeneous class or even to be arranged in consistent scales of rank (see Ehrenreich et al. 1995 for a discussion of heterarchy and the complexities of ranking).

Commoners, too, seem to have attained different levels of wealth, although always rather limited in status and power. An examination of the tribute census of Santa María Asunción in the Basin of Mexico reveals that some commoners held access to more land than others, sometimes by a factor of two or three (Williams 1991). Similarly, the analysis of wills and testaments from colonial Yucatán indicates gradients in household wealth based on land and material possessions (Restall 1997). Household members might also have differed in terms of their history of military service, their commercial success, and their ability to forge favorable interhousehold alliances (Brumfiel 2011). There is variability as well in the extent to which households participated in and hosted rituals and feasts involving other members of the community (Blackmore 2011; Gonlin and Lohse 2007). Studies of peasant agriculturalists suggest that some patterns of household organization promote more effective economic decision making than others, contributing to household prosperity (Netting 1993; Wilk 1991). Thus, it is not surprising that studies of commoner material culture also reveal continua of wealth and status (Evans 1988; Garraty 2000; Lohse and Valdez 2004; Masson and Peraza Lope 2004). Particularly during the Postclassic period, expanding market economies provided a basis for social mobility through economic activities (Freidel and Sabloff 1984; Masson 2000; Smith and Berdan 2003), although it is not clear if affluent commoners ever joined the ranks of the nobility in prehispanic times. By the colonial period, wealthy commoners could acquire almehen status (Chance 2008; Restall 1997). Some archaeologists consider the economic affluence of commoners as evidence for a middle class (Chase 1992; King and Potter 1994) while others regard it as evidence for difference within the commoner class (Marcus 1993, 2004; Smith and Masson 2000).

Finally, the ethnohistoric and archaeological data may capture different dimensions of social differentiation in Mesoamerica. The ethnohistoric literature may accurately reflect an ideological emphasis on the cultural distinctiveness of nobles and commoners in ancient Mesoamerica (Freidel et al. 1993; Inomata 2001; see Bourdieu 1984), while the material record faithfully registers the continuum of economic standing (but see Masson and Peraza Lope [2004] for evidence of cultural distinction between nobles and commoners).

THE HOUSE

Class differences in Mesoamerica were papered over by the inclusion of individuals of varying social statuses within corporate groups that constituted the basic building blocks of native society. Lockhart (1992: 15) describes these groups as "a series of relatively equal, relatively separate and self-contained constituent parts of the whole." Subgroups included both the noble houses (teccalli) and commoner groups (*calpulli*, or *tlaxilacalli*) (Carrasco 1971, 1976; Hicks 1986; Zorita 1963: 109–110). In the Maya area, the *cah* (community) articulated both noble and commoner statuses in a common identity (Farriss 1984; Restall 1997). At times, these subgroups coalesced to create larger political entities that exhibited a characteristic "modular organization" (Lockhart 1992; also see Daneels and Gutiérrez in press). When centralized political power waned, the subgroups might scatter, only to regroup in new polities, giving rise to cycles of centralization and decentralization (Marcus

1993; Martin and Grube 2008). Although widely distributed across time and space in ancient Mesoamerica, these entities drew on at least two different principles to supply ideological legitimation.

In most of Mesoamerica, and in central Mexico prior to the Postclassic, archaeological evidence suggests that subgroup identity was sustained by an ideology of common ancestry. For some Mayanists, clusters of houses surrounding a larger more elaborate and long-lived residence, which contains a shrine with evidence of ancestor veneration, suggest an ideology of patrilineal descent (Haviland 1968; McAnany 1995). Other Mayanists view these data as more consistent with an ideology of "the house," a corporate group that recruits its members through ties of both descent and affinity to share in and maintain an estate that includes lands, residence structures, valuables, and immaterial assets (Chance 2000; Gillespie 2000; Hendon 2002; also a special section of the journal *Ancient Mesoamerica* is dedicated to this debate: Fowler and Hageman 2004).

"Houses" of this sort may have existed by the Late Formative or even Early Formative in central Mexico (Grove and Gillespie 2002; Joyce 1999; Uruñuela and Plunket 2002). Some of the "apartment compounds" that were the basic residential unit at Classic Teotihuacan might also have subscribed to a lineage or "house" ideology (De Lucia 2008; Gillespie 2005; Manzanilla 2004; Spence 1974; Widmer and Storey 1993). Inequality existed both within and between these compounds, and it varied over time (Millon 1976; Sempowski 1987).

ETHNICITY

Ethnicity was another form of identity that cross-cut class lines. Ethnicity can be defined as social identity based upon the presumption of shared history and common cultural inheritance (Brumfiel 1994). Anthropologists have increasingly moved away from a primordial view of ethnic groups, which sees them as local cultures that developed in relative isolation from other such "cultures." Instead, anthropologists regard ethnicity as a strategic identity, mobilized to maintain access to resources and allies (Barth 1969; Stein 2002) or to justify economic and social dominance (Comaroff 1987; Voss 2005). Schortman and Nakamura (1991) remind us that ethnicity in ancient Mesoamerica was not a fixed identity but was instead a resource that was drawn on selectively, according to the demands of the situation.

At Teotihuacan, some apartment complexes maintained a clear ethnic identity, archaeologically evident in distinctive mortuary treatments, ceramic styles, and architecture (Price et al. 2000; Rattray 1990; Spence 1996). The Oaxaca enclave at Teotihuacan maintained a distinctive identity for over five centuries despite the fact that many of the enclave residents were born in Teotihuacan and spent much of their adult lives there (Spence et al. 2005). Such persistence suggests that ethnicity was actively maintained through distinctive practices for specific ends, perhaps to mark the identity of foreign trade ambassadors (Spence et al. 2005). Ethnic diversity was not simply due to the lingering habits of incompletely assimilated migrants to the city.

Ethnicity was a central motif in the native histories of the late prehispanic era. These histories are filled with the accounts of wandering ethnic groups, their settlements, and their conflicts and short-lived alliances. Archaeologists have used the historically documented movement of these groups to account for the spread of stylistic markers in Classic and Postclassic Mesoamerica. In some cases the archaeological evidence is consistent with these historical narratives and in other cases it is not (Masson and Peraza Lope 2010; McCafferty 2003; Santley et al. 1987; Smith 2007; Stark 2008).

In Postclassic central Mexico, ethnicity was used both to maintain access to resources and allies and to justify dominance. Many of the modular units mentioned above, the noble houses (teccalli) and commoner groups (calpulli or tlaxila-calli), maintained pictorial documents that recorded the events that brought them into being and supplied charters for their territorial claims, their tribute rights, and their right to rule (Boone 2000; Brumfiel 1994). Postclassic communities were often composite "multiethnic" groups (Zantwijk 1985) where ethnicity cross-cut class stratification, but elites representing different "ethnic" groups intermarried to advance their social positions. On the eve of the Spanish conquest, the Aztecs heightened ethnic consciousness by propagating ethnic stereotypes of themselves and of others, stereotypes that legitimated their rule over foreign "peoples" (Brumfiel 1994; Berdan 2008; Umberger 2008).

In the Maya area, scholars have questioned whether the term "Maya" is a form of native self-identification or an identity ascribed by others, such as by Spaniards or anthropologists (Castañeda 1996; Gabbert 2004). There does not appear to be any Pre-Columbian term for an overarching "Maya" group. Contemporary people often self-identify first with their particular language group. But at particular moments in history a Maya ethnicity has been foregrounded, such as for Caste War rebels in the mid-nineteenth century who self-identified as masewal'ob to distinguish themselves from both Yucatecans of Spanish descent and noncompliant people of Indian descent (Gabbert 2004).

Thus, class and ethnic distinctions existed in Mesoamerica for at least two millennia, but neither distinction refers to a fixed or bounded form of identity. The existence of classes was obscured by (1) the multiple variables that went into determining the status of any particular individual, either commoner or noble, and by (2) modular units with communal ideologies (lineages, "houses," and shared ethnicity) that brought together people of widely differing social status into relations of interdependence. Across their lives and in different social situations, people could have variably deployed or displayed their class or ethnic positions. As well, through time, ideas of class and ethnicity took on new meanings, such as the development of ethnic stereotyping in the Aztec Empire or the expansion of ethnic identity during the Caste War of Yucatán.

REFERENCES

Barth, Frederick. 1969. Introduction. In *Ethnic Groups and Boundaries*, edited by
    Frederick Barth, pp. 9–38. Little, Brown, Boston.

Berdan, Frances F. 2008. Concepts of Ethnicity and Class in Aztec-Period Mexico.
    In *Ethnic Identity in Nahua Mesoamerica*, edited by Frances F. Berdan, John K.
    Chance, Alan R. Sandstrom, Barbara Stark, James Taggert, and Emily Umberger,
    pp. 105–132. University of Utah Press, Salt Lake City.

Boone, Elizabeth Hill. 2000. *Stories in Red and Black*. University of Texas Press, Austin.

Bourdieu, Pierre. 1984. *Distinction*. Translated by R. Nice. Harvard University Press,
    Cambridge.

Blackmore, Chelsea. 2011. Ritual among the Masses: Deconstructing Identity and Class
    in an Ancient Maya Neighborhood. *Latin American Antiquity* 22(2):159-177.

Brumfiel, Elizabeth M. 1994. Ethnic Groups and Political Development in Ancient
    Mexico. In *Factional Competition and Political Development in the New World*,
    edited by Elizabeth M. Brumfiel and John W. Fox, pp. 89–102. Cambridge University
    Press, Cambridge.

Brumfiel, Elizabeth M. 2011. Technologies of Time: Calendrics and Commoners in
    Postclassic Mexico. *Ancient Mesoamerica* 22:53-70.

Brumfiel, Elizabeth M., and Enrique Rodríguez-Alegría. 2010. *Estrategias de las
    elites y cambios políticos en Xaltocan, México*. Informe al Instituto Nacional de
    Antropología e Historia, Evanston, Illinois.

Carrasco, Pedro. 1971. Social Organization of Ancient Mexico. In *Archaeology of
    Northern Mesoamerica, Part One*, edited by Gordon F. Ekholm and Ignacio Bernal,
    pp. 349–375. Handbook of Middle American Indians, Vol. 10. University of Texas
    Press, Austin.

Carrasco, Pedro. 1976. Los linajes nobles del México antiguo. In *Estratificación social
    en la Mesoamérica prehispánica* by Pedro Carrasco and Johanna Broda, pp. 29–36.
    Centro de Investigaciones Superiores and the Instituto Nacional de Antropología e
    Historia, Mexico City.

Castañeda, Quetzil. 1996. *In the Museum of Maya Culture: Touring Chichen Itza*.
    University of Minnesota Press, Minneapolis.

Chance, John K. 2000. The Noble Houses in Colonial Puebla, Mexico: Descent,
    Inheritance, and the Nahua Tradition. *American Anthropologist* 102(3):
    485–502.

Chance, John K. 2008. Indigenous Ethnicity in Colonial Central Mexico. In *Ethnic
    Identity in Nahua Mesoamerica*, edited by Frances F. Berdan, John K. Chance, Alan
    R. Sandstrom, Barbara Stark, James Taggert, and Emily Umberger, pp. 133–149.
    University of Utah Press, Salt Lake City.

Chase, Arlen F. 1992. Elites and the Changing Organization of Classic Maya Society.
    In *Mesoamerican Elites*, edited by Diane Z. Chase and Arlen R. Chase, pp. 30–49.
    University of Oklahoma Press, Norman.

Chase, Diane Z., and Arlen F. Chase, eds. 1992. *Mesoamerican Elites*. University of
    Oklahoma Press, Norman.

Comaroff, John L. 1987. Of Totemism and Ethnicity. *Ethnos* 52:301-323.

Daneels, Annick, and Gerardo Gutiérrez, eds. In press. *El poder compartido: Ensayos
    sobre la arqueología de organizaciones políticas segmentarias y oligárquicas*.
    Ediciones de la Casa Chata, CIESAS, Mexico City.

De Lucia, Kristin. 2008. Looking beyond Gender Hierarchy: Rethinking Gender at
    Teotihuacan, Mexico. In *Gender, Households, and Society*, edited by Cynthia Robin
    and Elizabeth M. Brumfiel. Archaeological Papers of the American Anthropological
    Association 18(1):17–36.
De Lucia, Kristin. 2010. Domestic Economies and Regional Transition: Household
    Production and Consumption in Early Postclassic Xaltocan, Mexico. PhD
    dissertation, Northwestern University, Evanston.
Ehrenreich, Robert M., Carole L. Crumley, and Janet E. Levy, eds. 1995. *Heterarchy
    and the Analysis of Complex Societies*. Archaeological Papers of the American
    Anthropological Association No. 6.
Evans, Susan T., ed. 1988. *Excavations at Cihuatecpan: An Aztec Village in the
    Teotihuacan Valley*. Vanderbilt University, Publications in Anthropology 36,
    Nashville.
Farriss, Nancy M. 1984. *Maya Society under Colonial Rule*. Princeton University Press,
    Princeton.
Fowler, William R., and Jon B. Hageman. 2004. Introduction, Special Section: New
    Perspectives on Ancient Lowland Maya Social Organization. *Ancient Mesoamerica*
    15:61–62.
Freidel, David A., and Jeremy A. Sabloff. 1984. *Cozumel: Late Maya Settlement Patterns*.
    Academic Press, New York.
Freidel, David, Linda Schele, and Joy Parker. 1993. *Maya Cosmos*. William Morrow, New
    York.
Fried, Morton H. 1960. On the Evolution of Social Stratification and the States. In *Culture
    in History*, edited by Stanley Diamond, pp. 713–731. Columbia University Press, New
    York.
Gabbert, Wolfgang. 2004. *Becoming Maya: Ethnicity and Social Inequality in Yucatán
    since 1500*. University of Arizona Press, Tucson.
Garraty, Christopher P. 2000. Ceramic Indices of Aztec Eliteness. *Ancient Mesoamerica*
    11:323–340.
Gillespie, Susan D. 2000. Rethinking Ancient Maya Social Organization: Replacing
    "Lineage" with "House." *American Anthropologist* 102(3):467–484.
Gillespie, Susan D. 2005. Place and Person at Teotihuacan, Mexico. Paper presented at the
    70th annual meeting, Society for American Archaeology, Salt Lake City.
Gonlin, Nancy, and Jon C. Lohse, eds. 2007. *Commoner Ritual and Ideology in Ancient
    Mesoamerica*. University Press of Colorado, Boulder.
Grove, David C., and Susan D. Gillespie. 2002. Middle Formative Domestic Ritual
    at Chalcatzingo, Morelos. In *Domestic Ritual in Ancient Mesoamerica*, edited
    by Patricia Plunket, pp. 11–19. Cotsen Institute of Archaeology, Monograph 46,
    University of California, Los Angeles.
Haviland, William A. 1968. *Ancient Lowland Maya Social Organization*. Middle
    American Research Institute Publication 26:93–117, Tulane University, New Orleans.
Hendon, Julia A. 2002. Social Relations and Collective Identities: Household and
    Community in Ancient Mesoamerica. In *The Dynamics of Power*, edited by Maria
    O'Donovan, pp. 273–300. Center for Archaeological Investigations Occasional Paper
    30, Southern Illinois University, Carbondale.
Hicks, Frederic. 1986. Prehispanic Background of Colonial Political and Economic
    Organization in Central Mexico. In *Ethnohistory Supplement to the Handbook of
    Middle American Indians*, Vol. 4, edited by Ronald Spores, pp. 35–54. University of
    Texas Press, Austin.

Inomata, Takeshi. 2001. The Power and Ideology of Artistic Creation: Elite Craft
    Specialists in Classic Maya Society. *Current Anthropology* 42:321–349.
Joyce, Rosemary A. 1999. Social Dimensions of Pre-Classic Burials. In *Social Patterns in
    Pre-Classic Mesoamerica*, edited by David C. Grove and Rosemary A. Joyce,
    pp. 15–47. Dumbarton Oaks Research Library and Collections, Washington, DC.
King, Eleanor, and Daniel R. Potter. 1994. Small Sites in Prehistoric Maya Socioeconomic
    Organization: A Perspective from Colha, Belize. In *Archaeological Views from
    the Countryside: Village Communities in Early Complex Societies*, edited by Glenn
    M. Schwartz and Stephen E. Falconer, pp. 64–90. Smithsonian Institution Press,
    Washington, DC.
Lockhart, James. 1992. *The Nahuas after the Conquest*. Stanford University Press,
    Stanford.
Lohse, Jon C., and Fred Valdez Jr., eds. 2004. *Ancient Maya Commoners*. University of
    Texas Press, Austin.
Manzanilla, Linda. 2004. Social Identity and Daily Life at Classic Teotihuacan. In
    Mesoamerican Archaeology, edited by Julia A. Hendon and Rosemary A. Joyce,
    pp. 124–147. Blackwell, Oxford.
Marcus, Joyce. 1992. Royal Families, Royal Texts: Examples from the Zapotec and Maya.
    In *Mesoamerican Elites*, edited by Diane Z. Chase and Arlen F. Chase, pp. 221–241.
    University of Oklahoma Press, Norman.
Marcus, Joyce. 1993. Ancient Maya Political Organization. In *Lowland Maya Civilization
    in the Eighth Century ad*, edited by Jeremy A. Sabloff and John S. Henderson, pp.
    111–184. Dumbarton Oaks Research Library and Collections, Washington, DC.
Marcus, Joyce. 2004. Maya Commoners: The Stereotype and the Reality. In *Ancient
    Maya Commoners*, edited by John C. Lohse and Fred Valdez Jr., pp. 255–283.
    University of Texas Press, Austin.
Martin, Simon, and Nikolai Grube. 2008. *Chronicle of the Maya Kings and Queens*.
    Thames and Hudson, London.
Martinez Hernández, Juan. 1929. *Diccionario de Motul: Maya-Español*. Compañía
    Tipográfica Yucateca, Mérida.
Masson, Marilyn A. 2000. *In the Realm of Nachan Kan: Postclassic Maya Archaeology at
    Laguna de On, Belize*. University of Colorado Press, Boulder.
Masson, Marilyn A., and Carlos Peraza Lope. 2004. Commoners in Postclassic Maya
    Society: Social versus Economic Class Constructs. In *Ancient Maya Commoners*,
    edited by John C. Lohse and Fred Valdez Jr., pp. 197–223. University of Texas Press,
    Austin.
Masson, Marilyn A., and Carlos Peraza Lope. 2010. Evidence for Maya-Mexican
    Interaction in the Archaeological Record of Mayapán. In *Astronomers, Scribes, and
    Priests*, edited by Gabriel Vail and Christine Hernández, pp. 77–113. Dumbarton
    Oaks Research Library and Collections, Washington, DC.
McAnany, Patricia A. 1995. *Living with the Ancestors: Kinship and Kingship in Ancient
    Maya Society*. University of Texas Press, Austin.
McCafferty, Geoffrey G. 2003. Ethnic Conflict in Postclassic Cholula, Mexico. In *Ancient
    Mesoamerican Warfare*, edited by M. Kathryn Brown and Travis Stanton, pp.
    219–244. Altamira, Walnut Creek, California.
Millon, René. 1976. Social Relations in Ancient Teotihuacan. In *The Valley of Mexico*,
    edited by Eric R. Wolf, pp. 205–248. University of New Mexico Press, Albuquerque.
Netting, Robert McC. 1993. *Smallholders, Householders: Farm Families and the Ecology of
    Intensive, Sustainable Agriculture*. Stanford University Press, Stanford.

Price, T. Douglas, Linda Manzanilla, and William Middleton. 2000. Immigration and the Ancient City of Teotihuacan in Mexico: A Study Using Strontium Isotope Ratios in Human Bone and Teeth. *Journal of Archaeological Science* 27(10):903–913.

Rattray, Evelyn C. 1990. The Identification of Ethnic Affiliation at the Merchants' Barrio, Teotihuacan. In *Etnoarqueología: Coloquio Bosch-Gimpera*, edited by Yoko Sugiura and Mari Carmen Serra, pp. 113–138. Instituto Nacional de Antropología e Historia, Mexico City.

Restall, Matthew. 1997. *The Maya World: Yucatec Culture and Society, 1550–1850*. Stanford University Press, Stanford.

Robin, Cynthia. 2001. Kin and Gender in Classic Maya Society: A Case Study from Yaxchilán, Mexico. In *New Directions in Anthropological Kinship*, edited by Linda Stone, pp. 204–228. Rowman and Littlefield, Lanham, Maryland.

Robin, Cynthia. 2003. New Directions in Classic Maya Household Archaeology. *Journal of Archaeological Research* 11:307–356.

Sanders, William T., and Barbara J. Price. 1968. *Mesoamerica: The Evolution of a Civilization*. Random House, New York.

Santley, Robert, Clare Yarborough, and Barbara Hall. 1987. Enclaves, Ethnicity, and the Archaeological Record at Matacapan. In *Ethnicity and Culture*, edited by R. Auger, M. F. Glass, S. MacEachern, and P. H. McCartney, pp. 85–100. Proceedings of the Eighteenth Annual Conference of the Archaeological Association of the University of Calgary, Department of Archaeology, University of Calgary.

Schortman, Edward, and Seiichi Nakamura. 1991. A Crisis of Identity: Late Classic Competition and Interaction on the Southeast Maya Periphery. *Latin American Antiquity* 2(4):311–336.

Sempowski, Martha L. 1987. Differential Mortuary Treatment: Its Implications for Social Status at Three Residential Compounds in Teotihuacan, Mexico. In *Teotihuacán: Nuevos datos, nuevas síntesis, nuevos problemas*, pp. 115–131. Universidad Autónoma de México, Mexico, D.F.

Service, Elman R. 1958. *Profiles in Primitive Culture*. Harper and Row, New York.

Sharer, Robert J. 1993. The Social Organization of the Late Classic Maya: Problems of Definitions and Approaches. In *Lowland Maya Civilization in the Eighth Century ad: A Symposium at Dumbarton Oaks*, edited by Jeremy A. Sabloff and John S. Henderson, pp. 91–109. Dumbarton Oaks Research Library and Collections, Washington, DC.

Sheets, Payson. 2002. *Before the Volcano Erupted: The Ancient Cerén Village in Central America*. University of Texas Press, Austin.

Smith, Michael E. 2007. Tula and Chichén Itzá: Are We Asking the Right Questions? In *Twin Tollans: Chichén Itzá, Tula, and the Epiclassic to Early Postclassic Mesoamerican World*, edited by Jeff K. Kowalski and Cynthia Kristan-Graham, pp. 579–618. Dumbarton Oaks Research Library and Collections, Washington, DC.

Smith, Michael E., and Frances F. Berdan, eds. 2003. *The Postclassic Mesoamerican World*. University of Utah Press, Salt Lake City.

Smith, Michael E., and Cynthia Heath-Smith. 1994. Rural Economy in late Postclassic Morelos. In *Economies and Polities in the Aztec Realm*, edited by Mary G. Hodge and Michael E. Smith, pp. 349–376. State University of New York, Institute for Mesoamerican Studies, Albany.

Smith, Michael E., and Marilyn A. Masson. 2000. *The Ancient Civilizations of Mesoamerica: A Reader*. Blackwell, Malden, Massachusetts.

Spence, Michael W. 1974. Residential Practices and the Distribution of Skeletal Traits in
    Teotihuacán, Mexico. *Man* 9:262–273.

Spence, Michael W. 1996. A Comparative Analysis of Ethnic Enclaves. In *Arqueología
    Mesoamericana: Homenaje a William T. Sanders*, edited by Alba Guadalup
    Mastache, Jeffrey Parsons, Robert S. Santley, and Mari Carmen Serra Puche, pp.
    333–353. Instituto Nacional de Antropología e Historia, Mexico, D.F.

Spence, Michael W., Christine D. White, Evelyn C. Rattray, and Fred J. Longstaffe. 2005.
    Past Lives in Different Places: The Origins and Relationships of Teotihuacan's
    Foreign Residents. In *Settlement, Subsistence, and Social Complexity: Essays
    Honoring the Legacy of Jeffrey R. Parsons*, edited by Richard E. Blanton, pp. 155–197.
    Cotsen Institute of Archaeology, University of California, Los Angeles.

Spores, Ronald. 1974. Marital Alliance in the Political Integration of Mixtec Kingdoms.
    American Anthropologist 76:297–311.

Stark, Barbara L. 2008. Archaeology and Ethnicity in Postclassic Mesoamerica. In *Ethnic
    Identity in Nahua Mesoamerica*, edited by F. Berdan, John Chance, Alan Sandstrom,
    Barbara Stark, James Taggert, and Emily Umberger., pp. 38–63. University of Utah
    Press, Salt Lake City.

Stein, Gil. 2002. Colonies without Colonialism: A Trade Diaspora Model of Fourth
    Millennium BC Mesopotamian Enclaves in Anatolia. In *The Archaeology of
    Colonialism*, edited by Claire L. Lyons and John K. Papadopoulos, pp. 26–64. Getty
    Research Institute Publications, Los Angeles.

Umberger, Emily. 2008. Ethnicity and Other Identities in the Sculptures of Tenochtitlan.
    In *Ethnic Identity in Nahua Mesoamerica*, edited by F. Berdan, John Chance,
    Alan Sandstrom, Barbara Stark, James Taggert, and Emily Umberger, pp. 64–104.
    University of Utah Press, Salt Lake City.

Uruñuela, Gabriela, and Patricia Plunket. 2002. Lineages and Ancestors: The Formative
    Mortuary Assemblages of Tetimpa, Puebla. In *Domestic Ritual in Ancient
    Mesoamerica*, edited by Patricia Plunket, pp. 20–30. Cotsen Institute of Archaeology
    Monograph 46, University of California, Los Angeles.

Voss, Barbara L. 2005. From *Casta* to *Californio*: Social Identity and the Archaeology of
    Culture Contact. *American Anthropologist* 107(3):461–474.

Widner, Randolph J., and Rebecca Storey. 1993. Social Organization and Household
    Structure of a Teotihuacán Apartment Compound: S3W1:33 of the Tlajinga Barrio.
    In *Prehispanic Domestic Units in Western Mesoamerica*, edited by Robert S. Santley
    and Kenneth G. Hirth, pp. 87–104. CRC Press, Boca Raton, Florida.

Wilk, Richard R. 1991. *Household Ecology: Economic Change and Domestic Life among the
    Kekchi Maya in Belize*. University of Arizona Press, Tucson.

Williams, Barbara J. 1991. The Lands and Political Organization of a Rural *Tlaxilacalli* in
    Tepetlaoztoc, AD 1540. In *Land and Politics in the Valley of Mexico*, edited by H. R.
    Harvey, pp. 187–208. University of New Mexico Press, Albuquerque.

Yoffee, Norman. 1993. Too Many Chiefs? (or, Safe Texts for the '90s). In *Archaeological
    Theory: Who Sets the Agenda?* edited by Norman Yoffee and Andrew Sherratt, pp.
    60–78. Cambridge University Press, Cambridge.

Zantwijk, Rudolph van. 1985. *The Aztec Arrangement*. University of Oklahoma Press,
    Norman.

Zorita, Alonso de. 1963. *Life and Labor in Ancient Mexico*. Translated by Benjamin Keen.
    Rutgers University Press, New Brunswick, New Jersey.

CHAPTER 51

HOUSEHOLDS IN ANCIENT MESOAMERICA

DOMESTIC SOCIAL ORGANIZATION, STATUS, ECONOMIES, AND RITUALS

DAVID M. CARBALLO

MESOAMERICAN peoples built for themselves a wide array of domestic units, ranging from modest wattle-and-daub structures in the earliest villages to Teotihuacan's highly planned urban apartment compounds, which were among the most populous residences of the ancient world. Household archaeology has been ongoing for the past six decades and has accelerated rapidly over the last three, as many investigators move away from monumental public buildings to address issues of status, identity, and production across the socioeconomic spectrum (e.g., Blanton 1994; Carballo 2011; Escalante Gonzalbo 2004; Flannery 1976; Hendon 2010; MacEachern et al. 1989; Manzanilla 1986; Robin 2003; Santley and Hirth 1993; Lohse and Valdez 2004; Wilk and Ashmore 1988). The result has been a refined appreciation for how most Mesoamericans once lived. Advances in analytical methods continue to improve our understanding of ancient domestic units, most notably through the reconstruction of activity patterns by means of floor- and soil-chemistry studies (Barba 2007; Hutson et al. 2007; Manzanilla and Barba

1990). This chapter outlines four broad dimensions of Mesoamerican households: their social organization, their variability related to status, their productive activities, and their ritual practices.

HOUSEHOLD SOCIAL ORGANIZATION

Archaeologists evaluate the remains of Mesoamerican households with reference to ethnohistoric and ethnographic accounts of social organization and indigenous conceptualizations of kinship and affiliation. The applicability of historically documented cultural patterns to earlier periods may be questioned on the grounds that texts from the sixteenth century onward record societies after the introduction of Spanish norms and institutions. They are also heavily biased to central Mexico, the heart of colonial New Spain (e.g., Carrasco 1971; Wright Carr 2008). Nevertheless, the presence of many overlapping terms for household organization among widely distributed languages suggests that Mesoamerican cultures shared much in the way of domestic concepts and practices. Careful attention to residential floor plans and the distribution of domestic artifacts within houses allows archaeologists to assess the fit between later domestic institutions and prehistoric contexts (e.g., Flannery and Marcus 2005; Hirth 2000; Manzanilla 1993; Sheets 2002; Smith 1992).

One of the pervasive similarities in Mesoamerican domestic organization is the manner in which households were linguistically referenced in terms of the spatial association of individuals sharing a built environment. Residences in Mesoamerica typically featured a central patio or were organized around an outside lot within which many domestic activities were undertaken, as is reflected in their Spanish name, *solares*. Domestic life was therefore often conducted in public except in densely populated cities, whose inhabitants constructed walled compounds for privacy, and in the case of the restricted access palaces owned by nobles. A shared residence was fundamental as the basis of households, which may be defined as the basic units of economic cooperation for mutual benefit, social competition for status, and integration through rituals to common ancestors and patron deities. This strong spatial association ensures that patio groups, house lots, apartment compounds, and comparable residential arrangements are meaningful analytical units.

A second general similarity in Mesoamerican domestic organization is the manner in which households articulated with larger society through corporate-kin groups such as the Aztec *calpolli*, the Mixtec *siqui*, and the Maya *chi'na* (Lockhart 1992: 59–93; Marcus 2004: 274; Monaghan 1996; Terraciano 2001: 102–132). Such groups could be spatially associated but were usually more dispersed than individual households; therefore, they are more difficult to reconstruct archaeologically.

Nevertheless, corporate-kin groups clearly possess a deep history in Mesoamerica, and they are suggested to be discernible among the sedentary villages of the second millennium BC (Flannery and Marcus 2005; Kowalewski et al. 2009). It is probable that the collective systems of land tenure and flexible affiliation that characterized corporate-kin groups during the sixteenth century apply to much earlier periods as well, though how far back remains uncertain.

Domestic groups of the sixteenth century were also commonly organized around noble houses or courtly systems that operated parallel to, or crosscut, more collective corporate-kin groupings (Carrasco 1976; Chance 2000, 2004; Gillespie 2000). Yet noble houses and courts arose later in Mesoamerican history, associated

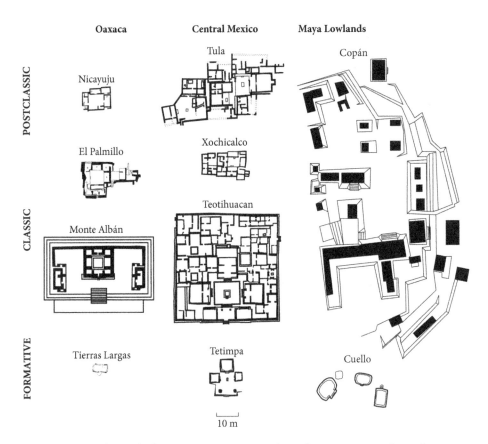

Figure 51.1 Plans of select Mesoamerican residential arrangements from Oaxaca, central Mexico, and the Maya lowlands. The examples from Monte Albán and Copán represent households headed by elites, while the rest would have housed families of commoner or intermediate status. Redrawn by the author and Cathryn Snyder from the following sources: Copán (Maca 2002: Fig. 5.2); Cuello (Hammond et al. 1991: Fig. 3.8); El Palmillo (Feinman and Nicholas 2007: Fig. 8.5); Monte Albán (Winter 2003: Fig. 8.7); Nicayuju (Pérez Rodríguez 2006: Fig.3); Teotihuacan (Manzanilla 1993: Fig. 11); Tetimpa (Plunket and Uruñuela 2003: Fig. 2.5); Tierras Largas (Flannery and Winter 1976: Fig. 2.17); Tula (Healan 2009: Fig. 4.4); Xochicalco (Hirth 2000: Fig. 7.5).

with patron-client relations within hierarchical societies and the balkanization of more centralized polities into smaller kingdoms. Significant variability in their roles is suggested by the differing urban residences of the Classic-period Maya and those of central Mexican societies such as the Aztecs, Toltecs, and Teotihuacanos. Within Classic Maya capitals, domestic units were commonly organized as spatially extensive residential aggregates whose inhabitants were strongly differentiated based on their relationship to the hereditary lord who occupied the largest residence. In contrast, urban residences in central Mexico tended to be organized as highly nucleated compounds with less exaggerated differentiation among their constituent residential blocks (compare the examples in Figure 51.1). These cases underscore one of the primary axes of variability in household archaeology: how social status varied within and between societies.

COMMONER AND ELITE HOUSEHOLDS

As the individuals depicted in Mesoamerican art and writing disproportionately represent elite segments of society, we have learned how commoners, the majority of prehispanic peoples, lived through household archaeology (Lohse and Valdez 2004). Investigations of domestic units permit assessment of how the lives of commoners differed from the lives of elites, as well as how the spectrum of status varied by region, time, degree of urbanization, and other factors. Understanding status variability requires the consideration of multiple lines of evidence, but certain indices, such as house size and elaboration, are more reliable indicators of household status than others (Blanton 1994; Hirth 1993; Rathje 1983). In general, construction materials marked household status along a continuum progressing from wattle-and-daub, to adobe bricks, to cut-stone masonry finished with lime plaster. Higher-status families also tended to have larger and more elevated residences, reflecting both their increased ability to mobilize labor and their larger membership, due to the tendency for polygamy among elites and their more abundant resource base. External decorations such as sculptures and painted motifs also served as conspicuous signals of household status.

The interior of a standard Mesoamerican home was organized around a hearth, usually located in the center of the living space and featuring three stones arranged orthogonally to support a pot or griddle. Dried maize and other foods were stored in subterranean pits, the rooms of attached platforms, or in daub granaries positioned in front of the house (Figure 51.2; Plunket and Uruñuela 1998). Because large domesticated animals like those of Eurasia were absent in Mesoamerica, residences did not include associated barns, but penned dogs, turkeys, and rabbits would have often occupied the confines of a house cluster, and access to meat is another reliable marker of household status (e.g., Emery 2003).

Figure 51.2 Reconstruction of a Terminal Formative residential platform from La Laguna, Tlaxcala. The wattle-and-daub house with roasting and storage pits in an earthen platform lined with stone would have corresponded to a family of commoner status (illustration by the author).

Nobles and rulers resided in palaces, which may be defined not only by their relative size and elaboration but also by their multifunctionality (Christie and Sarro 2006; Evans and Pillsbury 2004; Inomata and Houston 2001). Political relations such as patronage and diplomacy were negotiated within interior patios large enough to accommodate dozens of individuals or in rooms with thronelike benches that ensured a noble be positioned higher than guests (Figure 51.3). Mesoamerican palaces appear to have arisen with the strategies of governance characteristic of state polities (Flannery 1998), though they vary temporally and geographically in their size and importance for large-scale assembly. In certain societies palaces rivaled or exceeded major temple constructions, such as among the Classic Maya and the Mixtec and eastern Nahua of the Postclassic Mixteca-Puebla interaction sphere. In such cases semipublic rituals were undertaken within these grandest of residences, and courts headed by nobles were especially central to organizing social relations (Houston and McAnany 2003; Pohl 2003).

DOMESTIC CRAFT PRODUCTION

Cooperation in economic endeavors was one of the defining characteristics of Mesoamerican households, but great disparities exist in the archaeological visibility of past economic activities. Whereas systems of land tenure are extremely elusive to archaeologists lacking detailed texts, production activities involving perishable goods, such as textile or feather working, may be reconstructed indirectly based on the nonperishable tools used in their manufacture. Most conspicuous is the domestic production of nonperishable crafts such as ceramics, lithics, and shell or greenstone adornments, as they often result in the preservation of a detailed production sequence. Not surprisingly, those activities with greater visibility have been emphasized, but current understanding of domestic economies is imbalanced as a result.

Household craft production was usually intermittent and diversified (Hirth 2009). It was intermittent because domestic craftspeople also tended fields and had other labor obligations to their corporate-kin group, local elite, temple, or political capital. Crafting was diversified because household members strategized in order to distribute the risk associated with the procurement and distribution of goods and resources; therefore, forms of production were frequently interrelated. For instance, a household may have engaged in stone-tool production as well as activities in which those tools were put to use, such as plant processing or drilling beads (Haines et al. 2004). Diversified economic production both benefits from and encourages a gendered organization of domestic labor (Brumfiel and Nichols 2009; Hendon 1996) as well as interdependence among households, as one family looks to the next for partners in trade and in the procurement, production, or distribution of more involved craft industries. Economic interdependence and intermarriage, then, formed the foundation of Mesoamerica's corporate-kin groups (Watanabe 2007).

No straightforward relationship exists between domestic craft production and household status since subsistence, commercial, and prestige economies operated simultaneously, often intersecting to create variable modes of production between and within households (e.g., Pyburn 2008). Archaeologists have documented some households to have specialized in craft production due to their impoverished landholdings or their possession of land that was less suitable for agriculture (Evans 2005; McAnany 1993). Such forms of specialization tended to make use of resources that were abundant in that particular environment. In other cases, specialization within high-status households focused on prestige goods that circulated predominantly among elites (Inomata 2001; Manzanilla 2009). Such production usually involved scarce resources acquired from a distance, knowledge and abilities that not all community members possessed (e.g., literacy), or a combination of these variables. In these elite contexts, production may have been undertaken by relatives of nobles, who were not high enough in the social hierarchy to assume political leadership but were too high to engage in more menial tasks. Alternatively, retainers may have either lived within a noble's compound or visited one periodically to pay tribute labor by crafting. This latter form of production demonstrates how households were articulated within a larger political economy, and the manner in which political leaders may have prioritized either controlling production or simply taxing independent household production based on the relative ease and value of monopolization of the resources involved (e.g., Widmer 1996).

Figure 51.3 Reconstructed central patio of the Quezalpapalotl Palace at Teotihuacan
(photo by the author).

An important recent addition to household literature is the increased attention given to ritual economy—defined as the processes of provisioning and con-
suming that create, sustain, and shape worldviews and religious institutions (Wells
and Davis-Salazar 2007; Wells and McAnany 2008). A focus on ritual economy
helps to bridge formalist-substantivist dichotomies by considering the intersection
of rational choice and cultural meaning. Household ritual economies included the
production of goods used in rituals and the ritualization of production sequences
for goods used in quotidian, nonritual settings.

DOMESTIC RITUALS

Mesoamerican archaeologists have interpreted the significance of household rituals both in terms of their social functions—as a means of connecting individuals by
inculcating a sense of trust and common purpose—and in terms of their embodied
practice, allowing for the regeneration of and resistance to interpersonal relations,
meaning, and memory (e.g., Gonlin and Lohse 2007; Plunket 2002). For heuristic
purposes, domestic rituals may be classified in three general groups: (1) mortuary rituals for deceased household members; (2) general rituals undertaken within
houses, patios, or house lots; and (3) rituals that animated or deanimated domestic spaces (Grove and Gillespie 2002). Three corollary goals of such rituals, not
exclusive to any one group, were (1) communion and covenant with ancestors and

deities; (2) curing and welfare of household members; and (3) respecting the life force and interconnectivity of natural, supernatural, and cultural domains.

Ancestors were essential to Mesoamerican belief systems as individuals who connected the living to the physical world and who could intercede on their behalf in the spiritual world (McAnany 1995). By being physically interred underneath the floors of houses and other living spaces, ancestors tethered living households to domestic structures and land. Mortuary rituals thereby materialized household claims to structures and their associated property and entitlements. For instance, the iconic talud-tablero façade, seen at Teotihuacan and in the architecture of many public buildings throughout Mesoamerica, was first used in house construction, for which it is argued that the basal talud (talus) platform represented the dwelling of the buried ancestors while the upper tablero (tableaux) platform was inhabited by the living (Uruñuela and Plunket 2007). Within larger house groups and compounds, ancestors were often buried within the central altars of open patios, so that a number of assembled families could pay homage and make requests to them.

General domestic rituals could also involve ancestors in the case of clay figurines, which appear to have been made and used by women in certain settings to commune with, and divine from their ancestors (Cyphers Guillén 1993; Marcus 1998). In other settings, particularly associated with state societies, figurines tended to depict deities and may have been used in curing rituals or to make appeals for general household welfare (e.g., Halperin et al. 2009; Smith 2002). Deities venerated in domestic settings were also appealed to through rituals involving effigy incense burners (e.g., Carballo 2007), and blood offerings were made to them as rituals of communion by using needlelike implements shaped from obsidian or bone or by using natural spines provided by the maguey plant or stingrays.

Mesoamericans viewed houses as living entities that could be cosmically centered and imbued with symbolic significance or an animate personification (Mock 1998). Ethnographic accounts, such as for the Tzotzil Maya of Zinacantan (Vogt 1976), assist in comprehending the worldview expressed through house offerings. In Oaxaca, ceramic vessels and animals were frequently left as offerings under floors or within walls of residences during the dedication or termination of particular construction phases (Feinman et al. 2008). The termination and dedication of Teotihuacan's apartment compounds and palaces included a range of materials such as ceramic vessels, mica, figurines, small incense burners, stone tools, and slate-backed mirrors (Manzanilla 2003). Domestic mortuary offerings could also involve the burial of individuals or groups in a manner that was seen as "completing" or "ensouling" the structure (McAnany et al. 1999: 141).

In the above examples of household ritual the contents and degree of elaboration of offerings to the house relate to two previous sections in that they could serve to index the social identity and status of the household. Such examples demonstrate that Mesoamericans conceived of residences as living entities with a life cycle appropriately commemorated by rites of passage. Just as the individuals residing in a house possessed particular identities as well as collective identities based on corporate group, economic interdependence, and status, domestic units themselves were identified with their collective histories and their years of persistence and renewal.

REFERENCES

Barba, Luís. 2007. Chemical Residues in Lime-Plastered Archaeological Floors. *Geoarchaeology* 22:439–452.

Blanton, Richard E. 1994. *Houses and Households: A Comparative Study.* Plenum Press, New York.

Brumfiel, Elizabeth M., and Deborah L. Nichols. 2009. Bitumen, Blades, and Beads: Prehispanic Craft Production and the Domestic Economy. In *Housework: Specialization, Risk, and Domestic Craft Production in Mesoamerica*, edited by Kenneth G. Hirth, pp. 239–251. Archaeological Papers of the American Anthropological Association, Vol. 19, Washington, DC.

Carballo, David M. 2007. Effigy Vessels, Religious Integration, and the Origins of the Central Mexican Pantheon. *Ancient Mesoamerica* 18(1):53–67.

Carballo, David M. 2011. Advances in the Household Archaeology of Highland Mesoamerica. *Journal of Archaeological Research* 19:133–189.

Carrasco, Pedro. 1971. Social Organization of Ancient Mexico. In *Handbook of Middle American Indians, Vol. 10*, edited by Gordon Ekholm and Ignacio Bernal, pp. 349–375. University of Texas Press, Austin.

Carrasco, Pedro. 1976. Estratificación social indígena en Morelos durante el siglo XVI. In *Estratificación social en la Mesoamérica prehispánica*, edited by Pedro Carrasco and Johanna Broda, pp. 102–117. Centro de Investigaciones Superiores del Instituto Nacional de Antropología e Historia, México, D.F.

Chance, John K. 2000. The Noble House in Colonial Puebla, Mexico: Descent, Inheritance, and the Nahua Tradition. *American Anthropologist* 102:485–502.

Chance, John K. 2004. La casa noble mixteca: una hipótesis sobre el cacicazgo prehispánico y colonial. In *Estructuras políticas en el Oaxaca antiguo,* Memoria de la Tercera Mesa Redonda de Monte Albán, edited by Nelly M. Robles, pp. 1–26. Instituto Nacional de Antropología e Historia, México, D.F.

Christie, Jessica J., and Patricia J. Sarro eds. 2006. *Palaces and Power in the Americas: From Peru to the Northwest Coast.* University of Texas Press, Austin.

Cyphers Guillén, Ann. 1993. Women, Rituals, and Social Dynamics at Ancient Chalcatzingo. *Latin American Antiquity* 4:209–224.

Emery, Kitty F. 2003. The Noble Beast: Status and Differential Access to Animals in the Maya World. *World Archaeology* 34(3):498–515.

Escalante Gonzalbo, Pablo, ed. 2004. *Historia de la vida cotidiana en México, Tomo I, Mesoamérica y los ámbitos indígenas de la Nueva España*. El Colegio de México, Fondo de Cultura Económica, México, D.F.

Evans, Susan T. 2005. Men, Women, and Maguey: The Household Division of Labor among Aztec Farmers. In *Settlement, Subsistence, and Social Complexity: Essays Honoring the Legacy of Jeffrey R. Parsons*, edited by Richard E. Blanton, pp. 198–228. Cotsen Institute of Archaeology, University of California, Los Angeles.

Evans, Susan T., and Joanne Pillsbury, eds. 2004. *Palaces of the Ancient New World.* Dumbarton Oaks Research Library and Collection, Washington, DC.

Feinman, Gary M., and Linda M. Nicholas. 2007. The Socioeconomic Organization of
    the Classic Period Zapotec State. In *The Political Economy of Ancient Mesoamerica:
    Transformations during the Formative and Classic Periods*, edited by Vernon L.
    Scarborough and John E. Clark, pp. 135–147. University of New Mexico Press,
    Albuquerque.
Feinman, Gary M., Linda M. Nicholas, and Edward F. Maher. 2008. Domestic Offerings
    at El Palmillo: Implications for Community Organization. *Ancient Mesoamerica*
    19:175–194.
Flannery, Kent V., ed. 1976. *The Early Mesoamerican Village*. Academic Press, New York.
Flannery, Kent V. 1998. The Ground Plans of Archaic States. In *Archaic States*, edited by
    Gary M. Feinman and Joyce Marcus, pp. 15–57. School of American Research Press,
    Santa Fe.
Flannery, Kent V., and Joyce Marcus. 2005. *Excavations at San José Mogote 1: The
    Household Archaeology*. Museum of Anthropology, University of Michigan, Ann
    Arbor.
Flannery, Kent V., and Marcus C. Winter. 1976. Analyzing Household Activities. In *The
    Early Mesoamerican Village*, edited by Kent V. Flannery, pp. 34–47. Academic Press,
    New York.
Gillespie, Susan D. 2000. Rethinking Maya Social Organization: Replacing "Lineage"
    with "House." *American Anthropologist* 102(3):467–484.
Gonlin, Nancy, and John C. Lohse, eds. 2007. *Commoner Ritual and Ideology in Ancient
    Mesoamerica*. University Press of Colorado, Boulder.
Grove, David C., and Susan D. Gillespie. 2002. Middle Formative Domestic Ritual at
    Chalcatzingo, Morelos. In *Domestic Ritual in Ancient Mesoamerica*, edited by
    Patricia Plunket, pp. 11–19. Cotsen Institute of Archaeology, University of California,
    Los Angeles.
Haines, Helen R., Gary M. Feinman, and Linda M. Nicholas. 2004. Household Economic
    Specialization and Social Differentiation: The Stone-Tool Assemblage at El Palmillo,
    Oaxaca. *Ancient Mesoamerica* 15:251–266.
Halperin, Christina T., Katherine A. Faust, Rhonda Taube, and Aurore Giguet, eds.
    2009. *Mesoamerican Figurines: Small-Scale Indices of Large-Scale Social Phenomena*.
    University Press of Florida, Gainesville.
Hammond, Norman, Juliette Cartwright Gerhardt, and Sara Donaghey. 1991.
    Stratigraphy and Chronology in the Reconstruction of Preclassic Developments
    at Cuello. In *Cuello: An Early Maya Community in Belize*, edited by Norman
    Hammond, pp. 23–69. Cambridge University, Cambridge.
Healan, Dan M. 2009. Household, Neighborhood, and Urban Structure in an "Adobe
    City": Tula, Hidalgo, Mexico. In *Domestic Life in Prehispanic Capitals: A Study of
    Specialization, Hierarchy, and Ethnicity*, edited by Linda R. Manzanilla and Claude
    Chapdelaine, pp. 67–88. Museum of Anthropology, University of Michigan, Ann
    Arbor.
Hendon, Julia A. 1996. Archaeological Approaches to the Organization of Domestic
    Labor: Household Practice and Domestic Relations. *Annual Review of Anthropology*
    25:45–61.
Hendon, Julia A. 2010. *Houses in a Landscape: Memory and Everyday Life in
    Mesoamerica*. Duke University Press, Durham, North Carolina.
Hirth, Kenneth G. 1993. Identifying Rank and Socioeconomic Status in Domestic
    Contexts: An Example from Central Mexico. In *Prehispanic Domestic Units in
    Western Mesoamerica: Studies of the Household, Compound, and Residence*, edited

by Robert S. Santley and Kenneth G. Hirth, pp. 121–146. CRC Press, Boca Raton, Florida.

Hirth, Kenneth G. 2000. *Ancient Urbanism at Xochicalco: The Evolution and Organization of a Pre-Hispanic Society.* University of Utah Press, Salt Lake City.

Hirth, Kenneth G., ed. 2009. *Housework: Specialization, Risk, and Domestic Craft Production in Mesoamerica.* Archaeological Papers of the American Anthropological Association, Vol. 19, Washington, DC.

Houston, Stephen D., and Patricia A. McAnany. 2003. Bodies and Blood: Critiquing Social Construction in Maya Archaeology. *Journal of Anthropological Archaeology* 22(1):26–41.

Hutson, Scott R., Travis W. Stanton, Aline Magnoni, Richard Terry, and Jason Craner. 2007. Beyond the Buildings: Formation Processes of Ancient Maya Houselots and Methods for the Study of Non-architectural Space. *Journal of Anthropological Archaeology* 26(3): 442–473.

Inomata, Takeshi. 2001. The Power and Ideology of Artistic Creation: Elite Craft Specialists in Classic Maya Society. *Current Anthropology* 42:321–349.

Inomata, Takeshi, and Stephen D. Houston, eds. 2001. *Royal Courts of the Ancient Maya, Volumes 1 and 2.* Westview Press, Boulder, Colorado.

Kowalewski, Stephen A., Andrew K. Balkansky, Laura R. Stiver Walsh, Thomas J. Pluckhahn, John F. Chamblee, Verónica Pérez Rodríguez, Verenice Y. Heredia Espinoza, and Carol A. Smith. 2009. *Origins of the Ñuu: Archaeology in the Mixteca Alta, Mexico.* University Press of Colorado, Boulder.

Lockhart, James. 1992. *The Nahuas after the Conquest: A Social and Cultural History of the Indians of Central Mexico, Sixteenth through Eighteenth Centuries.* Stanford University Press, Stanford.

Lohse, John C., and Fred Valdez, eds. 2004. *Ancient Maya Commoners.* University of Texas Press, Austin.

Maca, Allan Leigh, Jr. 2002. Spatio-Temporal Boundaries in Classic Maya Settlement Systems: Copan's Urban Foothills and the Excavations at Group 9J-5. Unpublished doctoral dissertation, Department of Anthropology, Harvard University, Cambridge.

MacEachern, Scott, David J. Archer, and Richard D. Garvin, eds. 1989. *Households and Communities: Proceedings of the Twenty-First Annual Conference of the Archaeological Association of the University of Calgary.* University of Calgary Archaeological Association, Calgary.

Manzanilla, Linda R. 1993. Los conjuntos residenciales teotihuacanos. In *Anatomía de un conjunto residencial teotihuacano en Oztoyahualco, Vol. 1, Las excavaciones,* pp. 31–46. Universidad Nacional Autónoma de México, México, D.F.

Manzanilla, Linda R. 2003. The Abandonment of Teotihuacan. In *The Archaeology of Settlement Abandonment in Middle America,* edited by Takeshi Inomata and Ronald W. Webb, pp. 91–101. University of Utah Press, Salt Lake City.

Manzanilla, Linda R. 2009. Corporate Life in Apartment and Barrio Compounds at Teotihuacan, Central Mexico: Craft Specialization, Hierarchy, and Ethnicity. In *Domestic Life in Prehispanic Capitals: A Study of Specialization, Hierarchy, and Ethnicity,* edited by Linda R. Manzanilla and Claude Chapdelaine, pp. 21–42. Museum of Anthropology, University of Michigan, Ann Arbor.

Manzanilla, Linda, and Luís Barba. 1990. The Study of Activities in Classic Households: Two Case Studies from Coba and Teotihuacan. *Ancient Mesoamerica* 1:41–49.

Marcus, Joyce. 1998. *Women's Ritual in Formative Oaxaca: Figurine-making, Divination, Death and the Ancestors.* Museum of Anthropology Memoirs 33, University of Michigan, Ann Arbor.

Marcus, Joyce. 2004. Maya Commoners: The Stereotype and the Reality. In *Ancient Maya Commoners*, edited by John C. Lohse and Fred Valdez, pp. 255–284. University of Texas Press, Austin.

McAnany, Patricia A. 1993. Resources, Specialization, and Exchange in the Maya Lowlands. In *The American Southwest and Mesoamerica: Systems of Prehistoric Exchange*, edited by Jonathon E. Ericson and Timothy G. Baugh, pp. 213–245. Plenum Press, New York.

McAnany, Patricia A. 1995. *Living with the Ancestors: Kinship and Kingship in Ancient Maya Society.* University of Texas Press, Austin.

McAnany, Patricia A., Rebecca Storey, and Angela K. Lockhard. 1999. Mortuary Ritual and Family Politics at Formative and Early Classic K'axob, Belize. *Ancient Mesoamerica* 10:129–146.

Mock, Shirley Boteler, ed. 1998. *The Sowing and the Dawning: Termination, Dedication, and Transformation in the Archaeological and Ethnographic Record of Mesoamerica.* University of New Mexico Press, Albuquerque.

Monaghan, John. 1996. The Mesoamerican Community as a "Great House." *Ethnology* 35(3):181–194.

Pérez Rodríguez, Verónica. 2006. States and Households: The Social Organization of Terrace Agriculture in Postclassic Mixteca Alta, Oaxaca, Mexico. *Latin American Antiquity* 17:3–22.

Plunket, Patricia, ed. 2002. *Domestic Ritual in Ancient Mesoamerica.* Cotsen Institute of Archaeology, University of California, Los Angeles.

Plunket, Patricia, and Gabriela Uruñuela. 1998. Preclassic Household Patterns Preserved under Volcanic Ash at Tetimpa, Puebla. *Latin American Antiquity* 9:287–309.

Plunket, Patricia, and Gabriela Uruñuela. 2003. From Episodic to Permanent Abandonment: Responses to Volcanic Hazards at Tetimpa, Puebla, Mexico. In *The Archaeology of Settlement Abandonment in Middle America*, edited by Takeshi Inomata and Ronald W. Webb, pp. 13–27. University of Utah Press, Salt Lake City.

Pohl, John M. D. 2003. Royal Marriage and Confederacy Building among the Eastern Nahuas, Mixtecs, and Zapotecs. In *The Postclassic Mesoamerican World*, edited by Michael E. Smith and Frances F. Berdan, pp. 243–248. University of Utah Press, Salt Lake City.

Pyburn, K. Anne. 2008. Pomp and Circumstance before Belize: Ancient Maya Commerce and the New River Conurbation. In *The Ancient City: New Perspectives on Urbanism in the Old and New Worlds*, edited by Joyce Marcus and Jeremy A. Sabloff, pp. 247–272. School of American Research Press, Santa Fe.

Rathje, William L. 1983. To the Salt of the Earth: Some Comments on Household Archaeology among the Maya. In *Prehistoric Settlement Patterns: Essays in Honor of Gordon R. Willey*, edited by Evon Z. Vogt and Richard M. Leventhal, pp. 23–34. University of New Mexico Press and Peabody Museum of Archaeology and Ethnology, Albuquerque and Cambridge.

Robin, Cynthia. 2003. New Directions in Classic Maya Household Archaeology. *Journal of Archaeological Research* 11(4):307–356.

Santley, Robert S., and Kenneth G. Hirth, eds. 1993. *Prehispanic Domestic Units in Western Mesoamerica: Studies of the Household, Compound, and Residence.* CRC Press, Boca Raton, Florida.

Sheets, Payson, ed. 2002. *Before the Volcano Erupted: The Ancient Cerén Village in Central America*. University of Texas Press, Austin.

Smith, Michael E. 1992. *Archaeological Research at Aztec Period Rural Sites in Morelos, Mexico: Volume 1*. Memoirs in Latin American Archaeology, No. 4, University of Pittsburgh, Pittsburgh.

Smith, Michael E. 2002. Domestic Ritual at Aztec Provincial Sites in Morelos. In *Domestic Ritual in Ancient Mesoamerica*, edited by Patricia Plunket, pp. 93–114. Cotsen Institute of Archaeology, University of California, Los Angeles.

Terraciano, Kevin. 2001. *The Mixtecs of Colonial Oaxaca: Ñudzahui History, Sixteenth through Eighteenth Centuries*. Stanford University Press, Stanford.

Uruñuela, Gabriela, and Patricia Plunket. 2007. Tradition and Transformation: Village Ritual at Tetimpa as a Template for Early Teotihuacan. In *Commoner Ritual and Ideology in Ancient Mesoamerica*, edited by Nancy Gonlin and John C. Lohse, pp. 33–54. University Press of Colorado, Boulder.

Vogt, Evon Z. 1976. *Tortillas for the Gods: A Symbolic Analysis of Zinacanteco Rituals*. Harvard University Press, Cambridge.

Watanabe, John M. 2007. Ritual Economy and the Negotiation of Autarky and Interdependence in a Ritual Mode of Production. In *Mesoamerican Ritual Economy: Archaeological and Ethnological Perspectives*, edited by E. Christian Wells and Karla L. Davis-Salazar, pp. 301–322. University Press of Colorado, Boulder.

Wells, E. Christian, and Karla L. Davis-Salazar, eds. 2007. *Mesoamerican Ritual Economy: Archaeological and Ethnological Perspectives*. University Press of Colorado, Boulder.

Wells, E. Christian, and Patricia A. McAnany, eds. 2008. *Dimensions of Ritual Economy*. Research in Economic Anthropology, Volume 27, Emerald Group, Bingley, United Kingdom.

Widmer, Randolph J. 1996. Procurement, Exchange, and Production of Foreign Commodities at Teotihuacan: State Monopoly or Local Control. In *Arquelogía Mesoamericana: Homenaje a William T. Sanders I*, edited by Alba Guadalupe Mastache, Jeffery Parsons, Robert Santley, and Mari Carmen Serra Puche, pp. 271–280. Instituto Nacional de Antropología e Historia and Arqueología Mexicana, México, D.F.

Wilk, Richard R., and Wendy Ashmore, eds. 1988. *Household and Community in the Mesoamerican Past*. University of New Mexico, Albuquerque.

Winter, Marcus. 2003. Monte Albán and Late Classic Site Abandonment in Highland Oaxaca. In *The Archaeology of Settlement Abandonment in Middle America*, edited by Takeshi Inomata and Ronald W. Webb, pp. 103–119. University of Utah Press, Salt Lake City.

Wright Carr, David Charles. 2008. La sociedad prehispánica en las lenguas náhuatl y otomí. *Acta Universitaria* 18(1):15–23.

....

CHAPTER 52

COMMUNITIES
IN ANCIENT
MESOAMERICA

....

MARCELLO A. CANUTO AND
JASON YAEGER

THE term "community" seems straightforward, referring to a small town or village and the group of people who live together in that settlement and consequently inter-act regularly. Over the long sweep of Mesoamerican history, from Pre-Columbian times through the present, many people have lived in small settlements—hamlets, villages, towns—of the type that archaeologists often refer to as communities, drawing on this common-sense understanding of the term.

This view of community is similar to the more formal construct that Murdock (1949) defined. Inspired by sociology's growing interest in understanding how tra-ditional institutions of social cohesion accommodated change (e.g., Hollingshead 1948), Murdock operationalized the community as the maximal residential group that maintains face-to-face interactions. The community as enshrined in Murdock's definition occupied a central place in sociocultural anthropology for the first half of the twentieth century. In practical terms, communities commonly served as venues for the fieldwork through which ethnographers immersed themselves in other cultures. From a theoretical and interpretive standpoint, communities were idealized as primary loci for social and cultural reproduction (e.g., Arensberg 1961), conservative repositories of shared beliefs and knowledge that were being lost through acculturation in urban contexts (e.g., Gould 1959; Miner 1952; Mintz 1953; Redfield 1955; Tax 1951).

By the 1960s and 1970s, new theoretical concerns within anthropology and the impact of globalization on the societies that anthropologists studied led to a disenchantment with Murdock's notion of community. Its emphasis on homogeneity, social and political boundedness, and cultural conservatism smacked of naïve romanticism, and it was increasingly contravened by ethnographic research (e.g., Cancian 1972; Goldkind 1965; Rambo 1977). Whereas scholars once viewed the community as an enduring social fact and key site of cultural reproduction, the community came to be framed as a historically contingent institution, and its own reproduction was now problematized (Wolf 1957; 1986). As a result, although small communities continued to be the field sites for many anthropologists, the construct of community *sensu* Redfield and Murdock no longer factored strongly into the framing of their research or their interpretations.

Throughout the 1980s and 1990s, ethnography's emphasis on agency, structuration, place, and embodiment led to new understandings of community. As the theoretical focus shifted to the dialectic between practice and structure (Bourdieu 1977; Giddens 1979), social institutions such as communities were reinterpreted as emergent social forms arising out of repeated and intentional actions rather than preexisting ideal types. To paraphrase Cohen (1985), people thought themselves into difference and, by acting accordingly, realized social institutions that were consistent with their aggregate goals (Urban 1996). Social institutions, constituted in this manner, also proved consequential to individual action by subsequently structuring the actions of their members in such a way as to naturalize their existence. In this paradigm, communities came to be viewed as nodes of interaction, negotiation, and identity formation (e.g., Barth 1978). This redefinition of community expanded the scope of the term and its applicability to understanding the complex nature and role of non-kin social groups in society. However, its less empirical underpinnings and its divorce from face-to-face interactions and material preconditions also made it seem less applicable to archaeology.

In fact, archaeology in Mesoamerica and beyond had been influenced strongly by Murdock's view of community (e.g., Lipe 1992; Varien and Potter 2008b), perhaps unknowingly in some cases, as the overwhelming association in archaeology linked the community and the archaeological site (e.g., Coe 1965; Layton 1972; Sanders 1981; Willey et al. 1955). For archaeologists, sites were the material remains of ancient settlements and by inference the traces of a spatially delimited social group (i.e., the community of people who lived there).

Approaches to community derived from settlement studies that were burgeoning in Mesoamerican archaeology during the 1960s and 1970s were strongly informed by ecological and behavioralist paradigms. Communities were modeled as aggregates of households, themselves interpreted narrowly as society's smallest unit of socioeconomic production (Bawden 1982; Flannery 1976; Freter 2004; Hayden and Cannon 1982; Spencer-Wood 1989). Research on these constituent units, so narrowly defined in their own right, was deemed sufficient to understand the properties of the social unit they formed in aggregate. Consequently, communities were modeled as organizational entities that reflected the extent to which a particular domestic socioeconomic adaptation prompted supra-household modes of integration and cooperation. As such, the community was a mechanism that helped ensure household economic production and social reproduction.

But this approach had its limitations. As with the conflation of house and household (see Carballo, this volume; Wilk and Ashmore 1988), eliding an analytical unit in the archaeological record with a past social institution creates two epistemological problems. First, it appears to eliminate the need for bridging arguments that allow for empirical evaluation of whether those who lived in a particular spatial unit (i.e., house or settlement) indeed constituted a coherent social formation (household or community). Second, and perhaps more important, it does not problematize the social constitution of those institutions, treating them as self-evident units of social organization (Varien and Potter 2008b). In the last fifteen years, archaeology has increasingly emphasized the historically contingent nature of social institutions and their related foundational constructs, framing them as socially constituted formations. For the study of communities, this has entailed decoupling the notion of community from the archaeological site and opening the community "black box" to understand its inner workings and generative processes.

One concerted effort to develop the study of ancient communities in Mesoamerica was *The Archaeology of Communities* (Canuto and Yaeger 2000). We were struck that most paradigms for understanding social and political processes and dynamics, particularly in the Maya area, took as their frame of analysis either the household or the polity. Scholars working with households generally saw households as building blocks of society (Netting 1982; Wilk and Rathje 1982), and they adopted an epistemology of methodological individualism (de Montmollin 1988). In contrast, those who framed their analyses at the polity and regional level often employed epistemologies that fell under the rubric of methodological holism, espousing top-down models that framed social change as a response to macro-political processes or ecological and demographic changes. Like other scholars, we found neither extreme to be fully satisfying, and we believed that the community could serve as the central framing device for an approach that occupied the epistemological middle ground between methodological holism and methodological individualism.

We looked to John Watanabe (1992) for a definition of community. In his study of contemporary Mam Mayan society in highland Guatemala, Watanabe defined community as the intersection of people, place, and premise. This definition is explicit and clear, and it encompasses the social, cultural, and spatial dimensions of human experience. It is not deeply embedded in any particular theoretical perspective, and thus it has broad applicability. As archaeologists, we found the inclusion of place important, bridging concerns of the spatial and material dimensions of human action. Watanabe's definition is also implicitly temporal, as the intersection of people, place, and premise implies contemporaneity and a rhythm of interactions.

As scholars began developing more explicit notions of community in prehispanic Mesoamerica, some delved into the ethnographic and historic literature to identify indigenous constructs of community. Extensive written sources for central Mexico (e.g., Carrasco 1971; Gibson 1964; Lockhart 1992), Oaxaca (Monaghan 1995), and the Maya area (Marcus 1983; Restall 1997) provided archaeologists with many native terms that related to their notions of community and physical settlements. Through ethnohistoric analysis of these data, Marcus (2000), Hare (2000), and Robin (1999, 2003) were able to identify emic terms for co-residential communities of different scales. Two of these studies appeared in *The Archaeology of Communities.*

Other contributors to *The Archaeology of Communities* developed other facets of Watanabe's relatively unconstraining definition, emphasizing different aspects of community. So conceived, community has proven useful as a framing construct because it focuses our interpretive gaze firmly on interactions among certain people or categories of people, interactions that entailed particular kinds of practices that took place in certain locations (e.g., Hastorf 2003; Knapp 2003; Mathews 2004; Reeves 2003; Tarlow 2002; Varien and Potter 2008a; Varien and Wilshusen 2002).

Collectively, the contributors to *The Archaeology of Communities* shifted our research focus to the social construction of communities, emphasizing, in turn, the complex negotiations involved in their development (e.g., Isbell 2000). As archaeologists, though, most retained an abiding concern with the spatial and material aspects of community (see Lipe [1992] and Varien and Potter [2008b] for similar concerns). William Isbell (2000), for example, highlighted the issue of spatial scale and its effects on social interactions by introducing the heuristic terms of natural versus imagined communities (*sensu* Anderson 1991). The former is founded on frequent daily interactions by people living in close proximity, while the latter is constructed on notions of sameness and shared history, heritage, and purpose that are fostered through less frequent but socially powerful interactions and events.

This distinction is not evidence of a paradigmatic divide in the archaeological study of community, but rather it underscores the importance of considering the effects of scale on the nature and regularity of interaction among a community's members and the kinds of constructs that are more likely to serve as foundational logics for those communities. In studies of so-called natural communities, scholars have been particularly interested in everyday practices and frequent face-to-face interactions through which a community identity is constituted, reproduced, and contested and the ways in which difference is negotiated and naturalized within communities. In cases where the community entails a social group that is not co-resident, but whose members are more spatially dispersed, generative practices tend to occur more episodically (Joyce and Hendon 2000; Yaeger 2003b). We concur with Isbell that there are important differences between smaller, co-resident communities and more dispersed, non-co-resident communities in terms of the kinds of practices that are likely to constitute them and the rhetorical logics that justify and naturalize them. But while natural and imagined communities are useful heuristic terms, they should not be reified into distinct types, nor should the existence of the so-called natural community be problematized any less than that of the imagined community, as both extremes are equally constituted social forms.

Despite conceptualizing the community at different scales, archaeological interpretations of community in ancient Mesoamerica have largely acceded to two basic notions. First, the community as a social construct and social group is constituted by interpersonal interactions and negotiations that are rendered salient by a shared framework of expectations. Second, communities develop and exist within broader social and political contexts. Both these positions undermine the closed community model that characterized early research on this topic in Mesoamerican archaeology. These positions have indeed proven productive, as scholars in Mesoamerican archaeology have recently employed this paradigm to examine issues such as the formation of identity groups, socialization and the development of personhood, management of sociopolitical heterogeneity, practices of social affiliation, and creation of social memory.

Of all the topics recently addressed under the rubric of the archaeology of communities, identities and identity formation have been most salient (e.g., Barber 2005; Canuto 2002, 2004; Canuto and Fash 2004; Eberl 2007; Hutson 2010; Hutson et al. 2008; Johnson 2011; Yaeger 2000, 2003a, 2003b; Yaeger and Robin 2004). While such research often begins with an assessment of whether the residents of a local settlement considered themselves to be a community (e.g., Yaeger 2000), in most cases, scholars have focused even more attention on identity groups in which membership was not coterminous with a co-resident settlement. They have elucidated how identities enacted and affirmed through activities in small co-resident communities structured broader social and political dynamics, including the constitution of imagined communities that cross-cut smaller-scale communities.

In many cases, these studies examine how the constitution of local communities was entangled in the development of regional political entities, such as Classic-period Maya polities. Canuto (2002) at Copán, Eberl (2007) at Dos Pilas, Hutson et al. (2008) at Chunchucmil, and Johnson (2011) at Chichén Itzá all have investigated how practices of affiliation to local groups were delimited or impacted by regional (polity) forces. These studies help determine the processes whereby broad social cohesion was forged by investigating how social practices within one context—local communities—could be co-opted into generative processes that constituted more regional and physically dispersed social groups (i.e., political or imagined communities).

Different studies elucidate the various ways in which practices within the local community were imbricated within broader sociopolitical processes. Yaeger (2000, 2003a, 2003b) argues that local leaders in the village of San Lorenzo emulated the practices of the ruling elite at Xunantunich in order to create and reinforce inequalities within the local community, while at the same time hosting commensal feasts and other activities that helped reproduce the local community. Hutson (2010) at Chunchucmil and Barber (2005) in coastal Oaxaca investigate the socializing function of the local community (i.e., how it helps to impart meaning and provide access to salient identities). In an interesting turn, Robin (2003) employs a community focus to show how local institutions and practices rooted in the farming community of Chan provided a degree of self-sufficiency and resilience that allowed its members to push back against efforts by extra-community agents and state institutions to incorporate Chan into larger political and economic networks and appropriate its resources.

Most researchers working at the scale of the small or natural community draw heavily on practice theory, as employed by Hendon (2010), Hutson (2010) and Lopiparo (2003, 2007), for example. These scholars focus on the constitution of past social groups through dialogic relations to other subjects as well as the material world. In this approach, community is a social group with an explicit discursive identity that develops through participation in meaningful practices, at meaningful places, and using meaningful objects. Focus is placed on "the mutual engagement of a joint enterprise" (Hendon 2010: 60) in which people, places, and material culture are engaged in some common project (i.e., premise). This approach allows scholars to interpret how material patterns within co-residential groups were the outcome of practices aimed at constituting and rendering meaningful *sui generis* social constructs such as memory communities or houses (*sensu* Levi-Strauss 1982: 163-187).

Given the fact that popular connotations of community are broadly consonant with Murdock's definition and Isbell's natural community, it is perhaps unsurprising that the notion of community has been applied less frequently to larger-scale social groups in prehispanic Mesoamerica. There have been some exceptions, however. For example, Houston and his colleagues (2003) draw on Weber's notion of a moral community in their discussion of political authority and social solidarity at Piedras Negras. Yaeger (2003b) deploys the construct of imagined community (Anderson 1991) to argue that new rulers at Xunantunich who were poorly connected to preexisting social, political, and political-economic networks and institutions sought to encourage a new sense of belonging to the polity in order to smooth the flow of tribute to the rulers.

This brief review of the study of ancient Mesoamerican communities demonstrates that the use of a community approach has been productive, drawing our attention to new topics of interest and illuminating the roles played by everyday practices and interpersonal interactions in the constitution not only of local social entities, but also of larger social and political formations as well. To date, most scholars have emphasized intersubjectivity at various scales of interaction and the constitution of particular social groups, all of which can be glossed as communities. As the archaeology of communities in Mesoamerica continues to develop, we hope to see attention focused on several aspects that remain unexplored.

The first of these is the material dimension of the community. Some scholars (Hendon 2010; Hutson 2010) have begun to look more carefully at the dialectic between the social and the material, but community research stands to benefit from a more concerted effort to understand the way physical settings (community as place) frame and shape interactions and practices of affiliation (community as identity), and how those enduring settings structure subsequent generations of practice. We would also advocate a renewed emphasis on the social life of things (*sensu* Appadurai 1984), by looking at the manner in which objects are rendered socially meaningful through display, consumption, exchange, and curation in community settings. These approaches provide insight into how past groups not only constituted themselves but also conceived of themselves, a topic often avoided by archaeologists not benefiting from a rich written record.

The second relates to the study of the relation between the material and the social. We see a need to understand the temporality of socially constituted groups. It is not enough to provide evidence for communal interaction, shared practices, and mutual engagement without also appreciating the rhythm of interactions. Archaeological research often emphasizes historically contingent events to the detriment of the quotidian. We also should consider the extent to which repetition is required to ensure the ongoing reconstitution of a social group and its foundational constructs.

The research we have synthesized here shows the importance of an archaeology of communities for Mesoamerica. Methodologically, the community is situated between the scales of household and polity, which permits researchers to have new insights into the broader social and political dynamics through which these other social institutions were constituted and changed over time. As a paradigm, this approach treats communities as emergent social institutions in which local identities were constituted as a consequence of shared quotidian and extraordinary practices. Because they often were important nodes within regional political and economic structures, communities also become the key arenas for the negotiation of relationships and affiliations that linked its members with other social groups, institutions, and networks. Finally, epistemologically, this approach's focus on the relational, negotiated, and contested nature of the ancient Mesoamerican past helps avoid essentializing and normative interpretations.

REFERENCES

Anderson, Benedict. 1991. *Imagined Communities: Reflections on the Origin and Spread of Nationalism.* Verso, London.

Appadurai, Arjun, ed. 1984. *The Social Life of Things.* Cambridge University Press, Cambridge.

Arensberg, Conrad M. 1961. The Community as Object and as Sample. *American Anthropologist* 63:241–264.

Barber, Sarah B. 2005. Heterogeneity, Identity, and Complexity: Negotiating Status and Authority in Terminal Formative Coastal Oaxaca. PhD thesis, Department of Anthropology, University of Colorado, Boulder.

Barth, Frederick. 1978. Conclusions. In *Scale and Social Organization*, edited by Frederick Barth, pp. 253–273. Universitetsforlaget, Oslo.

Bawden, Garth. 1982. Community Organization Reflected by the Household: A Study of Pre-Columbian Social Dynamics. *Journal of Field Archaeology* 9(2):165–181.

Bourdieu, Pierre. 1977. *Outline of a Theory of Practice.* Cambridge University Press, Cambridge.

Cancian, Frank. 1972. *Change and Uncertainty in a Peasant Economy: The Maya Corn Farmers of Zinacantan*. Stanford University Press, Stanford.

Canuto, Marcello A. 2002. A Tale of Two Communities: The Role of the Rural Community in the Socio-Political Integration of the Copan Drainage in the Late Preclassic and Classic Periods. PhD thesis, Department of Anthropology, University of Pennsylvania.

Canuto, Marcello A. 2004. The Rural Settlement of Copan: Changes through the Early Classic. In *Understanding Early Classic Copan*, edited by Ellen E. Bell, Marcello A. Canuto, and Robert J. Sharer, pp. 29–53. University of Pennsylvania Museum, University of Pennsylvania, Philadelphia.

Canuto, Marcello A., and William L. Fash. 2004. The Blind Spot: Where the Elite and Non-Elite Meet. In *Continuities and Changes in Maya Archaeology: Perspectives at the Millennium*, edited by Charles W. Golden and Greg Borgstede, pp. 47–70. Routledge, New York.

Canuto, Marcello A., and Jason Yaeger, eds. 2000. *The Archaeology of Communities: A New World Perspective*. Routledge, London

Carrasco, Pedro. 1971. Social Organization of Ancient Mexico. In *Handbook of Middle American Indians: Archaeology of Northern Mesoamerica, Part 1*, edited by Gordon F. Ekholm and Ignacio Bernal, pp. 349–375. University of Texas Press, Austin.

Coe, Michael D. 1965. A Model of Ancient Community Structure in the Maya Lowlands. *Southwestern Journal of Anthropology* 21(2):97–114.

Cohen, Anthony P. 1985. *The Symbolic Construction of Community*. Routledge, London.

de Montmollin, Olivier. 1988. Settlement Scale and Theory in Maya Archaeology. In *Recent Studies in Pre-Columbian Archaeology*, edited by Nicholas J. Saunders and Olivier de Montmollin, pp. 63–104. BAR International Series 431. British Archaeological Reports, Oxford.

Eberl, Markus. 2007. Community Heterogeneity and Integration: The Maya Sites of Nacimiento, Dos Ceibas, and Cerro de Cheyo (El Peten, Guatemala) during the Late Classic. PhD thesis, Department of Anthropology, Tulane University.

Flannery, Kent V., ed. 1976. *The Early Mesoamerican Village*. Academic Press, New York

Freter, Anne. 2004. Multiscalar Model of Rural Households and Communities in Late Classic Copan Maya Society. *Ancient Mesoamerica* 15(1):93–106.

Gibson, Charles. 1964. *The Aztecs under Spanish Rule: A History of the Indians of the Valley of Mexico, 1519–1810*. Stanford University Press., Stanford.

Giddens, Anthony. 1979. *Central Problems in Social Theory: Action, Structure, and Contradiction in Social Analysis*. Macmillan, London.

Goldkind, Victor. 1965. Social Stratification in the Peasant Community: Redfield's Chan Kom Reinterpreted. *American Anthropologist* 67:863–884.

Gould, Harold A. 1959. The Peasant Village: Centripetal or Centrifugal? *Eastern Anthropologist* 13:3–17.

Hare, Timothy S. 2000. Between the Household and the Empire: Structural Relationships within and among Aztec Communities and Polities. In *The Archaeology of Communities: A New World Perspective*, edited by Marcello A. Canuto and Jason Yaeger, pp. 78–101. Routledge, London.

Hastorf, Christine A. 2003. Community with the Ancestors: Ceremonies and Social Memory in the Middle Formative at Chiripa, Bolivia. *Journal of Anthropological Archaeology* 22(4):305–332.

Hayden, Brian, and Aubrey Cannon. 1982. The Corporate Group as an Archaeological Unit. *Journal of Anthropological Archaeology* 1:132–158.

Hendon, Julia A. 2010. *Houses in a Landscape: Memory and Everyday Life in Mesoamerica*. Duke University Press, Durham, North Carolina.

Hollingshead, August B. 1948. Community Research: Development and Present Condition. *American Sociological Review* 13:136–155.

Houston, Stephen D., Héctor Escobedo, Mark Child, Charles Golden, and René Muñoz. 2003. The Moral Community: Maya Settlement Transformation at Piedras Negras, Guatemala. In *The Social Construction of Ancient Cities*, edited by Monica L. Smith, pp. 212–253. Smithsonian Institution Press, Washington, DC.

Hutson, Scott R. 2010. *Dwelling, Identity, and the Maya: Relational Archaeology at Chunchucmil*. Archaeology in Society Series. Altamira, Plymouth, United Kingdom.

Hutson, Scott R., David Hixson, Aline Magnoni, Daniel E. Mazeau, and Bruce H. Dahlin. 2008. Site and Community at Chunchucmil and Ancient Maya Urban Centers. *Journal of Field Archaeology* 33(1):19–40.

Isbell, William H. 2000. What We Should Be Studying: The "Imagined Community" and the "Natural Community." In *The Archaeology of Communities: A New World Perspective*, edited by Marcello A. Canuto and Jason Yaeger, pp. 243–266. Routledge, London.

Johnson, Scott. 2011. Popola, Yucatan, Mexico: Using Communities to Explore Regional Political Interaction. Paper presented at "Climates of Change," the 44th annual Chacmool conference, Calgary, Alberta, Canada.

Joyce, Rosemary A., and Julia A. Hendon. 2000. Heterarchy, History, and Material Reality: "Communities" in Late Classic Honduras. In *The Archaeology of Communities: A New World Perspective*, edited by Marcello A. Canuto and Jason Yaeger, pp. 143–160. Routledge, London.

Knapp, A. Bernard. 2003. The Archaeology of Community on Bronze Age Cyprus: Politiko Phorades in Context. *American Journal of Archaeology* 107(4):559–580.

Layton, Robert. 1972. Settlement and Community. In *Man, Settlement, and Urbanism*, edited by Peter J. Ucko, Ruth Tringham, and G. W. Dimbleby, pp. 377–381. Duckworth, London.

Levi-Strauss, Claude. 1982. *The Way of the Masks*. University of Washington Press, Seattle.

Lipe, William D. 1992. Introduction. In *The Sand Canyon Archaeological Project: A Progress Report*, pp. 1–10. Occasional Paper No. 2, Crow Canyon Archaeological Center, Cortez, Colorado.

Lockhart, James. 1992. *The Nahuas after the Conquest: A Social and Cultural History of the Indians of Central Mexico, Sixteenth through Eighteenth Centuries*. Stanford University Press, Stanford.

Lopiparo, Jeanne. 2003. Household Ceramic Production and the Crafting of Society in the Terminal Classic of the Ulúa Valley, Honduras. Department of Anthropology, University of California, Berkeley.

Lopiparo, Jeanne. 2007. House Societies and Heterarchy in the Terminal Classic Ulúa Valley, Honduras. In *The Durable House: House Society Models in Archaeology*, edited by Robin A. Beck, pp. 73–96. Center of Archaeological Investigations Occasional Paper No. 35, Southern Illinois University, Carbondale.

Marcus, Joyce. 1983. On the Nature of the Mesoamerican City. In *Prehistoric Settlement Patterns: Essays in Honor of Gordon R. Willey*, edited by Evon Z. Vogt and Richard M. Leventhal, pp. 195–242. University of New Mexico Press and Peabody Museum of Archaeology and Ethnology, Harvard University, Albuquerque and Cambridge.

Marcus, Joyce. 2000. Toward an Archaeology of Communities. In *The Archaeology of Communities: A New World Perspective*, edited by Marcello A. Canuto and Jason Yaeger, pp. 231–242. Routledge, London.

Mathews, Steven G. 2004. Gesture, Gender, Ethnicity: The Instantiated Communities of Bronze Age Europe. *Archaeological Review from Cambridge* 19(2):56–72.

Miner, Horace. 1952. The Folk-Urban Continuum. *American Sociological Review* 17(5):529–537.

Mintz, Sidney W. 1953. The Folk-Urban Continuum and the Rural Proletarian Community. *American Journal of Sociology* LIX:136–143.

Monaghan, John. 1995. *The Covenants with Earth and Rain: Exchange, Sacrifice, and Revelation in Mixtec Sociality*. University of Oklahoma Press, Norman.

Murdock, George P. 1949. *Social Structure*. Macmillan, New York.

Netting, Robert McC. 1982. Some Home Truths on Household Size and Wealth. *Archaeology of the Household: Building a Prehistory of Domestic Life* 25(6):641–662.

Rambo, A. Terry. 1977. Closed Corporate and Open Peasant Communities: Re-opening a Hastily Shut Case. *Comparative Studies in Society and History* 19:179–188.

Redfield, Robert. 1955. *The Little Community: Viewpoints for the Study of a Human Whole*. University of Chicago Press, Chicago.

Reeves, Matthew B. 2003. Reinterpreting Manassas: The Nineteenth-Century African American Community at Manassas National Battlefield Park. *Historical Archaeology* 37(3):124–137.

Restall, Matthew. 1997. *The Maya World: Yucatec Society and Culture, 1550–1850*. Stanford University Press, Stanford.

Robin, Cynthia. 1999. Toward an Archaeology of Everyday Life: Maya Farmers of Chan Nòhool and Dos Chombitos Cik'in, Belize. Department of Anthropology, University of Pennsylvania.

Robin, Cynthia. 2003. New Directions in Classic Maya Household Archaeology. *Journal of Archaeological Research* 11(4):307–356.

Sanders, William T. 1981. Classic Maya Settlement Patterns and Ethnographic Analogy. In *Lowland Maya Settlement Patterns*, edited by Wendy A. Ashmore, pp. 351–369. University of New Mexico Press, Albuquerque.

Spencer-Wood, Suzanne. 1989. Community as Household: Domestic Reform, Mid-Range Theory and the Domestication of Public Space. In *Households and Communities*, edited by Scott MacEachern, David J. W. Archer, and Richard D. Garvin, pp. 113–122. Chacmool annual conference, Archaeological Association, University of Calgary, Calgary.

Tarlow, Sarah. 2002. Excavating Utopia: Why Archaeologists Should Study "Ideal" Communities of the Nineteenth Century. *International Journal of Historical Archaeology* 6(4):299–323.

Tax, Sol. 1951. *Penny Capitalism, a Guatemalan Indian Economy*. Institute for Social Anthropology, Smithsonian Institute, Washington, DC.

Urban, Greg. 1996. *Metaphysical Community*. University of Texas Press, Austin.

Varien, Mark D., and James M. Potter, 2008a. *The Social Construction of Communities: Agency, Structure and Identity in the Prehispanic Southwest*. Archaeology in Society, Altamira, Plymouth, United Kingdom.

Varien, Mark D., and James M. Potter. 2008b. The Social Production of Communities: Structure, Agency, and Identity. In *The Social Construction of Communities: Agency, Structure and Identity in the Prehispanic Southwest*, edited by Mark D. Varien and James M. Potter, pp. 1–18. Altamira, Plymouth, United Kingdom.

Varien, Mark D., and Richard H. Wilshusen, eds. 2002. *Seeking the Center Place: Archaeology and Ancient Communities in the Mesa Verde Region*. University of Utah Press, Salt Lake City.

Watanabe, John M. 1992. *Maya Saints and Souls in a Changing World*. University of Texas Press, Austin.

Wilk, Richard R., and Wendy A. Ashmore, eds. 1988. *Household and Community in the Mesoamerican Past*. University of New Mexico Press, Albuquerque.

Wilk, Richard R., and William L. Rathje. 1982. Household Archaeology. *American Behavioral Scientist* 25(6):617–639.

Willey, Gordon R., William R. Bullard, and John B. Glass. 1955. The Maya Community of Prehistoric Times. *Archaeology* 8(1):18–25.

Wolf, Eric R. 1957. Closed Corporate Peasant Communities in Mesoamerica and Central Java. *Southwestern Journal of Anthropology* 13:1–18.

Wolf, Eric R. 1986. The Vicissitudes of the Closed Corporate Peasant Community. *American Ethnologist* 13:325–329.

Yaeger, Jason. 2000. The Social Construction of Communities in the Classic Maya Countryside. In *The Archaeology of Communities: A New World Perspective*, edited by Marcello A. Canuto and Jason Yaeger, pp. 123–142. Routledge, London.

Yaeger, Jason. 2003a. Small Settlements in the Upper Belize River Valley: Local Complexity, Household Strategies of Affiliation, and Changing Organization. In *Perspectives on Ancient Maya Rural Complexity*, edited by Gyles Iannone and Samuel V. Connell, pp. 42–58. Monograph 49, Cotsen Institute of Archaeology, University of California, Los Angeles.

Yaeger, Jason. 2003b. Untangling the Ties That Bind: The City, the Countryside, and the Nature of Maya Urbanism at Xunantunich, Belize. In *The Social Construction of Ancient Cities*, edited by Monica L. Smith, pp. 121–155. Smithsonian Books, Washington, DC.

Yaeger, Jason, and Cynthia Robin. 2004. Heterogeneous Hinterlands: The Social and Political Organization of Commoner Settlements Near Xunantunich, Belize. In *Ancient Maya Commoners*, edited by Jon C. Lohse and Fred Valdez, Jr., pp. 147–173. University of Texas Press, Austin.

CHAPTER 53

....

CITIES AND
URBANISM IN
PREHISPANIC
MESOAMERICA

....

RICHARD E. BLANTON

CITIES were an important and endurable characteristic of Mesoamerican civilization after 500 BC.[1] This aspect of the Mesoamerican past was not widely recognized until the 1960s and 1970s when settlement-pattern archaeologists initiated field research at Teotihuacan (Millon 1973), Monte Albán (Blanton 1978), and Dzibilchaltún (Kurjack 1974). Since these pioneering efforts, archaeologists and ethnohistorians not only have amassed an impressive body of data (summary and synthetic sources include Andrews 1975; Blanton et al. 1993; Ciudad Ruíz et al. 2001; Cowgill 1997; Iannone and Connell 2003; Joyce 2009; Kowalewski 1990; Kowalewski et al. 1989, 2009; Manzanilla and Chapdelaine 2009; Pollard 2003; Ringle 1999; Sanders, Parsons, and Santley 1979; Sanders et al. 2003; M. E. Smith 2005, 2008), but they also have turned to other disciplines, principally sociology and geography, for new methods and theories (e.g., Blanton et al. 1993; Joyce 2009; Marcus 1983; Sanders and Webster 1988). Some researchers have translated their Mesoamerican experiences into sources intended for a broader audience (Blanton 1976; Cowgill 2004; Smith 2007, 2010a 2010b), while general works on cities and urbanism in some cases include Mesoamerican cases or develop ideas stemming from Mesoamerican examples (e.g., Iglesias Ponce de Léon et al. 2006; Marcus and Sabloff 2008; M. L. Smith 2003; G. Storey 2006b).

---

1. Below, I distinguish between the related concepts of cities and urbanism.

"REGAL-RITUAL" MESOAMERICAN CITIES?

Were Mesoamerican cities comparable to premodern cities in the Old World? We do recognize several highly distinctive formal features of Mesoamerican cities: for one, Mesoamerican public buildings typically were connected by open plaza or patio spaces (Arancón García 1992), in some cases resulting in exceptionally large and spatially integrated concourses (Kubler 1962: 29). Also, most building complexes and, sometimes, whole city plans, mimic the widely shared Mesoamerican idea of a cosmos structured by cardinal directionality and multiple vertical levels (Figure 53.1).[2] William Sanders and David Webster (Sanders and Webster 1988; Webster and Sanders 2001) went beyond formal design features to argue that Mesoamerican cities can be contrasted with cities in other civilizations in that they most often served in an ideological capacity as the "regal-ritual" sites of cults and ritual cycles that certified the power of rulers (following the typology in Fox [1977]), and, as such, typically lacked the administrative and mercantile functions driving most city growth in the Old World. According to this scheme, regal-ritual cities, limited largely to ideological functions, would not attract the large, high-density resident populations that would denote true "urban" status (the latter argued to be two thousand persons per square kilometer and a minimum of five thousand to six thousand for the total population in Sanders and Price [1968: 47]); hence, Mesoamerica was not viewed as a highly urbanized civilization.[3]

2. Apart from three well-known central Mexican examples where we see orthogonal design aligning streets with cardinal directions, at Teotihuacan (Millon 1973), Tula (Guadalupe Mastache et al. 2002: Figure 6.9), and Tenochtitlan (Calnek 2003: 157), there is little other credible evidence of city planning in Mesoamerica beyond the scale of plaza-structure complexes, but this is currently a topic of research and debate (cf. Ashmore 2005; Ashmore and Sabloff 2002; Aveni 2001; Smith 2003, 2008: 10, 201–203).

3. By contrast, administrative cities are assumed to achieve urban status, with their large populations of administrators and support personnel, and mercantile cities would also feature large and dense populations of city-dwelling merchants and craft specialists. Sanders and Webster (1988) identify only two Mesoamerican cities as having been administrative, and, hence, truly urban: Teotihuacan and Tenochtitlan-Tlatelolco. They also argued that mercantile activities were not an important force in bringing city growth in Mesoamerica (ibid.: 539-540). These two authors attribute limited urban growth in Mesoamerica to the inherent constraints of prehispanic Mesoamerican transport technologies and biotechnologies that resulted in a lower potential for per capita production of surplus and transport of farm produce and other products to distant cities (Sanders and Santley 1983; Sanders and Webster 1988; Webster and Sanders 2001). This claim can be investigated, partially, based on a systematic comparison of Mediterranean and Mesoamerican premodern settlement patterns (Neolithic to Late Roman, and Early Formative through Late Postclassic, respectively) (Blanton 2004). Although Mediterranean urbanism cannot stand as a proxy for all Old World civilizations, the results of the comparison are still of interest. I found few inherent differences in biotechnological productivity or transport efficiency, and, from systematic settlement-pattern data, found that, on average, Mesoamerican cities were actually larger

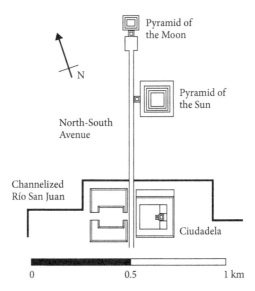

Figure 53.1 Central Teotihuacan, showing an east-west division created by the major north-south avenue, and a north-south division created by channeling the Río San Juan. As interpreted by Sugiyama (1993, 2005), Millon (1981), and Cowgill (2000), the north-south division symbolized a distinction between a watery underworld zone and a celestial realm symbolized by the origin myths of the sun and moon. Most Teotihuacan buildings adhered to an orientation 15.5 degrees east of astronomic north and 16.5 or 17 degrees south of true east (modified from Sugiyama 2005: Fig. 14; drawing by Kristin Sullivan).

The regal-ritual city concept does capture some of the variation found in pre-hispanic Mesoamerica, but only within the context of the comparatively "segmentary" (weakly bureaucratized) states found in certain Maya polities of the Classic period (e.g., Ball and Taschek 1991; Fash 2005) and the Postclassic (Fox 1987). These centers featured core complexes of plazas, palaces, ballcourts, and structures commemorating royal burials (e.g., McAnany 1998; Figure 53.2) where, to counter the prevailing centrifugal tendencies of weak political integration (Inomata 2006a: 206), theatrical-like spectacles were conducted that allowed sovereigns to display "wealth, sacrality, and gestures of generosity to courtiers" (Houston 2006: 139; cf. Inomata 2006b). And the idea of the regal-ritual city is perhaps consistent with the generally low population densities of lowland Classic Maya cities (Rice 2006). Tikal, for example, has been estimated at 517 people per square kilometer (Culbert et al. 1990), comparatively dense for a lowland Classic Maya city but less than the estimated 6,300 to 7,500 people per square kilometer for Teotihuacan (based on

than Mediterranean cities, although the population of Rome (estimated at three hundred thousand by G. Storey [1997]) was larger than the largest Mesoamerican cities—Teotihuacan and Tenochtitlan-Tlatelolco, each with an estimated population in the range of one hundred thousand to two hundred thousand (Cowgill 1997; Sanders 2003).

Figure 53.2 A probable example of a lowland Maya Classic-period regal-ritual center,
at Aguateca, Guatemala. A massive palace, causeway, and plaza-group complex is
surrounded by scattered elite residential plaza-structure groups and other residences
(from Inomata [2008: Fig. 1.8]; with permission of the author).

Drennan 1988: Table 13.1; Millon 1973: 45) or the 1,000 to 15,700 people per square
kilometer density of central Mexican Postclassic cities (Smith 2008: Table 2.1). Yet
not all lowland Maya cities of the Classic period had low densities, as we have
learned at the site of Chunchucmil (Figure 53.3). And a low population density
should not necessarily result from the social and demographic processes associated
with regal-ritual cities. Dispersed settlement patterns may have multiple causes,
including some forms of agricultural intensification in tropical lowland environments (Drennan 1988; Tourtellot 1993), as Stark (1999) discovered in her study of
the Classic period in the tropical lower Papaloapan Basin, where she encountered

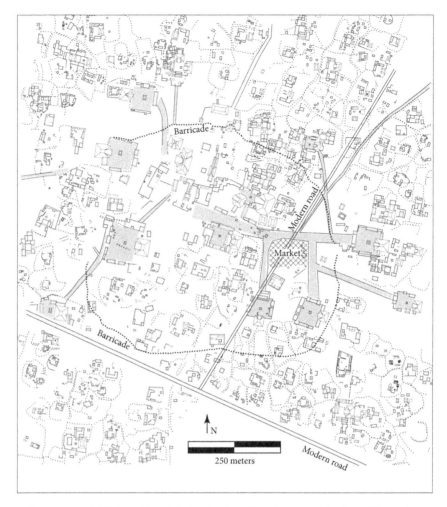

Figure 53.3 A high residential density in a Classic-period lowland Maya city, Chunchucmil, Mexico (Hutson et al. 2008; reproduced with permission of Scott Hutson).

a "dispersed capital zone" that appears to have resulted from an increase in cotton exports to highland cities.

The idea that the regal-ritual city was the dominant Mesoamerican pattern has been critically evaluated (e.g., D. Chase, A. Chase, and Haviland 1990; A. Chase and D. Chase 1996), and these arguments are convincing that Mesoamerican cities cannot be understood in relation to any predominant pattern. Even within the limited framework of the lowland Late Classic Maya area, archaeologists have discovered a surprising degree of variation in city size, form, and function (e.g., Demarest 2006). A wide range of estimated peak population sizes for Classic Maya cities has been discovered, up to an estimated 62,000 for central Tikal (Culbert et al. 1990: 116), 42,000 for Dzibilchaltún (Kurjack 1974: 94), 43,000 to 62,500 at Cobá (Kintz and Fletcher 1983: 197–200), 50,000 at Calakmul (Folan et al. 1995: 310), and 115,000 to 150,000 in 177 square kilometers at Caracol (A. Chase and D. Chase 2003). These population values are substantial compared with other Mesoamerican regions (Smith 2005) and Old World preindustrial cities (Chandler and Fox 1974), and these point to the possibility that, even in the lowland Maya Classic period, cities combined to varying degrees regal-ritual duties with administrative (e.g., at Caracol [A. Chase and D. Chase 2003]) and mercantile functions (e.g., at Chunchucmil [Dahlin et al. 2007; Hutson et al. 2008]). The possibility that mercantile functions were one important social force driving city growth in Mesoamerica is becoming more evident in the Maya area and elsewhere (Blanton 1996; Dahlin 2009; Dahlin et al. 2007; Hirth 1998; the growing interest in markets is evident in Garraty and Stark 2010). (I return to this issue below.)

CITIES, TOWNS, AND URBANISM IN SOCIETY

The typological comparative method pioneered by Fox (1977) is of limited utility when we consider the great diversity in prehispanic Mesoamerican cities, leading researchers to turn to a multiscalar approach that is more analytically suited to such a complex topic. In multiscalar theory, cities are seen as the product of the cumulative effects of social action found at various spatial scales of the household, neighborhood, community, region (a local network of cities and their hinterlands), macroregion (multiple interacting regions), and world-system (a multicultural political and economic system featuring a core-periphery hierarchy) (e.g., Blanton et al. 1999; Feinman and Nicholas 1991, 2010; Kepecs and Kohl 2003).[4] At the scale of regions, cities are viewed as nodes or nuclei (central places) where ideological as well as administrative, religious, and commercial activities are concentrated (e.g., Blanton 1976; Kowalewski 1990; Marcus 1983). This scale of analysis is well suited to asking questions about the nature of social interactions between the governing elites (and other urban groups such as mercantile organizations) and commoner and other hinterland populations (e.g., Nichols 2004). One expression of a regional perspective is found in Hirth (2003, 2008), A. Chase et al. (2009), and M. E. Smith (2008), in which cities are interpreted as nodes in the regional systems of taxation and political control. But to better understand the nature of rural-urban social

4. Millon (1973) and his colleagues first reported foreign enclaves at Teotihuacan, and this finding has stimulated interest in the role of long-distance migration in the social and cultural composition of urban populations. Recent advances in the analysis of bone chemistry have advanced this line of study greatly (e.g., Price et al. 2008; Spence et al. 2005; Spence and White 2009). Now that bone chemistry assays are becoming a more routine archaeological method, a surprising amount of long-distance migration has been discovered not only in foreign enclaves at Teotihuacan but also in multiethnic barrios there (summarized in Manzanilla 2009).

differentiation and economic change, regional analysts must also address how regional networks of cities provided rural and other provincial households with access to public goods and markets (e.g., Blanton and Fargher 2008).

Macroregional and world-system approaches bring to light multiple avenues of investigation relevant to understanding city formation and change. Balkansky (1998) points to cases where new cities are established as a defensive response to external enemies, similar to the *synoikism* in Classical Greek experience (Demand 1990), for example, in the origins of Monte Albán as proposed by Blanton and colleagues (Blanton 1978; Blanton et al. 1999: 63–65), and at Monte Negro in the Mixteca Alta region (Balkansky et al. 2004). The foundation of a new political regime and capital at Late Postclassic Tlaxcala, Mexico, was in response to pressure from the Aztec Empire (Fargher et al. 2010, 2011). In this case synoikism was a consideration in the foundation of the new capital; however, the staging of political change in an existing capital, where the urban infrastructure is replete with symbols and spaces associated with the old order, presents challenges to state builders. Political change is facilitated by moving the capital center to a new location or by substantially rebuilding an old city, as happened at Teotihuacan with the radical political restructuring and urban renewal of the third century CE (Millon 1992: 397).

A multiscalar perspective is a powerful tool for investigating urban change during the transition from the Classic to the Epiclassic (the Terminal Classic in the Maya area) and Postclassic periods that saw a reordering of Mesoamerica's world-system geography (Smith and Berdan, 2003a) and the widespread adoption of the Quetzalcoatl cult over a vast area from central Mexico to the Northern Maya area (Berlo and Diehl 1989, Ringle et al. 1998). Growing world-system interactions resulted in restructured regional and macroregional networks of cities across a wide zone from the Central Highlands to the Maya area (Kepecs and Masson 2003; Smith and Berdan 2003b). In Yucatán, Chichén Itzá (Kepecs 2007) and Mayapán (e.g., Masson et al. 2006; Paris 2008) emerged as prominent political and trade centers and like other Yucatán cities featured new kinds of civic spaces including open elevated plazas and "quadrangle" court complexes in sites such as Uxmal, and capacious open plazas and large sheltered spaces in the form of colonnaded halls (e.g., Ringle and Bey 2001; Stone 1999). These urban designs are consistent with the development of council-based governance and a growing degree of political participation across social sectors at a time when rule by divine kings was in decline (e.g., D. Chase and A. Chase 1988; Cobos 2007; Ringle and Bey 2001; Schele and Freidel 1990: 348–349; Stone 1999).

THE PROBLEMS WITH URBANISM

Regional and world-system perspectives contextualize city growth and form in relation to interactive networks of centers, but a large-scale perspective is fruitfully combined with the study of urbanism, or how persons and groups organize themselves, or are organized, to manage city living. In Mesoamerica, this question has been addressed principally by the study of occupational specialization, ethnic diversity, and urban neighborhoods (*barrios* and ethnic enclaves) and administrative districts, for example, at Monte Albán (Blanton 1978; González Licón 2009), Teotihuacan (Millon 1981; Cowgill et al. 1984; Spence 1996; Manzanilla 1996, 2004, 2009), Xochicalco (Hirth 2000, 2009), Tula (e.g., Healan 2009), and Tenochtitlan-Tlatelolco (Calnek 2003; van Zantwijk 1985) and other Aztec cities (Smith 2008). While city living provides amenities, especially propinquity to information networks and marketplaces, it also poses problems stemming from crowding, which brings threats to health and safety such as fire danger and disease (the "urban grave-yard effect" in G. Storey [2006a: 5–9]; cf. Nichols [2006]; Storey [1992]), competition for space, and social and cultural diversity that can enhance the potential for conflict and other social problems (Kostoff 1992: 102–110). Adapting to urban biosocial challenges is a generative force for social, technological, and cultural innovation and change (e.g., Fletcher 1995; Joyce 2009), perhaps even in situations of relatively low population density. For example, Stark (2003) proposes that in the context of the dispersed settlement pattern of the lower Papaloapan Basin in the Classic period, "urban gardening" and water management would have raised issues surrounding land value, land abundance, and land rights (cf. Scarborough and Gallopin 1990; Stark and Ossa 2007).

CITY AND MORAL COMMUNITY

The urban landscape plays a role in the creation of community when civic buildings and spaces are material expressions of the moral order of society (Kostoff 1991; Wheatley 1983: 1). To many Mesoamericanists, the central element of the ancient moral order was the sacred authority of ruling families (e.g., Ashmore 2009; Houston et al. 2003; Houston and Taube 2000; Kowalski 1999; Sanders and Webster 1988), but Rykwert (1998) takes on a different analytical task when he asks how city form creates a sacred space where originating dramas are played out that evoke a sense of civic identity and obligation to the city itself. Mesoamericanists would benefit by following this lead to entertain the possibility that civic or corporate goals informed urban design (e.g., Connell 2003: 40). In Classic-period Teotihuacan, where rulers were not named and dynastic mortuary cults were nonexistent (Manzanilla 2006), the city's design, as described in Figure 53.1, reflected the earth's four quarters, vertical divisions distinguishing between a zone of heaven (north) and a watery underworld (south), as well as numerology based on the significance of the 260-day ritual cycle (e.g., Cowgill 2000; Millon 1981; Sugiyama 1993, 2005). Cowgill (2003: 44–45) and Pasztory (1992, 1997) suggest

Figure 53.4 Folio 2r from the Codex Mendoza (Berdan and Anawalt 1992; redrawn by
Kristin Sullivan; reproduced with the permission of Frances Berdan).

that these expressions of cosmic themes made the city an object of devotion that
could evoke feelings of collective identity and obligation. An analogy is possibly
to be found in the representation of Tenochtitlan in the Codex Mendoza (e.g.,
in Berdan and Anawalt 1997; Figure 53.4). This image depicts the city's foundation, but with humans shown only as subordinate elements in a design concept
that situates ethnically diverse founding groups in relation to a cosmic structure
specifying each of their roles in the city's organizational structure and functions
(van Zantwijk 1985: Chapter 4; cf. Carrasco 1999: Chapter 1).

REFERENCES

Andrews, George F. 1975. *Maya Cities: Placemaking and Urbanization*. University of Oklahoma Press, Norman.

Arancón García, Ricardo. 1992. Las plaza: Generadora del espacio urbano Mesoamericano. *Cuadernos de Arquitectura Mesoamericana* 16:29–39.

Ashmore, Wendy. 2005. The Idea of a Maya Town. In *Structure and Meaning in Human Settlements*, edited by Tony Atkin and Joseph Rykwert, pp. 35–54. University Museum of Archaeology and Anthropology, Philadelphia.

Ashmore, Wendy. 2009. Mesoamerican Landscape Archaeologies. *Ancient Mesoamerica* 20:183–187.

Ashmore, Wendy, and Jeremy A. Sabloff. 2002. Spatial Orders in Maya Civic Plans. *Latin American Antiquity* 13:201–215.

Aveni, Anthony F. 2001. *Skywatchers: A Revised and Updated Version of Skywatchers of Ancient Mexico*. University of Texas Press, Austin.

Balkansky, Andrew K. 1998. Urbanism and Early State Formation in the Huamelulpan Valley of Southern Mexico. *Latin American Antiquity* 9:37–67.

Balkansky, Andrew K., Verónica Pérez Rodríguez, and Stephen A. Kowalewski. 2004. Monte Negro and the Urban Revolution in Oaxaca, Mexico. *Latin American Antiquity* 15:33–60.

Ball, Joseph W., and Jennifer T. Taschek. 1991. Late Classic Lowland Maya Political Organization and Central-Place Analysis: New Insights from the Upper Belize Valley. *Ancient Mesoamerica* 2:149–165.

Berdan, Frances F., and Patricia Rieff Anawalt. 1992. *The Codex Mendoza, Volume 4: A Facsimile Reproduction of the Codex Mendoza*. p. 11. University of California Press, Berkeley.

Berdan, Frances F., and Patricia Rieff Anawalt. 1997. *The Essential Codex Mendoza*. University of California Press, Berkeley.

Berlo, Janet Catherine, and Richard A. Diehl, eds. 1989. *Mesoamerica after the Decline of Teotihuacan, AD 700–900*. Dumbarton Oaks Research Library and Collection, Washington, DC.

Blanton, Richard E. 1976. Anthropological Studies of Cities. *Annual Review of Anthropology* 5:249–264.

Blanton, Richard E. 1978. *Monte Albán: Settlement Patterns at the Ancient Zapotec Capital*. Academic Press, New York.

Blanton, Richard E. 1996. The Basin of Mexico Market System and the Growth of Empire. In *Aztec Imperial Strategies*, edited by Frances F. Berdan, Richard E. Blanton, Elizabeth H. Boone, Mary G. Hodge, Michael E. Smith, and Emily Umberger, pp. 47–84. Dumbarton Oaks Research Library and Collection, Washington, DC.

Blanton, Richard E. 2004. Settlement Pattern and Population Change in Mesoamerican and Mediterranean Civilizations. In *Side-By-Side Survey: Comparative Regional Studies in the Mediterranean World*, edited by Susan E. Alcock and John F. Cherry, pp. 206–240. Oxbow Books, Oxford.

Blanton, Richard E., and Lane F. Fargher. 2008. *Collective Action in the Formation of Pre-Modern States*. Springer, New York.

Blanton, Richard E., Gary M. Feinman, Stephen A. Kowalewski, and Linda M. Nicholas. 1999. *Ancient Oaxaca: The Monte Albán State*. Cambridge University Press, Cambridge.

Blanton, Richard E., Stephen A. Kowalewski, Gary M. Feinman, and Laura Finsten. 1993. *Ancient Mesoamerica: A Comparison of Change in Three Regions*. Cambridge University Press, Cambridge.

Calnek, Edward. 2003. Tenochtitlan-Tlatelolco: The Natural History of a City. In *El urbanismo en Mésoamerica: Urbanism in Mesoamerica*, edited by William T. Sanders, Alba Guadalupe Mastache, and Robert H. Cobean, pp. 149–202. Instituto Nacional de Antropología e Historia, Mexico, D.F., and Pennsylvania State University, University Park.

Carrasco, David. 1999. *City of Sacrifice: The Aztec Empire and the Role of Violence in Civilization*. Beacon, Boston.

Chandler, Tertius, and Gerald Fox. 1974. *3,000 Years of Urban Growth*. Academic Press, New York.

Chase, Arlen F., and Diane Z. Chase. 1996. More Than Kin and King: Centralized Political Organization among the Late Classic Maya. *Current Anthropology* 37:803–810.

Chase, Arlen F., and Diane Z. Chase. 2003. Minor Centers, Complexity, and Scale in Lowland Maya Settlement Archaeology. In *Perspectives on Ancient Maya Rural Complexity*, edited by Gyles Iannone and Samuel V. Connell, pp. 27–41. Cotsen Institute of Archaeology, University of California, Los Angeles.

Chase, Arlen F., Diane Z. Chase, and Michael E. Smith. 2009. States and Empires in Ancient Mesoamerica. *Ancient Mesoamerica* 20:175–182.

Chase, Diane Z., and Arlen F. Chase. 1988. *A Postclassic Perspective: Excavations at the Maya Site of Santa Rita Corozal, Belize*. Monograph 4, Pre-Columbian Art Research Institute, San Francisco.

Chase, Diane Z., Arlen F. Chase, and William A. Haviland. 1990. The Classic Maya City: Reconsidering the "Mesoamerican" Urban Tradition. *American Anthropologist* 92:499–506.

Ciudad Ruíz, Andrés, Josefa Iglesias Ponce de Leon, and Carmen Martínez Martínez. 2001. *Reconstruyendo la ciudad Maya: El urbanismo en las sociedades antiguas*. Sociedad Española de Estudios Mayas, Madrid.

Cobos, Rafael. 2007. *Multepal* or Centralized Kingship? New Evidence on Governmental Organization at Chichén Itzá. In *Twin Tollans: Chichén Itzá, Tula, and the Epiclassic to Early Postclassic Mesoamerican World*, edited by Jeff Karl Kowalski and Cynthia Kristan-Graham, pp. 316–343. Dumbarton Oaks Library and Collection, Washington, DC.

Connell, Samuel V. 2003. Making Sense of Variability among Minor Centers: The Ancient Maya of Chaa Creek, Belize. In *Perspectives on Ancient Maya Rural Complexity*, edited by Gyles Iannone and Samuel V. Connell, pp. 27–42. Cotsen Institute of Archaeology, University of California, Los Angeles.

Cowgill, George L. 1997. State and Society at Teotihuacan, Mexico. *Annual Review of Anthropology* 26:129–161.

Cowgill, George L. 2000. Intentionality and Meaning in the Layout of Teotihuacan, Mexico. *Cambridge Journal of Archaeology* 10:358–365.

Cowgill, George L. 2003. Teotihuacan: Cosmic Glories and Mundane Needs. In *The Social Construction of Ancient Cities*, edited by Monica L. Smith, pp. 37–55. Smithsonian Books, Washington, DC.

Cowgill, George L. 2004. Origins and Development of Urbanism: Archaeological Perspectives. *Annual Review of Anthropology* 33:525–549.

Cowgill, George, Jeffrey H. Altschul, and Rebecca S. Sload. 1984. Spatial Analysis of Teotihuacan: A Mesoamerican Metropolis. In *Intrasite Spatial Analysis in*

Archaeology, edited by Harold J. Hietala, pp. 154–195. Cambridge University Press, Cambridge.

Culbert, T. Patrick, Laura J. Kosakowsky, Robert E. Fry, and William A. Haviland. 1990. The Population of Tikal, Guatemala. In *Pre-Columbian Population History in the Maya Lowlands*, edited by T. Patrick Culbert and Don S. Rice, pp. 103–122. University of New Mexico Press, Albuquerque.

Dahlin, Bruce H. 2009. Ahead of Its Time? The Remarkable Early Classic Maya Economy of Chunchucmil. *Journal of Social Archaeology* 9:341–367.

Dahlin, Bruce, H., Christopher T. Jensen, Richard E. Terry, David R. Wright, and Timothy Beach. 2007. In Search of an Ancient Maya Market. *Latin American Antiquity* 18:363–384.

Demand, Nancy H. 1990. *Urban Relocation in Archaic and Classical Greece: Flight and Consolidation*. University of Oklahoma Press, Norman.

Demarest, Arthur A. 2006. Sacred and Profane Mountains of the Pasión: Contrasting Architectural Paths to Power. In *Palaces and Power in the Americas: From Peru to the Northwest Coast*, edited by Jessica Joyce Christie and Patricia Joan Sarro, pp. 117–140. University of Texas Press, Austin.

Drennan, Robert D. 1988. Household Location and Compact versus Dispersed Settlement Pattern in Prehispanic Mesoamerica. In *Household and Community in the Mesoamerican Past*, edited by Richard R. Wilk and Wendy Ashmore, pp. 273–294. University of New Mexico Press, Albuquerque.

Fargher, Lane F. Richard E. Blanton, and Verenice Heredia Espinoza. 2010. Egalitarian Ideology and Political Power in Pre-Hispanic Central Mexico: The Case of Tlaxcallan. *Latin American Antiquity* 21:227–251.

Fargher, Lane F., Richard E. Blanton, Verenice Y. Heredia Espinoza, John Millhauser, Nezahualcoyotl Xiutecuhtli, and Lisa Overholtzer. 2011. Tlaxcallan: The Archaeology of an Ancient Republic in the New World. *Antiquity* 85:172-186.

Fash, William L. 2005. Toward a Social History of the Copán Valley. In *Copán: The History of an Ancient Maya Kingdom*, edited by E. Wyllys Andrews and William L. Fash, pp. 73–101. School of American Research Press, Santa Fe.

Feinman, Gary M., and Linda M. Nicholas. 1991. New Perspectives on Prehispanic Highland Mesoamerica: A Macroregional Approach. *Comparative Civilizations Review* 24:13–33.

Feinman, Gary M., and Linda M. Nicholas. 2010. A Multiscalar Perspective on Market Exchange in the Classic-Period Valley of Oaxaca. In *Archaeological Approaches to Market Exchange in Ancient Societies*, edited by Christopher P. Garraty and Barbara L. Stark, pp. 85–98. University Press of Colorado, Boulder.

Fletcher, Roland. 1995. *The Limits of Settlement Growth: A Theoretical Outline*. Cambridge University Press, Cambridge.

Folan, William J., Joyce Marcus, Sophia Pincemin, Maria del Rosario Dominguez Carrasco, Laraine Fletcher, and Abel Morales López. 1995. Calakmul: New Data from an Ancient Maya Capital in Campeche, Mexico. *Latin American Antiquity* 6:310–334.

Fox, John W. 1987. *Maya Postclassic State Formation: Segmentary Lineage Migration in Advancing Frontiers*. Cambridge University Press, Cambridge.

Fox, Richard G. 1977. *Urban Anthropology: Cities in Their Cultural Settings*. Prentice-Hall, Englewood Cliffs, New Jersey.

Garraty, Christopher P., and Barbara L. Stark, eds. 2010. *Archaeological Approaches to Market Exchange in Ancient Societies*. University Press of Colorado, Boulder.

González Licon, Ernesto. 2009. Ritual and Social Differentiation at Monte Albán,
    Oaxaca: Strategies from a Household Perspective. In *Domestic Life in Prehispanic
    Capitals: A Study of Specialization, Hierarchy, and Ethnicity*, edited by Linda R.
    Manzanilla and Claude Chapdelaine, pp. 7–20. Memoir 46 of the University of
    Michigan Museum of Anthropology, Ann Arbor.

Guadalupe Mastache, Alba, Robert H. Cobean, and Dan M. Healan. 2002. *Ancient
    Tollan: Tula and the Toltec Heartland*. University of Colorado Press, Boulder.

Healan, Dan M. 2009. Household, Neighborhood, and Urban Structure in an "Adobe
    City": Tula, Hidalgo, Mexico. In *Domestic Life in Prehispanic Capitals: A Study of
    Specialization, Hierarchy, and Ethnicity*, edited by Linda R. Manzanilla and Claude
    Chapdelaine, pp. 67–88. Memoir 46 of the University of Michigan Museum of
    Anthropology, Ann Arbor.

Hirth, Ken. 1998. The Distributional Approach: A New Way to Identify
    Marketplace Exchange in the Archaeological Record. *Current Anthropology*
    39:451–467.

Hirth, Ken. 2000. *Ancient Urbanism at Xochicalco: The Evolution and Organization of a
    Pre-Hispanic Society*. University of Utah Press, Salt Lake City.

Hirth, Ken. 2003. The Altepetl and Urban Structure in Prehispanic Mesoamerica. In
    El urbanismo en Mésoamerica: Urbanism in Mesoamerica, edited by William T.
    Sanders, Alba Guadalupe Mastache, and Robert H. Cobean, pp. 57–84. Instituto
    Nacional de Antropología e Historia, Mexico, D.F., and Pennsylvania State
    University, University Park.

Hirth, Ken. 2008. Incidental Urbanism: The Structure of the Prehispanic City in Central
    Mexico. In *The Ancient City: New Perspectives on Urbanism in the Old and New
    World*, edited by Joyce Marcus and Jeremy A. Sabloff, pp. 273–297. School for
    Advanced Research Press, Santa Fe.

Hirth, Ken. 2009. Household, Workshop, Guild, and Barrio: The Organization of Craft
    Production in a Prehispanic Urban Center. In *Domestic Life in Prehispanic Capitals:
    A Study of Specialization, Hierarchy, and Ethnicity*, edited by Linda R. Manzanilla
    and Claude Chapdelaine, pp. 43–66. Memoir 46 of the University of Michigan
    Museum of Anthropology, Ann Arbor.

Houston, Stephen D. 2006. Impersonation, Dance, and the Problem of Spectacle among
    the Classic Maya. In *Archaeology of Performance: Theaters of Power, Community,
    and Politics*, edited by Takeshi Inomata and Lawrence S. Coben, pp. 135–155.
    Altamira, Lanham, Maryland.

Houston, Stephen D., Héctor Escobedo, Mark Child, Charles Golden, and René Muñoz.
    2003. The Moral Community: Maya Settlement Transformation at Piedras Negras,
    Guatemala. In *The Social Construction of Ancient Cities*, edited by Monica L. Smith,
    pp. 212–253. Smithsonian Books, Washington, DC.

Houston, Stephen D., and Karl Taube. 2000. An Archaeology of the Senses: Perception
    and Cultural Expression in Ancient Mesoamerica. *Cambridge Journal of
    Archaeology* 10:261–294.

Hutson, Scott R., David R. Hixson, Aline Magnoni, Daniel Mazeau, and Bruce Dahlin.
    2008. Site and Community at Chunchucmil, and Ancient Maya Urban Centers.
    Journal of Field Archaeology 33:19–40.

Iannone, Gyles, and Samuel V. Connell, eds. 2003. *Perspectives on Ancient Maya Rural
    Complexity*. Cotsen Institute of Archaeology, University of California, Los Angeles.

Iglesias Ponce de León, Josefa, Rogelio Valencia Rivera, and Andrés Ciudad Ruíz, eds.
    2006. *Nuevas ciudades, nuevas patrias: Fundación y relocalización de ciudades en*

Mésoamerica y el Mediterráneo antiguo. Sociedad Española de Estudios Mayas, Madrid.

Inomata, Takeshi. 2006a. Politics and Theatricality in Mayan Society. In *Archaeology of Performance: Theaters of Power, Community, and Politics,* edited by Takeshi Inomata and Lawrence S. Coben, pp. 187–221. Altamira, Lanham, Maryland.

Inomata, Takeshi. 2006b. Plazas, Performers, and Spectators: Political Theaters of the Classic Maya. *Current Anthropology* 45:805–820.

Inomata, Takeshi. 2008. *Warfare and the Fall of a Fortified Center: Archaeological Investigations at Aguateca.* Vanderbilt Institute of Mesoamerican Archaeology Volume 3, Nashville.

Joyce, Arthur A. 2009. Theorizing Urbanism in Ancient Mesoamerica. *Ancient Mesoamerica* 20:189–196.

Kepecs, Susan. 2007. Chichén-Itzá, Tula, and the Epiclassic/Early Postclassic World-System. In *Twin Tollans: Chichén Itzá, Tula, and the Epiclassic to Early Postclassic Mesoamerican World,* edited by Jeff Karl Kowalski and Cynthia Kristan-Graham, pp. 129–150. Dumbarton Oaks Library and Collection, Washington, DC.

Kepecs, Susan, and Philip Kohl. 2003. Conceptualizing Macroregional Interaction: World-Systems Theory and the Archaeological Record. In *The Postclassic Mesoamerican World,* edited by Michael E. Smith and Frances F. Berdan, pp. 14–20. University of Utah Press, Salt Lake City.

Kepecs, Susan, and Marilyn Masson. 2003. Political Organization in Yucatán and Belize. In *The Postclassic Mesoamerican World,* edited by Michael E. Smith and Frances F. Berdan, pp. 40–44. University of Utah Press, Salt Lake City.

Kintz, Ellen R., and Laraine A. Fletcher. 1983. A Reconstruction of the Prehistoric Population at Coba. In *Coba: A Classic Maya Metropolis,* edited by William J. Folan, Ellen R. Kintz, and Laraine A. Fletcher, pp. 91–210. Academic Press, New York.

Kostoff, Spiro. 1991. *The City Shaped: Urban Patterns and Meanings through History.* Little, Brown, Boston.

Kostoff, Spiro. 1992. *The City Assembled: The Elements of Urban Form through History.* Little, Brown, Boston.

Kowalewski, Stephen A. 1990. The Evolution of Complexity in the Valley of Oaxaca. *Annual Review of Anthropology* 19:39–58.

Kowalewski, Stephen A., Andrew K. Balkansky, Laura R. Stiver Walsh, Thomas J. Pluckhahn, John F. Chamblee, Verónica Pérez Rodríguez, Verenice Y. Heredia Espinoza, and Charlotte A. Smith. 2009. *Origins of the Ñuu: Archaeology in the Mixteca Alta, Mexico.* University Press of Colorado, Boulder.

Kowalewski, Stephen A., Gary M. Feinman, Laura Finsten, Richard E. Blanton, and Linda Nicholas. 1989. *Monte Albán's Hinterland, Part II: Prehispanic Settlement Patterns in Tlacolula, Etla, and Ocotlán, the Valley of Oaxaca, Mexico.* Memoir 23 of the University of Michigan Museum of Anthropology, Ann Arbor.

Kowalski, Jeff K., ed. 1999. *Mesoamerican Architecture as a Cultural Symbol.* Oxford University Press, New York.

Kubler, George. 1962. *The Art and Architecture of Ancient America: The Mexican, Maya, and Andean Peoples.* Pelican History of Art, Baltimore.

Kurjack, Edward B. 1974. *Prehistoric Lowland Maya Community and Social Organization: A Case Study at Dzibilchaltun.* Tulane University Middle American Research Institute Publication 38, New Orleans.

Manzanilla, Linda. 1996. Corporate Groups and Domestic Activities at Teotihuacan. *Latin American Antiquity* 7:228–246.

Manzanilla, Linda. 2004. Social Identity and Daily Life at Classic Teotihuacan. In *Mesoamerican Archaeology: Theory and Practice*, edited by Julia A. Hendon and Rosemary A. Joyce, pp. 124–147. Blackwell, Oxford.

Manzanilla, Linda. 2006. Estados corporativos arcaicos: Organizaciones de excepción en escenarios excluyentes. *Cuicuilco* 13:13–45.

Manzanilla, Linda. 2009. Corporate Life in Apartment and Barrio Compounds at Teotihuacan, Central Mexico: Craft Specialization, Hierarchy, and Ethnicity. In *Domestic Life in Prehispanic Capitals: A Study of Specialization, Hierarchy, and Ethnicity*, edited by Linda R. Manzanilla and Claude Chapdelaine, pp. 21–42. Memoir 46 of the University of Michigan Museum of Anthropology, Ann Arbor.

Manzanilla, Linda R., and Claude Chapdelaine, eds. 2009. *Domestic Life in Prehispanic Capitals: A Study of Specialization, Hierarchy, and Ethnicity*. Memoir 46 of the University of Michigan Museum of Anthropology, Ann Arbor.

Marcus, Joyce. 1983. On the Nature of the Mesoamerican City. In *Prehistoric Settlement Patterns: Essays in Honor of Gordon Willey*, edited by Evon Z. Vogt and Richard M. Leventhal, pp. 195–242. University of New Mexico Press, Albuquerque, and the Peabody Museum of Archaeology and Ethnology, Harvard University, Cambridge.

Marcus, Joyce, and Jeremy A. Sabloff, eds. 2008. *The Ancient City: New Perspectives on Urbanism in the Old and New World*. School for Advanced Research Press, Santa Fe.

Masson, Marilyn A., Timothy S. Hare, and Carlos Peraza Lope. 2006. Postclassic Maya Society Regenerated at Mayapán. In *After Collapse: The Regeneration of Complex Societies*, edited by Glenn M. Schwartz and John J. Nichols, pp. 188–207. University of Arizona Press, Tucson.

McAnany, Patricia A. 1998. Ancestors and the Classic Maya Built Environment. In *Function and Meaning in Classic Maya Architecture*, edited by Stephen D. Houston, pp. 271–298. Dumbarton Oaks Research Library and Collection, Washington, DC.

Millon, René. 1973. *Urbanization at Teotihuacan, Mexico, Volume One: The Teotihuacan Map, Part One: Text*. University of Texas Press, Austin.

Millon, René. 1981. Teotihuacan: City, State, and Civilization. In *Supplement to the Handbook of Middle American Indians, Volume I: Archaeology*, edited by Jeremy A. Sabloff, pp. 198–243. University of Texas Press, Austin.

Millon, René. 1992. Teotihuacan Studies: From 1950 to 1990 and Beyond. In *Art, Ideology, and the City of Teotihuacan*, edited by Janet Catherine Berlo, pp. 339–430. Dumbarton Oaks Research Library and Collections, Washington, DC.

Nichols, Deborah L. 2004. The Rural and Urban Landscapes of the Aztec State. In *Mesoamerican Archaeology: Theory and Practice*, edited by Julia A. Hendon and Rosemary A. Joyce, pp. 265–295. Blackwell, Oxford.

Nichols, Deborah L. 2006. Shining Stars and Black Holes: Population and Preindustrial Cities. In *Urbanism in the Preindustrial World*, edited by Glenn R. Storey, pp. 330–340. University of Alabama Press, Tuscaloosa.

Paris, Elizabeth H. 2008. Metallurgy, Mayapán, and the Postclassic Mesoamerican World System. *Ancient Mesoamerica* 19:43–66.

Pasztory, Esther. 1992. Abstraction and the Rise of a Utopian State at Teotihuacan. In *Art, Ideology, and the City of Teotihuacan*, edited by Janet Catherine Berlo, pp. 281–320. Dumbarton Oaks Research Library and Collection, Washington, DC.

Pasztory, Esther. 1997. *Teotihuacan: An Experiment in Living*. University of Oklahoma Press, Norman.

Pollard, Helen P. 2003. Central Places in the Core of the Tarascan State. In *El urbanismo en Mésoamerica: Urbanism in Mesoamerica*, edited by William T. Sanders, Alba

Guadalupe Mastache, and Robert H. Cobean, pp. 345–390. Instituto Nacional de Antropología e Historia, Mexico, D.F., and Pennsylvania State University, University Park.

Price, T. Douglas, James H. Burton, Paul D. Fullagar, Lori E. Wright, Jane E. Buikstra, and Vera Tiesler. 2008. Strontium Isotopes and the Study of Human Mobility in Ancient Mesoamerica. *Latin American Antiquity* 19:167–180.

Rice, Don S. 2006. Late Classic Maya Population: Characteristics and Implications. In *Urbanism in the Preindustrial World*, edited by Glenn R. Storey, pp. 252–276. University of Alabama Press, Tuscaloosa.

Ringle, William M. 1999. Pre-Classic Cityscapes: Ritual Politics among the Early Lowland Maya. In *Social Patterns in Pre-Classic Mesoamerica*, edited by David C. Grove and Rosemary Joyce, pp. 183–223. Dumbarton Oaks Research Library and Collection, Washington, DC.

Ringle, William M., and George J. Bey III. 2001. Northern Maya Courts: Postclassic to Terminal Classic. In *Royal Courts of the Ancient Maya*, Volume 2, edited by Takeshi Inomata and Stephen D. Houston, pp. 266–307. Westview Press, Boulder, Colorado.

Ringle, William M., Tomás Gallareta Negrón, and George J. Bey III. 1998. The Return of Quetzalcoatl: Evidence for the Spread of a World Religion during the Epiclassic Period. *Ancient Mesoamerica* 9:183–232.

Rykwert, Joseph. 1998. *The Idea of a Town: The Anthropology of Urban Form in Rome, Italy and the Ancient World*. MIT Press, Cambridge.

Sanders, William T. 2003. The Population of Tenochtitlan-Tlatelolco. In *El urbanismo en Mésoamerica: Urbanism in Mesoamerica*, edited by William T. Sanders, Alba Guadalupe Mastache, and Robert H. Cobean, pp. 203–216. Instituto Nacional de Antropología e Historia, Mexico, D.F., and Pennsylvania State University, University Park.

Sanders, William T., Alba Guadalupe Mastache, and Robert H. Cobean. 2003. *El urbanismo en Mésoamerica: Urbanism in Mesoamerica*. Instituto Nacional de Antropología e Historia, Mexico, D.F., and Pennsylvania State University, University Park.

Sanders, William T., Jeffrey R. Parsons, and Robert S. Santley. 1979. *The Basin of Mexico: Ecological Processes in the Evolution of a Civilization*. Academic Press, New York.

Sanders, William T., and Barbara Price. 1968. *Mesoamerica: The Evolution of a Civilization*. Random House, New York.

Sanders, William T., and Robert S. Santley. 1983. A Tale of Three Cities: Energetics and Urbanization in Pre-Hispanic Central Mexico. In *Prehistoric Settlement Patterns: Essays in Honor of Gordon Willey*, edited by Evon Z. Vogt and Richard M. Leventhal, pp. 243–292. University of New Mexico Press, Albuquerque, and the Peabody Museum of Archaeology and Ethnology, Harvard University, Cambridge.

Sanders, William T., and David Webster. 1988. The Mesoamerican Urban Tradition. *American Anthropologist* 90:521–546.

Scarborough, Vernon L., and Gary G. Gallopin. 1990. A Water Storage Adaptation in the Maya Lowlands. *Science* 251:658–662.

Schele, Linda, and David Freidel. 1990. *A Forest of Kings: The Untold Story of the Ancient Maya*. William Morrow, New York.

Smith, Michael E. 2003. Can We Read Cosmology in Ancient Maya City Plans? Comment on Ashmore and Sabloff. *Latin American Antiquity* 14:221–228.

Smith, Michael E. 2005. City Size in Late Postclassic Mesoamerica. *Journal of Urban History* 31:403–434.

Smith, Michael E. 2007. Form and Meaning in the Earliest Cities: A New Approach to Ancient Urban Planning. *Journal of Planning History* 6:3–47.

Smith, Michael E. 2008. *Aztec City-State Capitals.* University Press of Florida, Gainesville.

Smith, Michael E. 2010a. The Archaeological Study of Neighborhoods and Districts in Ancient Cities. *Journal of Anthropological Archaeology* 29:137–154.

Smith, Michael E. 2010b. Sprawl, Squatters, and Sustainable Cities: Can Archaeological Data Shed Light on Modern Urban Issues? *Cambridge Archaeological Journal* 20:229–253.

Smith, Michael E., and Frances F. Berdan. 2003a. *The Postclassic Mesoamerican World.* University of Utah Press, Salt Lake City.

Smith, Michael E., and Frances F. Berdan. 2003b. Spatial Structure of the Mesoamerican World-System. In *The Postclassic Mesoamerican World,* edited by Michael E. Smith and Frances F. Berdan, pp. 21–31. University of Utah Press, Salt Lake City.

Smith, Monica L., ed. 2003. *The Social Construction of Ancient Cities.* Smithsonian Books, Washington, DC.

Spence, Michael W. 1996. A Comparative Analysis of Ethnic Enclaves. In *Arqueología Mesoamericana: Homenaje a William Sanders,* edited by Alba Guadalupe Mastache, Jeffrey R. Parsons, Robert S. Santley, and Marí Carmen Serra Puche, pp. 333–353. Instituto Nacional de Antropología e Historia, Mexico D.F.

Spence, Michael W., and Christine D. White. 2009. Mesoamerican Bioarchaeology: Past, Present, and Future. *Ancient Mesoamerica* 20:233–240.

Spence, Michael, W., Christine D. White, Evelyn C. Rattray, and Fred J. Longstaffe. 2005. Past Lives in Different Places: The Origins and Relationships of Teotihuacan's Foreign Residents. In *Settlement, Subsistence, and Social Complexity: Essays Honoring the Legacy of Jeffrey R. Parsons,* edited by Richard E. Blanton, pp. 155–197. Cotsen Institute of Archaeology, University of California, Los Angeles.

Stark, Barbara. 1999. Formal Architectural Complexes in South-Central Veracruz, Mexico: A Capital Zone? *Journal of Field Archaeology* 26:197–225.

Stark, Barbara. 2003. Cerro de las Mesas: Social and Economic Perspectives on a Gulf Center. In *El urbanismo en Mésoamerica: Urbanism in Mesoamerica,* edited by William T. Sanders, Alba Guadalupe Mastache, and Robert H. Cobean, pp. 391–426. Instituto Nacional de Antropología e Historia, Mexico, D.F., and Pennsylvania State University, University Park.

Stark, Barbara, and Alanna Ossa. 2007. Ancient Settlement, Urban Gardening, and Environment in the Gulf Lowlands of Mexico. *Latin American Antiquity* 18:385–406.

Stone, Andrea. 1999. Architectural Innovation in the Temple of the Warriors at Chichén Itzá. In *Mesoamerican Architecture as a Cultural Symbol,* edited by Jeff K. Kowalski, pp. 298–319. Oxford University Press, New York.

Storey, Glenn R. 1997. The Population of Ancient Rome. *Antiquity* 71:966–978.

Storey, Glenn R. 2006a. Introduction: Urban Demography of the Past. In *Urbanism in the Preindustrial World,* edited by Glenn R. Storey, pp. 1–26. University of Alabama Press, Tuscaloosa.

Storey, Glenn R., ed. 2006b. *Urbanism in the Preindustrial World.* University of Alabama Press, Tuscaloosa.

Storey, Rebecca. 1992. *Life and Death in the Ancient City of Teotihuacan: A Modern Paleodemographic Synthesis.* University of Alabama Press, Tuscaloosa.

Sugiyama, Saburo. 1993. Worldview Materialized at Teotihuacan. *Latin American Antiquity* 4:103–129.

Sugiyama, Saburo. 2005. *Human Sacrifice, Militarism, and Rulership: Materialization of State Ideology at the Feathered Serpent Pyramid, Teotihuacan.* Cambridge University Press, Cambridge.

Tourtellot, Gair III. 1993. A View of Ancient Maya Settlements in the Eighth Century. In *Lowland Maya Civilization in the Eighth Century AD*, edited by Jeremy A. Sabloff and John S. Henderson, pp. 219–242. Dumbarton Oaks Library and Collection, Washington, DC.

van Zantwijk, Rudolph. 1985. *The Aztec Arrangement: The Social History of Pre-Spanish Mexico.* University of Oklahoma Press, Norman.

Webster, David, and William T. Sanders. 2001. La antigua ciudad Mesoamericana: Teoría y concepto. In *Reconstruyendo la ciudad Maya: El urbanismo en las sociedades antiguas*, edited by Andrés Ciudad Ruíz, Josefa Iglesias Ponce de León, and Carmen Martínez Martínez, pp. 43–64. Sociedad Española de Estudios Mayas, Madrid.

Wheatley, Paul. 1983. *Negara and Commandery: Origins of the Southeast Asian Urban Traditions.* University of Chicago Department of Geography, Research Paper Numbers 207–208, Chicago.

CHAPTER 54

....

MESOAMERICAN
STATES AND EMPIRES

....

GARY M. FEINMAN

FOLLOWING more than a half-century of empirical and theoretical advances (Blanton et al. 1993: 1–27; Wolf 1994), our understanding of the nature and variability of prehispanic Mesoamerican states and empires has expanded significantly, but fundamental questions remain unresolved. Few still adhere to simple notions such as that earlier Mesoamerican states were "theocratic" while later polities were "militaristic" (e.g., Wolf 1959). Nor can we any longer use sixteenth-century documentary sources on the Aztec as the main prism (e.g., Peterson 1962) through which to view the long history of the prehispanic Mesoamerican polities that occupied this diverse physio-cultural landscape (Chase et al. 2009). One comparative essay (Wright 1989: 99) proposed Mesoamerica as "the most different of the world's early civilizations," arising where communication was often difficult, domestic animals few, and the economy reliant on stone as opposed to metal tools (Stark 2001). Yet the specific parameters of such global organizational distinctiveness remain largely undefined (Blanton 2004), while the diversity of prehispanic Mesoamerican states across space and over time is now demonstrable.

States are hierarchical sociopolitical formations that are characterized by several tiers of decision making above the household and internally specialized administrative organizations (Blanton et al. 1993: 19; Spencer 2010; Stark 2001; Wright 1977). Yet such definitions are not always easy for archaeologists to apply, especially when endeavoring to distinguish states from social forms of more intermediate scale and complexity (chiefdoms). These definitional issues lie at the crux of the debate (Pool 2009: 246–247) over when and where the earliest states arose in Mesoamerica (Spencer and Redmond 2004; cf. Clark 2007). Yet states and other hierarchically organized polities did not exist in isolation; they generally were part of macroregional networks (e.g., Balkansky 2006; Blanton and Feinman 1984; Flannery and Marcus 2000) over which people, goods, and information were exchanged and wars fought. Thus, while we may not soon achieve scholarly consensus on the precise location and date of Mesoamerica's earliest state (e.g., Sanders 1970: 441), we are apt to gain wider agreement on the dynamic cycling of hierarchically organized polities in the macroregion as well as some of the key axes of variation that characterized them.

The Rise and Historical Dynamics of Mesoamerican States

Hierarchically organized polities arose in both the highlands and lowlands of Mesoamerica not long after the advent of sedentary villages during the second millennium BC (Grove and Gillespie 1992). These polities were centered at head towns (of a few thousand inhabitants or fewer) that were characterized by monuments, elaborate residences, and civic-ceremonial constructions generally absent at smaller settlements (Marcus and Flannery 1996; Pool 2009). These early polities, and their networks of interaction, provided an economic, political, and ideological foundation for subsequent demographic growth (Feinman 1991; Ringle 1999; Smith 2002) and for political developments that coincided with the emergence of more populous communities across much of Mesoamerica during the last five hundred years of the first millennium BC. Some of these communities, such as Monte Albán (Blanton et al. 1999; Marcus and Flannery 1996; Spencer and Redmond 2004) and Teotihuacan (Cowgill 1997, 2004; Sanders et al. 1979), were the capitals of early states that continued for centuries as regional centers of power.

Military expansion has been advanced as central to the rise of early Mesoamerican states (Spencer 2003; Spencer and Redmond 2004), although a suite of other factors, including the organizational challenges and adjustments posed by more nucleated populations, were important as well (Blanton et al. 1999: 68–110). The harnessing of human labor through a diverse set of means was a key component of leadership and power in ancient Mesoamerica. Larger cities were generally at the centers of strong states. "The art of Mesoamerican politics is especially evident in ... grand urban designs" (Carrasco 2009: 449). At the same time, cycles of demographic growth and decline temporally coincided with the waxing and waning of political clout (e.g., Feinman 1998; Kowalewski 2003).

In the lowland Maya region where a landscape of competing states arose slightly later than in the highlands, rulers (and their polities) jockeyed for power for centuries, leaving archaeological and textual records of political and demographic fluctuations (Chase et al. 2009). The core regions of most Classic Maya polities are thought to have been relatively small (Adams and Jones 1981), approximately

8,000–11,000 square kilometers (Chase and Chase 1998; Folan et al. 1995). The reach of political power could be extended through both warfare and alliance (Martin and Grube 2008), although such episodes tended to be brief (Marcus 2003).

In the highlands, the early states centered on Monte Albán and Teotihuacan also exercised power primarily over the large valleys in which they were situated and adjacent regions, although short episodes of more distant expansion have been postulated (e.g., Millon 1988: Smith and Montiel 2001; Spencer 2003), particularly early in their histories. The decline and eventual abandonment of these long-dominating centers late in the Classic period (ca. 650–900 AD) was part of a reorganization of the Mesoamerican world that also was marked by the decline of many of the Classic Maya cities. At the same time, new centers arose, including in regions that had been more sparsely settled earlier during the Classic period (Diehl and Berlo 1989; Smith and Berdan 2003). Shifts in the demographic and political centers of power continued during the Postclassic period (ca. 900–1520 AD), although the eventual rise of the Aztec Empire after 1320 AD culminated in the largest and most populous political entity in the history of prehispanic Mesoamerica. Nevertheless, no polity ever came close to politically unifying this cultural area (Blanton and Feinman 1984). At the time of the Spanish invasion, resistance to Aztec imperial expansion was ongoing by both the Tarascan Empire to the west and the Tlaxcalans to the east (Berdan et al. 1996).

THE ECONOMIC UNDERPINNINGS
OF MESOAMERICAN STATES

Traditionally, non-Western states, including prehispanic Mesoamerican polities, have been modeled, often rather implicitly, as despotic (*sensu* Wittfogel 1957), with the direct control of economic resources and exchange (through redistribution) underpinning a self-aggrandizing ruling class (e.g., Carrasco 1978; Sanders and Price 1968; cf. Offner 1981). But as the long-standing foci on temples, tombs, and texts have been amplified by systematic investigations of houses and settlement patterns, a new perspective on ancient Mesoamerican economies has been advanced (e.g., Feinman 1999; Feinman and Nicholas 2004; Garraty and Stark 2010; Hirth 2009). This view, grounded more directly in empirical findings, emphasizes domestic craft production for exchange, multicrafting, a broader role for marketing (Carrasco Vargas et al. 2009), and, in general, less direct top-down management of storage, exchange, and agricultural production by rulers (Kowalewski et al. 2009: 342; Nichols 2008).

The different ways that specific Mesoamerican polities raised revenues remain to be deciphered. But through textual accounts, the Aztec Empire and the smaller petty states integrated by it provide a suite of potential revenue sources, including tribute following military conquests or political subordination, taxes on market participation, labor drafts/corvée, exactions from the gains of long-distance traders, and rents for the use of land (Berdan et al. 1996; Hicks 1984; Nichols 2008; Rojas Rabiela 1984; Smith 1993a). On theoretical grounds, the specific mix of these and other means of generating revenues has been proposed to be closely associated with varied forms of governance (Blanton and Fargher 2008, 2009; Levi 1988, 2006). More externally focused exactions (such as war tribute and long-distance exchange) have been associated with more autocratic governments, while the placement of high-revenue burdens on local populations (e.g., rent, labor drafts) required greater degrees of collectivity or corporate organization (*sensu* Blanton et al. 1996). So while the geographic location of large, dense, well-planned Mesoamerican cities with grand, centrally situated public spaces (such as at Teotihuacan, Monte Albán, Tula, Tenochtitlan-Tlatilolco) in broad fertile valleys (with ample opportunities for labor taxes and rent) fits the expectations of a range of theoretical perspectives, the relative rarity of artistic, architectural, or epigraphic indicators of highly individualized, autocratic rulers at these same centers (Feinman 2001) coincides more closely with framing expectations drawn from theories of collective action (Blanton and Fargher 2008, 2009).

Mesoamerican Statecraft and Its Diversity

To understand the organization and dynamics of prehispanic Mesoamerican states, scholars largely have relied on two primary sources: texts and the archaeological record, including architectural building plans and settlement layouts. Indigenous writing extends back in Mesoamerica to the middle of the first millennium BC (Marcus 1976). Yet ample prehispanic textual accounts remain geographically and temporally spotty, preserved and decipherable largely just for the Classic Maya and Late Postclassic highland societies, particularly the Mixtec (Marcus 1992). Indigenous Mesoamerican writing was principally political in content, focused on life-history events, legitimation, and sanctification of specific powerful persons (at times grading to propaganda) (Marcus 1992). Texts afford a unique and detailed vantage point on Mesoamerican political organization. Yet because the texts focus on times and places in which individual identities were a key aspect of rule, they should not be inherently privileged (e.g., Feinman 1997; Moreland 2006).

The consideration of epigraphic information in holistic archaeological context signals key axes of variation in Mesoamerican leadership and statecraft. In general for this cultural macroregion, the presence of rich indigenous texts coincides with political formations that focused on dynastic rulers who utilized personal networks of descent, marriage, and alliance as core bases of rule (Blanton et al. 1996; Feinman 2001). The Classic-period Maya states, particularly in the southern lowlands, illustrate this organizational dynamic in part through numerous and often dated (using the Mesoamerican Long Count) records of royal events (including the accessions, marriages, and military victories of named rulers) (Looper 1999; Marcus 1993; Martin and Grube 2008; Sabloff 2003) that were documented on carved stelae, polychrome ceramic vessels, and other media. Individualized public displays (Grube 1992; Inomata 2006) appear to have been an important means of attracting and rallying support. The personalized, exclusionary nature of Classic Maya political organization is not evidenced solely through hieroglyphic texts but is amplified by the discoveries of ornate royal burials housed in monumental funerary shrines (Fitzsimmons 2009; Jones 1991; Ruz Lhuiller 1973), large palatial courts and residences (Christie 2003; Harrison and Andrews 2004; Houston and Inomata 2009: 156–158; Inomata and Houston 2001, 2004), and a material record that features finely crafted trappings of elaborate ornamentation and dress frequently made with exotic resources (e.g., McAnany 1993, 2008). While not all Classic Maya states conformed to this organizational dynamic, it is informative that a period of greater "symbolic egalitarianism" and bureaucratized rule at Caracol coincided with the near absence of the site's rulers in the epigraphic record (Chase and Chase 2009; Chase et al. 2009: 176).

The Late Postclassic Mixtec/Zapotec *cacicazgos*, or hereditary kingdoms, also recorded glorified histories of specific named rulers, who gained and spread their power principally through descent, marriage, and conquest (Spores 1984). Elaborate personal ornamentation and wealth-filled tombs were associated with select rulers (Caso 1969; Gallegos Ruiz 1978). Commoners "voted with their feet," following successful dynasts, thereby setting off episodes of growth and decline at specific centers (Kowalewski et al. 2009). As with the Classic Maya, larger political entities could be formed by the joining of smaller petty states under a powerful ruler or through alliances; however, because they did not develop the bureaucratic infrastructures necessary to transform political relations, these entities did not endure. While states in the Mixteca Alta may have generally been small during Classic and Postclassic times (Kowalewski et al. 2009: 337–345), the small Late Postclassic polities in the Valley of Oaxaca (Kowalewski et al. 1989) stem from the breakdown of a larger Monte Albán polity beginning late in the Classic period (ca. 700–900 AD) (Feinman 2007; Marcus 1989). In the Valley of Oaxaca, this process was set off by the erection of a variety of small carved stones that trace the generational descent of distinct sets of named ruling pairs at roughly a dozen smaller valley centers (Marcus 2006; Urcid et al. 1994).

Although most (though not all) Mesoamerican states, like those of the Classic Maya and Postclassic Oaxaca, were relatively small (Smith 1993b: 18), the great majority did not regularly record dynastic exploits, and researchers have not found other markers of exclusionary or individualizing modes of leadership (*sensu* Blanton et al. 1996; Feinman 2001). For one of Mesoamerica's largest and most architecturally monumental capitals, Classic-period Teotihuacan, researchers cannot agree on the location of a ruler's palace (Cowgill 1983; Flannery 1998; Manzanilla 2002; Sanders and Evans 2006). Classic-period royal burials are absent at the site (Cowgill 2008: 966). Writing was known and artistic expression was ample (e.g., Taube 2000), yet individualized rulers were rarely if ever depicted or named at the site (Cowgill 1992, 1997; Manzanilla 1997, 2009; Sugiyama 2004: 116). Rather, representations of finely attired figures generally involved processions of multiple persons who were usually masked. Order and legitimacy were fostered by art, architecture, and ritual practices that emphasized collective themes and group identity (Blanton, this volume; Blanton et al. 1996; Feinman 2001; Manzanilla 1997).

For Classic-period Teotihuacan, the bases of power were not highly personalized, seemingly less directly tied to legitimation through patrimonial descent (Cowgill 1997; Hassig 1992: 190). Gender inequality was not highly developed (De Lucia 2008). Rather, power was somewhat shared or distributed, more collective, possibly drawing on representatives associated with the city's more than two thousand multifamily, multiroomed apartment compounds and the site's spatial segments (defined by a well-planned cruciform layout) (Blanton et al. 1996; Feinman 2001; Manzanilla 1997, 2004, 2009). Throughout the prehispanic Mesoamerican world, the strongest evidence for neighborhood or barrio organization (spatially defined social segments) has been noted where rulership was less personalized and power likely shared (e.g., Healan 2009; Smith 2010).

Although in regard to size, monumentality, and longevity as a center of power, Teotihuacan was anything but typical in prehispanic Mesoamerica; different forms of shared power (Ringle 2004) or corporate modes of governance may have been more prevalent in this macroregion than earlier envisioned. For example, venturing upon the sixteenth-century Tlaxcalans, archenemies of the Aztec, Cortés (1986: 68) observed that they did not have an "over-all ruler," comparing their governing system to an Italian republic, such as Venice. In late prehispanic Tlaxcala, political authority was vested in a governing council that was obligated to provide military as well as administrative services (Fargher et al. 2010, 2011). Dual rulership, governing councils, and other forms of shared governance have been postulated for other Late Classic and Postclassic Mesoamerican political capitals (Ringle 2004), including Cholula, Tula, Chichén Itzá, and Mayapán (Kepecs and Masson 2003), with access to power potentially shifting over time and in relation to circumstance. Yet even when political might became relatively concentrated, rulers of most Mesoamerican polities do not appear to have assumed the autocratic powers (or gained office through direct lineal descent in the manner) of the Classic-period southern lowland dynasts (e.g., Chase et al. 2009: 181; Ringle 2004: 213). For Mesoamerica, the legacy of such bilateral forms of descent seemingly extends into the postcolonial world (Burton et al. 1996).

RETROSPECT AND PROSPECT

Prehispanic Mesoamerican states were far from uniform over time and space, varying in both size and degree of political centralization. Whether (and how) the corpus of ancient Mesoamerican polities stands out from the preindustrial states in other global regions remains to be determined. Yet the macroregion's somewhat limited technological toolkit may have underpinned Mesoamerica's generally and comparatively small polity sizes as well as the development of sophisticated socioeconomic and ideological mechanisms that fostered interpersonal integration and collective action as opposed to strictly autocratic means of wielding power. In a socioenvironmental setting in which human labor may have been the critical resource, the largest and long-lasting polities appear to have relied less on autocratic means of social control or to have exhibited relatively narrow concentrations of wealth and power. Throughout the history of this ancient world, innovative socioeconomic and ideological mechanisms facilitated the foundation of urban agglomerations of culturally diverse populations that endured for many centuries, extensive empires (such as the Aztec), and networks of exchange and interdependence that regularly (and by significant distances) eclipsed the extent of political control.

Since the middle of the last century, our understandings of prehispanic Mesoamerican states and statecraft have moved from a heavy reliance on historical extrapolations and stereotypical models of non-Western societies to more empirically grounded and complex perspectives that endeavor to account for the inherent diversity. To build on these advances (and in the face of a disappearing archaeological record) requires even more concerted field, laboratory, and archival research along with the commitment to record and conceptualize these findings at multiple scales.

REFERENCES

Adams, Richard E. W., and Robert C. Jones. 1981. Spatial Patterns and Regional Growth among Classic Maya Cities. *American Antiquity* 46:301–322.

Balkansky, Andrew K. 2006. Surveys and Mesoamerican Archaeology: The Emerging Macroregional Paradigm. *Journal of Archaeological Research* 14:53–95.

Berdan, Frances F., Richard E. Blanton, Elizabeth Hill Boone, Mary G. Hodge, Michael E. Smith, and Emily Umberger. 1996. *Aztec Imperial Strategies*. Dumbarton Oaks, Washington, DC.

Blanton, Richard E. 2004. Settlement Pattern and Population Change in Mesoamerican and Mediterranean Civilizations: A Comparative Perspective. In *Side-by-Side Survey: Comparative Regional Studies in the Mediterranean World*, edited by Susan E. Alcock and John F. Cherry, pp. 206–240. Oxbow Books, Oxford.

Blanton, Richard E., and Lane F. Fargher. 2008. *Collective Action in the Formation of Pre-Modern States*. Springer, New York.

Blanton, Richard E., and Lane F. Fargher. 2009. Collective Action in the Evolution of Pre-Modern States. *Social Evolution and History* 8:133–166.

Blanton, Richard E., and Gary M. Feinman. 1984. The Mesoamerican World-System. *American Anthropologist* 86:673–692.

Blanton, Richard E., Stephen A. Kowalewski, Gary M. Feinman, and Laura M. Finsten. 1993. *Ancient Mesoamerica: A Comparison of Change in Three Regions*. 2nd ed. Cambridge University Press, Cambridge.

Blanton, Richard E., Gary M. Feinman, Stephen A. Kowalewski, and Linda M. Nicholas. 1999. *Ancient Oaxaca*. Cambridge University Press, Cambridge.

Blanton, Richard E., Gary M. Feinman, Stephen A. Kowalewski, and Peter N. Peregrine. 1996. A Dual-Processual Theory for the Evolution of Mesoamerican Civilization. *Current Anthropology* 37:1–14.

Burton, Michael L., Carmella C. Moore, John W. M. Whiting, and A. Kimball Romney. 1996. Regions Based on Social Structure. *Current Anthropology* 37:87–123.

Carrasco, David. 2009. Cities as Cosmological Art. In *The Art of Urbanism*, edited by William L. Fash and Leonardo López Luján, pp. 443–453. Dumbarton Oaks, Washington, DC.

Carrasco, Pedro. 1978. La economía del México prehispánico. In *Economía política e ideología en el México prehispánico*, edited by Pedro Carrasco and Johanna Broda, pp. 15–76. Centro de Investigaciones Superiores, Instituto Nacional de Antropología e Historia, Editorial Nueva Imagen, Mexico.

Carrasco Vargas, Ramón, Verónica A. Vázquez López, and Simon Martin. 2009. Daily Life of the Ancient Maya Recorded on Murals at Calakmul, Mexico. *Proceedings of the National Academy of Sciences* 106:19245–19249.

Caso, Alfonso. 1969. *El tesoro de Monte Albán*. Memorias 3, Instituto Nacional de Antropología e Historia, Mexico.

Chase, Arlen F., and Diane Z. Chase. 1998. Late Classic Maya Political Structure, Polity Size, and Warfare Arenas. In *Anatomia de una civilización: Aproximaciones interdisciplinarias de la cultura Maya*, edited by Andrés Ciudad Ruiz, Yolanda Fernández Marquínez, José Miguel García Campillo, María Josefa Iglesias Ponce de León, Alfonso Lacadena García-Gallo, and Luis T. Sanz Castro, pp. 11–29. Sociedad Española de Estudios Mayas, Madrid.

Chase, Arlen F., and Diane Z. Chase. 2009. Symbolic Egalitarianism and Homogenized Distributions in the Archaeological Record at Caracol, Belize: Method, Theory, and Complexity. *Research Reports in Belizean Archaeology* 6:15–24.

Chase, Arlen F., Diane Z. Chase, and Michael Smith. 2009. States and Empires in Ancient Mesoamerica. *Ancient Mesoamerica* 20:175–182.

Christie, Jessica J., ed. 2003. *Maya Palaces and Elite Residences: An Interdisciplinary Approach*. University of Texas Press, Austin.

Clark, John E. 2007. Mesoamerica's First State. In *The Political Economy of Ancient Mesoamerica: Transformations during the Formative and Classic Periods*, edited by Vernon L. Scarborough and John E. Clark, pp. 11–46. University of New Mexico Press, Albuquerque.

Cortés, Hernan. 1986. *Letters from Mexico*. Translated by Anthony Pagdan. Yale University Press, New Haven.

Cowgill, George L. 1983. Rulership and the Ciudadela: Political Inferences from Teotihuacan Architecture. In *Civilizations in the Ancient Americas: Essays in Honor of Gordon R. Willey*, edited by Richard M. Leventhal and Alan L. Kolata, pp. 313–343. University of New Mexico Press, Albuquerque.

Cowgill, George L. 1992. Social Differentiation at Teotihuacan. In *Mesoamerican Elites: An Archaeological Assessment*, edited by Diane Z. Chase and Arlen F. Chase, pp. 206–220. University of Oklahoma Press, Norman.

Cowgill, George L. 1997. State and Society at Teotihuacan, Mexico. *Annual Review of Anthropology* 26:129–161.

Cowgill, George L. 2004. Origins and Development of Urbanism: Archaeological Perspectives. *Annual Review of Anthropology* 33:525–549.

Cowgill, George L. 2008. An Update on Teotihuacan. *Antiquity* 82:962–975.

De Lucia, Kristin. 2008. Looking Beyond Gender Hierarchy: Rethinking Gender at Teotihuacan, Mexico. In *Gender, Households, and Society: Unraveling the Threads of the Past and the Present*, edited by Cynthia Robin and Elizabeth M. Brumfiel, pp. 17–36. Archeological Papers 18, American Anthropological Association, Blackwell, Malden, Massachusetts.

Diehl, Richard A., and Janet Catherine Berlo, eds. 1989. *Mesoamerica after the Decline of Teotihuacan AD 700-900*. Dumbarton Oaks, Washington, DC.

Fargher, Lane F., Richard E. Blanton, and Verenice Heredia Espinoza. 2010. Egalitarian Ideology and Political Power in Pre-Hispanic Central Mexico: The Case of Tlaxcallan. *Latin American Antiquity* 21:227–251.

Fargher, Lane F., Richard E. Blanton, Verenice Y. Heredia Espinosa, and John Millhauser. 2011. Tlaxcallan: The Archaeology of an Ancient Republic in the New World. *Antiquity* 85:172-186.

Feinman, Gary M. 1991. Demography, Surplus, and Inequality: Early Political Formations in Highland Mesoamerica. In *Chiefdoms: Power, Economy, and Ideology*, edited by Timothy Earle, pp. 229–262. Cambridge University Press, Cambridge.

Feinman, Gary M. 1997. Thoughts on New Approaches to Combining the Archaeological and Historical Records. *Journal of Archaeological Method and Theory* 4:367–377.

Feinman, Gary M. 1998. Scale and Social Organization: Perspectives on the Archaic State. In *Archaic States*, edited by Gary M. Feinman and Joyce Marcus, pp. 95–133. School of American Research Press, Santa Fe, New Mexico.

Feinman, Gary M. 1999. Rethinking Our Assumptions: Economic Specialization at the Household Scale in Ancient Ejutla, Oaxaca, Mexico. In *Pottery and People*, edited by James M. Skibo and Gary M. Feinman, pp. 81–98. University of Utah Press, Salt Lake City.

Feinman, Gary M. 2001. Mesoamerican Political Complexity: The Corporate-Network Dimension. In *From Leaders to Rulers*, edited by Jonathan Haas, pp. 151–175. Kluwer Academic/Plenum, New York.

Feinman, Gary M. 2007. The Last Quarter Century of Archaeological Research in the Central Valleys of Oaxaca. *Mexicon* 29:3–15.

Feinman, Gary M., and Linda M. Nicholas. 2004. Unraveling the Prehispanic Highland Mesoamerican Economy: Production, Exchange, and Consumption in the Classic Period Valley of Oaxaca. In *Archaeological Perspectives on Political Economies*, edited by Gary M. Feinman and Linda M. Nicholas, pp. 167–188. University of Utah Press, Salt Lake City.

Fitzsimmons, James L. 2009. *Death and the Classic Maya Kings*. University of Texas Press, Austin.

Flannery, Kent V. 1998. The Ground Plans of Archaic States. In *Archaic States*, edited by Gary M. Feinman and Joyce Marcus, pp. 15–57. School of American Research, Santa Fe, New Mexico.

Flannery, Kent V., and Joyce Marcus. 2000. Formative Mexican Chiefdoms and the Myth of the "Mother Culture." *Journal of Anthropological Archaeology* 19:1–37.

Folan, William J., Joyce Marcus, Sophia Pincemin, María del Rosario Domínguez Carrasco, Laraine Fletcher, and Abel Morales López. 1995. Calakmul: New Data from an Ancient Maya Capital in Campeche, Mexico. *Latin American Antiquity* 6:310–334.

Gallegos Ruiz, Roberto. 1978. *El Señor 9 Flor en Zaachila*. Universidad Nacional Autónoma de México, Mexico.

Garraty, Christopher P., and Barbara L. Stark, eds. 2010. *Archaeological Approaches to Market Exchange in Ancient Societies*. University Press of Colorado, Boulder.

Grove, David C., and Susan D. Gillespie. 1992. Ideology and Evolution at the Pre-State Level. In *Ideology and Pre-Columbian Civilizations*, edited by Arthur A. Demarest and Geoffrey W. Conrad, pp. 15–36. School of American Research Press, Santa Fe, New Mexico.

Grube, Nikolai. 1992. Classic Maya Dance: Evidence from Hieroglyphs and Iconography. *Ancient Mesoamerica* 3:201–218.

Harrison, Peter D., and E. Wyllys Andrews. 2004. Palaces of Tikal and Copán. In *Palaces of the Ancient New World*, edited by Susan T. Evans and Joanne Pillsbury, pp. 113–147. Dumbarton Oaks, Washington, DC.

Hassig, Ross. 1992. *War and Society in Ancient Mesoamerica*. University of California Press, Berkeley.

Healan, Dan M. 2009. Household, Neighborhood, and Urban Structure in an "Adobe City": Tula, Hidalgo, Mexico. In *Domestic Life in Prehispanic Capitals: A Study of Specialization, Hierarchy, and Ethnicity*, edited by Linda R. Manzanilla and Claude Chapdelaine, pp. 67–88. Memoirs 46, Museum of Anthropology, University of Michigan, Ann Arbor.

Hicks, Frederic. 1984. Rotational Labor and Urban Development in Prehispanic Tetzcoco. In *Explorations in Ethnohistory: Indians of Central Mexico in the Sixteenth Century*, edited by Herbert R. Harvey and Hanns J. Prem, pp. 147–174. University of New Mexico Press, Albuquerque.

Hirth, Kenneth G., ed. 2009. *Housework: Craft Production and Domestic Economy in Ancient Mesoamerica*. Archeological Papers 19, American Anthropological Association, Wiley Periodicals, Malden, Massachusetts.

Houston, Stephen D., and Takeshi Inomata. 2009. *The Classic Maya*. Cambridge University Press, Cambridge.

Inomata, Takeshi. 2006. Plazas, Performers, and Spectators: Political Theaters of the Classic Maya. *Current Anthropology* 47:805–842.

Inomata, Takeshi, and Stephen D. Houston, eds. 2001. *Royal Courts of the Ancient Maya: Theory, Comparison, and Synthesis*. Vol. I. Westview, Boulder, Colorado.

Inomata, Takeshi, and Stephen D. Houston, eds. 2004. *Royal Courts of the Ancient Maya:Data and Case Studies*. Vol. II. Westview, Boulder, Colorado.

Jones, Christopher. 1991. Cycles of Growth at Tikal. In *Classic Maya Political History: Hieroglyphic and Archaeological Evidence*, edited by T. Patrick Culbert, pp. 102–127. Cambridge University Press, Cambridge.

Kepecs, Susan, and Marilyn Masson. 2003. Political Organization in Yucatán and Belize. In *The Postclassic Mesoamerican World*, edited by Michael E. Smith and Francis F. Berdan, pp. 40–44. University of Utah Press, Salt Lake City.

Kowalewski, Stephen A. 2003. Scale and the Explanation of Demographic Change: 3,500 Years in the Valley of Oaxaca. *American Anthropologist* 105:313–325.

Kowalewski, Stephen A., Andrew K. Balkansky, Laura R. Stiver Walsh, Thomas J. Pluckhahn, John F. Chamblee, Verónica Pérez Rodríguez, Verenice Y. Heredia Espinoza, and Charlotte A. Smith. 2009. *Origins of the Ñuu: Archaeology in the Mixteca Alta, Mexico*. University Press of Colorado, Boulder.

Kowalewski, Stephen A., Gary M. Feinman, Laura Finsten, Richard E. Blanton, and Linda M. Nicholas. 1989. *Monte Albán's Hinterland, Part II: Prehispanic Settlement Patterns in Tlacolula, Etla, and Ocotlán, the Valley of Oaxaca, Mexico*. Memoirs 23, Museum of Anthropology, University of Michigan, Ann Arbor.

Levi, Margaret. 1988. *Of Rule and Revenue.* University of California Press, Berkeley.

Levi, Margaret. 2006. Why We Need a New Theory of Government. *Perspectives on Politics* 4:5–19.

Looper, Matthew G. 1999. New Perspectives on the Late Classic Political History of Quirigua, Guatemala. *Ancient Mesoamerica* 10:263–280.

Manzanilla, Linda. 1997. Teotihuacan: Urban Archetype, Cosmic Model. In *Emergence and Change in Early Urban Societies*, edited by Linda Manzanilla, pp. 109–131. Plenum, New York.

Manzanilla, Linda. 2002. Gobierno corporativo en Teotihuacan: una revisión del concepto "palacio" aplicado a la gran urbe prehispánica. *Anales de Antropología* 35:157–190.

Manzanilla, Linda. 2004. Social Identity and Daily Life at Classic Teotihuacan. In *Mesoamerican Archaeology: Theory and Practice*, edited by Julia A. Hendon and Rosemary A. Joyce, pp. 124–147. Blackwell, Oxford.

Manzanilla, Linda. 2009. Corporate Life in Apartment and Barrio Compounds at Teotihuacan, Central Mexico: Craft Specialization, Hierarchy, and Ethnicity. In *Domestic Life in Prehispanic Capitals: A Study of Specialization, Hierarchy, and Ethnicity*, edited by Linda R. Manzanilla and Claude Chapdelaine, pp. 21–42. Memoirs 46, Museum of Anthropology, University of Michigan, Ann Arbor.

Marcus, Joyce. 1976. The Origins of Mesoamerican Writing. *Annual Review of Anthropology* 5:35–67.

Marcus, Joyce. 1989. From Centralized Systems to City-States: Possible Models for the Epiclassic. In *Mesoamerica after the Decline of Teotihuacan AD 700–900*, edited by Richard A. Diehl and Janet Catherine Berlo, pp. 201–208. Dumbarton Oaks, Washington, DC.

Marcus, Joyce. 1992. *Mesoamerican Writing Systems: Propaganda, Myth, and History in Four Ancient Civilizations.* Princeton University Press, Princeton, New Jersey.

Marcus, Joyce. 1993. Ancient Maya Political Organization. In *Lowland Maya Civilization in the Eighth Century AD,* edited by Jeremy A. Sabloff and John S. Henderson, pp. 111–183. Dumbarton Oaks, Washington, DC.

Marcus, Joyce. 2003. Recent Advances in Maya Archaeology. *Journal of Archaeological Research* 11:71–148.

Marcus, Joyce. 2006. Identifying Elites and Their Strategies. In *Intermediate Elites in Pre-Columbian States and Empires,* edited by Christina M. Elson and R. Alan Covey, pp. 212–246. University of Arizona Press, Tucson.

Marcus, Joyce, and Kent V. Flannery. 1996. *Zapotec Civilization: How Urban Society Evolved in Mexico's Oaxaca Valley.* Thames and Hudson, London.

Martin, Simon, and Nikolai Grube. 2008. *Chronicle of the Maya Kings and Queens: Deciphering the Dynasties of the Ancient Maya.* 2nd ed. Thames and Hudson, New York.

McAnany, Patricia A. 1993. The Economies of Social Power and Wealth among Eighth-Century Maya Households. In *Lowland Maya Civilizations in the Eighth Century AD,* edited by Jeremy A. Sabloff and John S. Henderson, pp. 65–89. Dumbarton Oaks, Washington, DC.

McAnany, Patricia A. 2008. Shaping Social Difference: Political and Ritual Economy of Classic Maya Royal Courts. *Research in Economic Anthropology* 27:219–247.

Millon, René. 1988. The Last Years of Teotihuacan Dominance. In *The Collapse of Ancient States and Civilizations*, edited by Norman Yoffee and George L. Cowgill, pp. 102–164. University of Arizona Press, Tucson.

Moreland, John. 2006. Archaeology and Texts: Subservience or Enlightenment. *Annual Review of Anthropology* 35:135–151.

Nichols, Deborah L. 2008. Artisans, Markets, and Merchants. In *The Aztec World*, edited by Elizabeth M. Brumfiel and Gary M. Feinman, pp. 105–120. Abrams, New York.

Offner, Jerome A. 1981. On the Inapplicability of "Oriental Despotism" and the "Asiatic Mode of Production" to the Aztecs of Texcoco. *American Antiquity* 46:43–61.

Peterson, Frederick. 1962. *Ancient Mexico: An Introduction to the Pre-Hispanic Cultures.* Capricorn, New York.

Pool, Christopher A. 2009. Asking More and Better Questions: Olmec Archaeology for the Next Katun. *Ancient Mesoamerica* 20:241–252.

Ringle, William M. 1999. Pre-Classic Cityscapes: Ritual Politics among the Early Lowland Maya. In *Social Patterns in Pre-Classic Mesoamerica*, edited by David C. Grove and Rosemary A. Joyce, pp. 183–223. Dumbarton Oaks, Washington, DC.

Ringle, William M. 2004. On the Political Organization of Chichen Itza. *Ancient Mesoamerica* 15:167–218.

Rojas Rabiela, Teresa. 1984. El tributo en trabajo en la construcción de las obras públicas de México Tenochtitlan. In *El modo de producción tributario en Mesoamérica*, edited by Alfredo Barrera Rubio, pp. 51–76. Escuela de Ciencias Antropológicas, Universidad de Yucatán, Mérida.

Ruz Lhuiller, Alberto. 1973. *El templo de las inscripciones Palenque.* Instituto Nacional de Antropología e Historia, Mexico.

Sabloff, Jeremy A., ed. 2003. *Tikal: Dynasties, Foreigners, and Affairs of State.* School of American Research Press, Santa Fe, New Mexico.

Sanders, William T. 1970. Review of *Dumbarton Oaks Conference on the Olmec, October 28th and 29th, 1967*, edited by Elizabeth P. Benson. *American Anthropologist* 72:441–443.

Sanders, William T., and Susan T. Evans. 2006. Rulership and Palaces at Teotihuacan. In *Palaces and Power in the Americas: From Peru to the Northwest Coast*, edited by Jessica J. Christie and Patricia J. Sarro, pp. 256–284. University of Texas Press, Austin.

Sanders, William T., Jeffrey R. Parsons, and Robert S. Santley. 1979. *The Basin of Mexico: Ecological Processes in the Evolution of a Civilization.* Academic Press, New York.

Sanders, William T., and Barbara J. Price. 1968. *The Evolution of a Civilization.* Random House, New York.

Smith, Charlotte Ann. 2002. Concordant Change and Core-Periphery Dynamics: A Synthesis of Highland Mesoamerican Archaeological Survey Data. Unpublished PhD dissertation, Department of Anthropology, University of Georgia, Athens.

Smith, Michael E. 1993a. Houses and the Settlement Hierarchy in Late Postclassic Morelos: A Comparison of Archaeology and Ethnohistory. In *Prehispanic Domestic Units in Western Mesoamerica: Studies of the Household, Compound, and Residence*, edited by Robert S. Santley and Kenneth G. Hirth, pp. 191–206. CRC, Boca Raton, Florida.

Smith, Michael E. 1993b. New World Complex Societies: Recent Economic, Social, and Political Studies. *Journal of Archaeological Research* 1:5–41.

Smith, Michael E. 2010. The Archaeological Study of Neighborhoods and Districts in Ancient Cities. *Journal of Anthropological Archaeology* 29:137–154.

Smith, Michael E., and Frances F. Berdan, eds. 2003. *The Postclassic Mesoamerican World.* University of Utah Press, Salt Lake City.

Smith, Michael E., and Lisa Montiel. 2001. The Archaeological Study of Empires and Imperialism in Pre-Hispanic Central Mexico. *Journal of Anthropological Archaeology* 20:245–284.

Spencer, Charles S. 2003. War and Early State Formation in Oaxaca, Mexico. *Proceedings of the National Academy of Sciences* 100:11185–11187.

Spencer, Charles S. 2010. Territorial Expansion and Primary State Formation. *Proceedings of the National Academy of Sciences* 107:7119–7126.

Spencer, Charles S., and Elsa M. Redmond. 2004. Primary State Formation in Mesoamerica. *Annual Review of Anthropology* 33:173–199.

Spores, Ronald. 1984. *The Mixtecs in Ancient and Colonial Times.* University of Oklahoma Press, Norman.

Stark, Barbara L. 2001. States and Empires. In *The Oxford Encyclopedia of Mesoamerican Cultures: The Civilizations of Mexico and Central America.* 3rd ed. edited by David Carrasco, pp. 165–167. Oxford University Press, Oxford.

Sugiyama, Saburo. 2004. Governance and Polity at Classic Teotihuacan. In *Mesoamerican Archaeology: Theory and Practice,* edited by Julia A. Hendon and Rosemary A. Joyce, pp. 97–123. Blackwell, Oxford.

Taube, Karl A. 2000. *The Writing System of Ancient Teotihuacan.* Center for Ancient American Studies, Washington, DC.

Urcid, Javier, Marcus Winter, and Raúl Matadamas. 1994. Nuevos monumentos grabados en Monte Albán, Oaxaca. In *Escritura zapoteca prehispánica: Nuevas aportaciones,* edited by Marcus Winter, pp. 2–52. Contribución 4. Proyecto Especial Monte Albán 1992–1994, Centro INAH Oaxaca, Oaxaca.

Wittfogel, Karl A. 1957. *Oriental Despotism: A Comparative Study of Total Power.* Yale University Press, New Haven.

Wolf, Eric R. 1959. *Sons of the Shaking Earth.* University of Chicago Press, Chicago.

Wolf, Eric R. 1994. Explaining Mesoamerica. *Social Anthropology: The Journal of the European Association of Social Anthropologists* 2:1–17.

Wright, Henry T. 1977. Recent Research on the Origin of the State. *Annual Review of Anthropology* 6:379–397.

Wright, Henry T. 1989. Mesopotamia to Mesoamerica. *Archaeology* 42(1):46–48, 96–100.

Beliefs and Rituals

CHAPTER 55

....

CREATION AND COSMOLOGY

GODS AND MYTHIC ORIGINS IN ANCIENT MESOAMERICA

....

KARL A. TAUBE

In ancient Mesoamerican thought, the creation and maintenance of the ordered world was only achieved through a concerted effort by the gods, a weighty responsibility that continued through the sacrificial offerings and rituals of mortals. The myths and behavior of gods not only explained the origins of the world but also served as models for human behavior for commoners and elites alike. Given the time depth and many cultures of Mesoamerica, it is not surprising that there is an extensive and complex array of deities and myths pertaining to this region. Some myths, such as the Aztec (or Mexica) episode of the birth of Huitzilopochtli (see Matos Moctezuma 1987), are unique to a particular time, place, and people. However, certain cosmogonic episodes and types of deities are particularly salient, making it possible to discuss broad and basic patterns of belief. Among these, the relation of events of creation to calendrical cycles is fundamental, both in terms of ordering the world and, as such, timed moments and in socially replicating and reifying the original acts of deities in the world of mortals.

Not surprisingly, many of the more important accounts pertaining to ancient Mesoamerican religion derive from the contact period of the sixteenth century, when many beliefs in both native languages and Spanish were recorded with Latin orthography. In addition, prehispanic manuscripts, such as the Mixtec Codex Vindobonensis, the central Mexican Codex Borgia and the Maya Codex Dresden, also provide illuminating glimpses into the mythic doings of gods as well as calendrics and cosmology. However, such delicate documents of paper and vellum are largely limited to the Late Postclassic (1250–1521 AD); for the earlier Classic period (250–900 AD) information pertaining to ancient Mesoamerican religious systems is largely gleaned from writing and iconography appearing in more durable media, including ceramics, mural painting, and stone monuments. Classic Maya carved or painted ceramic vessels constitute a great resource for reconstructing ancient creation events virtually a millennium before the extant Maya codices and the sixteenth-century *Popol Vuh*, a corpus unique in comparison to the rest of Classic-period Mesoamerica, which remains generally lacking in narrative scenes of creation mythology. Due to recent and still ongoing breakthroughs in our understanding of ancient Maya writing and art, a great deal is known concerning Classic Maya religion and iconography. The 2001 discovery of the San Bartolo murals in the northern Petén of Guatemala has exponentially increased our understanding of early Maya creation mythology. Dating to the first century BC, they constitute the most developed artistic program concerning creation mythology known for ancient Mesoamerica (Saturno 2009; Saturno et al. 2005; Taube et al. 2010). Not only do these murals aid in our understanding of the Late Preclassic origins of Classic Maya religion, but they also provide a link to still more ancient religious traditions, including those of the Olmec (ca. 1150–500 BC). However, although it is increasingly possible to trace certain beliefs of the contact period to remote antiquity, many of these same traditions have continued to the present, including detailed accounts concerning the flood, horned or plumed serpents, the origin of the sun and maize, and the mythic doings of gods of rain and lightning (e.g., Alcorn 1984; Braakhuis 1990; López Austin 1990; Negrín 1975; Taggart 1983; Thompson 1970: 197–373).

In ancient Mesoamerican thought, creation was not a single event but occurred numerous times. For the K'iche' Maya *Popol Vuh*, the theme of multiple world creations and destructions is cast in terms of failed attempts to create humans capable of worshipping and sustaining the gods, with the people of mud followed by those of wood, who were converted in monkeys from the flood and a rain of fire. In sixteenth-century Aztec accounts, the concept of multiple creations is still more developed, with four previous races of people and worlds, or "suns," before the present fifth sun, Nahui Ollin, 4 Motion, the calendrical name of the sun god Tonatiuh. Underlying the cause of the series of world creations and destructions is a cosmic battle between two deities, Tezcatlipoca and Quetzalcoatl, who are often adversaries but also allies in Aztec creation mythology. Tezcatlipoca, or "smoking mirror," is an omnipotent being of earthly, physical phenomena, and as such, is an embodiment of violent chaos, conflict, and change. In contrast, Quetzalcoatl, the quetzal-plumed serpent, is the god of the sustaining rain-bringing winds and the ephemeral breath of life.

According to Aztec belief, the creation of the sun and moon occurred at Teotihuacan, when humble Nanahuatzin and the haughty but cowardly Tecuciztecatl threw themselves into a sacrificial pyre to become the sun and moon (Bierhorst

1992: 147–149; Garibay 1979: 109; Mendieta 1980: 79–80; Sahagún 1950-1982, bk. 7: 3–8, 42–58). In Mesoamerica today, versions of the fiery transformation of the diseased and humble Nanahuatzin into the sun continue in the mythology of the eastern Gulf Coast region as well as with the Huichol of the western Pacific coast of Jalisco (Alcorn 1984: 58; Negrín 1975: 50–51; Taggart 1983: 101–102). Rising from the ashes, Nanahuatzin was reborn as the sun, Tonatiuh, who was already ready to fight his waiting predecessor, the morning star, Tlahuizcalpantecuhtli. With his brighter solar dart, the sun transformed him into a god of stone and coldness. However, every 584 days during the heliacal rising of Venus as the Morning Star, Tlahuizcalpantecuhtli emerges once again from the eastern sea to do battle, with only the sun to protect the world and the intended victims of this still fierce and angry god (see Seler 1904). Following the first battle of the dawn at Teotihuacan, the gods sacrificed themselves for the victorious sun to move and follow his path. Just as the gods first offered their hearts at Teotihuacan, human beings also nourish the sun through human sacrifice. The Mixtec sun god, 1 Death, is also a warlike being who appears wielding a spearthrower, including within a scene on page 23 of the Codex Vindobonensis, where he rises on a road of sacrificial blood. However, the concept of the sun deity as a bellicose, bloodthirsty deity is by no means limited to Late Postclassic highland Mexico, and it is becoming increasingly clear that the Classic as well as Postclassic Maya sun god, K'inich Ajaw, was also a god of war and sacrifice (Taube 2009b, 2010a).

Among the most widespread and basic mythic episodes in ancient Mesoamerica is the slaying and dismemberment of a primordial earth monster that had crocodilian and sharklike attributes. Among the Aztec and other peoples of Late Postclassic central Mexico, this creature was known as Cipactli, or "spiny one," which also is the first of the twenty day names in the sacred 260-day divinatory calendar (Garibay 1979: 25–26). The relation of Cipactli to the calendar probably concerns not only the concept of beginnings but also sacrificial dismemberment as the cosmogonic ordering of time and space. As noted by Susan Gillespie (1991: 333), "Cutting up the body thereby symbolizes the division of the cosmos into its constituent parts, both spatial (geographical) and temporal (cyclical)." According to the *Histoyre du Mechique*, Quetzalcoatl and Tezcatlipoca transform themselves into great serpents to tear in half the earth monster—here referred to as Tlaltecuhtli—with one portion of her body becoming the sky and the other the earth (Garibay 1979: 108). For the contact-period Maya of Yucatán, there is Itzam Kab Ayiin, or "iguana earth crocodile," a creature identified with the flood as well as with the creation of the world. A recently discovered mural from Mayapán depicts this creature speared and bound, floating in the sea with other slain aquatic creatures (see Houston et al. 2006: Figure 2.31). In the Late Postclassic Yucatán, the earth crocodile appears with day names and dates on its body, again relating it to the 260-day calendar as well as other cycles of time (Taube 1989). A text on a recently discovered bench in Temple XIX at Palenque demonstrates that a version of this creation episode was also present among the Late Classic Maya, with the text mentioning the decapitation of a cosmic crocodile as well as writing on its back, again a possible reference to calendrics (Stuart 2005: 68–77). For the ancient Maya, the earth crocodile can be readily traced back to the fifth century BC. Carved from a prismatic basalt column, Kaminaljuyú Stela 9 portrays a human figure standing or dancing atop the earth crocodile (see Finamore and Houston 2010: Number 75). In addition, the late Olmec Monument 63 from La Venta probably portrays an early version of the Cipactli myth, here with a human figure grappling with a vertically oriented, sharklike creature (Arnold 2005).

The earth as a cosmic crocodile floating on and surrounded by the sea constitutes a basic cosmological model in ancient Mesoamerica, but it is also by no means the only one. Still another is the concept of the earth as a square, with the corners oriented to the inter-cardinal points, much like the limbs of a splayed crocodile (Taube 2010b). However, in contrast to the primordial crocodilian monster, the four-sided cosmic model relates closely to concepts pertaining to human, socially constructed space, especially the *milpa* and a house with four corner posts (see Taube 2003). The sky-sustaining posts can be personified as gods in both central Mexico and in the Maya region, and they were referred to as the Bakabs in sixteenth-century Yucatán, where they are described in relation to the mythic flood (Thompson 1934). The corner posts relate to the world trees, although these living entities primarily denote the cardinal rather than inter-cardinal points. The erection of the corner posts and world trees relates to both the creation and delineation of ordered space and the raising of the sky. According to an Aztec creation account appearing in the *Historia de los Mexicanos por sus pinturas*, after the dismemberment of Cipactli, four directional roads leading to the world center separated the earth into quadrants, with Tezcatlipoca and Quetzalcoatl transforming themselves into a pair of trees to raise the sky (Garibay 1979: 32). Similarly, in the three Yukatek Maya *Chilam Balam* accounts of the Itzam Kab Ayiin episode, the directional world trees rise after the flood and the slaying of the earth monster (Taube 1993: 70, 72). The introductory page to the directional new year pages in the Codex Dresden portrays a celestial crocodilian spewing water from its mouth and body in a probable scene of the flood. The four following pages portray the erection of the directional world trees with sacrificial offerings, in other words, quite like the episode following the flood and killing of Itzam Kab Ayiin (Taube 1993: 72; 2010b). An especially early version of this sequence appears in the West Wall mural of Pinturas Sub-1a at San Bartolo. Although in different sequential order, the offerings before the world trees—a fish, deer, turkey, and aromatic flowers— are notably similar to the series appearing in the Codex Dresden almost 1,500 years later (Saturno 2009; Taube et al. 2010). In addition, four youths let blood through their phalli before the trees, again a reference to sacrifice as a fundamental act of creation (see Taube 2004a).

The mythic erection of the four world trees concerns not only the raising of the sky and directions, but also the systematic ordering of the cosmos. Although they appear with such mundane topics as calendrical cycles, colors, and directional animals, they literally encompass the entire world, with even the day names having their own spectrum of associations and belief. In the Dresden new year pages, the world trees are identified with specific days naming each 365-day year and directional colors, which for the ancient Maya were red for east, north for white, black for west, and yellow for south. Each of the twenty day names had a cardinal direction and color running in counterclockwise order beginning with Imix—equivalent to the Aztec Cipactli—to the east, and the following day name Ik' to the north. Although it remains to be demonstrated for the ancient Maya, in central Mexico each day that had its own color and direction also had its patron god, along with a closely parallel cycle of the twenty *trecenas*, thirteen-day "weeks" each with a "God of the Day" and associated celestial creatures. Each god of the thirteen series was probably identified with a certain level of the sky (Caso 1971; Nicholson 1971). For the Late Classic Maya, the 819-day calendrical cycle orients the series of twenty day names to the same cardinal points and colors known for the Maya codices and colonial Yukatek Maya accounts (Berlin and Kelley 1961).

Along with the Maya Dresden Codex, series of directional world trees appear in other prehispanic codices, including the Codex Borgia and Vaticanus B. In these passages, the same day names of each direction are oriented in groups of five below the world trees. However, the most elaborate and elegant display of this cosmological concept appears on page 1 of the Fejérváry-Mayer Codex. On this square page, the four-sided world appears as four trees, each with a specific bird and the five directional day names to the left-hand side. Thrown to the four quarters is the dismembered body of Tezcatlipoca, his arm to the east, his mirror foot to the north, his rib cage to the west, and his head to his south, recalling the sacrificial blood with the four world trees at San Bartolo.

The center of the Fejérváry-Mayer scene of the four-sided cosmos is occupied Xiuhtecuhtli, meaning Turquoise Lord, the god of fire and the pivotal world center. In central Mexican thought, this being symbolically overlaps with another fire deity, Huehueteotl, the "Old God," as can be seen in the following Florentine Codex account of the pivotal navel of the world, or *tlalxicco*: "mother of the gods, father of the gods, who resideth in the navel of the earth, who is set in the turquoise enclosure, [enclosed] with the waters of the lovely cotinga, enclosed with clouds— Ueueteotl, he of Ayamictlan, Xiuhtecuhti (Sahagún 1950–1982, bk. 6: 88–89). Huehueteotl is indeed an ancient god in Mesoamerica and can be traced to at least the first century BC in central Mexico and even earlier in Middle Formative Olmec sculpture (Taube 2004b: 102–104). This middle place of fire clearly relates to the cosmological metaphor of the four-sided house, here in terms of the central hearth. Another central Mexican source, the *Anales de Cuauhtitlan*, describes the centering of the world in terms of color-directional symbolism and directional offerings as well of the setting up of three hearthstones as the *axis mundi* (Bierhorst 1992: 23). For the ancient Maya, the three hearthstones were also of great importance, and they frequently appear in Late Classic Maya texts in reference to the great long count cycle beginning on August 13, 3114 BC (Freidel et al. 1993: 65–71; Taube 1998; Van Stone 2010: 29–35, 52–57). Although the texts are quite laconic and poorly understood, this calendrical event also appears on two Late Classic vessels portraying the convening of gods before an enthroned merchant deity currently referred to as God L (Coe 1973: 106–109; Grube and Kerr 1998; Van Stone 2010: 36–40). It is surely no coincidence that one of the vases is four-sided, again referring to the cosmic house model (see Grube and Kerr 1998).

Aside from the cosmic crocodile and four-sided world, a turtle floating on the sea also served as a basis for the world in ancient Maya thought. A Late Postclassic scene from the Codex Madrid portrays a darkened sky raining upon the earth turtle with the three hearthstones atop its back, and roughly contemporaneous sculptures from the northern Maya lowlands depict a hole in the center of its carapace, again referring to the world center (see Taube 1988; Finamore and Houston 2010: Number 85). Many Late Classic Maya vessel scenes portray the maize god emerging from the center of the turtle's carapace (Taube 1985; Freidel et al. 1993). In ancient Maya thought, the maize god also embodied the central world axis, and Early Classic caches from Copán feature jade statuettes of the maize deity placed in the center of directionally oriented jade and spondylus caches (Taube 2005: 25). Similarly, both a stone box from Tizapán and page 31 of the Codex Borbonicus portray the Aztec maize goddess Chicomecoatl surrounded by four directional aspects of the rain god, Tlaloc, each denoted by a particular color (see Taube 2000: 318–319, Figures 22-23). For the aforementioned series of directional world trees appearing in the Codex Borgia, the fifth tree of the world center is a maize plant sprouting out of a pool of water (Codex Borgia: page 53).

The relation of maize to the central *axis mundi* can be readily traced to the Middle Formative Olmec (ca. 900-500 BC). A number of incised celts portray the Olmec maize god in the center of four evenly spaced directional signs placed at the inter-cardinal points, quite probably portraying the earth as a four-sided field with maize in the center (Taube 1996: 44, Figure 6; 2000: 303). Due to the recent discoveries at San Bartolo, the historic links between the Olmec and Classic Maya maize gods are becoming increasingly clear, with the Late Preclassic Maya maize god retaining many facial characteristics of his Olmec predecessor (Taube and Saturno 2008).

For the Classic Maya, the scenes of the maize god and the earth turtle are not only cosmological models but also constitute an important episode of creation mythology, the rebirth of the maize god out of the earth (Taube 1985). Classic Maya vessels provide a rich corpus of narrative information concerning the underworld watery journey and resurrection of the maize deity (Braakhuis 1990; Fitzimmons 2009: 35–39; Freidel et al. 1993: 89–94; Just 2009; Quenon and Le Forte 1997; Taube 1985, 1993). In many scenes, the god is accompanied and assisted by a pair of youths; commonly referred to as the Headband Twins, they are the Classic-period counterparts of Xbalanque and Hunahpu of the *Popol Vuh* (see Coe 1989). One salient episode that occurs in both the sixteenth-century K'ichean text and Classic Maya scenes is the shooting down of a monster bird by the Hero Twins, known as Vucub Caquix in the *Popol Vuh* and the Principal Bird Deity in current Classic Maya studies. Scenes pertaining to the defeat of the great bird by the Hero Twins can be traced still earlier to Late Preclassic Izapa (see Coe 1989). The West Wall mural from Pinturas Sub-1 at San Bartolo depicts a Late Preclassic version of the maize god emerging from the earth turtle, in this case flanked by the god of celestial rain and lightning, Chahk, and the god of terrestrial water (Taube and Saturno 2008; Taube et al. 2010). The appearance of a maize deity on a turtle carapace appears as early as the Middle Formative Olmec, this example being a serpentine pectoral from La Encrucijada, Tabasco, which depicts the head of the infant form of the Olmec maize god atop the underside of a turtle shell (see Taube 1996: 62, Figure 22c). However, in the Gulf Coast region today among the Tepehua, Sierra Totonac, Popoluca, and other peoples, there is a widespread and complex mythic account of an infant maize god who is slain, ground up, and thrown into water only to appear reborn on the back of a turtle, arguably making this the longest lived mythic episodes known for ancient Mesoamerica (Braakhuis 1990; Taube 1996: 62; Taube and Saturno 2008: 315).

In two Late Classic Maya vessel scenes, forms of Chahk—the god of rain and lightning—break open the turtle shell. In one example, two Chahks brandishing lightning weapons flank the carapace and the emerging maize god, while for the other, a single Chahk holds a stone behind his head in preparation to strike the shell to release the emerging maize god (Robicsek and Hales 1981: Figures 58–59; Taube 1993: 66–67). The mythic event of lightning gods breaking open the earth, often as a massive rock or mountain, is again one of the most widespread and enduring myths of Mesoamerica. Among the Aztec, the red, blue, yellow, and white Tlalocs of the four directions prepared to split the rock of sustenance with their lightning, but it was the humble Nanahuatzin who accomplished the task (Bierhorst 1992: 147). Among the Sierra Nahuat of Veracruz, this myth continues to the present, with Nanahuatzin also mentioned in the episode (Taggart 1983: 87–92). In addition, forms of the myth are also known for contemporary Maya peoples as well as the Zoque of Chiapas (Thompson 1970: 349–352; Villasana Benítez 2009).

Clearly, the gods of rain and lightning constitute one of the most widespread and ancient group of deities known for Mesoamerica. According to J. Eric S. Thompson (1970: 279), the Mesoamerican rain complex can be traced back to the early Olmec: "It is my opinion that the rain cult, with world color and directional features and with quadripartite deities deriving from or fused with snakes, had developed in all of its essentials in the Formative period, probably as an Olmec creation." In a well-known diagram, Miguel Covarrubias (1946: Fig. 4) traced Mesoamerican rain gods, including the central Mexican Tlaloc, Cocijo of the Zapotec, and Chahk of the Maya to an Olmec prototype. There is now increasing evidence that the Covarrubias diagram is largely correct, with early forms of Chahk, Cocijo, and Tlaloc sharing many striking traits, including a snarling mouth and a deeply furrowed brow, with the Olmec rain god (Taube 1995, 2009a). In addition, it is likely that directional rain symbolism was also present. Dating to roughly 600 BC, a recently discovered Olmec-style cache from Cival, Guatemala, was a cruciform pit containing five large urns: four at the cardinal points and one in the center. Below the central vessel there were five vertically oriented jade celts, with the finest example in the middle (Estrada-Belli 2006). Roughly a millennium later, at Early Classic Teotihuacan, an offering from the Pyramid of the Moon contained five urns with the face of Tlaloc, with four at the corners and one in the center (Sugiyama and Cabrera Castro 2004: Figures 35, 97–98). Both the Cival and Teotihuacan offerings recall scenes from the Late Postclassic Codex Borgia and Codex Vaticanus B, which feature four directional Tlalocs atop with a fifth in the center, all casting water down upon maize fields.

Many aspects of the Mesoamerican rain-god complex—their relation to world directions and mountains; water jars as symbolic rain clouds; serpents as lightning—are also present among the Puebloan peoples of the American Southwest, suggesting that these images are part of a very ancient agricultural tradition (Schaafsma and Taube 2006).

Although all too often the more sanguinary aspects of ancient Mesoamerican religions, such as Classic Maya bloodletting, human sacrifice, and the Aztec cult of sacred warfare, tend to be stressed, some of the most basic and enduring traits, including the four-sided world, sacred mountains, directional rain gods and the *axis mundi*, are about water and maize, which are the stuff of life.

REFERENCES

Alcorn, Janis B. 1984. *Huastec Mayan Ethnobotany*. University of Texas Press, Austin.

Arnold, Philip J. III. 2005. The Shark-Monster in Olmec Iconography. *Mesoamerican Voices* 2:5–36.

Berlin, Heinrich, and David Kelley. 1961. The 819-Day Count and Color-Direction Symbolism among the Classic Maya. *Middle American Research Series* 26:9–20. Middle American Research Institute, Tulane University, New Orleans.

Bierhorst, John. 1992. *History and Mythology of the Aztecs: The Codex Chimalpopoca*. University of Arizona Press, Tucson.

Braakhuis, H. E. M. 1990. The Bitter Flour: Birth Scenes of the Tonsured Maize God. In *Mesoamerican Dualism/Dualismo Mesoamericano*, edited by Rudolf van Zantwijk, Rob de Ridder, and Edwin Braakhuis, pp. 125–147. ISOR, Utrecht.

Caso, Alfonso. 1971. Calendrical Systems of Central Mexico. In *Handbook of Middle American Indians*, volume 10, part 1, edited by Robert Wauchope, pp. 333–348. University of Texas Press, Austin.

Coe, Michael D. 1973. *The Maya Scribe and His World*. Grolier Club, New York.

Coe, Michael D. 1989. The Hero Twins: Myth and Image. In *The Maya Vase Book* 1, edited by Justin Kerr, pp. 161–184. Kerr Associates, New York.

Covarrubias, Miguel. 1946. El arte olmeca de La Venta. *Cuadernos Americanos* 4:154–179.

Estrada-Belli, Francisco. 2006. Lightning, Sky, Rain and the Maize God: The Ideology of Preclassic Maya Rulers at Cival, Peten, Guatemala. *Ancient Mesoamerica* 17:57–78.

Finamore, Daniel, and Stephen Houston, eds. 2010. *The Fiery Pool: The Maya and the Mythic Sea*. Yale University Press, New Haven.

Fitzimmons, James L. 2009. *Death and the Classic Maya Kings*. University of Texas Press, Austin.

Freidel, David, Linda Schele, and Joy Parker. 1993. *Maya Cosmos: 3,000 Years on the Shaman's Path*. William Morrow, New York.

Garibay, Angel Maria. 1979. *Teogonía e historia de los Mexicanos: Tres opúsculos del siglo XVI.* Editorial Porrúa, Mexico City.

Gillespie, Susan D. 1991. Ballgames and Boundaries. In *The Mesoamerican Ballgame,* edited by Vernon L. Scarborough and David R. Wilcox, pp. 317–345. University of Arizona Press, Tucson.

Grube, Nikolai, and Justin Kerr. 1998. Two Sides of a Quadrangular Polychrome Classic Maya Vase. *Mexicon* 20(1):2.

Houston, Stephen, David Stuart, and Karl Taube. 2006. *The Memory of Bones: Body, Being, and Experience among the Classic Maya.* University of Texas Press, Austin.

Just, Brian. 2009. Mysteries of the Maize God. *Record: Princeton University Art Museum* 68:2–15.

López Austin, Alfredo. 1990. *Myths of the Opossum: Pathways of Mesoamerican Mythology.* Translated by Bernard Ortíz de Montellano and Thelma Ortíz de Montellano. University of New Mexico Press, Albuquerque.

Matos Moctezuma, Eduardo. 1987. Symbolism of the Templo Mayor. In *The Aztec Templo Mayor,* edited by Elizabeth H. Boone, pp. 185–209. Dumbarton Oaks, Washington, DC.

Mendieta, Geronimo de. 1980. *Historia eclesiastica indiana.* Editorial Porrua, Mexico City.

Negrín, Juan. 1975. *The Huichol Creation of the World.* E. B. Crocker Art Gallery, Sacramento.

Nicholson, Henry B. 1971. Religion in Pre-Hispanic Central Mexico. In *Handbook of Middle American Indians,* volume 10, part 1, edited by Robert Wauchope, pp. 395–446. University of Texas Press, Austin.

Quenon, Michel, and Geneviève Le Fort. 1997. Rebirth and Resurrection in Maize God Iconography. In *The Maya Vase Book,* vol. 5, edited by Justin Kerr, pp. 884–902. Kerr Associates, New York.

Robicsek, Francis, and Donald M. Hales. 1981. *The Maya Book of the Dead: The Ceramic Codex.* University of Virginia Art Museum, Charlottesville.

Sahagún, Fray Bernardino. 1950–1982. *Florentine Codex: General History of the Things of New Spain,* 13 vols. Translated by A. J. O. Anderson and C. E. Dibble. School of American Research, Santa Fe.

Saturno, William. 2009. Centering the Kingdom, Centering the King: Maya Creation and Legitimization at San Bartolo. In *The Art of Urbanism: How Mesoamerican Cities Represented Themselves in Architecture and Imagery,* edited by William L. Fash and Leonardo López Luján, pp. 111–134. Dumbarton Oaks Research Library and Collections, Washington, DC.

Saturno, William, David Stuart, and Karl Taube. 2005. *The Murals of San Bartolo, El Peten, Guatemala, Part 1: The North Wall.* Ancient America 7, Center for Ancient American Studies, Barnardsville.

Schaafsma, Polly, and Karl Taube. 2006. Bringing the Rain: An Ideology of Rain Making in the Pueblo Southwest and Mesoamerica. In *A Pre-Columbian World: Searching for a Unitary Vision of Ancient America,* edited by Jeffrey Quilter and Mary Miller, pp. 231–285. Dumbarton Oaks Research Library and Collections, Washington, DC.

Seler, Eduard E. 1904. Venus Period in the Picture Writings of the Borgian Codex Group. In *Mexican and Central Mexican Antiquities, Calendar Systems, and History,* edited by Charles P. Bowditch, pp. 355–391. Bureau of American Ethnology, Bulletin 28, Smithsonian Institution, Washington, DC.

Stuart, David. 2005. *The Inscriptions from Temple XIX: A Commentary*. Pre-Columbian Art Research Institute, San Francisco.

Sugiyama, Saburo, and Rubén Cabrero Castro. 2004. *Voyage to the Center of the Moon Pyramid: Recent Discoveries at Teotihuacan*. Arizona State University, Tempe, and Instituto Nacional de Antropología e Historia, Mexico, D.F.

Taggart, James M. 1983. *Nahuat Myth and Social Structure*. University of Texas, Austin.

Taube, Karl Andreas. 1985. The Classic Maya Maize God: A Reappraisal. In *Fifth Palenque Round Table, 1983*, edited by Merle Greene Robertson, pp. 171-181. Pre-Columbian Art Research Institute, San Francisco.

Taube, Karl Andreas. 1988. A Prehispanic Maya Katun Wheel. *Journal of Anthropological Research* 44(2):183–203.

Taube, Karl Andreas. 1989. Itzam Cab Ain: Caimans, Cosmology and Calendrics in Postclassic Yucatan. *Research Reports on Ancient Maya Writing*, no. 26.

Taube, Karl Andreas. 1993. *Aztec and Maya Myths*. British Museum, London, and University of Texas Press, Austin.

Taube, Karl Andreas. 1995. The Rainmakers: The Olmec and Their Contribution to Mesoamerican Belief and Ritual. In *The Olmec World, Ritual and Rulership*, edited by Gill Guthrie, pp. 82–103. Art Museum, Princeton University.

Taube, Karl Andreas. 1996. The Olmec Maize God: The Face of Corn in Formative Mesoamerica. *Res: Anthropology and Aesthetics* 29/30:39–81.

Taube, Karl Andreas. 1998. The Jade Hearth: Centrality, Rulership, and the Classic Maya Temple. In *Function and Meaning in Classic Maya Architecture*, edited by Stephen D. Houston, pp. 427–478. Dumbarton Oaks Research Library and Collections, Washington, DC.

Taube, Karl Andreas. 2000. Lightning Celts and Corn Fetishes: The Formative Olmec and the Development of Maize Symbolism in Mesoamerica and the American Southwest. *In Olmec Art and Archaeology: Social Complexity in the Formative Period*, edited by John E. Clark and Mary Pye, pp. 297–337. Studies in the History of Art, vol. 58, National Gallery of Art, Washington, DC.

Taube, Karl Andreas. 2003. Ancient and Contemporary Maya Conceptions about the Field and Forest. In *The Lowland Maya Area: Three Millennia at the Human-Wildland Interface*, edited by Arturo Gómez-Pompa, Michael F. Allen, Scott Fedick, and J. J. Jiménez-Osornio, pp. 461–492. Haworth Press, New York.

Taube, Karl Andreas. 2004a. Aztec Religion: Creation, Sacrifice, and Renewal. In *The Aztec Empire*, curated by Felipe Solís, pp. 168–177. Guggenheim Museum, New York.

Taube, Karl Andreas. 2004b. *Olmec Art at Dumbarton Oaks*. Dumbarton Oaks, Washington, DC.

Taube, Karl Andreas. 2005. The Symbolism of Jade in Classic Maya Religion. *Ancient Mesoamerica* 16:23–50.

Taube, Karl Andreas. 2009a. El dios de la lluvia Olmeca. *Arqueología Mexicana* 16(96):26–29.

Taube, Karl Andreas. 2009b. The Womb of the World: The *Cuauhxicalli* and Other Offering Bowls in Ancient and Contemporary Mesoamerica, *Maya Archaeology* 1:86–106. Precolumbia Mesoweb Press, San Francisco.

Taube, Karl Andreas. 2010a. At Dawn's Edge: Tulum, Santa Rita and Floral Symbolism of Late Postclassic Yucatan. In *Astronomers, Scribes, and Priests: Intellectual Interchange between the Northern Maya Lowlands and Highland Mexico in the Late Postclassic Period*, edited by Gabrielle Vail and Christine Hernandez, pp. 145–191. Dumbarton Oaks Research Library and Collections, Washington, DC.

Taube, Karl Andreas. 2010b. Where Earth and Sky Meet: The Sea in Ancient and Contemporary Maya Cosmology. In *The Fiery Pool: The Maya and the Mythic Sea*, edited by Daniel Finamore and Stephen Houston, pp. 202–219. Yale University Press, New Haven.

Taube, Karl, and William Saturno. 2008. Los murales de San Bartolo: Desarrollo temprano del simbolismo y del mito del maíz en la antigua Mesoamérica. In *Olmeca: Balance y perspectivas*, edited by María Teresa Uriarte and Rebecca B. González Lauck, pp. 287–318. Universidad Nacional Autónoma de México, Mexico City.

Taube, Karl, William Saturno, David Stuart, and Heather Hurst. 2010. *The Murals of San Bartolo, El Peten, Guatemala, Part 2: The West Wall*. Ancient America 11, Center for Ancient American Studies, Barnardsville.

Thompson, J. Eric S. 1934. *Sky Bearers, Colors, and Directions in Maya and Mexican Religion*. Carnegie Institution of Washington, Pub. 436, Contrib. 10. Washington, DC.

Thompson, J. Eric S. 1970. *Ancient Maya History and Religion*. University of Oklahoma Press, Norman.

Van Stone, Mark. 2010. *2012: Science and Prophecy of the Ancient Maya*. Tlacaélel Press, San Diego.

Villasana Benítez, Susana. 2009. The Presence of Corn in Myths. The *K'en miomo*. Zoques of Chiapas. *Latin American Indian Literatures Journal* 25(1):1–18.

CHAPTER 56

SACRED PLACES
AND SACRED
LANDSCAPES

KATHRYN REESE-TAYLOR

RECENT studies of ancient landscapes have matured into well-rounded inquiries regarding humanity's engagement with the environment. While many remain centered on topics such as the distribution of settlements throughout a region, the modification of the environment for agricultural purposes, and large-scale water-management projects, they are complemented by an array of newer studies focused on sacred landscapes, which Knapp and Ashmore (1999) term the "socio-symbolic aspects of human-environment interaction." What unites these seemingly disparate perspectives is the concept that landscapes, especially sacred landscapes, are the result of collective human activity and, as such, are culturally constructed.

Sacred places and landscapes can be found both in nature and in the built environment. What distinguishes such spaces is not the degree of human modification, but the acts that are performed there. A sacred place is created from a prosaic space by means of human action that is of a spiritual or religious nature, such as rituals or ceremonies. A sacred landscape is a temporal and spatial fabric spread over a geographic region, unifying all the rituals conducted at the various sacred places within a narrative framework.

Often the rituals performed in sacred places are commemorated by cultural materials, such as offerings, monuments, or buildings. However, material symbols are not necessary to consecrate a place, only actions. Further, the sanctity of a place endures as long as the actions performed there remain in the social memory of a people.

Paradigms of Sacred Geography

Perhaps the earliest investigation of sacred places in Mesoamerica was a study of the role of caves in Maya culture written by J. E. S. Thompson (1959). However, it was during the 1970s that interest in the concept of a sacred geography increased, due principally to two events in 1971: the discovery of a cave under the Pyramid of the Sun at Teotihuacan and the publication of *Pivot of the Four Quarters* by Paul Wheatley. Heyden (1975) recognized that the cave under the Pyramid of the Sun was a replica of Chicomoztoc, the Aztec cave of origin, linking a sacred place to the creation narrative. Wheatley (1971) argued that ancient people built cities and shaped sacred landscapes according to religious and ideological tenets, resulting in a cosmogram, the symbolic manifestation of the cosmic order of the universe (cf. Coggins 1967).

Following Wheatley, Townsend (1979) asserted that Tenochtitlan was conceived and built as a representation of the Aztec worldview and in 1988, Freidel and Schele expanded the concept of the cosmogram by applying the term to elements of sculpture and artwork found in Maya centers. Directional cosmology has been used to explain various features in Maya cities, including architectural arrangements, water reservoirs, and sacbeob (Ashmore 1989, 1991; Ashmore and Sabloff 2002; Demarest et al. 2003; Fash 1998; Houk 1996; Kowalski and Dunning 1999; Scarborough 1998; Shaw 2001; Tourtellot et al. 2002). Sugiyama (1993), Manzanilla (1997), Cowgill (Carl et al. 2000), and Headrick (2007) explored cosmological notions at Teotihuacan, and Joyce (2004) applied similar concepts to Monte Albán.

However, recently, the concept of the Mesoamerican city as a cosmogram has come under fire. This critique is best illustrated in the debate between Smith (2003, 2005) and Ashmore and Sabloff (2002, 2003). Smith criticizes the validity of the north-south axis proposed by Ashmore for Classic-period Maya cities and argues that Mesoamericanists indiscriminately employ the cosmogram model. Ashmore and Sabloff counter with examples of cosmological principles employed meaningfully in many cases. Ivan Šprajc (2005) also contests Smith's arguments, stating that the Maya used significant astronomical alignments to orient their buildings and cities.

Indeed, since Blom first suggested that the E-group at Uaxactun was used to track the movement of the sun, astronomical alignments have been an important focus of research (Ricketson and Ricketson 1937). Aveni's studies of archaeoastronomy in Mesoamerica provided the foundation for subsequent investigations in this area (Aveni 1981, 1983; Aveni et al. 1988; Aveni and Hartung 1982, 1986; Aveni et al. 1982). Schele (Freidel et al. 1993) explored Classic Maya astronomy and its relationship to creation narratives, such as the Popol Vuh, determining that several architectural complexes may replicate constellations and supernatural locales. Most recently, Šprajc (Šprajc et al. 2009) has identified several astronomical alignments in buildings from El Mirador.

Beyond astronomical alignments, sacred landscapes often replicated important features in the natural world. While Heyden (1975) stated that the Pyramid of the Sun was intentionally placed above a natural cave, recently Manzanilla (Manzanilla et al. 1996) has argued that the Teotihuacanos excavated the cave, (re)creating the entrance to the underworld.

Like the artificial cave under the Pyramid of the Sun, natural caves lie under the El Duende pyramid, the Bat Palace, and a number of residential structures at Dos Pilas (Brady 1997), where they also offer a sensory experience of the landscape. Every year at the onset of the rainy season, water discharges from the Cueva de los Murciélagos under the Bat Palace, causing a roar that can be heard for more than a half kilometer (Brady and Ashmore 1999: 129). This hierophany transcends the boundary between the natural and built environments, a distinction that is often blurred within Mesoamerican sacred places as natural features are incorporated into built environments and as built environments mimic natural features in the landscape.

Often, natural and constructed features separated by large distances are woven together into a sacred landscape that covers many square kilometers, as was the case in the Basin of Mexico during the Late Postclassic. The Templo Mayor of Tenochtitlan embodied state ideology, with both water/fertility and militarism represented in the twin temples dedicated to the deities Tlaloc and Huitzilopochtli, between which the sun rose on the equinox (Aveni et al. 1988). Moreover, the Templo Mayor was oriented so that the mountain dedicated to Tlaloc, located to the east, appeared behind it on the horizon (Umberger 2002: 190). A walled compound with a long passageway, representing the entrance to the underworld from which the sun rose each day, sat atop Mount Tlaloc; there, Aztec rulers performed ceremonies dedicated to the Storm God to ensure continued fertility at the beginning of the rainy season (Umberger 2002).

The sacred hill of Tetzcotzingo is also linked to Mount Tlaloc, as the springs that fed the aqueducts encircling the hill originate at the foot of the sacred mountain dedicated to the Storm God. Interestingly, the sculptural program located on the summit of Tetzcotzingo references the same state ideology as the Templo Mayor (Townsend 1982). To the east of the summit was a statue of a feathered wolf—now destroyed—that represented a metaphorical image of King Netzahualcoyotl of Texcoco, who commissioned the carving to commemorate his military achievements during the battles that established Texcoco's independence. Thus, martial ideology was complemented by the imagery of water and fecundity associated with Tlaloc.

Over an area of about 116 square miles, the Aztec created a cohesive sacred landscape marked by places encompassing natural, as well as human-constructed features, and which echoed the duality of state religious ideology (Townsend 1982). Yet the cohesiveness of the landscape is not based on the similarity in the sculpture or architecture found in each place, but on the meaning bestowed on these features by human performances reenacting significant mytho-historical narratives.

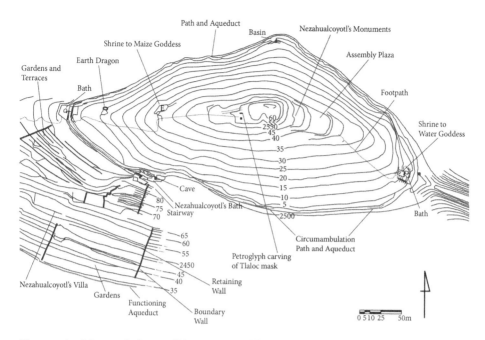

Figure 56.1 Map and photo of Tetzcotzingo (drawn by Kristin Sullivan and the author after Townsend 1982, Figure 7).

THE NARRATIVE STRUCTURE OF SACRED PLACE AND LANDSCAPE

Narrative frameworks give meaning to discrete human acts in various locales and embed a sacred landscape within the social memory of people. People culturally construct sacred locales by means of mytho-historical accounts that encompass neither an isolated report of a single event nor a chronological sequence of events. Instead, the narratives used to constitute sacred landscapes, and the places within them, selectively recount events and fragments of episodes that are important to a specific group. Events within narratives, therefore, are related to geographic locales with little attention paid to temporal flow.

Often it is the very acts associated with the recounting of past events, such as rituals performed in sacred places, that create the relationship between past and present, especially when people move into a new region. Migration tales, for example, give meaning to multiple landscapes to establish the right to inhabit a particular region (López Austin 1973: 98). Thus social groups create a relationship among themselves, the land, and the past through the narrative. They literally write themselves into the story by imprinting the narrative onto space.

A sacred landscape, then, is commonly infused with temporal significance. The present constantly crafts the past: Temporal qualities of landscape are bound

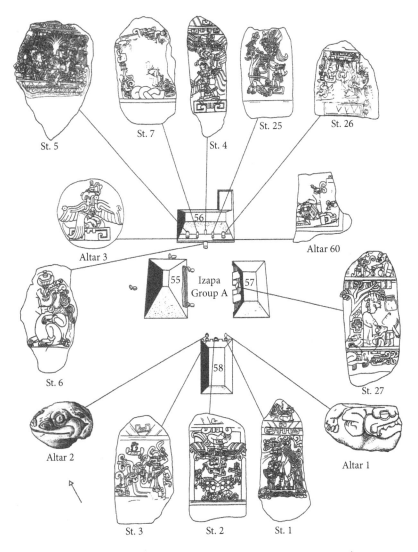

Figure 56.2 Group A, Izapa. (Guernsey 2006: Figure 1.4).

to the cultural construction of history through social memory. Specific actions are etched onto places and landscapes, and when the act is repeated or the locale seen again by an individual, the past event is recalled (Basso 1984). Viewing or recalling a sacred landscape recontextualizes the past in the present, thereby (re)creating a history.

Guernsey's (2006) study of the sacred landscape at Izapa illustrates this concept. Group A, located in the southwestern sector of Izapa's ceremonial zone, consists of a large plaza surrounded by four large platform mounds. The sculptural program within the plaza commemorates the ritual performances of a ruler's reenactment of passages of the creation narrative. In total, fourteen stelae and altars ring the plaza, most depicting scenes from the epic creation narrative of eastern

Mesoamerica, later recorded in the Popol Vuh (Guernsey 2006: 123). The place created through these performances was the supernatural location of the events that occurred during the creation of the world.

In addition, each stela was carefully placed within the compound in association with specific platforms and in precise relationship to one another, so that a storyline was created as actors moved through the plaza in a ritual circuit. Past and present were also fused at points: Stelae 2 and 4 and Altar 3 portray scenes from the narrative with the Izapan ruler inserted as the protagonist (Guernsey 2006: 122–123), performing in the guise of the Principal Bird Deity, one of the main characters in this early version of the creation myth. Accordingly, imagery of the ruler, the principal actor during ritual performances, punctuated the flow of the mythical timeline. Myth and history became intertwined within the landscape, and both were continuously recontextualized with each succeeding ceremony.

Naachtun offers a glimpse of how a narrative can structure ritual space throughout an entire civic center. Naachtun was a Classic-period city, the political and economic capital of a thriving polity with a dense urban and rural population. Sacred places within Naachtun, as elsewhere, were interspersed among, and at times coincided with, secular architecture. This, however, did not keep the citizens of Naachtun from creating a vivid and cohesive sacred landscape.

Naachtun grew by accretion from west to east. To the west lay Group C, the oldest sector of the site that included Structure 1, a triadic group located atop a truncated platform that also contained the remains of the earliest known tomb at its base, and Structure 5, a funerary acropolis. The E-group, the ballcourt, and the reservoir were located in Group A, situated at the center of the site to the east and connected to Group C via a long east-west sacbe. Further to the east and also linked to Group A by a wide east-west sacbe was Group B, which contained the radial pyramid (Morton 2007; Reese-Taylor et al. 2005).

Walking west to east through the cityscape, an individual moved from Structure 1, the First Three Stone Place, location of the three hearthstones of creation and the resting place of an important early ancestor, to Structure 5, a North Eight House Place, which marked the cardinal and inter-cardinal directions of the cosmos and was the burial location of several early ancestors (Reese-Taylor 2002). Events associated with the creation of the world—as recorded in Palenque's Temple of the Cross (Stuart 2005: 164–166)—occurred at these two locales.

Continuing east along the sacbe, an individual arrived at Naachtun's ballcourt, the mythic location of the ballgame between the Hero Twins and the Lords of the Underworld. The ballcourt, symbolizing an entrance to the underworld, was adjacent to the western entrance of the West Plaza. The reservoir, which also represented an entrance to the underworld in Maya cosmology, was located at the opposite, eastern end of the plaza. Moreover buildings and terraces surrounded the entire plaza, giving it the appearance of a large sunken courtyard. This built environment clearly identified the West Plaza as a location for public ceremonies set in the netherworld, perhaps the place where the Hero Twins struggled with the Lords of the Underworld.

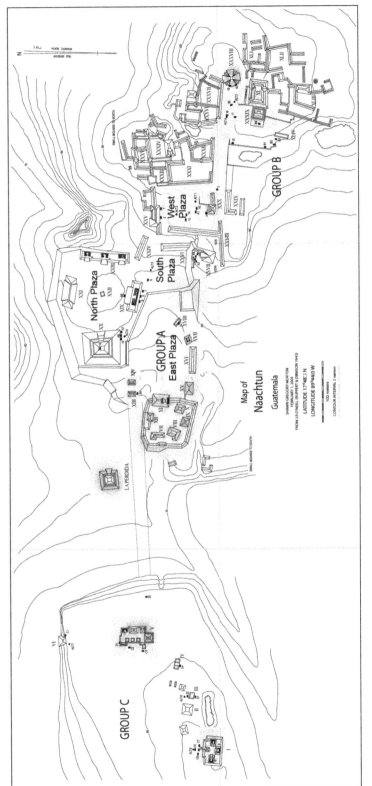

Figure 56.3 Map of Naachtun (drawing by Shawn Morton).

Just north of the West Plaza, the North Plaza contains the E-Group, which marked the passage of sun on pivotal days and contained at least three tombs of Early Classic rulers (Reese-Taylor et al. 2005). The four buildings surrounding the plaza were placed in the cardinal directions, and the entirety created a setting for the inaugural acts of the Maize God: just after the moment when he lifts the sky from the waters of the underworld, he lays out the four directions of the world and spins the sky, starting time (Reese 1996; Reese-Taylor 2002).

Finally, in the eastern sector of the site, a west-facing pyramid sits at the end of a wide sacbe, thereby linking it to the East Plaza: the stelae of Naachtun's Late Classic kings and queens line the causeway. This pyramid was a physical expression of Snake Mountain, which rose from the watery underworld and memorialized events involving the acquisition of military regalia and conquest of enemies (Reese-Taylor 2002; Reese-Taylor and Koontz 2001; Schele and Guernsey Kappelman 2001). Therefore, it is no accident that the stelae at the base of Structure 40 record an important victory over Calakmul (Mathews et al. 2005).

The narrative structure of the Naachtun landscape is not a chronological sequence of events, but rather episodes selectively woven together in a way that was meaningful to the city's inhabitants. The narrative grew by accretion, just as the city did; older episodes of the narrative performed in Group C were augmented with future events and flashbacks. At the heart of the landscape was the West Plaza, the realm of the underworld and the setting for primordial events of creation (Morton 2007), which was connected to the North Plaza via terraces and to Group C to the west and Group B to the east through sacbeob.

As at Izapa, the rulers of Naachtun inserted their stories into the narrative by means of tomb and stelae placement. History and mythology were inextricably intertwined in the sacred geography of the site, while rituals and commonplace events continuously revised the narrative embodied within the Naachtun landscape.

CONCLUSIONS

Sacred places and landscapes within Mesoamerica are created and evolve through human acts. While these places may reflect the cosmological organizing principles of society, they are not merely cosmograms but dynamic, complex landscapes created as settings for the reenactments of mytho-historical narratives. Narrative structure unifies the sacred places within broader landscapes and reinforces the social memory of the acts performed in them.

Like narratives, these landscapes are temporalized in several fashions. Events and places from the past are made relevant in the present by stressing aspects of the story that resonate with living populations or by inserting historical individuals and their acts into the narratives. Temporal flow is often suspended; sacred places are not ordered sequentially, but are contingent upon what is meaningful to populations at different points in history. Therefore, sacred landscapes grow by accretion and can seamlessly integrate flashbacks and flash forwards.

Sacred places and landscapes are also spatially liminal. Just as events in stories happen in a time before time, and are then reenacted in the present, sacred places coexist with prosaic places: a sacred place can be a plaza that both serves as the location of a market within a bustling city at one time and, at another time, is the location of the watery underworld.

Finally, like creation and migration narratives, sacred landscapes are religious and philosophical touchstones, as well as powerful sociopolitical statements. Because they embody the metanarratives of Mesoamerican people, sacred places and sacred landscapes are enduring in the social memory.

References

Ashmore, Wendy. 1989. Construction and Cosmology: Politics and Ideology in Lowland Maya Settlement Patterns. In *Word and Image in Maya Culture: Explorations in Language, Writing, and Representation*, edited by William F. Hanks and Don S. Rice, pp. 272–286. University of Utah Press, Salt Lake City.

Ashmore, Wendy. 1991. Site-Planning Principles and Concepts of Directionality among the Ancient Maya. *Latin American Antiquity* 2(3):199–226.

Ashmore, Wendy, and Jeremy A. Sabloff. 2002. Spatial Orders in Maya Civic Plans. *Latin American Antiquity* 13(2):201–215.

Ashmore, Wendy, and Jeremy A. Sabloff. 2003. Interpreting Ancient Maya Civic Plans: Reply to Smith. *Latin American Antiquity* 14(2):229–236.

Aveni, Anthony F. 1981. Archaeoastronomy in the Maya Region: A Review of the Past Decade. *Archaeoastronomy, no. 3 (Journal for the History of Astronomy Supplement* 12):S1–S16.

Aveni, Anthony F. 1983. *Skywatchers of Ancient Mexico*. University of Texas Press, Austin.

Aveni Anthony F., E. E. Calnek, and Horst Hartung. 1988. Myth, Environment, and the Orientation of the Templo Mayor of Tenochtitlan. *American Antiquity* 53(2):287–309.

Aveni, Anthony F., and Horst Hartung. 1982. Precision in the Layout of Maya Architecture. *Annals of the New York Academy of Sciences* 385:63–80.

Aveni, Anthony F., and Horst Hartung. 1986. Maya City Planning and the Calendar. *Transactions of the American Philosophical Society* 76(7):1–87.

Aveni, Anthony, Horst Hartung, and J. Charles Kelley. 1982. Alta Vista (Chalchihuites), Astronomical Implications of a Mesoamerican Ceremonial Outpost. *American Antiquity* 47(2):316–335.

Basso, Keith. 1984. "Stalking with Stories": Names, Places, and Moral Narratives among the Western Apache. In *Text, Play, and Story: The Construction and Reconstruction of Self and Society*, edited by E. Bruner, pp. 19–53. American Ethnological Society, Washington, DC.

Brady, James. 1997. Settlement Configuration and Cosmology: The Role of Caves at Dos Pilas. *American Anthropologist* 99(3):602–618.

Brady, James, and Wendy Ashmore. 1999. Mountains, Caves, Water: Ideational
    Landscapes of the Ancient Maya. In *Archaeologies of Landscape: Contemporary
    Perspectives*, edited by W. Ashmore and A. B. Knapp, pp. 124–145. Blackwell, Oxford.

Carl, Peter, Barry Kemp, Ray Laurence, Robin Coningham, Charles Higham, and George
    L. Cowgill. 2000. Viewpoint: Were Cities Built as Images? *Cambridge Archaeological
    Journal* 10(2):327–365.

Coggins, Clemency Chase. 1967. Palaces and the Planning of Ceremonial Centers in
    the Maya Lowlands. Unpublished manuscript, Tozzer Library, Peabody Museum,
    Harvard University.

Demarest, Arthur A., Kim Morgan, Claudia Wolley, and Hector L. Escobedo. 2003. The
    Political Acquisition of Sacred Geography: The Murciélagos Complex at Dos Pilas.
    In *Maya Palaces and Elite Residences: An Interdisciplinary Approach,* edited by
    Jessica Joyce Christie, pp. 120–153. University of Texas Press, Austin.

Fash, William L. 1998. Dynastic Architectural Programs: Intention and Design in Classic
    Maya Buildings at Copan and Other Sites. In *Function and Meaning in Classic
    Maya Architecture,* edited by Stephen D. Houston, pp. 223–270. Dumbarton Oaks,
    Washington, DC.

Freidel, David A., and Linda Schele. 1988. Symbol and Power: A History of the Lowland
    Maya Cosmogram. In *Maya Iconography,* edited by Elizabeth P. Benson and Gillette
    Griffin, pp. 44–93. Princeton University Press, Princeton.

Freidel, David A., Linda Schele, and Joy Parker. 1993. *Maya Cosmos: Three Thousand
    Years on the Shaman's Path.* William Morrow, New York.

Guernsey, Julia. 2006. *Ritual and Power in Stone: The Performance of Rulership in
    Mesoamerican Izapan Style Art.* University of Texas Press, Austin.

Headrick, Annabeth. 2007. *The Teotihuacan Trinity: The Sociopolitical Structure of an
    Ancient Mesoamerican City.* University of Texas Press, Austin.

Heydon, Doris. 1975. An Interpretation of the Cave underneath the Pyramid of the Sun in
    Teotihuacan, Mexico. *American Antiquity* 40:131–147.

Houk, Brett. 1996. The Archaeology of Site Planning: An Example from Dos Hombres,
    Belize. Unpublished PhD dissertation, Department of Anthropology, University of
    Texas at Austin.

Joyce, Arthur A. 2004. Sacred Space and Social Relations in the Valley of Oaxaca. In
    Mesoamerican Archaeology: Theory and Practice, edited by Julia A. Hendon and
    Rosemary Joyce, pp. 192–216. Blackwell, Oxford.

Knapp, A. Bernard, and Wendy Ashmore. 1999. Archaeological Landscapes: Constructed,
    Conceptualized, Ideational. In *Archaeologies of Landscape: Contemporary Perspectives*,
    edited by Wendy Ashmore and A. Bernard Knapp, pp. 1–32. Blackwell, Oxford.

Kowalski, Jeff Karl, and Nicholas P. Dunning. 1999. The Architecture of Uxmal: The
    Symbolics of Statemaking at a Puuc Maya Regional Capital. In *Mesoamerican
    Architecture as a Cultural Symbol,* edited by Jeff Karl Kowalski, pp. 274–297. Oxford
    University Press, New York.

López Austin, Alfredo. 1973. *Hombre-Dios: Religion y politica en el mundo náhuatl.*
    UNAM, Instituto de Investigaciones Históricas, Mexico, D. F.

Manzanilla, Linda. 1997. Teotihuacan: Urban Archetype, Cosmic Model. In *Emergence
    and Change in Early Urban Societies*, edited by Linda Manzanilla, pp. 109–131.
    Plenum, New York.

Manzanilla, Linda, Claudia Lopez, and Ann Corinne Freter. 1996. Dating Results from
    Excavations in Quarry Tunnels behind the Pyramid of the Sun at Teotihuacan.
    Ancient Mesoamerica 7:245–266.

Mathews, Peter, Kathryn Reese-Taylor, Marcelo Zamora, and Alexander Parmington. 2005. Los monumentos de Naachtun, Peten. In *XVIII simposio de investigaciones arqueológicas en Guatemala*, edited by Juan Pedro LaPorte, Bárbara Arroyo, and Héctor E. Mejía, pp. 691–696. Ministerio de Cultura y Deportes, Instituto de Antropología e Historia, Asociacíon Tikal, and Foundation for the Advancement of Mesoamerican Studies, Guatemala City.

Morton, Shawn G. 2007. Procession Ritual at Naachtun, Guatemala during the Late Classic Period. Unpublished MA thesis, Department of Archaeology, University of Calgary.

Reese, Kathryn V. 1996. Narratives of Power: Late Formative Public Architecture and Civic Center Design at Cerros, Belize. Unpublished PhD dissertation, Department of Anthropology, University of Texas at Austin.

Reese-Taylor, Kathryn. 2002. Ritual Circuits as Key Elements in Maya Civic Center Design. In *Heart of Creation: The Mesoamerican World and the Legacy of Linda Schele*, edited by Andrea Stone, pp. 143–165. University of Alabama Press, Tuscaloosa.

Reese-Taylor, Kathryn, and Rex Koontz. 2001. The Cultural Poetics of Space and Power in Ancient Mesoamerica. In *Landscape and Power in Ancient Mesoamerica*, edited by R. Koontz, K. Reese-Taylor, and A. Headrick, pp. 1–27. Westview Press, Boulder, Colorado.

Reese-Taylor, Kathryn, Peter Mathews, Marcelo Zamora Mejía, Debra Walter, Martin Rangel, Silvia Alvarado, Ernesto Arredondo, Shawn Morton, Alex Parmington, Roberta Parry, Baudilio Salazar, and Jeff Seibert. 2005. Proyecto arqueológico Naachtun: Resultados preliminares de la primera temporada de campo 2004. In *XVIII simposio de investigaciones arqueológicas en Guatemala*, edited by Juan Pedro LaPorte, Bárbara Arroyo, and Héctor E. Mejía, pp. 91–100. Ministerio de Cultura y Deportes, Instituto de Antropología e Historia, Asociación Tikal, and Foundation for the Advancement of Mesoamerican Studies, Guatemala City.

Ricketson, Oliver, and Elizabeth Ricketson. 1937. Uaxactun, Guatemala, Group E, 1926–31. Carnegie Institution of Washington, No. 477. Carnegie Institution of Washington, Washington, DC.

Scarborough,Vernon L. 1998. Ecology and Ritual: Water Management and the Maya. *Latin American Antiquity* 9(2):135–159.

Schele, Linda, and Julia Guernsey Kappelman. 2001. What the Heck's Coatepec? The Formative Roots of an Enduring Mythology. In *Landscape and Power in Ancient Mesoamerica*, edited by R. Koontz, K. Reese-Taylor, and A. Headrick, pp. 29–54. Westview Press, Boulder, Colorado.

Shaw, Justine M. 2001. Maya *Sacbeob*: Form and Function. *Ancient Mesoamerica* 12(2):261–272.

Smith, Michael E. 2003. Can We Read Cosmology in Ancient Maya City Plans? Comment on Ashmore and Sabloff. *Latin American Antiquity* 14(2):221–228.

Smith, Michael E. 2005. Did the Maya Build Architectural Cosmograms? *Latin American Antiquity* 16(2):217–224.

Šprajc, Ivan. 2005. More on Mesoamerican Cosmology and City Plans. *Latin American Antiquity* 16:209–216.

Šprajc, Ivan, Carlos Morales-Aguilar, and Richard D. Hansen. 2009. Early Maya Astronomy and Urban Planning at El Mirador, Peten, Guatemala. *Anthropological Notebooks* 15(3):79–101.

Stuart, David. 2005. *The Inscriptions from Temple XIX at Palenque: A Commentary.* Pre-Columbian Art Research Institute, San Francisco.

Sugiyama, Saburo. 1993. Worldview Materialized in Teotihuacan, Mexico. *Latin American Antiquity* 4(2):103–129.

Thompson, J. Eric S. 1959. The Role of Caves in Maya Culture. *Mitteilungen aus dem Museum für Völkerkunde in Hamburg* 25:122–129.

Tourtellot, Gair, Marc Wolf, Scott Smith, Kristen Gardella, and Norman Hammond. 2002. Exploring Heaven on Earth: Testing the Cosmological Model at La Milpa, Belize. *Antiquity* 76:633–634.

Townsend, Richard F. 1979. *State and Cosmos in the Art of Tenochtitlan.* Studies in Precolumbian Art and Archaeology, No. 20. Dumbarton Oaks, Washington DC.

Townsend, Richard F. 1982. Pyramid and Sacred Mountain. *Annals of the New York Academy of Science* 385:37–62.

Umberger, Emily. 2002. Imperial Inscriptions in the Aztec Landscape. In *Inscribed Landscapes: Marking and Making Place*, edited by B. David and M. Wilson, pp. 187–199. University of Hawaii Press, Honolulu.

Wheatley, Paul. 1971. *The Pivot of the Four Quarters: A Preliminary Enquiry into the Origins and Character of the Ancient Chinese City.* Aldine, Chicago.

CHAPTER 57

MESOAMERICAN RELIGIOUS BELIEFS

THE PRACTICES AND PRACTITIONERS

F. KENT REILLY III

MESOAMERICAN religion, as all the indigenous belief systems of ancient Americans, was firmly grounded in the need to ensure the necessities and of life and health and the balance of those oppositions inherent in the natural order. The primary methods of ensuring these objectives were those rites and ceremonies that obtained results through achieving supernatural access and contact with the ancestors. Though Mesoamerica was a cultural area consisting of a complex ethnic and political geography, it was unified by a commonly held, if not unified, system of religious practice.

Our knowledge and understanding of Mesoamerican religion is based on famous conquest and colonial records such as the Florentine Codex (1545–1590) compiled by Bernardo de Sahagún; *The Book of the Gods and Rites* (1574–1576), collected by Diego Durán; as well as many ethnographic sources, both colonial and modern. Finally, archaeological and iconographic evidence and interpretation contribute to this body of knowledge.

As with all known American belief systems, Mesoamerican religion possessed a cosmology that saw the visible world as multitiered, consisting of the Above Realm of the heavens; the middle Earthly Realm, the home of living humanity; and the watery Beneath Realm of the dead and thus of the ancestors. Within this layered cosmic model, directionality and coloration played pivotal roles. Each cosmic layer possessed its own deities, and they were linked by an axis-mundi that could take the form of a world tree or mountain, or a temple or sacred fire. At times this axis mundi could assume the personified form of a ruler or important religious practitioner. The deities and supernatural entities that inhabited these realms could and often did cross the three cosmic realms.

This cosmic model was organized on the principles of the unity of oppositions in tension and the perceived cycles of nature, both temporal and seasonal. Within the framework of this multitiered cosmos, rituals and the spaces where they were enacted served as stages or backdrops. Here shamans, priests, and, ultimately, rulers conducted those religious ceremonies through which the cosmos and its supernatural inhabitants were manifested publicly. Thus religious practitioners, whatever their complexity and organizational principles, were constantly using ceremonies and dances as fulcrums on which to balance and renew natural oppositions and temporal cycles (Reilly 2002, 2005). Undoubtedly for the ancient inhabitants of Mesoamerica, rites, rituals, and sacred ceremonies—as well as the individuals responsible for successfully performing them—were understood to be pivotal mechanisms for survival.

As David Jorelamon (1996: 52) has noted, the ritual roles and functions of religious practitioners changed over the course of Mesoamerican history, particularly as early political and economic systems became more complex. These religious practitioners can be defined loosely as shamans, priests, and rulers. Each age evidenced changes in the roles of religious practitioners. However, a close examination of all available evidence clearly shows that the offices of priests and ultimately of the rulers of state-level societies combined aspects of both shamanism and the early priesthood within their ritual functions. Thus Mesoamerican ritual practice and the function of religious practitioners became fused together within the person of the state-level divine ruler. To understand the ideological function of the rulers of the various Mesoamerican states, it is critical to understand the prestate religious functions and practices. This chapter restricts itself to those earlier religious rituals and to the category of religious specialists who developed and directed those ceremonies.

As one such religious category, shamanism is, of course, linked to the hunters and gatherers of the Paleolithic and Archaic periods (25,000-7,000 BC), and it broadly encompasses the earliest of the Mesoamerican religious systems. Shamans, as defined by Eliade (1964) and Furst (1994: 1–28), are part-time, charismatic, religious practitioners who serve as a community's healers and bear both the ability and responsibility of interacting with the primal spirits, such as fire and weather, as well as of traveling through the different cosmic realms as they perform their duties. Besides their practical function as healers, certainly one of their key ritual functions was safely escorting the spirits of the recently dead to their final abode, the Realm of the Dead, which was the home of the ancestors and the locus of ancestral power.

Throughout the Americas, the final journey to the Realm of the Dead, or indeed to any location within the supernatural otherworld, was understood to be fraught with danger for the shaman as well as for the spirits of the recently dead, whom he accompanies and guides. To prevail over these dangers, the shaman possesses the ability to summon or transform into powerful preternatural animals, whose salient attributes were mostly derived from beasts of prey such as harpy eagles, jaguars, or caimans. Such spirit companions, or *naguales*, aid the shaman to battle otherworldly dangers that face him and the souls during the journey to the Realm of the Dead. Both pivotal functions of supernatural and ancestral access thus become essential ritual practices of the part-time shamanic ritual practitioner through his ritual transformation from a human into a supernatural communicator mediator.

Undoubtedly, in ancient Mesoamerica, as they do today, shamans possessed ritual tools such as wands, sucking tubes, and soul containers, as well as transformation paraphernalia such as masks, rattles, and drums. All these objects served as props in the ritual performances that visualized the shaman's function and ritual practices, and they were key to properly understanding and performing the ritual. Despite their transcendental function, almost all such ancient Mesoamerican ritual objects were created from impermanent media and thus have perished (Pasztory 1982: 7–30), except in iconography. In one instance, however, at Gheo Shih in the Valley of Oaxaca, between 5000-4000 BC, archaeological evidence points to what appears to be a bolder bordered, ritual-specific space that perhaps was used for those dance rituals that gained prominence in later periods of Mesoamerican ritual development (Drennan 1976: 345–363).

In the Late Archaic and Early Formative periods (7000-1500 BC), technological breakthroughs occur in several cultural areas, including advances in pottery and the domestication of plants, which led to horticulture and ultimately agriculture. The archaeologist David Freidel (1995: 3–9) has proposed that shamans may have played a major role in achieving plant domestication, through their function as healers who collected medicinal plants. During this same dynamic period, permanent villages developed and larger populations became more settled than in the earlier Paleolithic and Early Archaic periods.

Plant domestication and its metaphysical dimensions became centered on maize, beans, and squash, and these were added to shamans' ceremonies and ritual practices. These new and evolving rituals focused on agricultural fecundity, rain making, the successful growth of plants, and greater agricultural yields. This new ritual focus did not replace the shamanic practices of the previous age; rather, it incorporated the hallowed rituals of ancestral contact and transformation into the new, complementary, agriculturally focused ritual cycles. The practitioners responsible for conducting and performing these also cyclically driven ritual practices for rain and agriculture fertility functioned fully as priests. Unlike the earlier part-time shamans, priests are full-time religious specialists who access the supernatural indirectly by focusing their religious practice on precisely conducted repetitive or formulaic rituals of renewal (Hultkrantz 1963).

With this greater specialization, priests usually are associated with religious structures or temples. Certainly the Late Archaic and Early Formative periods produce some of the first religious structures in Mesoamerica (Marcus 1989: 148–197).

Often these early temple sites are positioned within dramatic landscapes, taking symbolic advantage of naturally occurring, nearby formations such as mountains, caves, and springs: these undoubtedly served as portals of supernatural access to the otherworld and were fitting locations for ritual practice. One spectacular example that linked the natural landscape with Mesoamerican ritual practice has been the discovery of El Manatí, Veracruz, Mexico. Here, by 1600 BC, a hill and spring became the focus of intense ritual activity. The evidence of these ritual practices includes deposits within mineral-rich springs, of anthropomorphic wooden busts (the earliest surviving wood sculptures in Mesoamerica), jadeite and greenstone celts or axes, and the remains of human fetuses all carefully wrapped or bundled (Ortiz C. et al. 1997). The association of these deposits within the spring has led excavators to posit that the artifacts' ritual function was linked to rain procurement and, therefore, a long-lived fertility cult.

Also during this period, the earlier shamanic rituals of accessing ancestral power are expanded into a cult of the dead, demonstrated through the proliferation of elaborate burials, throughout much of Mesoamerica, and their accompanying grave goods (McAnany, 1995). Appearing for the first time during this period is a category of grave ritual objects that take the form of large hollow ceramic figures with infantlike features and elongated heads. Referred to in the literature as "Olmec babies" because of their naturalistic poses and expressions, these figures usually are crafted as unsexed and may have been dressed (Figure 57.1). This unique figure category may replace earlier shamanic soul catchers or containers that were intended to hold the souls of the departed. It is noteworthy that the eyes of many of these white-slipped figures are blank. In the grave, then, a soul was housed within

Figure 57.1 Olmec baby, Morelos, Mexico, hollow clay figure, ca. 1000–700 BC
(photograph by the author).

this infant-shaped container in order to await rebirth as a future lineage or family member. Also present in graves or ritual caches are stone and obsidian bloodletters that attest to the increasing importance of blood and human sacrifice within the expanded range of ritual practices during this period.

This era of priestly ritual performance is also when religious and ritual-specific art appears in permanent mediums (clay and stone) that can be recovered archaeologically. Certainly the earliest and most numerous of these objects are the clay figurines that become ubiquitous at this time (Flannery 1976, Niederberger 1996a, 1996b: 103–104). Significantly, Middle Formative Period clay figurines often are crafted as masked individuals. Furthermore, life-sized ceramic masks themselves, as well as clay masquettes, have been excavated from graves, strongly suggesting that significant portions of a given population were organized into sodalities, or dance and medicine societies, for public rituals during the same period. The archaeological recovery of conch-shell trumpets and turtle-shell rattles also from the Middle Formative Period is compelling evidence of increased ritual intensification, which required greater quantities of ritual objects and specialized regalia items (Flannery 1976: 333–345).

However, the most dynamic expressions of ritually focused art in the Middle Formative Period are to be viewed in the context of Olmec-style, sculpted-stone masterpieces, monumental and otherwise, that first appear along the Gulf Coast in the Mexican states of Tabasco and Veracruz. Also in this area of the Gulf Coast, a sophisticated symbol system first appears for use on both stone and clay objects. In many instances, the individual elements and motifs of this "Olmec symbol system" seem to combine the naguales of the earlier shamanically based rituals with the new and developing symbolic requirements of agriculturally driven rituals.

Certainly among the most important of the symbolic motifs expressed in this remarkably efficient symbol system is the zoomorphic supernatural identified as the Olmec Dragon (Joralemon 1976: 27–72). This image is derived from the form of the semiaquatic tropical caiman. Its symbolic import is attested by its expression both monumentally in stone, as well as in the many zoomorphic clay figurines that depict this supernatural creature. Within the symbol system, the Olmec Dragon also was reduced to schematic symbols that were incised or carved on pottery as well as on stone sculptures. This supernatural creature is depicted floating on water bands with its four legs extended outward, in a recognizably crocodilian resting posture. The Olmec Dragon is often artistically represented with a cleft brow ridge and eyes surmounted by flames or flanged eye ridges. While occasionally depicted with caiman fangs, the dragon is most frequently rendered fangless with gum brackets clearly marking the location of the removed dentition. In several instances the Olmec Dragon carries sprouting plants on its back, quite clearly identifying this specific creature as being the earth itself (Reilly 1994: 124–135) (Figure 57.2).

One particular clay figure is a work of art that dramatically illustrates the fusion of the shamanic ritual transformation from the Paleolithic and Early Archaic period with the agriculturally expanded priestly rituals of fertility and rain from the Late Archaic and Formative periods. Crafted in the form of a ceramic vessel,

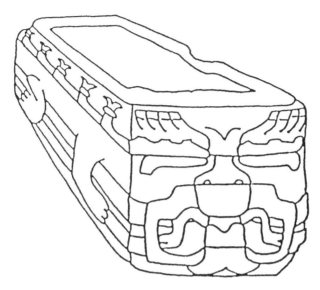

Figure 57.2 Sandstone sarcophagus, La Venta, Tabasco, Mexico, ca 800–600 BC, carved
in the shape of the Olmec Dragon (drawing by the author).

or an *incensario* (incense burner), the figure was recovered from Atlihuayán in the
highland Mexican state of Morelos (Piña Chan and López 1952). It depicts a seated,
crossed-legged individual who leans forward and whose features are rendered in
the Olmec style. The hollow clay figure wears a hooded cape that is clearly the full
hide of the Olmec Dragon (Figure 57.3). The skinned head of the Olmec Dragon
covers the head of the individual. At first glance the figure seems to have its eyes
closed in trance. However, upon more careful examination, the closed eyelids of the
human figure are incised so that they exactly replicate the Olmec Dragon's flanged
eye ridges as depicted on the cape this individual wears. It should be noted that the
richly emblematic Olmec Dragon cape that the transformation figure wears may
depict an actual, specific piece of ceremonial regalia, because the material remains
of what may be just such a cape have been recovered in excavations at the Fábrica
de San José in the Valley of Oaxaca (Flannery 1976: 339–340).

The entire composition of the Atlihuayán figure clearly represents an individual in a trancelike state. The fact that the figure itself bears Olmec Dragon
attributes strongly underscores his role as a ritual practitioner well into the process
of transforming into this major fertility symbol. The fusion of the eye elements
elegantly and economically represents the merged identities of the transformed
human ritualist with the supernatural being. Thus, the shamanic ritual of transformation is fused with the agricultural imagery of the Olmec Dragon. Notably, both
ritual concepts of transformation and horticultural fertility exist as major components of traditional belief and ritual practice in Mexico and Guatemala today.

Another aspect of ceremonial practice that is first depicted in the art of the
Formative period is the ritual bundle (Guernsey and Reilly 2007). Not only did religious practitioners bundle objects during ritual performances, but even large-scale

Figure 57.3 Ceramic hollow clay figure recovered from Atlihuayán, Morelos, Mexico, ca. 1000–700 BC. This hollow figure, or incensario, depicts a seated, crossed-legged individual whose features are rendered in the Olmec style (photograph by the author).

monuments also were kept wrapped or bundled (Reilly 2007: 1–21) by Mesoamerican religious practitioners. Werner Stenzel, one of the earliest researchers to explore the function of sacred bundles (1968), compared bundle use in the Mesoamerican highlands and in the Maya area. From his studies, he drew a series of basic premises that summarized how bundles function among the wider array of Mesoamerican ritual objects. Stenzel's specific points included these observations:

1. The wrappings of bundles function as more than mere packing cases.
2. Bundles contain a "secret and invisible energy."
3. Bundles are closely associated with creation and migration narratives.
4. Claims of rulership and authority are related to the "possession, preservation or taking care of sacred bundles."
5. The ritualized opening of bundles is "the only possible access to the contents," which means that their opening constitutes a major ritual event. (Stenzel, as summarized in Guernsey and Reilly 2007: vi)

Certainly, the fact that sacred bundles figure prominently in art and ritual during the Formative period strongly supports the interpretation of the pivotal role of the priesthood during this period. As previously stated, one identifier of the priestly ritual function lies in the fact that priests are full-time religious specialists who indirectly access the supernatural by focusing their religious practices on precisely conducted, repetitive, or formulaic rituals of renewal. Indeed, the widely diffused and highly significant activities of the wrapping and unwrapping of sacred bundles conform to this definition of priestly ritual —as precisely conducted repetitive and formulaic rites.

During the Formative period, the roles of priestly ritual practitioners and their ritual practices expanded, as is clear in their functions of fostering artistic production and contributing to the development of written language. Many of the individuals depicted on Olmec-style monuments have long been recognized as holding ritual implements, including torches, "knuckledusters," bloodletters, and maize vegetation. The discovery in 1998 or 1999 of the Cascajal Block near the great Olmec site of San Lorenzo (Veracruz) has sparked a great deal of speculation as to the nature and ritual function of early Mesoamerican writing and its origins (Skidmore 2006; Freidel and Reilly 2010).

Dating to the San Lorenzo B Phase (ca. 900 BC), the Cascajal Block is a roughly 15-inch-long block of greenish serpentine (Figure 57.4). The block bears sixty-two incised signs or symbols that can be interpreted as a record of the display of ritual

Figure 57.4 Cascajal Block, from the vicinity of San Lorenzo, Veracruz, Mexico, ca. 900 BC (drawing by the author).

objects contained within three opened or unwrapped ritual bundles (Freidel and Reilly 2010: 658–670). As such a depiction, the Cascajal Block is "a memorial to public prophecy and divination" (Freidel and Reilly 2010: 659). The Cascajal Block likely served as a permanent record, carved in stone, of a sacred bundle ritual: the assuredly positive effect of such a ritual is now permanently recorded in the enduring medium of stone; thus, the ritual results were intended to be permanent and ongoing.

Although the signs on the Cascajal Block are not writing itself, they most certainly represent an important step on the road to writing. The unique Cascajal Block, then, depicts how Mesoamerican ritual practitioners repetitively manipulated such objects in ceremonies to achieve ancestral contact and thus supernatural placation. Analogous to Chinese shamanistic symbols, the Mesoamerican signs evolved into hieroglyphs that depicted ritual objects that were used to communicate supernaturally between one cosmic realm and another. As with their Chinese analogues (Chang 1983: 81–94), ritual practitioners developed Mesoamerican writing as an important aid to their constant efforts to achieve harmony and balance in an unharmonious world.

The appearance of the Cascajal Block also signals a major shift in Mesoamerican religious practice in the form of a more rigid form of institutionalized ritual and the replacement of shamanic religious practitioners by priests. While a shaman depends greatly on personal charisma for effectively performing a ritual, a priest relies more specifically on the formally learned, clear standardization of ritual performance, as well as on the ability of a well-trained initiate to repeat, verbatim, specific incantations, ritual postures, and gestures. In succeeding Mesoamerican periods (Classic, 200-900 AD; Postclassic, 900-1521 AD), the artistic and archaeological evidence demonstrates that the combination of priestly ritual practitioners performing their rites and rituals, and their interactions with the deities and supernaturals themselves, became the transcendental focus of these rituals as they became institutionalized (Taube 1992). Certainly by the Postclassic period, priests were functioning as full-time specialists who had learned, often in formal institutions, specific ritual practices and had memorized an enormous corpus of esoteric lore that they also combined with an acute knowledge of what we now classify as natural history and astronomy.

Another clear difference between the religious practices and practitioners of later periods and those of the early Formative period is the widespread evidence of state cults in which rulers combined their political functions with the ideological functions of priests or religious practitioners. Artistic depictions at numerous Classic Maya cities—the great city of Teotihuacan, the Zapotec Monte Albán, and ultimately Aztec Tenochtitlan—represent the rulers of these sites as holding the supreme priestly office for these state cults, even at times merging their own priestly offices with the functions of the gods themselves.

As might be expected, in the Classic and Postclassic periods ritual spaces or stages become much more elaborate. For example, in the case of Teotihuacan, the entire central area of this enormous city is laid out and constructed as a cosmological stage on which the rituals of rulership are performed (Headrick 2007). Written evidence from the Classic-period Maya clearly shows that the functional identities of ritual spaces are recorded with regularity on epigraphic inscriptions (Stuart 1998). Because of the current understanding of Maya hieroglyphic texts, the importance of a complex religious calendar to these state cults (at least for the Maya but almost certainly for non-Maya peoples as well) was regularly marked by dedicating stelae whose incised images and texts meaningfully relate specific ritual events, both historical and mythic, as well as their individual practitioners, to specific cycles of time.

Certainly, our current understanding of the Mesoamerican priesthood, as previously stated, is based on such post-conquest books as the Florentine Codex and *The Book of the Gods and Rites*, as well as on many ethnographic sources that survived the conquest. These sources identify the existence of many orders of ritual-specific priests among the Mexica and other Postclassic peoples. Unfortunately, scholars do not agree among themselves as to whether a word for "priest" is identifiable in the Maya script. However, one should recall that the role of craftsperson or artificer is combined with that of priest in the Maya Classic period social order. Finally new archaeological and iconographic information and interpretations have contributed to the emerging evidence that, throughout its long and compelling history, Mesoamerica produced religious practitioners who, no matter the origin of their craft and skill, functioned for themselves and their peoples as mediators between the worlds of the gods and humankind.

References

Chang, K. C. 1983. *Art, Myth, and Ritual; The Path to Political Authority in Ancient China*. Harvard University Press, Cambridge.

Drennan, Robert D. 1976. Religion and Social Evolution in Formative Mesoamerica. In *The Early Mesoamerican Village*, edited by Kent V. Flannery, pp. 345–363. Academic Press, New York.

Eliade, Mircea. 1964. *Shamanism, Archaic Techniques of Ecstasy*. Princeton University Press, Princeton.

Flannery, Kent V. 1976. Interregional Religious Networks. In *The Early Mesoamerican Village*, edited by Kent V. Flannery, pp. 329–345. Academic Press, New York.

Freidel, David. 1995. Preparing the Way. In *The Olmec World: Ritual and Rulership*, edited by Jill Guthrie, pp. 3–10. The Art Museum, Princeton University, Princeton, New Jersey.

Freidel, David, and F. Kent Reilly III. 2010. The Flesh of God; Cosmology, Food and the Origins of Political Power in Ancient Southeastern Mesoamerica. In *Pre-Columbian Foodways: Interdisciplinary Approaches to Food, Culture, and Markets in Ancient Mesoamerica*, edited by John Edward Staller and Michael Carrasco, pp. 635–680. Springer Press, New York.

Furst, Peter T. 1994. Introduction: An Overview of Shamanism. In *Ancient Traditions: Shamanism in Central Asia and the Americas*, edited by Gary Seaman and Jane

S. Day, pp. 1–28. Denver Museum of Natural History and the University Press of Colorado, Niwot, Colorado.

Guernsey, Julia, and F. Kent Reilly III. 2007. *Sacred Bindings of the Cosmos: Ritual Acts of Bundling and Wrapping In Ancient Mesoamerica,* edited by Julia Guernsey and F. Kent Reilly III. Boundary End Archaeology Research Center Press, Barnardsville, North Carolina.

Headrick, Annabeth. 2007. *The Teotihuacan Trinity, The Sociopolitical Structure of an Ancient Mesoamerican City.* University of Texas Press, Austin

Hultkrantz, Anke. 1963. *Les religions des Indiens primitifs de l'Amerique.* Studies in Comparative Religion, No. 4, Stockholm.

Joralemon, Peter David. 1976. The Olmec Dragon: A Study in Pre-Columbian Iconography. In *Origins of Religious Art and Iconography in Preclassic Mesoamerica,* edited by H. B. Nicholson, pp. 27–72. UCLA Latin American Studies Series, Vol. 31, UCLA Latin American Center Publications, Los Angeles.

Joralemon, Peter David. 1996. In Search of the Olmec Cosmos: Reconstructing the World View of Mexico's First Civilization. In *Olmec Art of Ancient Mexico,* edited by Elizabeth P. Benson and Beatriz de la Fuente, pp. 51–60. National Gallery of Art, Washington, DC.

Marcus, Joyce. 1989. Zapotec Chiefdoms and the Nature of Formative Religions. In *Regional Perspectives on the Olmec,* edited by Robert J. Sharer and David C. Grove, pp. 148–197. School of American Research, Cambridge University Press, Cambridge.

McAnany, Patricia A. 1995. *Living with the Ancestors; Kinship and Kingship in Ancient Maya Society.* University of Texas Press, Austin.

Niederberger, Christine. 1996a. The Basin of Mexico: A Multimillennial Development Towards Cultural Complexity. In *Olmec Art of Ancient Mexico,* edited by Elizabeth P. Benson and Beatriz de la Fuente, pp. 83–94. National Gallery of Art, Washington, DC.

Niederberger, Christine. 1996b. Olmec Horizon Guerrero. In *Olmec Art of Ancient Mexico,* edited by Elizabeth P. Benson and Beatriz de la Fuente, pp. 61–95. National Gallery of Art, Washington, DC.

Ortiz C., Ponciano, Ma. del Carmen Rodríguez M., and Alfredo Delgado C. 1997. *Las investigaciones arqueológicas en El Cerro Sagrado Manatí.* Universidad Veracruzana, Xalapa, México.

Pasztory, Esther. 1982. Shamanism and North American Indian Art. In *Native North American Art History: Selected Readings,* edited by Zena P. Mathews and Aldona Jonaitis, pp. 7–30. Peek Publications, Palo Alto, California.

Piña Chan, Ramón, and Valetín López. 1952. Excavations at Atlihuayán, Morelos. *Tlatoani* 1:1, México, D.F.

Reilly, F. Kent III. 1994. Enclosed Ritual Spaces and the Watery Underworld in Formative Period Architecture: New Observations on the Function of La Venta Complex A. In *The Seventh Palenque Round Table,* 1989, Vol. IX, pp. 125–135, edited by Merle Green Robertson and Virginia M. Fields. Pre-Columbian Art Research Institute, San Francisco.

Reilly, F. Kent III. 2002. The Landscape of Creation: Architecture, Tomb and Monument Placement at the Olmec Site of La Venta. In *Heart of Creation: Issues in Mesoamerican Iconography and Art History: Essays in Honor of Linda Schele,* edited by Andrea Stone, pp. 34–65. University of Alabama Press, Tuscaloosa.

Reilly, F. Kent III. 2005. Olmec Origins of Classic Period Maya Symbols of Rulership. In *Lords of Creation: The Origin of Divine Kingship amongst The Classic Period Maya,* edited by Virginia Fields. pp. Los Angeles County Museum of Art, Los Angeles.

Reilly, F. Kent III. 2007. Middle Formative Origins of the Mesoamerican Ritual Act of Bundling. In *Sacred Bindings of the Cosmos: Ritual Acts of Bundling and Wrapping in Ancient Mesoamerica*, edited by Julia Guernsey and F. Kent Reilly III, pp. 1–21. Boundary End Archaeology Research Center Press, Barnardsville, North Carolina.

Skidmore, Joel J. 2006. The Cascajal Block: The Earliest Pre-Columbian Writing. Mesoweb Press. Electronic document, http://www.mesoweb.com/reports/cascajal.pdf (accessed August 23, 2011).

Stenzel, Werner. 1968. The Sacred Bundle in Mesoamerican Religion. *Thirty-eighth International Congress of Americanists, Stuttgart-Munchen, 1968* 2:347–352.

Stuart, David. 1998. "The Fire Enters His House": Architecture and Ritual in Classic Maya Texts. In *Function and Meaning in Classic Maya Architecture*, edited by Stephen D. Houston, pp. 373–426. Dumbarton Oaks Research Library and Collection, Washington, DC.

Taube, Karl A. 1992. *The Major Gods of Ancient Yucatan*. Dumbarton Oaks Studies in Pre-Columbian Art and Archaeology, No. 32, Dumbarton Oaks, Washington, DC.

CHAPTER 58

THE LIVING AND THE DEAD

JAMES L. FITZSIMMONS

THE archaeology of death has long provided scholars with a means of understanding not only the dead themselves but also the societies to which they once belonged. Interments are, after all, one of only a handful of archaeologically observable actions in which sociopolitical relationships are clearly expressed. Burials are the end result of a set of interactions between the individual and society, a discrete expression of a series of events in which the ties between people—living or dead— are initiated, renewed, or reinforced. In ancient Mesoamerica, the dead remained social actors and, as such, they often continued to play significant roles in the lives of everyday people. Biologically deceased, they were socially very much alive (Hallam et al. 1999). Unlike contemporary Western views of the dead, where even deceased political figures lack true agency, the dead of Pre-Columbian Mesoamerica were ever-present and were believed to be capable of making their influence tangible for the living. In addition to passively defining territorial boundaries and resource rights, for example, the dead could engage in a variety of more active exploits, ranging from "dancing" at weddings to "witnessing" royal accessions. In short, the dead were a vital part of life in Mesoamerica. Hence, we might view the death of an individual in ancient Mesoamerica as the beginning of a long process of social rebirth and reinvention.

As both a cause and a result of the influence the dead had upon the living, the ancient peoples of this culture area engaged in a variety of practices linking themselves to their forebears or even deceased enemies. From physically opening the tombs of ancestors and carrying ancestral heirlooms to periodic feasts, sacrifices, or other lavish ceremonies devoted to prominent individuals, the living revisited the dead on a regular basis. Even captives were occasionally given new "life" after death, proudly displayed as named spoils of war on monuments long after their physical demise. Yet these and other mortuary practices were more than just commemorative events or ways to display the human trophies taken in battle by prominent elites. Instead, we might view activities like these as points during which a particular event—for example, the death of a king—was remembered, reviewed, and reinterpreted. Over time, the mortuary activities and actions themselves became memories, subject to interpretation and potentially passed on to others in ways that changed their significance. This is the reason why memory is central to the study of death. As both archaeologists and ethnographers have noted cross-culturally, mortuary ritual is an opportunity for identity and social memory to be constructed, tested, and renegotiated (e.g., see Bloch 1982; Chesson 2001; Gillespie 2001, 2002; Metcalf and Huntington 1991; O'Shea 1996; Weiner 1976). In other words, death involves social drama. Given that the dead were literally omnipresent in ancient Mesoamerica, from the tombs of Classic Maya temple pyramids to the crypts beneath the floors of Zapotec houses, it is clear that the opportunities for such drama were frequent and likely involved struggle as well as cooperation among different interest groups.

THEMES AND TRENDS

Given the variability in Mesoamerican societies, the differences between elite and nonelite burial practices, and the sheer time span of Mesoamerican prehistory, the task of defining the various relationships between the living and the dead in this culture area would seem difficult, if not impossible. Nevertheless, one could say that many of the peoples of ancient Mesoamerica viewed their own mortalities in similar ways and that they shared ideas about why death occurred in the first place. Scholarship on Mesoamerican approaches to mortality stems primarily from Classic as well as Postclassic sources (e.g., Hunt 1977; López Austin 1984; Monaghan 2000; Houston, Stuart, and Taube 2006; Fitzsimmons 2009; Fitzsimmons and Shimada 2011), and has been most clearly spelled out for the K'iche', Kekchi, and Tzotzil in the Maya highlands, for the elites of lowland Classic Maya civilization, and for the Aztecs of central Mexico. In these ancient as well as contemporary groups, human mortality is viewed as the result of a kind of mutual obligation or covenant. The general theme is that two sides—god(s) and the "natural world" on one and humanity on the other—must suffer and die for each other so that fundamentals like agriculture, time, and civilization can function normally. Moreover, human death results not from something biological, such as disease or physical infirmity, but from a cause we might consider to be supernatural (Monaghan 2000). Such views on mortality strike, in many ways, at the heart of the relationship between the living and the dead in ancient Mesoamerica.

We can see these basic ideas on death, for example, expressed in Classic Maya elite conceptions of agriculture and mortality. Earth, or dirt, was viewed not only as a source of life but also as a place of death by the ancient Maya elites, who associated themselves with maize and their lives with the maize life cycle. In killing and eating products of the earth—whether maize or even wild creatures—the Maya incorporated death into their bodies (in the case of maize through a kind of anthropophagy) and, hence, took part in a larger system of reciprocal mortality. When we also note that an anthropomorphic earth deity was believed to literally eat the Maya dead or that death could be caused by, for example, a named, personified disease, we get a picture of Classic Maya mortality as being more than simply biological. Given that most Mesoamerican societies shared beliefs about maize, earth deities, and reciprocity, it would not at all be surprising to find similar ideas about mortality and death over a wide temporal and geographic spectrum.

In addition to shared ideas about mortality and what death was, there are a number of broad trends and themes that are characteristic of some, if not all, Mesoamerican societies, including (1) the use of what one might call the "honored dead" (e.g., individuals who were not sacrificed or otherwise desecrated) to define the social and political realms, particularly with respect to land rights and sacred space; (2) the manipulation of not only ancestral remains but also those of prominent enemies in mortuary rituals; and (3) the pervasive (and somewhat related) belief in the power and ability of ancestors to affect the living.

DEATH AND THE LANDSCAPE

Whether buried deep inside or below a large-scale funerary structure, such as a temple pyramid, or set within the basal platform for a simple house, the dead of ancient Mesoamerica played an integral role in creating what Patricia McAnany (1995) has termed for the Postclassic Maya a "genealogy of place": Mesoamericans drew on the physical spaces in which their dead were buried in order to establish their social or political positions, often using the dead to demonstrate ownership over particular lands, resource rights, and other crucial commodities.

This was done largely at the household level: despite the presence of cemeteries or more formal disposal areas in certain parts of Mesoamerica (e.g., as at Tomaltepec, Oaxaca, or El Opeño, Michoacán; see Marcus and Flannery 1996: 97; Oliveros 2006), the standard for many Mesoamerican peoples was to live above or near the structures in which their dead were housed. Because of this, the dead became ever-present, physical symbols of the "rights, privileges, and responsibilities" of the living, in ways similar to those reported for other parts of the world (Saxe 1970). Where funerary structures saw repetitive interments over multiple generations, as they often did, those "rights, privileges, and responsibilities"—and the social inequality they represented—could become more and more entrenched over time.

The earliest examples of the dead defining the Mesoamerican landscape in this way date to the Middle Preclassic (1500–600 BC). Perhaps the best-known Middle Preclassic example comes from Tlatilco, on the western shore of Lake Texcoco in the Basin of Mexico. The people of Tlatilco, burying their dead within house platforms, were certainly establishing lineage ties to particular locations. Patterns in the quantity and quality of grave goods with certain interments, particularly those belonging to females between fifteen and nineteen years of age, however, led Rosemary Joyce (2001) to suggest that more was at play here. Given that burials do not necessarily passively reflect social reality but can actively create that reality, Joyce suggested that the burials in this small village (perhaps one thousand to two thousand people in the late Preclassic) were being used to engender—at the time of interment—a collective memory of the deceased and their families, one that could have served the families involved as a means of engineering and reinforcing their desired perception in the larger community. Concerns with image and status reinforcement are, of course, reflected over a broad socioeconomic spectrum in most Mesoamerican societies well after the Middle Preclassic, from the southern lowlands to the Valley of Oaxaca to the Gulf Coast. Even in western Mexico, where funerary behavior and architecture are often considered atypical for Mesoamerica, one can find this common thread: shaft-and-chamber tombs, such as those encountered at Teuchtitlan or Huitzilapa, Jalisco, do appear to have been specifically designed for elites, were used by particular lineages repeatedly over time, and were often (but not always) superimposed by a structure associated with those lineages (Beekman 2000; Coe and Koontz 2008).

HUMAN REMAINS AND MORTUARY RITUALS

Human remains were used in ancient Mesoamerica in various ways, from the utilitarian to the ritual. Awls, rattles, and other objects frequently made from animal bones were occasionally made from human remains, as at the Classic Maya site of Tikal or at Postclassic Chichén Itzá (Moholy-Nagy and Ladd 1992). Unfortunately, the source material for these objects—that is, whether the bone was originally from a dishonored war captive or a prestigious ancestor—is usually unknown and so the specific ties between the living and their deceased's "utensils" are obscure. However, in cases where human remains are being used ritually, a much more detailed picture of the relationship between the living and the dead emerges. One can separate the specifics of that relationship into two basic categories: (1) the ties between the dead and their descendants and (2) the ties between deceased captives and a victorious captor.

In addition to serving as markers of lineage and royal authority in houses and temple pyramids across Mesoamerica, the bones of ancestors were occasionally employed for other purposes. The Classic and early Postclassic lowland Maya, for example, appear to have used ancestors' bones to conjure supernatural entities, giving names to the remains via inscriptions on monuments or on the bones themselves. Human remains were, for the Maya, markers of ancestral identity and charged symbols of ancient personhood that contained no small measure of ritual power (Fitzsimmons 2009). They were so charged, in fact, that some lowland Maya tombs and other burial chambers were opened for the purposes of modifying or removing body parts as well as grave goods. In most cases, from Tonina to Copán, the idea appears to have been to redefine and to reinforce the relationships between the living and the dead (Chase and Chase n.d.; Fitzsimmons 2009) as well as to obtain heirlooms for display or for ritual use.

Similar ideas can be found in the Valley of Oaxaca and the Mixteca Alta, where the possession, curation, and display of ancestral bodies—particularly skulls and long bones—provided legitimacy to Oaxacan elites across time in places like Huamelupan and Monte Albán (Gaxiola González 1986; Christensen and Winter 1997: 470–471; Blomster 2011). As Jeffrey Blomster (2011) has noted, during the Late Postclassic, tombs in Oaxaca were entered, bones were modified, and remains were displayed in ways that mirror the Maya example. Perhaps, as has been observed for the Postclassic Aztecs, there was even competition among groups for certain remains and parts of particular deceased individuals: the femurs of women who died in childbirth—equivalent to a warrior's death in the Aztec mind-set— "enhanced potency" on the battlefield and were so highly prized that "grieving families had to fight off attempts to steal these women's body parts" (Miller and Martin 2004: 172).

A much more pervasive Mesoamerican practice involved the creation and periodic exhibition of mummy bundles. In addition to the Maya area, the Valley of Oaxaca, and the Mixteca Alta, for which such objects are primarily limited to the Classic period onward, mummy bundles figured prominently in Classic Teotihuacano and Postclassic Tarascan mortuary rituals. They were also ubiquitous in highland Mexico among the Aztecs during the Postclassic. Such bundles, in addition to being interred, were also used across Mesoamerica as oracles and battle standards for dominant lineages (Headrick 1999; Pohl 1994; Fitzsimmons 2009). Hence, ancestral effigies were prime targets on a Mesoamerican battlefield, because their capture or destruction would spell disaster for an enemy who, bereft of the authority such ancestors provided, could no longer claim the protection or favor of the dead.

Ancestors were not, of course, the only deceased individuals to illustrate the relationship between the living and the dead in war. The sacrifice of war captives, and the bones such captives provided, also played a major role in Mesoamerican mortuary ritual. Individuals were commonly sacrificed to accompany primary, high-ranking interments in ancient Mesoamerica. Their treatment could range quite variably even within the same site and culture. As Saburo Sugiyama (2011) has noted, sacrificial interments in Classic Teotihuacan range from the apparently "honored" dead (such as the warriors sacrificed for the founding of the Pyramid of the Feathered Serpent) to seemingly dishonored individuals buried alive or bound (such as those found within the Moon Pyramid). Individual bones of war captives, moreover, served as trophies within many Mesoamerican cultures. Jaws, crania, shrunken heads, and whole, shrunken bodies were worn as trophies by warriors in the Maya area well into the colonial era, for example (Tozzer 1941: 120–123). Furthermore, to some Mesoamerican peoples such trophies were probably more than just reminders of success in battle or decorative, albeit fearsome, ornaments. It seems likely that the remains of certain sacrificed individuals, particularly the "honored" ones, were viewed as ritually potent and charged in ways similar to those mentioned earlier for ancestral remains (Fitzsimmons 2011).

ANCESTOR VENERATION

Ancestor veneration was common throughout ancient Mesoamerica (Palka 2000: 1). As anthropologists working in Africa, Asia, and the Americas have noted (e.g., see Freedman 1970; Fortes 1987), one of the primary characteristics of ancestor veneration is that it is usually exclusive to a particular subset of deceased individuals:

> The practices of ancestor veneration and the rituals surrounding the treatment of the dead are not extended equally to all members of a lineage; rather, they are employed preferentially when particularly important and influential members of a lineage die. (McAnany 1995: 11)

In ancient Mesoamerica, the dead can only be called "ancestors" if the qualities that lead to their exalted status in the afterlife are "maintained or reinvented through time and space" (Fitzsimmons 2009: 119). Social inequality is thus at the root of ancestor veneration in ancient Mesoamerica, and as such ancestors or figures believed to be ancestors emerge—at the very latest—with the first stratified societies of the Preclassic. Although ancestors are represented in nearly all socioeconomic and temporal strata within Mesoamerica, the majority of the scholarly research on ancestor veneration has been focused on peoples of the Valley of Oaxaca and the Maya area. In these regions, one finds specialized structures devoted to particular ancestors dating back to the early Preclassic (e.g., see Marcus 1999), continuing through the Classic and Postclassic (e.g., Maya *oratorios*; see Becker 1971; Haviland 1981; Leventhal 1983), and well into the colonial period (McAnany 1995).

Village and household-based ancestor veneration is, to date, of greatest antiquity among the Zapotecs, where figurines identified as ancestors and dating as early as 1150 BC have been found at sites like Abasolo, Huitzo, San José Mogote, Tierras Largas, and Tomaltepec (Marcus and Flannery 1996). Ancestors as major figures first appear in the Maya area in village shrines dating to the Late Preclassic, as at K'axob (McAnany 1995). The emergence of ancestors in both of these areas is, as mentioned earlier, connected to ideas about the landscape and land tenure. These regions, moreover, demonstrate a similar pattern when states and kingdoms emerge in the Late Preclassic and Early Classic: both undergo, as McAnany has noted, a transition from a village- and lineage-based kind of ancestor veneration—one that is an organizing principle of their respective societies—to a state-based system where royal ancestors are the foundation of public religious life. The transition is not accompanied by the abandonment of lineage-based ancestors per se, but it is one that subordinates lineage to kingship (McAnany 1995). Thus, ideas about power, land, lineage, kinship and kingship were all ultimately tied to the dead; future research will demonstrate the extent to which this model is valid for other regions of Mesoamerica.

Ancestor veneration involved more than just remembrance and the tensions between lineage- and state-based systems of religious organization. Feeding or otherwise presenting offerings to the dead was a necessary part of ancestor veneration, and it is particularly well documented for the Postclassic. Likewise, there were elite and commoner rituals connected to ancestor veneration that included caching, feasting, fasting, bloodletting, sacrifice, dedicatory and termination events, and even spectacles designed with large audiences in mind. None of these rituals were, of course, limited to ancestor veneration. This returns us to the larger point: the dead continued to play an active part in both normal, everyday life and in the special occasions removed from the norm. They were of both the sacred and the mundane, and they were thus an integral part of daily existence in ancient Mesoamerica.

REFERENCES

Becker, Marshall J. 1971. The Identification of a Second Plaza Plan at Tikal, Guatemala, and Its Implications for Ancient Maya Social Complexity. Unpublished PhD dissertation, Department of Anthropology, University of Pennsylvania.

Beekman, Christopher S. 2000. Correspondence of Regional Patterns and Local Strategies in Formative to Classic Period West Mexico. *Journal of Anthropological Archaeology* 19(4):385–412.

Bloch, Maurice. 1982. Death, Women and Power. In *Death and the Regeneration of Life*, edited by Maurice Bloch and Jonathan Parry, pp. 211–230. Cambridge University Press, Cambridge.

Blomster, Jeffrey P. 2011. Bodies, Bones, and Burials: Corporeal Constructs and Enduring Relationships in Oaxaca, Mexico. In *Living with the Dead: Mortuary Ritual in Mesoamerica*, edited by James Fitzsimmons and Izumi Shimada, pp. 102–160. University of Arizona Press, Tucson.

Chase, Diane Z., and Arlen F. Chase. 2011. Ghosts amid the Ruins: Analyzing Relationships between the Living and the Dead among the Ancient Maya at Caracol, Belize. In *Living with the Dead: Mortuary Ritual in Mesoamerica*, edited by James Fitzsimmons and Izumi Shimada, pp. 78–101. University of Arizona Press, Tucson.

Chesson, Meredith S., ed. 2001. *Social Memory, Identity, and Death: Anthropological Perspectives on Mortuary Rituals.* Archaeological Papers of the American Anthropological Association Number 10, University of California Press, Berkeley.

Christensen, Alexander F., and Marcus Winter. 1997. Culturally Modified Skeletal Remains from the Site of Huamelulpan, Oaxaca, Mexico. *International Journal of Osteoarchaeology* 7:467–480.

Coe, Michael, and Rex Koontz. 2008. *Mexico: From the Olmecs to the Aztecs.* 6th ed. Thames and Hudson, London.

Fitzsimmons, James L. 2009. *Death and the Classic Maya Kings.* University of Texas Press, Austin.

Fitzsimmons, James L. 2011. Perspectives on Death and Transformation in Maya Society: Human Remains as a Means to an End. In *Living with the Dead: Mortuary Ritual in Mesoamerica,* edited by James Fitzsimmons and Izumi Shimada, pp. 53–77. University of Arizona Press, Tucson.

Fortes, Meyer. 1987. *Religion, Morality and the Person: Essays on Tallensi Religion.* Cambridge University Press, Cambridge.

Freedman, Maurice. 1970. Ritual Aspects of Chinese Kinship and Marriage. In *Family and Kinship in Chinese Society,* edited by Maurice Freedman, pp. 163–188. Stanford University Press, Stanford.

Gaxiola González, Margarita. 1986. La arquitectura mixteca de Huamelupan. *Cuadernos de Arquitectura Mesoamericana* 7:70–74.

Gillespie, Susan. 2001. Personhood, Agency, and Mortuary Ritual: A Case Study from the Ancient Maya. *Journal of Anthropological Archaeology* 20:73–112.

Gillespie, Susan. 2002. Body and Soul among the Maya: Keeping the Spirits in Place. In *The Space and Place of Death,* edited by Helaine Silverman and David B. Small, pp. 67–78. Archaeological Papers of the American Anthropological Association No. 11, University of California Press, Berkeley.

Hallam, Elizabeth, Jenny Hockey, and Glennys Howarth. 1999. *Beyond the Body: Death and Social Identity.* Routledge, London.

Haviland, William A. 1981. Dower Houses and Minor Centers at Tikal, Guatemala: An Investigation into the Identification of Valid Units in Settlement Hierarchies. In *Lowland Maya Settlement Patterns,* edited by Wendy Ashmore, pp. 89–120. University of New Mexico Press, Albuquerque.

Headrick, Annabeth. 1999. The Street of the Dead...It Really Was: Mortuary Bundles at Teotihuacan. *Ancient Mesoamerica* 10(1):69–85.

Houston, Stephen, David Stuart, and Karl Taube. 2006. *The Memory of Bones: Body, Being, and Experience among the Classic Maya.* University of Texas Press, Austin.

Hunt, M. Eva. 1977. *Transformation of the Hummingbird: Cultural Roots of a Zinacantecan Mythical Poem.* Cornell University Press, Ithaca.

Joyce, Rosemary. 2001. Burying the Dead at Tlatilco: Social Memory and Social Identities. In *Social Memory, Identity, and Death: Anthropological Perspectives on Mortuary Rituals,* edited by Meredith S. Chesson, pp. 12–26. Archaeological Papers of the American Anthropological Association Number 10, University of California Press, Berkeley.

Leventhal, Richard M. 1983. Household Groups and Classic Maya Religion. In *Prehistoric Settlement Patterns,* edited by Evon Vogt and Richard Leventhal, pp. 55–76. University of New Mexico Press, Albuquerque.

López Austín, Alfredo. 1984. *Cuerpo humano e ideología: las concepciones de los antiguos Nahuas.* Universidad Nacional Autónoma de México, Instituto de Investigaciones Antropológicas, Mexico.

Marcus, Joyce. 1999. Early Architecture in the Valley of Oaxaca: 1350 BC–AD 500. In *Mesoamerican Architecture as a Cultural Symbol*, edited by J. Kowalski, pp. 58–75. Oxford University Press, Oxford.

Marcus, Joyce, and Kent V. Flannery. 1996. *Zapotec Civilization: How Urban Society Evolved in Mexico's Oaxaca Valley*. Thames and Hudson, New York.

McAnany, Patricia A. 1995. *Living with the Ancestors: Kinship and Kingship in Ancient Maya Society*. University of Texas Press, Austin.

Metcalf, Peter, and Richard Huntington. 1991. *Celebrations of Death: The Anthropology of Mortuary Ritual*. 2nd ed. Cambridge University Press, Cambridge.

Miller, Mary Ellen, and Simon Martin. 2004. *Courtly Art of the Ancient Maya*. Thames and Hudson, London.

Moholy-Nagy, Hattula, and John M. Ladd. 1992. Objects of Stone, Shell, and Bone. In *Artifacts from the Cenote of Sacrifice, Chichen Itza, Yucatan*, edited by C. Coggins, pp. 99–151. Peabody Museum Memoirs 10(3), Harvard University, Cambridge.

Monaghan, John. 2000. Theology and History in the Study of Mesoamerican Religions. In *Handbook of Middle American Indians, Supplement 6, Ethnology*. University of Texas Press, Austin.

Oliveros Morales, J. Arturo. 2006. El Opeño: un antiguo cementerio en el occidente mesoamericana. *Ancient Mesoamerica* 17(2):251–271.

O'Shea, John. 1996. *Villagers of the Maros: A Portrait of an Early Bronze Age Society*. Springer Verlag, New York.

Palka, Joel. 2000. *Historical Dictionary of Ancient Mesoamerica*. Scarecrow Press, Lanham, Maryland.

Pohl, John. 1994. *The Politics of Symbolism in Mixtec Codices*. Vanderbilt University Press, Nashville, Tennessee.

Saxe, Arthur A. 1970. Social Dimensions of Mortuary Practices. Unpublished PhD dissertation, Department of Anthropology, University of Michigan, Ann Arbor.

Sugiyama, Saburo. 2011. Interactions between the Living and the Dead at Major Monuments in Teotihuacan. In *Living with the Dead: Mortuary Ritual in Mesoamerica*, edited by James L. Fitzsimmons and Izumi Shimada, pp. 161–202. University of Arizona Press, Tucson.

Tozzer, Alfred Marston. 1941. *Landa's relación de las cosas de Yucatán*. Papers of the Peabody Museum of American Archaeology and Ethnology, Harvard University, Cambridge.

Weiner, Annette B. 1976. *Women of Value, Men of Renown: New Perspectives in Trobriand Exchange*. University of Texas Press, Austin.

Art and Iconography, Calendars, Writing, and Literature

CHAPTER 59

....

MESOAMERICAN CALENDARS AND ARCHAEOASTRONOMY

....

ANTHONY F. AVENI

In its complexity, precision, and sheer elegance, the Mesoamerican, and especially the Maya, calendar is at least on par with any of the timekeeping systems of the ancient Middle East and Mediterranean worlds. Among its hallmarks that facilitated the performance of mathematical operations were the invention of numerical place notation, zero, and the use of only three symbols, the dot (one), the bar (five), and the zero, or completion symbol, all likely derived from hand gestures, to represent time units, the day serving as the basic temporal currency. (Justeson 1989; Lounsbury 1978)

THE most significant intervallic reckoning period consisted of 260 days, called the *tzolkin*, or "count of days," by the Maya or the *tonalpohualli* by the Aztecs. Consisting of cycles of twenty named days, likely derived from the full body count of fingers and toes, and thirteen numerical coefficients, which may have signified the layers of heaven, this divinatory calendar very likely originated as early as the sixth century BC in the southern Zapotec region, when it was recognized that the commensuration of the two produced a cycle that resonated with natural rhythms. Mesoamerican daykeepers took particular advantage of commensurate numbers because they facilitated reckoning events in sacred time. Thus, 260 approximates both the human gestation period, nine lunar months, and the average duration of appearance of the closely watched planet Venus as the morning or evening star. Moreover, in mid-Mesoamerican latitudes, 260 is an excellent approximation to the agricultural cycle. It may also be more than mere coincidence that the two days of annual passage of the sun overhead in these latitudes divides the year into 260-day and 105-day periods. It is likely that, as in timekeeping systems in nonhierarchical cultures (cf. Aveni 2004), the agricultural cycle predated the seasonal, or solar-based, cycle of 365 days (ca. 300 BC), reckoning only the time interval during which subsistence activity took place and disregarding the remainder of the year.

Most Mesoamerican calendars measure a year as eighteen months, each consisting of twenty days, with an added month of only five unlucky days. There is no solid evidence that leap year was a valid Mesoamerican concept (cf. Prem 2008). Thus, the year count would have slowly backslided with respect to the seasons. Combinations of named days in the 260- and 365-day cycles would occur every 52 years, termed by investigators as a "calendar round." Evidence from the Aztec codices and chronicles suggests that at the time of the overturning of this cycle the world was vulnerable to destruction, for the time cycles themselves were thought to be reenactments of the ancient cosmic creation myth. On this occasion New Fire ceremonies were held to commemorate the completion of the cycle (Figure 59.1). Blood sacrifices were offered by drilling fire in the chest of a sacrificed victim as a debt payment to the gods, so that the sun, and therefore time, would continue on its course.

To reckon deep time, the Maya created the longest Mesoamerican calendar cycle by multiplying the basic unit of twenty to the fifth order, the exception being the multiplication of the 20-day count by 18 to form a cycle of 360 days, or one *tun*,

Figure 59.1 New Fire fifty-two-year-cycle celebration rites are exhibited in the Central Mexican Codex Borbonicus, 34.

which approximated the year; thus, 20 x 360 days = 7,200 days, or one *katun*, and 20 x 7,200 = one *baktun*. The Long Count cycle consisted of 13 baktuns, or 5,125.37 years. Dates are carved in prominent positions on hundreds of stelae situated in (likely) publicly accessible locations in open plazas fronting temples. Monumental Long Count dates appear from the first century BC to the mid-ninth century AD, or late baktun 7 to early baktun 10, alongside portrayals of rulers whose accessions, captures, alliances, and so on, are written in the accompanying hieroglyphs. These data imply that the cycle was employed as a conduit for political propaganda. As was the case in the Old World, such monuments served the purpose of anchoring dynastic lineage to the distant past, when the ancestor gods created the world. Subdivisions of the cycle (e.g., the thirteen katuns) may have been used to set up social order via a set of rotating geopolitical capitals (Rice 2004, 2007). The Long Count zero date, calculated back from baktun 7, is August 11, 3114 BC. The cycle will overturn on December 21, 2012 CE. That the first date was a solar zenith passage and the last a winter solstice may have played a role in setting up the cycle to be in tune with significant seasonal marking points; however, no other significant astronomical event matches either the starting or ending date.

The equivalent Christian dates in the Julian Calendar for events expressed in the Long Count are arrived at via the Goodman-Thompson-Martinez correlation family, which is based on a combination of ethnohistoric documentation and internal consistency with predicted dates of astronomical events verifiable both historically and via back calculation. The correlation constant, or the number of days one must add to a Long Count to arrive at a Julian date, is almost universally agreed upon to within two days (either 584,283 or 584,285). The former constant has been employed throughout this essay (cf. Bricker and Bricker 2011 for detailed arguments favoring this choice).

In addition to monumental texts, codices are the other major source of calendric information. In central Mexico some twenty precontact documents survive. Most of them are fashioned out of lime-coated, painted animal skin. Contents include narrative histories, or details regarding ritual procedures, such as what to sacrifice, to whom, and when, the latter couched almost exclusively in divisions and multiples of the 260-day cycle (cf. Boone 2007). Only three agreed-upon examples of codices survive the Maya conquest: most of these folded-screen, bark texts were destroyed by the early Spanish chroniclers, who regarded them as the work of the devil. Far more elaborate than their central Mexican counterparts, they consisted of hieroglyphic notation, *tzolkin* rounds, and some Long Count dates. They are exclusively divinatory in nature and incorporate the teachings of the elite daykeepers, whose courtly scribes were closely allied with the royal lineages.

Of particular interest among the some three hundred almanacs that make up the Maya codices are those that reveal the extraordinary sophistication of Maya astronomical practice. The Paris Codex, for example, contains a thirteen-constellation zodiac that implies that Maya astronomers tracked the movement of the sun, moon, and planets against the background of the stars (Figure 59.2). A Venus table in the Dresden Codex marks the first and last appearance of that planet in the morning and evening sky. An accompanying correction table allows the user to fit the canonic round of 584 days to the observed Venus cycle of 583.92 days to an accuracy of one day in five hundred years. That a similar table can be found in the central Mexican Codex Borgia may imply long-distance cross-cultural trafficking in ideas about the measure of time across ancient Mesoamerica (cf. Vail and Aveni 2004).

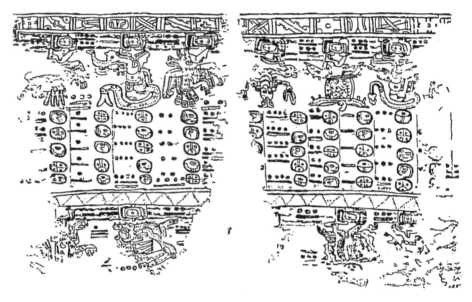

Figure 59.2 The Maya zodiac, a testimony to their interest in following celestial motions. Paris Codex, 23-4 (Vail and Hernández 2011).

Other almanacs in the Maya codices incorporate mathematical mechanisms for reckoning the motion of Mars and eclipse warnings. Recent investigations posit that a number of almanacs previously thought to refer to endless cycles of 260 days may also have been intended to indicate adjustable seasonal points in a historical ("real-time") framework (cf. Bricker and Bricker 2011, Vail and Aveni 2004). A similar example has also been proposed in the Borgia Codex (Milbrath 2007). While Mesoamerican astronomy is quantitative and precise, its end responds exclusively to astrological interests, namely securing predictions concerning crops, disease, rain, and so forth.

Though so much evidence relating to precontact calendrical practice has been destroyed, some information survives, though in modified form, in the post-conquest Books of Chilam Balam and Annals of the Cakchiquel in the Maya area. These several sacred historical books, housed in and named after towns that grew up around the Maya ruins, refer to particular ritual cycles, especially to prophecies that accompany katun endings. In addition, books by Spanish chroniclers (e.g., Durán and Sahagún in Mexico, and Landa in Yucatán) contain narratives that refer to calendrical divinatory procedures, calendar wheels, stars, names of constellations, planets, and eclipses. Though heavily corrupted by the Hispanic worldview, indigenous ideas and practices can nonetheless be extracted from these valuable data.

In addition to the excavation, restoration, and preservation of carved texts on the monuments, the archaeological record offers insight into the role of time, astronomy, and cosmology in urban planning, as well as in the architectural placement and orientation of particular structures. The interdisciplinary study of archaeoastronomy, lately renamed "cultural astronomy" (Ruggles and Saunders 1993), is the study of the practice of astronomy in ancient civilizations based on both written and unwritten records. A broad survey of the methodology and history of such studies is detailed in Aveni's work (2001, 2003, 2008). Because sky events offer the most reliable seasonal and longer-term timing devices, one might expect celestial axes and pivots to play a role in architectural planning, especially where ceremonial activities are conducted, and most especially in cultures known to have exhibited an interest in sky phenomena based on the written and pictorial record. Herewith are a few examples.

According to the Aztecs, Teotihuacan was regarded as the place where time began when the sun was born. The deviation from cardinality as well from the lay of the land, by some 15½° clockwise, of the rigid rectangular grid structure of the city is likely owed, at least in part, to an attempt to duplicate the cosmos in the built environment. The east-west orientation of the city is directed toward the setting point of the Pleiades star group, which passed the overhead point when Teotihuacan was founded, ca. 200 BC. Moreover, the predawn appearance of the Pleiades in the east coincided with the date of the first two annual passages of the sun overhead. This clever sun-and-star timing device, incorporated into the spatial fabric of the city, may have served as a way of both controlling and celebrating time, a response to the cosmic mandate connecting rulership to transcendence. The 15½° axis also coincides with sunset positions forty days after the spring equinox and twenty days before first solar zenith passage, which may imply an attempt to configure the basic twenty-day Mesoamerican calendrical count into a horizon-based calendar, further linking city and cosmos. Sugiyama (2010) has proposed that multiples of basic calendrical periods such as 260-day and the 584-day Venus cycle served as measuring units applied to the dimensions and relative spacing of many of Teotihuacan's basic structures. Local mountains and caves also appear to have played a role in the city plan. One can appreciate the problem confronting the architectural designers, who were faced with the practical problem of arranging their city to be in perfect harmony with the many manifestations of nature they believed lay at the source of their power.

The influence of Teotihuacan architectural tradition resonates in the skewed orientation plans of other sites in highland Mexico. The calendar is also reflected in the architects' plan. More than eighty pecked cross-circle petroglyphs found all over Mesoamerica, from the Tropic of Cancer to the Petén rain forest, appear to have served as calendric counting devices related to the calendar at Teotihuacan. Two of these devices, which consist (usually) of a double circle centered on a cross pecked into stucco floors or rock outcrops, mark the east-to-west Teotihuacan alignment. An interesting analog appears in the stucco subfloor of Structure A-V at the Maya site of Uaxactún. Its count of twenty on each axis of the cross follows that of several prototypes found at Teotihuacan; however, counts of the circular elements reflect aspects of both local and Teotihuacan solar seasonal timings (Aveni 2000). Whether this Teotihuacan connection resulted simply from an imitation of style or a direct imposition of some sort of "Teotihuacan Standard Time" in the Maya area is not clear, but the idea of employment of Mesoamerican time standards makes sense given the demands of economy and trade.

Evidence for the dissemination of Teotihuacan astronomy and the calendar 650 kilometers to the northwest appears in alignments at Alta Vista (Chalchihuites), a site exhibiting the ceramic influence of the Teotihuacan Tlamimilolpa-Xolalpan phase (ca. 250-550 CE). An equinox orientation defined by the east-west corner points of the principal temple points to the most important mountain on the eastern horizon, the site of an ancient turquoise mine. Alignment with the same mountain is duplicated on the June solstice from a backsight located on a plateau overlooking Alta Vista. The latter site is marked by a pair of pecked cross-circle petroglyphs. That the site is located at the Tropic of Cancer adds to the motive for cosmic preplanning, for this is where the sun stands overhead at noon on but one day of the year, the June solstice.

Maya cities also exhibit systematic deviations from cardinality, with more than 84 percent of them being skewed to the east of north. A peak at 14° is especially prominent in the Puuc (Terminal Classic, ca. 900 CE) alignments. This may have constituted an attempt to transform a twenty-day based seasonal calendar acquired from the Petén to one more suited to seasonal phenomena in the more northerly Puuc latitudes.

Other celestially aligned Maya complexes include Tikal's quadripartite Twin Pyramid groups, which invite comparison with cosmograms in the codices (but see the archaeological debate-discussion of "city as cosmogram" reported in Aveni [2008]). Oddly shaped and oriented individual Maya structures include the Caracol of Chichén Itzá and the House of the Governor at Uxmal, both likely dedicated to Venus, with rituals of the sort detailed in the Venus table in the Dresden Codex. Both align with eight-year standstill positions of Venus on the horizon.

The assemblages known as E-Groups, named for the prototype at Uaxactún, consist of a series of three small buildings (Structures EI-EII-EIII) located on a single platform fronting on the east a radial pyramid (EVII-sub). From the latter site the sun rises over EI and EIII on the solstices and over EII at the equinox (Figure 59.3). Among the more than thirty later complexes that fit this category, precise solar alignment may have become a minor consideration (Aimers and Rice 2006), subservient to metaphoric principles tying together concepts of sacred space and stressing ritual performance related to agricultural events. However, there is some evidence supported by alignments in the E-Group complexes that can be measured with some precision that points to a change in calendar orientation at about the beginning of the Classic (ca 200 CE), not unlike that which occurred in

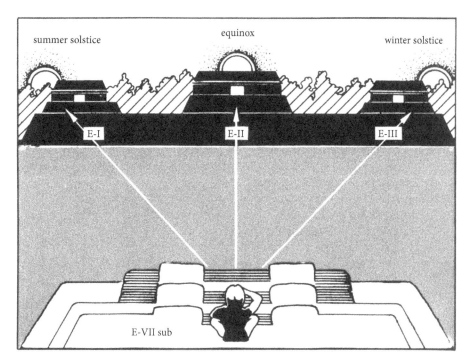

Figure 59.3 The E-Group Complex at Uaxactún, a prototype of solar-aligned Maya architectural assemblages (Aveni, 2001: Fig. 109).

the Puuc sites. Alignment dates focus on the beginning of the twenty-day months that lead up to the first solar zenith passage, which coincides with the period when the rainy season would have been anticipated (Aveni et al. 2003). One might better think of these astronomically aligned structures as theaters where sacred rites were conducted upon the timed arrival of the celestial deity, rather than as precise "scientific" observatories used by elite specialists.

References

Aimers, James, and Prudence Rice. 2006. Astronomy, Ritual, and the Interpretation of Maya "E-Group" Assemblage. *Ancient Mesoamerica* 17:79–96.

Aveni, Anthony. 2000. Out of Teotihuacan: Origins of the Celestial Canon in Mesoamerica. In *Mesoamerica's Classical Heritage: From Teotihuacan to the Aztecs*, edited by David Carrasco and Scott Sessions, pp. 253–268. University Press of Colorado, Niwot.

Aveni, Anthony. 2001. *Skywatchers: A Revised Updated Version of Skywatchers of Ancient Mexico.* University of Texas Press, Austin.

Aveni, Anthony. 2003. Archaeoastronomy in the Ancient Americas. *Journal of Archaeological Research* 11(2):149–191.

Aveni, Anthony. 2004. *Empires of Time: Calendars, Clocks, and Cultures*. Revised ed. University Press of Colorado, Boulder.

Aveni, Anthony. 2008. *Foundations of New World Cultural Astronomy: A Reader with Commentary*. University Press of Colorado, Boulder.

Aveni, Anthony, Anne Dowd, and Benjamin Vining. 2003. Maya Calendar Reform: Evidence from Orientations of Specialized Architectural Assemblages. *Latin American Antiquity* 14(2):159–178.

Boone, Elizabeth. 2007. *Cycles of Time and Meaning in the Mexican Books of Fate*. University of Texas Press, Austin.

Bricker, Victoria, and Harvey Bricker. 2011. *Astronomy in the Maya Codices*. American Philosophical Society, Philadelphia.

Codex Borbonicus. 1899. Foundation for the Advancement of Mesoamerican Studies. Electronic document, http://www.famsi.org/research/loubat/Borbonicus/images/Borbonicus_34.jpg. (accessed July 31, 2011).

Justeson, John. 1989. Ancient Maya Ethnoastronomy: An Overview of Hieroglyphic Sources. In *World Archaeoastronomy*, edited by Anthony Aveni, pp. 76–129. Cambridge University Press, Cambridge.

Lounsbury, Floyd. 1978. Maya Numeration, Calendar, and Astronomy. *Dictionary of Scientific Biography* 15, suppl. L, edited by Charles C. Gillespie, pp. 759–818. Scribner's, New York.

Milbrath, Susan. 2007. Astronomical Cycles in the Imagery of Codex Borgia 29–46. In *Cultural Astronomy in New World Cosmologies*, edited by Clive Ruggles and Gary Urton, pp. 157–207. University Press of Colorado, Boulder.

Prem, Hanns. 2008. *Manual de la antiqua cronología Mexicana*. CIESAS y Miguel Angel Porrua, Mexico.

Rice, Prudence. 2004. *Maya Political Science: Time, Astronomy, and the Cosmos*. University of Texas Press, Austin.

Rice, Prudence. 2007. *Maya Calendar Origins: Monuments, Mythistory, and the Materialization of Time*. University of Texas Press, Austin.

Ruggles, Clive, and Nicholas Saunders. 1993. *Astronomies and Cultures*. University Press of Colorado, Niwot.

Sugiyama, Saburo. 2010. Teotihuacan City Layout as a Cosmogram: Preliminary Results of the 2007 Measurement Unit Study. In *The Archaeology of Measurements, Comprehending Heaven, Earth and Time in Ancient Societies*, edited by Colin Renfrew and Iain Morley, pp. 208–231. Cambridge University Press, Cambridge.

Vail, Gabrielle, and Anthony Aveni, eds. 2004. *The Madrid Codex: New Approaches to Understanding an Ancient Maya Manuscript*. University Press of Colorado, Boulder.

Vail, Gabriell, and Christine Hernández. 2011. The Maya Codices Database Version 4.0. Electronic document, http://www.mayacodices.org/images/fig4.jpg (accessed July 31, 2011).

CHAPTER 60

....

THEMES IN THE ART
OF THE PRECLASSIC
PERIOD

....

MARY E. PYE

THIS short chapter on Preclassic-period art cannot fully do justice to the topic, and so I will only briefly treat some recurrent themes as well as discuss some new approaches and recent finds.

The concept of "art" is a critical aspect of human expression without easy parameters that can be applied across cultures and time. Here, I begin with a broad definition of art taken from the online Merriam-Webster's dictionary: "the quality, production, expression, or realm, according to aesthetic principles, of what is beautiful, appealing, or of more than ordinary significance." The current Western view of art was greatly influenced by the Enlightenment period, the era of reason, science, and a more secular approach in all aspects of society. Kant (1987), in his *Critique of Judgment*, argued that aesthetics are tied to cognitive reasoning and he highlighted the contemplation of forms and the need to stand apart from the object to appreciate its qualities. Today, works of art are commodities that are bought and sold, independent of their origins whether those were as a pure art object or as a functioning artifact, like a retable on the altar of a Catholic Church, for example.

The origins of Pre-Columbian art were far removed from Western concepts. In defining the difference between Western and Pre-Columbian "functions of the soul," George Kubler wrote that "religious, ethical, aesthetic, and social functions were experienced as a seamless entity" that could not be readily divided, while "men of today cannot bring them back together" (1975: 17). The creation of art and aesthetics of any culture are embedded in its environment, belief systems, societal norms, and particular history, and Pre-Columbian scholars studying art attempt to understand it as skillfully created, multivalent artifacts, sometimes lacking context but never without meaning.

CHRONOLOGY AND THE TRANSITION
FROM THE ARCHAIC TO PRECLASSIC PERIOD

Bracketed by the Late Archaic on one side and the Classic period on the other, the definition of "Preclassic" is a historical construct based on early ideas of Maya history. Classic Maya civilization (AD 300-900), widely publicized by the accounts of John Lloyd Stephen and beautiful drawings by Frederick Catherwood, was the focus of scholarly study in the late nineteenth century. The romantic scenes of abandoned stone cities, carved stelae depicting individuals with human proportions, hieroglyphic writing, a calendrical system, and so on, led to the christening of both this time period and art style as "florescent" (Miller 2006: 11). Hence, all developments that came before the Classic Maya were designated "Preclassic."[1]

Given our current knowledge of Mesoamerican prehistory, the Preclassic period is perhaps the true "florescent" era, at least for Mesoamerican civilization as a whole, given the appearance, development, and coalescence of arguably all of its major components and features long before Classic Maya civilization. What came before the Preclassic era is still poorly known, as seasonal mobility, depositional overburden, and the environments of Mesoamerica conspire to leave little evidence. Undoubtedly, Archaic peoples had artistic traditions that likely included bodily adornment, portable objects of perishable materials, and a decorative container technology. Some of this is indicated by what is found in the subsequent Preclassic period: for example, Tlatilco figurines with painted body designs (Piña Chan 1955: 50, Fig. 8) or the early polychrome Barra ceramics, which have been argued to be the adoption of a new ceramic technology to a well-developed preexisting decorative gourd tradition in the Soconusco (Clark and Gosser 1995).

But apart from the limited material record, the delimitation of the Archaic from the Preclassic is marked by a major shift in human adaptation from nomadic

---

1. Further substantive work on the Preclassic sites has led to more temporal subdivisions within this period. The major demarcations are Early (1800-1000 BC), Middle (1000-500 BC), and Late (500 BC-200 AD); however, this breakdown can vary by region and site. Such is also the case for the Archaic period. Here, I will use broad terms: Late Archaic, Early Preclassic, Middle Preclassic, and Late Preclassic to indicate temporality. See Evans (2008) for further details on Preclassic Mesoamerican chronology.

to sedentary existence, along with increasing dependence on certain cultigens and the creation of new societal arrangements. A few critical themes are immediately relevant for understanding Preclassic art. First, the relationship of individuals or groups to their identified and utilized landscapes would have changed, as the seasonal round collapsed into fewer locations occupied for longer time periods. As travel to and experiences with particular regions decreased, a few key sites—specific river crossings and prominent mountain peaks and passes—might have remained sacred. Rupestrian art is widely seen in Mesoamerica and, although difficult to date, seems to have existed from Paleo-Indian times (e.g., López Wario 2008). In eastern Guerrero and Morelos a carved and red-painted tradition of motifs is found throughout the region, on many mountain ridges, massifs, and alongside permanent rivers, and are believed to be from the Archaic (Figure 60.1) (Gutiérrez 2008). In the subsequent Preclassic, only three Olmec-style paintings have been found in caves and rockshelters, and all mark critical passes on the route between central Mexico and the Pacific coast (Pye and Gutiérrez 2007). The Cauadzidziqui rockshelter in particular presents a scene with an individual wearing Olmec-style iconography plastered over the paintings of the earlier tradition (Figure 60.2) (Gutiérrez 2008). This Preclassic graffito indicated the arrival of new artistic canons.

Another transformative theme is how individuals and groups experienced a new engagement with "things." Renfrew (1998, 2001) argues that sedentism brought about a major transition in human cognition—in technologies and the use of symbols. The shift to sedentism would have resulted in profound alterations to artistic expression and tradition, at the level of the individual and group, and a new identification with and creation of permanent residential nodes. Along with

Figure 60.1 Carved motifs on Piedra Pinta, Totomixtlahuaca, Guerrero
(photo by Gerardo Gutiérrez).

Figure 60.2 Cauadzidziqui rockshelter, Ocoapa, Guerrero
(photo by Gerardo Gutiérrez).

beautifully crafted ceramics and figurines of the Soconusco, the first ceremonial center at Paso de la Amada dates to early in the Preclassic period (Clark 2004). The implications of this shift to sedentism, and its relation to art, have been explored in works on cognition, agency, and material culture theory (e.g., Gell 1998; Hooper 2000; DeMarrais et al. 2004; Pasztory 2005; Morphy 2009).

Finally, there were new media available for use in the Preclassic. Finely worked ceramics and figurines are later joined by carved stone in a variety of types and sizes, from large basalt Olmec heads to jade earspools. Large stucco masks adorn Maya temples. Painting, woodworking, and other skills that leave few traces would have been part of this expanded repertoire, as demonstrated by the fortuitous finds of life-sized Olmec wooden busts at El Manatí (Ortiz and Rodríguez 2000), painted murals of San Bartolo (Saturno et al. 2005), or the colored clay quatrefoil sculpture of La Blanca (Love and Guernsey 2007). In addition, we see what were ritual acts creating art, such as the buried mosaic jaguar mask of carved greenstone and limestone axes seen at La Venta (Drucker et al. 1959: 94, Fig. 29), and more recent offerings uncovered at El Cival (Bauer 2005) and Chiapa de Corzo (Bachand et al. 2008).

OLMEC ART

Olmec art has captured scholarly and popular attention since the first report of a colossal Olmec head by Melgar (in 1871) and has since become a hallmark of Preclassic art.

Olmec origins have been the object of polemical debate since a 1942 Mesa Redonda in Chiapas, specifically focusing on the "Olmec problem" (Sociedad Mexicana de Antropología 1942). Mayanists argued against an early dating for Olmec archaeological culture, asserting Maya civilization as the oldest in Mesoamerica. With the first radiocarbon dates at La Venta in the 1950s, that debate was over (Taube 2004: 4–5). Controversy continues today about the origin of Olmec-style ceramics found outside the Gulf Coast; however, excavations at early sites like El Manatí (Rodríguez and Ortíz 2008) and continuing work at San Lorenzo (Di Castro and Cyphers 2006) suggest that this debate will eventually be resolved in favor of Gulf Coast primacy. "Mother" versus "sister" arguments of Preclassic interaction (Sharer and Grove 1989) seem to be waning in recognition of the extraordinary complexity of the Preclassic period, which requires researchers to understand the archaeological culture of specific sites and regions before postulating Olmec connections (Lesure 2004; Pool 2007). Even within Olman (the Olmec heartland of the southern Gulf Coast), differences between sites over time (e.g., San Lorenzo versus La Venta) are profound and have implications for understanding art and iconography.

Olmec-style monuments, ceramics, portable greenstone art, and figurines have been widely reported throughout Mexico, and scholars have been writing about them since the early twentieth century (see de la Fuente 1977; Taube 2004). The style presents many facets. The sculptures of Olman, from the colossal heads to the three-dimensional human and animal forms, have been described by many scholars as naturalistic and conceptual representations. Other objects present more abstract designs, like Early Preclassic Calzadas Carved ceramics with flame eyebrows, St. Andrew's cross, U-shaped elements, and others. These motifs are often grouped together for a pars pro toto representation of a dragon (Joralemon 1976) or an avian serpent (Taube 1994). Nonetheless, some of these abstract elements also appear on "naturalistic" sculptures: for example, Mon. SL-7, a sinuous feline with an inverted S-shaped motif on its side (Cyphers 2004: 56–57, Figs. 16-17). Olmec art was clearly more figurative than later Mesoamerican art styles, but its themes include supernatural narratives we do not understand, because early writing systems did not appear until later.

A notable feature of Olmec art was the rapid diffusion of certain elements over a wide area beginning at 1200 BC with carved ceramics and figurines, and later in the Middle Formative with portable greenstone axes and other objects, as well as sculptural styles and ritual practices. The impact of Olmec art on cultures outside of Olman varied greatly over time and from region to region. Hence, the replacement of the local Mokaya tradition of figurines and ceramics at Cantón Corralito with ceramics and figurine styles (and imports) from San Lorenzo (Cheetham 2010) contrasts greatly with the variable situation seen in the Basin of Mexico. In Tlatilco burials, possible Calzadas Carved imports are found together with local ceramics completely unrelated to those of the Gulf Coast, including local naturalistic animal effigy pots occasionally decorated with a random Olmec motif (Piña Chán 1958: lam.4). Later Early Preclassic whitewares and redwares with Olmec faces in profile similar to those on the Middle Preclassic jade celts seem to appear in the Basin of Mexico first (Niederberger 1976; Clark and Pye 2000) and indicate a changing dynamic of styles occurring rapidly in Central Mexico and spreading elsewhere. As regional and site chronologies improve and tighter classes of motifs and related objects are defined, the acceptance, mediation, and adaptation of the Olmec symbol set outside of Olman will become better understood and offer more nuanced insights into Preclassic interactions.

Many key themes of Olmec art continued into the Late Preclassic period. Rulership was one such critical theme. The colossal heads are believed to be portraits of rulers, perhaps later buried and transformed into important ancestors (Cyphers et al. 2006). The massive tabletop-style monuments have been argued to be thrones or ancestral altars (Figure 60.3) (Grove 1973; Gillespie 1999) and their distribution across the San Lorenzo region indicates their use as markers in the social and political hierarchy (Cyphers 2008). Both of these classes of sculpture were subject to mutilation, presumably to neutralize the power of a deceased ruler (Grove 1981) or to delegitimate claims by competing lineages upon the death of a ruler (Clark 1997). Bas-relief monuments, which became more numerous in the Middle and Late Preclassic, clearly depict rulers arrayed in all their costume and glory, like Mon. 1 at La Venta (de la Fuente 1977: pl. 52).

Another important theme is "art in space"—the confluence and arrangement of monuments, monument groupings, site layouts, natural features, and even buried objects in the creation of sacred landscapes, highlighted at San Lorenzo (Cyphers 1999; Cyphers et al. 2006). With the rise of many Middle Formative cities or kingdoms, a standard feature is the idea of these locales as nodes in the Mesoamerican cosmic landscape as presented in the requisite art, iconography, architecture, and layouts, illustrated by La Venta (González Lauck 2004); sites in Morelos and Guerrero, such as Chalcatzingo (Grove 2000) and Teopantecuanitlan (Martínez

Figure 60.3 Altar 4 at La Venta (photo by author).

Donjuan 2010); throughout Chiapas, from Chiapa de Corzo to La Libertad (Clark in press); and in the Maya lowlands at Nakbé (Clark et al. 2000).

Other themes concern deities and supernatural connections. The maize god and his personification of the growth stages of maize seem to be the focus of Middle Formative iconography on greenstone celts (Taube 2000). Covarrubias's (1957: 62, Fig. 22) depiction of an iconic jaguar mask evolving into regional rain gods is still debated. Taube has proposed further examples and insights to support this schema—particularly with reference to his ideas on Olmec rain gods (Taube 1994, 2004: 29–34). Clark (2008: 152–155) has argued that Covarrubias's schema is not about continuity without change, but rather the transformation of deities both in depiction and meaning over time. "Transformation" here has both an academic and emic viewpoint. In the academic sense, potential changes in the meaning of artistic forms and motifs over time have long been identified as problematic for understanding archaeological cultures that left no written records (Kubler 1970). Still, there seem to be key tenets of Mesoamerican religion that were represented in Preclassic art, one of them being "transformation," which was (and still is) a key concept, involving the ability of gods and men to transform into animals and natural forces (e.g., Guernsey 1997; Gutiérrez and Pye 2010).

Olmec art was not the only artistic tradition of the Preclassic period, but arguably it had the greatest impact in Mesoamerica, particularly in the Middle Preclassic. With the waning of La Venta's power and influence, many sites were in ascendance and became prominent in the late Middle Preclassic and Late Preclassic periods. Notably, they offer distinct regional differences in their art styles. While the classic Olmec style continued at Tres Zapotes in Olman, Kaminaljuyú, Izapa, Monte Albán, sites along the Guatemalan Pacific coast, and in the Maya lowlands, all presented vibrant artistic traditions in stone, painting, ceramics, and plaster, along with the inclusion of early writing systems into the sculpture, portable objects, and ceramics.

Finally, even as we improve our understanding of Preclassic archaeological cultures, with new sites excavated, new objects uncovered, and more nuanced interpretations, the presentations of these complicated ideas seem to be lost on the public, particularly in museum exhibitions that emphasize the most simplistic ideas. Most insidious is the lumping together of all Preclassic art under the rubric of "Olmec," such as the beautiful duck effigy from Tlapacoya exhibited in the National Gallery of Art (Benson and de la Fuente 1996: 391) or the jadeite earspool purportedly from Michoacán at a Princeton University Art Museum Olmec show (Art Museum 1995: 257). These examples highlight the fact that Pre-Columbian art has indeed become part of collectible and commodified Western art.

FURTHER READING

Because my frame of reference is as an archaeologist, I would like to call attention to art historical scholarship on Preclassic art, particularly with a different view on the anthropological/archaeological approach. Kubler's (1975) introduction in his landmark textbook on Pre-Columbian art and his article "Period, Style, and Meaning" (1970) remain sobering caveats for the archaeologist, as does a more recent piece by de la Fuente (2008). For examples of formalistic approaches to Preclassic art, see Pohorilenko (2004) and Quirarte (1976). A lively debate on the use of shamanism for understanding Mesoamerican art is offered by Klein and colleagues (2002), with commentary from a variety of scholars. A range of viewpoints on Olmec artistic expression can be found in a number of articles in *Olmeca: Balance y perspective* (Uriarte and González Lauck 2008), a two-volume set of articles with CDs of discussions based on a conference at the Museo Nacional de Antropología e Historia held in 2005. Finally, Boone (2006) offers an insightful essay on three icons of Pre-Columbian art and their impact on the societies and eras when they were found. In particular, she presents the Las Limas stone, an Olmec monument, as an illustration of the impact that a single artifact can have on academic scholarship.

REFERENCES

The Art Museum. 1995. *The Olmec World: Ritual and Rulership.* The Art Museum, Princeton, New Jersey.

Bachand, Bruce R., Emiliano Gallaga Murrieta, and Lynneth S. Lowe. 2008. Chiapa de Corzo Archaeological Project Report of the 2008 Field Season. Electronic document, http://chiapadecorzo.byu.edu/ (accessed May 2010).

Baur, Jeremy. 2005. Between Heaven and Earth: The Cival Cache and the Creation of the Mesoamerican Cosmos. In *Lords of Creation: The Origins of Sacred Maya Kingship*, edited by Virginia Fields and Dorie Reents-Budet, pp. 28–29. Los Angeles County Museum and Scala Publishers, Los Angeles and London.

Benson, Elizabeth P., and Beatriz de la Fuente, eds. 1996. *Olmec Art of Ancient Mexico.* National Gallery of Art, Washington, DC.

Boone, Elizabeth Hill. 2006. The Defining Sample: How We Parse the Pre-Columbian Past. In *A Pre-Columbian World*, edited by Jeffrey Quilter and Mary Miller, pp. 21–53. Dumbarton Oaks, Washington, DC.

Cheetham, David. 2010. Cultural Imperatives in Clay: Early Olmec Carved Pottery from San Lorenzo and Cantón Corralito. *Ancient Mesoamerica* 21(1):165–185.

Clark, John E. 1997. The Arts of Government in Early Mesoamerica. *Annual Review of Anthropology* 26:211–234.

Clark, John E. 2004. Mesoamerica Goes Public: Early Ceremonial Centers, Leaders, and Communities. In *Mesoamerican Archaeology*, edited by Julia Hendon and Rosemary Joyce, pp. 43–72. Blackwell, Oxford.

Clark, John E. 2008. Teogonía olmeca: perspectivas, problemas y propuestas. In *Olmeca: Balance y perspectivas. Memoria de la primera mesa redonda*, vol. 1, edited by María Teresa Uriarte and Rebecca González Lauck, pp. 145–183. Universidad Nacional Autónoma de México, Instituto Nacional de Antropología e Historia, New World Archaeological Foundation, Mexico.

Clark, John E. In press. Western Kingdoms of the Middle Preclassic. In *Early Maya States*, edited by Robert Sharer and Loa Traxler. University Museum, University of Pennsylvania, Philadelphia.

Clark, John E., and Dennis Gosser. 1995. Reinventing Mesoamerica's First Pottery. In *The Emergence of Pottery: Technology and Innovation in Ancient Societies*, edited by William Barnett and John Hoopes, pp. 209–221. Smithsonian Institution Press, Washington, DC.

Clark, John E., Richard Hansen, and Tomás Pérez Suárez. 2000. La zona maya en el Preclásico. In *Historia antigua de México*, Vol. 1, edited by Linda Manzanilla and Leonardo López Luján, pp. 437–510. Consejo Nacional para la Cultura y las Artes, Universidad Nacional Autónoma de México, Mexico.

Clark, John E., and Mary E. Pye. 2000. The Pacific Coast and the Olmec Question. In *Olmec Art and Archaeology in Mesoamerica*, edited by John Clark and Mary Pye, pp. 217–251. Studies in the History of Art, no. 58, National Gallery of Art, Washington, DC.

Covarrubias, Miguel. 1957. *Indian Art of Mexico and Central America*. Knopf, New York.

Cyphers, Ann. 1999. From Stone to Symbols: Olmec Art in Social Context at San Lorenzo Tenochtitlan. In *Social Patterns in Pre-Classic Mesoamerica*, edited by David Grove and Rosemary Joyce, pp. 155–181. Dumbarton Oaks, Washington, DC.

Cyphers, Ann. 2004. *Escultura olmeca de San Lorenzo Tenochtitlan*. Universidad Nacional Autónoma de México, Mexico.

Cyphers, Ann. 2008. Los tronos olmecas y la cambiante configuración de poder. In *Ideología política y sociedad en el periodo formativo: Ensayos en homenaje al doctor David C. Grove*, edited by Ann Cyphers and Kenneth Hirth, pp. 311–341. Universidad Nacional Autónoma de México, Mexico.

Cyphers, Ann, Alejandro Hernández-Portilla, Marisol Varela-Gómez, and Lilia Grégor-López. 2006. Cosmological and Sociopolitical Synergy in Preclassic Architectural Complexes. In *Precolumbian Water Management: Ideology, Ritual, and Power*, edited by Lisa Lucero and Barbara Fash, pp. 17–32. University of Arizona Press, Tucson.

de la Fuente, Beatriz. 1977. *Los hombres de piedra. Escultura olmeca*. Universidad Nacional Autónoma de México, Mexico.

de la Fuente, Beatriz. 2008. ¿Puede un estilo definir una cultura? In *Olmeca: Balance y perspectivas. Memoria de la primera mesa redonda*, Vol. 1, edited by María Teresa Uriarte and Rebecca González Lauck, pp. 25–37. Universidad Nacional Autónoma de México, Instituto Nacional de Antropología e Historia, New World Archaeological Foundation, Mexico.

DeMarrais, Elizabeth, Chris Gosden, and Colin Renfrew, eds. 2004. *Rethinking Materiality: The Engagement of Mind with the Material World*. McDonald Institute for Archaeological Research, University of Cambridge, Cambridge.

Di Castro, Anna, and Ann Cyphers. 2006. Iconografía de la cerámica de San Lorenzo. *Anales del Instituto de Investigaciones Estéticas* 28(80):29–58.

Drucker, Philip, Robert F. Heizer, and Robert H. Squier. 1959. *Excavations at La Venta, Tabasco, 1955*. Bureau of American Ethnology Bulletin, no. 170, Smithsonian Institution, Washington, DC.

Evans, Susan. 2008. *Ancient Mexico and Central America: Archaeology and Culture History*. Thames and Hudson, London.

Gell, Alfred. 1998. *Art and Agency*. Clarendon, Oxford.

Gillespie, Susan. 1999. Olmec Thrones as Ancestral Altars: The Two Sides of Power. In *Material Symbols: Culture and Economy in Prehistory*, edited by John Robb, pp. 224–253. Center for Archaeological Investigations, Occasional Paper no. 26, Southern Illinois University, Carbondale.

González Lauck, Rebecca. 2004. Observaciones en torno a contextos de la escultura olmeca en La Venta, Tabasco. In *Acercarse y mirar: Homenaje a Beatriz de la Fuente*, edited by María Teresa Uriarte and Leticia Staines Cicero, pp.75–106. Universidad Nacional Autónoma de México, Mexico.

Grove, David C. 1973. Olmec Altars and Myths. *Archaeology* 26:128–135.

Grove, David C. 1981. Olmec Monuments: Mutilation as a Clue to Meaning. In *The Olmec and Their Neighbors: Essays in Memory of Matthew W. Stirling*, pp. 48–68. Dumbarton Oaks, Washington, DC.

Grove, David C. 2000. Faces of the Earth at Chalcatzingo, Mexico: Serpents, Caves, and Mountains in Middle Formative Period Iconography. In *Olmec Art and Archaeology in Mesoamerica*, edited by John Clark and Mary Pye, pp. 277–295. Studies in the History of Art, no. 58, National Gallery of Art, Washington, DC.

Guernsey, Julia. 1997. *Ritual and Power in Stone: Performance of Rulership in Mesoamerican Izapan Style Art*. University of Texas Press, Austin.

Gutiérrez, Gerardo. 2008. Four Thousand Years of Communication Systems in the Mixteca-Tlapaneca-Nahua Region: From Cauadzidziqui Rock Shelter Murals to the Azoyú Codices. In *Mixtec Writing and Society. Escritura de Ñuu Dzau*, edited by Maarten Jansen and Laura van Broekhoven, pp. 67–103. Royal Netherlands Academy of Arts and Sciences, Amsterdam.

Gutiérrez, Gerardo, and Mary E. Pye. 2010. The Iconography of the Nahual: Human-Animal Transformations in Preclassic Guerrero and Morelos. In *The Place of Sculpture in Mesoamerica's Preclassic Transition: Context, Use, and Meaning*, edited by Julia Guernsey, John Clark, and Bárbara Arroyo, pp. 27–54. Dumbarton Oaks, Washington, DC.

Hooper, Steven. 2000. An Anthropologist Looks at Art. *Art History* 23(2):300–321.

Joralemon, Peter David. 1976. The Olmec Dragon: A Study in Pre-Columbian Iconography. In *Origins of Religious Art and Iconography in Preclassic Mesoamerica*, edited by H. B. Nicholson, pp. 27–71.University of California, Los Angeles.

Kant, Immanuel. 1987. *Critique of Judgment*. Translated by Werner Pluhar. Hackett Publishing, Indianapolis.

Klein, Cecilia, Eulogia Guzmán, Elisa C. Mandell, and Maya Stanfield-Mazzi. 2002. The Role of Shamanism in Mesoamerican Art. *Current Anthropology* 43(3):383–419.

Kubler, George. 1970. Period, Style and Meaning in Ancient American Art. *New Literary History* 1(2):127–144.

Kubler, George. 1975. *The Art and Architecture of Ancient America: The Mexican, Maya, and Andean People*. 2nd ed. Penguin, Middlesex.

Lesure, Richard. 2004. Shared Art Styles and Long-Distance Contact in Early Mesoamerica. In *Mesoamerican Archaeology: Theory and Practice*, edited by Julia Hendon and Rosemary Joyce, pp. 73–96. Blackwell, Oxford.

López Wario, Luis Alberto. 2008. *Lenguage en piedra: Manifestaciones gráfico rupestres registradas por la dirección de salvamento arqueológico*. Instituto Nacional de Antropología e Historia, Mexico.

Love, Michael W., and Julia Guernsey. 2007. Monument 3 from La Blanca, Guatemala: A Middle Preclassic Earthen Sculpture and its Ritual Associations. *Antiquity* 81:920–932.

Martínez Donjuan, Guadalupe. 2010. The Sculpture from Teopantecuanitlan, Guerrero, Mexico. In *The Place of Sculpture in Mesoamerica's Preclassic Transition: Context, Use, and Meaning*, edited by Julia Guernsey, John Clark, and Bárbara Arroyo, pp. 55–76. Dumbarton Oaks, Washington, DC.

Melgar, J. M. 1871. Estudio sobre la antigüedad y el origen de la cabeza colosal de tipo etiópico que existe en Hueyapan. *Boletín de la Sociedad Mexicana de Geografía y Estadística*, 3(2):104–109.

Miller, Mary Ellen. 2006. *The Art of Mesoamerica: From Olmec to Aztec*. 4th ed. Thames and Hudson, London.

Morphy, Howard. 2009. Art as Mode of Action: Some Problems with Gell's Art and Agency. *Journal of Material Culture* 14:5–28.

Niederberger, Christine. 1976. *Zohapilco: Cinco milenios de ocupación humana en un sitio lacustre de la Cuenca de México*. Instituto Nacional de Antropología e Historia, Mexico.

Ortiz, Ponciano, and María del Carmen Rodríguez. 2000. The Sacred Hill of El Manatí: A Preliminary Discussion of the Site's Ritual Paraphernalia. In *Olmec Art and Archaeology in Mesoamerica*, edited by John Clark and Mary Pye, pp. 75–93. Studies in the History of Art, no. 58, National Gallery of Art, Washington, DC.

Pasztory, Esther. 2005. *Thinking with Things: Toward a New Vision of Art*. University of Texas Press, Austin.

Piña Chan, Román. 1955. *Las culturas preclásicas de la Cuenca de México*. Fondo de Cultura Económica, Mexico.

Piña Chan, Román. 1958. *Tlatilco: A través de su cerámica*, vol. 2. Instituto Nacional de Antropología e Historia, Mexico.

Pohorilenko, Anatole. 2004. A Formalistic Approach to Olmec Representation: The Fundamental Themes. In *Acercarse y mirar: Homenaje a Beatriz de la Fuente*, edited by María Teresa Uriarte and Leticia Staines Cicero, pp.107–166. Universidad Nacional Autónoma de México, Mexico.

Pool, Christopher. 2007. *Olmec Archaeology and Early Mesoamerica*. Cambridge University Press, Cambridge.

Pye, Mary E., and Gerardo Gutiérrez. 2007. The Pacific Coast Trade Route of Mesoamerica: Iconographic Connections between Guatemala and Guerrero. In *Archaeology, Art, and Ethnogenesis in Mesoamerican Prehistory: Papers in Honor of Gareth W. Lowe*, edited by Lynneth Lowe and Mary Pye, pp. 229–246. Papers of the New World Archaeological Foundation, no. 68, Brigham Young University, Provo.

Quirarte, Jacinto. 1976. The Relationship of Izapan-Style Art to Olmec and Maya Art. In *Origins of Religious Art and Iconography in Preclassic Mesoamerica*, edited by H. B. Nicholson, pp. 73–86. University of California, Los Angeles.

Renfrew, Colin. 1998. Towards a Cognitive Archaeology. In *The Ancient Mind: Elements of Cognitive Archaeology*, edited by Colin Renfrew and Ezra Zubrow, pp. 3–12. Cambridge University Press, Cambridge.

Renfrew, Colin. 2001. Commodification and Institution in Group-Oriented and Individualizing Societies. In *The Origins of Human Social Institutions*, edited by W. G. Runciman, pp. 93–117. Proceedings of the British Academy, no. 110, Oxford University Press, Oxford.

Rodríguez, María del Carmen, and Ponciano Ortíz. 2008. Los asentamientos olmecas y preolmecas de la cuenca baja del río Coatzacoalcos, Veracruz. In *Olmeca: Balance y perspectivas. Memoria de la primera mesa redonda*, vol. 2, edited by María Teresa Uriarte and Rebecca González Lauck, pp. 445–469. Universidad Nacional Autónoma de México, Instituto Nacional de Antropología e Historia, New World Archaeological Foundation, Mexico.

Saturno, William A., Karl A. Taube, and David Stuart. 2005. Los murales de San Bartolo, El Petén, Guatemala. Parte 1. El mural del norte. *Ancient America* 7, Barnardsville, North Carolina.

Sharer, Robert F., and David C. Grove, eds. 1989. *Regional Perspectives on the Olmec*. University of Cambridge Press, Cambridge.

Sociedad Mexicana de Antropología. 1942. *Mayas y Olmecas: Segunda reunión de Mesa redonda sobre problemas antropológicas de México y Centro América*. Talleres de la Editorial Stylo, Mexico.

Taube, Karl A. 1994. The Rainmakers: The Olmec and Their Contribution to Mesoamerican Belief and Ritual. In *The Olmec World: Ritual and Rulership,* by the Art Museum, pp. 83–103. The Art Museum, Princeton.

Taube, Karl A. 2000. Lightning Celts and Corn Fetishes: The Formative Olmec and the Development of Maize Symbolism in Mesoamerica and the American Southwest. In *Olmec Art and Archaeology in Mesoamerica*, edited by John Clark and Mary Pye, pp. 297–337. Studies in the History of Art, no. 58, National Gallery of Art, Washington, DC.

Taube, Karl A. 2004. *Olmec Art at Dumbarton Oaks*. Dumbarton Oaks, Washington, DC.

Uriarte, María Teresa, and Rebecca González Lauck, eds. 2008. *Olmeca: Balance y perspectivas. Memoria de la primera mesa redonda*. 2 vols. Universidad Nacional Autónoma de México, Instituto Nacional de Antropología e Historia, New World Archaeological Foundation, Mexico.

CHAPTER 61

ART OF THE CLASSIC PERIOD

REX KOONTZ

THE Mesoamerican Classic period (ca. 250–900 AD) is characterized above all by the expansion of urban elite artistic cultures across the region. The basic characteristics of Classic-period elite art were first developed in the preceding Preclassic period. Essential Classic-period monument types such as the stela and the relief panel as well as fundamental urban architectural forms like the pyramid and plaza were all created in the Preclassic period. These and related forms were further developed with the expansion of Mesoamerican urbanism.

Monumental architecture was a critical element in elite visual programs, serving as a frame or backdrop for much Classic-period art. This was especially apparent during periodic festivals when the polity would gather in the central urban spaces to participate in rites, games, economic activities, and other events (Inomata 2006). Buildings and platforms defined the smaller open spaces and rooms for more intimate courtly activities (Inomata and Houston 2001). Classic-period architecture also provided much stylistic and iconographic information encoded in building form and decoration (Kowalski 1999; Miller 1998). The talud/tablero architectural motif is a case in point: although already in use in the Preclassic (Plunket and Uruñuela 1998), it became standard at Teotihuacan toward the end of that period and soon became an architectural marker of the metropolis. Other regional architectural styles appropriated the form in turn, integrating Teotihuacan's prestige into what were clearly independent regional norms (Kubler 1973).

SMALL-SCALE OBJECTS AND PRESTIGE MATERIALS

Jade was the most important prestige material throughout Classic Mesoamerica and thus it was a key material for small-scale elite objects. Many Classic-period jade objects mimic Preclassic forms and seem to have been directly associated with ideas of ancient legitimacy. There is some evidence that Classic elites obtained heirloom Preclassic jade objects that embodied ancient legitimating power for their owners or curators (Joyce 2000; Miller 1991: 35). Jade celts and earflares, key items of adornment throughout much of Mesoamerica, associated the wearers with sacred flowering trees, ancestors, and the animating breath of life (Taube 2005). Artists fashioned additional objects of jadeite or other greenstone that con-noted elite status, such as the greenstone masks and effigy figures associated with Teotihuacan and the greenstone yokes associated with Classic Veracruz. Like work in precious stones, featherwork would have been central to artistic practice but is almost completely absent from the archaeological record.

Jade and other prestige materials were the near-exclusive province of elites, but ceramic objects were made and distributed more widely. An important ele-ment in many commoner art traditions was the ceramic figurine, a form associ-ated mainly with household rites during the Preclassic, but during the Classic such figurines are found in more varied contexts. Figurine form also changed consid-erably over time, from the Preclassic near-nude female to the elaborately clothed and accoutered figurines of the Late Classic Maya and Gulf Coast (Halperin et al. 2009).

TEOTIHUACAN'S ART AND ARCHITECTURE

Teotihuacan was the largest city in Mesoamerica during the Early Classic period (c. 250–600 AD). The entire city was organized around two enormous avenues that formed perpendicular axes. The north-south avenue connected two monumental pyramids, now known as the Pyramids of the Sun and Moon. These took shape in the preceding Preclassic period and were largely complete at the opening of the Classic period. Each of these pyramids seems to have had specific symbolic asso-ciations: The Pyramid of the Sun was built over a series of modified caves often associated with the emergence of ancestors in Mesoamerican lore (Heyden 1975), while the Pyramid of the Moon was associated with the sacred mountain looming behind it (Tobriner 1972). Deposits inside the Pyramid of the Moon suggest that militaristic rites also played an important role in the dedication and symbolism of the building (Sugiyama and López Luján 2007).

A final major pyramid, smaller but elaborately decorated, was built along the same avenue at the beginning of the third century. The Feathered Serpent Pyramid preserves a large amount of architectural sculpture (Figure 61.1) in the form of repeating feathered serpents carrying a mosaic headdress associated with Teotihuacan warriors (Taube 1992). The scene takes place in a watery environment that may allude to the beginning of time (López Austin, López Luján, and Sugiyama 1991). More than two hundred humans were sacrificed during the dedication of the building, including a large number of victims dressed as warriors (Sugiyama 2005). The iconographic thrust of this last major pyramid was clearly militaristic.

In the early fourth century the sculptures of the Feathered Serpent Pyramid were ritually defaced on three sides, and the fourth side was covered by a large talud/tablero structure (Cowgill 1997: 155). These highly unusual actions may have signaled a change in the city's relationship to these symbols or the particular group responsible for the program. It is certain that there was a change in elite strategies involving monumentality around this time. After the construction of the Feathered Serpent Pyramid, the elites turned away from monumental pyramid construction and instead directed the building of residential complexes, many of which were elaborately decorated.

By the fourth century, Teotihuacanos were housed in apartment complexes that followed the same strict orientation seen for the main avenue and principal pyramids. The more elite residences clustered in groups near the main avenue. Murals decorated the walls of a whole range of residential buildings, and they were in no way limited to the elites. The most popular subject matter was the processing officiant with a great deal of costume detail and little interest in individuality or

Figure 61.1 West façade detail, Feathered Serpent Pyramid, Teotihuacan.

the human body underneath the costume. Representations of maguey spines and other indications of sacrifice are also widespread.

With a handful of important exceptions, sculpture in prestige materials was limited to idealized masks and rigidly posed effigy figures, the latter's schematic presentation of the human body likely dependent on perishable accouterments and dress for their effect. This same conventionalized and abstracting treatment of the human body is also seen in figurines that are found everywhere in Teotihuacan and used in household rites. Early in the Classic period figurines were handmade, but after about 400 AD figurines were fashioned in molds and often included more information on dress, rank, and identity (S. Scott 2001). The plaques used to adorn *incensarios* were also moldmade. Incensarios served as another focus of household ritual and were found throughout the site as well.

Teotihuacan's Place in Mesoamerica

Although Teotihuacan is the most important city in Mesoamerica during the Early Classic, at no time does it dominate artistic developments throughout the area (Pasztory 2005: 169–175). This can be most clearly seen in the Maya area, where elite Maya artists integrated Teotihuacan symbols and style into Maya artistic structures throughout the Classic period. The appropriation of Teotihuacan symbols would sometimes be accompanied by Maya texts referring to Teotihuacan political agents, suggesting a more intensive interaction between the two in the late fourth and early fifth centuries at major sites such as Tikal and Copán (Stuart 2000). The use of Teotihuacan iconography continued long after Teotihuacan could have maintained any real presence in the Maya area (Stone 1989).

Maya elite art traditions were already well established by the time Maya artists begin appropriating Teotihuacan symbol and style, and thus it is not surprising that Teotihuacan art did not overwhelm Maya practice. The same may be said for Monte Albán, which also appropriated specific elements from Teotihuacan and also cited possible Teotihuacano political actors in the monuments (Figure 61.2; Coggins 1993: 150–151; Winter 2001).

Many of the same stylistic and iconographic phenomena may also be found in south-central Veracruz, with the appropriation of Teotihuacan style and symbol by local elites, always in the context of regional developments and art traditions (Stark and Johns 2004: 326; Miller 1991). Another case in point is north-central Veracruz, which in the Early Classic created a regional elite art tradition with forms (candeleros, floreros, and others) and even symbols (mosaic serpent headdresses) related to Teotihuacan but combined in a distinctly regional fashion (Pascual Soto 2009).

Figure 61.2 Monte Albán, Stela 4.

IMAGE AND TEXT IN EASTERN
MESOAMERICA AND OAXACA

The stela format was well established by the beginning of this period in the burgeoning cities of the eastern lowlands (south-central Veracruz [Isthmian] and
Maya areas) as well as along the southern Pacific coast. Stelae were set in public
spaces and given complex combinations of hieroglyphic texts and detailed figural images (Figure 61.3). Many of the figural representations may be identified as
historical rulers or other high-ranking officials (Proskouriakoff 1960; Schele and
Freidel 1990). As with most Classic-period art, there was great interest in clothing
and jewelry details, but here those details were represented more naturalistically,
especially in the Maya area. This is especially true for representations of the prestigious jade and feather ensembles worn by rulers and other nobility. Often these
costumes were specifically tied to a dance or other performance (Grübe 1992). The
rise of Chichén Itzá toward the end of the Classic reversed this naturalistic trend
and downplayed the use of stelae.

The marriage of image and text on stelae and other media produced specific
narratives in Maya public art, with information on the exact date of the action

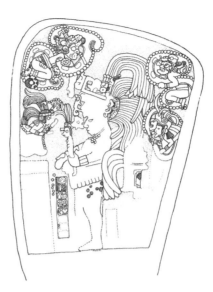

Figure 61.3 Ixlu Stela 2. Drawing by Linda Schele, © David Schele, courtesy of
the Foundation for the Advancement of Mesoamerican Studies, Inc., www.famsi.org.

and the identity of the participant(s) (Martin 2006; Reents-Budet 1989). While
Teotihuacan imagery may have depicted rulers (Headrick 2007), the stela tradition
in eastern Mesoamerican art specified the ruler's names, titles, and activities in
both image and text to a degree not seen elsewhere in Mesoamerica. In the Maya
area as elsewhere, public stone monuments would have been complemented by
semiprivate murals displaying more detailed accounts of elite rites, but few of these
programs remain (Miller 1986). More numerous are detailed presentations of elite
activities on Maya polychrome vases (Reents-Budet 1994).

Classic Maya texts on stelae and other art objects give us some idea of how they
conceptualized such objects. The more intimate private objects, such as precious
stone jewelry and finely painted vases, often contained inscriptions naming the
owner, vessel, or object class, vessel content, and other pertinent material information (Houston et al. 1989). Some vases were signed by the artist or scribe, certainly
as an important marker of artistry nestled beside the name of the patron and the
precious contents of the vessel (Stuart 1987; Reents-Budet 1994). Other texts maintain that sculpted images such as stelae and relief panels shared some vital quality
with the being represented, so that gods and kings were literally stored in these
public images (Houston et al. 2006: 76–81). A work of art's animate qualities may
go some way to explaining the common practice of resetting or mutilating monuments, not only for the Maya but across Mesoamerica (López Luján et al. 2006; Just
2005; O'Neil 2009).

Public monuments with figures and hieroglyphic texts were extensively reset
at Monte Albán (Oaxaca) and environs. It is likely that monument groups originally formed narrative ensembles that spoke to the legitimacy of elite power (Urcid

2001; Lind and Urcid 2010: 309). A remarkable amount of funerary mural art is preserved in situ, however. Murals of processing figures covered in costumes line the walls of several important tombs. These figures may be identified as ancestors who personified particular deities and may have legitimated the group's access to certain rituals, offices, and landholdings (Urcid 2008).

CENTRAL MEXICO AFTER TEOTIHUACAN: LATE CLASSIC INNOVATIONS

The decline of Teotihuacan at the beginning of the Late Classic period (ca. 600-900 AD) created an eclectic and innovative artistic environment in central Mexico at the same time that the Maya tradition was experiencing its most prolific phase. Elite artistic culture in central Mexico centered on the new cities that rose to fill the vacuum in trade and politics left by the retraction of Teotihuacan (Diehl and Berlo 1989). Cacaxtla in the Valley of Puebla was one of these new urban powers, occupying a defensible hilltop with a walled acropolis. The interior buildings contained many important murals on interior walls as well as on façades. The style of a great majority of these murals is clearly derived from Late Classic Maya canons, with the same detailed naturalism found in the depictions of ornaments and the human body (but see Brittenham 2009 for an important exception). The accompanying texts are not Maya, however, and the iconography is an eclectic mix of Teotihuacan archaisms, other appropriations, and local innovations (Foncerrada de Molina 1993; McVicker 1985; Nagao 1989). Just to the east of the acropolis was an abandoned Preclassic ceremonial center (Xochitécatl) that in the Late Classic was rededicated to a cult centered on female figurines in a style very different from that seen in the Cacaxtla murals. Xochitécatl and Cacaxtla functioned as a single cultural unit during the Late Classic, suggesting that the profound differences in style, iconography, material, and other cultural patterns indicate different sociocultural functions for each center (Serra Puche 2001). Cholula, a nearby complex already centered on an enormous pyramid, was revitalized in the Late Classic with monumental public art that borrowed scroll forms and other elements from the Gulf Coast (McCafferty 1996).

Xochicalco, Morelos, also rose with the decline of Teotihuacan and also drew on artistic practices across Mesoamerica to forge a unique and innovative art style (Nagao 1989). The site is centered on a pyramid with repeating feathered serpents, recalling the Pyramid of the Feathered Serpent at Teotihuacan. In the coils of this serpent are figures recalling seated Maya lords on portable jade and ceramic objects, again suggesting some relationship with the distant Maya or their agents (McVicker and Palka 2001; Ringle, Gallareta Negron, and Bey 1998).

Another important Late Classic highland center, Cantona (Puebla), did not participate in this eclectic and innovative borrowing. The ceramic system of Cantona

Figure 61.4 Avian palma. Museo de Antropología, Xalapa.

remained decisively local throughout the Classic, and the site cultivated a rather crude sculptural style (García Cook and Carrion 1998). It did erect monumental architecture including a great number of ballcourts for the playing of the rubber ballgame, but these were left with little sculpture or other extant decoration.

El Tajín, in the north-central Veracruz lowlands, developed a particularly harmonious architectural style based on the talud/tablero that added repeated niches and different proportions to the Teotihuacan standard. This site was vitally interested in the ballgame, with eleven courts in the urban center and more in the surrounding suburbs. Several of these courts were decorated with relief sculpture that give us one of the richest accounts of rites associated with the ballgame (Koontz 2009). El Tajín was closely associated with portable sculptures called *palmas* (Figure 61.4) that were worn in these rites, as were other finely carved portable stone objects called *yokes* and *hachas*. The latter two object types were found throughout the Gulf Coast during the Classic period (Proskouriakoff 1954; J. Scott 2001). Variations on all three of these object types are found on the Pacific coast of Guatemala and El Salvador, as are reliefs depicting ballcourt rites, although few if any are in a style that may be directly related to El Tajín (Chinchilla Mazariegos 2009; Shook and Marquis 1996).

References

Brittenham, Claudia. 2009. Style and Substance, or Why the Cacaxtla Paintings Were Buried. *Res: Anthropology and Aesthetics* 55/56:135–155.

Chinchilla Mazariegos, Oswald. 2009. Games, Courts, and Players at Cotzumalhuapa, Guatemala. In *Blood and Beauty: Organized Violence in the Art and Architecture of Mesoamerica and Central America*, edited by Heather Orr and Rex Koontz, pp. 139–160. UCLA Cotsen Institute of Archaeology, Los Angeles.

Coggins, Clemency. 1993. The Age of Teotihuacan and Its Mission Abroad. In *Teotihuacan: Art from the City of the Gods*, edited by Kathleen Berrin and Esther Pasztory, pp. 140–155. Thames and Hudson, London.

Cowgill, George L. 1997. State and Society at Teotihuacan, Mexico. *Annual Review of Anthropology* 26:129–161.

Diehl, Richard A., and Janet Catherine Berlo, eds. 1989. *Mesoamerica after the Decline of Teotihuacan, AD 700–900*. Dumbarton Oaks Research Library and Collection, Washington, DC.

Foncerrada de Molina, Marta. 1993. *Cacaxtla: La iconografía de los Olmeca-Xicalanca*. Universidad Nacional Autónoma de México, Mexico City.

García Cook, Angel, and Beatriz Leonor Merino Carrion. 1998. Cantona: Urbe Prehispanica en el altiplano central de Mexico. *Latin American Antiquity* 9(3):191–216.

Grübe, Nikolai. 1992. Classic Maya Dance: Evidence from Hieroglyphs and Iconography. *Ancient Mesoamerica* 3:201–218.

Halperin, Christina T., Katherine A. Faust, Rhonda Taube, and Aurore Giguet, eds. 2009. *Mesoamerican Figurines: Small-Scale Indices of Large-Scale Phenomena*. University Press of Florida, Gainesville.

Headrick, Annabeth. 2007. *The Teotihuacan Trinity: The Sociopolitical Structure of an Ancient Mesoamerican City*. University of Texas Press, Austin.

Heyden, Doris. 1975. An Interpretation of the Cave Underneath the Pyramid of the Sun in Teotihuacan, Mexico. *American Antiquity* 40(2):131–147.

Houston, Stephen, David Stuart, and Karl Taube. 2006. *The Memory of Bones: Body, Being and Experience among the Classic Maya*. University of Texas Press, Austin.

Houston, Stephen D., David Stuart, and Karl A. Taube. 1989. Folk Classification of Classic Maya Pottery. *American Anthropologist* 91(3):720–726.

Inomata, Takeshi. 2006. Plazas, Performers, and Spectators: Political Theaters of the Classic Maya. *Current Anthropology* 47(5):805–842.

Inomata, Takeshi, and Stephen D. Houston, eds. 2001. *Royal Courts of the Ancient Maya*. 2 vols. Westview, Boulder, Colorado.

Joyce, Rosemary A. 2000. Heirlooms and Houses: Materiality and Social Memory. In *Beyond Kinship: Social and Material Reproduction in House Societies*, edited by Rosemary A. Joyce and Susan D. Gillespie, pp. 189–212. University of Pennsylvania Press, Philadelphia.

Just, Bryan R. 2005. Modifications of Ancient Maya Sculpture. *Res: Anthropology and Aesthetics* 48:69–82.

Koontz, Rex. 2009. *Lightning Gods and Feathered Serpents: The Public Sculpture of El Tajín*. University of Texas Press, Austin.

Kowalski, Jeff K., ed. 1999. *Mesoamerican Architecture as a Cultural Symbol*. Oxford University Press, Oxford.

Kubler, George A. 1973. Iconographic Aspects of Architectural Profiles at Teotihuacan and in Mesoamerica. In *The Iconography of Middle American Sculpture*, edited by Elizabeth Kennedy Easby, 24–39. Metropolitan Museum of Art, New York.

Lind, Michael, and Javier Urcid. 2010. *The Lords of Lambityeco: Political Evolution in the Valley of Oaxaca during the Xoo Phase*. University Press of Colorado, Boulder.

López Austin, Alfredo, Leonardo López Luján, and Saburo Sugiyama. 1991. The Temple
    of Quetzalcoatl at Teotihuacan: Its Possible Ideological Significance. *Ancient
    Mesoamerica* 2(1):93–105.
López Luján, Leonardo, Laura Filloy Nadal, Barbara W. Fash, William L. Fash, and Pilar
    Hernández. 2006. The Destruction of Images in Teotihuacan: Anthropomorphic
    Sculpture, Elite Cults, and the End of a Civilization. *Res: Anthropology and
    Aesthetics* 49/50:12–39.
Martin, Simon. 2006. On Pre-Columbian Narrative: Representations across the
    Word-Image Divide. In *A Pre-Columbian World*, edited by Jeffrey Quilter and
    Mary Miller, pp. 55–106. Dumbarton Oaks Research Library and Collection,
    Washington, DC.
McCafferty, Geoffrey G. 1996. Reinterpreting the Great Pyramid of Cholula, Mexico.
    Ancient Mesoamerica 7:1–17.
McVicker, Donald. 1985. The "Mayanized" Mexicans. *American Antiquity* 50(1):82–101.
McVicker, Donald, and Joel W. Palka. 2001. A Maya Carved Shell Plaque from Tula,
    Hidalgo, Mexico: Comparative Study. *Ancient Mesoamerica* 12:175–197.
Miller, Mary Ellen. 1986. *The Murals of Bonampak*. Princeton University Press,
    Princeton, New Jersey.
Miller, Mary Ellen. 1991. Rethinking the Classic Sculptures of Cerro de las Mesas,
    Veracruz. In *Settlement Archaeology of Cerro de las Mesas, Veracruz, Mexico*, edited
    by Barbara L. Stark, pp. 26–38. Cotsen Institute of Archaeology, University of
    California, Los Angeles.
Miller, Mary Ellen. 1998. A Design for Meaning in Maya Architecture. In *Function and
    Meaning in Classic Maya Architecture*, edited by Stephen D. Houston, pp. 187–222.
    Dumbarton Oaks Research Library and Collection, Washington, DC.
Nagao, Debra. 1989. Public Proclamation in the Art of Cacaxtla and Xochicalco. In
    Mesoamerica after the Decline of Teotihuacan, AD 700–900, edited by Richard A.
    Diehl and Janet Catherine Berlo, pp. 83–104. Dumbarton Oaks Research Library and
    Collection, Washington, DC.
O'Neil, Megan E. 2009. Ancient Maya Sculptures of Tikal, Seen and Unseen. *Res:
    Anthropology and Aesthetics* 55/56:119–134.
Pascual Soto, Arturo. 2009. *El Tajín: Arte y poder*. Insituto Nacional de Antropología e
    Historia, Mexico City.
Pasztory, Esther. 2005. *Thinking with Things: Toward a New Vision of Art*. University of
    Texas Press, Austin.
Plunket, Patricia, and Gabriela Uruñuela. 1998. Preclassic Household Patterns Preserved
    under Volcanic Ash at Tetimpa, Puebla, Mexico. *Latin American Antiquity* 9(4):287–309.
Proskouriakoff, Tatiana. 1954. *Varieties of Classic Central Veracruz Sculpture*.
    Contributions to American Anthropology and History No. 58, Carnegie Institution
    of Washington, Washington, DC.
Proskouriakoff, Tatiana. 1960. Historical Implications of a Pattern of Dates at Piedras
    Negras, Guatemala. *American Antiquity* 25(4):454–475.
Reents-Budet, Dorie. 1989. Narrative in Classic Maya Art. In *Word and Image in Maya
    Culture: Explorations in Language, Writing, and Representation*, edited by William
    Hanks and Don Rice, pp. 189–197. University of Utah Press, Salt Lake City.
Reents-Budet, Dorie, ed. 1994. *Painting the Maya Universe: Royal Ceramics of the Classic
    Period*. Duke University Press in association with Duke University Museum of Art,
    Durham, North Carolina.

Ringle, William M., Tomás Gallareta Negron, and George J. Bey III. 1998. The Return
    of Quetzalcoatl: Evidence for the Spread of a World Religion during the Epiclassic
    Period. *Ancient Mesoamerica* 9(2):183–232.

Schele, Linda, and David A. Freidel. 1990. *A Forest of Kings: The Untold Story of the
    Ancient Maya*. Morrow, New York.

Scott, John F. 2001. Dressed to Kill: Stone Regalia of the Mesoamerican Ballgame. In
    The Sport of Life and Death: The Mesoamerican Ballgame, edited by E. Michael
    Whittington, pp. 50–63. Thames and Hudson, London.

Scott, Sue. 2001. *The Corpus of Terracotta Figurines from Sigvald Linné's Excavations
    at Teotihuacan, Mexico (1932 and 1934–35) and Comparative Material*. National
    Museum of Ethnography, Stockholm.

Serra Puche, Mari Carmen. 2001. The Concept of Feminine Places in Mesoamerica: The
    Case of Xochitécatl, Tlaxcala, Mexico. In *Gender in Pre-Hispanic America*, edited
    by Cecelia Klein, pp. 255–283. Dumbarton Oaks Research Library and Collection,
    Washington, DC.

Shook, Edwin M., and Elayne Marquis. 1996. *Secrets in Stone: Yokes, Hachas and
    Palmas from Southern Mesoamerica*. American Philosophical Society,
    Philadelphia.

Stark, Barbara L., and Kevin M. Johns. 2004. Veracruz sur-central en tiempos
    Teotihuacanos. In *La Costa del Golfo en tiempos Teotihuacanos: Propuestas y
    perspectivas*, edited by Maria E. Ruiz Gallut and Arturo Pascual Soto, pp. 307–328.
    Instituto Nacional de Antropología e Historia, Mexico City.

Stone, Andrea. 1989. Disconnection, Foreign Insignia, and Political Expansion:
    Teotihuacan and the Warrior Stelae of Piedras Negras. In *Mesoamerica after
    the Decline of Teotihuacan, AD 700-900*, edited by Richard A. Diehl and Janet
    Catherine Berlo, pp. 153–172. Dumbarton Oaks Research Library and Collection,
    Washington, DC.

Stuart, David. 1987. *Ten Phonetic Syllables*. Research Reports on Maya Hieroglyphic
    Writing 14, Center for Maya Research, Washington, DC.

Stuart, David. 2000. "The Arrival of Strangers": Teotihuacan and Tollan in Classic Maya
    History. In *Mesoamerica's Classic Heritage: From Teotihuacan to the Aztecs*, edited
    by Davíd Carrasco, Lindsay Jones, and Scott Sessions, pp. 465–514. University Press
    of Colorado, Boulder.

Sugiyama, Saburo. 2005. *Human Sacrifice, Militarism, and Rulership: Materialization of
    State Ideology at the Feathered Serpent Pyramid, Teotihuacan*. Cambridge University
    Press, Cambridge.

Sugiyama, Saburo, and Leonardo López Luján. 2007. Dedicatory Burial/Offering
    Complexes at the Moon Pyramid, Teotihuacan. *Ancient Mesoamerica* 18:127–146.

Taube, Karl A. 1992. Temple of Quetzalcóatl and the Cult of Sacred War at Teotihuacán.
    Res: Anthropology and Aesthetics 21:53–87.

Taube, Karl A. 2005. The Symbolism of Jade in Classic Maya Religion. *Ancient
    Mesoamerica* 16(1):23–50.

Tobriner, S. 1972. The Fertile Mountain: An Investigation of Cerro Gordo's Importance
    to the Town Plan and Iconography of Teotihuacan. *Teotihuacán: Onceava Mesa
    Redonda [México, DF, 7–13 agosto, 1966]*, Sociedad Mexicana de Antropología,
    México City.

Urcid, Javier. 2001. *Zapotec Hieroglyphic Writing*. Dumbarton Oaks Research Library and
    Collection, Washington, DC.

Urcid, Javier. 2008. El arte de pintar las tumbas: Sociedad e ideología Zapotecas (400-800
    d.c.). In *La pintura mural prehispanica en México III: Oaxaca*, 4 (Estudios),
    pp. 513–627. Univ. Nacional Autónoma de México, Instituto de Investigaciones
    Estéticas, Mexico City.
Winter, Marcus. 2001. Monte Albán. In *Oxford Encyclopedia of Mesoamerican Cultures*,
    2:336–340. Oxford University Press, Oxford.

CHAPTER 62

ART IN THE AZTEC EMPIRE

EMILY UMBERGER

ARCHAEOLOGICAL remains testify to the spread of goods and ideas over broad areas of Mesoamerica at different times throughout its prehispanic history (Rice 1993). However, most material expansions are unaccompanied by texts, so it is difficult to identify which resulted from empires, and which from other types of interaction, like trade, gift giving, and emulation (Stone-Miller 1993: 31–36). In contrast, the Aztec Empire, which dominated central Mexico during its final pre-conquest years, is known to us mostly through documents written during and after its overthrow by Spaniards in 1521 (Barlow 1949; Berdan et al. 1996; Carrasco Pizana 1996; Davies 1987; Hassig 1988). Ironically, the material remains do not match the expectations raised by the documents. More relics have been excavated and studied in the last few decades than previously, but relatively few scholars have yet engaged with their evidence (however, see Ohnersorgen 2001; Sergheraert 2009; Smith 1990, 2001; Smith and Montiel 2001; Umberger 1996, 2007b; Umberger and Klein 1993). The objective of this chapter is to show how the imagery of sculptures can supplement and refine our notions of Aztec strategies.

THE IMPERIAL CAPITAL

The capital of the Aztec Empire was Tenochtitlan, now under Mexico City, in the highland Valley of Mexico. The central precinct, the propagandistic focus of the empire, was decorated with a plethora of monumental sculptures explicating ideological issues at the time of their creation. The precinct's remains reveal Tenochtitlan to have been a true imperial capital (Broda, Carrasco, and Matos Moctezuma 1988; López Austin and López Luján 2009; López Luján 2006; Matos Moctezuma 1981). The Aztec Empire was established in 1431 after the defeat of the local Tepanec Empire by three allied city-states. By the late 1470s Tenochtitlan dominated its allies, as well as its "twin city" Tlatelolco, which it absorbed. During this time the Aztecs displayed their increasing power with public ceremonies featuring militaristic imagery and the sacrifice of captives from conquered areas (Brumfiel 1987, 2001).

The most important monuments in the ceremonial center visualized the Aztec charter myth. The main feature was the Templo Mayor, which symbolized the sacred mountain of the earth. In the myth, the actors were deified personifications of competing cosmic forces—the sun, moon, and stars—conceived as members of a royal family. Coatlicue, the mother of the gods, who, like the pyramid, personified the earth, gave birth to her youngest child, the Aztec patron god Huitzilopochtli, at the sacred mountain. Immediately after his birth this god defeated an enemy army of older siblings and sent them to the underworld. In his meteoric rise, Huitzilopochtli was compared to the sun, the defeated siblings became stars, and their leader, Coyolxauhqui, the moon.

In Tenochtitlan, these characters first appeared in sculptural form after 1450, in tandem with the reconception of the city as an imperial capital. The best-known

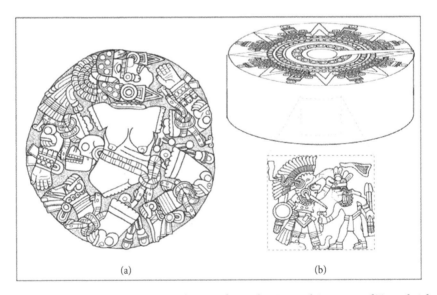

(a)   (b)

Figure 62.1 Monumental victory sculptures from the Central Precinct of Tenochtitlan, the Aztec imperial capital: (a) Great Coyolxauhqui Stone, carved ca. 1473 for Axayacatl, east-west diameter, 326 centimeters, Museo del Templo Mayor, Mexico. (b) Stone of Tizoc with a close-up of Tizoc grasping the ruler-god of Matlatzinco, the Matlatzinca area in the Toluca Valley, carved ca. 1485 for Tizoc, Museo Nacional de Antropología, Mexico (drawings by the author).

examples are the Great Coyolxauhqui Stone of 1473 and the Tizoc Stone of 1484, both of which used mythic and cosmic imagery to justify the defeat of contemporary enemies. The Coyolxauhqui Stone (Figure 62.1a), for instance, celebrated the defeat of the Tlatelolca, and the forms and imagery of the dismembered enemy leader referred to multiple metaphors about failed rulership. Because defeat revealed the enemy ruler's lack of the masculine qualities necessary for military dominance, the figure is of a woman wearing a male loincloth (Umberger 2007a).

The Stone of Tizoc (Figure 62.1b) expands the Huitzilopochtli myth to the greater world outside the Valley of Mexico by depicting the defeated ruler-gods of both the valley and far-flung territories (Umberger 2008). This giant vessel was first used in 1485 for the sacrificial blood of prisoners from the Matlatzinca area, and then again for the blood of captives from all over the empire, sacrificed to proclaim Tenochca dominance during the Templo Mayor dedication of 1487 (Umberger 2002). On it, conquered rulers are presented as landless Chichimecs (meaning barbarians, migrants, and commoners) in contrast to Tenochca warriors, whose ancient Toltec clothing signaled their noble heritage and right to control territories (Umberger 2008).

THE EMPIRE

The empire was a hegemonic empire, in which local hierarchies and cultures of formerly independent polities were left in place where possible (Berdan et al.1996; Calnek 1982; Hassig 1984; Scheidel 2006; Smith 2001). While Tenochtitlan remained the stage for demonstrations of military power, imperially sponsored projects in the empire emphasized the sacred, cosmic underpinnings of territorial expansion. In other words, although its objective was appropriation, the empire was aware of the supernatural powers of new lands as well as the traditional rulers, who negotiated with the sacred. As Alfredo López Austin (1997: 259) has stated, "When a town was established the patron gods occupied the hills or changed themselves into hills. ... Taking possession of a territory implied extending the different manifestations of divine force to it." Thus, the Aztecs did not create new administrative centers (cf. Schreiber 2001), but rather they installed shrines at sites of supernatural power, and high officials, tax collectors, and colonists alike moved into already existing communities and structures. They used whatever artists were available, whether skilled artists trained in imperial workshops or in foreign styles, less talented professionals, or part-time amateur carvers.

As elsewhere, the closer provinces formed an inner empire, more tightly linked to the center than more recently conquered, distant provinces. In areas to the north of the Valley of Mexico, sons and grandsons of the Tenochca royal family were installed as rulers, and the local Otomí, a group whose original culture was very different from the Nahuatl-speaking Aztecs, seem to have been converted to Aztec-style religious practices (Umberger 1996: 151). This type of conversion probably started with the valley Otomí who lived in close proximity to the Aztec Nahuatl-speaking groups, and conversion may have been limited to this group. In contrast, Aztec incorporation of areas to the south and east of the capital (the modern states of Morelos and Puebla) was based on similar preexisting practices among Nahuas, for instance, the traditional feasting and gift giving that tied allied and enemy elites together in a network of common interests (see Pohl 1998; Smith 1986). Motecuhzoma I himself was born from a dynastic intermarriage between a princess from this area (Cuernavaca) and a Tenochca prince. Early Aztec remains in the vicinity probably pertain to his reign; an example may be the rock art near a reported palace and tropical garden that he created at Huaxtepec in the 1440s or 1450s (Alvarado Tezozomoc 1975: 370–371). It is possible that the Tenochca dynasty also appropriated the famous Pulque God temple above Tepoztlan for use as a funerary monument.

To the west of the capital, after its conquest in the 1470s the Toluca Valley was made a territorial extension of the Valley of Mexico and a buffer zone between the Aztecs and the Tarascans further west. Aztec colonists settled in the Toluca Valley both to provide food for Valley of Mexico residents and to serve as part-time soldiers during Aztec warfare on people further west. Colonists came from different Valley of Mexico towns and settled on blocks of land distributed to these towns. Among these blocks were properties pertaining to Aztec administrators and tax collectors; others belonged to members of the Tenochca royal family, such as Motecuhzoma I's grandson Axayacatl and his relatives (Barlow 1950). Like the Otomí, the Matlatzinca who had controlled the Toluca Valley before Aztec arrival were not Nahuas (García Payón 1936). However, there is no evidence that they were Nahuatized by the Aztecs. In fact, it is unclear how they were incorporated into the heartland and whether conquest involved sudden, imposed cultural changes or the less choreographed changes that accompany close contact over time. This type of information is also lacking for the more distant provinces.

Examples of Aztec art are relatively abundant in this inner empire and along a territorial band that extends east through Puebla to the Gulf Coast of modern Veracruz. Remains are most numerous in the Toluca Valley and around the town of Castillo de Teayo in northern Veracruz (Seler 1960–1961b; Solís Olguín 1981; Umberger 1996, 2007b). They are found also in significant numbers as far south as central Veracruz (Medellín Zenil 1952; Ohnersorgen 2001; Stark 1990). Most images in these areas have little to do with the frightening and humiliating motifs of cosmic terror and sacrifice so prominent in the capital's ceremonial center. Rather, many depict nature and agricultural deities. Their creation can be divided, hypothetically, between commissions for Aztecs living in an area and commissions for the state. The former usually correspond to local concerns, while the latter show links to broader imperial concerns. Of course, the line between the two categories is blurry. Similar deity images are seen in both, but the imperial commissions are found at more prominent places, may include architectural structures, and may feature monuments in the distinctive imperial styles of the capital. They are located at ancient cities, on hills, at water sources, near caves, or locations that combine such features.

Some places in the inner empire, like Malinalco, Calixtlahuaca, and Tepoztlan, feature major temples built over older, locally important hill shrines. The shrines at all three places are obviously imperial productions for use by the empire. In the case of two other well-known pyramids in Veracruz, at Castillo de Teayo and Huatusco, it is unknown whether they were imperial commissions or were the productions of local communities for their only purposes. More archaeological research is required to determine the circumstances. At sites without architecture, the evidence of Aztec presence is within individual images on rocks (Krickeberg 1969). Some feature Aztec deity images newly installed at the places associated with their powers. An example is a water deity carved in 1507 on a rock at the

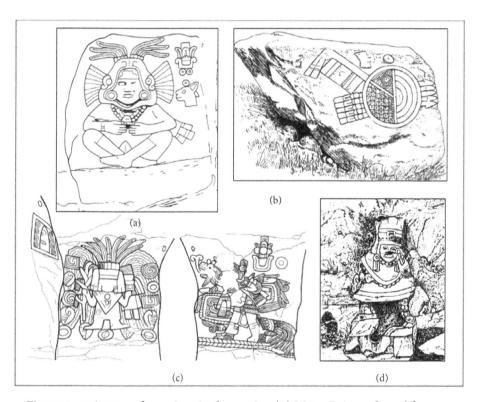

Figure 62.2 Aztec rock carvings in the empire: (A) Water Being enlarged from an antique picture plaque, 1506–1507, spring at Acacinco, southern Toluca Valley (drawing from photo in Barlow 1946); (B) Xipe shield on Chimalli Stone, probably ca. 1469, near Cuernavaca (drawing after Seler 1960–1961a: Figures 76–77) (now in front of the Palacio de Cortés, Cuernavaca); (C) Tula relief of Quetzalcoatl petitioning the water goddess Chalchiuhtlicue, 1500, in situ (drawing by author); (D) Image of the water goddess Chalchiuhtlicue over a fountain spring, at the site of Tusapan, 1450–1521, northern Veracruz, seen by Carl Nebel in the nineteenth century and now lost (drawing after a lithograph in Nebel 1836).

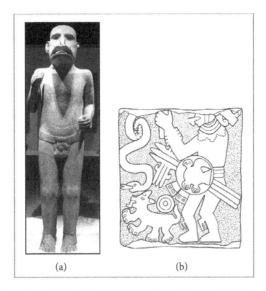

Figure 62.3 Wind gods at Calixtlahuaca, northern Toluca Valley: (A) Aztec Ehecatl,
after 1476, H. 176 centimeters (photograph by the author, courtesy of the Museo de
Antropología del Estado de México, Instituto Mexiquense de Cultura, Toluca). (B) One
of four reliefs of the Matlatzinca Wind God, before 1476, H. 89 centimeters
(drawing after a photo by Michael E. Smith; Museo de Antropología del Estado de
México, Toluca).

Acacinco spring in the Toluca Valley (Figure 62.2A). Some consist of accumula-
tions of symbols and dates relating to Aztec rituals (Cerro de la Campana, Acatlán,
Puebla); some are animals in the round (Huacachula, Puebla); and some feature
shields, the most famous being the Chimalli Stone near Cuernavaca (Figure 62.2B).
Images like the shields and ferocious animals were reminders of Aztec militarism,
but most others, although signaling Aztec appropriation, were not so obviously
intimidating.

The only life-sized Aztec temple image found in the empire is the free-stand-
ing Ehecatl (Figure 62.3A) that the Aztecs installed in the Wind God temple at
Calixtlahuaca. Images of the Wind God (Figure 62.3B) who occupied the temple
before the Aztec deity are very different in appearance and supply rare evidence of
a local cult at a conquered site.

Most remains in the empire lack obvious connections to the imperial heartland, but several refer to events in the capital through a combination of imagery and
hieroglyphic dates. Most notable is a series of reliefs on the Malinche Hill near the
ancient site of Tula (and in Figure 62.3C) northwest of Tenochtitlan. The principle
deity is the Aztec water goddess Chalchiuhtlicue in a frontal image. An inscribed
date next to her refers to the great flood that almost destroyed Tenochtitlan in
1500. To her right the legendary Quetzalcoatl, the prototypical model of Aztec ruler
behavior, draws blood from his ear, presumably a petition to the goddess to control

the flow of water. The key to the location of these images is nearby Tula, the ruined ancient city that Quetzalcoatl once ruled. Along with Teotihuacan, Xochicalco, and other ancient sites, Tula was visited by Aztec delegations seeking supernatural aid on important occasions (Umberger 1987; see Paso y Troncoso 1905-1906: 6:221–222). Motecuhzoma I reportedly sent sorcerers to the Tula area to find Coatlicue in the 1450s, and Motecuhzoma II sent Aztec priests to the same site with a piece of Spanish bread as a temple offering in about 1519 (Durán 1967: 2:217, 510–511). The extent to which the Aztecs used ancient and natural sites in these ways in the outer empire is unknown. Imperial-style rock carvings in Veracruz (Figure 62.2D) hint at similar concerns.

Most Aztec-style remains seem not to have been commissioned by imperial administrators, but rather were made for and by colonists. Colonists settled in groups of thousands in five large areas of the empire (for smaller enclaves, see Sergheraert 2009). In addition to the Toluca Valley, large groups were sent to Oaxaca to the far southeast of the capital and to Guerrero to the southwest after conquest of these areas in the 1450s and 1480s, respectively (Durán 1967: 2:238–239, 352–353). Motecuhzoma I's instructions to the colonists bound for Oaxaca were few and generalized. Selected from multiple towns in the heartland, they were told to resettle in barrios of the same composition in the new territory. Further, they were to move into existing structures, and, given the distance to Oaxaca, they were not to carry things that could be made for them locally (Durán 1967: 2:238). In contrast, the first colonies around Castillo de Teayo in northern Veracruz seem to have been founded by immigrants escaping the Valley of Mexico during the great famine of the 1450s (Durán 1967: 2:244). Later Castillo de Teayo was taken over by the state. Reportedly, areas in central Veracruz were colonized by imperial command on several occasions after depopulation by disease in these tropical areas (Stark 1990: 252).

The most intensively studied sculptural corpuses at colony areas to date are those from the Toluca and Castillo areas (García Payón 1979: 275–287; Seler 1960–1961b; Solís Olguin 1981; Umberger 1996, 2007b). Although the colonies had stratified societies, the majority of the inhabitants were commoner-farmers. Correspondingly, the great majority of the images are deities promoting agricultural fertility, but they are of less polished manufacture than the imperial shrines. In the Toluca area, sculptures are relatively small and probably pertained to individual house groups; strangely, no two are alike, meaning that there are no signs of ensembles or local workshops. In contrast, at Castillo de Teayo, the sculptures form a recognizable local style. Many figures are almost life-sized and can be paired (Figure 62.4A), meaning they were probably installed together at barrio shrines. Similar deity images have been found at humble hill shrines (Figure 62.4B).

Thus far, my arguments about patronage correlate imperial-style sculptures with the activities of the state, and less refined, or provincial-style, sculptures with resident colonists. Although generally appropriate, this distinction cannot be applied without other evidence. Exceptions are sculptures at imperial sites that were made by lesser artists: for instance, the exterior sculptures decorating the rock-cut temple at Malinalco. At Castillo de Teayo, the dates inscribed on a

Figure 62.4 Aztec sculptures at the colony site of Castillo de Teayo, northern Veracruz, 1450–1521, all made of local sandstone: (A) Pair of fertility goddesses, Earth Goddess with Paper Headdress, 156 centimeters, and the water goddess Chalchiuhtlicue, 146 centimeters (now in the central plaza of Castillo de Teayo). (B) Pair of fertility deities, Paper Headdress Goddess, carved surface of 152 centimeters, and Tlaloc, size unknown, found on a small pyramid on Cerro de Zapotitlan (present locations unknown, drawings after Seler 1960–1961b: Figures 19 and 30). (C) Four sides of a stela with dates 1 Crocodile, 13 Reed, 13 Flower, and 1 Flint, the years of the birth of the sun and the god Huitzilopochtli and the first and last days of the sacred 160-day count, all comparable to inscriptions on the Calendar Stone of Tenochtitlan, H. 311 centimeters (drawing after Seler 1960–1961b: Figure 8).

stela (Figure 62.4C) refer to imperial imagery in Tenochtitlan, but the style indicates a provincial artist. Finally, two deity sculptures found at Coxcatlán in the Tehuacán Valley closely resemble the Aztec deities Huitzilopochtli and his mother Coatlicue in style and imagery, but written evidence argues against their having been imposed by the empire. The Coxcateca were politically independent allies of the empire (Berdan et al. 1996), but because they shared the Aztecs' Nahua culture, their patron god, Xelhua, and his mother, Cihuacóatl, were functionally similar to their Aztec counterparts (Umberger 1996: 169–171; see also Pohl 2003). However, the Aztec style of the sculptures indicates a more complex situation. The Coxcateca apparently had access, through their alliance, to a trained Aztec artist.

ACKNOWLEDGMENTS

I thank Walter Scheidel for inspiring me to rethink the interrelationship of art and politics in hegemonic empires; Michael Smith and Barbara Stark for personal communications and discussions throughout the years; and Michael Smith and Maëlle Sergheraert for insightful comments on a draft of this chapter.

REFERENCES

Alvarado Tezozomoc, Hernando. 1975. *Cronica mexicana* [ca. 1598], annotated by Manuel Orozco y Berra. 2nd ed. Porrúa, Mexico.

Barlow, Robert H. 1946. The Malinche of Acacingo, Edo. de Mexico. *Notes on Middle American Archaeology and Ethnology* 65:31–32.

Barlow, Robert H. 1949. *The Extent of the Empire of the Culhua Mexica.* Ibero-Americana 28, University of California Press, Berkeley.

Barlow, Robert H. 1950. Documentos relacionados con San Bartolomé Tlatelolco. *Memorias de la Academía Mexicana de la Historia* 9(1):233–250.

Berdan, Frances F., Richard E. Blanton, Elizabeth Hill Boone, Mary G. Hodge, Michael E. Smith, and Emily Umberger. 1996. *Aztec Imperial Strategies.* Dumbarton Oaks, Washington, DC.

Broda, Johanna, David Carrasco, and Eduardo Matos Moctezuma. 1988. *The Great Temple of Tenochtitlan, Center and Periphery in the Aztec World.* University of California Press, Berkeley.

Brumfiel, Elizabeth M. 1987. Elite and Utilitarian Crafts in the Aztec State. In *Specialization, Exchange, and Complex Societies,* edited by Elizabeth M. Brumfiel and Timothy Earle, pp. 102–118. Cambridge University Press, New York.

Brumfiel, Elizabeth M. 2001. Aztec Hearts and Minds: Religion and the State in the Aztec Empire. In *Empires, Perspectives from Archaeology and History,* edited by Susan E. Alcock, Terence N. D'Altroy, Kathleen D. Morrison, and Carla M. Sinopoli, pp. 283–310. Cambridge University Press, New York.

Calnek, Edward E. 1982. Patterns of Empire Formation in the Valley of Mexico, Late Postclassic Period, 1120–1521. In *The Inca and Aztec States 1400–1800, Anthropology and History,* edited by George A. Collier, Renato I. Rosaldo, and John D. Wirth, pp. 43–62. Academic Press, New York.

Carrasco Pizana, Pedro. 1996. *Estructura político territorial del Imperio Tenochca: La Triple Alianza de Tenochtitlan, Tetzcoco, y Tlacopan.* Colégio de México/Fondo de Cultura Económica, Mexico.

Davies, Nigel. 1987. *The Aztec Empire: The Toltec Resurgence.* University of Oklahoma Press, Norman.

Durán, Diego. 1967. *Historia de las indias de Nueva España e islas de la Tierra Firme* [ca. 1580], edited by Angel María Garibay K. 2 vols. Editorial Porrúa, Mexico.

García Payón, José. 1936. *La zona arqueológica de Tecaxic-Calixtlahuaca y los matlatzincas, primera parte.* Talleres Gráficos de la Nación, Mexico.

García Payón, José. 1979. *La zona arqueologica de Tecaxic-Calixtlahuaca y los matlatzinca: etnología y arqueología (textos de la segunda parte),* edited by Wanda Tommasi de Magrelli and Leonardo Manrique Castañeda. Biblioteca Enciclopédica del Estado de México, tomo 30, Mexico.

Hassig, Ross. 1984. The Aztec Empire: A Reappraisal. In *Five Centuries of Law and Politics in Central Mexico,* edited by Ronald Spores and Ross Hassig, pp. 15–24. Publications in Anthropology 30, Vanderbilt University Press, Nashville, Tennessee.

Hassig, Ross. 1988. *Aztec Warfare, Imperial Expansion and Political Control.* University of Oklahoma Press, Norman.

Krickeberg, Walter. 1969. *Feldsplastik und Felsbilder Altamerikas,* Vol. II. Verlag von Dietrich Reimer, Berlin.

López Austin, Alfredo. 1997. *Tamoanchan, Tlalocan: Places of Mist.* University Press of Colorado, Niwot.

López Austin, Alfredo, and Leonardo López Luján. 2009. *Monte Sagrado-Templo Mayor.* Instituto Nacional de Antropología e Historia/Universidad Nacional Autónoma de México, Mexico, D.F.

López Luján, Leonardo. 2006. *La Casa de la Aguilas, Un ejemplo de la arquitectura religiosa de Tenochtitlán.* Conaculta/Instituto Nacional de Antropología e Historia/Fondo de Cultura Económica, Mexico.

Matos Moctezuma, Eduardo. 1981. *Una visita al Templo Mayor de Tenochtitlán.* Instituto Nacional de Antropología e Historia, Mexico, D.F.

Medellín Zenil, Alfonso. 1952. *Exploraciones en Quauhtochco.* Gobierno de Veracruz and Instituto Nacional de Antropología, Jalapa.

Nebel, Carl. 1836. *Voyage pittoresque et archéologique dans la partie la plus intéressante du Méxique.* Chez M. Moench, Paris.

Ohnersorgen, Michael Anthony. 2001. Social and Economic Organization of Cotaxtla in the Postclassic Gulf Lowlands. Unpublished Ph.D. dissertation, Department of Anthropology, Arizona State University, Tempe.

Paso y Troncoso, Francisco del. 1905-1906. *Papeles de Nueva España.* Segunda Serie, Geografía y Estadística, 6 vols. (vols. 1 and 3–7). Tipográfico Sucesores de Rivadeneyra, Madrid.

Pohl, John M. D. 1998. Themes of Drunkenness, Violence, and Factionalism in Tlaxcalan Altar Paintings. *Res: Anthropology and Aesthetics* 33:184–207.

Pohl, John M. D. 2003. Creation Stories, Hero Cults, and Alliance Building: Postclassic Confederacies of Central and Southern Mexico from AD 1150-1458. In *The Postclassic Mesoamerican World,* edited by Michael Smith and Frances Berdan, pp. 61–66. University of Utah Press, Salt Lake City.

Rice, Don Stephen, ed. 1993. *Latin American Horizons.* Dumbarton Oaks, Washington, DC.

Schreiber, Katharina. 2001. The Wari Empire of Middle Horizon Peru: The Epistemological Challenge of Documenting an Empire without Documentary Evidence. In *Empires, Perspectives from Archaeology and History,* edited by Susan E. Alcock, Terence N. D'Altroy, Kathleen D. Morrison, and Carla M. Sinopoli, pp. 70–92. Cambridge University Press, New York.

Scheidel, Walter. 2006. Republics between Hegemony and Empire: How Ancient City-States Built Empires and the USA Doesn't (Anymore). *Princeton/Stanford Working Papers in Classics.* Electronic document, http://www.princeton.edu/~pswpc (accessed May 10, 2010).

Seler, Eduard. 1960-1961a. Die Ruinen von Xochicalco. In *Gesammelte Abhandlungen zur Amerikanischen Sprach- und Alterthumskunde*, Vol. II, pp. 128–167. Akademische Druck- und Verlagsanstalt, Graz. Originally published 1902-1923, A. Asher und Co. and Behrend und Co., Berlin, from article of 1888.

Seler, Eduard. 1960-1961b. Die Alterthümer von Castillo de Teayo. In *Gesammelte Abhandlungen zur Amerikanischen Sprach- und Alterthumskunde*, Vol. III, pp. 410–449. Akademische Druck- und Verlagsanstalt, Graz. Originally published 1902-1923, A. Asher und Co. and Behrend und Co., Berlin, from article of 1904.

Sergheraert, Maëlle. 2009. L'expansion mexica (1430–1520 après J.-C.), La question du contrôle impérial dans les provinces extérieures de l'Empire. Unpublished PhD dissertation, Université de Paris I.

Smith, Michael E. 1986. The Role of Social Stratification in the Aztec Empire: A View from the Provinces. *American Anthropologist* 88(1):70–91.

Smith, Michael E. 1990. Long-Distance Trade under the Aztec Empire: The Archaeological Evidence. *Ancient Mesoamerica* 1:153–169.

Smith, Michael E. 2001. The Aztec Empire and the Mesoamerican World System. In *Empires, Perspectives from Archaeology and History,* edited by Susan E. Alcock, Terence N. D'Altroy, Kathleen D. Morrison, and Carla M. Sinopoli, pp. 128–154. Cambridge University Press, New York.

Smith, Michael E., and Lisa Montiel. 2001. The Archaeological Study of Empires and Imperialism in Prehispanic Central Mexico. *Journal of Anthropological Archaeology* 20:245–284.

Solís Olguin, Felipe R. 1981. *Escultura del Castillo de Teayo, Veracruz, México, Catálogo.* Instituto de Investigaciones Estéticas, Universidad Nacional Autónoma de México, Mexico, D.F.

Stark, Barbara. 1990. The Gulf Coast and the Central Highlands. *Research in Economic Anthropology* 12:243–285.

Stone-Miller, Rebecca. 1993. An Overview of "Horizon" and "Horizon Style" in the Study of Ancient American Objects. In *Latin American Horizons,* edited by Don Stephen Rice, pp. 15–39. Dumbarton Oaks, Washington, DC.

Umberger, Emily. 1987. Antiques, Revivals, and References to the Past in Aztec Art. *Res: Anthropology and Aesthetics* 18:62–105.

Umberger, Emily. 1996. Aztec Presence and Material Remains in the Outer Provinces. In *Aztec Imperial Strategies,* edited by Frances F. Berdan, Richard E. Blanton, Elizabeth Hill Boone, Mary G. Hodge, Michael E. Smith, and Emily Umberger, pp. 151–179. Dumbarton Oaks, Washington, DC.

Umberger, Emily. 2002. Notions of Aztec History: The Case of the 1487 Great Temple Dedication. *Res: Anthropology and Aesthetics* 42:86–108.

Umberger, Emily. 2007a. Metaphorical Underpinnings of Aztec History: The Case of the 1473 Civil War. *Ancient Mesoamerica* 18:11–29.

Umberger, Emily. 2007b. Historia del arte y el Imperio Azteca: La evidencia de las esculturas. *Revista Española de Antropología Americana* 37(2):165–202 [English translation: http://www.public.asu.edu/~mesmith9/calix.]

Umberger, Emily 2008. Ethnicity and Other Identities in the Sculptures of Tenochtitlan. In *Ethnic Identity in Nahua Mesoamerica: The View from Archaeology, Art History, Ethnohistory, and Contemporary Ethnography,* by Frances F. Berdan, John Chance, Alan Sandstrom, Barbara Stark, James Taggart, and Emily Umberger, pp. 64–104. University of Utah Press, Salt Lake City.

Umberger, Emily, and Cecelia F. Klein. 1993. Aztec Art and Imperial Expansion. In *Latin American Horizons,* edited by Don Stephen Rice, pp. 295–336. Dumbarton Oaks, Washington, DC.

CHAPTER 63

EARLY MESOAMERICAN WRITING SYSTEMS

JOHN JUSTESON

FROM a comparative perspective, the early development of writing in Mesoamerica is poorly preserved. In Mesopotamia, more than six thousand tablets attest the first two centuries of the archaic, proto-cuneiform stage of the world's most ancient writing system. In contrast, the first few centuries of Mesoamerican writing, up to about 400 BC, are probably represented by fewer than a dozen texts.

FORMATIVE-PERIOD SCRIPTS

There is no solid evidence for writing in Mesoamerica during the Early Formative period. During the late Middle Formative, Mesoamerica was home to probably four notational systems in which symbols were deployed in part in relation to a spoken language: Olmec, Zapotec, epi-Olmec (Zoquean), and Mayan.

Olmec

The only generally accepted Olmec text appears on La Venta Monument 13, dating to the Terminal Olmec period (ca. 450–300 BC). A column of three glyphs in front of the striding figure is widely thought to be a caption referring to that person.

However, Lacadena (2008) plausibly suggests that the footprint symbol behind the striding figure, an iconographic indicator of travel in Postclassic screenfolds, on this monument is a hieroglyph that represents a verb and that it completes a two-column text stating something like 'N traveled'—in Mixe-Zoquean word order.

A plausible one-glyph caption appears on a stela from San Miguel Amuco, Guerrero (600–500 BC; Grove and Paradis 1971: Fig. 2). A day name may be recorded on a jade "spoon" (evidently a paint/ink palette; Covarrubias 1946: Fig. 24), which might, for example, name its owner; there is another perhaps in a mural at Oxtotitlan (Grove 1970: Fig. 15). Other Middle Formative Olmec notations may be in an emerging writing system, but they are as likely to be part of specialized subsystems of Olmec iconography from which writing systems may have emerged (see "Precursors" below).

Zapotec

Zapotec is the best-attested Formative writing system (Caso 1947; Whittaker 1983; Urcid Serrano 2001), with well over one hundred known texts from before 200 CE. The earliest whose chronological placement is uncontroversial are from the first building phase of Monte Albán Structure L (Danibaan phase, 500–300 BC). Monuments that Urcid Serrano (2006) has shown to have formed part of the building's exterior wall include 130 known "danzantes"; 27 of them are inscribed with texts, most of them probably captions naming the associated figure. Building L also displayed five "stelae" and two glyphic slabs. Nineteen other danzante-like sculptures attributed to the same era also bear short texts, probably exclusively names. Only five texts are attributed to the Pe phase (300–100 BC). Remains of more than seventy, from Mound J, are attributable to the Niza phase (100 BC–200 CE). The script may be from the Rosario phase (600–500 BC), to which Flannery and Marcus (e.g., 2003: 11803) assign a danzante sculpture from San José Mogote bearing a calendrical name, but others (e.g., Cahn and Winter, 1993) argue that it dates to the Danibaan phase or later.

The geographical distribution of these and later texts in the same script has always suggested that they were linguistically Zapotecan. Kaufman and Justeson (1992–2008; Justeson and Kaufman 2010) provide substantial grammatical evidence establishing this, especially from verb constructions.

At least forty-two of the forty-eight Danibaan danzante texts appear to be captions naming the depicted individuals. Four or five of the other six texts each contain a logogram representing a verb for being seated (Figure 63.1; cf. Justeson 1986: 448; Urcid Serrano 2006: 14). These texts are analyzable grammatically as referring to someone sitting (Kaufman and Justeson 1992–2008); this is plausibly the posture of the depicted figures, which thereby suggest to Urcid and me a portrayal of bloodletting more than of human sacrifice.

Mound J was faced with at least seventy-four evidently reused wall panels ("tablets"), each organized around a hill symbol, they were dubbed "conquest slabs" based on their inferred theme (Caso 1947: 21–31). Usually (maybe always) a glyph

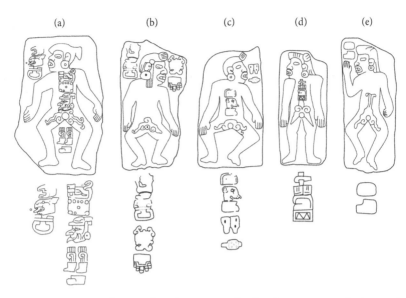

Figure 63.1 Danzante sculptures bearing texts referring to a person as being seated; the second plausibly states that he was sitting as lord, otherwise that 'Lord *N*' was sitting. Drawings by John Justeson and Justin P. Lowry: a–b after García Moll et al. 1986: plates 304, 306; c–e after drawings and a photo courtesy of Javier Urcid; hieroglyphic text in d after photograph in Scott 1978: monument M4.

or glyph group surmounts the hill symbol. Caso's suggestion that they are place names stimulated research concerned with military expansion and the consolidation of state authority at Monte Albán, beginning with Marcus (1976). However, they have since been shown to spell personal names (Justeson and Kaufman 1996; cf. Kaufman and Justeson 2004b; Carter 2007); some also appear as names of danzantes. At least eighteen end with titles, one or two of which also appear after danzante names (Figure 63.2).

Several Formative texts record a lunar day count via "Glyph W" (Justeson and Kaufman 1996), on whose basis absolute distances can be calculated for several of them; the Stela 12/13/14 text dates earliest, 275 years before Tablet 14, which is the latest.

Epi-Olmec

Currently just twelve epi-Olmec texts are known; six of these have substantially legible noncalendrical sign sequences. Although the earliest, on a potsherd from Chiapa de Corzo, dates to the Terminal Olmec period (450–300 BC), and some epi-Olmec signs plausibly have Olmec iconographic sources, there is no direct evidence that epi-Olmec writing is a later stage of an Olmec script.

During the Late Formative, the epi-Olmec script is associated with what has been traditionally recognized as the epi-Olmec cultural tradition (Lowe 1989: 61–65; Diehl 2004; Pool 2007). Cultural descendants of the Olmec tradition continued

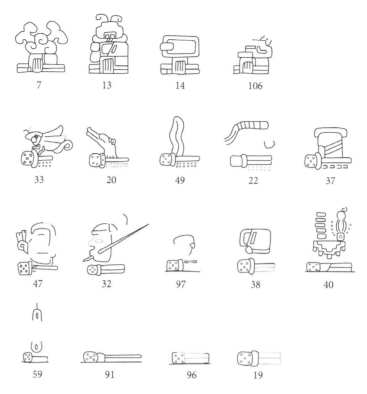

Figure 63.2 Titles and names on the Mound J wall panels. Numbers are the standard designators for each tablet: J-13, J-14, etc. Drawings by Justin P. Lowry after original drawings courtesy of Javier Urcid.

especially to the northwest, in the Tuxtlas and northward into the Papaloapan Basin, and in the southeast around Chiapa de Corzo. In the Isthmus—the zone of low elevation between the Gulf Coast and the Pacific—the Olmec tradition faded away. Epi-Olmec texts come exclusively from the two epi-Olmec zones; not one is known from the Isthmus proper.

During the Formative period, this script represented pre-proto-Zoquean, a Zoquean language descending from proto-Mixe-Zoquean but retaining archaic features lost by the proto-Zoquean stage (Justeson and Kaufman 1993; Kaufman and Justeson 2004: 1104). Two substantially legible texts dating to the Early Classic period—a brief text on Cerro de las Mesas Stela 6 dating to 468 AD, and a long text on a Teotihuacan-style mask arguably dating between 386 and 523 AD—provide no evidence concerning these archaisms.

Mayan

The earliest definitively Mayan texts—conforming throughout to Mayan grammar, phonology, and vocabulary (Mora-Marín 2001: Chapter 6)—date to the Late Formative period.

Several earlier texts are plausibly but not demonstrably Mayan. The earliest with signs in the Mayan tradition is on the El Portón stela (450–350 BC, Sharer and Sedat 1987; cf. Justeson and Mathews 1990: 97,115). More suggestive are texts from Takalik Abaj. Its recently discovered Altar 48, dating to ca. 350 BC, bears glyphs in definitively Mayan forms, but debate surrounds the identification of its language as Mixe-Zoquean versus Mayan. By the Late Formative, the site is pretty clearly Mayan. At 125 AD, Stela 5 from the same site has a sign for the title ʔaajaaw 'lord, ruler' whose pronunciation is verified by the syllabogram **wa** that follows; while the spelling for this title could have been borrowed, it is so far unknown within demonstrably non-Mayan texts, and the same monument exhibits a stage in the

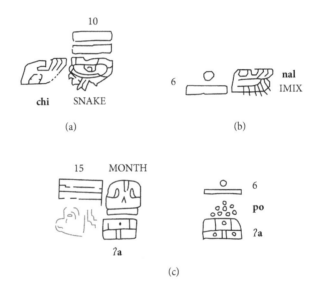

Figure 63.3 On Kaminaljuyú Stela 10, Mayan and Zoquean vocabulary items are implicated in the development of spellings for calendrical terms. (a) Stuart (cited by Mora-Marín 2005: 71) identified the spelling 10 chi-SNAKE as possibly phonetically reflecting the day name Chicchan (proto-Greater Tzeltalan *chij=chaan 'boa constrictor'; pGTz *chij 'deer' + *chaan 'snake'), reflecting the change of *k to GTz ch. (b) This plausible date is almost immediately preceded by a definite date 6 Imix, which precedes 10 Chicchan by just four days—circumstantial evidence for the correctness of Stuart's proposal. The spelling for Imix uses the Late Formative form of the logogram for that day, but, uniquely, surmounted by the sign nal; this relates to proto-Ch'olan name #nalchan for this day, documented in colonial Ch'ol, Ch'olti', and Chontal and known from no other language. (c) The lower text segment opens with 15-MONTH-??-ʔa, while on the epi-Olmec stela of La Mojarra, the same sign ʔa ends the spelling po-ʔa for the Zoquean word *po(:)yʔa 'month' (also 'moon'). Though possibly coincidental, the Kaminaljuyú sequence plausibly spells this Zoquean word. Kaminaljuyú glyph drawings by Justin P. Lowry, after Mora-Marín 2005: Fig. 2, with some corrections by Justeson based on published photographs (Doehring and Collins 2007); epi-Olmec text from a 1996 field drawing by Justeson.

development of a seemingly exclusively Mayan concept of zero out of a system of positional notation (Justeson 2010: 48–49).

Perhaps somewhat later are texts from Kaminaljuyú; the earliest, Kaminaljuyú "Stela" 10, dates to late in the Verbena phase (400–200 BC). Texts from San Bartolo, which date as early as 300–200 BC (Saturno et al. 2006), include not only signs but also sign groups that later have Mayan interpretations. The San Bartolo texts appear to be in the same or a closely related writing system as Kaminaljuyú Stela 10, given that so many signs in the tiny attested inventories are common to both; these include otherwise exclusively Mayan signs for the title ʔaajaaw 'lord, ruler' and a variant of the otherwise epi-Olmec syllabogram for *si*.

There is not enough internal evidence for reading any Kaminaljuyú or San Bartolo text in a particular language, but location and overall continuities in sign forms and style suggest that San Bartolo's texts represent a Mayan language. Vocabulary data so far are not definitive. Just three words seem relatively secure, all from Kaminaljuyú Stela 10 (Figure 63.3); each is calendrical and susceptible to borrowing in language or script. However, these words establish at least that a Greater Tzeltalan Mayan language, in or ancestral to the Ch'olan branch, was somewhere being written by 200 BC.

RELATIONSHIPS AMONG THE SCRIPTS

All of these scripts probably emerged during the Middle Formative period. The sharing of certain conventions and even signs, such as the logogram for being seated, make it plausible that they arose from one common script, but Zapotec writing, for example, could have emerged via interaction with others engaged either in writing or in representational practices that led to writing (see "Precursors" below). There is some evidence for diffusion of signs among Zapotec, epi-Olmec, and Mayan.

Olmec writing is too poorly attested to relate to any other script. Several organizational features suggest that Mayan and epi-Olmec writing, geographically circumscribing Olmec, are more closely related than either is to Zapotec writing. We can now be more specific. Mayan writing appears to have been written originally in a script whose syllabograms were developed in or modeled after a Mixe-Zoquean syllabary, given Lacadena's (2010) evidence that syllabograms for consonants unknown in early Mixe-Zoquean were devised to a great extent by modifying or combining signs for consonants found in both language families. The Mixe-Zoquean source of Mayan writing could have been the Olmec script, or it may have been a common ancestor of epi-Olmec and Mayan (there is evidence of a common origin for a small set of epi-Olmec and Mayan signs, some at least probably due to diffusion).

REPRESENTATIONAL PRINCIPLES

Conventions cited below for epi-Olmec and Zapotec are based on joint research by Justeson and Kaufman, applying models for the structures of early Mixe-Zoquean and Zapotecan languages as well as calendrical constraints.

Sign types

Most signs in all of these writing systems are *logograms*, representing whole words or their roots or stems. Conversely, in the Late Formative period almost all roots and stems are spelled by logograms in Zapotec and probably in Mayan; in Formative epi-Olmec texts, less than half of verb roots and stems are spelled logographically.

Almost all other signs are *syllabograms*. Zapotec syllabograms represent only consonant-vowel (CV) syllables. Correspondingly, proto-Zapotecan and early (pre-proto-)Zapotecan had only CV syllables, except that the consonant could be doubled (or lengthened); the script appears to have spelled doubled consonants as though they were single. The vast majority of epi-Olmec and Mayan syllabograms also represent CV syllables. All Zoquean and Mayan syllables begin with a CV sequence (where the vowel may be long or short), and in epi-Olmec many words contained only CV syllables. However, both languages included CVC and restricted types of CVCC syllables as well.

A few CVC syllabograms occur in both Mayan (e.g., **nah** spelling both *naah* 'house' and *nah* 'first', and **nal**, spelling both *nal* 'corn ear' and grammatical suffix sequences *-Vn-aal*) and epi-Olmec (e.g., **pɨk** spelling both *pɨk* 'hair, feathers' and *pɨk* 'to take'). Most CVC syllables were spelled CV-CV, where the last vowel was not pronounced—a common convention worldwide in syllabic and logosyllabic scripts that lack or make little use of CVC signs. However, in both scripts these syllables were spelled CV if the final consonant was "weak"—*ʔ*, *h*, or (in epi-Olmec only) *w* or *y*; in epi-Olmec these reduced spellings were the rule, while in Mayan, at the ends of words they were usually spelled by CV-CV sign sequences. In Mayan, other syllable-final consonants were sometimes not spelled, mainly resonants that end the first element of a compound word (e.g., *ʔihtz'iin=winik* 'younger sibling' can be spelled **ʔi-tz'i-WINIK**).

In epi-Olmec writing, the unpronounced final vowel in CV-CV spellings of CVC sequences was always *synharmonic* (the same as the preceding vowel), another common convention worldwide. In Mayan, some Mayanists (e.g., Houston, Robertson, and Stuart 1998; Lacadena and Wichmann 2004) believe that the unpronounced vowel, when not synharmonic, signaled differences among CVVC, CVhC, and CVʔC syllables; others (e.g., Kaufman with Justeson 2003: 29–33; Mora Marín 2001: 75–86) believe that they relate to grammatical differences in the suffixing patterns of words (a practice for which there is better comparative support, and which also accounts for synharmonic spellings).

Spelling Grammatical Morphemes

As in other partly logographic scripts, the spelling of almost all grammatical morphemes was by phonetic signs. The only clear exception is that Mayan writing had a logogram for the general preposition *ta*, seemingly attested already at San Bartolo; note that this morpheme is a full word.

Almost all grammatically required morphemes appear to have been explicitly represented in all three scripts. This is exceptionless for preposed grammatical morphemes: for Zapotec, aspect markers and derivational prefixes on verbs; for Mayan and epi-Olmec, prefixes that on nouns mark agreement with their possessors and that on transitive verbs mark agreement with their subjects (also on intransitive verbs in subordinate clauses in Zoquean).

Zapotec has no postposed grammatical affixes. Zoquean and Mayan do, and these postposed morphemes are explicitly represented (at least) starting with the first consonant, if any. Neither script necessarily spelled the vowel of a vowel-initial suffix when the stem was spelled by a logogram. The details are language- and script-specific.

(1) In epi-Olmec, the pronunciations of verb forms with vowel-initial aspect/ mood suffixes (*-i, -e, -tɨʔ, -aʔ*) were orthographically equivalent to those of nouns derived from the verb, such as *(ʔi) wuʔtz-i* 'when (he) pierces it' and *wuʔtz.iʔ* 'something pierced'. A verb logogram alone could spell such inflected verb forms; clear phonetic spellings of these suffixes are found only in cases such as **ʔi-ko-te** for *ʔi kot-e* 'when he was putting it away', when the verb stem was spelled phonetically.

(2) In Mayan, almost all verb suffixes ended in a consonant; syllabic spellings of such suffixes or suffix sequences began with the first consonant. For example, the *-aj* passivizer is spelled **ja** when word-final, and the sequence *-Vy-i* is typically spelled **yi**. A similar convention is found in especially the earlier stages of grammatical spelling in Sumerian; consonants and vowels that were not part of CV sequences were rarely spelled by Sumerian scribes until late in the third millennium BC.

The only common verb suffix consisting of a vowel only was the plain status suffix *-i* of intransitive verbs. The previously noted practice would suggest that such a form would not be spelled at all when the verb stem was spelled logographically. When the stem is spelled phonetically, the last syllabogram would spell the stem-final consonant + *i*, as in **ʔu-ti** for *ʔuht-i* 'it happened'. By the Early Classic period, this suffix was typically spelled syllabically after a logogram for the verb stem, just as in fully phonetic spellings. It is unclear whether this was an extension of the practice in fully phonetic spellings (and the practice could be defined differently).

(3) The Olmec text on La Venta Monument 13, if correctly interpreted by Lacadena, does not represent the grammatically required aspect/mood

suffix, which would probably have been a simple open syllable -*pa* or -*wɨ* (otherwise -*ʔi[n]*). This recalls the earliest stages of Sumerian writing.

Sign Forms, Names, and Values

Some Mesoamerican signs appear to be abstract, but many (perhaps most) in Formative scripts are highly depictive. Iconic signs for beings depict their heads, the synecdoche or pars pro toto principle; the use of full figures as signs is a later development, appearing only in Mayan writing and plausibly as a facet of Teotihuacan influence in Early Classic imagery and texts. More abstract signs tend to have a generally rectangular profile; in the Mayan tradition, perhaps by the end of the Late Formative, more eccentric sign forms began conventionalizing to a more compact profile.

Logograms for verbs often represent actions via images of objects, typically including a body part or implement in the process of performing the action.

Syllabograms often spell the CV sequence beginning a word associated with the concept. For example, the Zapotec sign for the syllable *ni* is based on pre-Zapotec **nisa* and the epi-Olmec sign for *nɨ* on pre-Zoquean **nɨtɨʔ*, both meaning 'water, liquid'. Like logograms for verbs, signs for syllables could be based on verb participles and nominalizations of verbs: for example, the Mayan sign for the syllable *ye*, depicting a hand, palm side forward in a posture of display, is presumably based on *yeʔ .eel* 'showing, displaying'.

PRECURSORS OF WRITING

It has long been suggested that writing in Mesoamerica emerged out of an Olmec iconographic system (e.g., Prem 1971: 127; Coe 1976: 111–112), and this seems all the more likely today. A twenty-five-year-old model for the emergence of writing in Mesoamerica (Justeson 1986; Justeson and Mathews 1990) seems to capture basic representational processes that may have introduced linguistic encoding into precursor systems of visual notation; these include most commonly a specialized variety of iconography appearing on some Olmec celts, most elaborately on the Humboldt celt.

Apart from masks, small-scale three-dimensional Olmec depictive sculptures most often represent entire beings—most commonly humans or anthropomorphic beings, ducks, or felines; less often, other mammals, reptiles, birds, fish, and insects.

Much two-dimensional art also represents entire beings. Incised on celts, by far the most common two-dimensional images are of human beings, relatively

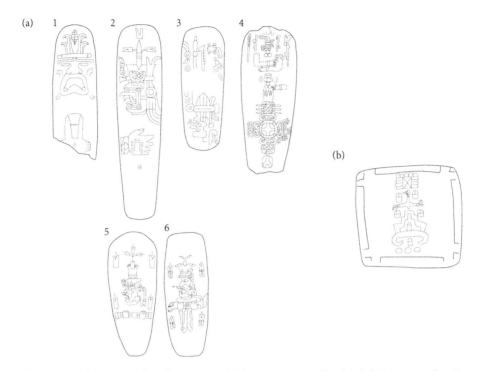

Figure 63.4 Two specialized variants of Olmec iconography. (a) *Celt iconography*: (1)
Late Olmec or epi-Olmec celt from El Sitio; (2) celt of unknown provenience; (3) celt
from Tlaltenco, Basin of Mexico; (4) the Humboldt celt. In a-2 and a-3, note the shared
elements of the complex of symbols above the head. (5–6) Two celts from Arroyo
Pesquero. (b) *Other media*: tablet from Ahuelican, Guerrero. Drawings by Justin P.
Lowry: (a 1–4) after Justeson and Mathews 1990: Fig. 1; (a 5–6) after Reilly 1990: Fig. 12;
(b) after Fields and Reents-Budet 2005: 190.

richly dressed and wearing or holding a variety of artifacts. Many of the artifacts
and costume elements recur across different celts; some do not appear in monumental reliefs or three-dimensional sculptures.

Some incised celts depart from usual conventions by representing only parts
of a figure, in free space (Figure 63.4a). Most often, a disembodied head appears,
sometimes with other isolated body parts in an approximately standard placement
relative to the head. Various elements that elsewhere accompany an incised figure
may be represented, often in groups. Some celts seem very abstract, marked only
with what Reilly (e.g., 1995) identifies as locational symbols.

These relate to writing in two ways. In a full-scale figural representation, a
knowledgeable viewer might glean such information as, among other things, the
identity of the person depicted; their rank, office, or role; the act they are performing; the place in which they are performing it. The *excised*, or abbreviated,
mode of representation—with many iconographic elements removed from a figural context—may have focused attention on these specific issues, with a given
symbolic unit corresponding to specific categories of information rather than a

holistic representation of beings in action, just as logograms focus on such issues via particular words. The celt as the vehicle for these representations, appropriate in the first instance for displaying human figures, produces a vertical layout of the discrete information categories, which may have set the stage for a linear layout and columnar format.

A few celts (Figure 63.4 [3, 4]) have multiple groupings of symbols, as though multiple related messages are being conveyed. Symbols within a group are associated both spatially and in that they represent functionally similar items, such as headgear elements or held paraphernalia.

This system seems to have coexisted with and to be related to full figural celt representations; a pair of celts from Rio Pesquero are closely similar, with one showing a full figural form and the other the abbreviated format (Figure 63.4a [5, 6]).

The recently discovered Cascajal tablet (Rodriguez Martínez et al. 2006) is a critical document in the history of Mesoamerican writing (Figure 63.5a). Based largely on a claimed consistency of linear symbol order in repeating sign groups, it has been proposed to be a writing system, representing features of a language (Rodriguez Martínez et al. 2006; Mora-Marín 2009); however, while certain symbol groups recur, sign order within them is not entirely consistent (Figure 63.5b). The frequency distribution of symbols is completely uncharacteristic of signs in writing: in Mesoamerican texts of comparable length (even excluding numerals), as in other script traditions, most signs by far occur only once, but only 25 percent of the Cascajal tablet's symbols do so. Unlike all early Mesoamerican texts of any length, they include no animal heads (nor pars pro toto symbols of any sort), and the complete absence of numerical notations is quite unusual.

The tablet shares far more with the specialized subsystem of abbreviated celt iconography, with its excised symbolic elements, than with writing. Notably, the tablet draws for the most part from the same vocabulary of symbols as do the incised celts; especially common are locational images, and accoutrements, including head and facial elements, that are worn or carried by figures. There are several spatially grouped sets of symbols, which are associated internally and distinguished from other groups by size and relative proximity. The associations among individual sequential symbols were sometimes clearly interpretable iconographically (Figure 63.5c). For example, figures in Olmec art often hold a "knuckleduster" in one hand and a "torch" in the other; a knuckleduster symbol appears adjacent to and facing a torch symbol on the tablet. (The quoted identifiers are nicknames only, the objects depicted by these symbols being unresolved; cf. Joralemon 1996: 218–219.) Similarly, two symbols on the tablet depict a right eye, each with different interior details and different facial markings above and below; the only two eye symbols on the tablet, they are placed adjacent to one another.

Curiously, not one symbol on the Cascajal tablet also occurs on the Humboldt celt, with which Rodriguez and colleagues (2006: 1613) associate its symbol system. It would appear that distinct subsystems of Olmec iconography had developed by the excision process; a tablet from Ahuelican, Guerrero (Figure 63.4b), may reflect further diversity. Such developments, all of which may date to roughly

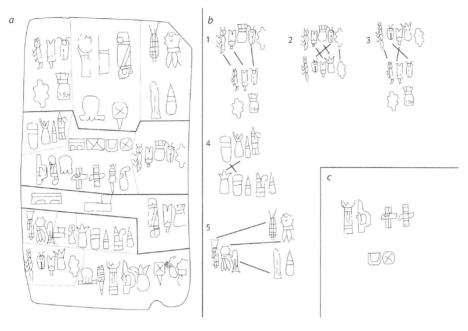

Figure 63.5 The Cascajal inscribed tablet. (a) Approximate breakdown into text segments: darker divisions separate areas with noticeably larger signs from areas with
noticeably smaller signs; finer divisions mark off repeating sign groups from others.
(b) Three sign groups contain three or more adjacent symbols; sign order in the longer
two is inconsistent; inconsistency is reflected by crossed lines in the symbol sequence
comparisons. In b-1, one group appears three times, in one instance in a grouping that occupies part of two lines; inconsistency is represented only for the linearly
organized sections of this sequence, though other inconsistencies are present. The
symbol sequencing in b-3, the shortest repeating symbol group, is probably the same
in both instances. (c) Iconographically motivated symbol pairings: "torch" + "knuckle-
duster"; a possible analogue of the U-bracket + crossed bands motif; and a pair of right
eyes. Drawings by John Justeson and Justin P. Lowry from photographs provided by
Ponciano Ortiz C. and María del Carmen Rodríguez; the most significant departure
from previous drawings is the correction to the third sign from the upper left.

900–600 BC, may be the ultimate sources of one or more systems of writing in
Mesoamerica.
    While it could be consistent for some excised symbols to be treated as correspond-
ing to words, the social context of the production and of the transmission of these
symbol systems within an iconographic framework must have reinforced their being
understood as iconography. The emergence of an intrinsic relationship to language
may have depended on the introduction of numeral symbols, which conflict with iconographic conventions for representing a number of entities, and names, which inherently refer to persons via words. These two features co-occur in calendrical names of
days or persons; the representation of the divinatory calendar may have played a critical role in the reinterpretation of these iconographic systems in terms of language.

REFERENCES

Cahn, Peter Robert, and Marcus Winter. 1993. The San José Mogote Danzante. *Indiana*
    13:39–64.
Carter, Nicholas Poole. 2007. The "Emblem" Monuments of Structure J at Monte Albán,
    Oaxaca, Mexico. MA thesis, Department of Art, University of Texas, Austin.
Caso, Alfonso. 1947. Calendario y escritura de las antiguas culturas de Monte Albán. In
    Obras completas de Miguel Othon de Mendizabal, vol. 1, pp. 5–102. Talleres gráficas
    de la nación, Mexico City.
Coe, Michael D. 1976. Early Steps in the Evolution of Maya Writing. In *The Origins
    of Religious Art and Iconography in Preclassic Mesoamerica*, edited by Henry B.
    Nicholson, pp. 109–122. UCLA Latin American Studies Series, vol. 31, UCLA Latin
    American Studies Center, Los Angeles.
Covarrubias, Miguel. 1946. El arte "olmeca," o de La Venta. *Cuadernos Americanos*
    28(4):153–179.
Diehl, Richard A. 2004. *The Olmecs: America's First Civilization*. Thames and Hudson,
    London.
Doehring, Travis, and Lori Collins. 2007. Mesoamerican Three-Dimensional
    Imaging Database. Published online by the Foundation for the Advancement of
    Mesoamerican Studies, http://research.famsi.org/3D_imaging/view_all_scans.
    php?id_number=M3D0005; accessed August 17, 2011.
Flannery, Kent V., and Joyce Marcus. 2003. The Origin of War: New ^{14}C Dates from
    Ancient Mexico. *Proceedings of the National Academy of Science* 100(20):
    11801–11805.
Fields, Virginia, and Dorie Reents-Budet. 2005. *Lords of Creation: The Origins of Sacred
    Maya Kinship. Olmec Art of Ancient Mexico*. Los Angeles County Museum of Art,
    Los Angeles.
García Moll, Roberto, Donald W. Patterson Brown, and Marcus C. Winter. 1986.
    Monumentos escultóricos de Monte Albán. Materialen zur Allgemeinen und
    Vergleichenden Archäologie, Band 37, Verlag C. H. Beck, Munich.
Grove, David C. 1970. *The Olmec Paintings of Oxtotitlan Cave, Guerrero, Mexico*. Studies
    in Pre-Columbian Art and Archaeology, 6, Dumbarton Oaks Research Library and
    Collections, Washington, DC.
Grove, David C., and Louise I. Paradis. 1971. An Olmec Stela from San Miguel Amuco,
    Guerrero. *American Antiquity* 36(1):95–102.
Houston, Stephen D., David Stuart, and John Robertson. 1998. Disharmony in Mayan
    Hieroglyphic Writing: Linguistic Change and Continuity in Classic Society. In
    Anatomía de una civilización: aproximaciones interdisciplinarias a la cultura maya,
    edited by Andrés Ciudad-Ruíz, Yolanda Fernández, José María García Campillo,
    María Josefa Iglesias Ponce de León, Alfonso Lacadena García-Gallo, and Luís T.
    Sanz Castro et al., pp. 275–296. Sociedad Española de Estudios Mayas, Madrid.
Joralemon, Peter David. 1996. Seated figure carrying torch and "knuckle-duster". In
    Olmec Art of Ancient Mexico, edited by Benson, Elizabeth P., and Beatriz de la
    Fuente, pp. 218–219. National Gallery of Art, Washington, DC.
Justeson, John. 1986. The Origin of Writing Systems: Preclassic Mesoamerica. *World
    Archaeology* 17(3):437–458.
Justeson, John. 2010. Numerical Cognition and the Origin of "Zero" in Mesoamerica.
    In *The Archaeology of Measurement: Comprehending Heaven, Earth and Time in*

Ancient Societies, edited by Iain Morley and Colin Renfrew, pp. 43–53. Cambridge
   University Press, New York.
Justeson, John, and Terrence Kaufman. 1993. A Decipherment of Epi-Olmec Hieroglyphic
   Writing. *Science* 259:1703–1711.
Justeson, John, and Terrence Kaufman. 1996. Warfare in the Preclassic Inscriptions of
   Monte Alban. Unpublished manuscript.
Justeson, John, and Terrence Kaufman. 2010. Zapotec Grammatical Constructions in
   the Preclassic Inscriptions of Monte Alban. Paper presented in the Coloquio sobre
   Lenguas Otomangues y Vecinas, IV: Thomas C. Smith-Stark, Biblioteca Burgoa,
   Oaxaca de Juárez, Oaxaca, April 16–18.
Justeson, John, and Peter Mathews. 1990. Evolutionary Trends in Mesoamerican
   Hieroglyphic Writing. *Visible Language* 24(1):88–132.
Kaufman, Terrence, and John Justeson. 1992–2008. The Decipherment of Zapotec
   Hieroglyphic Writing. Unpublished manuscript.
Kaufman, Terrence, and John Justeson. 2004a. Epi-Olmec. In *The Cambridge
   Encyclopedia of the World's Ancient Languages*, edited by Roger D. Woodard,
   pp. 1071–1108. Cambridge University Press, Cambridge.
Kaufman, Terrence, and John Justeson. 2004b. Zapotec. Appendix 3. In *The Cambridge
   Encyclopedia of the World's Ancient Languages*, edited by Roger D. Woodard,
   pp. 1109–1111. Cambridge University Press, Cambridge.
Kaufman, Terrence, with John Justeson. 2003. *A Preliminary Mayan
   Etymological Dictionary*. Published online at http://www.famsi.org/reports/
   01051/index.html.
Lacadena, Alfonso. 2008. La escritura olmeca y la hipótesis del Mixe-Zoque:
   implicaciones lingüísticas de un análisis estructural del Monumento 13 de La Venta.
   In *Olmeca: Balance y perspectivas: Memoria de la Primera Mesa Redonda*, edited
   by María Teresa Uriarte and Rebecca B. González Lauck, pp. 607–626. Universidad
   Nacional Autónoma de México, Mexico City.
Lacadena, Alfonso. 2010. Historical Implications of the Presence of Non-Mayan
   Linguistic Features in Maya Script. In *The Maya and Their Neighbours: Internal and
   External Contacts Through Time. Proceedings of the 10th European Maya Conference,
   Leiden, December 2005*, edited by Laura van Broekhoven, Rogelio Valencia Rivera,
   Benjamin Vis and Frauke Sachse, pp. *Acta Mesoamericana*, vol. 23, Verlag Anton
   Saurwein, Markt Schwaben.
Lacadena, Alfonso, and Søren Wichmann. 2004. On the Representation of the Glottal
   Stop in Maya Writing. In *The Linguistics of Maya Writing*, edited by Søren
   Wichmann, pp. 103–162. University of Utah Press, Salt Lake City.
Lowe, Gareth. 1989. The Heartland Olmec: Evolution of Material Culture. In *Regional
   Perspectives on the Olmec*, edited by Robert J. Sharer and David C. Grove, pp. 33–67.
   Cambridge University Press, Cambridge.
Marcus, Joyce. 1976. The Iconography of Militarism at Monte Albán and Neighboring
   Sites in the Valley of Oaxaca. In *The Origins of Religious Art and Iconography in
   Preclassic Mesoamerica*, edited by Henry B. Nicholson, pp. 123–139. UCLA Latin
   American Studies Series, vol. 31, UCLA Latin American Studies Center, Los Angeles.
Mora-Marín, David. 2001. The Grammar, Orthography, Content, and Social Context of
   Late Preclassic Mayan Portable Texts. PhD dissertation in Anthropology, University
   at Albany.
Mora-Marín, David. 2005. Kaminaljuyu Stela 10: Script Classification and Linguistic
   Affiliation. *Ancient Mesoamerica* 16(1):63–87.

Mora-Marín, David. 2009. Early Olmec Writing: Reading Format and Reading Order. *Latin American Antiquity* 20(3):395–412.

Pool, Christopher A. 2007. *Olmec Archaeology and Early Mesoamerica*. Cambridge University Press, Cambridge.

Prem, Hanns J. 1971. Calendrics and Writing. In *Observations on the Emergence of Civilization in Mesoamerica*, edited by Robert F. Heizer and John A. Graham, pp. 112–132. University of California Archaeological Research Facility Contributions, 11, Archaeological Research Facility, Berkeley.

Reilly, F. Kent 1990. Cosmos and Rulership: The Function of Olmec-Style Elements in Formative Period Mesoamerica. *Visible Language* 24(1):12–37.

Reilly, F. Kent 1995. Art, Ritual, and Rulership in the Olmec World. In *The Olmec World: Ritual and Rulership*, edited by Michael Coe, pp. 27–45. The Art Museum, Princeton University, Princeton, New Jersey.

Rodriguez Martínez, María del Carmen, Ponciano Ortíz Ceballos, Michael D. Coe, Richard A. Diehl, Stephen D. Houston, Karl A. Taube, and Alfredo Delgado Calderón. 2006. Oldest Writing in the New World. *Science* 313:1610.

Saturno, William A., David Stuart, and Boris Beltrán. 2006. Early Maya Writing at San Bartolo, Guatemala. *Science* 311:1281–1283.

Scott, John F. 1978. *The Danzantes of Monte Alban*. Part II: Catalogue, Dumbarton Oaks, Washington, DC.

Sharer, Robert J., and David W. Sedat. 1987. *Archaeological Investigations in the Northern Maya Highlands, Guatemala: Interaction and the Development of Maya Civilization*. University Museum, University of Pennsylvania, Philadelphia.

Urcid Serrano, Javier. 2001. *Zapotec Hieroglyphic Writing*. Dumbarton Oaks, Washington, DC.

Urcid Serrano, Javier. 2006. Oracles and Warfare: The Role of Pictorial Narratives in the Early Development of Monte Albán (500 BC–200 AD). Unpublished manuscript.

Whittaker, Gordon. 1983. The Hieroglyphs of Monte Alban. PhD dissertation, Department of Anthropology, Yale University, New Haven.

CHAPTER 64

....

MAYA WRITING

....

NIKOLAI GRUBE

ANCIENT Maya civilization is widely known for its hieroglyphic writing system. Although the Maya were not the only Mesoamerican civilization that had developed writing, Maya hieroglyphs have received major attention because of the sheer size of the script corpus as well as the fact that Maya writing has been deciphered during the last thirty years so that approximately 75 percent of its written texts can now be understood.

Maya hieroglyphic inscriptions are found in an area that corresponds to the geographic extension of classic Maya civilization, including archaeological sites in the Mexican states of Tabasco, Chiapas, Campeche, Yucatán and Quintana Roo; the Petén department of Guatemala; the western part of Honduras; and all of Belize. There are also inscriptions in earlier and probably related writing systems from the Pacific coast and the highlands of Chiapas, Guatemala, and El Salvador. It is disputed whether these writing systems were direct precursors to the script of the Maya lowlands or whether they were independent developments (Chinchilla Mazariegos 1999; Houston 2004).

The beginning of Maya hieroglyphic writing can now be dated to the second half of the Middle Preclassic period. The earliest archaeologically dated texts from ca. 300 BC have been found at San Bartolo, Petén, Guatemala (Saturno, Stuart, and Beltrán 2006). Their formal development and elaboration suggest that earlier forms of Maya writing must have developed centuries before. While texts from the Preclassic period are very few, the beginning of the Early Classic period is marked by a sudden increase of writing on stone monuments. The Classic period (250-900 AD) saw the apex of Maya writing. During this time, Maya writing was employed on many different media. Due to the decomposition of organic material, most Maya texts from the Classic period are preserved on stone monuments, such as stelae and altars as well as on architectural sculpture, such as lintels, doorjambs,

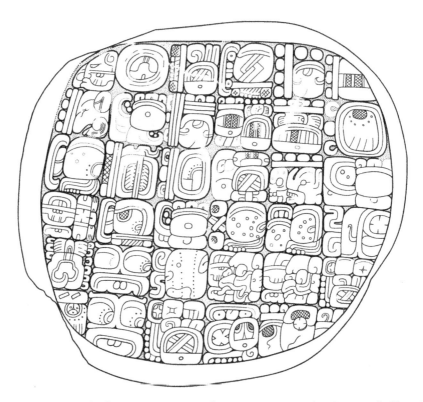

Figure 64.1 Hieroglyphic inscription on Altar 2, Naranjo, Petén, Guatemala (drawing
by Nikolai Grube).

and stairways (Figure 64.1). In addition to monumental inscriptions, the preserved
corpus also includes texts painted and carved on ceramics (Reents-Budet 1994).
Few painted inscriptions have survived apart from those on ceramics; those that
have been discovered are found in caves and on the walls of buildings. Finally, a
large number of small artifacts in bone, jade, or greenstone jewelry and shell have
also been used as media for Maya writing. With the end of dynastic kingship in
the ninth century and the transformation of Maya society during the Postclassic
period, writers went from recording monumental texts to creating screen-fold
books almost exclusively. Three books from the Postclassic period have survived
the tropical climate and destruction by the Spanish clergy: these are the Maya
codices housed today in European libraries in Dresden, Madrid, and Paris (Figure
64.2). Although the only Maya books that exist today were painted in the last centuries before the Spanish conquest, paintings and other secondary evidence leave
no doubt that paper books were in use from the very beginning of Maya writing.
The end of Maya writing came with the advent of the Spanish conquistadors and
priests, who forbade the use of the native, "pagan" writing system. Even though
hieroglyphic manuscripts were burnt and their owners punished, Maya writing
continued to be used secretly until the end of the eighteenth century (Chuchiak
2010).

Figure 64.2 Page 49 of the Dresden Codex.

THE STRUCTURE OF MAYA WRITING

Maya hieroglyphic writing is a logosyllabic script based on a corpus of approximately one thousand signs, although at any particular period of time scribes never used more than between approximately three hundred and five hundred signs (Grube 1990). The signs represent either syllables (syllabograms) or words (logograms). Syllabograms are signs that represent consonant-vowel (CV) syllables or simple vowels (V). Vowel-consonant (VC) signs or consonant-vowel-consonant (CVC) signs are not known. The sound values of syllabic signs are conventionally transcribed in lowercase boldface letters. Because most Maya roots have the structure CVC, two vowel signs can be combined to render a root. In such a CV-CV-spelling, the last vowel remains silent. Typically, the last vowel was the same as the root vowel. However, in the Classic Mayan, the language of the inscriptions, vowel quality (the distinction between long, short, aspirated, and glottalized vowels) was phonemic. Maya scribes marked long and glottalized vowels by vowel disharmony, so that the final silent vowel was different from the internal root vowel, such as in the spelling **b'a-ki** for the word *b'aak* "bone." How precisely disharmonic vowels correspond to glottalized and elongated root vowels has long been a matter of scholarly debate and still is not totally understood (Houston, Stuart, and Robertson 1997; Lacadena and Wichmann 2004).

The total number of syllabic signs in Maya script was above two hundred, although there are only five vowels and nineteen consonants that could be combined to form CV syllabic signs. The large number can be explained by the fact that many syllable combinations could be represented by more than one sign. For example, there were at least four different signs for the syllable **nu** and three different **na** signs. The reason for the overrepresentation of certain CV combinations seems to have been entirely of an aesthetic nature. The availability of signs of different sizes would have provided scribes more formal variability. Most syllabograms seem to have been derived originally from logograms by way of acrophonic reduction, where the last, usually weak, consonant of a CVC root, usually *a j, h, y*, or a glottal stop, had disappeared, for example, a mandible (*choj*) became the sign for the syllable **cho**, a fish (*kay*) became the syllable **ka**, and a fox (*jij*) became the syllable **ji** (Figure 64.3). More abstract syllabic signs were introduced into the writing system during the Classic period as a response to language change. These include signs for the writing of **t'V** and probably also **p'V** values, which were composed of preexisting signs that were combined in order to create new, discrete units.

Logograms are signs that represent word roots. Many of the logograms therefore have the syllable structure CVC, although there are also a few bisyllabic roots (*otoot* "house," *b'ahlam* "jaguar") (Figure 64.4). Logographic signs often have an iconic origin, in particular in those cases where the noun or verb referred to could easily be depicted. Logograms represent root morphemes of verbs (**CHOK** "scatter"), nouns (**MIHIN** "son of father"), adjectives (**CHAK** "red"), prepositions (**TI'** "at, on, with"), numerical classifiers and plural markers (**TAAK** "plural of human beings"), and numbers (**PIK** "eight thousand"). The sound values of logograms are conventionally transcribed in roman capital letters. Polyvalency was almost

Figure 64.3 The syllabic signs **ji, cho,** and **ka** (drawings by Nikolai Grube).

Figure 64.4 The logographic signs OTOCH "house" and B'AHLAM "jaguar" (drawings by Nikolai Grube).

nonexistent; with little exception there was a one-to-one correspondence between a sign and its sound value. Because of the great number of homophonic words, the sound value of a sign could be used for "rebus" spellings. The sign, which originally meant "eight thousand," had the value **PIK**, which could also stand for the semantically completely unrelated word *pik* ("dress").

Word signs and syllable signs could be combined to spell words and to combine words into sentences. Very often, word signs were attached to logograms in order to stress the appropriate pronunciation. Syllabic signs in this position are called phonetic complements. This was particularly necessary in roots that have suffered a sound shift over the long period of time the writing system was in use. In these cases, a syllabic sign was attached either to stress the "old" conservative (**OTOOT-ti** for *otoot* "house") or the new sound value (**OTOOT-che**, for *otooch* "house" in Yukatekan). Another function of attached syllabic signs was to determine the vowel length of a logogram based on the distinction between harmonic and disharmonic vowels. The addition of the syllabic sign **ni** to the word sign **TUUN**, for example, would stress the fact that the root vowel was long (Houston, Stuart, and Robertson 1997). Most phonetic complements are attached behind the word signs. Preposed phonetic complements are rare and restricted to vowel-initial words, words beginning with a semi-vowel, and words with *k* or *k'* as their initial consonant (Grube 2010). The explanation for the complementation of *k* or *k'* initial words may have been a phonemic shift from *k* (*k'*) to *ch* (*ch'*) in Classic Mayan, which occurred at some time during the Early Classic period. The prefixed complement in such case would fossilize the old, conservative pronunciation.

Phonetic complementation of word signs already was in use during the Early Classic period, but it became much more common with the beginning of the Late Classic. During the Terminal Classic, phonetic complementation lost much of its former significance, because the distinction between long, glottalized and short vowels disappeared (Houston, Stuart, and Robertson 1997). Prefixed complements, on the other side, became more prominent in order to disambiguate the sound values of complex or less common signs. Other than in its function as phonetic complements, syllable signs were attached to word signs to spell grammatical prefixes and suffixes, such as pronouns, derivational morphemes, and markers of tense and aspect.

Although Maya writing underwent considerable changes and even certain script reforms during the time of its use, there was never a tendency to reduce its complexity or to abandon word signs in favor of a completely syllabic script (Grube 1990). Even with the last expression of Maya writing in the three codices, word signs are much more prominent than syllabic signs in the spelling of words and sentences. This conservatism in regard to the structure of the script certainly results from notions of authenticity, ancient origin, and the sacred nature of Maya hieroglyphs. Another, more pragmatic reason for the continuous use of logograms was the way they facilitated the reading process. Logograms represent the most common roots, allowing the reader to locate verbs and nouns easily in a text.

SENTENCES AND TEXT STRUCTURE

The signs of the script were arranged in square or rectangular blocks. These glyph blocks in general correspond to semantic components such as verbs and nouns and probably reflect an emic understanding of words. Glyph blocks were then arranged in a doubled column that was read in pairs from left to right and from top to bottom. Shorter texts, such as captions to figures or dedication texts written on ceramic vessels, are placed in single lines that were read from top to bottom or from left to right.

The sentence structure of Classic Mayan was verb-object-subject (VOS) (Schele 1982). If necessary, the verb could be preceded by adverbs, which provided the chronological anchor for the sentence, and if several sentences were put together to a longer text, a series of adverbs provided the temporal frame for the entire narrative (Figure 64.5). The dates of the Maya Calendar, whether written as Long Count or Calendar Round dates, linguistically represent adverbs. Dates are often not taken into account as part of the actual sentence, but they should be analyzed in the same way as other components of a sentence. Dates function as adverbs of time, providing the chronological network both for the entire text as well as for a single verbal phrase located within.

Syntactically, dates are followed by verbs and are inflected to specify person, temporal aspect or deixis, and voice (Houston, Robertson, and Stuart 2000). Simple intransitive verbs only have a subject, such as in *i huli* "and then he arrived." More complex sentences based on full transitive verbs have a subject and an object as in *u chokoow ch'aaj* "he scattered incense." Most sentences include additional

(1) *ux k'an*
„on the day 3 K' an"

(2) *juun uniiw*
„on the first day of
the month
K' ank' in"

(3) *muhkaj*
„was buried"

(4) *tahn ch'een*
„in the center of the
cave"

(5) *?-ha' ux winik
haab' ajaw*
„of Dos Pilas, the
lord of 3 K'atun
periods"

itzamnaaj k'awiil
(name of the king)

y-ilaj waxak k'al
"its was observed by
twenty-eight"

ajawtaak, u tz'akaj
"lords, and then . . ."

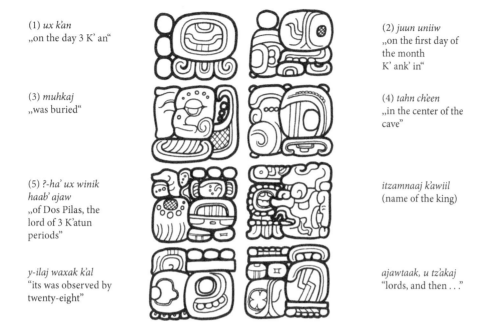

Figure 64.5 A text passage from Stela 8 at Dos Pilas, Petén, Guatemala,
with translation (drawing by Nikolai Grube).

information about the nouns involved; for example, if the subject was a king, we will find extensive title phrases following his name, including so-called emblem glyphs, which address the subject as the "divine king" (*k'uhul ajaw*) of a particular kingdom (Mathews 1991).

THE LANGUAGE OF MAYA INSCRIPTIONS

The identification of the language underlying Maya hieroglyphic writing has been an issue of constant debate since the beginning of hieroglyphic studies. Most of the early scholars were little explicit in regard to the linguistic affiliation of Maya writing, assuming that the Mayan languages spoken today in the lowlands were those that were recorded in the texts. More explicit theories about the role of Ch'olan languages emerged during the process of the decipherment of Maya writing in the 1970s and 1980s (Justeson and Campbell 1984). Contemporary researchers saw the inscriptions of the Maya lowlands as being written in Classic Mayan—a prestige language closely related to Eastern Ch'olan, and in particular to Ch'orti' Maya and its colonial precursor Ch'olti', although the language also preserves many linguistic forms that predate the split between Eastern and Western Ch'olan (Houston, Robertson, and Stuart 2000; Wichmann 2004). Classic Mayan was used as the language of literate elites all over the lowlands, from Copán to Chichén Itzá. Although the linguistic identification of Classic Mayan has been widely accepted, it had generated many new questions about how remote the prestige language was from the actual, spoken languages, as well as how vernacular languages (Yukatekan, Tzeltalan) affected the writing system (Lacadena and Wichmann 2002). There is no doubt that hieroglyphic writing was used to write Yukatek Maya at the time of the Spanish conquest.

SOCIAL DIMENSIONS OF MAYA WRITING AND LITERATURE

Maya hieroglyphic writing was strongly connected to the institution of kingship. It had developed in the Late Preclassic, contemporary with the rise of the first royal dynasties, and it disappeared almost completely from public monuments after the collapse of Maya kingship in the ninth and tenth centuries AD. It survived into the Colonial period as a medium of priestly communication in the form of bark-paper manuscripts. Maya writing was regarded to be of divine origin, conveying the words of gods, and also that of kings, the impersonators of gods on earth. The production of texts, therefore, was restricted to palaces and their immediate environments. It seems that most royal courts maintained their own workshop of literate painters and artisans; however, we also know that certain scribes worked at more than one palace (Coe and Kerr 1998). To what extent the people inhabiting a royal court were literate, or whether literacy was an obligatory component of elite education is still debated. Even more controversial is the question whether people outside of the court also had at least a limited knowledge of certain hieroglyphic signs, which may have included dates and the names of the current king (Houston 1994).

Maya artists occasionally signed their names on ceramics or even carved their signatures in the background of sculptures. In some instances we find as many as twelve signatures on a single stela, leaving no doubt that artists were organized in large workshops. The large numbers of signatures, all beginning with the same statement *y-uxulul* "this is the carving of," also suggests that craftsmanship and calligraphy were more important than the authorship of texts (Stuart 2001). Maya carvers and painters did not regard themselves as the authors of their writings. The messages they wrote were conceived as words of the gods or utterances of divine kings. Scribes had very little impact on the style and literary quality of the written messages, whose formal speech and constant repetitions often leave an impression of monotony.

The most common genres of Maya writing include self-referential texts and historical and mythological narratives. Self-referential texts include messages by which owners of artifacts express that the artifact is in their possession. Such texts can also include formulaic expressions by which an artifact or a building was dedicated to particular divinities. Historical texts are usually third-person narratives about the lives of kings and their predecessors and their ritual obligations to the gods (Martin and Grube 2008). Purely mythological narratives are found mostly on painted ceramics. We must not forget, however, that only tiny portions remain of the literary production of the Maya. The humid tropical climate has destroyed almost all organic materials, such as texts on wood and fabric, and above all the many books made from bark paper. All that remains is what the scribes wrote on stone and materials that have withstood the passage of time. Even though these texts only represent a fraction of ancient scribal production, the decipherment of these texts has provided us unique insights into Maya history, religion, cosmology, and thinking.

FURTHER READING

Coe, Michael D. 1992. *Breaking the Maya Code.* Thames and Hudson, London.

Coe, Michael D., and Mark van Stone. 2001. *Reading the Maya Glyphs.* Thames and Hudson, London.

REFERENCES

Chinchilla Mazariegos, Oswaldo. 1999. Desarrollo de la escritura en Mesoamerica durante el Preclásico. In *Historia General de Guatemala, Tomo* 1, edited by Marion Popenoe de Hatch, pp. 557–562. Fundación para la Cultura y el Desarrollo, Guatemala.

Chuchiak, John F. 2010. Writing as Resistance: Maya Graphic Pluralism and Indigenous Elite Strategies for Survival in Colonial Yucatán 1550–1750. *Ethnohistory* 57(1):87–116.

Coe, Michael D., and Justin Kerr. 1998. *The Art of the Maya Scribe.* Harry N. Abrams, New York.

Dresden Codex. N.d. Electronic document, http:// http://digital.slub-dresden.de/ fileadmin/data/280742827/280742827_tif/jpegs/280742827.pdf (accessed February 8, 2012).

Grube, Nikolai. 1990. *Die Entwicklung der Mayaschrift: Grundlagen zur Erforschung des Wandels der Mayaschrift von der Protoklassik bis zur Spanischen Eroberung.* Acta Mesoamericana 3, Verlag von Flemming, Berlin.

Grube, Nikolai. 2010. Preposed Phonetic Complements in Maya Hieroglyphic Writing. In *Linguistics and Archaeology in the Americas: The Historization of Language and Society,* edited by Eithne B. Carlin and Simon van de Kerke, pp. 27–43. Koninklijke Brill, Leiden.

Houston, Stephen D. 1994. Literacy among the Pre-Columbian Maya: A Comparative Perspective. In *Writing without Words,* edited by Elizabeth Hill Boone and Walter D. Mignolo, pp. 27–49. Duke University Press, Durham, North Carolina.

Houston, Stephen D. 2004. Writing in early Mesoamerica. In *The First Writing*, edited by
    Stephen D. Houston, pp. 274-309. Cambridge University Press, Cambridge.

Houston, Stephen D., John Robertson, and David Stuart. 2000. The Language of Classic
    Maya Inscriptions. *Current Anthropology* 41(3):321–356.

Houston, Stephen D., David Stuart, and John Robertson. 1997. Disharmony in Maya
    Hieroglyphic Writing: Linguistic Change and Continuity in Classic Society. In
    Anatomia de una civilización: Aproximaciones interdisciplinarias a la cultura maya,
    edited by Andres Ciudad Ruiz et al., pp. 275–296. Sociedad Española de Estudios
    Mayas, Madrid.

Justeson, John, and Lyle Campbell, eds. 1984. *Phoneticism in Maya Hieroglyphic Writing*.
    Institute of Mesoamerica Studies Pub. 9, State University of New York at Albany,
    Albany.

Lacadena, Alfonso, and Sören Wichmann. 2002. The Distribution of Lowland Maya
    Languages in the Classic Period. In *La organización social entre los maya. Memoria
    de la tercera mesa redonda de Palenque*, Vol. I, edited by Vera Tiesler Blos, Rafael
    Cobos, and Merle Greene Robertson, pp. 79–100. Instituto Nacional de Antropología
    e Historia and Universidad Autónoma de Yucatán, México and Mérida.

Lacadena, Alfonso, and Sören Wichmann. 2004. On the Representation of the Glottal
    Stop in Maya Writing. In *The Linguistics of Maya Writing*, edited by Sören
    Wichmann, pp. 103–162. University of Utah Press, Salt Lake City.

Martin, Simon, and Nikolai Grube. 2008. *Chronicle of the Maya Kings and Queens*. 2nd
    ed. Thames and Hudson, London.

Matthews, Peter. 1991. Classic Maya Emblem Glyphs. In *Classic Maya Political History*,
    edited by T. Patrick Culbert, pp. 19–29. Cambridge University Press, Cambridge.

Reents-Budet, Dorie, ed. 1994. *Painting the Maya Universe: Royal Ceramics of the Classic
    Period*. Duke University Press, Durham, North Carolina.

Saturno, William, David Stuart, and Boris Beltrán. 2006. Early Maya Writing at San
    Bartolo, Guatemala. *Science* 311(5765):1281–1283.

Schele, Linda. 1982. *Maya Glyphs: The Verbs*. University of Texas Press, Austin.

Stuart, David. 2001. Lectura y escritura en la corte maya. *Arqueología Mexicana*
    8(48):48–53.

Wichmann, Sören, ed. 2004. *The Linguistics of Maya Writing*. University of Utah Press,
    Salt Lake City.

CHAPTER 65

....

SCRIBAL TRADITIONS FROM HIGHLAND MESOAMERICA (300–1000 AD)

....

JAVIER URCID

In a synthesis of what was then known of Mesoamerican scribal traditions, Prem and Riese (1983) created a diagram to chart their temporal and geographical distribution, positing that they all were probably genealogically related, although their presumed common ancestral form was unknown. The earlier branch, starting ca. 400 BC, was the script of Monte Albán, which gave way to Zapotec writing, which in turn played a role in the development of the "Central Mexican writing horizon," a wide-ranging phenomenon that endured for five hundred years (700-1200 AD). Yet no evidence spanning the abandonment of Monte Albán and the inception of "Mixtec writing" supported the instantiation of such a horizon in Oaxaca, and because writing was construed as glottic forms only, the authors assumed that no such script existed in the Basin of Mexico prior to 1000 AD; hence, the omission in their discussion of writing at Teotihuacan.

Currently, the earliest presumed evidence of glottic writing—in the southern Gulf Coast lowlands—has been pushed back to ca. 900 BC (Rodríguez Martínez et al. 2006), although it is unclear how it may relate to subsequent traditions. Also, the division of Oaxacan scripts was unwarranted, for Zapotec writing constituted a single enduring tradition (Urcid 2001, 2005). Furthermore, by defining a writing system as a set of social practices associated with an inventory of written signs (Harris 1995: 56), there is evidence of at least four other systems not charted in their column for Oaxaca, namely Ñuiñe, Coastal, Chiapanec, and post-Monte Albán scripts (Urcid 2011). Most important, the model of Prem and Riese does not account for the genealogical development of scripts (inception, branching off, discontinuity) in terms of social processes. They simply impose the analogy of the "tracing of descent" onto the different scalar dimension of scripts.

The purpose of this chapter is to assess what we presently know of scribal practices between 300 and 1000 AD in "highland Mesoamerica."[1] Specifically, the focus is on reckonings of time, writing at Teotihuacan, scripts and historicity, and scribal emulations in the context of interregional interaction.

INDEXES OF ANCIENT CALENDARS

Writing practices in highland traditions commonly involved the rendering of glyphs accompanied by numerals. With few exceptions, their values range from 1 to 13. These numerals were represented using bar and dot graphic conventions, although by ca. 700 AD, Xochicalco scribes occasionally included dots only. Graphic conventions in the Cotzumalhuapa region stand as a novel approach, for carvers wrote numerals using predominantly the dots-only convention, replicating within each dot the glyph that was intended to be qualified by the numeral. Although many of the sign and numeral couplets stand for the calendrical names of people, these appellatives were drawn from the 20-day list that formed the core of both the divinatory calendar of 260 days and the solar calendar of 52 years. Thus, these signs serve as indexes to certain features of the ancient calendars. Using the Zapotec glyphic day list as the main guide, it is possible to reconstitute complete or partial lists from several scribal traditions (Figure 65.1).[2]

In these reconstructions the Ñuiñe list is almost complete; its day signs are practically identical to those from the Zapotec script. For the Teotihuacan day list, not much has changed since Caso's (1937) treatment of the problem. Glyphs for only ten of the twenty positions are known. Several of the known signs resemble those from Zapotec and Ñuiñe scripts. In the Xochicalco day list, the signs for two positions remain unattested, although one (day Maize/Eagle) can be filled in with data from Cacaxtla. About half of the glyphic day names share graphic conventions

1. The latter term is used arbitrarily to exclude the major lowland scribal traditions of Mixe-Zoquean and Mayan linguistic affiliation, although this study discusses instantiations of writing in several lowland regions.

2. The glyphs in the Zapotec list were anchored to their positions by matching the iconicity of signs with the meaning of Zapotec day names recorded in the second half of the sixteenth century by Fray Juan de Córdova (1987 [1578]), or by means of graphic comparisons with later glyphic lists from screenfolds painted in the Mixteca Alta and the Central Highlands.

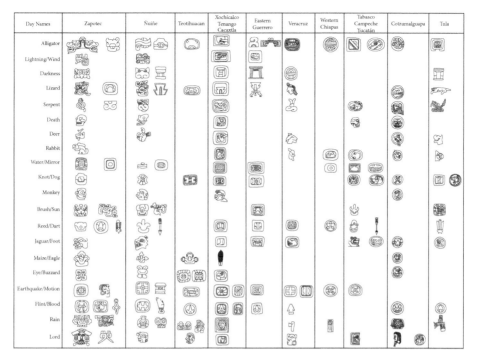

Figure 65.1 Reconstruction of glyphic day lists from several "highland" scribal traditions.

with the Ñuiñe and Zapotec scripts. The remaining signs presage the glyphic usages that became widespread in the highland scribal traditions of the thirteenth through sixteenth centuries. Thus, rather than being an amalgam of other traditions (Caso 1962; Sáenz 1964)—and unless these conventions were set by scribes at Teotihuacan—the Xochicalco script involved novel practices that became prestigious and worth emulating in later times. While the glyphic day list from western Chiapas is scantly accounted for (six of twenty positions), the remaining ones have eleven or twelve out of the twenty positions attested. There are other signs to fill in several positions to the Cotzumalhuapa series, but their forms are so unique that graphic comparisons with other lists are unproductive.[3]

Reckonings of time were represented in some of the highland scribal traditions in different ways, although they invariably deployed the Calendar Round (CR, or cycle of fifty-two vague, not tropical, solar years) to frame historical accounts. The lack of temporal records in terms of multiple concurrent cycles and a fixed point of departure (like the Long Count in the Epi-Olmec and southeastern regions of Mesoamerica) may reflect an ethos that emphasized an experiential sense of time rather than one based on mental manipulations. After all, individuals experienced no more than two celebrations marking the end of a fifty-two-year cycle.

3. Chinchilla Mazariegos (2008) has a more complete and in some cases different reconstruction of the Cotzumalhuapa glyphic day list.

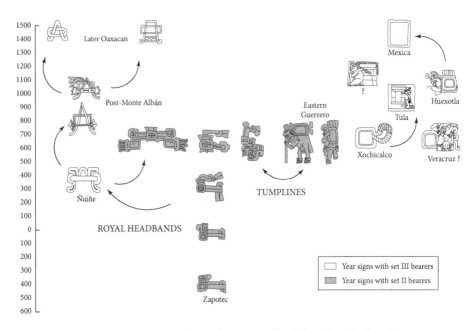

Figure 65.2 Year signs and year bearers in "highland" scribal traditions.

Because of the properties in the reckoning of the CR, which graphically dictate a syntagmatic relation between a sign indexing the "year" and four sign and numeral couplets signaling the "year name"—with the signs drawn from the twenty-day list being spaced five positions from each other—it is possible to trace in several traditions the recording of annual dates, dates that cannot be synchronized to the Gregorian calendar because these are not anchored to a fixed point of departure.

Charting the graphic conventions to render the year glyph across scripts and through time shows two trajectories based on slightly different metaphors linking the fulfillment of political duties and the passage of time (Figure 65.2). The most enduring trend, characterized by the icon of a royal headband to signal the year, appears to mark each of the corresponding year bearers as "the name of the year that rules any given cycle" (Stuart 1991). The other trend, based on the icon of a person carrying the year name on the back with a tumpline, seemingly marks each named year as "the bearer that carries the burden during the year." This trajectory substitutes at times the bearing person by an alter ego (e.g., a rabbit), or in the case of the known annual dates from Xochicalco/Tenango/Maltrata (n = 14), by the use of synecdoche (the tumpline tied to the cartouche that frames the year name). Eventually, in the scribal practices from the basin of Mexico between the thirteenth and sixteenth centuries AD, the year sign was connoted by rendering only the year name framed by a cartouche. Figure 65.2 also plots two main forms attested thus far of reckoning the CR: the oldest, based on set II year bearers, was deployed in the Zapotec and eastern Guerrero scribal traditions, and a later one, based on set

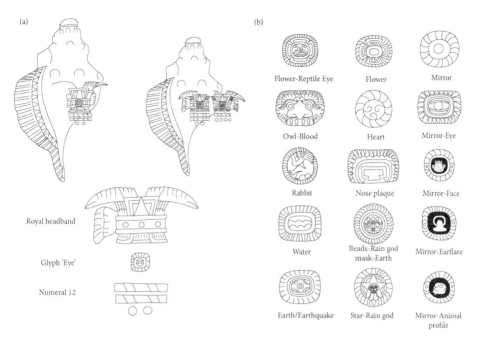

Figure 65.3 Teotihuacan graphic conventions. (a) Representations of royal headbands with sign and numeral couplets; (b) glyphs with feathered cartouches.

III year bearers, was used by scribes in the Ñuiñe and post-Teotihuacan Central Highland scribal traditions.[4]

Complicating the identification of annual dates is the use of glyphs representing royal headbands to mark a paramount political office and the accompanying sign and numeral couplets to signal the nominal identity of those who occupied it. Several examples have been attested in inscriptions from central Oaxaca and the Mixteca Baja. This evidence bears important implications for the only three instances of royal headbands accompanied by sign and numeral couplets traditionally attributed to Teotihuacan, even though the provenience of the shell trumpets upon which the signs were painted is unknown (Figure 65.3a). The associated sign and numeral combinations are '12 Eye' in the larger trumpet, and '12 Eye' and '9 Eye' in the smaller one, in all cases with the Eye glyph framed by a feathered cartouche. Although synecdochical, it is unlikely that the glyph and its cartouche have an iconic origin (the eye of a specific kind of bird) because other glyphs in the Teotihuacan sign repertoire are also framed by feathered cartouches (Figure 65.3b). On the other hand, the glyph anchored to the sixteenth position in the Zapotec and

4. Set II year bearers involved glyphs in day-name positions 2-7-12-17; set III year bearers were based on day-name positions 3-8-13-18. The CR at Monte Albán began with the year bearer Earthquake [17], although it is uncertain whether the numeral was 1 or 13. The year name/numeral with which the CR began in the other scribal traditions represented in Figure 65.2 remains to be determined with future epigraphic findings.

Ñuiñe glyphic day lists is the icon of a human eye. If that were to be the anchorage of the Teotihuacan Eye glyph, and if the royal headband in this context were to signal the year, it would mean that the reckoning of the CR at the great metropolis was based on set I year bearers. To confirm this interpretive alternative, examples of the royal headband would have to be accompanied by sign and numeral couplets with the day signs Alligator (RE glyph) [1], Death (Human skull) [6], and Monkey [11].[5] If in the context of the shell trumpets the royal headband were to signal a paramount political office, the inscriptions would name at least two rulers who were perhaps genealogically related. If so, no currently available epigraphic evidence would substantiate what many scholars refer to as the "Teotihuacan year sign."

TEOTIHUACAN WRITING AT
HOME AND ABROAD

In a brilliant study, Kubler (1967) implicitly criticized previous "mentalist" approaches for the unstated assumption that ancient Teotihuacanos cognitively internalized whatever came to their minds when apprehending the visual forms of communication displayed at the city and never spoke about their experiences. To him, viewing led people to verbally communicate with one another, positing that Teotihuacan imagery was logo-phonic and grammatically structured. Sign reiterations in the mural paintings, the paucity of what he construed as verbal markers, and the seeming proliferation of reputed nouns and adjectives, led Kubler to conclude that Teotihuacan writing was mostly liturgical litany. Subsequent analytic studies (von Winning 1987; Langley 1986, 1992; Taube 1999, 2003) focused on recognizing the iconicity of primary graphic units (although there are still disagreements on many identifications), ascertaining the repertoire of signs, understanding their degree of internal variability, eliciting the way primary graphic units form compounds, and defining several of the scribal rules. Because (1) signs are embedded in a multiplicity of aggregate units or in multilayered imagery, (2) many glyphs show increased hierarchical levels of recombination, (3) constitutive signs display varied orientations, and (4) there is much reiteration of larger units, the semantic values appear to be contingent on context and were most likely obtained by means of logo-phonic readings, the homophonic principle, and on conventional associations that involved metaphors and metonymy. Thus, a promising approach to elicit

---

5. If the Teotihuacan Eye glyph were to stand for the sign "Mirror" (9th position) (Taube 1992: 181–182), or be synecdochical of the Rain god (19th position), a chronological value of the royal headdress glyph would imply that the reckoning of the Teotihuacan CR was based on the equally unusual set IV year bearers.

the capacity for action generated by the inscriptions is to interpret them in relation to their supporting surfaces.

However, the poor degree of preservation of inscribed surfaces (painted murals, decorated vessels, stone assemblages, and sculptural tableaus) has been a major deterrent for conducting contextual approaches. In the case of murals, it is evident that entire interior and exterior walls in domestic and public settings were painted, and yet most of the known mural production remains only on the lower portions of some walls. The directionality of the surviving paintings, which pervasively display bilateral symmetry and line up entry-exit traffic routes, strongly suggests the role of inscribed walls in directing some of the movements of people within or between rooms, corridors, courtyards, and streets. A contextual approach would allow as well detecting patterns that convey narratives and multiple layers of meaning (Díaz Oyarzábal 2002), perhaps enabling an assessment of the possible uses of inhabited spaces or about the social constituencies that occupied them.

For example, the spatial configuration of the Zacuala apartment compound highlights the central sector as the most important because of its size, the presence on the east side of a structure atop a raised platform, and the paths converging into it (Figure 65.4). The vestibule of the compound includes an open, colonnaded shallow basin that captured rainy water, creating a pool (Séjourné 1959: 19). The porticos on the path to the Main Patio (nos. 1 and 8) have basal murals with representations

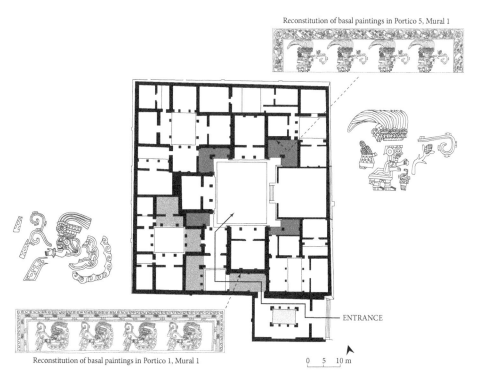

Reconstitution of basal paintings in Portico 5, Mural 1

Reconstitution of basal paintings in Portico 1, Mural 1

0   5   10 m

ENTRANCE

Figure 65.4 Agricultural themes painted on the surviving murals at the Zacuala apartment compound.

of the rain god, rendered amid a scalloped sky band and clouds. Their busts are shown scattering seeds unto the ground while "speaking" the lexeme "earth" two times. The rooms in the four corners of the Main Patio include basal murals depicting processions of rain god impersonators holding in their hands stalks with ripped ears of corn and "snake rattle" pouches (for planting seeds) and carrying on their backs woven baskets full of mature ears of corn. Thus, the kinesics from the street toward the Main Patio proceeds parallel to the timing of the agricultural cycle (beginning of the rainy season [the pool], planting [rain deity amid clouds scattering seeds], sowing [rain deity assistants carrying baskets with ripped corn]).

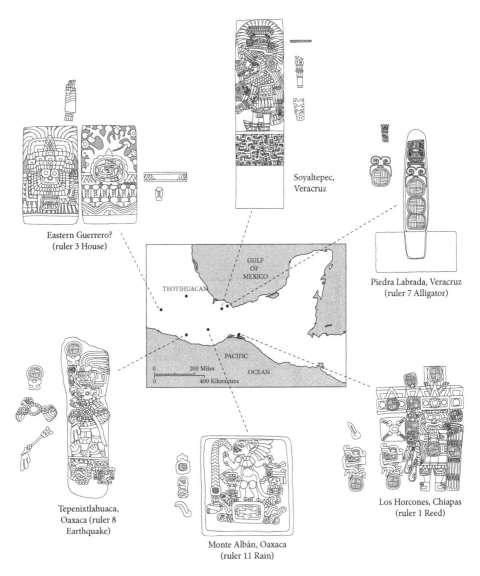

Figure 65.5 Enthronement monuments from distant regions carved with inscriptions that emulate Teotihuacan symbols in local styles.

The quadripartite pattern of the "sowing" theme in porticos 3-4-5-6 indexes the Mesoamerican paradigm of the four corners of the world, the mountain of sustenance, the origin of humans from maize, the deed of father-and-mother thunder in releasing the wealth contained within the mountain, and the role of rain deity attendants in disseminating corn to teach people how to cultivate it and gain sustenance from it. It seems unlikely that the Zacuala apartment compound housed peasants; rather, the thematic emphasis on agriculture in the surviving mural portions suggests that its inhabitants claimed property rights on hinterland estates.

During its economic and political heyday, Teotihuacan likely pursued various strategies in its interregional interactions, conquering and controlling some polities directly, ruling others indirectly, or maintaining mutually beneficial relations with others. Its prestige did not wane after the polity balkanized and became increasingly insular between 550 and 900 AD. Before and during these centuries, elites in many parts of Mesoamerica actively sought to appropriate, emulate, and reformulate aspects of its legacy, including highly charged symbols, in order to legitimate claims to local political power. Rulers in distant regions commissioned monuments to memorialize their enthronement, selecting certain Teotihuacan conventions and embedding them in local usages (Figure 65.5). The irony is that such leaders were keenly interested in proclaiming exclusionary ruling strategies, identifying themselves by name, at the same time that they were co-opting symbolic conventions that seemingly originated in the context of an inclusionary political ideology. A limited set of signs composed of the couplet "serpent-mat," "darts" (to symbolically define the territory or to proclaim warfare victories), "torches" (new fire drilling), or embodiments of the rain deity (the ruler as provider and social benefactor) appear in several stelae from distant regions, in some cases adhering to the corporate ideal of rulership, that is, without identifying the protagonist but embedding key signs in the paraphernalia of the officeholder.

DYNASTIC SUCCESSIONS AMID SACRED PROPOSITIONS

The study of scripts in the Central Highlands is riddled with ahistorical interpretations, claims that inscriptions exclusively allude to deities, calendrical adjustments and synchronizations, or idyllic stargazing. Few studies (Berlo 1989; Hirth 1989; Smith 2000a, 2000b; Urcid 2007) approach the inscribed record in terms of mortals, their motivations, and their claimed deeds. Expanding on earlier comments, the narrative program of the Building of the Feathered Serpents at Xochicalco appears to record, among other things, a dynastic succession of rulers and the boundaries of their proclaimed territory. One section of the narrative refers to the enthronement, on a CR date 6 Reed, of a ruler 9 House, a celebration that required taking a captive named 11 Monkey. Like in some Ñuiñe inscriptions, the representation of this ruler involves conflation (substituting his image by his calendrical name), and synecdoche (alluding to actions by depicting his arms stretching from the nominal cartouche) (Figure 65.6a). Other rulers in what survives of the narrative are identified as 2 Earthquake and 7 Serpent.

The study of painted murals at Cacaxtla has prompted various interpretations, most of them privileging discussions about the relationship between graphic style and ethnicity. Because the murals reveal continuities with the Teotihuacan scribal tradition but deploy as well Maya graphic conventions (excluding glottic writing), much attention has been given to their production in terms to the Olmeca-Xicallanca, an

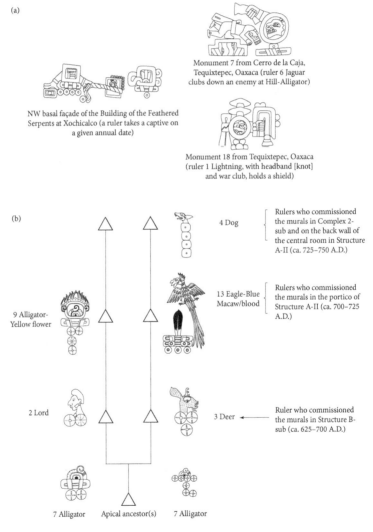

Figure 65.6 Rulers named in highland inscriptions. (a) Examples from Xochicalco and Ñuiñe scripts; (b) hypothesized dynastic succession of paired rulers at Cacaxtla.

exogenous group mentioned in sixteenth-century sources. In addition to the problem of critically correlating the legacy in the social memory of the early colonial period with social processes that unfolded almost a millennium before, another drawback in much of the scholarly production is the lack of an approach that highlights the agency of those who commissioned the paintings, as well as a semiotic perspective that takes into account the murals' architectural context. Following the latter paradigms, a case can be made that the murals from Buildings B-sub, A-II, and Complex 2-sub were commissioned by a succession of four paired rulers who held power at Cacaxtla through a span of about a century (Urcid and Domínguez Covarrubias 2012a, 2012b). This local dynasty deployed elements of a distant and exotic graphic style to increase their political clout (Robertson 1980; Figure 65.6b).

EMULATION THROUGH PROSELYTIZING AND TRADE

Between the eighth and tenth centuries AD, elites in the Central Highlands selectively imported foreign representational styles; so did elites in southeastern Mesoamerica. While the presence of exogenous-looking signs in settlements along the Usumacinta drainage and central Yucatán initially stirred the imagination of conquest and population replacement, a model of the development of a new religion (Ringle et al. 1998) posits that certain glottic and nonglottic scribal practices spread throughout large portions of Mesoamerica after the decline of Teotihuacan as the result of a messianic movement centered on the cult of a deity known as Feathered Serpent.

An example of the appropriation of nonlocal graphic conventions in the context of imagery of the Feathered Serpent is the sculpted bench from El Mercado, in Chichén Itzá (Figure 65.7a). It may well be that the template of the bench was later emulated at Tula, but what is significant in this case is the relationship between the representation of captives and nominal signs. The focal scene shows a warrior personifying an eagle holding a thrower and darts. He stands on a feathered serpent over two captives who offer their hearts, each one followed by processions of high-ranking captives bound to a rope. The people in the processions wrap around the sides of the bench. Each prisoner is identified by a name glyph, except for the main figure and the two sacrificial foes. It is as if foreign conventions, used as pseudo glyphs or to render pejorative names, were deployed to "depersonalize" and hence highlight the humiliation of captives, even though these most likely came from neighboring polities in the northern Maya lowlands.

But the adoption of foreign glyphic conventions may have also been facilitated by professional traders and the prestige that exotic-looking writing conveyed, as suggested by an incised travertine vessel with an unusual theme (Figure 65.7b). The provenience of the vessel is unknown, but the rendering of the human body

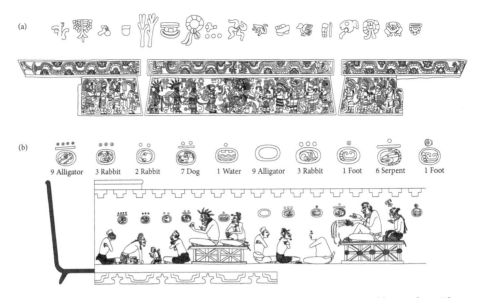

Figure 65.7 Inscribed surfaces with foreign glyphic conventions. (a) Bench in El Mercado, Chichén Itzá (redrawn from Ruppert 1943: Figures 23–25); (b) travertine vase (drawn after Kerr 2002: vase no. 319).

adheres more to the graphic conventions of southeastern Mesoamerica while the nominal glyphs do not. The imagery has two vignettes that seemingly represent legal disputes among a guild of long-distance merchants, with the same pair of plaintiffs (named 3 Rabbit and 9 Alligator) shown in two separate hearings.

ENTANGLED SUCCESSIONS OF SCRIPTS

While secondary scribal traditions are in part derivative of earlier ones, they all may not have had a single common ancestral form. Extricating their historical relations will be contingent on more epigraphic data on already known and still unknown scripts. Future studies may redefine the current monolithic construct of the "central Mexican writing horizon" and could model their diachronic trajectories in terms of varied social processes to account for script origins, transformations, and obsolescence.

ACKNOWLEDGMENT

Much gratitude is due to Elbis Domínguez Covarrubias for her creation of the figures.

REFERENCES

Berlo, Janet C. 1989. Early Writing in Central Mexico: In Tlilli, In Tlapilli before AD 1000. In *Mesoamerica after the Decline of Teotihuacan AD 700–900*, edited by Richard A. Diehl and Janet C. Berlo, pp. 19–47. Dumbarton Oaks, Washington, DC.

Caso, Alfonso. 1937. ¿Tenían los Teotihuacanos conocimiento del Tonalpohualli? *El México Antiguo* IV(3–4):131–143.

Caso, Alfonso. 1962. Calendario y escritura en Xochicalco. *Revista Mexicana de Estudios Antropológicos* XVIII:49–79.

Chinchilla Mazariegos, Oswaldo. 2008. La escritura de Cotzumalhuapa. Manuscript on file, Museo Popol Vuh, Universidad Francisco Marroquín, Guatemala.

Córdova, Fray Juan de. 1987 [1578]. *Vocabulario en lengua Çapoteca*. Pedro Bali, Imprenta del Gobierno de Morelia, Mexico.

Díaz Oyarzábal, Clara Luz. 2002. Las serpientes emplumadas de Techinantitla, Teotihuacan. *Arqueología Mexicana* X(55):40–43.

Harris, Roy. 1995. *Signs of Writing*. Routledge, London.

Hirth, Kenneth, G. 1989. Militarism and Social Organization at Xochicalco, Morelos. In *Mesoamerica after the decline of Teotihuacan AD 700–900*, edited by Richard A. Diehl and Janet C. Berlo, pp. 69–81. Dumbarton Oaks, Washington, DC.

Kerr, Justin. 2002. Maya Vase Database: An Archive of Rollout Photographs. Foundation for the Advancement of Mesoamerican Studies. Electonic document, http://www.mayavase.com (accessed February 24, 2003).

Kubler, George. 1967. *Iconography of the Art of Teotihuacan*. Studies in Pre-Columbian Art and Archaeology, number 4, Dumbarton Oaks, Washington, DC.

Langley, James C. 1986. *Symbolic Notation of Teotihuacan. Elements of Writing in a Mesoamerican Culture of the Classic Period*. BAR International Series no. 313, Oxford.

Langley, James C. 1992. Teotihuacan Sign Clusters: Emblem or Articulation? In *Art, Ideology, and the City of Teotihuacan*, edited by Janet C. Berlo, pp. 247–280. Dumbarton Oaks, Washington, DC.

Prem, Hanns J., and Berthold Riese. 1983. Autochthonous American Writing Systems: The Aztec and Maya Examples. In *Writing in Focus*, edited by Florian Coulmas and Konrad Ehlich, pp. 167–186. Mouton, Berlin.

Ringle, William M., Tomás Gallareta Negrón, and George J. Bey III. 1998. The Return of Quetzalcoatl: Evidence for the Spread of a World Religion during the Epiclassic Period. *Ancient Mesoamerica* 9:183–232.

Robertson, Donald. 1980. The Cacaxtla Murals. In *Fourth Palenque Round Table* (1979), edited by Merle Green Robertson, pp. 291–302. University of Texas Press, Austin.

Rodríguez Martínez, Ma. Del Carmen, Pociano Ortíz Ceballos, Michael D. Coe, Richard A. Diehl, Stephen D. Houston, Karl A. Taube, and Alfredo Delgado Calderón. 2006. Oldest Writing in the Old World. *Science* 313:1610–1614.

Ruppert, Karl. 1943. *The Mercado, Chichen Itza, Yucatan*. Carnegie Institution of Washington Publication 546, pp. 223–260, Washington, DC.

Sáenz, César, A. 1964. Las estelas de Xochicalco. *Actas y memorias del XXXV Congreso Internacional de Americanistas*, 1962, Mexico.

Séjourné, Laurette. 1959. *Un palacio en la ciudad de los dioses (Teotihuacán)*. Instituto Nacional de Antropología e Historia, Mexico.

Smith, Virginia. 2000a. The Iconography of Power at Xochicalco: The Pyramid of the Plumed Serpents. In *Archaeological Research at Xochicalco, Volume Two, The Xochicalco Mapping Project*, edited by Kenneth Hirth, pp. 57–82. The University of Utah Press, Salt Lake City.

Smith, Virginia. 2000b. The Art and Iconography of Xochicalco Stelae. In *Archaeological Research at Xochicalco, Volume Two, The Xochicalco Mapping Project*, edited by Kenneth Hirth, pp. 83–101. The University of Utah Press, Salt Lake City.

Stuart, David. 1991. Ruler Names in Zapotec Inscriptions. Paper presented at the roundtable "Art and Writing: Recording Knowledge in Pre-Columbian America," March 23–24, 1991, Dumbarton Oaks, Washington, DC.

Taube, Karl. 1992. The Iconography of Mirrors at Teotihuacan. In *Art, Ideology, and the City of Teotihuacan*, edited by Janet Catherine Berlo, pp. 169–204. Dumbarton Oaks Research Library and Collection, Washington, DC.

Taube, Karl. 1999. *The Writing System of Ancient Teotihuacan*. Ancient American Art and Writing, Washington, DC.

Taube, Karl. 2003. Tetitla and the Maya Presence at Teotihuacan. In *The Maya and Teotihuacan: Reinterpreting Early Classic Interaction*, edited by Geoffrey E. Braswell, pp. 273–314. University of Texas Press, Austin.

Urcid, Javier. 2001. *Zapotec Hieroglyphic Writing*. Studies in Pre-Columbian Art and Archaeology, no. 34, Dumbarton Oaks, Washington, DC.

Urcid, Javier. 2005. *Zapotec Writing: Knowledge, Power, and Memory in Ancient Oaxaca*. Foundation for the Advancement of Mesoamerican Studies. Electronic document, http://www.famsi.org/zapotecwriting/ (accessed May 16, 2005).

Urcid, Javier. 2007. A Stela of Unknown Provenience Inscribed in the Central Mexican Scribal Tradition. *Mexicon* XXIX(5):117–123.

Urcid, Javier. 2011. The Written Surface as a Cultural Code: A Comparative Perspective of Scribal Traditions from Southwestern Mesoamerica. In *Their Way of Writing: Scripts, Signs, and Notational Systems in Pre-Columbian America*, edited by Elizabeth Boone and Gary Urton, pp. 111–148. Dumbarton Oaks, Washington, DC.

Urcid, Javier, and Elbis Domínguez Covarrubias. 2012a. La casa de la tierra, la casa del cielo: los murales en el edificio A de Cacaxtla. In *La pintura mural prehispánica en México IV: Cacaxtla*, edited by Ma. Teresa Uriarte. Instituto de Investigaciones Estéticas, Universidad Nacional Autónoma de México, Mexico, D.F.

Urcid, Javier, and Elbis Domínguez Covarrubias. 2012b. El ascenso al poder del señor 4 perro: las pinturas murales del Conjunto 2-sub en Cacaxtla. In *La pintura mural prehispánica en México IV: Cacaxtla*, edited by Ma. Teresa Uriarte. Instituto de Investigaciones Estéticas, Universidad Nacional Autónoma de México, Mexico, D.F.

von Winning, Hasso. 1987. *La iconografía de Teotihuacan. Los dioses y los signos*. 2 vols. Instituto de Investigaciones Estéticas, Universidad Nacional Autónoma de México, Mexico, D.F.

CHAPTER 66

....

NAHUA AND MIXTEC PICTORIAL BOOKS

RELIGION AND HISTORY THROUGH VISUAL TEXT

....

LORI BOORNAZIAN DIEL

DURING the Late Postclassic period, Nahuas and Mixtecs kept pictorial books for multiple functions, with the two main genres being religion and history.[1] The Spaniards must have understood the significance of these books for the native peoples because they had specifically targeted the royal archives and temples, burning the books that were housed inside. So successful were they that few pre-conquest manuscripts from western Mesoamerica survive. Those that do, along with many others that were created after the conquest, provide a wealth of information on indigenous religion and history, and they do so by using a pictorial system of writing, whose main strength, I would argue, was its interpretive openness.

1. For comparative analyses of the pictorial books, see Robertson (1994), Boone (1994, 2000, 2007), and Marcus (1992).

THE CORPUS

....

The corpus of major pre-conquest codices includes five divinatory books that contain a series of religious almanacs and protocols and are collectively known as the Borgia Group (Codices Borgia, Cospi, Vaticanus B, Fejérváry-Mayer, and Laud).[2] Though their exact provenience is still debated, these writings are stylistically similar to works from the Mixtec region and the Puebla-Tlaxcala Valley and are accordingly described as "Mixteca-Puebla" (Nicholson 1982). Nevertheless, information is recorded in these Nahua codices in a pictorial system of writing that would have been understood throughout central Mexico, including the Aztec domain, which shared the religious ideology and divinatory system recorded in these books. In fact, two post-conquest divinatory manuscripts from the Aztec imperial core—the Codex Borbonicus and Tonalamatl Aubin—share some similarities to the Borgia Group works, though they have a different general focus. Hence, there was clearly a shared religious ideology and pictorial script throughout central Mexico, but the content and focus of the books varied based on local traditions and concerns (Jansen 1988: 102; Boone 2007: 230).

Four pre-conquest Mixtec books are also known (Codices Bodley, Colombino-Becker, Zouche-Nuttall, and Vienna) and these record information in a pictorial system of writing similar to that seen in the divinatories.[3] A number of other Mixtec documents were also painted after the conquest and in the native style, with the most extensive one being the Codex Selden. The Mixtec codices are historical genealogies presented chronologically, though key events and individuals take precedence over time; hence, they are often described as "event-oriented" histories (Boone 2000: 10; Williams 2009: 40). Mixtec books focus largely on local ruling lineages, beginning with ancestral origins and community foundations and then following key rulers and their military victories and diplomatic and marital alliances, before moving on to the alliances and exploits of their descendants.

By contrast, all known Aztec pictorial histories were created after the conquest, though many of these were painted in the native style and based on pre-conquest traditions. The histories could take various formats, but cartographic histories and time-based annals were most common, with the choice of format for the most part linked to content.[4] Thus, cartography was most useful for migration accounts

2. For overviews of the divinatory codices, see Boone (2007) and Nowotny (2005).

3. For key works on the Mixtec books, see Smith (1973), Troike (1982), Jansen (1988, 1992), King (1990, 1994), Jansen and Pérez Jiménez (2011), Monaghan (1990), Byland and Pohl (1994), and Williams (2009).

4. The major annals-formatted histories from the Aztec imperial core are the Codices Aubin, Azcatitlan, Boturini, Mendoza, Mexicanus, and Telleriano-Remensis. The Tira de Tepechpan and Codices Azoyu, en Cruz, Huichiapan, and Xicotepec are also annals-based and come from more provincial communities within the empire. The Mapa Sigüneza, with its focus on the Mexica migration, is fittingly cartographic, as are works from Texcoco, such as the Mapas Quinatzin and Tlotzin and the Codex Xolotl. The

because of the emphasis on place, while the annals format, with its emphasis on time, was preferred for imperial historical accounts (Boone 1994). In fact, Elizabeth Boone (1996) has argued that the annals format itself was a diagnostic trait of Aztec imperial control. By aligning their history with the calendar, Aztec rulers, as the major patrons of the histories, emphasized a link between the Aztec state and the progression of time, providing their history with a sense of divine providence.

THE BOOKS

The native books are often called codices, but these were not the inflexible bound books typical of Europe. Instead, Mesoamerican books were made of long sheets of paper—of deer hide or bark or maguey fiber—that were coated with gesso and then painted and folded accordion-style. A bound book can only reveal two pages at any one time, whereas a screenfold document can display any or all pages at once. Moreover, one can fold the leaves so as to make comparisons between non-sequential imagery or to omit information not deemed necessary in a particular reading. The screenfold format, then, allows for maximum flexibility in use and enhances the interpretive potential of the manuscripts.

The pictorial system of writing in which the bulk of information was recorded visually used standardized iconography and pictorial conventions.[5] Specific information, such as the names of people and places, was conveyed through hieroglyphic compounds that made use of logograms that worked as either signs or syllables and effectively "spelled" a word with little ambiguity. Because this script functioned as a visual communication system, the viewer's ease of understanding an image was paramount. Thus, native artists preferred conceptual representations that strived for clarity, depicting the human body in twisted perspective with black outlines defining forms and framing areas of color and making no attempt to show depth through modeling, shading, or the illusion of space (Robertson 1994: 15–23). By blurring the boundaries between art and text, and painting and writing, this pictorial system essentially was a visual text.

The Codex Mendoza, painted in the Aztec capital ca. 1541, exemplifies this writing system (Figure 66.1). A column of signs at the left represents time. In the Aztec (and Mixtec) calendar, years were designated by one of four signs—Rabbit, Reed,

Historia Tolteca-Chichimeca from Cuauhtinchan contains both annals and cartographic histories. Many of these books have been explicated; for some of the more recent studies, see Boone (1996, 2000), Castañeda de la Paz (2006), Diel (2008), Douglas (2010), Leibsohn (2009), Navarette (2004), and Quiñones Keber (1995).

5. For studies of the Aztec and Mixtec systems of writing, see Caso (1965), Dibble (1971), Nicholson (1973), Smith (1973), Galarza (1979), Prem (1992), Lacadena (2008), and Whitaker (2009).

Flint, and House—that cycled through coefficients from 1 to 13. Thus, the first year in the calendar was 1 Rabbit, followed by 2 Reed, 3 Flint, 4 House, 5 Rabbit…13 Rabbit, then 1 Reed, and so on. After cycling through fifty-two years, the count began anew. Here, the first year is written with one dot and a simplified flint knife, for 1 Flint, and the last year is 13 Flint. A man is pictured to the right, and his standardized iconography marks him as a ruler. A speech scroll issues from his mouth, conveying his role as *tlatoani*, or speaker, the official term for an Aztec ruler. Moreover, he wears a turquoise diadem and sits on a woven reed mat, more signs of rulership in the Aztec pictorial system. A hieroglyphic compound of an obsidian-encrusted serpent identifies the figure specifically as Itzcoatl (Obsidian Serpent), and he faces a shield

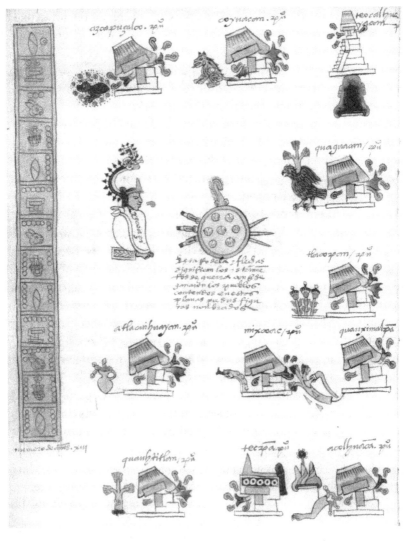

Figure 66.1 Codex Mendoza, folio 5r. Courtesy of the Bodleian Libraries, University of Oxford.

over three spears and a series of temples with smoking, overturned summits. These icons communicate warfare and conquest, and each of the temples is marked with a hieroglyphic compound that phonetically names the place conquered.

In the Mixtec codices, information is conveyed in a similar manner but with slight cultural and linguistic variation. In an excerpt from the Codex Zouche-Nuttall, the year 11 House is shown at bottom right (Figure 66.2). An "A-O" sign is superimposed on the date; this is a Mixtec convention that distinguishes the date as a year rather than a day. A red guideline to the left (another typical device in Mixtec pictorials) directs the reader upward to a place-name glyph for Hua Chino, rendered as a conventionalized hill sign with a red-and-white bundle inside. It is pierced by an arrow, a Mixtec convention for conquest that likely reflects the Mixtec language, whose word for "conquer" (*chihi nduvua ñuhu ñaha*) literally means "to put an arrow into the lands of another person" (Smith 1973: 33). Above is a battle scene, with one man grabbing another by the hair. The Mixtecs named people by the day on which they were born; hence, the "8 Deer" sign linked to the conquering warrior's head identifies him as the famous Mixtec culture hero, 8 Deer, who appears in most Mixtec codices. More information is conveyed through the elaborate clothing and poses of the figures, and a knowledgeable interpreter could certainly provide an embellished account if so desired.

The readings of religious codices are slightly different because these function on a more symbolic rather than narrative level. Focusing largely on the 260-day

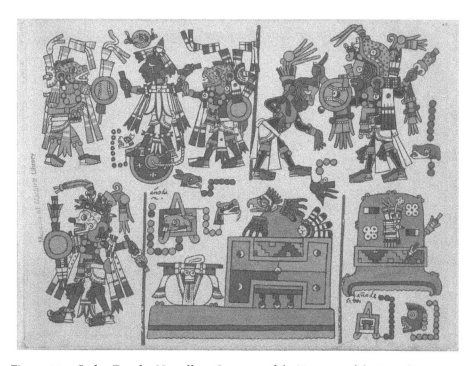

Figure 66.2 Codex Zouche-Nuttall 83. Courtesy of the Trustees of the British Museum, London.

sacred calendar (of twenty day names cycling through coefficients from 1 to 13), the divinatory books provide information about the days and associated ritual actions. In a page from the Codex Borgia, twenty day signs frame an image of back-to-back gods, whose accoutrements associate them, respectively, with life and death (Figure 66.3). The calendar sequence begins at the lower right corner with 1 Alligator, then, reading to the left, twelve dots indicate twelve more days, at which time we reach 1 Jaguar, then continuing back to the right we count ahead an additional twelve days and arrive at 1 Deer, and so on, through the entire 260-day ritual calendar. Thus, an interpreter of this page would use it in consultation with other almanacs to provide a reading for particular days and their supernatural associations.

READING THE BOOKS

The Aztec language distinguishes the painters of books (the *tlacuiloque*, who were seen more as craftsmen) from their readers (the *tlamatinime*, who were considered wise men) (Sahagún 1959–1982: 10:28–29), which suggests that the pictorial books were not silently read but were given voice by knowledgeable interpreters. In fact,

Figure 66.3 Codex Borgia 56. Courtesy of the Biblioteca Apostolica Vaticana.

the Mixtec word for book, *tacu*, also means "to hear" or "to listen," which implies a public context for the reading of books (King 1994: 105). Hung on palace or temple walls, the codices, then, likely functioned on one level as scripts or guides for performances that would have used a number of sensory devices—song, music, dance, costumes—to bring the recorded stories and rituals to life and to elevate them to a sacred level. The performances would have been facilitated through the composition of the manuscripts; as John Monaghan (1990: 134) has pointed out, the images in the Mixtec books are large enough to be easily read and the screenfold format allows for the reader to have an entire scene before him. Because Aztec and Mixtec histories were political rhetoric, such public performances would have been necessary to communicate the interests of the ruling class to the people (King 1994: 102–103). Furthermore, it seems that the strength of the arguments related in the histories was tied to a poetic rationale, which accordingly suggested sanctification. For the Mixtecs, the placement of the figures on the manuscript pages reflected the verbal arts of poetry (Monaghan 1990; King 1994), while Aztec histories were highly ordered and given divine legitimacy through links to the calendar (Umberger 1981). The implication is that the more elegant one's history is, the stronger its political argument will be.

Though surely brought to life through performance, it is unlikely that the codices were simple mnemonic devices, merely inspiring oral recitations already memorized. Pictorial writings were clearly capable of phonetic, unambiguous texts when and where precision was necessitated, which suggests that the texts were not simply memorized. Indeed, the important conquests of Itzcoatl's reign were recorded in the Codex Mendoza in an unambiguous manner, as was 8 Deer's conquest in the Codex Zouche-Nuttall, and one need not already know Aztec or Mixtec history to have a basic understanding of the content of these pages. Because pictorial writing is not language-dependent, these texts could also be understood and interpreted in their multiethnic and multilingual context. To see the books as simple mnemonic devices for singular oral performances, then, ignores their phonetic potential and also their interpretive strength; these manuscripts do not just call to mind a past event already memorized, but they guide the telling of that event and in so doing allow for elaboration and interpretation.

Indeed, recording a unique message was likely not the intention behind the historical or divinatory manuscripts. For the histories, which acted more as political arguments than objective records of the past, their brevity and lack of specificity allowed for varied readings based on political objectives and audience. As Federico Navarette (2004) has pointed out, the indeterminacy inherent in pictorial writing likely appealed to native scribes. Through ambiguity, interpretations were left open and fluid, allowing an interpreter to provide varied readings suitable for different audiences and political circumstances, a useful tool considering the shifting alliances that marked the Aztec and Mixtec domains. The pictorial form of these histories, then, fulfilled their political intentions. The same openness of interpretation was the intent of the divinatory manuscripts as well, but, here, the ambiguity would have enhanced the esoteric knowledge of the priests tasked with interpretation. Elizabeth Boone (2007: 32) has described divination as a dialogue, a "complex performance in which the patron, the diviner, and the codical *tonalamatl* all interacted." Thus, for indigenous scribes and wise men, the pictorial nature of their books was advantageous, privileging ambiguity and multiple meanings over univocal readings.

When considering the painted books as a whole, their multiplicity is striking, with many histories and religious books containing redundancies and contradictions. For example, the people of one town, Cuauhtinchan, kept multiple histories of the community that sometimes repeat each other and other times contradict each other (Leibsohn 1994). Camilla Townsend (2009) has made sense of this problem by showing that when native peoples needed to get at a historical truth, they consulted multiple histories in a cellular manner, essentially building their cases out of their interpretations of the painted books. Though this happened in a Spanish legal context, the books themselves and their interpretations were surely based on pre-conquest traditions. The same was likely true of the Mixtec histories, with multiple books needing to be consulted to get their larger messages (Byland and Pohl 1994: 8). The same was also true for priests working with the religious manuscripts; they, too, would have consulted numerous books and almanacs to arrive at a particular reading for a particular circumstance (Boone 2007: 32).

Ultimately, the screenfold format of the books and the pictorial nature of the writing system were ideally suited to the religious and historical traditions that they recorded because these traditions were not fixed or standardized. Instead, they were flexible and amenable to modification and interpretation, which was permitted and enhanced by a pictorial writing system. Though such writing systems are often considered limited or partial scripts because their exact meanings may be ambiguous, Nahua and Mixtec scribes and interpreters likely saw ambiguity as an advantage of their system. This would have been especially true of the religious and historical books, in which the elegance and openness of this visual communication system suggests an underlying poetic rationale that legitimized the information recorded and elevated it to a higher, sacred status. Though the books themselves were repositories for information, they necessitate an active reader (both in the past and present) to bring forth and build the interpretation most fitting for the time and place.

REFERENCES

Boone, Elizabeth Hill. 1994. Aztec Pictorial Histories: Records without Words. In *Writing without Words: Alternative Literacies in Mesoamerica and the Andes*, edited by Elizabeth Hill Boone and Walter D. Mignolo, pp. 50–76. Duke University Press, Durham, North Carolina.

Boone, Elizabeth Hill. 1996. Manuscript Painting in the Service of Imperial Ideology. In *Aztec Imperial Strategies*, edited by Frances F. Berdan, Richard E. Blanton, Elizabeth

Hill Boone, Mary G. Hodge, Michael E. Smith, and Emily Umberger, pp. 181–208. Dumbarton Oaks, Washington, DC.

Boone, Elizabeth Hill. 2000. *Stories in Red and Black: Pictorial Histories of the Aztecs and Mixtecs.* University of Texas Press, Austin.

Boone, Elizabeth Hill. 2007. *Cycles of Time and Meaning in the Mexican Book of Fates.* University of Texas Press, Austin.

Byland, Bruce E., and John M. D. Pohl. 1994. *In the Realm of 8 Deer: The Archaeology of the Mixtec Codices.* University of Oklahoma Press, Norman.

Caso, Alfonso. 1965. Mixtec Writing and Calendar. In *Handbook of Middle American Indians, Vol. 3, Archaeology of Southern Mesoamerica, Part 2,* edited by Gordon R. Willey, pp. 948–961. University of Texas Press, Austin.

Castañeda de la Paz, María. 2006. *Pintura de la peregrinación del los Culhuaque-Mexitin (el Mapa Sigüenza). Análisis de un documento de origen tenochca.* El Colegio Mexiquense and Instituto Nacional de Antropología e Historia, Mexico.

Dibble, Charles. 1971. Writing in Central Mexico. In *Handbook of Middle American Indians,* Vol. 10, edited by Gordon F. Ekholm and Ignacio Bernal, pp. 322–332. University of Texas Press, Austin.

Diel, Lori Boornazian. 2008. *The Tira de Tepechpan: Negotiating Place under Aztec and Spanish Rule.* University of Texas Press, Austin.

Douglas, Eduardo de J. 2010. *In the Palace of Nezahualcoyotl: Painting Manuscripts, Writing the Pre-Hispanic Past in Early Colonial Tetzcoco, Mexico.* University of Texas Press, Austin.

Galarza, Joaquin. 1979. *Estudios de escritura indígena tradicional (azteca-náhuatl).* Archivo General de la Nación, Mexico City.

Jansen, Maarten. 1988. The Art of Writing in Ancient Mexico: An Ethno-Iconological Perspective. *Visible Religion: Annual for Religious Iconography* 6:86–113.

Jansen, Maarten. 1992. Mixtec Pictography: Conventions and Contents. In *Supplement to the Handbook of Middle American Indians, Vol. 5, Epigraphy,* edited by Victoria Reifler Bricker, pp. 20–33. University of Texas Press, Austin.

Jansen, Maarten, and Gabina Aurora Pérez Jiménez. 2011. *The Mixtec Pictorial Manuscripts: Time, Agency and Memory in Ancient Mexico.* Brill, Leiden.

King, Mark. 1990. Rethinking Codices: Poetics and Metaphor in Mixtec Writing. *Ancient Mesoamerica* 1:141–151.

King, Mark. 1994. Hearing the Echoes of Verbal Art in Mixtec Writing. In *Writing without Words: Alternative Literacies in Mesoamerica and the Andes,* edited by Elizabeth Hill Boone and Walter D. Mignolo, pp. 102–136. Duke University Press, Durham, North Carolina.

Lacadena, Alfonso. 2008. Regional Scribal Traditions: Methodological Implications for the Decipherment of Nahuatl Writing. *PARI Journal* 8:1–21.

Leibsohn, Dana. 1994. Primers for Memory: Cartographic Histories and Nahua Identities. In *Writing without Words: Alternative Literacies in Mesoamerica and the Andes,* edited by Elizabeth Hill Boone and Walter D. Mignolo, pp. 161–187. Duke University Press, Durham, North Carolina.

Leibsohn, Dana. 2009. *Script and Glyph: Pre-Hispanic History, Colonial Bookmaking and the Historia Tolteca-Chichimeca.* Dumbarton Oaks Research Library, Washington, DC.

Marcus, Joyce. 1992. *Mesoamerican Writing Systems: Propaganda, Myth, and History in Four Ancient Civilizations.* Princeton University Press, Princeton, New Jersey.

Monaghan, John. 1990. Performance and the Structure of the Mixtec Codices. *Ancient Mesoamerica* 1:133–140.

Navarette, Federico. 2004. The Hidden Code of the Codex Azcatitlan. *Res* 45:145–160.

Nicholson, H. B. 1973. Phoneticism in the Late Pre-Hispanic Central Mexican Writing System. In *Mesoamerican Writing Systems*, edited by Elizabeth P. Benson, pp. 1–46. Dumbarton Oaks Research Library, Washington, DC.

Nicholson, H. B. 1982. The Mixteca-Puebla Concept Revisited. In *The Art and Iconography of Late Post-Classic Central Mexico*, edited by Elizabeth Hill Boone, pp. 227–254. Dumbarton Oaks, Washington, DC.

Nowotny, Karl Anton. 2005. *Tlacuilolli: Style and Contents of the Mexican Pictorial Manuscripts, with a Catalogue of the Borgia Group*, translated and edited by George A. Everett Jr. and Edward B. Sisson. University of Oklahoma Press, Norman.

Prem, Hanns J. 1992. Aztec Writing. In *Supplement to the Handbook of Middle American Indians, Vol. 5, Epigraphy*, edited by Victoria Reifler Bricker, pp. 53–69. University of Texas Press, Austin.

Quiñones Keber, Eloise. 1995. *The Codex Telleriano-Remensis: Ritual, Divination, and History in a Pictorial Aztec Manuscript*. University of Texas Press, Austin.

Robertson, Donald. 1994. *Mexican Manuscript Painting of the Early Colonial Period: The Metropolitan Schools*. Yale University Press, New Haven.

Sahagún, Bernardino de. 1959–1982. *Florentine Codex: General History of the Things of New Spain*, 13 vols., edited by Charles E. Dibble and Arthur J. O. Anderson. School of American Research, Santa Fe.

Smith, Mary Elizabeth. 1973. *Picture Writing from Ancient Southern Mexico*. University of Oklahoma Press, Norman.

Townsend, Camilla. 2009. Glimpsing Native American Historiography: The Cellular Principle in Sixteenth-Century Nahuatl Annals. *Ethnohistory* 56:625–650.

Troike, Nancy P. 1982. The Interpretation of Postures and Gestures in the Mixtec Codices. In *The Art and Iconography of Late Post-Classic Central Mexico*, edited by Elizabeth Hill Boone, pp. 175–206. Dumbarton Oaks, Washington, DC.

Umberger, Emily. 1981. The Structure of Aztec History. *Archaeoastronomy* 4:10–18.

Whitaker, Gordon. 2009. The Principles of Nahuatl Writing. *Göttinger Beiträge zur Sparchwissenschaft* 16:47–81.

Williams, Robert Lloyd. 2009. *Lord Eight Wind of Suchixtlan and the Heroes of Ancient Oaxaca: Reading History in the Codex Zouche-Nuttall*. University of Texas Press, Austin.

CHAPTER 67

COLONIAL DOCUMENTS

EDUARDO DE JESÚS DOUGLAS

AFTER 1521, the indigenous peoples of Mesoamerica became subjects of the Spanish king, thereby coming into contact with European cultural, economic, political, social, and technological practices. New forms of writing and record keeping as well as types of mundane and literary texts entered the Mesoamerican repertoire, eventually displacing the traditions of iconic script ("picture writing") inherited from the prehispanic past, which indigenous painter-scribes sustained and transformed throughout the first colonial century (Gruzinski 1993: 6–69; Leibsohn 2009; León-Portilla 1996; Lockhart 1992: 326–373). Once indigenous languages such as Nahuatl had been systematically transcribed into Roman alphabetic script, and when indigenous nobles and intellectuals had mastered not only the alphabet but also Spanish and Latin, linguistic and textual strategies then moved "beyond the codices," in the words of Arthur J. O. Anderson, Frances Berdan, and James Lockhart (Anderson, Berdan, and Lockhart 1976). New legal, political, and religious standards necessitated new forms of administration and supervision and generated new forms of archives, too.

Although all documents produced in Mesoamerica between 1521 and 1821 can be considered colonial documents, the origins, cultural and ethnic affiliations, and intentions of the authors and their perspectives and voices, and the documents' functions and social contexts, may be used to refine the category. Records and texts by and about indigenous Mesoamericans and their cultures and history, whether past or present, and perhaps those written specifically for them, might be qualified as indigenous, while records and texts by, about, or for the Spaniards, *criollos* (American-born people of European descent), and *castas* (mixed-race peoples) of New Spain could be labeled differently. Many works about Mesoamerican peoples, cultures, and history, especially those of the sixteenth and early seventeenth centuries, are fundamental to any study of Mesoamerica and its past, but they were written or compiled by Europeans, and arguably from a European perspective (Baudot 1995; Burrus 1975; Nicolau d'Olwer and Cline 1975; Warren 1975). At the same time, texts by indigenous authors were often written for and targeted to a Catholic or Spanish readership and to some degree accommodate the cultural biases and expectations of their intended audience. If the author, whether individual or corporate, is the determining factor, other problems arise. Is an author Mesoamerican by birth or by cultural affiliation, experience, and expression? Are Mesoamerican documents only those that communicate a message from an indigenous perspective, in an indigenous language and voice? What constitutes an indigenous perspective or voice in New Spain? What is the status of translated works? Which culture, perspective, or voice do they reflect? How do change, choice, and compulsion operate in a colonial situation and inflect authorial, linguistic, and textual identities or identifications? These are only the most basic questions, and none admits a simple or satisfactory answer. They do, however, alert one to the arbitrary nature of "colonial documents" and the need to specify what is intended by the term in any given context.

For the purposes of this chapter, colonial Mesoamerican documents will be understood as a subset of colonial New Spanish documents, namely those instances of graphic communication, whether mundane or purposely literary, or record keeping by, about, or for Mesoamerica's indigenous peoples that employ uniquely colonial forms of expression and address uniquely colonial practices or situations. Colonial forms of expression include native languages written in alphabetic script, texts written in or translated into or from Spanish or Latin, printed texts, and new archival and textual genres—for example, diaries, letters, and petitions to the Crown and its representatives; Inquisition and legal testimony; land litigation records, wills, and *cabildo* (municipal) records; and religious dramas, manuals, and tracts. While preconquest genres such as dynastic and noble genealogies, *altepetl* histories, poetry, religious songs, and tribute and census records could be and were translated into alphabetic script, in native and European languages, the new documentary genres satisfied specifically colonial concerns or needs. Even though iconic-script texts, especially "bilingual" codices such as the Codex Mendoza, can be said to be colonial in form and purpose, they are considered in a separate chapter (Diel, this volume) and treated as continuations and gradual adaptations of pre-conquest scripts and documentary genres (Boone 1998; Robertson 1994: 34–67). In contrast, pictorial documents created to satisfy royal, viceregal, or judicial queries or ends, for example, the maps and other illustrations produced for the 1579–1582 *Relaciones geográficas*, land litigation maps, and Techialoyan codices, often reflect change or difference more than continuation or adaptation (Acuña 1981–1988; Gruzinski 1987; Harvey 1986; Leibsohn 1995; Montes de Oca Vega 2003; Mundy 1996; Robertson 1975a, 1975b, 1994: 186–195; Russo 2005; Wood 1998a, 1998b). The criterion here is that although these works are pictorial, they are not always or necessarily iconic-script texts as such and can and often do function as illustrations to an alphabetic-script text either in a native language or Spanish.

Colonial Mesoamerican documents may be broadly but not categorically defined as private or public and nonofficial or official: a private document such as a will, for instance, has an official and public function, while a royal or vice-regal *cédula* (letter patent) or *provisión* (order) granted to an individual or a family affects private as well as public life. Official and public documents transact or record affairs in the purview of the state and its administrators, whether imperial, viceregal, regional, or municipal in origin and scope, and they address administrative, fiscal, judicial, legislative, political, and social matters. Although an official institution and an arm of the Crown subject to its authority because of the *patronato real*, the Church and its ministers are as much private as public agents, and ecclesiastical archives, ethnographic and linguistic studies, and reports to Crown or Church authorities are written by members of the clergy; religious texts, especially those composed in or translated into indigenous languages for ministering to indigenous congregations, negotiate both public and private spheres. Private and nonofficial documents and texts can be equally wide-ranging. Wills and inventories that concern personal and real property and their transfer require official execution and registration by notaries, and they are a matter of public record. Litigation undertaken by individuals over the disposition or ownership of property is likewise a matter of public record, which the state adjudicates through its laws and agents. Letters and petitions written by individuals can engage both private and public affairs, especially when they are addressed to and acted upon by the Crown and its representatives.

What one may call literature and literary texts is perhaps the most problematic of Mesoamerican colonial document types, as well as the best-known and most extensively published—for example, the *Cantares mexicanos*, the *Popol Vuh*, the *Relaciones de Juan Cano*, the *Leyenda de los soles*, the numerous Books of Chilam Balam, the Sahagún corpus, as well as the writings of Fernando de Alva Ixtlilxochitl, Gaspar Antonio Chi, Domingo Francisco de San Antón Muñón Chimalpahin Cuauhtlehuanitzin, Diego Muñoz Camargo, and Fernando Alvarado Tezozómoc. All forms of verbal and pictorial communication may be considered and treated as texts, of course, but the term "literature" implies, if not always a written form, then at least the author's awareness of a structure and style that differ from or exceed everyday speech and in so doing inflect the subject matter and affect the reader. Moreover, works of literature may not need to be rooted in and mimic, represent, or reflect lived experience. Whatever their relationship to life, literary texts are different from it, and they are different from documentation that explicitly and "objectively" administers, quantifies, or rationalizes it such as *cadastres*, censuses, deeds, fiscal ledgers, judicial testimony and transcripts, law codes, reports to ecclesiastical or state authorities, and wills, even though many of these are conceived in or ultimately take written form and can be and often are executed in polished prose. Stories, songs, sermons, prayers, poetry, philosophical essays, myths, letters, histories, dramas, and diaries are some but not all of the genres assumed by literary texts, and many of these pertain to numerous categories at the same time: private and public, official and nonofficial, ecclesiastical and secular, and so forth.

In all these cases, form and style are as important as, and in part shape or qualify, the content; and an author, reader, and critic are to varying degrees conscious of this symbiosis of the message and medium.

The scholarship on Mesoamerican literature is extensive, and new theoretical perspectives in the humanities and social sciences, new publications, new annotated editions of previously published texts, and more widespread interest in and accessibility to the study of indigenous languages enrich this corpus every year (Brotherston 1992; Garibay K. 1953–1954; León-Portilla 1992; Tedlock 2010). Because recent theoretical perspectives have brought into question binary oppositions such as Indian/non-Indian, Spanish-language texts written by indigenous or mestizo authors—and much of indigenous colonial experience—have been reclaimed from the interpretative limbo of "acculturation" and "deracination." At the same time, developments in social and cultural history have likewise shifted critical paradigms, which now engage bottom-up analyses sustained by archival research at the local level. The new approaches to colonial history and the consequent turn to archives and native languages have in effect created "Mesoamerican colonial documents" as a category and genus distinct from "Mesoamerican literature." In spite of the extent, importance, and artistic quality of Mesoamerica's literary traditions, and the wealth of the scholarship devoted to it, Mesoamerican colonial documents in the restricted sense here have made as great, if not greater, contributions to our understanding of New Spain's indigenous societies and cultures and their interactions with the colony's diverse peoples and fluid cultural traditions.

Study and publication of Mesoamerican colonial documents as opposed to literature began in the nineteenth century, as scholars combed archives, libraries, and private collections for primary sources relating to the history of Spanish America (Gibson 1975). The holdings of Spanish state archives such as the Archivo General de Indias (Seville) and the Archivo General de Simancas proved especially rich, as would the Archivo General de la Nación in Mexico City. Scholars collected, catalogued, and published documents, often in multivolume anthologies that made available, for instance, transcriptions of letters and petitions to the Crown and its agents penned by indigenous correspondents; royal *cédulas* and *provisiones* issued in response to such missives; viceregal reports to the Crown and the Council of the Indies; and demographic records and fiscal accounts (Archivo General de Indias 1928; Boban 1891; Compañia Ibero-Americana de Publicaciones 1927–1932; García Icazbalceta 1858–1866, 1941–1944; Paso y Troncoso 1905–1906, 1939–1942; Real Academia de la Historia 1864–1884, 1885–1932). Much of the material that concerns indigenous Mesoamerica hails from the sixteenth to early seventeenth centuries. Many of the documentary anthologies also included previously unpublished "literary" texts, manuscripts of which were "rediscovered" by the scholars who transcribed and edited state documents for publication.

The documents published in the nineteenth-century and early twentieth-century anthologies generally refer to matters transacted at the imperial or viceregal levels of administration. In the early to mid-twentieth century, historians began to study and publish documents from subregional, notarial, municipal, and parish archives in Spanish America, in addition to those from the Spanish state archives at Seville and Simancas (e.g., Actas de Cabildo de la Ciudad de México 1889–1916). A shift in historical focus from the imperial state and its larger administrative units—viceroyalties, captaincies, and *audiencias*—to its smaller political and social components—municipalities and ethnic groups—motivated the new research in national and, more important, in previously untapped local archives from indigenous communities, which were frequently penned in native languages. Scholars such as Charles Gibson, especially in his groundbreaking 1952 study (reissued in 1967), *Tlaxcala in the Sixteenth Century*, investigated and reconstructed the forms, processes, and personnel of indigenous self-government—to the extent that such was permitted and viable after 1521—in New Spain through contemporary records, primarily those generated by and for the purposes of municipal administration. In a later (1964) and equally influential study, *The Aztecs under Spanish Rule: A History of the Indians of the Valley of Mexico, 1519–1810*, Gibson mined, among other sources, the colonial section of the Archivo General de la Nación, the Mexican national archives, in order to tease out the broader economic, political, and social patterns of indigenous life in colonial central Mexico (that is, in the core region of western Mesoamerica). The documents preserved in the Archivo General de la Nación series denominated "Indios" and "Tierras" proved particularly fruitful for historical enquiry, and they continue to be catalogued and published (Carrera Stampa 1952; Chavez Orozco 1951–1953; Colín 1966, 1967; Méndez Martínez 1979a, 1979b; Reyes García and Gómez Z. 1979–1982; Spores and Saldaña 1975).

Two landmark publications, Donald Robertson's *Mexican Manuscript Painting of the Early Colonial Period: The Metropolitan Schools* (1994) and the four-part *Guide to Ethnohistorical Sources* edited by Howard F. Cline (1975, volumes 12–15 of the monumental *Handbook of Middle American Indians* [1964–1976], edited by Robert Wauchope) made colonial Mesoamerican documents more easily and widely accessible. Although both include and assess readily available primary and secondary sources—alphabetic and pictorial, manuscript and printed—such as the major prehispanic and early colonial iconic-script codices or the key sixteenth-century accounts of conquest and colonization, they also feature lesser-known, often previously unpublished, material by or about Mesoamerica's indigenous peoples. For example, in *Mexican Manuscript Painting* and in his contributions to the *Guide to Ethnohistorical Sources*, Robertson studied and catalogued the indigenous maps from the 1579–1582 *Relaciones geográficas* and the so-called Techialoyan manuscripts of the late seventeenth and eighteenth centuries. John B. Glass's "A Survey of Native Middle American Pictorial Manuscripts" in Part 3 of the *Guide to Ethnohistorical Sources* (volume 14 of the *Handbook*), in tandem with his and Charles Gibson's "A Census of Middle American Prose Manuscripts in the Native Historical Tradition" in Part 4 of the *Guide* (volume 15 of the *Handbook*), provided an annotated and authoritative listing of indigenous texts recorded or published up to that time.

The works of scholars such as Gibson, Robertson, and Glass, as well as other social historians, art historians, linguists, and anthropologists of the mid-twentieth century, demonstrated significant continuities as well as far-reaching changes in Mesoamerican cultures and societies from the prehispanic to the colonial periods and inspired further and more narrowly focused archival and linguistic research and publication. Scholars such as Nancy M. Farriss, James Lockhart, and John Chance and their students focused and continue to focus their investigations on local-level, indigenous-language archival sources, especially notarial and municipal records (e.g., Chance 1989; Cline 1986; Farriss 1984; Haskett 1991; Horn 1997; Kellogg 1995; Kellogg and Restall 1998; Lockhart 1991, 1992; Oudijk 2000; Pérez-Rocha 1982; Restall 1995, 1997; Schoeder 1991; Terraciano 2001; Whitecotton 1990; Wood 2003). The shift from documents about to documents generated by indigenous men and women themselves, in their own languages, to negotiate the economic, legal, political, religious, and social relations that ordered their lives revolutionized the study of colonial Mesoamerica and further challenged either/or interpretations of cultural change (Restall, Sousa, and Terraciano 2005). The painstaking analysis of the morphology and syntax of indigenous languages as written and spoken in the Colonial period, of the people's interactions with the Spanish, and of their patterns of change over time, exemplified by the work of Lockhart and collaborators such as Arthur J. O. Anderson, Frances Berdan, and Frances Karttunen on Nahuatl, engaged Mesoamerican history at its most fundamental level: the articulation of consciousness and experience in language (Anderson, Berdan, and Lockhart 1976; Karttunen and Lockhart 1987; Lockhart, Anderson, and Berdan 1986). The study of language as a system of meaning through the sustained investigation of and comparison of specific instances of signification, namely nonliterary native-language documents, facilitated an examination of Mesoamerican cultural forms—kinship, political structures, religious beliefs and practices, ethics, gender, and so forth.

Electronic and digital technologies have inspired new research possibilities. The Bibliothèque Nationale de France created electronic publications of alphabetic- and iconic-script Mesoamerican documents from its superb holdings. The Éditions sur Supports Informatique initiative (2011) in Paris has published dictionaries of indigenous languages, and the Wiki-Filología project, a revision of Glass's (1975) "A Survey of Native Middle American Pictorial Manuscripts," has made this material yet more accessible, at the same time updating the scholarship. Likewise, the Archivo General de Indias (http://www.mcu.es/archivos/MC/AGI/index.html) and the Archivo General de Simancas (http://www.mcu.es/archivos/MC/AGS/index.html) in Spain as well as the Archivo General de la Nación (http://www.agn.gob.mx/) have digitized their catalogues and scanned many of their documents, which are now accessible on-line. Thus, new technologies and new research paradigms have opened new views into indigenous life "beyond the codices."

References

Actas de Cabildo de la Ciudad de México. 1889–1916. *Actas de cabildo de la Ciudad de México*. 54 vols. Various publishers, Mexico City.

Acuña, René, ed. 1981–1988. *Relaciones geográficas del siglo XVI*. 10 vols. Universidad Nacional Autónoma de México, Instituto de Investigaciones Antropológicas, Mexico City.

Anderson, Arthur J. O., Frances Berdan, and James Lockhart, eds. and trans. 1976. *Beyond the Codices: The Nahua View of Colonial Mexico*. UCLA Latin American Studies 27, UCLA Latin American Center and University of California Press, Berkeley.

Archivo General de Indias. 2011. http://www.mcu.es/archivos/MC/AGI/index.html (accessed August 2, 2011).

Archivo General de Indias, Seville. 1928. *Indice de documentos de Nueva España existentes en el Archivo de Indias de Sevilla*. 4 vols. Monografías Bibliográficas Mexicanas 12, 14, 22–23, Imprenta de la Secretaría de Relaciones Exteriores, Mexico City.

Archivo General de Simancas. 2011. http://www.mcu.es/archivos/MC/AGS/index.html (accessed August 2, 2011).

Archivo General de la Nación, Mexico. 1979–1982. *Catálogo de ilustraciones*. 11 vols. Departamento de Publicaciones del Archivo General de la Nación, Mexico City.

Archivo General de la Nación, Mexico. 2011. http://www.agn.gob.mx/ (accessed August 2, 2011).

Baudot, George. 1995. *Utopia and History in Mexico: The First Chronicles of Mexican Civilization 1520–1569*. Translated by Bernard R. Ortiz de Montellano and Thelma Ortiz de Montellano. University Press of Colorado, Niwot.

Boban, Eugène. 1891. *Documents pour servir à l'histoire du Mexique: Catalogue raisonné de la collection de M. E.-Eugène Goupil (ancienne collection J.-M.-A. Aubin)*. 2 vols. and an atlas. Ernest Leroux, Paris.

Boone, Elizabeth Hill. 1998. Pictorial Documents and Visual Thinking in Postconquest Mexico. In *Native Traditions in the Postconquest World*, edited by Elizabeth Hill Boone and Tom Cummins, pp. 149–199. Dumbarton Oaks Research Library and Collection, Washington, DC.

Brotherston, Gordon. 1992. *Book of the Fourth World: Reading the Native Americas through Their Literature*. Cambridge University Press, Cambridge.

Burrus, Ernest J., S. J. 1975. Religious Chroniclers and Historians: A Summary with Annotated Bibliography. In *Guide to Ethnohistorical Sources*, Part 2, edited by Howard F. Cline, pp. 138–185. Handbook of Middle American Indians, vol. 13, Robert Wauchope, general editor, University of Texas Press, Austin.

Carrera Stampa, Manuel. 1952. *Archivalia mexicana*. Publicaciones del Instituto de Historia, 1st ser., 27, Instituto de Historia, Mexico City.

Chance, John K. 1989. *Conquest of the Sierra: Spaniards and Indians in Colonial Oaxaca*. University of Oklahoma Press, Norman.

Chavez Orozco, Luis, ed. 1951–1953. *Índice del ramo Indios, Archivo General de la Nación*. 2 vols. Instituto Indigenista Interamericano, Mexico City.

Cline, Howard F., ed. 1975. *Guide to Ethnohistorical Sources*, Parts 1–4. Handbook of Middle American Indians, vols. 12–15, Robert Wauchope, general editor, University of Texas Press, Austin.

Cline, Sarah L. 1986. *Colonial Culhuacan, 1580–1600: A Social History of an Aztec Town.* University of New Mexico Press, Albuquerque.

Colín, Mario, ed.1966. *Índice de documentos relativos a los pueblos del estado de México: Ramo de Tierras del Archivo General de la Nación.* Biblioteca Encyclopédica del Estado de México 7, Sociedad Mexicana de Geografía y Estadística, Mexico City.

Colín, Mario, ed. 1967. *Índice de documentos relativos a los pueblos del estado de México: Ramo de Mercedes del Archivo General de la Nación.* 2 vols. Biblioteca Encyclopédica del Estado de México 8–9, Estado de México, Mexico City.

Colín, Mario, ed. 1968. *Índice de documentos relativos a los pueblos del estado de México: Ramo de Indios del Archivo General de la Nación.* Biblioteca Encyclopédica del Estado de México 14, Sociedad Mexicana de Geografía y Estadística, Mexico City.

Compañía Ibero-Americana de Publicaciones. 1927–1932. *Colección de documentos inéditos para la historia de Ibero-América.* 14 vols. Compañía Ibero-Americana de Publicaciones, Madrid.

Éditions sur Supports Informatique. 2011. http://www.sup-infor.com/ (accessed August 2, 2011).

Farriss, Nancy M. 1984. *Maya Society under Colonial Rule: The Collective Enterprise of Survival.* Princeton University Press, Princeton, New Jersey.

García Icazbalceta, Joaquín, ed. 1858–1866. *Colección de documentos para la historia de México.* 2 vols. Librería de J. M. Andrade, Mexico City.

García Icazbalceta, Joaquín, ed. 1941–1944. *Nueva colección de documentos para la historia de México.* 3 vols. Editorial Chávez Hayhoe, Mexico City. [Originally published 1886–1892, 5 vols., Díaz de León, Mexico City]

Garibay K., Ángel María. 1953–1954. *Historia de la literatura náhuatl.* 2 vols. Editorial Porrúa, Mexico City.

Gibson, Charles. 1964. *The Aztecs under Spanish Rule: A History of the Indians of the Valley of Mexico, 1519–1810.* Stanford University Press, Stanford.

Gibson, Charles. 1967. *Tlaxcala in the Sixteenth Century.* Stanford University Press, Stanford.

Gibson, Charles. 1975. Published Collections of Documents Relating to Middle American Ethnohistory. In *Guide to Ethnohistorical Sources*, Part 2, edited by Howard F. Cline, pp. 3–41. Handbook of Middle American Indians, vol. 13, Robert Wauchope, general editor, University of Texas Press, Austin.

Gibson, Charles, and John B. Glass. 1975. A Census of Middle American Prose Manuscripts in the Native Historical Tradition. In *Guide to Ethnohistorical Sources*, Part 3, edited by Howard F. Cline, pp. 322–400. Handbook of Middle American Indians, vol. 14, Robert Wauchope, general editor, University of Texas Press, Austin.

Glass, John B. 1975. A Survey of Native Middle American Pictorial Manuscripts. In *Guide to Ethnohistorical Sources*, Part 3, edited by Howard F. Cline, pp. 3–80. Handbook of Middle American Indians, vol. 14, Robert Wauchope, general editor, University of Texas Press, Austin.

Gruzinski, Serge. 1987. Colonial Indian Maps in Sixteenth-Century Mexico: An Essay in Mixed Cartography. *Res* 13:46–61.

Gruzinski, Serge. 1993. *The Conquest of Mexico: The Incorporation of Indian Societies into the Western World, 16th–18th Centuries.* Translated by Eileen Corrigan. Polity Press, Cambridge, England.

Harvey, Herbert R. 1986. Techialoyan Codices: Seventeenth-Century Indian Land Titles in Central Mexico. In *Ethnohistory, Supplement to the Handbook of Middle American Indians*, vol. 4, edited by Ronald Spores, pp. 153–164. University of Texas Press, Austin.

Haskett, Robert. 1991. *Indigenous Rulers: An Ethnohistory of Town Government in Colonial Cuernavaca.* University of New Mexico Press, Albuquerque.

Horn, Rebecca. 1997. *Postconquest Coyoacan: Nahua-Spanish Relations in Central Mexico, 1519–1650.* Stanford University Press, Stanford.

Karttunen, Frances, and James Lockhart, eds. 1987. *The Art of Nahuatl Speech: The Bancroft Dialogues.* UCLA Latin American Studies 65, UCLA Latin American Center Publications, University of California, Los Angeles.

Kellogg, Susan. 1995. *Law and the Transformation of Aztec Culture, 1500–1700.* University of Oklahoma Press, Norman.

Kellogg, Susan, and Matthew Restall, eds. 1998. *Dead Giveaways: Indigenous Testaments of Colonial Mesoamerica and the Andes.* University of Utah Press, Salt Lake City.

Leibsohn, Dana. 1995. Colony and Cartography: Shifting Signs on Indigenous Maps of New Spain. In *Reframing the Renaissance: Visual Culture in Europe and Latin America, 1450–1650,* edited by Claire Farago, pp. 265–281. Yale University Press, New Haven.

Leibsohn, Dana. 2009. *Script and Glyph: Pre-Hispanic History, Colonial Bookmaking and the Historia Tolteca-Chichimeca.* Studies in Pre-Columbian Art and Archaeology 36, Dumbarton Oaks Research Library and Collection, Washington DC.

León-Portilla, Miguel. 1992. *Literaturas indígenas de México.* Editorial MAPFRE, Madrid.

León-Portilla, Miguel. 1996. *El destino de la palabra: De la oralidad y los glifos mesoamericanos a la escritura alfabética.* El Colegio Nacional and Fondo de Cultura Económica, Mexico City.

Lockhart, James. 1991. *Nahuas and Spaniards: Postconquest Central Mexican History and Philology.* UCLA Latin American Studies 76, Stanford University Press, Stanford.

Lockhart, James. 1992. *The Nahuas after the Conquest: A Social and Cultural History of the Indians of Central Mexico, Sixteenth through Eighteenth Centuries.* Stanford University Press, Stanford.

Lockhart, James, Arthur J. O. Anderson, and Frances Berdan, eds. and trans. 1986. *The Tlaxcalan Actas: A Compendium of the Records of the Cabildo of Tlaxcala, 1545–1627.* University of Utah Press, Salt Lake City.

Méndez Martínez, Enrique, ed. 1979a. *Índice de documentos relativos a los pueblos del Estado de Oaxaca: Ramo Tierras del Archivo General de la Nación.* Instituto Nacional de Antropología e Historia, Mexico City.

Méndez Martínez, Enrique, ed. 1979b. *Índice de documentos relativos a los pueblos del Estado de Puebla: Ramo Tierras del Archivo General de la Nación.* Instituto Nacional de Antropología e Historia, Mexico City.

Montes de Oca Vega, Mercedes, ed. 2003. *Cartografía de tradición hispanoindígena: Mapas de mercedes de tierra siglos xvi y xvii.* Universidad Nacional Autónoma de México, Instituto de Investigaciones Históricas, and Archivo General de la Nación, Mexico City.

Mundy, Barbara E. 1996. *The Mapping of New Spain: Indigenous Cartography and the Maps of the Relaciones Geográficas.* University of Chicago Press, Chicago.

Nicolau d'Olwer, Luis, and Howard F. Cline. 1975. Sahagún and His Works. In *Guide to Ethnohistorical Sources,* Part 2, edited by Howard F. Cline, pp. 186–206. Handbook of Middle American Indians, vol. 13, Robert Wauchope, general editor, University of Texas Press, Austin.

Oudijk, Michel. 2000. *Historiography of the Bènizàa: The Postclassic and Colonial Periods (1000–1600 ad).* CNWS Publications, Leiden University, Leiden.

Oudijk, Michel, and María Castañeda de la Paz. 2011. Wiki-Filología, http://132.248.101.214/wikfil/index.php/Portada (accessed August 2, 2011).

Paso y Troncoso, Francisco del, ed. 1905–1906. *Papeles de Nueva España publicados de orden y con fondos del gobierno mexicano por Francisco del Paso y Troncoso.* 2nd series, Geografía y Estadística, 7 vols., Sucesores de Rivadeneyra, Madrid.

Paso y Troncoso, Francisco del, ed. 1939–1942. *Epistolario de Nueva España, 1505–1818.* Biblioteca Histórica Mexicana de Obras Ineditas, 2nd series, 16 vols., Antigua Librería Robredo, de José Porrúa e Hijos, Mexico City.

Pérez-Rocha, Emma. 1982. *La tierra y el hombre en la villa de Tacuba durante la época colonial.* Instituto Nacional de Antropología e Historia, Mexico City.

Real Academia de la Historia. 1864–1884. *Colección de documentos inéditos relativos al descubrimiento, conquista y organización de las antiguas posesiones españolas de América y Oceanía, sacados de los archivos del reino, y muy especialmente del de Indias.* 42 vols. Imprenta de M. Bernaldo de Quirós, Madrid.

Real Academia de la Historia. 1885–1932. *Colección de documentos inéditos relativos al descubrimiento, conquista y organización de las antiguas posesiones españolas de ultramar.* 25 vols. Sucesores de Rivadeneyra, Madrid.

Restall, Matthew. 1995. *Life and Death in a Maya Community: The Ixil Testaments of the 1760s.* Labyrinthos, Lancaster, California.

Restall, Matthew. 1997. *The Maya World: Yucatec Culture and Society, 1550–1850.* Stanford University Press, Stanford.

Restall, Matthew, Lisa Sousa, and Kevin Terraciano, eds. 2005. *Mesoamerican Voices: Native-Language Writings from Colonial Mexico, Oaxaca, Yucatan and Guatemala.* Cambridge University Press, New York.

Robertson, Donald. 1975a. The Pinturas (Maps) of the Relaciones Geográficas, with a Catalog. In *Guide to Ethnohistorical Sources,* Part 1, edited by Howard F. Cline, pp. 243–278. Handbook of Middle American Indians, vol. 12, Robert Wauchope, general editor, University of Texas Press, Austin.

Robertson, Donald. 1975b. Techialoyan Manuscripts and Paintings, with a Catalog. In *Guide to Ethnohistorical Sources,* Part 3, edited by Howard F. Cline, pp. 253–280. Handbook of Middle American Indians, vol. 14, Robert Wauchope, general editor, University of Texas Press, Austin.

Robertson, Donald. 1994. *Mexican Manuscript Painting of the Early Colonial Period: The Metropolitan Schools.* University of Oklahoma Press, Norman.

Russo, Alessandra. 2005. *El realismo circular: Tierras, espacios y paisajes de la cartografía indígena novohispana siglos xvi y xvii.* Universidad Nacional Autónoma de México, Instituto de Investigaciones Estéticas, Mexico City.

Schroeder, Susan. 1991. *Chimalpahin and the Kingdoms of Chalco.* University of Arizona Press, Tucson.

Secretaría de Relaciones Exteriores and Archivo General y Público de la Nación. 1910. *Proceso inquisitorial del cacique de Tetzcoco.* Publicaciones de la Comisión Reorganizadora del Archivo General y Público de la Nación 1, Secretaría de Relaciones Exteriores and Archivo General y Público de la Nación, Mexico City.

Secretaría de Relaciones Exteriores and Archivo General y Público de la Nación. 1912. *Procesos de indios idolatras y hechiceros.* Publicaciones del Archivo General de la Nación 3, Secretaría de Relaciones Exteriores and Archivo General de la Nación, Mexico City.

Spores, Ronald, and Miguel Saldaña, eds. 1975. *Documentos para la etnohistoria del Estado de Oaxaca: índice del ramo de indios del Archivo General de la Nación,*

México. Vanderbilt University Publications in Anthropology 13, Department of Anthropology, Vanderbilt University, Nashville.

Tedlock, Dennis. 2010. *2000 Years of Mayan Literature.* University of California Press, Berkeley.

Terraciano, Kevin. 2001. *The Mixtecs of Colonial Oaxaca: Ñudzahui History, Sixteenth through Eighteenth Centuries.* Stanford University Press, Stanford.

Warren, J. Benedict. 1975. An Introductory Survey of Secular Writings in the European Tradition on Colonial Middle America, 1503–1818. In *Guide to Ethnohistorical Sources,* Part 2, edited by Howard F. Cline, pp. 42–137. Handbook of Middle American Indians, vol. 13, Robert Wauchope, general editor, University of Texas Press, Austin.

Wauchope, Robert, general ed. 1964–1975. *Handbook of Middle Americans.* 15 vols. University of Texas Press, Austin.

Whitecotton, Joseph W. 1990. *Zapotec Elite Ethnohistory: Pictorial Genealogies from Eastern Oaxaca.* Vanderbilt University Publications in Anthropology 39, Department of Anthropology, Vanderbilt University, Nashville.

Wood, Stephanie. 1998a. The Social vs. Legal Context of Nahuatl *Títulos.* In *Native Traditions in the Postconquest World,* edited by Elizabeth Hill Boone and Tom Cummins, pp. 201–231. Dumbarton Oaks Research Library and Collection, Washington, DC.

Wood, Stephanie. 1998b. El problema de la historicidad de los *Títulos* y los codices *Techialoyan.* In *De tlacuilos y escribanos: Estudios sobre documentos indígenas colonials del centro de México,* edited by Xavier Noguez and Stephanie Wood, pp. 167–221. El Colegio de Michoacán and El Colegio Mexiquense, Zamora and Zinacantepec.

Wood, Stephanie. 2003. *Transcending Conquest: Nahua Views of Spanish Colonial Mexico.* University of Oklahoma Press, Norman.

FURTHER READING

Arellano Hoffmann, Carmen, Peer Schmidt, and Xavier Noguez, eds. 2002. *Libros y escritura de tradición indígena: Ensayos sobre los códices prehispánicos y coloniales de México.* El Colegio Mexiquense and Katolische Universität Eichstätt, Toluca.

Boone, Elizabeth Hill. 2000. *Stories in Red and Black: Pictorial Histories of the Aztecs and Mixtecs.* University of Texas Press, Austin.

Boone, Elizabeth Hill, and Tom Cummins, eds. 1998. *Native Traditions in the Postconquest World.* Dumbarton Oaks Research Library and Collection, Washington, DC.

Boone, Elizabeth Hill, and Walter D. Mignolo, eds. 1994. *Writing without Words: Alternative Literacies in Mesoamerica and the Andes.* Duke University Press, Durham, North Carolina.

Borah, Woodrow. 1983. *Justice by Insurance: The General Indian Court of Colonial Mexico and the Legal Aides of the Half-Real.* University of California Press, Berkeley.

Brotherston, Gordon. 1995. *Painted Books from Mexico: Codices in UK Collections and the World They Represent.* British Museum Press, London.

Burkhart, Louise M. 1989. *The Slippery Earth: Nahua-Christian Moral Dialogue in Sixteenth-Century Mexico.* University of Arizona Press, Tucson.

Burkhart, Louise M. 1996. *Holy Wednesday: A Nahua Drama from Early Colonial Mexico.* University of Pennsylvania Press, Philadelphia.

Burkhart, Louise M. 2001. *Before Guadalupe: The Virgin Mary in Early Colonial Nahuatl Literature.* Institute for Mesoamerican Studies Monograph 13, University at Albany, Albany.

Carrasco, Davíd, and Scott Sessions, eds. 2007. *Cave, City, and Eagle's Nest: An Interpretive Journey through the Mapa de Cuauhtinchan No. 2.* University of New Mexico Press, Albuquerque.

Caso, Alfonso. 1949. El mapa de Teozacoalco. *Cuadernos Americanos* 47(5):145–181.

Chance, John K. 1978. *Índice del archivo del Juzgado de Villa Alta, Oaxaca: Época colonial.* Vanderbilt University Publications in Anthropology 21, Department of Anthropology, Vanderbilt University, Nashville.

Florescano, Enrique. 1994. *Myth, Memory, and Time in Mexico: From the Aztecs to Independence.* Translated by Albert G. Bork and Kathryn R. Bork. University of Texas Press, Austin.

Herrera Huerta, Juan Manuel, and Victoria San Vicente Tello, eds. 1990. *Archivo General de la Nación, Mexico, Guía General.* Departamento de Publicaciones del Archivo General de la Nación, Mexico City.

Horcasitas, Fernando. 1974. *El teatro náhuatl: Épocas novohispana y moderna.* Universidad Nacional Autónoma de México, Instituto de Investigaciones Históricas, Mexico City.

Horcasitas, Fernando. 1978. Los descendientes de Nezahualpilli: Documentos del cacicazgo de Tetzcoco (1545–1855). *Estudios de historia novohispana* 6:145–185.

Leibsohn, Dana. 1994. Primers for Memory: Cartographic Histories and Nahua Identity. In *Writing without Words: Alternative Literacies in Mesoamerica and the Andes,* edited by Elizabeth Hill Boone and Walter D. Mignolo, pp. 161–187. Duke University Press, Durham, North Carolina.

León-Portilla, Ascensión H. de. 1988. *Tepuztlahcuilolli Impresos en Náhuatl.* 2 vols. Universidad Nacional Autónoma de México, Mexico City.

León-Portilla, Miguel. 2003. *Códices: Los antiguos libros del Nuevo Mundo.* Aguilar, Mexico City.

Lockhart, James. 1993. *We People Here: Nahuatl Accounts of the Conquest of Mexico.* Repertorium Columbianum, vol. 1, Geoffrey Simcox, general editor, University of California Press, Berkeley.

Münch, Guido. 1976. *El cacicazgo de San Juan Teotihuacan durante la colonia, 1521–1821.* Instituto Nacional de Antropología e Historia, Mexico City.

Nicholson, Henry B. 1971. Pre-Hispanic Central Mexican Historiography. In *Investigaciones contemporáneas sobre historia de México: Memorias de la tercera reunión de historiadores mexicanos y norteamericanos, Oaxtepec, Morelos, 4–7 de noviembre de 1969,* pp. 38–81. Universidad Nacional Autónoma de México, El Colegio de México, and the University of Texas at Austin, Mexico City.

Nicholson, Henry B. 1998. The Native Tradition Pictorials in the Aubin-Goupil Collection of Mesoamerican Ethnohistorical Documents in the Bibliothèque Nationale de France: Major Reproductions and Studies. *Journal de la Société des Américanistes* 84(2):35–50.

Noguez, Xavier, and Stephanie Wood, eds. 1998. *De tlacuilos y escribanos: Estudios sobre documentos indígenas colonials del centro de México.* El Colegio de Michoacán and El Colegio Mexiquense, Zamora and Zinacantepec.

Paz, Julián. 1933. *Catálogo de manuscritos de América existentes en la Biblioteca Nacional.* Tipografía de Archivos, Madrid.

Peñafiel, Antonio, ed. 1979. *Manuscritos de Texcoco*. Editorial Innovación, Mexico City. [Originally published 1903, Colección de Documentos para la Historia Mexicana 6, Oficina Tipográfica de la Secretaría de Fomento, Mexico City]

Pérez-Rocha, Emma. 1998. *Privilegios en lucha: La información de doña Isabel Moctezuma*. Instituto Nacional de Antropología e Historia, Mexico City.

Pérez-Rocha, Emma, and Rafael Tena, eds. 2000. *La nobleza indígena del centro de México después de la Conquista*. Instituto Nacional de Antropología e Historia, Mexico City.

Pohl, John M. D. 1994. Mexican Codices, Maps, and Lienzos as Social Contracts. In *Writing without Words: Alternative Literacies in Mesoamerica and the Andes*, edited by Elizabeth Hill Boone and Walter D. Mignolo, pp. 137–160. Duke University Press, Durham, North Carolina.

Radin, Paul. 1920. *The Sources and Authenticity of the History of the Ancient Mexicans*. University of California Publications in American Archaeology and Ethnology 17, no. 1, University of California Press, Berkeley.

Reyes García, Cayetano, ed. 1981. *Ramo Tributos*. 2 vols. Serie Guías y Catálogos 15, Departamento de Publicaciones del Archivo General de la Nación, Mexico City.

Reyes García, Cayetano, ed. 1982. *Documentos mexicanos: Cacchiqueles, mayas, matlatzincas, mixtecos y nahuas*. 2 vols. Serie Guías y Catálogos 72, Departamento de Publicaciones del Archivo General de la Nación, Mexico City.

Reyes García, Cayetano, and Magdalena Gómez Z., eds. 1978–1982. *Catálogo del Ramo de Indios*. 6 vols. Serie Guías y Catálogos 19, Departamento de Publicaciones del Archivo General de la Nación, Mexico City.

Reyes García, Luis, Eustaquio Celestino Solís, Armando Valencia Ríos, Constantino Medina Lima, and Gregorio Guerrero Díaz. 1996. *Documentos nauas de la Ciudad de México del siglo XVI*. Archivo General de la Nación and Centro de Investigaciones y Estudios Superiores en Antropología Social, Mexico City.

Solís, Eustaquio Celestino, Armando Valencia R, and Constantino Medina Lima, eds. and trans. 1985. *Actas de cabildo de Tlaxcala 1547–1567*. Códices y Manuscritos de Tlaxcala 3, Archivo General de la Nación, Instituto Tlaxcalteca de la Cultura, and Centro de Investigaciones y Estudios Superiores en Antropología Social, Mexico City.

Spores, Ronald. 1964. The Genealogy of Tlazultepec: A Sixteenth-Century Mixtec Manuscript. *Southwestern Journal of Anthropology* 20:15–31.

Tudela de la Orden, José. 1954. *Los manuscritos de América en las bibliotecas de España*. Ediciones Cultura Hispánica, Madrid.

Williams, Barbara J. 1984. Mexican Pictorial Cadastral Registers: An Analysis of the *Códice de Santa María Asunción* and the *Codex Vergara*. In *Explorations in Ethnohistory: Indians of Central Mexico in the Sixteenth Century*, edited by H. R. Harvey and Hanns J. Prem, pp. 103–125. University of New Mexico Press, Albuquerque.

PART V

THE SPANISH CONQUEST AND ARCHAEOLOGY OF THE COLONIAL AND REPUBLICAN PERIODS

CHAPTER 68

THE SPANISH CONQUEST AND THE ARCHAEOLOGY OF THE COLONIAL AND REPUBLICAN PERIODS

JOHN M. D. POHL

THE development of historical archaeology as a social science is a relatively recent phenomenon in Mesoamerica. Most published studies have been limited to purely descriptive reports of investigations of salvage projects or the architectural restoration and conservation of churches, the houses of prominent officials, and haciendas, for example (Gasco, Smith, and Fournier-Garcia 1997). However, a growing number of archaeologists and historians have begun to formulate research designs that move beyond artifact description and architectural restoration to address broader concerns with acculturation, ethnicity, and shifting patterns of socioeconomic stratification (Carmack and Weeks 1981; Charlton et al. 2009; Fernández Dávila and Gómez Serafín 1998; Fournier-Garcia and Mondragon 2003; Kepecs and Alexander 2005; Lister and Lister 2002, Meyers 2005; Meyers and Carlson 2002; Palka 2009; Rice and Rice 2003; Zeitlin 2005). Some of the most innovative multidisciplinary field research has focused on the Mexican highlands in particular.

Despite widespread devastation after the Spaniards arrived in the early sixteenth century, not all of Mexico was "conquered." Many kingdoms throughout the southern Mexican highlands engaged the new colonial order peacefully under the leadership of *caciques* (indigenous nobles). The evangelization of the Children of Quetzalcoatl, as they had been known, was given largely to the Franciscan and later to the Dominican orders that sent missionaries to all of the ranking noble houses from Tlaxcala to Oaxaca. Before long, factional disputes emerged over the administration of Indian lands between Spanish nobles called encomenderos, the church, and the caciques. Acting as mediators between the crown and the caciques who actually controlled the land, the holy orders eventually succeeded in forming more lucrative partnerships (Spores 1984; Terraciano 2001).

Southern Mexico became a land of opportunity. Traditional forms of production, marketing, trade, and the collection of tribute continued. The cultivation of maize, beans, and squash was supplemented with the introduction of European domesticated plants and animals, and the region became integrated into the Habsburg world economy. Textile production thrived as a regional specialization, especially with the introduction of wool and silk together with native cotton. Dyed with precious scarlet cochineal, the garments were unsurpassed in quality and workmanship. The caciques capitalized on the new economy by engaging in lucrative long-distance trading ventures, gaining monopolies over the transportation of international goods moving from Manila to Spain via overland routes through Mexico, first from the port of Huatulco, Oaxaca, and later Acapulco, Guerrero. Caciques dressed as Spaniards, rode horses, and acquired new titles to suit their elevated positions, such as Domingo de Guzmán, who took the name of the founder

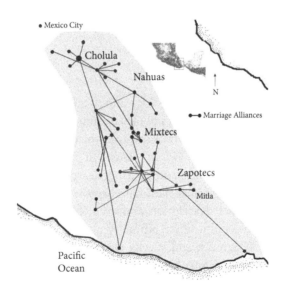

Figure 68.1 During the Postclassic and early Colonial periods, the southern Mexican highlands were dominated by a confederacy of kingdoms that extended from the modern state of Tlaxcala through Puebla to Pacific coastal Oaxaca. Alliances were formulated through strategic marriages that cross-cut ethnic differences maintained by fifteen different language groups of whom the eastern Nahaus, Mixtecs, and Zapotecs predominated (author's illustration).

of the Dominican order, while the cacique of Tilantongo became Felipe de Austría, one of the titles of the Holy Roman Emperor. They expanded their domains, built lavish palaces, dedicated churches, and yet were careful to preserve indigenous traditions, not the least of which was the continuing production of codices, maps, and *lienzos*, remarkable works of art that recorded royalty lists extending back to the ninth century, making them the longest continuous royal genealogies.

Research on the Postclassic and early Colonial periods in Mesoamerica over the past twenty years has forced us to reevaluate traditional evolutionary models (Figure 68.1). While there is basic agreement that the region experienced significant restructuring after the Classic period, the actual process of change remains poorly understood. For example, the Postclassic shift toward political decentralization has been traditionally equated with notions of "collapse" or "fall" but in fact we know that many social institutions actually became more complex. One problem has been the tendency by anthropologists to employ political centralization as a measure of state organization and by archaeologists to concentrate their research on sites that boasted large public buildings (Smith and Berdan 2003).

Rather than focusing on centralized systems, archaeologists have found that much of the Postclassic is better characterized by decentralized political structures and the emergence of new economic and political systems that served as primary integrative mechanisms for Mesoamerica. As the powerful Classic-period polities broke down in many regions after 800–900 AD, numerous small, petty states took their place. Archaeologists working in highland Guatemala with the kingdoms of the Quiché and Cakchiquel have even proposed the term "segmentary state" (Fox 1987; Braswell 2003a, 2003b). The composition of these polities was in a state of constant flux as alliances were forged, through marriage or conquest, only to dissolve and begin a new cycle of alliance and fragmentation. The geopolitical scene in Postclassic Mesoamerica was consequently dynamic and frequently bellicose. Despite factional tendencies, however, we also see Postclassic kingdoms and city-states being organized into flexible confederacies or leagues that created corridors of cultural and commercial exchanges, providing members with greater access to long-distance trade goods than ever before (Smith and Berdan 2003).

Confederacies have received little serious attention from archaeologists for many reasons. Confederacy implies social agendas that were shared between multiple political units of generally equal size and influence, a phenomenon that is difficult, if not impossible, to evaluate on any broad regional basis through archaeological study alone. Historical sources suggest that confederacies were more than a single response to a mutual threat such as the Aztec Empire of the Triple Alliance, but rather confederacies were institutional and rooted in shared religious, political, and economic institutions extending back over five hundred years. The question is how one would apply the different types of historical sources that might be regarded as simultaneously myth and history to the facts of the archaeological record.

The answer can be found in the application of inductive and deductive reasoning to the interdisciplinary study of peer polities (Pohl 2004: 217). Traditionally

archaeologists have examined material remains recovered in surveys and excavations and then used historical and ethnographic literature to produce plausible
interpretations. This presumes, however, that our knowledge of the past is only
as good as our present knowledge and, furthermore, the tendency is to apply only
those sources that best fit the data from a survey or excavation. The means for
avoiding this one-sided dependency is for archaeologists, art historians, ethnohistorians, and ethnographers to focus on problems that are of mutual interest
and to devise hypotheses in one field that can be tested with the approaches of
another field. Spatial relationships have been deemed particularly significant to
the study of cultural history in general. The way in which societies use space both
within a settlement and between settlements is directly related to their sociopolitical systems.

Surviving Late Postclassic and Colonial-period pictorial documents for which
highland Mexico is particularly well known reflect the concerns of the indigenous
elites with spatial relationships. Archaeologists have succeeded in applying these
resources to the study of highland confederacies in a number of innovative ways. The
Mixtec codices, for example, depict more than twenty-five generations of the ranking
families that dominated the Mixteca Alta between the ninth and sixteenth centuries.
While analyzing the complex kinship systems documented in the Codex Bodley, a
colonial manuscript probably associated with a late sixteenth-century inheritance
dispute, Alfonso Caso was the first to detect a pattern of geographical site shifting
(Caso 1960). The narrative of Tilantongo, a kingdom located in the eastern Mixteca
Alta, begins with a group of dynastic ancestors associated with one set of ninth-
century place signs; then, after a period of internecine warfare, the line of descent
continues but its members are depicted ruling at a second set of entirely different
place signs from the eleventh century through the end of the sixteenth century.

The fact that the conflict seemed to take place in the intervening tenth century
was later recognized as highly significant by archaeologists (Pohl 2004). It was at
this time that a period of actual site shifting had been detected during which populations of as many as ten thousand people, who had occupied major Classic-period
sites constructed atop high mountain ridges for the previous five hundred years,
abandoned these urban centers in favor of moving to the valley floors to reorganize themselves into scores of autonomous Postclassic royal houses that extended
from coastal Oaxaca to Puebla. Subsequent full coverage surveys have not only
confirmed the conjunction in the data between the historical and archaeological
phenomena indicative of community fissioning, but on-site interviews with local
farmers who maintain traditional indigenous place names for ruins along with
legends and religious stories that echo the pictorial accounts have led to the identification of many of the actual locations.

By focusing on questions of mutual concern, archaeologists and historians
have therefore concluded that the heroic legends depicted in the codices suggest
that political factionalism had been the primary reason for the abandonment of
Classic centers, at least from the perspective of the caciques who commissioned
documents like the Codex Bodley to advocate their inheritance to lands not only

throughout the Late Postclassic period but also in the sixteenth century in their dealings with Spanish courts. While an analysis of indigenous pictographic sources can contribute significantly to the archaeological identification of site hierarchies among peer polities, full coverage surveys and excavations in turn can help resolve what appear to be inconsistencies in different kinds of historical records.

Some historians have expressed concern over the relevance of pictographic codices, lienzos, and maps for reconstructing culture history, considering that they are created from a largely indigenous conception of the world that blends myth with history. They emphasize that the only truly factual accounts are to be found in documents like genealogies, wills, and trial testimonies created under Spanish colonial administrations that reflect the pragmatics of postmodern historical thought (see Anderson et al. 1976; Spores 1967; Terraciano 2001; Oudjik 2000 for discussion). For example, Tilantongo appears as the most prominent kingdom in the mytho-genealogical recounting portrayed in the codices and yet outside of a few references to its ranking royal line there is little documentation to support any comparable role that the *cacicazgo* (indigenous kingdom) played during the early Colonial period, and by the late Colonial and Republican periods Tilantongo existed only as a remote village, reflecting nothing of the social power that it had apparently once had.

Considering the amount of archival material that has survived for the administration of the Colonial cacicazgo of Teposcolula located 30 kilometers to the northwest, Tilantongo appears to present a conundrum (Spores 1967, 1984; Spores and Robles García 2007; Terraciano 2001). The consequent bias in the Pre-Columbian historical emphasis on Tilantongo and the eastern Mixteca Alta on the one hand and Colonial documentary emphasis on the western Mixteca Alta on the other is not coincidental. We see in the mytho-genealogical history portrayed in the codices a purposeful, even structured, formula by which all Mixtec caciques connected themselves to the remote past by showing their ancestors, priests, and oracles emerging out of the "pre-sunrise" world of the Classic-period sites documented in archaeological surveys of the Nochixtlán Valley (Hamann 2002, 2008; Fields, Pohl, and Lyall 2012). Archaeological surveys of the western Mixteca Alta, on the other hand, have demonstrated that the region experienced nothing of the same level of growth during the Classic period: instead, its dramatic florescence for which it became better known only occurred during the Late Postclassic and Colonial periods (Balkansky et al. 2000).

Consequently, we can see why the Mixtecs attributed their ninth-century dynasties to the more ancient eastern Mixteca Alta citadels well into the Colonial period (Pohl 2009). They really were the ranking Classic-period capitals of the Mixteca Alta at the time. The ensuing tenth- and eleventh-century conflicts then represent an *Iliad* of the Mixtec people that was played out in the Nochixtlán Valley documented archaeologically as site fissioning during the early Postclassic. The direct descendants of the Mixtecs were subsequently credited with establishing the principal alliance corridors by intermarriage throughout the greater Mixteca Alta, the Baja, the Costa, and the Valley of Oaxaca (Pohl 2003).

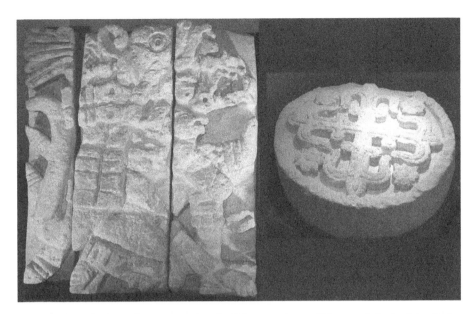

Figure 68.2 Relief panels excavated at the Mixtec palace of Teposcolula depict a fusion
of Pre-Columbian and Dominican traditions. The image at left depicts lord Eight Deer,
the eleventh-century Tilantongo warlord. The Dominican medallion at right
ornamented the convento constructed adjacent to the palace (author's photo; courtesy
of the Museo de Convento de Teposcolula).

Extensive excavations at the Postclassic Mixtec palace of Teposcolula in the
western Mixteca Alta confirm the prosperity of the cacicazgo regardless of what
rank its royal family may or may not have held in a larger confederacy (Figure 68.2).
Composing a community of between seven thousand and eight thousand people,
it was constructed atop a 2,400-meter-high hill called Yucundaa that overlooked
a broad fertile valley. Covering 450 hectares, the site consisted of a grand plaza, an
extensive royal palace, a ballcourt, and massive retaining walls that created broad
terraces occupied by the lesser ranking elite as well as a large supporting population of servants and farmers (Spores and Robles García 2007).

Even more remarkable was the discovery of one of the first Dominican conventos in Oaxaca. Consisting of a chapel and associated living quarters, it was constructed adjacent to the royal palace and clearly illustrates the importance of the
cacique's patronage on which the friars were totally dependent in their efforts to
missionize the region, obviously a very different scenario from that being played
out at the same time in the Valley of Mexico. The surprising degree of cultural
continuity is reflected in the artifactual record, particularly the continuance of
the Nahua-Mixteca Polychrome ceramic tradition recognized as the hallmark of
the systems of royal feasts that supported the marriage networks by which these
kingdoms maintained their alliance structures well in to the Colonial period (Pohl
2003, 2007). The discovery of a burial of an indigenous woman in the atrium of the

church could reflect the introduction of Spanish elite funerary customs except for the fact that she was covered in thousands of jade beads and small *penates*, green stone figurines representing the deceased spirits of indigenous gods and ancestors (Spores et al. 2009: 75–78).

Instead, the primary evidence for a break with the traditions of the Postclassic was the discovery of the burials of persons believed to have died in the epidemics that swept through the Mixteca Alta during the 1530s and 1540s AD. By 1550, the palace, the grand plaza, and the convento were abandoned and the community was relocated to the valley floor. Although Viceroy Antonio de Mendoza tried to prevent any further resettlement, the cacique Don Pedro Osorio had established himself within a new administrative headquarters constructed at the center of an aggregated colonial town while the Dominican friars had begun plans for what would become one of the most impressive religious structures in New Spain, the Convento de San Pedro y San Pablo Tepsocolula.

Significantly, Don Pedro Osorio arranged to have his daughter marry the cacique of Tilantongo, Don Felipe de Austría. However, when the unexpected deaths of his daughter, his son, and ultimately Don Pedro himself left the inheritance of this prosperous new community in dispute, Don Felipe claimed it through ancient tradition by which the *yya* of Tilantongo was entitled to either appoint an heir or usurp the kingdom himself, invoking the Pre-Columbian traditions rooted in the creation stories, heroic legends, and subsequent genealogies portrayed in codices like the Codex Bodley and ultimately rooted in the events of the Terminal Classic period (Megged 2010: 44–48).

From a purely archaeological perspective we would have no idea what the relationship between the two kingdoms was. By comparison of site size and architectural complexity alone, we would more than likely assume that Tilantongo was a minor cacicazgo at best. Consequently we learn that it is impossible to evaluate peer polity relationships among Postclassic and Colonial kingdoms without examining the systemic variables of social organization reflected both in the Colonial documentary sources and in Pre-Columbian indigenous thought as well. Although his attempts to invoke the remote Pre-Columbian past were ultimately checked by a rival claimant working through the Spanish courts, Felipe de Austría, like other Colonial-period caciques, had become a very powerful man in New Spain. Claiming titles of not just yya, or cacique, but even *rey*—"king"—these men used their traditional claims to lands to not only found new settlements that would eventually become the leading commercial centers of New Spain but also to capitalize on the new global Habsburg economy.

A crucial archaeological project for an interpretation of this new economic environment has been the excavations at the Convento de Santo Domingo, Oaxaca, the principal headquarters for the Dominican administration of much of southern Mexico (Gómez Serafín and Fernández Davíla 2009). Structural remains and artifacts associated with the production of iron are important indicators of industry, but a significant discovery that will continue to have a dramatic impact on future archaeological research throughout Mesoamerica was the identification of an entire sequence of ceramic forms that reflect not only two centuries of trade between Asia and Europe but also the recognition that southern Mexico was invested in the local production of glazed wares emulating many of these same forms and stylistic patterns as well. Further investigations will no doubt lead to confirmation of documentary accounts of Postclassic caciques controlling the production of not only their cacicazgos but even large *mestizo* and Spanish-occupied towns as well.

A good case in point is the multidisciplinary research being done at Cholula, Puebla (Lind 2012; Knab 2012; Uruñuela y Ladrón de Guevara and Plunket 2012). A Late Postclassic through contemporary pilgrimage and market center, the city was estimated to have had a population of thirty thousand at the time of the conquest, with a cult focusing on Quetzalcoatl, the city's "god of the merchants" (Figure 68.3). The colonial chronicler Diego Durán specifically warned his readers that the merchants of the city seemed to be promoting the cult of the Virgen de los Remedios through a system of *mayordomía*, or rotating stewardship, in much the same way as they had the cult of Quetzalcoatl in pre-conquest times by competing against one another. With their profits in long-distance trade, they vied for the right to sponsor the feast, in return for which they were rewarded with powerful positions

Figure 68.3 The church of San Gabriel de Cholula was built of masonry from the original temple of Quetzalcoatl, Mesoamerica's principal pilgrimage and market shrine during the Late Postclassic (author's photo).

in the governmental administration of the city. Using an extensive corpus of written histories as well as maps and pictographic documents, together with remote sensing imagery, archaeologists have succeeded in mapping the locations of many of the Pre-Columbian and Colonial structures in which these nobles functioned.

Ethnographic studies have demonstrated that, despite the ostensible image of a contemporary community administered by a constitutionally elected city government, the reality is very different. Political power continues to be rooted in the family structures of powerful men who hold positions in a "ladder" of mayordomía and work very closely with the Franciscan order whose headquarters remains the Convento de San Gabriel, actually constructed from the remains of the former pre-conquest temple of Quetzalcoatl. Cholula still sponsors the largest indigenous market in North America. It is held with the feast of the Virgen de los Remedios and it has more than 200,000 people in attendance each year. Projects of this kind can have tremendous implications for examining large-scale urban political organization in Mesoamerica as an alternative to the model of the Aztec imperial state.

Alliances among cacique families throughout highland Mexico persisted during the colonial period; after the sixteenth century, however, the caciques lost much of their political power to *gobernadores* and indigenous town councils. Archival research has indicated that despite the devastating effects of epidemics during the seventeenth century, cacique families succeeded in consolidating their family networks and reorganizing themselves as urban elites residing largely in the city of Puebla. For example, by the eighteenth through nineteenth centuries, the Villagómez family claimed to be the inheritors of many of the lands and titles of the cacicazgos of both Puebla and Oaxaca. They were also among the largest landowners in México in the second half of the colonial period through the late 1800s. Branches of the family had owned sugar haciendas, ranches, an inn, and other commercial enterprises; they also preserved a collection of Pre-Columbian codices, maps, and lienzos among other documents to demonstrate their claims in court cases (Monaghan et al. 2003; Chance 2009).

During the nineteenth century, haciendas and *fincas* flourished throughout Mesoamerica. Mexican haciendas in particular are better known from the portrayal of the cultural stereotype of the tyrant landowner in historical literature. Commonly considered as large estates, haciendas were operated by a dominant extended family together with a dependent labor force that by the nineteenth century tended to serve the social status aspirations of the owners as much as the rural market economy. Some haciendas became enormous landholding fiefdoms. Although hacienda workers were not legally slaves, a number of factors such as debt peonage created working environments among indigenous people comparable to plantation slaves in the Caribbean and southern United States (Meyers and Carlson 2002).

Nevertheless, archaeological investigations of hacienda remains have revealed some surprising contrasts between recorded oral histories by direct descendants of the workers as well as documentary sources about the living conditions of the estates. An interdisciplinary study of the Hacienda San Miguel Acocotla, Atlixco,

Puebla, for example has investigated the lives of Nahua workers who toiled on the estate from 1577 AD to the Mexican Revolution (Juli 2003; Juli et al. 2006). Instead of the ephemeral remains of impermanent architecture that the investigators expected to find, they discovered the remains of a substantial *calpaneria* of no less than thirty-seven structures along with an associated ceramic assemblage reflecting vessel forms, decorative styles, and functions related to a variety of subsistence and sociocultural activities, as well as extensive quantities of faunal and floral remains. The nonceramic artifacts, including metals, glass, and lithics, suggested a higher standard of living than had been expected.

Both archaeological and historical sources indicate that the period between 1200–1600 AD should be considered as a time of major societal transformation in southern Mexico that withstood Aztec conquest only to resurrect itself and expand upon a new early colonial Spanish foundation. Consequently, the strong distinction made between the Postclassic and early Colonial periods ought to be combined into a "Late Antiquity," the term applied by historians to Europe and other areas of the world that witnessed comparable developments (Brown 1971). These include the maintenance of decentralized political systems; the use of international communication systems (Nahua-Mixteca and Romanesque-Gothic) to foster an elite, multicultural identity; an emphasis on pilgrimage centers as coordinating

Figure 68.4 Constructed directly on the foundations of a fifteenth-century Zapotec palace, the Hacienda of Xaaga in the Mitla Valley, Oaxaca, is a testament to the enduring importance of Pre-Columbian traditions even into the nineteenth century. A tomb featuring carved relief panels of geometric design was preserved under the main entry (author's photo).

mechanisms; and the spread of a shared social and cultural ideology, that is to say Christianity, through the missionary efforts of monastic orders working with an indigenous pagan nobility (Pohl 2012; Zborover, and Kroefges 2011) (Figure 68.4).

Many estates in southern Mexico continued to be controlled by the descendants of indigenous nobles well into the second half of the nineteenth century. Rather than view these as the last gasp of the waning colonial order, archaeologists and historians now focus on their transformations by examining the connections between the cacicazgo and other key nineteenth-century rural institutions, such as the corporate community and the hacienda. Future archaeological research will demonstrate that their continuing existence ensured the survival of so many of the indigenous lifeways that continue to characterize the region today.

REFERENCES

Anderson, Arthur J. O., Frances Berdan, and James Lockhart. 1976. *Beyond the Codices: The Nahua View of Colonial Mexico.* University of California Press, Berkeley.

Balkansky, Andrew K., Stephen A. Kowalewski, Verónica Pérez Rodríguez, Thomas J. Pluckhahn, Charlotte A. Smith, Laura R. Stiver, Dmitri Beliaev, John F. Chamblee, Verenice Y. Heredia Espinoza, and Roberto Santos Pérez. 2000. Archaeological Survey in the Mixteca Alta of Oaxaca, Mexico. *Journal of Field Archaeology* 27(4):365–389.

Braswell, Geoffrey E. 2003a. Highland Maya Polities of the Postclassic Period. In *The Postclassic Mesoamerican World*, edited by Michael Smith and Frances Berdan, pp. 45–49. University of Utah Press, Salt Lake City.

Braswell, Geoffrey E. 2003b. K'iche'an Origins, Symbolic Emulation, and Ethnogenesis in the Maya Highlands: AD 1400–1524. In *The Postclassic Mesoamerican World*, edited by Michael Smith and Frances Berdan, pp. 297–303. University of Utah Press, Salt Lake City.

Brown, Peter. 1971. *The World of Late Antiquity: AD 150–750.* Harcourt Brace Jovanovich, New York.

Carmack, Robert M., and John M. Weeks. 1981. The Archaeology and Ethnohistory of Utatlan: A Conjunctive Approach. *American Antiquity* 46:323–341.

Caso, Alfonso. 1960. *Interpretation of the Codex Bodley 2858.* Sociedad Mexicana de Antropología, Mexico.

Chance, John K. 2009. Marriage Alliances among Colonial Mixtec Elites: The Villagómez Caciques of Acatlan-Petlalcingo. *Ethnohistory* 56(1):91–123.

Charlton, Thomas H., Patricia Fournier, and Cynthia L. Otis Charlton. 2009. Historical Archaeology in Central and Northern Mesoamerica: Development and Current Status. In *International Handbook of Historical Archaeology*, edited by Teresita Majewski and David Gaimster. pp. 409–427. Springer Science and Business Media, New York.

Fernández Dávila, Enrique, and Susana Gómez Serafín. 1998. *Primer Congreso Nacional de Arqueología Histórica: memoria: Oaxaca, 1996.* 1st ed. CONACULTA, INAH, México, D.F.

Fernández Dávila, Enrique, and Susana Gómez Serafín. 2009. Las ceramicas coloniales del ex Convento de Santo Domingo de Oaxaca: Pasado y presente de una tradicion. Instituto Nacional de Antropología, México.

Fields, Virginia M., John M.D. Pohl, and Victoria Lyall, eds. 2012. *Children of the Plumed Serpent: The Art and Ritual of Mesoamerica's Late Antiquity*. Los Angeles County Museum of Art, Los Angeles.

Fournier-Garcia, Patricia, and Lourdes Mondragon. 2003. Haciendas, Ranchos, and the Otomi Way of Life in the Mezquital Valley, Hidalgo, México. *Ethnohistory* 50:47–68.

Fox, John W. 1987. *Maya Postclassic State Formation Segmentary Lineage Migration in Advancing Frontiers*. Cambridge University Press, Cambridge.

Gasco, Janine, Greg Charles Smith, and Patricia Fournier-Garcia, eds. 1997. *Approaches to the Historical Archaeology of México, Central, and South America*. Institute of Archaeology, University of California, Los Angeles.

Juli, Harold. 2003. Perspectives on Mexican Hacienda Archaeology. *SAA Archaeological Record*: Vol. 3, No. 423–24.

Juli, Harold, Elizabeth Terese Newman, and S. S. Saenz. 2006. Arqueología histórica en la Hacienda San Miguel Acocotla, Atlixco Puebla: Informe de la primera temporada de excavaciones, 2005 y propuesta para la segunda temporada, 2006. Unpublished report to INAH, México.

Hamann, Byron. 2002. Social Life of Pre-Sunrise Things: Indigenous Mesoamerican Archaeology. *Current Anthropology* 43:351–382.

Hamann, Byron. 2008. Heirlooms and Ruins: High Culture, Mesoamerican Civilization, and the Postclassic Oaxacan Tradition. In *After Monte Alban: Transformation and Negotiation in Oaxaca, Mexico*, edited by Jeffrey P. Blomster, pp. 119–168. University Press of Colorado, Boulder.

Kepecs, Susan, and Rani T. Alexander. 2005. *The Postclassic to Spanish-Era Transition in Mesoamerica: Archaeological Perspectives*. University of New Mexico Press, Albuquerque.

Knab, Timothy. 2012. Mayordomía at Cholula, Puebla, Mexico. In *Children of the Plumed Serpent: Art and Ritual in Mesoamerica's Late Antiquity*, edited by Virginia M. Fields, John M. D. Pohl, and Victoria Lyall Los Angeles County Museum of Art, Los Angeles.

Lind, Michael. 2012. Cholula: A Sacred City and Pilgrimage Center in the Valley of Puebla, Mexico. In *Children of the Plumed Serpent: Art and Ritual in Mesoamerica's Late Antiquity*, edited by Virginia M. Fields, John M. D. Pohl, and Victoria Lyall. Los Angeles County Museum of Art, Los Angeles.

Lister, Florence C., and Robert H. Lister. 2002. *Maiolica Olé*. Museum of New Mexico Press, Santa Fe.

Megged, Amos. 2010. *Social Memory in Ancient and Colonial Mesoamerica*. Cambridge University Press, Cambridge.

Meyers, Allan. 2005. Material Expressions of Social Inequality on a Porfirian Sugar Hacienda in Yucatán, México. *Historical Archaeology* 39:112–137.

Meyers, Allan, and David L. Carlson. 2002. Peonage, Power Relations and the Built Environment at Hacienda Tabi, Yucatán, México. *International Journal of Historical Archaeology* 6:225–252.

Monaghan, John, Joyce Arthur A., and Ronald Spores. 2003. Transformations of the Indigenous Cacicazgo in the Nineteenth Century. *Ethnohistory* 50:131–150.

Newman, Elizabeth Terese, and Harold Juli. 2008. Historical Archaeology and Indigenous Identity at the Ex-Hacienda San Miguel Acocotla, Atlixco, Puebla, México. Foundation for the Advancement of Mesoamerican Studies Incorporated, Crystal River, Florida.

Oudijk, Michel R. 2000. *Historiography of the Benizaa: The Postclassic and Early Colonial Periods (1000–1600 AD)*. Research School of Asian, African, and Amerindian Studies (CNWS), Universiteit Leiden, Leiden.

Palka, Joel W. 2009. Historical Archaeology of Indigenous Culture Change in Mesoamerica. *Journal of Archaeological Research* 17: 297–346.

Pohl, John M. D. 2003. Royal Marriage and Confederacy Building among the Eastern Nahuas, Mixtecs, and Zapotecs. In *The Postclassic Mesoamerican World*, edited by Michael Smith and Frances Berdan, pp. 243–248. University of Utah Press, Salt Lake City.

Pohl, John M. D. 2004. The Archaeology of History in Postclassic Oaxaca. In *Mesoamerican Archaeology*, edited by Julia Hendon and Rosemary Joyce, pp. 217–238. Blackwell Publishers, Malden, Massachusetts.

Pohl, John M. D. 2007. Narrative Mixtec Ceramics of Ancient Mexico. Cuadernos 10, Princeton University Program in Latin American Studies, Princeton.

Pohl, John M. D. 2009. Lord Eight Wind of Suchixtlan and the Heroes of Ancient Oaxaca: Introduction. In *Lord Eight Wind of Suchixtlan and the Heroes of Ancient Oaxaca* by Robert Lloyd Williams, pp. 1–26. University of Texas Press, Austin.

Pohl, John M. D. 2012. *Children of the Plumed Serpent: The Art and Ritual of Mesoamerica's Late Antiquity*. Los Angeles County Museum of Art, Los Angeles.

Rice, Don S., and Prudence M. Rice. 2003. History in the Future: Historical Data and Investigations in Lowland Maya Studies. In *Continuities and Changes in Maya Archaeology: Perspectives at the Millennium*, edited by Charles W. Golden and Greg Borgstede, pp. 71–87. Routledge, New York.

Smith, Michael E., and Frances F. Berdan. 2003. *The Postclassic Mesoamerican World*. University of Utah Press, Salt Lake City.

Spores, Ronald. 1967. *Mixtec Kings and Their People*. University of Oklahoma Press, Norman.

Spores, Ronald. 1984. *The Mixtecs in Ancient and Colonial Times*. University of Oklahoma Press, Norman.

Spores, Ronald, and Nelly Robles García. 2007. A Prehispanic (Postclassic) Capital Center in Colonial Transition: Excavations at Yucundaa Pueblo Viejo de Teposcolula, Oaxaca, Mexico. *Latin American Antiquity* 18:333–353.

Spores, Ronald, Nelly Robles García, and Bertha Flores Canseco. 2009. *Yucundaa: Pueblo Viejo de Teposcolula*. Productos Gráficos El Castor, S.A., México.

Terraciano, Kevin. 2001. *The Mixtecs of Colonial Oaxaca Ñudzahui History, Sixteenth through Eighteenth Centuries*. Stanford University Press, Stanford.

Uruñuela y Ladrón de Guevara, Gabriela and Patricia Plunket 2012. In: Fields, Virginia M., John M.D. Pohl, and Victoria Lyall, eds. 2012. *Children of the Plumed Serpent: The Art and Ritual of Mesoamerica's Late Antiquity*. pp. 200–203. Los Angeles County Museum of Art, Los Angeles.

Zborover, Danny, and Peter Kroefges. 2011. *Integrating Archaeology and History in Oaxaca*. University of Colorado Press, Boulder.

Zeitlin, Judith F. 2005. *Cultural Politics in Colonial Tehuantepec: Community and State among the Isthmus Zapotec, 1500–1750*. Stanford University Press, Stanford.

CHAPTER 69

POPULATION DECLINE DURING AND AFTER CONQUEST

REBECCA STOREY

Two big controversies continue to be debated about what happened to Native Americans when Europeans arrived in the Western Hemisphere to conquer and colonize. The Columbian Quincentenary in 1992 was a spur to investigation and new perspectives. Evidence that this encounter was unfavorable to the Native Americans is strong. The depopulation and disappearance of groups was noted by many European observers for several centuries after contact. The scale of this loss depends on the size of that population before contact. Thus, the first controversy is over how many people were present and thus what was the scale of the depopulation. If there were many people present, then the scale of the loss is horrific. If the population was relatively small, the depopulation, while tragic, does not seem as unprecedented. Researchers on the issue fall into High Counters (Henige 1998), those who might be called Low Counters, and those who literally try to find a happy medium. Each position has its own rationale and has used Mesoamerica as a case study.

The second controversy is over what caused the depopulation. Most researchers agree that there are two main culprits: the introduction of new diseases from the Old World and the stresses caused by conquest and colonization. The controversy is which was the more damaging. It seems a little insensitive to argue about such things; no matter what the cause was, human beings suffered and died. However, the encounter of the Old and New Worlds, beginning in 1492, was one of the most important meetings of humans who had no previous knowledge of each other. Understanding what happened and why is important to knowing how the history of Mesoamerica and its modern nations unfolded.

This article will first look at the evidence for the pre-contact population of Mesoamerica. Then, the casualties of conquest will be discussed. The important controversy over the causes of depopulation after conquest will be investigated in depth. Research on this subject is still ongoing.

MESOAMERICA ON THE EVE OF
THE SPANISH CONQUEST

It really is a "numbers game." The only real evidence is archaeological, in the number and density of settlements in the Late Postclassic. There has not been found, and probably will not be, a single number from a Pre-Columbian text about any population. One reason for revisions to the population size in 1492 or 1519 is that as new archaeological information and context become available, there is more with which to work. However, the translation of archaeological evidence into population numbers is not simple; all ways require assumptions (Hassan 1981). Mesoamerica is fortunate to also have some ethnohistorical information as well. However, it seems to come down to the philosophy and intuitions of individual researchers.

Earlier in the twentieth century, the estimates for Mexico at contact were 3.2 million (Kroeber 1934) and Rosenblat (1954) at 4.5 million. Then in the 1960s, the estimates jumped to 25 million (Borah and Cook 1963) and Dobyns (1966) at 30–37.5 million in central Mexico alone. While more recent estimates of central Mexico are at 16 million (Whitmore 1992) and 17.2 (Denevan 1992), these are definitely higher than the original estimates. What changed? Whether one believes the Pre-Columbian populations were few or many seems to be affected by opinions on how complex or "civilized" Pre-Columbian societies were and how devastating European conquest and colonization were (Alchon 2003). Mesoamerica definitely had complex, hierarchical societies, so some dense populations and significant numbers of people would have been present.

Central Mexico has been the most common area for estimating the pre-contact population. The most famous is Borah and Cook's (1963) estimate of over 25 million, which has been accepted but also severely criticized. Using pre-conquest tribute lists (post-conquest copies) and other documents, they calculated the number of tributaries in central Mexico. For total population, one multiplies that figure by a probable average family size (4.5 people) and then adds the proportion exempt from tribute (35–40 percent). However, the relationship between Aztec tribute and population is rather tenuous, because there is no evidence that such tribute was based on the number of taxpayers in a province; it was levied on conquered rulers and how they collected it is unknown (Sanders 1976). The exempt proportion also seems inflated. Borah and Cook pile assumption on assumption and have received more support than warranted by any evidence (Henige 1998).

Sanders (1976; Sanders et al. 1979) criticized Borah and Cook but also did his own calculations based on documentary and archaeological evidence, especially for the Basin of Mexico. He began with numbers for 1568, the first reliable census evidence, and then calculated a depopulation ratio back to 1519 for an estimate of 1–1.2 million for the basin, and 2.6–3.1 million for the basin and adjacent areas. He also has archaeological evidence from the detailed survey of the basin (Sanders et al. 1979). The Aztec period had 1,636 sites, compared to only 398 the period before, indicating a dense settlement. Using artifact density and size of settlements, the calculation was 1–1.2 million at contact, very similar to his documentary estimate. Using Sanders's estimates, Denevan (1976) calculated a figure of 11.4 million for central Mexico (45 percent of Borah and Cook's figure).

Whitmore (1992) also tried to calculate the basin population in 1519 but used computer simulation based on censuses in 1530s and 1560s, while modeling fertility, mortality, and migration based on epidemiological models of morbidity and mortality for newly introduced diseases. He ran the model multiple times, varying the demographic and epidemiological parameters, and then compared with the historical data and what seemed probable. His figure was 1.5 million for the basin in 1519, close to Sanders, and 16 million for all of Mexico (64 percent of Borah and Cook's figure).

The rest of Mesoamerica (the Yucatán Peninsula and northern Central America) has received less attention. That is because the dense population is thought, on archaeological grounds and perhaps unjustly, to be present during the earlier Classic Maya times rather than in the early sixteenth century. Estimates here also vary widely, from 800,000 to 8 million for just the Yucatán (Denevan 1976). Frederic Lange (1971) used documentary evidence to count the large Maya cities, mostly coastal, for an estimate of almost 2.3 million for the northern Yucatán. An estimate for Guatemala (Lovell and Swezey 1982) was calculated three ways: by using a tribute assessment from the mid-sixteenth century, by using the average population density as calculated for central Mexico, and by aggregating available population data for subregions. This latter calculation is the most reasonable method and yields a figure of 2 million. Chiapas (275,000–200,000) and Soconusco (80,000–90,000) are based on similar methods, such as the use of early tribute documents and information on settlements and population from archives (Lovell and Lutz 1995). If all are added together, including that for Yucatán from Lange, the estimate is 4,665,000. As Lovell and Lutz (1995) note, this puts the estimates among the high numbers, but not at the extreme high end. The accumulating evidence that this part of Mesoamerica had complex, hierarchical societies at contact continues the trend toward higher population estimates.

The recent totals for Mesoamerica seem to range from 16 million to near 30 million, a rejection of the earlier small estimates. As Henige (1998) reminds us, many sources have not been critically evaluated. Much more archaeological research is also needed.

CASUALTIES DURING THE CONQUEST

The question of how much credence should be given to early accounts by the Spanish underlies the discussion of mortality during the conquest. Undoubtedly, the Spaniards were able to take over Mesoamerica with relatively few Spanish soldiers: the interest is in the details. Several accounts by eyewitness *conquistadors* contain estimations of the sizes of the armies faced as well as the sizes of towns and provinces. There are a few accounts by native Mesoamericans, mostly of the conquest of central Mexico, but these were written long after the events and are "sketchier" in detail (Hassig 2006). It is generally agreed that the Spanish accounts were written for self-serving reasons (Hassig 2006; Henige 1998). Thus, the numbers of warriors and sizes of settlements encountered come mostly from the Spaniards (and also influenced the estimation of pre-contact numbers), and there is no reason to think that any numbers were meant to be accurate, especially about native demography.

For example, Cortés faced and defeated armies at Tlaxcala he estimated to be at "more than 149,000" with only a few hundred Spaniards (Cortés 1988). Díaz del Castillo (1982) argued that such numbers are inflated; they faced only 30,000, 40,000, or 50,000. Henige (1998) questioned whether any of these numbers were reasonable or were just common battlefield inflations for the glory of the teller. After the conquest of Tenochtitlan, Cortés had nine hundred surviving Spaniards (Hassig 2006). However, "what made the conquest of Mexico possible was not the Spaniards' military might, which was always modest, but the assistance of tens and even hundreds of thousands of Indian allies—laborers, porters, cooks, and especially soldiers" (Hassig 2006: 175). Cortés's success was due to "the pivotal role...played by his two hundred thousand Indian allies, even though they went virtually unacknowledged and certainly unrewarded" (Hassig 2006: 178). While Hassig does depend on Cortés's account, exactly how these numbers were determined is not clear. More investigation of native archives and other Spanish sources resulted in a calculation of circa 24,000 native allies at the siege of Tenochtitlan (Oudijk and Restall 2007), a distinctly lower number. While Hassig (2006) does give credit, as do others, to the Spanish advantage in horses and metal technology, they were highly outnumbered by their allies and their adversaries. The native allies prevented the Spaniards from being overwhelmed. The bulk of the warrior casualties, as well as the number of residents wounded and killed by the attacks on settlements, would have been borne by the natives. There is just no information presently available to allow a quantification of the losses, but it probably was significant for some groups.

After the Fall of Tenochtitlan
and the Colonial Period

Throughout the sixteenth century, the Spanish noted the loss of the native population, which they depended on for labor and taxes. The scale of this loss and its
causes are still debated. The historical consensus is that the conquest and colonization of Mesoamerica were made possible by the introduction of new epidemic
diseases to "virgin-soil" populations (e.g., Crosby 1972; Diamond 1997). While Pre-
Columbian Mesoamerica certainly was not free of disease or famines (Verano and
Ubelaker 1992; Alchon 2003), the appearance of smallpox, measles, influenza, and
other infectious diseases wreaked havoc on natives and their societies who had no
experience, and thus no immunity, against these illnesses. In such "virgin-soil"
epidemics, all ages are infected and mortality is high, historically, around 30–40
percent for smallpox and 10–20 percent for measles (Whitmore 1992). Some have
felt that the mortality in Mesoamerica would be higher, because everyone would be
ill, and nurses and cooks would be lacking. There were as well the societal disruptions caused by the Spanish (Dobyns 1993).

The first Old World disease introduced to Mesoamerica was smallpox, in 1520,
during the conquest, documented by various eyewitness accounts. The outbreak
definitely interfered with the defense of Tenochtitlan (Hassig 2006; McCaa 1995),
and various sources and researchers claim that half the population of the basin
and adjacent areas died during this epidemic (e.g., Dobyns 1993). There are revi-
sionists who claim that it was only mild smallpox with effects similar to cases in
contemporary Europe (Brooks 1993). McCaa (1995) has investigated the sources
and found that the mortality is not recoverable, whether it was 10 or 50 percent
but it was a significant epidemic and more serious than any in Europe at that time.
He preferred a probable 30 percent loss, similar to historical examples. The sixteenth-century accounts also point to epidemics in 1545-1546 and 1576-1577 as more
deadly, but which are hard to diagnose (McCaa 1995; Prem 1991). These latter were
described as having profuse bleeding as in a hemorrhagic fever. Again, mortality
rates are calculated as 50–70 percent (Prem 1991), but no real count is possible.

The real controversy about the role of disease is not that new diseases were
introduced, but how widespread their effects turned out to be. Were they only
significant when there was sustained contact with Europeans, or did they spread
fast and wide to other populations, causing depopulation before any European
observer was present? The pre-contact High Counters favor the former, so that
the introduction of smallpox, first in Hispaniola in 1518 and then Mexico in 1520,
became a continentwide pandemic with very high mortality (Dobyns 1993). Thus,
no European ever saw how dense the pre-contact Mesoamerican population was,
and the colonization was already made of smaller and weaker societies. How
important these undocumented disease epidemics were affects the views of the
size of the pre-contact population and the course of conquest. Again, archaeology

would be of help, but the problems of coverage and the need for finer chronological control do not yet allow many areas of Mesoamerica to provide either positive or negative evidence. There is no documentary or archaeological evidence used to show a clear history of a pre-contact epidemic (Henige 1998). It is not that smallpox could have preceded the Spaniards; it is just that no one has really proved it. For example, the Cakchiquel Maya recorded a disease with high mortality five years before the Spanish entered (Lovell 1991), although diagnosis of the disease is unclear, let alone the actual amount of population loss.

Perhaps the most contentious part of the High Counters' reconstruction of Mesoamerican population dynamics is the depopulation ratio, which Dobyns (1993) had put at 90–95 percent for the Americas based partly on central Mexico, a terrible demographic catastrophe. Whitmore's (1992) simulations for the Basin of Mexico try to test what might be plausible depopulation patterns, using epidemiological and demographic modeling. His various simulations are compared with historical estimates, and he found that a depopulation ratio of near 90 percent is best almost a century after the conquest, with higher ones being unrealistic. However, one cannot really generalize this to all of Mesoamerica. One cannot really be sure how far the 1520 smallpox spread outside the Basin of Mexico, for example. Differences in settlement patterns and types, population densities, ecological constraints, social complexity, and frequency of contact are all likely to have influenced depopulation ratios. Too often, the Basin of Mexico is taken as the measure for all of Mesoamerica.

Although newly introduced Old World diseases are generally implicated as the main cause of Native American depopulation, recent researchers are implicating a wider variety of causes.

> There is agreement that a demographic catastrophe occurred and that epidemic disease was a dominant factor.... But the role of disease cannot be understood without taking to account the harsh treatment (forced migration, enslavement, abusive labor demands, and exorbitant tribute payments) and ecological devastation that accompanied Spanish colonization. Killing associated with war and conquest was clearly a secondary factor. (McCaa 1995: 429)

Whitmore (1992) also observed that famine added to the mortality because of disruptions to normal agricultural activities caused by widespread morbidity (especially if everyone is ill at harvest time) and labor demands. Alchon (2003) also wanted a multicausal explanation, that the depopulation of the Americas cannot be understood if disease is not coupled with the other effects of colonization. Her point is to show that Native Americans reacted to disease and other disruptions in a similar fashion as in the Old World. What is distinctive about the Mesoamerican case is the extent of population loss and the long time it took to begin to recover. Usually, a population recovers after the introduction of a new disease, but, here, with the introduction of so many new diseases within a century, the population never had time to rebound significantly. Added to the disruptions caused by the Spanish focus on native labor to extract and control the resources, the loss of native lands to the Spaniards, and lower economic opportunities for survivors, the Native Americans, in essence, lost most of their social, political, and economic institutions, a further hindrance to demographic recovery (Alchon 2003). Of course, eventually, the surviving Native American populations began to grow again, until some now number several million in the twenty-first century.

Understanding Pre-Columbian and colonial Mesoamerica population dynamics is a work in progress. The outlines of what happened do seem to be clear: a significant population was present, especially where there were complex, hierarchical societies. This population was then severely impacted by European diseases, conquest warfare, and Spanish colonial practices. It only took about a century after contact for much of the native population to be gone. The quantification of such terms as "significant," "severely impacted," and "depopulation ratio" is questionable. At this point, most researchers have simplistically used preconceptions of large, and sometimes small, populations to guide their choice of sources and numeric multipliers, too often unquestioningly using the previous estimates of High Counters (Henige 1998). The very high estimates of the precontact population and very high depopulation ratios have fallen out of favor. Better estimates will come from careful study and criticism of documents, the finding of new documents (McCaa 1995), and more complete archaeological surveys from many parts of Mesoamerica. Sanders's careful critique of documentary sources and archaeological data (1976; Sanders et al. 1979) provided a population estimate in the Basin of Mexico in 1568 (earliest good census information) at 404,000 to 407,000. The population at 1519 is estimated at 1–1.2 million. Taking these figures, the population was reduced to between 33–37 percent of the precontact size after just about fifty years. As several researchers have pointed out (Henige 1998; Alchon 2003), to argue about whether 66, 75, or 95 percent were lost is unimportant. The post-conquest demographic history of Mesoamerica is a tragic one, and it has provided evidence of how new contact between humans can have terrible consequences.

REFERENCES

Alchon, Suzanne A. 2003. *A Pest in the Land: New World Epidemics in a Global Perspective.* University of New Mexico Press, Albuquerque.

Borah, Woodrow W., and Sherbourne F. Cook. 1963. *The Aboriginal Population of Central Mexico on the Eve of the Spanish Conquest.* University of California Press, Berkeley.

Brooks, Francis J. 1993. Revising the Conquest of Mexico: Smallpox, Sources, and Populations. *Journal of Interdisciplinary History* 24:1–29.

Cortés, Hernan. 1988. *Cartas de relación.* Cisalpino-Goliardica, Milan.

Crosby, Alfred W. 1972. *The Columbian Exchange: Biological and Cultural Consequences of 1492.* Greenwood, Westport, Connecticut.

Denevan, William M. 1976. *The Native Population of the Americas in 1492.* University of Wisconsin Press, Madison.

Denevan, William M. 1992. *The Native Population of the Americas in 1492*. 2nd ed. University of Wisconsin Press, Madison.

Diamond, Jared M. 1997. *Guns, Germs, and Steel: The Fates of Human Societies*. W. W. Norton, New York.

Díaz del Castillo, Bernal. 1982. *Historía verdadera de la conquista de la Nueva España*. Instituto Gonzalo Fernández de Oviedo, Madrid.

Dobyns, Henry F. 1966. Estimating Aboriginal American Population: An Appraisal of Techniques with a New Hemispheric Estimate. *Current Anthropology* 7:395–416, 425–349.

Dobyns, Henry F. 1993. Disease Transfer at Contact. *Annual Review of Anthropology* 22:273–291.

Hassan, Fekri A. 1981. *Demographic Archaeology*. Academic Press, New York.

Hassig, Ross. 2006. *Mexico and the Spanish Conquest*. 2nd ed. University of Oklahoma Press, Norman.

Henige, David P. 1998. *Numbers from Nowhere: The American Indian Contact Population Debate*. University of Oklahoma Press, Norman.

Kroeber, Alfred L. 1934. Native American Population. *American Anthropologist* 36:1–25.

Lange, Frederic W. 1971. Una reevaluación de la población del norte de Yucatán en el tiempo del contacto español: 1528. *América Indígena* 31:117–139.

Lovell, W. George. 1991. Disease and Depopulation in Early Colonial Guatemala. In *"Secret Judgments of God": Old World Disease in Colonial Spanish America*, edited by N. David Cook and W. George Lovell, pp. 49–83. University of Oklahoma Press, Norman.

Lovell, W. George, and C. Lutz. 1995. *Demography and Empire: A Guide to the Population History of Spanish Central America, 1500–1821*. Westview Press, Boulder, Colorado.

Lovell, W. George, and William R. Swezey. 1982. The Population of Southern Guatemala at Spanish Contact. *Canadian Journal of Anthropology* 3(1):71–84.

McCaa, Robert. 1995. Spanish and Nahuatl Views on Smallpox and Demographic Catastrophe in Mexico. *Journal of Interdisciplinary History* 25:397–431.

Oudijk, Michel R., and Matthew Restall. 2007. Mesoamerican Conquistadors in the Sixteenth Century. In Matthew Laura E., and Michel R. Oudijk, *Indian Conquistadors: Indigenous Allies in the Conquest of Mesoamerica*, pp. 28–64. University of Oklahoma Press, Norman.

Prem, Hans J. 1991. Disease Outbreaks in Central Mexico during the Sixteenth Century. In *"Secret Judgments of God": Old World Disease in Colonial Spanish America*, edited by N. David Cook and W. G. Lovell, pp. 20–48. University of Oklahoma Press, Norman.

Rosenblat, Angel. 1954. *La población indígena y el mestizaje en América*. Editorial Nova, Buenos Aires.

Sanders, William T. 1976. The Population of the Central Mexican Symbiotic Region, the Basin of Mexico, and the Teotihuacan Valley in the Sixteenth Century. In *The Native Population of the Americas in 1492*, edited by W. M. Denevan, pp. 85–151. University of Wisconsin Press, Madison.

Sanders, William T., Jeffrey Parsons, and Robert S. Santley. 1979. *The Basin of Mexico: Ecological Processes in the Evolution of a Civilization*. Academic Press, New York.

Verano, John W., and Douglas H. Ubelaker, eds. 1992. *Disease and Demography in the Americas*. Smithsonian Institution, Washington, DC.

Whitmore, Thomas M. 1992. *Disease and Death in Early Colonial Mexico: Simulating Amerindian Depopulation*. Westview Press, Boulder, Colorado.

CHAPTER 70

....

HISTORICAL ARCHAEOLOGY IN CENTRAL AND WESTERN MESOAMERICA

....

PATRICIA FOURNIER G. AND THOMAS H. CHARLTON

RECENTLY there has been increasing interest in historical archaeology on a world-wide scale. We have published a number of papers dealing with the emergence and growth of historical archaeology in Mexico in general (Charlton and Fournier G. 2007; Fournier G. 2003; Fournier-G. and Miranda-Flores 1996), and in western and northern Mesoamerica specifically (Charlton et al. 2009), considering the characteristics of diverse research strategies and the incorporation of different approaches as used by historical archaeology in these regions. Other studies have addressed historical archaeology briefly or focused on particular topics of interest (e.g., Palka 2009; Van Buren 2010).

Here we briefly summarize background information relevant to the development of historical archaeology in Mexico, and we present key research themes to examine the current status of historical archaeology in central and western Mesoamerica (Figure 70.1).

Figure 70.1 Mesoamerica with subareas and important places mentioned in the text.

GENERAL BACKGROUND

Scholars studying the archaeology of the Late Postclassic period and relating the material remains to available textual sources are in essence practicing historical archaeology (e.g., Charlton and Fournier G. 2007). The term "historical archaeology" in the New World, however, is usually applied to periods following initial European contact. In the case of central Mesoamerica and particularly in the Basin of Mexico these would be the Colonial (1521–1820 AD) and the post-independence or Republican (1821 AD–present) periods.

    This field of inquiry has emerged and expanded as a new research strategy that parallels and connects with Mesoamerican archaeology's traditional focus on the rich Pre-Columbian cultural resources. It has been aided in Mexico by legislation that since 1972 has required that archaeologists protect and study pre-conquest and historical remains that are threatened by contemporary construction activities (Charlton et al. 2009), lending impetus to historical archaeology investigations, under the norms mandated by the Instituto Nacional de Antropología e Historia (INAH) and carried out under its supervision.

The focus of these studies is on the post-contact processes and outcomes of cultural changes in (1) indigenous Mesoamerican cultures; (2) the cultures of Hispanic and other Old World origins newly introduced to Mesoamerica; and (3) those emerging syncretic cultures with various combinations of Mesoamerican, Old World cultures, and new syntheses developing at any time from the Spanish conquest in the early sixteenth century to the present day (Charlton et al. 2009; Fournier G. 2003).

Investigative projects are often part of salvage or rescue archaeology involving a great deal of fieldwork, as well as an embrace of post-conquest studies including the viceregal era, the post-Independence nineteenth century up to the early 1900s, and rural and urban problem-oriented research topics.

There are many different trends within post-conquest historical archaeology research as practiced in Mexico today. Such diversity of approaches is due in part to the institutional contexts within which these activities are conducted. Such diversity is common in the current worldwide burgeoning field of historical archaeology. It reflects both a dynamic field and a recently emerging field (Charlton and Fournier G. 2007: 186).

During the past four decades research on historic sites has been carried out by many Mexican and foreign investigators. These studies can be grouped into three categories: (1) studies where the historic past is treated as an archaeological topic in the same manner as the prehispanic past; (2) studies where historic sites have been analyzed as part of major programs of architectural restoration; and (3) studies where investigators have shown interest in the development of a scientific form of historical archaeology focused on the inference of social processes (Fournier-G. and Miranda-Flores 1996) within different implicit or explicit theoretical frameworks, ranging from culture history to postprocessual approaches.

KEY RESEARCH THEMES

Conservation, Salvage, and Rescue Archaeology

The movement to preserve Colonial and Republican buildings stimulated the growth of institutional historical archaeology in Mexico. The number of projects undertaken increased substantially with the legislated need to conduct salvage and rescue operations. Much of the data derived from these projects have been used to examine general theoretical questions of culture contact and hybridity along with the construction of social systems, identity, and meaning.

Many historical archaeology projects have focused on the conservation and restoration of convents, monasteries, churches, chapels, hospitals, and palaces in urban centers, either to create tourist attractions or to remodel buildings for such public use as universities, government offices, banks, and museums. Mexico City, Oaxaca, Puebla, and Morelos have been the main centers for these types of projects that include research on the architectural history of the structural complex and basic or detailed studies of the archaeological materials recovered (e.g., Córdova Tello 1992; Gómez Serafín and Fernández Dávila 2007; Fournier G. 1990; Hernández Pons 1997; Juárez Cossio 1989; Salas Contreras 2006).

The archaeological record in urban sites often is very complex, due to the prevalence of disturbed deposits and the multiple transformations of spatial use over time (e.g., Fournier G. 1990; Gómez Goyzueta 2007). The discovery of the layout of coeval architectural features, such as houses and the recovery of artifacts that were left inside rooms or discarded into trash pits are seldom possible. Occasionally, at some sites, the ceramics recovered from domestic contexts have shown the potential to provide insights on household consumer patterns that may reflect dominant ideologies, identity, power structures, and negotiation (Rodríguez-Alegría 2005).

Salvage projects in rural areas seldom cover historic sites because Pre-Columbian sites are the priority. However, in the Soconusco region in Chiapas, a Dominican church was studied in detail prior to the construction of a dam (Beristáin Bravo 1996).

At the Santa Inés site, located close to the Augustinian monastery of Zempoala, Hidalgo, a sector of a Late Postclassic to early Colonial-period Otomí town was

Figure 70.2 Santa Inés site, Hidalgo. Excavation of early Colonial houses and patios, with the foundations of a *cuezcomatl*.

excavated as part of salvage operations. Architectural features associated with houses and patios included the foundations of several *cuezcomatl*, or barns for storing corn (Figure 70.2). Although a few metal artifacts and coins were found, ceramic evidence indicated that life continued after the conquest without major changes in material culture other than the introduction of a few glazed vessels.

Regional and Site Research Projects

Charlton's investigations in the eastern Teotihuacan Valley within the Basin of Mexico, near Otumba, included intensive surface survey with surface collections and excavations, along with a detailed ethnohistory of the region. During the early Colonial period (1521–1620), the major Hispanic cultural introductions consisted of churches, associated residential complexes, and cemeteries, associated with or separate from the churches. Aspects of contact, acculturation, demographic collapse, economics, and the development of ranchos and haciendas were documented. Land tenure and agricultural production, and the patterns of production, distribution, and consumption of ceramics were also included in the studies, as was the early Colonial production of obsidian tools (Borg 1975; Charlton 1972, 1986; Charlton and Fournier G. 1993; Charlton et al. 2005; Cressey 1974; Otis Charlton and Charlton 2007; Seifert 1977).

In rural Xaltocan, also in the Basin of Mexico, the use of Hispanic ceramics by some members of the indigenous population may mark status distinctions and the aspiration to power by people of lesser rank than the elites during the early Colonial period (Rodríguez-Alegría 2010). The use and production of obsidian tools was also documented for the post-conquest era as part of the change in labor and demographic patterns at the settlement (Rodríguez-Alegría 2008).

In a small hamlet with a Franciscan *visita*, or chapel, located at the obsidian mines of the Sierra de las Navajas, close to Pachuca, Hidalgo (Pastrana and Fournier G. 1998), obsidian use continued to the seventeenth century although the form and function of the chipped-stone tool production changed. Massive scrapers used to process cow hides and to extract agave fibers to produce cord required at regional silver mines are ubiquitous in the assemblage. Except for the introduction of plainwares that apparently were produced in the region, no major ceramic changes occurred in indigenous traditions.

Recent contributions emphasize post-conquest environmental degradation, changes in resource exploitation, and the introduction of new cultigens and cattle. These investigations address regional environmental history to understand anthropogenic landscape modifications from prehispanic to Republican times, based on demographic, geographical, and ethnoarchaeological studies in the Basin of Mexico (Parsons 2006), the Pátzcuaro Basin, Michoacán (Fisher 2005; Pollard 2005), and the Mezquital Valley, Hidalgo (Fournier G. 2007; Hunter 2009). In the latter region, an integrated study of the construction of indigenous identity and resistance attests to the impact of Colonial conquest and domination on the lives of the Otomí people, through consideration of the economic emphasis on agave exploitation. Included are the effects of intrusive ideological and economic systems marked by family chapels and oratories, ranchos, and haciendas (Charlton and Fournier G. 1993; Fournier G. 2007; Fournier G. and Mondragón 2003; Mondragón et al. 1997).

In an area composed of zones of northwest Puebla, southern Hidalgo, eastern Mexico, and most of Tlaxcala, surveys provided information on post-conquest settlement patterns and ceramic diversity and consumption up to the twentieth century (Müller 1981).

The examination of changes in economic inequality and land-tenure patterns, both within and among indigenous communities during the Colonial period, has been addressed for the Soconusco region in Chiapas (Gasco 2005).

The impact of Colonial aggregation systems on pre-conquest populations and on settlement patterns has also been discussed in detail for the Tehuantepec region in Oaxaca (Zeitlin 2005). Studies of population history, political economy, the ecological consequences of Colonial rule, and conflicts between indigenous Tarascan communities and European settlers in the Pátzcuaro Basin, Michoacán, illustrate the long-term effects of the Spanish intrusion in the region (Pollard 2005).

Recently, new research programs have been implemented in northwestern Mesoamerica. In Nayarit, the architectural and urban development of the port of San Blas, a major trading post connecting the Pacific Coast of New Spain with the mission sites in the Californias, was studied. Ongoing surveys, both in San Blas and in the earlier port established nearby at the Matanchel Bay, provide additional information about the daily life of both civilians and military inhabitants and insights into the transpacific trade network with Asia (Fournier G. and Bracamontes 2010).

In Sinaloa de Leiva, the Jesuit College of San Felipe and Santiago was recently excavated, uncovering the foundations of the old church (Santos Ramírez 2004), and different Jesuit mission sites have been surveyed as well. In northern Sinaloa, the former presidio settlement of El Fuerte and neighboring towns are under study (Carpenter Slavens and Sánchez Miranda 2007). Preliminary results provide information about the shift from prehispanic to historic indigenous ceramic traditions and about the way of life of the Mayo-Cahita native communities during the Colonial and Republican periods.

The investigation of ranchos and haciendas is attracting historical archaeologists after the first study in the Otumba area (Jones 1981), with isolated examples in Guerrero (Murrieta Flores 2008), the Mezquital Valley (Fournier G. and Mondragón 2003), and a major project in San Miguel Acocotla, Puebla (Juli 2003; Newman 2010) focusing on ethnic and class identity, the daily life of workers, and economic activities.

Ceramics

Mexican historical archaeology includes the study of ceramic artifacts not only for the development of sequences and the relative dating of archaeological sites and deposits, but also for indicating continuities and changes in cultural and social boundaries both within and between the Spanish and Indian-mestizo communities over time.

Multiple studies have addressed continuities, innovation, deterioration, and changes in production, styles, and exchange of indigenous ceramics, to investigate the impact of the Spanish conquest on Late Postclassic wares, craft production, and the market economy. Little is known about these processes except for at locations in the Basin of Mexico (Charlton and Fournier G. 1993, 2011; Charlton et al. 2007; Charlton et al. 2005), the Puebla-Tlaxcala area (Müller 1981), and the Tehuantepec region (Zeitlin 2005). These changes have been documented in detail on decorated vessels, plainwares (Figure 70.3), and figurines (Otis Charlton and Charlton 2007). Research results attest to the continuation and florescence of some indigenous ceramic wares while others show deterioration or disappearance. Different technological, stylistic, and formal modifications in the native traditions, including the adoption of lead glazing for the surface finish and updraft kilns, have been studied.

Shifts in market systems and economics have been explored by means of INAA (instrumental neutron activation analyses) (e.g., Charlton et al. 2005; Nichols et al. 2002). The variations in the archaeological record indicate an urban-rural dichotomy associated with an elite-commoner dichotomy, resulting in earlier and stronger acculturative processes in the cities and among the elites.

Figure 70.3 Early Colonial redware vessels from Mexico City.

European, European-style, and Asian pottery and chinaware were used as status symbols for visible display by members of Colonial and Republican society. These included lead-glazed ceramics, tin-opacified pottery, or majolica either imported or produced in Mexico City, Puebla, and Oaxaca; Chinese or French porcelains; and European creamwares, pearlwares, and whitewares mostly produced in England but also emulated in Mexico (e.g., Blackman et al. 2006; Borg 1975; Charlton et al. 2007; Fournier G. 1990; Fournier G. et al. 2009; Gómez Serafín and Fernández Dávila 2007; Lister and Lister 1982; Müller 1981; Seifert 1977).

Chinese porcelains dating to the Colonial period and European wares that mostly date from the late eighteenth century to the nineteenth century have been found to be the best chronological indicators. Usually these wares represent only a small percentage of recovered artifacts at historic sites. Imported ceramics evidence consumer behavior, in that they were a means of communicating the social status, wealth, and ethnicity of those who could afford these commodities (e.g., Borg 1975; Fournier G. 1990).

Lead-glazed earthenwares are ubiquitous in urban and rural historical archaeology sites. They exhibit a wide variety of wheel and mold-made forms, with limited changes in style through time except for those dating to the early Colonial period in the Basin of Mexico (Charlton et al. 2007; Sodi 1994). The manufacture of these wares has been attributed to multiple production centers and workshops in Mesoamerica from which they were distributed regionally (e.g., Fournier G. and Blackman 2008; Gómez Serafín and Fernández Dávila 2007).

Diagnostic decorated pottery such as majolica has attracted much interest and attention as a way to document chronology through changes in style and typological distinctions over time, starting with Goggin's seminal research on tin-opacified lead-glazed ceramics in the New World for types of the sixteenth to the nineteenth centuries (Goggin 1968; Lister and Lister 1982; Seifert 1977). A number of studies focus on the development of the majolica industry in Mexico City (e.g., Fournier G. et al. 2009; Gómez et al. 2001), Puebla (Lister and Lister 1984), Sayula, Jalisco (López Cervantes 1985), Oaxaca (Gómez Serafín and Fernández Dávila 2007), and Guanajuato (Cohen-Williams 1992).

As a result of analyses of numerous collections of majolica from urban centers, specifically Mexico City (Charlton and Fournier G. 1993; Lister and Lister 1982), Cuernavaca (Fournier G. and Charlton 2011), Puebla (Reynoso Ramos 2004), and Oaxaca (Gómez Serafín and Fernández Dávila 2007), it has become clear that while the cities possess a wide range of majolicas in terms of origins, types, and qualities, the rural areas possess few types in limited quantities and not always of the highest quality.

The effects of colonial rule, economics, and power structures on majolicas and glazed wares have been explored through chemical characterization of ceramic pastes by means of INAA and other analytical techniques, providing insights into production, commercialization, and the trade of pottery in different regions and periods (e.g., Blackman et al. 2006; Charlton et al. 2007; Fournier G. and Blackman 2008; Fournier G. et al. 2007, 2009; Nichols et al. 2002). New ethnoarchaeological and compositional studies about Tarascan-produced Colonial pseudo majolicas in the Pátzcuaro Basin have illustrated the adoption of European technological traditions among indigenous potters, influenced by the demand of the colonizers' markets and the popularity of these wares among urban and rural consumers of the viceroyalty (Fournier G. et al. 2007).

Other wares and particular vessel shapes have also been investigated, including Spanish olive jars used to ship foods across the Atlantic (Goggin 1960) and glazed chandeliers from Mexico City (López Palacios 1998). Slipped coarse brown *páteras* or *lebrillos* (bowls) that occur in Mexico City from about 1600–1650 to ca. 1850, and possibly employed as bowls for drinking pulque or for serving meals at hospitals (e.g., Lugo Ramírez 2006; Sánchez 1998), are present only from about 1621 to 1820 in rural areas of the Basin of Mexico. Fine burnished ceramics produced from the seventeenth century to the present in Tonalá, near Guadalajara, Jalisco, occur in low percentages in urban centers and rural areas of Mesoamerica (Charlton and Reiff Katz 1979; Gómez Serafín and Fernández Dávila 2007).

MINOR TOPICS

Little research has been conducted on the archaeology of the African diaspora in central and western Mesoamerica (e.g., Gallaga Murrieta 2010). Occasionally, Colonial burials such as some excavated in Mexico City (Meza and Báez 1994) include Afro-American individuals, as do some in Oaxaca at a sugar plantation cemetery for African slaves (Meza 2003).

Archaeologically recovered faunal and paleoethnobotanical data attest to the post-conquest prevalence of indigenous dietary customs and to the incorporation of European-introduced species, resulting in hybrid culinary traditions (Guzmán and Polaco 2003; Montúfar 1998, 2003; Newman 2010; Reynoso Ramos 2004; Valentín Maldonado 2003).

Osteological and bioarchaeological analyses, mostly in the Basin of Mexico and in Oaxaca, were usually carried out independently from archaeological studies. Such analyses bear witness to burial methods, general health conditions, life expectancy, morbidity, nutritional deficiencies, and the effects of toxic agents such as lead on individuals (e.g., Mansilla et al. 2000; Mansilla and Pijoan 1995; Meza 2003; Meza and Báez 1994; Moncada González and Mansilla 2005; Moncada González et al. 2006).

New projects are being developed with interdisciplinary approaches, advanced geophysical techniques are being used to evaluate the feasibility of potential archaeological excavations, and previous interpretations about social dynamics and consumer behavior are put to the test by taking into account the formation processes of the archaeological record (e.g., Ponce et al. 2004; Gómez Goyzueta 2007).

There is little systematic investigation of the physical remains of the industrial past in Mexico. Historians and architects alike tend to label some of their studies as "industrial archaeology," and they include mining centers as part of their research in surveys (Niccolai and Morales 2003; Oviedo 1998). Theoretical and methodological issues contributing to the development of industrial archaeology have been proposed (Litvak King and Rodríguez 2003) but little progress has been made under these considerations. Minor salvage projects in Mexico City at a paper factory (Moreno Cabrera et al. 1997), and other studies addressing leather tanneries and bottled soda factories in Puebla (Allende Carrera 2007; Reynoso Ramos 2005), are strictly industrial archaeology, contributing to the historical reconstruction of production processes and facilities through the artifacts associated with the end products.

FINAL CONSIDERATIONS

Starting in the late 1960s, historical archaeology in Mexico has been undertaken during a series of important research projects at sites all over Mesoamerica, in many instances with the integration of archaeological, ethnohistorical, and historical data into the analyses of the Colonial and Republican past, from the sixteenth century to the present day. This research strategy is well positioned and has generated a mass of significant publications as well as enormous databases in unpublished technical reports and theses (on file at the archaeology archives of the Instituto Nacional de Antropología e Historia), along with catalogues of architectural features and artifacts found at excavation sites. It contributes constantly to the extension and deepening of our understanding of past social life. Case studies have looked at material culture (ceramics, compositional analyses, lithics, and architecture), ethnicity and social identity, power, consumerism, subsistence, zooarchaeology, bioarchaeology, urbanization, ruralization, settlement patterns, land-tenure systems, the long-term impact of European culture on indigenous peoples, further developments among mestizo communities, and ecology.

Although the field of historical archaeology has matured, it should still be regarded as an expanding field of inquiry that primarily engages with salvage archaeology and architectural restoration of historical monuments in Mexican urban centers. Historical archaeology in Mesoamerica provides insights into the daily lives of the conquerors and the conquered and their descendants, with or without the aid of textual evidence. Documentary resources are only a single line of evidence to infer processes of social change during the post-conquest centuries in Mesoamerica. Historical archaeology provides the means to expand our understanding of such processes based on material correlates, considering Colonial and post-independence Mexico in the global context of the modern world system.

In any case, historical and archaeological datasets reflect different aspects of "reality" in different ways. Although they are complementary in many ways, archaeological data do more than simply support constructs based on historical data. Archaeological datasets propose one "reality" while historical datasets present another.

In the future, historical archaeology research projects with a regional scope and in rural settings in Mesoamerica will provide opportunities for more complete investigations that often are not feasible in salvage or rescue operations in urban archaeology. The richness of the archaeological record, historical documentation, and the presence of the descendants of both indigenous and intrusive societies in many instances mean that an enhanced study of social and cultural practices can be carried out within many differing contexts.

ACKNOWLEDGMENTS

Thomas H. Charlton and I discussed the general sketch of this contribution and started working on a rough draft of this chapter prior to his untimely death in June 2010. Unfortunately, he did not see the final product. As my mentor and long-time friend, I dedicate this contribution to his memory. We thank Patricia Castillo Peña, the director of the "Salvamento Arqueológico Gaseoducto Tuxpan-Atotonilco de Tula" project, for her invitation to visit the excavations at Santa Inés, Hidalgo, and to carry out preliminary studies of the archaeological collections. Cynthia Otis Charlton created the map included in this chapter.

REFERENCES

Allende Carrera, Arnulfo. 2007. Curtiduría "La piel de tigre": Arqueología en un sitio industrial de Puebla. *Dualidad* 7:8–13.

Beristáin Bravo, Francisco. 1996. *El templo dominico de Osumacinta, Chiapas.* Colección Científica 336, Instituto Nacional de Antropología e Historia, México, D.F.

Blackman, M. James, Patricia Fournier G., and Ronald L. Bishop. 2006. Complejidad e interacción social en el México colonial: La producción, intercambio y consumo de cerámicas vidriadas y esmaltadas con base en análisis de activación neutrónica. *Cuicuilco* 36:203–222.

Borg, Barbara E. 1975. Archaeological Whitewares of the Teotihuacan Valley, Mexico. MA thesis in Anthropology, University of Iowa, Iowa City.

Carpenter Slavens, John P., and Guadalupe Sánchez Miranda. 2007. Nuevos hallazgos arqueológicos en la región del valle del Río Fuerte, norte de Sinaloa. *Diario de Campo* 93:18–29.

Charlton, Thomas H. 1972. *Post-Conquest Developments in the Teotihuacan Valley, Mexico. Part 1. Excavations.* Report 5, Office of the State Archaeologist, Iowa City.

Charlton, Thomas H. 1986. Socioeconomic Dimensions of Urban-Rural Relations in the Colonial Period Basin of Mexico. In *Supplement to the Handbook of Middle American Indians*, vol. 4, edited by Ronald Spores and Patricia A. Andrews, pp. 122–133. University of Texas Press, Austin.

Charlton, Thomas H., and Patricia Fournier G. 1993. Urban and Rural Dimensions of the Contact Period: Central México, 1521–1620. In *Ethnohistory and Archaeology. Approaches to Postcontact Change in the Americas*, edited by J. Daniel Rogers and Samuel M. Wilson, pp. 201–220. Plenum Press, New York.

Charlton, Thomas H., and Patricia Fournier G. 2007. Geographic Overviews, The Americas (Central): Historical Archaeology in Mexico. In *Encyclopedia of Archaeology*, Vol. 1, edited by Deborah Pearsall, pp. 181–192. Academic Press, New York.

Charlton, Thomas H., and Patricia Fournier G. 2011. Pots and Plots. The Multiple Roles of Early Colonial Red Wares in the Basin of Mexico (Identity, Resistance, Negotiation, Accommodation, Aesthetic Creativity, or Just Plain Economics?). In *Enduring Conquests. Rethinking the Archaeology of Resistance to Spanish Colonialism in the Americas*, edited by Matthew Liebmann and Melissa S. Murphy, pp. 127–148. School for Advanced Research Press, Santa Fe, New Mexico.

Charlton, Thomas H., Patricia Fournier G., and Cynthia L. Otis Charlton. 2007. La cerámica del periodo colonial temprano en la cuenca de México. Permanencia y cambio en la cultura material. In *La producción alfarera en el México antiguo, Vol. V, La alfarería en el Posclásico (1200–1521 d. C.), el intercambio cultural y las permanencias,* edited by Beatriz Leonor Merino Carrión and Angel García Cook, pp. 429–496. Colección Científica 508, INAH, México, D.F.

Charlton, Thomas H., Patricia Fournier G., and Cynthia L. Otis Charlton. 2009. Historical Archaeology in Central and Northern Mesoamerica: Development and Current Status. In *International Handbook of Historical Archaeology*, edited by Teresita Majewski and David Gaimster, pp. 409–428. Springer, New York.

Charlton Thomas H., Cynthia L. Otis Charlton, and Patricia Fournier G. 2005. The Basin of Mexico AD 1450–1620. Archaeological Dimensions. In *The Postclassic to Spanish-Era Transition in Mesoamerica. Archaeological Perspectives*, edited by Susan Kepecs and Rani T. Alexander, pp. 49–63. University of New Mexico Press, Albuquerque.

Charlton, Thomas H., and Roberta Reiff Katz. 1979. Tonala Bruñida Ware: Past and Present. *Archaeology* 32:44–53.

Cohen-Williams, Anita G. 1992. Common Maiolica Types of Northern New Spain. *Historical Archaeology* 26(1):119–130.

Córdova Tello, Mario. 1992. *El convento de San Miguel de Huejotzingo, Pue.* Colección Científica 243, Instituto Nacional de Antropología e Historia, México, D.F.

Cressey, Pamela J. 1974. *Post-Conquest Developments in the Teotihuacan Valley, Mexico. Part 4. The Early Colonial Obsidian Industry.* Research Report No. 1, Mesoamerican Research Colloquium, Department of Anthropology, University of Iowa, Iowa City.

Fisher, Christopher T. 2005. Demographic and Landscape Change in the Lake Pátzcuaro Basin, Mexico: Abandoning the Garden. *American Anthropologist* 107(1):87–95.

Fournier G., Patricia. 1990. *Evidencias arqueológicas de la importación de cerámica en México, con base en los materiales del exconvento de San Jerónimo.* Colección Científica 213, Instituto Nacional de Antropología e Historia, México, D.F.

Fournier G., Patricia. 2003. Historical Archaeology in Mexico: A Reappraisal. *SAA Archaeological Record* 3(4):18–19, 39.

Fournier G., Patricia. 2007. *Los hñähñü del Valle del Mezquital: Maguey, pulque y alfarería*. Consejo Nacional para la Cultura y las Artes, Instituto Nacional de Antropología e Historia, México, D.F.

Fournier G., Patricia, and M. James Blackman. 2008. *Production, Exchange, and Use of Glazed Ceramics in New Spain: Development of an Elemental Composition Data Base by Means of Instrumental Neutron Activation Analysis*. Electronic document, http://www.famsi.org/reports/06014/ (accessed October 20, 2009).

Fournier G., Patricia, M. James Blackman, and Ronald L. Bishop. 2007. Los alfareros purépecha de la cuenca de Pátzcuaro: Producción, intercambio y consumo de cerámica vidriada durante la época virreinal. In *Arqueología y complejidad social*, edited by Patricia Fournier, Walburga Wiesheu, and Thomas H. Charlton, pp. 195–221. Escuela Nacional de Antropología e Historia, Instituto Nacional de Antropología e Historia, Programa del Mejoramiento del Profesorado, México, D.F.

Fournier G., Patricia, and Juan José G. Bracamontes. 2010. Matanchel, San Blas y el comercio transpacífico en Nueva Galicia: perspectivas desde la arqueología histórica. In *La Nueva Nao: De formosa a América Latina. Interacción cultural entre Asia y América: Reflexiones en torno al bicentenario de las independencias Latinoamericanas*, edited by Lucía Chen (Hsiao-Chuan Chen) and Alberto Saladino García, pp. 333–350. Universidad de Tamkang, Taipei.

Fournier G., Patricia, Karime Castillo, Ronald L. Bishop, and M. James Blackman. 2009. La loza blanca novohispana: Tecnohistoria de la mayólica en México. In *Arqueología colonial Latinoamericana. Modelos de estudio*, edited by Juan García Targa and Patricia Fournier G., pp. 99–114. BAR International Series 1988, Archaeopress, Oxford, England.

Fournier G., Patricia, and Thomas H. Charlton. 2011. Arqueología histórica de Cuauhnahuac-Cuernavaca. In *Perspectivas de la investigación arqueológica*, Vol. V, edited by Patricia Fournier G. and Walburga Wiesheu, pp. 129–164. Escuela Nacional de Antropología e Historia, Consejo Nacional de Ciencia y Tecnología, México, D.F.

Fournier-G., Patricia, and Fernando Miranda Flores. 1996. Historic Sites Archaeology in Mexico. In *Images of the Recent Past. Readings in Historical Archaeology*, edited by Charles E. Orser, pp. 440–452. Altamira, Walnut Creek, California.

Fournier G., Patricia, and Lourdes Mondragón. 2003. Haciendas, Ranches, and the Otomí Way of Life in the Mezquital Valley, Hidalgo, Mexico. *Ethnohistory* 50(1):47–68.

Gallaga Murrieta, Emiliano, ed. 2010. *¿Dónde están? Investigaciones sobre afromexicanos*. Universidad de Ciencias y Artes de Chiapas, Consejo Nacional Para la Cultura y las Artes, Instituto Nacional de Antropología e Historia, México, D.F.

Gasco, Janine. 2005. The Consequences of Spanish Colonial Rule for the Indigenous Peoples of Chiapas, Mexico. In *The Postclassic to Spanish-Era Transition in Mesoamerica. Archaeological Perspectives*, edited by Susan Kepecs and Rani T. Alexander, pp. 77–96. University of New Mexico Press, Albuquerque.

Goggin, John M. 1960. *The Spanish Olive Jar. An Introductory Study*. Yale University Publications in Anthropology, Number 62, Yale University, New Haven.

Goggin, John M. 1968. *Spanish Maiolica in the New World*. Yale Publications in Anthropology, Number 72, Yale University, New Haven.

Gómez, Pastor, Tony Pasinski, and Patricia Fournier G. 2001. Transferencia tecnológica y filiación étnica: El caso de los loceros Novohispanos del siglo XVI. *Amerística* 7:33–66.

Gómez Goyzueta, Fernando. 2007. Análisis crítico e interpretación de la estratigrafía arqueológica del ex templo jesuita de San Pedro y San Pablo de la ciudad de México.

In *Arqueología y complejidad social*, edited by Patricia Fournier G., Walburga Wiesheu, and Thomas H. Charlton, pp. 241–264. Escuela Nacional de Antropología e Historia, Instituto Nacional de Antropología e Historia, Programa para el Mejoramiento del Profesorado, México, D.F.

Gómez Serafín, Susana, and Enrique Fernández Dávila. 2007. *Las cerámicas coloniales del ex convento de Santo Domingo de Oaxaca. Pasado y presente de una tradición.* Colección Científica 496, Instituto Nacional de Antropología e Historia, México, D.F.

Guzmán, Ana F., and Oscar Polaco. 2003. El consumo de peces en una casa del siglo XVI en la ciudad de México. In *Excavaciones del programa de arqueología urbana*, edited by Eduardo Matos Moctezuma, pp. 39–73. Colección Científica 452, Instituto Nacional de Antropología e Historia, México.

Hernández Pons, Elsa, ed. 1997. *La antigua casa del Marqués del Apartado. Arqueología e historia.* Colección Científica 329, Instituto Nacional de Antropología e Historia, México, D.F.

Hunter, Richard. 2009. People, Sheep, and Landscape Change in Colonial Mexico: The Sixteenth-Century Transformation of the Valle del Mezquital. Unpublished PhD dissertation, Louisiana State University.

Jones, David M. 1981. The Importance of the Hacienda in 19th Century Otumba and Apan, Basin of Mexico. *Historical Archaeology* 15:87–116.

Juárez Cossio, Daniel. 1989. *El convento de San Jerónimo. Un ejemplo de arqueología histórica.* Colección Científica 178, Instituto Nacional de Antropología e Historia, México, D.F.

Juli, Harold. 2003. Perspectives on Mexican Hacienda Archaeology. *SAA Archaeological Record* 3(4):23–24, 44.

Lister, Florence C., and Robert H. Lister. 1982. *Sixteenth Century Maiolica Pottery in the Valley of Mexico.* Anthropological Papers of the University of Arizona 39, University of Arizona Press, Tucson.

Lister, Florence C., and Robert H. Lister. 1984. The Potter's Quarter of Colonial Puebla, Mexico. *Historical Archaeology* 18:87–102.

Litvak King, Jaime, and María de los Ángeles Rodríguez. 2003. Problemas y perspectivas de la arqueología industrial en México. In *La cultura industrial Mexicana. Primer encuentro nacional de arqueología industrial. Memoria*, edited by Sergio Niccolai and Humberto Morales Moreno, pp. 45–56. Benemérita Universidad Autónoma de Puebla, Comité Mexicano para la Conservación del Patrimonio Industrial, A. C., México.

López Cervantes, Gonzalo. 1985. Epigmenio Vargas, ceramista sayulense. *Antropología* 1:16–17.

López Palacios, José A. 1998. Cronología de la loza barniz plúmbeo: El caso de los candeleros novohispanos. In *Primer congreso nacional de arqueología histórica*, edited by Enrique Fernández Dávila and Susana Gómez Serafín, pp. 468–482. Instituto Nacional de Antropología e Historia, México, D.F.

Lugo Ramírez, Mónica. 2006. Los lebrillos o páteras de "El Pradito," ciudad de México. *Boletín de Monumentos Históricos* 8:36–46.

Mansilla, Josefina, and Carmen M. Pijoan. 1995. A Case of Congenital Syphilis during the Colonial Period in Mexico City. *American Journal of Physical Anthropology* 97:187–195.

Mansilla, Josefina, Corina Solís, and María E. Chávez. 2000. Lead Levels in Human Teeth from the Inhabitants of Mexico City from Three Different Historical Periods. *Antropología y Técnica* 6:81–84.

Meza, Abigail. 2003. Los angelitos de San Nicolás Ayotla, Oaxaca. *Estudios de Antropología Biológica* XI(2):549–560.

Meza, Abigail, and Socorro Báez. 1994. Paleopatología y demografía en el Hospital Real de los Naturales. In *De fragmentos y tiempos*, pp. 53–67. Subdirección de Salvamento Arqueológico, Instituto Nacional de Antropología e Historia, México, D.F.

Moncada González, Gisela C., Josefina Mansilla, and Martha Díaz de Kuri. 2006. Enfermedades dentales y alimentación en una muestra ósea de la capital de la Nueva España. *Revista de la Asociación Dental Mexicana* LXIII(3):93–96.

Mondragón, Lourdes, Patricia Fournier G., and Nahúm Noguera. 1997. Arqueología histórica de Sta. María del Pino, Hgo., México. In *Approaches to the Historical Archaeology of Middle and South America*, edited by Janine Gasco, Greg Ch. Smith, and Patricia Fournier G., pp. 17–28. Monograph 38, Institute of Archaeology, University of California, Los Angeles.

Montúfar, Aurora. 1998. Estudio botánico de un basurero colonial en el Templo Mayor, ciudad de México. *Arqueología* 19:173–177.

Montúfar, Aurora. 2003. Estudio arqueobotánico en el Palacio Nacional. En *Excavaciones del programa de arqueología urbana*, coordinated by Eduardo Matos Moctezuma, pp. 109–113. Colección Científica 452, Instituto Nacional de Antropología e Historia, México, D.F.

Moreno Cabrera, María de la Luz, Jaime Cedeño, and Luis F. Castro. 1997. Arqueología industrial en la Plaza Loreto, San Angel, Ciudad de México. In *Umbrales y veredas*, coordinated by Rubén Manzanilla, pp. 197–213. Dirección de Salvamento Arqueológico, Instituto Nacional de Antropología e Historia, México.

Müller, Florencia. 1981. *Estudio de la cerámica hispánica y moderna de Tlaxcala-Puebla*. Colección Científica 103, Instituto Nacional de Antropología e Historia, México, D.F.

Murrieta Flores, Patricia A. 2008. El proceso productivo del azúcar en época colonial y sus materiales arqueológicos: el caso de la Hacienda de Tecoyutla, Guerrero. *Arqueología* 38:90–111.

Newman, Elizabeth T. 2010. Butchers and Shamans: Zooarchaeology at a Central Mexican Hacienda. *Historical Archaeology* 44(2):33–50.

Niccolai, Sergio, and Humberto Morales, eds. 2003. *La cultura industrial Mexicana. Primer encuentro nacional de arqueología industrial. Memoria.* Benemérita Universidad Autónoma de Puebla, Comité Mexicano para la Conservación del Patrimonio Industrial, A. C., México.

Nichols, Deborah L., Elizabeth M. Brumfiel, Hector Neff, Mary Hodge, Thomas H. Charlton, and Michael D. Glascock. 2002. Neutrons, Markets, Cities, and Empires: A Thousand-Year Perspective on Ceramic Production and Distribution in the Postclassic Basin of Mexico at Cerro Portezuelo, Chalco, and Xaltocan. *Journal of Anthropological Archaeology* 21:25–83.

Otis Charlton, Cynthia L., and Thomas H. Charlton. 2007. Artesanos y barro: Figurillas y alfarería en Otompan, estado de México. *Arqueología Méxicana* 83:71–76.

Oviedo, Belem. 1998. La arqueología industrial en el distrito minero de Pachuca y Real del Monte. In *Primer congreso nacional de arqueología histórica. Memoria,* edited by Enrique Fernández Dávila and Susana Gómez Serafín, pp. 53–68. Instituto Nacional de Antropología e Historia, México, D.F.

Palka, Joel W. 2009. Historical Archaeology of Indigenous Culture Change in Mesoamerica. *Journal of Archaeological Research* 17:297–346.

Parsons, Jeffrey R. 2006. *The Last Pescadores of Chimalhuacan, Mexico: An Archaeological Ethnography*. Anthropological Paper No. 92, Museum of Anthropology, University of Michigan, Ann Arbor.

Pastrana, Alejandro, and Patricia Fournier G. 1998. Explotación colonial de obsidiana en el yacimiento de Sierra de las Navajas. In *Primer congreso nacional de arqueología histórica. Memoria,* coordinated by Enrique Fernández Dávila and Susana Gómez Serafín, pp. 486–496. Instituto Nacional de Antropología e Historia, México, D.F.

Pollard, Helen P. 2005. From Imperial Core to Colonial Periphery: The Lake Patzcuaro Basin 1400–1800. In *The Postclassic to Spanish-Era Transition in Mesoamerica: Archaeological Perspectives*, edited by Susan Kepecs and Rani T. Alexander, pp. 65–76. University of New Mexico Press, Albuquerque.

Ponce, Rocío, Denisse Argote, René E. Chávez, and M. Encarnación Cámara. 2004. Empleo de los métodos geofísicos en la prospección arqueológica urbana: La Basílica de Nuestra Señora de la Salud, Patzcuaro, México. *Trabajos de Prehistoria* 61(2):11–23.

Reynoso Ramos, Citlalli. 2004. Consumer Behaviour and Foodways in Colonial México: Archaeological Case Studies Comparing Puebla and Cholula. Unpublished MA thesis in Archaeology, University of Calgary, Canada.

Reynoso Ramos, Citlalli. 2005. Basura industrial: exploración arqueológica en la fabrica Latisnere, Puebla. Producción de bebidas de sabores, agua mineral y ¿vino? In *Memorias del II congreso nacional de patrimonio industrial*. http://www. granadacollection.org/Congreso_Nacional_Citlalli.pdf (accessed November 9, 2010).

Rodríguez-Alegría, Enrique. 2005. Consumption and the Varied Ideologies of Domination in Colonial Mexico City. In *The Postclassic to Spanish-Era Transition in Mesoamerica*, edited by Susan Kepecs and Rani T. Alexander, pp. 35–48. University of New Mexico Press, Albuquerque.

Rodríguez-Alegría, Enrique. 2008. Narratives of Conquest, Colonialism, and Cutting-Edge Technology. *American Anthropologist* 110(1):33–43.

Rodríguez-Alegría, Enrique. 2010. Incumbents and Challengers: Indigenous Politics and the Adoption of Spanish Material Culture in Colonial Xaltocan, Mexico. *Historical Archaeology* 44(2):51–71.

Salas Contreras, Carlos. 2006. *Arqueología del exconvento de La Encarnación. Edificio sede de la Secretaría de Educación Pública*. Colección Científica 493, Instituto Nacional de Antropología e Historia, México, D.F.

Santos Ramírez, V. Joel. 2004. Arqueología histórica del Colegio de la Compañía de Jesús de Sinaloa. In *Seminario sobre la religión en el noroeste novohispano*, edited by José Gaxiola López and José C. Zazueta Manjares, pp. 213–242. El Colegio de Sinaloa, Culiacán, Sinaloa, México.

Seifert, Donna J. 1977. Archaeological Majolicas of the Rural Teotihuacan Valley, Mexico. PhD dissertation in Anthropology, University of Iowa, Iowa City.

Sodi, Federica. 1994. *La cerámica novohispana vidriada y con decoración sellada del siglo XVI*. Colección Científica 291, Instituto Nacional de Antropología e Historia, México, D.F.

Temple Sánchez, John J. 1998. El cajete pulquero en la época colonial: Noticias para su cronología. In *Primer congreso nacional de arqueología histórica. Memoria,* edited by Enrique Fernández Dávila and Susana Gómez Serafín, pp. 221–227. Instituto Nacional de Antropología e Historia, México, D.F.

Valentín Maldonado, Norma. 2003. Análisis de material zoológico. In *Excavaciones del programa de arqueología urbana*, edited by Eduardo Matos Moctezuma, pp. 27–37. Colección Científica 452, Instituto Nacional de Antropología e Historia, México.

Van Buren, Mary. 2010. The Archaeological Study of Spanish Colonialism in the Americas. *Journal of Archaeological Research* 18:151–201.

Zeitlin, Judith Francis. 2005. *Cultural Politics in Colonial Tehuantepec. Community and State among the Isthmus Zapotec, 1500–1750.* Stanford University Press, Stanford, California.

CHAPTER 71

LANDSCAPE CHANGE IN THE MAYA REGION, 1450–1910 AD

RANI T. ALEXANDER

LANDSCAPE transformations are at the heart of archaeological debate over whether native cultural practices in the Maya region survived the Spanish invasion. Questions of change or continuity hinge on opposing assumptions about European contact (Alexander and Kepecs 2005). One side of the debate is dominated by the assertion that the conquest obliterated native societies and produced a clean slate on which Spain expanded her transoceanic empire. The opposing view is that the conquest was a catalyst for the transformation of native cultures, inspiring continuous and sometimes drastic social reconfigurations, as past practices were reinterpreted and modified to meet contemporary demands.

Resolution of these issues necessarily rests on evidence that bridges arbitrary scholarly divisions among the present, historic, and prehistoric periods (Lightfoot 1995). Because archaeology spans all time periods, it provides answers to questions about continuity and change in native societies before and after the European invasion. As a result, today's landscape archaeology reveals how the historical contingencies of the post-contact era shaped the choices and strategies of Maya households and communities to transform, not erase, earlier cultural traditions.

Below, I examine landscape change in the Maya region by using the theoretical lens of historical ecology (Crumley 2007). I compare two trajectories of change: (1) the period from 1450 to 1750, marked by the upheavals of conquest, demographic decline, and economic contraction, and (2) the period from 1750 to 1910, marked by the transition from colonial to postcolonial political regimes, demographic

growth, and economic expansion. The archaeological record reveals shifts in political-economic structures, agrarian ecology, the production of commodities for the
world market, and negotiations of native cultural autonomy for communities and
regions rarely mentioned in the documentary record.

LANDSCAPE ECOLOGY IN THE
POST-CONQUEST ERA

Historical ecology is a useful concept for framing questions about native people's
autonomy and how colonialism, capitalism, modernity, and globalization shape
fields of political, social, and economic relations (Orser 1996; Wolf 1982; Wolf 1990:
587). Landscapes are spatial manifestations of human-environmental relations in
the broadest sense (Crumley 2007). Landscape change unfolds as a historically
contingent process that binds together *spaces* that delimit physical experience and
places that attach meaning to locations (Smith 2003: 11). Consequently, material
transformations of places can be understood as shifts in human-environmental
relations, broadly conceived to include all those elements that make a difference
in people's decision making and strategizing, such as local environmental conditions, markets for goods and labor, consumption norms and needs, identity formation, local power structures, government programs, and macroregional economic
structure and commodity flows (Wilk 1991: 32–33). These processes create variation in the life histories of archaeological sites and associated material systems—
an *archaeology of place* (e.g., Basso 1996; Binford 1982; McAnany 1995).

Preservation of native cultural autonomy after European contact depends
on how native peoples relate to their ancestral homelands (Lightfoot 2004).
Resettlement programs are destructive to native identity because people are dis-
associated from the places of their ancestors' birth and burial, agricultural land,
water sources, shrines, and landmarks that are central to their experience. By contrast, colonial and national programs that allow flexibility in residential options
foster cultural autonomy and continuity of tradition.

The Maya region is an important test case for this proposition (Figure 71.1). The
Spanish conquest unfolded piecemeal between 1511 and 1697, as different areas were
brought under colonial administration. Fierce and protracted resistance prevailed in
eastern Yucatán, Guatemala, the Laguna de Términos, and the Petén, and many zones
remained unpacified (Chamberlain 1948; Jones 1998; Restall 1998; Scholes and Roys
1948). Areas that were brought under colonial authority formed a patchy archipelago
surrounded by a vast frontier, which still harbors fugitive and dissident groups in the
present day. Consequently, native ancestral homelands were not subject to wholesale
expropriation by Spanish colonists. The colonial regime and later national governments made significant inroads to native communities as policies were implemented

Figure 71.1 Locations of selected post-conquest sites in the Maya region.

to appropriate resources, control labor, and reorient the political economy to the production of commodities that could be lucratively exported on world markets. Yet, in many instances, control of arable land and water, agricultural production, and management of critical resources, such as salt and cacao, remained in native hands (Alexander 2012; Andrews 1983; Fowler 2006; Gasco 2006; Kepecs 2005).

Following the Spanish invasion, landscape change was driven by four principal factors: population density; the physical attributes of the environment; technological and managerial use strategies; and political-economic policies that encourage overexploitation or sustainability (Turner et al. 2003). Demographic decline influenced the numbers, size, distribution, and composition of settlements. Variation in population density, forced settlement nucleation, and new methods of transport, however, altered mobility patterns (Farriss 1978, 1984). Adjustments in travel time and transport costs between farmers' fields and residences and between rural communities and urban centers influenced settlement aggregation and dispersal, as well as cycles of habitation, abandonment, reoccupation, and post-abandonment activities on archaeological sites (Alexander 2006).

Additionally, the introduction of European cultigens and domestic animals altered preexisting mutualistic relationships among agriculture, wild game, and the husbandry of animals native to the region. Mesoamerica underwent a secondary products revolution (Sherratt 1981), which substituted animal traction and derivative second-ary products for human muscle power—the plough for the digging stick; the pack mule and the horse and oxcart transport for human burden bearers; and the promo-tion of higher energy-yielding secondary products (milk, wool) over meat and hides. Mutualisms were influenced by the demands of state and religious institutions for pay-ment of taxes and tribute in specific products, especially cloth, honey, wax, maize, and the "products of Castile." Animal husbandry strategies are traceable through fauna analysis and the distribution of infrastructure used to care for the animals. Raising pigs, poultry, sheep, goats, cattle, mules, and horses buffered Maya farmers from loss of land, excessive taxation, and changing markets. Animals were significant sources of wealth in Maya villages, and their comestible by-products figured prominently in feasts and festivals. Animals were exceptionally liquid commodities, and exchange of animal products helped to connect rural villages to urban markets.

Further, the introduction and development of new technology—transport techniques, firearms, metal tools, ceramics and glass, and new forms of currency and credit—meshed with population fluctuations and produced shifts in the social-environmental learning processes by which new innovations were introduced and adopted. Population loss, mobility, and migration affected the transmission, con-servation, and loss of traditional ecological knowledge (TEK). Changes in social and environmental learning are reflected in the production of material culture, the ways it is used to mark social boundaries, and the practice of daily routines (e.g., Lightfoot et al. 1998). Distribution of nonlocal items and new technological and stylistic innovations also reflected householders' participation in local and regional markets. Systems of production, distribution, and consumption vary, depending on how local commerce is connected to the macroregional economy.

Finally, changes in religious and administrative hierarchies, economic strati-fication, and forcible religious conversions restructured the built environment. Construction of new civic structures using costly materials often reflects an emerg-ing political autonomy. Variation in the size and cost of residential architecture and the segregation of residential space indicate increasing class divisions. Variations in the distribution, size, and configuration of religious architecture, shrines, cem-eteries, and religious objects suggest changes in orthodox and heterodox religious practices and the locales where they were performed (Chuchiak 2005, 2009).

THE SPANISH INVASION
AND ITS AFTERMATH, 1450-1750

As the Maya region became enmeshed in Spain's overseas empire during the six-teenth and seventeenth centuries, native populations experienced a drastic and protracted decline, resources were demanded of indigenous communities as tribute and taxes, settlements were forcibly relocated under the policy of *congregación*, and inhabitants were subjected to compulsory religious conversion (Farriss 1984; MacLeod 1973). Historians have projected an over 90 percent population decline between 1500 and 1550 (Farriss 1984; Lovell and Lutz 1994; Restall 1997). Poor climate, droughts, famines, and outbreaks of yellow fever caused continued population declines through the seventeenth century, and native populations reached a nadir around 1700. Under the colonial policy of congregación, hamlets and villages were combined into towns and local centers, leaving a two-tiered hierarchy of *cabeceras* (municipal seats) and *subjetos* (auxiliary towns) (Farriss 1984: 158). Relocated populations were required to arrange themselves along the colonial grid plan centered on a church, water source, and central plaza.

Archaeological evidence, however, indicates that these processes were variable. Two full-coverage archaeological surveys on the north coast of Yucatán, an area of early Spanish contact, suggest regional variability in rates of demographic decline (Andrews and Robles Castellanos 2009; Kepecs 1997, 1999). Ceramic evidence from Postclassic-period sites on the northeast coast indicates continued occupation into the mid- to late sixteenth century, which suggests that the demographic slide was less precipitous in some regions. Some Spanish settlements on Yucatán's northeast coast failed completely (Kepecs 2005). Other native communities in Yucatán, whose tribute was assigned as *encomienda*, were abandoned by the late sixteenth century (Andrews, Benavides Castillo, and Jones 2006; Roys 1952). Still others such as Tipu and Lamanai in Belize were abandoned and reoccupied during post-conquest revolts, whereas Nohpetén was not brought under colonial rule until 1697 (Jones 1989, 1998). The initial proselytizing efforts of the clergy are manifest in the distribution of open or perishable *ramada* chapels (Andrews 1991; Graham et al. 1989). Archaeological survey and excavation confirm that town planning in *congregaciones* was similar for communities in Chiapas, the Yucatán Peninsula, Soconusco, and El Salvador (Alexander 2005; Fowler 1995; Gallardo and Fowler 2002; García Targa 2000; Lee and Bryant 1988; Lee and Markman 1977). House lots were laid out on a grid centered on a church and main plaza. In native communities that survived sixteenth-century upheavals, perishable religious architecture gradually was replaced with more permanent construction. *Conventos*, religious complexes that also contained residential facilities for clergy, were constructed through the late sixteenth and seventeenth centuries (Hanson 1996).

Settlements in the frontier zones of southwestern Campeche, the Petén, Belize, and the Chiapas lowlands were often situated on islands, peninsulas, and lakes (Alexander 2005; Oland 2009; Palka 2009; Rice and Rice 2009). In the prehispanic era, farmers intensively cultivated wetlands and other hydrogeologic resources, such as *cenotes* (natural water sources) and *rejollas* (sinkholes), and they modified these landscapes with hydraulic infrastructure and terracing. As populations suffered additional declines, migrated, or were forcibly relocated to colonial towns after the Spanish invasion, wetlands, hydrogeologic features, and prime farmland reverted to extensive use. Because there was insufficient labor to maintain hydraulic infrastructure and terrace systems, soil erosion contributed to infilling lakes and bajos. Although many sites were abandoned in the sixteenth century, occupation in the Petén lakes area was continuous, and these polities attracted populations fleeing the Spanish invasion from Yucatán. Interactions among native groups and with the Spaniards in the frontier zone frequently were acrimonious and resulted in shifting alliances and violence. New ethnic boundaries were formed, marked by distinct differences in ceramics and architecture, as well as ritual practices (Rice and Rice 2009). Clandestine trade in metal tools, honey, wax, and cacao developed between frontier communities and colonial settlements (Caso Barrera 2002; Caso Barrera and Aliphat F. 2006; Jones 1998). Native communities in Belize intensively exploited aquatic resources with no adoptions of European cultigens or domesticated animals (Oland 2009; Wiewall 2009). In the Petén lake sites, however, cattle bones and European metal artifacts were found in ritual contexts (Pugh 2009).

Conditions of labor scarcity in colonized areas prompted a shift to extensive agricultural strategies. In some parts of Yucatán, native communities retained ownership of lands and hydrologic resources from which they were relocated (Roys 1939); as well, arable lands were cultivated extensively or scoured for resources that would allow native communities to meet tribute and tax levies. Animals and plants introduced from Europe, especially citrus, chickens, pigs, goats, horses, and cattle, were early adoptions in native communities and frequently cultivated and raised on house lots within the settlement (Alexander 2008; deFrance and Hanson 2008; Gallardo and Fowler 2002). In prime agricultural zones that supplied growing colonial cities, the activities of clergy and their household staff in rural conventos provided native groups with working examples of new European technologies, animal husbandry, and siviculture. Animal husbandry and the production of indigo dye in Yucatán fostered adoption of the waterwheel (*noria*), which pumped greater quantities of water to the surface by means of animal traction or wind power. Archaeological survey and excavation in conventos yielded imported glazed ceramics; metal artifacts; bones of European domesticates; wells and mechanical water-control facilities; and architectural features such as stables, water and feed troughs, *arriates* (planting beds), and animal pens (Alexander 2008, 2012; Burgos Villanueva et al. 2010).

In the cacao-producing regions of the Pacific coast and the saltworks of Yucatán's north coast, native groups successfully inserted themselves into Spain's global market by producing large quantities of labor-intensive bulk commodities (Andrews 1983; Fowler 2006; Gasco 2006; Kepecs 2005). Under conditions of demographic decline and labor scarcity, migration in and out of these regions by natives and Europeans produced changes in ethnic identity (Gasco 2005a). Archaeological evidence from Ocelocalco and sites in the Izalcos region of El Salvador also show rapid technological and material changes resulting from inhabitants' consumption of expensive imported goods, including majolicas and lead-glazed earthenware, metal goods, coinage, and Chinese porcelain (Gasco 2005b; Sampeck 2007). European ceramic forms that were typical of majolicas were adopted and replicated on indigenous vessels, producing distinct technological microstyles in Ciudad Vieja, El Salvador (Card 2007). The distribution of imported and local materials among residential groups suggests intensive market participation accompanied by the leveling of socioeconomic class within villages in some areas. Yet the vitality of cacao and salt production was progressively undermined by labor shortage, and native industries collapsed in the late sixteenth and seventeenth centuries (Fowler 2006; Kepecs 2005).

LATE COLONIAL TO POSTCOLONIAL
TRANSFORMATIONS, 1750–1910

As the Bourbon political reforms came into effect in the second half of the eighteenth century, new patterns of demographic and economic growth took hold in the Maya region. Mérida and other provincial capitals thrived under less restrictive trade policies, as archaeological evidence for imports of European ceramics, glass, tools, and technology attests (Burgos Villanueva 1995). Along Yucatán's north coast, Belize, and in the Laguna de Términos, Bourbon free-trade policies also fueled clandestine activity and piracy (Finamore 2002; Victoria Ojeda and Canto Alcocer 2006), which spurred increased migration and violence in the frontier zones (Palka 2005a, 2009). Rural populations near the centers of colonial authority recovered, fueled by internal growth and migration of Spanish creoles and people of African descent to the countryside.

The wars of independence (1821) left the fledgling nations of Mexico and Central America severely undercapitalized, and national governments sought new connections to world markets. New legislation revamped tax policy and encouraged privatization of land and production of lucrative exports. Cattle, sugar, and henequen were produced on *haciendas* (landed estates) in Yucatán and Campeche, and salt-production and logwood-extraction industries thrived along the peninsula's west coast (Alexander 2003; Andrews, Burgos Villanueva, and Millet Cámara 2006; Bracamonte and Sosa 1993). Coffee and cattle supplanted cacao production in Soconusco (Gasco 2006). Indigo dye and logwood production flourished in eastern Yucatán and Belize (Dumond 1997). Entrepreneurs launched a "second conquest" of the Petén in search of chicle and precious hardwoods (Palka 2005b).

The political developments of the Bourbon intendancy, the constitutional reforms of the Cortes de Cadiz (1812), and post-independence legislative agendas raised native people's expectations for social justice and equitable participation in the political process (Dumond 1997; Güemez Pineda 1994). In practice, however, the growth and redistribution of population in rural areas, accompanied by the expansion of the hacienda economy, deepened socioeconomic disparities. Rural revolts and resistance were common in Yucatán, Chiapas, and Guatemala and these fueled people's flight to the frontier (Bricker 1981; Patch 2002; Rugeley 2009). By the mid-nineteenth century, the invasiveness of national policies radically constrained community decision making and ignited the Caste War of Yucatán

(1847-1901), a revitalization movement that resulted in a new religion with its own priesthood and ritual practices (Dumond 1997; Reed 2001; Sullivan 1989). During the presidency of Porfírio Díaz (1877-1910), an influx of capital from the United States and Europe helped industrialize Mexico's economy, but in the Maya region economic imbalances, social inequality, and abusive labor practices contributed to widespread underdevelopment.

Radical landscape changes accompanied these processes and are clearly visible in the archaeological record. In Maya-speaking communities in central Yucatán, settlement dispersal to ranchos situated on parcels with cenotes and rejollas was a form of agricultural intensification, which allowed farmers to avoid the predations of civil and religious authorities (Alexander 2004, 2006). Spanish creoles formed small cattle-ranching and maize-producing haciendas staffed by few resident workers. Population growth in long-established cabeceras and pueblos was accompanied by the expansion of religious architecture, the construction of buildings that housed creole-dominated local governments, and the use of masonry residential architecture, which indicated increased class stratification. Archaeological evidence from house lots in pueblos, ranchos, and haciendas for the years before the onset of the Caste War shows that householders pursued different agropastoral strategies within the settlement zone to compensate for loss of land and for heavy taxation. They also consumed nonlocal ceramics and metal artifacts in variable quantities, which indicated differential market participation.

In the Izalcos region of El Salvador, eighteenth-century settlements also were dispersed, and small cattle haciendas were established. The production of cattle, balsam, indigo, pottery, and foodstuffs connected haciendas, small landholdings, and towns to world markets after the collapse of the cacao industry (Sampeck 2007). In the frontier areas of the Petén and lowlands of Chiapas, intrusions of mestizo traders and interactions with inhabitants at chicle and logging camps encouraged acquisition of glazed earthenwares, metal tools, and pharmaceuticals in glass containers (Palka 2005a). Yet some Lacandon groups abandoned settlements, leaving usable portable items behind, and moved further into the forest away from rivers and natural transportation routes. At the same time, the Lacandon also intensified ritual activities, depositing large quantities of incense burners at prehispanic archaeological sites used as shrines (Palka 2009). On Yucatán's north coast, fugitives of African descent settled the communities of San Fernando Aké and San Francisco de Paula alongside haciendas staffed by salaried workers and debt peons in the late eighteenth and nineteenth centuries (Andrews and Robles Castellanos 2009; Kepecs 1999).

Large, architecturally elaborate, haciendas that produced industrial quantities of sugar, henequen, and cattle typified the Porfiriato in Yucatán. They were staffed by native, African, and Asian indebted laborers, who sometimes occupied segregated residential zones. Excavations of the central buildings and house lots of estate workers at haciendas Pacabtún, San Pedro Cholul, Tabi, and Xucu illuminate how the severe, hierarchical labor organization was manifest in the built environment and in patterns of consumption (Andrews, Burgos Villanueva, and

Millet Cámera 2012; Burgos Villanueva et al. 2005; Fernández Souza et al. 2010; Meyers 2005, 2012; Meyers and Carlson 2002; Meyers et al. 2008). Rural farmers in central Yucatán continued to cultivate small landholdings after the Caste War, but in the late nineteenth century intensification and settlement dispersal were underway again. Native farmers established numerous privately owned ranchos, used for small-scale stock raising and for the production of maize, sugarcane, and henequen (Alexander 2012).

After the Mexican Revolution of 1910, redistribution of land to new and exist-ing farming communities (*ejido* grants) sparked widespread changes, and agrarian reform fused with a new *campesino* (peasant farmer) social identity (Eiss 2008b; Gabbert 2004; Wells and Joseph 1996). Ex-haciendas granted as ejidos to groups of agriculturalists were characterized by the crumbling disrepair of the architec-ture and facilities of the estates. By contrast, new municipalities formed after the Mexican Revolution often symbolized their legitimacy and political autonomy by building large and elaborate civic structures in a distinctive postrevolutionary style, which dominated the main plaza and dwarfed the religious architecture of the community.

Conclusions

Many investigators recognize that Maya speakers in Guatemala and Mexico share comparable experiences and a common heritage (Eiss 2008a; Fischer 1999; Watanabe and Fischer 2004), but no pan-Maya ethnic identity exists in the region. Today, Yucatán's inhabitants generally reject indigenous identities (Castañeda 2004), even though many native communities retained control of land. The Lacandon of the Petén and lowland Chiapas are not a unified cultural group; instead, current atti-tudes and practices were reconfigured through a long-term process of ethnogenesis (McGee 1990; Palka 2005a). Though many inhabitants of Guatemala and Chiapas are active participants in the pan-Maya and First Nations movements, the historical evidence is slim for a pan-Maya ethnogenesis in the postcolonial era or for the long-term maintenance of a Maya social identity from the time of the Spanish invasion (Gabbert 2004; Hervik 2001; Restall 2004). Place, rather than language, class, or ethnicity, remains the idiom for the expression of sociocultural identity in the Maya area, as it has in other Mesoamerican regions (Berdan et al. 2008).

The transformations discussed here reveal that conservation of cultural auton-omy relates to long-term trajectories of landscape change. The study of the forma-tion of anthropogenic landscapes from the perspectives of historical ecology and archaeology shows how variations in population density, adoption of European cultigens, animal husbandry practices, technological changes, political policies, and new macroregional economic structures tempered the loss or retention of ecological knowledge and reconfigured cultural practices. The ways in which native peoples related to places on the landscape in the past have shaped identity and practice in the present.

REFERENCES

Alexander, Rani T. 2003. Architecture, Haciendas, and Economic Change in Yaxcabá, Yucatán, Mexico. *Ethnohistory* 50(1/2):191–220.

Alexander, Rani T. 2004. *Yaxcabá and the Caste War of Yucatán: An Archaeological Perspective*. University of New Mexico Press, Albuquerque.

Alexander, Rani T. 2005. Isla Cilvituk and the Difficulties of Spanish Colonization in Southwestern Campeche. In *The Postclassic to Spanish-Era Transition in Mesoamerica: Archaeological Perspectives*, edited by Susan Kepecs and Rani T. Alexander, pp. 161–183. University of New Mexico Press, Albuquerque.

Alexander, Rani T. 2006. Maya Settlement Shifts and Agrarian Ecology in Yucatán, 1800–2000. *Journal of Anthropological Research* 62(4):449–470.

Alexander, Rani T. 2012. Prohibido Tocar este Cenote: The Archaeological Basis for the Titles of Ebtun. *International Journal of Historical Archaeology* 16(1):1–24.

Alexander, Rani T., and Susan Kepecs. 2005. The Postclassic to Spanish-Era Transition in Mesoamerica: An Introduction. In *The Postclassic to Spanish-Era Transition in Mesoamerica: Archaeological Perspectives*, edited by Susan Kepecs and Rani T. Alexander, pp. 1–12. University of New Mexico Press, Albuquerque.

Alexander, Rani T., with technical contributions by José Díaz Cruz, Adam Kaeding, Susan Kepecs, Ruth Martínez Cervantes, and Matthew Punke. 2008. *La arqueología colonial en los pueblos de Ebtún, Cuncunul, Kaua, Tekom, y Tixcacalcupul, Yucatán, México*. Informe técnico de campo para la temporada de 2006, presentada al Consejo de Arqueología, Instituto Nacional de Antropología e Historia, México, D.F.

Andrews, Anthony. 1983. *Maya Salt Production and Trade*. University of Arizona Press, Tucson.

Andrews, Anthony. 1991. The Rural Chapels and Churches of Early Colonial Yucatan and Belize: An Archaeological Perspective. In *The Spanish Borderlands in Pan-American Perspective*, edited by David H. Thomas, pp. 355–374. Columbian Consequences. vol. 3, Smithsonian Institution, Washington, DC.

Andrews, Anthony P., Antonio Benavides Castillo, and Grant D. Jones. 2006. Ecab: A Remote Encomienda of Early Colonial Yucatan. In *Reconstructing the Past. Studies in Mesoamerican and Central American Prehistory*, edited by David M. Pendergast and Anthony P. Andrews, pp. 5–32. British Archaeological Reports International Series S1529, Oxford.

Andrews, Anthony P., Rafael Burgos Villanueva, and Luis M. Millet Cámara. 2006. The Historic Port of El Real de Salinas in Campeche and the Role of Coastal Resources in the Emergence of Capitalism in Yucatan, Mexico. *International Journal of Historical Archaeology* 10(2):179–205.

Andrews, Anthony P., Rafael Burgos Villanueva, and Luis M. Millet Cámara. 2012. Henequen Ports of Yucatán's Gilded Age. *International Journal of Historical Archaeology* 16(1):25–46.

Andrews, Anthony P., and Fernando Robles Castellanos. 2009. La arqueología histórica del noroeste de Yucatán. In *Arqueología colonial Latinoamericano, modelos de estudio*, edited by Patricia Fournier García and Juan García Targa, pp. 115–131. BAR International Series 1988, British Archaeological Reports, Oxford.

Basso, Keith H. 1996. *Wisdom Sits in Places: Landscape and Language among the Western Apache*. University of New Mexico Press, Albuquerque.

Berdan, Frances F., John K. Chance, Alan R. Sandstrom, Barbara L. Stark, James Taggart, and Emily Umberger, eds. 2008. *Ethnic Identity in Nahua Mesoamerica: The View from Archaeology, Art History, Ethnohistory, and Contemporary Ethnography*. University of Utah Press, Salt Lake City.

Binford, Lewis. 1982. An Archaeology of Place. *Journal of Anthropological Archaeology* 1:5–31.

Bracamonte y Sosa, Pedro. 1993. *Amos y Sirvientes, Las Haciendas de Yucatán 1789–1860*. Universidad Autónoma de Yucatán, Mérida.

Bricker, Victoria R. 1981. *The Indian Christ, the Indian King*. University of Texas Press, Austin.

Burgos Villanueva, Rafael. 1995. *El Olimpio: un predio colonial en el lado poniente de la Plaza Mayor de Mérida, Yucatán y análisis cerámico comparativo*. Colección Científica, 216, Instituto Nacional de Antropología e Historia, México.

Burgos Villanueva, Rafael, Yoly Palomo Carrillo, and Sara Dzul Góngora. 2010. *El Camino Real a Campeche: una perspectiva arqueolgógica e histórica*. Instituto Nacional de Antropología e Historia, Mérida, Yucatán, México.

Burgos Villanueva, Rafael, Yoly Palomo, and Sara Dzul Góngora. 2005. *San Agustín de Pacabtún: Arqueología e historia de una hacienda henequenera*. Grupo Bepensa, Centro INAH Yucatán, Mérida, Yucatán.

Card, Jeb J. 2007. The Ceramics of Colonial Ciudad Vieja, El Salvador: Culture Contact and Social Change in Mesoamerica. PhD dissertation, Department of Anthropology, Tulane University, New Orleans.

Caso Barrera, Laura. 2002. *Caminos en la selva: Migración, comercio y resistencia. Mayas yucatecos e itzaes, siglos XVII-XIX*. El Colegio de México, Fondo de Cultura Económica, México.

Caso Barrera, Laura, and Mario Aliphat F. 2006. The Itza Maya Control over Cacao: Politics, Commerce, and War in the Sixteenth and Seventeenth Centuries. In *Chocolate in Mesoamerica: A Cultural History of Cacao*, edited by Cameron L. McNeil, pp. 289–306. University Press of Florida, Gainesville.

Castañeda, Quetzil. 2004. "We are not Indigenous!" An Introduction to the Maya Identity in Yucatan. *Journal of Latin American Anthropology* 9(1):36–63.

Chamberlain, Robert S. 1948. *The Conquest and Colonization of Yucatan 1517–1550*. Carnegie Institution of Washington Publication No. 582, Washington, DC.

Chuchiak, John F. 2005. In Servitio Dei: Fray Diego de Landa, the Franciscan Order, and the Return of the Extirpation of Idolatry in the Colonial Diocese of Yucatan, 1573–1579. *The Americas* 61(4):611–646.

Chuchiak, John F. 2009. De Descriptio Idolorum: An Ethnohistorical Examination of the Production, Imagery and Functions of Colonial Yucatec Maya Idols and Effigy Censers, 1540-1700. In *Maya Worldviews at Conquest*, edited by Leslie G. Cecil and Timothy W. Pugh, pp. 135–158. University of Colorado Press, Boulder.

Crumley, Carole L. 2007. Historical Ecology: Integrated Thinking at Multiple Temporal and Spatial Scales. In *The World System and the Earth System: Global Socioenvironmental Change and Sustainability since the Neolithic*, edited by

Alf Hornborg and Carole Crumley, pp. 15–28. Left Coast Press, Walnut Creek, California.

deFrance, Susan, and Craig Hanson. 2008. Labor, Population Movement, and Food in Sixteenth-Century Ek Balam, Yucatan. *Latin American Antiquity* 19(3):299–316.

Dumond, Don E. 1997. *The Machete and the Cross: Campesino Rebellion in Yucatan.* University of Nebraska Press, Lincoln.

Eiss, Paul K. 2008a. Constructing the Maya. *Ethnohistory: Special Issue, Constructing the Maya: Ethnicity, State Formation, and Material Culture in Yucatán, Chiapas, and Guatemala* 55(4):503–508.

Eiss, Paul K. 2008b. El Pueblo Mestizo: Modernity, Tradition and Statecraft in Yucatán, 1870–1907. *Ethnohistory* 55(4):525–552.

Farriss, Nancy M. 1978. Nucleation versus Dispersal: The Dynamics of Population Movement in Colonial Yucatan. *Hispanic American Historical Review* 58:187–216.

Farriss, Nancy M. 1984. *Maya Society under Colonial Rule: The Collective Enterprise of Survival.* Princeton University Press, Princeton, New Jersey.

Fernández Souza, Lilia, Héctor Hernández Álvarez, and Mario Zimmermann. 2010. *Informe preliminar proyecto arqueología histórica en la Hacienda San Pedro Cholul, temporada de campo Septiembre 2009-Mayo 2010.* Presentado al Consejo de Arqueología, Instituto Nacional de Antropología e Historia, México, D.F.

Finamore, Daniel. 2002. Pirates of the Barcadares. *Natural History* 111(9):58.

Fischer, Edward F. 1999. Cultural Logic and Maya Identity. *Current Anthropology* 40(4):473–449.

Fowler, William R. 1995. *Caluco, historia y arqueología de un pueblo pipil en el siglo XVI.* Consejo Nacional para la Cultura y el Arte, Dirección de Publicaciones e Impresos, CONCULTURA.

Fowler, William R. 2006. Cacao Production, Tribute, and Wealth in Sixteenth-Century Izalcos, El Salvador. In *Chocolate in Mesoamerica: A Cultural History of Cacao,* edited by Cameron L. McNeil, pp. 307–321. University Press of Florida, Gainesville.

Gabbert, Wolfgang. 2004. *Becoming Maya: Ethnicity and Social Inequality in Yucatan since 1500.* University of Arizona Press, Tucson.

Gallardo, Roberto, and William R. Fowler. 2002. *Investigaciones arqueológicas en Ciudad Vieja, El Salvador: la primigenia villa de San Salvador.* Consejo Nacional para la Cultura y el Arte, Dirección de Publicaciones e Impresos, CONCULTURA.

García Targa, Juan. 2000. Análisis histórico y arqueológico del asentamiento colonial de Tecoh [Estado de Yucatán, México], siglo XVI. *Ancient Mesoamerica* 11(2):231–243.

Gasco, Janine. 2005a. The Consequences of Spanish Colonial Rule for the Indigenous Peoples of Chiapas, Mexico. In *The Postclassic to Spanish-Era Transition in Mesoamerica: Archaeological Perspectives,* edited by Susan Kepecs and Rani T. Alexander, pp. 77–96. University of New Mexico Press, Albuquerque.

Gasco, Janine. 2005b. Spanish Colonialism and Processes of Social Change in Mesoamerica. In *The Archaeology of Colonial Encounters: Comparative Perspectives,* edited by Gil J. Stein, pp. 69–108. School of American Research Press, Santa Fe.

Gasco, Janine. 2006. Soconusco Cacao Farmers Past and Present. In *Chocolate in Mesoamerica: A Cultural History of Cacao,* edited by Cameron L. McNeil, pp. 322–337. University Press of Florida, Gainesville.

Graham, Elizabeth, David M. Pendergast, and Grant D. Jones. 1989. On the Fringes of Conquest: Maya-Spanish Contact in Colonial Belize. *Science* 246(4935):1254–1259.

Güemez Pineda, Arturo. 1994. *Liberalismo en Tierras del Caminante, Yucatan, 1812–1840.* El Colegio de Michoacán, Zamora.

Hanson, Craig A. 1996. The Hispanic Horizon in Yucatan: A Model of Franciscan Missionization. *Ancient Mesoamerica* 6:15–28.

Hervik, Peter. 2001. Narrations of Shifting Maya Identities. *Bulletin of Latin American Research* 20(3):342–359.

Jones, Grant D. 1989. *Maya Resistance to Spanish Rule: Time and History on a Colonial Frontier.* University of New Mexico Press, Albuquerque.

Jones, Grant D. 1998. *The Conquest of the Last Maya Kingdom.* Stanford University Press, Stanford.

Kepecs, Susan. 1997. Native Yucatán and Spanish Influence: The Archaeology and History of Chikinchel. *Journal of Archaeological Method and Theory* 4(3–4):307–333.

Kepecs, Susan. 1999. The Political Economy of Chikinchel, Yucatán, Mexico: A Diachronic Analysis from the Prehispanic Era through the Age of Spanish Administration. PhD dissertation, Department of Anthropology, University of Wisconsin, Madison.

Kepecs, Susan. 2005. Mayas, Spaniards, and Salt: World Systems Shifts in Sixteenth-Century Yucatán. In *The Postclassic to Spanish-Era Transition in Mesoamerica: Archaeological Perspectives*, edited by Susan Kepecs and Rani T. Alexander, pp. 117–137. University of New Mexico Press, Albuquerque.

Lee, Thomas A., Jr., and Douglas D. Bryant. 1988. The Colonial Coxoh Maya. In *Ethnoarchaeology among the Highland Maya of Chiapas, Mexico*, edited by Thomas A. L. Lee Jr. and Brian Hayden, pp. 5–20. Papers of the New World Archaeological Foundation No. 56, Brigham Young University, Provo, Utah.

Lee, Thomas A. Lee, Jr., and Sidney D. Markman. 1977. The Coxoh Colonial Project and Coneta, Chiapas, Mexico: A Provincial Maya Village under the Spanish Conquest. *Historical Archaeology* 11:56–66.

Lightfoot, Kent G. 1995. Culture Contact Studies: Redefining the Relationship between Prehistoric and Historical Archaeology. *American Antiquity* 60(2):199–217.

Lightfoot, Kent G. 2004. *Indians, Missionaries, and Merchants: The Legacy of Colonial Encounters on the California Frontiers.* University of California Press, Berkeley.

Lightfoot, Kent G., Antoinette Martinez, and Ann M. Schiff. 1998. Daily Practice and Material Culture in Pluralistic Social Settings: An Archaeological Study of Culture Change and Persistence from Fort Ross, California. *American Antiquity* 63(2):199–222.

Lovell, W. George, and Christopher H. Lutz. 1994. Conquest and Population: Maya Demography in Historical Perspective. *Latin American Research Review* 29(2):133–140.

MacLeod, Murdo J. 1973. *Spanish Central America: A Socio-Economic History.* University of California Press, Berkeley.

McAnany, Patricia A. 1995. *Living with the Ancestors: Kinship and Kingship in Ancient Maya Society.* University of Texas Press, Austin.

McGee, R. Jon. 1990. *Life, Ritual, and Religion among the Lacandon Maya.* Wadsworth, Belmont, California.

Meyers, Allan D. 2005. Material Expressions of Social Inequality on a Porfirian Sugar Hacienda in Yucatán, Mexico. *Historical Archaeology* 39(4):112–137.

Meyers, Allan D. 2012. *Outside the Hacienda Walls: The Archaeology of Plantation Peonage in Nineteenth-Century Yucatán.* University of Arizona Press, Tucson.

Meyers, Allan D., and David L. Carlson. 2002. Peonage, Power Relations, and the Built Environment at Hacienda Tabi, Yucatán, Mexico. *International Journal of Historical Archaeology* 6(4):225–252.

Meyers, Allan D., Allison S. Harvey, and Sarah A. Levithol. 2008. Houselot Refuse Disposal and Geochemistry at a Late 19th Century Hacienda Village in Yucatán, Mexico. *Journal of Field Archaeology* 33(4):371–388.

Oland, Maxine Heather. 2009. Long-Term Indigenous History on a Colonial Frontier: Archaeology at a 15th-17th Century Maya Village, Progresso Lagoon, Belize. PhD dissertation, Department of Anthropology, Northwestern University, Evanston, Illinois.

Orser, Charles, E., Jr. 1996. *A Historical Archaeology of the Modern World.* Plenum, New York.

Palka, Joel W. 2005a. *Unconquered Lacandon Maya: Ethnohistory and Archaeology of Indigenous Culture Change.* University of Florida Press, Gainesville.

Palka, Joel W. 2005b. Postcolonial Conquest of the Southern Maya Lowlands, Cross-Cutural Interaction, and Lacandon Maya Culture Change. In *The Postclassic to Spanish-Era Transition in Mesoamerica: Archaeological Approaches*, edited by Susan Kepecs and Rani T. Alexander, pp. 183–201. University of New Mexico Press, Albuquerque.

Palka, Joel W. 2009. Agency and Worldviews of the Unconquered Lacandon Maya. In *Maya Worldviews at Conquest*, edited by Leslie G. Cecil and Timothy W. Pugh, pp. 261–278. University of Colorado Press, Boulder.

Patch, Robert W. 2002. *Maya Revolt and Revolution in the Eighteenth Century.* M. E. Sharpe, Armonk, New York.

Pugh, Timothy W. 2009. Contagion and Alterity: Kowoj Maya Appropriations of European Objects *American Anthropologist* 111(3):373–386.

Reed, Nelson. 2001. *The Caste War of Yucatan.* Rev. ed. Stanford University Press, Stanford.

Restall, Matthew. 1997. *The Maya World: Yucatec Culture and Society 1550–1850.* Stanford University Press, Stanford.

Restall, Matthew. 1998. *Maya Conquistador.* Beacon, Boston.

Restall, Matthew. 2004. Maya Ethnogenesis. *Journal of Latin American Anthropology* 9(1):64–89.

Rice, Prudence M., and Don S. Rice, eds. 2009. *The Kowoj: Identity, Migration, and Geopolitics in Late Postclassic Petén, Guatemala.* University Press of Colorado, Boulder.

Roys, Ralph L. 1939. *The Titles of Ebtun.* Publication No. 505, Washington, DC.

Roys, Ralph L. 1952. *Conquest Sites and the Subsequent Destruction of Maya Architecture in the Interior of Northern Yucatan.* Contributions to American Anthropology and History No. 54, Carnegie Institution of Washington, Washington, DC.

Rugeley, Terry. 2009. *Rebellion Now and Forever: Mayas, Hispanics and Caste War Violence in Yucatán, 1800–1880.* Stanford University Press, Stanford.

Sampeck, Kathryn E. 2007. Late Postclassic to Colonial Landscapes and Political Economy of the Izalcos Region, El Salvador. PhD dissertation, Department of Anthropology, Tulane University, New Orleans.

Scholes, France V., and Ralph L. Roys. 1948. *The Maya Chontal Indians of Acalán-Tixchel.* Publication No. 560, Carnegie Institution of Washington, Washington, DC.

Sherratt, Andrew. 1981. Plough and Pastoralism:Aspects of the Secondary Products Revolution. In *Pattern of the Past: Studies in Honour of David Clarke*, edited by Ian Hodder, Glyn Isaac, and Norman Hammond, pp. 261–305. Cambridge University Press, Cambridge.

Smith, Adam T. 2003. *The Political Landscape: Constellations of Authority in Early Complex Polities.* University of California Press, Berkeley.

Sullivan, Paul. 1989. *Unfinished Conversations: Mayas and Foreigners between Two Wars.* University of California Press, Berkeley.

Turner, B. L., Peter Klepeis, and Laura L. Schneider. 2003. Three Millennia in the Southern Yucatán Peninsula: Implications for Occupancy, Use, and Carrying Capacity. In *The Lowland Maya Area: Three Millennia at the Human-Wildland Interface*, edited by Arturo Gómez Pompa, Michael Alle, Scott L. Fedick, and Juan J. Jiménez-Osornio, pp. 361–387. Haworth Press, Binghamton, New York.

Victoria Ojeda, Jorge, and Jorge Canto Alcocer. 2006. *San Fernando Aké: microhistoria de una comunidad afroamericana en Yucatán.* Ediciones de la Universidad Autónoma de Yucatán, Mérida, Yucatán, México.

Watanabe, John M., and Edward F. Fischer. 2004. Emergent Anthropologies and Pluricultural Ethnography in Two Postcolonial Nations. In *Pluralizing Ethnography: Comparison and Representation in Maya Cultures, Histories, and Identities*, edited by John M. Watanabe and Edward. F. Fischer, pp. 3–33. School of American Research Advanced Seminar Series, SAR Press, Santa Fe.

Wells, Alan, and Gilbert M. Joseph. 1996. *Summer of Discontent, Seasons of Upheaval: Elite Politics and Rural Insurgency in Yucatan, 1876–1915.* Stanford University Press, Stanford.

Wiewall, Darcy Lynn. 2009. Identifying the Impact of the Spanish Colonial Regime on Maya Household Production at Lamanai, Belize during the Terminal Postclassic to Early Colonial Transition. PhD dissertation, Department of Anthropology, University of California, Riverside.

Wilk, Richard R. 1991. *Household Ecology:Economic Change and Domestic Life among the Kekchi Maya in Belize.* University of Arizona Press, Tucson.

Wolf, Eric R. 1982. *Europe and the People without History.* University of California Press, Berkeley.

Wolf, Eric R. 1990. Distinguished Lecture: Facing Power—Old Insights, New Questions. *American Anthropologist* 92:586–596.

INDEX

....

Page numbers in italics indicate illustrations.